THE SCRIPTURES IN THE GOSPELS

BIBLIOTHECA EPHEMERIDUM THEOLOGICARUM LOVANIENSIUM

CXXXI

THE SCRIPTURES IN THE GOSPELS

EDITED BY

C.M. TUCKETT

LEUVEN
UNIVERSITY PRESS

UITGEVERIJ PEETERS
LEUVEN

1997

CIP KONINKLIJKE BIBLIOTHEEK ALBERT I, BRUSSEL

ISBN 90 6186 802 5 (Leuven University Press)
D/1997/1869/16
ISBN 90 6831 932 9 (Uitgeverij Peeters)
D/1997/0602/41

© Leuven University Press / Presses Universitaires de Louvain
Universitaire Pers Leuven
Blijde Inkomststraat 5, B-3000 Leuven-Louvain (Belgium)

Uitgeverij Peeters, Bondgenotenlaan 153, B-3000 Leuven (Belgium)

PREFACE

The present volume comprises the papers given at the 45th session of the Colloquium Biblicum Lovaniense (July 31 – August 2 1996), which was devoted to the study of "The Scriptures in the Gospels", with the sub-title "Intertextuality: The Use of the Old Testament in the Four Gospels".

Part I contains the papers of the invited speakers. There were two papers devoted to Q (Tuckett, Neirynck), one more broadly based paper on evidence from Qumran (Lust), together with papers on each of the four evangelists: two on Matthew (Senior, Weren), four on Mark (Focant, Marcus, Breytenbach, Collins), three on Luke (Bogaert, Denaux, Morgen), and three on John (Theobald, Menken, Busse). Part II contains twenty-one offered papers, covering a wide range of issues and subjects: the first deals with broader methodological questions (Rese), and this is followed by papers on Q (3), Matthew and Luke together (1), Matthew (3), Mark (2), Luke (7) and John (2), the volume being concluded by two more general papers on the possible relevance for 4Q521 and Isa 61 in studying the Jesus tradition.

About 150 participants at the Colloquium enjoyed the excellent hospitality offered by the Pope Adrian VI College, as well as invaluable administrative support provided by the Secretariat of the Faculty of Theology in the University of Leuven. All visitors to Leuven were once again very grateful to the local organisers for providing such a convivial atmosphere in which to engage in fruitful and enjoyable discussion at the Colloquium. The meeting was sponsored by the Universities of Leuven and Louvain-la-Neuve, and the National Fund for Scientific Research (FWO/FNRS, Brussels). The 35 contributors to this volume reflect the international nature of the Leuven Colloquium with scholars from ten countries: Belgium (9), Germany (8), United Kingdom (4), USA (4), the Netherlands (3), Austria (2), South Africa (2), with one each from France, Ireland and Swaziland.

I would like to express my gratitude to all who have helped in the many stages which have brought this volume to completion. I am grateful to the Committee of the Colloquium for electing me as President of the 1996 meeting. Professor Reimund Bieringer provided much assistance prior to the Colloquium. The Secretary of the Faculty of Theology in Leuven, Karel Dehuyvetters, and his colleagues were unfailingly helpful and supportive before and during the Colloquium. Finally, I am very grateful to Professor Frans Neirynck who has remained a tower of strength and support throughout the whole project, and without whose constant readiness to help and advise, the production of this volume would not have been possible.

Christopher M. TUCKETT

CONTENTS

MAIN PAPERS

OFFERED PAPERS

INDEXES

INTRODUCTION

The 45th session of the Colloquium Biblicum Lovaniense, July 31 – August 2, 1996, was devoted to the study of *The Scriptures in the Gospels*, with the sub-title *Intertextuality: The Use of the Old Testament in the Four Gospels*. The topic of the use of the so-called Old Testament scriptures in New Testament writings has formed the focus of several individual contributions to Leuven Colloquia in the past, although this was the first time that the whole Colloquium had been devoted to such a theme. Partly too such an undertaking was felt to be useful in the light of developments in the area of literary study, stressing the idea of "intertextuality" which places such emphasis on the claim that texts can only be understood in relation to a network, or matrix, of other texts. In the case of the gospels, one such network is of course provided by the texts of Jewish scripture. Fourteen scholars were invited to give main papers or to conduct seminars. In addition, a total of twenty-seven short papers were offered and read at the Colloquium.

The proceedings of the Colloquium are presented here in two parts. Part I contains the fourteen papers of the invited speakers who presented main papers or who made presentations at the four seminar sessions (in Dutch, French, English and German). Twenty-one of the twenty-six offered papers which were read at the Colloquium appear in Part II. The following Introduction focuses on the papers in the order in which they appear in this volume.

My opening address, *Scripture and Q*, sought to discuss some of the issues raised by recent studies of the phenomenon of "intertextuality". In particular, an author-centred approach to the topic is defended (though recognising the force of others' insistence on the importance of the reader). The main part of the paper discusses the possible influence of Isaiah on the Sayings Source Q. The servant song of Isa 53 may be related (perhaps indirectly) to Q's language about Jesus as Son of Man, and Isa 53 may also have influenced some of the language of the tirade against Capernaum in Q 10,14. The rest of the paper is devoted to a discussion of the influence of Isa 61 on Q. The Q beatitudes, it is argued, reflect such influence, and Isa 61 was an important text in interpreting and re-presenting Jesus' own preaching. However, while Isa 61 can only with difficulty explain the whole wording of Q's beatitudes, the recently published Qumran text 4Q521 may provide a missing link: here Isa 61 is linked with language from Ps 146 in describing the blessings of the new age, and it may be a similar exegetical tradition, whereby these two OT texts are regarded as mutually interpreting each other, that lies behind the Q tradition.

Much of the same material formed the basis of the other main contribution devoted to Q at the Colloquium, the paper of F. NEIRYNCK (Leuven) on *Q 6,20.21b, 7,22 and Isaiah 61*. The overlap in material had not been planned, but it provided an interesting alternative viewpoint, as the conclusions reached differed somewhat from my opening address. Neirynck is less willing to see very strong influence from that OT passage at the level of Q. In relation to the beatitudes in Q, Isa 61 cannot be clearly seen as influencing the first beatitude, where any verbal correspondence between the two texts is minimal. With regard to the possible parallel between Matthew's second beatitude (on the mourners) and similar diction in the Lukan woes (Lk 6,24-26), substantial Lukan redaction, if not entire Lukan composition, remains the most likely explanation of Luke's wording in the woes, especially the references to "consolation" and "mourning". Thus any parallels between Matthew and Luke here cannot be used to justify a theory of an origin in Q for such language. Thus the clear allusion to Isa 61,2 in Mt 5,4 is most likely due to Matthew's own redaction of the beatitude. It does not indicate any influence of Isa 61 at the level of Q. Further, any connection between Matthew's third beatitude (on the hungry) and Isa 61 is extremely tenuous.

Isa 61 is indeed reflected in Q 7,22, although this is not necessarily the dominant clause. However, the conjunction of the reference to Isa 61,1 with a reference to "raising the dead" is now strikingly paralleled in the Qumran text 4Q521. Nevertheless, the parallel must be properly interpreted, and the Qumran text should be read on its own terms, not in the light of Q 7,22 (or vice versa). Neirynck argues that in 4Q521, there is no idea that the tasks of "raising the dead" etc. are thought of as the activity of a "messianic" figure: they are solely the actions of God. Thus any direct link between Q and 4Q521 is unlikely. Influence of Isa 61 in Q should probably be limited to the clause in Q 7,22.

A wide-ranging paper was delivered by J. LUST (Leuven) on *Mic 5,1-3 in Qumran and in the NT, and Messianism in the Septuagint*. Here Lust deals with a large number of issues in the study of the Qumran texts and the NT and their common use of scripture, with particular reference to Mic 5,1-3. Lust discusses some of the introductory formulae in both sets of literature: such formulae as occur in the NT are mostly not the same as in Qumran, but the range of books introduced by such formulae is very similar. With regard to Mic 5, Lust examines the theory (of R. Fuller) that a fragment from Qumran may preserve a part of Mic 5,1-2; however, it is very doubtful if such an identification can be established on the basis of so small a text. The Micah passage is also preserved in the Greek Prophets scroll from Nahal Hever, and this leads to some discussion of the representation of the divine name in Greek texts.

Lust offers a detailed analysis of the text in Mic 5 in the MT, LXX, the Nahal Hever text, and (where relevant) the citation of Mic in Mt 2. Matthew's text shows a number of differences from both the Hebrew and Greek texts, and certainly seems to be independent of the LXX.

In a final section of his paper, Lust discusses the claim that the LXX tended to enhance the messianism in the MT, possible preparing the way for the messianic interpretation of the OT in the NT. Lust compares the MT and the LXX of Mic 5,1-3 with this question in mind, but finds no confirmation of the general theory. In fact, he claims that, for Mic 5, "in the Greek translation both its text and its context are less open to a messianic interpretation than in the NT".

In a supplementary discussion, Lust also introduced a discussion on *Tools for Septuagint Studies*, giving information about resources already available in the scholarly literature, and also giving details about the work currently underway in Leuven (under Lust's direction) to produce *A Greek-English Lexicon of the Septuagint*. This information is now published in *ETL* 73 (1997) 215-221.

Two presentations at the Colloquium focused on the Gospel of Matthew. In one, D. SENIOR (Chicago) discussed *The Lure of the Formula Quotations. Re-assessing Matthew's Use of the Old Testament with the Passion Narrative as a Test Case*. As well as all the well-known problems concerning the text form etc. of the formula quotations in Matthew, Senior draws attention to the phenomenon of their apparently uneven distribution throughout the gospel: a significant cluster of quotations occur in the birth narratives, some more in chs. 4–13, but relatively few later in the gospel with only two in the passion narrative.

Senior argues that it may be wrong to consider the formula quotations in isolation form the rest of the gospel. Matthew's whole theology is dominated by the idea of fulfilment, affecting his Christology, his ecclesiology, and his view of the Jewish opponents of Jesus, and this emerges in a wide variety of ways. "An entire repertoire of programmatic statements, direct quotations, biblical allusions, biblical typologies and the influence of the Old Testament on certain episodes in the gospel confront the reader with the rich brew of Matthew's theology of fulfilment" (p. 108). Senior argues that the passion narrative in Matthew is no exception. The narrative is full of programmatic statements (26,54.56), direct quotations (26,31; 27,9-10), biblical allusions and individual narrative elements generated by OT scripture. Explicit formula quotations may be relatively small, but the general motif of fulfilment, of which the formula quotations are part, dominate Matthew's passion narrative no less than the rest of the gospel. The only difference lies in the fact that in these instances, it is the author himself, rather than a character in the narrative, who is the speaker.

The second presentation on Matthew formed the basis of the Dutch speaking seminar and appears here in English form in the essay of W. WEREN (Utrecht) on *Jesus' Entry into Jerusalem: Matthew 21,1-17 in the Light of the Hebrew Bible and the Septuagint*. Two general hypotheses were proposed: first, that Mt 21,1-17 may have been influenced by the Hebrew OT text as well as the LXX, and second, that the Matthean story may be influenced by the wider OT context from which the texts actually cited are taken.

In relation to the quotation of Isa 62,11 + Zech 9,9 in Mt 21,5, it is argued that this may be influenced by the Hebrew OT text; also the substitution of Isa 62,11 at the start may be connected with the distinction drawn between the inhabitants of Jerusalem and the crowds from Galilee who recognise Jesus as a prophet. Moreover, the double reference to the ass and the foal may allude to yet further OT passages and contexts, viz. Gen 49,11.14. Similar arguments are deployed in relation to the quotation of Ps 118,25-26 (in Mt 21,9.15) and of Isa 56,7 + Jer 7,11 (in Mt 21,13). Again the suggestion is made that interpreters should look beyond the boundaries of the quotation in the strict sense to find clues about how Matthew may have taken note of the broader context of the quotations as well. For example, in relation to the Isa 56 + Jer 7 quotation, a further dimension can be added to this polemic against the temple by referring to the hypocrisy of certain categories of the people. In each case, therefore, the "pretext" has to be analyzed before one sees how it is re-used by a later writer. Intertextuality has to do with relations between text units and not merely between isolated verses.

Four papers were devoted to the Gospel of Mark. In *La recontextualisation de Is 6,9-10 en Mc 4,10-12, ou un example de non-citation*, C. FOCANT (Louvain-la-Neuve) reviews the many attempts to make sense of the well-known crux in Mk 4,10-12, with its apparently predestinarian language placed on the lips of Jesus. Focant argues that the verses from Isa 6, apparently alluded to here, are used by Mark in a way which is unlike the way they are used by other early Christian writers. There the focus is usually on the rejection of Jesus by Israel. For Mark, it is more of a direct address to the reader. Mark does not even introduce the saying as an explicit citation of scripture. For him, it is rather a way of challenging the listener to ask whether s/he is, or wishes to be, one of those to whom the "mystery of the kingdom" has been given, or remain one of "those outside". For the characteristic feature of "those outside" is that they do *not* ask about the parables. Those to whom the mystery has been given are certainly not those to whom a body of knowledge has been given, for they still have to ask about the parables. Rather than communicating a theory of divine hardening of others, the allusion to Isa 6 in Mk 4 thus serves to describe the catastrophic situation of those who separate themselves in their blindness.

The English speaking seminar was led by J. MARCUS (Glasgow) and discussed his paper *Scripture and Tradition in Mark 7*, focusing on the debates recorded in Mk 7,1-15. Marcus starts from the extremely sharp polemic of vv. 8, 9, 13, contrasting the oral tradition with the written law. Such an attack strikes at the heart of Pharisaic thinking. Indeed the reverence for ancestral traditions was very widespread in antiquity. By contrast, some of the rest of the material in this section presents the Pharisaic viewpoint in terms that can be read quite positively (cf. "holding fast to the tradition"). So too the debates about clean hands, purity, and honouring parents, would all have been grist to any Pharisaic mill. Marcus thus suggests that Mk 7 contains, just below the surface, some of the *Jewish* arguments deployed *against* Jesus and his followers: it is Jesus who is accused of breaking the Law and of threatening family relationships; and the citation of Isa 29,13 may originally have been part of the arsenal of the opponents of Jesus. Mark 7 thus represents an attempt by the Markan Jesus to take up, and reverse, this attack by throwing it back at the opponents and charging them with the same accusations.

For Mark the true nature of evil and defilement comes from the heart and evil thoughts (possible akin to the "evil inclination" of Judaism). The response of the Markan Jesus is similar to Paul in Rom 8,3: God's Law has been unable to accomplish what it promised, because it has been weakened by the flesh; but that purpose is now achieved in and through the person of Jesus.

The paper given by C. BREYTENBACH (Berlin) was on *Das Markusevangelium, Psalm 110,1 und 118,22f. Folgetext und Prätext*. Breytenbach starts by proposing a taxonomy of the phenomenon of the ways in which a later text (a Folgetext) can relate to an earlier one (a Prätext): the former can replace the latter, it can abbreviate, it can expand, or it can simply repeat. And within the last category one can distinguish allusions from quotations. In his paper, Breytenbach chooses two examples of this last category, the explicit citations via repetition of Ps 110,1 in Mk 12,35-37 and Ps 118,22f. in Mk 12,10f.

Repetition of words does not necessarily imply identity of meaning. The relationship between a Prätext and a Folgetext is more complex. Above all, the repetition of words from a Prätext in a Folgetext must be interpreted on the basis of the signals within the Folgetext itself. Thus Breytenbach analyses in his paper the ways in which the two Psalm verses are to be interpreted within the Gospel of Mark. He argues that both are to be interpreted primarily Christologically. The debate in Mk 12,35-37 concerns the nature of Jesus as the Christ, the Jewish Messiah. It is assumed that the Psalm verse refers to the Jewish Messiah, and the question is then how that messiahship is to be understood: whether in terms of Davidic sonship (so the scribes) or in terms of the one who is the exalted and coming *Kyrios* (Mark). The second Psalm considered here (Ps 118) is explicitly cited in Mk 12, but, Breytenbach argues, is also alluded to in Mk 8,31. The citation is to be interpreted primarily in relation to Jesus' own death and resurrection. Any ecclesiological interpretation, or any added allusions to Isa 28,16, is unlikely. Both Psalm verses are now integral parts of the wider Folgetext into which they have been incorporated from the Prätext. Mark takes up the interpretation, widespread in early Christianity, that the verses are to be seen as messianic, and incorporates them into his own narrative Christology developed in his story.

The final essay in this volume on Mark is the paper given by A.Y. COLLINS (Chicago) on *The Appropriation of the Psalms of Individual Lament by Mark*. She places her paper within the broader problem of how far Christian appropriation of OT scripture constitutes an illegitimate misreading of the text. How far is Christian appropriation of Jewish scripture at the same time a disappropriation of the Jews? Collins focuses on the Psalms of individual lament, arguing that these Psalms were frequently read, re-read, and then re-applied, by Jews over the course of time to different situations and appropriated by different individuals or groups. Thus some Qumran texts clearly adopt the language of these Psalms and apply them to the community's present position, or to the Teacher of Righteousness. So too, Collins argues, several of these texts may have been applied to a Jewish eschatological ("messianic") figure. The Gospel of Mark makes extensive use of these Psalms in its account of the suffering of Jesus: the use of these Psalms in Mark's passion narrative is well known; but such Psalms probably also lie behind Mark's diction in Mk 9,11-13 (cf. Ps 22,7) and 3,20-21 (cf. Ps 69,9).

With the Jewish background in mind, Collins claims that Mark cannot be accused of disappropriation in his use of these Psalms. By applying these texts to the experiences of a "messianic" figure such as Jesus, Mark is doing exactly what other Jews of the time also did. "The messianic interpretation of the individual psalms of lament found in the Gospel of Mark is well within the boundaries of acceptable Jewish exegesis, certainly in terms of method and also, generally speaking, with regard to content ... The act of re-reading the psalms in this way was not in itself an act of disappropriation or a violent theft of part of the Jewish heritage" (p. 240). Both Jewish and Christian re-readings of the Psalms are in one way equally legitimate; what is problematic is the ways texts have been used in power struggles in subsequent history.

An approach which some might regard as more genuinely "intertextual" is adopted in the first of the essays on Luke here: P.-M. BOGAERT (Louvain-la-Neuve) on *Luc et les Écritures dans l'évangile de l'enfance à la lumière des Antiquités Bibliques: Histoire sainte et livres saints*. Bogaert here places side by side for comparison Luke's narrative, especially his infancy narratives, on the one hand, and the *Biblical Antiquities* (so-called "Pseudo-Philo") on the other. In relation to the latter, Bogaert focuses on the narrative of the birth of Samuel (1 Sa 1–2), a text where the various textual witnesses (MT, LXX, Qumran) are notoriously divergent. Bogaert discusses all these differences and also the way in which the story is treated by the author of the *Biblical Antiquities*, who seems to show agreement with different versions at different points.

Bogaert then compares the Lukan narrative, and shows a number of similarities between Luke's work and the *Biblical Antiquities*. Both are deeply indebted to scripture, and both share the view that God, in directing the course of human history, gives to special men and women the gift of the Spirit for certain specific tasks and for understanding His will. There are of course also the well-known similarities between Luke's birth narrative and the Samuel story (cf. especially the similarity between the Magnificat and the song of Hannah). Yet despite similarities, there are also differences. Luke does not offer a rewritten version of the birth of a figure of Israel's sacred history such as Samuel: he writes about the birth of a figure of the recent past, Jesus, albeit evoking the Samuel story "typologically". "Luc lit la Bible à la façon de l'auteur des *Ant. Bibl.*, mais sa lecture est orientée, non d'Abraham à David, mais d'Abraham par David à Jésus Sauveur" (p. 270).

The topic of A. DENAUX (Leuven) was *Old Testament Models for the Lukan Travel Narrative*. Denaux here takes up a number of recent suggestions that the basis for Lukan Travel Narrative (here assumed to be 9,51–18,14) lies in the OT. Denaux discusses the various theories of C.F. Evans (Luke is almost a rewriting of the book of Deuteronomy)

D. Moessner (Luke is dominated by the idea of Jesus as the prophet like Moses), W.M. Swartley (on the influence of OT way-conquest traditions), M.L. Strauss (Luke is influenced by Deutero-Isaiah and an idea of a new Exodus of the King Messiah), and E. Mayer (on the influence of the OT motif of the wilderness wanderings). In each case, Denaux argues that, although some correspondence with Luke's travel narrative can be shown, none of the proposals is fully satisfactory as a comprehensive explanation of the Lukan text.

Denaux concludes by saying that Christology is clearly important for Luke, with the idea of Jesus as a Moses-like prophet clearly significant. But perhaps the Christology shifts from a stress on the rejected prophet idea in the first part of the travel narrative to more that of a rejected king in the second half. So too the Mosaic typology is more explicit in Acts than in the gospel. Further, source-critical factors should not be ignored. Whatever the nature and extent of the influence of (parts of) the OT on Luke, the fact remains that the primary model for Luke is the Gospel of Mark. So too any influence of OT ideas and patterns may have been mediated through his sources Mark and Q (cf. the rejected prophet motif in Lk 11,49-51; 13,34f.). Any alleged OT influence on Luke's travel narrative should therefore be regarded with some critical caution.

The focus of the French speaking seminar was the paper by M. MORGEN (Strasbourg), *L'arrière-fond scripturaire des deux apocalypses lucaniennes (Lc 17 et Lc 21)*, in which Luke's references to scripture in the two Lukan "apocalypses" were discussed. In Lk 17, Morgan argues, the focus of attention is the motif of destructive and absolute judgement in the comparisons of the day of the Son of Man with lightning, and with the days of Noah and Lot. But with vv. 25 and 37, Luke draws attention to the true place of revelation of the Son of Man, viz. the passion of Jesus, v. 37 being interpreted as a reference to the body of Jesus: it is here that the real locus of revelation and of salvation are to be found.

In Lk 21, a key element is the question of the time (v. 7). In vv. 8-11 Luke uses the OT allusions (Dan 2,28 in v. 9, Isa 19,2 and 2 Chr 15,6 in v. 10) to develop a different scheme to that of Mark, warning about false interpretations of the *kairos* and implying that all that happens is in accordance with the divine will. In vv. 20-24, Luke is to be aligned with a number of other theological reflections on the devastation of Jerusalem, such as one finds in Jeremiah, the Chronicler and other midrashic literature. These various texts see in the fate of Jerusalem a fulfilment of God's plan whereby the nations become the instruments of divine judgement. In these verses, Luke thus invites the readers to subscribe to such a view in order to understand the present situation.

The German speaking seminar met to discuss the paper of M. THEOBALD (Tübingen), *Schriftzitate im "Lebensbrot"-Dialog Jesu (Joh 6). Ein Paradigma für den Schriftgebrauch des vierten Evangelisten.* The Bread of Life discourse of Jn 6 contains two OT citations: Ps 77,24 LXX is cited in 6,31, and Isa 54,13 in 6,45. Both texts are adapted for their purpose by the evangelist. Theobald argues that the discourse is not to be seen as some kind of midrash or homily on the scriptural text Ps 77,24 LXX (so Borgen), but rather as an exposition of the meaning of the "I am" saying in v. 35. (Hence too the eucharistic section in vv. 51c-58 is somewhat surplus.) The two scriptural quotations in Jn 6 are thus not the primary texts, but are subsidiary to the central saying of v. 35. The citation in v. 31 (from the crowds) is subordinated to Jesus' authoritative counter-statement in v. 32 (cf. "Amen amen I say to you"). Jesus is thus presented here not as an interpreter of scripture, but as the authoritative "Son of God" and "Son of Man".

Further, it is only in the light of Jesus as the one authoritative revealer that scripture can be properly interpreted. Scripture apart from Jesus will lead to misunderstanding. Thus Ps 78,24 is now interpreted Christologically and is no longer to be related to the history of Israel in the wilderness. Similarly the use of Isa 54,13 by John refers only to the time of Jesus. These results are paradigmatic for John's use of scripture elsewhere. Scripture for John is of interest primarily as a written text, not as a witness to the history underlying it; and it is for John a text that can only be interpreted in relation to Jesus.

Two further main papers at the Colloquium were devoted to the Gospel of John. In the first of these, M.J.J. MENKEN (Utrecht) analyzes *The Use of the Septuagint in Three Quotations in John: Jn 10,34; 12,38; 19,24.* In each of these three citations, John cites the version of the LXX exactly. Elsewhere, Menken argues, any deviations by John from the LXX are deliberate; hence, in these three case, he suggests that the LXX text form fits precisely with the use John wishes to make of them.

In Jn 10,34, Ps 81,6 LXX is cited to provide scriptural justification for Jesus' right to be called "Son of God". The background of thought here may be the idea of a special human being taken up into the heavenly court, the scenario presupposed by Ps 81 LXX. If such people can rightly be called "gods", then how much more can Jesus rightly be termed "Son of God". In Jn 12,38, the use of the LXX of Isa 53,1 with the addition of κύριε, enables the words to be taken as an address to God by Jesus. The verse is then to be taken as a reference to Jesus' signs (not his words), and the two parts of the verse should be read as concessive: people did not believe the report about Jesus, *although* the arm of the Lord was revealed to them. Finally, the quotation of Ps 21,19 LXX in Jn 19,24 is used by John in a way that ignores any possible parallelism in the Psalm verse to refer to two separate incidents: the division of Jesus' clothes and casting lots for his tunic. John thus carefully chooses precisely the text he wants for his purposes; moreover, his procedures are fully in line with other exegetical methods which are evidenced in the first century.

The second main paper on John was given by U. BUSSE (Essen) on *"Und sie glaubten der Schrift und dem Wort Jesus" (Joh 2,22). Impliziter Rekurs auf die biblische Tradition im Johannesevangelium.* Busse adopts a rather different approach to that of Menken. Whereas Menken looks at explicit quotations, Busse considers much more implicit use of the scriptural tradition. His primary focus of attention is the Jewish temple and all ideas associated with the temple in Judaism. Busse argues that such ideas are prevalent throughout John's gospel, as John takes up a whole range of motifs and concepts associated with the temple and reapplies them to Jesus and the situation of Jesus' followers in the Christian church. Thus the temple as the dwelling place of God with his people is echoed in the prologue (cf. Jn 1,14); Jesus is the lamb of God (1,29), alluding to the cultic praxis of atonement rites focused on the temple in Jerusalem; so too Jesus as the link between heaven and earth (1,51) takes over the role associated with the temple. Other passages in the gospels, and other concepts associated with the temple, include the locus of true worship (cf. Jn 4), the place of study of the law which replaced the temple after the latter's destruction (cf. Jn 6–7), the image of the vine (Jn 15) etc. Imagery and ideas associated with the temple, Busse argues, are thus absolutely central to John's presentation and ultimately give authority to his theological convictions (cf. Jn 2,22).

The reports on the seminars were given at the final plenary session by J. Verheyden, J.M. van Cangh, J. Kremer and R.L. Brawley respectively.

A total of twenty-seven short papers were read at the Colloquium. Twenty-one are published here in Part II of this volume. Six essays (by Cimosa, Heil, Magne, Poirier, Swancutt and Van Aarde) could not be included here but are all likely to be published elsewhere. A more general methodological discussion is given by M. RESE (Münster), *"Intertextualität" – Ein Beispiel für Sinn und Unsinn "neuer" Methoden.* Papers on the Sayings source Q include: Chr. HEIL (Bamberg), *Die Rezeption von Mi 7,6 in der Logienquelle und im Lukasevangelium*; J. SCHRÖTER (Berlin), *Erwägungen zum Gesetzverständnis in Q anhand von Q 16,16-18*; T.L. BRODIE (Dublin), *Intertextuality and Its Use in Tracing Proto-Luke and Q*; Mark and Q are compared in N. TAYLOR

(Swaziland), *Interpretation of Scripture as an Indicator of Socio-Historical Context. the Case of the Eschatological Sections of Mark and Q.* One paper discusses both Matthew and Luke: G. GEIGER (Wien), *Falsche Zitate bei Matthäus und Lukas.* There were four papers devoted to Matthew's gospel: M. HASITSCHKA (Innsbruck), *Die Verwendung der Schrift in Mt 4,1-11*; Lena LYBAEK (Durham), *Matthew's Use of Hosea 6,6 in the Context of the Sabbath Controversies*; Susan GRAHAM (Sheffield), *A Strange Salvation: Intertextual Allusion in Mt 27,39-43*; A.G. VAN AARDE (Pretoria), *The "Temporal" Function of the Old Testament in the Gospel of Matthew*; three on Mark: J.C. POIRIER (New York), *Two Transfigurations (Mark 8,31–9,10 and Zech 3–4)*; B.J. KOET (Amsterdam), *Mk 12,28-34: Übereinstimmung im Kern der Sache*; J. VERHEYDEN (Leuven), *Describing the Parousia: The Cosmic Phenomena in Mk 13, 24-27*; eight on Luke: G. STEYN (South Africa), *Luke's Use of "Mimesis" as an Ancient Rhetorical Technique*; F. NOËL (Leuven), *The Double Commandment of Love in Lk 10,27. A Deuteronomic Pillar or Lukan Redaction of Mk 12,29-33?*; E. VERHOEF (Hollandsche Rading), *Eternal Life and Following the Commandments. Lev 18,5 and Lk 10,28*; S. VON STEMM (Berlin), *Der betende Sünder vor Gott. Zur Rezeption von Psalm 51(50),19 im griechisch sprechenden Judentum und Urchristentum*; R.L. BRAWLEY (Chicago), *Scripture Resisting the Carnivalesque in the Lucan Passion*; H.A.J. KRUGER (Durban), *A Sword over His Head or in His Hand? (Luke 22,35-38)*; G.P. CARRAS (Berkeley), *A Pentateuchal Echo in Jesus' Prayer on the Cross: Intertextuality between Numbers 15,22-31 and Luke 23,34a*; five on John: M. CIMOSA (Rome), *L'utilisation de la Septante dans l'évangile de Jean*; J. MAGNE (Paris), *Jésus parlant et agissant dans l'Ancien Testament, principalement d'après Jn 5,39-46; 8,14; 8,37-50; 8,56-58; 12,37-41*; Diane Marie SWANCUTT (Durham, NC), *Isaiah Saw His Glory. The Interrelation of Isa 40 and Isa 52–53 in Jn 12,12-50*; G. VAN BELLE (Leuven), *L'accomplissement de la parole de Jésus. La parenthèse de Jn 18,9*; W. KRAUS (Erlangen), *Die Vollendung der Schrift nach Joh 19,28. Überlegungen zum Umgang mit der Schrift im Johannesevangelium.* Two final papers consider the use of Isa 61 and the possible significance of the Qumran text 4Q521: K.-W. NIEBUHR (Dresden), *Die Werke des eschatologischen Freudenboten. 4Q521 und die Jesusüberlieferung*, and P.J. TOMSON (Brussels), *The Core of Jesus' Evangel: Isa 61*, εὐαγγελίσασθαι πτωχοῖς.

The papers given showed a wide range in the understanding of what was meant by the term "intertextuality", though most preferred to retain a historical critical approach and to focus on the author of the New Testament texts concerned, rather than adopt a more radical reader-response approach.

Further, there was a common realisation that our understanding of Jewish scripture at the time of the writing of the New Testament texts is itself undergoing change as new evidence, especially from some of the hitherto unpublished Qumran scrolls, becomes available. (Cf. the frequent reference to the newly available 4Q521 text.) Nevertheless, all were agreed upon the great importance of understanding the potential significance of the background in Jewish scriptures, and the subsequent interpretation of those scriptures by other contemporary writers, for interpreting the New Testament gospels and the traditions they contain.

Christopher M. TUCKETT

MAIN PAPERS

SCRIPTURE AND Q

The first paper which I offered at a Leuven Colloquium was in 1981 on a subject in fact closely related to the general topic of this year's meeting[1]. When originally invited to read a main paper to this meeting, the general topic of "The Scriptures in Q" was provisionally suggested. When subsequently, and to my astonishment, I was very kindly invited to act as President of the Colloquium this year, it seemed appropriate to keep the same general topic, and to pick up some of the threads, together hopefully with a few new ones, of my paper of 15 years ago. Hence I propose to consider some of the ways in which Old Testament scripture, and in particular the book of Isaiah, may be related to the Sayings Source Q.

But first, a very few brief, and rather amateurish, remarks on the sub-title of the subject for our Colloquium: "Intertextuality".

I. INTERTEXTUALITY

"What's in a name?"

"When I use a word, it means just what I choose it to mean – neither more nor less"[2].

The word "intertextuality" has become something of an "in word" for New Testament studies in recent years. In part its usage reflects the ever growing sensitivity of New Testament exegetes to the insights of literary critics and an awareness that New Testament study must learn from, and engage with, the study of texts in other academic disciplines. Yet, just as we have learnt (at times to our cost) that language is never a static entity, and that the meanings of words change over the course of time, so the same may be the case for "in words" such as "intertextuality" which Biblical scholars appropriate from time to time from secular literary criticism. What the word may mean when used in one context may not be the same when used by others in another context.

---

1. *Luke 4, 16-30 Isaiah and Q*, in J. DELOBEL (ed.), *Logia. Les Paroles de Jésus – The Sayings of Jesus* (BETL, 59), Leuven, 1982, pp. 343-354.
2. Humpty Dumpty to Alice in Lewis Carroll's *Alice through the Looking Glass*.

As far as I am aware, the term "intertextuality" was first coined by Julia Kristeva, and has been used by others literary critics since, notably Roland Barthes[3]. The term has also been appropriated by a number of Biblical scholars to describe their work, for example by Richard Hays in his study of allusion to Old Testament scripture in Paul, and by the authors in the Festschrift published in honour of B. van Iersel[4].

In the work of Kristeva and Barthes, however, the term really has little to do with the explicit interpretation of a particular text as such. Rather it refers to the theory that texts in general gain meaning only in relation to a potentially never ending series of other texts. Reacting in part against the view that a text could be an independent and a totally new production by its author, the proponents of an approach of intertextuality would claim that all texts are dependent for their meaning on their place within a matrix of other texts. Part of this is the way in which texts echo, or allude to, earlier texts, either by way of explicit citation, or deliberate allusion, or even by semi-conscious or unconscious echo; but "intertextuality" as defined by Kristeva and Barthes would go wider than this and see the way in which other texts give meaning and significance to a text as potentially far more than this historical, diachronic way (which traditional Biblical scholarship has affirmed ever since the rise of critical Biblical scholarship). Thus intertextuality focuses quite as much on the *reader* as on the author of a text[5]. Jonathan Culler says:

> Intertextuality thus becomes less a name for a work's relation to particular prior texts than a designation of its participation in the discursive space of a culture: the relation between a text and the various languages or signifying practices for a culture and its relation to those texts which articulate for it the possibilities of that culture[6].

---

3. J. KRISTEVA, *Semiotiké*, Paris, 1969; *La révolution du langage poétique*, Paris, 1974; R. BARTHES, *S/Z. Essais*, Paris, 1970. For good summaries, see J. CULLER, *Presupposition and Intertextuality*, in *The Pursuit of Signs. Semiotics, Literature, Deconstruction*, Ithaca, 1981, pp. 100-118; J. STILL & M. WORTON, *Introduction*, in IBID. (eds.), *Intertextuality: Theories and Practices*, Manchester & New York, 1990; A.C. THISELTON, *New Horizons in Hermeneutics*, London, 1992, esp. pp. 495-508.

4. R.B. HAYS, *Echoes of Scripture in the Letters of Paul*, New Haven & London, 1989, cf. esp. pp. 14-21; S. DRAISMA (ed.), *Intertextuality in Biblical Writings. Essays in Honour of Bas van Iersel*, Kampen, 1989.

5. This is strongly emphasised by Thiselton. See too E. VAN WOLDE, *Trendy Intertextuality?*, in DRAISMA (ed.), *Intertextuality* (n. 4), pp. 43-49, on p. 47: "In an intertextual analysis or interpretation of a text it is the reader and not the writer who is the centre of attention, because it is the reader who makes a text interfere with other texts".

6. CULLER, *Presupposition and Intertextuality* (n. 3), p. 103 (also cited in part by HAYS, *Echoes* [n. 4], p. 15).

Nevertheless the twin poles of author and reader can perhaps still be quite legitimately maintained, even in an understanding of intertextuality[7].

Now in fact, as Still and Worman say, "although the term *intertextuality* dates from the 1960s, the phenomenon, in some form, is at least as old as recorded society"[8]. They consider the discussion of, and attitudes to, imitation and novelty in writers such as Plato, Aristotle and other classical authors as well as in more recent figures in the history of literature and literary theory. Certainly in Biblical studies, the idea that older traditions are taken up by later writers within the Biblical tradition is something with which any student of the New Testament is familiar. So too the idea that, as well as explicit citations of earlier traditions, there may be less explicit allusions, and indeed less conscious adoption of earlier "texts", is a familiar one for New Testament studies. The question whether it is then open to a later reader to identify such an allusion and read in a "meaning" that was not originally "intended" by the author, or even to bring in texts originally written after the time of the text in question to illuminate the latter, is more debatable; and certainly some New Testament scholars would argue that, at least in the case of many (if not all) New Testament texts, authorial intention is vitally important[9]. The situation is of course potentially quite different in relation to some products of "literature", "literature" being often taken as rather narrower in scope than the set of all written texts[10]. And even in the case of a narrower range of "literature" (however defined), those who accuse others of being guilty of the "intentional fallacy" should not lose sight of the fact that the original essay concerning this "fallacy" attacked not the principle of whether the original author's intent was discoverable, but only whether this should be the sole criterion for judging "the success of a work of literary art"[11]. In the case

---

7. Cf. STILL & WORMAN, *Intertextuality* (n. 3), p. 1. Speaking about why a text is not a closed system, they write: "First, *the writer* is a reader of texts (in the broadest sense) before s/he is a creator of texts, and therefore the work of art is inevitably shot through with references, quotations and influences of every kind... Secondly, a text is available only through some process of *reading*; what is produced at the moment of reading is due to the cross-fertilisation of the packaged textual material (say, a book) by all the texts which the reader brings to it". Hence they go on to talk about "*both* axes of intertextuality, texts entering via *authors* and texts entering via *readers*" (my italics).

8. *Ibid.*, p. 2.

9. See, for example, J.D.G. DUNN, *Historical Text as Historical Text: Some Basic Hermeneutical Reflections in Relation to the New Testament*, in J. DAVIES, G. HARVEY, W.G.E. WATSON (eds.), *Words Remembered, Texts Renewed. Essays in Honour of John F.A. Sawyer* (JSOTSup, 195), Sheffield, 1995, pp. 340-359.

10. See my *Reading the New Testament*, London, 1987, pp. 175-176.

11. W.K. WIMSATT & M.C. BEARDSLEY, *The Intentional Fallacy*, in *The Verbal Icon. Studies in Meaning*, Lexington, 1954, p. 3.

of New Testament texts, it is dubious how far we should be regarding them as "works of literary art" and seeking to assess their "success" in this capacity. Of course it is open to us to do so; but then we need to raise the question of *genre*, and of whether it is appropriate for us to use the texts in this way (though we could of course make different decisions in relation to different parts of the New Testament)[12].

In fact the way in which "intertextuality" has been appropriated by New Testament scholars has often been at the level of the author of a text and his use of earlier texts and traditions[13]. I am aware that such an approach may be guilty in part of misappropriating the term, or simply "us[ing] intertextuality as a modern literary theoretical coat of veneer over the old comparative approach" in some kind of "trendy intertextuality"[14]. Nevertheless, it may be appropriate to restrict ourselves in this way, at least in relation to the New Testament texts. Despite the attractiveness in many ways and in many contexts of a reader-response approach to the New Testament texts, New Testament scholars generally have wished to focus on the author quite as much as on the reader. Further, for those who would wish to see the New Testament texts as playing a significant role within a broader theological enterprise, this has generally been within a context where the Biblical text has been conceived as something which speaks *to* the reader quite as much as being something which is entirely at the reader's disposal[15]. Whilst aware then of the dangers of being guilty of the charge of misappropriating (and probably misunderstanding!) the word, I intend to relate "intertextuality" in the rest of this paper to the echoes and allusions to scripture one finds in the New Testament at the level of the "authors" concerned, and I propose to focus here on one strand of the gospel tradition, viz. the sayings source Q.

12. The fundamental importance of an understanding of genre for intepretation is universally recognised. Cf. J. BARTON & R. MORGAN, *Biblical Interpretation*, Oxford, 1988, p. 4: "It is important to recognize what kind of a text one is reading and what literary devices are being employed. How we classify it (the literary 'genre') will decide how we read it". The perils of wrongly applying methods and criteria appropriate to "literary" works to other "texts" are neatly summed up by Barton and Morgan in relation to legal, or quasi-legal, codes: "A thousand interpretations of [Shakespeare's play *King*] *Lear* may be enriching, even two of the *Highway Code* disastrous" (p. 12).
13. So, for example, Hays's work on Paul (n. 4 above).
14. See VAN WOLDE, *Trendy Intertextuality?* (n. 5), p. 43.
15. On reader response approaches, see THISELTON, *New Horizons* (n. 3), pp. 546-550; also his *On Models and Methods: A Conversation with Robert Morgan*, in D.J.A. CLINES, S.C. FOWL, S.E. PORTER (eds.), *The Bible in Three Dimensions. Essays in Celebration of Forty Years of Biblical Studies in the University of Sheffield*, Sheffield, 1990, pp. 337-356.

II. SCRIPTURE IN Q

That reference is made to the Old Testament in Q is accepted by all (or at least by all those who hold to some kind of "Q hypothesis"!)[16]. The extent and significance of such reference and allusion is however debated.

The total extent of the Jewish scripture presupposed by Q is almost impossible to determine with any precision. The fact that Q's references to the Old Testament are, for the most part, by way of relatively general allusions, combined with the fact that Q itself is relatively small in size, means that we cannot put precise limits around the body of literature regarded by Q as "scriptural" with any degree of confidence. We know that the limits of the Jewish canon of scripture were still somewhat fluid in the first century CE. We may however just note here the reference in Q 11,51 ("from the blood of Abel to the blood of Zachariah who perished between the altar and the sanctuary")[17], specifying the acts of violence in the past for which the present generation will be held responsible. The time span covered in the reference appears to be a closed one, covering the period from the start of Biblical history (Abel) to the end ("Zachariah" here is usually taken as the prophet whose murder is recounted in 2 Chr 24)[18]. This particular Q saying thus seems to envisage a body of sacred scripture whose limits are fixed chronologically: there is a beginning and there is also a chronological end[19]. There may be, and probably were, debates about the precise limits of the canon; but the presupposition of this Q saying seems to be that the era of "biblical" history is one on which to look back, as a closed era of the past.

If then it is probably reasonably sensible to think of a fairly fixed entity in talking about the "Scripture" in Q, what of the other pole in the title of my paper: what is the "Q" we are talking about in this context?

---

16. There is not enough space here to argue for the existence of "Q". For some attempt to do so, together with discussions of the possible nature of Q (written/oral, single "text"/multiple traditions, Greek/Aramaic), see my *Q and the History of Early Christianity*, Edinburgh, 1996, chs. 1, 3.

17. The Lukan version here is widely regarded as more original, in particular in referring to Zachariah *simpliciter*, and not, as in Matthew, to "Zachariah son of Barachiah". See O.H. STECK, *Israel und das gewaltsame Geschick der Propheten* (WMANT, 23), Neukirchen-Vluyn, 1967, pp. 39-40; also my *The Revival of the Griesbach Hypothesis* (SNTS MS, 44), Cambridge, 1983, pp. 160-161, with further literature. As is now standard, I refer to verses in Q by their Lukan chapter and verse numbers.

18. See previous note.

19. In itself this is not of course a startling result: cf. the similar view implied in Josephus, *c.Ap.* 1.39; also the evident belief of the writer of 1 Maccabees that the era of prophecy was now ended, at least for the present (1 Macc 14,41).

1. *Strata in Q?*

The question is by no means trite, and not only in relation to those who would deny the existence of a Q source completely. Even amongst those who would fully accept some kind of Q hypothesis, i.e. by explaining the Matthew-Luke agreements as due to dependence on a prior source, there is now a widely held belief that this "Q" source underwent a quite complex history of development and growth, so that instead of a simple "Q", we should think of a Q^1, a Q^2, and a Q^3 at least (if not more) as stages in the growth of the document Q. The model proposed by John Kloppenborg has gained widespread support in recent years[20]; but before Kloppenborg's work, there were other related theories, for example in the studies of S. Schulz and A. Polag[21]. Moreover, in many such theories, the apparent use of the Old Testament in Q has sometimes played a significant role in distinguishing between proposed strata in Q. Thus, in Schulz's essentially two-stage division of Q^{22}, one of the criteria proposed for distinguishing between an earlier and a later stratum was the use of the LXX in the latter[23]. In a related way, Polag argues that the relatively few explicit citations of the Old Testament – the three citations in the temptation narrative, and the mixed citation of Mal 3,1 and Exod 23,20 in Q 7,27 – are so unlike the rest of Q, simply by virtue of being explicit citations with an introductory formula, that they must be assigned to a late stage in the development of Q, a postulated "späte Redaktion"[24]. Others have made similar deductions or observations. M. Sato has argued, in a way similar to Polag, that the explicit citations in the temptation narrative and in Q 7,27 are unlike the rest of Q and hence come from a later stage in the redactional history of Q^{25}. So too, A. Jacobson, in his delineation of the development of Q, and in his attempt to assign Q 7,18-23 to a later stage in that developmental history, appeals to the use of the LXX in the allusion in Q 7,22 as one of the criteria for assigning the pericope as a whole to a later stage[26].

20. J.S. KLOPPENBORG, *The Formation of Q*, Philadelphia, 1987.

21. S. SCHULZ, *Q – Die Spruchquelle der Evangelisten*, Zürich, 1971; A. POLAG, *Die Christologie der Logienquelle* (WMANT, 45), Neukirchen-Vluyn, 1977.

22. Schulz proposes also a further stage in the growth of Q (cf. his *Q* [n. 21], pp. 481, 484), though he assigns virtually nothing to it: see my *Q and the History* (n. 16), p. 60; also J.S. KLOPPENBORG, *Tradition and Redaction in the Synoptic Sayings Source*, in *CBQ* 46 (1984) 34-62, on p. 39.

23. SCHULZ, *Q* (n. 21), p. 49.

24. POLAG, *Christologie* (n. 21), p. 9.

25. M. SATO, *Q und Prophetie* (WUNT, 2.29), Tübingen, 1988, pp. 35-6.

26. A.D. JACOBSON, *The First Gospel*, Sonoma, 1992, p. 112.

Slightly different is the approach of Kloppenborg and others influenced by his model for the development of Q. Kloppenborg, as is well known, distinguishes between an early, "sapiential" Q^1, where the exhortations are influenced by wisdom traditions and directed to insiders in the community, and a "prophetic" Q^2, where the polemic is much sharper and the sayings are directed (at least ostensibly) to outsiders. In a further stage in the development of Q, a "Q^3", the temptation narrative is added with its explicit references to scripture, and a few further glosses in the material are added, glosses which emphasize the loyalty of the Q Christians to the Torah and their commitment to Torah observance (Q 11,42d and 16,17)[27]. Although the existence or otherwise of Old Testament allusions was not an explicit part of Kloppenborg's argument distinguishing between "Q^1" and "Q^2"[28], Kloppenborg has subsequently pointed out that his Q^1 contains virtually no reference to the Old Testament; virtually all the Old Testament allusions come in the material assigned to the later Q^2 stage, and this is used by Kloppenborg as part of his evidence to construct a social history of the Q community[29]. Burton Mack's theories are similar: the explicit appropriation of Israel's "epic history" is a feature of a later stage in the history of the Q people, reflecting a change in their situation where opposition from the Jewish establishment became more explicit and overt[30].

Such general theories and/or criteria are however not compelling. With regard to the proposed stratification of Q into separable and identifiable stages in the history of Q, I remain unconvinced that our extant evidence (the texts of two subsequent "readers"/users of Q, viz. Matthew and Luke) is really sufficient for us to be able to make such confident proposals. Undoubtedly, the Q tradition represents the end-point of what may well have been quite a complex history of the development of the tradition. However, whether we can be so confident about tracing the precise stages

27. For the latter, see especially KLOPPENBORG, *Nomos and Ethos in Q*, in J.E. GOEHRING *et al.* (eds.), *Gospel Origins and Christian Beginnings*, FS J.M. Robinson, Sonoma, 1990, pp. 35-48.

28. Though it becomes virtually so in the case of "Q^3". (Although Kloppenborg does not use the nomenclature of "Q^1", "Q^2", and "Q^3" in his seminal book, it has now become widely used, and, as far as I am aware, Kloppenborg himself has no objection to using such terminology. I use it here therefore simply for the sake of convenience.)

29. Cf. his *Literary Convention, Self-Evidence and the Social History of the Q People*, in *Semeia* 55 (1991) 77-102, on p. 84; also his Introduction in KLOPPENBORG (ed.), *Conflict and Invention. Literary, Rhetorical and Social Studies on the Sayings Gospel Q*, Valley Forge, 1995, p. 9.

30. B. MACK, *The Lost Gospel*, San Francisco, 1993, p. 132 and also the whole chapter there on "Singing a Dirge". Cf. too W. COTTER, *"Yes, I Tell You, and More Than A Prophet". The Function of John in Q*, in KLOPPENBORG (ed.), *Conflict*, pp. 135-150, on pp. 135-136.

in that development by isolating specific stages in the formation of the document Q (i.e. in a Q^1, Q^2 and Q^3) seems to me much more dubious, as I have sought to argue elsewhere[31]. We may well be able to isolate earlier and later stages within single traditions, or perhaps within individual pericopes; but that is quite a different matter from claiming that earlier stages of some, but not all, of these individual traditions were collected together in an earlier, written form of the "document" we now call "Q". Hence I have argued that we should preserve the siglum "Q" for the "final" form of the tradition, i.e. the latest stage of any tradition common to Matthew and Luke[32]. Earlier stages of Q traditions undoubtedly existed; but precisely how and where they existed is much harder to say.

With this in mind, it seems to me problematic to make a clear qualitative distinction between a "Q^1" and a "Q^2", or indeed "Q^3", in relation to any use of the Old Testament. It is true that there are some parts of Q that are more polemical, other parts that are less polemical; and a large part of the more overt allusions to the Old Testament in Q occurs in the context of the polemic mounted by Q, usually against other Jews. But whether we can simply equate these parts with two separate, and chronologically distinct, strata in Q seems to me more doubtful. In fact, some parts of Q which refer to the Old Testament may well be earlier rather than later. I have argued elsewhere that the explicit citation in Q 7,27 (of Mal 3,1 and Exod 23,20) represents an earlier, not a later, stage in the growth of the whole unit in Q 7,18-35[33]. Indeed v. 27 may well be the earliest conclusion to the unit in vv. 24-26. Verse 28 would then be a secondary comment, glossing v. 27 and perhaps implying some critique of John. But any such critique is then totally overshadowed by the section in vv. 31-35 where John and Jesus appear in parallel alongside each other, as messengers of Wisdom in a hostile environment[34]. It is clear that, in literary terms, vv. 31-35 form the climax of the unit in vv. 18-35 as a whole, and as such probably reflect the view of the (final) Q editor. Thus

---

31. See my *On the Stratification of Q*, in *Semeia* 55 (1991) 213-222; also my *Q and the History* (n. 16), pp. 70-74.

32. See my *Q and the History* (n. 16), pp. 75-82.

33. See my *Mark and Q*, in C. FOCANT (ed.), *The Synoptic Gospels* (BETL, 110), Leuven, 1993, pp. 149-175, on p. 165. Others have pointed out that the form of the OT cited here is not that of the LXX: cf. K. STENDAHL, *The School of St Matthew and Its Use of the Old Testament*, Philadelphia, 1968, p. 51; D.S. NEW, *Old Testament Quotations in the Synoptic Gospels and the Two-Document Hypothesis* (SBL Septuagint and Cognate Studies Series, 37), Atlanta, 1993, pp. 60-63. *If* conformity to the LXX is a sign of a later date, then the form of this citation would suggest that it is earlier, not later, in the tradition history of Q. (It is though a big "if": cf. below!)

34. *Mark and Q* (n. 33), pp. 165-166.

the explicit appeal to the Old Testament in v.27 is not a feature of a late stage in Q, but of an earlier, pre-redactional stage[35].

Other appeals to scripture in Q are not necessarily confined to later strands of the material. In part such a claim must depend on other decisions about the contents of Q. But if, for example, one accepts that Q may have contained a version of the double love command (Matt 22,34-40 // Luke 10,25-28), as I have argued elsewhere[36], then this is a further instance of an explicit reference to scripture in Q, with no clear indication that it is to be assigned to a later, rather than an earlier, stage in Q[37]. Nor is the concern about Torah observance clearly the concern only of a later "Q[3]" editor (cf. above), as I have tried to show elsewhere[38]. We shall see later that large parts of the inaugural sermon in Q (Q 6,20-49), usually assigned to "Q[1]" by those who opt for such theories, are significantly influenced by Old Testament allusions and echoes.

The alleged use of the LXX as a criterion for distinguishing between earlier and later elements of Q is also not entirely convincing. In the first place, one must remember that Q was probably a Greek text: the close verbal agreement between the Greek texts of Matthew and Luke is at times so close that a Greek *Vorlage*, not just an Aramaic original, seems to be presupposed[39]. Use of a Greek version of the Old Testament would thus not be strange in a Greek text such as Q. One must however also note that any evidence for a specifically Septuagintal version of the Old Testament as used by Q is extremely thin. Schulz's claim about the Septuagintal nature of the Old Testament allusions in Q was searchingly examined by Paul Hoffmann in his extensive and very detailed review of Schulz's book[40]. Hoffmann showed clearly that in virtually the instances

---

35. For Kloppenborg, any such elements here are not part of Q[1]: the whole of Q 7,18-35 is taken as Q[2], though Kloppenborg readily grants that the Q[2] material is not all unitary.

36. In *Q and the History* (n. 16), pp. 416-418; cf. the contrasting views of J. LAMBRECHT, *The Great Commandment Pericope and Q*, in R.A. PIPER (ed.), *The Gospel and the Gospels. Current Studies on Q* (NTSup, 75), Leiden, 1995, pp. 73-96, and F. NEIRYNCK, *The Minor Agreements and Q*, in PIPER (ed.), *The Gospel and the Gospels*, pp. 49-72, esp. pp. 61-64.

37. Unless of course the reference to the fact that the lawyer is "testing" Jesus (one of the Matthew-Luke agreements here which is part of the evidence for suggesting the possible existence of a Q version) implies that this is part of the more "polemical" parts of Q, i.e. "Q[2]". The passage is not included by Kloppenborg in his discussion and therefore not assigned to one particular stratum.

38. Cf. *Q and the History* (n. 16), pp. 404-424; also my *Q, the Law and Judaism*, in B. LINDARS (ed.), *Law and Religion. Essays on the Place of the Law in Israel and Early Christianity*, Cambridge, 1988, pp. 90-101.

39. See KLOPPENBORG, *Formation* (n. 20), pp. 51-64; also my *Q and the History* (n. 16), pp. 83-92.

40. In *BZ* 19 (1975) 104-115, esp. pp. 108-9.

where Q seems to allude to the Old Testament, an allusion to the LXX version could adequately explain the evidence; but equally, the text of the LXX is as often as not indistinguishable from that of the Hebrew MT at the relevant points: hence one cannot claim with any degree of certainty that the allusion was to the LXX and not to the MT.

The one exception often cited is the phenomenon of the three explicit citations in the temptation narrative. I have however examined these in detail elsewhere and sought to show that any alleged LXX influence is at best marginal[41]. Q 4,12 agrees with the LXX against the MT in having a second person singular ἐκπειράσεις for the MT's plural תנסו, though the context (Jesus speaking to a singular Devil) really demands such a difference. The other allegedly clear LXX features are the use of προσκυνήσεις in Q 4,8 (MT תירא) and the addition of μόνῳ here. But in both cases, the Q version agrees with at most one or two LXX manu-scripts[42], and the reading cannot be regarded as peculiarly Septuagintal. Apart from these, the LXX and MT agree with each other so that it is impossible to distinguish between dependence on one as opposed to the other.

We should of course also remember the fluid state of the Old Testament text at this period, shown above all by the evidence of the Qumran texts. Allegedly Septuagintal readings have now been shown to occur in Hebrew MSS of this period, so that we certainly cannot make a neat, over-schematic division between "Hebrew/MT = Palestinian = early", and "Greek/LXX = non-Palestinian = late". Nor should we forget the obvious facts about the complexity of the history of "the" so-called LXX. Perhaps New Testament scholars are guilty of perpetuating a caricature whereby Jews of the ancient world are divided into two totally distinct, and never-overlapping groups, one speaking Greek and carrying (printed?!) copies of Rahlfs' LXX under their arms, the other speaking Aramaic and carrying copies of Kittel's *Biblia Hebraica*, and whenever they refer to scripture, they open up their versions of the Bible at the relevant point and cite with deadly accuracy. Clearly such a model is a total caricature, but one wonders if sometimes sómething not far removed is presupposed when New Testament scholars start to discuss the question of the version of the text presupposed by a first century writer or speaker. The fact

---

41. See my *The Temptation Narrative in Q*, in F. VAN SEGBROECK, C.M. TUCKETT, J. VERHEYDEN, G. VAN BELLE (eds.), *The Four Gospels 1992*, FS F. Neirynck (BETL, 100), Leuven, 1992, pp. 479-507, on p. 484.

42. προσκυνήσεις agrees with codex A, μόνῳ with A and P[963]. See my *Temptation Narrative* (n. 41), p. 484; also NEW, *Old Testament Quotations* (n. 33), pp. 58-59.

that an odd element or two in Q's reference to the Old Testament agrees with what is regarded by later scholars as "the" LXX version, which might differ from "the" MT, should not be allowed to become the basis for too far-reaching theories regarding the geographical provenance or the relative date of the tradition in question[43].

2. Texts and "Contexts"

In referring to, or citing, Old Testament texts, how far were New Testament writers aware of the broader context from which the text cited was taken? The question is a very wide-ranging one, and one to which very diverse answers have been given. Thus, for example, C.H. Dodd argued that New Testament writers were aware of the broader contexts and indeed expected their readers to be equally aware[44]; others have argued that the New Testament's use of the Old Testament was far more atomistic[45].

The question is however posed in far too black-and-white terms when put in this way. One probably cannot make a blanket simple decision of either yes or no covering all cases of all New Testament writers' reference to all Old Testament texts to which allusion is made. One writer may differ from another. A reference to a text at one point by a writer may be different from a reference to another text at another point by the same writer. So too we can, and probably should, distinguish between writers and readers, and indeed between readers and readers. Some broader allusions may have been intended by a writer, and may have been picked up by some readers but not others; sometimes such broader allusions may have provided some readers with a "bonus" for those "with ears to hear", even though the text can still make good and adequate sense for those who miss the broader allusion[46].

43. Cf. H. MAHNKE, *Die Versuchungsgeschichte im Rahmen der synoptischen Evangelien* (BEvT, 9), Franfurt, 1978, p. 186, who claims that the existence of LXX influence on the temptation narrative implies that the latter could not have belonged to the "original" Sayings Source. See my *Temptation Narrative* (n. 41), p. 481.

44. C.H. DODD, *According to the Scriptures: The Sub-Structure of New Testament Theology*, London, 1952.

45. Cf. M.J. SUGGS, *On Testimonies*, in *NovT* 3 (1959) 268-281. See the discussion by I.H. MARSHALL, *An Assessment of Recent Developments*, in D.A. CARSON, H.G.M. WILLIAMSON (eds.), *It Is Written: Scripture Citing Scripture*, FS Barnabas Lindars SSF, Cambridge, 1988, pp. 7-8.

46. Cf. R.T. FRANCE, *The Formula Quotations of Matthew 2 and the Problem of Communication*, in *NTS* 27 (1981) 252-281, on the quotations in Matt 2.

Further, the nature of the "broader context" may need further definition. Clearly any allusion to scripture as scripture assumes the broader context of a collection of writings having some religious authority for the person using it. Other "contexts" can be narrower: an allusion to one verse of Isa 53 could be intended to evoke the whole of the chapter in which it is embedded in the present form of the book. But can we or should we limit ourselves to this chapter (perhaps considered within the relatively narrow compass of the four so-called "servant songs" which modern scholarship has claimed to isolate)? Or should we also see it as part of the whole context of the prophecies now collected under the name of "Isaiah"? Perhaps too we need to take account of the fact that some texts, or contexts, were already interpreted in other interpretative schemes in the first century, schemes which involved other literary contexts brought in to illuminate and develop ideas in the texts being cited or alluded to. Some of this I hope to show in the case of Q.

But first it may be worth referring to one instance where any wider context of two Old Testament quotations is apparently notably absent from view. I refer to the use of Ps 91,11.12 (LXX 90,11.12), quoted by the Devil in the scene in the temptation narrative in Q 4,10-11. What is so striking about this is the fact that we have here two adjacent verses of the Psalm cited: Ps 91,11 is cited in Q 4,10, Ps 91,12 in Q 4,11. However, both Matthew's version and Luke's version separate the two with an extra καί. (Luke has an additional ὅτι, almost certainly a ὅτι *recitativum*)[47]. Almost certainly therefore Q separated the two verses with a καί, perhaps even with the καὶ ὅτι of Luke. It would appear that Q was not aware that the two verses were in fact directly connected in the original of Ps 91. Rather, it looks as if the verses were assumed to be isolated verses, brought together here and connected with an extra καί[48]. The person who adduced this quotation thus seems to have been unaware of any broader literary context from which these two verses were taken.

Such a theory is however difficult, if not impossible, to show elsewhere. Indeed any negative theory asserting ignorance of a wider context will inevitably be harder to defend than a theory claiming knowledge of such wider context: ingenious theories claiming such knowledge

---

47. See J.A. FITZMYER, *The Gospel according to Luke I-IX* (AB, 28), Garden City NY, 1981, p. 517.

48. I find this more convincing than the claim that the καί shows awareness of what is left *out* from the end of Ps 91,10, as is assumed by a number of commentators: cf. I.H. MARSHALL, *The Gospel of Luke*, Exeter, 1978, p. 173, following T. HOLTZ, *Untersuchungen über die alttestamentlichen Zitate bei Lukas* (TU, 104), Berlin, 1968, pp. 57-58; also W.D. DAVIES & D.C. ALLISON, *The Gospel according to Saint Matthew I*, Edinburgh, 1988, p. 366.

can always be developed, with varying degrees of plausibility; but absence of knowledge or intention is very difficult, if not impossible, to establish.

In one set of cases, however, some such wider knowledge is really demanded and essential. I refer to the use of names. As we have already noted, much of Q's reference to the Old Testament is at the level of fairly general allusions and indirect references rather than direct explicit citations. And sometimes the reference consists of a name together with a brief reference to the wider context. Thus when Q 11,51 says that this generation will be responsible for all the blood shed "from the blood of Abel to the blood of Zachariah", some knowledge by the reader is presumed of the story of the murder of Abel in Gen 4, and (probably) of the murder of the prophet Zechariah in 2 Chr 24[49]. Similarly, references to Solomon (Q 11,31; 12,27), Jonah (Q 11,30. 32), Tyre and Sidon (Q 10,13-14), or Noah (Q 17,26) all demand some awareness of the context in which these names are mentioned in the Old Testament[50]. In these cases, the claims of an approach of intertextuality are self-evident: the language of the Q text requires a network of other texts for its meaning to be understood.

3. *Isaiah 53 and Related Texts*

In the case of proper names such as Noah or Solomon, such an intertextual approach is both appropriate and necessary. With other terms the issue is heavily debated. I refer, for example, to the self-reference by Q's Jesus to himself (at least for Q!) as "Son of Man". I would argue that the use of the phrase in Q (as indeed in the finished gospels of Matthew, Mark and Luke) is a reference to the phrase in Dan 7,13: the "Son of Man" description is deliberately intended to evoke the Danielic scene by focusing on the theme of vindication and triumph, and also that of suffering and obedience (though I am fully aware that such an overall theory is heavily disputed!)[51].

I have further argued elsewhere that the Q sayings about the Son of Man show a number of important links with other texts, some of which relate to Dan 7, some of which do not, at least directly. In particular, as Nickelsburg has convincingly argued, there is evidenced in Judaism a

---

49. See nn. 17, 18 above.
50. Though some of course are notoriously ambiguous: cf. the reference to Jonah in Q 11,30!
51. See *Q and the History* (n. 16), ch. 8.

developing tradition whereby the servant song of Isa 52,13–53 has been taken up and developed in texts such as 1 En 62 and Wisd 2–5. Here the righteous man/men is/are persecuted by human figures, the Isaianic poem being reinterpreted so that those who are aghast and amazed at the new appearance of the once despised figure (cf. Isa 52,13) are now the active persecutors whose opposition has led to the figure's temporary demise; however, in a *post-mortem* scene, the erstwhile persecutors are confronted by their one time victim(s) and are then condemned[52]. Indeed Isa 53 may have partly influenced the language of Daniel itself (though more likely Dan 12,3 rather than Dan 7 itself)[53]. As I have tried to argue elsewhere, the Q Son of Man sayings may show a similar set of ideas. The reference to Isa 53 is mostly left behind (though see below), but some basic ideas remain common to the complex of Son of Man sayings in Q and the traditions reflected in 1 En 62 and Wisd 2-5: as a suffering and persecuted figure (cf Q 7,34; 9,58), the Q Son of Man will be vindicated and will be an active agent in the final judgement (cf. Q 12,8; 17,26-30).

In the course of his discussion, Nickelsburg notes in passing that both 1 Enoch and Wisdom may use the language of the fall of the king of Babylon in Isa 14 to refer to the downfall of the persecutors[54]. It is perhaps a further striking coincidence of ideas and language that Q too uses the language of the fall of the king of Babylon in Isa 14: in Q 10,15 the woes against the Galilean cities are concluded with the tirade against Capernaum in language that is clearly intended to echo the taunt song of Isa 14 ("And you Capernaum, will you be exalted to heaven? You will be brought down to Hades": cf. Isa 14,13.15). The allusion is so close as to qualify almost for the description "quotation", though there is no explicit introductory formula[55]. The wording of Q is similar to that of the LXX of Isa 14, though there is little difference between the LXX and the MT here. Schulz refers to the use of καταβήσῃ here[56], and the absence

52. See G.W.E. NICKELSBURG, *Resurrection, Immortality and Eternal Life in Intertestamental Judaism*, London, 1972, pp. 62-78; also my *Q and the History* (n. 16), pp. 271-272.
53. Cf. *Q and the History* (n. 16), p. 271, for details
54. NICKELSBURG, *Resurrection* (n. 52), p. 69 (cf. Wisd 4,18f.), p. 75 (cf. 1 En 46,6f). For the Wisdom parallel, cf. too P. SKEHAN, *Isaias and the Teaching of the Book of Wisdom*, in *CBQ* 2 (1940) 289-299, on p. 296.
55. For discussion of what might count as a "quotation", cf. C.D. STANLEY, *Paul and the Language of Scripture. Citation Technique in the Pauline Epistles and Contemporary Literature* (SNTS MS, 74), Cambridge, 1992, pp. 33-37. However, this text is not discussed by NEW, *Old Testament Quotations* (n. 33).
56. The variant reading καταβιβασθήσῃ in Luke is probably due to assimilation to the form of the ὑψωθήσῃ at the start of the saying: cf. A.H. MCNEILE, *The Gospel according to St Matthew*, London, 1915, p. 161; R.H. GUNDRY, *The Use of the Old Testament in St. Matthew's Gospel* (NTSup, 18), Leiden, 1967, p. 81; J.A. FITZMYER, *The Gospel according to Luke X-XXIV* (AB, 28A), New York, 1985, p. 855.

of any article with ᾅδου as evidence of Septuagintal influence[57], but this seems very weak evidence. Stendahl's comment is probably more accurate when he refers to this as "another example of biblical allusion in apocalyptic language without the exact nature of a citation and without definite indications of influence from either the LXX or the M.T."[58].

However, one notable feature of Q's diction remains unexplained. This is the use of ὑψωθήσῃ (common to Matthew and Luke and hence secure as the Q wording). This agrees neither with the LXX's ἀναβαίνω, nor with the MT's אעלה, which correspond closely to each other. In fact the LXX never uses ὑψόω for עלה, though ἀναβαίνω is very frequently used as the translation equivalent. It has been argued that ὑψόω has come into the Q wording under the influence of the next clause in Isa 14,13 ("I will exalt [ארים] my throne above the stars of God")[59], but this seems improbable since there is no other evidence of influence of this clause in Q. Although there are always dangers of over-interpreting, and misreading in non-existent allusions, it is possible that the use of ὑψωθήσῃ here could be evoking the language of the fourth servant song in Isa 52,13 (LXX ὑψωθήσεται)[60].

If this parallel were accepted, it might go some way to explaining one or two odd features of the verse. The first half of the verse is couched in the form of a question expecting the answer no (cf. μή)[61]. Why though the town of Capernaum would ever have thought that it could or should exalt itself to heaven has always been a puzzle to commentators. Davies & Allison mention as possibilities Jesus' exalting Capernaum by his presence, or a reference to Capernaum's geographical situation, its prosperity, or its pride[62]. Yet none of these is easy to see evidenced here or really very satisfactory as an explanation for the language used[63]. Perhaps though, with the allusion to Isa 52,13, the passage is easier to interpret. The force

57. SCHULZ, Q (n. 21), p. 363.

58. STENDAHL, School (n. 33), p. 91. Cf. too HOFFMANN, Review (n. 39), p. 109: "...ohne daß LXX- oder MT-Einfluß unterschieden werden können".

59. So GUNDRY, Use of the Old Testament (n. 56), p. 81.

60. I realise that some might regard this as somewhat speculative, especially since ὑψόω is not that uncommon in the LXX, and a closer parallel might be thought to be in Ezek 28,5 or 31,14. On the other hand, practitioners of an "intertextual" approach would need little justification for adopting such an interpretative approach to this text in Q!

61. The variant reading ἡ... ὑψωθεῖσα may be due to one of two consecutive μ's dropping out accidentally: cf. MARSHALL, Luke (n. 48), p. 425; FITZMYER, Luke X-XXIV (n. 56), pp. 854-855.

62. W.D. DAVIES & D.C. ALLISON, The Gospel according to Saint Matthew II, Edinburgh, 1991, pp. 268-269.

63. Cf. U. LUZ, Das Evangelium nach Matthäus (Mt 8-17) (EKK, 1/2), Zürich & Neukirchen-Vluyn, 1990, p. 194.

of the saying may not be to highlight a particular sin of arrogance as such on the part of Capernaum; rather, the question expresses negative astonishment at the implied claim that Capernaum, *rather than someone else*, should be exalted. This is probably also the force of the emphatic σύ (again present in both Matthew and Luke and hence probably in Q). The question is thus "Do you think that *you* will be exalted?" The hidden unexpressed item is then not so much "you will not be *exalted* but brought low", but rather, "*you* will not be exalted, because that is the destiny of another person". By implication it is Jesus as the figure of the servant song who will be exalted; and Capernaum, which has done nothing to respond positively to Jesus, will be brought down to Hades[64].

If this "allusion" is accepted, then it may have some significance within the slightly wider literary context in Q. The woes against the Galilean cities in Q 10,13-15 come at the end of the mission charge in Q 10,2-12 + 16; that mission charge is probably preceded in Q by the sayings in Q 9,57-60. Preeminent in the latter is the Son of Man saying in Q 9,58. Indeed many would see here a piece of deliberate editing by the Q compiler: the Son of Man who has nowhere or lay his head acts as a paradigm for the follower of Jesus who will also experience similar rejection and (possibly) homelessness[65]. If then it is right to see the designation "Son of Man" as reflecting both the immediate literary context of Dan 7 and also the wider interpretative context of a broader interpretation and development of the Isaianic servant song as evidenced (probably independently) in 1 En 62-63 and Wisd 2-5[66], then the reference in Q to Jesus as "Son of Man" at the start of the unit comprising Q 9,57–10,16 and the possible implicit allusion to Isa 52,13 at the end of the unit may form a significant *inclusio*.

The Son of Man sayings in Q are, as I have tried to show elsewhere, closely connected with themes of suffering, and also with the related themes of Wisdom, or rather rejected Wisdom, and prophecy, since it is a highly characteristic feature of Q to refer to Wisdom sending the prophets, all of whom suffer violence and persecution[67]. Certainly these two themes – of Wisdom, and of the prophets suffering violence – occur separately or together on several occasions, and there is often in the

64. Luz, *ibid*. For the critical significance in Q of failing to respond to Jesus, cf. my *Q and the History* (n. 16), pp. 284-296.

65. See my *Q and the History* (n. 16), pp. 180-183. I am fully aware that the statement above begs a large number of exegetical questions!

66. 1 Enoch uses Son of Man language, Wisdom does not.

67. See *Q and the History* (n. 16), ch. 6; Steck, *Israel* (n. 17). For the combination of the theme of the violence suffered by the prophets and Wisdom as the agent who sends out such prophets as a characteristic and distinctive feature of the Q tradition, see my *Revival* (n. 17), pp. 164-6.

same context a reference to Jesus as Son of Man. Q 9,58 itself is probably an example of Wisdom motifs (the saying is redolent of the "myth" of Wisdom seeking a home and finding none, as e.g. in 1 En 42), and it may be significant that the Q saying is couched in the form of a Son of Man saying. Similarly, the final beatitude in Q (Q 6,22-23) refers to the violence suffered by the prophets, and is coupled again with a reference to the Son of Man[68].

It is then perhaps not surprising to find further parallels in these Q contexts to the complex of texts relating to the interpretative development of the Isaianic servant song which we can see now perhaps in Daniel itself, in 1 Enoch and in Wisd 2–5. In particular, there is a notable cluster of such parallels in the language of the beatitudes and perhaps also the corresponding woes, if indeed these did belong to Q, as a number of scholars have argued[69]. For example, the maltreatment which followers of Jesus can expect, as spelt out in the final beatitude, is differently worded in Matthew and Luke; however, one word which they share in common, and which therefore was almost certainly present in Q, is ὀνειδίσωσιν ("revile"). The diction is similar to that of Wisd 5,4 and the words of the one-time persecutors of the righteous man who look back to what they did, saying "This is the man whom we once held in derision, and made a byword of reproach" (παραβολὴν ὀνειδισμοῦ)[70]. One may also note in this context the persecutors' belated realisation that being "rich" has brought them no profit at all (Wisd 5,8: "What good has our boasted wealth brought us?"), and their (also belated) realisation of the folly of their "laughter" or "derision" (cf. 5,4 cited above: "whom we held in derision [εἰς γέλωτα]"). The language is close to that of the Lukan woes which pronounce doom on the "rich" (Luke 6,24) and on "those who laugh now" (Luke 6,25)[71]. The language of the beatitude and the

68. The Lukan wording here ("for the sake of Son of Man") is widely regarded as more original than Matthew's parallel ("for the sake of me"). See *Q and the History* (n. 16), p. 180, with further references.

69. See my *The Beatitudes: A Source-Critical Study*, in *NT* 25 (1983) 193-207, on p. 199; also H. SCHÜRMANN, *Das Lukasevangelium. Erster Teil* (HTKNT, 3/1), Freiburg, 1969, pp. 339-40; D.R. CATCHPOLE, *The Quest for Q*, Edinburgh, 1993, pp. 87-90.

70. In turn this echoes their earlier claims that the righteous man has "reproached" them for their transgressions of the Law: cf. Wisd 2,12.

71. The reference to laughter here in Luke seems to have been misunderstood by Luke himself, and brought back into his version of the corresponding beatitude; but "laughing" is almost certainly regarded negatively, as scornful and disreputable activity. Luke perhaps is unaware of this, but the slight mismatch here confirms both the secondary wording of Luke's version of the beatitude in Lk 6,21 and also possibly the presence of the woe in a pre-Lukan tradition, possibly Q. Hence part of the force of the argument that the woes are probably pre-Lukan and may have been present in Q. See my *Beatitudes* (n. 69), pp. 197-198.

woes thus shows a close affinity with that of Wisd 5 in relation to the suffering of the righteous in the present and the actions and behaviour of "opponents". The language is not so close as to suggest a direct quotation necessarily of the text of Wisdom itself by Q (or by the author of the Lukan woes, if not Q). Nevertheless, the verbal echoes and links may reinforce the theory that, in the Q context dealing with the suffering of the followers of Jesus at the hands of (or in contrast to the fate of) others and in the description in Wisd 2–5, we have a common network of ideas and Old Testament texts reflected[72].

So too, we may note in this connection the reference to Q Christians as being "sons" of God (the "Most High" in Luke, "your Father" in Matthew) in Q 6,35, and the similar implication in Q 6,36 with the reference to "your Father". These are clearly similar to the claim of the righteous sufferer of Wisdom to be a/the son of God, echoed in Wisd 2,18; 5,5.

4. Isaiah 61 and Q[73]

Now the beatitudes in Q are influenced not only by the complex of texts associated with "Son of Man" and Isa 53. Behind the first beatitudes in Q almost certainly lies the programmatic text of Isa 61,1-2. The wording of the first two Q beatitudes is probably heavily aligned to the wording of Isa 61,1-2, as I have tried to argue elsewhere, especially the wording of the second beatitude on the mourners in Matt 5,4, which is very close to the language of Isa 61,2 (LXX παρακαλέσαι πάντας τοὺς πενθοῦντας) and where the Matthean form of the beatitude probably reflects the Q wording rather than being due to MattR[74].

Certainly too a relation between Isa 61,1-2 and the Son of Man complex of ideas is not confined in Q to their collocation in the beatitudes. The unit in Q 7,18-23, and perhaps 7,18-35, shows an even closer link.

---

72. It is perhaps surprising that none of these parallels is noted by P. DOBLE, *The Paradox of Salvation. Luke's Theology of the Cross* (SNTS MS, 87), Cambridge, 1996, despite his general theory that allusions to the book of Wisdom, and in particular the idea of Jesus as the righteous sufferer of Wisd 2–5, permeate Luke's writings in a very wide-ranging way. (The verbal parallels with Wisdom are all in Luke's gospel, even if, as I have argued here, they are in Q as well.)

73. A very similar general topic forms the basis of the essay of F. Neirynck in this volume, there with rather different conclusions. The present essay was written before I was aware of Neirynck's discussion. I have not attempted to alter it substantively, or to engage directly with Neirynck's argument: readers may however be interested to compare the two approaches offered here.

74. See my *Beatitudes* (n. 69), pp. 197-199.

The question put to Jesus by (the messengers of) John the Baptist is "Are you ὁ ἐρχόμενος?" (v. 20). For Q the "one who is to come" is almost certainly Jesus in his role as Son of Man[75], and hence the question of v. 20 is not unrelated to the end of the Q unit where we have explicitly a reference to Jesus as Son of Man (Q 7,34)[76]. However, in Q the immediate response to the question of John the Baptist by Q's Jesus comes in v. 22: "The blind receive their sight, the lame walk, the lepers are cleansed, the deaf hear, the dead are raised, and the poor are evangelised". Here we have, by common consent, a series of clauses that (at least in part: see below) reflect Isaianic passages, notably Isa 29,18; 35,5-6, and climaxing in the final clause which alludes to Isa 61,1 with its claim that the poor are being evangelised. Thus the question of whether Jesus is truly "the coming one" is answered in part by the implied assertion that he is the one fulfilling the prophecy of Isa 61. The significance of Isa 61 for Q is increasingly recognised[77], and such a theory would of course be considerably enhanced if it could be established that the rejection scene at Nazareth in Lk 4,16-30, with its explicit citation of Isa 61,1-2, also emanates, at least in part, from Q. I have proposed such a view, and sought to defend it again against recent criticism[78], though I will not discuss the issue explicitly here. Suffice it to say that at at least two other points in Q, both of which have considerable significance in the literary structure of Q as a whole, the language of Isa 61 is used to inform and delineate the teaching of Jesus (Q 6,20-21) and his own interpretation of his work (Q 7,22).

Now as with Dan 7 and Isa 53, Isa 61 itself is not a text existing in isolation. It has its own intertextual links in relation to prior texts (it may, for example, have been regarded as of a piece with the "servant songs" elsewhere in the "book" of Isaiah). So too the verse probably takes up of the ideas and the language of the jubilee[79]. Yet it is also now

75. See CATCHPOLE, *Quest* (n. 69), p. 78.
76. Cf. *ibid*, p. 239.
77. See J.M. ROBINSON, *The Sayings Gospel Q*, in VAN SEGBROECK et al. (eds.) *The Four Gospels 1992* (n. 40), pp. 361-388, on the importance of πτωχοί and εὐαγγελίζομαι in the framing of (at least the first part of) Q; also CATCHPOLE, *Quest* (n. 69), pp. 86-88 (at least on the beatitudes, as well as the programmatic significance of the beatitudes themselves for the rest of Q).
78. Cf. n. 1 and also my *Q and the History* (n. 16), pp. 226-237.
79. See R.B. SLOAN, *The Favorable Year of the Lord. A Study of Jubilary Theology in the Gospel of Luke*, Austin, 1977, pp. 36-7; B.J. KOET, *Five Studies on Interpretation of Scripture in Luke-Acts* (SNTA, 14), Leuven, 1989, p. 31; C.J. SCHRECK, *The Nazareth Pericope. Luke 4,16-30 in Recent Study*, in F. NEIRYNCK (ed.), *L'Évangile de Luc. The Gospel of Luke* (BETL, 32), revised and enlarged edition, Leuven, 1989, pp. 399-471, on p. 450, with further literature.

clear that Isa 61 became a generative text for other later texts, especially in Judaism. In particular, this has become clear from some of the Qumran scrolls. The 11QMelch text has been known for some time, and the influence of Isa 61 on that text is well recognised, as well as its possible relevance for the study of texts such as Lk 4,18-19[80]. Isa 61 is also clearly important in another Qumran text which has only been published relatively recently, viz. 4Q521 "On Resurrection"[81]. This new text, sadly fragmentary, may offer some insight and background to some of the Q passages we have been considering.

The most substantial fragment of 4Q521 appears to have a reference to a "Messiah" figure in the first line ("the heavens and the earth will obey his Messiah"), before going on to describe some of the blessings which will come to God's faithful followers. (It is however notoriously uncertain and unclear who is the intended subject of the actions involved in bringing such blessings: is it God? Or is it an agent, a "messianic" figure?) One of the arresting features of the fragment is that there is an allusion (universally recognised) to Isa 61,1 at one point. Line 12 of the main fragment reads "He will heal the wounded, give life to the dead and preach good news to the poor". The allusion in the last phrase to Isa 61,1 is clear. What is also striking is the similarity of the text to Q 7,22: both texts juxtapose an allusion to Isa 61,1 with a reference to giving life to the dead, and this has been noted by a number of scholars[82].

However, perhaps just as noteworthy is the influence of another Old Testament text in the fragment, viz. Ps 146. J.J.Collins says that "in lines 1-8, this passage is heavily dependent on Psalm 146"[83], though the dependence is clearly one of intertextual allusions and interweaving of language, not of formal explicit quotation. The opening line's reference to "heaven and earth... [and all that] is in them" recalls Ps 146,6[84]; and

---

80. See M. DE JONGE & A.S. VAN DER WOUDE, *11Q Melchizedek and the New Testament*, in *NTS* 12 (1966) 301-326; M.P. MILLER, *The Function of Isa 61:1-2 in 11Q Melchizedek*, in *JBL* 88 (1969) 467-469.

81. See É. PUECH, *Une apocalypse messianique (4Q521)*, in *RQ* 15 (1992) 475-519; also in R. EISENMAN & M. WISE, *The Dead Sea Scrolls Uncovered*, Shaftesbury & Rockport, 1992), pp. 19-23 (though with some controversial readings and interpretations!).

82. See PUECH, *Apocalypse* (n. 81), p. 493 (with many other parallels as well); J.D. TABOR & M.O. WISE, *4Q521 'On Resurrection' and the Synoptic Gospel Tradition: A Preliminary Study*, in *JSP* 10 (1992) 149-162, on pp. 157-162; J.J. COLLINS, *The Works of the Messiah*, in *DSD* 1 (1994) 98-112, on pp. 106-107.

83. COLLINS, *Works* (n. 82), p. 2. Cf. too TABOR & WISE, *4Q521* (n. 82), p. 151: "This Psalm [Ps 146)] was very influential on the author's thinking".

84. Though in part this is a reconstruction whose precise wording depends on the presumed allusion! The argument, as so often, is in danger of becoming circular.

line 8 of the fragment ("releasing captives, giving sight to the blind, and raising up those who are bo[wed down]") is virtually a verbatim quotation of Ps 146,8[85]. It seems then that the eschatological promise of good news for the poor has been heavily interpreted by reference to the promises articulated in Ps 146. Or, more probably, it is the other way round: in 4Q521, Ps 146 has been taken up and its promises extended via Isa 61,1 to refer to the eschatological blessings of the future.

The parallel between 4Q521 and Q 7,22 has already been noted. Collins argues persuasively that what may be in mind both in line 12 of 4Q521 and elsewhere in the text is a belief in an Elijah-type prophetic figure, "raising the dead" as Elijah did: hence what is in view is above all a prophetic messianic figure after the pattern of Elijah, a fact which he believes throws important light on the gospel tradition[86]. The parallel is certainly important, though the suggestion that Q 7,22 has in mind a prophetic figure similar to Elijah in the reference to raising the dead is not new[87]. Further, it is clear that an Elijah typology is not the only such parallel in mind in Q 7,22: the reference to "cleansing lepers" is equally hard to deduce from the Isaianic prophecies of Isa 29, 35 or 61, and may derive from significance seen in the parallel between Jesus' activity and that of the prophet Elisha (cf. 2 Kings 4)[88]. Hence, whilst in no sense denying the powerful prophetic thrust of the passage, the typology may be rather broader than Collins suggests[89].

The use of Isa 61 in 4Q521 may also throw light on the other main reference in Q to Isa 61, viz. the opening beatitudes in Q 6,20-21. Such an allusion is denied by some, partly because of the lack of clear reference to Isa 61 in the first beatitude apart from the common use of the word

85. Only the explicit subject of the divine name is lacking. Cf. PUECH, *Apocalypse* (n. 81), p. 490: "citation presque littérale de *Ps* 146,7b-8a-b, avec omission de YHWH à chaque stique mais le sujet 'DNY, 1.5, est son équivalent et son *ersatz*".

86. He even suggests that Q may have known 4Q521: "It is quite possible that the author of the Sayings Source knew 4Q521; at the least he drew on a common tradition". (*Works* [n. 82], p. 107). It is however not at all certain who the subject of the verb in line 12 of the fragment really is. Cf. above, and also the discussion by F. Neirynck in this volume (p. 000).

87. Cf. my *Luke 4,16-30* (n. 1), p. 353.

88. *Ibid.*; also MARSHALL, *Luke* (n. 48), p. 292; P. HOFFMANN, *Studien zur Theologie der Logienquelle* (NTAbh, 8), Münster, 1971, p. 209.

89. The fact though that the two clauses in Q 7,22 which are hard to parallel from the general Isaianic prophecies show Jesus to be similar specifically to the prophets Elijah and Elisha provides a remarkable parallel to the situation in Lk 4,25-27 where again Jesus refers to his own mission and claims precedent from the examples of Elijah and Elisha. This might suggest a common traditio-historical origin for the two passages and hence strengthen the argument for Lk 4,16-30 stemming, at least in part, from Q. See my *Luke 4, 16-30* (n. 1), p. 353.

"poor"[90]. It may be however that the way in which Isa 61 is used in 4Q521 may throw a little more light here. *If* Isa 61 were being interpreted alongside, and with, Ps 146, then perhaps this broader tradition of these two texts taken together may illuminate the Q beatitudes a little more. For example, the third Q beatitude (on the hungry being fed) can relate to Isa 61 alone at best only somewhat tangentially and indirectly[91]. However, the conjunction with Ps 146 provides a closer parallel here: in Ps 146,7, the verse just before that quoted in the virtual citation in line 8 of the most extensive extant fragment of 4Q521, there is the promise that as well as "releasing prisoners"[92], the Lord "gives food to the hungry". Thus the exegetical tradition evidenced in 4Q521, linking Ps 146 with Isa 61, may also be reflected in the Q beatitudes which speak of the blessings of the new age for the poor and the hungry as well as those who mourn.

Indeed it may be that the beatitude form itself in Q 6 owes something to Ps 146. Although the beatitude form is by no means unique to these two contexts, it is present in Ps 146,5 ("Happy is the man who has the God of Jacob for himself": MT אַשְׁרֵי, LXX μακάριος)[93]. And the reference to the "Kingdom of God" as the "reward" promised to the poor in the first

---

90. Cf. most recently F. NEIRYNCK, *Q: From Source to Gospel*, in *ETL* 71 (1995) 421-430, on p. 426: "The Q Beatitudes show no cogent evidence of contacts with Isa 61,1-2", citing Frankemölle: "Wer wollte einen Bezug zur messianischen Prophezeiung in Jes 61,1f einzig und allein durch das Wort 'die Armen' als erwiesen ansehen?" (H. FRANKEMÖLLE, *Evangelium – Begriff und Gattung: Ein Forschungsbericht*, Stuttgart, 1994, p. 146). However, see above for the wording of the second beatitude in Matt 5,4, with its clear intertextual echo of Isa 61,2, as reflecting the Q wording more accurately.

91. Cf. Isa 61,5-6: "Strangers shall stand and feed your flocks,... You will eat the wealth of the nations". The parallel is explicitly drawn by K. KOCH, *Was ist Formgeschichte?*, Neukirchen, 1967, p. 52; also A. FINKEL, *Jesus' Sermon at Nazareth*, in *Abraham unser Vater*, FS O. Michel, Leiden, 1963, p. 113. Others claim more generally that the three groups of the poor, the mourners and the hungry are in reality a single group to whom the promise of Isa 61 is addressed (cf. SCHÜRMANN, *Lukasevangelium* (n. 69), p. 327; J. DUPONT, *Les Béatitudes II*, Paris, 1969, p. 13; CATCHPOLE, *Quest* (n. 69), p. 86). However, the difficulty of finding an exact parallel to the "hungry" in Isa 61 is highlighted by G. STRECKER, *Die Makarismen der Bergpredigt*, in *NTS* 17 (1971) 255-275, on p. 261 n. 7; cf. too DAVIES & ALLISON, *Matthew I* (n. 48), pp. 437-438, who print all the possible parallels between the beatitudes and Isa 61 (including Matt 5,6 as parallel to Isa 61,6), but say that the "most persuasive" parallels concern only vv. 3, 4 and 5 in Matthew: "the rest of the allusions or parallels are hardly striking and should be considered fortuitous".

92. אֲסוּרִים in Ps 146,7 provides a verbal link with Isa 61,1, in particular with the difficult Hebrew phrase there פְּקַח קוֹחַ וְלַאֲסוּרִים. *If* this Stichwort link was in any way instrumental in linking the two texts, it must have been in Hebrew, not via any Greek version such as the LXX.

93. Cf. CATCHPOLE, *Quest* (n. 69), p. 87 n. 25: "...Ps 146:5, which is particularly close to the trio of Q beatitudes" (though with no reference to the existence of 4Q521).

beatitude is not so far removed from the language of the final verse of Ps 146 which says that the "the Lord will reign for ever" (LXX βασιλεύσει κύριος εἰς τὸν αἰῶνα). The language and form of the Q beatitudes may thus be significantly influenced not just by Isa 61 but also by an exegetical tradition in which Isa 61 and Ps 146 had already been allowed to influence and interpret each other.

Whether the complex of texts can find further echo in Q is not certain and would certainly repay further study. In the next section of the Great Sermon in Q, it may be that at least some of the exhortations echo allusively the two complexes I have tried to isolate here. Thus Catchpole has pointed to the way in which the exhortation to lend freely in Q 6,30[94] may well be heavily influenced by the Isa 61 allusion: insofar as Isa 61 itself is proclaiming "release", it is taking up ideas associated with that of the sabbath year and/or the jubilee, and hence focusing on the demand in that legislation for an end to the imposition of debts[95]. So too the immediately preceding exhortation to turn the other cheek *may* be an echo of part of the language about the servant in Isaiah: the use of ῥαπίζειν in Q 6,29[96] recalls the ῥαπίσματα of Isa 50,6; and the command στρέψον[97] is similar to the ἀπέστρεψα of Isa 50,6[98]. So too, as already noted, the "reward" for those who follow the way laid down by Q's Jesus is that they will be "sons" of God (Q 6,35), as is implied in Wisd 2,18; 5,5.

At a broader level, we may also note the way in which the whole section on love of enemies in Q 6,31-35 has been deeply influenced by the command to love one's neighbour as oneself (Lev 19,18), as Catchpole has shown[99]. What seems to be presupposed is a community consciousness, an awareness of an "us/them" mentality, where those outside the community are assumed to be Gentiles (Matt 5,47)[100]. The exhortation of the section

94. Taking the Matthean wording as more original: Luke may betray knowledge of the Q wording here by his reminiscence in Lk 6,34. See SCHÜRMANN, *Lukasevangelium* (n. 69), pp. 345-7; also my *Q and the History* (n. 16), p. 302, with further references.

95. See CATCHPOLE, *Quest* (n. 69), p. 113.

96. Luke's τύπτω is probably secondary here: cf. SCHULZ, *Q* (n. 21), p. 122; CATCHPOLE, *Quest* (n. 69), p. 110, with further details regarding statistics and preferred usage by the evangelists: ῥαπίζειν occurs only here and in Matt 26,67 (cf. ῥάπισμα in Mk 14,65); τύπτω (2-1-4+5) is adequately explicable as LkR on the basis of word statistics. This is also the decision of the International Q Project: see M.C. MORELAND & J.M. ROBINSON, *The International Q Project: Work Sessions 6-8 August, 18-19 November 1993*, in *JBL* 113 (1994) 495-499, on p. 497.

97. Again Luke's πάρεχε is probably secondary: see SCHULZ, *ibid*; also *International Q Project* (n. 95), *ibid*.

98. Cf. CATCHPOLE, *Quest* (n. 69), p. 110.

99. *Ibid*, p. 115.

100. Matthew's reference to "Gentiles" here is almost universally regarded as more original than the more general "sinners" of Lk 6,33.

are then dominated by the three ideas of love (cf. 6,27), the neighbour (6,32-35) and one's self (6,31). Although not directly related to the texts from Isaiah discussed earlier, the passage in Q shows again the vital importance of scripture as the driving force behind its ethical teaching and the powerful Israel/covenant awareness that is constantly presupposed. So too, the implied exhortations to have regard to the Mosaic Law are not just a feature of an odd verse or two to be consigned to a small and insignificant "Q^3" layer.

III. Conclusion

Enough has hopefully been said to show that allusions to scripture go deeper and further in Q than has sometimes been allowed. Certainly, if any of the suggestions in the last section of this paper are accepted, they indicate that references to the Old Testament are present in an alleged Q^1 layer quite as much as in any Q^2 stratum[101]. But the way in which different sets of allusions are interrelated here, and moreover seem to straddle any of the proposed stratifications of the Q material, may suggest that the Q material is both more unified, and more scripturally oriented, than some in the past have allowed. There may be relatively few explicit quotations of scripture in Q with introductory formulae. But a sensitivity to the possibility of slightly more allusive intertextual echoes should make us aware that scripture is far more fundamental in Q than first impressions might imply; and such influence pervades the Q material across any alleged boundaries between different possible strata.

Theology Faculty Centre   Christopher M. Tuckett
41 St Giles
Oxford OX1 3LW

---

101. Virtually all of the Great Sermon is assigned by Kloppenborg to the earlier stratum in Q.

Q 6,20b-21; 7,22 AND ISAIAH 61

When, in 1994, I submitted to our president-elect the title of my lecture, *Scriptural Quotations and Interrelationship of the Gospels*, my choice was influenced by reading a dissertation entitled *Old Testament Quotations in the Synoptic Gospels, and the Two-Document Hypothesis*, written by David S. New and published in the SBL series "Septuagint and Cognate Studies" (1993)[1]. This study was limited to the explicit Old Testament quotations, and the examination of their appearance and of their text-type led the author to conclude that (I summarize) the pattern of the quotations in the Synoptic Gospels favours the two-document hypothesis and offers "embarrassing" difficulties for advocates of the Griesbach theory. The priority of Mark versus originality of Matthew remains of course the basic question of interrelationship of the Gospels, though one can hardly say that it constitutes the central discussion in present-day gospel studies. D. New's treatment also includes quotations in Q material (Mt 4,4.6.7.10 / Lk 4,4.10-11.12.8; Mt 11,10 / Lk 7,27)[2], and it is fair to say, I think, that the second source Q is one of the Gospel issues which now appear to inspire NT scholarship more particularly. In recent years, there is an extraordinary proliferation of studies on Q[3]. In the programme of lectures and seminars at our Colloquium on Scriptures in the (Four) Gospels there was no explicit reference to Q[4], and it struck me that the article "Old Testament in the Gospels" in a Dictionary of the Gospels treats Jesus, Mk, Mt, Lk, Jn, but has nothing on Q[5]. Therefore,

---

1. D.S. New, *Old Testament Quotations in the Synoptic Gospels, and the Two-Document Hypothesis* (Septuagint and Cognate Studies, 37), Atlanta, GA, Scholars Press, 1993. Doctoral dissertation at McMaster University, under S.R. Westerholm, 1990. See my review in *ETL* 70 (1994) 167-168.

2. *Ibid.*, pp. 54-64.

3. It can suffice, for the moment, to refer to one of the latest published volumes on Q: C.M. Tuckett, *Q and the History of Early Christianity: Studies on Q*, Edinburgh, Clark, 1996. See now also the first volume of *The Database of the International Q Project* (Documenta Q), *Q 11:2b-4*, by S. Carruth, A. Garsky, and S.D. Anderson, Leuven, Peeters, 1996; cf. my review in *ETL* 72 (1996) 418-424.

4. I refer here to the programme as it was announced in December 1995 with unspecified mention of the "Presidential Address". In fact, at the Colloquium, C.M. Tuckett's opening paper was devoted to "Scripture and Q" (in this volume, pp. 3-26) and Q texts were treated in offered papers by T.L. Brodie, M. Hasitschka, C. Heil, and J. Schröter.

5. C.A. Evans, *Old Testament in the Gospels*, in J.B. Green – S. McKnight (eds.), *Dictionary of Jesus and the Gospels*, Downers Grove, IL – Leicester, Intervarsity, 1992, pp. 579-590. The quotations in Q 4,1-13; 7,27; 10,15; 12,53; 13,27.35 are mentioned (with reference to Mt) in the section on "Jesus' Use of the OT" (pp. 579-583).

I decided to concentrate in this last lecture on scriptural quotations in Q
(or, as some would now prefer to call it, the Sayings Gospel Q).

I begin with a preliminary observation on the extent of Q[6]. I think we
can exclude from Q triple-tradition texts such as the quotation of Isa 40,3
in Lk 3,4 / Mt 3,3 (par. Mk 1,2-3)[7], and the quotation of Deut 6,5; Lev
19,18 in the pericope of the great commandment (Lk 10,27 / Mt 22,37.39,
par. Mk 12,30.31 and 33)[8], and also the Lukan Sondergut in Lk 4,18-19[9].
As a provisional list of quotations and allusions (*) in Q[10] I refer to the
"quotations" printed in italics in the N-A text at Lk 4,4.8.10-11.12;
7,22*.27; 12,53*; 13,19*.27*.35[c]; and in addition four phrases in Lk
10,15; 13,29.35[a]; 17,27, marked in N (= H) but now printed in normal
type in N-A (1979[26], 1993[27])[11]. Apart from a few minor differences else-

6. Cf. *Recent Developments in the Study of Q* (1982), in *Evangelica II: 1982-1991*
(BETL, 99), Leuven, 1991, esp. pp. 415-419; *Q-Synopsis* (SNTA, 13), Leuven, [2]1995.
7. *The First Synoptic Pericope: The Appearance of John the Baptist?*, in *ETL* 72
(1996) 41-74.
8. *Luke 10:25-28: A Foreign Body in Luke?*, in S.E. PORTER – P. JOYCE – D.E.
ORTON (eds.), *Crossing the Boundaries. Essays in Biblical Interpretation*. FS M.D. Goulder (Biblical Interpretation Series, 8), Leiden, Brill, 1994, pp. 149-165; *The Minor Agreements and Lk 10,25-28*, in *ETL* 71 (1995) 151-160. See also in this volume, F. NOËL, *The
Double Command of Love in Lk 10,27*, pp. 559-570. Contrast C.M. TUCKETT, *Q and the
History* (n. 3), pp. 416-418 (cf. *Revival*, 1983, pp. 125-133: Mk and Q two forms of this
pericope in the tradition).
9. On this case, see C.J. SCHRECK, *The Nazareth Pericope: Luke 4,16-30 in Recent
Study*, in F. NEIRYNCK (ed.), *L'évangile de Luc – The Gospel of Luke* (BETL, 32),
Leuven, [2]1989, pp. 399-471, esp. 414-417: "Tuckett's Proposal: Q" (cf. below, n. 17). R.
Hodgson includes Lk 4,18-19 (and 6,27c-28a; 9,61; 17,32 as well) in his list of twenty-
two OT citations and allusions. Cf. R. HODGSON, *On the* Gattung *of Q: A Dialogue with
James M. Robinson*, in *Bib* 66 (1985) 73-95, esp. pp. 77-85 ("Q and the Old Testament").
10. On quotations in Q, cf. S. SCHULZ, *Q: Die Spruchquelle der Evangelisten*, Zürich,
Theologischer Verlag, 1972, pp. 27-28 ("Die Septuaginta-Benutzung"), with references
to P. Wernle (1899), S.E. Johnson (1943), K. Stendahl (1954). See also A.W. ARGYLE,
The Accounts of the Temptations of Jesus in Relation to the Q Hypothesis, in *ExpT* 64
(1952-53) 382; ID., *Scriptural Quotations in Q Material*, in *ExpT* 65 (1953-54) 285-286;
H.T. FLEDDERMANN, *Mark and Q* (BETL, 122), Leuven, 1995, p. 27 n. 10 (and my comment: p. 269 nn. 26-30). – For a full discussion of OT quotations and allusions in Q see
now J. SCHLOSSER, *L'utilisation des Écritures dans la source Q*, in *L'Évangile exploré*.
Mélanges offerts à Simon Légasse (LD, 166), Paris, Cerf, 1966, pp. 126-146.
11. "Allusions" (here marked *) are printed in normal type in GNT[3.4]. For a list of
OT allusions on the basis of N-A, see J.J. O'ROURKE, *Possible Uses of the Old Testament in the Gospels: An Overview*, in C.A. EVANS – W.R. STEGNER, *The Gospels and
the Scriptures of Israel* (JSNT SS, 104), Sheffield, Academic, 1994, pp. 15-25; C.A.
KIMBALL, *Jesus' Exposition of the Old Testament in Luke's Gospel* (JSNT SS, 94),
Sheffield, Academic, 1994, pp. 204-205 (quotations in Lk), 206-212 (allusions in Lk).
For a more complete (over-complete?) list of "Biblische Zitate, Anspielungen und
Motive im Matthäusevangelium", see H. FRANKEMÖLLE, *Die matthäische Kirche
als Gemeinschaft des Glaubens*, in R. KAMPLING – T. SÖDING (eds.), *Ekklesiologie
des Neuen Testaments*. FS K. Kertelge, Freiburg, Herder, 1996, pp. 85-132, esp. 127-
132. The following verses with Q-material can be selected from his list: Mt 3,11;

where[12], there seems to be some confusion in the presentation of Q 7,22: in Mt 11,5 and in Lk κωφοὶ ἀκούουσιν and νεκροὶ ἐγείρονται are now printed in italics, but πτωχοὶ εὐαγγελίζονται is printed in normal type, and such is the case also with οἱ πτωχοί in Mt 5,3 and Lk 6,20 and πενθοῦντες, παρακληθήσονται in Mt 5,4 (diff. Lk 6,21b), in contrast to N (= H)[13].

I

It cannot be a surprise that I start with the first three Beatitudes (Q 6,20b.21a.b). Here in Leuven, and elsewhere, we are all familiar with Jacques Dupont's essential studies on this topic[14] and with his special emphasis on the significance of Isa 61. Those who were not acquainted with Dupont's work are now reminded of it by the *DBS* article on the Sermon on the Mount[15] and by numerous references in H.D. Betz's massive commentary[16]. Most recently, C.M. Tuckett's book on Q has a section on "Isa 61 and Q", in which he recapitulates and updates the two

4,2.3.4.5.6.7.8.10.11; 5,3.4.6.11.12.18.39.42.44.48; 6,9.10.11.12.13.19.20.22.23.26.27.28. 29.33; 7,1.7.8.12.20.21.22.23.24.25.27; 8,11.12.20.21; 9,38; 10,8.10-11.15.16.19.30.32. 35.37; 11,3.5.10.11.17.19.21.22.23.25.27; 12,39.40.41.42; 13,32.33; 18,12.15; 19,28; 22,3.4; 23,12.13.34.36.38.39; 24,28.37.38. For allusions to OT figures in Q, see D. Lührmann, *Die Redaktion der Logienquelle* (WMANT, 33), Neukirchen, Neukirchener, 1969, p. 98. See now also J. Schlosser (n. 10), pp. 127-132.

12. Words printed in normal type in N: Lk 4,8 μόνῳ, 7,27 σου[2]; but 12,53 ἐπὶ (ante πατρί).

13. With the exception of οἱ πτωχοί in Lk 6,20 (normal type in H).

14. J. Dupont, *Les Béatitudes*, first edition, Bruges, 1954; new edition in three volumes: I. *Le problème littéraire*, 1958; II. *La Bonne Nouvelle*, 1969; III. *Les évangélistes* (Études Bibliques), Paris, Gabalda, 1973. Cf. *Introduction aux Béatitudes*, in *NRT* 108 (1976) 97-108. See also Id., *L'ambassade de Jean-Baptiste (Matthieu 11,2-6; Luc 7,18-23)*, in *NRT* 83 (1961) 805-821, 943-959; *Jésus annonce la bonne nouvelle aux pauvres*, in *Evangelizare pauperibus. Atti della XXIV Settimana biblica*, Brescia, Paideia, 1978, pp. 127-189; = Id., *Études sur les évangiles synoptiques* (BETL, 70-A), Leuven, 1985, pp. 23-85.

15. M. Dumais, *Sermon sur la montagne*, in *DBS* fasc. 68-69 (1993-1994) 699-938, esp. cc. 776-817 ("Les Béatitudes"). Cf. c. 778: "Parmi tous ceux qui ont écrit sur le sujet, l'exégète belge J. Dupont demeure le maître par excellence... De nombreux commentateurs des béatitudes puisent largement dans ces études de J. Dupont". Dumais's article now appeared in a revised format: *Le Sermon sur la montagne. État de la recherche, interprétation, bibliographie*, Paris, Letouzey et Ané, 1995, 331 p.

16. H.D. Betz, *The Sermon on the Mount* (Hermeneia), Minneapolis, MN, Fortress, 1995, pp. 91-153 (Mt 5,3-12), 571-589 (Lk 6,20b-26). See the references to J. Dupont (mostly vol. III) in the section on Mt: nn. 135, 147, 154, 169, 174, 178, 179, 207, 209, 271, 273, 286, 289, 290, 292, 293, 294, 298, 304, 311, 331, 332, 334, 360, 402, 403, 406, 426, 440, 446, 453, 496, 498, 514; less frequent, and only to vol. I, in the section on Lk (nn. 6, 55, 118).

Contrast H. Frankemölle, *Die Makarismen (Mt 5,1-12; Lk 6,20-23): Motive und Umfang der redaktionellen Komposition*, in *BZ* 15 (1971) 52-75; cf. Dupont's reaction: "l'information... est exclusivement limitée aux publications de langue allemande; un pareil isolationnisme interdit évidemment toute discussion scientifique sérieuse" (*Béatitudes* III, p. 41 n. 2; but on Frankemölle's view on the evangelist's redaction, see p. 13 n. 1: "foncière-

papers on this topic he delivered in the early 1980's[17]. The clause
πτωχοὶ εὐαγγελίζονται is at the centre of J.M. Robinson's attempt to
justify the designation "Gospel" in the text of Q itself[18]. I wrote a short
reply[19], calling for a more cautious reading of Q 7,22; a too short statement, which needs further elaboration.

Q 6,20b-21

J. Dupont[20]

[3]μακάριοι οἱ πτωχοί,
  ὅτι αὐτῶν ἐστιν ἡ βασιλεία τοῦ θεοῦ[22].
[4]μακάριοι οἱ πενθοῦντες,
  ὅτι αὐτοὶ παρακληθήσονται.
[6]μακάριοι οἱ πεινῶντες (καὶ διψῶντες)[22],
  ὅτι αὐτοὶ χορτασθήσονται.

H. Schürmann[21]

[20b]μακάριοι οἱ πτωχοί,
  ὅτι ὑμῶν* ἐστιν ἡ βασιλεία τοῦ θεοῦ.
[21a]μακάριοι οἱ πεινῶντες,
  ὅτι χορτασθήσεσθε.
[21b]μακάριοι οἱ κλαίοντες,
  ὅτι γελάσετε.

ment saine"; p. 308 n. 5: "quelques remarques justes"). For a discussion of the Beatitudes
in constant dialogue with "dem Autor des dreibändigen Werkes über die Seligpreisungen"
(p. 18), see I. BROER, *Die Seligpreisungen der Bergpredigt. Studien zu ihrer Überlieferung
und Interpretation* (BBB, 61), Königstein/Ts.–Bonn, Hanstein, 1986. For an earlier survey
of studies "published since Dupont's magisterial work appeared", cf. N.J. McELENEY, *The
Beatitudes of the Sermon on the Mount/Plain*, in *CBQ* 43 (1981) 1-13; with critique of con-
jectural reconstructions by G. Schwarz, D. Flusser, and S. Lachs (pp. 6, 8, 11).

17. C.M. TUCKETT, *Q and the History* (n. 3), pp. 221-237: "Isa 61 and Q" (Q 7,22;
6,20-21; Lk 4,16ff.). Cf. *The Beatitudes: A Source-Critical Study*, in *NT* 25 (1983) 193-
207 (with "A Reply" by M. Goulder, pp. 207-216), a paper read at the SNTS Seminar on
the Synoptic Problem (Toronto, 1980); *Luke 4,16-30, Isaiah and Q*, in J. DELOBEL (ed.),
Logia. Les paroles de Jésus – The Sayings of Jesus (BETL, 59), Leuven, 1982, pp. 343-
354 (paper read at the Colloquium Biblicum Lovaniense, 1981). Cf. below, n. 79. See
now his *Scripture and Q* in this volume, pp. 3-26, esp. 20-26 ("Isaiah 61 and Q").

18. J.M. ROBINSON, *The Sayings Gospel Q*, in *The Four Gospels 1992*. FS F. Neirynck
(BETL, 100), Leuven, 1992, pp. 361-388, esp. 368-372; *The Incipit of the Sayings Gospel
Q*, in *RHPR* 75 (1995) 9-33, esp. pp. 31-33.

19. Cf. *Q: From Source to Gospel*, in *ETL* 71 (1995) 421-430, pp. 425-427.

20. *Béatitudes* I, p. 343 (= 1954, p. 127). Compare (without καὶ διψῶντες): A. HAR-
NACK, 1907, p. 89; K. KOCH, *Was ist Formgeschichte?*, Neukirchen, Neukirchener, 1964,
p. 247 (cf. pp. 46-47); J. SCHLOSSER, *Le règne de Dieu dans les dits de Jésus* (Études
Bibliques), Paris, Gabalda, 1980, II, pp. 423-450 ("La béatitude des pauvres [Lc 6,20 par.
Mt 5,3]"), esp. 425-430; D.R. CATCHPOLE, *The Quest for Q*, Edinburgh, Clark, 1993,
pp. 81-94 ("The Beatitudes and Woes. Q 6:20b-23,24-26"), here 86; *et al.* Cf. M.
DUMAIS, *Sermon* (n. 16), p. 784: "le texte de base des béatitudes dans la source Q… à
partir de la reconstruction proposée par J. Dupont et reprise presque textuellement par
J. Lambrecht" (but see below, n. 51).

21. H. SCHÜRMANN, *Die Warnung des Lukas vor der Falschlehre in der "Predigt am
Berge" Lk 6,20-49*, in *BZ* 10 (1966) 59-81, esp. pp. 74-78 ("Lk 6,20-26"); = *Traditionsgeschichtliche Untersuchungen zu den synoptischen Evangelien*, Düsseldorf, Patmos, 1968,
pp. 290-309, esp. 303-307; *Das Lukasevangelium* I (HTK, 3/1), Freiburg, Herder, 1969,
pp. 325-341, esp. 329-330. Lk's ὑμετέρα "hat vielleicht ein ὑμῶν verdrängt" (p. 329
n. 24). The second person (= Q) is possibly not the original form and then the change to the
third person in Mt would be "eine Wiederherstellung des Ursprünglichen" (p. 328).

22. Τῶν οὐρανῶν (1954, p. 80); cf. I, pp. 209-210: "question ouverte". Καὶ
διψῶντες: "Pas de raison suffisante pour écarter les 'assoiffés'" (I, p. 223); G.

With regard to the original three beatitudes, J. Dupont and H. Schürmann represent two different types of reconstruction of the Q text: in the
third person (*Aussage*) for Dupont and in the second person (*Anrede*) for
Schürmann. Dupont's Matthean type of reconstruction has Mt 5,4 in the
order of Mt as the second beatitude and in the wording of Mt: πενθοῦντες and παρακληθήσονται. Schürmann has the Lukan type of reconstruction: Lk 6,21b as the third beatitude and in the vocabulary of Lk:
κλαίοντες and γελάσετε. This is now also the IQP text, printed here in
contrast to A. Polag's compromise (Polag has Mt's third person but the
Lukan order; and, in the third beatitude, Mt's παρακληθήσονται but
Lk's κλαίοντες):

A. Polag[23]

μακάριοι οἱ πτωχοί,
  ὅτι αὐτῶν ἐστιν ἡ βασιλεία τοῦ θεοῦ.
μακάριοι οἱ πεινῶντες νῦν,
  ὅτι χορτασθήσονται.
μακάριοι οἱ κλαίοντες νῦν,
  ὅτι παρακληθήσονται.

IQP (1992)[24]

20b μακάριοι οἱ πτωχοί,
  ὅτι ⟦ὑμετέρα⟧ ἐστιν ἡ βασιλεία τοῦ θεοῦ.
21a μακάριοι οἱ πεινῶντες,
  ὅτι χορτασθήσεσθε.
21b μακάριοι οἱ ⟦κλαί⟧οντες,
  ὅτι γελάσετε.

There is almost a consensus on the Lukan addition of the adverb νῦν in
6,21a.b (but see Polag), on the substitution of τῶν οὐρανῶν (for τοῦ
θεοῦ) in Mt 5,3 and the Matthean additions τῷ πνεύματι in v. 3 and
(καὶ διψῶντες) τὴν δικαιοσύνην in v. 6. It is widely agreed that the
fourth beatitude (Lk 6,22-23 / Mt 5,11-12, on persecution) was already

STRECKER, *Makarismen* (n. 25), p. 264: "zweifelhaft"; J.A. FITZMYER, *Luke* I, 1981,
p. 634: "'and thirst'... comes to Matthew from 'Q'". But see above, n. 20. Note that
διψῶντες in Mt has no matching term besides χορτασθήσονται.
    23. A. POLAG, *Fragmenta Q. Textheft zur Logienquelle*, Neukirchen, Neukirchener,
1979, ²1982, p. 32. For the combination of κλαίοντες (Lk) and παρακληθήσονται (Mt),
see W. Grimm (1976), I.H. Marshall (*Lk*, 1978), and M.E. BORING, *Criteria of Authenticity: The Lucan Beatitudes as a Test Case*, in *Forum* 1/4 (1985) 3-38, here p. 20 (contrast
IQP!); ID., *The Continuing Voice of Jesus*, St. Louis, KY, Westminster/John Knox, 1991,
pp. 192-206 ("Q 6:20b-23"). For the Lukan order combined with the third person (Mt),
see S. Schulz (1972), H. Merklein (1978), W. Schenk (1981), J. Lambrecht (1983), M.E.
Boring (1985), *et al*. Cf. Dupont's "base commune" in *Introduction* (n. 14), p. 99! Undecided: J. SCHLOSSER (n. 20), p. 424: "il paraît préférable... de laisser la question
ouverte"; W.D. DAVIES & D.C. ALLISON, *The Gospel according to Saint Matthew*, Edinburgh, Clark, vol. I, 1988, pp. 445-446: "No agreement has been reached... we still await
a decisive observation".
    24. Cf. *JBL* 111 (1992), pp. 501-502. Cf. U. LUZ, *Das Evangelium nach Matthäus* I
(EKK, 1/1), Zürich, Benziger – Neukirchen, Neukirchener, 1985, p. 200 (and 201); ET,
1989, p. 227; M. SATO, *Q und Prophetie. Studien zur Gattungs- und Traditionsgeschichte
der Quelle Q* (WUNT, 2/29), Tübingen, Mohr, 1988, p. 254 (= 1984, p. 297); J.S. KLOP-
PENBORG, *Q Thomas Reader*, Sonoma, CA, Polebridge, 1990, p. 38; E. SEVENICH-BAX,
*Israels Konfrontation mit den letzten Boten der Weisheit. Form, Funktion und Interde-
pendenz der Weisheitselemente in der Logienquelle* (MThA, 21), Altenberge, Oros, 1993,
pp. 95-98, 103.

added to the original three in the common source Q and that the additional beatitudes in Mt 5,5.7-9.10 are later insertions (Q[mt] or, more likely, MtR)[25].

There are of course opponents to the Q hypothesis. Thus, D.A. Hagner writes in his *Matthew* (1993), "It may well be that each evangelist follows an independent, though overlapping, oral tradition" (cf. I.H. Marshall: "two different forms of the tradition; an original bifurcation in the tradition")[26]. For H.D. Betz, the SM and the SP existed first apart from Q and, in the beatitudes, the differences "seem to be original to the (presynoptic) compositions and reflect fundamentally different presuppositions"[27]. Redactional interventions of the evangelists are radically excluded: "there is nothing within the SM that has the specific character of Matthew's redaction"; and even: "I do not see any place within the SM where I would be able to recognize sufficient reasons for assuming the interferring hand of the Gospel writer Matthew"[28]. Quite opposite to Betz, but in his own way also emphasizing the unitary composition of the beatitudes, M.D. Goulder proposes that Matthew is responsible for the creation of the beatitudes and Mt 5,3-12 was the

25. For most authors Mt 5,10 is due to MtR. In defence of the Q[mt] hypothesis (Mt 5,5.7-9: R.A. Guelich [n. 56], 1976; U. Luz, 1985; M. Sato, 1984=1988; *et al.*), G. Strecker's lecture at our 1970 Colloquium has been most influential: *Die Makarismen der Bergpredigt*, in *NTS* 17 (1970-71) 255-275, p. 259; = *Les macarismes du Discours sur la montagne*, in M. DIDIER (ed.), *L'évangile selon Matthieu* (BETL, 29), 1972, pp. 185-208, esp. 190. See also *Die Bergpredigt*, Göttingen, Vandenhoeck & Ruprecht, 1984; ET: *The Sermon on the Mount: An Exegetical Commentary*, Edinburgh, Clark, 1988, p. 30. But see, e.g., D.R. CATCHPOLE, *Quest* (n. 20), pp. 81-83, for the attribution to the evangelist.

26. D.A. HAGNER, *Matthew 1–13* (WBC, 33A), Dallas, TX, Word, 1993, p. 89; I.H. MARSHALL, *The Gospel of Luke*, Exeter, Paternoster, 1978, p. 247; D.L. BOCK, *Luke* I, Grand Rapids, MI, Baker, 1994, p. 550. Cf. H.-T. WREGE, *Die Überlieferungsgeschichte der Bergpredigt*, Tübingen, Mohr, 1968.

27. *The Sermon on the Mount* (n. 16), esp. p. 571. On the "relationship" between SM and SP, see also pp. 109-110: "the Sermons operate with different views about what these beatitudes mean" (p. 109). Betz is extremely critical of redaction criticism; see p. 94, on the second- and third-person form (n. 13); pp. 577-578, on Lk 6,21b / Mt 5,4: "Scholars have done their best to show how Matthew may have reformulated the Q-version found in Luke, but with little success. If Matthew had the Lukan version or something similar in front of him, no convincing reason has been presented for changing the wording to what is Matthew's second beatitude". Cf. below, n. 69.

28. BETZ, *The Sermon on the Mount in Matthew's Interpretation*, in B.A. PEARSON (ed.), *The Future of Early Christianity*. FS H. Koester, Minneapolis, MN, Fortress, 1991, pp. 258-275, here 260 (referring to his forthcoming commentary). See, e.g., *Sermon*, 1995, p. 131: "This interpretation of the notion of righteousness, central as it is for the SM, differs from that of the evangelist Matthew"; p. 127: on πραεῖς (5,5) and Jesus' meekness in Mt "different from the SM". For critical reactions to Betz's hypothesis, see J.S. KLOPPENBORG (ed.), *Conflict and Invention*, 1995, pp. 7-8 (cf. *ETL* 72, 1996, p. 442); P. HOFFMANN, in *AAR/SBL Abstracts 1996*, pp. 246-247: "One may ask whether Betz does not underestimate the work of the evangelists" (p. 247).

unique source of Lk 6,20-26²⁹. With É. Puech the restoration of the traditional Matthean hypothesis comes to completion: the source-text of
Mt includes τῷ πνεύματι, τῶν οὐρανῶν, τὴν δικαιοσύνην, in an original composition of the beatitudes, (4+4)+1: "Le nombre primitif de
cette composition n'est pas de 3 ou 4 (= 3+1) béatitudes comme en Luc
ou le prétendu document *Q(uelle)*, mais de 8"³⁰.

There is one element that opponents of Q have in common with its
defenders: in their comments on the Beatitudes, at some stage, traditional or redactional, they all refer to Isa 61. The reference is usually
connected with the theme of the πτωχοί in the first beatitude (Isa 61,1
εὐαγγελίσασθαι πτωχοῖς)³¹, but can be extended to the second beatitude in Mt 5,4 with πενθοῦντες and παρακληθήσονται, diff. Lk 6,21b
(Isa 61,2 παρακαλέσαι πάντας τοὺς πενθοῦντας). For Dupont and
many others Mt 5,3-4 clearly alludes to Isa 61,1-2 and this is one of the
reasons for considering the pairing of πενθεῖν (mourn) and
παρακαλεῖσθαι (being comforted) the original wording of the beatitude. Those who, like Dupont, argue that the woe-sayings in Lk 6,24-26

---

29. M.D. GOULDER, *Midrash and Lection in Matthew*, London, SPCK, 1974, esp.
pp. 252-254: "The simplest explanation must be that Matthew wrote the Beatitudes, and
that Luke rewrote them" (p. 254); *Luke: A New Paradigm* (JSNT SS, 20), Sheffield,
Academic, 1989, pp. 346-360, esp. 356-358. Cf. above, n. 17, Goulder's "Reply" to
Tuckett (1983). See D.R. Catchpole's response in *Quest* (n. 20), ch. 1: "Did Q Exist?",
pp. 1-59, esp. 16-23 ("The Beatitudes"); 43-45 ("The Baptist's Question"). See also
C.M. TUCKETT, *Q and the History* (n. 3), pp. 1-39, ch. 1: "The Existence of Q".

30. É. PUECH, *Un hymne essénien en partie retrouvé et les Béatitudes. 1QH v 12 – VI
18 (= col. XIII-XIV 7) et 4QBéat*, in *RQ* 13 (1988) 59-88, esp. p. 87; *4Q525 et les péricopes
des Béatitudes en Ben Sira et Matthieu*, in *RB* 98 (1991) 80-106 (here p. 97). For a reaction with reservations, see J.A. FITZMYER, *A Palestinian Collection of Beatitudes*, in *The
Four Gospels 1992*. FS F. Neirynck (BETL, 100), 1992, pp. 509-515. Puech adopts the
structure suggested by A. Di Lella on the basis of the number of words: the original
group of eight Beatitudes in Mt 5,3-10 with two sections of exactly thirty-six words (vv.
3.5.4.6 and 7-10). Cf. A.A. DI LELLA, *The Structure and Composition of the Matthean
Beatitudes*, in M.P. HORGAN – P.J. KOBELSKI (eds.), *To Touch the Text*. FS J.A. Fitzmyer,
New York, Crossroad, 1989, pp. 237-242. I cite here a few examples of this author's
argument of the word counts: "one of the reasons for the addition of the phrase τῷ πνεύματι was to give v. 3 the twelve words it would need in order to correspond to the twelve
words in v. 10" (p. 239); one of the reasons for the inclusion of the πραεῖς beatitude:
"its eight words were required for the sum of thirty-six words that comprise the first stro-
phe" (p. 240). Note that Di Lella's article is written to help scholars avoid "subjectivity
and circular arguments" (p. 242)! Compare M. Dumais's comment on Puech's hypothesis: "l'argument principal qui la fonde n'évite pas le cercle vicieux: en effet, la séquence
de huit macarismes du fragment incomplet 4Q525 est établie à partir de Mt v,3-10, vu
comme parallèle. De plus, l'A. ne considère pas les autres arguments qui militent en
faveur d'une activité rédactionnelle de Mt en v,3-10" (*Sermon* [n. 15], c. 785). Cf. B.T.
VIVIANO, *Eight Beatitudes at Qumran and in Matthew? A New Publication from Cave
Four*, in *SEÅ* 58 (1993) 71-84; *BAR* 18/6 (1992) 53-55.66.

31. DUPONT, *Introduction* (n. 14), p. 100: "La première béatitude donne le ton. C'est
aussi celle qui rappelle le mieux la prophétie d'Isaïe".

were not part of Q but are due to LkR (or Q^lk)[32], can explain the Lukan parallel(s) without too much difficulty: the verbs κλαίειν and γελᾶν are Luke's substitutes for πενθεῖν and παρακαλεῖσθαι (Q), in the beatitude (6,21b κλαίοντες – γελάσετε) and in the corresponding woe (6,25b γελῶντες – κλαύσετε), and πενθήσετε in the double phrase πενθήσετε καὶ κλαύσετε is regarded as a reminiscence of the original wording of the beatitude in Q. Likewise, τὴν *παράκλησιν* ὑμῶν (6,24) is supposed to be a reminiscence of παρακληθήσονται in the Q-beatitude.

Defenders of the pre-Lukan origin of the woes can reverse the argument of the reminiscences and assign the use of the verbs πενθεῖν and παρακαλεῖσθαι in Mt 5,4 to Matthean redaction influenced by the tradition of the woes. In reply to H. Schürmann[33] (followed by H. Frankemölle, R.H. Gundry, *et al.*)[34] it has been observed that, if Matthew picked up his two verbs in the woes, then the "allusion" to Isa 61 was mere coincidence ("rein zufällig entstanden")[35]. It can be asked, however, whether it is likely that πενθοῦντες in the beatitude would come from the corresponding woe-saying in Lk 6,25b and παρακληθήσονται, in the same beatitude, would derive from a different woe-saying (6,24, on the rich) and from a quite different phrase: ὅτι ἀπέχετε τὴν παράκλησιν ὑμῶν. Moreover, the question of Lukan authorship can be raised, if not (as I think it should) for the whole complex of the four woes (Lk 6,24-26), at least for the terms παράκλησιν and πενθήσετε (6,24.25b). For Schürmann, the pre-Lukan origin of πενθήσετε (in combination with καὶ κλαύσετε) can be explained as stereotyped usage, and J.A. Fitzmyer who argues for Lukan composition

32. Cf. U. LUZ, *Matthäus* (n. 24), pp. 200-201: "Die von Jes 61,2 her erfolgte Neuformulierung der zweiten Seligpreisung ist... eindeutig vormatthäisch. [n. 9] Die Weherufe Lk 6,24.25b setzen V4 in der mt Fassung wohl bereits voraus" (p. 200). Compare G. STRECKER, *Makarismen* (n. 25), p. 263 n. 1; reprinted in ID., *Eschaton und Historie*, Göttingen, Vandenhoeck & Ruprecht, 1979, pp. 108-131, here 117, n. 27 (= *Macarismes*, p. 195 n. 27); cf. *Sermon*, pp. 34-35.

33. *Warnung* (n. 21), 1966, p. 77 (= *TrU*, p. 305); *Lukasevangelium*, p. 339: "Das πενθήσετε Lk 6,25 wird Matth mitbestimmt haben, Mt 5,4 die κλαίοντες in die πενθοῦντες zu ändern [p. 331 n. 42]. Wahrscheinlich hat Mt in 5,4 auch entsprechend das γελάσετε in παρακληθήσονται geglättet, wobei ihm eine Vorlage wie 6,24 (παράκλησις) half [pp. 332 n. 45; 336 n. 84]".

34. H. FRANKEMÖLLE, *Makarismen* (n. 16), p. 64; R.H. GUNDRY, *Matthew*, Grand Rapids, MI, Eerdmans, 1982, ²1994, p. 68. Cf. J. NOLLAND, *Luke 1–9:20* (WBC, 35A), Dallas, TX, Word, 1989, pp. 287, and 280: "Matthew will have the verb he uses here ('mourn') from the corresponding Lukan woe".

35. E. SCHWEIZER, *Formgeschichtliches zu den Seligpreisungen Jesu*, in *NTS* 19 (1972-73) 121-126, p. 122 n. 4; = *Matthäus und seine Gemeinde* (SBS, 71), Stuttgart, KBW, 1974, pp. 69-76, esp. 71 n. 9.

can repeat this same explanation[36]. One may add that the emphatic pleonasm is used quite fittingly in this third woe-saying[37]. Fitzmyer's comment is even more explicit on παράκλησις in 6,24: "*Paraklesis* is used by Luke alone among the evangelists... This is a sign that the woes were not part of 'Q'"[38]. More recently, D.R. Catchpole, in *The Quest for Q*, has inserted an analysis and reconstruction of the first three woes, which he considers to be pre-Lukan:

Lk 6,24-25	Catchpole
[24]πλὴν οὐαὶ ὑμῖν τοῖς πλουσίοις,	οὐαὶ τοῖς πλουσίοις,
ὅτι ἀπέχετε τὴν **παράκλησιν** ὑμῶν.	ὅτι ἀπέχουσιν τὸν **μισθὸν** αὐτῶν.
[25a]οὐαὶ ὑμῖν, οἱ ἐμπεπλησμένοι νῦν,	οὐαὶ τοῖς (?γελῶσιν/**χαίρουσιν**),
ὅτι πεινάσετε	ὅτι πενθήσουσιν.
[25b]οὐαί, οἱ γελῶντες νῦν,	οὐαὶ τοῖς ἐμπεπλησμένοις,
ὅτι **πενθήσετε** καὶ κλαύσετε.	ὅτι πεινάσουσιν.

I quote: "The one difficulty is the woe on the rich which ought to function as a heading for the other two woes and which is unlikely to have

---

36. SCHÜRMANN, *Lukasevangelium*, p. 331 n. 42: "Es ist Lk 6,25 wohl durch das stereotyp-gewohnheitsmäßige Nebeneinander der beiden Verben... vorluk in den Weheruf geraten und von dort in die matth Seligpreisung"; cf. *Warnung*, p. 75 n. 65. FITZMYER, *Luke* I, 1981, p. 637 (cf. 627): "The pair, 'weep and mourn' (*penthein* and *klaiein*), is found in Greek papyri (MM, 502-503 [POxy 528,9]) and in the LXX (2 Sam 19:2; 2 Esdr 18:19). See further Mark 16:10; Jas 4:9; Rev 18:11,15,19". Cf. J. GNILKA, *Matthäusevangelium* I, 1986, p. 122: "eine manchmal fast floskelhafte Verbindung"; H.-D. BETZ, *Sermon* (n. 16), p. 588: "The combination of the two verbs is traditional, so that one should rule out redactional operations on this point". See also H.-T. WREGE, *Bergpredigt* (n. 26), p. 16, with reference to TJud 25,5; TJos 3,9 (ἐπένθησα, A[ab] add καὶ ἔκλαυσα); add: TZeb 4,8 μὴ κλαῖε μηδὲ πένθει (*v.l.* λυποῦ). In reply to Wrege, Dupont observes that πενθεῖν καὶ κλαίειν in this order occurs only once in the LXX (Neh 8,9 = 2 Esdr 18,19), and in the NT: Jas 4,9; Mk 16,10; in inverted order: Rev 18,11.15.19. It may suffice to note here: "on les [les deux verbes] rencontre plus souvent en parallélisme synonymique (Gen 37,35; 2 S 19,1 [= 2]; Neh 1,4 [2 Esdr 11,4]; Ps 77,63-64; Is 16,8-9; Si 7,34)... probable en *Hen* 96,2" (*Béatitudes* III, p. 75 n. 2). For Tuckett, "Luke's πενθήσετε καὶ κλαύσετε... looks overloaded, and if κλαίω is redactional, this would confirm the use of πενθέω in Luke's tradition here" (*Q and the History*, p. 225). If overloaded, πενθεῖν may have been added redactionally to the traditional κλαίειν (cf. 6,21b οἱ κλαίοντες). In *Beatitudes* (n. 17) Tuckett replies to Schürmann and Wrege: "the coupling is not that common and relatively rare in the LXX", and "if πενθέω is an addition to an original κλαίω, one would expect πενθέω to come second" (p. 199 n. 24). But since "there is no fixed order to the coupling" (*ibid.*), the argument "from order" is at least reversible in the light of the first member of the woe-saying (οἱ γελῶντες): "Luke's use of κλαίω may also be partly occasioned by the presence of γελάω, since 'weeping' might be seen as a natural antithesis to 'laughing'" (p. 199).

37. P. KLEIN, *Die lukanischen Weherufe Lk 6,24-26*, in ZNW 71 (1980) 150-159 (on Lukan redaction), here p. 156: "die stärkere Betonung des bejammernswerten Zustandes der jetzt Privilegierten in der Zukunft durch die pleonastische Ausdrucksweise".

38. *Luke*, p. 636. Cf. Lk 2,25; Acts 4,36; 9,31; 13,15; 15,31. Cf. H. KLEIN, in *NTS* 42 (1996), p. 422: "die Weherufe (standen) nicht in der Logienquelle". On Luke's use of παράκλησις in 6,24 in the light of Lk 2,25, cf. P. KLEIN, *Weherufe*, p. 155.

included the very Lukan word παράκλησις"[39] (compare Goulder: "a perfectly Lukan word"[40]). Therefore, in the *pre-Q* tradition of the woes, he proposes to read τὸν μισθόν instead of τὴν παράκλησιν[41].

If, in the woes, we can explain παράκλησιν (6,24) and πενθήσετε (6,25b) as redactional without necessarily referring to Mt 5,4, there remains in Lk no positive evidence for a Q (or Q^{mt}) origin of Mt's verbs πενθεῖν and παρακαλεῖν. Lukan redaction of κλαίειν and γελᾶν is Catchpole's second argument. But the statistics are rather confusing: apart from Lk 6,21b.25b there are in Lk-Acts ten (or eleven)[42] occurrences of κλαίειν and none of γελᾶν. For Catchpole, this can be "no problem in view of the profusion of *hapax legomena* in Luke-Acts"[43], though for οἱ γελῶντες in the woe (Lk 6,25b) the possibility of tradition is left open in his reconstruction: οὐαὶ τοῖς (?γελῶσιν/χαίρουσιν)[44]. Tuckett's option for tradition is less ambiguous. Because of the pejorative use of γελᾶν (derision) in the LXX, he concludes that "the usage in the woe is more original and that [less appropriate] in the beatitude is due to LkR"[45]. However, the whole argument is very much relativized by Tuckett's final observation that Luke "may have been unaware of the slightly specialised use of the verb in the OT"[46]. In this connection,

39. *Quest* (n. 20), p. 90. Catchpole seems to correct his argument when he notes that Luke's παρακαλεῖν/παράκλησις "never (represents) the original prosperity of the rich as such" and "the contrivedness of the παράκλησις usage in Luke 6:24" can be an echo of the "natural" usage in Mt 5,4 (p. 85 n. 17). But see n. 38.

40. "Reply" (n. 17), p. 215.

41. *Quest*, p. 90. Cf. Mt 6,2.5.16: "Matthew appears to know Luke 6:24" (p. 89), which is an inversion of Dupont's suggestion (I, p. 163 n. 1). Compare the theme in Lk 15,27 ἀπέλαβες τὰ ἀγαθά σου ἐν τῇ ζωῇ σου. The verb ἀπέχετε can be Lk's variation for the other commercial term ἀπολαμβάνειν. There is no need for a source-text with μισθός (for the Lukan παράκλησις).

42. If Lk 22,62 (par. Mk 14,72) is included; on the textual problem, cf. *Evangelica* II, pp. 109 n. 85, 135. Cf. Tuckett, *Beatitudes* (n. 17), p. 198: 2–4–10+3 (correction: Acts 9,39; 21,13). The occurrences in Mk are: 5,38.39 (diff. Mt); 14,72 (= Mt); [16,10]; in Mt 2,18 (quotation); 26,75 (= Mk). On Luke's use of κλαίειν, cf. Dupont, *Béatitudes* III, pp. 69-74.

43. *Quest*, p. 85.

44. *Ibid.*, p. 90.

45. Cf. above, n. 17: *Luke 4,16-30*, p. 343 n. 1; *Beatitudes*, p. 198; *Q*, pp. 224-225. Compare J. Schlosser (n. 20), 1980, p. 428: "De la malédiction (Lc 6,25b), dans laquelle ils sont bien en situation, les vocables [κλαίω, γελάω] auront passé dans la béatitude correspondante (Lc 6,21b), où ils conviennent beaucoup moins".

46. *Ibid.* Cf. *Scripture and Q*, p. 19, n. 71: "The reference to laughter here in Luke [6,25] seems to have been misunderstood by Luke himself... Luke perhaps is unaware of this...". But see Dupont, *Béatitudes* III, p. 69: "Il reste donc à prendre le 'rire' dans le sens du vocabulaire grec courant"; in the beatitude, and in the woe-saying: "Inutile d'y chercher une attitude hostile à l'égard de ceux dont ils se moqueraient. On s'en prend à leur bonheur satisfait et sûr de lui-même".

Goulder refers to Ecclesiastes 3,4a (καιρὸς τοῦ κλαῦσαι καὶ καιρὸς τοῦ γελάσαι): "Luke takes the word [γελᾶν] as an obvious converse to κλαίειν in the light of Eccl. 3.4"[47]. Tuckett reverses this observation: "given the slightly more unusual idea of laughter [γελᾶν], one can see how 'weeping' (κλαίειν) might arise as an antithesis on the basis of Eccles. 3"[48]. But do we really need to think, in one sense or another, of dependence on Qohelet in the case of οἱ κλαίοντες and the antithetic γελᾶν, preceded here by οἱ πεινῶντες and its antithesis χορτασθῆναι? There can be no dispute that this last pair comes from Q (Lk 6,21a; Mt 5,6).

By saying "preceded by the πεινῶντες" I am expressing a provisional option for the order of Lk 6,21a.b as the order of Q. Of course, the possibility of a Lukan reordering of the second and third beatitudes can be envisaged. It has been suggested by Dupont that Luke moved the πεινῶντες from the third place to the second (after πτωχοί) because he associated hunger with poverty[49]. But this association can be traditional and there is an elementary logic in the order of πτωχοί and πεινῶντες – κλαίοντες which Luke may have found in the original three beatitudes. Catchpole proposes that the beatitude on the κλαίοντες is placed last by Luke as a transition to the fourth beatitude on persecution[50]. But if it is agreed that the combination of the fourth beatitude with the first three already took place in Q, it is less evident that we can still speak of a specific Lukan interest. The integration of the final beatitude with those preceding is clearly Matthew's concern, as appears from the creation of the bridge saying on the persecuted in Mt 5,10, without parallel in Lk. Mt 5,10 forms an *inclusio* with 5,3 (second line: ὅτι αὐτῶν ἐστιν ἡ βασιλεία τῶν οὐρανῶν), and its phrase ἕνεκεν δικαιοσύνης in the first line echoes the theme of Matthew's reformulation of the πεινῶντες beatitude in 5,6. Matthew added (καὶ διψῶντες) τὴν

47. *Luke*, p. 359. Cf. SCHULZ, p. 78: "entspricht genau καλεῖν".
48. *Beatitudes*, p. 199 n. 25. Cf. above, n. 36. Note that for Tuckett (in contrast to Strecker) the acceptance of a traditional γελᾶν in 6,25 does not imply that κλαίειν in the same woe is also traditional. Compare G. STRECKER, *Sermon*, p. 34: "The opposition of laughing and weeping occurs also in the woe of Luke 6:25, and it is conceivable that Luke found it present in his copy of Q (Q^Luke) and on that basis changed the language of the second beatitude".
49. *Béatitudes* I, pp. 271-272: "Un lien étroit s'établit dans la pensée de l'évangéliste entre la pauvreté et la privation de nourriture". But see III, p. 46: "Les 'affamés' sont traditionnellement mentionnés en parallélisme synonymique avec les pauvres (voir Is 58,7...). ... ce sont ces mêmes pauvres considérés dans la réalité concrète de leur détresse".
50. Cf. D. CATCHPOLE, *Quest*, p. 85; ID., *Beatitudes*, in R.J. COGGINS – J.L. HOULDEN (eds.), *A Dictionary of Biblical Interpretation*, London, SCM – Philadelphia, TPI, 1990, pp. 79-82, here 81.

δικαιοσύνην and, very probably, relocated this beatitude at the end of the first set of four[51].

The question of the order in Mt is complicated by the textual problem concerning the inversion of 5,5 πραεῖς and 5,4 πενθοῦντες (D 33 lat sy^c bo^ms; Or Eus). It is now less usual that Mt 5,5 is treated as a later gloss (μακάριοι **οἱ πραεῖς**, ὅτι αὐτοὶ **κληρονομήσουσιν** τὴν **γῆν**, cf. Ps 36,11a LXX)[52], though N.J. McEleney (1981) still invented a post-Matthean redactor in charge of v. 5[53]. J. Dupont in 1958 defended the originality of the order 5,3.5.4 (πτωχοί immediately followed by πραεῖς) in the text of Mt[54]. For others, this order is pre-Matthean and the evangelist is responsible for the relocation of πενθοῦντες (v. 4) before πραεῖς (v. 5). Thus, for Davies & Allison, Mt 5,5 was originally "added by an editor of Q^mt in order to explicate the first beatitude (which it at some time immediately followed)"[55]. Compare R.A. Guelich's statement: "The two Beatitudes would then have been transmitted together in the tradition until Matthew... rearranged them"[56]. The influence of Dupont, which is undeniable, goes here far beyond his own intention by positing a pre-Matthean origin of Mt 5,5 and by using in this regard the text-critical evidence[57]. In this case one may regret that

---

51. Compare J. Lambrecht's reconstruction of the beatitude in Q: the wording of Mt 5,4 but in the Lukan order. See *Maar ik zeg u. De programmatische rede van Jezus (Mt. 5–7; Lc. 6,20-49)*, Leuven, VBS-Acco, 1983, p. 53 (GT, 1984, p. 46; ET, 1985, p. 43; FT, 1986, p. 44). Cf. above, n. 23. Less convincing is S. Schulz's distinction between Mt 5,3-4 ("menschliche Notlage") and 5,5-10 ("christliche Tugenden"), including v. 6 (p. 76).

52. J. Wellhausen (1904), followed by A. Harnack (1907), E. Klostermann (1909), R. Bultmann (1921), C.H. Dodd (1955). More recently, and now rather exceptionally, M.-É. BOISMARD, *Synopse* II, 1972, p. 127; K.C. HANSON, *"How Honorable! How Shameful!" A Cultural Analysis of Matthew's Makarisms and Reproaches*, in *Semeia* 68 (1996) 81-111, here p. 99. See also the footnote that appears in all editions of the Jerusalem Bible: "Le v. 4 [*les doux*] pourrait n'être qu'une glose du v. 3; son omission ramènerait le nombre des béatitudes à sept" (1955, p. 1294; 1973, p. 1420, n. *i*; cf. P. Benoit, 1950, p. 51, note).

53. *Beatitudes* (n. 16), p. 12; see also p. 13: addition of τὴν δικαιοσύνην in v. 6.

54. *Béatitudes* I, pp. 251-257, esp. 253: "les hésitations de la tradition textuelle s'expliquent à partir d'une rédaction primitive plaçant les 'doux' en deuxième rang". The strength (and the weakness!) of Dupont's argument lies in the concentration on πτωχοί/πραεῖς (= ʿănāwîm) as the link between the two beatitudes: "un copiste grec ne pouvait plus le percevoir" (p. 253). See also III, pp. 473-474 ("cette question reste discutée...").

55. *Matthew* I, p. 449. But see p. 447 n. 30, on the textual witnesses.

56. R.A. GUELICH, *The Sermon on the Mount*, Dallas, TX, Word, 1982, p. 82. Cf. ID., *The Matthean Beatitudes: 'Entrance-Requirements' or Eschatological Blessings?*, in *JBL* 95 (1976) 415-434, p. 426.

57. Cf. GUELICH, *Beatitudes* (n. 56), p. 426: "Text-critically, however, there is ample witness to indicate that originally there was no intervening Beatitude [between 5,3 and 5]". "Originally" here means in the pre-Mt tradition different from the text of Mt.

the readers of Dupont's *Béatitudes* almost never refer to its first edition. I quote from the 1954 volume[58]:

> Inspirée du psaume 36, elle [la béatitude des doux] a été insérée par l'éditeur du premier évangile après la béatitude des affligés.
> Nous préférons nous en remettre au témoignage de la tradition manuscrite et laisser la béatitude des doux en troisième place.

With only a few exceptions[59] modern text editions prefer this more common reading of the Greek manuscripts (with good reason, I think)[60]. Nevertheless we can retain from Guelich's approach at least one valid observation: the order of the beatitudes πτωχοί – πενθοῦντες in Mt 5,3.4 is due to MtR, more particularly, to Matthew's "desire to align the initial Beatitudes more closely to the language and order of Isa 61:1-2"[61]. In addition to the arrangement of the πεινῶντες beatitude in Mt 5,6 (mentioned above) this alignment to Isa 61,1-2 can be another, and perhaps more important, reason for Matthew's reordering of the second and third Q-beatitudes.

The influence of Isa 61,1-2 on Matthew's relocation of Mt 5,4 (cf. Lk 6,21b) is accepted by Schürmann and even extended by him to the influence of Isa 61 on Mt 5,6: χορτασθήσονται has a parallel in Isa 61,6

---

58. *Béatitudes*, 1954, pp. 292 and 87-90 (here, p. 89 n. 2). Contrast vol. I, 1958, pp. 252-253.

59. Lachmann, Tischendorf, Lagrange, Bover. See also the French translations in the Jerusalem Bible (ET: NJB, 1990) and TOB. Cf. P. Benoit's commentary (1950), with a famous lapsus in the note on "les doux": "Rejeté après le v. 5 par D 33..." ([3]1961, p. 54).

60. "If verses 3 and 5 had originally stood together, with their rhetorical antithesis of heaven and earth, it is unlikely that any scribe would have thrust ver. 4 between them" (B.M. METZGER, *Textual Commentary*, [2]1994, p. 10). Cf. H. FRANKEMÖLLE, *Makarismen* (n. 16), p. 70 n. 71: "nicht nur die handschriftliche Überlieferung, sondern auch der enge Bezug in V 3f auf Js 61,1f". See also U. LUZ, *Matthäus* I, p. 199 n. 1: "V 4 und 5 sind in westlichen Textzeugen umgestellt, vermutlich um der so entstehenden Parallelität in der Apodosis willen" (3/5: οὐρανοί – γῆ; 4/6 Schluß auf -θήσονται)". On this last parallel, see also J. GNILKA, *Matthäusevangelium* I, p. 119 n. 17. – A.A. Di Lella (n. 30) strangely argues for the originality of Mt 5,3.5 by referring to the phrase τὸν οὐρανὸν καὶ τὴν γῆν in Gen 1,1 and 2,4a (p. 242; followed by É. Puech, p. 98). No more convincing is their argument based on the number of words (Di Lella, p. 241; Puech, p. 97). M. Dumais (n. 15) presents the "Béatitudes matthéennes" (cc. 797-817) in the order: "a) Les 'pauvres en esprit' (v,3); b) Les 'doux' (v,4); c) Les 'affligés' (v,5)...", without really discussing the location of πραεῖς. He notes that "la béatitude des 'doux' [his 5,4] a essentiellement le même sens que celle des 'pauvres en esprit'" and seems to rely on J. Dupont (c. 800).

61. GUELICH, *Sermon*, p. 82. See also W. GRUNDMANN, *Das Evangelium nach Matthäus* (THKNT, 1), Berlin, Evangelische Verlagsanstalt, 1968, p. 123: "Die dritte lukanische Seligpreisung rückt bei Matthäus an die zweite Stelle; diese Stellung ist bestimmt durch Jes. 61,1-3".

κατέδεσθε (you shall *eat*...); "Die Sättigung der Hungernden mußte umgestellt werden, wenn Is 61,6 κατέδεσθε anklingen sollte"[62]. My comment can be brief. I subscribe to Tuckett's statement saying that "the verbal agreement is not at all close and one should probably not lay any great value [or any value at all] on such a possible parallel"[63]. Unlike the parallel with Mt 5,4 in Isa 61,2, the Greek word in 61,6 is not the same and the theme is different: "you shall eat the wealth of the nations". Moreover, Schürmann also considers the following v. 7: κληρονομήσουσιν τὴν γῆν, par. Mt 5,5; this would imply that Mt 5,6 is once more "umgestellt", now with reference to the parallels in Isa 61,6.7 (Mt 5,6.5).

Mt 5,5 has a much closer parallel in Ps 36(LXX),11a, with the subject οἱ πραεῖς[64]. For M. Hengel one may find there the key for understanding the relocation of Mt 5,6: the Q-beatitudes "werden von ihm [Mt] umgestellt... dem Tenor von Jes 61 und Ps 37 entsprechend. Mt 5,3 und 4 läßt deutlich Jes 61,1-3 anklingen, Mt 5,5 und 6 Ps 37,11 und [19]"[65].

---

62. *Lukasevangelium*, p. 336 n. 84. Cf. p. 330 n. 30: "unter Einfluß von Is 61,1ff.6f[!]". Quoted by Schulz (p. 76 n. 124).

63. *Q and the History*, p. 226. The conjunction with Ps 146,7b, "the Lord gives food to the hungry", in *Scripture and Q* (p. 24) illustrates anew that for Tuckett the parallel in Isa 61,6 has no great value. Contrast J. DUPONT, *Béatitudes* II, p. 94.

64. Cf. above, n. 52. See also DAVIES & ALLISON, *Matthew* I, p. 451: "Given the other allusions to Isa 61 in the other beatitudes, perhaps 5.5 should recall Isa 61.7 even though 5.5 clearly quotes Ps 37.11—especially since both Matthew and Isaiah agree, against the psalm, in having the definite article before γῆν". Contrast I. BROER (n. 16), p. 67 n. 16: "Da Mt 5,5 auf Ps 36,11 LXX basiert, ist eine doppelte Vermittlung unwahrscheinlich und auch unnötig" (cf. below, n. 74); here in reply to D. Flusser.

In Flusser's theory the original saying (in Hebrew) is preserved in Mt 5,3-5. He prefers the order 3-5-4 because in his view v. 3 (on the poor "endowed with the Holy Spirit": theirs is the kingdom of heaven) is an explanation (*pesher*) of v. 5 (= Ps 37,11: the meek shall inherit the earth); at the same time it is "the explanation of עניים in Isa. 61,1" (nn. 5 and 9). This order is also closer to a parallel passage in 1QH. Since Mt 5,3-5-4 and 1QH 23(18),14-15 are based on the same combination of Isa 61,1-2 and 66,2, there is "some literary connection" between the two passages and "the source of the three first Beatitudes (probably) originated in the Dead Sea Sect or in some milieu close to it". Cf. *Blessed are the Poor in Spirit...*, in *Israel Exploration Journal* 10 (1960) 1-13; reprinted in his *Judaism and the Origins of Christianity*, Jerusalem, Magnes, 1988, pp. 102-114 (passim). Note that for Flusser Luke has no parallel to Mt 5,4: Lk 6,21b is a different beatitude, which is omitted by Matthew. The original number of beatitudes was probably ten (9 + 1) and they all had their counterpart in the woes (pp. 11-12 = 112-113). For criticism see e.g. J. DUPONT, *Béatitudes* II, p. 98 n. 3. In particular, Dupont rejects the influence of Isa 66,2 on Matthew's addition of τῷ πνεύματι in 5,3: "Cet appel à *Is* 66 nous paraît parfaitement inutile". Contrast GUNDRY, *Matthew*, p. 67: "Matthew adds 'in spirit' from Isa 66:2 ('poor and contrite of spirit')". Flusser has further developed his construction in *Some Notes to the Beatitudes*, in *Immanuel* 8 (1978) 37-47 (= *Judaism*, pp. 115-125), esp. pp. 42-44 (= 120-122) on Mt 5,6.

65. M. HENGEL, *Zur matthäischen Bergpredigt und ihrem jüdischen Hintergrund*, in *TR* 52 (1987) 327-400, esp. pp. 348-357 (on the beatitudes), here p. 354. Hengel refers to

Hengel seems to neglect that the case of Mt 5,6 is quite different from
Mt 5,4. Without discussing here the parallel in Ps 36,19b (καὶ ἐν
ἡμέραις λιμοῦ χορτασθήσονται)[66], one should note that the refrain
κληρονομήσουσιν γῆν is repeated throughout the psalm (vv.
9.11.22.29; cf. 34), before and after v. 19; this is of course an unsuitable
basis for an argument "from order".

The influence of Isa 61,2 on the wording and location of Mt 5,4 can
be acknowledged without reserve and, in accord with Hengel, can be
assigned to MtR (and not to Q or Q^mt)[67]. Word statistics of the Synoptics
alone (as practiced by T. Bergemann)[68] can hardly demonstrate redactional usage in Mt 5,4 (diff. Q 6,21b), though the occurrence of πενθεῖν
in 9,15 (Mk νηστεύειν) and the use of παρακληθῆναι in the sense "be
comforted" in 2,18 (Jer 31[38],15) should not be neglected in a statisti-
cal analysis. As indicated above, Matthew's dependence on the woe-say-

Ps 37,11 and "17-18" (my correction: "19"). Cf. pp. 351-353: "Das Problem des Ein-
flusses von Jes 61", esp. 352: "in 5,3-6 (werden) Textstücke, Begriffe und Motive aus Jes
61,1-8 und Ps 37 (vor allem V. 11.14.19) miteinander 'verwoben'"; and "Die Verheißung
κληρονομήσουσιν τὴν γῆν nimmt Jes 61,7 zusammen mit Ps 37,11 in 5,5 auf".
    Compare G.W. Buchanan's "midrashic" analysis: *Matthean Beatitudes and Tradi-
tional Promises*, in W.R. FARMER (ed.), *New Synoptic Studies*, Macon, GA, Mercer, 1983,
pp. 161-184; on parallels in Ps 37(36), see esp. 166-168. Cf. DAVIES & ALLISON, p. 438
n. 16: "Most of these [parallels] must..., *pace* Buchanan, be regarded as insignificant".
    66. Cf. M.-É. BOISMARD, *Synopse* II, 1972, p. 128; D.A. HAGNER, *Matthew* I, p. 93:
Mt 5,6 may reflect the language of Ps 106(LXX),5a πεινῶντες καὶ διψῶντες, 9 ὅτι
ἐχόρτασεν ψυχὴν κενὴν καὶ ψυχὴν πεινῶσαν ἐνέπλησεν ἀγαθῶν. See also Isa
49,10 οὐ πεινάσουσιν οὐδὲ διψήσουσιν.
    67. Contrast DAVIES & ALLISON, *Matthew* I, p. 438: "the strongest links with Isa 61
[in Mt 5,3-4] are to be assigned not to Q^mt but to an earlier stage of Q"; "the farther back
we go, the greater the impact of Isa 61 seems to be... Matthew has not done much if anything to accentuate the connexions between Isa 61 and Mt 5.3-12"; "the connexion with
Isa 61... gradually weakened over time" (p. 437; cf. W. Grimm; J. DUPONT, *Jésus,
messie des pauvres, messie pauvre* (1984), in *Études* (n. 14), pp. 86-130: "Ce n'est pas
au niveau de la rédaction des deux évangélistes (que le texte d'Is 61,1 a exercé son influence sur la formulation de la première béatitude): ni l'un ni l'autre n'ont perçu la
référence, et les retouches que chacun d'eux a apportées au texte de base ont éloigné la
béatitude de l'oracle qui l'inspirait" (p. 99). – On Q^mt, cf. above, nn. 25 and 32. See also
M. SATO, *Q*, p. 47 (1984, p. 54). The π-alliteration in Mt 5,3-6 (Luz, Sato: cf. C.
Michaelis) can be coincidental: πτωχοί (from Q), πενθοῦντες (from Isa 61,2), πραεῖς
(from Ps 36,11), πεινῶντες (from Q) + καὶ διψῶντες (MtR).
    68. T. BERGEMANN, *Q auf dem Prüfstand. Die Zuordnung des Mt/Lk-Stoffes zu Q am
Beispiel der Bergpredigt* (FRLANT, 158), Göttingen, Vandenhoeck & Ruprecht, 1993.
For critique, cf. A. DENAUX, *Criteria for Identifying Q-Passages*, in *NT* 37 (1995) 105-
129. On πενθέω Bergemann expresses "eine gewisse Unsicherheit" (p. 76); with quotation of Sato's remark on Mt 9,15: "damit *muss* dasselbe Wort in Mt 5,4 nicht redaktionell sein" (n. 7), but no reference to Isa 61,2! On παρακαλέω (pp. 79-80), n. 43:
"Schulz... vermutet... eine matthäische Formulierung in Anlehnung an Jes 61,2, ohne
dies wahrscheinlich machen zu können"; without further discussion.

ings (6,24 παράκλησιν; 6,25 πενθήσετε) is doubtful, for more than one reason. On the contrary, Isa 61,2 παρακαλέσαι πάντας τοὺς πενθοῦντας (together with the reference to πτωχοί in v. 1) provides a satisfactory explanation of Matthew's changing κλαίοντες – γελάσετε to πενθοῦντες – παρακληθήσονται. The influence of Isa 61,2 can be the "convincing reason" H.D. Betz is looking for[69].

However, with the allusion to Isa 61,2 in Mt 5,4 new problems arise. Our discussion of possible influences on the location of Mt 5,6 has shown that for Schürmann and Hengel the parallels to the Matthean beatitudes are not restricted to Isa 61,1-2. Hengel emphasizes that "ein Zitat den ganzen Kontext, aus dem er stammt, miteinbringen kann", and: "Man darf bei Mt nicht nur 'platte' Zitate erwarten, vielmehr wird aus wenigen Zitate und mancherlei Anspielungen ein bunter Teppich geflochten, der den Schriftkundigen erfreut"[70]. All sorts of parallels from Isa 61 (or at least 61,1-8), "Textstücke, Begriffe, Motive", are recorded by both Schürmann (1969)[71] and Hengel[72]:

Isa 61 LXX	Mt 5,3-12
1 πνεῦμα κυρίου ἐπ' ἐμέ, οὗ εἵνεκεν ἔχρισέν με·	
εὐαγγελίσασθαι πτωχοῖς ἀπέσταλκέν με,	**3**
ἰάσασθαι τοὺς **συντετριμμένους τῇ καρδίᾳ**,	(3a)8a
κηρύξαι αἰχμαλώτοις ἄφεσιν καὶ τυφλοῖς ἀνάβλεψιν,	
2 καλέσαι ἐνιαυτὸν κυρίου δεκτὸν καὶ ἡμέραν ἀνταποδόσεως,	(3b)
παρακαλέσαι πάντας τοὺς **πενθοῦντας**[a],	**4**
3 δοθῆναι τοῖς **πενθοῦσιν**[b] Σιων	
δόξαν[a] ἀντὶ σποδοῦ,	(8b.9b)
ἄλειμμα εὐφροσύνης ⌜τοῖς **πενθοῦσιν**[c],	⌜ἀντὶ πένθους (Ziegler)

69. Cf. above, n. 27.
70. *Bergpredigt* (n. 65), p. 351.
71. List of parallels in *Lukasevangelium*, p. 336 n. 84. See also Davies & Allison's list (pp. 436-437), with reference to W. Grimm: "some less certain than others". Cf. W. GRIMM, *Die Verkündigung Jesu und Deuterojesaja* (ANTJ, 1), Frankfurt, P. Lang, 1976 (first title: *Weil Ich dich liebe*), pp. 68-77; [2]1981, pp. 68-77 (revised). See also K. KOCH, *Formgeschichte* (n. 20), p. 247: Mt 5,3.4 (Isa 61,1.2), and "weitere Bezugnahme auf Jes. 61" in Mt 5,5 (Isa 61,7); 5,6 (Isa 61,6); same references in GUNDRY, *Matthew*, at Mt 5,3.4.5.6.
72. *Bergpredigt*, p. 352: "die Umformung von Lk 6,21 (Q) unter dem Einfluß von Jes 61,2f. in 5,4 und außerdem... weitere Anspielungen... In dem πτωχοὶ τῷ πνεύματι klingt das συντετριμμένους τῇ καρδίᾳ von Jes 61,1 mit an (vgl. auch 5,8). Die Verheißung κληρονομήσουσιν τὴν γῆν nimmt Jes 61,7 zusammen mit Ps 37,11 in 5,5 auf, das Stichwort 'Gerechtigkeit' von Jes 61,3 und 8 findet sich wieder in 5,6.10. Jes 61,6: ὑμεῖς δὲ ἱερεῖς κυρίου κληθήσεσθε, λειτουργοὶ θεοῦ klingt in 5,9 ὅτι αὐτοὶ υἱοὶ θεοῦ κληθήσονται an... Sachlich ist 'das angenehme Jahr des Herrn' und 'der Tag der Vergeltung' (61,2) identisch mit dem Anbruch der Gottesherrschaft, und die dreimalige Nennung der δόξα in 61,3, das dann ausklingt in dem φύτευμα κυρίου εἰς δόξαν, mit der eschatologischen Gottesschau und Gottessohnschaft".

καταστολὴν δόξης[b] ἀντὶ πνεύματος ἀκηδίας·   3a
καὶ κληθήσονται[a] γενεαὶ δικαιοσύνης[a], φύτευμα κυρίου εἰς δόξαν[c].   6.10
9b.6a=10a
6 ὑμεῖς δὲ ἱερεῖς κυρίου κληθήσεσθε[b], λειτουργοὶ θεοῦ·   9b
ἰσχὺν ἐθνῶν κατέδεσθε   6b
καὶ ἐν τῷ πλούτῳ αὐτῶν θαυμασθήσεσθε.
7 οὕτως ἐκ δευτέρας κληρονομήσουσιν τὴν γῆν,   5
καὶ εὐφροσύνη αἰώνιος ὑπὲρ κεφαλῆς αὐτῶν.
8 ἐγὼ γάρ εἰμι κύριος ὁ ἀγαπῶν δικαιοσύνην[b]
καὶ μισῶν ἁρπάγματα ἐξ ἀδικίας·...
10 ... ἀγαλλιάσθω[a] ἡ ψυχή μου ἐπὶ τῷ κυρίῳ...   12
11 ... οὕτως ἀνατελεῖ κύριος δικαιοσύνην[c]
καὶ ἀγαλλίαμα[b] ἐναντίον πάντων τῶν ἐθνῶν.

The section on Isa 61 in Hengel's survey article (*TR*, 1987) was written in response to I. Broer (*Seligpreisungen*, 1986). Broer's thesis is the extreme opposite to Hengel's approach: "der Einfluß von Jes 61 beschränkt sich auf Mt 5,4"; "über Mt 5,4 hinaus sind in der matthäischen Makarismenreihe keine zusätzliche Elemente zu finden, die auf Jes 61 hinweisen"[73]. Broer defends, in the line of Schürmann and Frankemölle, the pre-Lukan origin of the woe-sayings, but he is critical of what he calls "eine doppelte Vermittlung", i.e., the acceptance of a double dependence in Mt 5,4 on both the Isaiah prophecy (61,2) and the woe-sayings (Lk 6,24.25b): "eine Ableitung aus Jes 61,2 (ist) völlig ausreichend"[74]. His method of neutralizing the parallels in the woes, παράκλησιν and πενθήσετε, is not completely my way of arguing but it leads to the same result.

Broer shows the contingency of parallels (other than with Mt 5,4 in Isa 61,2) such as τῇ καρδίᾳ in 61,1 (Mt 5,8: cf. Ps 23 LXX,4), the word πνεύματος in 61,3 (Mt 5,3), κληθήσονται in 61,3 (Mt 5,9), κατέδεσθε in 61,6 (Mt 5,6), κληρονομήσουσιν τὴν γῆν in 61,7 (Mt 5,5; cf. Ps 36 LXX,11: another "doppelte Vermittlung")[75]. With regard to the beatitudes in Q, Broer cites with approval the much-quoted passage in Frankemölle's 1971 article[76]:

---

73. *Seligpreisungen* (n. 16), pp. 64-67 ("Der Zusammenhang der Makarismen mit Jes 61"), here 67 and 65.
74. *Ibid.*, p. 20. See also U. LUZ, *Matthäus*, p. 200 n. 9; E. SEVENICH-BAX, *Konfrontation* (n. 24), p. 76 (ctr. SCHÜRMANN, *Lukasevangelium*, p. 336 n. 84).
75. *Ibid.*, pp. 65-66. Frankemölle prefers to retain this last parallel (61,7: Mt 5,5), as well as δικαιοσύνη (61,5.6.8: Mt 5,6.10): *Makarismen*, p. 69; ID., *Matthäus Kommentar I*, Düsseldorf, Patmos, 1994, pp. 210-211. See also R.A. GUELICH, *Matthean Beatitudes*, pp. 427-428; J.M. ROBINSON, *The Sayings Gospel Q* (n. 18), p. 369: Mt 5,5 and Isa 61,6 (= 7); 60,21 (no mention of Ps 36 LXX); Mt 5,10 and Isa 60,21 ("may have supplied δίκαιος to suggest δικαιοσύνη as an addition..."); on Mt 5,4 and Isa 61,2, *ibid.* (and n. 8: in his view, the woes in Lk 6,24.25 "may reflect also the influence of Isa 61,2").
76. *Makarismen*, p. 60; quoted by Broer (p. 64). Cf. below, n. 81.

Unter der Voraussetzung, daß Lk der Q-Tradition in den VV. 20b-21b ziemlich nahesteht..., darf man die These wagen, daß... kein Bezug zur messianischen Prophezeiung Jes 61,1f. vorlag. Wer wollte dies einzig und allein durch das Wort οἱ πτωχοί (die Armen) als erwiesen ansehen?

Unlike οἱ πτωχοί (τῷ πνεύματι)[77] in Mt 5,3, the word οἱ πτωχοί in Lk is not supported by a further parallel with Isa 61 in the second or third beatitude: "As Luke's Beatitudes now stand they reflect little or no connection with Isa 61:1-3" (Guelich)[78]. For those who argue that the wording of Mt 5,4 comes closer to Q than that of Lk 6,21b, "it may be significant [I quote Tuckett] that Luke may have redacted the beatitudes in such a way that the allusion to Isa 61 is diminished rather than increased"[79]. The alternative solution proposes that Matthew may have seen in οἱ πτωχοί (Q) an allusion to Isa 61,1 and may have increased the parallelism with Isa in the redaction of his second beatitude (5,4). I refer here to a note on Q 6,20b by M. Sato, which goes in the same direction[80]:

> Unser Text ist nicht auf Jes 61,1ff zu beziehen. Das Wort "Arme" reicht dafür nicht aus. Die Anspielung auf Jes 61,1ff geschah in unseren Makarismen erst im Stadium von Q-Matthäus (Mt 5,4: πενθέω/παρακαλέω wie Jes 61,2f).

Οἱ πτωχοί in Q 6,20b (= Lk) is only an incomplete parallel to the phrase in Isa 61,1 (εὐαγγελίσασθαι πτωχοῖς)[81] and the evidence for an allu-

---

77. For an (exceptional) interpretation of ἐν πνεύματι in the light of Isa 61,1 (πνεῦμα κυρίου), see the recent suggestion of an instrumental sense: M. LATTKE, *Glückselig durch den Geist (Matthäus 5,3)*, in C. MAYER, et al. (eds.), *Nach den Anfängen fragen*. FS G. Dautzenberg, Gießen, 1994, pp. 363-382.
78. *Matthean Beatitudes*, p. 424.
79. C.M. TUCKETT, *The Lukan Son of Man*, in ID. (ed.), *Luke's Literary Achievement. Collected Essays* (JSNT SS, 116), Sheffield, Academic, 1995, pp. 198-217, p. 217 n. 65. Compare DAVIES & ALLISON and DUPONT (above, n. 67).
80. *Q und Prophetie* (n. 23), 1988, p. 255 n. 449 (1984, p. 530 n. 491). I would say: at the stage of MtR.
81. Cf. H. FRANKEMÖLLE, *Evangelium, Begriff und Gattung. Ein Forschungsbericht* (SBB, 15), Stuttgart, KBW, ²1994, p. 129: "allein das Wort οἱ πτωχοί, das hier wie dort auftaucht (dazu noch in einem anderen Kasus), belegt noch keine Abhängigkeit" (with reference to Broer in n. 156; and again, p. 146 n. 193); ID., *Jesus als deuterojesajanischer Freudenbote? Zur Rezeption von Jes 52,7 und 61,1 im Neuen Testament, durch Jesus und in den Targumim*, in ID. – K. KERTELGE (eds.), *Vom Urchristentum zu Jesus*. FS J. Gnilka, Freiburg, Herder, 1989, pp. 34-67, esp. 49-50: "Mt 5,3 par Lk 6,20" (cf. *Evangelium*, pp. 145-146). See also ID., *Evangelium und Wirkungsgeschichte*, in L. OBERLINNER – P. FIEDLER (eds.), *Salz der Erde – Licht der Welt. Exegetische Studien zum Matthäusevangelium*. FS A. Vögtle, Stuttgart, KBW, 1991, pp. 31-89, here 51-52. Frankemölle comes closer to Hengel than would be suggested by his rather tendentious assimilation of Hengel's position with the "Konsens der Forscher" [?], i.e., "die These, wonach in Lk 6,21b [Q] bereits auch schon Jes 61,2 rezipiert sei" (p. 52); see also his critique of Broer (p. 52 n. 73; cf. above, n. 75).
By suggesting "more light" from a "broader tradition" of Isa 61 and Ps 146 "taken together", C. Tuckett (*Scripture and Q*, p. 24) seems to recognize that there is a problem with οἱ πτωχοί as reference to Isa 61,1 (see his n. 90).

sion to Isa 61,1 is usually taken from Q 7,22 πτωχοὶ εὐαγγελίζονται (if not from the quotation in Lk 4,18-19)[82]. It is to this factor, external to the beatitudes, that I will turn in the second part of this lecture.

II

Except for the opening phrase, which is probably redactional in both versions[83], Mt 11,2-6 represents the text of the common source Q, possibly with a few minor changes:

82. Cf. SCHÜRMANN, *Lukasevangelium*, p. 341: "in Bezugnahme auf Is 61,1 und von Lk 4,18 und 7,22 her" (see also pp. 326, 328). Note however that, in contrast to Davies & Allison, *et al.* (nn. 67, 79), Schürmann stresses that "Matth erkennt und verdeutlicht ergänzend... die Is-Anspielung der Heilrufe Jesu" (p. 336 n. 84).

In his 1981 Leuven paper Schürmann has reformulated his position: *Das Zeugnis der Redenquelle für die Basileia-Verkündigung*, in J. DELOBEL (ed.), *Logia*, 1982, pp. 121-200, esp. 136-140; reprinted in his *Gottes Reich – Jesu Geschick*, Freiburg, 1983, pp. 65-152, esp. 83-88. He still maintains that in the original version (= Lk 6,20b-21) "die Vermeldung an die 'Armen' immerhin an Jes 61,1 anklingen mag", but: "hier wird nicht ein Jesaja-Text zitiert in der Art, wie das Lk 7,22 par Mt, dann auch Lk 4,18f geschieht. Es ist auch nicht in Anspielung auf Jesaja vom εὐαγγελίζεσθαι Jesu die Rede... Hier wird das dem 'Lachen' entprechende 'Weinen' noch nicht (wie dann Mt 5,4) durch 'Tröstung' der 'Trauernden' (in Wortlaut und Stellung!) von Jes 61,2 gebracht... Wo, wie Lk 7,22 par und 4,18.21, ein deutlicher Rückverweis auf Jes 61,1 vorliegt, wird... die Basileia nicht ins Spiel gebracht" (pp. 138-139 = 85-86).

83. Mt 11,2a ἀκούσας ἐν τῷ δεσμωτηρίῳ τὰ ἔργα τοῦ Χριστοῦ / Lk 7,18a ἀπήγγειλαν Ἰωάννῃ οἱ μαθηταὶ αὐτοῦ περὶ πάντων τούτων. See P. HOFFMANN, *Studien*, pp. 192-193 (undecided: ἐν τῷ δεσμωτηρίῳ); S. SCHULZ, *Q*, pp. 190-191; W. SCHENK, *Synopse*, p. 40; *IQP*, in *JBL* 113 (1994), pp. 497-498; *et al.* Contrast the combination of both versions in ἀκούσας + περὶ πάντων τούτων: A. POLAG, *Fragmenta Q*, p. 41; E. SEVENICH-BAX, *Konfrontation* (n. 24), p. 195 (and 239); R.L. WEBB, *John the Baptizer*, p. 280; D. CATCHPOLE, *Quest*, p. 239 (πάντων LkR). In reply to M.D. Goulder, Catchpole shows that it would be natural for Luke to retain the phrase τὰ ἔργα τοῦ χριστοῦ if he were using Matthew (pp. 43-45). The preceding context in Q is the Centurion's Son (Q 7,1-10) and, as noted by Catchpole, the alternative responses to Jesus are present in the two adjacent passages: πίστις in 7,9 and σκανδαλίζεσθαι in 7,23 (p. 281).

For recent study of Q 7,18-23, cf. V. SCHÖNLE, *Johannes, Jesus und die Juden. Die theologische Position des Matthäus und des Verfassers der Redenquelle im Lichte von Mt. 11* (BEvT, 17), Frankfurt, Lang, 1982, pp. 38-41, 57-64, 97-100; D. VERSEPUT, *The Rejection of the Humble Messianic King. A Study of the Composition of Matthew 11–12* (EHS, 23/291), Frankfurt, Lang, 1989, esp. pp. 56-76; J. ERNST, *Johannes der Täufer. Interpretation – Geschichte – Wirkungsgeschichte* (BZNW, 53), Berlin – New York, de Gruyter, 1989, pp. 56-60; K. BACKHAUS, *Die "Jüngerkreise" des Täufers Johannes. Eine Studie zu den religionsgeschichtlichen Ursprüngen des Christentums* (Paderborner Theologische Studien, 19), Paderborn, Schöningh, 1991, pp. 116-137; R.L. WEBB, *John the Baptizer and Prophet. A Socio-Historical Study* (JSNT SS, 62), Sheffield, Academic, 1991, pp. 278-282; G. HÄFNER, *Der verheißene Vorläufer. Redaktionskritische Untersuchung zur Darstellung Johannes des Täufers im Matthäusevangelium* (SBB, 27), Stuttgart, KBW, 1994, pp. 159-191.

On the reconstruction of the introduction, see HÄFNER, pp. 166-168: "Eine entsprechende Aussage in der Logienquelle [the common content: 'Kenntnisnahme vom Wirken Jesu'] ist also wahrscheinlich, auch wenn der genaue Wortlaut nicht mehr rekon-

19a ὁ Ἰωάννης... πέμψας διὰ τῶν μαθητῶν αὐτοῦ εἶπεν αὐτῷ·
 b σὺ εἶ ὁ ἐρχόμενος ἢ ἕτερον προσδοκῶμεν;
22a καὶ ἀποκριθεὶς ὁ Ἰησοῦς εἶπεν αὐτοῖς·
 b πορευθέντες ἀπαγγείλατε Ἰωάννῃ ἃ ἀκούετε **καὶ βλέπετε**·
 c **τυφλοὶ ἀναβλέπουσιν** καὶ **χωλοὶ περιπατοῦσιν,**   (1) (2)
 d **λεπροὶ καθαρίζονται** καὶ **κωφοὶ ἀκούουσιν**   (3) (4)
 e καὶ **νεκροὶ ἐγείρονται** καὶ **πτωχοὶ εὐαγγελίζονται**·   (5) (6)
23 καὶ μακάριός ἐστιν ὃς ἐὰν μὴ σκανδαλισθῇ ἐν ἐμοί[84].

It is undisputed that several phrases in Jesus' answer to John (Q 7,22cde) allude to Isaianic passages. The primary parallels are Isa 35,5-6 and 61,1 but the recent literature on Q 7,22 from J. Dupont (1961) to G. Häfner (1994)[85] also refers to a number of secondary parallels:

Isa 26,19   ἀναστήσονται οἱ **νεκροί,**   (5)
        καὶ **ἐγερθήσονται** οἱ ἐν τοῖς μνημείοις,
        καὶ εὐφρανθήσονται οἱ ἐν τῇ γῇ

   29,18   καὶ **ἀκούσονται**... **κωφοὶ** λόγους βιβλίου,   (4)
        καὶ οἱ ἐν τῷ σκότει... ὀφθαλμοὶ **τυφλῶν** βλέψονται.   (1)
   19   καὶ ἀγαλλιάσονται **πτωχοὶ** διὰ κύριον ἐν εὐφροσύνῃ   (6)
        καὶ οἱ ἀπηλπισμένοι τ. ἀ. ἐμπλησθήσονται εὐφροσύνης.

   35,5   τότε ἀνοιχθήσονται ὀφθαλμοὶ **τυφλῶν,**   (1)
        καὶ ὦτα **κωφῶν ἀκούσονται.**   (4)
   6   τότε ἁλεῖται ὡς ἔλαφος ὁ **χωλός,**   (2)
        καὶ τρανὴ ἔσται γλῶσσα μογιλάλων,...

   8   ἐκεῖ ἔσται ὁδὸς καθαρὰ καὶ ὁδὸς ἁγία κληθήσεται,   (3)
        καὶ οὐ μὴ παρέλθῃ ἐκεῖ ἀκάθαρτος, οὐδὲ ἔσται ἐκεῖ ὁδὸς ἀκάθαρτος

   42,7   ἀνοῖξαι ὀφθαλμοὺς **τυφλῶν,**   (1)
        ἐξαγαγεῖν ἐκ δεσμῶν δεδεμένους
        καὶ ἐξ οἴκου φυλακῆς καθημένους ἐν σκοτεῖ

struiert werden kann" (p. 168). On ἐν τῷ δεσμωτηρίῳ in Q (Webb, *et al.*), see *ibid.*: "... wahrscheinlicher, daß Mt an eine prinzipiell vorausgesetzte Situation noch einmal ausdrücklich erinnert" (pp. 167-168); undecided: Hoffmann, Polag ("possible"), Ernst (p. 57), Backhaus (p. 117; cf. p. 130: "zumindest... implizite"). But Schürmann rightly observes: "Lk 7,18 dürfte darauf hinweisen, daß die Redequelle die Gefangensetzung des Johannes noch nicht erzählt hatte" (*Lukasevangelium*, p. 184). See also SCHÖNLE, p. 40: not in Q.
    84. Words in verbatim agreement with Lk appear in bold type in the text above. The differences (in normal type) are: πέμψας... εἶπεν αὐτῷ / ἔπεμψεν... λέγων, διὰ / δύο (v. 18b), ἕτερον / ἄλλον, ὁ Ἰησοῦς / om., ἀκούετε κ. βλέπετε / εἴδετε κ. ἠκούσατε (but see p. 62) καὶ ter / om. (cf. below, n. 88 on καί in Q 7,22). The pluses in Lk 7,20.21 (and v. 18b: calling two of his disciples) can be assigned to the evangelist (ctr. Gundry, Hagner, *et al.*: Mt's characteristic abbreviation). On Lk 7,20, cf. KLOPPENBORG, *Q Parallels*, p. 52; HÄFNER, *Vorläufer*, pp. 165-166.
    85. DUPONT, *L'ambassade* (n. 14), pp. 948-950; *Jésus annonce*, pp. 177-178 (= 73-74): "Attaches dans le Livre d'Isaïe"; HÄFNER, *Vorläufer*, pp. 179-180 (with references).

18   οἱ κωφοί, ἀκούσατε,   (4)
      καὶ οἱ τυφλοί, ἀναβλέψατε ἰδεῖν   (1)

61,1 εὐαγγελίσασθαι πτωχοῖς ἀπέσταλκέν με,   (6)
      ἰάσασθαι τοὺς συντετριμμένους τῇ καρδίᾳ,
      κηρύξαι αἰχμαλώτοις ἄφεσιν
      καὶ τυφλοῖς ἀνάβλεψιν   (1)

It has been observed that the allusion to Isa 61,1 has a climactic position at the conclusion of the sixfold series in Q 7,22. But is it correct to
say that both the first item in the list (τυφλοὶ ἀναβλέπουσιν) and the
last item (πτωχοὶ εὐαγγελίζονται) come from Isa 61,1[86]? Isa 61,1 LXX
reads τυφλοῖς ἀνάβλεψιν (text cited in Lk 4,18)[87], but the association
of τυφλοί with κωφοί that appears in other passages is perhaps a more
notable parallel: Isa 35,5; 42,18 (with the verb ἀναβλέπειν); 29,18. If
the καί's in Mt 11,5 (diff. Lk) stem from Q, including the καί before
νεκροί[88], then the healing miracles in Q 7,22 form one group of four
specific classes of sufferers, in two pairs, beginning with τυφλοί and
ending with κωφοί[89].

86. Cf. below, n. 92. See also J.M. ROBINSON, *The Sayings Gospel Q* (n. 18), pp. 363-
364: the first and last items "in chiastic order" in Q 7,22 and even the healings "perhaps
triggered by an intervening phrase in Isa 61,1: ἰάσασθαι...". J.S. KLOPPENBORG, *The
Formation of Q*, Philadelphia, Fortress, 1987, p. 108 n. 24: "The phrase τυφλοὶ
ἀναβλέπουσιν reveals dependence on the LXX of Isa 61:1-2". See however TUCKETT, *Q
and the History*, p. 129 n. 77: "The reference to the 'blind seeing' could derive from Isa
35:5 rather than Isa 61 LXX" (cf. n. 75); see also p. 232 n. 81: "more likely".
    On E. Hirsch's reconstruction of the original saying (τυφλοί, πτωχοί), see A. Stro-
bel's comment in his *Untersuchungen zum eschatologischen Verzögerungsproblem*
(NTSup, 2), Leiden, Brill, 1961, p. 274 n. 2: "So hypothetisch dieser Vorschlag auch sein
mag, die Bedeutung von Jes 61 wird mit ihm besonders augenfällig unterstrichen".
    87. On the Hebrew text, פקח־קוח ולאסורים "and to those who are bound opening"
(liberation of prisoners), cf. W.A.M. BEUKEN, *Servant and Herald of Good Things. Isaiah
61 as an Interpretation of Isaiah 40-55*, in J. VERMEYLEN (ed.), *The Book of Isaiah – Le
Livre d'Isaïe* (BETL, 81), Leuven, 1989, pp. 410-442, esp. 419-420; W. LAU, *Schriftgelehrte Prophetie in Jes 56-66* (BZAW, 225), Berlin – New York, de Gruyter, 1994,
p. 74 n. 232.
    88. Most authors assign Mt's four καί's to Q and regard Lk's one καί and the two
groups of three asyndetic clauses joined by this καί before κωφοί as stylistic improvement. Exceptions are (besides Polag who deletes the καί before νεκροί in his Q text)
Schenk (p. 40), Gundry (p. 206) and Kloppenborg (*Q – Thomas* [n. 24], p. 44), who opt
for Lk's single καί before κωφοί. The καί in Lk is omitted in the Majority text (TR T S
V B Greeven).
    89. Cf. J. GNILKA, *Matthäusevangelium* I, p. 405: "In formaler Hinsicht werden die
ersten 4 Tätigkeiten paarweise zusammengeschlossen. Tätigkeit 5 und 6 erscheinen dann
(mit καί angefügt) wie eine Steigerung". It is less clear whether items 5 and 6 in Q are
taken individually (VERSEPUT, pp. 67-68 and 71: "After listing in pairs the healing miracles Jesus builds to a polysyndetic climax"; SEVENICH-BAX, pp. 201, 239; cf. GUNDRY,
p. 206: MtR) or form a third and last pair introduced with καί (DAVIES & ALLISON, II,
p. 242 n. 29).

In his comment on τυφλοὶ ἀναβλέπουσιν in Lk 7,22 Fitzmyer notes that "interpreters debate whether Jesus' words allude to Isa 61:1 or 35:5". He then refers to the quotation of Isa 61,1 in Lk 4,18 and concludes: "it should be so understood here"[90]. This is a valuable observation in a commentary on Lk, though the argument is less serviceable with regard to Q if, as he maintains, Lk 4,17-21 is "better ascribed to Luke's own pen"[91]. It is not uncommon that the use of Isa 35,5-6 in Q 7,22 is seen as an extension of the allusion to Isa 61,1[92]:

Is. 61,1 fournit le premier et le dernier terme de la liste évangélique; mais la mention initiale des 'aveugles' permet un rapprochement avec Is. 35,5, qui rend compte de la mention des 'sourds' en quatrième place, et aussi de celle des 'impotents' en deuxième place.

Dupont can hardly be blamed for minimizing the importance of Isa 35,5-6. Not only, like many others, he refers to this passage for parallels to χωλοί ("la mention peut être suggérée par Is. 35,6")[93] and κωφοί ("Le parallèle le plus intéressant est Is. 35,5"), he even attempts to explain λεπροὶ καθαρίζονται in reference to the context of this same passage (35,8)[94]. But does he not show too much reserve in the case of τυφλοί? If "the most interesting parallel" to κωφοὶ ἀκούουσιν is found in Isa

---

90. *Luke* I, p. 668. Cf. p. 664: "Luke 7:22 is to be understood as an echo of the quotation of Isa 61:1, as presented by Luke in 4:18".

91. *Ibid.*, p. 527.

92. DUPONT, *Jésus annonce*, p. 178 (= 74). Cf. p. 177 (= 73): "Le premier terme… semble donc emprunté au dernier terme d'*Is.* 61,1, le verset dont le premier terme fournit le dernier de la liste évangélique. Celle-ci doit donc son cadre à *Is.* 61,1". See also SCHÜRMANN, *Lukasevangelium* I, p. 411: "isaianische Prophetien – rahmend Is 61,1 [*n.* 26: Aber in umgekehrter Folge], formiert durch Is 35,5f"; R. PESCH, *Jesu ureigene Taten? Ein Beitrag zur Wunderfrage* (QD, 52), Freiburg, Herder, 1970, pp. 36-44, esp. 42: "Jes 61,1 (scheint) den Rahmen, Jes 35,5-6 die Reihenfolge der Aufzählung zu bestimmen"; A. VÖGTLE, *Wunder und Wort in urchristlicher Glaubenswerbung (Mt 11,2-5 / Lk 7,18-23)*, in ID., *Das Evangelium und die Evangelien*, Düsseldorf, Patmos, 1971, pp. 219-242, esp. 232: "Den eigentlichen Basistext dürfte Jes 61,1 stellen", with reference to K. Stendahl (1962: "The quotation is basically from Isa 61:1") and P. Stuhlmacher (1968: " Jes. 61,1 ist tatsächlich das Oberthema").

93. The allusion to Isa 35,6 (ὁ χωλός) is accepted by most commentators. Contrast Fitzmyer's statement: not related to any promise of the OT (*Luke*, p. 668). The verb used in Q 7,22 is περιπατοῦσιν (cf. Mk 2,9 par. Mt, Lk, Jn). The verbs ἅλλεσθαι and περιπατεῖν are combined in Acts 3,8 and 14,10.

94. *L'ambassade*, p. 950; *Jésus annonce*, p. 178 (= 74). Dupont's suggestion is now mentioned, after R. Pesch (p. 42: "vielleicht") and D. Verseput (p. 69), by Häfner: "Wenn ich recht sehe, hat auf diesen möglichen Bezugspunkt erstmals *J. Dupont* hingewiesen. Sein Vorschlag ist aber kaum beachtet worden" (*Vorläufer*, p. 180 n. 4, with reference to *L'ambassade* only). But see already B. WEISS, *Das Matthäus-Evangelium* (KEK, 1/1), Göttingen, ⁸1890, p. 210 n. 1: "dass nach V. 8 kein Unreiner auf dem heiligen Wege gehen wird, hat mit der Reinigung der Aussätzigen nichts zu thun". See also E. SEVENICH-BAX, *Konfrontation* (n. 24), p. 328: "eine entfernte Analogie".

35,5b (the ears of the deaf), how can he be critical with regard to the parallel in Isa 35,5a (the eyes of the blind), where "the blind" comes first in the list like τυφλοὶ ἀναβλέπουσιν comes first in Q 7,22? The same form is adopted in all six clauses of the gospel saying (in the third person plural: anarthrous subject and verb) and none of the supposed Isaianic parallels is strictly identical. Assertions that τυφλοὶ ἀναβλέπουσιν draws on Is 61,1 "in the use of ἀναβλέπειν"[95] seem to neglect that the verb is not used in Isa 61,1 (τυφλοῖς ἀνάβλεψιν) and restrict the Isaianic background to Isa 61,1 and 35,5-6. Parallels such as 29,18-19; 42,7; and 42,18 (οἱ τυφλοί, ἀναβλέψατε ἰδεῖν) are explicitly refused by J. Gnilka "weil an diesen Stellen das Blind- und Taubsein metaphorisch gemeint ist"[96]. But there is at least some truth in G. Häfner's reply: "Der ursprüngliche Sinn einer atl Stelle war kein Kriterium für die urchristliche Bezugnahme auf das AT"[97].

The 19th-century consensus, still represented in some later commentaries[98], combines allusions to Isa 35,5-6 (the blind, the deaf, the lame) and Isa 61,1 (the poor), together with the two additional clauses, "lepers are cleansed" and "dead are raised". More recent studies generally include the parallels Isa 29,18-19 (cf. 35,5-6) and Isa 26,19 (the raising of the dead)[99]. Only the cleansing of the lepers is not related to an Isaianic parallel and the traditional solution that the raising of the dead and the cleansing of the lepers were added in reference to the miracles of the historical Jesus[100] is now applied to the cleansing of the lepers

95. R.H. GUNDRY, *The Use of the Old Testament in St. Matthew's Gospel* (NTSup, 18), Leiden, Brill, 1967, p. 79.

96. J. GNILKA, *Matthäusevangelium* I, p. 408. See also H. GIESEN, *Jesu Krankenheilungen im Verständnis des Matthäusevangeliums*, in L. SCHENKE (ed.), *Studien zum Matthäusevangelium*. FS W. Pesch, Stuttgart, KBW, 1988, pp. 79-106, esp. 100 n. 72 (with reference to Gnilka: "mit Recht"). See also P. BONNARD, *L'évangile selon saint Matthieu* (CNT, 1), Neuchâtel, 1963, p. 161: Isa 29,18 rejected because of its "sens figuré".

97. *Vorläufer*, p. 180 n. 2.

98. See the commentaries on Mt 11,5: W.M.L. de Wette ("bezieht sich offenbar auf Jes. 35,5f. 61,1"), B. Weiss, P. Schanz, *et al.* See also J. Knabenbauer, J. Weiss, E. Klostermann, P. Gaechter, P. Bonnard, W. Trilling, D. Hill, H.B. Green, F.W. Beare, M. Davies.

99. Isa 26,19 and 29,18-19 are included in commentaries (besides special studies: J. Dupont, R. Pesch, A. Vögtle; P. Hoffmann, *Studien*, p. 204): P. Benoit, H. Schürmann, F.W. Danker, I.H. Marshall, R.H. Gundry, W.D. Davies – D.C. Allison, F. Bovon, R. Schnackenburg, D.A. Hagner; Isa 26,19 only: J.A. Fitzmyer, J. Gnilka; Isa 29,18-19 only: B.W. Bacon, J.C. Fenton, M.-É. Boismard, U. Luz.
This development can be seen in the marginal annotations of the Nestle editions at Mt 11,5: Isa 35,5-6; 61,1; 1927[13]: + 29,18-19; 1979[26]: + 26,19 and 42,7.18.

100. Cf. P. SCHANZ, *Matthäus*, 1879, p. 306: "nimmt auf Jes. 35,5; 61,1 Rücksicht, erweitert aber die Prophetie nach der Erfüllung"; J. JEREMIAS, *Die Gleichnisse Jesu*, Göttingen, Vandenhoeck & Ruprecht, [4]1956, p. 99 (= [8]1970, p. 116): "Wenn dabei die Nen-

alone[101]. Others prefer the alternative explanation that the cleansing of the lepers was added to the list because of the impact of leprosy in the environment of the gospel tradition[102]. Still others think that the cleansing of the lepers has a link with the OT, not with Isa 35,8 (Dupont) but with 2 Kgs 5 as an Elisha typology[103]. Finally some do not mention Isa 26,19 and join again raising the dead and cleansing the lepers by extending the OT background to the stories of Elijah and Elisha in 1 Kgs 17,17-24; 2 Kgs 4,18-37 (raising the dead) and 2 Kgs 5,1-27 (cure of Naaman's leprosy)[104].

nung der Aussätzigen und der Toten über Jes. 35,5f. hinausgeht, so heißt das: die Erfüllung transzendiert alle Hoffnungen, Erwartungen, Verheißungen" (Theologie, below n. 106, p. 107: "... weit übersteigt"); GUNDRY, The Use (n. 95), p. 80: "Jesus adds references to his cleansing the lepers and raising the dead to show that his ministry surpasses the prophetic expectation" (but see below, n. 101); P. STUHLMACHER, Das paulinische Evangelium, I (FRLANT, 95), Göttingen, Vandenhoeck & Ruprecht, 1968, p. 221: "dem irdischen Jesus (war) die Heilung Aussätziger und die Erweckung Toter nachzurühmen".
See also, on this basis, the conclusion on the tradition history of Q 7,22: A. VÖGTLE, Wunder und Wort (n. 92), p. 242: "nicht alle der jetzt aufgezählten Wunder (wie etwa Totenerweckungen und Aussätzigenheilungen) mußten schon von Anfang an genannt worden sein"; cf. p. 233: "könnten später zur Vervollständigung des Wunderkatalogs hinzugefügt worden sein"; A. STROBEL, Verzögerungsproblem (n. 86), p. 274 n. 1: "womöglich hinzugesetzte Elemente"; D. FLUSSER, Jesus in Selbstzeugnissen und Bilddokumenten, Hamburg, 1968, Rowohlt, p. 36; E. SCHWEIZER, Matthäus, 1973, p. 165: "Die bei Jesaja fehlenden Wunder... sind vielleicht in Q im Blick auf die von Jesus berichteten Taten zugefügt worden"; CATCHPOLE, Quest, p. 239 n. 30: "Of course, we cannot rule out the further possibility, even probability, that some of the actions listed are additions to the original list. This applies particularly to 'lepers are cleansed' and 'the dead are raised up'".
101. P. HOFFMANN, Studien, pp. 208-209: "möglicherweise... eine Reminiszenz an Jesu Tätigkeit", and: "Die Totenerweckungen sind aber hier eher durch Jes 26,19 angeregt worden"; GUNDRY, Matthew, p. 206: "Raising the dead... does appear in Isa 26:19. Cleansing lepers does not appear in any of these passages or others of similar kind. This surplus shows that Jesus' deeds exceed the demands of John's question..."; DAVIES & ALLISON, Matthew II, p. 243: "Perhaps one is to infer that Jesus' works go even beyond what the OT anticipates" (cf. SCHÜRMANN, Lukasevangelium, p. 412).
The case of the cleansing of the lepers leads to a more general conclusion, "Die Formulierungen scheinen daher mehr von den Ereignissen des Auftretens Jesu geprägt zu sein als vom Wortlaut der Schrift": A. POLAG, Die Christologie der Logienquelle (WMANT, 45), Neukirchen, Neukirchen, 1977, p. 36 n. 100; A. SAND, Das Evangelium nach Matthäus (RNT), Regensburg, Pustet, 1986, p. 238.
102. H.-W. KUHN, Enderwartung und gegenwärtiges Heil (SUNT, 4), Göttingen, Vandenhoeck & Ruprecht, 1966, p. 196 n. 4: "eine häufige Krankheit im Palästina der Zeit Jesu"; P. HOFFMANN, Studien, p. 209 (as a possibility); J. GNILKA, Matthäusevangelium I, p. 408: "Die nicht schriftgemäße Erwähnung der Reinigung der Aussätzigen erklärt sich am besten daraus, daß der Aussatz eine häufig auftretende Krankheit gewesen ist".
103. As a possibility ("perhaps"): I.H. MARSHALL, Luke, p. 292; DAVIES & ALLISON, Matthew II, p. 243.
104. LUZ, Matthäus II, p. 169 (no mention of Isa 26,19; see n. 37: "die 'unbiblische' Aufnahme von Aussätzigenheilung und Totenerweckung"); M. SATO, Q und Prophetie, p. 142 (= 167). Cf. TUCKETT, Luke 4,16-30 (n. 17), p. 353: "part of the significance of

The inclusion of Isa 29,18-19 among the parallels may also have some consequences. Isa 61,1 and 29,18-19 are cited at the top of U. Luz's list of Isaianic parallels (before 35,5-6 and 42,18) with the following comment: "Beide Stellen bilden so den Rahmen für Mt 11,5. Es ist also voreilig, einseitig Jes 61,1 zum 'Oberthema' der Antwort Jesu zu machen"[105]. The specific role of Isa 29,18-19 probably receives a more satisfactory presentation in J. Jeremias's approach[106]:

> Jesus zitiert in freier Wiedergabe die prophetische Verheißung Jes. 35,5f. (Blinde, Taube, Lahme) und fügt (*wohl unter dem Einfluß von Jes. 29,18f*.: Taube, Blinde, *Arme* und Elende) Jes. 61,1 hinzu: 'Den Armen wird die Frohbotschaft verkündigt'.

The implication of Jeremias's reading seems to be that Isa 61,1 is not to be regarded as the *Rahmen* of the list in Q 7,22. But before we reach any conclusion we have to consider the new parallel to Q 7,22 in a Dead Sea fragment.

The manuscript 4Q521 (seventeen fragments) was published in 1992 by É. Puech and is known under the title Messianic Apocalypse[107]. The

---

these extra activities [not in Isa 29,18-19; 35,5-6] may be that they show Jesus continuing in the line of Elijah and Elisha"; *Q and the History*, p. 222 (though influence of Isa 26,19 is "not quite impossible").

105. Luz, *ibid.*, n. 38 (in reply to P. Stuhlmacher).

106. *Jesu Verheißung an die Völker*, Stuttgart, 1956, p. 39 (emphasis mine). See also his *Neutestamentliche Theologie. I. Die Verkündigung Jesu*, Gütersloh, Mohn, 1971, p. 106: "eine freie Zitatkombination von Jes 35,5ff. und 29,18f. mit 61,1f."; p. 107: "Mit allen drei Jesajastellen teilt Lk 7,22f. par. in formaler Hinsicht den Listencharakter" (n. 29: "Auch Jes 26,19 spielt herein"). – J. Dupont has drawn attention to Isa 29,18-19, in *Jésus annonce*, p. 177 (= 73) n. 9: "mérite une attention particulière, parce qu'il y est question successivement de sourds, d'aveugles et de pauvres". Dupont's conclusion is extremely brief: "Les contacts littéraires ne s'imposent cependant pas" (*ibid.*). Looking for "literary contacts" was he expecting too much from this parallel? Compare P. Grelot, *"Celui qui vient" (Mt 11,3 et Lc 7,19)*, in *Mélanges B. Renaud* (cf. below, n. 111), 1995, pp. 275-290, esp. 282, on the parallel in Isa 29,18-19: "La chose est d'autant plus remarquable que la suite [au v. 19] mentionne explicitement 'les pauvres', qu'on retrouve dans l'énumération analysée ici: il y a une affinité entre le fait qu'ils 'se réjouiront en YHWH' et le fait qu'ils 'soient évangélisés'".

I noted however some confusion in Grelot's description of the Isaianic parallels (pp. 280-283). Cf. p. 282 n. 7: "pour les aveugles mentionnés dans Is 35,5..., le texte évangélique semble renvoyer au texte de la Bible grecque plutôt qu'à l'hébreu", and p. 281: "La Septante porte ἀνοιχθήσονται, où le préfixe verbal rappelle celui de ἀναβλέπουσιν" (sic). But see p. 282, on κωφοί in Isa 35,5: "mais on n'a pas le verbe entendre en cet endroit"; contrast Isa 35,5b καὶ ὦτα κωφῶν ἀκούσονται! On the other hand Grelot is perhaps too certain about the parallel to τυφλοί in Isa 61,1: "L'allusion à Is 60,1 [read 61,1] est donc certaine" (p. 281).

107. É. Puech, *Une apocalypse messianique (4Q521)*, in *RQ* 15/60 (1992) 475-522; Id., *La croyance des Esséniens en la vie future* (Études Bibliques, NS 22), Paris, Gabalda, 1993, vol. II, pp. 627-669: "Une apocalypse messianique (4Q521)" (followed by "Com-

longest and most important fragment (frags. 2 col. ii + 4) runs as follows (English translation by J.A. Fitzmyer)[108]:

1 [the hea]vens and the earth will listen to His Messiah,
2 [and all th]at is in them will not swerve from the commandments of holy ones.
3 Be strengthened in his service, all you who seek the Lord!
4 Shall you not find the Lord in this, all those who hope in their hearts?
5 For the Lord will visit pious ones, and righteous ones he will call by name.
6 Over lowly ones will His Spirit hover, and faithful ones will He restore with His power.
7 He will honor (the) pious ones on a throne of eternal kingship,
8 as He frees prisoners, gives sight to the blind, straightens up those be[nt over].
9 For[ev]er shall I cling [to tho]se who hope, and in His steadfast love He will recompense;
10 and the frui[t of a] good [dee]d will be delayed for no one.
11 Wond<r>ous things, such as have never been, the Lord will do, as He s[aid].
12 For He will heal (the) wounded, revive the dead, (and) announce good news to lowly ones;
13 (the) [po]or He will satisfy, (the) uprooted He will guide, and on (the) hungry He will bestow riches;
14 and (the) intel[ligent], and all of them (shall be) like hol[y ones].

mentaire général", pp. 669-692); Hebrew text and translation, pp. 485-486 (= 632-633). See also ID., *Messianism, Resurrection, and Eschatology at Qumran and in the New Testament*, in E. ULRICH – J. VANDERKAM (eds.), *The Community of the Renewed Covenant. The Notre Dame Symposium on the Dead Sea Scrolls* (CJAS, 10), Notre Dame, IN, 1994, pp. 235-256, esp. 243-246.

    Previously to Puech's edition the fragment was entitled "On Resurrection" because of its reference to revivifying in line 12. Cf. TABOR & WISE (below n. 109), p. 149 n. 1. For Fitzmyer (n. 108), "this is a misuse of the term, especially with its Christian connotation" (p. 315). On the use of the term "apocalypse", cf. PUECH, p. 515 n. 63 (= 664 n. 71); *Messianism*, p. 241 n. 20: "I use 'apocalypse' in its broad sense". But see COLLINS, *Works* (below n. 114), p. 98: "The extant fragments show none of the formal marks of apocalyptic revelation". The term "messianic" refers to the mention of "his messiah" (or anointed ones?) in line 1: cf. below. A more acceptable designation of the genre would be to call it an eschatological psalm. Cf. R. BERGMEIER, *Beobachtungen* (below n. 120): "Sprechen wir also lieber von einem Psalm eschatologischen Inhalts!" (p. 41). See now also K.-W. Niebuhr, in this volume pp. 637-646.

    108. J.A. FITZMYER, *The Dead Sea Scrolls and Early Christianity*, in *Theology Digest* 42 (1995) 303-319, esp. p. 314. – F. GARCÍA MARTÍNEZ, *The Dead Sea Scrolls Translated. The Qumran Text in English* (ET: W.G.E. Watson), Leiden, Brill, 1994, p. 394; ID. – A.S. VAN DER WOUDE, *De rollen van de Dode Zee ingeleid en in het Nederlands vertaald*, I, Kampen, Kok – Tielt, Lannoo, 1994, pp. 420-424 ("Over de Opstanding"). Cf. F. GARCÍA MARTÍNEZ, *Los Mesías de Qumrân. Problemas de un traductor*, in *Sefarad* 53 (1993) 345-360; ID., *Messianische Erwartungen in den Qumranschriften*, in *Jahrbuch für Biblische Theologie* 8 (1993) 171-208, esp. pp. 180-185 (GT: G. Stemberger); = *Messianic Hopes in the Qumran Writings* (ET: W.G.E. Watson), in ID. – J. TREBOLLE BARRERA, *The People of the Dead Scrolls*, Leiden, Brill, 1995, pp. 159-189, esp. 168-170 (original: *Los Hombres de Qumrân*, Madrid, 1993). – J. MAIER, *Die Qumran-Essener: Die Texte vom Toten Meer, II: Die Texte der Höhle 4* (UTB, 1863), München-Basel, Reinhardt, 1995, pp. 683-687 (..."On Resurrection").

Already before Puech's *editio princeps* R.H. Eisenman had published in 1991 a photograph and translation of the text, and preliminary studies by M.O. Wise and J.D. Tabor had appeared in 1992[109]. In "The Messiah at Qumran" the lines 1 and 12 of this "extremely important text" are excerpted and printed in boldface: *The heavens and the earth will obey His Messiah... He will heal the sick, resurrect the dead, and to the poor announce glad things.* By combining lines 1 and 12 Wise & Tabor suggest that the author of 4Q521 intends to say that it is the Messiah who will raise the dead. I summarize here their argument: Jews who believed in resurrection apparently thought that it was something God, not the Messiah, would do. But in this text the last phrase of line 12 "to the poor announce glad things" is a direct quotation of Isa 61,1 which tells of an anointed one (i.e. Messiah) who will work various signs before the Day of the Lord. Although in the entire Hebrew Bible there is nothing at all about a messianic figure raising the dead, in 4Q521 "raising the dead" is linked to glad tidings for the poor: the two phrases are linked as "signs of the Messiah". This language is "virtually identical" to that of Q 7,22: healing the sick and, in identical order, νεκροὶ ἐγείρονται and πτωχοὶ εὐαγγελίζονται. Q 7,22 and 4Q521 share "the same technical list of criteria for identification of the Messiah".

The problem is however that the Messiah is mentioned only in the first line ("His Messiah"). Lines 3ff. explicitly refer to God (אדני, the Lord) and the works described in line 8 are works of God. Therefore it was suggested that the text returns to the messianic figure with an explicit mention prior to line 12: *[10]... His] holy [Messiah] will not be slow [in coming.] [11] And as for the wonders that are not the work of the Lord, when he* (i.e. the Messiah) *[come]s*[110]. Critical misfortune awaited this conjecture "His Messiah" (line 10) and the notion "not the work of the Lord" (line 11): "paleographically impossible" and "an idea which

109. R.H. EISENMAN, *A Messianic Vision*, in *BAR* 17/6 (1991), p. 65; ID. – M.O. WISE, *The Dead Sea Scrolls Uncovered*, Shaftesbury – Rockport, MA – Brisbane, Element, 1992, pp. 19-23: "The Messiah of Heaven and Earth" (GT: *Jesus und die Urchristen: Die Qumran-Rollen entschlüsselt*, München, 1992); M.O. WISE – J.D. TABOR, *The Messiah at Qumran*, in *BAR* 18/6 (1992) 60-65; TABOR & WISE, *4Q521 'On Resurrection' and the Synoptic Gospel Tradition: A Preliminary Study*, in *Journal for the Study of Pseudepigrapha* 10 (1992) 149-162, esp. pp. 158-162; reprinted in J.H. CHARLESWORTH (ed.), *Qumran Questions* (The Biblical Seminar, 36), Sheffield, Academic, 1995, pp. 151-163.

110. Cf. *BAR*, p. 62; *JSP*, p. 151 (= 1995, p. 153). See also EISENMAN & WISE, *The Dead Sea Scrolls Uncovered*, p. 23: same text in line 11, but more hesitant regarding line 10: "...] of Holiness will not delay..."; cf. p. 20: "in Lines 11-13, it is possible that a shift occurs, and the reference could be to 'His Messiah'. The editors were unable to agree on the reconstruction here".

does not appear in the text if read correctly" (F. García Martínez)[111]. For J.J. Collins, "To suggest that the works of the messiah are 'not the works of the Lord' makes no sense"[112]. Puech's quite different text of lines 10-11 is now accepted by almost all translators[113].

Apart from his critique of the Wise & Tabor reading of lines 10 and 11, Collins proposes an interpretation of line 12 that can be seen as a corrected version of their approach[114]:

111. *Messianic Hopes*, pp. 169, 170 (= *Messianische Erwartungen*, pp. 184-185). *Ibid.*, p. 170: "all these speculations are unnecessary if the text is read correctly. In it, the Messiah does not raise up the dead, nor are there wonderful deeds which are not the work of God". See also, with reference to García Martínez, J. DUHAIME, *Le messie et les saints dans un fragment apocalyptique de Qumrân (4Q521 2)*, in R. KUNTZMANN (ed.), *Ce Dieu qui vient*. FS B. Renaud (Lectio Divina, 159), Paris, Cerf, 1995, pp. 265-274, esp. 273, on the mention of Messiah in line 10: "il s'agit là d'une pure spéculation".

112. On Collins's contribution see below n. 114; here, *Works*, p. 100 n. 6; *Scepter*, p. 132 n. 83.

113. In line 11 Puech reads יעשה (the Lord *will do*), and not מעשה (the *work* of the Lord). Cf. above, Fitzmyer's translation. Compare, e.g., the translations by Puech, García Martínez, and J. Maier (see also below, n. 160):
10 et le fru[it d'une] bonne [œuvr]e ne sera différé pour personne,
  11 et des actions glorieuses qui n'ont jamais eu lieu, le Seigneur réalisera comme il l'a d[it].
10 and from no-one shall the fruit [of] good [deeds] be delayed,
  11 and the Lord will perform marvellous acts such as have not existed, just as he sa[id].
10 und die Fruch[t guter Ta]t wird sich einem Mann nicht verzögern,
  11 und die glorreiche Dinge, die (so noch) nicht gewesen, wird der Herr tun, wie Er ges[agt hat].

114. J.J. COLLINS, *The Works of the Messiah*, in *Dead Sea Discoveries* 1 (1994) 98-112 (here p. 100); slightly revised in ID., *The Scepter and the Star: The Messiahs of the Dead Sea Scrolls and Other Ancient Literature*, New York, Doubleday, 1995, pp. 117-122 ("Q4521"), here pp. 118, 132 n. 85 ("not... as mutually exclusive"). Compare however TABOR & WISE, p. 158: "The Messiah resurrects the dead as God's agent" and COLLINS, *Works*, p. 101, on the possibility that "God should use an agent in the resurrection". Compare É. PUECH, in *Messianism* (n. 107), pp. 245-246: "In 4Q521, God himself accomplishes these signs (probably in the days of the Messiah and through his messenger)... In the gospels, by contrast, Jesus ... acts by himself as the Elect, the Son of God". The first sentence is now quoted by Collins in *Jesus* (cf. below), p. 297 n. 52.
See also COLLINS, *"He shall not judge by what his eyes see"*: *Messianic Authority in the Dead Sea Scrolls*, in *Dead Sea Discoveries* 2 (1995) 145-164, esp. pp. 161-163; *Jesus and the Messiahs of Israel*, in H. LICHTENBERGER (ed.), *Geschichte – Tradition – Reflexion*. FS M. Hengel, III. *Frühes Christentum*, Tübingen, Mohr, 1996, pp. 287-302, esp. 296-298. Collins's first essay in *Dead Sea Discoveries* originally circulated as a Sample Issue (1994), pp. 1-15. It was written in dialogue with Wise & Tabor (see p. 98 n. 1: "The text is discussed..."); compare: "an exceptionally interesting text" (an extremely important text); "Three aspects of the text are especially interesting" (Three striking features of this text are significant), i.e., mention of a messiah, reference to resurrection, and close parallel in Q 7,22.
Several other contributions on 4Q521 were written in reference to Wise & Tabor. Cf. F. GARCÍA MARTÍNEZ, *Messianic Hopes* (n. 108), pp. 169-170 ("The only study of this manuscript which has appeared so far"); with reference to Eisenman & Wise: K.

In view of the introduction of a 'messiah' in the first line of the fragment, it is likely that God acts through the agency of a prophetic messiah in line 12. [n. 9:] My position here differs from that of Wise and Tabor in so far as I do not see the agency of God and of the messiah as alternatives to each other.

But how certain is their common starting point: the mention of "His Messiah" in line 1? First, although משיחו is read by Puech as a singular ("très probablement"), his translation indicates the possibility of a plural: "Son (/Ses?) Messie(s)"[115]. For M.G. Abegg, Jr., there is a need for further reflection because "the word is situated on the left margin of the fragment; the right margin having been eroded. Given Qumran paleography and orthography, the text could also be read 'his messiahs' (משיחיו), or perhaps more likely, 'the anointed of...' (משיחי)"[116]. Second, the word occurs in the plural in 4Q521 frag. 8: "and all her [Zion's?] anointed ones" (line 9: וכל משיחיה)[117]. This plural, probably referring to the priests (cf. line 8: "holy vessels")[118], has been used against reading the plural in frag. 2 (Puech, García Martínez, Duhaime) but also as a confirmation of the plural in frag. 2 (Abegg, Maier). Third, the parallelism of lines 1 and 2 should not be neglected:

¹ *the heavens and the earth will listen to* משיחו
² *and all that is in them will not turn away from the commandment(s) of* קדושים.

Fitzmyer's translation: *His Messiah and holy ones*[119] is accompanied with the following comment: "Because the text is fragmentary it is not

Berger, *Qumran und Jesus. Wahrheit unter Verschluß?* Stuttgart, Quell, 1993, esp. pp. 99-100 (cf. below, n. 134); O. Betz, in Id. – R. Riesner, *Jesus, Qumran und der Vatikan. Klarstellungen*, Gießen/Basel, Brunnen – Freiburg, Herder, 1993, pp. 111-115: "Gott und der helfende Messias (4Q521)". Cf. below, n. 119.

115. *RQ*, p. 486; see p. 487 n. 14 (= *Croyance*, pp. 633, 634): "Une orthographe mšyhw peut être lue au pluriel, 'ses messies'; pour une trentaine de cas dans les textes déjà publiés, voir E. Qimron, *The Hebrew of the Dead Sea Scrolls* (HSS, 29), 1986, p. 59".

116. M.G. Abegg, Jr., *The Messiah at Qumran: Are We Still Seeing Double?*, in *Dead Sea Discoveries* 2 (1995) 125-144, esp. pp. 141-143 (here 142).

117. Puech, p. 508 (= 659): "et tous ses oints"; Maier, p. 686: "und alle ihre Gesalbten" (n. 655: the feminine suffix = Jerusalem). – The plural can possibly be read in frag. 9: "you will abandon into the power of (your) messiah (or messiahs?)" (line 3: [משיח). Cf. Puech, p. 509 (= 660): "[son/ses] oint(s)".

118. Puech, et al.; García Martínez: the prophets. Cf. Collins, *Scepter*, p. 118.

119. This is the most usual translation of קדושים: "of (the) holy ones", "des saints", "Heiliger" (sometimes identified as "angels"). Contrast García Martínez: "the holy precepts" ("de heilige geboden").

Note the translation of line 2 by Wise & Tabor (Eisenman & Wise and Tabor & Wise): "[The sea and all th]at is in them. He will not turn aside from the commandment of the Holy Ones" (He = the Messiah). This translation is adopted by O. Betz: "Auch der

possible to be certain about who those are who are called *qĕdôšîm*"[120]. What is important for us here is the synonymous parallelism which may recommend the reading of the plural in line 1: "the anointed ones"[121]. The text is fragmentary indeed and one of our uncertainties concerns the possible connection with a preceding context. Puech proposes the restoration of a two-letter word at the opening of the first line: כי, translated in French: "car(?)" (García Martínez: "for")[122]. This conjecture presupposes a context of which we can only guess that it could explain the reading "His Messiah" or "the anointed ones" in line 1 of the fragment[123]. What we know is the fact that, if "his messiah" is to be read, this "anomalous reference in the adaptation of Psalm 146" (Collins) is never mentioned again in lines 3-14[124].

The second argument Collins has in common with Wise & Tabor is the allusion to Isa 61,1. "In view of the role of the anointed prophet in Isaiah 61" line 12c becomes the key for the messianic interpretation. His basic observation concerns ענוים יבשר: "It is surprising to find God as the subject of preaching good news. This is the work of a herald or messenger. The phrase in question is taken from Isa. 61:1…"[125]. Three

---

Messias wird nicht von den Geboten weichen, an die sich selbst die Engel halten". Cf. *Jesus* (n. 114), p. 115; see also pp. 111, 112 ("d.h. von den Weisungen Gottes, die auch die Engel, die besonderen und himmlischen Diener Gottes, befolgen").

120. *Scrolls* (n. 108), p. 314. See, e.g., J. Duhaime's suggestion "qu'il s'agisse d'un messie royal (angélique?) dont *les fidèles* partageraient le pouvoir". Cf. *Le messie et les saints* (n. 111), pp. 272, 274. A peculiar solution is suggested by R. BERGMEIER, *Beobachtungen zu 4 Q 521 f 2, II, 1-13*, in ZDMG 145 (1995) 38-48, here pp. 39 (n. 9), 44. In parallel to the singular in the first line he proposes to read קדשים "als Hoheitsname Gottes (= der Hochheilige)": "seinen Gesalbten" and "den Geboten des Hochheiligen".

121. Cf. J. MAIER, p. 683 n. 651: "Hier scheint ein Parallelismus mit 'Heiligen' (Engeln?) im Sinne von hohen Amtsträgern vorzuliegen". In a short paper delivered at the Colloquium the reading "the anointed ones" (for priestly figures of the end-time) was defended by K.-W. Niebuhr on the basis of the synonymous parallelism. See in this volume: K.-W. NIEBUHR, *Die Werke des eschatologischen Freudenboten: 4Q521 und die Jesusüberlieferung*, pp. 637-646.

122. Cf. *Rollen* (n. 108): "want". See also L.H. SCHIFFMAN, *Reclaiming the Dead Sea Scrolls*, Philadelphia – Jerusalem, Jewish Publication Society, 1994, pp. 347-350 ("The Messianic Apocalypse"), here p. 347: "For…".

123. Cf. J. VANDERKAM, *Messianism in the Scrolls*, in *Community* (n. 107), pp. 211-234, here 215: "the unknown factor is what came before the heavens and the earth – the angels?". The possibility is suggested by R. Bergmeier (n. 120) "daß Z. 1-2 Schlußzeilen eines vorausgehenden Psalms wären" (p. 39 n. 7).

124. Therefore scholars who accept the reading "His Messiah" remain reticent about the subject in line 12. See, e.g., J. VANDERKAM, *Messianism* (n. 123), p. 215: "It remains unclear whether the messiah of the first line or the Lord who is mentioned several times thereafter is the one who does these miracles. The context favors the latter option". – Collins's phrase (in the text) is from *Messianic Authority* (n. 114), p. 162.

125. *Works*, p. 100; repeated in *Scepter*, p. 118; *Messianic Authority*, p. 162. Compare TABOR & WISE, p. 157: "ענוים יבשר is a modified quotation of Isa. 61.1 and a critical phrase

reflections can be made. First, defining by virtue of biblical quotation the identity of the agent of the third activity in line 12 can become problematic if it implies making him (the Messiah) responsible for all activities in line 12 (and 13). In particular, Collins knows quite well that to give life to the dead (12b מתים יחיה) is a function that is usually reserved for God. In 4Q521 frag. 7, "the one who gives life to the dead of this people" (line 6: המחיה את מתי עמו), "the reference is presumably to God"[126]. Second, the fact that in Isa 61,1 the "prophet" who has to announce-good-news is sent by God makes it less difficult to integrate this action in "the works of the Lord"[127]. Third, line 12 cannot be treated in isolation from its context in the fragment. The influence of Psalm 146 is generally recognised. Collins calls it "the base-text"[128], and for Tabor & Wise "this Psalm was very influential on the author's thinking, both verbally and conceptually"[129]. One can observe already in line 1 (and 2) the influence of Ps 146,6: "(his hope is in Yahweh his God) who made *heaven and earth*, the sea *and all that is in them*". The text of line 8, "freeing the prisoners, giving sight to the blind, lifting up those who are bo[wed down]", is a quotation of Ps 146,7c.8a.b:

יהוה מתיר אסורים
יהוה פקח עורים
יהוה זקף כפופים

The explicit mention of the subject Yahweh (omitted in line 8)[130] is typical of Ps 146 (vv. 1.2.5.7c.8a.b.c.9a.10). The substitute אדני is used in lines 3, 4, and 5: "The Lord will visit..." governing the following lines 6-8, and is used again in line 11: "the *mirabilia* the Lord will do". Since there is no change of subject the text of line 12 (and 13)[131] should be

in answering the question who is the agent responsible for the actions in l. 12" (p. 158: "Note that the Bible never uses בשר of God"). See also O. Betz, *Jesus* (n. 114), p. 113.

126. *Works*, p. 101. Cf. Puech, *Croyance*, p. 687: "La résurrection, un des actes de justice de Dieu (fg 7,7), est clairement l'œuvre de Dieu lui-même, créateur, fg 7,1-3, vivificateur, fg 7,6, qui ouvre (les tombeaux / les livres?), fg 7,8".

127. In this sense J. Duhaime, in *Le messie et les saints* (above, n. 111), can speak of harmonization "faisant de Dieu lui-même le sujet de toutes ces actions" (p. 273).

128. *Works*, p. 100.

129. *4Q521*, p. 151 (= 153). Cf. Puech, p. 515 (= 664): "une sorte de midrash du *Ps* 146, hymne au Dieu secourable, qui a fourni quelques thèmes centraux, Dieu créateur et sauveur, distinction entre justes et impies". Cf. below, nn. 130-131.

130. Cf. Tabor & Wise, p. 153 (= 155): "This line is a slightly modified quotation of Ps 146,7-8, dropping only the Tetragrammaton"; Puech, p. 490 (= 637): "citation presque littérale de Ps 146,7b-8a-b, avec omission de yhwh à chaque stique mais le sujet 'dny est son équivalent et son *ersatz*". Cf. Collins, *Works*, p. 99: "In lines 1-8, this passage is heavily dependent on Psalm 146".

131. Compare the last phrase in line 13 on the רעבים ("the hungry he will enrich") with Ps 146,7b: "he gives food to the hungry". Cf. Wise & Tabor, p. 62: "This psalm

read in the spirit of Ps 146. Interpretations emphasizing the parallel to Isa 61,1 in line 12c seem to read 4Q521 (too much) in light of Q 7,22.

Q 7,22 is no doubt "the most fascinating parallel" to 4Q521: "the parallel... is intriguing since both go beyond Isaiah 61 in referring to the raising of the dead"[132]. On the side of 4Q521, Q 7,22 is adduced as decisive evidence for the messianic interpretation. In itself a remarkable parallel to line 12 (... νεκροὶ ἐγείρονται, πτωχοὶ εὐαγγελίζονται)[133] it has been enlarged with the introduction to John's question including Mt 11,2 τὰ ἔργα τοῦ Χριστοῦ, The Works of the Messiah (title of Collins's essay)[134]. On the side of Q 7,22, the parallel gives rise to suggestions on tradition history: "This can hardly be coincidental. It is quite possible that the author of the Sayings source knew 4Q521; at the least he drew on a common tradition"[135].

It is time now to come back to Q 7,22. We can no longer speak of the uniqueness of its reference to raising the dead followed by evangelizing the poor. It would be too rash a conclusion, however, to suggest that "New Testament writers"[136] may have known 4Q521. But one can

was apparently quite important for the author of our text. Both the psalm and our text reflect a concern for the destitute – the poor and the hungry".

132. COLLINS, *Works*, pp. 106, 107.

133. Recognised as such for instance by García Martínez: "the combination in a single phrase of the resurrection of the dead with the announcement of good news to the ʿanawim, which comes from Is 61:1, was not previously documented outside the New Testament" (*Messianic Hopes*, n. 108, p. 169). Cf. below, n. 135.

134. Compare K. BERGER, *Qumran und Jesus* (n. 114), p. 100: "Überdies bezeichnet Matthäus in Mt 11,2 diese Liste als 'Werke des Christus', dem entspricht vielleicht in Zeile 11 des hier zitierten Dokuments der Ausdruck 'Werke Gottes'" (on line 11, see above n. 113). In the same passage one can read, p. 99: "Totenerweckungen kommen bei Jesaja nicht vor" (no reference to Isa 26,19); and p. 100: "In der gemeinsamen Quelle für Matthäus und Lukas, der sogenannten Logienquelle, wo die Liste vielleicht zuerst stand, hatte es eine Totenerweckung als Tat Jesu auch nicht gegeben" (sic).

135. COLLINS, *Works*, p. 107; with an echo in G. BROOKE, *Luke-Acts and the Qumran Scrolls: The Case of MMT*, in C.M. TUCKETT (ed.), *Luke's Literary Achievement* (n. 79), 1995, pp. 72-90, esp. 75-76 (here 76). Compare TABOR & WISE, *4Q521*, p. 161: "Although it is unlikely that Luke knew the Qumran text directly, it seems that he shares with its author a common set of messianic expectations"; BERGER (n. 134), p. 100: "Hier liegt eine gemeinsame (wohl: mündliche) Auslegungstradition vor" ("eine Form der Jesaja-Interpretation").

136. GARCÍA MARTÍNEZ, *Rollen* (n. 108), p. 421: "Mogelijk kenden de Nieuwtestamentische schrijvers de tekst van 4Q521. Tenminste is een gemeenschappelijke traditie aan te nemen". – I may refer here to his recent essay, *Two Messianic Figures in the Qumran Texts*, in D.W. PARRY – S.D. RICKS (eds.), *Current Research and Technological Developments on the Dead Sea Scrolls* (Studies on the Texts of the Desert of Judah, 20), Leiden, Brill, 1996, pp. 14-40. The text of 4Q521, "one of the most beautiful fragments of the Qumran texts", is quoted on pp. 39-40. Although "the ambiguity of the fragmentary text cannot be resolved", he maintains his identification of the messiah in line 1 as

expect that the comparison with the parallel in 4Q521 will have some effect in judgments on the originality of Q 7,22. The association of νεκροὶ ἐγείρονται with "lepers are cleansed" as non-Isaianic and possibly secondary item in Q 7,22[137] does not, to say the least, receive confirmation in the presence of "reviving the dead" in 4Q521.

As indicated above, the climactic position of πτωχοὶ εὐαγγελίζονται in Q 7,22 is widely acknowledged. The parallel in 4Q521 is found in line 12, in the same order (healing the sick – raising the dead – evangelizing the poor), but the list continues in line 13 and עניים יבשר does not represent that same climax. The allusion to Isa 61 takes its place among the blessings of salvation. The distinctiveness of the last phrase in Q 7,22 has to do with its content (after the deeds comes the word: preaching-good-news)[138] and with its specific background in Isa 61,1[139]:

> The first two passages [Isa 29,18-19; 35,5-6] provide the general theme of an eschatological time when the deaf will hear, the blind see and the lame walk. But the climax clearly comes with the allusion to Isa. 61:1, πτωχοὶ εὐαγγελίζονται. Only with these words do we have a hint of a more specific answer to John's question about the person of Jesus... For the Q community this was the point of Jesus' reply... There is now clear evidence that at the time of Jesus Isa. 61:1 was being interpreted in a quite specific way as referring to *the* eschatological prophet.

This alludes of course to 11QMelch 2,18 [ח]הרו שיח[מ אה]הו והמבשר, "and the herald [Isa 52,7] is the one anointed with the Spirit [cf. Isa 61,1]"[140]. In his comment on 11QMelch M. de Jonge could refer to Q

the Royal Messiah (n. 40) and is "not sure that this messiah should be identified with the expected eschatological Prophet" (p. 39).

137. Cf. above, nn. 100, 104.

138. Possibly in a chiastic correspondence to the introductory phrase ἃ ἀκούετε καὶ βλέπετε (= Mt). Cf. GNILKA, *Matthäusevangelium* I, p. 407: "Hören/Sehen – Wunder/Wort"; HÄFNER, *Vorläufer*, p. 179: "der Bezug auf das Wort Jesu rahmt die Aussagen über die Wundertaten": MtR? (cf. below, p. 62). J.M. ROBINSON (cf. above, n. 86) does not consider this chiastic order; he apparently reads Q 7,22b ἃ εἴδετε καὶ ἠκούσατε (= Lk). Cf. *The Sayings Gospel Q* (n. 18), p. 364. On chiastic arrangement in Q, see *ibid.*, p. 365; *The* Incipit, p. 32:

Inaugural Sermon ⟋⟍ Healings (7,22)
Centurion ⟋⟍ Evangelizing the poor (7,22)

139. Quotation from G.N. STANTON, *On the Christology of Q*, in B. LINDARS, et al. (eds.), *Christ and the Spirit in the New Testament*. FS C.F.D. Moule, Cambridge, University Press, 1973, pp. 27-42, esp. 29-30.

140. "Der Textzusammenhang fordert, daß dies eine endzeitlich-prophetische Figur (der endzeitliche Prophet?) ist": P. STUHLMACHER, *Das paulinische Evangelium*, I (n. 100), 1968, pp. 142-147 (1QH 18,14; 11QMelch), here p. 145; see also pp. 218-225 (Q 7,18-23), esp. p. 219. But see his retraction in *Das paulinische Evangelium*, in ID. (ed.), *Das Evangelium und die Evangelien* (WUNT, 28), Tübingen, Mohr, 1983, pp. 157-182 (ET: *The Gospel and the Gospels*, Grand Rapids, MI, Eerdmans, 1991, pp. 148-172):

7,22: "This passage deals with Jesus' deeds and words; implicitly it is said that he [Jesus] is the εὐαγγελιζόμενος" (1966)[141]. Some twenty years later this statement was supplemented[142]:

> I cannot find any sign that Jesus' preaching of good news to the poor was connected with 'anointing through the Spirit' before Luke. In Jesus' answer to the question of John the Baptist in Q the word χριστός did not occur. [n. 101:] χριστός is never used in Q.

Collins has now replied in "The Works of the Messiah"[143]:

> We now have in 4Q521 a remarkable parallel to Jesus' answer to the Baptist, which also refers to a messiah, whom heaven and earth obey.
> There is good reason to think that actions described in Isaiah 61, with the addition of the raising of the dead, were already viewed as 'works of the messiah' in some Jewish circles before the career of Jesus.

The works-of-the-messiah interpretation goes not uncontested and an alternative reading of 4Q521 may imply a different view on the comparison with Q 7,22. There is first of all the problem of the literary unity of Q 7,18-23[144], which seems to be neglected in the studies on 4Q521.

"J.A. Fitzmyer [*JBL*, 1967], in my opinion very appropriately, points out that in 11QMelch 4ff. both Isa. 61:1f. and Isa. 52:7 must be related to the eschatological appearance of Melchizedek as heavenly redeemer" (p. 173 = 164, n. 37); "The interpretation I proposed... as referring to a (or the) end-time prophet is much less probable" (p. 171 = 162, n. 32); ID., *Biblische Theologie des Neuen Testaments*, I, Göttingen, Vandenhoeck & Ruprecht, 1992, p. 112: "In 11QMelch werden der Freudenbote von Jes 52,7 und der Geistgesalbte von Jes 61,1-2 auf *Melchisedek* als himmlischen Erlöser gedeutet". See also, e.g., J. BECKER, *Johannes der Täufer und Jesus von Nazareth* (BSt, 63), Neukirchen, Neukirchener, 1972, pp. 53-54.

141. M. DE JONGE – A.S. VAN DER WOUDE, *11Q Melchizedek and New Testament*, in *NTS* 12 (1965-66) 301-326, esp. pp. 309-312 ("The Use of Isa. LII.7 and LXI.1f. in the New Testament"), here p. 309. – In the same passage the authors refer to the first beatitude: in Mt 5,3 they find "a clear allusion" to Isa 61,1 and in Lk 6,20 "the connexion is even clearer because this evangelist writes οἱ πτωχοί without the addition τῷ πνεύματι...". But on this question see Part I of my paper.

142. *The Earliest Christian Use of Christos: Some Suggestions*, in *NTS* 32 (1986) 321-343; = ID., *Jewish Eschatology, Early Christian Christology and the Testaments of the Twelve Patriarchs. Collected Essays* (NTSup, 63), Leiden, Brill, 1991, pp. 102-124, esp. 116-117.

143. *Works*, pp. 110, 112; *Scepter*, p. 205.

144. Those who are in favour of the historicity of the Baptist's question and Jesus' response defend the unity of Q 7,18-23. See, e.g., W.G. KÜMMEL, *Jesu Antwort an Johannes den Täufer. Ein Beispiel zum Methodenproblem in der Jesusforschung*, Wiesbaden, Steiner, 1974. The unitary composition is also maintained by scholars like A. VÖGTLE, *Wunder und Wort* (n. 92; p. 242: "eine erst urchristliche Bildung", with the missionary purpose "noch abseitsstehende Täuferkreise für den Christusglauben zu gewinnen"); and, more recently, K. BACKHAUS, *Die "Jüngerkreise"* (n. 83), esp. pp. 118-119: "im ganzen (darf) die literarische Einheitlichkeit der Perikope als gesichert gelten; die weitere Analyse ergibt, daß diese Einheit sich im wesentlichen auf die Q-Gemeinde zurückführen läßt" (p. 119). Cf. J.S. KLOPPENBORG, *Formation* (n. 86), pp. 107-108:

Researchers on Q are more readily inclined to separate Q 7,22 (without direct reference to the question σύ εῖ;)[145] from its present framework. I may refer to Tuckett's statement: "The best explanation is that the putting together of Jesus' claims with John's question is a secondary composition by a later editor"[146], and to Catchpole's recent discussion of the secondariness of the framework: "The necessary conclusion seems to be that everything in this tradition apart from the six-fold list in Q 7:22 is Q-editorial"[147]. For Sato too the list in 7,22 is "als eigenständiges Stück isolierbar"[148]. Although there is a scholarly tradition[149] in favour of the authenticity of the Jesus saying Q 7,22+23, I consider here "the list of miracles"[150] in

"It is more likely ... that the entire pronouncement story is a post-Easter creation", and 7,22 "a post-Easter interpretation of Jesus' deeds as evidence of the presence of the kingdom". But see below, n. 151.

145. For a particular analysis of Q 7,18-23 see R. CAMERON, *"What Have You Come Out To See?" Characterizations of John and Jesus in the Gospels*, in *Semeia* 49 (1990) 35-69, esp. pp. 51-55. The original chreia comprised a question (v. 19b) and a response (v. 23): "When asked, 'Are you the one who is to come or should we expect another?' Jesus replied, 'Whoever is not offended by me is blessed'" (p. 52). In a later stage another response to the original question was substituted (v. 22) and John and his disciples were introduced into the narrative (vv. 18-19). Now, "the allusions to Isaiah... permit 'Jesus' to construct an argument that turns not simply on a saying attributed to him, but on a chreia that makes reference to a known, biblical authority" (p. 55); "the references to scripture... fit the developing portraits that are made in the elaboration pattern" in Q 7,18-35 (p. 51). Apart from the characterization of John and Jesus as "Cynic figures" and the construction of an original chreia, one may consider here Cameron's basic observation on linking 7,19b.23 (σὺ εῖ...; ... ἐν ἐμοί).

146. *Q and the History*, p. 126. With reference to Bultmann, *et al.*: "According to many, the reply in v. 22 ... can confidently be regarded as an authentic saying of the historical Jesus" (*ibid.*).

147. *Quest*, p. 239. Cf. W. SCHENK, *Synopse*, p. 40.

148. *Q und Prophetie* (n. 24), 1988, pp. 140-144 (1984, pp. 165-169), here 141 (165); "Lk 7,23 par ist erst mit dem Apophthegma entstanden; Lk 7,22 par ist dagegen älter" (*ibid.*). See also J. SCHÜLING, *Studien zum Verhältnis von Logienquelle und Markus-evangelium* (FzB, 65), Würzburg, Echter, 1991, p. 80: "Endzeitschilderung und Makarismus waren wahrscheinlich zunächst isoliert überliefert und später sekundär als Antwort auf die Täuferfrage zusammengestellt worden"; M. TILLY, *Johannes der Täufer und die Biographie der Propheten. Die synoptische Täuferüberlieferung und das jüdische Prophetenbild zur Zeit des Täufers* (BWANT, 137), Stuttgart, Kohlhammer, 1994, p. 86 n. 220: "Ursprünglich wurde wohl die zunächst isoliert tradierte Zusammenfassung der eschatologischen Heilszeichen Jesu nicht mit der als sekundäre christliche Bildung anzusehenden Täuferfrage verknüpft".

149. Named after Bultmann, *Geschichte*, ²1931, pp. 22.115; cf. 133.135.136 (= 1921, pp. 11.66; cf. 76-78). See, e.g., H. MERKLEIN, *Die Gottesherrschaft als Handlungsprinzip. Untersuchung zur Ethik Jesu* (FzB, 34), Würzburg, Echter, 1978, pp. 162-163.

150. Though with some reservation about supposed "independence of the miracle-list form in early Christian tradition", I refer here to D.T.M. FRANKFURTER, *The Origin of the Miracle-List Tradition and Its Medium of Circulation*, in *SBL 1990 Seminar Papers*, pp. 344-374, esp. 351-352: the list in Q 7,22 "more likely circulated originally independently of the oral miracle stories"; cf. J.D. CROSSAN, *Lists in Early Christianity*, in *Semeia* 55 (1992) 235-343, esp. pp. 238-240 ("Miracle Lists").

Q 7,22^{cde} and its original independence. In defining the genre of the logion itself, the parallel in 4Q521 can be helpful as an example of the *topos* of a description of the time of salvation[151]. The integration of "evangelizing the poor" in the glorious works of the Lord should perhaps prevent from dividing Q 7,22 into "deeds" and "words". As noted already[152], Isa 29,19a ("The *'anawim* shall obtain fresh joy in Jahweh") may withhold from dichotomizing the Isaianic allusions.

I conclude with a corollary on Q 7,22^b. Mt's ἀκούετε κ. βλέπετε is adopted in the IQP text[153] and in many other reconstructions of Q[154], but the word order of Lk's εἴδετε κ. ἠκούσατε also has its defenders, in the aorist (Gundry) or, with greater probability, in the present tense: βλέπετε κ. ἀκούετε (Vögtle, Polag, Schenk). Those who opt for Mt's order are well aware that the evidence is reversible[155]. Schürmann recognises: "Die Vorordnung des Sehens entspricht besser V 22"[156], and Sevenich-Bax even proposes the dubious argument that the order hearing and seeing is the *lectio difficilior* (and therefore "zu bevorzugen")[157]. For the point I made in my lecture at the Colloquium I was happy to find confirmation in B. Kollmann's study (1996)[158].

151. Cf. BULTMANN, *Geschichte*, p. 22: "das Wort (will) eigentlich nur mit den Farben des (Deutero-)Jesajas die selige Endzeit schildern"; J. JEREMIAS, *Die Gleichnisse Jesu* (n. 100), p. 99 (= 116); *Neutestamentliche Theologie* (n. 106), p. 107; ET, p. 104: "all age-old phrases for the time of salvation, when there will be no more sorrow, no more crying and no more grief"; H.-W. KUHN, *Enderwartung* (n. 102), p. 196: "Mit Motiven des Jesajabuches wird die eschatologische Heilszeit geschildert". Cf. H. MERKLEIN, n. 149, p. 163: "es (geht) um eine (allgemeine) Charakterisierung der Heilszeit". Compare now P. GRELOT, *"Celui qui vient"* (n. 106), p. 284: "c'est Dieu qui vient accomplir ici-bas le renversement eschatologique de la situation à laquelle étaient liés tous les maux humains"; J.S. KLOPPENBORG, *The Sayings Gospel Q and the Quest of the Historical Jesus*, in *HTR* 89 (1996) 307-344, p. 330 n. 101: on the list in 4Q521 which "bears an uncanny resemblance to the deeds of Jesus listed in Q 7:22"; and 331: "One cannot even be sure that the wonders to which Q alludes were meant to be understood as Jesus' own works"; "nothing in Q 7:22; 10:13-14 or 10:23-24 requires that Jesus was the only performer of wonders".

152. Cf. above, n. 106.

153. Cf. *JBL* 113 (1994), p. 498. Contrast KLOPPENBORG, in *Q – Thomas Reader*, p. 44 (cf. p. 34).

154. Harnack, Schürmann, Hoffmann, Schulz, Bovon, Gnilka, Catchpole, Sevenich-Bax, *et al.*

155. See, e.g., HOFFMANN, *Studien*, p. 193 n. 14: "Allerdings zeigt Matthäus umgekehrt ein Interesse am Hören (vgl. z.B. Mt 13,16f); er könnte die Reihenfolge der Verben hier dem Aufbau seines Evangeliums angepaßt haben".

156. *Lukasevangelium* I, p. 410 n. 20.

157. *Konfrontation*, p. 201.

158. B. KOLLMANN, *Jesus und die Christen als Wundertäter. Studien zu Magie, Medizin und Schamanismus in Antike und Christentum* (FRLANT, 170), Göttingen, Vandenhoeck & Ruprecht, 1996, pp. 216-221: "Die Wunder stehen im Vordergrund, bevor mit πτωχοὶ εὐαγγελίζονται im nachhinein die Verkündigung Erwähnung findet... [H]ier

Conclusion

The significance of Q 7,18-23 (Mt 11,2-6) for the composition of the Gospel of Matthew is undisputed[159]. In the Gospel of Luke too the insertion of 7,11-17 after 7,1-10 and the creation of 7,21 are rightly connected with the answer of Jesus in 7,22. It is less clear, however, whether similar conclusions can be drawn with regard to the composition of Q. The allusion to Isa 61,1 in Q 7,22 may on the one hand have influenced Matthew's redaction of the beatitudes (Mt 5,3-4) and on the other the quotation in the Nazareth pericope (Lk 4,18-19), both at the post-Q level of the evangelists' redaction.

SUPPLEMENTARY NOTE: J.M. Robinson has now reformulated his view in a recent article, *Building Blocks in the Social History of Q*, in E.A. CASTELLI – H. TAUSSIG (eds.), *Reimagining Christian Origins*. FS B.L. Mack, Valley Forge, PA, Trinity Press International, 1996, pp. 87-112, esp. 92-93: "Indeed there was hardly a time in the Q trajectory when Isaiah 61:1-2 was not in view" (p. 93); "already the formative stage of Q used Isaiah 61:1-2 to compose the Beatitudes" (*ibid.*); "Q 7:22 plays for the Q redaction the decisive role of a summary of, or a *post factum* organizing principle for, the first major section of Q, Q 3–7" (p. 92).

At least on two points Robinson is now more assertive than he was before. First, his position on the question whether the Baptism of Jesus is to be included in Q is well known, but it is new that the minor agreement ἐπ' αὐτόν (for εἰς αὐτόν in Mk) is no longer "notoriously inconclusive" (*The Sayings Gospel Q*, p. 383; referring to Kloppenborg): "It is in fact a very significant agreement. For the point is that the Q redactor was fully aware of Q 3–7 fulfilling Isa. 61:1" (p. 108 n. 20). Second, in my comment on his *The Sayings Gospel Q* I could still note that "Robinson himself does not suggest that πενθοῦντες and παρακληθήσονται in Mt 5,4 are from Q" (*ETL* 71, p. 426), with reference to his phrase "if it originally read κλαίοντες" (p. 369) and the IQP reconstruction ⟦κλαί⟧ οντες (Robinson being one of the respondents at the discussion of Q 6,20-21). Robinson now says that here he diverges from the IQP text but follows "the revision by the General Editors in the forthcoming critical edition" (p. 109 n. 21). Note: the three general editors are Robinson, Kloppenborg (but see above, n. 24) and P. Hoffmann. Hoffmann was undecided in *Bibel und Leben* 10 (1969), p. 114: "die älteste Textgestalt: die Armen, die Hungernden, die Trauernden (Weinenden?)" (in Mt's third person but in the Lukan order).

(erhielt) Jes 29,18f. gegenüber Jes 61,1f. mit der umgekehrten Rangordnung von Wundergeschichten und Verkündigung den Vorzug. Zudem ist auch Lk 7,22 (Q) mit ἃ εἴδετε καὶ ἀκούσατε eine formale Vorordnung der Tat gegenüber dem Wort gegeben" (p. 220).

159. On the Matthean composition of Mt 4,23–11,1, cf. D.L. DUNGAN (ed.), *The Interrelations of the Gospels* (BETL, 95), Leuven, 1990, pp. 23-46. Compare J.M. ROBINSON, *The Incipit*, p. 33. However, Matthew's redactional coordination of the Sermon and Healing in Mt 5–7 and 8–9 (cf. 11,4b: hear and see) hardly justifies retroactive extension to Q 6,20-49 and 7,1-10 (cf. above, n. 138).

Luke used Isa 61,1-2 in his new Inaugural Sermon (4,18-19). But the same Luke is supposed to have shifted the Isaianic mourn/comfort language in 6,21b to the weep/laugh of the woe. "Mourn" and "be comforted" in Mt 5,4 stems from Q and Matthew only used the context of Isa 61,1-2 in creating new Beatitudes (p. 93: Isa 61,3 "righteousness"; 61,7 "inherit the earth"). For a different view on Q 6,21b / Mt 5,4 I may refer to Part I of this paper (and to a forthcoming note in *ETL* on "The Baptism of Jesus in Q?").

With regard to Q 7,22 Robinson repeats the statement that "Q 7:22, in chiastic order, begins with the conclusion of Isaiah 61:1 (the blind see) and ends with the first item listed in Isaiah 61:1 (the evangelizing of the poor)" (p. 92). But see above in Part II of this paper[160].

Tiensevest 27   Frans NEIRYNCK
B-3010 Leuven

---

160. Addition to n. 113 (p. 54): M. WISE – M. ABEGG Jr. – E. COOK, *The Dead Sea Scrolls. A New Translation*, San Francisco, HarperCollins, 1996, pp. 420-422: "Redemption and Resurrection (4Q521)". Translation: "[10] [...] shall not be delayed [...] [11] and the Lord shall do glorious things which have not been done, just as He said" (p. 421).

MIC 5,1-3 IN QUMRAN AND IN THE NEW TESTAMENT AND MESSIANISM IN THE SEPTUAGINT

The purpose of this paper is not to give an exhaustive investigation of the Hebrew or Aramaic and Greek OT texts found in the neighbourhood of the Dead Sea. Good surveys of the available materials can be found in the works of E. Tov, E. Ulrich, J.A. Fitzmyer, and others[1]. It is well known that, apart from Esther[2], fragments of all the books of the Hebrew Bible have been discovered at Qumran, and that, in recent years, the publication of these data goes at a good pace[3].

The findings of biblical scrolls and the use of biblical quotations in the writings of the Qumran community had a major influence on biblical studies in general[4], and on textual criticism in particular[5]. Two major text

---

1. E. Tov, *Textual Criticism of the Hebrew Bible*, Minneapolis, Fortress; Assen, Gorcum, 1992, esp. 100-121 (*The Biblical Texts Found in Qumran*); E. Ulrich, *An Index of the Passages in the Biblical Manuscripts from the Judean Desert*, in *DSD* 1 (1994) 113-129 and 2 (1995) 86-107; J.A. Fitzmyer, *The Dead Sea Scrolls. Major Publications and Tools for Study* (SBL Resources for Biblical Study), Atlanta, GA, Scholars, ²1990; see also U. Glessmer, *Liste der biblischen Texte aus Qumran*, in *RQ* 16 (1993) 153-192; S.A. Reed, *The Dead Sea Scrolls Catalogue* (SBL Resources for Biblical Study), Atlanta, GA, Scholars, 1994.

2. See J.T. Milik, *Les modèles araméens du livre d'Esther dans la grotte 4 de Qumran*, in *RQ* 15 (1992) 321-399; S. Talmon, *Was the Book of Esther Known at Qumran?* in *DSD* 2 (1995) 249-267: "the Book of Esther was known, read, and cited, but not included among the circumscribed collection of books recognized as Holy Scripture". Milik's 4QProtoEsther has been given the sigle 4Q550: it can be found in R. Eisenman & M. Wise, *The Dead Sea Scrolls Uncovered*, London, 1992, under the title *Stories from the Persian Court* (pp. 99-103); see also the translation in F. García Martínez & A.S. van der Woude, *De rollen van de Dode Zee,* deel II, Kampen, Kok, 1995, 441-443.

3. The critical publication of the documents is given in *Discoveries in the Judaean Desert* (DJD, Oxford, Clarendon Press). Recent biblical volumes in the series are: E. Tov, *The Greek Minor Prophets Scroll from Nahal Hever* (DJD, viii), 1992; P.W. Skehan, E. Ulrich & J.E. Sanderson, *Paleo-Hebrew and Greek Biblical Manuscripts* (DJD, ix, Qumran Cave 4, iv), 1993; E. Ulrich a.o., *Genesis to Numbers* (DJD, xii, Qumran Cave 4, vii), 1994; Id., *Deuteronomy, Joshua, Judges, Kings* (DJD, xiv, Qumran Cave 4, ix), 1995.

4. See, e.g., J.A. Sanders, *The Dead Sea Scrolls and Biblical Studies*, in M. Fishbane & E. Tov (eds.), *"Sha'arei Talmon"*, Winona Lake, Eisenbrauns, 1992, 323-336.

5. See, e.g., F.M. Cross & S. Talmon (eds.), *Qumran and the History of the Biblical Text*, Cambridge MA, Harvard Univ. Press, 1975, with the collected reprints of essays by S. Talmon, M. Goshen-Gottstein, J. Ziegler, D. Barthélemy, W. Albright, F.M. Cross, D.N. Freedman, P.W. Skehan, E. Tov, together with the still stimulating new contributions by F.M. Cross, *The Evolution of a Theory of Local Texts* (306-320); S. Talmon, *The Textual Study of the Bible – A New Outlook* (321-400); and the (at that time up to date) lists of the materials so far published, by J.A. Sanders, *Palestinian Manuscripts, 1947-1972* (401-414).

critical projects reflect the impact of the discovery of the scrolls: the Hebrew University Bible Project (HUBP) with its main product: the edition of *The Hebrew University Bible*[6], and the United Bible Societies' Hebrew Old Testament Text Project (HOTTP) with its sequel, the *Biblia Hebraica Quinta* (BHQ), a revised edition of the *Biblia Hebraica Stuttgartensia*[7].

The aim of this paper is fourfold. Using Mic 5,1-3 and its quotation in Matthew as anchorage, I propose, first, to deal with some questions concerning the canon of the Scriptures in Qumran and in the NT, and second, to survey the available Qumranic materials in as far as Mic 5,1-3 is concerned, paying special attention to one Hebrew fragment, and to the Greek scroll of the Twelve Prophets with its transliteration of the tetragrammaton. The third section is a discussion of textual and literary critical data, based on a comparison of the MT, the Septuagint, and the New Testament quotation of Mic 5,1-3. The fourth section is devoted to an investigation of the messianic interpretation of Micah's prophecy, especially in the Septuagint.

I. QUOTATION FORMULAE AND CANON[8]

Matthew introduces his citation of Micah with an explicit introductory formula: οὕτως γὰρ γέγραπται διὰ τοῦ προφήτου. Similar quotation formulae can be found in the writings of Qumran and elsewhere in the New Testament. In Matthew the quotation is part of the fifth and final episode of the Infancy Narrative. Each of these episodes culminates in an OT quotation, and of these all but Mt 2,5-6 are introduced by the so-called fulfilment formula. The exception may be due to the fact that the

---

6. See M. GOSHEN-GOTTSTEIN, *The Book of Isaiah: Sample Edition with Introduction*, Jerusalem, 1965; ID., *The Book of Isaiah* (The Hebrew University Bible), Jerusalem, Magnes Press, 1995.

7. The results of the HOTTP are published by D. BARTHÉLEMY, *Critique textuelle de l'Ancien Testament*, Fribourg, Éd. Univ.; Göttingen, Vandenhoeck & Ruprecht, vol. 1 dealing with the so-called historical books (OBO, 50/1, 1982), vol. 2 with Isaiah, Jeremiah and Lamentations (OBO, 50/2, 1986), vol. 3 with Ezekiel, Daniel, and the Twelve Prophets (OBO, 50/3, 1992). For a presentation of BHQ see A. SCHENKER, *Eine geplante Neuausgabe der hebräischen Bibel*, in *Judaica* 50 (1994) 151-155.

8. About the canon of "Holy Scriptures" in Qumran and in the NT, see especially D. BARTHÉLEMY, *L'état de la Bible juive depuis le début de notre ère jusqu'à la deuxième révolte contre Rome (131-135)*, in S. AMSLER e.a. (ed.), *Le canon de L'Ancien Testament*, Genève, Labor et Fides, 1984, 9-45; J.A. SANDERS, *Text and Canon*, in P. CASSETTI a.o. (ed.), *Mél. D. Barthélemy* (OBO, 38), Fribourg, Éd. Univ., 1981; P. SKEHAN, *Qumran et le Canon de l'Ancien Testament*, in *DBS* 9 (1978) 818-822.

quotation in 2,5-6 is presented not as a comment of the evangelist, but as a proof from Scripture given by the Jewish leaders[9]. A comparison with the contemporary Qumranic data leads to the following observations.

1. The Qumranic authors never use the formula of "fulfilment". They simply use the verbs אמר and כתב in turnings such as כאשר כתוב "as it was written", and כאשר אמר "as it said" or "as he said", which find their Greek counterparts in the NT, e.g., οὕτως γὰρ γέγραπται as in our passage (Mt 2,5), or καθὼς γέγραπται (Luke 2,23), and κατὰ τὸ εἰρημένον (Luke 2,24)[10]. According to Fitzmyer the main reason for the presence or absence of fulfilment formulae is to be found in the difference of outlook which characterizes the two groups. The Qumran theology is still dominated by a forward look, whereas the Christian theology is more characterized by a backward glance, seeing the culmination of all that preceded in the advent of Christ[11].

In his leading contribution on the subject, Fitzmyer observes that the use of these formulae indicates a conscious and deliberate appeal to the Old Testament as the "Scriptures". It is true that the Qumranic authors, like those of the NT, appear to use the quotation formulae exclusively

---

9. ἵνα πληρωθῇ τὸ ῥηθὲν ὑπὸ κυρίου διὰ τοῦ προφήτου λέγοντος. See G.M. SOARES PRABHU, *The Formula Quotations in the Infancy Narrative of Matthew* (Analecta Biblica, 63), Rome, Pontif. Inst. Bibl., 1976, esp. p. 36; F. VAN SEGBROECK, *De Formulecitaten in het Mattheusevangelie. Bijdrage tot de Christologie van Mt.,4-13*, unpublished dissertation, Leuven, 1964; J.A. FITZMYER, *The Use of Explicit Old Testament Quotations in Qumran Literature and in the New Testament*, in *NTS* 7 (1960-61) 297-333, slightly updated reprint in *Essays on the Semitic Background of the New Testament*, London, Chapman, 1971.

10. About the explicit quotations of the "Old Testament" in the NT and in the Qumran writings, see especially FITZMYER 1960-61, 297-333 (see our note 9); F.M. HORTON, *Formulas of Introduction in the Qumran Literature*, in *RQ* 7 (1969-1971) 505-514; a list of the OT quotations in the documents of Qumran can be found in FITZMYER 1990, 205-237. On the interpretation of these biblical texts, see G. BROOKE, *Exegesis at Qumran* (JSOT SS, 29), Sheffield, JSOT Press, 1985, 302-309; M. FISHBANE, *Use, Authority and Interpretation of Mikra at Qumran*, in M.J. MULDER (ed.), *Mikra*, Assen, Gorcum, Philadelphia, Fortress, 1988, 339-378; G. VERMES, *Bible Interpretation at Qumran*, in *Eretz-Israel* 20 (1989) 184-191; ID., *Biblical Proof-Texts in Qumran Literature*, in *JSS* 34 (1989) 493-508; see also M.J. BERNSTEIN, *Introductory Formula for Citation and Re-citation of Biblical Verses in the Qumran Pesharim: Observations on a Pesher Technique*, in *DSD* 1 (1994) 30-70; J.M. BAUMGARTEN, *A 'Scriptural' Citation in 4Q Fragments of the Damascus Document*, in *JJS* 43 (1992) 95-98; L. GINZBERG, *An Unknown Sect*, New York, The Jewish Theological Seminary of America, 1976, 192-200; O.J.R. SCHWARZ, *Der erste Teil der Damascusschrift und das Alte Testament*, Diest, Lichtland, 1965; J. DE WAARD, *A Comparative Study of the Old Testament in the Dead Sea Scrolls and in the New Testament*, Leiden, Brill, 1965.

11. FITZMYER 1960-61, 303-304.

when citing writings which we now call "biblical" books[12]. This provides us with one of the rare indications telling us which books were considered as authoritative or canonical in the eyes of the members of the early Christian church and of the Qumran community. The list of the books that are quoted with a quotation formula is about the same in both communities[13]. Almost all of them belong to the Torah and to the Later Prophets. Hardly any quotations are found of the so-called Former Prophets or Historical Books, and from the Writings. The only exceptions seem to be: 1 Sam 25,26 in CD 9,9; 2 Sam 7,11.14 in 4QFlor 1,10-11; and Prov 15,8 in CD 11,20-21. The Psalms are cited most frequently, but almost always without introductory formula[14].

In an effort to delimit his research topic, Fitzmyer deliberately excluded the *pešarîm*, although they use the quotation formulae rather frequently. Filling in the gap, M.J. Bernstein devoted a penetrating study to that topic[15]. His main preoccupation is to demonstrate that 1QpHab and its use of quotation formulae are unique among the *pešarîm*. They are the exception rather than the rule. For our investigation it is perhaps more important to note that the *pešarîm* and the *pešer* method used in Qumran seem to offer a supplementary indication concerning the canon of the "Scriptures". All of the 17 identified *pešarîm* are commentaries of the Prophets or of the Psalms[16]. Nowhere does the *pešer* method seem to be applied to another biblical book, nor to any other type of writing. It should perhaps also be observed that no *pešer* of the books of the Torah seems to be preserved. This may be accidental. It is more plausible, however, that the absence of the Pentateuchal books among the *pešarîm* is due to the special character of these writings.

In this context we have to mention the somewhat distinctive use of the introductory כתוב in 4QMMT[17]. This recently published document could not yet be included in Fitzmyer's study. Qimron rightly notes that in this scroll the introductory כתוב never introduces literal quotations. It sometimes precedes a paraphrase of a biblical verse, as in "And concerning

12. In contrast with the New Testament, the Qumran literature never seems to use expressions such as ἡ γραφή or αἱ γραφαί as a designation for the OT as a whole.

13. See, e.g., BARTHÉLEMY 1984, 15-19.

14. Ps 7,8-9 and 82,1.2 quoted in 11QMelch 10-11 seem to be exceptions.

15. BERNSTEIN 1994, 30-70, see our note 10.

16. The identified *pešarîm* are: 1QpHab; 1QpMic; 1QpZeph; 1QpPs; 3QpIs? 4QpIs[a,b,c,d,e]; 4QpHos[a,b]; 4QMic?; 4QpNah; 4QpZeph; 4QpPs[a,b]. See M.P. HORGAN, *Pesharim: Qumran Interpretations of Biblical Books* (CBQ MS, 8), Washington, CBAA, 1979.

17. E. QIMRON & J. STRUGNELL, *Miqṣat Ma'aśe Ha-Torah* (DJD, x, Qumran Cave 4, v), Oxford, Clarendon, 1994.

him who purposely transgresses the precepts it is written (כתוב) that he despises (God) and blasphemes (Him)", which seems to present a paraphrase of Num 15,30[18]. This usage is not exceptional. Similar free quotations can be found in other Qumranic writings[19]. In some passages in 4QMMT, however, formulaic כתוב does not refer to any specific verse at all: "And the ruling refers to (כתוב) a pregnant animal"[20]. Qimron observes that in this and in similar instances, כתוב is not intended to introduce a verbal quotation from Scripture, but rather to introduce the statement which was derived from such a verse.

2. The Damascus or Cairo Document (CD) provides the richest harvest of explicit quotations[21]. One of them draws our special attention: CD 4,15-16 seems to quote Levi, son of Jacob. Before we discuss it, it may be useful to present its text and context:

ובכל השנים האלה יהיה 13בליעל משולח בישראל
כאשר דבר אל ביד ישעיה הנביא בן 14אמוץ לאמר
פחד בפחת ופח עליך יושב הארץ פשרו 15שלושת מצודות בליעל
אשר אמר עליהם לוי בן יעקב 16אשר הוא תפש בהם בישראל

*And during all these years shall[13] Belial be released against Israel
as God has spoken by the hand of Isaiah the prophet, son[14] of Amoz, saying*
terror, pit and snare are against you, inhabitant of the land (Is 24,17),
 *its interpretation:[15] the three nets of Belial
concerning which Levi son of Jacob has spoken,*
[16]that he, by means of them, catches Israel....

The exact source of the alleged quotation from Levi son of Jacob cannot be traced. According to Becker[22] it must be an allusion to the Testament of Levi. Others[23] find in it an allusion to TestDan 4,2. J.Greenfield suggests that the reference is indeed to the Testament of Levi, not in the extant Greek version, but to the Aramaic text of which fragments have

---

18. See B 70 in the edition and translation of E. QIMRON & J. STRUGNELL 1994, 54-55 and 140. Similar examples can be found in B 66-67 (a paraphrase of Lev 14,8) and 76-77 (a paraphrase of Lev 19,19?).

19. See L. GINZBERG 1976, 192-200; J.M. BAUMGARTEN 1992, 95-98.

20. 4QMMT B 38 in *ibidem*, 51 and 141.

21. M.A. KNIBB, *The Interpretation of* Damascus Document *vii,9b-8,2a and xix,5b-14*, in *RQ* 15 (1991) 243-251; J.M. BAUMGARTEN, *A Scriptural Citation in 4Q Fragments of the Damascus Document*, in *JJS* 43 (1992) 95-98; J.G. CAMPBELL, *Scripture in the Damascus Document 1:1-2:1* in *JJS* 44 (1993) 83-99; ID., *The Use of Scripture in the Damascus Document 1-8, 19-20* (BZAW, 228), Berlin, 1995.

22. *Testamente der zwölf Patriarchen*, 93, n. 4. See however the typical remark of C. RABIN in his *The Zadokite Fragments*, Oxford, Clarendon, 1954, 16: "Not in the extant T.Levi".

23. E. LOHSE, *Die Texte aus Qumran*, Darmstadt, Wissensch. Buchges., 288; RABIN 1954, 16.

been found in Qumran and in the Cairo Geniza[24]. But even there no exact source of the quotation can be identified. In our view the reason may be that the formula in CD 4,15 is not really a quotation formula, but rather a simple reference, telling the reader that Levi spoke about the plagues (עליהם) mentioned in the previous sentence taken from Isaiah. Originally, the reference may have been a marginal note, to be compared with CD 8,20 where a similar aside seems to refer to sayings from unknown writings of Jeremiah and Elisha without quoting them. Some further observations support this hypothesis. The so-called quotation of Levi in CD 4,16 is not formulated as a quotation. It opens with the relative pronoun אשר. None of the quotations in the Damascus Document begins that way. The relative pronoun occurs again after the verb אמר. Nowhere else in the Qumran writings is the verb אמר of the quotation formula followed by the relative pronoun אשר. The marginal note may have begun at the end of line 14, where the interpretation of Is 24,17 is introduced with the term *pešer*. Although many other Qumran scrolls use this term frequently in their biblical interpretations, it is found nowhere else in the Damascus Document. This supports the suggestion that the passage as a whole may be due to the hand of a copyist adding a marginal note.

3. Nowhere do the Qumranic authors give explicit directives concerning what they considered to be their Holy Scriptures, nor do they seem to have been particularly preoccupied with the correct transmission of the biblical text. The manuscripts of Isaiah, e.g., do not display one uniform text. Corrections are brought in in most of the biblical scrolls[25]. More remarkably, books such as the Temple Scroll seem to have been given a biblical, or nearly biblical authority. According to Wacholder, the morphology and orthography of that scroll are fused with syntax to produce an impression that the text emanates from God, as dictated to Moses from Sinai[26]. Most importantly, the tetragrammaton is written in square script, which seems to be a prerogative of biblical manuscripts[27].

No lists of authoritative biblical books are given. Nevertheless, the MMT document seems to have preserved some sort of canon. It encourages its

---

24. *The Words of Levi Son of Jacob in Damascus Document iv, 15-19*, in *RQ* 13 (1988) 319-322.

25. Tov 1992, 213-216.

26. See B.Z. WACHOLDER, *The Dawn of Qumran. The Sectarian Torah and the Teacher of Righteousness* (Monographs of the HUC), Cincinnati, HUC Press, 1983, 9; P. SIEGEL, *The Employment of Paleo-Hebrew Characters for the Divine Names at Qumran in the light of Tannaitic Sources*, in *HUCA* 42 (1971) 159-172.

27. See, however, the following section: *The Twelve Prophets Scroll and the Tetragrammaton*.

readers to study "the book of Moses and the books of the Prophets and (the book) of David" [ד]בספר[י הנ[ביאים ובדוי]ו] [ו]בספר מושה[28. It is well known that similar tripartite lists are mentioned in the prologue to the Greek Wisdom of Sira written about 135 BCE. MMT seems to limit the third part of the list to the "book of David", which probably refers to the Psalms, whereas the prologue of Sira refers to a collection of books[29], probably corresponding to Psalms and Writings. This strengthens the conviction, deduced from a survey of biblical quotations, that the third part of the "Scriptures" accepted as authoritative by the Qumran community was limited to the Psalms. Interestingly, the same restriction appears to be witnessed to in Lk 24,44: "... the Law of Moses and the Prophets and the Psalms".

II. Micah 5,1-3 in Qumran

1. The Hebrew Text and 4QMic 5,1-2. The non-biblical Qumran documents do not quote Mic 5,1-3. The Twelve Prophets scroll from Murabba'at hardly preserved a trace of the passage[30]. The Micah *pešer* from the first cave is extremely lacunous and has only minimal parts of 1,2-9; 6,14-16; 7,8-9.17, and the fragment of the *pešer* of the fourth cave deals only with 4,8-12. These data would not leave us much to discuss were it not that R. Fuller claims to have identified a leather fragment partially preserving Mic 5,1-2[31]. It cannot be assigned to any of the other manuscripts of the Minor Prophets presently known from Qumran[32]. It contains the ends of three lines on the right hand margin of a column. On the first line only the bottom of two vertical strokes are visible. Fuller

28. E. QIMRON & J. STRUGNELL, *Miqṣat Ma'a'se Ha-Torah* (n. 17), 1994, 111-112.
29. Και των αλλων των κατ αυτους ηκολουθηκοτων (2); και των αλλων πατριων βιβλιων (10); και τα λοιπα των βιβλιων (25).
30. The official publication of the scroll is to be found in DJD 2 (1961) 181-205. On p.194 and on the photographs one can see that perhaps the final ם of בית לחם may be preserved.
31. R. FULLER, *4QMicah: A Small Fragment of a Manuscript of the Minor Prophets from Qumran, Cave iv*, in *RQ* 16 (1993) 193-202.
32. A survey of the available texts can be found in U. GLESSMER, *Liste der biblischen Texte aus Qumran*, in *RQ* 16 (1993) 153-192, esp. 179-180. Glessmer lists the fragment as belonging to 4QXII[a] and mentions its PAM-number 43.161 as well as its unofficial photographic edition number 1216. The preliminary publication by Fuller follows immediately after Glessmer's list in *RQ* but does not refer to it. Fuller states that the fragment is not included in either the official or unofficial publication of the photographs. The editor rightly notes (p.193) that it is included in the microfiche 132 of *The Dead Sea Scrolls on Microfiche* but omits to mention microfiche 66 with PAM-number 43.161 signalled in Glessmer's list.

reconstructs a *he* (ה). On lines 2 and 3 all readings are certain. With the help of MT, Fuller reconstructs the text as follows:

ואת]ה [בית לחם אפרתה צעיר להיות באלפי יהודה ממך לי]
לא יצ[א להיות מושל בישראל ומוצאתיו מקדם מימי עולם]
לכן ית]נם עד עת יולדת ילדה ויתר אחיו ישובון על בני ישראל]

Although line 1 of the fragment is of no help, and lines 2 and 3 each pre-served only a particle and the first two characters of a verb, Fuller does not seem to hesitate much in as far as its identification is concerned. His assumption is that it belongs to a biblical scroll of Micah or of a scroll of the Minor Prophets. He does not discuss alternative possibilities. As far as I can see, the fragment could equally well belong to a biblical quotation in a non-biblical manuscript[33]. Theoretically it could also pertain to a hitherto unknown non-biblical text. One must admit, however, that the particle לכן (*therefore*) on the third line, hardly ever occurs in Qumran outside the biblical scrolls and the biblical quotations in the *pešarîm*. Even then it is not immediately obvious that the nine preserved characters are to be identified with parts of Mic 5,1-2. Fuller observes that the fragment contains only one variant, לא יצ[א on line two, but this variant amounts to almost half of the text actually preserved[34]. The result is that line 2 does not directly support the identification proposed by Fuller. This leaves us line 3. Supposing that the five preserved characters on that line are a literal rendition of the biblical text and no variant, one has to mention that this sequence also occurs in Isa 7,14. Line 3 could then be reconstructed as follows:

לכן ית]ן אדני הוא לכם אות

One must admit though, that it is rather difficult to read in line 2 of the fragment a variant of the immediately preceding Isaiah text. But that is no problem when one assumes that the line taken from Isa 7,14 may be a biblical quotation, or part of it, used in a non-biblical text. Indeed, the concordances easily allow us to verify that the sequence of line two (...לא יצ) occurs in several instances in the non-biblical scrolls[35].

If one accepts Fuller's reconstruction, the question of interpretation arises. In his option, the most straightforward way to understand the particle לא on line 2 (Mic 5,1) is to parse it as the negative particle. In a translation based on the RSV this would yield the following sense: "from you shall *not* come forth for me one who is to rule in Israel". Fuller

33. On p. 194 Fuller seems to admit this possibility, but does not discuss it.
34. See the editor's note on p. 200.
35. לא יצדק 1QH 9,14; 16,11; לא יצליחו CD 13,21.

notes that this would run contrary to the meaning of the passage in its context. He prefers to understand לא as the "counterfactual conditional particle, normally spelled לו, with the meaning 'would that' or 'if only', introducing a wish or an irreal conditional clause"[36]. He then translates line 2 as follows, "would that one came forth for me...", and proposes to understand this utterance against the background of the eschatological expectations of the Qumran community.

Fuller's reconstruction and interpretation are not very convincing. It is rather unlikely that the conditional particle לא or לו should occur in the middle of a sentence, ... ממך לי לא, "Out of you, for me, would that..." The biblical parallels adduced by Fuller clearly demonstrate that, as a rule, the particle figures at the beginning of a clause[37]. A minor modification of Fuller's proposal might make it slightly more acceptable, and help to solve another problem. It is well known that in Mic 5,1 according to MT, the first person suffix in לי does not fit the context, moreover, the position of לי before the verb יצא is grammatically unusual. The conditional particle לא in the Qumranic fragment, normally spelled לו, might preserve a trace of the original text reading לא, or לו, instead of לי. The beginning of the sentence would then read as follows: ממך לו יצא "Out of you would that came forth..." In this reconstruction, the position of ממך at the beginning of the phrase, preceding the conditional particle, is still unusual. This uncommon feature might, however, be intentional, emphasizing the origin of the new ruler.

2. The Greek Text and the Tetragrammaton. Our Micah passage is also partly preserved in the Greek Prophets scroll from Naḥal Ḥever[38]. In his innovating examination of this scroll, Barthélemy convincingly demonstrated that its text is a recension of the Septuagint, correcting it towards the MT. He gave it the label καίγε because of its typical translation of Hebrew גם(ו) by καίγε[39].

Of special interest for us is its transcription of the tetragrammaton using Hebrew characters. It shares this characteristic with p848 (pFouad 266), another pre-Christian Greek biblical Ms. Several scholars deduced

36. FULLER 1993, 201.

37. 1 Sam 14,30; 2 Sam 18,12; 19,7; Isa 48,18; 63,19. See also GESENIUS-KAUTZSCH §151e; MEYER §121 4a.

38. Preliminary publications by B. LIFSHITZ, *The Greek Documents of the Cave of Horror*, in *IEJ* 12 (1962) 201-207; *Yedi'ot* 26 (1962) 183-190; D. BARTHÉLEMY, *Les devanciers d'Aquila* (VTS, 10), Leiden, Brill, 1963; official publication: E. Tov, in DJD 8 (1990).

39. BARTHÉLEMY 1963, 31.

from these data that, in the original pre-Christian version of the Septuagint, the divine name YHWH was not rendered by κύριος, as so
often has been thought since the works of Baudissin[40], but in Hebrew
characters[41].

A new exploration of the available data led Pietersma to conclusions
returning to those of Baudissin[42]. In Pietersma's view, the tetragrammaton
is not original but a replacement of the original κύριος and a symptom
of an early archaizing recension. In a previous contribution[43] we drew
attention to another early Greek biblical MS from Qumran (p4Q120
Lev[b] or p802) in which the Hebrew tetragram is rendered by the Greek
trigram ΙΑΩ. In contrast with the Greek Prophets scroll from Naḥal
Ḥever and p848 (pFouad 266) it does not display recensional tendencies
and thus seems to be the better representant of the original Septuagint.
This implies that its trigram can hardly be a symptom of an early
archaizing recension. Its spelling seems to imply that the translator or
copyist knew, or thought he knew, the vocalisation of the tetragram, and
was probably not opposed to pronouncing it. It is tempting to suggest
that the trigram was the original transliteration of the vocalised Name,
dating from a time in which the pronunciation was not yet forbidden or
unusual. A closer look at the photographs, however, makes one hesitate.
The fragments are written in uncial script, without blanks between the
words. The trigram is an exception. It is preceded and followed by a
small blank space. This suggests that it may be a later insertion. The
original writer probably followed a procedure similar to that detected in
p848 (pFouad 266). Where the Hebrew had the tetragrammaton, he left
an open space larger than that due for the trigram. This does not necessarily imply that he had κύριος in mind. The space hardly suffices for the
six characters of κύριος. It may simply signify that the Hebrew *Vorlage*

---

40. W. GRAF BAUDISSIN, *Kyrios als Gottesname im Judentum und seine Stelle in der
Religionsgeschichte*, Giessen, 1929.
41. See especially P. SKEHAN, *The Divine Name at Qumran*, in *BIOSCS* 13 (1980) 14-
44. See also W.G. WADDELL, *The Tetragrammaton in the LXX*, in *JTS* 45 (1944) 158-161;
H. CONZELMANN, *An Outline of the Theology of the New Testament*, New York, 1969;
German original, 1967; H. STEGEMANN 1978, 210; G. HOWARD, *The Tetragram and the New
Testament*, in *JBL* 96 (1977) 63-68; J.A. FITZMYER, *The Semitic Background of the New
Testament Kyrios-Title*, in ID., *A Wandering Aramean*, Missoula, Scholars Press, 115-
142, a somewhat revised and expanded edition of the original German version *Der semi-
tische Hintergrund des neutestamentlichen Kyriostitels*, in *FS Conzelmann*, Tübingen,
Mohr, 1975, 267-298; see also J. LUST, אדני יהוה *in Ezekiel and Its Counterpart in the Old
Greek*, in *ETL* 72 (1996) 138-156.
42. A. PIETERSMA, *Kyrios or Tetragram: A Renewed Quest for the Original LXX*, in
FS J.W.Wevers, Mississauga, 1988, 85-101,
43. See our note 41.

also had a blank where the Name was to occur, as in 4QpIs[e] quoting Is 32,6, or that it had four dots, as in several other instances[44].

Concluding these remarks on the tetragrammaton, we may note that in the Greek Twelve Prophets scroll it is written in Paleohebrew characters. In Qumran, the writing of the Name in square characters seems to have been increasingly reserved for the purely biblical manuscripts written in Hebrew and for the Temple scroll[45]. The tetragrammaton in Paleo-hebrew script is found in many of the *pešarîm*[46]. Other *pešarîm* use square characters, but only when they quote a biblical text[47]. This practice, reserving the use of the Name written in square characters to the "Scrip-tures", may offer us another criterion allowing us to distinguish between canonical and non-canonical writings in the Qumran community. Because of the many exceptions to the rule, this criterion should be used with much restraint[48].

After the survey of the available data at Qumran, we turn to a text and literary critical reading of the major witnesses of Mic 5,1-3.

III. MICAH 5,1-3. TEXTUAL AND LITERARY CRITICAL NOTES[49]

In the following notes we focus mainly on textual matters that may have a bearing on the interpretation of the passage in the MT, the LXX, and the

---

44. See 1QS 8,14; 4Q175,1 and 19; 4Q176 passim. The four dots repeatedly found under or above the tetragrammaton in 1QIs[a] may have had the same function.

45. See SKEHAN 1980, 20-25; HOWARD 1977, 66-70; about the exceptional character of the Temple scroll, see WACHOLDER 1983, 9 and our note 26; other exceptional uses of the tetragrammaton in square characters may include 1Q29 1.7; 3.2; 2Q30 1,1; 2QapMos 1,4; 4Q185 1,ii,3; 4Q370 i,2.3; 4Q375 1,ii,8; 4Q380 1,i,5.8.9; 2,4.5; 4Q381 1,2; 24,8; 76,12; 4Q385 2,i,3.4.8.9; 3,i,4.7; 4Q386 ii,2.3, but most of these texts are very fragmen-tary and may use the tetragrammaton in (free) quotations.

46. 1QpMic 1,1.2; 1QpZeph 3,4; 1QpHab 1,1; 6,14; 10,7 and 14; 11,10; 4QpPs[a] or 4Q171 1-10 ii 4.13.25; iii 14; iv 7.10; 4QpIs[a] 7-10 iii 14 17, in the catena 4Q183 2,2 and 3, and repeatedly in the Psalm composition from cave 11 (11QPs).

47. See M.P. HORGAN, *Pesharim: Qumran Interpretations of Biblical Books* (CBQ MS, 8), Washington, CBAA, 1979, 21.

48. For the exceptions see note 45.

49. V. RYSSEL, *Die Textgestalt und die Echtheit des Buches Micha. Ein kritischer Commentar zu Micha*, Leipzig, Hirzel, 1887, 83-87; A. VAN HOONACKER, *Les douze petits prophètes traduits et commentés* (Études bibliques), Paris, Gabalda, 1908, 388-391; J.M. POWIS SMITH, *Micah* (ICC), Edinburgh, Clark, 1911, 100-106; W. RUDOLPH, *Micha-Nahum-Habakuk-Zephanja* (KAT, 13/3), Gütersloh, Gerd Mohn, 1975, 87-95; A.S. VAN DER WOUDE, *Micha* (POT), Nijkerk, Callenbach, 1976, 165-172; L.C. ALLEN, *The Books of Joel, Obadja, Jonah and Micah* (NICOT), Grand Rapids, Zondervan, 1976, 339-347; J.L. MAYS, *Micah* (OTL), London, SCM, 1976; H.W. WOLFF, *Micha* (BKAT, xiv/4), Neukirchen, Neukirchener Verlag, 1982, 100-122; R.L. SMITH, *Micah-Maleachi* (Word

NT. In order to facilitate the discussion we present the text of each verse in four versions. First we print the text of the Septuagint, alongside with that of the Twelve Prophets scroll from Naḥal Ḥever. Underneath these, we render the masoretic text, alongside with the New Testament quotation.

a. Mic 5,1

LXX
και συ Βηθλεεμ οικος του Εφραθα
ολιγοστος *ει* του ειναι εν χιλιασιν Ιουδα
εκ σου μοι εξελευσεται του ειναι
εις αρχοντα εν τω Ισραηλ και αι εξοδοι αυτου
απ'αρχης εξ ημερων αιωνος

Naḥal Ḥever
και συ οικο[ς του? αρτου? ε]φραθα
ολιγοστος του ειναι εν χ[ιλιασιν Ιο]υδα
εκ σου μοι εξ[ελευσε]ται του ειναι
αρχοντα εν τω Ι[σραηλ και αι] εξοδοι αυτ
απ'αρχης <u>αφ'</u>ημ[ερων αιωνος]

MT
ואתה בית לחם אפראתה
צעיר להיות באלפי יהודה
ממך לי יצא להיות
מושל בישראל ומוצאתיו
מקדם מימי עולם

NT
και συ Βηθλεεμ *γη(ς) Ιουδα(ς)*
ουδαμως ελαχιστη ει εν τοις *ηγεμοσιν* Ιου
εκ σου *γαρ* εξελευσεται
ηγουμενος

– בית לחם אפרתה. This MT reading is supported by Syp., Vulg., Targ., but not by LXX. In the critical edition the latter has βηθλεεμ οἶκος τοῦ εφραθα. The early Codex W (followed by Ach and Sa) has οἶκος τοῦ Βαιθλεεμ. τοῦ εφραθα· Even when in so old a manuscript freedom from Origen's influence· may safely be assumed, it is generally accepted that it inclines to accommodate to the Hebrew text. Here it probably preserved part of a double translation of בית לחם. The Naḥal Ḥever Manuscript is defective. It has: οικο[ ]φραθα. According to Barthélemy the lacuna is large enough to include Βηθλεεμ. In Tov's view the lacuna may equally well have read (τοῦ) ἄρτοῦ. In as far as the

Biblical Commentary, 32), Waco, Word Books, 1984, 42-44; D.R. HILLERS, *Micah* (Hermeneia), Philadelphia, Fortress, 1984, 64-67; A.W. DEISSLER, *Zwölf Propheten II, Obadja, Jona, Micha, Nahum* (Die neue Echter Bibel), Würzburg, Echter, 1984, 186-187; D. SCHIBLER, *Le livre de Michée* (CEB, 11), Vaux-sur-Seine, Fac. Libre de Théol. Prot., 1989, 105-111; W. HARRELSON, *Nonroyal Motifs in the Royal Eshatology*, in B.W. ANDERSON & W. HARRELSON (ed.), *Israel's Prophetic Heritage*, London, SCM, 1966, 147-165, esp. 155-159; T. LESCOW, *Der Geburtsmotiv in den messianischen Weissagungen bei Jesaja und Micha*, in ZAW 79 (1967) 172-207, esp. 192-207; J. COPPENS, *Le messianisme royal. Ses origines, son développement, son accomplissement* (Lectio divina, 54), Paris, Cerf, 1968, esp. 85-88; B. RENAUD, *La formation du livre de Michée. Tradition et Actualisation* (études bibliques), Paris, Gabalda, 1977, 219-254; D.G. HAGSTROM, *The Coherence of the Book of Micah* (SBL DS, 89), Atlanta, GA, Scholars, 1988, esp. 63-67; H. STRAUSS, *Messianisch ohne Messias* (Europ. Hochschulschriften, xxiii/232), Frankfurt, Lang, 1988, 53-60; about the Micah quotation in the NT, see esp. R.H. GUNDRY, *The Use of the Old Testament in St Matthew's Gospel* (NTSup, 18), Leiden, Brill, 1967; W. ROTHFUCHS, *Die Erfüllungszitate des Matthäus-Evangeliums* (BWANT, 88), Stuttgart, Kohlhammer, 1969; SOARES PRABHU 1976 (see note 9), 261-268; A.J. PETROTTA, *A Closer look at Matt. 2,6 and Its Old Testament Sources* in *JETS* (1985) 47-52; see also A. VAN DER WAL, *Micah, A Classified Bibliography* (Applicatio), Amsterdam, Free Univ. Press, 1990, esp. 141-153.

photographs allow us to make our own judgment, the size of the lacuna seems to be large enough for ἄρτου, but not for Βηθλεεμ. The restored reading οἶκος ἄρτου is in agreement with the scroll's tendency to bring the text closer to MT.

The Hebrew expression, juxtaposing Bethlehem and Ephrathah, is a hapax. The double name may have served to signal the close relation of both entities. LXX's 'insert' of οἶκος (τοῦ) between the two proper nouns Βηθλεεμ and εφραθα has led many commentators to take בית אפרתה as original and "Beth-lehem" as an explanatory gloss. In this hypothesis, the original text had בית אפרתה only, thus referring to the *gens* and not the city of Bethlehem. The protago-nists of this view find support in the use of the term אלפי ("thousands", "tribes"), and in the use of the 2nd person masculine in the address. Normally, cities are considered to be feminine whereas tribes are masculine. More recent commentaries tend to accept the MT. Apart from the fact that the deletion of Bethlehem has no direct textual basis, it must be noted that Beth-Ephrathah is attested nowhere. The masculine form of the address is no problem since geo-graphical names beginning with בית are often masculine[50].

In his quotation of Mic 5,1 Matthew does not mention the term οἶκος nor the 'clan' notion behind it, typical of the LXX. This strongly suggests that he used a Hebrew text. His γῆ(ς) Ιουδα(ιας) is taken to be a contemporisation of the antique אפרתה[51]. This rephrasing is probably due to the style of the author of the Gospel and to the context[52]. Prabhu wants to be more specific and suggests that Judah in the gospel text is a theological reference alluding to 1 Sam 17,12 where David is described as the "son of an Ephrathite of Bethlehem in Judah". It is by no means clear, however, why Matthew's Judah would obtain a more explicit reference to David and to 1 Sam 17,12, than the more original Ephrathah, since that same verse calls him an Ephrathite.

– צעיר. It is possible that the unvocalized text read הצעיר ("the smallest", or "are (you) small?"). There is no need to assume that the ה disappeared through haplography (Rudolph). It is more likely that the ה which in the MT is connected with אפרת was understood as prefixed to צעיר. The translator of the Septuagint seems to have read it that way since he rendered this term by the superlative ὀλιγοστός[53]. Although in several instances he correctly understood the adjec-tive without the article as a superlative[54], here the awkward turning of the Greek sentence suggests that here he felt forced by the Hebrew הצעיר. The superlative ὀλιγοστός followed by the article and the infinitive gives an unusual construc-tion in Greek. A literal translation would be: "least numerous to be among the tribes of Judah". The Naḥal Ḥever text shows traces of its recensional character. It preserves the term ὀλιγοστός and the infinitive form τοῦ εἶναι, but not the intervening verbal form εἶ which has no counterpart in the Hebrew. We will dis-cuss Matthew's version of this part of the verse when dealing with its messianic

50. JOÜON & MURAOKA 1993, § 134g.
51. See GUNDRY 1967, 91. It is not clear to me how Gundry can adduce Seligmann's notes on Isa 8,23 (1956, 80) in support of his views saying that this contemporisation is often found in the LXX.
52. See, e.g., Mt 10,15; 14,34; 2,20; 4,15, and ROTHFUCHS 1969, 60-61; SOARES PRABHU 1976, 262.
53. See also the *Vetus Latina* (La): *minima*, compare Vulg. *parvulus*.
54. See, e.g., Ob 2 where קתן is rendered by ὀλιγοστος (against Rudolph).

interpretation. Here it may suffice to say that the author of the gospel most likely did not use the Septuagint since he chose ἐλαχίστη as a translation of צעיר and not Septuagint's ὀλιγοστός which is an unusual equivalent of the Hebrew term in question.

Matthew's emphatic negative οὐδαμῶς ἐλαχίστη εἶ may be due to free interpretation, or to the reading of הצעיר as a rhetorical question, or to a different *Vorlage*[55]. The first option is the most probable one since the choice of the term ἐλαχίστη and the other deviations from LXX and MT also point in that direction.

– להיות. This verb has no equivalent in the Vulgar text and in Matthew's quotation. It is often deleted as an insert caused by the occurrence of the same verb form in the next line (Hitzig, Rudolph, Renaud, a.o.). A comparison with the *incipit* of the parallel verse 4,8 supports this correction. Others propose to read מהיות. It is true that the usual translation of expression צעיר להיות "too little to be," would demand צעיר מהיות[56]. This proposed correction, however, does not find a support in the Mss. According to Fitzmyer the problem is solved when one accepts that the preposition ל is here used in a comparative sense similar to מין[57]. In a paper published in 1967 Lescow suggests a similar solution. In his view, צעיר is not a superlative. It simply means "little, small". The preposition ל indicates some kind of direction or relation. The translation then should be "little in as far as its being among the clans of Judah is concerned". Both Fitzmyer and Lescow seem to be unable to adduce biblical examples of such a use. In a more recent contribution, Lescow revoked his earlier proposal and joined the position of those who consider the first occurrence of להיות as a secondary insert[58]. Barthélemy accepts MT as the *lectio difficilior*[59].

– באלפי. Matthew's ἐν τοῖς ἡγεμόσιν seems to be based on the reading אלופי "leaders of thousands" and is a personification of the cities of Judah in the persons of the clanheads.

– ממך לי יצא. This phrase has its own problems. A nominal subject for the verb יצא seems to be lacking. The first person suffix of the particle לי, referring to the Lord, seems to be in disagreement with vv. 2-3 where the Lord is spoken of in the third person. Moreover, לי is most often treated as a *dativus commodi* or ethical dative. According to Fitzmyer[60], the problem is here that no instances can be found of such a dative preceding the verb. The first problem is solved in the Targum through the insert of the term 'messiah', and in some Mss of the Septuagint and in the NT through the insert of the noun ἡγούμενος. Without any support of the Mss, some exegetes declare the particle לי to be a corruption of an original ילד: "From you a child will come forth". Another proposal is more in agreement with the textual data. It understands the 'jod' in לי as the well known abbreviation of the tetragrammaton. The main objection against this

---

55. See GUNDRY 1967, 91.

56. FITZMYER 1956, 10, referring to ROBINSON 1942, 142, and others.

57. LESCOW 1969, rejects Fitzmyer's biblical examples or interprets them differently. In fact, the examples of the preposition ל used as מין, taken from Gordon and Dahood, are criticized by Fitzmyer himself. In his view, all of them are instances of ל in the sense of an ablative מין, meaning "far away from".

58. *Redaktionsgeschichtliche Analyse von Micha 1-5*, in ZAW 84 (1972) 73, note 100.

59. 1992, 749.

60. 1956, 11-12.

tempting suggestion is that it does not explain why the Name should be abbreviated in Mic 5,1 whereas it is not in the immediate context. With Sellin, Fitzmyer brings another solution to the fore. He explains the "yod" as a dittograph, and construes the ל as a particle, of the intensive or emphatic sort. Accordingly he reads the sentence as follows: ממך [מלך] ליצא: "from you (a king) shall indeed go forth". A problem with this suggestion is that a biblical example of such a use of the ל before a verb is hard to find.

An alternative solution has been proposed by Willis[61]. He accepts the wordings of the MT. In his opinion there is good reason for the exceptional word order in this phrase. The author intended a type of polarity: "from... to". He puts this polarity before the verb for the sake of emphasis. In this context, the verb יצא "to go out (from... to)" means to publicly acknowledge the superiority of, and to submit to, another.

Finally, a solution can be distilled from the reconstruction of 4QMic 5,1-2 discussed above. The fragment in question suggests that the original text may have read the conditional particle לו or לא. This minor correction, with an admittedly weak textual support, allows the following translation: "out of you, would that came forth..." It eliminates the tensions caused by the first person personal pronoun, as well as the unusual character of the *dativus commodi* before the verb. The absence of a nominal subject for the verb יצא is not a major problem. An implicit subject is not an exceptional feature. Its explicitation in the Targum (משיח) and in the NT (ἡγούμενος) are facilitating readings.

Matthew's omission of לי is probably another symptom of the free character of his quotation. However, in light of the restored reading of 4QMic 5,1-2 ממך לו יצא, it can be understood as a free rendition of the particle לו.

– מושל. The Septuagint reads εἰς ἄρχοντα. Here again the Naḥal Ḥever scroll corrects the Septuagint towards MT. It accepts the wordings of the Septuagint, but leaves out the preposition εἰς before ἄρχοντα which has no counterpart in the Hebrew. The omission of להיות allows Matthew to interpret the term as a subject of the verb יצא. Note that his choice of ἡγούμενος demonstrates once more his independency of LXX.

b. Mic 5,2

LXX	Naḥal Ḥever
2. δια τουτο δωσει αυτους	δια τουτο δω[σει αυτους
εως καιρου τικτουσης τεξεται	εως καιρου τικτου]σης τεξεται
και οι επιλοιποι των αδελφων αυτων	και [οι επιλοιποι των αδελφων] αυτου
επιστρεψουσιν επι τους υιους Ισραηλ	επιστρεψουσιν επι το[υς υιους Ισραηλ]

MT

לכן יתנם
עד עת יולדת ילדה
ויתר אחיו
ישבון על בני ישראל

Verse 2 is not reflected in the NT quotation. The MT text does not display many textual difficulties. The Septuagint presents a fairly literal translation, corresponding word for word to the MT. Two possible exceptions are worth noting.

---

61. J.T. WILLIS, ממך לי יצא *in Micah 5,1*, in *JQR* 58 (1968) 317-322.

First, the early codex W and several other witnesses have δώσεις (second person singular) αὐτούς for Hebrew יתנם (third person singular). Second, the Lucianic Mss and other witnesses read ἀδελφῶν αὐτοῦ, corresponding with the Hebrew אחיו, whereas the critical edition, based on the oldest and best Greek Mss and supported by the Targum, has ἀδελφῶν αὐτῶν, probably influenced by the plural suffix in יתנם. The lacunous Naḥal Ḥever scroll seems to agree to a large extent with the Septuagint. The end of the verb δώσει(ς), however, has not been preserved. As expected, the scroll clearly reads ἀδελφῶν αὐτοῦ, in agreement with MT.

The literary problems are more numerous. The verse as a whole has often been considered to be a gloss or a late addition. The reasons are conveniently summarized by Lescow[62]. 1. The verse is prosaic. 2. It disturbs the line of thought of vv. 1 and 3 where the Messiah is the subject, whereas in v. 2 the Lord appears to be the subject. 3. The introductory לכן "therefore" in v. 2 is only loosely connected with the foregoing. The meaning cannot be that, because the new saviour-ruler will come forth from one of the clans of Judah, "therefore" the Lord will "give them up". The inserted gloss rather intends to explain why the coming of the new leader is delayed. It should be noted that the argument works also the other way round. The tensions between 5,2 and its immediate context are solved when one assumes that 5,1 and perhaps also 5,3, belong to a later layer added together with 4,8 as a framework to the three oracles in 4,9-5,2. We will return to this suggestion when dealing with the messianic interpretation of our passage.

c. Mic 5,3

LXX	Naḥal Ḥever
και στησεται *και οψεται* και ποιμανει	και στησεται και ποιμανει
το ποιμνιον αυτου εν ισχυι κυριος	εν ισχυι יהוה
και εν τη δοξη του ονοματος	*και εν τη επαρσει* ονοματος
κυριου *του θεου αυτων* υπαρξουσιν	יהוה θεου [αυτου?] *και επιστραφησονται*
διοτι νυν μεγαλυνθησονται εως ακρων της γης	οτι νυν μεγαλυνθησονται εως περατων της

MT	NT (2 Sam 5,2)
ועמד ורעה	οστις ποιμανει
בעז יהוה	τον λαον μου τον Ισραηλ
בגאון שם	
יהוה אלהיו וישבו	
כי עתה יגדל עד אפסי ארץ	

In verse 3 the textual problems of the MT are again minimal. More important are the differences with LXX. It adds καὶ ὄψεται, apparently from וראה, a variant of ורעה. Inserting τὸ ποίμνιον αὐτοῦ, it makes explicit the object of the latter verb.

Most of the witnesses, including the uncials B S V as well as A Q, translate the tetragrammaton in its first occurrence by the nominative κύριος, turning it

---

62. See LESCOW 1967, 192-193; see also J. COPPENS, *Le messianisme royal*, 1968, 85-88; *Le cadre littéraire de Michée 5:1-5*, in *Near Eastern Studies*, FS W.F. Albright, Baltimore, 1971, 57-62.

into the subject of the sentence. This is obviously not in agreement with MT which demands a genitive: "in the strength *of* the Lord". The main witnesses to the genitive are codex W, which often corrects LXX towards MT, and part of the Mss belonging to the Lucianic recension[63]. In their critical editions, Rahlfs and Ziegler prefer the genitive. This goes against the basic principle stipulated in the introduction to Ziegler's critical edition: "When the two main branches of the tradition, with their main representatives A Q and B S V, coincide, that reading is accepted in the text of the edition"[64]. It is not easy to see why this policy has not been followed in the present case[65]. Perhaps the editor assumed that the original LXX transliterated the tetragrammaton, and that later copyists, who were no longer aware of the Hebrew *status constructus* preceding it, erroneously replaced it by the nominative κύριος. This would, however, be most exceptional, since no such error can be found in one of the other 158 passages in the Twelve Prophets in which the tetragrammaton occurs in a similar grammatical construction. Moreover, the Greek Naḥal Ḥever text, which has the tetragrammaton in ancient Hebrew characters, is a recension towards MT. Taking the witnesses seriously, and accepting Pietersma's suggestion, holding that the original LXX probably did not transliterate the tetragrammaton, then one has to admit that in its first occurrence in Mic 5,3 the translator most likely used the nominative κύριος. The implications of this option are to be considered in light of the other interpreting elements in the Greek translation of the verse in question.

Inserting καί after the first occurrence of κύριος, the Greek translator breaks the *parallelismus membrorum* of MT and begins a new sentence with a new subject: "*And* they shall dwell in the glory of the name of the Lord *their God*". In order to obtain this sentence the *copula* before the verb יֵשְׁבוּ is omitted, and "*his* God" (אלהיו) is changed into "*their* God". The preceding context (v. 2) makes it clear that the plural subject is the people of Israel and/or the "remnant of their brothers".

In most Mss the next verb (μεγαλυνθήσονται) is also in the plural, whereas MT has the singular. The Greek Mss that read the nominative κύριος in its first appearance in the sentence, i.e., codex W and some of the Mss belonging to the Lucianic group, bring the translation closer to MT, and read the singular μεγαλυνθήσεται. Again, the editions of Rahlfs and Ziegler follow these Mss[66]. All the deviations from MT found in the majority text of the Septuagint are probably intentional. They offer an interpretative reading in which the tensions between vv.2 and 3 are smoothened. We will return to this topic when discussing the messianic connotations of the passage.

63. The remaining witnesses to the genitive are La^c, Aeth^p, Aug.civ.18,30.
64. *Duodecim prophetae* (Septuaginta, xiii), Göttingen, Vandenhoeck & Ruprecht, 1984³, 125.
65. A similar deviation from the policy is adopted by Rahlfs and Ziegler in the same verse where they prefer to read μεγαλυνθησεται (W, *L'*) and not μεγαλυνθησονται found in most of the uncials. In the beginning of the same verse, however, where W and *L'* read the plural στησονται και οψονται, Rahlfs and Ziegler prefer the singular attested to in the two main branches of the tradition.
66. Both editions mention B* among the witnesses to the singular. As far as I could see, B* has μεγαλυνθησοται and not μεγαλυνθησεται; a "v" is added between the lines. La^c has the plural.

The verse in the Greek Qumranic scroll displays many recensional elements. They are analysed by D. Barthélemy[67]. (a) The doublet καὶ ὄψεται of the LXX is omitted by the Qumran scroll which preserves only καὶ ποιμανεῖ corresponding to ורעה of MT. (b) The scroll also omits the gloss τὸ ποίμνιον αὐτοῦ. (c) After ἐν ἰσχύι it has the tetragrammaton. (d) The scroll has ἔπαρσις, correcting LXX where it freely translates גאון by δόξα. (e) The scroll omits the article before ὀνόματος and θεοῦ because it has no counterpart in MT[68]. (f) The scroll renders the conjunction of וְיָשְׁבוּ, omitted in LXX. The latter seems to have read יֵשְׁבוּ, translating freely ὑπάρξουσι. The scroll vocalized the verb differently reading וְיָשֻׁבוּ. In its translation it uses a medial form ἐπιστραφήσονται which usualy has the connotation of conversion. (g) In the Twelve Prophets LXX most frequently renders כי by διότι. Here and everywhere else the scroll changes this into ὅτι. (h) The author of the scroll preserved the plural μεγαλυνθήσονται, against MT. In doing so he witnesses to the ancient character of this reading found in most Mss of the Septuagint. (i) Finally the scroll corrects ἄκρων into περάτων in its rendition of the stereotyped expression עד אפסי ארץ. Most of these observations confirm the hypothesis that the scroll is a recension of the Septuagint which it corrects towards MT.

Matthew does not directly quote Mic 5,3. The reference to "shepherding" in Mic 5,3, along with Matthew's ἡγούμενος provides a link with 2 Sam 5,2. The author of the gospel attaches the latter quotation to Mic 5,1 by means of a relative pronoun with a consequent changing of the person of the verb, but otherwise he agrees with both MT and LXX[69].

IV. Messianism in Mic 5,1-3 in MT and in LXX[70]

It is generally accepted that the Masoretic text of Mic 5,1-3 announces the coming of a messianic king who will govern as a lieutenant of the Lord. He is seen in connection with the house of David. Matthew's quotation of Micah leads us to questions about the accentuation of the messianic character of this passage in the Septuagint and in the New Testament. It is often suggested that, in general, the Septuagint shows signs of a developing messianism[71], preparing the way for the messianic interpretation of the Old Testament in the New. Here we intend to check how far

---

67. 1963, 180-182.

68. Barthélemy notes that the scroll did not omit the article before ἔπαρσει and before γῆς although there also MT has no counterpart.

69. GUNDRY 1967, 92-93.

70. See esp. M. REHM, Der königliche Messias (Eichstätter Studien), Mainz, Butzon & Bercker, 1968, 267-276; J. COPPENS, Le messianisme royal (n. 49), 85-88; ID., Le cadre littéraire de Michée 5,1-5 (n. 62); B. RENAUD, La formation du livre de Michée (Études bibliques), Paris, Gabalda, 1977, 219-254.

71. For references see J. LUST, Messianism and Septuagint, in Congress Volume Salamanca (VTS, 36), Leiden, Brill, 1985, 174.

this assertion applies to the prophecy in Mic 5,1-3. Our textual and literary critical notes paved the way for this endeavour. Although the Septuagint proved to offer a fairly literal translation of the Hebrew, it displays quite some deviations from MT, especially in verse 3. It is our contention that these deviations weaken, rather than reinforce, the messianic message of Mic 5,1-3[72]. In order to underpin this assertion we will first turn to the immediate context, and then to the oracle itself.

a. *The Context*

The structure of Mic 4-5 has been a much debated issue[73]. It is not our intention to present a precise structural outline of this composition, but rather to examine its impact on the interpretation of Mic 5,1-3.

1. We take the study of H.W. Wolff as our starting point. In his view, Mic 4,9–5,4a.5b presents a collection of 3 oracles addressing Jerusalem[74]. They all open with עתה(ו) "(and) now". Mic 5,1-3 is part of the third of these sayings which begins in 4,14. For our purpose it is important to notice that this unit contrasts mighty Jerusalem and its leader which are besieged and beaten (4,14), with little Bethlehem out of which a new saviour-ruler is to come forth (5,1.3). The latter is obviously depicted as a new David whose call, described in 1 Sam 16, emphasized his littleness and his Bethlehemite origin.

How are these data reflected in the Greek translation? The Septuagint does not seem to preserve the contrast between Jerusalem with its leader in 4,14, and Bethlehem with its expected ruler in 5,1.3. In the Greek text

---

72. It should be clear that the theory in question and its critique presuppose a definition of messianism that suits the NT and its picture of the individual Davidic Messiah: Jesus. See LUST 1985, 175. For other contributions on Messianism in the Septuagint see J. LUST, *The Greek Verson of Balaam's Third and Fourth Oracles. The* ανθρωπος *in Num 24:7 and 17. Messianism and Lexicography,* in L. GREENSPOON & O. MUNNICH (ed.), *VIII Congress of the IOSCS* (SCS, 41), Atlanta, Scholars, 1995, 233-257; ID., *Messianism and the Greek Version of Jeremiah,* in C.E. COX (ed.), *VII Congress of the International Organisation for Septuagint and Cognate Studies 1989, Leuven* (SCS), Atlanta, GA, Scholars, 1991, pp. 87-122; *The Diverse Text forms of Jeremiah and History Writing with Jer 33 as a Test Case,* in *Journal of Northwest Semitic Languages* 20 (1994) 31-48; *Le Messianisme et la Septante d'Ézéchiel,* in *Tsafon* 2/3 (1990) 3-14.

73. Hagstrom's critique of the "major contributions to that discussion" (1988, 72-84) disregards important views such as those of VAN DER WOUDE 1976, esp. 125-127; WOLFF 1982, esp. xxix-xxxii and 104, RUDOLPH 1975, 87-95.

74. WOLFF 1982, 104; see also DEISSLER 1989, 98.111 DEISSLER 1984, 185; ALLEN 1976, 339.

of 4,14 Jerusalem is no longer directly addressed but is spoken about in the third person. The Hebrew term שֹׁפֵט denoting its leader has probably been read as שֵׁבֶט and been interpreted as a plural (שְׁבָטֵי) and rendered by τὰς φυλάς "the tribes". The result is that the MT-context is broken, a context in which a Davidic Messiah with his humble origins is contrasted with the actual leader of Jerusalem.

The final part of the third oracle has provoked many discussions. In MT the meaning of 5,4a is ambiguous, and it is not clear whether it concludes our oracle or whether it opens a new one. Without discussing it in detail we propose to follow H.W. Wolff, combining his interpretation with that of A. van der Woude[75]. In their view, the sentence rounds off the oracle, referring to the announced new ruler and contrasting his fate with that of the leader of Jerusalem mentioned in 4,14. Whereas the present leader is beaten, the expected ruler shall be successful: וְהָיָה זֶה שָׁלוֹם "and he shall be safe".

The Septuagint excludes this interpretation. Its translation does certainly not enhance the possible messianic characteristics of the passage: καὶ ἔσται αὕτη εἰρήνη "and this shall be peace". The feminine personal pronoun does not refer to the new ruler announced in the foregoing verses, but to "peace". The sentence begins a new oracle in which this peace is described.

2. Breaking through the limits and through the threepartite structure of the collection in 4,9–5,4a.5b, the section in 5,1 clearly shows links with 4,8. Both verses begin with the same direct address וְאַתָּה ("and you") and a description of the addressee in two parallel expressions: "tower of the flock, hill of the daughter of Zion" (4,8), and "Bethlehem of Ephrathah, a little one (to be) among the clans of Judah" (5,1). In contrasting sentences it is said to the daughter of Zion that the former "dominion" or "rule" (מֶמְשָׁלָה) shall come to her, and to Bethlehem of Ephrathah it is announced that the one who is to bring this "dominion", or the new "ruler" (מוֹשֵׁל), shall come from her. His origins "from of old" correspond to the "former" character of the rule that is promised to Zion. The two parallel verses obviously allude to a new David who is to restore the kingdom of Jerusalem. In a similar way 4,6-7 corresponds to 5,3. In both passages the theme of shepherding dominates. In language reminiscent of Ez 34[76], Mic 4,6-7 presents the Lord as the one who will take care of the flock, assembling the lame and gathering those who

75. VAN DER WOUDE 1976, 173-174.
76. Ez 34,11-16.

have been driven away. Again in consonance with Ez 34[77], Mic 5,3 suggests that the Lord will set up over them a new David who will pasture the flock in the strength of the Lord[78]. These data strongly invite the reader of the Book of Micah to consider 4,6-8 and 5,1-3 as two corresponding sections that form an envelope around the three oracles introduced by the particle עתה(ו) in 4,9.11.14[79].

What happened to the envelope and to its messianic implications in the Septuagint? The Greek translation seems to interrupt the parallelism between 4,8 and 5,1, and to weaken the messianic allusions to a new David. Indeed, in 4,8 it inserts a reference to Babylon as the origin of the restored kingdom. This hardly agrees with 5,1 where the source of the restoration is Bethlehem of Ephrata. It must be admitted, though, that one does not exclude the other. The reference may be to a descendant of David returning from the exile in Babylon.

b. *Mic 5,1-3*

Verse 1. According to MT, the origins of the new ruler are situated in "Bethlehem of Ephrathah". This recalls the Ephrathite David from Bethlehem: see 1 Sam 17,12. In the story of his election (1 Sam 16) the "littleness" of David was emphasized. Similarly, in Micah 5,1, his birthplace, Bethlehem, is described as a small village, in contrast with the capital and its leader (שפט) under siege (4,14). Here, as in 1 Sam, God chooses the small in order to shame the great. He shall come forth "for me", says the Lord. This unusual expression probably indicates that the Lord will be the real king and that the new human ruler will be his lieutenant.

The Septuagint provides a rather wooden translation of this verse. Deviations are rare. We noted the puzzling rendition of בית לחם. The Greek text inserts οἶκος (τοῦ) between the two proper nouns Βηθλεεμ and Εφραθα, extending to Ephrathah the notion of בית found in בית לחם[80].

---

77. Ez 34,22-24.

78. Both in Mic 4,7 and 5,2 the ones that are brought back or gathered are called the "remnant": Mic 4,7: שארית; 5,2: יתר. This may have facilitated the insertion of 5,1.3.

79. These framing elements, or part of them, may belong to a later layer in the composition of the book. Originally, the threatening opening of the oracle in 4,14 continued with 5,2 and its particle לכן. This hypothesis about the history of redaction open interesting perspectives. They are, however, not immediately relevant for our inquiry about the development of the messianic implications of the text in the Septuagint and the New Testament.

80. See BARTHÉLEMY 1992, 748; RYSSEL 1887, 83. According to Lescow (1967, 193) the Septuagint may have inserted οἶκος in order to save the notion of a "house" which gets lost in the transliteration Bethlehem.

This probably implies that he understood Ephrathah as a name of a clan or tribe. It does not seem to have any direct implications on his grasping of the messianic character of the text. On the other hand, it probably influenced his rendition of the term צעיר "little".

The preference given to the term ὀλιγοστός is remarkable. Nowhere else does it occur as an equivalent of צעיר. With its most current meaning "least numerous", its choice must have been inspired by the connotation of "tribe" recognized in "Bethlehem, house of Ephratha". The Hebrew צעיר recalls the story of the Lord's election of Gideon and the latter's objection: "But sir, how can I deliver Israel? My clan is the weakest in Manasseh, and I am the least (הצעיר, A: μικρός, B: ὁ μικρότερος) in my family" (Judg 6,15), and the account of Saul's election and his objection: "I am only a Benjaminite, from the least of the tribes of Israel, and my family is the humblest (הצעירה, τῆς ἐλαχίστης) of all the families of the tribe of Benjamin" (1 Sam 9,21)[81]. Without overemphasizing the point, it may be noted that the selection of the Greek term ὀλιγοστός does not help the reader to recognize the allusions to these stories featuring saviours who can be seen as models of the Messiah.

Verse 2. According to Wellhausen and many others, such as Westermann[82], verse 2 is to be understood as an allusion to Is 7,14 and to the birth of an individual Messiah. Lescow is of an other opinion. In his view, the one in labour is Zion. Her birth pangs symbolize the oppression by the enemy, and the end of these pangs refers to the deliverance characterized by the return of the exiles. A similar imagery, mingled with its interpretation, occurs in the immediate context, especially in 4,9.10. Note that, according to Lescow, the term יולדה is always used in the metaphorical sense[83]. Lescow's collectivising interpretation is probably correct. Nevertheless, the puzzling third person singular pronoun in "*his* brothers" or "*his* kindred" most likely alludes to the individual saviour announced in v. 1.

The Septuagint does not facilitate the individual messianic interpretation. One should perhaps not give too much attention to the fact that the translation speaks about "the time of the one in travail, (when) she shall give birth" rather than "the time that she who is in travail shall give birth". It is more significant that the Septuagint, using the plural form of

81. See LESCOW 1967, 197; the Hebrew term is used elsewhere, again in the context of the Lord's exaltation of the humble: see Is 60,22: "The least (הקטן, ὁ ὀλιγοστός) of them shall become a clan, and the smallest one (הצעיר, ὁ ἐλάχιστος) mighty nation". Compare Gen 25,23; 43,33; Ps 68,28.

82. 1964, 145f.; see LESCOW 1967, 199.

83. LESCOW 1967, 197.

the pronoun αὐτῶν, changes MT's "*his* brothers" into "*their* brothers", thus eliminating a possible reference to the new leader. The translation rather alludes to the return of the exiles announced in 4,8. They will bring back the "dominion" and the "sovereignty" to their brothers who remained in Jerusalem.

Verse 3. We already noticed that in this part of the oracle, the Septuagint shows numerous deviations from MT. For our inquest it is important to find out in how far these particularities enhance or diminish the messianic connotations of the passage. In that perspective some more attention should be given to the first occurrence of the name of the Lord. Opting in favour of the nominative κύριος, the translator made it clear that in his view God, and not the new ruler, was the subject of the verbs στήσεται and ποιμανεῖ. With this interpretation he diminished the tension with v. 2 where the Lord is also the subject. More important for us is that it implies a shift in the attention, away from the new leader, and towards the Lord God. In the Septuagint, God himself is going to be the shepherd of his people, not the Messiah.

The second part of the first distich confirms this shift. In MT it continues the thought of the first part, announcing that the new ruler will feed his flock "in the majesty of the name of the Lord *his* God". The translator again discards the reference to the coming saviour, changing the personal pronoun *his* into *their*. He breaks the parallelism and begins a new sentence through the insert of the conjunction καί: "*and* in the glory of the name of the Lord *their* God they shall dwell". In this sentence, the glory of the name of the Lord is no longer connected with the expected leader, but with the people who will be pastured by the Lord himself. In MT the end of the verse also refers to the new ruler of whom it is said that "he will be great (יגדל)". In the LXX it most likely describes the nation, or more exactly, those who "returned": "They shall be magnified (μεγαλυνθή- σονται) to the end of the earth".

The conclusion of this reading of Mic 5,1-3 is that the Septuagint does not enhance the alleged messianic connotations of the Hebrew text. The Greek translation is less open to an individual messianic interpretation than the MT.

GENERAL CONCLUSIONS

1. A comparison of the quotation formulae at Qumran and in the New Testament revealed that the early Christians and the Qumran community

recognized the same books as authoritative. The formula אשר אמר in CD 4,13 which might seem to introduce a quotation of the book of Levi is not necessarily an exception.

2. The harvest of Micah texts in Qumran did not prove to be very rich in as far as chapter 5,1-3 is concerned. Nevertheless, some interesting observations could be made. Although the identification of 4QMic 5,1-2 is very hypothetical, it may preserve a trace of the original text suggesting that the textcritically problematic לי יצא of MT should perhaps be corrected into לו יצא. Also, the Greek scroll of Naḥal Ḥever leads to useful remarks on the rendition of the tetragram.

3. The text and literary critical reading of Mic 5,1-3 allowed us to list several differences between LXX and MT. It also questioned the preference given to the genitive κυρίου and the singular μεγαλυνθήσεται in Mic 5,3 in the critical editions of the Septuagint. The quotation in the NT proved to be independent from LXX.

4. The often explicitly or implicitly accepted thesis that the Septuagint accentuates the individual messianic connotations of the relevant passages in MT, preparing for the New Testament, cannot be supported by Mic 5,1-3.

Van 't Sestichstraat 34   Johan LUST
B-3000 Leuven

THE LURE OF THE FORMULA QUOTATIONS
RE-ASSESSING MATTHEW'S USE OF THE OLD TESTAMENT
WITH THE PASSION NARRATIVE AS TEST CASE

INTRODUCTION

It is well known that Matthew's gospel interacts extensively with the Old Testament. A cursory review of the statistics bears this out. Matthew incorporates Old Testament quotations some sixty-one times in his gospel, forty of these are explicit citations and twenty-one are direct quotations but without explicit citation[1]. Of these sixty-one quotations, twenty-four are from Mark and nine from Q. Matthew never omits an Old Testament quotation found in a Markan or Q parallel but adds twenty-eight quotations of his own. Of these additions, ten are to Markan material, three are to Q and fifteen are in special Matthean material. Most of these sixty-one quotations are found on the lips of Jesus (43 times) or the narrator (13 times). Determining the number of allusions to Old Testament passages is a much less precise science but here, too, Matthew's use is extensive. The Nestle-Aland appendix lists 294 implicit citations or allusions in Matthew.

While there have been innumerable studies attempting to understand the purpose and meaning of Matthew's appeals to the Old Testament, the most characteristic note in recent scholarship has been an emphasis on the so-called "formula quotations" in Matthew[2]. In fact, with few exceptions, virtually all studies of Matthew's use of the Old Testament concentrate on the formula quotations as the most characteristic and

---

1. The statistics are drawn from the list of citations and allusions in K. ALAND et al., *Novum Testamentum Graece*, 27th rev. ed., Stuttgart, Deutsche Bibelgesellschaft, 1993, Appendix IV, pp. 770-806. Using the criteria suggested by D. MOO, *The Old Testament in the Gospel Passion Narratives*, Sheffield, Almond Press, 1983, "explicit quotations" are those that employ an "introductory formula" to set them off from the context; "implicit quotations" are "relatively lengthy, word-for-word parallels to the OT"; "allusions" are present where the text "utilizes Scriptural words and phrases without introduction and without disrupting the flow of the narrative". See D. MOO, pp. 18-21.

2. The term "formula quotation", taking its cue from the characteristic introduction to these quotations, has been the standard modern designation for this material in Matthew. German scholarship has tended to use the terminology *Reflexionszitate* to distinguish these texts from the standard *Kontextzitate*, although more recently the term *Erfüllungs-zitate* or "fulfillment quotations" suggested by Wilhelm Rothfuchs has been used by some scholars, expressing the specific theological purpose of the quotations.

revealing feature of the gospel's perspective in this matter. This paper
will briefly review the past quarter century of Matthean scholarship
on this issue and then suggest that the formula quotations have been
something of a "siren song", with attention to the peculiar features of
the formula quotations skewing a fuller appreciation of the role of the
Old Testament in Matthew's narrative. To make the latter point, I will
appeal in particular to Matthew's use of the Old Testament in the
passion narrative, a major segment of the gospel in which the formula
quotations are scarce and yet where Matthew's characteristic use of the
Old Testament is transparent.

I. THE LURE OF THE FORMULA QUOTATIONS

Two summations of this issue can help us chart the course of scholarship over the past twenty five years concerning the formula quotations.
At the University of Louvain's Journées Bibliques in 1970, Frans Van
Segbroeck had provided a state of the question entitled, "Les citations
d'accomplissement dans l'Évangile selon saint Matthieu d'après trois
ouvrages récent"[3]. The "three recent works" referred to in his title were
three major studies that appeared in the late sixties, R. H. Gundry's, *The
Use of the Old Testament in St. Matthew's Gospel*, R. S. McConnell's
study on *Law and Prophecy in Matthew's Gospel* and W. Rothfuchs',
Die Erfüllungszitate des Matthäus-Evangeliums[4]. Van Segbroeck's
summation came in the wake of the great resurgence of redaction critical
studies on Matthew begun in post-war Germany and dominating European
and North American scholarship for the past several decades. An earlier,
landmark study of the formula quotations was that of Krister Stendahl,
The School of St. Matthew and Its Use of the Old Testament, first
published in 1954 and reissued in 1968 with a new preface modifying
some of his views in the light of subsequent research[5]. Van Segbroeck,
too, uses Stendahl as his starting point.

3. F. VAN SEGBROECK, *Les citations d'accomplissement dans l'Évangile selon saint
Matthieu d'après trois ouvrages récents*, in M. DIDIER (ed.), *L'Évangile selon Matthieu:
Rédaction et Théologie* (BETL, 29), Gembloux, Duculot, 1972, pp. 107-30.
4. R.H. GUNDRY, *The Use of the Old Testament in St. Matthew's Gospel with Special
Reference to the Messianic Hope* (NTSup, 18), Leiden, Brill, 1967; R.S. MCCONNELL,
*Law and Prophecy in Matthew's Gospel. The Authority and Use of the Old Testament in
the Gospel of St. Matthew* (Theologische Dissertationen, 2), Basel, Friedrich Reinhardt,
1969; W. ROTHFUCHS, *Die Erfüllungszitate des Matthäus-Evangeliums* (BWANT, 8), Kohlhammer, Stuttgart, 1969.
5. K. STENDAHL, *The School of St. Matthew and Its Use of the Old Testament*, Philadelphia, Fortress, 1968.

A "bookend" for Van Segbroeck's assessment is provided by the recent study of Graham Stanton entitled "Matthew's Use of the Old Testament" which first appeared in the Festschrift, *It is Written: Scripture Citing Scripture*, honoring Barnabas Lindars and is now available as a chapter in his 1992 monograph on Matthew's gospel entitled *A Gospel for a New People*[6]. Stanton covers some of the same ground as Van Segbroeck but is in a position to survey the subsequent years of research. Monographs on Matthew's use of the Old Testament have not been numerous in recent years but in articles, commentaries and other studies on the full spectrum of Matthew's gospel advances have been made[7]. Stanton, it should be noted, writes from the same redaction critical perspective as that of Van Segbroeck; the influx of literary critical studies on Matthew do not figure prominently in his assessment.

Van Segbroeck's basic approach was to test the landmark thesis of K. Stendahl concerning Matthew's quotations on the basis of the three major works cited above. The essentials of Stendahl's thesis could be summarized as follows: (1) The formula quotations represent a distinct group of quotations within Matthew's gospel, different in form from the other citations. Whereas most of his other direct quotations reflect a Septuagintal form, the formula quotations exhibit a "mixed" form identifiable with no single known Hebrew, Aramaic or Greek version. (2) The formula quotations may have been the product of a Matthean "school" which exhibited a distinct style of biblical interpretation or adaptation of biblical texts which interpreted the life of Jesus as the fulfillment of the Old Testament, not unlike the Pesher technique found in the Qumran materials, specifically the interpretation of Habakkuk in relationship to the Teacher of Righteousness. (3) Together with its unique application

---

6. G.N. Stanton, *A Gospel for a New People. Studies in Matthew*, Edinburgh, T. & T. Clark, 1992, pp. 346-363.

7. Other works on Matthew's use of the Old Testament and the formula quotations would include: R. Brown, *The Birth of the Messiah*, Garden City, Doubleday, 1977, pp. 96-103; J.-M. van Cangh, *La Bible de Matthieu: Les citations d'accomplissement*, in *ETL* 6 (1975) 205-11; O. L. Cope, *Matthew: A Scribe Trained for the Kingdom of Heaven* (CBQ MS, 5), Washington, DC, Catholic Biblical Association of America, 1976; R.T. France, *The Formula Quotations of Matthew 2 and the Problem of Communication*, in *NTS* 27 (1981) 233-51, and his monograph, *Matthew: Evangelist and Teacher*, Grand Rapids, MI, Zondervan, 1989, pp. 166-185; L. Hartman, *Scriptural Exegesis in the Gospel of St. Matthew and the Problem of Communication*, in M. Didier (ed.), *L'Évangile selon Matthieu*, pp. 131-152; U. Luz, *Matthew 1-7: A Commentary*, Minneapolis, Fortress, 1989, pp. 156-64; A. Sand, *Das Gesetz und die Propheten. Untersuchungen zur Theologie des Evangeliums nach Matthäus* (BU, 11), Regensburg, Pustet, 1974; G.M. Soares Prabhu, *The Formula Quotations in the Infancy Narrative of Matthew* (AnBib, 63), Rome, Biblical Institute, 1976. A survey of recent studies is found in D. Senior, *What Are They Saying About Matthew?*, New York, Paulist, rev. ed., 1996, pp. 51-61.

of Old Testament quotations to the life of Jesus, the ordered nature of Matthew's gospel as a whole gave it the character of a "handbook" for use in forming church teachers and administrators.

Van Segbroeck's survey of subsequent Matthean research concluded that Stendahl's thesis had received a mixed judgment. His conclusion that the formula quotations were a distinct "mixed" text type in contrast to other, more Septuagintal quotations in Matthew was generally approved. A significant dissenting voice, however, was that of R. H. Gundry. According to Gundry, conformity to the Septuagint was found primarily in those quotations that Matthew derived from Mark, who does show a strong preference for the Septuagint. In other Matthean quotations and allusions not in parallel with Mark, however, no consistent bias for the Septuagint is found and there is evidence of the same "mixed" form detectable in the formula quotations. The impact of Gundry's meticulous examination of the evidence was blunted, however, for at least two reasons. First of all, some of his conclusions were based on an examination of the biblical allusions; the fragility of drawing inferences about text type from a few words or phrases made Gundry's conclusions less decisive. Also Gundry defended a very conservative thesis about the authorship of the gospel. He asserted that the mixed text type found in Matthew's non-Markan quotations reflected the tri-lingual context of first century Palestinian Judaism and concluded that Matthew's gospel depended in part on notes taken by the Apostle Matthew. For many interpreters of Matthew, therefore, Stendahl's thesis about the distinct form of the formula quotations and his inclination to the Septuagint in quotations other than the formula quotations continued to hold sway.

Other aspects of Stendahl's thesis, however, fared less well. The suggestion that Matthew's "school" was engaged in a kind of interpretation similar to that of Qumran's Pesher commentaries on Habbakuk was not generally accepted. Whereas the focus of Qumran materials was on the interpretation of the prophetic texts, Matthew's focus was on the life of Jesus. Nor was the hypothesis of a "school" received with enthusiasm. McConnell, for example, agreed with the thesis of Gärtner that a more likely milieu was in a missionary context, so that the formula quotations derived from the kind of interpretation done in Christian preaching and catechesis which showed the harmony between the scriptures and the life and ministry of Jesus[8]. In the new preface to his 1967 edition, Stendahl

---

8. R. McCONNELL, *Law and Prophecy in Matthew's Gospel*, p. 138; he refers to the study of B. GÄRTNER, *The Habakkuk Commentary (DSH) and the Gospel of Matthew*, in *ST* (1954), 1-24. A similar thesis had already been proposed by G. KILPATRICK, *The Origins of the Gospel According to St. Matthew*, Oxford, Clarendon Press, 1946.

took note of these mixed reviews. He also was willing to qualify his original thesis that the mixed text form of Matthew's formula quotations – while distinct from the other direct and more Septuagintal quotations in the gospel – was a unique creation of Matthew's community. The recognition of additional variants in our known Masoretic and Septuagintal texts and the fact that textual transmission may have been more fluid than originally thought caution interpreters not to draw premature conclusions about "uniqueness" concerning Matthew's or any other Old Testament citations.

The scholarship that Van Segbroeck reviewed had also gone beyond Stendahl's work on other issues. For example, Georg Strecker's hypothesis that Matthew drew the formula quotations from a pre-existing collection of Old Testament citations and applied them to the story of Jesus' life for historicizing purposes, that is, to show that Jesus' life belonged to a past sacred epoch, was not convincing to most scholars[9]. More persuasive was the thesis that Matthew himself was responsible for selecting the formula quotations and adapting them to the context of the gospel, and even at times adapting the narrative to fit the quotation. This latter conviction of redaction critics was strongly proposed by both McConnell and particularly Rothfuchs. Without question the introductory formulae were Matthean in both language and theology, serving Matthew's christology which viewed Jesus as the fulfillment of the Hebrew Scriptures. Likewise the quotations themselves were carefully selected and adapted to the context to illustrate this fundamental christology. Thus cumulatively the formula quotations were linked to a deep current of Matthean theology.

Rothfuchs and Van Segbroeck himself took up one final issue that continued to baffle Matthean scholarship, namely the rationale for the distribution of the formula quotations in the gospel. If the formula quotations were key to Matthew's effort to relate the life of Jesus to the Old Testament, then the uneven distribution of the quotations was puzzling. Of the ten formula quotations that fit the usually agreed upon criteria, four were found in the Infancy Narrative, four more in chapters 4-13, and only 2 in the remaining 15 chapters of the gospel (21,4-5; 27,9-10)[10]. Rothfuchs

---

9. G. STRECKER, *Der Weg der Gerechtigkeit: Untersuchung zur Theologie des Matthäus* (FRLANT, 82), Göttingen, Vandenhoeck & Ruprecht, 1966, pp. 49-85; see also his article, *Matthew's Understanding of History*, in *JAAR* 35 (1967) 219-30.

10. The designation "formula quotation" is usually applied to those Matthean quotations that: (1) include the introductory formula (ἵνα [ὅπως] πληρωθῇ τὸ ῥηθὲν διὰ τοῦ προφήτου λέγοντος); (2) are statements of the narrator; (3) include an explicit quotation. The texts that fit these criteria are: 1,22-23; 2,15; 2,17-18; 2,23; 4,14-16; 8,17; 12,17-21; 13,35; 21,4-5; 27,9-10. The citation in 2,5-6 is tantalizingly close but does not include the standard introductory fulfillment formula. Mt 26,54.56 emphasize fulfillment but do not meet the other two criteria.

suggested that, in fact, the formula quotations were grouped at the beginning of the gospel even more radically than the statistics suggested. The
quotation that concluded the Judas story (27,9-10) had probably already
been attached to this story before Matthew included it in his passion
account and appended his formulaic introduction. Likewise the citation
of Isa 62,11 attached to the entrance into Jerusalem in 21,4-5 may also
be traditional, as suggested by its use in John 12,15. The four quotations
in chapters 4-13 also form a distinct group: each of them is attributed to
Isaiah, each is attached to a summary of Jesus' ministry and all of them
are applied to his public ministry[11]. By means of the Isaiah quotations
Matthew wanted to draw attention to Jesus' mission to the "lost sheep"
of the house of Israel. Therefore the remaining four quotations in chapters 1-2 serve as orientation for the reader; in these opening chapters the
main themes of Jesus' mission are sounded and by means of the formula
quotations the evangelist immediately asserts that all of Jesus' mission is
a fulfillment of the Old Testament.

Van Segbroeck himself added further nuance to the observations of
Rothfuchs. The clustering of most of the formula quotations in chapters
1-13 may also reflect Matthew's use of sources in the construction of his
narrative. In these chapters Matthew inserts himself most forcefully in
comparison to Mark, incorporating a large block of Q material and freely
rearranging Mark's narrative sequence[12]. From chapter 14 on Matthew
follows the narrative framework of Mark much more closely. Thus it is
not surprising that Matthew's most distinctive Old Testament quotations
should appear in a portion of the gospel in which the evangelist was most
invested. Van Segbroeck also offered a further suggestion about the four
quotations attributed to Isaiah found in chapters 4-13. These citations did
not apply simply to material illustrating Jesus' mission to the lost sheep of
Israel, as Rothfuch had suggested, but also included the mounting opposition to Jesus from the religious authorities. This, too, provided a
rationale for quotations from Isaiah for the prophet was remembered as
experiencing rejection. Thus, too, the quotation of Isaiah 6,9-10 in the
parable chapter which Matthew draws from Mark and which is applied

---

11. Mt. 4,14-16 cites Isa 8,23-9,1; 8,17 cites Isa 53,4; 12,17-21 cites Isa 42,1-4; the
citation in 13,35 is actually from Ps 78,2 yet there is good reason to believe that
Matthew's attribution of this citation to Isaiah (13,35) is original. Thereby the evangelist
extends the name of Isaiah to Jesus' employment of parables (as already in 13,14-15, a
parallel to Mark where Isa 6,9 is quoted).

12. From 4,23 to the end of the parable discourse in 13,58, Matthew freely rearranges
Markan material in order to portray Jesus as teacher and healer; see F. NEIRYNCK, *La
rédaction matthéenne et la structure du premier évangile*, in *ETL* 43 (1967) 41-73.

both to the proclamation of the mystery of the Kingdom of God and its rejection fits into place.

If the studies of Rothfuchs and Van Segbroeck are to be credited for beginning to consider a rationale for the placement of the formula quotations in Matthew, their answers were still only partial. If Matthew was capable of adding Isaian quotations to interpret a substantial portion of Jesus' public ministry in chapters 4 to 13, why could he not do so for the rest of the gospel, including the passion narrative in which the issue of scriptural fulfillment would seem to be most acutely posed? And if Matthew's more radical reworking of his sources in chapters 1-13 provides part of the answer for the presence of the formula quotations in the first half of the gospel, how can one explain the seemingly errant quotations in 21,4-5 and 27,9-10? Even if one concedes that the Old Testament quotations were traditionally connected to these two stories, this does not explain why Matthew would introduce his fulfillment formula at these points and no other.

Graham Stanton's study complements that of Van Segbroeck, able as it is to survey the more than twenty years of Matthean research that had accumulated since the Journées Bibliques of 1970 and to make his own contribution to the discussion. At the outset, Stanton observes, as I have suggested above, that focus on the formula quotations has dominated studies on the use of the Old Testament in Matthew, to the neglect of other features[13]. Even so the lure of the formula quotations continues to hold sway in his own work, commanding the major part of his focus.

Stanton asks some of the same questions posed by Van Segbroeck but offers somewhat different answers. In considering whether or not Matthew, apart from the formula quotations, favored the Septuagint, Stanton aligns himself with Gundry's thesis and challenges the working assumptions of such influential Matthean scholars as Ulrich Luz and Georg Strecker. These and other scholars still accepted the groundwork of Stendahl who claimed that when Matthew introduced changes in the wording of Old Testament quotations derived from Mark, such changes moved further in the direction of conformity with the Septuagint. In reviewing the four

---

13. "They (i.e., the formula quotations) have dominated discussion of Matthew's use of the OT and have frequently been appealed to in attempts to elucidate the origin and purpose of the gospel. In addition, there is a further important aspect of the use of the OT in Matthew which has often been neglected: the evangelist's modifications of the quotations found in his sources and the additional references he includes without using his 'introductory formula.'" G. STANTON, *A Gospel for a New People*, p. 346; see also, U. LUZ, *Matthew 1-7*: "...one may not consider the formula quotations as a unique theological problem; they have to be interpreted in connection with the other quotations". (p. 157).

examples offered as evidence of this by Stendahl, Stanton believes a more plausible explanation is that such changes are typical stylistic or theological features of Matthew rather than attempts to align the quotations with the Septuagint[14]. For example in Matthew 19,18-19, the change from the Markan (10,9) formulation of μή plus the subjunctive to Matthew's οὐ plus the future indicative in the series of prohibitions is probably to be understood as a stylistic improvement to "balance more precisely the negative commandments with the positive commandment ἀγαπήσεις τὸν πλησίον σου ὡς σεαυτόν which the evangelist adds here, the wording of which corresponds exactly both with the MT and with the LXX of Lev 19,18"[15]. He also notes that the addition of the phrase about love of neighbor in Mt 19,19b fits well with Matthew's theological perspective which sees love of neighbor as fulfilling the law and the prophets (comp. 7,12b and 22,40). Similarly none of the other examples cited by Stendahl offers compelling evidence that Matthew is more in conformity with the LXX than the Markan parallels.

Stanton's conclusion about Matthew's adaptation of Old Testament quotations drawn from Mark or Q is significant: the changes Matthew makes in these Old Testament quotations are similar to those he consistently makes in his sources elsewhere[16]. "Matthew's primary allegiance is to the textual form of the quotations in his sources rather than to the LXX as such"[17].

Stanton's assessment of the formula quotations also emphasizes the redactional activity of the evangelist rather than reliance on traditional material. He makes several points:

(1) Without doubt, the introductory formulae themselves are creations of Matthew, reflecting his literary style and, with their emphasis on fulfillment, the theological perspective of the gospel. The original inspiration for the formula can be traced to Matthew's redaction of Mk 14,49c where two of the three elements found in all of the introductory formulae are already present, namely the emphasis on fulfillment of scripture and the fact that this is a comment of the "narrator"[18].

(2) Concerning the mixed form of the quotations themselves, Stanton thinks the usual attempt to find a single source for the quotations, whether in a school setting (Stendahl) or "testimony books" (Strecker) is misguided.

14. G. STANTON, *A Gospel for a New People*, pp. 354-58; see K. STENDAHL, *The School of St. Matthew*, pp. 147-148.
15. G. STANTON, *A Gospel for a New People*, p. 354.
16. *Ibid.*, p. 355; he examines Mt. 3,3; 9,13; 12,7; 16,9; 21,13; 24,15; 26,56.
17. *Ibid.*, p. 358.
18. *Ibid.*, p. 359.

He contends that in some instances Matthew may have drawn the citations from an existing source or tradition but in other cases the close fit between the surrounding narrative context and the quotation itself suggests that Matthew himself has shaped the quotation in his own manner. Two examples he notes of the latter type are the quotation of Isa 9,1-2 in Mt 4,14-16 and that of Isa 42,1-4 in Mt 12,17-21.

(3) Stanton's comments on the distribution of the formula quotations in Matthew do not go far beyond the observations of Rothfuchs and Van Segbroeck. There is, he concedes, "no clear answer" (p. 359). Mt 26, 54.56 – although not strictly a formula quotation – spread the mantle of scriptural fulfillment to the passion narrative. The function of chapters 1-2 as a prologue to the narrative as a whole probably explains why there are several formula quotations in these opening chapters. Stanton believes that the infancy narrative is composed of mainly traditional material to which Matthew added the formula quotations. He argues for this hypothesis on the premise that (1) 1,18-2,23 can be read coherently without the formula quotations (only 2,5-6 seems tightly woven to the context); (2) five of the six remaining quotations are added to pre-existing, i.e. Markan materials; (3) and the Old Testament texts quoted are not used elsewhere in the New Testament, suggesting that Matthew himself was the first to make these particular applications to the life of Jesus[19].

Stanton believes that even though there is evidence that Matthew adapted the quotations to fit into the narrative context of the gospel (e.g., the plural form of καλέσουσιν in 1,23 to indicate that the "they" are the Christian community who confess Jesus as Emmanuel; the addition of οὐδαμῶς in 2,6 to fit the new circumstance of Bethlehem as the birthplace of Jesus), and in some cases the introductory formula is also adapted in the light of the quotation (e.g., the references to Jesus as υἱός in 1,23 and 2,15 explain why in these instances the formula refers to the word spoken ὑπὸ κυρίου), still only to a limited degree, in Stanton's view, does the quotation shape the narrative (he cites the influence of the quotation from Jer 31,15 on Mt 2,16).

---

19. *Ibid*, pp. 360-361. Stanton's arguments are not particularly decisive for determining the traditional nature of chapters 1–2, however. The fact that Matthew adds formula quotations to Markan material in the body of the gospel does not mean that he can only add quotations to pre-existing material elsewhere. The ability to read the text coherently without the presence of the formula quotations could probably be said in every instance of the formula quotations in the Gospel, particularly since they are comments of the narrator and not intrinsic to the story. And the fact that the Old Testament quotations are not used elsewhere in the New Testament could be just as much an argument for the Matthean composition of the chapters 1–2 as for its traditional nature.

(4) Stanton is emphatic about the christological intent of the formula quotations. Their function throughout the gospel is to wrap Jesus in the mantle of scriptural fulfillment. At first blush the quotations in chapter 2 seem to undergird the geographical places mentioned (e.g., Bethlehem, Egypt, Bethlehem/Ramah, Nazareth) but even in these instances it is christology that holds sway: the citation of Mic 5,1,3 in reference to Bethlehem because Jesus will shepherd God's people (2,6); the citation of Hos 11,1 in the reference to Egypt for thereby Jesus is called God's son (2,15); and in both 2,15 and 2,17-18 Jesus is linked with the exodus experience of Israel through the citations of Hos 11,1 and Jer 31,15 plus Gen 35,19. The baffling quotation in 2,23 is probably a reference to Isa 11,1 and thereby affirms Jesus' messianic identity as the *nezir*[20]. The same holds true for the rest of the citations in the body of the gospel: 4,15-16 proclaims Jesus as the savior of the Gentiles; 8,17 and 13,35 underscore his God-given mission as healer and teacher; 12,17-21 his role as God's servant; and 21,4-5 his role as humble king.

Other recent studies of Matthew's quotations expand the picture presented by Stanton. In the introduction to their massive commentary on Matthew, W. D. Davies and D. Allison, Jr. devote considerable attention to Matthew's use of the Old Testament in their attempt to demonstrate that the evangelist was Jewish and knew Hebrew[21]. After reexamining each of the direct quotations and possible allusions in Matthew and noting that the evangelist appeals to the Old Testament much more than either Mark or Luke, their conclusions about Matthew's text type are emphatic:

a) In the 17 quotations Matthew shares with Mark, Matthew generally retains Mark's preference for the Septuagint but in those few cases in which he does introduce minor changes they are not uniformly in the direction of closer alignment with the LXX. Here Davies and Allison are in agreement with the conclusions of G. Stanton.

b) Matthew's redactional expansions or changes in allusions parallel with Mark and Luke, as well as his own unique redactional allusions, frequently depart from the LXX and often agree with the Masoretic text.

c) Mattthew's unique quotations exhibit the same mixed text form as the synoptic allusions and should be attributed to the evangelist's own redactional activity rather than to any source or pre-Matthean tradition.

---

20. On this text, see J.A. SANDERS, Ναζωραῖος in Matthew 2.23, in C.A. EVANS & W. R. STEGNER (eds.), *The Gospels and the Scriptures of Israel* (JSNT SS, 104), Sheffield, Academic Press, 1994, pp. 116-128; also in the same volume, R. PESCH, 'He will be Called a Nazorean': Messianic Exegesis in Matthew 1-2, pp. 129-178.

21. W. D. DAVIES & D. C. ALLISON, Jr., *The Gospel According to Saint Matthew*. Volume 1 (ICC), Edinburgh, T. & T. Clark, 1988, pp. 29-58.

Davies and Allison are much less hesitant than Stanton to assign the unique features of the evangelist's quotations to Matthew's own redactional activity and his knowledge of Hebrew rather than to some no longer extant version of the Septuagint or Masoretic text. They note that the Old Testament citations and allusions in Mark, Luke, John as well as in Paul, do not "give us any reason to suppose that their authors were familiar with anything but a Greek OT very similar to what we have in our hands today"[22]. Matthew, they assert, is "the only NT writer frequently to agree with the MT against the LXX...and because we lack any corroboration for the hypothesis that our evangelist had a now defunct Greek OT, we must strongly suspect not that the author of the First Gospel alone among early Christians had a non-LXX OT that has altogether disappeared but rather that he could read the scriptures in their original languages"[23].

Note that while underscoring Matthew's capacity to utilize the Hebrew text in his adaptation of Old Testament quotations, Davies and Allison confirm the important principle stated by Stanton: Matthew treats the Old Testament quotations in the same way he treats all of his source material. As is true throughout his gospel Matthew generally respects the material provided by Mark and therefore quotations and allusions taken over from Mark are more Septuagintal in character. Where he does make changes in Mark or Q, as well as in uniquely Matthean material, his composition is consistent with his characteristic style and redactional perspective.

Narrative critical studies of Matthew also complement and expand on Stanton's assessment. One of the more elaborate works dealing in part with Matthew's use of the Old Testament is that of David B. Howell, *Matthew's Inclusive Story: A Study in the Narrative Rhetoric of the First Gospel*[24]. Howell also concentrates on the formula quotations in assessing Matthew's use of the Old Testament. These quotations fall under the general category of "direct commentary" which is "one of the most visible ways a narrator/implied author's ideological point of view can be expressed since it is in direct commentary that the narrator explicitly addresses the implied reader" (p. 179). Using the categories of Seymour

---

22. *Ibid*, p. 45.
23. *Ibid*.
24. D.B. HOWELL, *Matthew's Inclusive Story: A Study in the Narrative Rhetoric of the First Gospel* (JSNT SS, 42), Sheffield, JSOT Press, 1990. See also J.D. KINGSBURY, *Matthew as Story*, Philadelphia, Fortress, 2nd ed., 1988, who, similar to Howell, locates the formula quotations as "narrative commentary" on the part of the implied author (p. 33) but does not give great attention to this feature of Matthew's gospel.

Chatman, Howell identifies three types of direct commentary: (1) "Interpretation" is a broad category that provides an explanation of the "gist, relevance, or significance of a story element" such as the meaning of Jesus' name in Mt 1,23 or the translation of "Golgotha" in 27,33; (2) "judgment" is an explanation or commentary on the basis of a moral judgment made by the implied author/narrator such as the information that Joseph is a "just man" in Mt 1,19 or that Jesus teaches with authority (7,29); (3) "generalization" is commentary or explanation which "makes reference outward from the fictional to the real world, either to 'universal truths' or to actual historical facts"[25].

Howell situates the formula quotations under the category of "generalizations". As he observes, "The Old Testament and its authority as the word of God (1,22; 2,15) exist independently of the narrative world of the gospel. When Matthew appeals to prophecies which lie outside of his gospel's narrative world (prophecies whose authority is accepted by the implied reader), and when he shows how the events in Jesus' life which he is narrating fulfilled the Old Testament messianic hopes, he thereby gives his narrative plausibility and reinforces the truthfulness of his claims about who Jesus is. Since the Old Testament formula quotations are cited by the narrator, his trustworthiness is also established for the implied reader" (p. 186). Thus for Howell the rhetorical function of the formula quotations supports both Matthew's christology and reinforces the authority of the gospel itself.

Howell briefly addresses the issue of the distribution of the formula quotations. Although bunched in the opening chapters of the gospel, they "highlight almost every aspect of Jesus and his ministry" (p. 186). Placing the quotations at the beginning of the narrative sets the stage for reading the rest of the story "by establishing the implied reader's initial understanding of Jesus' identity as the Son of God and promised Messiah" and also preparing for the theme of rejection by underlining "the gravity of the choice whether to accept or reject Jesus and his teaching" (p. 188). In fact, Howell notes, some of the formula quotations deal explicitly with the rejection of Jesus, particularly the Isaian quotations in chapters 4-13 which, as Van Segbroeck had already noted, evoke the prophet as both proclaimer of salvation to Israel and one who indicted Israel for its failure to respond to his preaching.

Howell adds a significant comment about 26,54.56 to which we will return. Jesus' statement about fulfillment of the prophets at the moment of his arrest not only extends scriptural fulfillment and the theme of

25. Chatman as cited by Howell, *Matthew's Inclusive Story*, p. 181.

rejection to the passion narrative but also is the only time in the gospel in which the character Jesus expresses the same words the narrator has been stating in the fulfillment quotations[26].

More recent studies have also given considerable attention to the social context of Matthew's gospel and here, too, there are implications for understanding Matthew's use of the Old Testament. Debate continues about the relationship of Matthew's community and formative Judaism. For some authors, following the early lead of W. D. Davies, the break between Matthew's community and Pharisaic Judaism was already decisive[27]. Others, however, consider Matthew to be still within the orbit of Judaism even if in considerable tension with its dominant group[28]. Despite these diverse assessments, authors at both ends of the spectrum relate Matthew's "fulfillment" theology and his use of scripture to the proposed social context of the community. Matthew's assignment of biblical fulfillment to the person and ministry of Jesus is also a legitimization of the teaching of his community and a claim upon the traditional authority of the scriptures over against the claims of the community's opponents – whether those opponents are viewed across the chasm of an already severed relationship or a relationship still existing but under serious strain. Thus Luz will note, "Matthew lived at a time when the bonds connecting his community with Israel's synagogues had been severed. His community did not view itself as a new 'Christian' congregation but as the true core of the nation of Israel, summoned by Jesus to God. This led him to reformulate, in a programmatic spirit, Mark's incidental Christian notion of the fulfillment of Scripture... The Christian communities raised claims to the legacy of Israel just as did the synagogues of the Pharisees"[29]. Overman, who contends that Matthew's community was still within the boundaries of formative Judaism, reaches a

26. D. B. HOWELL, *Matthew's Inclusive Story*, p. 189.
27. This view was strongly articulated by W. D. DAVIES in his classic study, *The Setting of the Sermon on the Mount*, Cambridge, University, 1964. Recent scholarship tends to believe that Davies overestimates the role of Jamnia in the formation of post-70 Pharisaic Judaism; however many would accept his judgment that Matthew's community had already experienced a definitive separation from the synagogue and was in tension with it; see, for example, H. FRANKEMÖLLE, *Jahwebund und Kirche Christi* (NTAbh NF, 10), Münster, Aschendorf, 1974, and U. LUZ, in his commentary and more recently in *The Theology of the Gospel of Matthew*, Cambridge, University, 1995, pp. 11-17.
28. See, for example, J. A. OVERMAN, *Matthew's Gospel and Formative Judaism*, Minneapolis, Fortress, 1990; G. N. STANTON, *A Gospel for a New People*; and A. J. SALDARINI, *Matthew's Christian-Jewish Community*, Chicago, University of Chicago, 1994. The latter describes Matthew's community in sociological terms as a "deviant" group attempting to assert its validity vis à vis the dominant majority.
29. U. LUZ, *The Theology of the Gospel of Matthew*, p. 40.

similar conclusion about the purpose of Matthew's emphasis on scriptural fulfillment: "The particular use of the notion of fulfillment, as it is expressed in the fulfillment citations, is an attempt by Matthew to lend antiquity and authority to the beliefs and life of his community. The use of Scripture and the interpretation of certain prophecies in light of the history of Jesus of Nazareth make the claim, in the face of contention and competition from the Jewish leadership in Matthew's setting, that the beliefs and actions of his community are neither spurious, new, nor innovative"[30].

Therefore Matthew's social context, specifically the need to legitimate the religious claims of his community, also contributed significantly to the gospel's emphasis on scriptural fulfillment.

This survey enables us to offer the following assessment of current scholarship on Matthew's use of the Old Testament:

1. Most scholars concentrate on the formula quotations as the most distinctive and revealing feature of Matthew's use of the Old Testament.

2. There is a strong consensus that the introductory formulae themselves are compositions of the evangelist. They have characteristic Matthean language, are in harmony with Matthew's theological perspective as a whole, and show evidence of being adapted both to their context in the gospel and to the content of the quotations they introduce.

3. Consensus is less strong here but perhaps a majority of scholars are also willing to attribute the particular form of the quotations themselves to the evangelist who adapted them to the narrative context in which they are introduced or to other overriding concerns of Matthew's theology. For those who speculate that at least some of the quotations may have been formulated prior to Matthew, most are not convinced that the quotations come from a single source such as the testimony books suggested by Strecker and others but derive in a more generic way from the preaching and teaching activity of the early pre-Matthean community.

4. There is less inclination than before to consider the text type of the formula quotations as unique in contrast to Matthew's supposed preference elsewhere for the Septuagint. In quotations Matthew draws from Mark he generally follows the Septuagintal form preferred by his source. Where he deviates from his source or in quotations and allusions that are non-Markan, Matthew exhibits a "mixed" form of quotation similar to that of the formula quotations. For some such as Davies and Allison this is evidence that Matthew composed these quotations on his own, drawing in part on his knowledge of Hebrew. For Stanton and others (including

30. J. A. OVERMAN, *Matthew's Gospel and Formative Judaism*, p. 78.

the later Stendahl), such mixed texts might be evidence of a Greek version unknown to us.

5. Commentators increasingly emphasize that the formula quotations serve Matthew's christology, underscoring his messianic authority by appeal to Old Testament fulfillment.

6. Similarly, renewed discussion of the social context of the gospel and the relationship of Matthew's community to formative Judaism have provided further rationale for the particular shape and emphasis in Matthew's appeal to the Old Testament. Therefore Matthew's ecclesiology as well as his christology are significant motivations for his stress on Old Testament fulfillment.

7. The rationale for the distribution of the formula quotations in Matthew's gospel remains difficult to understand. Most interpreters explain the profusion of quotations in the opening chapters of the gospel as the evangelist's means of orienting the reader to his particular theological perspective[31]. In this prelude to the gospel most of the major motifs of Matthew's narrative are already sounded. Some would detect a thematic rationale for the four Isaiah quotations in chapters 4-13, relating Jesus' public ministry to the prophet's proclamation of salvation to Israel as well as the motif of rejection. Van Segbroeck also connected the distribution to Matthew's more emphatic editing of his source material in the first thirteen chapters of the gospel. While these suggestions are all helpful and offer partial explanations, they are not completely satisfying. The two quotations in 21,4-5 and 27,9-10 appear orphaned in Matthew's scheme. And although there is something of a turning point in Mt 13,35, as Jesus leaves the crowds and turns to private instruction of the disciples, it is hardly the end of Jesus' public ministry to Israel nor the finale of the motif of rejection. Likewise the fact that Matthew was free to add formula quotations in chapters 21 and 27 at least blunts Van Segbroeck's explanation about the quotations appearing where Matthew takes a freer hand with his source material.

II. Situating the Formula Quotations in the Overall Context of Matthew's Gospel and Its Use of the Old Testament

Stanton's observation about the tendency of recent scholarship to focus on the formula quotations to the neglect of other features of Matthew's

---

31. "The formula quotations are notably frequent in the prologue, because here the evangelist introduces those viewpoints and accents which are important for the whole Gospel and which the reader must keep in mind while perusing the entire Gospel. The formula quotations which are scattered in the rest of the Gospel are then reminders." U. Luz, *Matthew 1-7*, p. 162.

appeal to the Old Testament is worth taking seriously. The evangelist's application of the Old Testament to Jesus is obviously not confined to ten or twelve verses of the gospel. Even if one concentrates on direct quotations and evident allusions, Matthew's use of the Old Testament is a substantial feature of his gospel. The formula quotations, in fact, make explicit a theological perspective that emerges in several ways through-out the gospel. Allow me to first illustrate this in a more generic fashion for the gospel as a whole and then concentrate on the passion narrative for more detailed illustration.

By means of the formula quotations Matthew asserts that the person and mission of Jesus "fulfills" the plan or promise of God expressed in the Hebrew scriptures. For Matthew – as was true of virtually all New Testament interaction with the Old Testament – the relationship to the Hebrew scriptures is dialogic rather than linear. "Fulfillment" does not mean simply a matter of applying Old Testament quotations to events in the life of Jesus. The events of Jesus' life are illuminated and their authority revealed in the light of the Old Testament and, at the same time, new understandings of the voice of God in the scriptures and the history of Israel are revealed in the light of Jesus' person and mission. Thus Jesus "fulfills" the scriptures both by being in harmony with the scriptures and revealing their intended meaning.

This fulfillment theology first of all serves Matthew's christology by extending the mantle of scriptural fulfillment to significant features of Jesus' history: his origin (chs. 1-2); his entry into Galilee and his mes-sianic mission to Jew and Gentile (4,14-16); his healings (chs. 8, 12); his teaching in parables (13), his entry into Jerusalem (21); his rejection (27,9-10). Thereby Matthew is able to underscore the authority of Jesus as Son of God and Messiah and to express a "Christian" reading of the scriptures. And, as discussed earlier, the formula quotations also serve Matthew's ecclesiology in that the community formed in Jesus' name and faithful to his teaching is assured of its own legitimacy and author-ity, an assertion of capital importance assuming that Matthew's commu-nity was still in tension with Pharisaic Judaism[32].

However, this fundamental appeal to the authority of Old Testament fulfillment is by no means confined to the formula quotations, a simple fact that should not be ignored. Along with the formula quotations there are at least three other means Matthew uses to assert that Jesus fulfills the Old Testament:

32. See above, pp. 101-102.

(1) *Programmatic statements.* In three instances in Matthew's narrative Jesus himself utters what might be called "programmatic statements" that connect the notion of scriptural fulfillment to his mission without explicit citation of any specific biblical passage. The first occurs in 3,15: Ἄφες ἄρτι, οὕτως γὰρ πρέπον ἐστὶν ἡμῖν πληρῶσαι πᾶσαν δικαιοσύνην. The use of πᾶσαν δικαιοσύνην gives the statement a strong ethical emphasis and therefore is applicable to Jesus' own faithfulness to the will of God, a fidelity to be exemplified in the desert test that takes place in the next scene (4,1-11) and throughout the gospel[33]. At the same time, the connotation of Matthew's key word πληρῶσαι and its link to the notion of πᾶσαν δικαιοσύνην also suggest to the reader that Jesus' obedience is a fulfillment of the justice asked of Israel in the scriptures.

Another evident programmatic statement is Matthew's key text in 5,17, Μὴ νομίσητε ὅτι ἦλθον καταλῦσαι τὸν νόμον ἢ τοὺς προφήτας· οὐκ ἦλθον καταλῦσαι ἀλλὰ πληρῶσαι. In the context of the Sermon this statement of Jesus affirms that his teaching is a fulfillment of the Old Testament viewed in its entirety, that is, "the law and the prophets" – a traditional designation for the scriptures[34]. It should be noted that in the scheme of Matthew's gospel, the Sermon on the Mount of chapters 5-7 is not simply one in a series of discourses but lays the foundation for all of Jesus' teaching in the remainder of the gospel, affirming Jesus' authority as teacher and, equally important for Matthew, affirming that all of his teaching and interpretation of law is both in continuity with the scriptures and brings them to fulfillment.

To these two "programmatic statements" we might also add a third, namely the statement of Jesus in 26,56 at the moment of his arrest: τοῦτο δὲ ὅλον γέγονεν ἵνα πληρωθῶσιν αἱ γραφαὶ τῶν προφητῶν.[35] As Howell had observed, this is the only text in the gospel where the Matthean Jesus uses the phraseology of the formula quotations. This text is programmatic in the sense that it extends scriptural fulfillment (again without any explicit citation) to the entire event of Jesus' rejection and death, complementing in effect the previous programmatic statements applied to his life and teaching.

From the vantage point of the rhetorical strategy of Matthew, the placement of these programmatic statements on the lips of Jesus puts

33. See U. LUZ, *The Theology of the Gospel of Matthew* (n. 27), p. 35.
34. See the references provided in W. D. DAVIES & D. C. ALLISON, Jr., *The Gospel According to Saint Matthew*, vol. 1, p. 484. Note that Matthew will use this same formulation with the same collective sense in 7,12 (οὗτος γάρ ἐστιν ὁ νόμος καὶ οἱ προφῆται); 11,13 (πάντες γὰρ οἱ προφῆται καὶ ὁ νόμος ἕως Ἰωάννου ἐπροφήτευσαν); 22,40 (ἐν ταύταις ταῖς δυσίν ἐντολαῖς ὅλος ὁ νόμος κρέμαται καὶ οἱ προφῆται).
35. See further below, p. 109.

them in a category comparable to the formula quotations themselves. That Jesus "fulfills" and illumines the Old Testament is now testimony provided not only by the narrator by means of the formula quotations but also by one who along with the divine voice (see 3,17; 17,5), is the narrative's most reliable and authoritative character, Jesus himself.

(2) *Direct Quotations and Allusions other than formula quotations.* Alongside the formula quotations there are a substantial number of other direct Old Testament quotations which Matthew either has in common with his sources Mark and Q or which are attributable to the evangelist[36]. Add to these the numerous biblical *allusions* which Matthew draws from his sources or adds himself and one is faced with an overwhelming number of examples where the evangelist links the Old Testament to the story of Jesus[37]. Not all of these Old Testament quotations or allusions in Matthew's gospel advance the motif of scriptural fulfillment in the sense that they either directly state or imply that aspects of Jesus' person or mission fulfill the scriptures, as, for example, Jesus' citation of the decalogue in his discussion with the rich young man (19,18-19) or his reference to Deut 24,1-3 and the citation of Gen 2,24 in the conflict with the Pharisees over divorce (19,4-5). The same might be said of the implicit citations of scripture in the antitheses of 5,21-48 which illustrate received teaching (such as that of Exod 30,13 in 5,21).

But in other instances, texts taken over from sources or introduced by Matthew do affirm, at least implicitly, the notion of "fulfillment": see, for example, the Markan material retained in Mt 3,3; 11,10; 15,8-9 and 21,42. Or the Q passages in the story of the desert test: see Mt 4,4. 6.7.10. In addition to the formula quotations other passages containing quotations unique to Matthew are particularly illustrative of this theology: the application of the combined quotations from Mic 5,1; 2 Sam 5,2 and 1 Chron 11,2 in Mt 2,6[38]; the use of Hos 6,6 in the Markan texts of Mt 9,13 and 12,7; the application of Isa 6,9-10 in the Markan parallel of Mt 13,14-15; and the use of Ps 8,3 in the Markan parallel of Mt 21,16.

Matthew's gospel also contains numerous biblical allusions which imply a theology of fulfillment. To those Matthew incorporates from his

---

36. See the chart of references provided by W.D. DAVIES and D.C. ALLISON, *The Gospel According to Saint Matthew*, pp. 34-57. They list 17 quotations common to Matthew and Mark, 4 quotations common to Matthew and Luke, and 21 quotations peculiar to Matthew.

37. Davies and Allison identify 39 possible allusions common to Matthew and Mark and 50 allusions peculiar to Matthew.

38. Some list 2,6 as a formula quotation even though its introductory formula is not consistent with the other examples.

sources, he adds others and in several instances, reinforces or expands allusions found in his sources[39].

(3) *Incidents or entire Episodes within the narrative that appear to be inspired in whole or part by Old Testament passages, events or personages*: This category is more difficult to define yet remains an important element in Matthew's repertoire of fulfillment theology. Included here would be categories of "typology" whereby descriptions of Jesus would evoke Old Testament figures, as well as what Douglas Moo referred to as "structural" citations, where Old Testament passages or episodes provide the basic structure or inspiration for a narrative or parts of a narrative[40].

An evident example of typology or the influence of an Old Testament personage on Matthew's text would be his use of Moses typology. Although the extent of Matthew's appeal to the figure of Moses is debated, few interpreters would deny Matthew evokes Moses typology in portions of the infancy narrative (the threat posed by Herod; the advent of the Magi; the appearance of the star; the killing of the children in Bethlehem; the exile of Jesus and his family)[41] and in the presentation of Jesus as teacher in the Sermon on the Mount. D. Allison has argued that Moses typology plays a far more extensive role in Matthew's portrayal of Jesus than usually conceded[42]. Other typologies which the evangelist employs either through his source material or in his own additions would be the Isaian servant, the figure of David (e.g., Matthew's more frequent use of the Son of David title), the prophet Jeremiah[43], the Suffering Just one, and so on.

It is also apparent that interplay with events from the Old Testament has played a role in the shaping of particular episodes in the gospel and thereby serves Matthew's perspective that in Jesus the promises of the Hebrew scriptures were fulfilled. This is certainly reflected in the stories of the infancy narrative which evoke not only the cycle of Moses stories but other paradigmatic events in the biblical history such as the exodus (the citation of Hos 11,1 in 2,15) and the exile (the citation of Jer 31,15 in 2,17-18). This "structural" influence of Old Testament stories can also

---

39. See the illustrations given by W.D. Davies and D.C. Allison, *The Gospel According to Saint Matthew*, pp. 44-45.

40. See above, n. 1.

41. See, for example, the analysis of R. Brown, *The Birth of the Messiah*, who notes, "As Matthew narrates the infancy narrative, it is the place where the OT and the Gospel meet" (p. 231).

42. D.C. Allison, Jr., *The New Moses: A Matthean Typology*, Minneapolis, Fortress, 1993.

43. On Matthew's use of Jeremiah, see M. Knowles, *Jeremiah in Matthew's Gospel: The Rejected-Prophet Motif in Matthean Redaction* (JSNT SS, 68), Sheffield, JSOT Press, 1993.

be detected in such episodes as the desert test (4,1-11), the sea stories (8, 23-27; 14,22-33), and the two miraculous feedings (14,14-21; 15,32-39), to name just a few incidents from the body of the gospel.

In other words, the formula quotations stand out in Matthew because they are statements of the narrator/implied author and make explicit for the reader Matthew's theology of fulfillment. But the formula quotations do not stand alone nor is Matthew's theology of fulfillment dependent on them alone or confined to those parts of the gospel where they appear. An entire repertoire of programmatic statements, direct quotations, biblical allusions, biblical typologies and the influence of the Old Testament on certain episodes in the gospel confront the reader with the rich brew of Matthew's theology of fulfillment.

To examine in detail all of these texts throughout the gospel would turn this paper into a monograph. Allow me to settle for the familiar terrain of the passion narrative to illustrate Matthew at work.

III. THE USE OF THE OLD TESTAMENT IN THE PASSION NARRATIVE

In recent assessments of Matthew's use of the Old Testament, the scarcity of the formula quotations in the latter part of the gospel has been something of a conundrum. In the passion story one could also note that apart from the formula quotation of 27,9-10 there is only one other direct quotation of the Old Testament (see 26,31). Only by scanning the full range of Matthew's repertoire for appealing to the Old Testament does the harmony of Matthew's composition of the passion narrative with the rest of his gospel become clear[44].

1. *Programmatic statements.* In 26,54 and 26,56 Matthew inserts into the passion narrative "programmatic" references to scriptural fulfillment on a par with those in 5,17 and 3,15. Although Matthew finds the inspiration for these statements in Mk 14,49 (ἀλλ᾽ ἵνα πληρωθῶσιν αἱ γραφαί) he goes beyond his source. In 26,54, in a phrase undoubtedly inspired by Mk 14,49, Matthew first applies the notion of scriptural

44. Recent studies of Matthew's use of the Old Testament in the passion narrative would include in addition to the work of D. Moo cited above (n. 1): R. BROWN, *The Death of the Messiah*, vol. 2, Garden City, NY, Doubleday, 1993, esp. pp. 1445-1467; R. J. DILLON, *The Psalms of the Suffering Just in the Accounts of the Jesus' Passion*, in *Worship* 61 (1987) 430-440; J. B. GREEN, *The Death of Jesus: Tradition and Interpretation in the Passion Narrative* (WUNT, 33), Tübingen, Mohr, 1988; J. MARCUS, *The Old Testament and the Death of Jesus: The Role of Scripture in the Gospel Passion Narratives*, in J. T. CARROLL and J. B. GREEN (eds.), *The Death of Jesus in Early Christianity*, Peabody, MA, Hendrickson, 1995, pp. 205-233.

fulfillment to Jesus' prohibition against armed intervention on his behalf: πῶς οὖν πληρωθῶσιν αἱ γραφαὶ ὅτι οὕτως δεῖ γενέσθαι. And in 26,56, the parallel to Mk 14,49, Matthew's version, by adding the emphatic phrase τοῦτο δὲ ὅλον γέγονεν applies the principle of scriptural fulfillment not simply to the episode of the arrest but by implication to the entire passion as the hostility of Jesus' opponents on display throughout the gospel now comes to a head and will lead to his death: τοῦτο δὲ ὅλον γέγονεν ἵνα πληρωθῶσιν αἱ γραφαὶ τῶν προφητῶν (compare Mk 14,49: ἀλλ᾽ ἵνα πληρωθῶσιν αἱ γραφαί)[45]. The addition of the phrase τῶν προφητῶν also moves this programmatic statement closer to the phraseology of the formula quotations themselves which typically cite the prophetic literature. Coming on the lips of Jesus within the narrative, the statement in 26,56 applies the mantle of scriptural fulfillment to the passion in an authoritative manner, certainly on a par with the narrator's voice in the formula quotations.

2. *Direct Quotations.* Direct quotations of the Old Testament in Matthew's passion narrative are spare[46]. There are two examples in Matthew, one in parallel with Mark and the other in special material. The first is 26,31 where Matthew, following Mk 14,27, quotes Zech 13,7 in reference to the scattering of the disciples. Neither Mark's nor Matthew's version coincides completely with the Masoretic text or with known Septuagintal forms. Matthew's quotation is slightly different from Mark, notably the addition of τῆς ποίμνης (and the accompanying inversion of the object τὰ πρόβατα after the verb). Matthew's addition is probably intended to emphasize the breaking up of the community of the disciples, coinciding with other similar changes in this direction[47]. We may note the connection between this reference to scriptural fulfillment in 26,31 (once again on the lips of the authoritative character Jesus) and the reference in 26,56; in both instances the moment of the arrest, where Jesus the shepherd is assaulted and the disciples are scattered, is immediately in view.

The other explicit quotation is found in the formula quotation of 27,9-10[48]. Here an explicit citation of scriptural fulfillment is applied not simply to

45. See D. SENIOR, *The Passion Narrative According to Matthew: A Redactional Study* (BETL, 39), Leuven, University Press – Peeters, 1975, pp. 153-156.

46. Some would trace this to the origin of the passion narrative in a context of scriptural reflection, with the result that biblical allusions are more tightly woven into the fabric of the narrative, offsetting the need for additional direct quotations; see R. BROWN, *The Death of the Messiah*, vol. 1, pp. 14-17; vol. 2, pp. 1445-1446.

47. D. SENIOR, *The Passion Narrative*, p. 92; this explanation was already suggested by K. STENDAHL, *The School of St. Matthew*, p. 81.

48. On this text, see D. SENIOR, *The Fate of the Betrayer: A Redactional Study of Matthew XXVII, 3-10*, in *ETL* 48 (1972) 372-426, and an updated discussion in *Matthew's Special Material in the Passion Story: Implications for the Evangelist's Redactional Technique and Theological Perspective*, in *ETL* 63 (1987) 272-294.

the fate of Judas but, more fundamentally, to the accountability of the chief priests and elders for the "blood money" used to betray the innocent Jesus, money which despite their efforts is returned to them by the despairing Judas. Matthew connects to this moment the prophecy of "Jeremiah", evoking the judgment of this prophet against the temple personnel even though the quotation itself is an adaptation of Zech 11,13. As we will note below, the entire episode of Judas' remorse, his attempt to return the blood money, and the subsequent purchase and naming of the "field of blood" is a Matthean passage strongly influenced by Old Testament reflection[49]. The fate of Judas in 27,2-10 also relates to 26,14-16 where Matthew had added a reference to the "thirty pieces of silver", also an allusion to Zech 11,12. Thus for Matthew the motif of the betrayal of "innocent blood", already prepared for in 23,30-36 (see especially 23,35), which comes to term in the betrayal of Judas and his collusion with the priests and elders, is thoroughly rooted in scriptural fulfillment.

3. *Biblical Allusions*. Control regarding the number of possible biblical allusions in the passion narrative is difficult. Building on the list of references in Nestle-Aland, one could cite as many as thirty allusions (distinct from direct quotations and what we are calling "structural" references)[50]. Of these thirty, ten are allusions that Matthew absorbs virtually unchanged from Mark, but eleven are instances where the allusion is either more emphatic in Matthew's version or added to a Markan parallel and six are special to Matthew:

a) *Instances in which Matthew expands or adds a biblical allusion to a Markan parallel*:

26,15 the addition of οἱ δὲ ἔστησαν αὐτῷ τριάκοντα ἀργύρια, a reference to Zech 11,12.

26,28b the addition of εἰς ἄφεσιν ἁμαρτιῶν, a reference to Jer 31,34.

26,36 the formulation Καθίσατε αὐτοῦ, a possible reference to Gen 22,5.

26,51 the addition of ἐκτείνας τὴν χεῖρα, a possible reference to Gen 22,10 (and numerous other OT texts that use this stereotype phrase).

49. See below, pp. 113-114.
50. 26,1 (Deut 32,45); 26,11 (Deut 15,11); 26,15 (Zech 11,12); 26,28a (Exod 24,8; Zech 9,11); 26,28b (Jer 31,31; Exod 24,8); 26,36 (Gen 22,5); 26,38 (Ps 42,6); 26,39 (Isa 51,17, 22); 26,41 (Ps 51,12); 26,45 (2 Sam 24,14); 26,51 (Gen 22,10); 26,52 (Gen 9,6); 26,53 (Ps 91,11-12); 26,59 (Ps 27,12); 26,60 (Deut 19,15); 26,64 (Dan 7,13; Ps 110,1; Ezek 1,26); 26,75 (Isa 22,4; 33,7); 27,12 (Isa 53,7); 27,24 (Deut 21,6-8; Ps 25,6; 72,13); 27,25 (2 Sam 1,16; 14,9); 27,29 (Isa 50,6); 27,34 (Ps 69,22); 27,42 (Zeph 3,15); 27,43 (Ps 22,9; Wis 2,13, 18-20; 16,16); 27,45 (Amos 8,9; Exod 10,22); 27,46 (Ps 22,2); 27,48 (Ps 69,22); 27,49 (Ps 69,22; Ps 22,2,6); 27,50 (Ps 22); 27,57 (Isa 53,9); 27,59 (1 Kings 13,29).

26,60 the reference to two witnesses, a possible reference to Deut 19,15 (see also Mt 18,16b).

26,75 the addition of πικρῶς, a reference to Isa 22,4; 33,7.

27,12 the addition of οὐδὲν ἀπεκρίνατο, a probable reference to Isa 53,7.

27,34 the formulation μετὰ χολῆς μεμιγμένον, aligning the text with Ps 69,22.

27,45 the formulation ἐπὶ πᾶσαν τὴν γῆν, a probable reference to Exod 10,22.

27,49 the use of the verb σώσων in place of Mark's καθελεῖν, a possible reference to the repeated use of σῴζειν in Ps 22 (see Ps 22, 6.9.22).

27,50 the verb κράξας, reflective of this verb's use in Psalm 22 (see 22,3.6.25).

b) *Allusions special to Matthew:*

26,1 the addition of the final transition formula καὶ ἐγένετο ὅτε ἐτέλεσεν ὁ Ἰησοῦς πάντας τοὺς λόγους τούτους, a probable reference to Deut 32,45.

26,52 the aphorism about perishing by the sword, a possible reference to Gen 9,6.

26,53 the saying about the protection of the angels, a reference to Ps 91,11-12.

27,24 Pilate's gesture of washing his hands, recalling Deut 21,6-8, as well as Ps 25,6; 72,13.

27,25 the cry of the people, recalling 2 Sam 1,16; 14,9.

27,43 the words of mockery, citing Ps 22,9; Wis 2,13.

The extent of these allusions confirms that Matthew, either drawing on Markan material or by additions of his own, casts a biblical aura over virtually every aspect of the passion story.

4. *Elements of the narrative inspired in whole or part by reference to Old Testament passages.* As in the case of some biblical allusions, a precise determination of the influence of Old Testament material on the narrative is often difficult. There is also some overlap with the categories above. For example, the words used by the mockers in 27,43 are clearly drawn from Ps 22,8 (also Wis 2,18); thus they could be considered a direct quotation. But by placing them on the lips of the chief priests, scribes and elders (27,41) Matthew now utilizes the biblical quotation as a structural element of the story itself. A similar case could be made for texts we have already counted as "allusions" such as the "thirty pieces

of silver" in Mt 26,14, a reference to Zech 11,12 that has now become an element in the story.

There are approximately fourteen such uses of "structural" references in Matthew, nine of them in common with Mark, two added to Markan material, and three in special Matthean material[51]. For example, there is little question that the mock homage given to Jesus by the Roman soldiers already found in Mark's narrative is inspired at least in part by the portrayal of the Suffering Servant of Isaiah 50-53, thus an influence of typology along with certain textual details such as striking and spitting at the servant (Isa 50,6; see Mk 15,17-20; Mt 27,28-31). Likewise interaction with Psalm 22 has undoubtedly had a strong influence on the crucifixion scene in Mark and is also carried over into Matthew's account, including the reference to such details as the division of garments (Mk 15,24; Mt 27,35; Ps 22,19), the mockers' "wagging their heads" (Mk 15,29; Mt 27,39; Ps 22,8), and the final words of Jesus (Mk 15,34; Mt 27,46; Ps 22,2). It is possible that the influence of Psalm 22 on the narrative extends to the fundamental structure of this scene with this classical lament's psalm's movement from lament to vindication reflected in the Mark and Matthean crucifixion scenes where there is also a movement from lament and derision with the mockery and Jesus' final words to a sense of vindication in the acclamation of the centurion and, particularly in Matthew's account, with the accompanying events that erupt at the moment of Jesus' death and trigger the reaction of the centurion and his companions (Mt 27,51-54)[52].

The influence of the Old Testament on Matthew's special material is remarkably strong, particularly in the major segments 27,3-10; 27,24-25 and 27,51-53. In earlier studies concerning the tradition history of these passages I have argued that Matthew is primarily responsible for the

---

51. Examples held in common with Mark are the betrayer's kiss in Mt 26,48 (2 Sam 20,9); the tearing of the High Priest's robe, 26,65 (Lev 10,6); the striking and spitting, 26,67 (Isa 50,6); the mock homage of Jesus, 27,27-31a (Isa 50-53); the offering of wine and gall, 27,34 (Ps 69,22); the mockery from the bystanders, 27,38-44 (Wisdom 2-5); the darkness, 27,45 (Amos 8,9); the offering of wine, 27,48 (Ps 69,22); the burial, 27,59 (1 Kings 13,29-30). Instances added to Mark are the reference to thirty pieces of silver in 26,25 (Zech 11,12) and the OT obedience formula in 26,17-19. Examples peculiar to Matthew are the death of Judas in 27,3-10, Pilate's washing of his hands and the cry of the people in 27,24-25, and the events that happen immediately after Jesus' death in 27,51-53.

52. I have suggested this influence in my discussion of the crucifixion scene; see D. SENIOR, The Passion Narrative According to Matthew, pp. 292-334; also, The Passion of Jesus in the Gospel of Matthew, (Passion Series, 1), Collegeville, MN, Liturgical Press, 1985, pp. 127-142. R. BROWN is skeptical, however, that the influence of the Psalm extends to the vindication of Jesus; The Death of the Messiah, Vol. 2, pp. 1079-1080; but see J. MARCUS, The Role of Scripture in the Gospel Passion Narrative, p. 210.

formulation of this special material, taking his cue from leads in the narrative potential of the Markan parallels and building narrative expansions on the basis of Old Testament reflections, reflections that may well have had precedent in the traditions of the Matthean community but had not yet taken on the literary format as now found in Matthew[53]. Each of these passages strongly reflects Matthew's theology and literary style and each is deeply entwined with Old Testament allusions. In 27,3-10 and 27,24-25 Matthew deals with the issue of the rejection of Jesus by the leaders of Israel. While 27,3-10 is immediately concerned with the fate of Judas, a fate predicted by Jesus in 26,20-25, a passage drawn from Mark (14,26-31), Matthew's traces a motif with more fundamental significance for his gospel, that of "innocent blood"[54]. The "blood money" used to purchase the innocent blood of Jesus that had been paid out to Judas by the leaders in 26,15 now returns to them as Judas flings the coins into the sanctuary. The money is taken by the leaders and used to purchase a potter's field where strangers will be buried. A number of Old Testament passages seem to be reflected in this tragic story. Judas's death recalls the suicide of Ahithophel, the betrayer of David, in 2 Sam 17,23. Much of the wording in 27,10 concerning the casting of the coins into the sanctuary is taken from Zech 11,13. But Matthew's introductory formula attributes the passage to Jeremiah. The link here seems to be the purchase of the "potter's field" which enables Matthew to tie the story to Jeremiah and his message of judgment upon the temple leadership, probably on the basis of Jeremiah 19 where the elements of a potter, a burial field for strangers and the key motif of "innocent blood" all coincide – a clear instance in which Matthew freely interacts with the scriptures rather than mechanistically apply Old Testament texts to events in the gospel.

Pilate's handwashing and the people's declaration in 27,24-25 continue the motif of "innocent blood" found in 27,3-10. Pilate's gesture and his declaration of innocence evoke Deut 21,1-9 where the ritual for dealing with the spilling of "innocent blood" is described[55]. Conversely, the "entire people" accept responsibility for the blood "on us and on our children", again evoking Old Testament formulas as found in 2 Sam 1,16 and 14,9.

---

53. See, D. SENIOR, *Matthew's Special Material in the Passion Story*, and, more recently, *Revisiting Matthew's Special Material in the Passion Narrative: A Dialogue with Raymond Brown*, in *ETL* 70 (1994) 417-24.

54. On this motif in Matthew, see, J. CARROLL and J. GREEN, *The Death of Jesus in Early Christianity*, pp. 45-48.

55. This connection had been forcefully made in the classic study of W. TRILLING, *Das wahre Israel: Studien zur Theologie des Matthäus-Evangeliums* (SANT, 10), München, Kösel Verlag, ³1964, pp. 60-74.

Therefore in two of Matthew's most elaborate examples of "structural" Old Testament allusions, he extends the canopy of scriptural fulfillment to what is a major concern of his gospel, namely the rejection of Jesus by the religious leaders (and in 27,24-25 by the people themselves). In Matthew's perspective this opposition is neither simply a tragic accident nor an unforeseen consequence of Jesus' mission. The backdrop of scriptural fulfillment certifies that such opposition is, however paradoxically, within the scope of God's plan of salvation revealed in the Scriptures. Thus neither Jesus' messianic authority nor the legitimacy of the Christian community are diminished by such opposition.

The special material in 27,51-53 extends the notion of scriptural fulfillment to the salvific meaning of Jesus' death, a theme that Matthew had announced early in his gospel (i.e., the name of Jesus in 1,21), connected with Jesus' healings (8,17; 12,17-21), and predicted in conjunction with his death (the reference to forgiveness of sins added by Matthew in 26,28). The core of this passage is the reference to the opening of the graves and the release of the bodies of the holy ones – the earthquake and sundering of the rocks as well as the subsequent visitation of the now raised saints are preparation and consequence of this core liberation. The Old Testament reference here is the vision of the dry bones in Ezekiel 37 (particularly 37,11-14), although a similar reference to the liberation of the dead is found in Dan 12,1-2[56]. The eschatological tone of these extraordinary events vindicates the trust of Jesus put in question by his death (see 27,43), underscores the historic significance of his death and resurrection as the decisive turning point in salvation history, and illustrates the salvific consequences of that death in restoring life to the holy ones. Articulating this in reference to the vision of Ezekiel enables Matthew to situate the meaning of Jesus' death in relationship to the Old Testament and to reaffirm his unique messianic authority. In so doing Matthew serves not only his christology but, in the face of contention about the manner of Jesus' death from opponents, serves the ecclesiological and apologetic concerns of his community by interpreting key Old Testament texts in a messianic key.

---

56. See D. SENIOR, *The Death of Jesus and the Resurrection of the Holy Ones (Mt 27,51-53)*, in *CBQ* 38 (1976) 312-29. In addition to Ezekiel 37, R. Aus has suggested that I Samuel 28 also has an influence on the passage (see *Samuel, Saul and Jesus*, Atlanta, GA, Scholars Press, 1994), and M. GOURGUES has appealed to 2 Sam 22,1-51 on the entire crucifixion scene as well as 27,51-53, see *'Il entendit de son temple ma voix': Échos du 'Cantique de David' (Ps 18-2 S 22) en Mt 27,50-51 et dans le Nouveau Testament*, in J.-C PETIT (ed.), *Où demeures-tu? La maison depuis le monde biblique* (Festschrift Guy Couturier), Montreal, Fides, 1994, pp. 323-341.

CONCLUSION

The depth and variety of Matthew's appeals to the Old Testament in the passion narrative put into perspective the function of the formula quotations within the gospel as a whole. The formula quotations take their place within the full repertoire of ways Matthew uses the Old Testament to underwrite the story of Jesus for his community and, at the same time, to provide his community with a new reading of their scriptures in the light of the faith in Jesus' identity as Messiah and Son of God: a) programmatic statements by Jesus affirming that his life and mission "fulfill" the scriptures; b) direct quotations connected with specific aspects of Jesus' life; c) numerous allusions that tie the details of the narrative to Old Testament texts and perspectives; d) several key events that are, in effect, shadow stories from the Old Testament suggesting that events and motifs of the Hebrew scriptures are being fulfilled in the life of Jesus. This stream of biblical interplay is carried out by all of the major characters in the narrative: Jesus himself, the disciples, the opponents, Pilate, the crowds, the narrator. For Matthew the appeal to scriptural fulfillment serves his christology by demonstrating that Jesus is the fulfillment of God's plan revealed to Israel. It also serves his ecclesiology by accruing to the Matthean community the authority of the scriptures for their allegiance to Jesus and for the teaching and interpretation of law they carry out in Jesus' name. Conversely, Matthew is able to assert that the opponents of Jesus erred grievously in rejecting the messianic authority of Jesus but in so doing they, too, fulfilled the plan foreseen by God and reflected in the scriptures. The contemporary opponents of Matthew's community, the gospel implies, continue in the same erroneous ways of their forebears from Jesus' day. Thus Matthew's theology and rhetorical strategy are inseparable from his emphatic use of the Old Testament.

Viewed within this overall context of Matthew's use of the Old Testament, the formula quotations are exceptional not because of their theology (scriptural fulfillment is characteristic of Matthew), nor even for their placement (scriptural fulfillment is asserted throughout the gospel in a variety of ways), but mainly because in these instances it is the narrator rather than other characters in the narrative world of Matthew who makes this recurring and fundamental affirmation.

Catholic Theological Union   Donald SENIOR, C.P.
5401 S. Cornell Avenue
Chicago, IL 60615, USA

JESUS' ENTRY INTO JERUSALEM

Mt 21,1-17 in the Light of the Hebrew Bible and the Septuagint

Mt 21,1-17 is rich in citations from the Old Testament. This text is therefore very suitable as the subject for a study of the use of Scripture by the first evangelist. This paper wants to contribute to that study. More in particular it is aimed at testing the hypothesis that the citations which we find in Mt 21,1-17 must also be understood in the light of the texts from the Hebrew Bible and the Septuagint (LXX) from which the quoted words and sentences originate.

This contribution is structured as follows. In the first section I argue that Mt 21,1-17 must be understood as a textual unit. Subsequently I will concentrate on the explicit citations which this text contains. In section two I will examine these citations by means of a literary-historical analysis to enable us to determine their textual form. Next, I will broaden my methodological perspective by linking up with the recently developed theory of intertextuality (section 3). In sections 4-7 the separate citations from Mt 21,1-17 will also be explored in the light of this theory. I will conclude my paper with some reflections on the way in which the various citations are connected (section 8).

1. Mt 21,1-17: A Textual Unit

In the synopsis by Aland Mt 21,1-17 is cut in two[1]. The first part (21,1-9) is about Jesus' entry into Jerusalem, the second (21,10-17) about his actions in the temple. This division was inspired by the parallel text in Mark. In that text, the arrival in Jerusalem and the cleansing of the temple take place on two separate days. In Matthew this is not the case. Not until v. 17 does Jesus leave the city to spend the night in Bethany. One could therefore agree with Gnilka when he writes: "Man könnte von einem Tag Jesu in Jerusalem sprechen, der durch Einzug und Tempelprotest gekennzeichnet ist"[2].

---

1. *Synopsis Quattuor Evangeliorum*, edidit K. Aland, editio tertia decima revisa, Stuttgart, 1985, pp. 365-371: Nr. 269: Der Einzug in Jerusalem; Nr. 271: Jesus in Jerusalem (Tempelreinigung), Rückkehr nach Bethanien.
2. Cf. J. Gnilka, *Das Matthäusevangelium. II. Teil* (HTKNT, I/2), Freiburg – Basel – Wien, 1988, p. 209. The statement in Mk 11,11a (καὶ εἰσῆλθεν εἰς Ἱεροσόλυμα εἰς τὸ

The locations mentioned in 21,1.10.12.17, which are all in line with one another and which together present a continuous movement, also argue in favour of the unity of Mt 21,1-17. In the first nine verses Jesus is near Jerusalem, in v. 10 he enters the city, in v. 12 he enters the temple precincts and in v. 17 he leaves the city to re-enter it the next day. Furthermore I would like to point out that the text contains a number of repetitions. The first example of this is the combination of κράζω and λέγω, followed by the exclamation "Hosanna to the Son of David" (21,9.15). In v. 9 this exclamation is uttered by the crowd that accompanies Jesus on the road to the city; in v. 15 we learn that the children of Jerusalem have adopted this cry of joy and let it resound among the temple walls. Together these pieces of information suggest that the cries of Hosanna continue uninterrupted. There is another repetition in the text. I refer to the fact that verses 10-11 contain a pattern that reappears with a number of variations in vv. 15-16. The hosanna of the crowd causes a question to arise among the inhabitants of Jerusalem and it is answered by the multitudes. Similarly, the jubilation of the children in the temple causes a question to arise among the high priests and scribes and the answer is supplied by Jesus.

I can be brief about the structure of the passage. The text is a kind of diptych. The first part is comprised of 21,1-9, the second 21,12-17, verses 10-11 functioning as the hinge. In a chart:

I	21,1-9	Jesus approaches Jerusalem
Hinge	21,10-11	Arrival in the city
II	21,12-17	Jesus in the temple

2. The Textual Form of the Citations in Mt 21,1-17

Mt 21,1-17 contains a number of explicit citations from the Old Testament, regularly scattered through the entire text:

ἱερόν) is divided into two separate events in Matthew: καὶ εἰσελθόντος αὐτοῦ εἰς Ἱεροσόλυμα (21,10) and καὶ εἰσῆλθεν Ἰησοῦς εἰς τὸ ἱερόν (21,12). We encounter the reverse in Mt 21,17 (ἐξῆλθεν ἔξω τῆς πόλεως εἰς Βηθανίαν): this verse shows a combination of elements from Mk 11,11b (ἐξῆλθεν εἰς Βηθανίαν) and Mk 11,19 (ἔξω τῆς πόλεως). See N. LOHFINK, Der Messiaskönig und seine Armen kommen zum Zion. Beobachtungen zu Mt 21,1-17, in L. SCHENKE (ed.), Studien zum Matthäusevangelium. FS W. Pesch (SBS), Stuttgart, 1988, p. 183 n. 10 (also published in N. LOHFINK, Studien zur biblischen Theologie (Stuttgarter Biblische Aufsatzbände, 16), Stuttgart, 1988, pp. 294-314.

21,4-5   The narrator comments on the narrated history by means of citations
         from Isa 62,11 and Zech 9,9.
21,9   The crowd uses words from Ps 118,25-26.
21,13   Jesus illustrates his actions in the temple by means of citations from
         Isa 56,7 and Jer 7,11.
21,15   The children repeat part of the words of the crowd (Ps 118,25).
21,16   Jesus answers the question of his opponents with a citation from Ps
         8,3.

With the exception of the quotations from Ps 118, all these citations are
preceded by an introductory formula. In v. 4 we find the formula that is
characteristic for the formula quotations by Matthew; the citations in
v. 13 are introduced by γέγραπται; the citation from Ps 8,3 is preceded
by the question οὐδέποτε ἀνέγνωτε.

Of the quotations mentioned Matthew shares a number with Mark,
namely the citation from Ps 118,25-26 (see Mk 11,9-10) and the mixed
citation from Isa 56,7 and Jer 7,11 (see Mk 11,17). In his representation
of these quotations, the first evangelist relies on Mark's version. In both
gospels Ps 118,26 is represented in the formulation of the LXX: εὐλογ-
ημένος ὁ ἐρχόμενος ἐν ὀνόματι κυρίου. It is remarkable that Matthew
repeats this sentence in 23,39 (cf. Lk 13,35), thus creating an *inclusio*
framing the long passage of the story set in the temple (Mt 21-23). By
using the joyful cry ὡσαννά the evangelists deviate from the psalm in a
similar way. In order to intensify the christological orientation of the
crowd's exclamation, Matthew has combined this word with the dative
τῷ υἱῷ Δαυίδ, which is clearly based on the reference in Mk 11,10a to
the coming kingdom of David. Also in the formulation of the mixed
citation from Isa 56,7 and Jer 7,11 Matthew corresponds to Mark, the
only difference being that the reference to "all the nations" is omitted.
Also in this case, the formulation in Mark goes back to the LXX.

Mt 21,1-17 also contains a number of citations which cannot be found
in Mark. In 21,15 Matthew repeats the ὡσαννὰ τῷ υἱῷ Δαυίδ created in
21,9; thus he recalls to mind the quotation from Ps 118. In 21,16 he
inserts a quotation from Ps 8,3. This is the only place in the New Testament
where this psalm verse (in the formulation of the LXX) can be found.
The origin of the formula quotation in Mt 21,5 is disputed. The first line
(εἴπατε τῇ θυγατρὶ Σιών) literally links up with the LXX version of
Isa 62,11 (which here closely follows the Hebrew text). In Mark this
reference to Isaiah is missing. Mt 21,5 continues with a quotation from
Zech 9,9 which can also be found in Jn 12,15. Mark's version does
not contain this quotation; however, the possibility that Matthew
has inserted the citation from Zech 9,9 into his story on the basis of
reminiscences of this text in Mark cannot be entirely ruled out. After all,

in Mk 11,2 a πῶλος is mentioned, a term which also occurs in the LXX version of Zech 9,9. In addition, the LXX mentions a πῶλος νέος at this point. This reference may have inspired the description in Mark: "a colt which no one has yet ridden"[3]. Still, the question concerning the origin of the citation from Zech 9,9 in Mt 21,5 has not been conclusively answered, for the formulation offered there initially runs parallel to that of the LXX, but toward the end this is no longer the case. In Matthew it is the king of Zion who mounts ἐπὶ ὄνον καὶ ἐπὶ πῶλον υἱὸν ὑπο-ζυγίου[4]. This formulation shows three similarities with the Hebrew text (על־חמור ועל־עיר בן־אתנות): a) ὄνος is a correct translation of חמור; b) υἱόν corresponds to בן; c) the twofold ἐπί is an accurate rendering of על, which is used twice. The LXX differs on all these points (ἐπὶ ὑποζύγιον καὶ πῶλον νέον).

Are these sufficient reasons to assume a direct link with the Hebrew text? A number of authors do not think so[5]. They prefer the hypothesis that at the end of 21,5 Matthew reverts to a Greek translation, already in existence in his time, which differs from the LXX and must be seen as a precursor of Aquila, Symmachus, Theodotion and the Quinta. Their hypothesis is based on the fact that also in those later *versiones* חמור is translated as ὄνος and בן as υἱός[6]. Another relevant point is that the singular ὑποζυγίου from Mt 21,5 differs from the plural form in the

---

3. J.D. CROSSAN, *Redaction and Citation in Mark 11:9-10 and 11:17*, in *Papers of the Chicago Society of Biblical Research, Vol. 17*, Chicago, 1972, pp. 33-50, offers an explanation of the reminiscences in Mark 11,1-11 of Zech 9,9 which is hardly convincing. Originally the text would have contained an explicit citation from Zech 9,9, later to be deleted by the redactor (Mark), while Matthew, who was also familiar with the tradition handed down to Mark, is supposed to have put it back in again.

4. The omission of the second ἐπί in a number of manuscripts indicates adaptation to the LXX.

5. M. WILCOX, *Text Form*, in D.A. CARSON – H.G.M. WILLIAMSON (eds.), *It is Written. Scripture Citing Scripture*. FS B. Lindars, Cambridge, 1988, pp. 193-204; M. MENKEN, *The Quotations from Zech 9,9 in Mt 21,5 and in Jn 12,15*, in A. DENAUX (ed.), *John and the Synoptics* (BETL, 101), Leuven, 1992, pp. 571-578 (here p. 574). See also M. MENKEN, *"Do Not Fear, Daughter Zion..." John 12:15*, in ID., *Old Testament Quotations in the Fourth Gospel. Studies in Textual Form* (Contributions to Biblical Exegesis and Theology, 15), Kampen, 1996, pp. 79-97.

6. Cf. W. ROTHFUCHS, *Die Erfüllungszitate des Matthäus-Evangeliums. Eine biblisch-theologische Untersuchung* (BWANT, 88), Stuttgart – Berlin – Köln – Mainz, 1969, p. 80, note 84. His presentation of the *versiones* must, in the light of J. ZIEGLER (ed.), *Duodecim Prophetae* (Göttinger LXX, 13), Göttingen, ²1967, pp. 310-311, be corrected as follows:

Aquila ἐπιβεβηκὼς ἐπὶ ὄνου καὶ πῶλου υἱοῦ ὀνάδων
Symmachus ἐπιβεβηκὼς ἐπὶ ὄνον καὶ πῶλον υἱὸν ὀναδός
Theodotion ἐπιβεβηκὼς ἐπὶ ὄνον καὶ πῶλον υἱὸν ὄνου.

Hebrew text (אתנות) and corresponds to the singular form in the LXX, Symmachus, Theodotion and the Targum[7].

Still, I do not support this hypothesis. Why resort to a postulated Greek textual form that is supposed to have circulated in the first century when the above-mentioned phenomena can adequately be explained on the basis of the correspondence with the Hebrew text? Furthermore, this hypothesis does not offer a solution for the twofold ἐπί. This latter point cannot be explained in any other way than as an accurate translation of the words from the Hebrew text. Therefore I consider it more accurate to argue that the conclusion of the citation is a literal translation of the Hebrew text.

On the basis of these observations about the textual form I draw the following conclusion. Most citations in Mt 21,1-17 are formulated in correspondence with the LXX. In a number of cases Matthew explicitly draws on the phrasing of the citations in Mark, but also when he inserts citations which do not occur in Mark (21,15 and specifically 21,17), he uses the formulation known to us from the LXX. The citation from Zech 9,9 forms the only exception to this rule. This citation is linked to both the LXX and the Hebrew text.

3. Methodological Intermezzo

The study of Old Testament citations in the New Testament is developing rapidly. Until recently this field of research was strongly dominated by a diachronic approach: scholars tried to trace the source from which a citation originated. This type of research is of a rather atomistic nature, which is inherent to the method used. Generally it can be characterised as follows. In order to determine the precise limits of the citation, it is necessary to make as sharp a distinction as possible between the quoted words or sentences and the New Testament text into which they have been incorporated. Thus isolated, the formulation of the elements is compared with their phrasing in the Hebrew text, in the Septuagint and the other *versiones* and in the early Jewish and early Christian texts. The verbal similarities are decisive for the question concerning the origin of the citation. Any other explanations may only be considered when there are few or no similarities at all. Examples of such explanations are that the author has directly translated the citation from Hebrew, or has taken

---

7. Aquila (υἱοῦ ὀνάδων) and the Quinta (υἱὸν ὄνων) follow the plural from the Hebrew text.

it from a source unknown to us, or has cited the relevant words or sentences from memory. Also in comparing quoted words and sentences with their source texts, scholars focus on exactly those elements that are quoted in the New Testament. This means that at that particular level those elements are also disconnected from the surrounding textual data: they are again isolated, now with regard to the Old Testament text to which they originally belonged.

In the above-mentioned method for studying citations, the role of both the present and the original literary context is negligible. As concerns the connection between the citations and their new literary context, this changed with the development of the *redaktionsgeschichtliche Methode* (redaction criticism). This approach focuses on the question of whether the differences between the phrasing of the citation and its original formulation might be attributed to the redactor, who after all may have adapted the citation to the text into which he has woven it, and to the function he makes it fulfil in that text; conversely it is also possible that he has adapted the literary context to fit the formulation of the citation. At this point the atomistic approach of the earlier method is renounced: the connections between the quotation and its literary context now fully enter the spotlight. The emphasis here is on those elements which can almost certainly be attributed to the redactor.

The correlation of citations with their new context is also central in the recently developed theory of intertextuality[8], which focuses on the phenomenon that almost every text has absorbed parts of other texts. Most prominent among these are the explicit citations[9]. Such citations to a certain extent form a kind of foreign body in their new literary context because of the sudden transition to a different language level or to a different style and through content similarities with older texts, but still they have been firmly integrated. The concept of "intertextuality" greatly

8. For a survey of that theory and an analysis of the way in which it can benefit biblical exegesis, see: W. WEREN, *Intertextualiteit en Bijbel*, Kampen, 1993, especially pp. 9-33.

9. I speak of an explicit citation when the text itself contains demonstrable indications that one or more parts of another text have been incorporated into that text. H. PLETT, *Intertextualities*, in H. PLETT (ed.), *Intertextuality* (Research in Text Theory, 15), Berlin – New York, 1991, p. 9, defines an explicit citation as follows: "A quotation repeats a segment derived from a pre-text within a subsequent text, where it replaces a proprie-segment". S. MORAWSKI, *The Basic Functions of Quotation*, in A. GREIMAS et al. (eds.), *Sign, Language, Culture*, Den Haag etc., 1970, pp. 690-705 (here p. 691), offers a broader description: "Quotation is the literal reproduction of a verbal text of a certain length or of a set of images, notes, sounds, movements, or a combination of all or some of these elements or some of them with a verbal text, wherein what is reproduced forms an integral part of some work and can easily be detached from the new whole in which it is incorporated".

emphasizes this correlation, even more so than redaction criticism. This approach is after all restricted to the relations between the citation and its new setting which have been consciously designed by the redactor.

An even newer development is that supporters of the theory of intertextuality advocate also studying the *original* context of the quoted words and sentences. Many New Testament scholars will not endorse this option[10]. It runs counter to a tendency they have repeatedly observed, that New Testament authors give no further thought to the original context of the elements they quote and concentrate exclusively on the particular segment that can fulfil a relevant function in their own argument or story. In addition, these authors often quote sentences which already form part of the tradition they assimilated into their own text. Is it not therefore unnecessarily complicating to argue that the text from which a citation is derived should be included in the study of citations?

I would not answer that question with a straight yes. This reserve springs from two remarkable features of explicit citations. The first feature is that explicit citations function as a powerful signal that the text must be read in the light of an earlier text. This is the case *a fortiori* when a text contains more than one explicit citation. For the experienced reader the presence of an explicit citation raises the question of whether the text contains other, more implicit references to the text from which the quoted segment originates. We can trace these more hidden connections by closely comparing the New Testament text in which we find the citation with the Old Testament pre-text from which it is taken. In this comparison we must be aware of the possibility that elements from the pre-text may turn up in a later text in a strongly altered fashion. A second feature of the explicit citation is that it initiates interaction between (at least) two texts. It acquires a new meaning and a new function within the text into which it is now integrated, but it will nonetheless continue to refer back to the inherent semantic configuration of the original text.

On the basis of these features I will not restrict myself in the analysis of the citations in Mt 21,1-17 to the relations between separate words or sentences. I will broaden the study by relating the cited elements to the entire text of Mt 21,1-17 and to the texts from the Old Testament. The explicit citations in Mt 21,1-17 form the point of departure in the choice of those Old Testament texts. The scheme presented below specifies which texts are involved:

---

10. This option was already supported by C.H. DODD, *According to the Scriptures. The Sub-Structure of New Testament Theology*, London, 1953, p. 126: "... in the fundamental passages it is the *total context* that is in view, and is the basis of the argument".

Mt 21,1-17	explicit citations	texts from the OT
Mt 21,5	Isa 62,11	Isa 62,1-11
	Zech 9,9	Zech 9,1-10
Mt 21,9	Ps 118,25-26	Ps 118
Mt 21,15	Ps 118,25	
Mt 21,13	Isa 56,7	Isa 56,1-8
	Jer 7,11	Jer 7,1-15
Mt 21,16	Ps 8,3	Ps 8

The remaining question is which version of those Old Testament texts should be used in the analysis. In the case of the citation from Zech 9,9 it is natural, in view of my observations about the textual form of this citation, to assume a kind of delta connection, within which the Hebrew text, the version of the Septuagint and Mt 21,1-17 occupy equivalent positions. In the case of the other citations, a comparison of Mt 21,1-17 with the LXX version of the above-mentioned Old Testament texts will suffice, since Matthew – via Mark or otherwise – goes back to this version. Still, even in this case one cannot ignore the Hebrew text. The reason is not that Matthew should have drawn from that text but the choice is inspired by the fact that the LXX version is a translation of the Hebrew text and therefore stands in a special intertextual relation to that text. The LXX here forms a link between the Hebrew text and Mt 21,1-17. One could thus speak of a linear relation (Hebrew text $\rightarrow$ LXX $\rightarrow$ Mt 21,1-17).

On the basis of these methodological observations I will be guided in this analysis by the following questions: a) which meaning do the quoted words and sentences have within the Old Testament text from which they originate?; b) which semantic changes arise as a result of the translation of the Hebrew text into Greek (the LXX)?; c) which meaning do the quotations acquire as a result of their incorporation into the whole of Mt 21,1-17?

4. The Citations from Isa 62,11 and Zech 9,9 in Mt 21,5

a. The Combination of Isa 62,11 and Zech 9,9

Verses 4-5 of Mt 21 do not belong to the direct speech that is pronounced by Jesus (character text) but to the narrator's text. This is characteristic of all formula quotations in Matthew: they function as a comment of the narrator on the narrated history. It is remarkable here that this comment is not presented at the end of the episode but is placed exactly between the description of Jesus' order to his two disciples (21,1-3) and the subsequent execution of his order (21,6-9)[11].

Mt 21,5 opens with the order to speak to the daughter of Zion; after that the words to be addressed to Zion are stated. This order is carried out in vv. 10-11 by the crowd, which informs "the whole city" that the man who is entering Jerusalem is a prophet, that his name is Jesus and that he comes from Nazareth in Galilee. In v. 9 the same crowd was introduced as speaker. Also in the words they speak there they carry out the order of v. 5. "The crowd" does not refer to the citizens of Jerusalem, but to the people who have travelled with Jesus from Galilee. This is clear from the division of roles in vv. 10-11.

The order of Mt 21,5 is formulated with words taken from Isa 62,11: "Tell the daughter of Zion". The continuation of this verse contains a citation from Zech 9,9. It is remarkable that the opening of Zech 9,9 ("Rejoice greatly, O daughter Zion! Shout aloud, O daughter Jerusalem!")[12] is not quoted in Mt 21,5. This part of Zech 9,9 (Zion must joyfully welcome the messianic king) is substituted with a citation from Isa 62,11 (a plural subject must speak to Zion). The reason for that replacement is revealed in the continuation of the story. There it becomes clear that it is not Zion that rejoices at the coming of Jesus. No, it is the crowd from Galilee that sets up the jubilant cry. Jerusalem's reaction is of a much less positive nature: according to Mt 21,10 the whole city was in turmoil[13].

However, is it correct to state that the opening of Zech 9,9 in Mt 21,5 has been substituted by Isa 62,11? Is not the relation between the two citations exactly the other way around? Would not it rather be the case that the original continuation of Isa 62,11 has here been replaced by the quoted words from Zech 9,9? This second option deserves preference to the first. This can be confirmed in the following way. Isa 62,11 (including the continuation of this verse that is not cited in Mt 21,5) consists of two segments: a) the order to speak to Zion; b) the content of the joyful message that Zion receives. This pattern also recurs frequently in other parts of Isaiah (e.g. 12,6; 40,9-10; 41,27; 52,1-2.6-8). The continuation of Isa 62,11 that is not quoted in Mt 21,5 runs as follows: "See, your

---

11. A similar composition can be found in Mt 1,18-23, where the formula quotation from Isa 7,14 is flanked by the order of the angel to Joseph and the execution of that order. The equivalence of the order and its execution is emphasised in Mt 21,1-9 by πορεύεσθε (v. 3) and πορευθέντες (v. 6).

12. In the LXX הריעי ("rejoice") is replaced by κήρυσσε ("tell").

13. This detail recalls the stir in Jerusalem (1 Kings 1,41.45) when Solomon rode to Gihon on David's (female) mule (פרדה: 1 Kings 1,33.38.44) to be anointed king there.

salvation (in the LXX: "saviour"[14]) comes; his reward is with him, and his recompense before him". The "reward" and "recompense" refer to the exiles God will take with him when he returns to Zion. This part of Isa 62,11 is a citation from Isa 40,10: the message to Zion in Isa 62,11 corresponds to the message which in Isa 40,10 Zion itself must pass on to the cities of Judah. There is also a difference between the two texts: that which is announced in Isa 40,10 is fulfilled in Isa 62,11[15]. The pattern described can also be found in Isa 52,1-2.6-8. Here, too, Zion is addressed (indeed by God himself: vv. 1-2); the content of the message is that God is king and that he will return to Zion. The words chosen here bring Isa 40,9-10 to mind. In view of all this one could say that Isa 62,11 forms a link in a chain of texts from Isaiah, which have two constant elements in common: speaking to Zion and the joyful tidings that God will return to Zion to become king over his people.

It is this complex of associations that is evoked in Mt 21,5 by the incomplete citation from Isa 62,11. In this setting, however, we only encounter the first part of the well-known bipartite Isaian scheme. The second part is replaced by a partial citation from Zech 9,9[16]. This substitution implies that the announcement from Isa 62,11 is rewritten in the light of the statement in Zech 9,9: God's kingship in Zion (Isa 62,11) is realised when the messianic king, who will rule in God's name, enters the city (Zech 9,9)[17]. Because of this interpretative modification the combined citations can be applied to Jesus to particularly good effect.

Must the modification described above be attributed to Matthew himself or is it conceivable that he discovered it in the tradition handed down to him? The latter possibility is not an unlikely one. The fact that we also find a combined citation in Jn 12,15 is already an indication.

14. Through the substitution of ישעך by ὁ σωτήρ the LXX provides the pronouns ἑαυτοῦ and αὐτοῦ with an antecedent. In the Hebrew text the pronouns refer to God (four times the suffix ו-), who is mentioned at the beginning of v. 11.

15. Cf. W. BEUKEN, *Jesaja. Deel III A* (De Prediking van het Oude Testament), Nijkerk, 1989, p. 239: "Een ombuiging vindt wel in deze zin plaats dat de komst van YHWH in 40:10 futurisch is geformuleerd, de komst van het heil hier (i.e. in 62,11, WW) perfectisch. TJ ensceneert hier de voltooiing van wat daar is beloofd".

16. Because of their correspondences, it is understandable that Isa 62,11 and Zech 9,9 have been combined in Matthew. In both texts the "daughter of Zion" is mentioned. The similarity between the two passages increases when we also note the non-quoted continuation of Isa 62,11. The following parallels can then be observed: הנה / ἰδού, בא / ἔρχομαι (Zech 9,9) or παραγίνομαι (Isa 62,11). Cf. M. MENKEN, *The Quotations* (n. 5), p. 571, note 2. Also consider the possessive pronouns in the Hebrew text: מלכך (Zech 9,9) and ישעך (Isa 62,11).

17. A similar interpretative adaptation is revealed when comparing Zech 2,10 (in the Hebrew text: Zech 2,14) with Zech 9,9.

The beginning of the citation (μὴ φοβοῦ) might derive from various texts (Isa 35,4; 40,9-10; 41,10; 44,2; Zeph 3,16). It is interesting that in this series there is a passage (Isa 40,9-10) that forms part of the Isaian association complex described above. In this framework a number of lines from Zech 9,9 are also quoted in Jn 12,15. Perhaps here again we come across the already described intertextual procedure: the second part of the Isaian pattern has been replaced by words from Zech 9,9. If this is correct, chances are that in their presentation of the combined citation from Isa 62,11 and Zech 9,9, Matthew as well as John are drawing on tradition.

b. Interpretations of Zech 9,9

We have already observed that Zech 9,9 is only partly quoted in Mt 21,5. The following verse (Zech 9,10) is missing in Matthew. This is re-markable, for the two verses in Zechariah are inextricably bound up with each other. Together they form a song that in total covers six lines. Each line contains two hemistiches, which reveal a *parallelismus membrorum*[18]. The song is structured concentrically[19]. In the first line "Zion" or "Jerusalem" is mentioned, in the last line "the ends of the earth". According to the second line the new future is heralded by the arrival of the messianic king; in line 5 it is said that he shall command peace to the nations. The third and fourth lines are concerned with the contrast between the donkey and the horses: by riding a donkey, the mount used in times of peace, the king shows his love of peace, whereas the horses together with the chariots and other weaponry stand for the war material that has been dominating matters in Jerusalem and Ephraim up till then. The line of thought in the text is that the former Northern and Southern kingdom will be reunited and that the peace which is to be realised in the new kingdom, will spread over all the earth.

The Hebrew text of Zech 9,1-10 makes a clear distinction between the role of God and of the messianic king. It is up to God to break the existing tyranny: according to 9,1-8 he will destroy the military strongholds that surround Israel and his victory march will finally lead him to Jerusalem, which he will purify of the implements of war to be found there. The messianic king will only enter the scene after that battle has been fought. He will spread the peace that has been achieved to the nations and his

---

18. See A.S. VAN DER WOUDE, *Zacharia* (De Prediking van het Oude Testament), Nijkerk, 1984, p. 173.

19. See A. LACOCQUE, *Zacharie 9-14* (Commentaire de l'Ancien Testament, 11c), Genève, ²1988, p. 156.

dominion will extend to the ends of the earth. That peace is accomplished by the work of God, and the messianic king also experiences the positive results of this work of God. This can be concluded from צדיק ונושע. The king is a just person because he is the subject of God's justice. The *participium niphal* נושע points in the same direction; it has a passive meaning and expresses that the king is not himself the saviour but that he has been saved by God and that he can enter Jerusalem with God's help[20].

This clear distinction of roles has been abandoned in the LXX. There the *participium activum* σῴζων is mentioned[21]: the king himself is a saviour or liberator, he fulfils the same role that in the Hebrew text is God's due (cf. Isa 45,21-25). A transformation at the beginning of v. 10 is along the same line. At this point in the Hebrew text we come across a sudden change of subject by the introduction of a first-person character: I (that is God) will wipe out the chariots and war horses. The LXX here opts for the third person (ἐξολεθρεύσει) to link up with v. 9, thus making the above-mentioned action an activity of the messianic king.

Now we are sufficiently equipped for a closer analysis of the changes undergone by Zech 9,9 through its integration into Mt 21,1-17. The statement that the king is just and is a saviour (or: has been saved), is missing in Mt 21,5. This is surprising since this assertion would have fitted very well into the portrait of Jesus as painted by Matthew[22]. Since this clause is missing, the emphasis is entirely on the assertion that the king of Zion is gentle (πραΰς), that he is a humble figure who is on the side of the needy. I also observe that the sharp allocation of activities between God and the messianic king, which was already under pressure in the LXX, has left no traces in Matthew's text. The various activities displayed by God in Zech 9 are now transferred to Jesus. In Zech 9,1-10 God undertakes a victory march which ends in Jerusalem; in Matthew this role has been transferred to Jesus, who has come travelling from Galilee to Jerusalem. In Zechariah God cleanses Jerusalem of the available implements of war; in Matthew Jesus throws the buyers and sellers out of the temple[23].

20. W. RUDOLPH, *Haggai, Sacharja 1-8, Sacharja 9-14, Maleachi* (KAT, 13/4), Gütersloh, 1976, p. 177, translates this part of Zech 9,9 as follows: "begnadet und reich an erfahrener Hilfe ist er".

21. The participle σῴζων in the LXX corresponds with the *participium hiphil* (מושיע) that has an active meaning (see also the textual variants in *BHS*, p. 1074).

22. See K. STENDAHL, *The School of St. Matthew and Its Use of the Old Testament* (ASNU, 20), Lund, ²1968, p. 119: "the omission of the adjectives δίκαιος καὶ σῴζων is surprising since these words... would constitute the very epitome of Matthew's Christology".

23. C. ROTH, *The Cleansing of the Temple and Zechariah XIV.21*, in *NT* 4 (1960) 174-181, sees a relation between the last sentence of the book of Zechariah and the activities of Jesus as described in Mt 21,12.

c. Two Donkeys

In Zech 9,9 the king is riding עַל־חֲמוֹר וְעַל־עַיִר בֶּן־אֲתֹנוֹת. He is there-fore riding on a donkey, which is a royal mount, indicating the dignity of its rider[24]. Both חֲמוֹר and עַיִר are masculine. An apposition follows (בֶּן־אֲתֹנוֹת), in which אֲתֹנוֹת serves as a plural of kind, which indicates that the animal is pure-bred, a noble thoroughbred and not a mule, born from crossbreeding a donkey and a mare[25]. The three descriptions apply to one and the same animal. The *waw* in עַל־חֲמוֹר וְעַל־עַיִר is not a *waw-copulativum* but a *waw-explicativum*. Zech 9,9 is probably best trans-lated as: "on a donkey, on a colt, the foal of a donkey (or: pure of race / a noble thoroughbred)".

A study by S. Talmon shows that an interesting parallel of the *waw-explicativum* in Zech 9,9 can be found in Gen 15,9[26]. There too an animal is presented that is referred to in two different ways. Gen 15,9 describes the sacrifice that Abram must offer. It consists of three animals (a heifer, a female goat, and a ram), all three years old, and of a fourth sacrificial animal that is referred to as תֹר וְגוֹזָל. According to Talmon this is a case of a hendiadys, in which the second noun supplies a further description of the first. This part of Gen 15,9 is to be translated as follows: "a pigeon, namely a young pigeon". Already in the LXX this one sacrificial animal has been doubled: τρυγόνα καὶ περιστεράν ("a turtledove and a young dove"; cf. the Vulgate: *turturum quoque et columbam*). Talmon is of the opinion that his interpretation is confirmed by Gen 15,10. There we find a singular צִפּוֹר (in the LXX and the Vulgate there is a plural at this point: τὰ δὲ ὄρνεα and *aves* respectively). The term צִפּוֹר refers back to the bird mentioned in 15,9. This bird – contrary to the three other sacrificial animals – is not to be divided in two. In Gen 15,9-10, therefore, not two different sorts of pigeons are concerned but only one single pigeon.

When comparing the Hebrew text of Zech 9,9 with Mt 21,5, we see that חֲמוֹר is represented as ὄνος and עַיִר as πῶλος. Also in the LXX these two Hebrew words are usually translated like this. Although ἐπὶ ὄνον καὶ ἐπὶ πῶλον is a correct translation of the Hebrew text, an ambiguity arises nonetheless as a result of the transition from Hebrew to Greek. This is caused by the fact that חֲמוֹר can only apply to a male animal

---

24. See G. HANFMAN, *The Donkey and the King*, in *HTR* 78 (1985) 421-426.
25. See A.S. VAN DER WOUDE (n. 18), p. 175.
26. S. TALMON, *"400 Jahre" oder "vier Generationen" (Gen 15,13-15): Geschichtliche Zeitangaben oder literarische Motive?*, in E. BLUM – C. MACHOLZ – E.W. STEGEMANN (eds.), *Die Hebräische Bibel und ihre zweifache Nachgeschichte*, FS R. Rendtorff, Neukirchen, 1990, pp. 13-25.

(she-ass = אָתוֹן), while the anarthrous ὄνος can apply to both a male and a female animal[27]. The quotation can therefore be read in two ways. The first option is that it expresses exactly the same as the Hebrew text: one animal is concerned, described in three different ways (καί then has the function of a καί-*epexegeticum*[28]): a (male) donkey, in fact a colt, the foal of a beast of burden[29]. The second option is that ὄνος applies to a she-ass and πῶλος to its foal. In that case two animals are concerned. The synonymous parallelism in the Hebrew text and the LXX version of Zech 9,9 is then replaced by a synthetic parallelism.

The quotation itself therefore leaves much to be desired as far as clarity is concerned. This is not the case with the direct context into which it has been incorporated. There, obviously two animals are concerned. In 21,2 Jesus speaks about "a donkey tied, and a colt with her" (δεδεμένην... μετ' αὐτῆς: always the feminine; cf. also the plural pronouns αὐτῶν and αὐτούς in v. 3). Also in v. 7 two animals are concerned. The two disciples put covers (saddle gear) ἐπ' αὐτῶν, i.e. on the two animals, and then Jesus mounts ἐπάνω αὐτῶν. These latter words can again be understood in two ways. One can read that Jesus rides two animals at the same time, but also that he sits on the saddle cloths, in which case it remains unclear whether he sits on the mother or on the foal[30].

Must we therefore conclude that the quotation and the surrounding verses are not in complete harmony with each other? If we adopt this assumption we must also accept that ὄνος in the quotation refers to a male animal and that the same term in vv. 2.7 refers to a she-ass. The quotation then gives a threefold description of one and the same animal. In addition, verses 2-3 and 7 inform us that during the entry into Jerusalem this (male) mount is accompanied by the she-ass. This proposal is rather awkward. It not only assumes that the one term ὄνος

---

27. L. KOEHLER – W. BAUMGARTNER, *Lexicon in Veteris Testamenti Libros*, Leiden, 1958, p. 310; BAUER-ALAND *Wörterbuch*, [6]1988, c. 1163. In the LXX ὄνος is used to translate both חֲמוֹר and אָתוֹן.

28. BDR, [15]1979, §442[18]: "Mt 21,5 (= Sach 9,9) ἐπιβεβηκὼς ἐπὶ ὄνον καὶ ("und zwar") ἐπὶ πῶλον". What is said about Mt 21,5 here, is more likely to apply to the LXX version of Zech 9,9. It is highly unlikely that the LXX should speak about two animals in view of the single use of ἐπί.

29. On the basis of a choice of arguments, R.H. GUNDRY, *The Use of the Old Testament in St. Matthew's Gospel. With Special Reference to the Messianic Hope* (NTSup, 18), Leiden, 1967, pp. 197-199, opts for this interpretation.

30. Some exegetes think that Jesus sits on the foal (this is the case in Mk) and that the she-ass stays close to its young to put it at ease (see for instance R.H. GUNDRY [n. 29], pp. 197ff). Others are of the opinion that Jesus must have preferred the adult animal to the unbroken foal (see for example P. NEPPER-CHRISTENSEN, *Das Matthäusevangelium ein judenchristliches Evangelium?* [Acta Theol. Dan., 1], Aarhus, 1958, p. 147). In both cases information is used that is not in the text.

is used for both animals, it also ignores the remarkable phenomenon that the she-ass in vv. 2.7 is always mentioned first. These complications are removed when the terms ὄνος and πῶλος from the citation are read in the light of vv. 2-3.7. The author must also have had two animals in mind in 21,5. This view is also to be preferred since the word ἐπί is mentioned twice in the citation and because the narrator attaches a great deal of importance to words of Scripture literally being fulfilled in Jesus' activities.

In mentioning two animals Matthew not only differs from the Hebrew and the Greek text of Zech 9,9 but also from the tradition that is embodied in the other gospels (Mk 11,1-10; Lk 19,29-36; Jn 12,14-15). How is his unusual choice to be explained? Many solutions to this problem have been offered: a) according to Jerome the two animals have an allegorical significance: the she-ass (*asina*) stands for Israel and the young foal (*pullus asinae*) for the gentiles[31]; b) Matthew has a predilection for pairs (cf. the two blind men in 20,29-34 and the two demoniacs in 8,28-34); c) the problem can be solved from a diachronic perspective: apart from Mark, the redactor has also used a pre-Mark tradition that has retained the historical fact that Jesus used two donkeys during his entry into Jerusalem[32].

These explanations are somewhat unsatisfactory. It is even more unsatisfactory that Matthew should have overlooked the synonymous parallelism in Zech 9,9[33]. This is very difficult to reconcile with the fact that it is exactly in this part of the citation that he so consciously seeks to link up with the Hebrew text. In order to resolve this quandary we could consider the possibility that Matthew read Zech 9,9 in the light of a different text from the Scripture in which two donkeys are explicitly

---

31. Hieronymus, *Commentaria in Evangelium S. Matthaei* 3,21 (*PL* 26,147).

32. According to K. STENDAHL (n. 22), pp. 119-120, Matthew was familiar with a tradition in which there were two donkeys; he was to have brought the citation from Zech 9,9 into agreement with this tradition. Also P. NEPPER-CHRISTENSEN (n. 30), R.H. GUNDRY (*Matthew. A Commentary on His Literary and Theological Art*, Grand Rapids, MI, 1982, p. 409) and R. BARTNICKI (*Das Zitat von Zach 9,9-10 und die Tiere im Bericht von Matthäus über den Einzug Jesu in Jerusalem*, in *NT* 18 [1976] 161- 166) are of the opinion that the redactor used a tradition that is older than the tradition that is at the basis of the versions of Mark, Luke and John. This solution fails on the grounds that there is no further evidence in the text that, apart from Mark, Matthew also drew on another source. It is also problematic that none of the authors who support this solution makes any attempt to textually border off the tradition material. See C.-P. MÄRZ, "*Siehe, dein König kommt zu dir...*". *Eine traditionsgeschichtliche Untersuchung zur Einzugsperikope* (ErfTSt, 43), Leipzig, 1981, pp. 4-8.

33. E. KLOSTERMANN, *Das Matthäusevangelium* (HNT, 4), Tübingen, [4]1971, p. 165; J. SCHNIEWIND, *Das Evangelium nach Matthäus* (NTD, 2), Göttingen, [12]1968, p. 212.

mentioned. Menken seeks a solution to the problem in that direction[34]. Given the fact that the crowd typifies Jesus as the Son of David (21,9 diff. Mk 11,10), he refers to 2 Sam 16,1-4. Because of the rebellion of Absalom, David must leave the city. Near the top of the Mount of Olives (cf. 2 Sam 15,30) Ziba provides him with a pair of saddled donkeys. This story corresponds with Mt 21,1-9 on a number of points: in both texts two donkeys are referred to, both animals are saddled, they are described as beasts of burden (ὑποζύγια: 2 Kgdms 16,2), and the scene is set on the Mount of Olives[35].

A weak point is that 2 Sam 16,1-4 has no evident connection with Zech 9,9. Are there any texts in which such a connection is manifest? This is indeed the case. In 1961 Blenkinsopp showed that already in the early Jewish literature, Zech 9,9 was associated with the oracle of Judah in Gen 49,8-12[36]. Of Judah it is said in verse 11 that he will tether his (male) ass (עיר) to the vine and the colt of his ass or his noble thoroughbred (בני אתנו) to the grapevine. These two lines reveal a synonymous parallelism. The similarities with Zech 9,9 are striking. In addition, מלכך יבוא from Zech 9,9 is a (clarifying) reflection of the cryptic phrase from Gen 49,10 (עד כי־יבא שילה) According to Blenkinsopp Zech 9,9 is a later messianic interpretation of the oracle of Judah. In this context he points out that in the LXX, the sceptre and the staff mentioned in the Hebrew text of Gen 49,10 have been replaced by a person who is referred to as an ἄρχων and a ἡγούμενος respectively, and that in the Targum the phrase "until Silo comes" is replaced with "until the king comes" (an allusion to David) or "until the Messiah comes". Matthew was probably also familiar with the traditional connection between Gen 49,10-11 and Zech 9,9. An indication is that δεδεμένην in Mt 21,2 (cf. Mk 11,2) corresponds with "tethering" in Gen 49,11. It is also interesting that the LXX in Gen 49,11a speaks of τὸν πῶλον αὐτοῦ and in 49,11b of τὸν πῶλον τῆς ὄνου αὐτοῦ: the same distinction between a colt and its mother as is made in Mt 21,2.7!

This intertextual network becomes even more intriguing when we also consider the fact that in Gen 49,14-15 Issachar is compared to a bony donkey (חמור) that must carry heavy burdens. In the LXX and in early Jewish texts a positive interpretation is given to this statement: Issachar

---

34. See M. MENKEN, The Quotations (n. 5), pp. 574-575.
35. In the Old Testament the Mount of Olives is only mentioned in 2 Sam 15,30 and in Zech 14,4.
36. J. BLENKINSOPP, The Oracle of Judah and the Messianic Entry, in JBL 80 (1961) 55-64.

has desired good things and he shoulders the Torah[37]. In the Hebrew text Gen 49,11 and 49,14 together contain precisely the three words which are also used in Zech 9,9 to describe the messianic king's mount. However, in the tradition a correlation was made between Zech 9,9 and the oracle of Judah, not with the oracle of Issachar. As I said, there are sufficient reasons to suppose that *that* correlation was also known to Matthew. I do not consider it impossible that on the basis of that existing association he made a similar connection with the blessing of Issachar. Indicative of this is the fact that he has modified the ending of Zech 9,9 (בן־אתנות) to read υἱὸν ὑποζυγίου, in other words: he describes the mother, the she-ass, as a beast of burden. In this way a connection is made between Zech 9,9 and Gen 49,14-15 where Issachar (at least in the Hebrew text) is compared to such an animal.

By linking Zech 9,9 to both Gen 49,8-12 and Gen 49,14-15, Matthew shows that Jesus, the messianic king in the sense of Zechariah, also unites the qualities associated with Judah and Issachar in himself. As king he is of the line of Judah and David, but his kingship is coloured in a very special way by the references to Issachar. Like Issachar, Jesus is someone who takes the burdens of others upon himself (cf. Mt 8,17). In this situation he is particularly concerned about the fate of the little ones and of the needy; accordingly, after his arrival in the temple we see that he especially gathers these groups around him, while rejecting the other groups[38].

I will wind up this section with the following conclusion. The scene of Jesus' entry contains implicit citations from Gen 49,8-12.14, and these, in turn, influence the formulation and meaning of the explicit citation from Zech 9,9. Also, they prepare the reader for 21,9 where Jesus is explicitly called the Son of David.

5. *The Citation from Ps 118,25-26 in Mt 21,9.15*

The crowd's jubilation in Mt 21,9 consists of three lines, the first of which is repeated in v. 15. The hosanna in line 1 refers to Jesus, the Son

---

37. J.D.M. DERRETT, *Law in the New Testament: The Palm Sunday Colt*, in *NT* 13 (1971) 241-258, esp. pp. 255-258.

38. According to D.E. GARLAND, *Reading Matthew. A Literary and Theological Commentary on the First Gospel*, New York, 1993, pp. 210-211, the two donkeys serve to illustrate two aspects of Jesus' identity: "Mounted on a donkey, a coronation animal, Jesus enters Jerusalem as the royal son of David, the messiah. Mounted on the son of a pack animal, he comes as the meek, suffering servant who will take away our weakness and bear our diseases (12:19). The king messiah of Israel will rule by virtue of his humble suffering and death".

of David, and in line 3 it refers to God or to the angels in the highest
heaven. The second line is derived from Ps 118,26 and corresponds to
the LXX in formulation. This blessing is flanked by ὡσαννά, repeated
twice; through the Aramaic הוֹשַׁע נא it can be considered as a phonetic
citation from Ps 118,25 (הוֹשִׁיעה נה). Such a citation of sound is a
phonetic repetition of a segment from an earlier text in a later one without repeating the meaning[39]. In Ps 118,25 הוֹשִׁיעה נה functions as a prayer
for help addressed to God (cf. the LXX: σῶσον δή). In the gospels
(Mt 21,9.15; Mk 11,9-10; Jn 12,13) this prayer is converted into a
salutation. This can be gathered from the use of the dative in Mt 21,9.15
(see also Did 10,6: ὡσαννὰ τῷ θεῷ Δαυίδ). This transformation may
have developed in early judaism, but when or where this happened cannot be established[40].

That the original context of the citation is conveyed in the new text
into which it has been woven, can be illustrated very appropriately
by means of the quotation in Mt 21,9[41]. Psalm 118 offers a description
of a festive procession to the temple. The last part of the psalm is
situated there. In v. 19 "the gates of righteousness" are mentioned, in
v. 20 "the gate of the LORD" and in v. 26 "the house of the LORD".
The temple is God's domain and may only be entered by the righteous. The group that enters through the gates, is welcomed by the
priests with the words: "Blessed is the one who comes in the name
of the LORD. We bless you (plural!) from the house of the LORD".
The arrival in the temple is followed by the offering of a sacrifice,
while at the same time people dance about with green twigs in their
hands.

In view of these data it is easy to ascertain that the psalm has left
many more traces in Matthew's text than just the citation of v. 9. People
cutting twigs from the trees and spreading them along the path is re-

39. P. CLAES, Echo's Echo's. De kunst van de allusie (Leven en Letteren), Amsterdam,
1988, pp. 55.57.207.
40. See E. LOHSE, Hosianna, in NT 6 (1963) 113-119; J.A. FITZMYER, Aramaic Evidence
Affecting the Interpretation of Hosanna in the New Testament, in G.F. HAWTHORNE –
O. BETZ (eds.), Tradition and Interpretation in the New Testament. FS E.E. Ellis, Grand
Rapids, MI – Tübingen, 1987, pp. 110-118. One might argue that the shout of joy
ὡσαννά was created by Greek-speaking pilgrims trying to pronounce the Aramaic הוֹשַׁע נא.
We cannot be certain about this because we come across "hosanna" for the first time in
the Greek text of the gospels.
41. See also J.A. SANDERS, A New Testament Hermeneutic Fabric: Psalm 118 in
the Entrance Narrative, in C.A. EVANS – W.F. STINESPRING (eds.), Early Jewish and
Christian Exegesis. Studies in Memory of W.H. Brownlee (Homage Series, 10), Atlanta,
1987, pp. 177-190.

miniscent of Ps 118,27[42]. Another parallel with Ps 118 is that in Matthew there is a continuous movement that ends only after the temple has been entered, where Jesus is confronted with the commercial activities associated with the sacrifice cult. I also want to point out that the entry into the temple, both in Ps 118,19 (LXX) and in Mt 21,10.12, is expressed by the verb εἰσέρχομαι.

Focusing on the original context of the citation, we see that in Matthew also a number of elements from the psalm have been rather drastically changed. In Ps 118 the officiating priests welcome the crowd at the temple gates; they pronounce the words from v. 26. In Matthew, however, this blessing is uttered by the crowd and refers to Jesus. The high priests are not mentioned until after Jesus has entered the temple. They and the scribes become agitated when they learn that the jubilation of the crowd has spread to the children of Jerusalem. Another discrepancy is that in the psalm the entry into the temple leads to a sacrifice being offered, whereas in Matthew Jesus displays activities which totally disrupt the religious sacrifice.

I will conclude these observations with some remarks on the citation itself. In the Hebrew text the priests bless the people who take part in the religious festival, invoking the name of God (cf. Num 6,22-27). In the LXX "in the name of the LORD" more unequivocally refers to "come". This is also the case in Matthew. Here Jesus is praised by the crowd as someone who comes in the name of, as the representative of, God. The ὁ ἐρχόμενος used here is also used in John's question in Mt 11,3. In his answer to that question Jesus draws from Isa 35. Interestingly, it is exactly this chapter that speaks about the coming of God (Isa 35,4: "He will come and save you") and about the curing of the blind and the lame (Isa 35,5-6), the same groups that are mentioned in our text (Mt 21,14). "He who comes" therefore refers to someone who makes available God's eschatological salvation.

6. The Citations from Isa 56,7 and Jer 7,11 in Mt 21,13

The mixed citation in Mt 21,13 is a combination of a positive and a negative statement. The positive statement is an abbreviated formulation

---

42. See also Lev 23,40 or 2 Macc 10,7. This latter text is about the purification of the temple on the 25th kislev of the year 164. Verse 7 reads: "Therefore, carrying ivy-wreathed wands and beautiful branches and also fronds of palm, they offered hymns of thanksgiving to him who had given success to the purifying of his own holy place". (NRSV).

of Isa 56,7; the negative statement contains two words from Jer 7,11. In both cases therefore, only a partial representation of the original is concerned.

The clause from Isa 56,7 in the original context runs as follows: "Truly, my house shall be called a house of prayer for all peoples". The text is in the prologue of Trito-Isaiah and speaks of the time shortly after the Babylonian captivity. God announces that his house, the temple, must have a new purpose, expressed in a new name: house of prayer for all peoples. The emphasis is on "for all peoples", rather than on "a house of prayer"[43]. The peoples will gather on Zion together with Israel, so that a new cult community will arise. This promise forms the conclusion of 56,4-7 in which God ensures that eunuchs and foreigners, two groups with a position in the margin of Israel's society, will positively have access to worship, at least if they are righteous. On the same condition gentiles or proselytes too can share in God's salvation.

In Mt 21,13 "for all peoples" is omitted (diff. Mk 11,17). The effect is that this verse formulates a pure contrast between "a house of prayer" and "a den of robbers". Now the emphasis is on "a house of prayer". What this description involves becomes clear from Jesus' activities. He chases all traders and buyers away and overturns the tables of the money-changers and the seats of the pigeon dealers. In this way he disrupts the commercial activities necessary for the continuity of the cult. He turns himself against the usual function of the temple as a cult centre and he brings about a situation in which the temple can no longer fulfil that function. Thus a distinction exists between the temple as a house of prayer and the temple as a cult centre. This differentiation is not made in Isaiah. There, "a house of prayer" is not meant to diminish the importance of sacrificial observances; on the contrary, in Isa 56,7 God states that especially sacrifices and burnt offerings of the fringe groups shall be acceptable to him[44].

The citation in Mt 21,13 functions primarily as a justification of Jesus' activities mentioned in verse 12. Given the original context of the Isaiah citation, this quotation can also be applied to verse 14, where Jesus cures the blind and the lame and gives them a position as full members in a community of which he himself is the centre. The blind

---

43. See W.A.M. Beuken, *Jesaja. Deel IIIA* (De Prediking van het Oude Testament), Nijkerk, 1989, p. 33.

44. R.J. Bauckham, *Jesus' Demonstration in the Temple*, in B. Lindars (ed.), *Law and Religion*, Cambridge, 1988, p. 83: "Isa 56:7 clearly uses the term 'house of prayer' to describe the temple precisely as a place of sacrifice".

and the lame are indeed substitutes for the eunuchs and the foreigners in Isaiah. Matthew's text and Isa 56 share the feature that the fringe groups acquire a full place as members of the community[45].

The reference to Jer 7,11 is based on two words: σπήλαιον λῃστῶν. In Jeremiah, the sentence in which these words occur is formulated as an interrogative sentence: "Has this house, which is called by my name, become a den of robbers in your sight?" In Matthew the interrogative is transformed into a positive assertion: "you are making it a den of robbers". Opting for the use of the present tense (ποιεῖτε) emphatically underlines that the text from Isaiah is still very relevant many centuries later. The syntagm σπήλαιον λῃστῶν, drawn from the LXX, has metaphoric significance: Jeremiah compares the temple with a hiding place where people imagine they are safe, and he characterises the inhabitants of Jerusalem as thieves who commit crimes and are not afraid to use violence (cf. Jer 7,6.9). In Matthew this prophetic censure is aimed specifically at those who are responsible for the management of the temple. The priesthood also belong to that category (cf. "the high priests" in 21,15). The religious system as perpetuated by them requires considerable financial sacrifices from the templegoers. By curing the blind and the lame in the temple, Jesus performs an activity which indicates in which direction the alternative is to be found for the practices he condemns. His act forms a beautiful illustration of the motto from Hos 6,6: "I desire mercy and not sacrifice" (cf. Mt 9,13; 12,7).

7. The Citation from Ps 8,3 in Mt 21,16

The citation from Ps 8,3 corresponds literally to the version of the LXX. This is especially clear from the term αἶνος ("hymn of praise"). The Hebrew text has עז ("bulwark") at this point, although this word too may have to do with a hymn of praise (cf. Ps 29,1; 96,7).

The first part of Ps 8 describes God's dominion over the monsters of chaos which form a constant threat to his creation. This is expressed most eloquently in the Hebrew text; in verse 3 it does not speak of a song of praise but of a bulwark, raised by God to keep the monsters under control. This bulwark also serves as God's throne. The second part

---

45. Mt 21,14 implies that the Son of David will break with the tradition that the blind and the lame were not allowed to enter the house of God, a custom which the LXX dates back to David's time (2 Sam 5,8). See also: D. GEWALT, *Die Heilung Blinder und Lahmer im Tempel (Matthäus 21,14)*, in *Dielheimer Blätter zum Alten Testament* 23 (1986) 156-173, especially p. 167.

is a meditative reflection on the position of man. God has put everything under his feet. Verses 8-9 explain that this especially refers to man's care for the animal-world. In his dominion over the animals, man resembles God, who dominates the monsters of chaos[46]. In the New Testament this second part is frequently applied to Jesus, preeminently the man to whom everything is submitted (1 Cor 15,27; Eph 1,22; Heb 2,6-8a; 1 Pet 3,22).

The remarkable thing about Mt 21,16 is that here also the first part of the psalm is applied to Jesus. In that interpretation process Matthew lets Jesus take the initiative. In his answer to the question of the high priests and the scribes, Jesus repeats the words from Ps 8,3 in the formulation of the LXX, and their meaning is changed by his quoting them. In the psalm itself, the song of the babes and infants is addressed to God, but Jesus declares that *he* is the object of that song. As a result of this provocative interpretation, other elements from the psalm likewise acquire a new significance. The νήπιοι are taken figuratively to refer to Jesus' disciples to whom the Father reveals the identity of his Son (cf. 11,25). It is God himself who has caused the children to sing. In the psalm the song is meant to stay the destructive power of the monsters of chaos. This dubious position is now applied to the high priests and the scribes. With this citation Jesus effectively shuts them up.

The story of Matthew thus very accurately reflects the constellation in the first part of the psalm. On the other hand, a transformation occurs: the struggle between God and the monsters of chaos is transposed to the bitter conflict between Jesus and the Jewish leaders in Jerusalem[47].

8. Conclusion

The hypothesis that an explicit citation generates interaction between the text from which it originates and the text into which it is incorporated,

---

46. This exegesis is strongly inspired by J. HOLMAN, *A Gentleman's Psalm. Genesis 1,26 naar het beeld van Psalm 8*, in C. VERDEGAAL – W. WEREN (eds.), *Stromen uit Eden*. FS N. Poulssen, Boxtel – Brugge, 1992, pp. 75-86.

47. I fully agree with H. Klein when he writes: "Wahrscheinlich ist [...], dass Mt das angeführte Zitat in seinem unmittelbaren Kontext ernst nahm: 'wegen deiner Feinde, um zum Schweigen zu bringen Feind und Widersacher.' Dieser Abschnitt wird zwar nicht zitiert, aber es geschieht ihm entsprechend: Das Lob der Kinder und der Hinweis auf die Schrift, macht die Feinde Jesu zunächst mundtot". See H. KLEIN, *Zur Wirkungsgeschichte von Ps 8*, in R. BARTELMUS – T. KRÜGER – H. UTZSCHNEIDER (eds.), *Konsequente Traditionsgeschichte*. FS K. Baltzer (OBO, 126), Freiburg – Göttingen, 1993, p. 197.

has proved to be particularly productive. We have repeatedly been able to observe that the original context of the citations reverberates in Mt 21,1-17. In their new setting the quoted words and sentences continue to refer to contextual data with which they were originally associated. These original connections are not merely repeated as to form or content, nor are they completely erased in the process; they usually reappear transformed. It also appears that the explicit citations are strongly integrated into their new literary setting, even to such an extent that one could ask whether the continuation of the story is not at least co-determined by the course of events in the Old Testament texts that have been assimilated in Mt 21,1-17.

For the sake of convenience I have discussed the citations one after another. In the process it sometimes appeared that they are strongly interconnected. In his story Matthew has used parts of various Old Testament texts and as a result those texts, in their new setting in Matthew, mutually illuminate each other. In conclusion of my contribution I will go a little further into this phenomenon.

The Old Testament citations in Mt 21,1-17 have been partially attuned to each other. The connection between Isa 62,11 and Zech 9,9 is based on literal and substantive similarities between the two texts. The verb ἔρχομαι from Zech 9,9 reappears in the quotation from Ps 118,25-26. This latter quotation is repeated in an abbreviated form in 21,15. In the LXX, the two citations in Mt 21,13 are linked by the syntagm ὁ οἶκός μου (in the Hebrew text of Isa 56,7 ביתי occurs and in Jer 7,11 הבית הזה is used). The term "praise" in Ps 8,3 refers to the acclamation of the children and the crowd, itself in its turn taken from Ps 118. Psalm 8 is flanked by the sentence: "O Lord, our Sovereign, how majestic is your name in all the earth!". This sentence establishes a connection with Ps 118,26: in both contexts the name of the Lord is mentioned.

From a substantive point of view it is important that the majority of the quoted passages already referred to Jerusalem or the temple in their Old Testament setting[48]. This becomes even more significant when we realise that in 21,1-17 Matthew shows his preference for texts from Trito-Isaiah and for other texts that refer to the time shortly after the captivity, which show that after a time of terrible misfortune God will again – and now definitively – settle in Zion and will establish a new

---

48. R. BRANDSCHEIDT, *Messias und Tempel. Die alttestamentliche Zitate in Mt* 21,1-17, in *TTZ* 99 (1990) 37, quite rightly observes that the citations "im Rahmen der alttestamentlichen Offenbarung Zeugnisse [sind] für Jahwehs Heilshandeln auf Zion, das ja nicht einfach die Stadt Jerusalem meint, sondern den Ort des Tempels als den Ort einer besonderen Offenbarungsgegenwart Gottes".

community there. The composition of this new community is heterogeneous: it is formed by returning deportees who ally themselves to persons and groups who remained behind in the wrecked city; also, the new community is open to righteous people from among the gentiles. The new future acquires a concrete form in salvation figures such as the servant from Deutero-Isaiah, the servants from Trito-Isaiah or the king of Zion from Zechariah.

Like the salvation figures from the post-exilic texts, Jesus is the leader or the centre of the new community which is going to develop in Jerusalem. The many citations also emphasize Jesus' bond with God: elements which in the Old Testament refer to God, are applied to Jesus as a result of their re-use in Matthew.

It is also interesting what the citations are saying about Jerusalem. At the beginning of Mt 21,1-17 Zion is a rather undifferentiated entity: the joyful message of 21,5 is meant for all the inhabitants of the city; in 21,10-11 it is said that "the whole city" is in turmoil. Subsequently the initially undifferentiated city is arranged into two groups. The one group is formed by the merchants and their clients, the money-changers and the pigeon sellers, the scribes and the high priests. They are depicted as Jesus' antipodes. The other group consists of the enthusiastic crowd, the blind and the lame, and the children of Jerusalem. The crowd and the children give voice to the response which actually one might have expected of all Jerusalem. Now that Jesus enters Jerusalem, a new community develops, just as it did in the time after the captivity, but now that community is formed around his person[49].

A final point of connection between Matthew and the post-exilic texts is that in both cases there is earnest meditation on the position of the temple. The rebuilding of the temple after the captivity gave renewed energy to innovative insights concerning the participation in public worship of members of fringe groups in Israel's society and of righteous people from all the inhabited world. It is significant that in Matthew, Jesus' journey to Jerusalem culminates in his action in the temple. I emphasized that his activities there in fact cause a disruption of the sacrificial practices. Little justice is done to the text in asserting that Jesus is only concerned about restoring the purity of the cult. Nor is opening Israel's worship to the nations within the scope of the text: the

---

49. As a result of Jesus' entry into Jerusalem, a dichotomy arises, but perhaps it is only of a temporary nature; at the end of Mt 23 the hope is voiced that a moment will come when Jesus' opponents too will fall in with the song of praise from Ps 118.

omission of the reference to "all nations" is incompatible with this interpretation. By expelling all (!) buyers and merchants from the temple, Jesus demonstrates that the role of the temple as a cult centre is a thing of the past. Note, however, that especially in Matthew's version Jesus' actions in the temple are twofold: immediately after his negative action in verse 12, Jesus gives the temple a new purpose by making it a place where the blind and the lame are healed and where through God, children become acquainted with the true identity of Jesus[50].

In the exegesis of Matthew's gospel it is commonplace to say that in Jesus the history of Israel is revived. This revival also involves certain corrections or is accompanied by transformations. However, the new meanings which result, are not the patent of Matthew or of the New Testament. The re-evaluation has already begun in Old Testament itself. The post-exilic texts are an eloquent example. By integrating those texts into his book, Matthew revives an important period from the history of Israel.

Tilburg Faculty of Theology   Wim WEREN
Academielaan 9
NL-5037 ET Tilburg

---

50. See also T. SÖDING, *Die Tempelaktion Jesu. Redaktionskritik – Überlieferungs-geschichte – historische Rückfrage (Mk 11,15-19; Mt 21,12-17; Lk 19,45-48; Joh 2,13-22)*, in *TTZ* 101 (1992) 36-64, especially pp. 41-43.

LA RECONTEXTUALISATION D'IS 6,9-10 EN MC 4,10-12
OU UN EXEMPLE DE NON-CITATION

L'utilisation du texte d'Is 6,9-10 par les quatre évangélistes et l'auteur du livre des Actes relève de la problématique générale de l'intertextualité. Cette phrase est une parole de mission adressée à Isaïe et qui résume le message du prophète. Elle a la forme d'une menace et d'un avertissement adressé au peuple infidèle à l'alliance conclue avec YHWH. Les auteurs du N.T. font habituellement référence à ce texte pour signifier que le rejet de Jésus par les juifs résulte d'un aveuglement prévu dans le dessein de Dieu, puisqu'il est inscrit dans les Écritures. Par rapport à ce traitement généralisé d'Is 6,9-10, Marc se singularise. En effet, chez lui, les aveuglés ne sont pas clairement identifiés comme juifs par rapport aux païens; ils sont désignés comme «ceux-là qui sont au dehors»[1], sans plus de précision. Par ailleurs, il n'introduit pas explicitement la citation et son texte ne suit exactement ni le texte hébreu, ni le texte de la LXX. L'objet de cet article sera de comprendre la façon si particulière selon laquelle le texte d'Isaïe est utilisé en Mc.

Cette question peut être traitée de deux manières, selon qu'on l'examine du point de vue de l'auteur de l'évangile ou du point de vue de son lecteur.

L'exégèse historico-critique aborde la question du côté de l'auteur-rédacteur. Elle examine ce qui le précède (les sources qu'il utilise), le contexte religieux, philosophique, littéraire, social dans lequel il écrit, mais aussi la personnalité littéraire et théologique qui se dégage de l'œuvre. À partir de ces recherches, diverses hypothèses peuvent être émises quant à la genèse de la composition du texte. Dans notre cas, on se demandera, par exemple, quelle était la forme du texte d'Isaïe dont Mc ou sa source disposait. A-t-il eu recours au texte hébreu ou au texte grec de la LXX ou encore à un Targum? Dans ce dernier cas, pourrait-il avoir mal compris et mal traduit le texte araméen? A-t-il construit son chapitre des paraboles à partir de ce logion sur le mystère du Royaume ou ce logion est-il, au contraire, intégré tant bien que mal dans un ensemble préalablement constitué? Telles sont quelques-unes des questions qui ont requis l'essentiel des efforts exégétiques au cours des

---

1. Traduction littérale de ἐκείνοις τοῖς ἔξω. Dorénavant je donnerai en traduction abrégée «ceux du dehors».

récentes décennies. Ma première partie fera rapidement le point sur les résultats de ces efforts.

Mais ceux-ci n'épuisent pas le sens du texte. Ainsi, on peut supposer, par exemple, que Mc a utilisé le Tg et l'a mal traduit, en interprétant dans le sens d'une finale ce qui devait être entendu comme une consécutive. Une telle considération peut certes aider à comprendre la manière dont cet auteur a conçu et composé son texte. Cependant, mis à part l'exégète érudit du XXe siècle, quel lecteur peut l'avoir lu avec une telle clé de lecture? De plus, la recherche de l'intention de l'auteur, si elle pouvait aboutir de manière assurée, ne condamnerait-elle pas le lecteur à répéter inlassablement le sens ainsi déterminé? Certes l'auteur a produit le texte qui reste la norme de toute interprétation. Mais, à partir de cette norme, le lecteur est lui-même invité à produire. L'acte de lecture est alors considéré «comme une activité dynamique qui ne se borne pas à répéter des significations à tout jamais fixées, mais qui se place dans le prolongement d'itinéraires de sens, ouverts sur un travail d'interprétation»[2]. De ces constatations ressort l'intérêt d'une autre démarche, à savoir analyser le texte du point de vue de son lecteur[3], sans se centrer sur son mode de production. Comment le lecteur du texte grec de Mc comprend-il la fonction du logion sur le mystère du Royaume et celle de la citation d'Isaïe qu'il inclut? Dans la nouvelle critique littéraire, l'intention de l'auteur et celles de ses sources sont mises entre parenthèses au profit de recherches basées sur l'hypothèse de la cohérence de l'œuvre finale. C'est la piste que j'explorerai dans ma seconde partie, en étant particulièrement attentif à l'impact qu'a eu sur le texte d'Is 6 sa recontextualisation en Mc.

I. RAPPEL DE L'ANALYSE HISTORICO-CRITIQUE

Au cœur de Mc 4, les vv. 10-12 sont considérés comme une *crux interpretationis*, en raison de la rigueur de la théorie de l'endurcissement qu'ils semblent attribuer à Jésus. L'allusion à Is 6,9-10 dans les versets de Lc et Mt parallèles à Mc 4,12, est moins dure. En effet, la finale de

---

2. P. RICŒUR, *La Bible et l'imagination*, in *RHPR* 62 (1982) 339-360, voir p. 340.
3. Il s'agit du lecteur implicite au sens où l'entend le *reader-response criticism*. Pour une analyse centrée sur le lecteur du premier siècle habitué à certaines méthodes rhétoriques, voir M. A. BEAVIS, *Mark's Audience. The Literary and Social Setting of Mark 4.11-12* (JSNT SS, 33), Sheffield, 1989. Dans le cadre de la *Wirkungsgeschichte*, on peut aussi s'interroger sur la compréhension de Mc 4,12 par les lecteurs de l'histoire chrétienne. Mais tel ne sera pas mon propos.

Mc 4,12 (μήποτε ἐπιστρέψωσιν καὶ ἀφεθῇ αὐτοῖς) ne se retrouve ni en Lc 8,10, ni en Mt 13,13. En outre, dans ce dernier cas, l'allusion à Isaïe est introduite par ὅτι et non par ἵνα. Du coup, elle intervient comme explication et non comme intention[4]. Pour sa part, Mt poursuit par une citation d'accomplissement reprenant le texte complet d'Is 6,9-10. Mais cette citation, comme celle du même texte en Ac 28,26-27, suit littéralement la LXX, si ce n'est l'omission de αὐτῶν après le premier τοῖς ὠσίν. Or, le texte de la LXX est beaucoup moins dur que le texte massorétique[5]. En effet, en Is 6,9, les indicatifs futurs ἀκούσετε et βλέψετε surprennent là où on attendrait des impératifs, à l'instar des impératifs qal שִׁמְעוּ et רְאוּ du TM. Au v. 10, l'impératif hifil הַשְׁמֵן est rendu par ἐπαχύνθη[6] suivi par la conjonction γάρ. La LXX remplace ainsi un commandement d'endurcissement donné par Dieu au prophète par une clause destinée à expliquer l'aveuglement dénoncé au v. 9. Les deux

---

4. Pour être complet, il faut ajouter que Mt 13,13 pousse le paradoxe à son comble: ce n'est pas seulement la compréhension qui fait défaut aux destinataires du logion; en fait, bien que voyant ils ne voient pas et bien qu'entendant ils n'entendent pas. En Lc 8,10, la citation est abrégée au maximum. Comme Mt, Lc oppose simplement voir et ne pas voir. Mais, comme Mc, il oppose entendre et ne pas comprendre. Par ailleurs, il conserve à la phrase son sens final, en l'introduisant, comme Mc, par ἵνα. Sur tout ceci, voir J. GNILKA, *Die Verstockung Israels. Isaias 6,9-10 in der Theologie der Synoptiker* (SANT, 3), München, 1961, pp. 16-17. La différence entre les conceptions de Mc et de Mt a été très finement exposée par D. MARGUERAT, *La construction du lecteur par le texte*, in C. FOCANT (éd.), *The Synoptic Gospels. Source Criticism and the New Literary Criticism* (BETL, 110), Leuven, Peeters – University Press, 1993, pp. 239-262, voir pp. 253-259.

5. C.A. EVANS, *The Text of Isaiah 6:9-10*, in ZAW 94 (1982) 415-418, a montré qu'à l'exception notable de la Vulgate, les traductions ont eu tendance à atténuer la dureté du texte d'Isaïe tel qu'il se lit dans le TM en remplaçant les indicatifs par des impératifs. Cela vaut pour la LXX, le Targum et la Peshitta. Mais aussi pour 1QIs^a 6,9-10 qui présente plusieurs variantes textuelles sans doute voulues par rapport au TM et dans un sens passablement différent: «In the second and third lines of v. 9 (what the prophet is to speak) the text reads על instead of אל. In v.10 the final ן of השמן has been omitted and in the last line of the verse ולבבו has become בלבבו. W.H. Brownlee has argued, and I think correctly, that these textual variants are not accidental, but are deliberate. As the text now stands the meaning is completely transformed. The prophet is to urge the people to listen *because* (על) they may understand and to look *because* (על) they may perceive. The purpose is to make the heart of the people *appalled* (השם) at evil lest they see evil with their eyes and hear of murder with their ears. In the case of the last variant because of the omission of the connective ו (which is replaced by sound-alike ב) the syntactical connection to פן ('lest') is broken. The final lines now take on imperative force: let the people understand in their heart and return and be healed. Thus, according to the Qumran version the prophet is no longer speaking an oracle of judgment in order to promote obduracy. Rather, the prophet admonishes the righteous (i.e. the Qumran convenanters) to take heed lest they fall prey to evil. Of all the text traditions 1QIsa^a 6,9-10 represents the most unusual textual modification» (p. 416).

6. Symmaque a traduit ἐλιπάνθη. Contrairement à ce qu'avance C.A. EVANS, *The Text* (n. 4), p. 416, c'est bien הַשְׁמֵן qui est rendu par ἐπαχύνθη et non הַכְבֵּד.

impératifs hifil suivants הַכְבֵּד et הָשַׁע sont remplacés dans la LXX par les indicatifs βαρέως ἤκουσαν et ἐκάμμυσαν. En conséquence, alors que, selon le TM, c'est la prédication du prophète qui doit provoquer l'endurcissement de cœur du peuple, selon la LXX, c'est le peuple qui ne comprendra pas parce que son cœur est déjà endurci. Cette reprise du texte de la LXX donne à Mt 13,10-17 une tonalité d'explication: le rejet de Jésus fait partie d'une dureté de cœur qu'Isaïe déjà reprochait au peuple élu[7]. On se trouve dans le cadre de l'histoire du salut[8] et on se réfère à l'histoire d'Israël comme à un temps révolu. Par contre, Mc applique le texte d'Isaïe au présent, tout en lui donnant une tonalité finale qui fait beaucoup plus difficulté.

Est-il possible que Jésus ait voulu parler de façon incompréhensible à une catégorie de personnes enfoncées délibérément dans l'incompréhension de peur qu'elles ne se convertissent et qu'il ne leur soit pardonné? Déjà A. Jülicher jugeait impensable d'attribuer à Jésus une telle intention[9]. Aussi considérait-il ce texte comme une théorie élaborée par la communauté chrétienne primitive, lorsque celle-ci ne comprit plus les paraboles pour ce qu'elles étaient au départ dans le chef de Jésus, à savoir un enseignement simple et imagé avec une pointe unique, mais les interpréta comme des allégories compliquées. J. Jeremias refuse, lui aussi, d'attribuer à Jésus la dureté du logion d'endurcissement[10]. Jésus aurait cité Is 6,9-10 selon la version araméenne du Tg où Dieu paraît souhaiter la conversion qui déboucherait sur le pardon. Un malentendu, lors de la traduction du Tg en grec, aurait malencontreusement introduit l'idée d'une finalité négative: «pour qu'ils… ne comprennent pas, de peur qu'ils ne se convertissent et qu'il ne leur soit pardonné».

La question historique de la continuité ou de la discontinuité entre la pensée de Jésus et celle de la communauté primitive et des évangélistes était ainsi posée. Elle ne manque pas d'intérêt, même si elle est difficile

---

7. Dans cette logique, il est difficile de penser qu'au v. 13 Mt aurait eu primitivement ἵνα et non ὅτι, hypothèse défendue par R. GRYSON, sur base de manuscrits de la vieille latine et de citations patristiques: *La vieille-latine, témoin privilégié du texte du Nouveau Testament. L'exemple de Matthieu 13,13-15*, in *RTL* 19 (1988) 413-432. Son étude doit venir en complément de celle de C.A. EVANS, *The Text* (n. 4), car, contrairement à ce qu'il annonce au départ (p. 416), ce dernier n'a pas tenu compte de la Vetus Latina.

8. C'est à juste titre que C. DIETERLÉ, *Le jeu entre l'espace et le temps en Marc 4,1-34*, in D. MARGUERAT – J. ZUMSTEIN (éd.), *La mémoire et le temps*. FS P. Bonnard (Le monde de la Bible, 23), Genève, 1991, pp. 127-140, voir p. 136, refuse d'attribuer à Mc une perspective d'histoire du salut qui est matthéenne.

9. A. JÜLICHER, *Die Gleichnisreden Jesu*, I, Leipzig-Tübingen, ²1899. Voir aussi M.-J. LAGRANGE, *Évangile selon saint Marc* (EBib), Paris ⁶1942, pp. 102-103.

10. J. JEREMIAS, *Die Gleichnisse Jesu* (ATANT, 11), Göttingen, ⁸1970, pp. 12-18.

à trancher. Elle a marqué l'exégèse de Mc 4,10-12 tout au long de ce siècle et toutes les possibilités d'explication à partir de l'intention de l'auteur et de ses sources semblent avoir été explorées: elles partent généralement de l'hypothèse d'une discontinuité.

1. Tradition et rédaction

Je me limite à résumer les positions classiques en ce qui concerne les vv. 10-12, sans reprendre la question de la composition de l'ensemble des vv. 1-34[11].

Au v. 10, il est admis que Mc reprend un donné traditionnel. Cependant, d'une part, il ajoute σὺν τοῖς δώδεκα à οἱ περὶ αὐτόν, constituant ainsi une formule unique dans son évangile[12]. D'autre part, il transforme le singulier παραβολήν de sa source en παραβολάς. Le singulier s'accordait bien avec la narration par Jésus de la seule parabole du semeur. Mais, au niveau de l'ensemble du ch. 4, le pluriel correspond au v. 2 et à la discussion concernant ceux à qui tout arrive en paraboles (v. 11)[13]. Le reste du verset serait traditionnel, même si le thème de l'enseignement en privé aux disciples est un thème de la prédication marcienne. En effet, le vocabulaire n'est pas marcien: κατὰ μόνας est un hapax chez Mc, la formule marcienne étant κατ' ἰδίαν (7 emplois); le verbe marcien de l'interrogation est ἐπερωτάω (25 emplois) et non ἐρωτάω (3 emplois).

Quant aux vv. 11-12, ils sont le plus souvent considérés comme un logion isolé ajouté par Marc au moyen de sa formule favorite καὶ

---

11. Pour un état de la question récent sur la genèse de la composition de cet ensemble, on peut voir, par exemple, C. BREYTENBACH, *Nachfolge und Zukunftserwartung nach Markus. Eine methodenkritische Studie* (ATANT, 71), Zürich, 1984, pp. 133-143 et 187-188; H.-J. KLAUCK, *Allegorie und Allegorese in synoptischen Gleichnistexten* (NTAbh, n.f. 13), Münster, ²1986, pp. 240-259; C.M. TUCKETT, *Mark's Concerns in the Parables Chapter (Mark 4,1-34)*, in *Bib* 69 (1988) 1-26, voir pp. 2-5.

12. Selon H.-J. KLAUCK, *Allegorie* (n. 11), p. 243, la formule οἱ περὶ αὐτόν désignait la foule (3,32.34) et Mc y a ajouté σὺν τοῖς δώδεκα pour marquer que les paroles suivantes de Jésus sont adressées à une partie de la foule, mais avant tout aux disciples. Voir dans le même sens F. NEIRYNCK, *Réponse à P. Rolland*, in *ETL* 60 (1984) 363-366, voir p. 365, citant les commentaires de Pesch, Gnilka, Schmithals; J.R. KIRKLAND, *The Earliest Understanding of Jesus' Use of Parables: Mark IV 10-12 in Context*, in *NT* 19 (1977) 1-21, voir p. 4; E. CUVILLIER, *Le concept de παραβολη dans le second évangile. Son arrière-plan littéraire. Sa signification dans le cadre de la rédaction marcienne. Son utilisation dans la tradition de Jésus* (EBib n.s., 19), Paris, 1993, p. 96.

13. J. DUPONT, *Le chapitre des paraboles*, in *NRT* 99 (1967) 800-820, voir p. 803.

ἔλεγεν αὐτοῖς[14]. À côté de cette opinion majoritaire, d'autres pensent que, dans la source de Mc, ces versets étaient déjà insérés dans leur contexte actuel[15]. En fait, le v. 11 ne reflète guère le vocabulaire habituel de Mc, puisque des expressions telles que τὸ μυστήριον δέδοται, τὸ μυστήριον τῆς βασιλείας τοῦ θεοῦ ou encore ἐν παραβολαῖς τὰ πάντα γίνεται constituent autant d'hapax[16]. Aussi n'a-t-on guère d'arguments pour l'attribuer à la rédaction marcienne[17]. Dans la tradition antérieure à Mc, il pourrait provenir d'un contexte liturgique[18]. Par contre, il n'en va pas de même du v. 12. Plusieurs auteurs, en effet, attribuent à Mc le fait d'avoir fait suivre le v. 11 par une citation d'Is 6,9-10[19], si toutefois il faut en ce cas parler de citation[20].

14. On peut lire une liste d'auteurs allant en ce sens dans H.-J. KLAUCK, *Allegorie* (n. 11), p. 245, n. 300. Voir aussi C. BREYTENBACH, *Nachfolge* (n. 11), pp. 140 et 142-143; E. CUVILLIER, *Le concept de παραβολή* (n. 12), p. 96, n. 39. Selon J. JEREMIAS, *Die Gleichnisse* (n. 10), pp. 13-14, Mc a inséré ce logion entre la parabole du semeur et son explication, suite à un malentendu, tandis qu'il l'a fait consciemment et intentionnellement, selon W. MARXSEN, *Redaktionsgeschichtliche Erklärung der sogenannten Parabeltheorie des Markus*, in *ZTK* 52 (1955) 255-271, voir pp. 264-270 (= ID., *Der Exeget als Theologe. Vorträge zum Neuen Testament*, Gütersloh, 1968, pp. 13-28, voir pp. 21-26).

15. E. SCHWEIZER, *Das Evangelium nach Markus* (NTD, 1), Göttingen, ²1968, p. 51; H. RÄISÄNEN, *Die Parabeltheorie im Markusevangelium* (Schriften der Finnischen Exegetischen Gesellschaft, 26), Helsinki, 1973, p. 46.

16. Je ne vois dès lors pas pourquoi E. CUVILLIER, *Le concept de παραβολή* (n. 12), pp. 97-98, considère le singulier μυστήριον et l'expression ἐν παραβολαῖς τὰ πάντα γίνεται comme des retouches de Mc.

17. J. LAMBRECHT, *Redaction and Theology in Mc., IV*, in M. SABBE (éd.), *L'Évangile selon Marc. Tradition et rédaction* (BETL, 34), Leuven, ²1988, pp. 282-285, pense pourtant pouvoir attribuer à la rédaction marcienne l'ensemble des vv. 10-13, tout en admettant de petits restes de tradition pré-marcienne aux vv. 10 et 12, peut-être au v. 11, mais pas au v. 13. Tout en renonçant à délimiter avec précision la tradition prémarcienne dans les vv. 10-13, C.M. TUCKETT, *Mark's Concerns* (n. 11), a montré que la plupart des idées présentes dans ces versets «can be incorporated into a reasonably coherent Markan scheme» (p. 20).

18. H.-J. KLAUCK, *Allegorie* (n. 11), p. 246 (se référant à l'étude de P. MERENDINO, *Gleichnisrede und Wortliturgie. Zu Mk 4,1-34*, in *Archiv für Liturgiewissenschaft* 16 [1974] 7-31, voir pp. 9-11), écrit: «Man kann sich V. 11 als isoliertes Logion vorstellen, das etwa in der Gemeindeversammlung als liturgischer Zuruf Verwendung fand». E. CUVILLIER, *Le concept de παραβολή* (n. 12), p. 105, semble plutôt favorable à cette opinion.

19. A. SUHL, *Die Funktion der alttestamentlichen Zitate und Anspielungen im Marcusevangelium*, Gütersloh, 1965, pp. 150-151: «Somit könnte Markus selbst die Targum-Paraphrase als das ihm geläufige 'Jes-Zitat' hier aufgegriffen haben. Diese Annahme hat zumindest die größere Wahrscheinlichkeit für sich». Voir dans le même sens P. LAMPE, *Die markinische Deutung des Gleichnisses vom Sämann Markus 4,10-12*, in *ZNW* 65 (1974) 140-150, voir p. 147; H.-J. KLAUCK, *Allegorie* (n. 11), pp. 249-252. Ce dernier auteur souligne que le texte d'Is 6,9-10 n'a joué aucun rôle dans la pensée prédestinationiste liée à l'apocalyptique. Selon lui, Mc aurait recouru à ce texte d'Isaïe en fonction de sa proximité thématique avec les différents types d'écoute présentés en 4,14-20. On trouvera un développement en sens exactement inverse dans J. MARCUS, *Mark 4:10-12 and Marcan Epistemology*, in *JBL* 103 (1984) 557-574, qui souligne le parallélisme avec l'apocalyptique, et particulièrement Qumrân; pour Is 6,9-10, il cite 1QS 4,11 (p. 561).

20. Il n'y a pas citation à proprement parler. Voir ci-dessous, pp. 169-170 et 174.

2. *Signification de* ἐκείνοις τοῖς ἔξω *(v. 11)*

Avec des nuances diverses, les exégètes ont proposé deux grands types d'interprétation pour l'expression ἐκείνοις δὲ τοῖς ἔξω.

Pour les premiers, même si, ailleurs dans le N.T., l'expression οἱ ἔξω employée absolument désigne toujours les non-chrétiens (1 Co 5,12-13; 1 Th 4,12; Col 4,5)[21], en Mc 4,11, elle ne pourrait se référer qu'à la foule[22]. Les paraboles sont alors conçues comme «un enseignement ésotérique, qui doit être compréhensible seulement pour les Douze choisis et pour ceux qui se réunissent à eux et sont avec eux»[23]. Selon ces auteurs, c'est ce qu'impose le contexte immédiat, puisque, aux vv. 1-2, Jésus est mis en scène comme enseignant une foule nombreuse rassemblée au bord du lac; cet enseignement leur est donné ἐν παραβολαῖς, idée reprise dans les vv. 33-34. Dès lors, ce doit être à la même foule que ἐν παραβολαῖς τὰ πάντα γίνεται. Cette interprétation s'accorde bien avec celles de Mt et Lc, qui n'ont pas la mention de ἔξω: Mt 13,11 a seulement ἐκείνοις δέ et Lc 8,10 τοῖς δὲ λοιποῖς. Ces deux expressions renvoient certainement à la foule dans les contextes, respectivement, de Mt et de Lc.

Cependant, la plupart des exégètes excluent cette interprétation et pensent que l'expression ἐκείνοις τοῖς ἔξω renvoie à des adversaires de Jésus et/ou du christianisme. Elle pourrait être inspirée par l'expression juive הַחִיצוֹנִים qui désignait les païens et les juifs incrédules[24]. En l'utilisant, le rédacteur viserait les non-chrétiens de son temps, ceux qui ne font pas partie de la communauté chrétienne[25]. Cependant, J. Gnilka, par exemple,

---

21. J. BEHM, art. ἔξω, in *TWNT* II, Stuttgart, 1935, pp. 572-573, voir p. 573.

22. E.P. GOULD, *A Critical and Exegetical Commentary on the Gospel according to St. Mark* (ICC), Edinburgh, 1897, p. 72; J. BEHM, art. ἔξω (n. 17), p. 573 («die nicht zu den Anhängern Jesu gehörige breite Masse des Volkes»); V. TAYLOR, *The Gospel according to St. Mark*, London, ²1966, p. 255; J.D. KINGSBURY, *The Parables of Jesus in Matthew 13. A Study in Redaction-Criticism*, London, 1969, p. 157, n. 228, estime que «in 4.11f., Mark states that Jesus spoke to the crowds in parables 'in order that' they may not see, hear or understand». Dans le même sens, H. RÄISÄNEN, *Die Parabeltheorie* (n. 15), p. 7; M.I. BOUCHER, *The Mysterious Parable. A Literary Study* (CBQ MS, 6), Washington, DC, 1977, pp. 56-57; J. MARCUS, *Mark 4:10-12* (n. 19), p. 560 («the general public»). Cette vue est explicitement rejetée par A. LOISY, *Les évangiles synoptiques*, I, Ceffonds, 1907, p. 742. Tout en étant d'une autre opinion, C. BREYTENBACH, *Nachfolge* (n. 11), p. 135, n. 9, constate: «ἐκεῖνοι οἱ ἔξω werden meistens mit dem Volk gleichgesetzt».

23. E. CUVILLIER, *Le concept de παραβολη* (n. 12), p. 108.

24. Str-B, II, ²1956, p. 7.

25. A. LOISY, *Les évangiles synoptiques* (n. 22), I, p. 742; W. MARXSEN, *Redaktionsgeschichtliche Erklärung* (n. 14), pp. 268-269 (= ID., *Der Exeget*, p. 25); T.W. MANSON, *The Purpose of the Parables: A Re-Examination of St. Mark 4,10-12*, in *ExpT* 68 (1956-57) 132-135, voir p. 133; D.E. NINEHAM, *The Gospel of St Mark* (The Pelican Gospel Commentaries), Baltimore, 1963, p. 135; E. LOHMEYER, *Das Evangelium nach Markus übersetzt und*

estime que cette interprétation est trop liée à une «konsequent redaktions-geschichtlichen Interpretation»[26]. Aussi bien, de nombreux auteurs estiment-ils que le rédacteur a en vue les adversaires de Jésus, soit une troisième catégorie bien différenciée par rapport aux disciples, d'une part, et à la foule, d'autre part[27]. Dans ce cadre, le rapprochement entre 3,20-35 et 4,10-12 est souvent mis en valeur, d'autant plus que la parenté des expressions est frappante: ἐκείνοις δὲ τοῖς ἔξω (4,11) fait penser à ἔξω στήκοντες (3,31) et ἔξω ζητοῦσίν σε (3,32), tandis que οἱ περὶ αὐτὸν

erklärt, Göttingen, [17]1967, p. 83; G. MINETTE DE TILLESSE, Le secret messianique dans l'évangile de Marc (LD, 47), Paris, 1968, pp. 176-177, s'appuyant à tort sur Gnilka qui exclut explicitement cette interprétation dans son commentaire (voir n. 26); W. GRUND-MANN, Das Evangelium nach Markus (THKNT, 2), Berlin, [3]1965, p. 92; E. SCHWEIZER, Markus (n. 15), p. 51; G. HAUFE, Erwägungen zum Ursprung der sogenannten Parabel-theorie Markus 4,11-12, in EvT 32 (1972) 413-421, voir p. 416; A.M. AMBROZIC, The Hidden Kingdom. A Redaction-Critical Study of the References to the Kingdom of God in Mark's Gospel (CBQ MS, 2), Washington, DC, 1972, pp. 53-72; R. PESCH, Das Marku-sevangelium, I, Freiburg, 1976, p. 238 (mais il ajoute que, dans le contexte de Mc, l'expression désigne les adversaires de Jésus mentionnés en 3,20ss.); J.R. KIRKLAND, The Earliest Understanding (n. 12), p. 5; V. FUSCO, Parola e Regno. La sezione delle para-bole (Mc. 4,1-34) nella prospettiva marciana (Aloisiana, 13), Brescia, 1980, pp. 224-229 (voir aussi ID., La section des paraboles. Mc 4,1-34, in J. DELORME [éd.], Les paraboles évangéliques. Perspectives nouvelles [LD, 135], Paris, 1989, pp. 219-234, voir 225).

26. J. GNILKA, Das Evangelium nach Markus, I, Mk 1-8,26 (EKK, II/1), Zürich-Ein-siedeln-Köln-Neukirchen-Vluyn, 1978, p. 165. M.A. BEAVIS, Mark's Audience (n. 3), p. 154, se refuse à trancher, lorsqu'elle écrit: «'Those outside' (v. 11) are those outside the kingdom of God, both in the narrative (Jewish leaders, Jesus' family and compatriots), and those outside the Marcan audience».

27. M.-J. LAGRANGE, Le but des paraboles d'après l'évangile selon saint Marc, in RB 7 (1910) 5-35, voir p. 26; J. GNILKA, Die Verstockung (n. 4), p. 85 (aussi ID., Markus [n. 26], p. 165); J. LAMBRECHT, De vijf parabels van Mc. 4. Structuur en theologie van de parabel-rede, in Bijdragen 29 (1968) 25-53, voir p. 37 (= ID., Marcus Interpretator. Stijl en bood-schap in Mc. 3,20-4,34, Brugge-Utrecht, 1969, pp. 101-134, voir p. 113); R. PESCH, Das Markusevangelium, I (n. 25), p. 238; H.J. KLAUCK, Allegorie (n. 11), p. 248, pour qui «ceux du dehors» regroupe les propres parents de Jésus (3,21), ses concitoyens (6,4), mais surtout les adversaires décidés de Jésus de différents groupes officiels ou semi-officiels du judaïsme, notamment les scribes et les grands-prêtres auxquels Mc dit explicitement à deux reprises que Jésus parle en paraboles (3,21; 12,1); C. BREYTENBACH, Nachfolge (n. 11), pp. 157, 159 et 188; D. LÜHRMANN, Das Markusevangelium (HNT, 3), Tübingen, 1987, pp. 86-87 (qui étend cependant la porté de l'expression à tous ceux qui refusent l'Évangile); C.M. TUCKETT, Mark's Concerns (n. 11), p. 14; B. VAN IERSEL, Reading Mark, Edinburgh, 1989, p. 81; H.-J. ECKSTEIN, Markus 10,46-52 als Schlüsseltext des Markusevangeliums, in ZNW 87 (1996) 33-50, voir p. 47. Pour sa part, J. COUTTS, «Those Outside» (Mark 4,10-12), in Studia Evangelica 2 (1964) 155-157, pense aussi aux adversaires de Jésus, mais c'est dans le cadre de son hypothèse suivant laquelle, primitivement, 4,10 aurait suivi 3,20-35 et non 4,1-9. Avec C. BREYTENBACH, Nachfolge (n. 11), p. 188, n. 357, je pense qu'il est trop restrictif d'identifier «ceux du dehors» à la famille de Jésus, comme le propose É. TROCMÉ, Why Parables? A Study of Mark IV, in BJRL 59 (1976-77) 458-471, voir pp. 462-463 et 465. J.-C. GIROUD, La parabole ou l'opacité incontournable: à propos de Mc 4,1-34, in J. DELORME (éd.), Les paraboles évangéliques. Perspectives nouvelles (LD, 135), Paris, 1989, pp. 235-246, voir p. 243, estime que «ceux du dehors» ne désigne pas les adversaires qui refusent, mais sa position n'est pas vraiment argumentée.

σὺν τοῖς δώδεκα (4,10) peut facilement être rapproché de ἐκάθητο περὶ αὐτὸν ὄχλος (3,32) et τοὺς περὶ αὐτὸν κύκλῳ καθημένους (3,34)[28].

3. Portée de la citation faite au v. 12

Le texte de Mc 4,12 diffère sensiblement du texte d'Is 6,9-10, tel qu'on le trouve dans le TM, la LXX et le Tg. D'abord, en Mc à l'inverse du texte d'Isaïe, le voir précède l'entendre. Ensuite, Mc ne mentionne pas le cœur, les oreilles et les yeux, à la différence du texte d'Isaïe où on les retrouve deux fois, avant et après μήποτε (פֶּן [TM], דלמא [Tg]). Aux impératifs qal du TM (שְׁמְעוּ et רְאוּ) correspondent des indicatifs futurs dans la LXX (ἀκούσετε et βλέψετε) et des participes introduits par ד (דשמען et וחזן) dans le Tg, alors que Mc a des subjonctifs introduits par ἵνα. Toutes ces différences font poser la question: de quel texte d'Isaïe Mc pouvait-il bien s'inspirer?

Il est devenu habituel, malgré toutes les différences relevées ci-dessus, d'affirmer qu'il s'agissait du texte du Tg[29]. Trois rapprochements sont, en effet, possibles, entre Mc 4,12 et le Tg. Premièrement, tous deux ont les verbes «voir, entendre, comprendre» à la 3ème personne du pluriel, tandis que le TM et la LXX les présentent à la 2ème personne dans un discours direct. Deuxièmement, comme le Tg, Mc utilise les participes βλέποντες et ἀκούοντες, alors que le TM a des impératifs. Il faut cependant remarquer que la LXX a aussi βλέποντες. Troisièmement, Mc n'a pas d'allusion à la guérison, comme dans le TM et la LXX; par contre, son καὶ ἀφεθῇ αὐτοῖς rappelle וישתביק להון du Tg. Il y a peut-être eu confusion entre les verbes hébreux רפא (guérir) et רפה (relâcher), verbe auquel le Tg a donné la forme passive (itpe'el). Mc l'aurait suivi sur ce point. C'est évidemment le point de rapprochement le plus fort entre les deux textes.

L'élément le plus controversé pour la compréhension du v. 12 de Mc est sans conteste le sens des conjonctions ἵνα et μήποτε. L'idée qu'on

---

28. À juste titre, V. Fusco, *Parola* (n. 25), p. 228, souligne que «le notazioni spaziali assumono una dimensione simbolico-spirituale: il gruppo che resta fuori è il parentado incredulo». Et il ajoute: «Questo parallelismo tra le due pericopi contigue (3,20-35 e 4,1-34) conferma ulteriormente che la contrapposizione in gioco è quella fra credenti e non credenti». E. Cuvillier, *Le concept de παραβολη* (n. 12), pp. 90-91, souligne bien que la thématique περὶ αὐτόν / ἔξω est propre à Mc et absente chez Mt et Lc.

29. Voir une liste des auteurs dans C.A. Evans, *The Function of Isaiah 6:9-10 in Mark and John*, in *NT* 24 (1982) 124-138, voir p. 127, n. 10. Cet auteur relève aussi trois rapprochements avec le Tg, mais nous différons sur le deuxième. Evans ne parle pas des participes, mais affirme que, comme dans le Tg, les verbes sont à l'indicatif au lieu de l'impératif; en fait, les verbes de Mc sont au subjonctif.

pourrait comprendre la phrase introduite par ἵνα comme une pointe ironique soit de Jésus[30], soit de l'évangéliste[31] n'a pratiquement pas rencontré d'écho. L'immense majorité des exégètes donne à ἵνα le sens final, qui paraît grammaticalement le plus obvie[32]. La suggestion de sous-entendre πληρωθῇ derrière ἵνα et de lire le v. 12 comme une citation d'accomplissement n'est plus guère suivie aujourd'hui[33]. Ceux pour qui le sens final ne paraît guère acceptable ont risqué d'autres solutions. Par exemple, comme la particule ד utilisée dans le Tg peut introduire soit une phrase finale, soit une phrase relative, l'hypothèse a été émise que Mc 4,12 résulterait d'une mauvaise compréhension des paroles dites par Jésus. Celui-ci aurait dit approximativement: ἐκείνοις δὲ τοῖς ἔξω ἐν παραβολαῖς τὰ πάντα γίνεται, οἳ βλέποντες βλέπουσιν καὶ οὐκ οἴδασιν, καὶ ἀκούοντες ἀκούουσιν καὶ οὐ συνίουσιν, μήποτε ἐπιστρέψωσιν καὶ ἀφεθῇ αὐτοῖς. Dans ce cas, Jésus aurait fait de la dureté de cœur la cause de la non-compréhension des paraboles, tandis que Marc aurait fait de cette dernière le but poursuivi par Jésus[34]. Cette hypothèse est restée isolée. Sur base du grec de la Koinè, certains veulent donner à ἵνα un sens consécutif[35], causal[36] ou explicatif[37].

30. C.A. MOORE, *Mark 4.12: More Like the Irony of Micaiah than Isaiah*, in H.N. BREAM – R.D. HEIM – C.A. MOORE (éd.), *A Light unto My Path*. FS J.M. Myers (Gettysbury Theological Studies, 4), Philadelphia, PA, 1974, pp. 336-344, cité par M.A. BEAVIS, *Mark's Audience* (n. 3), p. 212, n. 88.

31. L.W. HURTADO, *Mark* (A Good News Commentary), San Francisco, 1983, pp. 59-60.

32. Voir en ce sens toutes les traductions de la Bible. Sans vouloir être exhaustif, aux auteurs cités par J. GNILKA, *Die Verstockung* (n. 4), p. 47, n. 17, j'ajouterais: H.-J. KLAUCK, *Allegorie* (n. 11), p. 250; V. FUSCO, *Parola* (n. 25), pp. 243-246 (voir ID., *La fonction* [n. 25], p. 230); C.A. EVANS, *The Function* (n. 29), pp. 130-132; C.M. TUCKETT, *Mark's Concerns* (n. 11), p. 19; M.A. BEAVIS, *Mark's Audience* (n. 3), pp. 78-81; E. CUVILLIER, *Le concept de παραβολη* (n. 12), p. 105.

33. Voir ci-dessous, p. 170, n. 91.

34. T.W. MANSON, *The Teaching of Jesus. Studies in its Form and Content*, Cambridge, 1951, pp. 78-79. Bien qu'il la juge de prime abord attirante, M. BLACK, *An Aramaic Approach to the Gospels and Acts*, Oxford, ³1967, pp. 212-216, opte en définitive pour le sens final, plus compatible, à son avis, avec l'ensemble du texte de Mc.

35. H. PERNOT, *Études sur la langue des évangiles*, Paris, 1927, pp. 90-91; A. CHARUE, *L'incrédulité des Juifs dans le Nouveau Testament. Étude historique, exégétique et théologique*, Gembloux, 1929, pp. 139-140; C.H. PEISKER, *Konsekutives ἵνα in Markus 4,12*, in *ZNW* 59 (1968) 126-127; A. SUHL, *Die Funktion* (n. 19), pp. 149-150, qui parle, à la suite de Bl.-Debr. §391,5 d'une «Verwischung des Unterschieds zwischen Absicht und Folge».

36. A.T. ROBINSON, *The Causal Use of ἵνα*, in S.J. CASE (ed.), *Studies in Early Christianity*. FS F.C. Porter – B.W. Bacon, New York – London, 1928, pp. 51-57; T.A. SINCLAIR, *Note on an Apparent Mistranslation (Mk. 4:12)*, in *BibT* 5 (1954) 18; E. LOHMEYER, *Markus* (n. 25), pp. 83-84. Par contre, H. WINDISCH, *Die Verstockungsidee in Mc 4,12 und das kausale der späteren Koine*, in *ZNW* 26 (1927) 203-209, n'est pas favorable à cette interprétation.

37. P. LAMPE, *Die markinische Deutung* (n. 19), p. 141-142; D. LÜHRMANN, *Das Markusevangelium* (n. 27), p. 86; R. PESCH, *Das Markusevangelium*, I (n. 25), p. 239. Cette interprétation est rejetée par C.M. TUCKETT, *Mark's Concern* (n. 11), p. 19, car «the combination of both the ἵνα and the μήποτε together does seem to suggest a final meaning».

Mais ces propositions sont le plus souvent jugées comme des tentatives désespérées pour échapper au sens final qui reste le plus probable.

Ceux qui donnent un sens final à ἵνα comprennent μήποτε dans la même ligne, comme introduisant une intentionalité négative: «de peur que»[38]. Cependant il y a plus d'hésitation en ce qui concerne l'interprétation de μήποτε. Comme Mc semble bien s'être inspiré du Tg et que דלמא peut avoir le sens de «à moins que» ou «peut-être», un certain nombre d'auteurs, à la suite de T.W. Manson et J. Jeremias, sont favorables au sens conditionnel («à moins que»)[39]. La critique la plus forte à cette position est que ce sens n'est pas attesté pour μήποτε dans la Koinè[40]. Par contre, l'attestation de μήποτε dans un sens dubitatif («peut-être») se retrouve dans la Koinè. Cette interprétation a, dès lors, la faveur également d'exégètes qui récusent le recours au Tg pour interpréter μήποτε[41]. Elle a une certaine plausibilité, même si le sens final est le plus couramment admis. Les subjonctifs qui suivent μήποτε plaident peut-être en faveur du sens dubitatif. En effet, ils sont d'autant plus frappants que le seul autre emploi de μήποτε en Mc 14,2, au sens final cette fois, est suivi d'un indicatif futur[42].

Finalement, quant au sens, le v. 12 est le plus souvent perçu comme exprimant une finalité. Mais la façon suivant laquelle cette intentionalité est comprise varie: soit il s'agit de la présentation par Jésus du but de son ministère ou, à tout le moins, de sa prédication en paraboles[43], soit il s'agit

38. L'immense majorité des auteurs va dans ce sens, ainsi que les traductions des Bibles. Parmi les auteurs récents, voir notamment J. GNILKA, *Die Verstockung* (n.4), p. 49; H. RÄISÄNEN, *Die Parabeltheorie* (n. 15), p. 15; H.-J. KLAUCK, *Allegorie* (n. 11), p. 250; V. FUSCO, *Parola* (n. 25), pp. 246-250 (voir ID., *La section* [n. 25], p. 230); C.A. EVANS, *The Function* (n. 29), p. 130; C.M. TUCKETT, *Mark's Concern* (n. 11), p. 19. Par contre, C. BREYTENBACH, *Nachfolge* (n. 11), p. 160-163, s'oppose à cette interprétation.

39. J. JEREMIAS, *Die Gleichnisse* (n. 10), p. 13, qui se base notamment sur l'exégèse rabbinique qui interprète Is 6,10 comme une promesse de pardon; T.W. MANSON, *The Teaching* (n. 34), p. 78; W. MARXSEN, *Redaktionsgeschichtliche Erklärung* (n. 14), p. 269 (= *Der Exeget*, pp. 25-26); J. KIRKLAND, *The Earliest Understanding* (n. 12), p. 7; D. LÜHRMANN, *Das Markusevangelium* (n. 27), p. 87.

40. H. RÄISÄNEN, *Die Parabeltheorie* (n. 15), p. 15.

41. Cette interprétation est jugée possible par T.W. MANSON, *The Teaching* (n. 34), p. 79. Elle est reprise par E. LOHMEYER, *Markus* (n. 25), p. 83; P. LAMPE, *Die markinische Deutung* (n. 19), p. 143: «μήποτε ist hier das dubitative μή (durch ποτε verstärkt), das eine indirekte Frage einleitet». Cette possibilité est confirmée par Bl.-Debr. §370,3, même si Mc 4,12 n'est pas cité en exemple. C'est la solution que préfère C. BREYTENBACH, *Nachfolge* (n. 11), p. 161, car l'omission en Mc 4,12 de Is 6,10a-b altère le lien entre Mc 4,12c et 12d.

42. Bien que non permise en grec classique, cette tournure est plusieurs fois attestée dans le N.T. (Bl.-Debr. §369,2). L'objection la plus forte à la lecture de μήποτε dans un sens dubitatif réside dans le fait que cette conjonction vienne à la suite de ἵνα.

43. Voir, notamment, C.A. EVANS, *A Note on the Function of Isaiah, VI,9-10 in Mark, IV*, in *RB* 88 (1981) 234-235; ID., *The Function* (n. 29), pp. 137-138.

de l'intention de Dieu[44]. Les exégètes suggèrent alors que la pensée prédestinationiste sous-jacente ne posait pas problème à Mc et à ses premiers lecteurs[45]. Ou encore, ils montrent qu'une telle pensée est dans l'esprit du temps
et qu'on en retrouve la trace, par exemple, à Qumrân[46]. Le but poursuivi
par Mc est alors le plus souvent perçu comme une tentative pour expliquer
le scandale du rejet par Israël de Jésus et des chrétiens[47], et même, plus précisément, comme une réponse directe à la question que la communauté de
Mc se pose dans un contexte de persécution[48]. Les auteurs qui récusent la
portée finale de ἵνα et μήποτε proposent une autre interprétation: le texte
d'Isaïe ne viserait pas à faire saisir le but poursuivi par Jésus lorsqu'il parle
en paraboles; il définirait plutôt ce qui empêche un être humain de devenir
apte à recevoir le mystère du Royaume et donc de se convertir[49].

II. Analyse littéraire

Il n'est pas rare que les commentateurs de Mc 4,10-12 interprètent ces
versets comme exprimant dans le chef de Jésus la volonté d'une communication réservée à des auditeurs sélectionnés, en quelque sorte prédestinés,
puisque la citation d'Is 6,9-10 exprimerait à cet égard la volonté divine[50].

---

44. Ainsi, par exemple, V. Fusco, *La fonction* (n. 25), p. 230.
45. M.A. Beavis, *Mark's Audience* (n. 3), pp. 148-151.
46. J. Marcus, *Mark 4:10-12* (n. 19), pp. 561-562.
47. U. Luz, *Das Evangelium nach Matthäus* II (EKK I/2), Zürich – Braunschweig –
Neukirchen-Vluyn, 1990, p. 312.
48. J. Marcus, *Mark 4:10-12* (n. 19), pp. 572-573.
49. T.W. Manson, *The Teaching* (n. 34), pp. 78-79: «The quotation from Isaiah is not
introduced by Jesus to explain the purpose of teaching in parables, but to illustrate what
is meant by οἱ ἔξω: it is in fact a definition of the sort of character which prevents a man
from becoming one of those to whom the secret of the Kingdom is given, a description in
language borrowed from the Jewish Bible of those people who did not produce the things
for which Jesus was constantly seeking – insight, repentance, and faith».
50. Ainsi, par exemple, H. Anderson, *The Old Testament in Mark's Gospel*, in J.M.
Efird (ed.), *The Use of the Old Testament in the New and Other Essays*. FS W.F. Stinespring, Durham, NC, 1972, pp. 280-306, voir p. 297, n'hésite pas à écrire: «Mark 4:12
echoes the words of Isa. 6:9-10, which describe those people whose sin and ignorance
make it impossible for them to absorb the word of God through the prophet and who are
in fact condemned by it. In Mark's view verses 10-12 appear then to regard the teaching
of Jesus in parables as a means of carrying over God's will and design toward the ultimate division between those who are not destined for salvation and so cannot bear the
truth, and the elect to whom the mystery of the kingdom is revealed». Par contre, B.
Standaert, *L'évangile selon Marc. Composition et genre littéraire*, Brugge, 1978, p.
218, n. 1: «Il est clair que pour Marc Jésus ne cherche pas à voiler sa pensée au moyen
des paraboles. Si donc l'expression 'théorie parabolique' implique l'idée que le Jésus de
Marc cache intentionnellement et systématiquement sa pensée par le procédé des paraboles, il faut dire qu'il n'y a pas de 'théorie parabolique' dans le second évangile».

Les paraboles apparaissent dès lors comme une sorte de piège éliminant les foules loin du mystère du Royaume de Dieu. Cette image des foules comme destinataires des paraboles et des disciples comme destinataires du sens est la plupart du temps rejetée dans l'exégèse historico-critique récente[51]. Elle est souvent jugée simpliste par ceux qui abordent le texte dans une perspective structurale[52].

Pour ma part, une telle vision d'une théorie parabolique me paraît négliger plusieurs faits pourtant éclairants. D'abord elle place la responsabilité de cet état de choses du côté de l'instance d'émission, à savoir Jésus, alors que, dans le contexte, l'accent est mis sur l'instance de réception. Ensuite, elle prête trop peu d'attention à la recontextualisation que Mc opère de la citation d'Isaïe; plutôt que d'une théorie générale, il s'agit en 4,10-12 d'une réflexion de type métalinguistique sur la communication parabolique de la parole où on «explique pourquoi Jésus parle en paraboles et pourquoi ce genre particulier est le seul mode de discours qui puisse annoncer le Royaume des Cieux aux hommes»[53]. Enfin, l'idée d'un piège destiné à enfermer les foules dans l'incompréhension et la non-conversion semble exclue dans le contexte par 4,33 où le narrateur précise que Jésus «leur parlait la parole par de nombreuses paraboles semblables καθὼς ἠδύναντο ἀκούειν»[54]. Mon hypothèse sera que le texte de 4,1-34 élabore une réflexion sur le sort de la parole divine (mystère du Royaume de Dieu) et sur la capacité à l'entendre. C'est un élément clé d'un évangile qui opère un décodage de l'avenir de la parole divine (mystère du royaume de Dieu), en ce compris l'avenir non seulement des personnes qui l'entendent, mais aussi de celui qui dit, prononce cette parole.

Pour clarifier le sens de 4,10-12, il importe d'analyser d'abord le fonctionnement de ces versets dans le contexte du chapitre 4 de Mc, appelé

---

51. C. BREYTENBACH, *Nachfolge* (n. 11), p. 159: «Daß im Markusevangelium τοῖς ἔξω nicht auf das Volk referiert, sondern ein Ausdruck für diejenigen ist, die die Botschaft und Person Jesu ablehnen, ist in der neueren Forschung deutlich herausgestellt worden und braucht nicht noch einmal nachgewiesen zu werden».

52. Ainsi C. MELLON, *La parabole, manière de parler, manière d'entendre*, in C. CHABROL – L. MARIN (éd.), *Le récit évangélique* (Bibliothèque de Sciences Religieuses), Paris, 1974, pp. 147-161, voir p. 147; F. MARTIN, *Parler. Matthieu 13*, in *SémBib* nº 52 (1988) 17-34, voir pp. 17-18.

53. F. MARTIN, *Parler* (n. 52), p. 17. D. MARGUERAT, *La construction du lecteur* (n. 4), p. 254, note: «Marc ne s'interroge pas sur la coupure entre l'Église et Israël, mais sur la parabole comme mode de communication de la parole. (...) C'est le processus de communication de l'Évangile qui intéresse ici Marc».

54. On ne retrouve pas cette précision dans le texte parallèle, en Mt 13,34. Mais, au v. 35, Mt ajoute une citation du Ps 78,2 précisant que parler en paraboles aux foules revient à proclamer des choses cachées depuis la fondation du monde.

chapitre des paraboles, et particulièrement dans son contexte immédiat (4,1-20). Il convient ensuite d'élargir la perspective pour examiner le rapport des vv. 10-12 avec l'ensemble de l'évangile.

1. Rôle des vv. 10-12 dans Mc 4,1-34

a. La place des vv. 10-12 dans la structure de Mc 4,1-34

La structure concentrique de ce passage a été souvent mise en valeur par les approches de type rhétorique surtout. Je la vois comme suit[55]:

```
A  Introduction (vv.1-2)
      B  Parabole et mystère du Royaume de Dieu (vv. 3-20)
                  a  Parabole de celui qui sème le grain (vv. 3-9)
                    b  Mystère et paraboles (vv. 10-12)
                  a'  Parabole de celui qui sème la parole (vv. 13-20)
            C  Images de la manifestation et de la réception (vv. 21-25)
                  a  La lampe (vv. 21-23)
                  b  La mesure (vv. 24-25)
      B'  Deux paraboles du Royaume de Dieu (vv. 26-32)
                  a  Le grain qui pousse tout seul (vv. 26-29)
                  b  Le grain de sénevé (vv. 30-32)
A'  Conclusion (vv. 33-34)
```

Par ailleurs, d'un autre point de vue et pour faciliter l'analyse, il n'est pas inutile de distinguer les divers niveaux d'énonciation[56] dans le texte.

---

55. Le découpage correspond à celui que propose B. STANDAERT, *Marc* (n. 50), p. 209. On trouve déjà une proposition très proche chez J. LAMBRECHT, *Redaction* (n. 17), pp. 269-308, voir p. 303; la seule différence est qu'il propose pour le point central C trois parties et non deux: «a) Lamp (vv. 21-22), b) Exhortation to listen (vv. 23-24a), c) Measure (vv. 24b-25)». Il distingue mieux de cette manière les deux rappels du codage qui sépare les deux paroles imagées. Mais faut-il pour autant faire de ces vv. 23-24a le centre du centre de la structure? On retrouve la division en cinq parties découpées de la même façon dans l'hypothèse d'une structure concentrique proposée par J. DEWEY, *Markan Public Debate*, p. 150. Les cinq parties proposées par B. VAN IERSEL, *Reading Mark* (n. 27), p. 70, sont différentes (A vv. 1-2, B vv. 3-9, C vv. 10-20 et 21-25, B' vv. 26-32, A' vv. 33-34); ce découpage basé sur la distinction entre l'enseignement de Jésus aux foules et son enseignement privé me paraît beaucoup moins convaincant. Quant à M.A. BEAVIS, *Mark's Audience* (n. 3), p. 134, elle porte un jugement caricatural sur ces recherches de structure concentrique, lorsqu'elle affirme: «Attempts to find a concentric structure in Mark 4, then, do little more than prove that it has a beginning, a middle and an ending». Elle juge, à tort, je pense, qu'une structure inspirée du modèle rabbinique (enseignement public, question de disciples, explication en privé), inspiré d'un schème prophético-apocalyptique présent dans l'A.T. et les pseudépigraphes, rend mieux compte de Mc 4 (voir pp. 134-136).

56. I. ALMEIDA, *L'opérativité sémantique des récits-paraboles. Sémiotique narrative et textuelle. Herméneutique du discours religieux* (Bibliothèque des cahiers de l'institut de linguistique de Louvain, 13), Leuven – Paris, 1978, p. 211: «En disant qu'un récit-parabole se situe à l'intérieur d'un discours prononcé par un personnage d'un autre récit,

Il est aisé d'en repérer au moins trois, ce qu'a fait J. Delorme dont je m'inspire dans la présentation du tableau suivant[57]:

Récit 1
     Discours
         Récit 2

1 Καὶ πάλιν ἤρξατο διδάσκειν παρὰ τὴν θάλασσαν· καὶ συνάγεται πρὸς αὐτὸν ὄχλος πλεῖστος, ὥστε αὐτὸν εἰς πλοῖον ἐμβάντα καθῆσθαι ἐν τῇ θαλάσσῃ, καὶ πᾶς ὁ ὄχλος πρὸς τὴν θάλασσαν ἐπὶ τῆς γῆς ἦσαν. 2 καὶ ἐδίδασκεν αὐτοὺς ἐν παραβολαῖς πολλά καὶ ἔλεγεν αὐτοῖς ἐν τῇ διδαχῇ αὐτοῦ,
     3 Ἀκούετε.
         ἰδοὺ ἐξῆλθεν ὁ σπείρων σπεῖραι. 4 καὶ ἐγένετο ἐν τῷ σπείρειν ὃ μὲν ἔπεσεν παρὰ τὴν ὁδόν, καὶ ἦλθεν τὰ πετεινὰ καὶ κατέφαγεν αὐτό. 5 καὶ ἄλλο ἔπεσεν ἐπὶ τὸ πετρῶδες ὅπου οὐκ εἶχεν γῆν πολλήν, καὶ εὐθὺς ἐξανέτειλεν διὰ τὸ μὴ ἔχειν βάθος γῆς· 6 καὶ ὅτε ἀνέτειλεν ὁ ἥλιος ἐκαυματίσθη καὶ διὰ τὸ μὴ ἔχειν ῥίζαν ἐξηράνθη. 7 καὶ ἄλλο ἔπεσεν εἰς τὰς ἀκάνθας, καὶ ἀνέβησαν αἱ ἄκανθαι καὶ συνέπνιξαν αὐτό, καὶ καρπὸν οὐκ ἔδωκεν. 8 καὶ ἄλλα ἔπεσεν εἰς τὴν γῆν τὴν καλήν καὶ ἐδίδου καρπὸν ἀναβαίνοντα καὶ αὐξανόμενα καὶ ἔφερεν ἐν τριάκοντα καὶ ἐν ἑξήκοντα καὶ ἐν ἑκατόν.
9 καὶ ἔλεγεν,
     Ὃς ἔχει ὦτα ἀκούειν ἀκουέτω.
10 Καὶ ὅτε ἐγένετο κατὰ μόνας, ἠρώτων αὐτὸν οἱ περὶ αὐτὸν σὺν τοῖς δώδεκα τὰς παραβολάς. 11 καὶ ἔλεγεν αὐτοῖς,
     Ὑμῖν τὸ μυστήριον δέδοται τῆς βασιλείας τοῦ θεοῦ· ἐκείνοις δὲ τοῖς ἔξω ἐν παραβολαῖς τὰ πάντα γίνεται, 12 ἵνα βλέποντες βλέπωσιν καὶ μὴ ἴδωσιν, καὶ ἀκούοντες ἀκούωσιν καὶ μὴ συνιῶσιν, μήποτε ἐπιστρέψωσιν καὶ ἀφεθῇ αὐτοῖς.
13 Καὶ λέγει αὐτοῖς,
     οὐκ οἴδατε τὴν παραβολὴν ταύτην, καὶ πῶς πάσας τὰς παραβολὰς γνώσεσθε;
         14 ὁ σπείρων τὸν λόγον σπείρει. 15 οὗτοι δέ εἰσιν οἱ παρὰ τὴν ὁδόν· ὅπου σπείρεται ὁ λόγος, καὶ ὅταν ἀκούσωσιν, εὐθὺς ἔρχεται ὁ Σατανᾶς καὶ αἴρει τὸν λόγον τὸν ἐσπαρμένον εἰς αὐτούς. 16 καὶ οὗτοί εἰσιν οἱ ἐπὶ τὰ πετρώδη σπειρόμενοι, οἳ ὅταν ἀκούσωσιν τὸν λόγον εὐθὺς

appelé primaire ou principal, nous supposons l'existence de plusieurs circuits ou instances d'intégration discursive qui s'enchâssent les unes dans les autres (…). Chacune de ces instances suppose un système de relations qui correspondent à ce que l'on appelle le *fait d'énonciation*, par lequel chaque instance s'incorpore à celle qui lui est immédiatement supérieure». À la p. 212, Almeida propose un tableau mettant en valeur par des cercles l'enchâssement des différentes instances.
     57. J. DELORME, *La communication parabolique d'après Marc 4*, in *SémBib* n° 48 (1987) 1-17, voir pp. 2-4. Je le corrige pour le v. 26a qui a été malencontreusement placé en retrait.

μετὰ χαρᾶς λαμβάνουσιν αὐτόν, 17 καὶ οὐκ ἔχουσιν ῥίζαν
ἐν ἑαυτοῖς ἀλλὰ πρόσκαιροί εἰσιν, εἶτα γενομένης θλίψε-
ως ἢ διωγμοῦ διὰ τὸν λόγον εὐθὺς σκανδαλίζονται. 18 καὶ
ἄλλοι εἰσὶν οἱ εἰς τὰς ἀκάνθας σπειρόμενοι· οὗτοί εἰσιν
οἱ τὸν λόγον ἀκούσαντες, 19 καὶ αἱ μέριμναι τοῦ αἰῶνος
καὶ ἡ ἀπάτη τοῦ πλούτου καὶ αἱ περὶ τὰ λοιπὰ ἐπιθυμίαι
εἰσπορευόμεναι συμπνίγουσιν τὸν λόγον καὶ ἄκαρπος
γίνεται. 20 καὶ ἐκεῖνοί εἰσιν οἱ ἐπὶ τὴν γῆν τὴν καλὴν
σπαρέντες, οἵτινες ἀκούουσιν τὸν λόγον καὶ παραδέχον-
ται καὶ καρποφοροῦσιν ἓν τριάκοντα καὶ ἓν ἑξήκοντα καὶ
ἓν ἑκατόν.
21 Καὶ ἔλεγεν αὐτοῖς,
    μήτι ἔρχεται ὁ λύχνος ἵνα ὑπὸ τὸν μόδιον τεθῇ ἢ ὑπὸ τὴν κλίνην;
    οὐχ ἵνα ἐπὶ τὴν λυχνίαν τεθῇ;
    22 οὐ γάρ ἐστιν κρυπτὸν ἐὰν μὴ ἵνα φανερωθῇ, οὐδὲ ἐγένετο ἀπό-
    κρυφον ἀλλ᾽ ἵνα ἔλθῃ εἰς φανερόν.
    23 εἴ τις ἔχει ὦτα ἀκούειν ἀκουέτω.
24 Καὶ ἔλεγεν αὐτοῖς,
    βλέπετε τί ἀκούετε.
    ἐν ᾧ μέτρῳ μετρεῖτε μετρηθήσεται ὑμῖν καὶ προστεθήσεται ὑμῖν.
    25 ὃς γὰρ ἔχει, δοθήσεται αὐτῷ· καὶ ὃς οὐκ ἔχει, καὶ ὃ ἔχει ἀρθή-
    σεται ἀπ᾽ αὐτοῦ.
26 Καὶ ἔλεγεν,
    οὕτως ἐστὶν ἡ βασιλεία τοῦ θεοῦ ὡς ἄνθρωπος βάλῃ τὸν σπόρον
    ἐπὶ τῆς γῆς 27 καὶ καθεύδῃ καὶ ἐγείρηται νύκτα καὶ ἡμέραν, καὶ ὁ
    σπόρος βλαστᾷ καὶ μηκύνηται ὡς οὐκ οἶδεν αὐτός. 28 αὐτομάτη ἡ
    γῆ καρποφορεῖ, πρῶτον χόρτον εἶτα στάχυν εἶτα πλήρη[ς] σῖτον
    ἐν τῷ στάχυϊ. 29 ὅταν δὲ παραδοῖ ὁ καρπός, εὐθὺς ἀποστέλλει τὸ
    δρέπανον, ὅτι παρέστηκεν ὁ θερισμός.
30 Καὶ ἔλεγεν,
    πῶς ὁμοιώσωμεν τὴν βασιλείαν τοῦ θεοῦ ἢ ἐν τίνι αὐτὴν παρα-
    βολῇ θῶμεν; 31 ὡς κόκκῳ σινάπεως, ὃς ὅταν σπαρῇ ἐπὶ τῆς γῆς,
    μικρότερον ὂν πάντων τῶν σπερμάτων τῶν ἐπὶ τῆς γῆς, 32 καὶ
    ὅταν σπαρῇ, ἀναβαίνει καὶ γίνεται μεῖζον πάντων τῶν λαχάνων
    καὶ ποιεῖ κλάδους μεγάλους, ὥστε δύνασθαι ὑπὸ τὴν σκιὰν αὐτοῦ
    τὰ πετεινὰ τοῦ οὐρανοῦ κατασκηνοῦν.
33 Καὶ τοιαύταις παραβολαῖς πολλαῖς ἐλάλει αὐτοῖς τὸν λόγον καθὼς
ἠδύναντο ἀκούειν· 34 χωρὶς δὲ παραβολῆς οὐκ ἐλάλει αὐτοῖς, κατ᾽ ἰδίαν
δὲ τοῖς ἰδίοις μαθηταῖς ἐπέλυεν πάντα.

Si on reprend les trois grandes catégories de texte ainsi distinguées, il
est possible de faire quelques constatations sur chacune d'elles.
– Le récit primaire (R1) raconte à la troisième personne les actions de
  Jésus et des autres acteurs de l'évangile. Outre l'introduction et la conclusion (vv. 1-2a.33-34), il est composé des formules introduisant diverses parties de discours toujours tenu par Jésus (vv. 2b.9a.11a.13a.21a.
  24a.26a.30a) et de la mise en scène d'une question générale posée par
  les disciples à l'écart (v. 10).

– Un récit dans le récit (R2a) narré par un acteur du R1 et mettant en scène
des acteurs nouveaux, différents de ceux du R1. Ce récit-parabole du
semeur (vv. 3b-8) est encadré de deux appels à entendre (vv. 3a.9b)
qui sont comme des affirmations d'un codage. Dans les vv. 14-20 on
lit un nouveau récit-parabole (R2b) provoqué par une question d'une
partie de l'auditoire et précédé lui aussi d'une affirmation du codage
(v. 13b). Il ne s'agit pas d'une explication, d'un déchiffrement en clair
de la parabole première (v. 3b-8), comme si celle-ci n'était pas déjà
claire[58]. Il s'agit plutôt d'une transposition d'une parabole du semeur
de grain à une parabole du semeur de parole, transposition à l'occasion de laquelle l'accent est mis sur l'instance de réception (ἀκούω).
– Le reste relève du discours de Jésus, acteur principal du R1 et chaque
morceau est introduit par une des formules d'introduction relevées ci-
dessus. Il s'agit d'abord des vv. 3a et 9b qui, sous forme d'exhortation
à entendre, affirment le codage, tout en encadrant le R2a. Les vv. 11b-
12 explicitent le codage et en donnent une justification. Au v. 13b, le
codage est à nouveau affirmé, bien que sur le mode interrogatif, et
cela introduit le R2b. Les vv. 21b-22 et 24c-25 offrent deux paroles
imagées suivies d'une réflexion de type proverbial introduite par γάρ;
la première est suivie d'une affirmation du codage (v. 23) qui ressemble
à celle du v. 9b, tandis qu'une autre affirmation du codage, proche
cette fois du v. 3a, précède la seconde parole imagée au v. 24b. Enfin,
le discours se termine par deux comparaisons du Royaume de Dieu:
la première (vv. 26b-29) est introduite par une formule curieuse
(οὕτως…ὡς) insistant sur le codage, tandis que la seconde est introduite par une question à la première personne du pluriel qui semble
impliquer les destinataires dans le codage (vv. 30b-32).

b. Les deux groupes des vv. 10-12 par rapport au «parler en paraboles»

La structure concentrique met les vv. 10-12 en relief comme charnière
entre les deux récits-paraboles du semeur[59]. Le tableau des divers niveaux

---

58. Ceci est bien mis en valeur par I. ALMEIDA, *La structure conversationnelle de la
parabole*, in J. DELORME (éd.), *Parole – figure – parabole*, Lyon, 1987, pp. 61-84, voir p.
68: «Le premier récit est, pour ainsi dire, clair et unilinéaire, c'est la soi-disant 'explication' qui apparaît métaphorique». Dans un décodage on aurait, par exemple, dû préciser
qui était le semeur. On a un bon exemple de décodage au sens strict dans l'explication de
la parabole de l'ivraie en Mt 13,36-43. Par contre, dans le même chapitre 13 de Mt, la soi-
disant explication de la parabole du semeur est introduite par Ὑμεῖς οὖν ἀκούσατε τὴν
παραβολὴν τοῦ σπείραντος (v. 18).

59. Dans ce cadre, on s'interdit toute interprétation qui détacherait les vv. 10-12 de leur
contexte, comme celle proposée, par exemple, par E.F. SIEGMAN, *Teaching in Parables (Mk
4,10-12; Lk 8,9-10; Mt 13,10-15)*, in *CBQ* 23 (1961) 161-181, selon qui «it is commonly

d'énonciation, tout en respectant ce rôle de charnière, permet de distinguer dans ces versets ce qui relève du récit primaire (vv. 10-11a) ou du discours (vv. 11b-12). Dans ce discours, il est question de «mystère donné» et de ce qui «arrive en paraboles». Autrement dit, on a affaire à un discours métalinguistique offrant une réflexion sur ce qui se passe dans le parler en paraboles[60]. Il ne s'agit pas d'un simple retour au récit primaire, mais d'un effort pour articuler les paraboles avec les acteurs de ce récit primaire. C'est au cœur de cette réflexion métalinguistique qu'apparaît une allusion à Is 6,9-10 permettant d'illustrer l'attitude de «ceux du dehors» à qui tout arrive en paraboles et dont la non-conversion atteste la non-compréhension.

S'il en est ainsi, il importe d'abord de préciser le sens des mots ἐκείνοις τοῖς ἔξω. Dans le cadre de l'analyse historico-critique, nous l'avons vu, la solution la plus couramment admise est que le rédacteur vise les adversaires de Jésus, catégorie à ne pas confondre avec la foule[61].

Du point de vue de l'analyse littéraire, cette dernière solution paraît la plus respectueuse du contexte de Mc. Cependant, M.-J. Lagrange attirait déjà l'attention sur un fait important, lorsqu'il écrivait à propos de ἐκείνοις τοῖς ἔξω: «Jésus nomme ainsi ceux qui ne sont pas des siens, qui ne montrent pour sa doctrine que de l'hostilité, de l'indifférence ou une curiosité toute profane. Ce ne sont pas ceux qui sont sur le rivage, par opposition à ceux qui sont dans la barque, répartition de pure circonstance, car ici il est question d'une répartition de principes»[62]. Plus explicitement, je pense qu'il ne s'agit pas tellement de désigner par cette expression une catégorie précise d'acteurs appartenant au récit principal, mais bien d'introduire une distinction métalinguistique entre deux catégories d'auditeurs ne recoupant pas les distinctions narratives. D'ailleurs la catégorie opposée à ἐκείνοις τοῖς ἔξω ne recouvre pas davantage un groupe clairement identifié d'acteurs auquel on ferait allusion ailleurs

recognized that Mk 4,11-12 is a logion without a real connection with its present context» (p. 162). Une des thèses essentielles de M.A. BEAVIS, *Mark's Audience* (n. 3), est de défendre, contre Schweizer, Weeden, Räisänen, l'idée que le ch. 4 de Mc est structuré autour des vv. 11-12, dont les thèmes s'accordent bien avec le reste de l'évangile.

60. F. MARTIN, *Parler* (n. 52), p. 17, estime qu'il s'agit d'un passage où le narrateur «fait retour sur les conditions et les effets de la communication parabolique pour y mener une réflexion de type métalinguistique».

61. Voir ci-dessus, pp. 149-151.

62. M.J. LAGRANGE, *Le but* (n. 27), p. 26. C.F.D. MOULE, *Mark 4,1-20 Yet Once More*, in E.E. ELLIS – M. WILCOX (eds.), *Neotestamentica et Semitica*. FS M. Black, Edinburgh, 1969, pp. 95-113, voir 99, semble s'orienter dans la même direction, lorsqu'il écrit: «In short, there is nothing to prevent our regarding the two positions – namely, 'inside'... and 'outside' – as descriptions merely of the result of ways of responding to parables on a given occasion».

dans l'évangile. Tout se passe comme si, en utilisant une expression un peu complexe (οἱ περὶ αὐτὸν σὺν τοῖς δώδεκα) et non, par exemple, son terme favori οἱ μαθηταί, Mc voulait attirer l'attention du lecteur: on n'est pas en présence des divisions habituelles[63]. À travers cette expression sont visés ceux qui ont une attitude positive envers l'enseignement de Jésus et cela ne recouvre pas adéquatement un seul des groupes du récit évangélique principal. Dès lors, l'impression d'une certaine imprécision quant à la délimitation des groupes est tout à fait normale[64].

La situation peut se résumer dans le tableau suivant où, dans la colonne de gauche, se trouvent les groupes précis et habituels du récit évangélique global, tandis que la colonne de droite reprend les expressions qui sortent de ce cadre:

	Mentions habituelles du récit global	Expressions hors cadre
v. 1	ὄχλος πλεῖστος	
v. 2	πᾶς ὁ ὄχλος	
v. 10		οἱ περὶ αὐτὸν σὺν τοῖς δώδεκα
v. 11		ἐκείνοις δὲ τοῖς ἔξω
v. 33	αὐτοῖς[65]	
v. 34	αὐτοῖς (...) δὲ τοῖς ἰδίοις μαθηταῖς	

63. Contre P. ROLLAND, *L'arrière-fond sémitique des évangiles synoptiques*, in *ETL* 60 (1984) 358-362, voir p. 360, qui voit dans cette expression un «exemple typique de leçon double de Mc correspondant à un texte simple identique chez Mt et chez Lc» et juge que «personne ne pourrait penser, si nous ne connaissions pas le deuxième évangile, qu'ils dépendent d'un texte aussi complexe que Mc 4,10: 'Ceux qui étaient autour de lui avec les Douze'». En fait, ces deux évangélistes ont profondément transformé le texte de Mc 4,10-12 et, dans leur logique, il était tout à fait normal de reprendre ici l'habituel οἱ μαθηταί. Même si on suit l'hypothèse très répandue que Mc aurait repris οἱ περὶ αὐτόν à sa source et y aurait ajouté de sa main σὺν τοῖς δώδεκα (voir ci-dessus, p. 147, n. 12), l'expression ainsi créée par Mc est suffisamment originale pour que l'on attribue à son auteur une intention particulière.

64. Celle-ci a été notée par C.M. TUCKETT, *Mark's Concerns* (n. 11), p. 14: «It seems difficult to deny that for Mark οἱ περὶ αὐτόν has quite a wide reference. (...) Mark's terminology is thus somewhat imprecise in his description of who constitutes the in group and the out group, especially in relation to members of the crowd». Selon H.J. KLAUCK, *Allegorie* (n. 11), pp. 243-244, l'expression οἱ περὶ αὐτόν désigne la partie de la foule qui constitue la «familia Dei», et, en y ajoutant σὺν τοῖς δώδεκα, Mc veut indiquer que les paroles de Jésus s'adressent non exclusivement, mais d'abord, aux disciples. Pour sa part, C.F.D. MOULE, *Mark 4:1-20* (n. 62), p. 99, estime que les deux positions «inside» et «outside» sont à considérer «as descriptions merely of the result of ways of responding to parables on a given occasion. (...) At most it indicates a *character* rather than a *fixed class*».

65. De nombreux autres αὐτοῖς se retrouvent entre le v. 11 et le v. 33. Si, vu le parallèle avec les vv. 1-2, ceux des vv. 33-34 désignent assez certainement les foules, il est beaucoup plus difficile de savoir à qui précisément renvoient les αὐτοῖς des vv. 13.21.24.

Le fait que les groupes mentionnés aux vv. 10-11 échappent au dispositif narratif habituel est corroboré par l'observation souvent faite de l'impossibilité de représenter spatialement ce qui est décrit dans ce ch. 4[66]. En effet, le κατὰ μόνας du v. 10, où se retrouve un groupe assez large, est peu compatible avec la situation de Jésus en barque (v. 1). De plus, aux vv. 33-34, on retrouve la mention de Jésus parlant en paraboles à la foule, mention qui fait inclusion avec le v. 2, sans qu'on ait jamais fait allusion après les vv. 10-12 à un retour de Jésus vers cette foule.

Du point de vue littéraire, il est donc fondé de lire les vv. 10-12 comme sortant du cadre narratif proprement dit. Il s'agit d'une sorte de réflexion métalinguistique mise en exposant par rapport à ce cadre, en quelque sorte hors scène et hors temps.

Au plan narratif, les deux groupes des vv. 10-11 ont en commun d'être des gens à qui il arrive quelque chose: aux premiers le mystère du Royaume a été donné, tandis qu'aux seconds tout arrive en paraboles. Ces derniers ne sont sujets d'aucun verbe à l'actif. Par contre, les premiers sont présentés comme interrogeant (ἠρώτων) Jésus sur les paraboles. Donc, au plan narratif, ce qui distingue les deux groupes, c'est le fait de poser ou non des questions. Mais l'interprétation donnée de ce fait dans les vv. 10-12 est paradoxale. En effet, dans la vie courante, celui qui pose une question manifeste qu'il ne comprend pas bien et qu'il souhaite mieux comprendre. Or, d'après le v. 12, ce sont plutôt ceux qui n'interrogent pas qui ne comprennent pas: tout leur arrive en paraboles et ils voient sans voir et entendent sans comprendre. Par contre, au moment même où ceux qui sont autour de Jésus avec les Douze l'interrogent, celui-ci leur annonce: le mystère du Royaume de Dieu vous a été donné. Tout se passe comme si le fait de poser des questions sur les paraboles servait de révélateur de ce que l'on a reçu le mystère. «L'interrogation présuppose que l'objet verbal transmis précédemment a été reçu comme 'parabole', c'est-à-dire au moins comme énoncé faisant question. (…) Leur début de réception positive des paraboles est reconnu et mis au niveau des valeurs qui définissent 'le mystère du Règne de Dieu'. Cela est d'autant plus remarquable que ce don coexiste avec un non-'savoir' ou 'connaître' les paraboles, c'est-à-dire ici avec l'incapacité de les interpréter ou de les expliquer' (v. 34) comme Jésus va le faire pour le récit du grain semé. (…) Ce don (…) représente une forme d'intelligence non sue d'un objet de savoir ('le Règne de Dieu') qui échappe au

---

66. Ceci est encore appuyé par une autre constatation de J. DELORME, *La communication* (n. 57), p. 6: «L'effet de réception du discours de Jésus et du récit qu'il comporte n'est pas noté pour la foule. D'ailleurs il ne saurait l'être puisque l'écoute demandée est individualisée»(v. 9).

savoir et que le langage ne maîtrise pas, sauf à le désigner par une ex-
pression-énigme. Ce don met le destinataire en connivence avec l'objet
qui constitue l'horizon de sens en fonction duquel le discours parabolique s'organise et se donne à comprendre comme quête avant toute ac-
quisition d'un sens exploitable en discours»[67].

Par ailleurs, l'expression τὸ μυστήριον δέδοται est originale et paradoxale. Dire que le mystère du Royaume a été donné aux proches de
Jésus n'entraîne pas qu'il leur soit dévoilé, puisque ce n'est pas dit. Or,
d'un mystère, on dit habituellement qu'il est caché ou dévoilé, mais pas
donné. Les verbes conventionnels sont: ἀποκαλύπτω, ἀνακαλύπτω,
ἐκφαίνω, δηλόω, γνωρίζω, καταγγέλλω, λαλέω, λέγω[68]. Outre le fait
que l'expression μυστήριον τῆς βασιλείας τοῦ θεοῦ constitue un *hapax
legomenon*[69], la combinaison directe de μυστήριον avec le verbe δίδωμι
en constitue un second. D'ailleurs, Mt aussi bien que Lc ont modifié l'expression marcienne en ajoutant γνῶναι après δέδοται et en faisant passer
le mot μυστήριον du singulier au pluriel[70], ce qui est aussi plus courant.

67. J.DELORME, *La communication* (n. 57), pp. 6-8.
68. On trouvera les références bibliques dans B. VAN IERSEL, *Les récits-paraboles et
la fonction du secret pour le destinataire de Marc*, in *SémBib* n° 45 (1987) 23-35, voir
p. 24. À la p. 25 du même article, van Iersel relève qu'il n'a trouvé dans la littérature comparable qu'un seul cas analogue, à savoir Hénoch 68,1, cité d'après R.H. CHARLES, *The
Apocrypha and Pseudepigrapha of the Old Testament*, II, Oxford, 1913, p. 232: «And
after that my grandfather Henoch gave me the teaching of all the secrets in the book of all
the parables which had been given to him, and put them together for me in the words of
the book of the parables». Le même passage est repris dans B. VAN IERSEL, *Reading Mark*
(n. 27), p. 79. Il faut cependant noter deux différences importantes avec le texte de Mc:
d'abord le mot «mystère» est au pluriel; ensuite, les mystères ne sont pas l'objet direct
du don, mais bien l'enseignement (ou l'explication, ou encore les signes [en éthiopien =
te'emert]) des mystères.
69. V. FUSCO, *La section* (n. 25), p. 229, parle d'expression unique dans le N.T.
70. Déjà M.-J LAGRANGE, *Le but* (n. 27), p. 26 souligne que le pluriel donne à «mystères» une connotation plus notionnelle, tandis que le singulier de Mc est plus fort et présente le Royaume comme «un événement auquel on prend part». H. RÄISÄNEN, *Das
«Messiasgeheimnis» im Markusevangelium. Ein redaktionskritischer Versuch* (Schriften
der Finnischen Exegetischen Gesellschaft, 28), Helsinki, 1976, pp. 53-54, parle d'une
expression synthétique où se résume toute la révélation réalisée à travers la personne de
Jésus. Ainsi aussi, C. BREYTENBACH, *Nachfolge* (n. 11), p. 159 (pour un état de la question, voir pp. 134-135, n. 8). Pour J. KINGSBURY, *The Parables* (n. 22), p. 45, le terme (au
singulier) de Mc est eschatologique et christologique au sens strict (il proclame que le
Royaume de Dieu est advenu dans la personne, les paroles et les œuvres de Jésus), tandis
que le pluriel de Mt exprime une pensée plus large incluant non seulement l'eschatologie,
mais aussi l'éthique. Dans un sens proche, U. LUZ, *Matthäus* II (n. 47), p. 312. Pour sa
part, J. MARCUS, *Mark 4:10-12* (n. 19), p. 565, estime que le parfait δέδοται exclut que
le mystère du Royaume puisse consister dans l'identité de Jésus, puisque, à ce point du
récit, celle-ci n'est pas encore révélée aux disciples. Aussi propose-t-il, curieusement,
d'ajouter «en paraboles» à l'expression «à vous le mystère du Royaume de Dieu a été
donné». Et il en déduit que «Jesus indicates that his parables are a two-edged sword: to
his disciples they reveal 'the mystery of the kingdom of God', but to those outside they

L'expression de Mc était trop originale et a suscité une modification rédactionnelle de la part des deux autres synoptiques. Il est d'autant plus intéressant de chercher à voir ce que cette expression curieuse veut dire d'original dans le contexte littéraire où elle est incluse. Notant que «le syntagme
de Mc. n'est pas conventionnel», B. van Iersel ajoute: «La différence
entre les disciples et ceux qui sont dehors est que les premiers savent au
moins qu'il existe un secret, une énigme à résoudre, tandis que les autres
ne sont même pas au courant de son existence»[71]. Les proches reçoivent
comme don ce que les paraboles feraient subir à ceux du dehors comme
une perte radicale, s'ils voulaient bien les entendre: ils devraient perdre
l'illusion de comprendre et ils pourraient alors recevoir l'explication de
Jésus. Les proches, pour leur part, sont loin de l'évidence. Les vv. 10-12
suggèrent au lecteur qu'il vaut mieux ne pas comprendre ou croire comprendre trop vite. Et les constants rappels de l'incompréhension des disciples dans la suite de l'intrigue narrative montrent au lecteur combien est
long «le chemin à suivre pour accueillir la possibilité de comprendre»[72].

Lorsqu'il parle en paraboles, Jésus offre une voie de vérité, mais paradoxale, car le Royaume ne peut être appréhendé positivement que comme
mystère. D'ailleurs, les proches de Jésus sont appelés, eux aussi, à présenter le Royaume de la même manière, c'est-à-dire en paraboles, si, du
moins, on interprète au sens littéral la première personne du pluriel au
v. 30: πῶς ὁμοιώσωμεν τὴν βασιλείαν τοῦ θεοῦ ἢ ἐν τίνι αὐτὴν παρα-
βολῇ θῶμεν; Si la question est réelle et non pas rhétorique, cela revient

---

are weapons of blinding» (pp. 565-566). Ceci correspond à la thèse générale de cet article
qui interprète Mc 4,10-12 sur l'arrière-fond d'une pensée dualiste liée à l'apocalyptique
et particulièrement à Qumrân. Cependant, même si le mot μυστήριον a une saveur apocalyptique, cette façon de voir ne tient pas assez compte, à mon avis, de l'opposition marcienne entre δέδοται et ἐν παραβολαῖς γίνεται (même critique chez C.M. TUCKETT,
Mark's Concerns [n. 11], p. 16, soulignant, après un état de la question, combien «majority opinion today is undoubtedly in favour of the view that the 'secret' of 4,11 is, in some
sense at least, Christological»; voir aussi pp. 17-18). Par contre, je souscris volontiers à
l'affirmation: «As spoken to the Marcan community, the words of 4:11 'to you has been
given the mystery of the kingdom of God', imply more than mere *knowledge* of the mystery (although that factor is certainly included); they also suggest the community's participation in the mystery through its suffering» (MARCUS, p. 573). Selon D. LÜHRMANN, *Das
Markusevangelium* (n. 27), pp. 86-87, le mystère désigne moins une connaissance que
la réalité salvifique du Royaume proprement dite. M.A. BEAVIS, *Mark's Audience* (n. 3),
pp. 143-146, défend, à partir d'un point de vue de *reader response criticism*, que le mot
μυστήριον serait à comprendre dans une perspective grecque comme discipline philosophique ésotérique accessible uniquement aux membres du groupe. Cette vue semble peu
vraisemblable, si on tient compte de l'ensemble de l'expression μυστήριον τῆς βασιλείας τοῦ θεοῦ.

71. B. VAN IERSEL, *Les récits-paraboles* (n. 68), p. 25.
72. C. DIETERLÉ, *Le jeu* (n. 8), p. 139. Sur le développement narratif de ce point de
vue en Mc, voir D. MARGUERAT, *La construction du lecteur* (n. 4), pp. 255-256.

à dire que le don du mystère ne consiste pas en un savoir tout fait; il crée plutôt les conditions d'aptitude à être serviteurs de la parole et à «mettre» avec Jésus le Royaume dans une parabole[73]. Ce n'est pas une connaissance supérieure qui est donnée, mais la condition de l'accès à une explication supplémentaire où celui qui la reçoit ne s'imagine pas épuiser le sens du mystère. Que le mystère leur soit donné ne signifie pas qu'un contenu de savoir leur aurait été révélé. Ce serait d'ailleurs contradictoire avec la juxtaposition que fait Mc à deux versets d'intervalle entre ὑμῖν τὸ μυστήριον δέδοται τῆς βασιλείας τοῦ θεοῦ (v. 11) et οὐκ οἴδατε τὴν παραβολὴν ταύτην, καὶ πῶς πάσας τὰς παραβολὰς γνώσεσθε; (v. 13): le don du mystère n'a pas aboli la déficience au plan de la connaissance[74]. L'expression marcienne doit être prise au sens littéral et dans le contraste où elle se trouve avec le sort de «ceux du dehors»: les proches savent qu'il existe un mystère et donc une clé des paraboles-énigmes, mais ils n'en connaissent pas le contenu[75]. Cette situation fait d'eux des questionneurs. Dans l'ordre du récit global, on s'attend à ce que la clé soit dévoilée plus tard et, en tout cas, avant la fin du récit.

Le malheur de «ceux du dehors» consiste en ce qu'ils ne sont même pas conscients de l'existence du mystère du Royaume de Dieu. Dès lors, tout ce qui est du Royaume de Dieu[76] leur arrive en paraboles-énigmes, dont ils ne peuvent chercher la clé, puisqu'ils n'en soupçonnent pas l'existence. Ils ne sont pas conscients de ce que le Royaume de Dieu est un mystère qui échappe à un savoir total. Ils ont trop de savoir pour s'ouvrir au mystère. Comme le suggèrent les controverses de Mc 2,1–3,6,

73. Alors que, curieusement, la plupart des commentateurs semblent à peine remarquer ce «nous» étonnant, M.-J. LAGRANGE, *Marc* (n. 9), p. 118, y relève «une très intime communication avec l'auditoire. On dirait qu'on va chercher ensemble». Dans le même sens, R. PESCH, *Das Markusevangelium*, I (n. 25), p. 261. En fait donc, deux questions introduites par πῶς sont posées aux proches de Jésus. Alors que la première (v. 13) reproche un manque de compréhension, la seconde (v. 30) invite à la créativité. Celle-ci ne se retrouve pas dans les textes parallèles de Mt 13,31 et Lc 13,18 qui n'ont pas repris les verbes à la première personne du pluriel.

74. D. MARGUERAT, *La construction du lecteur* (n. 4), p. 255, souligne que «l'évangéliste crée aussitôt le paradoxe dont Matthieu ne veut pas: le don du μυστήριον n'équivaut pas au don de la compréhension». Aussi, «le récit de Marc (…) tour à tour désoriente et réoriente le lecteur, lui apprenant la vulnérabilité de toute connaissance par la dramatisation narrative de l'échec des disciples» (p. 256).

75. B. VAN IERSEL, *Reading Mark* (n. 27), p. 79: «I am convinced that the expression in Mark means what it says, namely that those who are addressed by Jesus here have definitively been given a secret but do not know its content. As with a document enclosed in an envelope, they know that the secret exists, but not what it contains». Voir aussi J. DELORME, *La communication* (n. 57), p. 8, cité ci-dessus, p. 15.

76. C. BREYTENBACH, *Nachfolge* (n. 11), p. 165, identifie, à juste titre, τὰ πάντα avec le mystère du Royaume de Dieu.

leur rapport à une loi absolutisée les détourne de la vie du Royaume de Dieu et les oriente vers des œuvres de mort[77]. L'interprétation que donne T.W. Manson du v. 12 va dans la même ligne: «the real cause of the blindness of those outside is that they do not wish to repent and be forgiven: a deadly self-satisfaction is the real hindrance to the efficacy of parabolic teaching»[78]. L'idéal serait que les paraboles fassent saisir à «ceux du dehors» qu'ils ne comprennent pas et sont ainsi sur la voie de la non-conversion, du non-salut; elles doivent dérégler leur fausse compréhension et, pour cela, d'abord obscurcir l'excessive clarté de leur savoir. Aussi longtemps qu'ils croient comprendre, la voie de la conversion et de la réception positive du mystère leur reste fermée[79].

c. Le v. 12 dans le cadre des vv. 1-20

La caractérisation de «ceux du dehors» au v. 12, par le biais d'une allusion à Is 6,9-10, comme gens qui voient sans voir et entendent sans comprendre s'intègre bien au contexte immédiat des deux récits-paraboles du semeur. Le premier récit, pourtant apparemment simple, est encadré par des appels, dont la répétition tout à fait inhabituelle empêche de penser qu'ils viseraient seulement à susciter l'attention: ἀκούετε (v. 3), ὃς ἔχει ὦτα ἀκούειν ἀκουέτω (v. 9). Tout se passe plutôt comme si les auditeurs/lecteurs étaient incités à une écoute d'un type particulier, une écoute au second degré, une écoute incluant une compréhension particulière. Suite au second de ces appels, les proches de Jésus l'interrogent. Cela conduit ce dernier à reconnaître que le mystère du Royaume leur a été donné, par opposition à «ceux du dehors» dont il dit que tout leur arrive en paraboles pour que ἀκούοντες ἀκούωσιν καὶ μὴ συνιῶσιν (v. 12). En même temps, cependant, Jésus se demande comment ses proches pourront comprendre (γνώσεσθε) toutes les paraboles (v. 13). Suit le récit-parabole de celui qui sème la parole. Il apparaît comme une sorte de décodage du premier récit, si ce n'est que la figure du semeur n'est pas décodée. Autrement dit, l'attention est centrée sur l'instance de

---

77. C. FOCANT, *Les implications du neuf dans le permis (Mc 2,1-3,6)*, dans R. MEYNET – P. BOVATI (éd.), *Ouvrir les Écritures*. FS P. Beauchamp (LD, 162), Paris, 1995, pp. 201-223, voir 215-223. Je suis assez d'accord avec F. MARTIN, *Parler* (n. 52), p. 27, lorsqu'il écrit: «l'auditoire de Jésus, comme le peuple d'autrefois, a du mal à entendre une parole prophétique ou parabolique parce qu'il s'est lui-même aveuglé et rendu sourd par sa propre identification à un énoncé qui, détaché de son énonciateur, peut se faire passer pour la vérité à l'état pur. Dans ce contexte, un tel énoncé renvoie vraisemblablement au discours de la loi».

78. T.W. MANSON, *The Teaching* (n. 34), p. 78 (pour une citation plus complète, voir ci-dessous, p. 169, n. 86).

79. La même idée se trouve explicitée d'une autre manière en Jn 9,41.

réception et non sur celle d'émission[80]. Ce qui caractérise la croissance et la fructification de la parole, ce n'est pas la manière dont elle
est semée, mais son rapport avec le type de terrain humain dans lequel
elle tombe. Les premiers entendent, mais se font aussitôt enlever la
parole par Satan (v. 15). Les deuxièmes entendent et reçoivent aussitôt
avec joie, mais le manque de racine les fait succomber aux épreuves
(vv. 16-17). Les troisièmes entendent, mais laissent étouffer la parole
par les soucis et les convoitises (vv. 18-19). C'est seulement dans le
quatrième cas que l'écoute débouche sur un accueil (προσδέχονται)
et une fructification (v. 20). Dans chacun des quatre cas, le verbe
ἀκούω est utilisé, mais, dans un seul, il débouche sur l'accueil-com-
préhension[81] qui permet de porter des fruits. Bref, le contexte immédiat invite à lire le v. 12 comme réflexion sur la qualité de la réception, plutôt que comme exprimant une volonté de l'instance d'émission,
même si ce verset débutant par ἵνα est formulé sur le mode de l'intentionnalité.

d. Le v. 12 par rapport aux vv. 21-25 et 26-32

La volonté de l'instance d'émission n'est cependant pas négligée dans le
ch. 4. Elle se trouve explicitée dans la première des deux images (vv. 21-25)
qui suivent le récit-parabole de celui qui sème la parole. Elle est exprimée
par le second ἵνα (répété 4 fois dans les vv. 21-22) du ch. 4[82]. Ce qua-
druple ἵνα reflète un vouloir immanent: il ne correspond pas à la nature
de la lampe d'être cachée sous le boisseau ou sous le lit. Par l'image de
cette lampe, quasi personnalisée par l'emploi du verbe ἔρχεται, Jésus
signifie que rien de ce qui vient n'est caché ou secret, si ce n'est pour
être manifesté, venir au jour. Bref, «du côté de l'émission, il n'y a rien
de caché qu'en vue de sa manifestation. (…) On ne saurait évacuer plus
nettement l'idée d'un secret à garder, comme si la communication parabolique avait pour stratégie de réserver un savoir aux initiés. Là est la
différence entre le 'secret' et le 'mystère' qui manifeste le 'caché' sans

---

80. J. DELORME, La communication (n. 57), p. 10: «C'est la qualité du récepteur qui
conditionne la fructification. La réception de l'objet ne suffit pas: tous entendent, mais il
n'y a de fruits que dans le dernier cas».
81. Par cette expression, je veux signifier qu'il ne s'agit pas, ou du moins pas uniquement, d'une compréhension intellectuelle. Comme le souligne GROUPE D'ENTREVERNES,
Signes et paraboles. Sémiotique et texte évangélique, Paris, 1977, p. 202: «La compréhension ne se laisse dériver d'aucune explication, elle s'atteste dans son fruit: la conversion».
82. C'est, selon C.M. TUCKETT, Mark's Concerns (n. 11), p. 20, l'un des points qui
met en évidence le parallèle entre les vv. 11-12 et 21-23.

échapper au langage parabolique»[83]. Nous trouvons dans ces versets une confirmation supplémentaire de ce que, sous peine de contradiction avec les vv. 21-22, le ἵνα du v. 12 ne dévoile pas l'intention de l'instance d'émission, mais concerne la participation active de l'auditeur. Les versets suivants insistent aussi sur cet engagement de l'auditeur: εἴ τις ἔχει ὦτα ἀκούειν ἀκουέτω (v. 23) et βλέπετε τί ἀκούετε (v. 24b). Dans ce dernier cas, on retrouve dans une formule paradoxale les deux verbes utilisés au v. 12, comme si les paraboles donnaient à voir ce qu'il faut entendre.

Quant aux vv. 24c-25, ils reviennent sur l'instance de réception. L'utilisation par deux fois de ὑμῖν suivi d'un verbe au passif (v. 24c) rappelle clairement le ὑμῖν δέδοται du v. 12: ce que les auditeurs reçoivent est à la mesure de leur écoute compétente et même il leur sera donné de surcroît. Ce rapprochement est encore confirmé par l'utilisation du verbe δοθήσεται au v. 25a. Si, selon l'interprétation commune, les passifs δέδοται (v. 12), προστεθήσεται (v. 24) et δοθήσεται (v. 25) sont des passifs divins, il faut peut-être parler de passif «satanique» pour ἀρθήσεται (v. 25b), au vu du seul autre emploi du verbe αἴρω dans le ch. 4: il désigne l'action de Satan qui enlève la parole chez ceux qui l'ont seulement entendue (v. 15). Selon le v. 25, l'écoute incompétente entraîne la perte même de ce qu'on a entendu. Écouter mal, sans comprendre, revient finalement au même que n'avoir pas entendu.

Tenues ensemble, les deux paroles imagées des vv. 21-25 insistent à la fois sur la nécessaire implication de l'auditeur qui doit mesurer largement et sur le dynamisme immanent du mystère qui n'est caché que pour devenir manifeste. La double parabole du semeur qui précédait ces versets ayant largement traité de la responsabilité de l'auditeur, les deux paraboles qui les suivent (vv. 26-29 et 30-32) n'auront plus qu'à mettre en valeur le parallèle entre le Royaume de Dieu et l'énergie surprenante et inexpliquée de la graine jetée sur le sol. Par le biais du v. 30, les auditeurs compétents, à savoir les proches de Jésus, sont d'ailleurs invités à participer à cette mise du Royaume en paraboles.

---

83. J. DELORME, *La communication* (n. 57), p. 11. On peut reprendre dans ce cadre la judicieuse remarque de J. KÖGEL, *Der Zweck der Gleichnisse Jesu im Rahmen seiner Verkündigung*, Gütersloh, 1915, p. 45, citée par H.-J. KLAUCK, *Allegorie* (n. 11), p. 251, n. 331: «Nicht Verhüllung und Verstockung gehören zusammen, sondern vielmehr Enthüllung und Verstockung». C'est lorsqu'il y a révélation que l'endurcissement vient au jour. Pour Mc, ce n'est pas la parabole comme telle qui est énigmatique, mais bien le comportement qu'elle suscite. Voir aussi la remarque de D. MARGUERAT, *La construction du lecteur* (n. 4), p. 256: «L'évangile de Marc n'est pas l'évangile gnostique de Thomas; il ne protège pas un secret, mais narrativise sa dissolution».

Des réflexions précédentes il ressort qu'en Mc 4,1-34 il n'y a guère d'élaboration sur l'instance d'émission proprement dite. On n'y trouve d'ailleurs pas d'anti-programme d'émission, comme c'est le cas, par exemple, chez Mt dans la parabole de l'ivraie et du bon grain (Mt 13,24-30.36-43). Certes, chez Mc aussi, on retrouve la figure de l'Adversaire, puisqu'il est question d'une action de Satan (Mc 4,15). Mais celui-ci agit dans le cadre d'un anti-programme de réception et non d'émission: son action consiste à enlever ce qui a été entendu sans être reçu[84].

e. La portée du v. 12 introduit par ἵνα

Dans un tel cadre, comment bien entendre le ἵνα du v. 12? Il est souvent compris comme manifestant une intention divine puisqu'il introduirait une citation d'Isaïe[85]. Mais est-ce bien le cas? Certes Mc 4,12 s'inspire du texte d'Is 6,9-10. Mais, d'une part, il le fait très librement et on est très loin d'une citation littérale de quelque version que ce soit d'Is 6,9-10[86]. Les mots qui, dans le texte d'Isaïe, suggèrent le plus clairement la volonté d'endurcir les cœurs sont d'ailleurs omis en Mc[87]. D'autre part, le texte n'est pas introduit explicitement comme une citation[88]; il caractérise plutôt une situation à l'aide d'expressions de saveur vétérotestamentaire[89]. Et, même si Mc n'est pas familier des citations d'accomplissement,

---

84. J. DELORME, *La communication* (n. 57), p. 14.

85. Voir, à titre d'exemple, J. DUPONT, *Le chapitre* (n. 13), p. 806: «La finalité dont il est question dans ces lignes concerne le but poursuivi, non pas directement par Jésus lui-même, mais par Dieu, sujet réel de toute cette déclaration. (…) L'enseignement parabolique de Jésus est le moyen par lequel Dieu exerce son jugement contre le peuple qu'il veut aveugler».

86. On a vu ci-dessus (p. 151) que le texte de Mc 4,12 ne correspond ni au TM, ni à la LXX, ni au Tg.

87. Ceci a été bien vu par T.W. MANSON, *The Teaching* (n. 34), pp. 78-79: «If the object of the quotation were to show that parabolic teaching was calculated to harden the hearts of the hearers, it is curious that the words in Is. VI.9f. which would most strongly suggest this are precisely those which are omitted in Mark: 'Make the heart of this people fat and make their ears heavy, and shut their eyes, lest they see with their eyes and hear with their ears, and understand with their heart'. These would surely be more apt to the purpose than what we actually have in Mark: and it seems to me significant that they are *not* quoted. With the omission of these words the conjunction דילמא is left in the air: and at once two possibilities emerge. Either it may be taken in the sense suggested above [= for if they did, they would repent and receive forgiveness], in which case it will appear that the real cause of the blindness of those outside is that they do not wish to repent and be forgiven: a deadly self-satisfaction is the real hindrance to the efficacy of parabolic teaching. Or, though this seems to me less probable, we may place a full stop after 'understand' and take דילמא in its other sense of 'perhaps'».

88. Le fait est noté par C. DIETERLÉ, *Le jeu* (n. 8), p. 136, n. 23. Avec elle, on peut parler d'échos de l'A.T.

89. Avec A. SUHL, *Die Funktion* (n. 19), p. 149: «Es zeigte sich uns schon mehrfach, daß Markus seine Gegenwart mit atl. Farben charakterisiert. Dasselbe dürfte auch hier wieder der Fall sein».

il est tout à fait à même d'introduire une référence explicite à l'A.T., lorsqu'il entend le faire[90]. C'est pourquoi il ne semble pas *ad rem* de sous-entendre derrière ἵνα le verbe πληρωθῇ, en vue de faire du v. 12 une citation d'accomplissement[91]. Mc connaissait cette thématique de l'accomplissement des Écritures (14,49)[92] et, s'il avait voulu l'introduire dans son ch. 4, il aurait dû le faire de manière explicite.

Suivant l'opinion générale, le sens final de ἵνα n'est cependant pas à mettre en doute[93]. Mais le contexte n'implique pas que s'y dévoile une intention de l'émetteur[94]. Il indique plutôt que, pour ceux du dehors, dont l'attitude révèle que le mystère du Royaume ne leur a pas été donné, tout arrive en paraboles dans un but, à savoir qu'ils ne comprennent pas. Il ne peut en aller autrement, non pas à cause de l'émetteur qui voudrait émettre un message brouillé, incompréhensible, mais parce que l'attitude de ces récepteurs ne leur permet pas de comprendre les paraboles, alors que celles-ci constituent pour l'heure le seul moyen de communication approprié pour transmettre le mystère du Royaume de Dieu. Si tout leur arrive en paraboles, c'est que leur but, sans le savoir, est de ne pas comprendre, vu la conversion que cela exigerait. Le ἵνα abrupt de Mc 4,12 n'est-il pas elliptique? Il pourrait être là pour choquer le lecteur[95] et l'amener à s'interroger sur un but caché aux yeux de ceux du dehors: ceux-ci agissent dans le sens du but décrit, mais à leur insu.

90. Voir Mc 1,2; 7,6; 11,17; 14,27.

91. Sur ce point, je suis d'acord avec H.-J. KLAUCK, *Allegorie* (n. 11), p. 250; C. BREYTENBACH, *Nachfolge* (n. 11), pp. 162-163; C.M. TUCKETT, *Mark's Concerns* (n. 11), p. 19. L'hypothèse de sous-entendre πληρωθῇ est retenue, notamment, par M.-J. LAGRANGE, *Marc* (n. 9), p. 99; J. HORST, art. οὖς, in *TWNT*, V, Stuttgart, 1954, pp. 543-557, voir p. 554 (par contre, E. STAUFFER, art. ἵνα, in *TWNT*, III, 1938, pp. 324-334, voir 328, opte pour le sens final sans plus); J. JEREMIAS, *Die Gleichnisse* (n. 10), p. 13; W. MARXSEN, *Redaktionsgeschichtliche Erklärung* (n. 14), p. 269 (= ID., *Der Exeget*, p. 25); J. GNILKA, *Die Verstockung* (n. 4), pp. 47-48; E.F. SIEGMAN, *Teaching* (n. 59), p. 176. J.R. KIRKLAND, *The Earliest Understanding* (n. 12), tout en optant personnellement pour la traduction peu précise «so it is that» qui peut couvrir à la fois un sens consécutif ou explicatif, prétend que «the most widely accepted view is that ἵνα here refers to the fulfillment of the OT text which follows» (pp. 6-7). Or, cette vue est loin d'être généralement admise. L'opinion la plus courante lit ἵνα au sens final, mais pas comme introduisant une citation d'accomplissement.

92. Mal attesté, Mc 15,28 est sans doute une reprise de Lc 22,37.

93. Voir l'état de la question ci-dessus, p. 152, n. 32.

94. Dans la discussion qui a suivi l'exposé, P. Beauchamp a proposé un rapprochement suggestif de ἵνα avec δεῖ. Sans autre précision, le ἵνα peut très bien être impersonnel et souligner une intentionnalité immanente. Les choses suivent leur cours, mais la parole introduit une crise en les dévoilant.

95. L'analyse narrative est particulièrement attentive à ce qui choque le lecteur à première lecture. Dans ces cas, elle se demande s'il n'y a pas là invitation pour le lecteur à un approfondissement de son approche, autrement dit à une lecture au second degré.

2. Mc 4,10-12 dans le cadre global de l'évangile

Le reste de l'évangile corrobore-t-il l'interprétation qui vient d'être donnée[96]? Il me semble que plusieurs indices vont en ce sens.

D'abord, l'usage de l'expression ἐν παραβολαῖς en Mc est assez frappant. On la retrouve quatre fois dans le second évangile. Sauf en 4,2, où l'expression concerne la foule, elle est habituellement liée à une attitude des adversaires de Jésus. Si en 4,11 cette attitude n'est pas explicitée, les deux autres cas sont plus clairs. En 3,23, Jésus parle aux scribes en paraboles, alors que ceux-ci donnent de ses exorcismes une interprétation qualifiée de blasphème contre l'Esprit: ils veulent les attribuer à Satan. En 12,1, l'expression ἐν παραβολαῖς introduit la parabole des vignerons homicides adressée aux grands prêtres, aux scribes et aux anciens. Or, cette parabole dénonce leur volonté d'accaparer l'héritage qui les mène au meurtre de l'héritier. Bref, tout se passe comme si le discours ἐν παραβολαῖς servait à réfuter une interprétation de l'action de Jésus contraire à l'Esprit (3,23), une compréhension de tout (τὰ πάντα) qui est contraire au mystère du Royaume de Dieu (4,11), ou encore une œuvre de mort qui se cache sous l'apparence de soins à la vigne (12,1), mais qui se révèle en fait contraire à l'Écriture (Ps 118,22-23). Bien qu'il soit compris par les autorités juives, ce dernier discours ne les détourne pas de leur projet d'arrêter Jésus (12,12).

Or, ce récit-parabole des vignerons homicides entretient un rapport particulier avec le récit-parabole du semeur. D'abord ce sont les deux seuls récits-paraboles au sens strict en Mc, comme l'a bien souligné I. Almeida[97]. Son analyse montre combien ces deux récits s'appellent pour opérer au sein de l'évangile un décodage de l'avenir de la parole divine (ou du mystère du Royaume de Dieu), y compris de ceux qui entendent cette parole et de celui qui la dit[98]. Le récit-parabole des vignerons homicides pourrait bien expliciter ce que signifie «voir et entendre sans comprendre». Lorsque le père-propriétaire envoie son υἱὸν ἀγαπητόν (12,6) chercher une part des fruits de la vigne (v. 2), les vignerons réduisent ce dernier à sa fonction économique et ne voient en lui que le κληρονόμος (v. 7) à tuer pour accaparer l'héritage. Si on s'interroge sur sa fonction dans le cadre évangélique global, la parabole des vignerons homicides

---

96. Avec C. BREYTENBACH, *Nachfolge* (n. 11), p. 158, je pense que la portée de ces versets est plus large qu'une éventuelle théorie parabolique et qu'une bonne interprétation doit permettre de les situer dans la cohérence d'ensemble de Mc.

97. I. ALMEIDA, *L'opérativité sémantique* (n. 56), p. 122.

98. Son analyse a inspiré l'article déjà cité de P. RICŒUR, *La Bible et l'imagination* (n. 2).

n'a pas pour but, comme on le dit souvent, de mettre en valeur l'intention meurtrière des autorités juives, puisque celle-ci est déjà connue du lecteur depuis 3,6. En fait la parabole décode plutôt le sens de cette intention meurtrière. S'inspirant du chant de la vigne d'Is 5[99], la parabole en décrit l'histoire ultérieure. Le malheur vient de ce que ceux à qui Dieu a confié la vigne veulent en garder les fruits et accaparer l'héritage. «Les pharisiens croient rendre honneur à Dieu en supprimant un blasphémateur. Or ce meurtre, la parabole le situe dans une autre histoire et lui donne, en l'insérant dans un autre schéma narratif, une signification totalement inversée. Elle situe ce meurtre au cœur d'une entreprise d'accaparement de l'héritage, c'est-à-dire du pouvoir religieux, par les pharisiens. C'est pour rester maîtres de l'interprétation de la loi qu'ils veulent supprimer Jésus, non pour rendre honneur à Dieu»[100]. Et, s'ils comprennent le but de la parabole (v. 12), le type de compréhension qui est le leur ne les conduit pas à la conversion, mais confirme leur intention meurtrière. Cependant la citation explicite du Ps 118,22-23 qui prolonge la parabole (vv. 10-11) annonce que cette intention sera contrariée par Dieu, dont l'œuvre admirable annoncée par l'Écriture consistera à faire du rejeté la pierre de faîte. Une part du mystère du Royaume se dévoile là. Il sera tout à fait dévoilé lors de la Passion, au moment où, selon Mc, les Écritures s'accomplissent: c'est de son arrestation que Jésus dit ἀλλ' ἵνα πληρωθῶσιν αἱ γραφαί (14,29)[101].

La phrase «à ceux du dehors tout arrive en paraboles» (4,11) ne concerne sans doute pas uniquement les discours de Jésus; τὰ πάντα inclut aussi ses actions, notamment les guérisons, surtout si elles sont pratiquées en transgression de la loi. Mais le «parler en paraboles» n'est pas sans fin, puisque la lampe vient pour être manifestée (4,21-22). En 8,32, la première annonce de la nécessité de la passion est suivie d'une

---

99. Il semble donc bien y avoir une ambiance isaïenne des deux récits-paraboles de Mc. Celle-ci est encore plus importante si, avec C.A. Evans, *On the Isaianic Background of the Sower Parable*, in *CBQ* 47 (1985) 464-468, on admet que «these passages in Isaiah (i.e., 6:9-13 and 55:10-11), linked by the catchword 'seed', provide the basis for a skillfully developed midrash in Mark 4:1-20» (p. 466). Dans le même sens, B. Standaert, *Marc* (n. 50), p. 214: «Au livre d'Isaïe, on rencontre déjà un recours identique aux phénomènes de croissance naturelle pour traduire la certitude de l'efficacité de la parole de Dieu (Is 55,10-11)».

100. Groupe d'Entrevernes, *Signes et paraboles* (n. 81), p. 204. Remarquons que les interlocuteurs de Jésus dans la parabole des vignerons homicides ne sont pas désignés comme pharisiens, ainsi que le suggère le groupe d'Entrevernes; il s'agit plutôt, selon Mc 11,27, des grands prêtres, des scribes et des anciens.

101. Le parallèle johannique est frappant: juste avant le discours d'adieu et l'arrestation, Jn clôture le livre des signes par une double citation d'Isaïe (53,1 et 6,9-10), dont la première est présentée comme citation d'accomplissement (Jn 12,38-40).

constatation du narrateur: παρρησίᾳ τὸν λόγον ἐλάλει. Le contraste est patent avec 4,33: τοιαύταις παραβολαῖς πολλαῖς ἐλάλει αὐτοῖς τὸν λόγον. L'écho entre la première annonce de la passion et la section des paraboles est encore renforcé par la présence dans les deux contextes du verbe διδάσκω (4,2 et 8,31). La parole dite mystérieusement dans les paraboles se dit ouvertement dans la passion. Ou encore, comme l'écrit P. Beauchamp, «les paraboles du Royaume et les miracles mettent sur le chemin d'une crise et 'l'enseignement de la Passion' est le dénouement de cette crise»[102]. Si ce qui s'annonçait paraboliquement à travers tout l'évangile se dévoile ouvertement dans la passion, parallèlement, la passion, en tant qu'accomplissement des Écritures (14,29), constitue la clé de lecture de celles-ci.

Ce qui chez Mc s'énonçait de façon cachée est explicité chez Jn, lorsque, à la fin du livre des signes et avant la passion, il écrit: «si le grain de blé ne tombe en terre, il reste seul; s'il meurt, il porte beaucoup de fruit» (Jn 12,24). Cette parole a, selon P. Beauchamp, une double fonction: «1) En reprenant le thème central des paraboles du Royaume – le grain –, elle en bâtit une sorte de sommaire qu'elle fait déboucher directement sur la croix, sur cette «heure» qui angoisse Jésus. 2) De surcroît, elle identifie brusquement le contenu de la parabole et le locuteur qui l'a enseignée: le grain c'est Jésus, ce sera le disciple éventuel. Marc disait: 'Le semeur sème la parole' (Mc 4,14). Pour Jean, le semeur *est* la parole, il se sème lui-même»[103].

CONCLUSION

Lorsque Mc s'inspire du texte d'Is 6,9-10, il le fait d'une manière tout à fait personnelle, qui le singularise par rapport aux autres auteurs du N.T. Ces derniers citent Is 6,9-10 pour éclairer le rejet de Jésus par Israël en le présentant comme une des péripéties de l'endurcissement d'Israël qui a sa place dans l'histoire du salut. Mc, par contre, ne semble pas s'intéresser à l'endurcissement d'Israël en tant que tel comme étape de l'histoire du salut. Sa perspective est différente. Il veut plutôt interroger son

---

102. P. BEAUCHAMP, *Paraboles de Jésus, vie de Jésus. L'encadrement évangélique et scripturaire des paraboles (Mc 4,1-34)*, in J. DELORME (éd.), *Les paraboles évangéliques. Perspectives nouvelles* (LD, 135), Paris, 1989, pp. 151-170, voir p. 159; son paragraphe sur le sujet est intitulé «la crise illuminative: des parabolai à la parrêsia».
103. P. BEAUCHAMP, *Paraboles* (n. 102), p. 161. Dans le même article, l'auteur fait remarquer, à propos de l'absence de récits d'enfance dans deux évangiles: «À leur place Jean enseigne qu''Au commencement était la parole' et Marc, sur un mode *plus* caché, rejoint cette affirmation» (p. 155). Il la rejoint au ch. 4 à travers la semence symbole de la parole.

lecteur, l'inviter à se poser la question de savoir s'il fait ou non partie de ceux à qui le mystère a été donné. Son attitude révèle-t-elle qu'il est «du dehors» ou qu'il est de ceux qui commencent à entrer dans le mystère? Le point de vue de Mc est donc bien celui du travail sur le lecteur[104].

Dans un tel cadre, il est compréhensible que Mc n'ait pas fait une citation explicite d'Is 6,9-10. Non seulement il tronque le texte d'Isaïe, mais de plus il ne reproduit aucune version connue de ce texte, ni le TM, ni le Tg, ni la LXX. En outre, il n'introduit pas comme citation l'allusion qu'il fait à ce texte. En un certain sens, il faut donc parler de non-citation. En effet, alors même qu'il y a une allusion claire à un texte vétéro-testamentaire reconnu ailleurs par Mc et les auteurs du N.T. comme Écriture faisant autorité, Mc ne recourt à aucun des indices d'extériorité manifestant l'appel qui serait fait à une autorité[105].

C'est qu'il n'entend pas déployer une théorie théologique sur la volonté divine d'endurcir le cœur d'une catégorie de gens. L'allusion à Is 6 lui sert plutôt à décrire la situation catastrophique de ceux qui s'enferment dans l'aveuglement. En conséquence, l'accès leur est barré au mystère du Royaume de Dieu, ainsi qu'à la conversion et au pardon qui lui sont liés. L'allusion à Is 6 introduite par un ἵνα déroutant pour le lecteur a une fonction phatique[106]: elle provoque, sollicite, invite à une lecture au second degré. Les paraboles énoncent métaphoriquement[107] une

104. Ce point de vue a été magistralement mis en lumière par D. MARGUERAT, *La construction du lecteur* (n. 4), pp. 253-259.

105. I. ALMEIDA, *Trois cas de rapports intra-textuels: la citation, la parabolisation, le commentaire*, in *SémBib* n° 15 (1979) 23-42, rappelle, à juste titre, que «c'est *l'extériorité* de la fiction *énonciative* qui définit le propre de la citation» (p. 24). Selon lui, «ce qui distingue la citation de la parabolisation et du commentaire c'est la marque d'*extériorité* attribuée au texte ou fragment cité. (…) Des énoncés sont transcrits comme venant d'une autre instance énonciative, par l'allusion à celui qui les a énoncés, mais sans que l'on dise *comment* cela a été énoncé (ce qui serait inclure son discours dans le mien = parabolisation) ni *de quoi* il parle (ce qui ferait de mon discours son commentaire). Seul le *quoi* et le nom de l'autre restent à l'intérieur du champ textuel. (…) Ce qui est cité l'est en tant que dit par quelqu'un» (p. 30).

106. C'est la fonction reconnue à la citation par A. COMPAGNON, *La seconde main ou le travail de la citation*, Paris, 1970, p. 23, dans la ligne des recherches linguistiques de Jakobson.

107. On sait que, à propos des paraboles, deux grands types de lectures se sont développées. La lecture inspirée de la rhétorique les approche comme des moyens de persuasion: le paraboliste recourt à des récits imagés fictifs qui éloignent en apparence l'auditeur de la situation conflictuelle où il se trouve avec le locuteur; sa méfiance est ainsi atténuée en sorte qu'il peut se laisser convaincre par le jugement auquel le récit même le conduit. Une autre lecture s'inspire de la poétique et tient les paraboles pour des moyens de révélation. Il s'agit alors non plus de persuader, mais de créer un récit qui révèle au-delà de lui-même le mystère du Royaume de Dieu. À vrai dire, les paraboles ne sont pas toutes du même genre et certaines relèvent plutôt de la persuasion, tandis que les autres se situent sur le registre de la révélation. Tel semble bien être le cas des paraboles de Mc 4.

crise qui se dénouera dans la passion, point où culminera l'aveuglement de
«ceux du dehors». Elles sont le seul langage apte au mystère du Royaume,
un langage qui relève de ce que J.-P. Manigne a appelé la «poétique ger-
minale»[108]. Parler de poétique (ποίησις) revient à souligner qu'il s'agit
d'un langage performatif qui «instaure le Royaume en le disant»[109],
mais en mystère.

Rue des Sarts 2   Camille FOCANT
B-5380 Franc-waret

---

108. J.-P. MANIGNE, *Le maître des signes* (Théologies), Paris, 1987, pp. 110-125.
109. D. MARGUERAT, *Parabole* (Cahiers Évangile, n° 75), Paris, 1991, p. 41.

SCRIPTURE AND TRADITION IN MARK 7

Introduction: The Tradition of the Elders

"You forsake the commandment of God and hold fast to the tradition of human beings" (Mark 7,8). "You annul the commandment of God, in order that you may establish your tradition" (Mark 7,9). "You void the word of God for the sake of your tradition which you have passed down" (Mark 7,13)[1]. Three times within the first few verses of Mark's seventh chapter, Jesus repeats the charge that the oral tradition of his Pharisaic opponents eclipses the word and commandment of God and empties it of its force.

A sharper attack on the Pharisaic, and later rabbinic, conception of the relationship between the divine word and tradition could scarcely be imagined. As that relationship is classically formulated in the first two chapters of the Mishnaic tractate 'Abot[2], God delivered to Moses, along with the Written Law, the true interpretation of the divine will and way, and Moses delivered it to Joshua, and Joshua to the elders, and the elders to the prophets – and on and on, in a continuous chain of tradition down to the Pharisaic houses of Hillel and Shammai, and from them to R. Johanan b. Zakkai, who reconstituted Judaism after the catastrophe of the Great Revolt of 66-72 C.E., and his disciples. The "tradition of the elders", then, is not just something that the Pharisees and rabbis have made up, but a treasured inheritance from Sinai, and far from representing a disfigurement of the word of God, it represents its vital preservation for later generations. This is because no Jewish group could live by scripture alone; some sort of tradition was necessary, if only to throw light on what was vague or seemingly contradictory in the scripture[3]. As Gershom Scholem emphasizes, therefore, in Judaism the categories of revelation

---

1. All translations are mine unless otherwise noted.
2. M. HERR (*Continuum in the Chain of Torah Transmission* [Hebrew], in *Zion* 44 [1979] 43-56, p. 50) estimates that the document at the core of *m. 'Abot* 1 was composed between the beginning of the first century B.C.E. and the end of the first century C.E. A. I. BAUMGARTEN (*The Pharisaic Paradosis*, in *HTR* 80 [1987] 63-77, p. 67, n. 16) asserts that this core document was Pharisaic, but that it has undergone substantial revision before becoming the text of *m. 'Abot* 1 as we know it. This qualification, however, does not affect the use that this study makes of *m. 'Abot* 1-2, since the study is concerned only with the basic idea of transmission of tradition that undergirds those chapters.
3. See BAUMGARTEN (n. 2), p. 65.

and tradition do not stand in a relationship of mutual hostility to each other but in one of complementarity. This complementarity is well illustrated by the fact that the term for Jewish mysticism, the stream of Judaism that above all others stresses revelation, and whose devotees aspire to a direct encounter with the divine presence, is precisely Kabbalah, which means "tradition"[4].

As Michael Fishbane has argued, however, the idea of tradition has two sides, the *traditum* or that which is transmitted, and the *traditio* or the process of transmission, which includes the elaboration of the *traditum*[5]. The concept, then, involves both continuity and discontinuity with what has gone before[6]. The Pharisees, for example, while claiming that their regulations came down from Moses, recognized the incontrovertible fact that these regulations were not explicitly written down in the Mosaic Law[7] – although they would have viewed them as the faithful elaboration of the written Torah[8]. It was the same with the later rabbis, who frankly acknowledged, for example, that the point initially at issue in our passage (Mark 7,2.5), the extension of the Bible's priestly handwashing rules to the laity, is not explicitly mandated by the written Torah[9].

Indeed, the Talmudic rabbis could even be jocular in their recognition of the apparent audacity of their claim that their regulations expressed the true intention of the written law. This is illustrated in the superb story in *b. Men.* 29b about Moses, God, and R. Akiba, the Tannaitic sage who was known for his elaborate interpretations of small scriptural details. In this story, when Moses ascends to God at Mt. Sinai, he finds

---

4. G. SCHOLEM, *Revelation and Tradition as Religious Categories in Judaism*, in *The Messianic Idea in Judaism and Other Essays on Jewish Spirituality,* London, George Allen & Unwin, 1971, orig. 1962, pp. 282-303.

5. M. FISHBANE, *Biblical Interpretation in Ancient Israel,* Oxford, Clarendon Press, 1985, pp. 6-19 et passim.

6. Cf. BAUMGARTEN (n. 2), p. 73

7. See Josephus, *Ant.* 13,297; cf. BAUMGARTEN (n. 2), pp. 64-65.

8. See BAUMGARTEN (n. 2), p. 73, who points out that the term מסרת = tradition originally meant letter or sign, and is sometimes used in rabbinic sources for the written text of the Bible; "thus, when the Pharisees chose מסרת as the name of the laws they observed not written in the Bible they were investing their traditions with the prestige of the written word". On the derivation of Pharisaic legal traditions from scripture, see D. W. HALIVNI, *Midrash, Mishnah, and Gemara: The Jewish Predilection for Justified Law,* Cambridge, Mass./London, Harvard University Press, 1986, pp. 38-40.

9. See e.g. *b. Ber.* 52b: אין נטילת ידים לחולין מן התורה ("washing of hands for ordinary food is not taught in the Torah"). As Billerbeck points out, the general opinion of the rabbis is that handwashing for lay people is one of the seven מצוות דרבנן, "commandments of our masters", which were added to the 613 commandments of the written Torah (H.L. STRACK and P. BILLERBECK, *Kommentar zum Neuen Testament aus Talmud und Midrasch* [6 vols.] München, Beck, 1922-1965, vol. 1, pp. 695-696).

him decorating the Hebrew letters of the Torah with tiny flourishes – the jots and tittles referred to in Matt 5,18. When Moses asks him the reason for this strange procedure, God replies that in later generations there will arise a man named Akiba, who will expound heaps and heaps of laws on the basis of every tittle. Moses asks to be shown this extraordinary teacher, and suddenly finds himself transported to Akiba's Talmudic academy, where he sits down in the back row. He is bewildered, however, to find that he does not understand a word of what Akiba and his students are saying, even though they are supposedly interpreting the Torah that Moses himself wrote. But then Akiba's students ask him the reason for a particular ruling, and Akiba replies, "It is a teaching given to Moses at Sinai". Moses, greatly comforted, returns to God and says, "Master of the Universe, you have a man like that and yet you give the Torah by me?" God replies: "Be silent, for this is the way I have determined it". The story ends like this:

> Then Moses said, "Master of the Universe, you have shown me his knowledge of the Torah, show me also his reward". God answered: "Turn around". He turned around and saw that Akiba's flesh was being weighed at the market stalls [his flesh was being torn by the tortures of the executioners]. Then Moses said to God: "Master of the Universe, this is the Torah and this is its reward?" He replied: "Be silent, for this is the way I have determined it"[10].

This story, in its portrayal of Moses' astonishment at Akiba's convoluted interpretations of the Torah, in its richly comic picture of God himself decorating the letters of the Torah in order to make those very interpretations possible, and in its equally comic description of Moses' credulous reaction at hearing from Akiba that these interpretations are "Torah given to Moses at Sinai", charmingly recognizes the stretch of imagination that is required to see the Pharisaic/rabbinic tradition as the direct continuation of the biblical revelation. At the same time, however, the story in another way takes that claim with the utmost seriousness, for it concludes with a description of Akiba's martyrdom, thus movingly presenting the tradition as something worth dying for.

To return to the Markan text with this Pharisaic/rabbinic background in mind is to be surprised at it in a new way. For in spite of the antithesis in Mark 7,6-13 between Pharisaic tradition and divine revelation, it is remarkable how much the previous verses concede to the Pharisaic/rabbinic view of tradition just described. As Mark portrays them, the Pharisees are not just making up out of thin air the requirement that people wash

---

10. Translation slightly altered from that of SCHOLEM (n. 4), p. 283.

their hands before eating; the Pharisees, rather, and "all the Jews"[11], observe this requirement because they are intent on "holding fast to the tradition of the elders". This tradition, Mark goes on to say, includes not only handwashing but also many other things "which they have received in order to hold them fast" (ἃ παρέλαβον κρατεῖν)[12]. In an ancient environment that prized connections with the past[13], these are remarkably positive statements for an opponent to make. The normal assumption in antiquity would have been that a group lucky enough to have inherited a venerable tradition stretching back into the distant past should continue to pass that tradition on to its posterity – an assumption with which the Markan clause "which they have received in order to hold them fast" seems to be in perfect accord. The word "elders" itself, moreover, implies a connection with the tried and tested wisdom of the ages[14].

The positive tone of this description can be more readily appreciated by contrasting it with the description in a section of Josephus' *Antiquities* dependent on the anti-Pharisaic Nicolaus of Damascus (17,41): The Pharisees are "a group of Jews *priding itself* (μέγα φρονοῦν) on its adherence to ancestral custom and *pretending* (προποιούμενον) to observe the Laws of which the Deity approves". On the one hand, this passage is remarkably similar to the overall portrayal of the Pharisees in Mark 7,1-13 in its reference to ancestral tradition, in its insinuated contrast between that tradition and the divine Law, and in its implied charge of hypocrisy ("pretending")[15]. On the other hand, if we just compare it to Mark 7,1-5, the latter seems to be much more positive than Nicolaus' description: instead of *priding themselves* on their adherence to ancestral custom, as Nicolaus would have it, Mark's Pharisees simply hold fast to the tradition

11. This phrase is a generalization, since Pharisaic purity rules were not universally observed even in the post-70 period (see E. SCHÜRER, *The History of the Jewish People in the Age of Jesus Christ (175 B.C.-A.D. 135)*, rev. and ed. by G. VERMES et al., 3 vols, Edinburgh, T. & T. Clark, 1973-1987, vol. 2, pp. 386-387, 396-400). But it is an implicit recognition of the great influence and popularity of the Pharisees (cf. Josephus, *Ant.* 18,15). See also *Ep. Arist.* 305, which approximates the language of our passage by saying, "Following the custom of *all the Jews*, they washed their hands in the sea in the course of their prayers to God" (OTP trans.; cf. *Sib. Or.* 3.591-593 and see E. P. SANDERS, *Jewish Law from Jesus to the Mishnah: Five Studies,* London/Philadelphia, SCM/Trinity Press International, 1990, pp. 228, 260).

12. Κρατεῖν is an infinitive of purpose according to H. B. SWETE (*The Gospel According to St Mark* [London/New York: Macmillan, 1898], p. 137) and A. T. ROBERTSON (*A Grammar of the Greek New Testament in the Light of Historical Research* [Nashville: Broadman Press, 1934; orig. 1914], p. 1087).

13. See P. PILHOFER, *Presbyteron Kreitton: Der Alterbeweis der jüdischen und christlichen Apologeten und seine Vorgeschichte* (WUNT 2.Reihe, 39), Tübingen, Mohr, 1990.

14. See R. A. CAMPBELL, *The Elders: Seniority Within Earliest Christianity* (Studies in the New Testament and Its World), Edinburgh, T. & T. Clark, 1994, passim.

15. Cf. BAUMGARTEN (n. 2), pp. 70-71.

of the elders, which they have received for that very purpose. Nicolaus' implication of the arrogance of the Pharisaic claim to a connection with antiquity is missing in Mark 7,1-5; instead, the Markan Pharisees seem to be doing just what an ancient reader would have expected them to do – standing fast by the tradition of their elders. Moreover, some of the traditions mentioned in 7,4 – the washing of cups, pitchers, and copper utensils – are biblical requirements (see e.g. Lev 11,32; 15,12)[16], and thus should presumably be observed by anyone claiming to be committed to "the commandment of God" (cf. Mark 7,8-9).

Why does Mark give so many hostages to fortune in 7,3-4? And why does the evaluation of the Pharisaic tradition change so sharply in 7,6-13? Why does Jesus respond to the Pharisees' perfectly legitimate question with such a harsh assault ("you hypocrites")? This discrepancy between the positive-sounding description of the Pharisees in 7,3-4 and the subsequent condemnation of them is a first indication that Mark is appropriating Pharisaic terminology and arguments and attempting to utilize them polemically for his own purposes.

The Commandment of God vs. the Teaching of Human Beings

This impression of reverse polemic is strengthened when we begin to examine 7,6-13 carefully. For if we ask ourselves dispassionately who really stands to profit from the scriptural principles and passages adduced here, we will be forced to conclude that they support the Pharisaic position as well as or even better than they do the Christian position[17].

This potential support for the Pharisaic position can be seen first of all from the general flow of the argument. As K. Berger points out[18], in our passage the Markan Jesus implies that the following witnesses testify

16. It would only have been the *way* in which these washings were performed that would have needed to be specified by Pharisaic tradition, as in the later Mishnaic tractate *Kelim*.

17. The method and conclusions here are similar to those of Pauline scholars who have argued that behind Paul's comments on Abraham in Gal 3,6-29 and on Hagar and Sarah in Gal 4,21-31 there lie midrashim on these subjects by Paul's Jewish Christian opponents; see C. K. BARRETT, *The Allegory of Abraham, Sarah, and Hagar in the Argument of Galatians*, in *Rechtfertigung: Festschrift für Ernst Käsemann zum 70. Geburtstag* eds. J. FRIEDRICH et al., Tübingen, J. B. Mohr/Paul Siebeck, 1976, pp. 1-16; J. L. MARTYN, *A Law-Observant Mission to Gentiles: The Background of Galatians*, in *SJT* 38 (1985), pp. 307-324; ID., *The Covenants of Hagar and Sarah*, in *Faith and History: Essays in Honor of Paul W. Meyer*, ed. J. T. CARROLL et al., (Scholars Press Homage Series) Atlanta, Scholars Press, 1990, pp. 160-192.

18. K. BERGER, *Die Gesetzesauslegung Jesu. Ihr historischer Hintergrund im Judentum und im Alten Testament. Teil I: Markus und Parallelen* (WMANT, 40), Neukirchen, Neukirchener Verlag, 1972, p. 487.

both to the validity of his position and to the hypocrisy of the Pharisees:

1) The hearts of people who have not turned away from God (7,6)
2) God's commandment (7,8. 9)
3) Moses (7,10)
4) The word of God (7,13)

But these "witnesses" might as easily, indeed more easily, be used by the Pharisaic side to support their own position and to refute the stance of freedom from Pharisaic regulations and from the ritual requirements of the Law that is developed in Mark 7,1-23. Although the "word of God", for example, does not contain any specific rule about the need for lay people to wash their hands before eating, it does contain several passages, especially in the Psalms, in which handwashing is a symbol of innocence or repentance (e.g. Deut 21,6-7; Ps 18,20.24; 26,6; 73,13)[19]. Based on this symbolism, Ps 24,4 says that only a person with clean hands and a pure heart can ascend to the hill of the Lord and stand in his holy place (the Temple). This passage seems to apply to everyone the Pentateuchal requirement that priests wash their hands before offering a sacrifice (cf. Exod 30,18-21; 40,31) and thus to be a forerunner of the Pharisaic program of extending priestly purity laws to the laity, which was probably the chief motive for Pharisaic handwashing[20]. Far from being opposites, then, as they are in Mark 7,1-23, clean hands and a pure heart belong together scripturally[21]; although the first may be symbolic of the second, this does not imply that the hands should *not be* literally washed[22].

19. See Sanders (n. 11), pp. 228, 262. The same concept, of course, lies behind Pilate's action in Matt 27,24.

20. See J. Neusner, *The Idea of Purity in Ancient Judaism* (SJLA, 1), Leiden, Brill, 1973, p. 3. In recent years Sanders has expressed reservations about the idea that the basis of the Pharisaic program was the desire to extend priestly purity rules to lay people (see e.g. *Jewish Law* [n. 11], 131-254); see however the ripostes from Neusner (*Mr. Sanders' Pharisees and Mine*, in *SJT* 44 [1991], 73-95), D. R. de Lacey (*In Search of a Pharisee*, in *TynB* 43 [1992], 353-72), R. Deines (*Jüdische Steingefässe und pharisäische Frömmigkeit* [WUNT, 2/52], Tübingen, Mohr, 1993, pp. 268-274), and H. H. Harrington (*Did the Pharisees Eat Ordinary Food in a State of Ritual Purity?*, in *JSJ* 26 [1995], 42-54).

21. Cf. James 4,8: καθαρίσατε χεῖρας, ἁμαρτωλοί, καὶ ἁγνίσατε καρδίας, δίψυχοι ("cleanse your hands, you sinners, and purify your hearts, you people of double mind"; cf. Sir 38,10). Δίψυχοι, people of double mind, are people torn between their evil and their good impulse (cf. J. Marcus, *The Evil Inclination in the Epistle of James*, in *CBQ* 44 [1982] 606-621, p. 617). In this Jewish-Christian work, then, cleanliness of hands is part of the battle against the Evil Inclination, whereas in Mark 7,1-23 the two things have nothing to do with each other (cf. the final section of this essay on οἱ διαλογισμοὶ οἱ κακοί in Mark 7,21 as a reference to the Evil Inclination[s]).

22. Cf. Josephus, *Ant.* 18,117 and especially the Jewish-Christian *Ap. Const.* 8,11,12, which says that handwashing is symbolic of purity of soul and assumes that it should still be performed. This is the general Jewish attitude toward the ritual practices mandated by the Law: the fact that they have a deeper symbolism does not dispense Jews from their literal observance; see e.g. Philo, *Migration of Abraham* 16,89-94.

Although "Moses" himself, therefore, does not explicitly mandate hand-washing for lay people before regular meals, it might be argued that to do so is in keeping with the spirit in which the Mosaic purity laws are already being reinterpreted within the Old Testament.

It was, moreover, a basic principle of God's written word, the Torah delivered to Moses, that Israel was "to make a distinction between the unclean and the clean, and between the living creature that may be eaten and the living creature that may not be eaten" (Lev 11,47). Anyone who did what Jesus, according to the Markan interpretation, does in our passage, sweeping away this dietary distinction and declaring all foods to be clean (7,19), ran the risk of being identified as a seducer who led the people's heart astray from the true God (cf. 7,6) and from the holy commandment he had given to Moses (cf. 7,8-9.13)[23]. Indeed, the antithesis that Mark's Jesus draws in 7,10-11 between what Moses said and what "you" say[24] could with just as much justice be applied to the Markan Jesus himself, since he sovereignly abrogates the Mosaic distinction between clean and unclean foods[25]. *Jesus* then might easily be accused of substituting human commandments, i.e. his own precepts, for the

---

23. It is unlikely that the historical Jesus explicitly revoked the Levitical food laws; as has often been pointed out, if he had, it would be difficult to explain why this revocation is never cited in the subsequent early church controversies about the food issue (see e.g. H. RÄISÄNEN, *Jesus and the Food Laws: Reflections on Mark 7.15*, in *Jesus, Paul and Torah: Collected Essays* [JSNT SS, 43], Sheffield, Academic Press, 1992; orig. 1982, pp. 127-148, pp. 142-143). Indeed, in Mark Jesus does not *say* that the OT food laws are passé; this is only Mark's editorial comment (7,19c) on 7,15. The latter is an open-ended statement that is capable of, and receives, more and less radical interpretations within the NT: Mark and Paul (Rom 14,20), perhaps relying on a common tradition, interpret it in an antinomian direction, whereas Matthew 15,10-20 interprets it in a more conservative manner. See J. D. G. DUNN, *Jesus and Ritual Purity: A Study of the Tradition-History of Mark 7.15*, in *Jesus, Paul and the Law: Studies in Mark and Galatians*, London/Louisville, SPCK/Westminster-John Knox, 1990, orig. 1985, pp. 37-60.

24. This antithesis is strikingly reminiscent of the Matthean Jesus' "Antitheses" in Matt 5,17-48, except that in Mark Jesus says, "Moses said...but *you* say", whereas in Matthew he himself in effect says, "Moses said,...but *I* say".

25. Cf. RÄISÄNEN (n. 23), pp. 137-138, n. 2. Against the apparent assumption of most exegetes, καθαρίζων in 7,19 does not imply that all foods have *always* been clean. Καθαρίζειν is never used in ritual contexts in the OT with the meaning of "declaring that something has always been pure"; besides, if all foods have always been pure, why did Moses say that some were impure? It is better, therefore, to interpret καθαρίζων πάντα τὰ βρώματα as "declaring that all foods have now become pure". In Mark's view, Jesus' saying about purity in 7,15 is a performative pronouncement, one which *accomplishes* the purification of foods that it announces. Καθαρίζειν probably also has this performative sense in Acts 10,15; 11,9.

clear mandates of God, and thus of falling under the judgment of Isa 29,13 – the passage that he himself cites in Mark 7,7[26].

We may very well suspect that Jesus and his followers *were* being accused of such abandonment of God's laws in the Markan environment, and that these accusations provide the background to the counterattack in 7,6-13. This hypothesis is supported by Berger's observation[27] that, in a variety of apocalyptic Jewish and Jewish-Christian texts, it is "prophesied" that in the endtime Jews will fall away from God and will prefer the commandments of human beings to the divine, Mosaic laws[28]. Some of these "prophecies", strikingly, include allusions to Isa 29,13. *Testament of Asher* 7,5, for example, accuses the disobedient descendants of Asher of "not paying attention to God's Law but to human commandments" (μὴ προσέχοντες τὸν νόμον τοῦ θεοῦ ἀλλ᾽ ἐντολαῖς ἀνθρώπων). Another passage from the *Testaments*, *T. Levi* 14,4-8, is worthy of more extended quotation, with the allusions to Isaiah 29,13 underlined[29]:

> 14:4) What will all the Gentiles do, if you are darkened through ungodliness and bring a curse upon our race – because of which the light of the law (came) which was given among you to enlighten every man?...[You will be] *teaching commandments contrary to the ordinances of God* (ἐναντίας ἐντολὰς διδάσκοντες τοῖς τοῦ θεοῦ δικαιώμασι). 5) You will rob the offerings of the Lord and steal from his portions...6) You will *teach the commandments*

26. C. G. MONTEFIORE (*The Synoptic Gospels*, 2 vols., London, Macmillan, 1927, vol. 1, pp. 156-60) points up the internal tension within 7,6-15, charging that it is illogical for Jesus on one occasion to appeal to the Law of God violated by rabbinical enactment (7,9-13) and on another to enunciate a principle antagonistic to the Law (7,15). "If the wise and perfect God has ordered [the dietary rules], they too are wise and perfect. If the wise and perfect God has said that what enters into man's mouth can and does defile him, then *He* must be right and Jesus must be wrong". The alternative, which Jesus seems to champion in 7,15, is to "imply that God made a mistake".

27. BERGER (n. 18), pp. 489-490.

28. E.g. CD 4,5; Jub 23,21; *T. Asher* 7,5; *T. Levi* 14,4; 16,2; cf. also the prophecies about the increase of ἀνομία in the end time in Matt 24,12; 2 Thess 2,3; and Did 16,4. Also of interest is the short apocalyptic passage in Acts of Philip K 142, which includes the prophecy that in the endtime the people will serve heathen gods and forsake the commandments that have been passed down to them (καταλείψουσιν τὰς παραδεδομέ-νας αὐτοῖς ἐντολάς; cited by Berger [n. 18], p. 490). As Berger points out, here the idea of tradition (παραδεδομένας is a cognate of παράδοσις) is positively evaluated and *connected* with God's commandments, rather than being divorced from them as in Mark 7. As F. BOVON notes (*Les Actes de Philippe*, in ANRW II.25.6 [1988], pp. 4518-4519), apocalyptic passages are unusual in apostolic novels such as the Acts of Philip, and it has been suggested that the text under discussion was not an original part of this work; might it have come from a Jewish-Christian circle?

29. 2 Clem 3,4-5 also, in a very "Jewish" way, combines a quotation of Isa 29,13 with an allusion to the *Shema* and an exhortation not to disregard the commandments. Although here the commandments to be obeyed are those of Jesus, this passage probably takes up a common Jewish way of interpreting Isa 29,13.

of the Lord out of covetousness, pollute married women, defile virgins of Jerusalem, be joined with harlots and adulteresses, take to wives daughters of the Gentiles, purifying them with an unlawful purification, and your union will be like Sodom and Gomorrah in ungodliness. 7)...*Puffed up also against the commandments of God* 8) you will mock the holy things, jesting contemptuously[30].

The theme of ritual purity, which so dominates Mark 7,1-23, is explicit in this and the *Testament of Asher* passage in the references to pollution and uncleanness, and it is implicit in the references to Sodom and Gomorrah. It is, moreover, intriguing that, among the sins of those who substitute human teachings for God's laws and thus bring down upon themselves the reproach of Isa 29,13, is that they take Gentile women for their wives and therefore make themselves unclean[31]. The student of Mark is here reminded of the way in which Jesus' abrogation of biblical and Pharisaic purity restrictions in our passage (7,1-23) is followed by a passage in which he is prevailed upon to heal the daughter of a Gentile woman, overcoming his natural resistance to "feeding" impure Gentile "dogs" (7,24-30). This juxtaposition may very well mirror and refute the Pharisaic charge that Jewish Christians such as Mark himself, who live in mixed Jewish/Gentile communities where the ritual prescriptions of the Law are ignored and mixed marriages are countenanced, thereby make themselves impure.

The whole issue of ritual purity probably had a very sharp relevance for Mark and some members of his community, since it seems to have been a consuming concern of the Jewish revolutionaries whose war against Rome provides the background for our Gospel's composition[32]. Although, for example, *Psalms of Solomon* was composed considerably before the revolt broke out (probably shortly after Pompey's invasion of Jerusalem in 63 B.C.E.), the following lines from *Pss. Sol.* 17 probably express something very close to the sort of purificatory holy war theology that catalyzed the revolt and kept it going even when all earthly hope of

---

30. Translation by H. W. HOLLANDER and M. DE JONGE, *The Testaments of the Twelve Patriarchs: A Commentary* (SVTP, 8), Leiden, Brill, 1985.

31. This is a natural connection in a Jewish usage of Isa 29,13, given the standard polemic against heathen gods as a human invention (e.g. Isa 44,9-20; Jer 10,1-16; Wis 13,10-19) and the frequent association of worship of those gods with marriages to foreign women or with sexual intercourse with them (e.g. Deut 7,1-6; 1 Kings 11,1-8; 16,31-34; cf. BERGER [n. 18], p. 485).

32. See M. HENGEL, *The Zealots: Investigations into the Jewish Freedom Movement in the Period from Herod I until 70 A.D.*, Edinburgh, T. & T. Clark, 1989, orig. 1961, pp. 198-200, 272; H. SCHWIER, *Tempel und Tempelzerstörung: Untersuchungen zu den theologischen und ideologischen Faktoren im ersten jüdisch-römischen Krieg (66-74 n.Chr.)* (NTOA, 11), Freiburg/Göttingen, Universitätsverlag/Vandenhoeck & Ruprecht, 1989, pp. 55-74, 90-101.

its success seemed to have vanished[33]:

> 22 Undergird [the son of David] with the strength to destroy the unright-
> eous rulers, to purge Jerusalem from gentiles who trample her to destruc-
> tion; in wisdom and in righteousness to drive out the sinners from the
> inheritance...
>
> 24 to destroy the unlawful nations with the word of his mouth...
>
> 26 He will gather a holy people whom he will lead in righteousness; and
> he will judge the tribes of the people that have been made holy by the
> Lord their God.
>
> 27 He will not tolerate unrighteousness (even) to pause among them, and
> any person who knows wickedness shall not live with them...
>
> 28 The alien and the foreigner will no longer live near them...
>
> 30 And he will purge Jerusalem (and make it) holy as it was even from the
> beginning...
>
> 32 There will be no unrighteousness among them in his days, for all shall
> be holy...
>
> 41 He will lead them all in holiness and there will be no arrogance among
> them, that any should be oppressed...
>
> 43 His words will be as the words of the holy ones, among sanctified peoples
> ...
>
> 45 May God dispatch his mercy to Israel; may he deliver us from the pol-
> lution of profane enemies. (R. B. Wright trans. from OTP)

Here the purity of the holy land and of the holy people form a unity, and
both are violated by the presence of unclean Gentiles in their midst. In
such a polarized atmosphere, in which ritual purity was deemed to be
essential for success in holy war, great hostility was probably shown to
groups like the Christians, who were perceived to compromise that
purity by violation of food laws and rupture of the dividing wall between
God's people and the impure Gentiles.

It begins to seem especially likely that Isa 29,13 was of interest to
those involved in the Jewish revolutionary effort when the context of that
verse is considered[34]. For Isa 29 begins with a graphic prophecy of Jerusalem ("Ariel") besieged by foreign armies and surrounded by their siege-
works, a description that would certainly have struck deep chords among
those familiar with the Roman siege of Jerusalem in the late sixties C.E.

---

33. Cf. HENGEL (n. 32), pp. 271-290. The likelihood that many of the rebels were driven by a theology of pollution is increased by Josephus' use of the same theme to counter
them; see e.g. *War* 6,110 and *Ant.* 20,166-167, and on Josephus' reverse polemics here
and elsewhere see D. M. RHOADS, *Israel in Revolution 6-74 C.E.: A Political History
Based on the Writings of Josephus,* Philadelphia, Fortress, 1976, pp. 168-170. Cf. also J.
MARCUS, *Modern and Ancient Jewish Apocalypticism,* in *JR* 76 (1996) 1-27, pp. 12-17,
where this theology of pollution is compared to that prevalent in the virulently anti-Arab,
anti-"Hellenistic" Kach movement in modern-day Israel.

34. I am grateful to Richard Hays for making this suggestion in the discussion of my
paper at the Louvain seminar.

(Isa 29,1-3). But, the Isaian passage continues, when Ariel cries out to God in her distress, he will scatter her enemies like chaff, coming and fighting on her behalf with his traditional storm-weapons of thunder, earthquake, whirlwind, tempest, and fire (Isa 29,4-8). In this context, the denunciation in Isa 29,13-14 of those who honor God with their lips but depart from him through disobedience of his commandments describes the sort of sinfulness that will bring Israel, and especially Jerusalem, to the brink of destruction, but from which she will be saved at the last moment by her repentance (Isa 29,4) and God's sudden appearance on her behalf. Pharisees involved in the war effort, then[35], may very well have seen in Isaiah 29 both an astonishingly accurate prophecy of their nation's current, dire situation and a clear pointer to the sole way of escape from it – a full-fledged return to the commandments of God's Law.

Honor Your Father and Your Mother

So Isaiah 29,13, with its denunciation of those who substitute human ordinances for the divine command, would serve the Pharisees' argument as well as or better than it would serve the Christians', and it may be suspected that Mark's citation of the verse responds to a Pharisaic argument about it[36]. Similar remarks apply to the citation of the Fourth Commandment ("Honor your father and your mother") in Mark 7,10.

---

35. On the involvement of Pharisees in the revolutionary cause, see HENGEL (n. 32), pp. 80-81, 86-88; SCHWIER (n. 32), pp. 128, 190-201. Josephus emphasizes the links between Pharisaic theology and the "Fourth Philosophy" of the revolutionaries (*Ant.* 18,23). Not all Pharisees were as quietistic as Johannan ben Zakkai at the time of the revolt; Simon b. Gamaliel, for example, was active in the revolutionary cause (Josephus, *Life* 190-198). Even the reference in *War* 2.411 to the opposition to the revolt from "the most notable of the Pharisees" would seem to imply that other Pharisees (the majority?) supported it.

36. At the Louvain seminar, Richard Hays pointed to the two citations of Isa 29 in Romans (Isa 29,10 in Rom 11,8 and Isa 29,16 in Rom 9,20), and another participant mentioned that Isa 29,13 itself is alluded to in the (Deutero-Pauline?) letter to the Colossians (Col 2,22). The citations in Romans, at least, make it clear that Isaiah 29 was already a subject of Christian reflection in the pre-Markan period, and even if Colossians is Deutero-Pauline, it may antedate Mark. All of this might suggest that Isaiah 29 was a standard Christian *testimonium* in C. H. Dodd's sense of the term, i.e. a connected OT passage to which Christians again and again had recourse in the explication of their faith (Dodd indeed discusses Isa 29,9-14 as a *testimonium* in *According to the Scriptures: The Sub-structure of New Testament Theology*, London, Fontana, 1965, orig. 1952, pp. 83-84). If this were true, would it falsify the contention that the Markan citation of Isa 29,13 is a response to a Pharisaic usage of that verse? Not necessarily; Isaiah 29 was probably the subject of continuing reflection both by Christians and by non-Christian Jews, and the reflections of both parties were probably stimulated by the exegesis of the text by the other side. Mark's mobilization of Isa 29,13, therefore, could well be a response to Pharisaic usage of that verse.

As Montefiore notes[37], it is a bit startling for Jesus to invoke the commandment to honor parents against the Pharisees, since earlier in the Gospel he has not exactly been a model of filial piety in his treatment of his own mother (3,31-35). At the beginning of his public ministry, moreover, the Markan Jesus called the two sons of Zebedee to abandon their father in his fishing boat in order to follow him (1,19-20), and later he will speak approvingly of those who leave their parents for his sake and the gospel's (10,29). This saying occurs in an even harsher version in Luke 14,26, which speaks of hating father and mother for Jesus' sake; elsewhere in the Synoptic tradition, moreover, Jesus imperiously orders a prospective disciple to forego the basic filial duty to bury his dead father (Matt 8,21-22//Luke 9,60-61). Certainly, therefore, anyone who wished to accuse Jesus of a breach of the Fourth Commandment would find within the Synoptic tradition plenty of ammunition for doing so.

On the positive side, filial piety might be mobilized by the Pharisees as an argument for observing both the "tradition of the elders" handed down from generation to generation and the written laws of Moses. With regard to the elders, there is a profound intrinsic connection between reverence for one's own parents and reverence for old people generally, and in postbiblical Judaism the two are often conflated, the point of departure being the injunction in Lev 19,32 to rise up before the hoary head and revere the face of the old man (והדרת פני זקן). Significantly, the Septuagint translates the latter clause καὶ τιμήσεις πρόσωπον πρεσβυτέρου ("and you shall honor the face of the elder"), thus forging a connection between the language of the Fourth Commandment and the term "elder". This connection becomes explicit in Josephus, who says that the Law requires the young "to have honor for every elder" (παντὸς τοῦ πρεσβυτέρου τιμὴν ἔχειν; Apion 2,206); Philo, similarly, declares that "one who pays respect to an aged man or woman who is not of his kin may be regarded as having remembrance of his father and mother" (Special Laws 2,237-238, LCL trans.; cf. also Pseudo-Phocyclides 221-22 and Pseudo-Menander 1,2; 2,10-14)[38].

This respect for one's parents and other elders often involved respect for the traditions, both biblical and non-biblical, that these elders had handed down. As G.K. Chesterton put it, "Tradition means giving votes to the most obscure of all classes, our ancestors"[39]. This linkage between the parental relation and tradition is, as J.M.G. Barclay has observed, built into Judaism's central creed, for according to the Shema the father

37. MONTEFIORE (n. 26), vol. 1, p. 95.
38. See BERGER (n. 18), p. 287.
39. G. K. CHESTERTON, Orthodoxy, London, Bodley Head, 1908, p. 83 (chapter 4).

is to teach the commandment of the Law diligently to his children "when you sit in your house, and when you walk by the way, and when you lie down, and when you rise up" (Deut 6,7; cf. 11,19; RSV alt.)[40]. In a rabbinic tradition (*b. Qidd.* 30b), the related commandment to teach Torah to one's children and one's children's children (Deut 4,9) is interpreted to imply that a father who teaches his son Torah is regarded as though he had taught it to his son, his son's son, and so on to the end of time; the parental relation, then, is linked to a teaching that is passed down from generation to generation.

The linkage between tradition and the parent/child relation continues to be strongly emphasized in post-biblical Jewish writings – sometimes, one suspects, out of anxiety that both are under threat. Sirach, for example, enjoins his hearers, "Do not despise the tradition of the old, which they have received from their fathers" (Sir 8,9)[41]. And *2 Enoch* 52,9-10 applies the age-old contrast between the "two ways" to people's divergent attitudes toward ancestral tradition: "Happy is he who preserves the foundations of the fathers, where they have been made sure. Cursed is he who destroys the rules and restrictions of his fathers" (OTP trans.). The Pharisees seem to have particularly emphasized the connection between filial piety and respect for their tradition; Paul and Josephus agree in referring to the Pharisaic tradition as "the tradition of the fathers" or "the law of the fathers" (Gal 1,14; Josephus, *Ant.* 13,297.408).

If the Pharisees linked filial piety with the conservation and transmission of their own, nonbiblical traditions, they would naturally have linked it also with observance of the biblical laws, such as the avoidance of non-kosher foods, that Jews had observed for centuries. These dietary restrictions were, of course, one of the best-known societal identity markers of ancient Jews; even if outsiders knew little else about Jews, they at least knew that they rested one day a week, circumcised their male children, and refused to eat pork[42]. These ancestral identity markers had become so important partly because they had been flashpoints of conflict since the time of the Maccabean Revolt; as one of the seven sons arrested and tortured by Antiochus Epiphanes, forced to choose between eating pork

---

40. See J.M.G. BARCLAY, *The Family as the Bearer of Religious Culture in Judaism and Early Christianity*, forthcoming in *The Family in Early Christianity*, ed. H. MOXNES et al., London, Routledge, 1997.

41. For this translation, and for the following passages, cf. F. MUSSNER, *Der Galaterbrief* (HTKNT, 9), Freiburg/Basel/Wien, Herder, 1974, p. 80.

42. See the remarks on these subjects by the Greco-Roman writers cited in M. WHITTAKER, *Jews and Christians: Graeco-Roman Views* (Cambridge Commentaries on Writings of the Jewish and Christian World 200 BC to AD 200, Vol. 6), Cambridge, University Press, 1984, pp. 63-85.

and execution, vows in 2 Macc 7,2, "We are ready to die rather than transgress the laws of our fathers (τοὺς πατρίους νόμους)".

The purity restrictions that Mark so casually sweeps aside with his editorial parenthesis in 7,19, therefore, were not an invention of yesterday but a venerable inheritance from fathers, grandfathers, and other elders, an inheritance whose supreme value had been sealed with the blood of the Jewish martyrs and whose preservation and transmission to the next generation not only symbolized but actually *was* the continuance of Judaism in an alien and frequently hostile pagan world. That such a linkage between the Old Testament dietary laws and the commandment to honor parents is natural is shown again by Josephus, who says in *Apion* 2,174 that the Law prescribes which meats should be eaten and which avoided, and thus acts as a father and master to its adherents. The Pharisees, then, would have been on very firm ground in asserting that Jesus' offenses against ritual purity, capped by his "cleansing" of non-kosher food, violated not only clear or implicit biblical teaching about foods but also the commandment to honor one's father and mother.

Taking our point of departure, then, from hints within Mark itself, especially from chapter 7, and from what we know about the Pharisees from other sources, we may with some confidence reconstruct the main lines of the Pharisaic attack to which Mark 7,1-23 is a response. I suggest that it ran something like this:

A Reconstructed Pharisaic Attack on the Christian Attitude Toward Scripture and Tradition

Woe to us! For there has come upon us, and upon all Israel, the great catastrophe prophesied in God's word – a falling away from God in the end time, and the corruption of the people through the lying words of blasphemous deceivers. What a good job Isaiah did of prophesying about you heretics: "This people honors me with their lips, but their heart stands far off from me; they worship me pointlessly, teaching as divine teachings the commandments of human beings" (Isa 29,13). For in these latter days you have arisen, you who take the name of the holy God upon your lips, but whose heart is far from him. You presume to speak in the name of God, but your teaching is a human one that springs from your own corrupted hearts and from the Evil One, as is shown by its blatant contradiction to the commandments that God gave to Moses. For you are filled with all unrighteousness, and you lead Israel astray, causing them to drift into paths of impurity and defilement, and to forget God's holy Law.

Like ravening wolves who devour their food in impurity, you eat with defiled hands. You presume to speak in the name of God, but you are not fit to stand in his holy place or to take his sacred name upon your unclean lips. For "who shall ascend the hill of the Lord? And who shall stand in his holy place? He who has clean hands and a pure heart, who does not lift up his soul to what is false, and does not swear deceitfully" (Ps 24,4). But your soul is filled with falsity and unrighteousness, and lies are on your lips, and you demonstrate it to the world by eating with unclean hands. For you break down the fence of tradition, which God gave at Sinai to stand guard over his inviolable Law, and which the holy men of old have passed down to us for the sanctifying of all Israel.

Nor is this the limit of your presumption – alas, if only it were! For you claim to speak for the holy God, but you eat swine's flesh and all unclean foods, and entice others to join with you in your apostasy. Thus you transgress the holy commandment that God gave to Moses when He revealed Himself on Sinai, and which Moses passed on to the people. For *Moses* said, "You shall not eat these foods; they are unclean to you" (Lev 11,8); but *you* say, "All foods are clean". Woe, woe to you, and woe to those whom you lead to destruction with your deceitful words, claiming in your madness that, because the days of the Messiah have come, everything is permitted!

Thus you defile all that is holy, break down every wall, and destroy the ancient foundations. The tradition that has been passed down to us from our fathers you treat with scorn, despising the wisdom of the ancients and abhorring the counsel of the elders. No wonder, then, that you justify your wild actions by the godless example of that upstart, may his name be blotted out, who treated his elders with open contempt, and who called his deluded followers to do likewise. For *Moses* said, "Honor your father and your mother", and "The person who curses father or mother, let him die the death" (Exod 20,12//Deut 5,16; Exod 21,17//Lev 20,9). But *he* said, "There is no one who abandons...mother or father ...for my sake,...who will not receive a hundredfold". He enticed those who followed him to turn their backs on their parents and to leave them without support, thus cursing them with poverty and degregation. But his curse came back upon his own head, as yours will certainly come back on yours; may all God's enemies perish so!

The Markan Response

I have tried to show that Mark 7,1-23 is a rejoinder to a serious theological challenge. Indeed, it may seem that the Pharisees' scriptural case is so good as to be nearly overwhelming and that Mark has been wise to impart to his readers only the barest hints of it. What would he say if forced to confront this searching challenge head-on in a systematic way? What does he consider to be wrong with the Pharisaic tradition? And what does he consider to be wrong with the purity regulations of the written Law, including the kosher laws[43]? Although it must remain speculative exactly how Mark would have answered these questions, Mark 7 and related passages point in the following direction:

1) Although, as we have seen, in the Pharisees' self-understanding their tradition had the benificent purpose of preserving and elaborating God's revelation for their own contemporaries, the Markan Pharisees invoke it with a hostile intent, namely to trip Jesus up and to alienate the people from him by presenting him as a violator of customs that have been hallowed by time and patrimony ("the tradition of the elders")[44]. In this hostile atmosphere, tradition ceases to be a lifeline for revelation and becomes instead a bludgeon to be used against transgressors; indeed, for Mark and his community, who have perhaps suffered physically at the

43. It will be noticed that our story concerns Jesus' attack *both* on the Pharisaic tradition (handwashing) *and* on the Mosaic Law itself (eating non-kosher food), or, rather, that what begins with a challenge by the Pharisees about Jesus' neglect of their tradition (7,1-5) ends with his revocation of a significant aspect of the Law itself (7,19). MONTEFIORE (n. 26) vol. 1, p. 156 charges Jesus with inconsistency because of this shifting of the subject. It is more likely, however, that the modulation of theme is due to the development of the narrative; the original controversy concerned only how ritual purity is affected by handwashing (7,1-2.5.15), but in the early church it was expanded to take in the broader issue of whether or not certain foods are unclean (see the list of scholars who support this reconstruction in RÄISÄNEN [n. 23], p. 129, n. 3). It is significant that the explicit revocation of the OT food laws comes in an editorial aside by Mark himself, and that it occurs in a short appended scene (7,17-23) in which Jesus privately explains to the disciples his previous proverb-like statement about purity (7,15), which as we have noted is capable of more or less radical interpretations (see above, n. 23). This seclusion with the disciples to explain a saying of Jesus is a typical Markan device to bring out the contemporary significance of a traditional *Jesuslogion* (cf. 4,10-20; 10,10-12; 13,3-37). Mark 7,1-23 is thus what J. L. MARTYN has called a "two-level narrative" (*History and Theology in the Fourth Gospel,* Nashville, Abingdon, ²1979, pp. 27-30): it begins with a question that arose in Jesus' own day, but ends with one that only became an issue in the later church. It is even possible that the Pharisaic position is represented within Mark's own community; see 7,18-19, in which Jesus' initial response to the disciples' question about his purity logion is to say, "Then are you also without understanding?" (RSV trans.).

44. Already the description in 7,1, "The Pharisees and some of the scribes who had come from Jerusalem gathered together against him", implies hostility, especially in view of the scriptural echo of Ps 2,2, in which συνάγεσθαι is used of rulers gathering together against the Lord and his Messiah, and of other Psalms (30[31],13; 34[35],15) in which it is used of the wicked gathering together against the righteous. The lumping of the Pharisees with the scribes, moreover, recalls 3,6, where the Pharisees joined with another group to plot against Jesus' life. Furthermore, the scribes seem to have come from Jerusalem with the express purpose of catching Jesus out. And the Pharisees' διὰ τί οὐ ("why do they not?") in 7,5 recalls similar hostile refrains in 2,1–3,6.

hands of Pharisees and other zealous Jews (cf. 13,9-13)[45], Pharisaic protestations of high theological purpose would probably ring hollow[46]. It is even possible that Mark intends a pun between two senses of παράδοσις, "tradition" and "betrayal": the Pharisaic παράδοσις, which understands itself as a faithful handing on of the divine word, has actually betrayed that word (cf. esp. 7,13)[47].

2) How has this subversion come about? Mark would doubtless answer: through the evil thoughts (οἱ διαλογισμοὶ οἱ κακοί) that come out of the human heart and defile everything that humanity touches (7, 21) – including the word of God. It is probable that the phrase οἱ διαλογισμοὶ οἱ κακοί is the Markan counterpart to the biblically rooted Jewish conception of יצר הרע, "the Evil Inclination"[48], a phrase which can sometimes appear in the plural. This inclination is the inner enemy of God lodged within the human heart[49], a wild force that is endemic to the human situation and that propels people willy-nilly into actions that are opposed to God's will. It is therefore no accident that the Markan Jesus' response to the Pharisees, which begins with his referring to the Pharisaic regulations as a tradition *of human beings* (τῶν ἀνθρώπων, 7,7-8), ends with him pointing repeatedly to the defilement that proceeds from the heart *of the human being* (τοῦ ἀνθρώπου, 7,15.18.20-21.23). These pervasive usages of ἄνθρωπος are conceptually as well as literarily linked: tradition inevitably ends up choking the revelation of God because it participates in the human sphere in which the Evil Inclination holds sway. Mark's diagnosis, then, is similar to that of Paul in Rom 8,3: God's Law has been unable to accomplish what it had promised, since it has been weakened by the flesh[50].

45. On Pharisaic participation in the Jewish Revolt which provides the background to the composition of Mark's Gospel, see above, n. 35.

46. This is natural; religious groups anathematized by other groups are rarely able to enter sympathetically into their persecutors' theological justifications for their actions, but tend to see those actions as being motivated solely by hostility on the human level and demonic incitement on the superhuman level.

47. Elsewhere in the Gospel the cognate verb παραδιδόναι is used with the sense of "to betray" (3,19; 9,31; 10,33; 13,9.11-12; 14,10-11.18.21.41-42.44).

48. On the Evil Inclination in the New Testament, see MARCUS, *Evil Inclination in James* [n. 21], pp. 606-621 and idem, *The Evil Inclination in the Letters of Paul*, in *IBS* 8 (1986), 8-21. As Joseph Fitzmyer pointed out to me in Louvain, a form of the term יצר רע has now turned up in a Qumran document, 4Q422 (4QParaphrase of Gen-Exod) col. 1 frag 1 (I am grateful to James Davila for the exact citation). This attestation increases the probability that already in the first century the Evil Inclination was a standard Jewish concept.

49. Gen 6,5; 8,21; cf. Mark's "from the heart of human beings".

50. On the Law as the antidote to the Evil Inclination in Judaism, see already Sir 21,11 and cf. F. C. PORTER, *The Yeçer hara: A Study in the Jewish Doctrine of Sin*, in *Biblical and Semitic Studies* (Yale Bicentennial Publications), New York, Scribners, 1901, pp. 93-156, p. 128. On Rom 8,3, see MARCUS, *Evil Inclination in Paul* (n. 48), pp. 15-16.

3) Mark's prognosis is also similar to Paul's: what God's Law could not do, God himself has done in the eschatological action of sending Jesus. As we learn in the later Markan discussion of divorce (10,5-6), the commandments of the Law were given with a view to checking the Evil Inclination (πρὸς τὴν σκληροκαρδίαν ὑμῶν)[51], but the era of their ultimately unsuccessful battle with it is now at an end. This is because, through Jesus, the "hardness of heart" which made the Law necessary, that is, the Inclination itself, has finally been dealt a death-blow by God's eschatological action, which restores the paradisiacal conditions that prevailed "in the beginning"[52].

4) That divine blow has overcome what is, from Mark's point of view, a further tragic consequence both of the written Law and of the Pharisaic tradition that elaborates it, namely the divisions that Law and tradition had created within the human family. As Mary Douglas has shown, distinctions between pure and impure things, such as are mandated in the Torah, necessarily imply divisions between pure and impure people and have far-reaching social consequences[53]. The Law separates Israel from the nations, and the Pharisaic tradition further subdivides Israel into observers and non-observers of that tradition. True, the purpose of both Law and tradition is not first and foremost to ostracize outsiders but to sanctify Israel, but that which is sanctified is necessarily separated from something else[54]. The kosher laws and other purity regulations of the Old Testament made meaningful social intercourse between Jews and Gentiles difficult, just as the supererogatory Pharisaic traditions discouraged socializing between Pharisees and other Jews who were not members of their pure-eating-clubs; if you cannot eat with someone, it is very difficult to become his friend, or really to understand him[55]. It is

51. On the equivalence of "hardness of heart" to the Evil Inclination in the Dead Sea Scrolls, see 1QS 5,4-5; cf. Marcus, *Evil Inclination in Paul* (n. 48), p. 9.

52. Cf. D. O. Via, *The Ethics of Mark's Gospel – In the Middle of Time,* Philadelphia, Fortress, 1985, p. 101.

53. M. Douglas, *Purity and Danger: An Analysis of the Concepts of Pollution and Taboo,* London, Ark Paperbacks, 1984; orig. 1966.

54. The etymology of the word "Pharisee" may reflect this idea of separation; see Schürer (n. 11), vol. 2, pp. 396-398.

55. See *Apion* 2.174, which says that the Law dictates "what meats one should abstain from, and what enjoy; and with what persons one should associate" (LCL trans. alt.); the juxtaposition of the subjects of diet and society is scarcely fortuitous. Indeed, it is a commonplace in Greco-Roman accounts that the Jewish dietary laws (which are often viewed polemically as an expression of hatred of humankind) deliberately separate Jews from foreigners. See e.g. Diodorus, *World History*, 34.2, a passage reflecting the views of Posidonius of Apamea: "The refugees [from Egypt] had occupied the territory around Jerusalem, and having organized the nation of the Jews had made their hatred of mankind into a tradition (παραδόσιμον ποιῆσαι τὸ μῖσος τὸ πρὸς τοὺς ἀνθρώπους), and on this

no accident, then, that in the Markan narrative, Jesus overcomes his initial reluctance to help the Syro-Phoenician woman, whom he at first characterizes as an impure Gentile "dog" (7,24-30), immediately after he revokes the separating dietary laws (7,19). The OT food laws, then, which had formed a dividing wall of hostility between Jews and Gentiles, have now been eschatologically breached, and as a consequence all God's children are able to enjoy the bread of life together (cf. Mark 8,1-10; Eph 2,14-15; John 6,51)[56].

Behind the sometimes puzzling polemic of Mark 7,1-15, therefore[57], there lies a serious theological challenge that Mark would have needed to confront in a serious way. If this study has enabled a deeper perception both of the gravity of that challenge and of the profundity of Mark's response, it will have achieved its purpose.

Dept. of Theology & Religious Studies   Joel MARCUS
University of Glasgow
Glasgow G12 8QQ

account had introduced utterly outlandish laws: not to break bread with any other race, nor to show any good will at all" (τὸ μηδενὶ ἄλλῳ ἔθνει τραπέζης κοινωνεῖν μηδ᾽ εὐνοεῖν τὸ παράπαν; trans. M. STERN from *Greek and Latin Authors on Jews and Judaism* [3 vols.], Jerusalem, Israel Academy of Sciences and Humanities, 1976-1984 vol. 1, p. 183). This passage comes especially close to Mark 7,1-30 by combining the themes of food laws and separation from foreigners with the vocabulary of "tradition" and the "table".

56. For a fascinating meditation by a contemporary Jewish scholar on the tension between Jewish Law, Jewish ethnicity, and the universalistic tendencies of early Christianity, especially in its Pauline incarnation, see D. BOYARIN, *A Radical Jew: Paul and the Politics of Identity* (Contraversions 1), Berkeley/Los Angeles/London, University of California Press, 1994.

57. I do not claim to have solved all the puzzles. For example, we know nothing about immersion of beds in early Judaism, so that 7,4 is cryptic if καὶ κλινῶν ("and of beds") is part of the original text. And the description of the Pharisees' *korban* practice does not correspond to what we know of later Mishnaic law (see e.g. *m. Ned.* 9,1 and cf. MONTEFIORE, [n. 26], 1.149); for a sensitive treatment of the issues, see A. I. BAUMGARTEN, *Korban and the Pharisaic Paradosis*, in *Journal of the Ancient Near Eastern Society* 16 (1984) 5-17.

— I wish to thank the British Academy for a travel grant and all the members of the Seminar for a lively and instructive discussion.

DAS MARKUSEVANGELIUM, PSALM 110,1 UND 118,22f.
FOLGETEXT UND PRÄTEXT

In memoriam Willem S. Vorster

1. Einführung: Zur Intertextualitätsdebatte[1]

Die Intertextualitätsdebatte, die seit den achtziger Jahren Hochkonjunktur in der Text- und Literaturwissenschaft hat[2] und zu einer Flut literaturtheoretischer Beiträge führte[3], ist, wenn auch verspätet, nicht spurlos an der Bibelwissenschaft[4] und der Judaistik[5] vorübergegangen[6]. Man

---

1. Die Abkürzungen richten sich nach den Vorgaben der BETL, sonst nach S.M. Schwertner, *Theologische Realenzyklopädie* [=*TRE*]. *Abkürzungsverzeichnis*, Berlin, de Gruyter, ²1994 [=*IATG²*]. Biblische Schriften werden nach dem *ÖVBE* abgekürzt. Sonst: *BAA*: W. Bauer, *Griechisch-deutsches Wörterbuch zu den Schriften des Neuen Testaments und der frühchristlichen Literatur*, K. Aland & B. Aland (eds.), Berlin, de Gruyter, ⁶1988; *BDR*: F. Blass & A. Debrunner, *Grammatik des neutestamentlichen Griechisch*, F. Rehkopf (ed.), Göttingen, Vandenhoeck & Ruprecht, ¹⁷1990; *GELS: A Greek-English Lexicon of the Septuagint*. Part I, A-I, J. Lust, E. Eynikel & K. Hauspie (eds.), Stuttgart, Deutsche Bibelgesellschaft, 1992; *Gesenius*: W. Gesenius, *Hebräisches und Aramäisches Handwörterbuch*, Berlin, Springer, ¹⁷1962; *HAL: Hebräisches und aramäisches Lexikon zum Alten Testament, Dritte Auflage*, Lieferung I-V, L. Koehler, W. Baumgartner, J.J. Stamm et al. (eds.), Leiden, Brill, 1967-1995; *LN: Greek-English Lexicon of the New Testament based on Semantic Domains*, Volume 1 and 2, J.P. Louw & E.A. Nida (eds.), New York, United Bible Societies, 1988; *LSJM: A Greek-English Lexicon*, H.G. Liddell, R. Scott, H.S. Jones & R. McKenzie (eds.), Oxford, Clarendon, 1968 (=⁹1940).
2. Vgl. den Forschungsbericht von O. Ette, *Intertextualität: Ein Forschungsbericht mit literatursoziologischen Anmerkungen*, in *Romanische Zeitschrift für Literaturgeschichte* 9 (1985) 497-522.
3. Vgl. die Bibliographie von H.-P. Mai, *Intertextual Theory – A Bibliography*, in H.F. Plett (ed.), *Intertextuality* (Research in Text Theory, 15), Berlin, de Gruyter, 1991, pp. 237-250.
4. Vgl. u.a. die Beiträge in: *Sémiotique et Bible* 15 (1979) und S. Draisma (ed.), *Intertextuality in Biblical Writings. Essays in Honour of Bas van Iersel*, Kampen, Kok, 1989; D.N. Fewell (ed.), *Reading between Texts. Intertextuality and the Hebrew Bible*, Louisville, Westminster Press, 1992 sowie K. Nielsen, *Intertextuality and Biblical Scholarship*, in *SJOT* 4/2 (1990) 89-95; I.R. Kitzberger, *Love and Footwashing. John 13:1-20 and Luke 7:36-50 Read Intertextually*, in *Biblical Interpretation* 2 (1994) 190-206; R.B. Hays, *Echoes of Scripture in the Letters of Paul*, New Haven & London, Yale University Press, 1989, bes. pp. 1-33.
5. Vgl. D. Boyarin, *Intertextuality and the Reading of Midrash*, Bloomington, Indianapolis, Indiana University Press, 1990.
6. Daß man noch 1991 den Bibelwissenschaftlern auf einem textwissenschaftlichen Forum vorwerfen konnte, sie würden sich von einer positivistischen Grundhaltung her gegen Reflexion anhand der Intertextualitätsdebatte sperren, liegt nicht nur an der Ausblendung

kann sich nun auf den Standpunkt stellen, daß die Exegese sich von alters her mit den Beziehungen zwischen Texten, mit dem »... was sich zwischen Texten abspielt...«[7], beschäftigt habe. Und zu Recht. Exegeten kennen verschiedene Formen der Intertextualität, auch wenn sie in der Regel nicht »Intertextualitäten«[8] genannt und im Rahmen einer Intertextualitätstheorie bedacht werden. »Intertextualität ... bezeichnet als theoretischer Begriff zunächst nichts mehr [als] das Phänomen einer wie auch immer festzulegenden Relation zwischen Texten«[9].

Nehmen wir als erstes Beispiel referentieller Intertextualität das Phänomen, daß ein Text einen Prätext *ersetzen* kann. In diesem Zusammenhang untersucht die Exegese schon immer den Sprachwechsel zwischen den griechischen bzw. hebräischen Originaltexten und den sie in fast allen jemals bekannten Sprachen ersetzenden Übersetzungen. Sie kennt ebenfalls die intertextuelle Relation, die durch den Gattungswechsel zwischen z.b. den narrativen Evangelientexten und den Homilien der Kirchenväter oder einem Gleichnis und dessen allegorisierender Auslegung entsteht.

Bibelwissenschaftler kennen eine zweite Form der Intertextualität, nämlich daß ein sekundärer Text einen primären Prätext *ergänzen* kann. Die Annotationes eines Erasmus von Rotterdam[10] oder eines Grotius aus Delft[11] zu den Bibeltexten stehen nicht nur an der Wiege der Bibelwissenschaft[12], sondern sind, wie die viel früheren Midraschim und die Gemara, Beispiele für die Kategorie »Epitext«, die von Gérard Genette in die literaturtheoretische

---

der Hermeneutikdebatte seit Bultmann, sondern auch an der mangelhaften Literaturrecherche von G.A. PHILLIPS (*Sign/Text/Différance. The Contribution of Intertextual Theory to Biblical Criticism*, in PLETT, *Intertextuality* (n. 3), pp. 78-97, bes. pp. 79f.) im Bereich der Exegese und deutschsprachigen Literaturwissenschaft.

7. »... d.h. de[m] Bezug von Text auf andere Texte.« So die Umschreibung des Begriffes »Intertextualität« bei U. BROICH & M. PFISTER (eds.), *Intertextualität. Formen, Funktionen, anglistische Fallstudien*, Tübingen, Niemeyer, 1985, p. IX.

8. Zu den Formen der intertextuellen Beziehung vgl. H.F. PLETT, *Intertextualities*, in ID., *Intertextuality* (n. 3), pp. 3-29, bes. pp. 17ff.; sowie die von U. BROICH eingeleiteten Beiträge *Zu den Versetzungsformen der Intertextualität*, in BROICH & PFISTER, *Intertextualität* (n. 7), pp. 135-196. Grundlegend: G. GENETTE, *Palimpsestes. La littérature au second degré*, Paris, Éditions du Seuil, 1982.

9. S. HOLTHUIS, *Intertextualität. Aspekte einer rezeptionsorientierten Konzeption*, Tübingen, Stauffenburg Verlag, 1993, p. 29.

10. Vgl. A. REEVE & M.A. SCREECH (eds.), *Erasmus' Annotations on the New Testament (Acts – Romans – I and II Corinthians). Facsimile of the final Latin text with all earlier variants*, Leiden, Brill, 1990.

11. Vgl. H. GROTIUS, *Annotationes in Novum Testamentum, Tomus I (Quatuor Evangelia et Explicationem Decalogi continens)*, Halle, 1769.

12. Zu Grotius vgl. u.a. H.J.M. NELLEN & E. RABBIE (eds.), *Hugo Grotius Theologian. FS G.H.M. Posthumus Meyjes*, Leiden, Brill, 1994. Zu Erasmus vgl. die Bibliographie in REEVE & SCREECH, *Annotations* (n. 10), pp. XXVII-XXXII.

Diskussion gebracht wurde[13]. Der allseits bekannte und so beliebte Bibelkommentar kann in diesem Zusammenhang als »Metatext« zum Bibeltext eingestuft werden.

Selbstverständlich kennt die Bibelwissenschaft auch ein drittes Intertextualitätsphänomen, bei dem der sekundäre Text den Prätext *verkürzt*, eine Form der intertextuellen Beziehung, die unter der Redaktionsgeschichte[14] bei der Interpretation der Verkürzung der markinischen Wundergeschichten durch Matthäus seit Bornkamms und Helds grundlegenden Studien für die Interpretation nutzbar gemacht wurde. Auch die intertextuelle Relation der Permutation ist der biblischen Exegese vertraut[15].

In diesem Beitrag möchte ich mich mit einer vierten intertextuellen Relation beschäftigen, die auf Wiederholung aufbaut. In diesem Zusammenhang ist Intertextualität eng zu fassen und zwar als »referentielle Intertextualität«, d.h. als Bezugnahme von Texten auf Einzeltexte. Ausgeklammert bleibt das Feld der »typologischen Intertextualität«, d.h. der Beziehung zwischen Text und Textklassen[16]. Der Text, hier das Markusevangelium, wiederholt einen Teil eines Prätextes. Nun kann diese Wiederholung sehr unterschiedlich ausfallen. Da ist zunächst die Allusion[17], in der die Oberflächenstruktur des Prätextes, auf den Bezug genommen wird, nicht wiederholt wird. Durch den Hinweis in Mk 2,25f. z.B. wird auf den Inhalt der Erzählung in 1 Sam 21,1-7 angespielt. Durch die Nennung des Namens Moses in Mk 10,3 wird auf den Inhalt und die Funktion des Gesetzes in Dtn 24,1.3 angespielt, ohne daß Jesus das Gebot zitiert. Dies tun erst die Pharisäer. Mehrere Stellen im Markusevangelium, besonders in der Passionserzählung[18], aber nicht nur in ihr[19], lassen

13. Vgl. PLETT, *Intertextualities* (n. 8), p. 22; G. GENETTE, *Seuils*, Paris, Éditions du Seuil, 1987.

14. Vgl. W.S. VORSTER, *Intertextuality and Redaktionsgeschichte*, in DRAISMA, *Intertextuality* (n. 4), pp. 15-26, bes. pp. 19-22.

15. William Wrede z.B. beschreibt den 2. Thessalonicherbrief als eine neuangeordnete Wiederverwendung der Bruchstücke des 1. Thessalonicherbriefes. Auch wenn man nicht so weit gehen will, bieten das Chronistische Werk, die Biblischen Antiquitates eines Flavius Josephus und eines Pseudo-Philon ausreichend Beispiele für diese Form der intertextuellen Relation.

16. Für diese Unterscheidung vgl. HOLTHUIS, *Intertextualität* (n. 9), pp. 48f. Im letztgenannten Zusammenhang könnte z.B. die traditionelle Frage nach der Gattung des Markusevangeliums gestellt werden. Ahmt das Markusevangelium die Tragödie, die Biographie oder den hellenistischen Roman nach?

17. Zu Anspielungen vgl. U.J. HEBEL, *Towards a Descriptive Poetics of Allusion*, in PLETT, *Intertextuality* (n. 3), pp. 135-164, bes. pp. 135f.

18. Vgl. Mk 14,34 (Ps 42,6.12; 43,5); Mk 14,57f. (Ps 35,11; 27,12); Mk 14,62 (Ps 110,1; Dan 7,13); Mk 15,24 (Ps 22,19); Mk 15,29 (Ps 22,8); Mk 15,34 (Ps 22,2); Mk 15,36 (Ps 69,22).

19. Vgl. Mk 1,11 (Ps 2,7); Mk 4,32 (Ps 104,2); Mk 8,31 (eventuell Ps 118,22); Mk 8,37 (Ps 49,8f.); Mk 11,9.10 (Ps 118,25; 148,1).

sich als Anspielungen auf Psalmtexte lesen und auslegen[20]. In Mk 10,6-8 finden wir eine Wiederholung, die als intertextuelle Paraphrase[21] klassifiziert werden kann. In einem Zitationsverfahren[22] dagegen wird die Oberflächenstruktur des Prätextes im Folgetext wiederholt. In diesem Beitrag soll das Augenmerk auf die Teile des Markusevangeliums gerichtet werden, die zitierende Texte sind. Aus Praktikabilitätsgründen werden lediglich die intertextuellen Relationen zwischen dem Markusevangelium als »Folgetext« und einigen Psalmtexten als »Prätexten« untersucht. Es gibt bekanntlich nur zwei solche Fälle, in denen sich das Markusevangelium als Folgetext mit expliziter Markierung der Zitate auf Psalmen als Prätexte bezieht: Mk 12,10f. bezieht sich auf Ps 118 als Prätext und zitiert V.22f.; Mk 12,36 bezieht sich auf Ps 110 als Prätext und zitiert V.1[23]. Im Falle dieser zwei Psalmzitate werden einige weitere Zitate und Anspielungen auf die zitierten Verse, die anderweitig im Evangelium vorkommen (Mk 8,31; 14,62), in die Untersuchung einbezogen[24].

Die vier obengenannten Formen der Intertextualität[25] sollen nicht verschleiern, daß die Intertextualitätsdebatte der letzten zwei Jahrzehnte verschiedene, zum Teil nicht miteinander zu vereinbarende Ansätze geliefert hat[26]. Deswegen soll der Rahmen des hier verfolgten Ansatzes in aller

20. Vgl. hier bes. den Kommentar von H.B. SWETE, *The Gospel According to St. Mark*, London, Macmillan, 1902 und die einschlägigen Untersuchungen von H.-J. STEICHELE, *Der leidende Sohn Gottes. Eine Untersuchung einiger alttestamentlicher Motive in der Christologie des Markusevangeliums* (BU, 14), Regensburg, Pustet, 1980; D.J. MOO, *The Old Testament in the Gospel Passion Narratives*, Sheffield, The Almond Press, 1983; J. MARCUS, *The Way of the Lord. Christological Exegesis of the Old Testament in the Gospel of Mark*, Louisville, Westminster Press, 1992, pp. 69f. 111-152. 172-186; sowie D. JUEL, *Messianic Exegesis. Christological Interpretation of the Old Testament in Early Christianity*, Philadelphia, Fortress Press, 1988, pp. 93-103. 110-117.

21. Vgl. dazu HOLTHUIS, *Intertextualität* (n. 9), pp. 136-147.

22. Zum Zitat vgl. H.F. PLETT, *The Poetics of Quotation*, in J.S. PETŐFI & T. OLIVI (eds.), *Von der verbalen Konstitution zur symbolischen Bedeutung*, Hamburg, Buske, 1988, pp. 313-334.

23. Die Literatur hierzu ist umfangreich. Vgl. neben den einschlägigen Kommentaren die bibliographischen Angaben bei F. NEIRYNCK et al. (eds.), *The Gospel of Mark 1950-1990* (BETL, 102), Leuven, University Press-Peeters, 1992. Unter den neueren Beiträgen zur mkn. Aufnahme von Ps 110,1 sei erwähnt: JUEL, *Exegesis* (n. 20), pp. 135-150; MARCUS, *Way* (n. 20), pp. 130-152; M. DE JONGE, *Jesus, Son of David and Son of God*, in DRAISMA (ed.), *Intertextuality* (n. 4), pp. 95-104. Unter den neueren Beiträgen zur Aufnahme von Ps 118,22 durch das Markusevangelium sei genannt: MARCUS, *Way* (n. 20), pp. 111-129; U. MELL, *Die »anderen« Winzer. Eine exegetische Studie zur Vollmacht Jesu Christi nach Markus 11,27-12,34* (WUNT, 77), Tübingen, Mohr, 1994.

24. Aus Raumgründen ist das unmarkierte Zitat LXX Ps 117,25f. in Mk 11,9 zu übergehen.

25. Es gibt sicher auch andere Taxonomien und noch mehrere Unterformen; vgl. GENETTE, *Palimpsestes* (n. 8).

26. Vgl. neben ETTE, *Intertextualität* (n. 2), auch: M. PFISTER, *Konzepte der Intertextualität*, in BROICH & PFISTER, *Intertextualität* (n. 7), pp. 1-30; HOLTHUIS, *Intertextualität* (n. 9), pp. 12-28.

Kürze gezeichnet und zu herkömmlichen exegetischen Fragestellungen in Beziehung gesetzt werden. Mit Susanne Holthuis verstehen wir die Intertextualität als Phänomen der Textverarbeitung[27], sie gehört zum Bereich der Textinterpretation. Die Quintessenz von diesem Ansatz ist, daß es, abhängig von *im* Text vorliegenden Intertextualitätssignalen, dem Leser und der Leserin obliegt, diese Signale als solche zu erkennen und den Text in Relation zu anderen Texten auszulegen. Intertextuelle Bezüge sind also keine textinhärente Eigenschaft. Holthuis meint zu Recht, daß intertextuelle Qualitäten zwar vom Text motiviert sein können, sie werden aber vollzogen »... in der Interaktion zwischen Text und Leser, seinen Kenntnismengen und Rezeptionserwartungen. Mit anderen Worten konstituiert sich Intertextualität als Relation zwischen Texten erst im Kontinuum der Rezeption«[28]. Dies hat besondere Konsequenzen für Ansätze, die sich an dem Autor bzw. der Rekonstruktion der Abfassungsverhältnisse des Textes orientieren und somit von der Textproduktion ausgehen, wie es in der Regel in der Exegese geschieht. Man kann aber nicht beim erst zu rekonstruierenden Ergebnis anfangen, sondern es ist beim Text anzusetzen. Die intertextuellen Bezüge, in die der zweite Evangelist bei der Abfassung seines Evangeliums seine Hörerschaft einbeziehen wollte, hat er mittels Intertextualitätssignalen im Text angelegt. Es obliegt aber dem Interpreten, diese Signale als solche zu erkennen und die Bezüge zu anderen Texten herzustellen. Als Rezipient des Textes kann der Exeget in einem zweiten Schritt aufgrund seiner Wertung der Signale im Text über die vom Autor bei der Textherstellung anvisierten intertextuellen Bezüge Vermutungen anstellen[29].

2. Ps 110,1 (LXX Ps 109,1) im Folgetext Mk 12,35-37

Zunächst sind die vom Verfasser markierten und unmarkierten Zitate aus Ps 110 im Markusevangelium zu untersuchen. Unter »zitieren« wird hier verstanden, daß ein Teil der Oberflächenstruktur des Prätextes in dem Folgetext wiederholt wird. In der Wiederholung kann der Prätext quantitativ verkürzt oder verlängert werden. Größere oder kleinere quantitative Übereinstimmung in der Wiederholung sagt aber noch wenig

27. Vgl. *ibid.*, p. 32. Zur Textverarbeitungstheorie vgl. T.A. van Dijk & W. Kintsch, *Strategies of Discourse Comprehension*, New York, Academic Press, 1983; G. Rickheit & H. Strohner, *Grundlagen der kognitiven Sprachverarbeitung. Modelle. Methoden. Ergebnisse* (UTB, 1735), Tübingen & Basel, Francke, 1993.
28. Holthuis, *Intertextualität* (n. 9), p. 31.
29. Vgl. *ibid.*, pp. 33f.; vgl. hierzu auch Vorster, *Intertextuality* (n. 14), pp. 16. 22.

über die inhaltliche Qualität der Wiederholung. Sowohl die quantitativen als auch die qualitativen Aspekte der Wiederholung eines Prätextes in einem Folgetext sind zu untersuchen, damit die intertextuelle Beziehung zwischen den Texten für die Interpretation fruchtbar gemacht werden kann[30]. Da das Zitat aus dem Prätext, in diesem Fall LXX Ps 109, nun aber als integraler Teil des Folgetextes Mk 12,35-37 zu verstehen ist, ist zuerst der Folgetext für sich zu analysieren. Es ist somit mit einer synchronen Analyse des vorliegenden Folgetextes anzusetzen und nicht bei dem Zitat im Psalm, auch nicht redaktionskritisch bei den Veränderungen, die der Evangelist in der Rezeption des Zitates vorgenommen hat. Sie sind später in einem zweiten Schritt zu verwerten. Da der Text durch V.36a den Leser explizit auf das, was David sagte, hinweist, gehört der intertextuelle Bezug zum Psalm mit zur Textwelt und zur kommunikativen Strategie und ist von Anfang an in die synchrone Analyse einzubeziehen.

2.1 *Markus 12,35-37 als Argument*

Vorab ein kurzer Überblick über den Text. In Mk 11,27-12,34[31] reagierte Jesus auf Fragen, und zwar die der Hohenpriester, Schriftgelehrten und Ältesten (11,27ff.), die der Pharisäer und Herodianer (12,13ff.), die der Sadduzäer (12,18ff.) und die eines Schriftgelehrten (12,28ff.). Dieser Teil ist mit der Bemerkung beendet worden, daß keiner mehr wagte, ihm eine Frage zu stellen (12,34b). Ab 12,35 ergreift Jesus die Initiative und setzt sich mit den Schriftgelehrten auseinander. Das Volk hört zu.

Das Thema der Davidssohnschaft ist in bezug auf Jesus schon angesprochen worden in 10,48 und 11,10. Daß Jesus aber der Christus ist, ist dem Leser seit 1,1 und den Jüngern seit dem Petrusbekenntnis klar. Das Petrusbekenntnis, daß Jesus der Christus sei (8,29), wird zwar von Jesus von der Vorstellung her, daß der Menschensohn zu leiden habe, verworfen werden und wieder auferstehen werde, kommentiert (8,31), aber nicht abgelehnt. Später in der Erzählung wird Jesus auf die Frage des Hohenpriesters, ob er nun der Christus, der Sohn des Hochgelobten sei, bestätigend antworten (14,61f.). Nach den Schweigegeboten von 8,30 und 9,9 versuchen die Jünger, Bartimäus davon abzuhalten, Jesus als υἱὸς Δαυίδ anzureden. Zunächst nehmen weder Jesus noch der Erzähler

---

30. Zu diesem Verständnis von »Zitat« vgl. PLETT, *Quotation* (n. 22); HOLTHUIS, *Intertextualität* (n. 9), pp. 91-114, bes. pp. 99f. 101f. 109f.
31. Vgl. unten 3.2.

Stellung zu dieser Bezeichnung. Auch das Volk darf Jesus unkommentiert beim Einzug als Erben Davids feiern (11,1-11)[32].

In 12,35-37 wird nun Stellung zu Jesu Davidssohnschaft bezogen. Wie bei dem Christusbekenntnis Petri, wo Jesus die Jünger fragt: »Ihr aber, wer sagt ihr, daß ich bin?« (Mk 8,29), geht auch hier die Initiative von Jesus aus[33]. Als Auftakt der kleinen Rede[34] stellt er selbst die Meinung der Schriftgelehrten, daß der Christus ein Sohn Davids sei (V.35b), in Frage. Es folgt eine asyndetisch angeschlossene Darstellung der abweichenden Meinung Davids (V.36-37a). Die Rede schließt mit einer mit καί angebundenen Schlußfrage, in der die Meinung der Schriftgelehrten angesichts Davids Aussage über den Messias problematisiert wird[35]. Auf die genaue Absicht des Argumentes wird nach Klärung einiger Detailfragen eingegangen.

Untersucht man das deutlich markierte Zitat in V.36, ist zunächst *quantitativ* offensichtlich, daß nur ein Vers aus dem Prätext zitiert wurde. Angesichts des Kontextes, in den das Zitat eingebunden ist, ist auch nicht zu erkennen, daß das Zitat für den ganzen Psalmtext steht. Dies wird klar, wenn man die Funktion des Folgetextes und die Rolle des Zitates in diesem Zusammenhang betrachtet. Wozu steht das Zitat in Mk 12,35-37? Was soll das Zitat beim Hörer des Markusevangeliums erreichen? Bei der Rede handelt es sich um ein Argument, das als argumentativer Text zu behandeln ist[36]. Seine Funktion ist von seinem intratextuellen Zusammenhang her zu bestimmen. Zunächst nimmt der markinische Jesus Stellung zu der Auffassung der Schriftgelehrten, daß der Christus ein Sohn Davids sein soll. Damit das Argument verständlich wird, ist auf die zeitgenössischen Voraussetzungen, die das Zitieren bedingen, einzugehen[37]. LXX Ps 109,1 wird unter zwei ungenannten Voraussetzungen zitiert[38]:

---

32. »... die Erwartung des Volkes wird in der Schwebe gehalten.« R. SCHNACKENBURG, *Die Person Jesu Christi im Spiegel der Evangelien* (HTK.S, 4), Freiburg, Herder, 1993, p. 77.

33. Mit M. HOOKER, *The Gospel according to St Mark* (BNTC), London, Black, 1991, p. 292.

34. Sie wird gerahmt von einer Situationsangabe (V.35a) und einem Kommentar des Erzählers (V.37c), in dem er die Reaktion der Menge auf Jesu Lehre darstellt. Dieser Kommentar bezieht sich nicht nur auf V.35-37b, sondern hat den ganzen Abschnitt ab 11,27ff. im Blick.

35. πόθεν ist Adverb der Frage – »woher«. Es kann wie hier eine verwunderte Frage einleiten und nach der Ursache – »aus welchem Grund?, wieso?, inwiefern?« – fragen. Vgl. *BAA*, c.1364.

36. Er ist nicht in ein A, B, C, D, C', B', A' Schema zu pressen. Anders MARCUS, *Way* (n. 20), pp. 130f.

37. Es ist notwendig, Intertextualitäten nicht zeitlos, sondern in einem sozio-kulturellen Kontext zu sehen; sie sind somit zeitgebunden. Vgl. PLETT, *Intertextualities* (n. 8), pp. 25f.

38. Vgl. auch E. LOHMEYER, *Das Evangelium des Markus* (KEK, I/2[17]), Göttingen, Vandenhoeck & Ruprecht [10]1963, pp. 261f.

Erstens sei der Psalm von David selbst gedichtet. Daß David Psalmendichter war, war eine im Judentum des Zweiten Tempels und im Urchristentum verbreitete Ansicht[39]. Sie stützte sich letztlich auf die Überschrift, den Epitext zu einigen Psalmen, auch zu Psalm 110. Die LXX-Tradition übersetzte in mehreren Fällen[40] das hebräische ל-auctoris[41] bei לְדָוִד mit τῷ Δαυιδ[42]. Von daher wurde in LXX Ps 109 das μοῦ in V.1 in der Auslegung auf Δαυιδ in der Überschrift zurückbezogen.

Die zweite implizierte Voraussetzung für das Argument, nämlich daß der Psalm von Christus handle, liegt zwar von V.2f. her nahe, wurde aber in der jüdischen Auslegungstradition nicht vollzogen. D.h. es gibt keine zeitrelevante jüdische Auslegungstradition, die den Psalm auf den Messias bezieht. Die Davidssohnfrage wird somit hier im *christlichen* Kontext behandelt[43], denn das Argument setzt, wie die Verbindung des Zitates mit der Einleitungsfrage zeigt, voraus, daß es im zitierten Psalmvers um den Christus geht. Dies sieht man deutlich, wenn man die markinische Kontextualisierung unter die Lupe nimmt und nach dem Referenten von τῷ κυρίῳ μου in V.36 bzw. von αὐτὸν κύριον in V.37 fragt. Beide Ausdrücke beziehen sich zurück auf ὁ χριστός in V.35. Die Ansicht, daß es im Psalm um den Christus geht, teilt das Markusevangelium mit anderen Strömungen des Urchristentums, wie die mehrfache Anwendung des Psalms auf den zur Herrschaft kommenden Χριστός bzw. Gottessohn in der urchristlichen Literatur zeigt[44]. Durch Aufnahme

---

39. Vgl. die Rezeption von 1 Sam 16,14-23 in Pseudo-Philons *LibAnt* 59f. und Josephus' *Ant* 6,166-168 (dazu DE JONGE, *Jesus* (n. 23), pp. 99f.). David als Psalmist: 11QPsᵃ; Mt 22,43.45; Lk 20,42.44; Apg 2,25; Röm 4,6; 11,9; Hebr 4,7.

40. Vgl. nur LXX Ps 3,1; 7,1; 50,1.

41. Vgl. dazu H.-J. KRAUS, *Psalmen* (BK, XV/1), Neukirchen-Vluyn, Neukirchener, ⁵1978, pp. 15f.

42. Der Artikel zeigt den Dativ bei dem im Griechischen in der Regel indeklinablen Eigennamen Δαυιδ an.

43. So zu Recht J. GNILKA, *Das Evangelium nach Markus* (EKK, II/2), Zürich, Benziger & Neukirchen-Vluyn, Neukirchener, 1979, p. 169.

44. Vgl. Röm 8,34; 1 Kor 15,25; Hebr 1,3.13; Barn 12,10f. und weitere Stellen bei M. HENGEL, »*Setze dich zu meiner Rechten!*« *Die Inthronisation Christi zur Rechten Gottes und Psalm 110,1*, in M. PHILONENKO (ed.), *Le Trône de Dieu* (WUNT, 69), Tübingen, Mohr, 1993, pp. 105-152. Der zwischen 130-132 entstandene Barnabasbrief zeigt weiterhin, daß man auch noch in der ersten Hälfte des 2. Jhs. LXX Ps 109,1 verwendete, um damit die jüdische Meinung, der Christus müsse Davidide sein, mit Davids eigener prophetischer Aussage zu widerlegen. »10. Siehe: Wiederum Jesus, nicht Sohn eines Menschen, sondern Sohn Gottes, durch ein Abbild aber im Fleisch offenbart. Da man aber sagen wird, daß Christus Sohn Davids ist, prophezeit David selbst, weil er den Irrtum der Sünder befürchtete und durchschaute: 'Es sprach der Herr zu meinem Herrn: Setze dich zu meiner Rechten, bis daß ich deine Feinde niederlege als Schemel deiner Füße.' 11. Und ferner spricht Jesaja folgendermaßen: 'Es sprach der Herr zu Christus, meinem Herrn: Dessen Rechte habe ich ergriffen, damit die Völker vor ihm gehorsam

von LXX Ps 109,1 unter der Fragestellung nach der Davidssohnschaft des Χριστός wurde der aus dem Psalmtext zitierte Vers seiner wörtlichen Formulierung nach zwar kaum, *qualitativ* auf der semantischen Ebene aber grundlegend verändert, indem vorausgesetzt wird, daß der 109. Psalm in der LXX mit τῷ κυρίῳ μου in V.1 den Χριστός meint. Der intertextuelle Bezug besteht gar nicht zwischen dem Markusfolgetext und LXX Ps 109 an sich, sondern zwischen dem Markustext und dem Psalmvers, wie der Vers nach der Schriftinterpretation des Urchristentums in der Rezeption verstanden und angewandt wurde. Unter dieser Voraussetzung kann der Leser des Markusevangeliums nun das Zitat im Zusammenhang des Folgetextes Mk 12,35-37 lesen.

Jesus als Christus wird in Beziehung zu der vermeintlichen Davidssohnschaft des Christus gesetzt, d.h. der bislang mißverstandene Christus selbst nimmt in Mk 12,35ff. Stellung zu der Frage, ob der Messias, der er ja ist, von David abzustammen hat. In seiner Stellungnahme geht der Erzähler nicht den Weg, den mkn. Jesus sagen zu lassen: Ich bin der Christus, ich bin kein Davidide, deswegen kann der Christus kein Davidssohn sein. Jesu Messianität wird nicht der Auffassung der Schriftgelehrten gegenübergestellt, sondern die Prämisse des Argumentes der Schriftgelehrten wird in Frage gestellt. Um sie zu gewinnen, wird es dem Verfasser des Markusevangeliums nichts nützen, auf die christliche Überzeugung, daß Jesus der Christus sei, hinzuweisen. Solange die Voraussetzung, daß der Christus Sohn Davids sei, gilt, kann Jesus, der nach dem Markusevangelium aus Nazaret stammt und Sohn der Maria ist (Mk 6,3), nicht der Christus sein.

---

sind, und ich werde die Macht von Königen zerbrechen.' Siehe, wie David ihn 'Herrn' nennt, und nicht Sohn nennt.« (Barn 12,10f. nach der Übers. von D.-A. Koch, in A. LINDEMANN & H. PAULSEN, *Die Apostolischen Väter*, Tübingen, Mohr, 1992, p.59). Nebenbei bemerkt, die Wendung αὐτὸς προφητεύει Δαυίδ sowie die Struktur des Argumentes in Barn 12,10f. zeigen auf, daß es sich um das gleiche Argument wie in Mk 12,35-37 handelt. Da der Barnabasbrief das Zitat nach der Septuaginta korrigiert hat, bleibt nur die erste Hälfte der Schlußfolgerung (Δαυίδ λέγει αὐτὸν κύριον) als teilweise wörtliche Übereinstimmung mit Mk 12,37a und Parallelen. Dies genügt nicht, um eine literarische Abhängigkeit des Barnabasbriefes von den Synoptikern zu postulieren. Da der Barnabasbrief jedoch mit καὶ υἱὸν οὐ λέγει die Folgerung des mkn. Argumentes explizit formuliert, kann man voraussetzen, daß der Verfasser des Barnabasbriefes dasselbe Argument in Verbindung mit LXX Ps 109,1 kannte. Ob er das Argument einer Rezeption der synoptischen Evangelien verdankt oder Markus und der Barnabasbrief zwei voneinander unabhängige Aufnahmen des gleichen Argumentes bieten, läßt sich nicht entscheiden. Die Ergänzung des Psalmzitates durch Jes 45,1 zeigt jedoch auf, daß der Verfasser des Barnabasbriefes mit dem schriftbezogenen Argument selbständig umging. Aber auch diese Beobachtung reicht nicht aus, Barn 12,10f. als Hilfe zur Rekonstruktion der von Markus verarbeiteten Tradition zu verwenden (anders MARCUS, *Way* (n. 20), pp. 131f.). Der Autor des Barnabasbriefes hätte das Argument aus den Synoptikern auch nach der LXX korrigiert und ergänzt in seinen eigenen Argumentationsduktus aufnehmen können.

Daß Gruppierungen innerhalb des Judentums des Zweiten Tempels einen
Gesalbten aus der Davidslinie erwarteten, ersieht man aus einigen Qumranschriften[45] und aus den Psalmen Salomos[46]. Um die Prämisse der
Schriftgelehrten, mit denen sie im Judentum des Zweiten Tempels keineswegs allein standen, auszuhebeln, führt der markinische Jesus David selbst
an. Was hat er zu der Davidssohnschaft des Christus gesagt? Hierzu
wird LXX Ps 109,1 zitiert. Es geht in dem zweiteiligen Argumentations-
abschnitt in V.36f., wie die zweimal gebrauchte Wendung αὐτὸς Δαυίδ
zeigt, um das, was David selbst zu dem Problem sagte, seine Autorität
wird hier mittels LXX Ps 109,1 von dem Jesus des Markusevangeliums
in V.36b-c ins Feld geführt. V.36a fügt das Zitat in das Argument ein, so
daß V.36 eine erste Einheit bildet. Dadurch wird unterstrichen, daß David
diese Aussage mit Unterstützung des Heiligen Geistes machte, es handelt
sich um prophetische, inspirierte Rede[47]. Dies macht die Aussage Davids
verbindlich, für Jesus, aber wahrscheinlich auch für die Schriftgelehrten.
D.h., entscheidend ist nicht, daß Jesus ein Schriftzitat der Meinung der
Schriftgelehrten entgegenstellt[48], sondern daß die prophetische Aussage
Davids selbst der Meinung der Schriftgelehrten über die vermeintliche
Davidssohnschaft des Christus gegenübergestellt wird.

Die zweite Einheit, V.37b, zieht eine Folgerung aus dem Zitat. David
selbst, um dessen Sohn es schließlich gehen soll, wurde zitiert. Der Text
schließt mit einer Frage: καὶ πόθεν αὐτοῦ (sc. Δαυίδ) ἐστιν υἱός; Angesichts dessen, daß David selbst den zur Herrschaft bestimmten Christus

---

45. Es will aber erstens bedacht werden, daß selbst in Qumran, wo der herrschende
Messias der Gerechtigkeit (4QpGen^a V,1 [=4Q252]; vgl. 4QFlor I,10-13 [=4Q174]) oder
der richtende Geistträger (4QpJes^a 8-10 III,11-25 [=4Q161]) dem Zweige Davids bzw.
Isais (vgl. 4QM^g V,2f. [=4Q285]) entstammt, auch ein levitischer Messias als Nach-
komme Aarons Erwähnung fand (vgl. 1Q Sa II,11-22 [=1Q28a]; vgl. 1QS IX,11). Zweitens ist zu bedenken, daß an den zwei Qumranstellen, an denen die Wirkung des Gottes-
geistes in Zusammenhang mit dem Gesalbten gebracht wird, seine davidische Herkunft
nicht im Hintergrund steht (vgl. 4QBer^b; 4Q Hymnen zur Endzeit I,1.6 [=4Q 521 I,1.6]).
Mit diesen Einschränkungen kann man aber sagen, daß es unter den verschiedenen Mes-
siaserwartungen des Judentums des Zweiten Tempels auch die gab, daß der Gesalbte aus
dem Hause Davids stammen werde. Vgl. hierzu insgesamt, H. STEGEMANN, Die Essener,
Qumran, Johannes der Täufer und Jesus, Freiburg, Herder, ⁴1994, p. 288; J.J. COLLINS,
The Scepter and the Star. The Messiahs of the Dead Sea Scrolls and Other Ancient Literature (AncB.RL), New York, Doubleday, 1995.

46. Bes. 17,21; vgl. hierzu M. DE JONGE, The Expectation of the Future in the Psalms
of Solomon, in: ID., Jewish Eschatology, Early Christian Christology and the Testaments
of the Twelve Patriarchs. Collected Essays of Marinus de Jonge (NTSup, 53), Leiden,
Brill, 1991, pp. 3-27.

47. Mit PLETT, Intertextualities (n. 8), p. 13, kann man hier von einer »authoritative
quotation« reden.

48. So u.a. D. LÜHRMANN, Das Markusevangelium (HNT, 3), Tübingen, Mohr, 1987,
p. 208.

seinen κύριον nennt, sei es unverständlich, wie der zur Erhöhung bestimmte Christus »Sohn Davids« sein könne. Markus setzt dabei voraus, daß ein Sohn seinen Vater κύριος nennt, aber nicht umgekehrt. »The implicit logic of our passage is that no father refers to his own son as 'my lord'«[49]. Da David – der vermeintliche Vater – nun aber eindeutig den Christus seinen Herrn nennt, kann der Christus nicht Davids Sohn sein[50]. Es liegt aber noch mehr im Text.

Aber vorher eine kleine philologische Bemerkung. Wie wir bereits sahen, sind Veränderungen des Zitatinhaltes im Markustext gegenüber dem im Psalmtext nicht nur auf Transformationen der Textoberfläche zurückzuführen, sondern auch auf die Veränderung in den intratextuellen Bezügen, in die das Zitat hineingenommen wurde. Dabei ist es entscheidend, die jeweilige Bedeutung des mehrfach vorkommenden Ausdrucks κύριος zu klären. Das absolute κύριος im Folgetext Mk 12,36b bezeichnet, wie schon das hebr. יהוה im Prätext, Gott. Das τῷ κυρίῳ μου bezeichnet im Psalmtext – wie sowohl das hebräische לַאדֹנִי sowie das τῇ δεσπότῃ μου des christlichen Übersetzers Symmachus (σ') zeigen – einen »Höherstehenden, Verfügungsberechtigten«[51]. Was bedeuten die Ausdrücke τῷ κυρίῳ μου in Mk 12,36 und κύριον in 12,37? Bedeutet κύριος hier im Folgetext, wie im Prätext LXX Ps 109,1, lediglich »master, lord, superior«[52], oder setzt der Text Mk 12,36f. eine Identifikation des Christus mit dem erhöhten Kyrios, wie etwa in Röm 10,9, voraus[53]? Vom markinischen Gesamtkontext her ist die Frage kaum zu lösen, denn in Mk 2,28; 11,3; 12,9 und 13,35 ist κύριος als »Höflichkeitsanrede« zu werten.

Es ist entscheidend, daran festzuhalten, daß die Eingangsfrage in Mk 12,35 zeigt, daß das Zitat in Mk 12,36 nicht verwendet wurde, um eine Aussage über die Davidssohnschaft des Κύριος[54], sondern des Χριστός zu machen. Es ist der zur Rechten Gottes sitzende Christus, der zur Herrschaft über seine Feinde bestimmt ist, dem David sich unterordnete. Der Evangelist stellt somit die Offenbarung der Herrschaft des Christus, nicht des Κύριος, unter eine zukünftige Perspektive. Wie die Wendung ἕως ἂν θῶ zeigt, liegt die Machtübernahme über die Feinde noch in der

---

49. MARCUS, *Way* (n. 20), p. 140.

50. So bereits W. WREDE, *Jesus als Davidssohn*, in ID., *Vorträge und Studien*, Göttingen, Vandenhoeck & Ruprecht 1907, pp. 147-177, bes. p. 168; weitere Vertreter dieser Position bei C. BURGER, *Jesus als Davidssohn. Eine traditionsgeschichtliche Untersuchung* (FRLANT, 98), Göttingen, Vandenhoeck & Ruprecht, 1970, pp. 56f.

51. Vgl. *BAA*, cc.932f.; *TWNT* III, pp. 1043f.

52. Vgl G.D. KILPATRICK, *»Kurios« in the Gospels*, in *L'Évangile hier et aujourd'hui*. Mélanges offerts au F.-J. Leenhardt, Genève, Éditions Labor et Fides, 1968, pp. 65-70, pp. 65. 69.

53. So F. HAHN, *Christologische Hoheitstitel* (UTB, 1873), Göttingen, Vandenhoeck & Ruprecht, ⁵1995, pp. 260f.; JUEL, *Exegesis* (n. 20), pp. 143f.

54. Anders HOOKER, *Gospel* (n. 33), p. 292; mit LÜHRMANN, *Markusevangelium* (n. 48), p. 209.

Zukunft. Der Χριστός ist dazu bestimmt, über seine von Gott ihm un-
terworfenen Feinde zu herrschen, bis dahin sitzt er zur Rechten Gottes.
Das Κύριος-Bekenntnis spielt hier keine Rolle, die Wendungen κυρίῳ
μου und κύριον verweisen auf den Christus als den Vorgesetzten Davids.
Das dem Psalm entnommene Verständnis des Christus als künftigem
Herrscher über seine Feinde und bis dahin Erhöhtem, hebt die Möglichkeit auf, ihn als Davidssohn zu verstehen[55]. Es ist aber dennoch wichtig
zu sehen, daß es sich hier um den Christus handelt. Er wird als zur Rechten Gottes Erhöhter gesehen. D.h., daß die Messianität nicht von der
davidischen Abstammung her gedacht wird, sie wird von der zukünftigen Machtübernahme des Christus her verstanden. Markus kontrastiert
nicht vordergründig die Gottessohnschaft Jesu mit seiner behaupteten
Davidssohnschaft[56]. Er kontrastiert mittels des Psalmzitates die Behauptung, der Christus sei Davidssohn, mit der in dem Psalm von David mit
prophetischer Vollmacht vorausgesagten Machtausübung des zur Rechten Gottes sitzenden Christus.

2.2 Zitate aus dem Prätext LXX Ps 109,1

Bislang haben wir es unterlassen, das *qualitative Verhältnis* zwischen
dem Zitat als Teil des Psalmtextes, der als Quelle diente, und dem gleichen Zitat als Teil des Markustextes, in den es aufgenommen wurde, zu
untersuchen. Dabei ist nicht nur auf Übereinstimmungen und Abweichungen in der Oberflächenform zu achten, sondern auch auf die Aus-
wirkung der Transformationen auf den Inhalt des Zitates[57]. Eine solche
»diachrone« Untersuchung ist hilfreich, denn sie kann uns noch einiges
über das Werden des Folgetextes verraten. Die traditionellen »diachro-
nen« Fragen nach der Entstehung eines Textes können zu interessanten
Interpretationsfragen führen, aber erst jetzt, da wir das Argument rekonstruiert haben. Dabei wird die Wiederholung einer Wendung aus LXX
Ps 109,1 in Mk 14,62 zwar berücksichtigt, aus Platzgründen aber nur
gestreift.

(1) Zunächst eine erste Transformation auf der Ausdrucksebene. *Mk 12,36*
zitiert Ps 110,1 nach der LXX (109,1). Unter den Zeugen zum Markustext

---

55. Vgl. auch D.M. HAY, *Glory at the Right Hand. Psalm 110 in Early Christianity*
(SBL MS, 18), New York, Abingdon Press, p. 114.
56. Anders MARCUS, *Way* (n. 20), pp. 141f.
57. Vgl. hierzu PLETT, *Intertextualities* (n. 8), pp. 9f.

gibt es aber wichtige Abweichungen von der in Nestle-Aland[27] übernommenen und besser bezeugten, kürzeren und schwieriger zu erklären-
den Lesart[58]. Etliche Manuskripte zu Mk 12,36[59] haben nach der ihnen
bekannten Version der LXX korrigiert. Sie ergänzen ὁ vor κύριος. Diese
Zeugen sind alle erst ab dem 4. Jh. zu datieren und benutzen somit eine
christlich überlieferte Version des LXX-Psalmtextes. Die Psalmtexte der
Vollbibeln, z.B. ℵ und A, enthalten also nicht den Quellentext des zweiten Evangelisten. Er schrieb schon um 70 n.Chr. und verwendete wahrscheinlich eine griechische Übersetzung des hebräischen Textes aus den
Kreisen des hellenistischen Judentums. Solche prächristlichen, griechischen Versionen der hebräischen Schriften ließen den undeterminierten
Gottesnamen יהוה, wie bei 8ḤevXIIgr zu beobachten ist, entweder unü-
bersetzt in althebräischen Buchstaben stehen oder transkribierten, wie
bei pap4QLXXLev[b] (Frag. 20,4 zu Lev 4,27) zu beobachten ist, mit ΙΑω;
in beiden Fällen also ohne Artikel. Oder es wurde, wie bei P. Fouad 266
zu Dtn (aus dem 1. Jh. v.Chr. – z.B. 31,26)[60], anstelle des Tetragram-
mons einfach eine Lücke im griechischen Text gelassen[61]. Der Artikel in
den uns vorliegenden LXX-Manuskripten zu Ps 109,1, in denen der Gottesname mit κύριος übersetzt wurde, dient zur Unterscheidung von dem
darauf folgenden τῷ κυρίῳ μου. Er wäre in den frühen Manuskripten
mit hebräischem Gottesnamen oder ΙΑω überflüssig[62]. Der Markustext
ist wahrscheinlich ein sehr früher Beleg dafür, daß griechischsprechende
Judenchristen den Gottesnamen mit κύριος übersetzten. Sie folgten damit
wahrscheinlich einer Praxis der griechischsprechenden Juden.

Daß diese Transformation nicht die einzige mögliche Wiedergabe des
Prätextes war, zeigt ein Blick auf *Mk 14,62*, wo LXX Ps 109,1 nochmals

---

58. Lesung von B und D.

59. Die Codices ℵ, A, L, W, Θ, Ψ, *f*[1.13], 33 und der Mehrheitstext.

60. Vgl. Z. ALY, *Three Rolls of the Early Septuagint: Genesis and Deuteronomy* (PTA, 27), Bonn, Habelt, 1980; P.Oxy. 656 (aus dem 3. Jh. n.Chr.) zu Gen 15,8; 24,31.40.42.

61. Zum Problem, vgl. A. PIETERSMA, *Kyrios or Tetragramm. A Renewed Quest for the Original LXX*, in ID. & C. COX, *De Septuaginta*. Studies in Honour of John William Wevers on his sixty-fifth birthday, Benben, 1984, pp. 85-101; M. RÖSEL, *Die Überset-zung der Gottesnamen in der Genesis-Septuaginta*, in D.R. DANIELS et al. (eds.), *Ernten, was man sät*. FS für Klaus Koch zu seinem 65. Geburtstag, Neukirchen-Vluyn, Neukir-chener, 1991, pp. 357-377.

62. Leider gibt es unter den Textzeugen zum LXX-Text von Psalm 109 keine vor-christlichen Zeugen. In B fehlen Ps 105,27-137,6, so daß die Hauptzeugen, A und S, die-selben sind wie bei der Lesart dieser »Vollbibel«-Codices zu Mk 12,36. Unter den Text-zeugen zu LXX Ps 109,1 läßt lediglich das griechisch-lateinische Verona-Manuskript (R) aus dem 6. Jh., das dem abendländischen Texttypus zu den Psalmen zuzuordnen ist, das ὁ vor κύριος in LXX Ps 109,1 weg und steht somit dem HT näher. Der Judenchrist σ′ vermeidet später bei seiner Übertragung von Ps 110,1 eine Verwirrung, indem er das hebr. לַאדֹנִי mit τῷ δεσπότῃ μου übersetzt; vgl. F. FIELD (ed.), *Origenis Hexaplorum. Tomus II*, Oxford, Clarendon Press, 1875, p. 266.

aufgegriffen wird. Das ἐκ δεξιῶν καθήμενον zeigt eine veränderte Aufnahme von Ps 110,1. Das καθήμενον greift den Imperativ κάθου des Prätextes auf, wurde aber wegen des Kontextes abgewandelt und nachgestellt[63]. Das zusätzliche τῆς δυνάμεως in Mk 14,62, die Kraft, die Macht des Herrn, steht anstelle von μοῦ nach dem δεξιῶν im LXX-Text. Es unterscheidet sich von Mk 12,36, denn dort ist das Bezugsnomen für μοῦ das absolute κύριος in V.36b. Es ist also unwahrscheinlich, daß das Zitat im Folgetext Mk 12,36 den Prätext von Mk 14,62 bildet. Der Prätext ist auch hier V.1 in LXX Psalm 109. Was stand aber im Prätext, in LXX Psalm 109,1, als Bezugsnomen für μοῦ? Wie wir sahen, wahrscheinlich das Tetragrammon in althebräischen Buchstaben oder Griechisch ΙΑω oder sogar eine Lücke! Die Konsequenz ist klar: δύναμις, »der, der die Macht ausübt«[64], wird in Mk 14,62 verwendet als Umschreibung für יהוה, das in LXX Ps 109,1 wohl ursprünglich in althebräischen Buchstaben stand, und das Mk in 12,36 mit κύριος wiedergegeben hatte.

In Mk 14,62 geht es also um die Umschreibung des Gottesnamens in Ps 109,1 mit δύναμις. Damit steht Mk in der jüdischen Tradition, wie man an der Anrede beim Kreuzeswort aus Ps 22,2 erkennen kann[65]. Der jüdische Übersetzer Aquila (α') übersetzt das אֵלִי אֵלִי von Ps 22,2 mit ἰσχυρέ μου, ἰσχυρέ μου[66]. Das Petrusevangelium folgt ebenfalls einer solchen Tradition, denn seine Version der Anrede lautet: ἡ δύναμίς μου, ἡ δύναμίς μου. Die Anrede Gottes mit δύναμις bzw. ἰσχυρός in den griechischen Übersetzungen von Ps 22,2 steht nicht allein[67]. Die Umschreibung des Gottesnamens mit δύναμις (PtEv) und ἰσχυρέ (α') in der Rezeption des Ps 22 greift auf eine Übersetzungspraxis »der« LXX zurück[68].

---

63. Nach HOLTHUIS, *Intertextualität* (n. 9), p. 92, wäre dies eine Form von modifizierender Re-Linearisierung.

64. Vgl. *BAA*, c. 417; *LN* 37,62.

65. Aus der Perspektive der Intertextualitätstheorie kann das Folgende als eine »textarchäologische« Rekonstruktion des Potentials der Anspielung gesehen werden; vgl. HEBEL, *Poetics* (n. 17), pp. 140-141, 156.

66. Bei Eusebius, DE, X 8, zitiert bei FIELD, *Origenis* (n. 62), p. 117.

67. Die Textzeugen zu der LXX-Überlieferung von Num 24,4a (נְאֻם שֹׁמֵעַ אִמְרֵי אֵל) schwanken in der Übersetzung von אִמְרֵי אֵל zwischen λόγια θεοῦ (B, F, V) λόγια ἰσχυροῦ (G, M, mehrere Gruppen Minuskelhandschriften, Euseb und Origenis Numeri Homilie bei Rufinus) und λόγια θεοῦ ἰσχυροῦ (A). Die Übersetzung von אֵל mit ἰσχυρός zeigt sich auch bei der Übersetzung von 2 Sam 22,18.31.32f.48; Neh 1,5; 9,31f. und Hiob 22,13; 33,29.31; 34,31; 36,22.26; 37,5.10.

68. Nach der Übersetzung von Ex 9,16 führt der Erweis der Kraft Gottes (ἰσχύς) zur Verbreitung seines Namens. Wichtig sind in unserem Zusammenhang die Psalmen. Die Textüberlieferung von LXX Ps 41,2 schwankt wie bei Numeri 24,4a zwischen θεός und ἰσχυρός als Übersetzung für אֵל. In LXX Ps 53,3 stehen Gottes Name und seine Kraft parallel: ὁ θεός, ἐν τῷ ὀνόματί σου σῶσόν με καὶ ἐν τῇ δυνάμει σου κρῖνόν με (vgl. auch LXX Jer 14,21).

Was für eine inhaltliche Verschiebung bewirkt diese Änderung in Mk 14,62? Die Vorstellung von Gottes δύναμις hat in der LXX durchaus »militärische« Konnotationen. Das Wort wird nicht nur verwendet, um auf Streitkräfte zu verweisen (Jos 5,14), sondern gelegentlich wird auch יהוה אֱלֹהֵי הַצְּבָאוֹת nicht mit κύριος παντοκράτωρ, sondern mit κύριος τῶν δυνάμεων[69] übersetzt. »Es ist anzunehmen, daß die Übersetzer mit dieser mehr wörtlichen Wiedergabe wie mit παντοκράτωρ dasselbe gemeint haben: die Herrschaft Jahwes über alle irdischen und himmlischen Kräfte«[70]. Im griechischsprechenden Judentum wurde es ohnehin üblich, von der δύναμις Gottes zu reden. Fest in der Tradition der Psalmen[71] betet z.B. die fromme Judit κύριε ὁ θεὸς πάσης δυνάμεως (13,4); er ist Gott, Gott aller Macht und Stärke (9,14)[72]. Die Tendenz, zur Vermeidung des Gottesnamens δύναμις absolut zu gebrauchen, läßt sich zwar außer in Mk 14,62 nicht nachweisen, die Paralipomena Jeremiae setzen aber in der Anrede absolut gebrauchtes δύναμις und θεός parallel: ἡ δύναμις ἡμῶν, ὁ θεὸς ἡμῶν κύριε (ParJer 6,9)[73]. Daneben hat der Brauch im griechischsprechenden Judentum, von Gottes δύναμις zu reden, auch eine Parallele im aramäischen Sprachgebrauch, wo das Wort גְּבוּרְתָא eingesetzt wird. Die aramäischen Fragmente zu Henoch 1,4 aus Qumran[74] formulieren eingangs, daß der große Heilige, wenn er auf die Erde herabsteigen wird, »...strahlend erscheinen wird in [der Macht seiner] Stärke«[75]. Die Targumtradition zeigt[76], daß der einzige Gott seine Stärke (תְּפֹף) im höchsten Himmel hat[77]. Die Umschreibung von יְמִין, auch ohne יַד »rechte Hand«, mit גְּבוּרָה, »Macht, Stärke« in dem Prophetentargum[78] trägt weiter dazu bei, die Wendung in Mk 14,62 vor ihrem Hintergrund zu sehen, nämlich der Umschreibung des Gottesnamens mit גְּבוּרָה. Daß Markus in seiner zweiten Aufnahme von LXX Ps

---

69. Vgl. LXX Ps 45,12; 79,5.8f.15; Amos 6,14 [B].

70. E. FASCHER, Art. *Dynamis*, in *RAC* IV, cc. 415-458, c. 428.

71. Vgl. LXX Ps 45,2; 139,7.

72. Eine Formulierung, die ihre urchristlichen Parallelen in 1 Klem 11,2 und Herm vis I 3,4 hat.

73. Vgl. auch das absolute ὁ ἱκανός für Gott in ParJer 6,3. Die beiden Hinweise auf die ParJer verdanke ich meinem Kollegen K.W. Niebuhr.

74. Vgl. 4QEnᵃar 1,4 (=4Q201), um 170 v.Chr. zu datieren.

75. בתקף [וגבורה] Übersetzung nach K. BEYER, *Die aramäischen Texte vom Toten Meer*, Göttingen, Vandenhoeck & Ruprecht, 1984, p. 232. Das griechische Fragment z.St. übersetzt: καὶ φανήσεται ἐν τῇ δυνάμει τῆς ἰσχύος αὐτοῦ ἀπὸ τοῦ οὐρανοῦ τῶν οὐρανῶν.

76. Vgl. G. DALMAN, *Die Worte Jesu*, Leipzig, Hinrichs, ²1930, pp. 164f.

77. Vgl. TO zu Dtn 33,26.

78. Vgl. TJon zu Jes 48,13. Das Targum übersetzt »meine Rechte«, mit der Gott den Himmel ausspannte im HT (מִינִי טִפְּחָה שָׁמַיִם) mit »durch meine Macht streckte ich den Himmel aus« (בגבורתי תלית שמיא).

109,1 δύναμις in der Wiederholung der Wendung aufnimmt, geht auf den Kontext der Verhörszene bei Markus zurück. Die »militärischen« Konnotationen der Vorstellung wurden aktiviert. Der Christus-Gottessohn wird unter der herrschenden Macht Gottes zur Verurteilung des Hohenpriesters und des ganzen Synhedrions kommen. Sie werden sehen.

(2) Es gibt aber noch eine zweite Änderung des Zitates aus dem Prätext Psalm 109 im Folgetext in Mk 12,35-37. Sie hilft dabei, die bislang gegebene Interpretationslinie weiterzuverfolgen. In LXX Ps 109,1 wurde das הֲדֹם in Ps 110,1 mit ὑποπόδιον gut übersetzt. Wieso verwendet Markus hier bloß ein Adverb, ὑποκάτω[79]? Im Zitat von LXX Ps 109,1 in Mk 12,36 korrigierte die mkn. Textüberlieferung nach der gängigen LXX-Lesart und ersetzte das Adverb ὑποκάτω durch das Substantiv ὑποπόδιον. Was ist aus dem Schemel geworden? Ein Blick auf 1 Kor 15 hilft. In 1 Kor 15,25 zitiert Paulus ebenfalls LXX Ps 109,1b. Dabei fallen zwei Berührungspunkte mit dem Markuszitat auf. Erstens begrenzt auch Paulus die Herrschaft des erhöhten Christus bis zu dem Zeitpunkt, an dem Gott ihm alle seine Feinde unter die Füße gelegt hat. Zweitens fehlt auch bei Paulus das Motiv des Schemels. Wie ist dies nun zu verstehen? Zwei Verse weiter, 1 Kor 15,27, zitiert Paulus Ps 8,7 und gibt zu erkennen, daß auch dieser Psalm auf den erhöhten Christus bezogen wurde[80]. Paulus mischt sogar die Zitate und nimmt das πάντα aus Ps 8,7 in das Zitat aus LXX Ps 109,1b in 1 Kor 15,25 auf. Vergleicht man nun Mk 12,36 mit Ps 8,7, ist zu erwägen, ob das ὑποκάτω nicht zeigt, daß V.36e auch von Ps 8,7 her beeinflußt wurde. Warum diese Möglichkeit? Markus benutzt doch ὑποκάτω sonst auch[81]. Aber sowohl Paulus (1 Kor 15,25-27) und der Epheserbrief (Eph 1,20.22) als auch der Hebräerbrief (1,13; 2,6-8) wenden Ps 8,7 und Ps 110,1 auf den erhöhten Christus-Gottessohn an[82]. Es gibt zumindest – abgesehen von dem ὑποκάτω – ein weiteres Argument, warum Markus mit Ps 8,7 hätte vertraut sein können. In Mk 14,62 wird die Erhöhungsvorstellung aus Ps 110,1 mit einem »wie ein Menschensohn« aus Dan 7,13 verbunden. Beide, »die« LXX und Theodotion (θ'), schreiben nur ὡς υἱὸς ἀνθρώπου. Markus seinerseits identifiziert den Christus-Gottessohn mit dem Menschensohn. Die Erhöhung des Christus zum endzeitlichen Herrscher wird in Mk 12, 35-37 vorausgesetzt. In LXX Ps 8 muß man das αὐτόν/αὐτοῦ in V.6f.

---

79. Bzw. eine uneigentliche Präposition.
80. Vgl. Hebr 2,6-8.
81. Vgl. Mk 6,11; 7,28.
82. Vgl. HENGEL, »Setze dich...« (n. 44), pp. 143-150.

auf υἱὸς ἀνθρώπου in V.5 beziehen. Bei einer christologischen Interpretation des Psalms, wie in 1 Kor 15,27 oder Hebr 2,8, ist der Menschensohn in LXX Ps 8,5b mit dem erhöhten Christus zu identifizieren.
Auch Markus 12,36 setzt m.E. eine Rezeption von Ps 110,1 voraus, die
bereits von Ps 8,7 beeinflußt wurde.

Mk 14,62 bestätigt diese Auslegung. Der Evangelist läßt Jesus dem
Hohenpriester so antworten, daß beide, der Gesalbte und der Sohn des
Hochgelobten, mit dem zum Gericht kommenden Menschensohn identifiziert werden. Der Leser weiß, daß Jesus der mit Geist gesalbte Gottes-
sohn ist, er weiß auch, daß Jesus der Christus ist, der zur Herrschaft zur
Rechten Gottes bestimmt ist. Neu an Mk 14,62 ist, daß er in der Zukunft
in der Gestalt des vom Himmel kommenden Menschensohnes zum
Richten seiner eigenen Richter kommen wird. Sie werden in der Zukunft
(ὄψεσθε) sehen, wer er wirklich ist. Er wird, wie in 12,36 gesagt, seine
Feinde unterwerfen. Er wird, wie 8,38 und 13,26 aussagten, zum Gericht
kommen. Ausgehend von der Erhöhung des Christus zum endzeitlichen
Herrscher und Richter wird die Danielstelle auf ihn angewandt[83].

Setzen wir aufgrund der zweiten textkritischen Beobachtung zum Zitat
für das Markusevangelium voraus, daß Markus Ps 110,1 und Ps 8,7 vermischt hat oder aus einer Tradition zitiert, in der beide Psalmtexte auf
den Erhöhten angewandt wurden, ist Mk 14,62 konsequent von 12,36 her
zu verstehen (vgl. auch Apg 7,55f.). Die Menschensohnbezeichnung wird
auf den erhöhten Christus-Gottessohn übertragen (14,61f.). So wird auch
die Bezugnahme auf Dan 7,13 in Mk 14,62 verständlich. Die Verbindung
zwischen Gottessohn und eschatologischem Menschensohn ist jedoch nicht
auf Mk 14,61f. begrenzt. In allen drei Fällen im Markusevangelium, an
denen von dem vom Himmel zum Gericht kommenden Menschensohn
die Rede ist, Mk 8,38; 13,26 und 14,62, setzt Markus die Gottessohnschaft Jesu im näheren Kontext voraus (8,38; 13,32; 14,61f.) und geht
davon aus, daß der Gottessohn zuvor in den Himmel erhöht werden wird.
Dies wird in 13,26 durch das das Danielzitat ergänzende μετὰ δυνάμεως πολλῆς καὶ δόξης und in 14,62 durch die Bezugnahme auf LXX
Ps 109,1 bestätigt. In Mk 14,62 wird das Zitat nicht abgewandelt, so daß
eine Aussage über das Kommen des erhöhten Κύριος gemacht würde,
sondern über den Christus, den Sohn des Hochgelobten. Dabei ist zu
beachten, daß die Unterwerfung der Feinde noch in der Zukunft liegt.

---

83. ἐρχόμενον μετὰ τῶν νεφελῶν τοῦ οὐρανοῦ· Die ganze Wendung lehnt
sich an θ´ Dan 7,13 an, der wie Mk 14,62 im Unterschied zum LXX-Text und dem
Kölner Teil des Papyrus 967 konsequent mit μετά anstelle von ἐπί überliefert wurde.
Die Funktion von Ps 110,1 in Mk 14,62 hat Juel gut erfaßt; vgl. JUEL, *Exegesis* (n. 20),
pp. 145f.

Die Erhöhung wird aber noch ganz unter dem Aspekt der zukünftigen Unterwerfung der Feinde und des Kommens zum Gericht gesehen[84]. Die Christologie des Markusevangeliums wird nicht von dem Gedanken bestimmt, daß der erhöhte Κύριος gegenwärtig präsent sei und direkt in das Leben der Gemeinde eingreife, sondern die Zukunftserwartung bestimmt die Gegenwart. Man bereitet sich auf das Kommen des Hausherrn vor und wartet auf das Kommen des herrschenden Christus als richtender Menschensohn[85].

3. Ps 118,22F. (LXX Ps 117,22F.) IM FOLGETEXT MK 8,31 UND 12,10F.

Der zweite Hauptteil des Markusevangeliums beginnt mit dem Petrusbekenntnis in Mk 8,27f.[86]. Mitten in dieser Perikope, sozusagen als Reaktion des markinischen Jesus auf das Petrusbekenntnis, finden wir die sogenannte erste Leidensweissagung. Hier ist einzusetzen, wenn man sich an den Textsignalen, die auf Ps 118,22f. hinweisen, orientieren will.

3.1 Markus 8,31 als »Sammelbericht«

Das ἤρξατο διδάσκειν hat auch die meisten derjenigen Kommentatoren, die vormarkinische Tradition hinter V.31 rekonstruieren möchten, überzeugen können, daß zumindest die ganze Einleitungswendung in V. 31a vom Evangelisten selber stammt und daß er den ὅτι-Satz in V.31b bearbeitet hat[87]. Es spricht aber einiges dafür, daß der ganze V.31 vom Evangelisten als eine Art erster Sammelbericht des zweiten Hauptteiles des Evangeliums gedacht war[88]. Diese Sammelberichte, dazuzurechnen sind noch die zwei anderen Leidensweissagungen in 9,31 und 10,33f., unterscheiden sich von den Sammelberichten im ersten Hauptteil, indem sie auf noch zu Erzählendes vorausblicken.

---

84. Vgl. H. CONZELMANN, *Geschichte und Eschaton nach Mk 13* (1959), in ID., *Theologie als Schriftauslegung* (BEvT, 65), München, Kaiser, 1974, pp. 62-73, p. 63.

85. Vgl. dazu C. BREYTENBACH, *Grundzüge markinischer Gottessohn-Christologie*, in ID. *et al.* (eds.), *Anfänge der Christologie. FS für Ferdinand Hahn zum 65. Geburtstag*, Göttingen, Vandenhoeck & Ruprecht, 1991, pp. 169-184.

86. Den breiteren Kontext von Mk 8,31, d.h. Mk 8,27-33, habe ich anderswo analysiert; vgl. C. BREYTENBACH, *Nachfolge und Zukunftserwartung nach Markus* (ATANT, 71), Zürich, TVZ, 1984, §7.1.

87. Vgl. C.H. TURNER, *Marcan Usage*, in J.K ELLIOTT (ed.), *The Language and Style of the Gospel of Mark* (NTSup, 71), Leiden, Brill, 1993, pp. 93f.

88. Das nicht-adverbial gebrauchte πολλά muß nicht dagegen sprechen.

Der syntaktische Aufbau von V.31 gibt Leitlinien für die Interpretation. Nach dem einleitenden Hauptsatz (31a) sind alle Aussagen von der mit ὅτι eingeleiteten Aussage (31b) δεῖ τὸν υἱὸν τοῦ ἀνθρώπου abhängig. Die generelle Aussage von 8,31cα, daß der Menschensohn viel leiden müsse, richtet den Blick auf die ganze bevorstehende Passion und reiht sich mit dem eschatologischen δεῖ unter die von Gott in der Schrift vorherbestimmten Endzeitereignisse ein[89]. Dies gilt aber auch für die mehr spezifischen Einzelaussagen, die erläutern, worin das von Gott vorherbestimmte Leiden des Menschensohnes bestehen wird. Mk 8,31cβ greift nun, wie sogleich zu begründen ist, vor allem auf Mk 12,1-12 – das Winzergleichnis –, insbesondere auf V.10f., das Zitat aus LXX Ps 117, 22f., und auf Mk 14,53-15,1 – das Verhör Jesu durch das Synhedrion – vor. Mk 8,31cγ (καὶ ἀποκτανθῆναι) greift auf die Kreuzigung in Kap. 15 vor, während Mk 8,31cδ (καὶ μετὰ τρεῖς ἡμέρας ἀναστῆναι) auf Mk 16,1-8 vorgreift.

Der Vorgriff auf das Winzergleichnis und die Verhörszene wird in Mk 8,31cβ zunächst durch den Infinitiv Passiv ἀποδοκιμασθῆναι signalisiert. Der Leser kann dies als Signal werten, als Anspielung[90] auf LXX Ps 117,22a, sofern ihm dieser Psalmvers geläufig ist. Dies ist nicht unwahrscheinlich, denn LXX Ps 117,22 wurde auch sonst im Urchristentum in Zusammenhang mit der Verwerfung Jesu durch die jüdische Führung zitiert[91]. Wie dem auch sei, spätestens bei einer Zweitlektüre des Markusevangeliums, oder wenn es dem Hörer zum zweiten Mal vorgelesen wird, wird er Mk 8,31 im Lichte des später im Text folgenden Zitates (in Mk 12,10f.) verstehen und eine intratextuelle Beziehung zum Kontext des Winzergleichnisses sowie eine intertextuelle Beziehung zum christlich interpretierten Psalmvers 117,22 der LXX herstellen. Aus diesem Psalm stammt bekanntlich der Begriff ἀποδοκιμασθῆναι in Mk 8,31, dessen Vorkommen in Mk 12,10f. und Parallelen[92] ebenfalls mit der Zitation von LXX Ps 117,22 zusammenhängt.

Ein Vergleich des Psalmverses mit den Stellen, an denen er in der urchristlichen Literatur zitiert wird, einerseits, und Mk 8,31 im besonderen andererseits, zeigt nun Zweierlei auf: Erstens ist mit dem Stein immer Jesus Christus gemeint. Zweitens ist das Geschick des Steines

---

89. Vgl. E. FASCHER, *Theologische Beobachtungen zu δεῖ*, in W. ELTESTER (ed.), *Neutestamentliche Studien für Rudolf Bultmann zu seinem siebzigsten Geburtstag* (BZNW, 21), Berlin, Töpelmann, 1954, pp. 228-254.

90. Zu diesem Verständnis von »Anspielung« vgl. HOLTHUIS, *Intertextualiät* (n. 9), pp. 128f. 131-133.

91. Vgl. Apg 4,11; 1 Petr 2,4.7; Barn 6,4.

92. Sowie in 1 Petr 2,7 und Barn 6,4. In allen Fällen in der Form ἀπεδοκίμασαν. Apg 4,11 wandelt ab und schreibt ὁ λίθος, ὁ ἐξουθενηθείς.

von LXX Ps 117,22f. in der urchristlichen Schriftauslegung auf die Verwerfung *und* Auferweckung Christi bezogen worden. Im Gegensatz zu allen anderen urchristlichen Autoren, die LXX Ps 117 zitieren, nimmt Mk 8,31 aber nur die erste Hälfte von V.22, nur das ἀποδοκιμασθῆναι, auf. So entsteht die Frage, ob, auch wenn der Gedanke von V.22b und V.23, daß Gott den verworfenen Stein zum Schlußstein machte, nicht an der Textoberfläche von Mk 8,31 durch eine Wiederholung dieses Teiles des Psalmverses angezeigt wird, dieser Gedanke mitgemeint ist. Inhaltlich, d.h. auf semantischer Ebene, ist der Gedanke m.E. in dem δεῖ τὸν υἱὸν τοῦ ἀνθρώπου ... ἀναστῆναι in Mk 8,31cδ enthalten. Dies zeigt sich, wenn man Mk 8,31 mit den anderen Folgetexten, die auf Ps 117,22 als Prätext zurückgreifen, in Beziehung setzt. In 1 Petr 2,4.7 steht die Auferweckung des Gekreuzigten im Hintergrund; von Barn 5,6f. her könnte auch 6,3 unmittelbar vor dem Zitat aus LXX Ps 117,22 als Hinweis auf die Auferweckung verstanden werden. Eindeutig ist Apg 4,11: Wegen der Parallelität zwischen ὃν ὁ θεὸς ἤγειρεν ἐκ νεκρῶν in V.10 und ὁ γενόμενος εἰς κεφαλὴν γωνίας in V.11 ist zu folgern, daß Gott den Gekreuzigten durch die Auferweckung zum Schlußstein machte.

Mit diesen intertextuellen Bezügen zwischen Mk 8,31 und der Rezeption von LXX Ps 117,22f. im Urchristentum im Hintergrund sind die drei Textabschnitte, auf die Mk 8,31cβ und 31cδ vorgreifen, das Winzergleichnis Mk 12,1-12 sowie die Verhörszene Mk 14,53-15,1 und Mk 16,1-8 in Beziehung zu Ps 117,22f. zu untersuchen.

3.2 *Markus 12,10f. als Teil der Rede Jesu (12,1-12)*

Markus 11-13 sind nach einem Drei-Tage-Schema abgefaßt worden. Am ersten Tag geschah der Einzug in Jerusalem (Mk 11,1-11), am zweiten Tag fand die Verfluchung des Feigenbaums und die Tempelaustreibung statt (Mk 11,12-11,19), am dritten Tag wird eine Auseinandersetzung im bzw. über den Tempel (Mk 11,20-13,37) geschildert. Dieser Teil ist genauer anzuschauen. Zunächst geht es um eine Jüngerbelehrung unterwegs, das Thema ist »Gebet und Glaube« (Mk 11,20-25); als dann Jesus und die Jünger am Tempel ankommen, beginnt die Auseinandersetzung auf dem Tempelplatz (Mk 11,27-12,44). Der Abschnitt, an dessen Ende das Zitat aus LXX Ps 117,22f. steht, beginnt mit einer Frage nach Jesu Vollmacht (11,27-33) und geht über in eine Rede Jesu (12,1-11). Für das Verständnis dieses Teils empfiehlt es sich, die erzählerischen Bemerkungen in V.12 zu beherzigen. Der Abschnitt wird zusammengehalten durch die Hohenpriester, Schriftgelehrten und Ältesten, die

Jesu Vollmacht in Frage stellen und denen dann ab 12,1ff. Jesu Rede gilt[93]. Der Abschnitt bringt zunächst die Auseinandersetzung mit den Hohenpriestern, Schriftgelehrten und Ältesten auf dem Tempelplatz, die in 11,27 einsetzte, zum Abschluß. Aus Angst vor der Volksmenge (vgl. auch 11,18.32) bleibt es nur bei ihrer Absicht, Jesus zu töten, und zum Schluß verlassen sie den Tempelplatz. Jesus bleibt und andere Kontrahenten kommen. Durch diese Bemerkung nach dem Schriftzitat werden Zitat und Gleichnis eindeutig aufeinander bezogen. Sie sind aber auch Teil derselben Episode, die in 11,27 anfing. »Markus interpretiert Gleichnis und Schriftzitat vor allem durch den Kontext«[94].

Die bislang aufgearbeiteten intratextuellen Bezüge zu Mk 8,31 und 12,12 sowie die Anbindung des Zitates an das Gleichnis liefern die Voraussetzungen dafür, daß das Zitat als Teil des Folgetextes Mk 12,1-12 verstanden werden kann. Von 8,31 her wurde bereits deutlich, daß die Bauleute, die den Stein verwerfen werden, die Hohenpriester, Schriftgelehrten und Ältesten sind. Über V.12 werden nun die Winzer im Gleichnis mit den Sanhedristen identifiziert. Die erneute Anrede markiert aber einen neuen Redeabschnitt und trennt V.10f. somit von der Parabel, so daß die Interpretation zunächst hier einsetzen darf[95]. Es wird erzählt, daß sie nach der Rede Jesu den Tempelplatz verlassen. In V.12 gibt der Erzähler durch seinen Kommentar den Grund an und gibt zugleich eine Hilfe zum Verständnis des Winzergleichnisses. Es wird ausdrücklich gesagt, daß mit den Weingärtnern in der Parabel die Hohenpriester, Schriftgelehrten und Ältesten gemeint waren. Sie sind aber auch mit den Bauleuten im Zitat gemeint. Die Hohenpriester, Schriftgelehrten und Ältesten werden von Jesus gefragt, ob sie nicht das Schriftwort kennen. Dabei wird impliziert, daß sie eigentlich hätten merken müssen, daß es hier um sie geht. Das Markusevangelium kontextualisiert die Psalmverse gerade angesichts einer auch in Apg 4,11 erkennbaren christlichen Auslegung von Ps 117,22. Bei diesem Gebrauch des Psalmverses wurden die Bauleute auf die jüdische Führung bezogen. Dieser Bezug liegt nahe, denn etwa nach grHen 99,13f. sind »die Bauenden« (οἱ οἰκοδομοῦντες) diejenigen, die das Volk im religiös-moralischen Sinn unterrichten. In der Tradition von Ez 13,10 sind die, die Mauern bauen, für die Essener diejenigen, die falsch lehren[96]. Die Hohenpriester, Schriftgelehrten und

---

93. Sie sind mit der 2. Pers. Plural in ἀνέγνωτε (V.10) gemeint.
94. GNILKA, *Markus* (n. 43), p. 149.
95. Mit LOHMEYER, *Evangelium* (n. 38), p. 246.
96. Vgl. CD 4,19; 8,12.18. Vgl. die הַבּוֹנִין in späteren rabbinischen Schriften. Belege bei Bill. I, p. 876.

Ältesten sind in diesem Sinne die Lehrer, die Bauleute, die den Stein verwerfen. Von Mk 8,31 her ist der Stein, der verworfen wird, der Menschensohn. Die Verschiebung der Referenz des λίθος von dem danksagenden Einzelnen im Prätext LXX Ps 117,21[97] auf Christus wird nicht erst durch die Rezeption im Folgetext Mk 12,10f. verursacht. Auch wenn es unsicher bleibt, ob das Judentum des Zweiten Tempels das Steinmotiv, ob nun aus Ps 118,22 oder aus Dan 2,34ff., auf den Messias übertragen hat[98], die urchristliche Deutung des Psalmverses in Zusammenhang mit der Verwerfung Jesu durch die jüdische Führung[99] ist geradezu Voraussetzung für die Verknüpfung von LXX Ps 117,22 mit dem Winzergleichnis[100]. Dadurch, daß der Sohn im Gleichnis als »einziggeliebter« Sohn bezeichnet wird, so wie Jesus bei der Taufe und Verklärung (Mk 1,11; 9,7), wird klar, daß der getötete Sohn in dem Gleichnis der zu tötende Jesus, d.h. der zu prüfende und zu verwerfende Stein ist. Die Geschichte des Sohnes ist aber in dem Gleichnis nicht einmal offen geblieben. Er wurde ermordet.

3.3 *Mk 12,10f. als Ausblick auf die Passion und Auferweckung Jesu*

An dieser Stelle wird nun deutlich, was das dem Gleichnis angeschlossene Schriftzitat leistet. Zunächst zu der negativen Seite. Der markinische Jesus, der das Wort hat, redet in V.10a die Hohenpriester, Schriftgelehrten und Ältesten an. Sie sind mit den Weingärtnern und mit den Bauleuten gemeint. Blicken wir von hier zu der mit der Verleugnung durch Petrus (Mk 14,54.66-72) verschachtelten Verhörszene (Mk 14,53.55-65+15,1), zeigt sich, wie in der Verhörszene immer wieder formuliert wird, daß die Gegner Jesu, der Hohepriester, alle Hohenpriester, Schriftgelehrten und Ältesten (14,53.55; 15,1), als ganzes Synhedrion (14,55) alle zusammen handeln (14,64c; 15,1)[101]. Wie die Winzer beraten sie sich miteinander, bevor sie Jesus, nachdem er die Frage, ob er der

---

97. Vgl. H. GUNKEL, *Die Psalmen*, Göttingen, Vandenhoeck & Ruprecht, [6]1986, p. 509; H.-J. KRAUS, *Psalmen. 2. Teilband* (BK, XV/2), Neukirchen-Vluyn, Neukirchener, [5]1978, p. 984.
98. Vgl. das spärliche bzw. späte Belegmaterial bei J. JEREMIAS, Art. λίθος, in *TWNT* IV, pp. 276-277.
99. Vgl. Apg 4,11; 1 Petr 2,4.6. Ab dem 2. Jh. Barn 6,4f.; Justin, *Dialogus*, 34,2; 36,1; 100,4; Irenäus, *AH*, III 21,7; Tertullian, *Adv. Marc.*, V 5,9; Hippolyt, *Ref.*, V 7,35.
100. Eine Verknüpfung, die ohne erkennbaren Einfluß des Markusevangeliums auch in der spät bezeugten koptischen Überlieferung des Thomasevangeliums zu erkennen ist.
101. Das καί ist epexegetisch, mit M. ZERWICK, *Biblical Greek. English Edition Adapted from the Fourth Latin Edition by Joseph Smith* (SPIB, 114), Rom 1963, §455ζ.

Christus, der Sohn des Hochgelobten sei, bejaht hatte, des Todes würdig erklären (14,64) und zur Vollstreckung eines diesbezüglichen Urteils an Pilatus ausliefern (15,1). Sie prüfen und verwerfen den Stein.

Das Zitat hat aber auch eine positive Seite, die dadurch verstärkt wird, daß das Markusevangelium, anders als der erste Petrus- und der Barnabasbrief, LXX Ps 117,22 *und* 23[102] zitiert. Im Unterschied zu diesen beiden ist die markinische Rezeption des Psalmzitates nicht mit einer Rezeption von Jes 28,16 vermischt, so daß der Gedanke des Ecksteines im Fundamentteil des Baues, über den gestolpert werden kann (1 Petr 2,7f.), oder der Gedanke des Ecksteines im Fundament, auf dem aufgebaut wird (Eph 2,20), nicht die markinische Rezeption prägt[103]. Das Zitat in Mk 12,10f. und die Anspielung in Apg 4,11 sind sich ähnlich. Bei beiden zeigt sich kein Einfluß von Jes 28,16. Wegen der Parallelität zwischen ὃν ὁ θεὸς ἤγειρεν ἐκ νεκρῶν in V.10 und ὁ γενόμενος εἰς κεφαλὴν γωνίας in V.11 in Apg 4 ist zu folgern, daß der Gekreuzigte durch die Auferweckung zum Schlußstein wurde. Hier wird der Psalmvers nicht in Zusammenhang mit dem Grund- oder Eckstein-Gedanken eines Fundamentes gedeutet, sondern der Kontrast zwischen dem verworfenen Stein und dem Schlußstein wird mit dem Gegensatz zwischen Tötung und Auferweckung Jesu parallelisiert. In diese Auslegungslinie ist auch die markinische Rezeption einzureihen. Der Streit, ob es sich bei der κεφαλὴ γωνίας um den Schlußstein eines Torbogens oder um den Eckstein auf dem Fundament handelt, kann offengelassen werden[104]. Er ist in der Tat unwichtig[105], solange man hier nicht den Gedanken des Stolperns hineinträgt und eine vom Markustext nicht signalisierte intertextuelle Relation zur urchristlichen Auslegungstradition von Jes 28,16 oder zu den neutestamentlichen Texten über die Kirche als Bauwerk herstellt. Bei der Deutung des Zitates sollte man folglich von einer ekklesiologischen Deutung Abstand nehmen[106]. Das Zitat im Folgetext Mk

---

102. Barn 6,4 übergeht V.23 und läßt V.24 auf V.22 folgen.

103. Wie stark Jes 28,16 sonst auf die christliche Rezeption von LXX Ps 117,22 einwirkte, zeigt zum Beispiel die Übersetzung von σ΄. Der Judenchrist übersetzte Ende des 2. Jhs. laut einer Bemerkung Theodorets (in *Interpretatio Psalmi*; cf. FIELD, *Origenis* [n. 62], p. 270.) seinen Psalmtext erklärend mit dem Adj. ἀκρογωνιαῖος, »an der äußersten Ecke liegend« (*BAA*, c.65). Das Wort entstammt LXX Jes 28,16 und ist ein Neologismus (von ἀκρός, -ά, -όν, »outermost«; *LSJM*, p. 57 – das NT kennt die Substantivierung τὸ ἄκρον »die äußerste Grenze«; z.B. Mk 13,27, und γωνία »Ecke«, d.h. an der äußersten Ecke; vgl. *BDR* §123.1₄).

104. Mit E. KLOSTERMANN, *Das Markusevangelium* (HNT, 3), Tübingen, Mohr, ⁴1950, p. 123.

105. Mit GNILKA, *Markus* (n. 43), p. 148.

106. Anders R. PESCH, *Das Markusevangelium. II. Teil* (HTKNT, II/2), Freiburg, Herder, 1977, p. 222; HOOKER, *Gospel* (n. 33), p. 277; MARCUS, *Way* (n. 20), pp. 122-124.

12,10f. ist von 8,31 her und in der Verbindung von LXX Ps 117,22 und 23 anders zu lesen. V.11 bei Markus wiederholt LXX Ps 117,23 ohne Änderung. Gott ist Urheber der Aktion, die zum Umschwung im Geschick des Steines führt[107]. Dieses geschah von ihm her: Damit ist auf den Umschwung in der Rolle des λίθος V.10b (bzw. LXX Ps 117,22)[108] Bezug genommen, denn nicht der Eckstein selbst, sondern der Umschwung ist das Erstaunliche[109]. Gerade das Stichwort θαυμαστή[110] zeigt an, daß die Gottestat, den verworfenen Stein an die äußerste Spitze zu stellen, etwas war, was Bewunderung und Erstaunen hervorgerufen hat. Die gängige deutsche Übersetzung mit dem Substantiv »Wunder«[111] ist irreführend. Bei der adjektivischen Wiedergabe mit »wunderbar«[112] erhebt sich die semantische Frage, ob θαυμαστή damit getroffen ist. Besser ist »marvellous«[113] oder »amazing«[114]. Der christliche Übersetzer σ′ zeigt die Interpretationsrichtung auf. Er übersetzte das hebräische Niphal Partizip נִפְלָאת[115] in Ps 118,23 akkurat mit παράδοξον. Worin liegt nun aber das παράδοξον, bzw. was ist θαυμαστή?

Entscheidend ist nun die bereits in Mk 8,31 aufgezeigte Verbindung der Verwerfung mit der Auferstehung des Menschensohnes[116]. Gott macht etwas ganz anderes aus dem Gekreuzigten. Zu Recht kommentiert Lührmann: »Der verworfene Baustein ist der getötete Sohn; wie Gott diesem Stein eine neue Funktion gegeben hat, so wird er auch den Sohn aufwecken ... die Verschlüsselung dieses Zitates weist voraus auf die

---

107. παρά mit Genitiv bezeichnet den Urheber der Aktion (vgl. *BAA*, c. 1233). κύριος bezeichnet als Übersetzung von יהוה Gott. Das übersetzte hebr. מֵאֵת (von מִן und אֵת) bedeutet »von jemandem her«. Das αὕτη hat den Umschwung in V.10 als Thema; nicht die Verwerfung des Steines ist vom Herrn her geschehen. So aber K. BACKHAUS, »*Lösepreis für viele*« *(Mk 10,45)*, in T. SÖDING (ed.), *Der Evangelist als Theologe* (SBS, 163), Stuttgart, KBW, 1995, pp. 91-118, hier p. 100.

108. ἐγένετο αὕτη ist ein Übersetzungssemitismus wegen des hebr. Demonstrativums זֹאת (Fem.). Bezöge man das αὕτη auf das Geschehen in V.10b, müßte im Griechischen, wie σ′ zu Recht korrigiert, τοῦτο stehen (vgl. *BDR* §4₃). E.P. GOULD, *The Gospel according to St. Mark* (ICC), Edinburgh, T. & T. Clark, 1986, p. 222, bezieht (wie übrigens schon α′), das αὕτη auf κεφαλὴν γωνίας. Dies ist zwar nicht unmöglich, aber zugunsten des Rückbezuges auf V.10b zu unterlassen (mit SWETE, *Mark* (n. 20), p. 272; *BDR* §138.2).

109. Vgl. KLOSTERMANN, *Markusevangelium* (n. 104), p. 123.

110. »Wonderful, marvellous«, *GELS* I, p. 202.

111. So die Luther- und die Einheitsübersetzung.

112. So *BAA*, c. 717 und die Kommentatoren.

113. So die KJV und die RSV, die sich für die Wiedergabe auf *LSJM*, p. 786, berufen könnten.

114. So die NRSV.

115. »Außerordentlich, ungewöhnlich«; Gesenius, p. 641; *HAL*, p. 876: »ungewöhnlich, wunderbar sein«.

116. So auch MARCUS, *Way* (n. 20), p. 114.

Botschaft des Engels in 16,6«[117]. Es ließe sich aber noch mehr aus dem Text ablesen. Die erstaunte, verwunderte Reaktion auf die Auferstehung, auf die das Zitat in seinem markinischen Kontext vorausweist, erinnert an die Jünger, die die Machttaten des verborgenen Gottessohnes nicht erfassen konnten[118], bei denen die Frage »Wer ist dieser?« unbeantwortet blieb[119]. Die Verwunderung, mit der dem Stein begegnet wird, greift aber auch auf Mk 16,5f. und 8 vor, wo die Frauen mit Furcht und Zittern auf die Osternachricht reagieren[120]. Gerade die von den Jüngern mit Unverständnis aufgenommene Ankündigung der Auferstehung (9,10) geschah vom Herrn her »und ist eine θαυμαστή in unseren Augen«.

4. Schluß

Auch wenn die Verwendung beider Psalmzitate bereits eine christologische Deutung der Psalmverse voraussetzt, unterscheidet sich die Art der Aufnahme des Psalmzitates am Schluß der Rede Mk 12,1-11 erheblich von der Weise, in der das Zitat aus LXX Ps 109,1 in das Argument Mk 12,35-37 integriert wurde. Beide Psalmzitate sind allerdings wiederum in den breiteren narrativen Kontext des Evangeliums eingebunden: Mk 12,10f. wird in 8,31 vorbereitet und greift über sich hinaus, über die Verhörszene hinweg bis zum Schluß des Evangeliums. Mk 12,36 steht im thematischen Zusammenhang der Davidssohnschaft des Christus und wird in 14,62 im Rahmen der Verhörszene aufgegriffen. Der Markustext setzt die auch sonst bei Paulus und in der urchristlichen Literatur zu beobachtende christologische Verwertung der Psalmverse voraus. Er rezipiert sie aber so, daß die Themen, die mit den Zitaten im Urchristentum in Verbindung standen, nämlich die endzeitliche Herrschaft des Christus zur Rechten des Mächtigen und die Verwerfung und Wiederherstellung Jesu nach meiner Lektüre fest mit den erzählerisch entfalteten christologischen Linien verbunden sind. Eine Untersuchung weiterer Zitate wird zeigen müssen, wie variabel Rezeptionsweise und -bedingungen von Zitaten aus den Heiligen Schriften im Evangelium

117. LÜHRMANN, *Markusevangelium* (n. 48), p. 199.

118. Vgl. die »buchstäblichen« intratextuellen Beziehungen, die durch die Verwendung von θαυμάζειν (5,20) und ἐκθαυμάζειν (12,17) sowie sinnverwandter Wörter wie θαμβεῖσθαι (1,27; 10,24.32), ἐκθαμβεῖσθαι (9,15; 14,33), ἐξίστασθαι (2,12) und ἐξιστάναι (5,42) entstehen.

119. Vgl. hierzu P. MÜLLER, *»Wer ist dieser?« Jesus im Markusevangelium* (BTSt, 27), Neukirchen-Vluyn, Neukirchener, 1995.

120. Mk 16,5f. (ἐκθαμβεῖσθαι); Mk 16,8 (τρόμος καὶ ἔκστασις).

sind. Erst dann, wenn überhaupt, werden weitergreifende Hypothesen über den vormarkinischen Überlieferungszusammenhang, den der Autor den Schriftzitaten entnommen hatte, aufgestellt werden können[121].

Institut für Urchristentum und Antike   Cilliers BREYTENBACH
Theologische Fakultät
Humboldt-Universität zu Berlin
Waisenstraße 28
D-10179 Berlin

121. Hiermit wäre das 1992 während des CBL Anvisierte weiter verfolgt. Vgl. C. BREYTENBACH, *Das Markusevangelium als traditionsgebundene Erzählung? Anfragen an die Markusforschung der achtziger Jahre*, in C. FOCANT (ed.), *The Synoptic Gospels. Source Criticism and the New Literary Criticism* (BETL, 110), Leuven, University Press-Peeters, 1993, pp. 77-110, p. 98. Dank gebührt zwei Mitarbeiterinnen am Institut für Urchristentum und Antike: Dott. Silvia Pellegrini (für wichtige Hinweise zur Intertextualitätsdebatte) und Angela Müller (für die sprachliche Durchsicht des Manuskriptes).

THE APPROPRIATION OF THE PSALMS
OF INDIVIDUAL LAMENT BY MARK

Julia Kristeva introduced the term and concept "intertextualité" in an essay entitled *Word, Dialogue, and Novel*, which appeared in 1969[1]. She created the term in order to elucidate and carry further a model developed by Mikhail Bakhtin. According to her, he was one of the first to employ a model in which "literary structure does not simply *exist* but is generated in relation to *another* structure"[2]. He gave a dynamic dimension to structuralism by conceiving of the "literary word" as a dialogue among several writings: that of the writer, the addressee, and the contemporary or earlier cultural context. In this model, history and society are seen as texts read by the writer, into which he inserts himself by rewriting them. Poetic language, therefore, is an act of social and political protest because it challenges official linguistic codes.

From this point of view, the very act of writing is political; it is a matter of power. Kristeva, who lived the first phase of her life under a totalitarian regime in Bulgaria, admired Bakhtin's refusal to conform to official Soviet aesthetic standards. The issues are less clear-cut in modern Western democracies, not least with regard to the relations of Jews and Christians. We live in a context in which Jews and Christians claim the same texts as foundational, while reading them in radically different ways. Such diversity would not be disturbing except for the fact that a significant degree of responsibility for anti-Semitism has been laid at the door of Christian exegesis. The fact that Christians came to call the Jewish scriptures the Old Testament and to read them as predicting and finding their fulfillment in Jesus as the Christ has led to strongly supersecessionist Christian attitudes. The Church has claimed that the Synagogue is blind and that Jews do not understand their own scriptures[3]. This intolerant

---

1. This article was first published in the volume of her essays entitled Σημειωτιχὴ: *Recherches pour une sémanalyse* (1969); it was reprinted in an English translation in J. KRISTEVA, *Desire in Language: A Semiotic Approach to Literature and Art*, ed. with an introduction by L. S. Roudiez, New York, Columbia University Press, 1980, pp. 64-91.

2. *Ibid.*, pp. 64-65.

3. See Justin Martyr, *1 Apol.* 31. Justin draws the conclusion that, since the Jews do not understand their scriptures, they have no right to keep them; see the discussion by Michael MACH, *Justin Martyr's* Dialogus cum Tryphone Iudaeo *and the Development of Christian Anti-Judaism*, ed. O. Limor and G. G. Stroumsa, *Contra Iudaeos: Ancient and Medieval Polemics between Christians and Jews*, Tübingen, Mohr, 1996, pp. 27-47, esp. pp. 41, 43.

attitude is the product of a long and complex historical process. Many Christian denominations have examined it critically and are attempting to eliminate it. In any case, the Christian appropriation of Jewish scripture must be seen in historical context. In this paper, the appropriation of an important group of Jewish texts by the author of the Gospel of Mark will be examined.

It is well known that the Gospel of Mark makes extensive use of older scripture in telling the story of Jesus[4]. The psalms of individual lament constitute an important group of passages that are appropriated in this way. Was Mark's appropriation of the psalms of individual lament, texts belonging to the Jewish collection of scriptures, a disappropriation of the Jews? Was Mark's rewriting an act of violence, a theft of a cultural heritage, an illegitimate misreading? To answer these questions, we must try to reconstruct the older literary structure and the earlier as well as the contemporary cultural context, and then discern how Mark rewrote them.

1. *The Psalms of Individual Lament*

Form-critical research has established that the oldest psalms of individual lament or complaint served the daily needs of common people within their respective small social groups in pre-exilic Israel[5]. Psalm 22, for example, was recited in its earliest usage within communal offices for afflicted members. The psalm may have served for cases of extreme and prolonged suffering. The proximity of death lent urgency to the prayer (v. 16.21). Thus the original intention of the psalm was to save members of the congregation from certain death[6]. A significant transformation of

See also the statues of the personifed "Church" and "Synagogue" from the south portal of the cathedral in Strasbourg which date to about 1230. Copies now stand in the south portal; the originals are in the Musée de l'Œuvre Notre Dame, which is across from the cathedral at 3, place du Château. The "Synagogue" is pictured blindfolded and with a broken lance.

4. W. S. Vorster rightly emphasized that the author of the Gospel of Mark used older scripture as a literary means to put across a narrative point of view; see *The Function of the Use of the Old Testament in Mark*, in *Neotestamentica* 14 (1980) 62-72, esp. pp. 62 and 68-69.

5. E. S. GERSTENBERGER, *Psalms: Part I with an Introduction to Cultic Poetry* (FOTL, 14), Grand Rapids, MI, Eerdmans, 1988, pp. 7-10, 29-34. The individual lament or complaint is the most common of the types of song found in the Psalter; the category includes Pss 3-7; 11-12; 13; 17; 22; 26-28; 31; 35; 38-39; 41; 42-43; 51; 54-57; 59; 61; 63-70; 71; 86; 88; 102; 109; 120; 130; 140-43. See GERSTENBERGER (*ibid.*, p. 14), who follows H. Gunkel and J. Begrich. Note, however, that Ps 41 was inadvertently omitted from Gerstenberger's list (*ibid.*, p. 174).

6. *Ibid.*, pp. 112-113. H.-J. Kraus assigns Ps 22 to the more general category "prayer song" and describes it as an instance of the "archetypal affliction" of God-forsakenness as suffered in mortal sickness; see *Psalms 1-59: A Commentary*, Minneapolis, MN, Augsburg, 1988, ET from the 5th Germ. ed., 1978, pp. 293-294.

the social context and manner of reading Psalm 22 occurred in the exilic
period, when authorship of the psalm was attributed to David in the super-
scription and it was included in the Davidic collection (Psalms 3–41). Although it is not explicitly connected to a particular incident in the life of
David, as some of the other psalms came to be, the indication of authorship is evidence that it was no longer understood as the utterance of an
ordinary member of the community in distress, but of the ideal king of the
past, David[7].

A further transformation occurred during the post-exilic period, between
500 and 200 BCE, when the Psalter, the *sēper těhillîm*, or "book of
praises", was compiled. In the Persian and Hellenistic periods, the Psalter
was the hymnbook of the many local Jewish communities[8]. In this context, the idea that David was the speaker in Psalm 22 probably continued
to be accepted. This re-reading was supplemented by other re-readings
which gave the psalm meaning in its new social context. On the one hand,
the original intention was retrieved, which identified the speaker with suffering individuals in the community. On the other hand, a new re-reading
most likely emerged, in which the speaker was identified with the local
community, or with Israel as a whole, thus giving meaning to the various
hardships encountered by the Jews in their changed and precarious social
situation. The eschatological conclusion of the psalm (vv. 28-32) seems to
presuppose late post-exilic life and theology and thus probably dates from
this period[9].

The texts from Qumran contain some indications regarding how the
psalms of individual lament were read by the community associated with
the scrolls. In the *Commentary on the Psalms*, Psalm 37 is interpreted in
terms of the history of the community and its opponents[10]. The citation
of vv. 12-13, "The wicked plots against the righteous, and gnashes his

---

7. GERSTENBERGER (n. 5), pp. 29-30. For a discussion of the theory that Ps 22 reflects
a cultic ritual in which the king represented the dying and reviving deity, see KRAUS (n. 6),
pp. 293-294. According to J. Becker, Ps 22 was originally a cultic complaint and thanksgiving of the individual; the addition of vv. 28-32 in the exilic period transformed it into
a prayer of the people; see *Israel deutet seine Psalmen: Urform und Neuinterpretation in
den Psalmen* (SBS, 18), Stuttgart, Katholisches Bibelwerk, 1966, pp. 39, 49-53.

8. GERSTENBERGER (n. 5), pp. 27-28. BECKER (n. 7, p. 31), however, takes the position
that the Psalter was created by collectors in a wisdom context for private reading.

9. GERSTENBERGER (n. 5), p. 112; see also BECKER (n. 7), pp. 39, 49-53.

10. Since the element of lament in Ps 37 is replaced by teaching, it is often classified
as a "wisdom psalm" or "liturgical instruction", but the two descriptive parts (vv. 12-15
and 16-26) are very similar to the laments or complaints; see GERSTENBERGER (n. 5), p. 159.
The document was at first entitled 4QpPs 37, but when it became clear that other psalms
were interpreted as well, the designation was changed to 4QpPs (4Q *171*); see M. P. HOR-
GAN, *Pesharim: Qumran Interpretations of Biblical Books* (CBQ MS, 8), Washington,
DC, Catholic Biblical Association of America, 1979, p. 193.

teeth at him; but the Lord laughs at the wicked, for he sees that his day is coming", is followed by the interpretation: "Interpreted, this concerns the violent of the Covenant who are in the house of Judah, who have plotted to destroy those who practise the law, who are in the Council of the Community. And God will not forsake them to their hands"[11]. We find here the typical post-exilic communal interpretation transformed in the context of the experiences of a persecuted, sectarian group[12].

A strikingly new re-reading of the psalms of individual lament, however, is manifest in the *Thanksgiving Hymns* which have been attributed to the "Teacher of Righteousness" by Gert Jeremias[13]. In one of these, Ps 41,10[14] is cited in a way that implies that the Teacher re-wrote the psalm with himself as the speaker: "But I have been [iniquity to] those who contend with me, dispute and quarrelling to my friends, wrath to the members of my Covenant and murmuring and protest to all my companions. *[All who have ea]ten my bread have lifted their heel against me*, and all those joined to my Council have mocked me with wicked lips"[15]. This transformation is analogous to the one posited for Psalm 22 in the exilic period, when David was written into the text as speaker. The occasion here for the move from the ordinary individual speaker or the suffering community as speaker to the special individual, the Teacher, is due to the self-understanding of the Teacher as an eschatological catalyst[16]. This self-understanding emerges clearly in 1QH 15 (7),12: "For Thou wilt condemn in Judgement all those who assail me, distinguishing through

11. The translation of Ps 37,12-13 is from the RSV; that of 4QpPs from G. Vermes, *The Dead Sea Scrolls in English*, London/New York, Penguin Books, [4]1995, p. 349.

12. L. Ruppert describes this text as the oldest explicitly attested identification of the persecuted righteous of the psalms with the distressed covenant-community; see *Der leidende Gerechte: Eine motivgeschichtliche Untersuchung zum Alten Testament und zwischentestamentlichen Judentum* (FzB, 5), Würzburg, Echter Verlag/Katholisches Bibelwerk, 1972, p. 118.

13. Jeremias used the older numbering of the columns devised by E. L. Sukenik. When fragments from Cave 4 were found, indicating that there was material prior to col. 1 of the copy found in Cave 1, É. Puech devised a new numbering system. In what follows, the numbers of Puech are given first, with those of Sukenik (also used in G. Vermes's translation [n. 11]) in parentheses. The hymns attributed to the Teacher by Jeremias are 1QH 10 (2),1-19; 10 (2),31-39; 11 (3),1-18; 12 (4),5-13 (5),4; 13 (5),5-19; 13 (5),20-15 (7),5; 15 (7),6-25; 16 (8),4-40; see G. Jeremias, *Der Lehrer der Gerechtigkeit* (SUNT, 2), Göttingen, Vandenhoeck & Ruprecht, 1963, p. 171; see also the discussion by Ruppert (n. 12), p. 123.

14. Ps 41,10 MT (41,9 RSV).

15. 1QH 13 (5),23-24; trans. from VERMES (n. 11), p. 205. Italics have been added to highlight the words alluding to Ps 41,10. Similarly, the Teacher is the speaker in the allusion to Ps 22,15-16 MT (22,14-15 RSV) in 1QH 13 (5),31; cf. RUPPERT (n. 12), p. 126.

16. The term was suggested by RUPPERT (n. 12), p. 116.

me between the just and the wicked"[17]. This passage suggests that the suffering of the Teacher has meaning as part of the divine eschatological plan. As is well known, the Teacher was not a messianic figure, but he did assimilate his suffering to the prophetic role, as his appropriation of the laments of Jeremiah shows[18].

Between two of the hymns attributed by Jeremias to the Teacher is a text which shares many themes and terms with the Teacher-hymns, but is more likely to be a later composition and is thus classified as a "community-hymn"[19]. It reads in part, "Violent men have sought after my life because I have clung to your Covenant.... From Thee it is that they assail my life, that Thou mayest be glorified by the judgment of the wicked, and manifest Thy might through me in the presence of the sons of men; for it is by Thy mercy that I stand"[20]. In this passage the speaker is the ideal or individual member of the community. Because of their association with the Teacher and their loyal membership in the community, the members share in his destiny, suffering to be followed by vindication.

2. The Gospel of Mark

Eight of the psalms of individual lament or complaint are cited or echoed in twelve passages of the Gospel of Mark[21]. In one case, the psalm-text

17. Trans. from VERMES (n. 11), p. 211.

18. See the discussion in RUPPERT (n. 12), pp. 126-127. The similarity in terminology between the laments of Jeremiah and the psalms of individual lament suggests that the confessions are, in part at least, a re-writing of the older psalms; see W. L. HOLLADAY, *Jeremiah 1: A Commentary on the Book of the Prophet Jeremiah Chapters 1-25* (Hermeneia), Philadelphia, PA, Fortress, 1986, p. 360 on Jeremiah's appropriation of the genre of individual laments and pp. 363-566 for detailed discussion of the texts. See also M. S. SMITH, *The Laments of Jeremiah and Their Contexts: A Literary and Redactional Study of Jeremiah 11-20* (SBL MS, 42), Atlanta, GA, Scholars Press, 1990, and the literature discussed on pp. xiii-xxi.

19. 1QH 10 (2),20-30; JEREMIAS (n. 13), without mentioning this text explicitly, speaks of "Schülerpsalmen" and describes them as epigones (p. 171). See the discussion in RUPPERT (n. 12), pp. 128-130.

20. 1QH 10 (2),21-22.23-25; trans. from VERMES (n. 11), pp. 194-195.

21. Ps 22,2 in Mk 15,34; 22,7 in Mk 9,12; 22,8 in Mk 15,29; cf. Ps 109,25; Ps 22,19 in Mk 15,24; Ps 41,10 in Mk 14,18; Ps 42,6.12 in Mk 14,34; cf. Ps 43,5; Ps 51,14 in Mk 14,38; Ps 65,8 in Mk 4,39; Ps 69,9 in Mk 3,21; Ps 69,22 in Mk 15,23 and 15,36; and Ps 130,4 in Mk 2,7. If Pss 42 and 43 are counted as one psalm, then seven are cited or echoed in Mark. On the notion of intertexual echoes, see R. B. HAYS, *Echoes of Scripture in the Letters of Paul*, New Haven, CT/London, Yale University Press, 1989, pp. 18-24.

refers to God's power over the sea[22]. In another, the reference is to forgiveness of sins by God[23]. In the rest, the speaker in the psalm complains, describes his mistreatment, or prays for divine support. In Mark, this speaker is implicitly identified with Jesus[24].

Eight of the ten allusions in the latter group occur in chapters 14–15 of Mark. Three of these may be attributed to Markan redaction[25], four are pre-Markan[26], and one is of doubtful origin[27]. The concentration of such allusions in the passion narrative and their largely pre-Markan origin has led to hypotheses about the understanding of the suffering and death of Jesus in the earliest community of his followers. Friedrich Feigel argued that the use of the proof from prophecy and the interpretation of types from older scripture were uncritical and merely formal[28]. Martin Dibelius took a similar position. He argued that the proof from Scripture was at first only a postulate; then in certain scriptural passages, namely Psalms 22; 31; 69; and Isaiah 53, the passion of Jesus was found depicted in advance. Motifs which had been at home in the Hebrew bible came into the text of the Passion. This took place without quoting the scriptural words; the motifs were simply adopted in the form of a narrative. He concluded that even the earliest record told events from the Passion which only had significance because they were known to be announced by scripture. Then everything shameful and dishonoring done to Jesus was legitimized in the Passion story, for it happened according to God's will[29]. Although Dibelius stated in passing, with reference to Luke 24,26, that the point of this early passion apologetic was that the "Christ had to suffer such things", he did not pursue this point, but focused on the question of historical reliability[30].

22. Ps 65,8 MT; 64,8 LXX (Rahlfs); 65,7 RSV; Mk 4,39.
23. Ps 130,4 MT RSV; 129,4 LXX (Rahlfs); cf. Mk 2,7.
24. In one case, Ps 51,14 MT; 50,14 LXX (Rahlfs); 51,12 RSV, Jesus is admonishing the disciples (Mk 14,38), but the context shows that the principle applies to him as well.
25. Mk 14,38; 15,34; 15,36. See A. Y. COLLINS, *The Beginning of the Gospel: Probings of Mark in Context*, Minneapolis, MN, Fortress, 1992, pp. 92-118.
26. Mk 14,34; 15,23; 15:24; 15,29. See COLLINS (n. 25).
27. Mk 14,18. See the discussion in J. GNILKA, *Das Evangelium nach Markus*, 2. Teilband, *(Mk 8,27-16,20)* (EKK II/2), Zürich/Neukirchen-Vluyn, Benziger Verlag/Neukirchener Verlag, ³1989, pp. 235-236. The argument that 14,18 is pre-Markan because Ps 41,10 is alluded to in a similar context in Jn 13,18 is only persuasive to those who conclude that the Gospel of John is independent of Mark, e.g., J. MARCUS, *The Way of the Lord: Christological Exegesis of the Old Testament in the Gospel of Mark*, Louisville, KY, Westminster/John Knox Press, 1992, pp. 175-176.
28. F. K. FEIGEL, *Der Einfluss des Weissagungsbeweises und anderer Motive auf die Leidensgeschichte*, Tübingen, Mohr, 1910, esp. p. 117.
29. M. DIBELIUS, *From Tradition to Gospel* (trans. from 2nd German ed.), New York, Charles Scribner's Sons, 1935, pp. 184-185.
30. *Ibid.*, pp. 185-217.

Emphasis on the formal character and the legitimating function of the allusions also characterized the work of Rudolf Bultmann and Eta Linnemann[31].

Later, scholars began to inquire more deeply about the logic of allusion to the psalms and to re-open the question about Jesus' own understanding of his destiny. In his book *Erniedrigung und Erhöhung bei Jesus und seinen Nachfolgern*, Eduard Schweizer observed that Jesus taught his disciples that the way they had to walk would lead through suffering and hardships to glory; the discussion at Caesarea Philippi shows that he saw his own destiny in similar terms. Jesus and his followers, confronted with his ignominious death, must have had a conception by means of which they could make sense of this way. Schweizer found such a conception in a schema which he abstracted from Jewish scripture and especially from Jewish apocalyptic and rabbinic texts, namely, a schema of the abasement and exaltation of the suffering righteous one. He found evidence that this schema actually served to make sense of the destiny of Jesus in the passion narrative, which is full of allusions to what he called "the psalms of the suffering righteous", whereas Isaiah 53 only comes into play later. He concluded that the schema of abasement and exaltation is the key to the understanding of the oldest Christology as well as to the self-understanding of the historical Jesus[32].

Lothar Ruppert criticized Schweizer's hypothesis on several grounds. The most telling is his conclusion that the Jewish motif posited by Schweizer regarding the abasement and exaltation of the righteous one is an unacceptable combination of different motifs and is not equivalent to the idea of the suffering (unto death) and eschatological glorification of the righteous which appears in Jewish apocalypticism and has roots in the Hebrew bible[33]. Nevertheless, Ruppert agreed with Schweizer that the passion narrative in Mark presents Jesus's destiny in terms of the suffering and rescued righteous[34]. He admitted, however, that the general

---

31. See the discussion by L. RUPPERT, *Jesus als der leidende Gerechte?: Der Weg Jesu im Lichte eines alt- und zwischentestamentlichen Motivs* (SBS, 59), Stuttgart, Katholisches Bibelwerk, 1972, pp. 12-13, 49. Bultmann, like Dibelius, assumed that the starting point was the problem of the crucified Messiah, but he did not pursue the point; see *The History of the Synoptic Tradition*, rev. ed., New York, Harper & Row, 1968; trans. of the 2nd Germ. ed., 1931, p. 280.

32. E. SCHWEIZER, *Erniedrigung und Erhöhung bei Jesus und seinen Nachfolgern* (ATANT, 28), Zürich, Zwingli-Verlag, ²1962, esp. pp. 21-33, 44-48, 50. See also the ET, ID., *Lordship and Discipleship* (SBT), Naperville, IL, Allenson, 1960.

33. Ruppert (n. 31), p. 44.

34. *Ibid.*, pp. 50-52.

recognition that the passion narrative was definitively shaped by related texts from the Hebrew bible or Septuagint is not proof that the evangelists or the early community understood the suffering of Jesus in terms of the suffering of the righteous[35]. He then proceeded to make a case for his position, arguing that the allusions to the psalms are not merely formal; rather, the analogy between the situation of the speaker of the psalm and that of Jesus is preserved[36]. This is an accurate observation and an important one. But it still does not prove that the suffering of Jesus was understood primarily as the suffering of the righteous in Mark or in the pre-Markan tradition.

In the course of his argument, Ruppert offered a criticism of the view of Dibelius and company. Ruppert thought it unlikely that members of the earliest community would have looked through the scriptures in order to find passages with which they could deal with the scandal of the cross[37]. The implied counter-argument seems to be that the motif of the suffering righteous, on the other hand, was part of the living culture of their social context. In response, it can be said that the canonical psalms, as the prayer-book of the local Jewish communities, were also part of that living culture. In fact, it is likely that the psalms played a role in the emerging communal rituals of the followers of Jesus after his death. They certainly had an important role in the liturgy by the end of the second century. In the *Apostolic Tradition*, a text attributed to Hippolytus which dates to c. 200 CE, there is a description of the communal supper, that takes place in the evening. A deacon brings in a lamp, and then the bishop says a prayer of thanksgiving. After the meal, further prayers are said. Then the boys, the virgins, and the deacon say psalms. That at least some of these are from the scriptures is indicated by the remark that one of them should be "from those in which 'Alleluia' is written"[38]. Tertullian describes a Christian feast which he calls *agape*. The ritual begins with prayer; then enough food is eaten to satisfy hunger and a modest amount is drunk. Next hands are washed, lamps lit, and each who is able is called into the center to chant praise to God either from the holy scriptures or his own talents. The ceremony concludes with prayer[39]. If the reading, singing, or chanting of the psalms was part of the communal worship of

---

35. *Ibid.*, pp. 48-49.
36. *Ibid.*, pp. 49-52.
37. *Ibid.*, p. 13.
38. *Apostolic Tradition* 25; see G. J. CUMING, *Hippolytus: A Text for Students* (Grove Liturgical Studies, 8), Bramcote Notts., UK, Grove Books, 1976, pp. 23-24.
39. Tertullian, *Apology* 39.

the followers of Jesus from the time of his death onward, these oral per-
formances of the psalms, perhaps associated with homilies or other
forms of teaching, may have been the occasion for the re-reading of the
psalms of individual lament with reference to the death of Jesus. Feigel,
Dibelius and Bultmann were probably right in their assumption that the
starting point was the conviction that Jesus was the Messiah. A messianic re-reading of passages describing suffering as prediction of the
suffering of the Messiah then followed[40].

The presentation of Jesus as a suffering righteous man clearly occurs
in Luke-Acts, as Ruppert pointed out[41]. In Mark, however, it is as "Son
of Man" (8,31; 9,31; 10,33) or "Son of God" (15,39) that Jesus must
suffer[42]. That Jesus was condemned to death unjustly is an important
point made in an indirect manner by the account of the trial before the
High Priest and his advisers (14,55-64)[43]. But the main point made by
the passion narrative in the context of Mark as a whole is that Jesus suffered as the Messiah because this messianic suffering is part of the divine
plan revealed in scripture. Although each has its own special range of connotations, "Son of Man" and "Son of God" in Mark are messianic epi-
thets[44].

Although my main concern here is with the presentation of this suffering in Mark, I would suggest that the allusions to the psalms of individual lament in the pre-Markan passion narrative already aim at making
sense of Jesus' death, not merely as foretold, but as the predetermined
suffering of the messiah[45]. As the "Teacher of Righteousness" viewed

40. D. Juel has attempted to reconstruct the logic of this process, suggesting that Ps 89
was the starting point for the messianic interpretation of the psalms by the followers of
Jesus; see *Messianic Exegesis: Christological Interpretation of the Old Testament in
Early Christianity*, Philadelphia, PA, Fortress, 1988, pp. 89-117.

41. Ruppert (n. 31), pp. 13, 47-48.

42. Ruppert recognized this point; see *ibid.*, p. 56. Although John the Baptist is
described as δίκαιος (Mk 6,20), Jesus is never given this epithet in Mark. Furthermore,
the most important of the psalms of individual lament in Mark, Ps 22, does not include
the motif of the righteousness of the one who suffers; Ruppert noted this point also
(n. 12), pp. 39, 206, nn. 99-100.

43. Cf. the discussion by RUPPERT (n. 31), pp. 53-56.

44. On the equivalence of "Son of Man" and "Christos" or "Messiah" in Jewish and
Christian tradition of the first century CE, see A. Y. COLLINS, *The Influence of Daniel on
the New Testament*, in J. J. COLLINS, *Daniel: A Commentary on the Book of Daniel*
(Hermeneia), Minneapolis, MN, Fortress, 1993, pp. 90-105.

45. This hypothesis is supported by the question of Pilate, "Are you the king of the
Jews?" (Mk 15,2), the mocking of Jesus as a king by the Roman soldiers (15,16-20), and
the statement that "the inscription of the charge against him was posted: the king of the
Jews" (15,26). These three elements were probably part of the pre-Markan passion narrative;
see COLLINS (n. 25), esp. pp. 109-113.

himself as the eschatological catalyst whose suffering was divinely ordained, the followers of Jesus understood his death as an important element in the predestined eschatological scenario. In both cases, a real analogy between the situation of the speaker in the psalm and that of the rejected and persecuted later eschatological leader was perceived and preserved. At the same time, the older psalms were re-read as predicting or at least pre-figuring the suffering of a special individual, whose destiny has universal significance.

As is well known, there is little explicit commentary or interpretation in the passion narrative in Mark. The exception is of course the exclamation of the centurion which interprets the death of Jesus as the death of God's son, an epithet with messianic connotations in a Jewish cultural context. In the next section of my presentation, I would like to support the hypothesis of the messianic re-reading of the psalms of individual lament in the Gospel of Mark by discussing the two passages outside the passion narrative which allude to such psalms.

3. *Mk 9,11-13*

V. 9 is set off from the account of the transfiguration by the change in location: "And as they were coming down from the mountain" (Mk 9,9). What follows in the rest of v. 9 is Jesus's command that the three disciples who witnessed the transfiguration say nothing about it until "the Son of Man has risen from the dead". The import of v. 10 is that Jesus's remark has impressed the disciples, but also thrown them into confusion. V. 11, rather than beginning a new pericope, then follows naturally as a question aimed at dispelling, or at least reducing, this confusion, "Why do the experts in the law say that Elijah must come first?" As many scholars have pointed out, this question alludes to Mal 3,22-23[46]. With reference to the passage in Malachi, the significance of the word "first" is that Elijah must come "before the great and glorious Day of the Lord"[47]. But in the context of Mark, the event before which Elijah must come is "the resurrection from the dead"[48]. The classic meaning of "the Day of the Lord" is the "day of judgment". By the late Second Temple

---

46. Mal 3,22-23 LXX (Rahlfs); 3,23-24 MT; 4,5-6 RSV. See, e.g., J. MARCUS (n. 27), p. 94; R. LIEBERS, *"Wie geschrieben steht"; Studien zu einer besonderen Art frühchristlichen Schriftbezuges*, Berlin/New York, de Gruyter, 1993, p. 75.

47. Mal 3,22 LXX.

48. Mk 9,10.

period, the notion of the day of judgment evoked a complex of eschatological ideas that included the resurrection from the dead. The disciples thus associate "the Day of the Lord" with the resurrection of the righteous or the general resurrection of the dead and assume that the Son of Man will rise on such an occasion. Their confusion is caused by the implied imminence of the resurrection, in spite of the fact that Elijah has apparently not yet come[49]. Jesus's response then comes in v. 12, which should be translated, "He said to them, 'Elijah does come first and restores all things; and yet how is it written with reference to the Son of Man that he is to suffer much and be treated with contempt?'"[50] The first part of his response confirms the contemporary Jewish tradition, based on Malachi, that Elijah would return in the last days. Jesus not only alludes to scripture here but also expands it, so that Elijah "restores" not only "hearts", but "all things". The second part of his response introduces a new theme: the suffering and rejection of the Son of Man. It is this theme that is of primary interest here.

Scholars disagree whether this statement about the Son of Man alludes to a specific passage, and if so, whether to one or several[51]. The epithet "Son of Man" most likely derives ultimately from Dan 7,13, but the link between that epithet and suffering does not derive from Daniel 7[52]. The idea that the Son of Man, or the Messiah, must suffer much could equally well be based on Isaiah 53 as on the psalms of individual lament,

---

49. The Gospel presents the disciples as unaware that the Son of Man would rise *before* the general resurrection from the dead. There is thus insufficient tension between the question of the disciples in v. 11, on the one hand, and the dialogue in vv. 9-10, on the other, to warrant the conclusion that vv. 11-13 contain a traditional, pre-Markan unit; *contra* LIEBERS (n. 46), p. 76.

50. The first part of the response should be translated as an affirmation and not as a question; with LIEBERS (n. 46), pp. 73-74, and against MARCUS (n. 27), pp. 94, 99.

51. A. Suhl concluded that the suffering of the Son of Man is merely asserted to be in accordance with the scriptures here, without allusion to any particular passage; see *Die Funktion der alttestamentlichen Zitate und Anspielungen im Markusevangelium*, Gütersloh, Mohn, 1965, p. 44; see the critique by J. MARCUS (n. 27), p. 95, n. 4 and by H. ANDERSON, *The Old Testament in Mark's Gospel*, in J. M. EFIRD (ed.), *The Use of the Old Testament in the New and Other Essays: Studies in Honor of W. F. Stinespring*, Durham, NC, Duke University Press, 1972, pp. 280-306, esp. pp. 286, 306. C.E.B. Cranfield saw a reference here primarily to Isa 52,13–53,12 and interpreted the suffering of the Son of Man as modeled on the suffering of the Servant of the Lord; he also mentioned Pss 22,6 (21,7 LXX); 123,3 (122,3 LXX); 119,22 (118,22 LXX); see *The Gospel according to Saint Mark* (rev. ed.; CGTC), Cambridge/New York, Cambridge University Press, 1977 (1st ed., 1959), p. 298. R. Pesch concluded that allusion is made to Pss 118,22; 22,6.25; 69,33 and especially to Ps 89,39 and interpreted the suffering of the Son of Man here as modeled primarily on that of the suffering righteous; see *Das Markusevangelium*, II. Teil, *Kommentar zu Kap. 8,27-16,20* (HTK NT, 2.2), Freiburg, Herder, [4]1991, (1st ed., 1977), p. 79.

52. See the discussion in A. Y. COLLINS (n. 44).

on the assumption of a messianic re-reading in each case. The use of the verb ἐξουδενηθῇ ("be treated with contempt") in Mk 9,12 makes it somewhat more likely that the allusion is to Ps 22,7, which reads, translated from the Greek version, "But I am a worm and no man, an object of reproach for men and an object of contempt for the people"[53].

The statement regarding the Son of Man in Mk 9,12b is probably a Markan composition[54]. This line of argumentation leads to a very important conclusion. A classic psalm of individual lament, Psalm 22, which is cited three times in Mark 15 in connection with the crucifixion of Jesus[55], is cited here in a way that does not limit the significance of the psalm to its prophecy of the physical suffering and death of Jesus. In Mk 9,12, Psalm 22 is re-read in such a way that it becomes a prophecy of the rejection of the person and message of Jesus as the Messiah.

This interpretation is supported by the conclusion of this unit, Mk 9,13, which reads, "But I say to you that Elijah has indeed come, and they did to him what they wanted, as it is written with reference to him". It is well known that the chief problem in the interpretation of this statement is that the motif that the returned Elijah would be persecuted is not attested in Jewish tradition prior to or contemporary with the Gospel of Mark[56]. It is likely, however, that the clause "as it is written with reference

53 ἐγὼ δέ εἰμι σκώληξ καὶ οὐκ ἄνθρωπος, ὄνειδος ἀνθρώπου καὶ ἐξουδένημα λαοῦ (Ps 21,7 LXX [Rahlfs]); italics added. Although the verb ἐξουδενοῦν or ἐξου-θενοῦν occurs in the translations of Isa 53,3 attributed to Aquila, Symmachus, and Theodotion, as Cranfield pointed out (n. 51, p. 298), neither verb occurs in the Old Greek (LXX) translation of this vs or anywhere in Isa 52,13–53,12. The noun ἐξουδένωσις occurs in Pss 123,3 (122,3 LXX); 119,22 (118,22 LXX), as Cranfield pointed out (ibid.), but the analogy between the situations of the speakers in these psalms and that of Jesus is less striking; more significantly, neither of these psalms is cited elsewhere in Mark. Ps 22,25 (21,25 LXX), mentioned by PESCH (n. 51), p. 79, belongs to the thanksgiving part of the prayer and thus does not fit the situation of Jesus in Mk 9,12 as well as Ps 22,6 (21,7 LXX). The same holds for Ps 69,33 (68,34 LXX), also mentioned by Pesch (ibid.). There is indeed an analogy between Mk 9,12 and Ps 89,39 (88,39 LXX) (PESCH, ibid.), and it is striking that the "anointed" is mentioned, but the speaker is not the anointed himself; rather, a representative of the people addresses God concerning an event of the past.

54. Few would agree with PESCH (n. 51), p. 1, that Mk 9,2-13 belongs to the pre-Markan passion narrative; more convincing are the arguments in favor of Markan redaction, presented by LIEBERS (n. 46), p. 83.

55. Ps 22,2 is alluded to in Mk 15,34; Ps 22,8 in Mk 15,29; and Ps 22,19 in Mk 15,24.

56. See MARCUS (n. 27), p. 97 and LIEBERS (n. 46), pp. 87-91. Although MARCUS minimizes this possibility (pp. 97-98, n. 19), it could be that the witness who resembles Elijah in Rev 11,3-13 reflects a contemporary Jewish tradition that the returned Elijah would indeed be persecuted. It seems more likely, however, that this motif is Christian in origin. The idea that Elijah would be the forerunner of the Messiah may, however, be an inner-Jewish tradition, since it is attested in the Pesikta Rabbati, Piska 35.4; see W. G. BRAUDE, Pesikta Rabbati: Discourses for Feasts, Fasts, and Special Sabbaths, 2 vols., (YJS), 18

to him" refers to established scripture, rather than to Jesus's immediately preceding affirmation concerning Elijah[57]. Unlike most inner-biblical and post-biblical references, this one does not seem to allude to a single, specific passage. Rather, on the assumption that John the Baptist was a prophet, it alludes to a pervasive scriptural motif, namely, the rejection of the person and message of the prophet, which sometimes involves the threat or even the actuality of his death[58]. Thus, the passage affirms two similarities between Jesus and John the Baptist. A formal parallel lies in the application of the phrase "it is written with reference to him" to each figure. A parallel in destiny is manifest in that each is a divinely sent eschatological agent who meets with resistance and rejection[59].

4. *Mark 3,20-21*

The passage reads, "And he went home. And the crowd gathered again, so that they were not even able to eat. And when his family heard (about it)[60], they went out to restrain him; for they said, 'He has lost his senses'". Although this passage does not allude in an obvious way to any specific passage in scripture, it echoes a motif which occurs in Ps 69,9. The psalm passage, translated from the Greek version, reads,

New Haven, CT/London, Yale University Press, 1968, vol. 2, pp. 674-675. Piska 35 has been dated to the third or early fourth century CE; see H. L. STRACK and G. STEMBERGER, *Introduction to the Talmud and Midrash*, (Edinburgh, T. & T. Clark, 1991; ET of the 1982 Germ. ed., p. 328. In this passage, Elijah is identified with "the messenger of good tidings" in Isa 52,7. On the debate whether there was a Jewish expectation in the first century CE that Elijah would act as a forerunner of the Messiah, see MARCUS (n. 27), p. 110.

57. I disagree with MARCUS (n. 27), p. 107, on this point.

58. See Jer 11,19.21; 20,2; 26,8-11.20-23; 37,14-16; 38,4-6; 2 Chron 16,10; 24,21; 1 Kings 19,2.10.14; 22,27. Although I disagree with Liebers' conclusion that the καί preceding Ἠλίας in Mk 9,13 should be translated "auch" ("also"; I translate "indeed", in keeping with the affirmatory character of the statement as a response to a question), his argument concerning the reference to scripture at the end of that verse is persuasive and his discussion of the motif of the rejection of the prophets in biblical and post-biblical literature is excellent; see LIEBERS (n. 46), pp. 369-376.

59. LIEBERS (n. 46), pp. 84-85, notes the two parallels, but describes them in such a way that John the Baptist is subordinated to Jesus. It is not so clear that such is the intention of the Gospel of Mark; on this topic with reference to the Gospel of Matthew, see H. FRANKEMÖLLE, *Johannes der Täufer und Jesus im Matthäusevangelium: Jesus als Nachfolger des Täufers*, in *NTS* 42 (1996) 196-218.

60. Some MSS (D W it) read ἀκούσαντες (ὅτε ἤκουσαν D) περὶ αὐτοῦ οἱ γραμματεῖς καὶ οἱ λοιποὶ ("when the experts in the law and the rest heard about him"). Clearly the original reading οἱ παρ' αὐτοῦ ("his family") was so offensive that some copyists changed it, so that the standard opponents of Jesus, rather than his family, said that he had lost his senses.

"I became alienated from my brothers and a stranger to the sons of my mother"[61]. Even though the brothers of Jesus are not mentioned explicitly in v. 21, his family, οἱ παρ' αὐτοῦ, is further defined in v. 31 as his mother and his brothers. Like Psalm 22, Psalm 69 is a psalm of individual lament which is also cited in the Markan passion narrative[62]. Here, however, it echoes in a quite different way. The reproach and shame borne by the speaker[63] are not connected primarily with the physical suffering and death of Jesus, but with the misunderstanding of his charismatic activity. This misunderstanding is tantamount to a rejection of his divine mission, and thus, in the context of Mark as a whole, of his messianic role[64].

5. When is Appropriation Disappropriation?

We have seen that the psalms of individual lament were re-read during the period of the second Temple so that the speaker was identified with personified Israel[65]. In the texts from Qumran, the collective re-reading was narrowed to the members of the new covenant. The one case in which the speaker was identified with a special individual is the re-reading of these psalms reflected in the poems of thanksgiving apparently written by the "Teacher of Righteousness", who understood himself as persecuted because of his eschatological role.

In the classical rabbinic period, the speaker was understood often either as an ordinary individual or as collective Israel. For example, in one of the few citations of Psalm 22 in the *Midrash Rabbah* which reveals how the speaker of the psalm is understood, "the afflicted" or "the poor" is interpreted literally, as the man who can only afford to make an offering of meal or cereal[66]. In another citation, "he who cannot keep

---

61. Ps 69,9 MT; ἀπηλλοτριωμένος ἐγενήθην τοῖς ἀδελφοῖς μου καὶ ξένος τοῖς υἱοῖς τῆς μητρός μου according to 68,9 LXX (Rahlfs); 69,8 RSV.

62. Ps 69,22 is alluded to in Mk 15,23.36.

63. Cf. Ps 69,8 MT; 68,8 LXX (Ráhlfs); 69,7 RSV.

64. J. Gnilka doubted that the evangelist had scriptural models in mind, but thought it appropriate to point out that similar motifs were associated with the prophet; see *Das Evangelium nach Markus*, 1. Teilband, *Mk 1-8,26* (EKK II/1), Zürich/Neukirchen-Vluyn, Benziger Verlag/Neukirchener Verlag, ³1989, p. 148, n. 23, with reference to Jer 12,6; 11,21; Zech 13,3. Jer 12,6 is the only one of these three to which allusion could be made in Mk 3,21. It is a more distant parallel to the latter passage than Ps 69,9, since it refers to the father, rather than the mother, and emphasizes the element of treachery, an element missing in Mark.

65. See further J. BECKER (n. 7), pp. 22-26.

66. Ps 22,24-25 MT (22,23-24 RSV) is cited in the comments on Lev 2,1, "And when one bringeth a meal-offering unto the Lord"; see H. FREEDMAN and M. SIMON, (eds), *Midrash Rabbah*, vol. 4, *Leviticus*, London/New York, Soncino Press, ³1983) pp. 36-37.

himself alive" is interpreted of all the dead[67]. These two citations are interpreted in the same way in the *Midrash on Psalms* (*Midrash Tĕhillîm*)[68]. The statement "But I am a worm and no man" in v. 7 is attributed to David in some manuscripts of the *Misdrash on Psalms*, as an example of the reaction of a righteous man to the divine conferral of greatness. Most manuscripts, however, understand collective Israel to be the speaker of the entire verse[69]. In most of the rest of the psalm, the speaker is understood to be Esther or Esther and Mordecai[70].

There is evidence, however, that Psalm 22 was read messianically by a Jewish group, perhaps as early as the third century CE, who called themselves "Mourners of Zion" in allusion to Isa 61,2-3[71]. They were characterized by perpetual supplication of divine mercy and unabated hope in divine salvation. They claimed that their mourning rituals were more important to God than the law, because they were sharing in the divine pathos. This stance may have had the effect of non-fulfillment of

67. Ps 22,30 MT (22,29 RSV) is cited in the comments on Num 7,89, "from above the ark-cover that was upon the ark of the testimony": "R. Dosa observed: It says, *For man shall not see Me and live* (Ex. XXXIII, 20). This implies that men cannot see God when they are alive but that they can see him at their death; in this strain it says, *All they that go down to the dust shall kneel before Him, even he that cannot keep his soul alive* (Ps. XXII, 30)". See FREEDMAN and SIMON (n. 66), vol. 6, *Numbers II*, p. 640.

68. *Midr. Tĕh.* on Ps 22, sections 30-31 and 32; see W. G. BRAUDE (ed), *The Midrash on Psalms (Midrash Tehillim)*, vol. 1, containing Book I (Pss 1-41) and Book II (Pss 42-72) (YJS, 13), New Haven, CT, Yale University Press, 1959, vol. 1, pp. 323-25, 326. The speaker in Ps 69 is consistently understood as collective Israel in the *Midrash on Psalms*. V. 4 (v. 3 RSV) is interpreted in terms of "the oppression of the present exile"; see BRAUDE, vol. 1, pp. 550-51.

69. *Midr. Tĕh.* on Ps 22, section 20; see BRAUDE (n. 68), pp. 315-16 and p. 315, note.

70. See BRAUDE (n. 68), pp. 297-326.

71. A. Marmorstein argued that *Pesikta Rabbati* 34 derived from a messianic movement of the third century CE; see *Eine messianische Bewegung im dritten Jahrhundert*, in *Jeschurun* 13 (1926) 16-28, 171-86, 369-83. The foundation of his argument is the reference to an opponent of the group who later became persuaded of the validity of their position. Marmorstein used the edition by Friedmann (M. FRIEDMANN, *Pesikta Rabbati: Midrasche für den Fest-Cyclus und die ausgezeichneten Sabbathe*, Wien, 1880, repr. Tel Aviv, 1963, which referred simply to Rabbi, son of Hanina, in 34.1. Following Friedmann, MARMORSTEIN concluded that the scholar in question was R. Jose b. Hanina, who was active in Tiberias from 240-260 CE; see Marmorstein, pp. 19-20, 22. The Parma MS, to which Friedmann did not have access, refers to "Jose the son of R"; see BRAUDE (n. 56), vol. 1, pp. 27-28; vol. 2, 665, n. 6. Then Marmorstein analyzed the evidence for the life and teachings of R. Jose b. Hanina, as well as his historical context, and made a plausible case for the movement in question as a part of his milieu. A. Goldberg emphasized the difficulty of dating the text, but concluded that *Pesikta Rabbati* 34 originated some time after the middle of the third century CE; ID., *Erlösung durch Leiden: Drei rabbinische Homilien über die Trauernden Zions und den leidenden Messias Efraim (PesR 34. 36. 37)* (FJS, 4), Frankfurt a. M., Gesellschaft zur Förderung Judaistischer Studien, 1978, p. 142. See also the discussion and literature cited by STRACK and STEMBERGER (n. 56), pp. 327-328.

some positive commandments. Such an effect could be the reason why they were persecuted by other Jews[72]. Some of their beliefs and traditions are preserved in *Pesikta Rabbati* 34-37. According to this text, during the seven year period preceding the coming of the son of David, iron beams will be loaded upon his neck until the Messiah's body is bent low. Then he will cry and weep and complain to God. With regard to his complaint, the comment is made, "It was because of the ordeal of the son of David that David wept, saying 'My strength is dried up like a potsherd'", a citation of Ps 22,16[73]. This comment takes the historical king David to be the speaker of the psalm, but understands him to be speaking, not of his own suffering, but of that of his descendant, the Messiah. Then, when the Messiah appears, the patriarchs will arise and say to him, "Ephraim[74], our true Messiah, even though we are your forbears, you are greater than we because you suffered for the iniquities of our children, and terrible ordeals befell you, such ordeals as did not befall earlier generations or later ones; for the sake of Israel you became a laughingstock and a derision among the nations of the earth...."[75]. In this context, the suffering of the Messiah when he will be shut up in prison is described: "a time when the nations of the earth will gnash their teeth at him every day, wink their eyes at one another in derision of him, nod their heads at him in contempt, open wide their lips to guffaw, as is said *All they that see me laugh me to scorn; they shoot out the lip, they shake the head* (Ps 22,8); *My strength is dried up like a potsherd; and my tongue cleaves to my throat; and you lay me in the dust of death* (Ps 22,16). Moreover, they will roar over him like lions, as is said *They open wide their mouth against me, as a ravening and roaring lion. I am poured out like water, and all my bones are out of joint; my heart is become like wax; it is melted in my inmost parts* (Ps 22, 14-15)"[76].

---

72. According to *Pesikta Rabbati*, Piska 34.1 (BRAUDE [n. 56], pp. 663-65), the group suffered great distress because the children of Israel both mocked and scorned them. My colleague, Michael Fishbane, has a very helpful discussion of this group in his essay, *Midrash and Messianism: Some Theologies of Suffering and Salvation*, in Mark COHEN and Peter SCHÄFER (eds), *Jewish Messianism* (NumenSup), Leiden, Brill, forthcoming.

73. Ps 22,16 MT; 21,16 LXX (Rahlfs); 22,15 RSV. This verse is cited in *Pesikta Rabbati*, Piska 36.2 (BRAUDE [n. 56], p. 680).

74. The assignment of the name "Ephraim" to the Messiah is apparently due to exegetical reflection on Jer 31,9.20; so FISHBANE (n. 72), pp. 11-12, 18-19. Jer 31,20 is cited in *Pesikta Rabbati*, Piska 37.1; see BRAUDE (n. 56), p. 686.

75. *Pesikta Rabbati*, Piska 37.1; trans. taken and modified from BRAUDE (n. 56), p. 685.

76. *Pesikta Rabbati*, Piska 37.1; trans. taken and modified from BRAUDE (n. 56), pp. 686-687.

For various reasons, including the fact that the "Mourners of Zion" did not expect the Messiah to die for the iniquities of Israel, but only to suffer, it is unlikely that this tradition is due to Christian influence[77]. The "Teacher-Hodayot" provide evidence that the psalms of individual lament could be and in fact were re-read in a pre-Christian Jewish context as expressing the distress of a special individual, an eschatological agent of God, whose suffering was part of and necessary for the fulfillment of the divine plan. The traditions of the "Mourners of Zion" show that these psalms could be and were re-read in a Jewish context as describing the sufferings of the Messiah. A similar tradition is preserved in the *Yalkut* on Isa 60,1, in which Psalm 22 is interpreted with reference to the suffering of the Messiah[78].

The Jewish tradition of a suffering Messiah is also occasionally found in interpretations of Isaiah 53. A passage in the Babylonian Talmud reads, "The Messiah – what is his name?... The Rabbis say, The leprous one [; those] of the house of Rabbi [say, The sick one], as it is said, 'Surely he hath borne our sicknesses'", etc[79]. Further evidence may be found in the statement attributed to the Jewish interlocutor of Justin Martyr in the latter's *Dialogue with Trypho* 89, "It is quite clear, indeed, that the scriptures announce that the Messiah had to suffer; but we wish to learn if you can prove to us whether it was by the suffering cursed in the law". According to Trypho, the idea of a suffering Messiah was not a problem for the Jews of his time, but the notion of a *crucified* Messiah was indeed problematic because of Deut 21,23, "for a hanged man is accursed by God"[80]. The skepticism of A.J.B. Higgins on the reliability of this statement with regard to contemporary Jewish belief is unwarranted; if Justin had seriously misrepresented the views of Jews, the rhetorical force of the work would have been significantly undermined[81].

77. So also FISHBANE (n. 72), pp. 23-24, n. 41.

78. The *Yalkut* is a midrashic thesaurus on the entire Hebrew bible, compiled from more than fifty works, some of which are otherwise lost; see STRACK and STEMBERGER (n. 56), p. 383. The passage on Isa 60,1 and Ps 22 is mentioned by JUEL (n. 40), p. 112.

79. *b. Sanhedrin* 98[b] with citation of Isa 53,4; trans. from S. R. DRIVER and A. NEUBAUER, *The Fifty-Third Chapter of Isaiah according to the Jewish Interpreters*, vol. 2, *Translations*, with an introduction by E. B. Pusey and a prolegomenon by R. Loewe, New York, Ktav, 1969, 1st ed., 1877, p. 7. FISHBANE (n. 72), pp. 3-4, has argued in favor of the restoration of the name "The Afflicted One" (which involves a play on words with Isa 53,4) to the text.

80. Trans. from the RSV; cf. Gal 3,13.

81. A. J. B. HIGGINS, *Jewish Messianic Belief in Justin Martyr's* Dialogue with Trypho, in *NT* 9 (1967) pp. 298-305, esp. pp. 302-303; similarly, JUEL (n. 40), pp. 111-112. FISHBANE (n. 72), p. 23, n. 36, finds Higgins' argument unconvincing. Michael MACH (n. 3), pp. 34-35, and n. 37, leaves open the question whether there was an expectation of a suffering messiah among Jews at this time, although he argues that the *Dialogue* should not be taken as a summary of a historical conversation.

Even if his intended audience included only other Christians and as yet unconverted Gentiles, he would have had to take into account the knowledge that the members of his audience had of contemporary Jewish traditions, beliefs, and practices. He may have misrepresented Judaism unintentionally from time to time, but the possibility of a challenge from contemporary scholarly Jews would have restrained him from fabricating and attributing to the Jews beliefs that he knew they did not in fact hold.

Even if Psalm 22 and Isaiah 53 had not yet been interpreted messianically in Jewish circles at the time Mark was written, it is clear that the messianic application of the individual psalms of lament found in the Gospel of Mark is well within the boundaries of acceptable Jewish exegesis, certainly in terms of method and also, generally speaking, with regard to content. The crucial point of difference between Jewish followers of Jesus and other Jews was the affirmation or the denial of the messiahship of Jesus. Thus, the act of re-reading the psalms in this way was not in itself an act of disappropriation or a violent theft of part of the Jewish heritage.

Why then does such an appropriation so easily appear to be disappropriation? The answer of course lies in the historical development after Mark which includes first of all the gradual separation of followers of Jesus from the institutions of Judaism and later the establishment of the Christian religion as the dominant religion of the Roman empire, a process which began in the fourth century. Mark and other Christians of the first century, however, laid a foundation for this development by the way in which they appropriated Jewish scripture. Mark did not choose to write a scriptural commentary or to confine himself to genres closely based on biblical precedents. He wrote in Greek and created a new literary genre which resembled Hellenistic and Roman biographical and historiographical writings. Many Jews of the Second Temple period also wrote in Greek and adopted Hellenistic literary genres, but after the destruction of the temple, the tendency to use the Hebrew language and specifically Jewish genres gradually became dominant in scholarly circles[82].

From the historical-critical point of view, Jewish and Christian messianic re-readings of the psalms are equally problematic. From the postmodern point of view of intertextuality, they are equally legitimate. What is ethically problematic, in any case, is not the exegetical methods

---

82. M. Hirshman has observed this distinction between Jewish and Christian writers from the second to the fourth century; see *A Rivalry of Genius: Jewish and Christian Biblical Interpretation in Late Antiquity* (SUNY Series in Judaica, Albany, NY, State University of New York Press, 1996, esp. p. 10.

or conclusions or the fact that the Jewish and Christian communities have separate histories and institutions, but the inhumane ways in which texts have unfortunately been used in struggles for power and dominance.

The Divinity School   Adela Yarbro COLLINS
The University of Chicago
Chicago, IL 60637, USA

LUC ET LES ÉCRITURES DANS L'ÉVANGILE DE L'ENFANCE À LA LUMIÈRE DES «ANTIQUITÉS BIBLIQUES»

HISTOIRE SAINTE ET LIVRES SAINTS

Au terme d'un chapitre solidement documenté sur l'interprétation de l'Ancien Testament par Luc, François Bovon proposait en 1978 deux tâches à la recherche: «la première, dont on sent déjà l'annonce, serait de préciser le milieu exégétique, juif et hellénistique et chrétien, dans lequel baigne Luc et de déterminer quel genre d'exégèse a eu le plus d'influence sur lui (…). La seconde serait de voir de manière méticuleuse la fonction littéraire des citations»[1]. Ne faut-il pas aujourd'hui associer ces deux tâches et viser à montrer que Luc, soucieux de donner un histoire des origines chrétiennes, vise simultanément à y inclure, à l'occasion des discours principalement, des résumés de l'histoire d'Israël qui préparent l'avènement de Jésus et la prédication apostolique?

Cette façon de comprendre Luc et d'expliquer simultanément des aspects de sa technique littéraire et de sa vision d'historien, je voudrais la recommander plus que la démontrer en attirant une fois de plus l'attention sur les *Antiquités Bibliques* (*Antiquitates Biblicae*; en abrégé: *Ant.Bibl.*), dites du Pseudo-Philon[2]. Recommander, non démontrer. Des lectures, même bien dirigées, ne peuvent donner à un visiteur de l'exégèse néotestamentaire la compétence nécessaire pour disserter sur l'œuvre lucanienne de façon originale. En revanche, l'absence presque totale des *Ant. Bibl.* dans les travaux et les commentaires sur Luc m'avait été depuis longtemps un sujet d'étonnement.

Certes, dès 1956 Paul Winter[3] et Charles Perrot[4] en 1967 avaient signalé des ressemblances surprenantes dans le récit de l'enfance, mais c'est surtout en préparant le commentaire des *Ant.Bibl.* dans la collection *Sources Chrétiennes* que j'avais été frappé par les observations de ce

---

1. Fr. Bovon, *Luc le théologien. Vingt-cinq ans de recherches (1950-1975)*, Neuchâtel, 1978; Genève, Labor et Fides, 1988², p. 117.

2. J'évite le titre assez répandu *Liber Antiquitatum Biblicarum* que les manuscrits n'autorisent pas et qui introduit le mot *liber*, utilisé limitativement et techniquement par la librairie antique.

3. P. Winter, *The Proto-Source of Luke I*, in *NT* 1 (1956) 184-199.

4. Ch. Perrot, *Les récits de l'enfance dans la haggada antérieure au IIᵉ siècle de notre ère*, in *Recherches de science religieuse* 55 (1967) 481-518.

dernier[5] sur la parenté de Luc, ce qui m'amena ensuite à étudier les hymnes et la technique narrative de l'historien juif[6]. Ce n'est que tout récemment qu'une thèse défendue durant l'hiver 1992-93 et publiée en 1994 annonce franchement la couleur dans son titre, *Pseudo-Philo und Lukas*, de Eckart Reinmuth[7]. Il est temps que les exégètes de Luc relisent les *Antiquités Bibliques*.

Le peu d'intérêt porté aux *Ant.Bibl.* a quelque chose à voir avec la datation assez tardive – postérieure à la destruction de Jérusalem en 70 – communément proposée et reçue. Je crois avoir fait bonne justice, dès 1969, de l'argument de Leopold Cohn qui rendait cette datation inéluctable[8]. Et une fois ce verrou ouvert, les vraisemblances vont toutes pour une datation antérieure à 70. Petit à petit cette nouvelle datation fait son chemin.

En un temps où la «narrativité» prend une place importante dans l'exégèse et dans la théologie, l'étude des ressemblances entre Luc (Lc, Ac) et les *Ant.Bibl.* est de saison. Mais quelque chose de plus est en jeu. Dans un premier temps, je rappellerai ce que les travaux récents ont mis en évidence au sujet des *Ant.Bibl.*, et cela en fonction des nécessités de la suite de l'exposé: l'établissement du texte, la date de l'œuvre et de ses versions, la technique littéraire et ses fondements théologiques. Dans un deuxième temps, j'examinerai l'histoire de la naissance de Samuel dans

---

5. PSEUDO-PHILON, *Les Antiquités Bibliques. T. I. Introduction et texte critique*, par D.J. HARRINGTON. *Traduction* par J. CAZEAUX. T. II. *Introduction littéraire, commentaire et index*, par Ch. PERROT et P.-M. BOGAERT (Sources Chrétiennes, 229 et 230), Paris, Cerf, 1976; voir t. II, p. 30 en haut, pp. 51-52.

6. P.-M. BOGAERT, *Pour une phénoménologie de l'appropriation de la prière. Le cantique d'Anne dans le Ier livre de Samuel, dans les Antiquités Bibliques et dans le Nouveau Testament*, in H. LIMET et J. RIES (ed.), *L'expérience de la prière dans les grandes religions. Actes du colloque de Louvain-la-Neuve et Liège (22-23 nov. 1978)* (Homo religiosus, 5), Louvain-la-Neuve, Centre Cerfaux-Lefort, 1980, pp. 245-259; ID., *Histoire et prophétie dans la composition des Antiquités Bibliques du Pseudo-Philon*, in *À cause de l'Évangile. Mélanges offerts à dom Jacques Dupont* (Lectio Divina, 123), Paris, Cerf, 1985, pp. 361-376.

7. E. REINMUTH, *Pseudo-Philo und Lukas. Studien zum Liber Antiquitatum Biblicarum und seiner Bedeutung für die Interpretation des lukanischen Doppelwerks* (WUNT, I,74), Tübingen, Mohr, 1994.— Sauf erreur, ni R. BROWN (*The Birth of the Messiah. A Commentary on the Infancy Narratives in Matthew and Luke*, Londres, Chapman, 1977), ni R. LAURENTIN (*Les Évangiles de l'Enfance du Christ*, Paris, Desclée, 1982), ni M.L. STRAUSS (*The Davidic Messiah in Luke-Acts. The Promise and Fulfillment in Lukan Christology* [JSNT SS, 110], Sheffield, 1995) ne font mention de façon précise d'une ressemblance avec les *Ant.Bibl.*, qu'ils ne dissocient pas des autres récits juifs de naissance.

8. L. COHN, *An Apocryphal Work Ascribed to Philo of Alexandria*, dans *JQR*, Old Series, 10 (1898) 277-332; P.[-M.] BOGAERT, *L'Apocalypse syriaque de Baruch* (Sources Chrétiennes, 144 et 145), Paris, Cerf, 1969; voir t. I, pp. 253-257; ID., dans PSEUDO-PHILON, *Les Antiquités Bibliques* (ci-dessus, n. 5), t. II, 1976, pp. 66-74.

le récit biblique – qui présente diverses formes – et dans les *Ant.Bibl.* Dans la troisième partie, je considérerai l'évangile de l'enfance selon Luc en relation avec 1 S 2 et avec les *Ant.Bibl.*, à l'intérieur de l'ensemble de l'œuvre lucanienne.

Étant acquis que les *Ant.Bibl.* et Luc mettent en œuvre une vision historique et une technique narrative comparables, pourrait-on montrer que les *Ant.Bibl.* constituent le chaînon manquant entre le récit biblique et Luc? Quoi qu'il en soit d'une dépendance, la définition du rapport de Luc à l'Écriture peut se préciser au terme d'une comparaison avec les *Ant.Bibl*[9].

I. LES «ANTIQUITÉS BIBLIQUES»

A. *La consolidation du texte latin*

Au départ de la tradition manuscrite des *Ant.Bibl.* se trouve un seul témoin latin qui proposait successivement d'une part les *Antiquitates Biblicae*, et d'autre part – le traducteur est différent – les *Quaestiones in Genesim* et le *De Essaeis*, de Philon. Et c'est de l'édition des œuvres proprement philoniennes qu'est venue la preuve de l'excellence de l'édition princeps de Ioannes Sichardus (Bâle, 1527), fondée sur un manuscrit de Lorsch et un autre de Fulda, celui-ci conservé intégralement (Kassel, Landesbibliothek, Theol. 4°, 3). Éditrice des *Quaestiones in Genesim*, Françoise Petit a pu établir dès 1973 la tête du stemma[10] qui vaut aussi pour les *Ant.Bibl.*

Au moment de l'édition des *Quaestiones* par Fr. Petit (1973) et des *Ant.Bibl.* par D.J. Harrington (1976), le manuscrit de Lorsch était tenu pour perdu. Depuis 1983 il n'en est plus totalement ainsi. Douze fragments de parchemin découverts dans une reliure du XVIe siècle et rajustés ont permis de reconstituer un bifeuillet écrit en une vénérable onciale de la première moitié du VIIe siècle. Et ce feuillet comporte précisément la fin des *Quaestiones*, manquante dans le manuscrit de Fulda (sans que celui-ci soit mutilé), mais présente dans l'édition de Sichard et donc dans son deuxième témoin. On reconnaît sur les fragments les indications typographiques destinées à l'imprimeur (distinction des mots de la

---

9. Sur les pseudépigraphes latins en général et sur les *Ant.Bibl.* en particulier, voir J. VERHEYDEN, *Les Pseudépigraphes d'Ancien Testament: Textes latins. À propos d'une Concordance*, in *ETL* 71 (1995) 383-420; pp. 386-387.

10. Fr. PETIT, *L'ancienne version latine des Questions sur la Genèse de Philon d'Alexandrie*. I. *Édition critique*. II. *Commentaire* (TU, 113 et 114), Berlin, 1973.

scriptio continua). Le bifeuillet appartenait donc au manuscrit de Lorsch utilisé par Sichard en complément de celui de Fulda[11].

À partir de la trouvaille de Vera Sack, Françoise Petit a pu apporter une confirmation de son stemma; elle peut aussi envisager de le perfectionner. Car le manuscrit de Lorsch, abbaye fondée en 777, n'a pas pu y être copié. Il venait peut-être de Saint-Riquier et, finalement, d'Italie du Nord. Il est dès lors très vraisemblable que le manuscrit de Lorsch, proche de celui Fulda au dire de Sichard (*ut ouum...ouo*), soit l'archétype de toute la tradition du Philon latin et donc des *Ant. Bibl.*

Cette étonnante découverte ne modifie pas dans son principe la constitution du texte proposée par D.J. Harrington. Mais on en tirera des conséquences pratiques pour une révision possible de certains choix et de meilleures lectures.

1. L'édition de Sichard doit être considérée avec le plus grand respect. Le *Laurissensis* et le *Fuldensis* se ressemblaient «comme un œuf à un œuf», et Lorsch, perdu pour les *Ant.Bibl.*, est très ancien, *peruetustus*, d'après le premier éditeur[12].

2. Les conjectures déjà faites et à faire pour donner un sens au texte et une vraisemblance quelconque aux noms propres impossibles peuvent s'appuyer désormais sur l'existence d'un modèle en onciale. Ce n'est pas le lieu d'insister, mais au passage nous tirerons parti de ce nouvel acquis.

B. *La date de composition*

1. Les *Ant.Bibl.* en latin

La traduction latine des *Ant.Bibl.* doit maintenant être datée antérieurement aux fragments conservés du manuscrit de Lorsch (première moitié du VIIe siècle). D'autre part, le poète Prudence fait de Orpha, sœur de Ruth, l'ancêtre de Goliath (*Hamartigenia*, v. 782-784), ce qu'il n'a guère pu trouver que dans les *Ant.Bibl.* 61,6, en latin plus

---

11. Fr. Petit, *Le fragment 63 de la Bibliothèque de l'Université de Fribourg-en-Brisgau*, in *Codices Manuscripti* 9 (1983) 164-172, 2 pl.; V. Sack, *Fundbericht zu Fragment 63 der Universitätsbibliothek Freiburg i. Br.*, in *Codices Manuscripti* 9 (1983) 173-174. – Sur la datation, et l'origine, voir B. Bischoff et V. Brown, *Addenda to Codices Latini Antiquiores*, in *Mediaeval Studies* 47 (1985) 317-368, 18 pl; p. 327 et pl. v b.

12. L'édition princeps de Sichardus a été l'objet d'une réimpression (Rome, Klaraeavgia, 1983) en petit format (17 x 12,2); distrib.: Libreria già Nardecchia, Piazza Cavour 25, Roma.

vraisemblablement qu'en grec. La version latine remonte donc sans doute avant 400[13]. Il est à penser que des références patristiques aux *Ant.Bibl.* n'ont pas été observées, car peu d'éditeurs sont au fait de l'existence de cette source possible.

Hermann Josef Frede est plus précis lorsqu'il observe la parenté des citations de la Genèse avec celles d'Ambroise, ce qui pointerait vers le Nord de l'Italie[14].

2. Les *Ant.Bibl.* en grec

Il n'y a jamais eu d'hésitation sur ce point: le latin des *Ant.Bibl.* est une traduction du grec. On n'a cependant pas identifié de citations des *Ant.Bibl.* chez les écrivains grecs, même pas chez les Chronographes qui utilisent les *Jubilés*. Mais pour les Pères grecs comme pour les Pères latins a-t-on vraiment cherché?

Divers indices donnent à penser que le grec était lui-même une traduction de l'hébreu (plutôt que de l'araméen). Dès lors, deux voies s'ouvrent pour proposer une datation de la version grecque. Le texte biblique cité est-il la plus ancienne Septante (Old Greek) ou une révision de celle-ci? La méthode de traduction ne rappelle-t-elle pas l'une de celles que l'on observe pour les livres bibliques?

À la première question, D.J. Harrington a cherché à répondre, et il n'est pas aisé d'aller plus loin[15]. Le sol se dérobe vite quand l'on veut distinguer le contenu du texte, qui peut remonter au modèle hébreu des *Ant.Bibl.*, et le vocabulaire grec sous-jacent au latin, révélateur d'une méthode de traduction de l'hébreu en grec.

En revanche, il est des termes du vocabulaire biblique, mais employés par les *Ant.Bibl.* dans des passages de sa composition, qui peuvent nous éclairer sur le milieu et la date de la traduction grecque. Les trois cas orientent vers la méthode de traduction et de révision dite Théodotion-kaige mise en lumière par Dominique Barthélemy. Dans l'étymologie du nom de Samuel (51,1), *'el* est rendu par ἰσχυρός[16]. Le hifil de *yrh* est

---

13. P.-M. BOGAERT, dans *Bulletin de la Bible latine*, t. VI, n° 31, p. [9], annexé à la *Revue bénédictine* 85 (1975).

14. H.J. FREDE, *Probleme des ambrosianischen Bibeltextes*, dans G. LAZZATI (éd.), *Ambrosius Episcopus. Atti del Congresso internazionale di studi ambrosiani... Milano 2-7 dic. 1974* (Studia Patristica Mediolanensia, 6), Milan, Vita e Pensiero, 1976, t. I, pp. 365-392; voir p. 386, n. 54.

15. D.J. HARRINGTON, *The Biblical Text of Pseudo-Philo's* Liber Antiquitatum Biblicarum, in *CBQ* 33 (1971) 1-17.

16. D. BARTHÉLEMY, *Les Devanciers d'Aquila* (Supplements to Vetus Testamentum, 10), Leyde, Brill, 1963, p. 83.

rendu par φωτίζω, en latin *illumino* (voir aussi *lucerna*). Cette caractéristique, reconnue depuis assez longtemps[17], a été appliquée récemment aux *Ant.Bibl.* par Sebastian Brock[18]. Mais la particularité la plus étonnante a échappé jusqu'ici. Plusieurs fois, en relation avec le don de l'alliance ou de la loi, les *Ant.Bibl.* emploient le terme *superexcellentia* (9,8; 12,2; 30,2) à quoi il faut associer *superexcelsa* (19,4) et vraisemblablement en raison du contexte *excelsa* (11,1; 44,6). Tout s'explique si le traducteur latin a rendu ainsi les substantifs ἀκριβασμός ou ἀκρίβασμα et leur pluriel, peut-être en fonction d'une étymologie les faisant dériver de ἄκρος. Chez Aquila, en effet, mais certainement avant lui, et probablement dans la recension Théodotion-kaige, les mots de la racine *ḥqq* sont rendus par des dérivés de ἀκριβ-[19]. L'association *superexcel-* et *iustitiae* (9,8; 12,2; 30,2) est décisive. En fait, le traducteur latin n'a pas reconnu le sens spécifique du mot grec, à savoir «commandements (précis)».

Il est donc assuré que la traduction grecque des *Ant.Bibl.* a été faite dans le milieu palestinien des réviseurs de la Bible grecque, selon une méthode attestée au moins depuis le début de notre ère. Cette conclusion corrobore sur une base plus ferme celle faite à partir des citations bibliques.

3. Les *Ant.Bibl.* en hébreu

Après ce qui a été dit, il faut écarter, pour des raisons de critique externe, les datations tardives telles que celle proposée en 1980 par A. Zeron: «Auf Grund der Vergleiche mit rabbinischem Material und der Verwandtschaft mit byzantinischen Quellen aus dem 2. und 3. Jahrhundert müsste man annehmen, dass das *LAB* nach dem 2. Jahrhundert, möglicherweise sogar nach dem 4. Jahrhundert, befasst wurde»[20]. Tout récemment le même auteur a observé des ressemblances avec l'inscription de Deir 'Alla qui, si elles étaient avérées, iraient dans un tout autre sens[21].

---

17. M. SMITH, *Another Criterion for the* καιγε *Recension*, in *Bib* 48 (1967) 443-445.

18. S. BROCK, *To revise or not to revise: Attitudes to Jewish Biblical Translation*, in G.J. BROOKE et B. LINDARS (éd.), *Septuagint, Scrolls and Cognate Writings. Papers ... (Manchester, 1990)* (Septuagint and Cognate Studies, 33), Atlanta, GA, Scholars Press, 1992, pp. 301-338; spéc. pp. 317-319; voir aussi ce qu'il dit de Gn 6,2 cité par *Ant.Bibl.* 3,1.

19. P. WALTERS (KATZ), *The Text of the Septuagint. Its Corruptions and their Emendation*, Cambridge, Cambridge University Press, 1973, pp. 205-210, 336-337.

20. A. ZERON, *Erwägungen zu Pseudo-Philos Quellen und Zeit*, in *Journal for the Study of Judaism* 11 (1980) 38-52, p. 50. A. Zeron ne paraît pas connaître les travaux de Harrington et Perrot.

21. A. ZERON, *Pseudo-Philonic Parallels to the Inscriptions of Deir 'Alla*, in *VT* 41 (1991) 186-191.

Leopold Cohn avait proposé un interprétation de *Ant.Bibl.* 19,7 qui rendait inévitable une datation après la Guerre Juive de 70[22]. Mais ce verrou ne résiste pas. Dès lors, bien des indices internes poussent à une datation avant 70. C'est dans ce sens que vont actuellement D.J. Harrington[23] et Frederick J. Murphy[24]. Eckart Reinmuth ne tranche pas[25].

On se souviendra aussi que le roi des Ammonites opposé à Jephté est appelé Getal (39,8 et 9), forme sémitique du nom connu sous sa forme hellénisée de Kotylas, tyran de Philadelphie (Amman), chez Flavius Josèphe. Kotylas d'Ammon est à situer entre 134 et 80 av. J.-C.; les *Ant.Bibl.* ne peuvent lui être antérieures[26]. Mais le récit fortement hellénisé du sacrifice de la fille de Jephté sur le modèle d'Iphigénie ne peut pas être daté trop loin du règne de ce roitelet qui n'a guère laissé de souvenir[27].

Une datation avant 70 s'impose donc pour l'œuvre en hébreu et elle se recommande pour la traduction en grec. Dans la question des rapports entre l'œuvre lucanienne et les *Ant.Bibl.*, il faudra distinguer original hébreu et traduction grecque.

C. *Un commentaire scripturaire très particulier*

S'il est justifié de ranger les *Ant.Bibl.* dans la catégorie du midrash, il est sans doute plus important encore de souligner l'originalité de sa technique narrative et de sa théologie de l'histoire. En cette matière, le pionnier fut Otto Eissfeldt en 1955[28] qui mit en évidence les procédés littéraires par lesquels l'auteur raconte, récapitule et anticipe les faits d'histoire. L'ouvrage déjà cité de Frederick J. Murphy pousse la recherche aussi

22. L. Cohn, *An Apocryphal Work* (ci-dessus, n. 8).
23. D.J. Harrington, dans J.H. Charlesworth (éd.), *The Old Testament Pseudepigrapha*, Garden City, NY, Doubleday, t. 2, 1985, pp. 298-299.
24. Fr. J. Murphy, *Pseudo-Philo. Rewriting the Bible*, New York et Oxford, Oxford University Press, 1993, p. 6.
25. E. Reinmuth, *Pseudo-Philo und Lukas* (cité à la n. 7), pp. 17-26 (bon état de la question).
26. P.-M. Bogaert, *Les «Antiquités Bibliques» du Pseudo-Philon. Quelques observations sur les chapitres 39 et 40 à l'occasion d'une réimpression*, in *RTL* 3 (1972) 334-344, p. 342.
27. M. Alexiou et P. Dronke, *The Lament of Jephta's Daughter: Themes, Traditions, Originality*, in *Studi medievali* III,12 (1971) 819-863.
28. O. Eissfeldt, *Zur Kompositionstechnik des Pseudo-Philonischen Liber Antiquitatum Biblicarum*, in *Norsk Teologisk Tidsskrift* 56 (1955) 53-71; = Id., *Kleine Schriften*, t. III, Tübingen, Mohr, 1966, pp. 340-353.

loin que possible dans cette direction[29]: *Rewriting the Bible* est le sous-titre; le mot *narrative* vient dans le titre du chap. 2, le principal, de son prologue, qui annonce un *narrative commentary*.

Bien que sensibles à cet aspect, les commentaires des *Ant.Bibl.* récemment publiés n'ont pas la place de développer l'application à l'histoire sainte de procédés narratifs particuliers. On trouve des observations utiles de la main de Ch. Perrot, qui distingue deux types de lecture, «texte expliqué» et «texte continué». Dans le premier cas, la référence est le texte même de la Bible; dans le second, elle est l'histoire sainte connue tant par la Bible que par des traditions parallèles (orales ou autres)[30].

Mieux encore qu'en 1976, on perçoit aujourd'hui l'implication mutuelle de trois phénomènes au tournant de notre ère:

1. la fixation (progressive) du texte hébreu de la Bible;
2. les révisions de la Septante sur le texte hébreu qui va se standardisant;
3. la disparition progressive des midrashim du second type (texte continué), trop libres vis-à-vis du texte désormais reçu, au profit des midrashim fonctionnant sur un texte biblique tenu pour fixé.

Ce qu'il importe cependant de voir, c'est que la technique narrative décrite depuis Eissfeldt sert une vision de l'histoire qu'elle veut mettre en évidence[31].

Au terme d'une analyse poussée des procédés, E. Reinmuth a bien montré que le Pseudo-Philon n'a pas pour but de reformuler le contenu narratif de la Bible et de l'aggada biblique, mais qu'il veut proposer une interprétation des éléments qui la composent en manifestant leurs rapports[32]. Son objectif n'est pas de tout raconter (il reste loin du compte), mais de mettre en évidence un fil d'Ariane.

Ce fil conducteur, c'est le dessein divin qui préside à l'histoire sainte. Comment se fait-il connaître pour que s'explique après coup le sens des événements ou pour les annoncer à l'avance? C'est ici que l'autorité prophétique et l'Esprit interviennent pour rendre possible dans la bouche des inspirés un discours sur la continuité de l'action de Dieu dans l'histoire d'Israël. La prophétie n'est pas regardée d'abord comme un acte de

---

29. Fr. J. MURPHY, *Pseudo-Philo* (ci-dessus, n. 24).
30. Ch. PERROT, in PSEUDO-PHILON, *Les Antiquités Bibliques* (ci-dessus, n. 5), t. II, pp. 22-28.
31. C'est ce que j'ai cherché à montrer dans *Histoire et prophétie* (ci-dessus, n. 6).
32. E. REINMUTH, *Pseudo-Philo und Lukas* (ci-dessus, n. 7), pp. 126-127. – Cet ouvrage contient nombre de remarques utiles sur la théologie des *Ant.Bibl.* On les trouve moins dans la première partie, qui porte sur les *Ant.Bibl.* proprement dites, que dans la seconde, qui porte sur la comparaison entre Luc (Lc-Ac) et les *Ant.Bibl.*

discernement spirituel (*entweder... oder*), ni comme une annonce du futur (*vorher... nachher*), mais comme l'éclairage révélant la signification de l'histoire voulue par Dieu, ce qui comporte l'annonce de l'avenir et l'interprétation du passé et du présent.

Avant de faire intervenir une comparaison avec l'œuvre lucanienne – comparaison qui s'impose désormais –, il importe de préciser l'originalité des *Ant.Bibl.* lorsqu'elles font intervenir l'Esprit et la prophétie comme éléments de la conduite divine de l'histoire. Entre de nombreux autres exemples de chaînes prophétiques, de concaténations, sur lesquelles j'avais attiré l'attention il y a une dizaine d'années, on peut retenir celui-ci. C'est Cenez (Kenaz) qui parle (*Ant.Bibl.* 28,6)[33] :

> Et dum sederent, insiluit spiritus sanctus, habitans in Cenez, et extulit sensum eius et coepit prophetare, dicens: Ecce nunc uideo quae non sperabam, et considero quae non cognoscebam. Audite nunc, qui habitatis super terram: Sicut commorantes in ea prophetauerunt, ante me uidentes horam hanc, priusquam corrumperetur terra, ut cognoscatis praedestinatas prophetationes omnes uos qui habitatis in ea.

> «Et lorsqu'ils furent assis, l'Esprit Saint habitant en Cenez bondit et dilata son intelligence, et il se mit à prophétiser en disant: Voici, je vois maintenant des réalités que je n'espérais pas et je contemple des réalités que je ne connaissais pas. Écoutez maintenant, vous qui habitez sur la terre, comment[34] ceux qui y ont demeuré ont prophétisé avant moi à la vue de cette heure, avant que la Terre ne se corrompe, afin que vous reconnaissiez les prophéties annoncées antérieurement, vous tous qui habitez en elle».

J'interprète. Cenez prophétise (il voit la création du monde et sa fin, 28,7-9). D'autres ont prophétisé avant lui sur le même objet. Le peuple est invité à reconnaître la concordance des prophéties antérieures avec celle de Cenez. Le lecteur sait d'ailleurs que l'autorité de Cenez a déjà été fondée antérieurement sur le choix de Juda par Jacob (21,5) et sur la faveur de Josué (20,10) à la demande de Caleb son père.

De même, les *Ant.Bibl.* s'achèvent par une sorte de *non obstat* prononcé par Saül sur la succession davidique, lorsqu'il implore son pardon: *non memor sis odii mei neque iniustitiae meae* (65,5). Avant cela, Samuel a joué un rôle décisif dans l'intronisation de Saül, puis de David (56-57; 59,1). Saül et Jonathan annoncent le règne de David (62,2.9). Saül et Samuel prédisent la fin de la «première race» (62,2; 64,8), tandis que David annonce lui-même l'avènement de Salomon (60,3fin). Ouverture sur l'avenir: Samuel évoque Jérémie dont Saül a emprunté à

---

33. Je cite selon l'édition princeps (ci-dessus, n. 12), p. 32.
34. Je tiens le *sicut* du latin pour la traduction d'un ὡς grec qu'il faut rendre non comme le corrélatif d'une apodose inexistante, mais au sens de *quomodo*.

l'avance les premières paroles (56,6; cf. Jr 1,6), autre façon sans doute d'annoncer la destruction du premier temple (voir aussi 19,7).

Ainsi toute l'histoire s'oriente vers la lignée davidique. La passation du relais se fait de manière ininterrompue, confirmée par des déclarations prophétiques sur le sens du passé et sur l'avenir. Ces déclarations soulignent la trame de la narration.

En prévision d'une comparaison avec l'œuvre lucanienne, il faudrait dire aussi toute l'importance accordée au patriarche Abraham, dont les faits et gestes sont mis en relation avec David[35].

II. LA NAISSANCE DE SAMUEL DE LA BIBLE AUX *ANT.BIBL.*

Chacun peut savoir aujourd'hui que la fixation du texte de 1 Samuel a été lente et tardive. En regard du texte massorétique, celui de la plus ancienne Septante est sensiblement différent. De plus, les fragments de la grotte 4 de Qumrân attestent une configuration souvent distincte, et la tradition rabbinique a gardé, précisément à propos d'Elcana, la trace d'une leçon non attestée par ailleurs.

Diverses façons d'aborder l'examen des différences ont été tentées. Les uns, Dominique Barthélemy[36] et Steven Pisano[37] par exemple, se sont efforcés surtout de proposer un texte homogène en soulignant les qualités et la logique du texte massorétique attesté au moins depuis Aquila; d'autres, c'est le cas des commentateurs, pratiquent l'éclectisme et recourent occasionnellement à la Septante pour sortir des difficultés de l'hébreu; d'autres enfin s'efforcent de retrouver la logique des différentes formes de texte. D'un point de vue pratique, les deux premières façons de faire sont acceptables. La troisième seule, au moins lorsqu'elle débouche sur des résultats, est pleinement satisfaisante, car les différences observées ne sont pas habituellement le résultat d'accidents de transmission, mais des changements délibérés.

---

35. Sur les épisodes des pierres inscrites (6,2; 61,5) et la *turrificatio* (construction de la tour, 32,1.15; cf. 23,7), voir P.-M. BOGAERT, *La figure d'Abraham dans les Antiquités Bibliques du Pseudo-Philon*, in P.-M. BOGAERT (éd.), *Abraham dans la Bible et dans la tradition juive* (Publications de l'Institutum Iudaicum, 2), Bruxelles, 1979, pp. 40-61.

36. D. BARTHÉLEMY, *Critique textuelle de l'Ancien Testament. I. Josué… Esther. Rapport final du Comité pour l'analyse textuelle de l'Ancien Testament hébreu* (OBO, 50/1), Fribourg (Suisse), Éditions universitaires; Göttingen, Vandenhoeck & Ruprecht, 1982, pp. 137-150.

37. St. PISANO, *Additions or Omissions in the Books of Samuel. The Significant Pluses and Minuses in the Massoretic, LXX and Qumran Texts* (OBO, 57), Fribourg (Suisse), Éditions universitaires; Göttingen, Vandenhoeck & Ruprecht, 1984, pp. 17-29, 71-75, 157-163.

Lorsque, au tout début de notre ère vraisemblablement, les *Ant.Bibl.*
proposent une version narrative nouvelle de la naissance de Samuel, leur
auteur pouvait encore être sensible à certaines «vibrations» dans la tradition textuelle, et il importe de voir non seulement quel texte il connaît,
mais quelle interprétation il favorise. Les *Ant.Bibl.*, par leur date, peuvent constituer une clé dans l'examen des diverses formes de l'enfance
de Samuel (1 S 1-2). Certaines occultations et certaines insistances
seront aussi significatives au moment de se tourner vers la narration
lucanienne.

A. *Les diverses formes de 1 S 1-2*

Il n'y a pas lieu d'entreprendre ici une étude systématique de 1 S 1-2.
Rappelons que deux textes anciens sont intégralement disponibles: le
texte massorétique (appuyé presque constamment par la version hiéro-
nymienne) et la Septante selon le *Vaticanus*, appuyé constamment par
un témoin vieux latin, le palimpseste de Vienne (sigle VL: 115)[38]. De
4QSam[a], très lacuneux, on peut affirmer qu'il est habituellement proche
de la Septante et qu'il en diffère quelques fois sans se rapprocher pour
autant du texte reçu[39]. Il emploie le mot *nāzîr* pour Samuel (col. I, ligne
3; 1 S 1,22); avant le dernier départ de Silo, Anne seule se prosterne
(col. I, ligne 15; 1 S 1,28). L'offrande comporte un taureau de trois ans
(non trois taureaux) et du pain (col. I, ligne 7; 1 S 1,24). Surtout, en
1,23, 4QSam[a] va clairement avec la Septante: *hywṣ' mpyk* (col. I, ligne
5) correspond à τὸ ἐξελθὸν ἐκ τοῦ στόματός σου.

Dans le Talmud de Babylone (*Berakôt* 61a), deux Rabbi Nahman (IVe
s.) discutent la question de savoir si Manoah était un *'am hā-'ārèṣ* (sans
éducation), puisqu'il marchait derrière sa femme (Jg 13,11), alors que la

---

38. Pour le grec, utiliser: A.E. Brooke, N. McLean et H.St J. Thackeray, *The Old
Testament in Greek*. II,1. *I-II Samuel*, Cambridge, Cambridge University Press, 1927. Le
texte lucianique ou antiochien a été republié récemment: N. Fernandez Marcos et J.R.
Busto Saiz, *El texto antioqueno de la Biblia Griega*. I. *1-2 Samuel* (Textos y Estudios
«Cardenal Cisneros», 50), Madrid, C.S.I.C., 1989; B.A. Taylor, *The Lucianic Manus-
cripts of 1 Reigns*. I. *Majority Text* (Harvard Semitic Monographs, 50), Atlanta, GA,
Scholars Press, 1992. Pour la vieille version latine, voir surtout B. Fischer, *Palimpsestus
Vindobonensis*, in B. Fischer, *Beiträge zur Geschichte der lateinischen Bibeltexte* (Aus
der Geschichte der lateinischen Bibel, 12), Fribourg-en-Br., Herder 1986, pp. 308-438;
spéc. pp. 334-337 (cf. aussi la note suivante).

39. E.Ch. Ulrich, *The Qumran Text of Samuel and Josephus* (Harvard Semitic Monographs, 19), Missoula, MT, Scholars Press, 1978; Id., *The Old Latin Translation of the LXX
and the Hebrew Scrolls from Qumran*, in E. Tov (éd.), *The Hebrew and Greek Texts of
Samuel (1980 Proceedings IOSCS – Vienna)*, Jérusalem, Academon, 1980, p. 123-165. On
trouvera une photographie de 4QSam[a] dans l'article *Qumrân* du DBS, t. 9, 1979, col. 893-894.

même expression est employée à propos d'Élisée (2 R 4,30) et d'Elcana. Pour Elcana, la référence est introuvable, mais on ne peut écarter le témoignage de deux rabbis s'accordant sur un détail du texte. C'est une autre question de savoir où se plaçait cette variante[40].

Examinons séparément le récit, le cantique et la place du cantique dans le récit.

1. Le récit

Je ferai fond ici sur l'article de Stanley D. Walters[41]. Son étude comparative de 1 S 1,4-8.22-25.27-28; 2,11 dans la Septante et le texte hébreu reçu conduit à reconnaître l'existence de deux récits voisins, mais distincts.

En 1 S 1,23, après qu'Anne a déclaré qu'elle ne confierait Samuel au sanctuaire qu'une fois sevré, Elcana consentant répond dans le grec: «mais que le Seigneur accomplisse ce qui est sorti de ta bouche» (ἀλλὰ στήσαι Κύριος τὸ ἐξελθὸν ἐκ τοῦ στόματός σου). Ce devait être aussi le texte de 4QSam[a] partiellement conservé. En revanche, le texte massorétique lit: 'ak yāqém YHWH 'èt-dᵉbārô «mais que YHWH accomplisse sa parole» – sa propre parole divine.

Selon Walters, la formule de la Septante, qui n'a d'équivalent qu'en Is 44,26 et Jr 28,6, suppose qu'Anne soit tenue pour prophétesse[42]. Si l'on s'en tient au grec confirmé par Qumrân, ce qui sort de la bouche d'Anne est soit sa prière, soit son vœu. Et dans ce cas, Elcana souhaite seulement que Dieu exauce la prière (accompagnée d'un vœu) de son épouse. Quant au texte hébreu reçu, il se réfère lui à une parole de Dieu antérieure, et Walters estime que c'est à Dt 18,18 (sur le prophète). Les *Ant.Bibl.* ont une autre proposition, nous le verrons.

Toujours selon Walters, la Septante vise à reporter les initiatives d'Anne sur Elcana. Il n'apparaît jamais clairement qu'elle va faire ce qu'elle a promis ni, jusqu'à la dernière ligne, qu'elle l'a effectivement fait. La Septante cherche à éloigner Anne de toute participation au culte et attribue au mari toutes les responsabilités, en particulier celle du vœu. En

---

40. En 2,11, selon V. Aptowitzer, *Das Schriftwort in der rabbinischen Literatur*, 1906-1915; réimpr. New York, Ktav Publ. House, 1970, pp. 68-69. Je penserais aussi à 2,20 et même à 1,9 ('aḥᵃréy šātoh lu 'aḥᵃréy 'ištāh, mais il faudrait qu'Elcana soit sujet). Voir de plus H.M. Orlinsky, *The Masoretic Text. A Critical Evaluation*. Prolegomenon à la réimpr. de Chr.D. Ginsburg, *Introduction to the Massoretico-critical Edition of the Hebrew Bible*, New York, Ktav Publ. House, 1966, pp. xxii-xxiii.

41. St.D. Walters, *Hannah and Anna: The Greek and Hebrew Texts of 1 Samuel 1*, in *JBL* 107 (1988) 385-412.

42. *Ibid.*, p. 410.

revanche, le texte hébreu reçu, sans dénigrer Elcana, insiste sur Anne: elle participe au sacrifice; elle a un rôle décisif dans la présentation de l'enfant au sanctuaire. Anne vit dignement et pieusement en dépit des provocations de l'autre épouse; c'est une personne de plein droit qui fait un vœu et l'accomplit sans réserve[43].

On notera encore que toute insistance sur le naziréat de l'enfant à naître est estompée dans l'hébreu reçu. D'une part, le mot *nazîr*, présent en 4QSam[a] (col. I, ligne 3; 1 S 1,22) est absent; d'autre part, au v. 11, l'hébreu reçu n'a rien à la place du grec δότος[44] et il ne mentionne pas l'abstinence de vin et de boisson fermentée signalée dans le grec.

2. Le cantique d'Anne

Dans le cantique biblique, seul le v. 5 rappelle la situation particulière d'Anne vis-à-vis de sa rivale: «la stérile enfante sept fois, et la mère d'enfants nombreux se flétrit». Encore n'est-il question en contexte que d'une seule naissance. Pour le reste, il s'agit plus d'un chant de victoire sur la bouche d'un opprimé que d'un chant de naissance. L'évocation finale du roi et du oint (v. 10) va dans ce sens.

Seule la Septante, au v. 9, se réfère clairement à un vœu, ce qui a pour effet d'insérer le cantique dans son contexte: διδοὺς εὐχὴν τῷ εὐχο-μένῳ «il exauce le vœu en faveur de qui fait un vœu». En revanche, l'hébreu reçu accentue l'aspects cosmique: la partie propre du v. 8 vient confirmer le v. 10 commun.

LXX	TM
8. [...]	8. [...]
	Car à YHWH sont les colonnes de la terre, et il a posé sur elles le monde.
9. Il exauce le vœu en faveur de qui fait un vœu, et il a béni les années du juste.	
	9. Il garde les pas de ses fidèles, et les méchants périront dans les ténèbres.
Car ce n'est pas de la force que l'homme est puissant.	Car ce n'est pas dans sa (propre) force que l'homme est fort.

Mais surtout la Septante introduit dans le v. 10 une longue addition parallèle à Jr 9,22-23. Les différences de vocabulaire assez nettes dans le grec plaident pour situer l'addition dans le modèle hébreu de la Septante.

---

43. *Ibid.*, pp. 408-409.
44. Δότος correspond sans doute à un *nātîn* non attesté (*n*ᵉ*tînîm* = δεδομένοι en 1 Ch 9,2).

Nous verrons plus loin que les *Ant.Bibl.* la connaissent. Pour mémoire, en voici la traduction:

> Que le sage ne se glorifie pas de sa sagesse;
> et que le puissant ne se glorifie pas de sa puissance;
> et que le riche ne se glorifie pas de sa richesse.
> Mais qu'en cela se glorifie celui qui se glorifie:
> comprendre et connaître le Seigneur,
> et accomplir jugement et justice au milieu de la terre.

Depuis longtemps, Thackeray avait noté que le cantique grec comportait un triple ἅγιος (v. 2bis.10) qu'il explique, ici et dans le Ps 99 LXX, par une utilisation liturgique[45].

On peut donc tenir qu'une hymne royale de victoire a été adoptée et plus ou moins adaptée par l'historien de Samuel. L'appropriation au contexte de naissance s'est ensuite continuée et renouvelée. À partir de l'observation de parallèles entre 1 S 2,1-10 et 2 S 22 (Ps 18 TM = 17 LXX), faite par Thackeray, je suis tenté de lier l'introduction de ces deux cantiques à la mise en évidence éditoriale de l'ensemble 1-2 Samuel (la division en deux livres étant conditionnée seulement par la longueur).

3. L'insertion du cantique dans le récit

Toute la tradition attribue le cantique à Anne. D'autres cantiques, qui sont aussi des cantiques de victoire, sont attribués à des femmes, Miryam (Ex 15,21; cf. v. 1), Débora (Jg 5), la fille de Jephté (Jg 11,34), Judith (Jdt 16).

La place du cantique, elle, n'est pas exactement fixée ou, du moins, les versets 1,28 et 2,11 qui l'encadrent présentent des différences attestant divers essais de lier le cantique au contexte[46]. Selon la Septante, l'épilogue (1,28; 2,11) souligne le rôle d'Anne accomplissant son vœu, laissant l'enfant à Silo et retournant chez elle. En revanche, le texte massorétique revient à Elcana dès la fin du v. 28 et en 2,11. Grammaticalement, cela paraît l'inverse de ce que Walters a noté pour l'ensemble du chapitre 1er, mais ce n'est pas illogique si l'on poursuit sa perspective. Selon la Septante, Anne accomplit son vœu sous l'autorité incontestée de son mari. Dans l'hébreu reçu, Elcana revient seul; on pourrait même

---

45. H.St J. THACKERAY, *The Song of Hannah and Other Lessons and Psalms for the Jewish New Year's Day*, in *JTS* 16 (1914-15) 177-204, pp. 190 et 201-202.

46. H.B. SWETE, *An Introduction to the Old Testament in Greek*, Cambridge, Cambridge University Press, 1902, p. 245; P.-M. BOGAERT, *Pour une phénoménologie* (ci-dessus, n. 6), p. 249. – Il faut faire intervenir ici le texte lucianique, mais 4QSam^a est de peu de secours; en 1,28, il lit «...]là et elle se prosterna[...».

croire qu'Anne reste à Silo si la suite (2,18-21) n'indiquait le contraire. Mais c'est bien elle qui offre son fils.

Conclusion

Notre but n'était pas de déterminer une généalogie des textes disponibles, mais de mettre en évidence les enjeux possibles des différences pour l'interprétation ultérieure. Anne est bien une prophétesse, de par le cantique qui annonce un roi et un oint. Le contexte souligne, soit le caractère naziréen de l'enfant attendu et le mécanisme du vœu, reconnu par l'époux comme l'exige le droit – c'est le texte de la Septante et vraisemblablement plus nettement encore celui de 4QSam[a] –, soit la volonté divine déjà à l'œuvre avant la naissance du prophète – c'est l'hébreu reçu. Dans la première lecture, Samuel, nazîr, est un autre Samson, le dernier des Juges; dans la seconde, Samuel est le prophète accordé pour accomplir une promesse antérieure de Dieu.

B. *La naissance de Samuel dans les Antiquités Bibliques*

1. Le récit

Les *Ant.Bibl.* racontent la naissance et l'enfance de Samuel de façon originale et selon une logique propre. Avant d'en préciser les sources bibliques, il convient de bien comprendre le propos général. Voici un résumé:

49. Le peuple cherche un successeur à Finees (Pinhas) qui soit du type de Cenez (Qenaz). Le tirage au sort pour l'ensemble, puis par tribu reste sans résultat. Finalement le sort tombe sur la ville d'Armathem (Ramathaïm), puis sur Elcana, qui refuse. Suite à une prière du peuple, Dieu annonce qu'un fils d'Elcana, mais non de Fenenna (Penina), l'une de ses épouses, détiendra l'autorité et la prophétie.

50. Fenenna dénigre Anne, la seconde épouse, stérile. Elle récidive lorsque Elcana monte au temple pour la Pâque, dans les termes inversés du cantique (1 S 2,10 LXX). Anne va alors au temple de Silo prier à voix basse – il n'est pas question de vœu –, mais elle évoque déjà les termes du cantique (1 S 2,5). Héli, prêtre établi légitimement, annonce qu'elle aura un fils, mais taît délibérément que l'enfant sera le prophète annoncé. Après quoi, Anne revient chez elle.

51. Anne met au monde Samuel et, après l'avoir sevré, elle le place devant Héli qui reconnaît celui pour lequel le peuple a prié et en qui s'accomplit la prophétie (il n'y pas de vœu). Anne et un chœur chantent alors un cantique de naissance célébrant celui qui sera lumière et prophète pour le peuple et qui donnera l'onction royale. Après quoi, Anne et Elcana se retirent. Et le peuple venu à Silo reconnaît à son tour Samuel comme lumière et prophète.

52. Les fils de Héli, indignes, reçoivent une mise en garde de leur père. Mais Dieu est irrité contre Héli.

53. À l'âge de huit ans, Samuel reçoit la première parole de Dieu lui annonçant la punition de Héli et de toute sa famille. Il hésite à la rapporter. Mais Héli lui raconte alors sa naissance.

54. Les Allophyles (Philistins) s'emparent de l'arche. Héli, ses fils, et la femme de Héli[47] meurent. Seul survit le dernier-né de celle-ci.

Ce résumé met en relief quelques détails que je reprends ici, pour la clarté.

1. Le peuple joue un rôle important. Il demande un chef (49,1-8); c'est lui, le peuple, qui au terme, célèbre la prière exaucée en Samuel enfant (51,7).

2. Anne n'a pas prononcé de vœu mais a prié. Elle le fait à voix basse de sorte que, si elle n'est pas exaucée, Dieu ne soit pas en même temps qu'elle la risée de Fenenna (*ubi est deus tuus in quo confidis?*)[48]. Manifestement l'auteur veut éviter le vœu et le vœu inconsidéré, problématique qu'il connaît dans le cas de Jephté[49]. Il se place dans la logique du texte reçu.

3. Il n'y a pas de vœu, mais un oracle divin annonçant un chef prophète (49,8) et, face à Anne, Héli sait que ce chef sera son fils à naître (50,8). Il le dira clairement lorsque Anne lui présentera son fils (51,2). Anne et le peuple le confirmeront: Samuel est bien le prophète annoncé. Encore une fois, c'est la perspective du texte reçu, non de la Septante. Le cantique ouvre en plus la perspective d'une onction royale et voit donc au-delà de Samuel.

4. La légitimité des acteurs est soulignée. Le sacerdoce de Héli est établi: *quem praeposuerat Finees filius Eleazari sacerdotis sicut praeceptum ei fuerat* (50,3). Ce sera une autre prophétie, de Samuel, qui annoncera la fin de cette légitimité (chap. 53). De même, le peuple cherche un nouveau Cenez pour succéder à Finees. Ce personnage est annoncé par Dieu, reconnu par Héli et par Anne, finalement par le peuple, et il oindra le roi à venir. Dès lors que Samuel est là, Elcana son père ne joue plus aucun rôle. La prophétie divine (49,8) est d'ailleurs confortée par la référence du cantique (51,6 milieu) au psaume d'Asaph (Ps 99[98 LXX],6)[50] qui met Samuel au rang de Moïse et d'Aaron.

---

47. On lit habituellement *Finees* (un des fils de Héli) au lieu de *Heli*, mais cette dernière leçon, très solidement attestée, peut se défendre.

48. Cf. Ps 42(41),4; Is 37,10.

49. Sur le vœu inconsidéré de Jephté, voir P.-M. BOGAERT, Les «*Antiquités Bibliques*» (ci-dessus, n. 26).

50. Plusieurs psaumes canoniques sont attribués à Asaph: les Ps 50 (49 LXX) et 73 à 83 (72 LXX à 82 LXX).

2. Les cantiques

À l'intérieur du récit est enchâssé le long cantique d'Anne, encadré de deux pièces courtes qui se répondent, une bénédiction de Héli (51,2) et une acclamation du peuple (51,7 fin).

Tout en gardant certaines traces précises de son modèle biblique, le cantique des *Ant.Bibl.* s'en distingue très nettement. Il est, en effet, totalement intégré dans la trame narrative, un cantique de naissance dans un récit de naissance. Les thèmes caractéristiques du contexte s'y retrouvent, à tel point que l'unité d'auteur et de composition saute aux yeux.

Quelques éléments sont repris au cantique biblique: *exaltabitur cornu* (51,3 fin), *nolite... magna eloqui nec eicere de ore uestro alta... sterilis enim pariens saturata est, quae autem multiplicata fuerat in filiis euacuata est* (51,4), *mortificat... uiuificat... iniquos... tenebris* (51,5), *cornu christo suo... potentia... regis* (51,6 fin). On observera surtout, comme en 1 S 2,1-10, la répétition du mot *cornu* vers le début et à la fin. Dans les *Ant.Bibl.*, le oint peut être Samuel (voir 51,7) ou David.

Par ailleurs, des images telles que lumière et illuminer, lait et mamelles, ainsi que l'évocation du peuple, des tribus et de la prophétie rattachent l'hymne au contexte.

Au regard du cantique biblique, celui des *Ant.Bibl.* paraît bien être dialogué et comporter un aspect choral. D'une part, la parole de Héli en 51,2[51] et l'acclamation du peuple en 51,7 ont un caractère lyrique et se répondent. D'autre part, le cantique principal se termine par une adresse à Anne, une réponse modeste d'Anne (*Quae est Anna...*), une adresse à Elcana et finalement une parole attribuable à Anne (*Stet autem filius meus...*). Un phénomène semblable se retrouve dans le discours-hymne de Débora selon les *Ant.Bibl.* (40,5-6).

Mais la comparaison doit encore tenir compte du fait suivant. L'un ou l'autre élément du cantique biblique est repris par les *Ant.Bibl.* non dans le cantique, mais dans la narration. Ainsi Anne cite 1 S 2,5 en *Ant. Bibl.* 50,5, dans la prière qu'elle fait au temple pour avoir un enfant. Et surtout Fenenna dénigre Anne en *Ant.Bibl.* 50,2 en des termes empruntés à l'addition grecque de 1 S 2,10: *ne glorietur in specie sua Anna sed qui gloriatur glorietur cum uidet semen suum...*, ce qui évoque à l'évidence

---

51. *Non tu sola petisti, sed populus orauit pro hoc, non est petitio tuae solius, sed in tribus antea promissum erat, et per hunc iustificata est metra tua, ut statuas prophetiam populis, et lac mamillarum tuarum constituas in fontem duodecim tribuum.* La leçon *prophetiam*, déformée progressivement en *profeciam, profectum, proficiam, proficuum*, est de loin préférable. On traduira donc: «... et par lui ton ventre a reçu justice pour que tu accomplisses la prophétie en faveur du peuple et pour faire du lait de tes mamelles une fontaine pour les douze tribus».

μὴ καυχάσθω… ἀλλ᾽ ἢ ἐν τούτῳ καυχάσθω ὁ καυχώμενος. Voilà qui confirme d'une part la cohérence du récit et du cantique et qui établit d'autre part la présence du supplément grec dans la Bible hébraïque de l'auteur des *Ant.Bibl.*

De l'examen des parties narratives et lyriques, il ressort d'abord, au plan littéraire, que l'œuvre constitue une relecture libre du texte biblique. La partie lyrique est désormais intégrée dans la narration pour la soutenir. L'une et l'autre véhiculent des thèmes nouveaux, ceux de lumière et de prophétie pour le peuple en particulier. Les personnages qui entourent l'enfance de Samuel, Elcana, Héli, Anne, le peuple, jouent un rôle nouveau, celui d'établir la légitimité de Samuel. Ce midrash sur Samuel s'intègre étroitement dans une vision d'ensemble de l'histoire.

Peut-on préciser davantage? Les *Ant.Bibl.* s'appuient-elles sur un texte biblique déjà identique au texte reçu, ou non? Les constatations sont contradictoires.

D'un côté, certains détails s'expliquent mieux en référence à la Septante (ou à son modèle hébreu), on vient de le voir. De l'autre, les *Ant.Bibl.* paraissent plus proches de l'hébreu reçu que de la Septante en ce qui touche à la problématique fondamentale. C'est Anne qui a presque constamment l'initiative; Samuel n'est pas le fils d'un vœu, mais la réponse à une prière et l'accomplissement d'une parole divine. Le vœu, encore mentionné dans l'hébreu reçu, est totalement gommé. En définitive, nous ne pouvons rejoindre avec certitude le modèle hébreu des *Ant.Bibl.*; son témoignage se joint à d'autres pour confirmer la non-fixation du texte biblique de 1 Samuel au tournant de notre ère.

III. LES ENFANCES SELON LUC, ET LEUR MODÈLE

Si je me risque sur le terrain néotestamentaire, c'est dans la conviction qu'une comparaison avec les *Ant.Bibl.* s'impose plus encore qu'on ne l'a fait jusqu'ici. La façon dont Luc se sert de la Bible est conditionnée foncièrement par un rapport à l'histoire sainte dont les *Ant.Bibl.* sont un témoin pour nous après avoir été peut-être le modèle de Luc.

A. *Les enfances dans l'histoire sainte selon Luc*

1. Une partie intégrante de l'ensemble

Le récit des enfances de Jean et de Jésus est une partie intégrante de l'histoire sainte selon Luc. S'il est légitime de distinguer le genre littéraire des récits d'enfance, ce souci est moderne et n'implique pas que pour Luc ces chapitres aient une importance fonctionnelle différente du reste[52]. S'il utilise pour les enfances d'autres sources ou d'autres modèles que pour le ministère de Jésus ou l'histoire des apôtres, cela ne comporte pas qu'il attache moins de prix à ce début.

Il y a, en effet, des ressemblances importantes entre les récits d'enfance et la suite de l'œuvre lucanienne: le rapport de Jean-Baptiste à Jésus, le rôle de la prophétie et l'intervention de l'Esprit, la figure d'Abraham, et la fonction des cantiques, comparable pour une part à celle des discours dans les Actes. Certaines de ces ressemblances apparaissent mieux entre les enfances et les Actes. Le ministère et la passion de Jésus sont conditionnés chez Luc par l'emploi de sources (Mc, Q) qui laissent moins de champ à son invention. Toutefois, là aussi des ressemblances sont notables[53].

a. Jean-Baptiste et Jésus[54]

Les commentateurs observent que, selon les termes de Lc 3,19-22, Jésus ne peut être baptisé par Jean. Le baptême a lieu après l'emprisonnement de Jean, et Jean n'est pas mentionné lors du baptême. Mais, d'une façon générale, la place de Jean-Baptiste est très grande chez Luc, et elle est constante, depuis les enfances parallèles jusque loin dans les Actes (Apollos: Ac 18,24-28; Paul à Éphèse: 19,1-7). Un des thèmes récurrents est celui de la supériorité du baptême de Jésus sur celui de Jean (Lc 3,3.7.12.15.21; 7,29-30; 20,4; Ac 1,5; 11,16; 18,25; 19,3-4); et la mention des disciples de Jean (Lc 5,33; 7,18.19; 11,1; cf. 3,1-19; Ac 19,1) nous éclaire sur l'actualité de ce thème dans la prédication lucanienne. La succession Apollos-Paul à Éphèse (Ac 18-19), plus explicitement que le discours de Paul à Antioche de Pisidie (13,24-25), fait écho au relais Jean-Jésus dans l'évangile de l'enfance et au cours de leur prédication.

52. On pourrait tenir que le prologue lucanien va jusqu'au chap. 4 inclusivement: F.Ó. FEARGHAIL, *The Introduction to Luke-Acts. A Study of the Role of Lk 1,1–4,44 in the Composition of Luke's Two-Volume Work* (Analecta Biblica, 126), Rome, Pontificio Ist. Biblico, 1991.

53. Sur la cohérence littéraire de l'œuvre lucanienne, voir maintenant Th. BERGHOLZ, *Der Aufbau des lukanischen Doppelwerkes. Untersuchungen zur formalliterarischen Charakter von Lukasevangelium und Apostelgeschichte* (Europäische Hochschulschriften, 23, 545), Berne, P. Lang, 1995.

54. O. BÖCHER, art. *Johannes der Taüfer*, in *TRE* 17 (1988) 172-181, p. 174, oppose les chap. 1-2, qui induisent selon lui un parallélisme d'égalité entre Jean et Jésus, au reste de l'œuvre lucanienne qui vise à limiter l'importance du ministère de Jean. – Le parallélisme est présent dans toute l'œuvre et il est d'opposition.

Luc souligne que la course (δρόμος Ac 13,25) de Jean s'achève au moment où Jésus entame son chemin (ὁδός). Paul reprend alors la forte parole de Jean-Baptiste se disant indigne de délier la lanière des sandales de son successeur (Lc 3,16; Ac 13,25).

Si nous nous tournons vers les récits des enfances, nous retrouvons la même distinction:

a. Élisabeth, remplie de l'Esprit Saint, salue Marie, non l'inverse (Lc 1,41-45);

b. Zacharie doute de la parole de l'ange et demande un signe, comme Achaz (Lc 1,18), tandis que Marie, bien qu'elle soit inquiète, croit (Lc 1,34.45); sans l'avoir demandé, elle reçoit un signe: Élisabeth est enceinte (Lc 1,36).

c. Jean marche devant le Seigneur; Jésus est le Seigneur (Lc 1,16-17; 2,11); sur Jean est la main du Seigneur, sur Jésus sa faveur (Lc 1,66; 2,40)[55].

b. Esprit et prophétie

Les mentions corrélatives d'Esprit et de prophétie sont présentes partout chez Luc et particulièrement dans les enfances parallèles. L'intervention de l'Esprit est le fil conducteur d'une histoire qui commence dans les temps anciens. François Bovon a résumé à cet égard les acquis, et je retiens le premier point qui importe ici: «Les liens que Luc établit entre le Saint-Esprit et l'histoire du salut sont évidents: dès Pentecôte, tous les croyants reçoivent un don qui n'avait atteint dans l'Ancien Testament que quelques prophètes et qui s'était concentré sur le seul Jésus dans la deuxième étape de l'Histoire du salut»[56].

Il est moins aisé de définir la notion de prophète chez Luc, qu'il s'agisse des prophètes de l'Ancien Testament, de Jésus lui-même[57], et des prophètes de l'Église naissante[58]. Mais on accordera sans peine, je crois, que le prophète n'est pas seulement celui qui, parlant sous la mouvance de l'Esprit, annonce l'avenir, mais aussi celui qui, sous la mouvance du même Esprit, reconnaît la réalisation des prophéties antiques.

La fonction prophétique de Jésus est une nécessité corrélative à l'importance de l'Esprit. Le titre et la fonction prophétiques sont effectivement

---

55. Plus de détails dans J.A. FITZMYER, *The Gospel according to Luke (I-IX). Introduction, Translation and Notes* (The Anchor Bible, 28), Garden City, NY, Doubleday, 1981, p. 315.

56. Fr. BOVON, *Luc le Théologien* (cité à la n. 1), p. 234.

57. *Ibid.*, pp. 191-193.

58. *Ibid.*, p. 392.

insuffisants pour décrire la mission et la personne de Jésus, mais ils sont indispensables pour établir la nouveauté sur le fond d'une continuité[59].

Appliquée aux enfances, cette façon de lire Luc est confirmée.

Jean reçoit l'Esprit-Saint dès le sein de sa mère (1,15); l'esprit et la puissance d'Élie, un prophète, sont sur lui (1,17). Élisabeth est remplie de l'Esprit Saint lorsqu'elle reconnaît la mère de son Seigneur, et Jean Baptiste remue dans son sein, autre forme de reconnaissance. Zacharie son père est également rempli de l'Esprit Saint lorsqu'il prononce prophétiquement le cantique. Annoncé par les prophètes de jadis, Jean est lui-même prophète pour préparer la voie. Luc applique Is 40,3-5 à Jean (Lc 3,4-6) préparant la voie de Jésus, mais Jésus s'applique à lui-même l'accomplissement de Is 61,1 (Lc 4,18-19): prophète, il s'applique une prophétie.

Jésus est reconnu par Élisabeth et par Jean, par Syméon, au sujet duquel l'Esprit Saint est mentionné trois fois (2,25-27), et par Anne appelée prophétesse (2,36). L'Esprit Saint et la puissance du Très-Haut viennent sur Marie (1,35) pour la conception de Jésus. Son baptême sera dans l'Esprit Saint et le feu, et l'Esprit Saint descend sur lui sous une forme corporelle en une véritable investiture. Après quoi, l'Esprit Saint le conduit au désert (4,1) et le fait revenir en Galilée (4,14). Jésus se reconnaît comme prophète à ce qu'il n'est plus reçu dans sa patrie et il doit s'expatrier pour faire des miracles comme Élie et Élisée (4,24-27).

En définitive, l'articulation des deux enfances comporte que l'Esprit intervienne abondamment dans l'une et dans l'autre, et supérieurement dans la seconde. Ses interventions conduisent en bonne partie à des reconnaissances plus qu'à des initiatives.

c. Abraham

L'importance d'Abraham dans l'histoire sainte lucanienne été mise en évidence par Nils A. Dahl en 1966[60]. Si l'on part des mentions contenues dans Lc 1–4, deux registres apparaissent.

1. «Des pierres que voici Dieu peut susciter des enfants à Abraham» (Lc 3,8). Tel est déjà le message de Jean. La notion d'enfants d'Abraham est récurrente (Lc 13,16; 19,9), mais ce sont aussi les auditeurs de Pierre (Ac 3,25), une partie de l'auditoire de Paul à Antioche de Pisidie

59. *Ibid.*, p. 193.

60. N.A. DAHL, *The Story of Abraham in Luke-Acts*, in L.E. KECK et J.L. MARTYN (éd.), *Studies in Luke-Acts. Essays Presented in Honor of P. Schubert*, Nashville, TN, Abingdon, 1966, pp. 139-158.

(Ac 13,26); d'abord donc et essentiellement des juifs: on a noté en Ac 3,25, citant Gn 22,18, le remplacement de ἔθνη par πατριαί.

2. L'accomplissement actuel porte sur la promesse faite à Abraham. C'est la fin du cantique de Marie (Lc 1,55), le nœud du cantique de Zacharie (Lc 1,72-73). Et, dans les Actes, Pierre et surtout Étienne s'y réfèrent comme à un début (Ac 3,25; 7,2-8.16-17). On pourrait tenir que pour Luc l'histoire sainte commence avec Abraham. En aidant à mieux comprendre la logique propre du discours d'Étienne sur la base de la promesse au patriarche, Dahl ouvre la voie à une interprétation riche de la référence à Abraham dans le récit des enfances. Le temple et le culte salomoniens ne constituent pas, selon les termes des cantiques et selon l'interprétation de la prophétie de Nathan (Ac 7,46), le but de l'Exode.

d. Cantiques et discours

Personne ne doute plus que les discours soient des compositions lucaniennes, même si l'on peut y déceler des sources, johannites par exemple selon M.-É. Boismard et A. Lamouille[61]. La question est plus délicate pour les cantiques, que leur forme poétique distingue nettement du contexte. Les caractéristiques générales du style de Luc ne font cependant que s'y manifester avec une plus grande netteté, les septantismes entre autres. Nous ne rappellerons ici que la parenté des thèmes et la similitude de fonction. Qu'elles soient ou non de Luc, les hymnes font partie de la démonstration lucanienne.

Au même titre que le discours d'Étienne et que les autres grands discours des Actes, le cantique inspiré de Zacharie prophète parcourt à sa façon l'histoire de l'intervention salvifique de Dieu. Une promesse à venir dans la famille de David a été annoncée par les prophètes d'autrefois et promise à Abraham. La naissance de Jean Baptiste, prophète, prépare la voie de l'accomplissement de cette promesse.

Du thème à la fonction le passage est facile, mais il faut le noter. Le cantique de Zacharie met d'emblée le lecteur de Luc en présence d'une perspective historique d'ensemble. Le cantique de Marie atteste l'accomplissement effectif, et ceux des anges et de Syméon achèvent le registre des reconnaissances.

La référence au cantique biblique d'Anne est particulièrement nette et continue dans le cantique lucanien de Marie. La correspondance de Lc 1,48 (ἐπέβλεψεν ἐπὶ τὴν ταπείνωσιν τῆς δούλης αὐτοῦ) avec le

---

61. M.-É. BOISMARD et A. LAMOUILLE, *Les Actes des deux Apôtres*. I. *Introduction – Textes* (Études bibliques, N.S., 12), Paris, Gabalda, 1990, p. 24-26.

contexte en prose du cantique biblique en 1 S 1,11 (ἐπιβλέπων ἐπιβλέ-ψῃς ἐπὶ τὴν ταπείνωσιν τῆς δούλης σου) en est une confirmation. En revanche, le cantique de Zacharie n'a retenu en claire du cantique biblique qu'une mention de la «corne» (Lc 1,69 et 1 S 2,10; voir 1 S 2,1). Il y a donc une diffraction du cantique biblique. Mais surtout, les deux cantiques de Luc se réfèrent à la promesse faite à Abraham.

Si l'on revient alors aux *Ant.Bibl.*, la parenté du cantique lucanien de Zacharie avec celui d'Anne selon le Pseudo-Philon saute aux yeux. Dans l'un comme dans l'autre, le prophète ou la prophétesse salue l'accomplissement *partiel*, dans une naissance, d'une promesse faite autrefois.

e. Conclusion

Les hymnes, surtout celle de Zacharie, jouent donc un rôle comparable à celui des discours dans les Actes. De plus, ils se trouvent étroitement mêlés à la trame générale de la narration dans laquelle ils sont enchâssés. Certes Luc doit connaître le récit biblique. Mais ce que nous venons de dire sur la prophétie, sur Abraham, sur la fonction et la place des hymnes dans son évangile de l'enfance ressemble davantage aux *Ant.Bibl.* Puisque Luc s'est inspiré de la naissance de Samuel pour sa propre rédaction des enfances, autant croire qu'il a connu un récit proche de celui des *Ant.Bibl.*, sinon celui-là même.

Une particularité cependant reste à documenter. Luc entremêle savamment deux récits de naissance, la merveille annonçant le mystère.

B. *Les naissances dans les* Antiquités bibliques

Trois naissances sont longuement évoquées dans les *Ant.Bibl.*, celles de Moïse, de Samson et de Samuel[62]. Une autre est signalée en passant (Isaac)[63].

1. Samson

Compte tenu de la liberté très grande que s'accorde l'auteur des *Ant. Bibl.*, le rappel détaillé qu'il fait de la naissance merveilleuse de Samson, largement emprunté à la Bible, surprend un peu, car le personnage

---

62. D.J. HARRINGTON, *Birth Narratives in Pseudo-Philo's Biblical Antiquities and the Gospels*, in M.P. HORGAN et P.J. KOBELSKI (éd.), *To Touch the Text. Biblical and Related Studies in Honor of Joseph A. Fitzmyer, S.J.*, New York, Crossroad, 1989, pp. 316-324. – Je suis surpris que cette étude ne cite pas la naissance de Samuel selon les *Ant.Bibl.*

63. P.-W. VAN DER HORST, *Seven Months' Children in Jewish and Christian Tradition*, in *ETL* 54 (1978) pp. 346-360.

n'est pas édifiant et il ne paraît pas occuper un rôle fonctionnel dans la succession des envoyés divins. Mais lisons-nous bien? Je propose ici une lecture nouvelle.

Immédiatement après la carrière de Samson (*Ant.Bibl.* 42 et 43), vient l'épisode de Michas (*Ant.Bibl.* 44; cf. Jg 17). D'après *Ant.Bibl.* 44,2, Michas est le fils de Dedila, mère de Heliu. Cette généalogie n'est pas biblique, et elle a dû surprendre les scribes grecs avant les copistes latins. Si l'on se souvient que dans l'écriture onciale Λ et Δ sont facilement confondus et que les manuscrits grecs écrivent presque toujours $\Delta\alpha\lambda(\varepsilon)\iota\delta\alpha$ pour désigner la femme de Samson, je crois non seulement possible mais probable qu'il s'agit d'elle ici. Restitué, ce nom établit un lien entre l'histoire de Samson et celle de Michas.

Mais l'étrangère est dite aussi mère de Heliu. Donc Michas, prêtre, et Heliu sont frères (ou demi-frères). Serait-il croyable que ce Heliu soit le Héli qui recevra Samuel à Silo? Notons d'abord que les *Ant.Bibl.*, comme les vieilles versions latines, écrivent bien *Heli* (non *Eli*) pour désigner le prêtre de Silo. Les noms propres rares étant souvent déformés et l'identification avec Héli de Silo n'étant pas du tout obvie, il n'y aurait pas à être surpris que *Heliu* soit une déformation de *Heli*. On pourrait même penser au génitif grec de *Helias*[64]. Mais l'identité est-elle intrinsèquement vraisemblable? Les difficultés de convenance seraient ici plus importantes que celles qui résulteraient de la logique ou de la chronologie, car ces dernières n'arrêtent pas notre auteur. Mais Heli et Micha sont prêtres; il est bien écrit: … *in Sylon… ubi Heli sacerdos sedebat quem praeposuerat Finees filius Elezazari sacerdotis, sicut praeceptum ei fuerat* (*Ant.Bibl.* 50,3). Le titre *sacerdos*, employé aussi pour Michas (44,2), est porté indignement, mais rien ne dit qu'il est usurpé.

Supposons acquises ces deux identifications, il en résulte un lien étroit entre les naissances de Samson et de Samuel. Dalila, femme de Samson, a pour fils Michas et Héli. La fin des deux familles est racontée (en 44,9 pour Samson), tandis que Samuel est adopté par Héli: *Et dixit Heli ad eum* (Samuelem): *Audi nunc fili* (*Ant.Bibl.* 53,12)[65].

---

64. Le nom du prêtre Héli n'est décliné ni dans la Septante ni dans les *Ant. Bibl.* Le nom du prophète Élie est habituellement $H\lambda(\varepsilon)\iota ov$, indéclinable dans la Septante, mais ce nom est déclinable dans les manuscrits lucianiques ($H\lambda(\varepsilon)\iota\alpha\varsigma$; gén. $H\lambda(\varepsilon)\iota ov$) et chez Flavius Josèphe ($H\lambda(\varepsilon)\iota\alpha$; gén. $H\lambda(\varepsilon)\iota ov$). Voir aussi en Lc 1,17 le gén. $H\lambda\iota ov$, mais de très anciens témoins ont $H\lambda(\varepsilon)\iota\alpha$: S($\aleph$) B* L W 565. On a *Helias* (avec h) en latin. Dès lors, si le traducteur grec n'a pas reconnu l'identité du prêtre de Silo et du fils de Dalila, il peut s'être laissé influencer par le nom du prophète (soit par la forme non déclinable en -ov, soit pas le gén. en -ov).

65. Ce n'est pas un hasard si Flavius Josèphe donne au nom de Samson l'étymologie qui convient au nom de Samuel: $\iota\sigma\chi\upsilon\rho\delta\nu$ (*A.J.* V,iv,285); voir *Ant.Bibl.* 51,1, et ci-dessus n. 16.

On l'a compris, s'il convient de mettre en évidence cet enchaînement de naissances, c'est que le contraste Samson-Samuel rentre parfaitement dans la logique propre des *Ant.Bibl.* Mais c'est aussi qu'il peut préfigurer de loin le contraste Jean-Jésus chez Luc. Le mutisme de Zacharie n'a-t-il pas été comparé à celui de Eluma mère de Samson (*Ant.Bibl.* 42,4)?

2. Samuel

Il n'y a plus à revenir sur la naissance de Samuel, sinon pour rappeler:
1. la présence de plusieurs pièces lyriques dont la principale est une cantate à plusieurs voix (un oratorio déjà?);
2. l'importance des concaténations en amont établissant l'autorité de Samuel.

Les enchaînements en aval de Samuel méritent aussi l'attention. Samuel intrônise Saül (*Ant.Bibl.* 56,4) et David (*Ant.Bibl.* 59). Mais Saül a péché en laissant Agag en vie; il périra donc par le fils d'Agag (58,3). Après que Saül a cherché à tuer David, Edab[66] fils d'Agag tue Saül dont les derniers mots, qui achèvent aussi l'œuvre conservée, sont pacifiques: *Non memor sis odii mei neque iniustitiae meae* (65,5). Par cet aveu Saül reconnaît la succession davidique.

Cette passation de pouvoir peut faire penser à la succession Jean-Jésus (Jean en prison, puis décapité par Hérode); elle invite à regarder aussi du côté des Actes. Ici un autre Saul participe comme témoin à la lapidation d'Étienne qui pardonne à ses bourreaux, donc à Saul que l'on retrouvera bientôt persécuteur «retourné».

Même si l'on tient pour accidentelles ces ressemblances, d'ailleurs imparfaites, il reste que la méthode des *Ant.Bibl.* et celle de Luc se recoupent. La concaténation comporte que les personnages soient introduits sur la scène avant d'y jouer un rôle. Barnabé nommé en 4,36 intervient à partir de 11,26, tandis que Saul nommé en 7,58 et 8,1 entre en scène au côté de Barnabé, d'abord en second (11,30). Barnabé lance Saul qui devient bientôt le premier de la paire (14,13.42). Jean-Marc entre en scène en 12,24 et revient à Jérusalem (13,13) avant de suivre Barnabé (15,37-40), tandis que Paul prend avec lui Silas et Timothée (15,40-16,1). Au chapitre 15, le débat entre Jacques et Paul est arbitré par Pierre à Jérusalem; en 21,17, Paul retrouve Jacques à Jérusalem. Pierre n'est plus là, mais Paul entame son itinéraire vers Rome. En cours de route interviennent des prophètes, tels Ananias (9,10-18) et Agabus (11,27-28; 21,10-11).

---

66. *Ant.Bibl.* 65,4; lire *Edab* avec les meilleurs témoins. *Edabus* paraît une latinisation.

Cette façon de présenter la diffusion de l'évangile comme une course de relais dont chaque segment est parcouru simultanément par deux coureurs, la paire se renouvelant de moitié à chaque passage du «témoin», manifeste la continuité de l'histoire sous la providence divine.

Faut-il s'étonner alors si Luc, dès le début de son œuvre, noue soigneusement la fin de la carrière du Précurseur avec le début de celle du Sauveur?

C. *Les modèles de Luc*

Luc a des sources: Mc, Q et d'autres à l'évidence, en particulier pour les Actes. Ce n'est pas ce dont nous voulons parler ici. Mais Luc a pu avoir aussi des modèles dans la composition de son œuvre, choisi dans ses sources principales ou en dehors d'elles.

La source johannite que des auteurs sont prêts à reconnaître dans les grands discours des Actes et dans l'évangile de l'enfance selon Luc pourraient alors avoir servi, non seulement de source mais aussi de modèle, à supposer qu'elle présentât déjà, dans les discours, et peut-être dans les cantiques, une conception de l'histoire du type de celle que nous avons mise en évidence dans les *Ant.Bibl.* et connaissons chez Luc. Je préfère toutefois abandonner le terrain discuté d'une source johannite intermédiaire, pour m'en tenir à la ressemblance entre les deux termes connus de la comparaison, les *Ant.Bibl.* et Luc.

Si les *Antiquités Bibliques* sont antérieures à 70 – ce qui est la seule position vraisemblable après ce que nous avons dit –, si elles ont été traduites très tôt, et même avant 70 – ce qui est au moins probable –, alors rien n'empêche que Luc les ait tenues en main. En l'absence d'un détail qui trahirait une dépendance certaine, il faut rester prudent. Mais il n'est pas moins raisonnable de proposer une dépendance de Luc par rapport aux *Ant.Bibl.* que de conjecturer l'existence d'une œuvre qui lui serait assez semblable. *Entia non sunt multiplicanda.*

CONCLUSION

On l'aura noté, nous avons évité de revenir sur les comparaisons de détail avec les récits de naissance des héros de l'Ancien Testament autres que ceux des *Ant.Bibl.* En privilégiant celles-ci, nous avons voulu mettre en évidence une certaine façon de raconter l'«histoire sainte». Certes la parenté stylistique et rédactionnelle avec Luc n'est pas négligeable, certains épisodes sont étonnamment semblables, certains détails curieusement proches; mais c'est leur historiographie et leur façon de l'imprimer dans la rédaction qui est aussi à souligner. La parenté n'est pas seulement extérieure; elle est profonde.

Luc et les *Ant.Bibl.* citent tous deux l'Écriture. Il arrive même que Luc la cite selon la révision Théodotion-kaige, ce qui peut le rapprocher des *Ant.Bibl.* Ce point de détail est à signaler, car il rentre exactement dans la définition de ces Journées. En Ac 2,18, la citation de Jl 3,2 (2,29) comporte la leçon καίγε[67].

Luc cite la Bible de façon originale. Mais pour lui, comme pour l'auteur des *Ant.Bibl.*, l'autorité est celle de Dieu qui, conduisant l'histoire, donne à des hommes de Dieu et à des «femmes de Dieu»[68] l'Esprit en vue de diverses tâches et aussi pour écrire, mais plus encore pour lire l'Écriture et en saisir le sens dans la continuité de son dessein.

Ceci pour la ressemblance. Il faut noter aussi la différence. Luc applique à des événements récents, tout proches de lui, une méthode que les *Ant. Bibl.* appliquent à des événements antiques. Le centre de gravité pour Luc est bien l'événement-Jésus. Raconter la naissance de Jean et de Jésus dans les termes où la tradition juive de son temps racontait celles de Samson et de Samuel n'est pas du tout la même chose que de raconter la naissance de Samson et de Samuel en dévelopant, sous forme de midrash aggadique, les récits bibliques. Dans les deux cas, il s'agit de rendre manifeste la continuité et la cohérence du dessein divin. Mais dans le premier, il s'agit de montrer a posteriori, *ex eventu*, un dessein en progrès; dans le second, chez Luc, il s'agit de constater un accomplissement et de l'exprimer littérairement[69]. S'il faut donc renoncer à définir les récits lucaniens comme midrash[70], car

---

67. D'une façon générale, on se référera à Tr. HOLTZ, *Untersuchungen über die alttestamentlichen Zitate bei Lukas* (TU, 104), Berlin, Akademie-Verlag, 1968. Mais il n'utilise pas encore les ressources de la découverte de la recension Théodotion-kaige par D. BARTHÉLEMY (*Les Devanciers d'Aquila*, Leyde, Brill, 1963) qu'il ne fait que citer. Se référer à la famille textuelle de l'*Alexandrinus* ne signifie rien pour l'époque où Luc écrit. À cette date, la Septante est encore transmise en rouleaux, sans garantie d'homogénéité entre eux, et l'*Alexandrinus* représente une édition chrétienne, non un type de texte. En revanche Luc a pu connaître la révision Théodotion-kaige, au moins pour certains livres, le Dodecapropheton par exemple, car il cite Jl 3,2 (2,29) avec καίγε pour un *gam* de l'hébreu. Les deux autres emplois de καίγε par Luc, viennent hors de citations bibliques (Lc 19,42; Ac 17,27). Cette recherche serait à poursuivre.

68. P.W. VAN DER HORST, *Portraits of Biblical Women in Pseudo-Philo's Liber Antiquitatum Biblicarum*, in ID., *Essays on the Jewish World of Early Christianity* (NTOA, 14), Göttingen, Vandenhoeck & Ruprecht, 1990, pp. 111-122.

69. E. REINMUTH, *Pseudo-Philo und Lukas* (ci-dessus, n. 7), p. 248.

70. Ch. PERROT, *Les récits de l'enfance* (ci-dessus, n. 4), p.515: «Le midrash est en quelque sorte 'retourné' sur lui-même par des gens qui, délibérément substituèrent Jésus à la Tora. On ne peut donc pas parler de midrash pour cataloguer les récits évangéliques».

ils ne commentent pas le texte biblique, je soulignerais en revanche la parenté des conceptions historiques et, partant, des méthodes narratives chez Luc et dans les *Ant.Bibl.*[71].

Le cantique de Marie, le Magnificat[72], est très proche du cantique biblique d'Anne, tandis que celui de Zacharie, le Benedictus, atteste la perspective historique typique des *Ant.Bibl.* Les deux faits doivent être considérés simultanément, sans être dissociés. Les *Ant.Bibl.* (ou une œuvre similaire) ne se trouvent pas entre Luc et 1 Samuel au point de cacher le texte biblique. Luc, en colorant son œuvre de «septantismes», plus ou moins abondamment selon les parties, et abondamment dans les enfances, manifeste son souci de s'inscrire dans le prolongement de l'Écriture juive de langue grecque au même titre que 1 Maccabées s'inscrivait dans le prolongement stylistique des livres historiques hébreux[73]. Luc lit la Bible à la façon de l'auteur des *Ant.Bibl.*, mais sa lecture est orientée, non d'Abraham à David, mais d'Abraham par David à Jésus Sauveur.

Abbaye de Maredsous　　　　　　　　　　Pierre-Maurice BOGAERT
B-5537 Denée

---

71. D.J. HARRINGTON, *Birth Narratives* (ci-dessus, n. 62), p. 324, est sur ce point restrictif à l'extrême. Il montre bien l'inadéquation des mots midrash et aggada, mais il ne perçoit pas l'insistance commune de Luc et des *Ant.Bibl.* sur la continuité du dessein divin par des procédés littéraires presque identiques.

72. Il est certain qu'une partie non négligeable de la tradition latine et déjà Irénée de Lyon attribuent le Magnificat à Élisabeth, mais cela ne règle pas la question de fond (P.-M. BOGAERT, *Épisode de la controverse sur le «Magnificat». À propos d'un article inédit de Donatien De Bruyne (1906)*, in *Revue bénédictine* 94 [1984] 38-49, p. 45, note d). R. BROWN, *The Birth of the Messiah* (ci-dessus, n. 7), pp. 335-336, estime que le meilleur argument en faveur de l'attribution à Marie est le fait que les deux bénéficiaires des annonciations sont aussi les deux à prononcer un cantique.

73. F.-M. ABEL et J. STARCKY, *Les livres des Maccabées*, Paris, Cerf, 3e éd. revue, 1961, p. 15.

OLD TESTAMENT MODELS
FOR THE LUKAN TRAVEL NARRATIVE

A CRITICAL SURVEY

Introductory Remarks

The purpose of this paper is to examine whether the Old Testament can in one way or another offer an explanation for the existence, the nature and organisation of the second main part of Luke's Gospel, which is usually called the "Central Section" or the "Lukan Travel Narrative" (LkTN). We hope to do this by offering a survey of the extant literature and by making our critical comments on it. Before entering into my subject, I would like to make two introductory remarks. The first one concerns the so-called "Lukan Travel Narrative". In scholarly discussion, the delineation and even the existence of the LkTN is a matter of dispute. Nevertheless, one cannot deny (i) that in the third Gospel there is somehow a "central section" (9,51–18,14) where Luke leaves the order of Mark and inserts mainly material of different origin, and (ii) that this central part is put within the framework of Jesus' journey to Jerusalem, with the obvious result that there is a tension between the content (didactic saying traditions) and the frame (journey motif) of this section, a dissonance of form from content. The so-called "central section" forms a characteristic feature of the structure of Luke's Gospel, it distinguishes Luke's structure from that of the other two Synoptic Gospels. Whether this narrative "journey-section" ends with 18,14, 19,27/28 or 19,44/46/48 is a matter of dispute[1]. The problem of the end of the travel narrative is secondary in comparison with that of its very existence. Indeed, the travel narrative has always puzzled Lukan scholars. Several questions may be raised: where does this central part in Luke come from? What is its origin? Was it inspired by his main source, Mark, and elaborated by Luke? Were other sources available which can explain the existence of the central section and which sources would

---

1. See A. DENAUX, *The Delineation of the Lukan Travel Narrative within the Overall Structure of the Gospel of Luke*, in C. FOCANT (ed.), *The Synoptic Gospels. Source Criticism and the New Literary Criticism* (BETL, 110), Leuven, 1993, pp. 359-392, where we argued that the entry story Lk 19,29-44 forms an integral part of the Travel Narrative and that Lk 19,45-48 interlaces the TN and the temple section (Lk 19,45–21,38).

these be (traditional travel stories; Q; L; ProtoLk; Mt)? Or should the main stimulus be searched for in the Old Testament (a book, a tradition, etc.)? What constitutes the organizing principle and hence the meaning and coherence of the entire section?

My second remark has to do with intertextuality, more precisely the nature and different forms of the relationship between Old and New Testament texts. How did the NT writers make use of the OT and what understanding did they have of it? It is quite clear that a variety of types of use must be recognised. Marshall distinguishes at least seven possibilities: influence of language and of style; (literal) references to events, to divine commands, to passages which were understood as prophecies; and typological and allegorical uses of the OT, which transcend a literal use[2]. Even when one may question which organizing principle lies behind this enumeration (philological considerations, literal or non literal use, exegetical methods used by the NT author), Marshall's list shows how varied and multiple the influence of the OT on the NT can be. There is a problem of an epistemological nature here. Can every use or influence be detected by the reader/exegete? First of all, one should distinguish between use and influence. The distinction depends on whether the NT author (use) or the OT (influence) is the dominant element within the intertextual relationship. By "use" we mean a conscious use of the OT by the NT

---

2. See I.H. MARSHALL, *An Assessment of Recent Developments*, in D.A. CARSON & H.G.M. WILLIAMSON (eds.), *It is Written: Scripture Citing Scripture*. FS B. Lindars, Cambridge, 1988, pp. 9-10: "(1) The influence of the *language* of the OT in the diction of the NT authors, with the result that they write a 'biblical Greek' distinguished by its secondary Semitisms (i.e. Semitisms which have been transmitted through the LXX). (2) The influence of the *style* of the OT. This emerges specifically in the case of Luke whose use of a LXX style must raise the question whether he thought of himself as writing a work of the same kind and thus continuing the 'salvation historical' story which he found in it. (3) The use of the OT in a straightforward 'literal' manner when *reference* is being made *to events described in it*. This use is so 'obvious' that it is often passed over without comment, and yet it may demand further attention. (4) The use of the OT again in a 'literal' manner to *refer to the divine commands, etc.*, which are found in it and which are believed to be still valid (or which may be cited in order to be brought up to date or even abrogated). (5) The use of the OT yet again in a 'literal' manner to *refer to passages which were understood as prophecies* and which found their literal meaning in the events now taking place. 'About whom does the prophet say this?' Then Philip 'told him the good news of Jesus' (Acts 8,34f.). (6) The use of the OT *typologically* to show a correspondence between a contemporary event and an event in the OT so that understanding of the former (and sometimes the latter) may be enhanced. (7) The use of the OT *allegorically* to draw parallels between an OT story and a contemporary situation or piece of teaching". Douglas J. Moo (*The Old Testament in the Gospel Passion Narratives*, Sheffield, 1983, pp. 17-24), distinguishes seven types of "citation procedures": general linguistic influence, explicit quotations, implicit quotations, allusions, structural style, conceptual influence, summaries of OT history and teaching.

writer, a process which can take different forms[3]. By "influence" we mean rather the fact that the OT is exerting influence in one way or another on the redactional activity of the NT author. Secondly, one should be aware of what kind of OT element or part one is dealing with. The following enumeration shows that there are many possibilities indeed: quotations, allusions, themes or motifs (e.g. the hardness of heart; the rejection of God's messengers), characters (prophet: Moses, Elijah; Davidic King; Suffering Servant), events or "faith traditions" (i.e. exodus, conquest, temple, and kingship traditions), books (e.g. Deuteronomy in Lk) or group of books (e.g. Pentateuch in Mt). In other words, the OT could have been used consciously by the NT author or even have influenced the NT writer unconsciously. What criteria are there to "prove" that the NT author consciously made use of the OT or to establish an OT influence of some kind on his work? It is rather easy in the case of quotations, because the author explicitly mentions it through an introductory formula. It is more difficult with respect to allusions: "Unfortunately the works that list the OT citations and allusions in the NT do not agree completely on definitions or on the identification of such references in Luke and the NT"[4]. It is still more risky to detect the influence of "motifs", "faith traditions" or whole books of the OT on NT authors, texts or books. The border between a conscious intertextual use of the OT by a NT author, an unconscious influence of the OT upon the mind, the language and the style of a NT author, and the intertextual exegesis practised by the modern interpreter is not always easy to draw. The exegete can play it safe and limit him- or herself to the study of quotations, in accordance with the famous principle of Wittgenstein: "Worüber man nicht reden kann, muss man schweigen". Nevertheless, it is quite certain that Luke knew the Septuagint better than anyone of us, be it only for the reason that it was his "Scripture" and that it was written in his mother tongue. Hence it is obvious that the OT plays a prominent part in his writings and that its

---

3. According to D.L. Bock (*Proclamation from Prophecy and Pattern. Lucan Old Testament Christology* [JSNT SS, 12], Sheffield, 1987, pp. 49-51), Luke's hermeneutical use of the OT involves the classification of the passage's function. He distinguishes seven classifications: (i) typology or better typological-prophetic usage; (ii) analogy; (iii) illustration; (iv) legal proof; (v) proof passage; (vi) an explanatory or hermeneutical use which specifically explains the nature or significance of an event, and (vii) prophetic category or direct prophecy. D.J. Moo (*Passion Narratives* [n. 2], pp. 56-78) states that the process through which the appropriation of Scripture took place can be described in terms of three basic alternatives: direct appropriation, re-orientation of the text, and modification in the point of application (see esp. pp. 76-77).

4. C.A. Kimball, *Jesus' Exposition of the Old Testament in Luke's Gospel* (JSNT SS, 94), Sheffield, 1994, p. 47.

influence is much more radical than what is displayed by quotations[5]. Therefore, one should not a priori disapprove research done concerning OT influence on Luke other than by way of explicit citations. Of course, the exegete who has the courage to set foot in these more difficult fields of study should remain aware that he/she is sometimes skating over thin ice. So let us now examine the attempts which have been made to clarify the existence and meaning of the LkTN by referring to the OT.

1. The Lukan Travel Narrative a "Christian Deuteronomy"

The first line of thought sees the LkTN as a "Christian Deuteronomy". Christopher F. Evans has initiated the idea in his seminal study "The Central Section of St. Luke's Gospel"[6]. He suggested that the content of Jesus' journey is modelled on the content of instruction given during Israel's journey narrated in the Book of Deuteronomy. This suggestion is based on the following considerations. First, verses Lk 9,51-53; 10,1 suggest a situation analogous to that of Moses who, in leading Israel towards the Promised Land, sends out one emissary for each tribe to explore the land, and who also appoints seventy elders to receive of his spirit and to share his work. Secondly, the presence of the term ἀνάλημψις in Lk 9,51 could be an indication of Luke's knowledge of the Jewish apocalyptic work Ἀνάλημψις Μωυσέως[7], where not only Moses' mysterious transition from earth to heaven is narrated, but also a series of addresses and commandments is given. Thirdly, in the light of all this it is not impossible that Luke, for whom the identification of Jesus with 'the prophet like unto Moses' (Dt 18,15; Acts 3,22) was axiomatic, has

---

5. Surveys of the study of the OT in Lk can be found in D.L. BOCK, Proclamation (n. 3), pp. 13-53; F. BOVON, Luc le théologien. Vingt-cinq ans de recherches (1950-75) (Le Monde de la Bible), Neuchâtel, 1978; Genève, ²1988, pp. 85-117; Engl.: Luke the Theologian. Thirty-Three Years of Research (1950-1983) (transl. K. McKinney), Allison Park, 1987, pp. 78-108; C.A. KIMBALL, Jesus' Exposition (n. 4), pp. 13-44. See also J.A. FITZMYER, The Use of the Old Testament in Luke-Acts, in SBL Seminar Papers 1992, p. 524-538, esp. p. 525, n. 2.

6. C.F. EVANS, The Central Section of St. Luke's Gospel, in D.E. NINEHAM (ed.), Studies in the Gospels. Essays in Memory of R.H. Lightfoot, Oxford, 1955, pp. 37-53. He takes up his proposal in his commentary Saint Luke (TPI N.T. Commentaries), London/Philadelphia, 1990, pp. 34-36: "one principle of its selection and organization could have been supplied by the book of Deuteronomy, also a book of teaching in the context of a journey" (p. 34).

7. Evans relies on R.H. Charles (The Apocrypha and Pseudepigrapha of the Old Testament in English, II, Oxford, 1913, pp. 407-413), who thinks that the Assumptio Moysis must be older than the letter of Jude, because Jd 9 refers to it, and that Luke was possibly acquainted with the book in its final form.

selected and ordered his material with a view to presenting it as a Christian Deuteronomy. C.F. Evans then sets out in detail a number of parallels between the book of Deuteronomy and Lk 9,51–18,14. There are not only resemblances of content and vocabulary (some of which may be fortuitous, Evans concedes), but especially the coincidence of order is striking[8]. The conclusion is difficult to resist that Lk has selected and arranged his material in such a way as to present it in a deuteronomistic sequence. Thus far Evans.

Several scholars have endorsed Evans' view, be it in different ways[9]. One recent voice is that of Willard Swartley (1994). Evans' view, he says, that the content of Luke's Central Section is modelled on Deuteronomy merits careful analysis. Relatively few criticisms of his ingenious contribution have been made, and those put forward are minor in comparison to the weight of evidence. So "Luke uses Deuteronomy as a literary model" and this phenomenon calls for analysis at the level of theological significance[10]. Later on, we will come back to Swartley's monograph. Craig A. Evans has supported C.F. Evans' view by examining some of the deuteronomistic parallels more closely (Lk 16,1-18/Dt 23, 15–24,4; Lk 18,9-14/Dt 26)[11].

---

8. C.F. Evans (*Central Section* [n. 6], pp. 42-50) sees the following coincidences of order: Dt 1/Lk 10,1-3.17-20; Dt 2–3,22/Lk 10,4-16; Dt 3,23–4,10/Lk 10,21-24; Dt 5–6/Lk 10,25-27; Dt 7/Lk 10,29-37; Dt 8,1-3/Lk 10,38-42; Dt 8,4-20/Lk 11,1-13; Dt 9,1–10,11/Lk 11,14-26; Dt 10,12–11,32/Lk 11,27-36; Dt 12,1-16/Lk 11,37–12,12; Dt 12,17-32/Lk 12,13-34; Dt 13,1-11/Lk 12,35-53; Dt 13,12-18/Lk 12,54–13,5; // Dt 14,28/Lk 13,6-9; Dt 15,1-18/Lk 13,10-21; [Dt 16,1–17,7/Lk 13,22-25; Dt 17,8–18,22/Lk 14,1-14 (cf. Lk 9,35)]; // Dt 20/Lk 14,15-35; // Dt 21,15–22,4/Lk 15,1-32; // Dt 23,15–24,4/Lk 16,1-18; Dt 24,6–25,3/Lk 16,19–18,8; // [Dt 26/Lk 18,9-14]. // points to text-units which are not inserted in the series of parallels; for square brackets see n. 10. See Appendix I.

9. J. BLIGH, *Christian Deuteronomy (Luke 9-18)*, Langley, Bucks, 1970, and A.J. TANKERSLEY, *Preaching the Christian Deuteronomy; Luke 9,51–18,14* (Diss. School of Theology), Claremont, 1983, have popularised Evans' theory for homiletic purposes. See also C.H. CAVE, *Lazarus and the Lukan Deuteronomy*, in *NTS* 15 (1969) 319-325; J.D.M. DERRETT, *Law in the New Testament*, London, 1970, pp. 100.129.226; J.A. SANDERS, *The Ethics of Election in Luke's Great Parable Banquet*, in J.L. CRENSHAW and J.T. WILLIS (eds.), *Essays on Old Testament Ethics*, New York, 1974, pp. 245-271; rev. and repr. in C.A. EVANS and J.A. SANDERS, *Luke and Scripture. The Function of Sacred Tradition in Luke-Acts*, Minneapolis, MN, 1993, pp. 70-83; S.H. RINGE, *Luke 9:28-36: The Beginning of An Exodus*, in M.A. TOLBERT (ed.), *The Bible and Feminist Hermeneutics* (Semeia, 28), Chico, CA, 1983, pp. 83-99.

10. W.M. SWARTLEY, *Israel's Scripture Traditions and the Synoptic Gospels*, Peabody, MA, 1994, pp. 130-131; on pp. 151-153 he takes over the list of Evans (see n. 8), except the texts between square brackets.

11. C.A. EVANS, *Luke's Use of the Elijah/Elisha Narratives and the Ethic of Election*, in *JBL* 106 (1987) 75-83; rev. and repr. in C.A. EVANS and J.A. SANDERS, *Luke and Scripture. The Function of Sacred Tradition in Luke-Acts*, Minneapolis, MN, 1993, pp. 70-83; *Luke 16:1-18 and the Deuteronomy Hypothesis*, in ibid., pp. 121-139; *The Pharisee and the Publican: Luke 18.9-14 and Deuteronomy 26*, in C.A. EVANS & W.R. STEGNER (eds.), *The Gospels and the Scriptures of Israel* (JSNT SS, 104), Sheffield, 1994, pp. 342-355.

Other scholars are impressed by the similarities of form between the *Assumptio Moysis* and the LkTN which they call therefore a "farewell discourse" or "Jesus' testament for the time of the Church" (thus Gerhard Sellin)[12]. In the line of Jewish testamentary literature, Jesus' teaching to his disciples in the LkTN has the characteristics of a testament (last will: *Vermächtnis*), thus Ulrich Busse[13].

Still other writers build on the essay of C.F. Evans and use the term "midrash" to describe a method allegedly employed by Luke for a fictional creation of NT narratives from OT stories. They combine this character-isation of Luke with an alternative source theory: one does not need hypothetical sources like Q or L to explain the origin of the third Gospel; it suffices to see Luke's work as a free midrash on Mt, Mk and the LXX. In this approach, the LXX receives almost the status of a source of the same kind as Mt and Mk. In his 1955 article *On Dispensing with Q*, Austin M. Farrer already suggested that Luke is dependent on Matthew's overall hexateuchal structure, but that in the section 10,25–18,30 Luke gives more weight to Deut[14]. John Drury calls Luke 9,51–18,14 a "Christian Deuteronomy", and thinks that in this section Lk is more dependent on Dt than on Mt: "The thread through the labyrinth is Deuteronomy. Matthew is secondary"[15]. Michael Goulder combines Luke's dependence on Mt with a more extreme lectionary hypothesis. The latter explains the big changes of the Mt order in Luke: "only whereas Matthew had been concerned principally to provide discourses to fit the themes of the Jewish-Christian Feasts, Luke was attempting something more elaborate in a weekly story 'fulfilling' the Saturday Old

---

12. G. SELLIN, *Komposition, Quellen und Funktion des lukanischen Reiseberichtes (Lk. IX 51 – XIX 28)*, in *NT* 20 (1978) 100-135, esp. 133-135: However, Sellin does not agree with Evans concerning the resemblances of order between Deut and LkTN.

13. U. BUSSE, *Die Wunder des Propheten Jesus. Die Rezeption, Komposition und Interpretation der Wundertradition im Evangelium des Lukas* (FzB, 24), Stuttgart, 1977, pp. 271-274; cf. G. NEBE, *Prophetische Züge im Bild Jesu bei Lukas* (BWANT, 127), Stuttgart/Berlin/Köln, 1989, pp. 180-181.

14. A.M. FARRER, *On Dispensing with Q* in D.E. NINEHAM (ed.), *Studies in the Gospels. Essays in Memory of R.H. Lighfoot*, Oxford, 1955, pp. 55-86, esp. pp. 75-79: Mt 1–17/Genesis; Mt 5–7/Exodus; Mt 10/Leviticus; Mt 13/Numbers; Mt 18/Deuteron-omy; Mt 24–25/Joshua; and pp. 79-81: Lk 1–2/Genesis; Lk 3,1–4,44/Exodus; Lk 6/Leviticus ("St. Matthew's Sermon on the Mount, i.e. his Exodus, becomes St. Luke's Sermon after the Mount, i.e. his Leviticus, p. 80); Lk 9,1–10,24/Numbers; Lk 10,25–18,30/Deuteronomy;"It is hardly necessary to say anything about St. Luke's Joshua. For in any case the triumphant passion and resurrection compose the 'Book of Jesus' *par excellence*"(p. 81). C.F. Evans (*Luke*, p. 34, n. j) comments:"Evidence that 1^5-9^{50} is arranged on the basis of Genesis – Numbers is tenuous in the extreme".

15. J. DRURY, *Tradition and Design in Luke's Gospel*, London, 1976, pp. 138-164: "A Christian Deuteronomy (Luke 9:51–18:14; Matthew 8:18–24:41)"; and p. 140.

Testament lesson" (p. vii). But Goulder's set of parallels between Deuteronomy and Luke differs considerably from the one suggested by C.F. Evans[16], as is the case with other similar attempts[17].

With regard to this first variant of an OT model for the LkTN, some critical considerations can be made.

1. Luke's knowledge of the early Jewish literature, more specifically the Ἀνάλημψις Μωυσέως can be questioned (contra Evans)[18]. Would it not be more natural to relate the characteristic Lukan vocabulary concerning Jesus' bodily ascension into heaven ἀνάλημψις/ἀναλαμβάνεσθαι (Lk 9,51; Acts 1,2.11.22) to the Septuagint rather than to remote non biblical texts? The verb ἀναλαμβάνεσθαι is used in the LXX to describe the "assumption" of Enoch (Sir 49,14) and especially of Elijah (4 Kgs 2,9-11; 1 Macc 2,58; Sir 48,9), who is at the background of the whole pericope Lk 9,51-56 in a subtle but real way[19].

---

16. M. GOULDER, *The Evangelists' Calendar: A Lectionary Explanation of the Development of Scripture*, London, 1978, esp. pp. 95-104.: Dt 1,1–3,22/Lk 9,51–10,24; Dt 3,23–7,11/Lk 10,25–11,13; Dt 7,12–11,25/Lk 11,14-54; Dt 11,26–16,17/Lk 12,1–13,9; Dt 16,18–21,9/Lk 13,10–14,24; Dt 21,10–25,19/Lk 14,25–16,13; Dt 26,1–29,9/Lk 16,14–17,4; Dt 29,10–30,20/Lk 17,20–18,14; Dt 31,1-30/Lk 18,15-43; Dt 32,1-52/Lk 19,1–20,18. See Appendix II.

17. W.J. BARNARD & P. VAN 'T RIET, *Lukas, de Jood. Een joodse inleiding op het evangelie van Lukas en de Handelingen der Apostelen*, Kampen, 1984, pp. 103-117: "Het reisverhaal (Luk. 9:51–19:28)", esp. pp. 108 and 110-111: Dt 4,1-40; 5,1-32/Lk 9,51-56; Dt 6,5/Lk 10,27; Dt 7,1-26/Lk 10,30-37; Dt 8,3/Lk 10,38-42; Dt 8,9/Lk 11,3; Dt 8,11-18/Lk 11,5-13; Dt 9,1-11/Lk 11,14-20; Dt 13,1-5/Lk 11,29-32; Dt 14,1-2/Lk 11,33-36; Dt 12,1-17; 14,3-29/Lk 11,37-52; Dt 13,6-11/Lk 12,2-3; Dt 12,17-19/Lk 12,16-21; Dt 15,7-18/Lk 12,22-34; Dt 13,6-11/Lk 12,51-53; Dt 16,18-20/Lk 12,57-59; Dt 16,21; 17,1.2-7/Lk 13,1-5; Dt 15,1-8/Lk 13,10-17; Dt 17,14-20/Lk 13,31-35; Dt 15,1-8/Lk 14,1-6; Dt 20,1-9/Lk 14,16-20; Dt 20,10-11/Lk 14,31-32; Dt 21,18-21/Lk 15,11-32; Dt 22,1-4/Lk 16,1-8; Dt 22,5-12/Lk 16,10-13; Dt 22,13-20; 24,1-5/Lk 16,18; Dt 24,6-15/Lk 16,19-31; Dt 26,16-19/Lk 7,7-10. According to these authors, the third gospel was not only written by a Jewish author, but was also written for a Jewish audience. The LkTN can be read as a midrash on Deuteronomy.

18. See J.H. CHARLESWORTH, *The Old Testament Pseudepigrapha and the New Testament. Prolegomena for the Study of Christian Origins* (SNTS MS, 54), Cambridge, 1985, pp. 70-90; J. TROMP, *The Assumption of Moses. A Critical Edition with Commentary* (Studia in Veteris Testamenti Pseudepigrapha, 10), Leiden/New York/Köln, 1993, esp. pp. 115-123: "Summary and Conclusions". In his introduction to the *Testament of Moses* (ed. J.H. CHARLESWORTH, *The Old Testament Pseudepigraphia*. Vol. I, London, 1983, pp. 919-934, esp. p. 924), J. Priest states that: "...the strongest case for possible knowledge of the Testament of Moses by a New Testament author is with the letter of Jude. The other proposals are not compelling. The possibility exists that some New Testament authors were familiar with the Testament of Moses, but it would be better to say that both the Testament of Moses and certain New Testament texts show familiarity with common traditional material".

19. Cf. A. DENAUX, *Delineation* (n. 1), p. 373-74, n. 53.

2. The existence and the precise content of Jewish liturgical calendars is much debated. Goulder's highly speculative hypothesis has met with much scepticism[20].

3. My third remark relates to "midrash" as commentary technique and pattern. Several authors argue that Drury's and Goulder's use of midrash as narrative creation is an improper employment of the term, which originally refers to a rabbinical literary genre. Blomberg gives a much more precise definition of the term: "Regardless of disagreement on finer points of definition, most agree that a fundamental characteristic of Jewish midrash is that it interprets the Old Testament. The biblical text is primary; the midrash merely comments on, embellishes and applies it. This implies that the presence of an Old Testament quotation or allusion in a piece of literature does not automatically make that writing midrashic, although this restriction is not always observed". Similar critical remarks can be found with P.S. Alexander (1984) and G. Teugels (1994)[21]. Charles A. Kimball mentions that, in contrast to this improper use of the term midrash, other scholars like J.W. Doeve, R.N. Longenecker and E.E. Ellis use the term according to its traditional meaning of biblical commentary based on Jewish techniques and patterns for interpreting Scripture and have analyzed some Lukan passages along these lines[22].

4. What kind and what measure of agreements are needed in order to accept that an OT *book* forms the model or pattern of a NT book or part

---

20. C.F. EVANS, *Goulder and the Gospels*, in *Theology* 82 (1979) 425-432; C.L. BLOMBERG, *Midrash, Chiasmus, and the Outline of Luke's Central Section*, in R.T. FRANCE & D. WENHAM (eds.), *Gospel Perspectives* III, Sheffield, 1983, pp. 217-261, esp. 229-233; A.D. BAUM, *Lukas als Historiker der letzten Jesusreise*, Wuppertal/Zürich, 1993, pp. 29-32; NOLLAND, *Luke II*, pp. 529-530; C.A. KIMBALL, *Jesus' Exposition* (n. 4), p. 21; and especially L. MORRIS, *The New Testament and the Jewish Lectionaries*, London, 1964; ID., *The Gospels and the Jewish Lectionaries*, in R.T. FRANCE & D. WENHAM (eds.), *Gospel Perspectives* III, Sheffield, 1983, pp. 129-156, esp. 132-149.

21. C.F. BLOMBERG, *Central Section* (n. 20), p. 223; P.S. ALEXANDER, *Midrash and the Gospels*, in C.M. TUCKETT (ed.), *Synoptic Gospels. The Ampleforth Conferences of 1982 and 1983* (JSNT SS, 7), Sheffield, 1984, pp. 1-18, esp. p. 1: "[…] a survey of recent contributions to New Testament studies has forced me to conclude that the nature and function of midrash is often misunderstood by New Testament scholars, and as a result the term midrash is tending to generate more confusion than light"; G. TEUGELS, *Midrasj in, en, op de bijbel? Kritische kanttekeningen bij het onkritische gebruik van een term*, in *NTT* 49 (1995) 273-290.

22. C.A. KIMBALL, *Jesus' Exposition* (n. 4), pp. 22-23, with reference to J.W. DOEVE, *Jewish Hermeneutics in the Synoptic Gospels and Acts*, Assen, 1954, pp. 91-167; R.N. LONGENECKER, *Biblical Exegesis in the Apostolic Period*, Grand Rapids, 1975, pp. 19-78,133-140; E.E. ELLIS, *Prophecy and Hermeneutic in Early Christianity*, Grand Rapids, 1978, pp. 147-172, 188-197, 237-253; ID., *The Old Testament in Early Christianity* (WUNT, 54), Tübingen, 1990, pp. 77-138.

of a book (in our case, the Lukan travel narrative)? One could think of agreements of vocabulary, content, order and literary genre. However, on each of these points a doubt arises whether the alleged parallels between the LkTN and Dt are sufficient or real.

– With respect to the vocabulary, C.L. Blomberg remarks that in most instances of the fourteen verbal parallels (within the twenty-two parallel pairs of texts), "the words and expressions that he [i.e. Evans] cites occur so often in Deuteronomy (and elsewhere in the Old Testament) that equally convincing parallels could have been drawn from a wide variety of other texts"[23]. Thus the criterion of verbal coherence is hardly relevant.

– With respect to content, Blomberg thinks that the set of parallels fares no better. Only for five cases can one defend the view that Luke had Dt in mind: 14,15-24 (the great supper), 14,28-33 (the warring king), 16,1-9 (the unjust steward), 15,1-7 (wandering sheep), 15,11-32 (rebellious children?). Beyond these five cases, the parallels are generally quite vague[24]. The criterion of thematic coherence has some probability for some passages.

– The agreements of order depend largely on the agreements in content. A comparison of the different lists made up by Evans, Drury, Goulder, Barnard & van 't Riet "confirms how the parallels between Luke and Deuteronomy are often so general as to allow for equally plausible (or implausible) parallels to be drawn elsewhere"[25]. In some lists (Evans, Barnard & van 't Riet), the final part of the LkTN (18,15–19,44) is not taken into consideration. Moreover, the explicit quotations and allusions of the LkTN do not fit very well within the proposed parallels. In the margins of NA[26], ninety verses of Lk 9,51–19,44 are said to allude to or to quote an OT text or passage[26]. Only ten of them are referring to Dt[27]. The references do not follow the order of Dt. Moreover, the only two explicit quotations of Dt in Lk 10,27 (= Dt 6,5) and 18,20 (= Dt 5,16-20),

23. C.F. BLOMBERG, *Central Section* (n. 20), pp. 225-226.

24. C.F. BLOMBERG, *Central Section* (n. 20), pp. 227-228; on p. 253, n. 63, he refers to Glenn H. WILMS, *Deuteronomic Traditions in St. Luke's Gospel* (Ph.D. Diss. Edinburgh), 1972, pp. 17-32, who concludes that 16 of the 22 "parallels" show no correspondence of subject matter at all.

25. C.F. BLOMBERG, *Central Section* (n. 20), p. 230.

26. Cf. a list in C.A. KIMBALL, *Jesus' Exposition* (n. 4), pp. 206-212.

27. O.T **quotations** and allusions of Dt in Lk 9,51–19,44 according to UBS[3] and NA[26]: Lk 10,27 (cf. **Dt 6,5**; 10,12; Lev 19,18) (= Mt 22,27-39 = Mk 12,29-31); 13,14 (cf. Ex 20,9-10; Dt 5,13-14); 13,34 (cf. Dt 32,11); 14,5 (cf. Dt 22,4); 14,13 (cf. Dt 14,29); 14,20 (cf. Dt 24,5); 14,26 (cf. Dt 33,9); 18,18 (cf. Dt 14,22-23); 18,20 (cf. **Dt 5,16-20**; Ex 20,12-16) (= Mt 19,18-19 = Mk 10,19); 19,42 (cf. Dt 32,28-29).

which seem to have a structural correspondence in the LkTN, are not taken into consideration by these authors.

– Is there an agreement in literary genre between Dt and the LkTN? It seems not. In Dt, Moses, standing on the edge of the Promised Land, looks back on the past events and gives a long farewell address in the face of death, preparing the people for their stay in the Promised Land. In the LkTN there is a narrative progress: Jesus goes up to Jerusalem and looks to the future. Therefore, the LkTN as a whole cannot be considered to be a "testamentary genre". If there is something like a farewell discourse or "testament" of Jesus in Luke, it should be confined to the smaller text unit of Lk 22,15-38.

Within the framework of the hypothesis of the Markan priority vis-à-vis Luke, one can easily argue that Mark's gospel was Luke's real model: there are striking agreements on the four points mentioned. When the relationship Mk/Lk is compared with that between Dt and Lk (with respect to these four areas), it seems difficult to maintain that the book of Dt functioned as the model of Luke's Gospel or the Lukan Travel Narrative. It could be objected that Mark, being Luke's main source, is of course also his model, but that Dt is only said to be a model for Luke, not his source. This would imply that not all of the four criteria mentioned above must be fulfilled to qualify Dt as a model of the LkTN. In response to this it should be remarked that for some scholars at least Dt functions as an alternative source for Luke. And even when this is not the case, there should be at least a substantial correspondence with respect to the literary genre and the content (in a more or less similar order) before one can speak of Dt as a model. However, a closer look at the alleged parallels has proved that this is not the case. My conclusion would then be that the assertion that the LkTN is modelled on the *book* of Dt is a case which should be closed. However, this conclusion does not imply that Dt played no role at all in the LkTN or in Lk-Acts. Therefore, we could almost agree with Craig A. Evans, when he says: "…Luke has neither rewritten nor incorporated Deuteronomy. At most he has alluded to portions of it, followed the order of its content, and selected dominical tradition that touches on larger theological issues (such as election) with which Deuteronomy and its interpreters were concerned"[28]. But this can

---

28. C.A. EVANS, *Luke 16:1-18 and the Deuteronomy Hypothesis* (n. 11), p. 123. But is it not too much to say that "the evangelist has produced a 'commentary' on Deuteronomy only in the most general sense" and that "Luke wishes his readers to study the materials of the central section in the light of the parallel passages and themes from Deuteronomy" (*ibid.*, p. 133)?

be established only by a detailed analysis of possible verbal, thematic and exegetical coherences between the proposed parallels Lk/Dt[29].

2. The deuteronomistic view on the mission of the prophet Moses and on the history of Israel as the generative paradigm of the LkTN

In an important study, David P. Moessner (1989)[30] undertakes to solve the well-known problem of "dissonance of form from content" within the LkTN (9,51–19,44). His main thesis is that the deuteronomistic view on the mission and fate of the prophet Moses and on the history of Israel is the generative paradigm of Luke's depiction of Jesus' journey to Jerusalem in the Travel Narrative and that it gives a literary and theological coherence to this section. Moessner is well aware of the weaknesses of former attempts[31]. So for him, it is not the *book* of Deuteronomy as such which functions as the model of the LkTN (as it is for Evans, Goulder, Swartley), but two important deuteronomistic *patterns* or *motifs* which together function as the literary and theological model for both the teaching and the journey of the Lukan Jesus[32]. Moessner's method is not historical-critical but literary-critical.

29. In addition to the studies of J.A. Sanders (Lk 14,15-24/Dt 20,5-8) and C.A. Evans (Lk 16,1-18/Dt 23,15–24,4; Lk 18,9-14/Dt 26) mentioned in n. 9 and 11, we refer to R.W. WALL, *The Finger of God. Deuteronomy 9.10 and Luke 11.20*, in *NTS* 33 (1987) 144-150; ID., *Martha and Mary (Luke 10.38-42) in the Context of a Christian Deuteronomy*, in *JSNT* 35 (1989) 19-35. C.A. Evans proposes three criteria for evaluating the Deuteronomy Hypothesis: dictional, thematic and exegetical coherence (see his *Luke 16:1-18 and the Deuteronomy Hypothesis* [n. 11], pp. 137-138).

30. D.P. MOESSNER, *Lord of the Banquet. The Literary and Theological Significance of the Lukan Travel Narrative*, Minneapolis, MN, 1989.

31. *Ibid.*, p. 32: "Of the various patterns proposed, the analogy to Deuteronomy would appear to be the most promising, since a great mass of teaching is presented in the form of a journey to the Promised Land. Yet in the exposés thus far, no attempt has been made to relate the peculiar tension between the teaching and the course of the journey in Deuteronomy to that of the Central Section. Rather, Jesus, the 'prophet like Moses' of Deut. 18:15-19, is a teacher, now delivering a 'new Torah' which in sequence and substance parallels that of the 'old' (Deuteronomy 1–26). A number of parallels are indeed startlingly close; others, consisting of verbal and catchword connections without substantial similarity in either correspondence or contrast, are tenuous at best. The result as before is either a functional cohesion within the edifice of the church or a literary model which at crucial joints collapses under scrutinizing stress".

32. Moessner (*ibid.*, p. 60) considers the fourfold exodus typology of the prophetic calling of Jesus as the organizing principle for the form and content of the whole of the Central section, but then he goes on with the caution: "As the scheme is set out, it is important to bear in mind that the correspondence in type is not a function of a mechanical, rote-like parallelism in the sequence of events or description of details. It is *not* suggested that a one-to-one analogy in the chronology of episodes in Deuteronomy exists in Luke 9:1-50 or that every event or subject in the one has a mirror image in the other".

In Part 2[33], Moessner describes the prophetic mission of Moses according to Deuteronomy. Moses emerges as a suffering mediator, sent from Horeb to lead the faithless and crooked generation of "children" to the promised salvation by dying outside the land. More precisely, he distinguishes a fourfold dynamic in his prophetic vocation. (i) On the mountain Moses' calling to be the mediator of God's life-giving words (the Law) on the Exodus journey is revealed most formidably by the *voice* out of the fiery cloud to the gathered assembly of *all* Israel. (ii) From the mountain the persistent *stubborness* of the people to hearken to this voice is divulged through the distortion of this voice in the image of the molten calf; this defiance in turn illustrates the unwillingness of the people to "hear" this voice from the beginning. (iii) Accordingly, while Moses is still on the mountain and as he descends and is *sent* on the Exodus his calling is disclosed to be *a suffering journey* to *death*. (iv) As a result, his calling does not effect deliverance for all those who follow him to the Promised Land but only for the renewed people of the land, the *"children* of the mountain". At the core of this dynamic is the double stroke of Israel's stiff-necked opposition to the voice of the Lord through Moses and the consequent tragic fate of this prophet.

In Lk 9,1-50, which functions as a preview of the LkTN, this fourfold exodus-typology of the prophetic vocation of Moses is transfered to Jesus. Like Moses in Deuteronomy, Jesus here (i) is called to mediate the voice of God (9,35), (ii) confronts a warped generation afraid of hearing that voice (9,32-33.41), (iii) is destined to suffer for his people (9,22-25.32.51), and (iv) through his death the children who submit to the authority of the prophet will enter the "land of deliverance" and receive the blessing of the covenant promised to Abraham (Acts 3,22.24-25).

In Part 3, the heart of the study[34], Moessner contends that Luke was dependent on the deuteronomistic view of Israel's history in shaping his travel narrative. For the description of this view, Moessner relies on the monumental study of Odil Hannes Steck[35]. This author claims that for the Palestinian Judaism of about 200 B.C.E. to 100 C.E. one overriding framework of understanding permeated all of its extant literary activity, whether explicit or presupposed. He delineates four tenets of what he

---

33. *Ibid.*, pp. 45-79.
34. *Ibid.*, pp. 81-257.
35. O.H. STECK, *Israel und das gewaltsame Geschick der Propheten. Untersuchungen zur Überlieferung des deuteronomistischen Geschichtsbildes im Alten Testament, Spätjudentum und Urchristentum* (WMANT, 23), Neukirchen-Vluyn, 1967, esp. pp. 60-64.

calls a deuteronomistic conception of the prophetic sayings within the deuteronomistic comprehensive view of Israel's history: (A) The history of Israel is one long, persistent story of a "stiff-necked", rebellious and disobedient people (cf. Jer 7,25-26). (B) God sent his messengers, the prophets, (i) to mediate his will (i.e. the Law), (ii) to instruct and admonish them about this will (parenesis), and (iii) to exhort them to repentance lest they bring upon themselves judgment and destruction (cf. Jer 33,4-5a LXX). (C) Nevertheless, Israel *en masse* rejected all these prophets, even persecuting and killing them out of their stubborn "stiff-neckedness" (2 Esd 19,26 = Neh 9,26). (D) Therefore, Israel's God had "rained" destruction upon them in 722 and 587 B.C.E. and would destroy them in a similar way if they did not heed his word (Zech 7,14 LXX). The oldest attestation of this conception is Neh 9,26f. (see also 2 Kgs 17,7-41; 21,1-16; 2 Chron 30,1-2.6.10; 33,1-17). And it is still present in writings more or less contemporary with Luke, like Flavius Josephus (*Ant* 9,265-267; 10,38-39) and the Qumran covenanters (CD 1,3–2,4; 1Q 2,5-10 on Hab 1,5). Moessner's thesis in Part 3 is that this deuteronomistic understanding provides the conceptual world in which the disparate traditions of the Central Section of Luke become coherent and present a cohesive picture of a prophet rejected by the unmitigating obduracy of Israel. In intensely argued fashion, Moessner goes over the ground of the LkTN four times, once for each tenet, to collect all possible elements which bring its content to expression[36]. The result of Moessner's application of this paradigm to the LkTN is a Lukan portrait of Jesus as a travelling guest prophet on his way to Jerusalem, bearing with him the dynamic presence of God. "As guest along the way, he turns out to be a host, indeed the Lord of the Banquet of the divine kingdom. But he is not received. Apart from a few 'child-like' (penitent sinners) who receive Jesus, he meets monolithic rejection. The λαός of Israel, their perception corrupted by Pharisaic 'leaven', fail to repent, refuse to receive Jesus, and so are destined for judgment"[37].

In Part 4[38] Moessner tries to show that Luke integrates the deuteronomistic view of Israel's history (part 3) and the Moses typology (part 2) to present, in the travel narrative, "a coherent drama of a New Exodus for the Prophet Jesus who is the prophet like Moses" (p. 260).

Moessner has certainly written an important and stimulating (but also a very difficult) book, which has set the agenda for future research on

36. See Appendix nr. III.
37. J.T. CARROLL, review of Moessner in *JBL* 110 (1991) 165.
38. D. MOESSNER, *Lord of the Banquet* (n. 30), pp. 259-288.

the LkTN[39]. Nevertheless, however intriguing his thesis may be, ultimately it remains unconvincing. The main reason is that it takes the form of a somewhat forced combination of several elements which do not find a sufficient basis in the text of the OT itself. To begin with, it is doubtful whether the fourfold portrait of the prophetic mission of Moses (Part 2) could be easily found as such by Luke in the book of Dt and then transfered to Jesus in his ninth chapter. The Moses/Jesus typology (Dt/Lk 9) seems to be an intertextual construct present in the mind of Moessner rather than in that of Luke[40]. Secondly, even more problematic are the four tenets of the deuteronomistic view of Israel's history (Part 3) which Moessner borrows from Steck and takes for granted. A closer look at the texts which, according to Steck, establish this deuteronomistic pattern[41], shows that (i) the basis of OT texts is rather small, that (ii) the order of the four tenets is not fixed (only 2 Kgs 17,7-20 has the A,B,C,D order[42]), that (iii) in Neh 9,26-31 MT (= 2 Esdras 19,26-31 LXX) there is a more complex sequence of six tenets, that (iv) the so called four-fold paradigm is present outside of the Deuteronomists' writings (Fl. Josephus and Qumran) and therefore not distinctively deuteronomistic, and (v) that therefore it is not sure that Luke perceived it in the way Moessner and Steck do[43]. And even when he did, it is not sure that Lk had the same

---

39. His book has received much attention, which is shown by the high number of reviews: *BTB* 22 (1992) 41- 42 (J. Topel); *Bijdragen* 55 (1994) 209-210 (B.J. Koet); *Cumberland Sem* 28 (1990) 53-54 (R.L. Brawley); *EvQ* 63 (1991) 271-273 (J. Weatherly); *ExpT* 101 (1991) 346 (M. Davies); *FilNT* 3 (1990) 81-82 (J. Mateos); *HBT* 12 (1990) 99-101 (C.S. LaHurd); *Int* 45 (1991) 197 (M. Salmon); *JBL* 110 (1991) 165-167 (J.T. Carroll); *JES* 27 (1991) 611 (J.M. Dawsey); *JTSA* 77 (1991) 89-90 (J. Draper); *LTJ* 25 (1991) 185-186 (V.C. Pfitzner); *NT* 34 (1992) 101-102 (L.T. Johnson); *Perkins Journal* 43 (1990) 29-30 (C.C. Black); *RExp* 87 (1990) 492 (J.E. Jones); *TS* 51 (1990) 515-517 (D. Hamm); *TToday* 47 (1990) 208-209 (J.M. Hamilton); *SJT* 44 (1991) 406-407 (I.H. Marshall); *SWJT* 32 (1990) 56 (E. Ellis); *TZ* 47 (1991) 366-368 (R.B. Sloan).

40. Problematic also is Moessner's assertion that Moses' death is vicarious and that Mosaic typology highlights the atoning significance of Jesus' death (pp. 322-323). Dt 32,50-51 asserts that Moses dies outside the land because of his own sin. See the critical comments of Jon Weatherly (in *EvQ* 63 [1991] 272) and E. MAYER, *Die Reiseerzählung des Lukas (Lk 9,51–19,10): Entscheidung in der Wüste* (Europäische Hochschulschriften, 23/554), Frankfurt am Main, 1996, p. 33-34.

41. See Appendix IV.

42. See also Eva Osswald's remark: "Nach seiner [i.e. O.H. Steck's] Ansicht beruht Neh. 9,26 auf der generellen deuteronomistischen Prophetenaussage (dtrPA), die allerdings im deuteronomistischen Geschichtswerk nur einmal in 2. Kö. 17,7-20 vorkommt. Von einem generell gewaltsamen Geschick ist freilich in 2. Kö. 17,13f. nicht die Rede" (in her review of Steck in *TLZ* 93 [1968], p. 830).

43. Cf. C.C. Black's review in *Perkins Journal* 43 (1990,3-4), p. 29: "On what basis, other than concurrence with O.H. Steak [sic] (pp. 83-84), are these and not other "tenets" abstracted? Not only do modern *Alttestamentlicher* [sic] differ in their assessments of Deuteronomic theology; there are structural and thematic variances between Deuteron-

monolithic view of rebellious Israel as in tenet C[44]. Thirdly, the way Moessner combines the fourfold typology of the prophet Moses in Dt (cf. Lk 9,1-50) and the four tenets of the popular deuteronomistic view of Israel's prophetic history (cf. Lk 9,51–19,44) is rather cumbersome[45]. Fourthly, a similar problem arises with Moessner's combination of the notion of a prophet like Moses journeying on a new exodus with the notion of a guest at meals[46]. In short, we fully agree with John T. Carroll when he states: "In my judgment, the author (i.e. D. Moessner) finds too much coherence in the Lucan travel narrative, now and then forcing the data to fit the interpretative grid being placed upon Luke's story (the grid provided by the deuteronomistic pattern of Israel's history and the Moses/Jesus typology)"[47]. This may explain why Moessner himself is not always consistent concerning what motif finally forms the organizing principle of the LkTN[48].

omy and the Deuteronomic History, as well as among the components of that History (e.g. Judges and 1-2 Kings). Even if a simplified Deuteronomic pattern is perceptible in the Third Gospel, who is perceiving the correspondences: Luke or Moessner?". Cf. H. WEIPPERT, *Das deuteronomistische Geschichtswerk. Sein Ziel und Ende in der neuren Forschung*, in *ThRu* 50 (1985) 213-249; H.D. PREUSCH, *Zum deuteronomistischen Geschichtswerk*, in *ThRu* 58 (1983) 229-264.341-395.

44. Cf. C.C. BLACK, review in *Perkins Journal* 43 (1990), p. 30: "Can Luke be said to adjudge Israel as monolithically repudiative of Jesus (pp. 113-18; 191-99 *et passim*) if some in that nation, even some Pharisees, are favorably disposed or at least partially friendly toward him (cf. Luke 6:17-19; 13:31; Acts 5:34-39; 23:6-10)"; J.T. CARROLL, review in *JBL* 110 (1991) 167: "Moessner tends to lump the people – and even the apostles and disciples – with the Pharisees, as one wicked, rebellious generation. In the end, Luke depicts monolitic rejection of Jesus (with the exception of a few child-like who penitently receive him). Does this analysis miss important nuances in Luke's characterisation of the people, Pharisees, and disciples – particularly in view of the developments in the first part of Acts?".

45. See esp. D. MOESSNER, *Lord of the Banquet* (n. 30), pp. 260-262, and the critical comment of E. Mayer (*Die Reiseerzählung* [n. 40], pp. 34-35).

46. See John Topel's review in *BTB* 22 (1992), p. 42: "Although Moessner developed this suggestion of Grundmann, I am still uncertain of the relation between these concepts either in Dt or in Lk-Ac. If they are to serve as a unifying motif in the CS, the concept itself has to be more unified than it appears here. Consequently I am still more impressed with Grundmann's notion of Jesus as a teacher of the way to Luke's Church as the central organizing motif of the CS"; and a similar remark of J.T. Carroll in his review in *JBL* 110 (1991), p. 167: "Indeed, is it legitimate to link so closely the motifs of meal and journey (Moessner speaks of the 'journeying guest' motif), so that the one motif may be seen as implying also the other? This linkage of meal and travel is crucial to Moessner's claim that sayings and journeying cohere in Luke's central section, yet it is questionable whether that connection is firmly established".

47. *Ibid*. (n. 46), p. 166.

48. Thus writes C. Clifton Black in his review in *Perkins Journal* 43 (1990,3-4), p. 30: "Not only is the portrait of Moses proposed as '*the organizing principle* for the whole of [Luke's] Central Section' (p. 60, author's emphasis; cf. p. 285); 'the journeying guest who eats and drinks as Lord of the Banquet' is also identified as this material's 'Integrating Motif' (pp. 173-86). Though consolidated by Moessner into a putative Deuteronomic

3. *The formative influence of the Old Testament way-conquest (and exodus) traditions on the Synoptic journey narrative*

Building further on the work of Evans and Moessner, Willard M. Swartley (1994) has developed another type of OT influence on the journey narrative of Luke (9,51–19,44) within an overall structuring influence of OT traditions on the structure of the Synoptic Gospels[49]. The Synoptic Gospels have a common structure, he says, which consists of a Galilean section, a Journey to Jerusalem section, and a Jerusalem section[50]. John gives a different outline of Jesus' movements between Jerusalem and Galilee – showing three trips north and south. There have been several efforts to explain why the Synoptics present Jesus' ministry within the distinctive "Galilee–journey–Jerusalem" structure.

Swartley proposes a rationale for the distinctive macro-structure of the Synoptics, as opposed to that of the Johannine and non-canonical Gospels. He argues that Israel's fundamental faith traditions have shaped the content and structure of the Synoptics' stories of Jesus[51]. He even contends that the case for a sequential, formative influence (i.e. exodus, conquest, temple, and kingship) upon the structural and theological design of the Synoptics is very strong[52].

Within the Old Testament, there are two sets of traditions: the Exodus/Sinai and the conquest traditions on the one hand, and the temple and kingship traditions on the other[53]. The four themes of divine redemptive activity that shape the Synoptic story (exodus, way-conquest, temple, and kingship) already appear in one of Israel's earliest poetic articulations of faith, the famous Song of the Sea in Exodus 15,1-18: vv. 1a-12: the Lord's salvation at the sea; vv. 13-16: the Lord leads the conquest; v. 17: the Lord brings his people to the sanctuary; v. 18: the Lord will reign for ever and ever (pp. 32-33). These respective sets of traditions,

schema, may not these and other themes have been juggled by Luke throughout the travel account, without systematic synthesis? Would such a possibility have been as offensive to an ancient historian as it may seem to some modern, literary-critical sensibilities?"

49. W.M. SWARTLEY, *Israel's Scripture* (n. 10).

50. Swartley admits that within this common design there is also variation (*ibid.*, p. 39, n. 27).

51. *Ibid.*, pp. 4-5.

52. *Ibid.*, p. 6.

53. The exodus-Sinai and conquest traditions (the first set) were developed in pre-monarchical Israel and were nurtured in the north (countryside) before there ever was a Zion; they are, among other texts, reflected in Psalms 75, 77, 78, 80, 81, 105, 106, 114, 136. The temple and kingship traditions (the second set) seem to be more recent: they were developed during the monarchy or even earlier, they had an original southern (city) setting and were in various ways promulgated throughout Israel; they are represented by Psalms 20, 46, 48, 76, 84, 87, 89, 97, 99, 101, 132 (*ibid.*, p. 37).

however different in origin and distinct in meaning they may have been, could not remain completely isolated. In the course of history, they were blended together in complementary, and sometimes critical, relationship (e.g. Jer 7,1-15; Ps 50). Second Isaiah played a major role in revitalizing and blending these traditions. His use of both the older and younger faith traditions of Israel sets a structural model for the Synoptics' story of Jesus[54].

In chapters 3-6, Swartley develops his thesis that the theological emphases of the Synoptics' Galilean and journey sections correlate with the Old Testament (northern) theological traditions: the exodus and conquest traditions. Similarly, the Synoptic portraits of Jesus' Jerusalem ministry, in both the pre-passion and passion phases, correspond to the Old Testament (southern) traditions: the temple and kingship traditions. He then proposes that the four major streams of Old Testament tradition, in an overall sequential order, shaped the synoptic pattern of the Gospel tradition[55].

Swartley agrees with Evans, Drury, Goulder and Moessner that Luke's central section is a Christian Deuteronomy and that the content of Jesus' journey is modelled after the content of instruction given during Israel's journey narrated in the book of Deuteronomy[56]. Six themes permeate the narrative and are developed as three couplets. Echoing the emphases of the older story (Deut), Luke discloses Jesus as: the journeying guest/ Lord of the Banquet and rejected prophet, the bringer of peace and justice, and the disarmer of evil and agent of divine judgment. These themes are prominent in the structural design of Luke's travel narrative and disclose the influence of the deuteronomistic "entrance" and conquest traditions[57]. Yet Luke's use of Deuteronomy shows both continuity and change between the orders of Moses and those of Jesus[58]. Of the four intertextual relationships that a literary work might have to a predecessor – imitative, eclectic, heuristic, or dialectical, according to Thomas Greene[59] – Luke's central section is related to Deuteronomy in different ways: there may

---

54. *Ibid.*, pp. 37-39.

55. *Ibid.*, p. 7. This gives the following scheme: the formative influence of Old Testament exodus and Sinai traditions on the Synoptic Galilean Narrative (ch. 3); the formative influence of the Old Testament way-conquest (and exodus) traditions on the Synoptic journey narrative (ch. 4); the formative influence of Old Testament Temple traditions on the Synoptic prepassion (and passion) narrative (ch. 5); the formative influence of Old Testament kingship traditions on the Synoptic passion narrative (ch. 6).

56. *Ibid.*, p. 130.

57. *Ibid.*, pp. 132-133.

58. *Ibid.*, p. 131.

59. T.M. GREENE, *The Light in Troy: Imitation and Discovery in Renaissance Poetry*, New Haven, CT, 1982.

be a correspondence of parallel thought (P), a transformation in thought (T) or even a reversal of the thought structure, i.e. contrast (C)[60].

Swartley's study is another example of growing scholarly interest in the phenomenon of intertextuality in NT literature. His project is more ambitious than that of Moessner. He not only tries to throw light on a larger text unit within Luke (i.e. the LkTN) against the background of the OT, he even aims to demonstrate that the macro-structure of the Synoptic Gospels has been shaped by OT traditions. As to the methodology used, he describes his work as a "narrative compositional study", although redaction criticism helps him to discover the variations each evangelist introduces in this fundamental Synoptic structure. Swartley has a thorough knowledge of previous scholarly work, on which he sometimes relies too easily[61]. He is at home in finding biblical correspondences and correlations between OT types and NT antitypes. His lively interest in biblical theological motifs, themes and traditions can bring relief for scholars used to painstaking study of exegetical details. Nevertheless, the question of the validity of his main thesis cannot be avoided. One cannot deny that the four OT traditions, taken separately, have shaped the Gospels in varied ways[62]. But Swartley's overall thesis, that these OT traditions have had a sequential, formative influence upon the structural and theological design of all three Synoptics simultaneously, is too schematic to be ultimately convincing. His starting point is the postulate of a common threefold structure in each of the Synoptic Gospels[63]. He then accepts the existence of a sequential fourfold pattern of OT traditions. Next, this fourfold pattern is accommodated to the threefold (or fourfold?) Synoptic structure. But is it possible to link each OT tradition to a

60. W.M. SWARTLEY, *Israel's Scripture* (n. 10), p. 139, n. 117.

61. Cf. J.T. CARROLL, review of W.M. Swartley in *CBQ* 57 (1995), p. 610: "Frequently, he [i.e. W.M. Swartley] advances a controversial interpretation, depending on the work of another scholar but failing to make a case for the view (e.g., Jesus in Luke as 'journeying guest and banquet host' [Moessner]; Jesus in Matthew as 'Wisdom and Shekinah' [Burnett]; the imagery of blind and lame in Matt 21:15 implying their status as 'Israel's Jebusite enemies' [Gundry]; Christ as Zion [adapted from Donaldson])".

62. See e.g. U. MAUSER, *Christ in the Wilderness: The Wilderness Theme in the Second Gospel and its Basis in the Biblical Tradition*, London, 1963; J.B. CHANCE, *Jerusalem, the Temple and the New Age in Luke-Acts*, Macon, GA, 1988; F.D. WEINERT, *The Meaning of the Temple in Luke-Acts*, in *BTB* 11 (1981) 85-89.

63. Swartley is not consistent in his division of the Synoptic basic structure: on p. 39 he speaks of a "Galilee–journey–Jerusalem"–structure, later of the "Galilee–Jerusalem structure" (e.g. p. 43), and p. 38 it is said that "the Synoptic structure is not simply 'Galilee–Jerusalem,' but 'Galilee–Jerusalem–Return to Galilee' (in Mark and Matthew)"; but in chapters 3-6 he distinguishes in fact a fourfold Synoptic structure: Galilean Narrative–Journey Narrative–Prepassion Narrative–Passion Narrative. How this view (these views) relates to the numerous studies on the structure of respectively Mk, Mt, Lk and Jn, is not clear or at least not sufficiently treated (pp. 39-43).

specific part of the Gospel Narrative[64]? And should not alternative explanations for the Synoptic structural pattern be considered more carefully[65]? As regards the LkTN, it remains difficult to equate Jesus' journey to Jerusalem, as narrated by Luke, with the journey to the Promised Land, let alone with the conquest of the Promised Land. Jesus' journey takes place within the borders of the Promised Land. He does not walk towards the Promised Land, but to Jerusalem, the place of death and ascension[66].

4. The Influence of Deutero-Isaiah and the New Exodus of the King-Messiah

In a recent monograph on the Davidic Messiah in Luke-Acts (1995)[67], Mark L. Strauss rightly criticizes the Deuteronomy hypothesis as it was developed by Moessner and others. Moessner puts too much stress on the Moses typology and, furthermore, he links the motif of the rejected prophet too exclusively with the Book of Deuteronomy. Luke sees Jesus' role and destiny in the line of the whole prophetic tradition (cf. the parallels with Elijah in Lk 7,11-17; 9,10-17.38-43, and with Elisha in 5,12-16;

---

64. Cf. J. MARCUS, review of W.M. Swartley in *The Princeton Seminary Bulletin* 16 (1995,1), p. 88: "For example, Jesus' kingship (= messiahship) is announced in each Gospel from the word go, not just in the final section, and it becomes a major theme already in the Matthean and Lukan birth narratives. It is also a more serious problem than Swartley acknowledges that the temple is a leitmotif throughout Luke's Gospel, not just in the penultimate section. And if in all three Synoptics Jesus is the divine warrior, as Swartley persuasively argues, then this real victory, his 'conquest', is achieved in his death and resurrection, not in the way up to Jerusalem in the central section".

65. J.T. CARROLL (n. 61), p. 610: "Especially problematic in a consideration of historical issues (notably, the emergence of the synoptic structure) is the author's neglect of a basic question: To what extent was the 'synoptic design' shaped by an early Christian tradition informed by historical memory? (For example, did Jesus actually carry out – in Galilee – a ministry resonating with liberation themes from the exodus? Did Jesus provoke his arrest with his action in the temple? Did the issue of kingship figure in his crucifixion?) To be sure, S. eschews reductionism on this score, but he cannot make his case that the synoptic pattern is determined by OT traditions without considering such alternative explanations".

66. Cf. J.M. DAWSEY, *Jesus' Pilgrimage to Jerusalem*, in *Perspectives in Religious Studies* 14 (1987) 217-232, p. 221: "...the view that the central section of the gospel is modelled on the Exodus event remains difficult. In spite of many similarities, the journey-motif in Luke is of an inherently different type than the Old Testament Exodus. The Lucan journey takes place in its entirety in the traditional Promised Land. In this regard, it might be significant that Peter's messianic confession was moved from the far northern reaches of Galilee to Jerusalem. Jesus does not walk toward the Promised Land, but resolutely walks through it toward his death".

67. M.L. STRAUSS, *The Davidic Messiah in Luke-Acts. The Promise and its Fulfillment in Lukan Christology* (JSNT SS, 110), Sheffield, 1995.

7,2-10). All important biblical characters, like Moses, Elijah, David and the Suffering Servant, have affected Luke's christology. On the other hand Luke's redaction of Jesus' approach to, and entrance into, Jerusalem has strong royal and Davidic implications: Jesus enters the city not primarily as a Mosaic but as a royal-Davidic figure.

Strauss also thinks that Luke's model is not the book Deuteronomy, but Deutero-Isaiah. In the Book of Consolation (Isa 40–55) the exodus memory has undergone a prophetic transformation and reinterpretation: the imagery recalling the Exodus from Egypt is used to describe the eschatological return of the exiles from Babylon to Jerusalem. This return is pictured as a "new exodus" to the promised land[68]. Isaiah's wording of the eschatological new exodus is the primary OT model for Luke's exodus' motif: "As the Isaianic eschatological deliverer, Jesus acts as God's instrument in both announcing and bringing to fulfillment God's eschatological reign and kingdom. Empowered by the Spirit, he defeats the forces of sin and Satan and leads God's people in an eschatological new exodus"[69]. Luke understands the Travel Narrative as a "new exodus" where Jesus guides God's people, according to the model of Isa 40–55. In Isa 55,3, but still more explicitly in Isa 11, the coming Davidic King plays a key role in the eschatological regathering, or "new exodus".

Luke's work is permeated with imagery drawn from Isaiah's portrait of eschatological salvation. It is not surprising, then, that Luke would also pick up the Isaianic theme of an eschatological new exodus, according to Strauss. The first exodus centered on Yahweh leading his people out of Egypt to the promised land. The Isaianic new exodus begins with the glorious return of Yahweh to his people (Isa 40,3-5), after which he gathers and leads them (Isa 40,11). The latter is closer to Luke's presentation. The quotation of Isa 40,3-5 in Lk 3,4-6 sets the universalist tune (Isa 40,5; Lk 3,6), which points to the Gentile mission. When Jesus has fulfilled his Exodus, the Gentiles will receive salvation (σωτήριον in Isa 40,5; Lk 3,6, Acts 28,28; cf. Lk 2,30-32). The reference to a road prepared for the coming of the Lord who brings salvation (Isa 40,5; Lk 3,6) recalls the theme of God visiting his people (ἐπισκέπτομαι in Lk 1,68.78; 7,16; cf. 7,18-23; 19,41-44). This description remarkably parallels the Isaianic description of the new exodus: Yahweh himself comes to his people, delivering them through his messianic envoy. Moreover, in Isaiah, the goal of the new exodus is Jerusalem/Zion, where Yahweh's

68. *Ibid.*, pp. 285-305.
69. *Ibid.*, p. 284.

glory will be revealed (Isa 40,5; 52,10) and where he will reign as king (Isa 52,7; cf. 41,21; 43,15; 44,6). In Luke, too, the emphasis is on Jerusalem as Jesus' goal. It is there he fulfills his ἔξοδος, resulting in his exaltation and heavenly enthronement[70].

If the new exodus refers to a time of salvation which begins with the coming of Jesus, then the notion of "exodus" (explicitly mentioned in Lk 9,31) possibly encompasses the whole way of Jesus (ὁδός in Lk 1,76; 3,4; 7,27) and not only the Lukan travel narrative, although the focus is on the events in Jerusalem. In Luke, the term thus becomes a metaphor for the eschatological time of salvation inaugurated with the coming of Jesus, according to Strauss[71].

Strauss' work deals with Luke's christology, not with the LkTN. He nevertheless rightly stresses the christological aspect of this section and the preponderant role of Deutero-Isaiah in Luke's biblical thinking[72]. Strauss is not the only author who thinks that Luke describes Jesus' journey to Jerusalem as a New Exodus, of which the exodus of the people of Israel from Egypt under Moses' leadership is a proto-type. The link can be made either with reference to Exodus–Deuteronomy (Ringe, Dawsey, Moessner), or with reference to Deutero-Isaiah (Strauss[73]). This typological interpretation of Jesus' journey is often linked to Lk 9,31, where the term ἔξοδος is said to have a larger meaning than just a reference to "death". That ἔξοδος can refer to death is clear from other texts like 2 Pet 1,15; Wis 3,2; 7,6; and Jos. *Ant.* 4,8,2,189. That this "departure" is to take place ἐν Ἰερουσαλήμ pleads for this meaning in Lk 9,31 too. Nevertheless, the fact that Lk also says that Jesus ἤμελλεν πληροῦν his exodus has brought some authors to the idea that the subsequent events of resurrection and ascension, which also take place in Jerusalem, are an

---

70. *Ibid.*, pp. 298-300.

71. *Ibid.*, p. 304.

72. Cf. J.A. SANDERS, *Isaiah in Luke*, in C.A. EVANS and J.A. SANDERS, *Luke and Scripture. The Function of Sacred Tradition in Luke-Acts*, Minneapolis, MN, 1993, pp. 14-25. This becomes clear when one compares the number of citations or allusions of the OT books in Luke (according to NA[26]) (for each book, we give the number of chapters and the number of quotations and allusions in Luke: Gen: 50/53; Exod: 40/30; Lev: 27/20; Num: 35/6; Deut: 34/27; Josh: 24/1; Judg: 19/9; Ruth: 4/3; 1 Sam: 25/15; 2 Sam: 24/13; 1 Kings: 22/17; 2 Kings: 23/11; 1 Chron: 29/6; 2 Chron: 36/4; Ezra: 10/3; Neh: 13/2; Esther: 10/1; Job: 42/7; Ps: 150/76; Prov: 31/7 Eccles: 12/1; Cant: 8/0; Isa: 66/80 (Isa: ch. 40-66: 17/46); Jer: 51/21; Lam: 5/1; Ezek: 48/16; Dan: 12/25; Hos: 14/7; Joel: 3/2; Amos: 1/3; Obad: 1/0; Jonah: 4/3; Micah: 7/7; Nahum: 3/1; Hab: 3/2; Zeph: 3/0; Hag: 2/2; Zech: 14/6; Mal: 4/6; 3 Esdras: /0; 4 Esdras: /1; 1 Macc: 16/2; 2 Macc: 15/2; Tob: 14/8; Jdt: 16/2; Bar: 5/1; Eccles: 51/10.

73. STRAUSS, *Davidic Messiah* (n. 67), chapter 6, pp. 285-305.

integral part of this "departure"[74], or even that Jesus, like Moses, leads forth on a journey, an ἔξοδος, a journey of liberation[75]. However, we think that Lk 9,31 is not a reference to the OT exodus tradition, but simply an euphemism for death. In the LXX the term ἔξοδος sometimes refers to the exodus event (Ex 19,1; Num 33,38; 1 Kgs 6,1; Ps 113,1), but the word then is occurring within a rather fixed formula ἐξόδος (τῶν υἱῶν) Ἰσραηλ ἐξ (ἐκ γῆς) Αἰγύπτου, which stresses the moment of leaving Egypt[76]. Moreover, in Acts 13,24: the beginning of Jesus' ministry is called ἔισοδος[77], to which "his" departure, i.e. his death, in Jerusalem corresponds. "We need to recognize that our text (Lk 9,31) is concerned with 'his exodus', rather than an exodus of which he is moving force or leader"[78].

74. Cf. J. FITZMYER, *Luke II*, p. 800; S.R. GARRETT, *Exodus from Bondage: Luke 9:31 and Acts 12:1-24*, in *CBQ* 52 (1990) 656-680, esp. p. 677: "In his account of the transfiguration Luke remarks that Jesus discussed with Moses and Elijah the 'exodus' that Jesus was to complete in Jerusalem. Luke's use of this term was neither casual nor insignificant, but a pointed allusion to Jesus' death and exaltation, conceptualized as a deliverance of 'the people who sat in darkness' from bondage to Satan, the prince of darkness and ruler of this world". Another application of the exodus-typology is given by J. MANEK, *The New Exodus in the Books of Luke*, in *NT* 2 (1957-58) 8-23: "the exodus in Luke's account is the leaving of the sepulchre, the realm of death, and not in any way Jesus' end, His death, His crucifixion" (p. 12). "Originally the word 'exodus' means only 'going out'. In the history of Israel, however, it became a covering concept of the way out of Egypt to Palestine in all its phases" (p. 13). "Moses led his people into the Promised Land and on the way out of Egypt he had to cross the Red Sea. Jesus led the new Israel from the earthly Jerusalem (= Egypt) to the heavenly Jerusalem and had to go through suffering and the cross" (p. 15). The fall of Jerusalem corresponds to the annihilation of the Egyptians (in the red sea) (p. 15). "the presence of the Resurrected Lord for forty days (between the resurrection and ascension) has as prototype the forty years' journey of Israel to the Promised Land" (p. 19); "The entrance into the Promised Land, Palestine, has its analogy in the New exodus in Jesus' ascent to heaven, which is the conclusion of the entire New Testament Exodus in Luke's conception" (p. 19).

75. Cf. S.H. RINGE, *Luke 9:28-36: The Beginning of An Exodus*, in M.A. TOLBERT (ed.), *The Bible and Feminist Hermeneutics* (Semeia, 28), Chico, CA, 1983, pp. 83-99, esp. p. 94, with reference to Lk 9,31-32: "It is this journey itself which appears to be the ἔξοδος to which the splendid visitors refer".

76. Thus S.H. RINGE, *art. cit.* (n. 75), p. 93 rightly states: "Mánek's recognition that the word ἔξοδος clearly recalls the journey on which Moses led the Israelites to freedom is important, but he overlooks the fact that in the biblical traditions themselves ἔξοδος refers particularly to the beginning event of that journey (going out from Egypt) and not to its conclusion"; in n. 24 she refers to the four texts mentioned (except Ps 105,37 [LXX 104,38] instead of Ps 113,1) and to Philo, *Migr. Abr.* 15,151 and *Vit. Mos.* I,105,122; II (III) 248; Fl. Josephus, *Ant* 2,271; 3,305; 5,72; 8,61; *Test.Sol.* 25,5; Heb 11,2; 2 Pet 1,15. J. Nolland (*Luke II*, p. 449) agrees with Ringe's remark: "It is surely…an excess to embrace in 'exodus' the whole Mosaic saga of deliverance from Egypt through to possession of the promised land".

77. W.C. ROBINSON, Jr., *The Theological Context for Interpreting Luke's Travel Narrative*, in *JBL* 79 (1960) 20-31 (= *Der theologische Interpretationszusammenhang des lukanischen Reiseberichtes*, in G. BRAUMANN [ed.], *Das Lukas-Evangelium*, Darmstadt, 1974, pp. 115-134), p. 23, points to this connection.

78. J. NOLLAND, *Luke II*, p. 500, who further says: "Feuillet (*RevThom* 77 [1977] 191) helpfully correlates 'exodus' here with ἀνάλημψις, 'receiving up', in 9:51. Both terms des-

5. The typological use of the Old Testament motif of the "Wandering in the Wilderness" in Luke's Travel Narrative

In his doctoral dissertation *Die Reiseerzählung des Lukas (Lk 9,51-19,10): Entscheidung in der Wüste*, published in the Series Theology of the European University Studies (1996), Edgar Mayer explores another possible Old Testament background for Luke's Travel Narrative[79]. Along the lines of Darrell L. Bock and others, he points to the phenomenon of typology in Luke-Acts. Although it is not easy to offer a generally accepted definition of typology, it is possible to give a description of the way it functions in a literary work[80]. In Luke-Acts, there are some clear examples of typology: one can point to the typology between John the Baptist and Jesus in the Infancy Narrative, the typological use of Jesus' passion as a model (typos) for the post-resurrection experiences of the disciples (Stephen, Peter and Paul), and to the OT typologies in short passages like Lk 4,24-27 and 11,29-32 and in the longer episode of Acts 7,2-53 (where the Moses/Jesus typology is worked out). This leads to the question how other examples of typology can be detected in Luke's work[81].

Building further on a suggestion made by David A.S. Ravens, that the three pericopes of the feeding, the transfiguration and the healing of the

ignate the end of the earthly career of Jesus; where the former puts the accent on his death (but in the context of what is to follow), the latter focuses on his ascension to glory".

79. E. MAYER, *Die Reiseerzählung des Lukas (Lk 9,51-19,10): Entscheidung in der Wüste* (Europäische Hochschulschriften, 23/554), Frankfurt am Main, 1996.

80. *Ibid.*, p. 49: "Unter Berücksichtigung der besprochenen sechs Problemfelder, die bei einer Definition des Begriffes 'Typologie' beachtet werden müssen, soll nun der Sachverhalt der Typologie wie folgt bestimmt werden: Eine Typologie ist die intendierte Ausrichtung auf Vorherbilder. Die Vorherbilder oder Typen bestehen beispielsweise aus Gestalten, Einrichtungen oder Handlungsabläufen. Sie dienen als Verstehenshintergrund der entsprechenden Gegebenheiten oder Antitypen, die auf sie ausgerichtet sind. Die Vorherbilder oder Typen werden dabei zunächts in ihrem ursprünglichen Kontext (historischer oder literarischer Kontext) belassen und ernst genommen, aber die Korrespondenz zwischen Typen und Antitypen kann dann vor allem bei den neutestamentlichen Autoren noch eine intensivere Interpretation erfahren (z. B.: Steigerung, beauftragte Nachahmung, Prophetie)".

81. *Ibid.*, p. 58: "Zusammenfassend bleibt zu wiederholen, dass nur eine entsprechende Anhäufung von Einzelhinweisen eine sachgemässe Erfassung von Typologien erlaubt. Dabei sind bezüglich der Einzelhinweise fünf Fragestellungen wichtig. Erstens: Gibt der lukanische Text konkrete Anstazpunkte, die eine typologische Ausführung erwarten lassen? Zweitens: Kann ein längerer Handlungsablauf auf typologische Vorbilder zurückgeführt werden und lassen sich dabei überzeugende Indizienketten vorweisen? Drittens: Zeigen Wortsignale die Verwendung von literarischen Vorlagen an, aus denen Typen gewonnen worden sind? Viertens: Hat Lukas alttestamentliche Typen bereits durch eine eigene Darstellung der alttestamentlichen Heilsgeschichte skizziert? Fünftens: Üben bei Lukas alttestamentliche Zitate mit programmatischem Charakter einen typologischen Einfluss aus?".

possessed boy after the disciples' lack of faith in Lk 9 are intended to recall Israel's wilderness experiences of the feeding with manna, Moses on Sinai and Israel's lack of faith in making the golden calf[82], Mayer argues that even a larger series of typological correspondences can be detected in Luke's Gospel:

Luke	Exodus
1. The feeding of 5000 teaches the people about Jesus and they hear the preaching of the Kingdom of God (Lk 9,10b-17).	1. The feeding with manna teaches the people about God and is linked with teachings to them (Exod 16);
2. In front of the mountain of transfiguration and on it Jesus is fully revealed and the teaching about his person forms the basis of the teaching of following Jesus (Lk 9,18-36).	2. In front of the mountain Sinai and on the mountain, God is revealed and the teaching about his person forms the basis of the commandments toward Israel (Exod 19,3-6; 20–24).
3. After the events on the mountain of transfiguration the people acts against the christological revelation and against Jesus' teaching of following him (Lk 9,37-50).	3. After the revelation of God on the mountain Sinai the people acts against the divine revelation and against God's commandments (Exod 32).
4. Jesus' journey to Jerusalem (Lk 9,51–19,10).	4. The wandering of the people in the wilderness.
5. Jesus' passion and resurrection as a transition to glory, as a victory over the demonic powers and a hope for a future resurrection for all (Lk 19,11-24,53).	5. The exodus from Egypt as a liberation of the people from the slavery in Egypt and the entrance into the promised land.

According to Mayer, the Travel Narrative forms the missing link of a consequent, typological chain of events in Luke's Gospel. Mayer first establishes the threefold typological reference of Lk 9[83]. He then argues that Jesus' passion and resurrection in Jerusalem can be understood as a salvific Exodus event (cf. Lk 9,31)[84]. And finally, he develops the thesis

82. D.A.S. RAVENS, *Luke 9.7-62 and the Prophetic Role of Jesus*, in *NTS* 36 (1990) 119-129, esp. p. 121: "The Three miracles of the feeding (9.12-17), the transfiguration (9.28-36) and the healing of the possessed boy after the disciples' lack of faith (9.38-43) are presumably intended to recall Israel's wilderness experiences of the manna feeding, Moses on Sinai and Israel's lack of faith by making the golden calf. These events are described in detail in Exodus and, more briefly, in Deuteronomy where the order is different. Deuteronomy places the Sinai–Horeb incidents (Deut 4.10-15; 5.22-31) before the manna feeding (8.3,16) but Luke's order follows that of Exodus (chaps. 16,19,24 and 34,32)".

83. MAYER, *Reiseerzählung* (n. 79), pp. 118-134.

84. *Ibid.*, pp. 134-173, esp. p. 172: "Der in Lk 9,31 erwähnte Exodus/ἔξοδος, den Jesus in Jerusalem vollbringen wird, konnte aufgrund einer sprachlichen Untersuchung des Begriffs ἔξοδος, einer Untersuchung des Abrahammotivs bei Lukas, der acht Tage in

that the wandering in the wilderness forms the hermeneutical context of Luke's Travel Narrative. The last thesis is not new[85], but Mayer argues it comprehensively[86]. The problem with this sequence is that it is composed of five parallels of quite different nature: the first three belong to the same context (Lk 9) and refer to a pericope (in Lk) and specific texts in Exod, the fifth one is rather an interpretation of the fundamental Christ event (his passion and resurrection) in the light of an OT motif

Lk 9,28, sowie der beiden proleptischen Abschnitte Lk 4,28-30 und 8,22-9,6 als ein heilbringender Exodus durch Jesu Leiden und Auferstehung bestimmt werden. Dieses Resultat überzeugt, weil ja nur genügend Hinweise gefunden werden mussten, um den konkreten Hinweis auf Jesu ἔξοδος in Lk 9,31 tatsächlich als einen heilbringenden Exodus aufzufassen".

85. Cf. DRURY, *Tradition* (n. 15), p. 140: "…a handbook on the Christian life in the historical setting of a journey to Jerusalem, just as Deuteronomy is a guide for the devout Jew set in the historical perspective of the journey into the promised land with Jerusalem…"; J.M. DAWSEY, *Jesus' Pilgrimage* (n. 66), pp. 218-224, has suggested that the central section of Luke was organized with the pilgrimage experience in mind; he tried to show that it joins Jesus' journey to the festival in Jerusalem to a specific memory of the Exodus event found in Moses' speeches in Deuteronomy and in the theme of the wandering in the wilderness; see p. 220: "…the impression of aimless wandering in Luke parallels the experience of the people of Israel in the wilderness; the sense of timelessness and the indefinite geography of both end at Jericho; the conflict between Jesus and his followers in the travel narrative is reminiscent of the confrontations between Moses and the congregation of Israel; and a community of the elect arises in each narrative out of the midst of a large multitude of followers"; cf. MOESSNER, *Lord of the Banquet* (n. 30), p. 280: "In Deuteronomy…a dynamic, bifocal tension is sustained, moving the story from Moses' ascent of Horeb to his ascent of Mt. Nebo… We have charted the same bifocal tension in the chain of travel notices which reach back to Jesus' ascent of the mountain in Luke 9 and sending to Jerusalem, where, again, he ascends a mountain to climax the journey (Luke 24 – Acts 1)"; cf. W. ROTH, *Disclosure at Emmaus*, in *Bible Today* 31 (1993) 46-51, esp. p. 48: "From Luke 9:51 on, Moses' and his people's wandering is evidently the foil for what Jesus and his followers do and say, until they reach Jerusalem".

86. E. MAYER, *Reiseerzählung* (n. 79), pp. 288-320. He develops three arguments for this thesis: (1) There are some smaller striking indications ("verschiedene Einzelhinweise"): an agreement at the beginning (the seventy [two] and their power to tread upon serpents and scorpions in Lk 10,1.17; cf. the seventy elders after the departure from Sinai Num 11) and the end (Jericho in Lk 18,35-19,10 and Jos 6). The motifs of grumbling (Lk 15,2; 19,7) and wandering (of Jesus Lk 9,51 and the multitudes with him Lk 11,29-32; 14,25) could well be integrated in a typology of "wandering in the wilderness" (cf. διαγογγύζω in LXX Exod 15,24; 16,2.7.8; 17,3; Num 14,2.36; 16,11; Dt 1,27; Jos 9,18). (2) Luke's interpretation of the OT wandering in the wilderness (Acts 7,2-53) and the LkTN have in common the deuteronomistic view of history in connection with a wandering motif. From this it seems plausible that the LkTN is written in the light of the OT wandering in the wilderness (cf. Moessner). (3) The description of Christianity as the way/ὁδός (Acts 9,1-2; 18,25-26; 19,9.23; 22,4; 24,14.22) refers to the Lukan use of Isa 40,3-5 in Lk 3,3-6. The Isaianic passage, which speaks of a preparation of the way in the wilderness, can offer an interpretative frame for the LkTN. This OT background of the LkTN gives room for a typological interpretation: Jesus and the people are wandering in the wilderness, during which Jesus calls the people to repentance, thus to preparing the way in the wilderness, in order to prepare the coming of the Lord, i.e. Jesus' coming to Jerusalem, and finally his parousia.

becoming a fundamental theological paradigma (i.e. the exodus concept), the fourth parallel is between two larger sections (in Lk and the Pentateuch). There is also a problem with the order of the sequence: the "exodus", which in the OT is the starting event of the whole narration, forms the last element in Luke's sequence. Mayer stresses the fact that for the first three parallels, Lk does not follow the order of Dt, but the (historical) order of Exodus. But if the nature and the position of the fifth correspondence is questionable, then the insertion of the fourth typological parallelism also becomes doubtful.

CONCLUSION

We have presented five proposals which claim to offer an explanation for the existence and specific nature of the central section of Luke. It is time now to draw some conclusions from our investigation or to formulate some observations.

At first sight, it looks as if the results of our survey are rather negative. We have indeed expressed some critical comments about the deuteronomistic hypothesis in its different forms (Evans, Moessner, Swartley), on the concept of the "New Exodus" (Strauss), and on the typological use of the OT motif of the "wandering in the wilderness" (Mayer) as a means of explaining the existence and the specific nature of the LkTN. This does not mean that the discussion initiated by C.F. Evans' stimulating essay has not borne fruit. A growing awareness of the great variety of OT influence on Lk or of Lukan use of the OT, a wealth of detailed studies on certain passages, an insight into the way Lk rethinks and rewrites the traditional Jesus story in the light of OT texts, motifs and figures, the preponderant role of Dt-Isa on Lk–Acts: all these issues have been spelt out and enriched in the course of forty years of scholarly discussion. Let me make three more observations, which at the same time are suggestions for further research.

Christological aspects

Christology is an important aspect of the LkTN. Studies of Lukan christology have pointed to the "basic christological category of Messiah–Servant–Prophet" in Luke's work[87], which is a confluence of

___

87. Cf. D.L. BOCK, *Proclamation from Prophecy and Pattern: Luke's Use of The Old Testament for Christology and Mission*, in C.A. EVANS & W.R. STEGNER (eds.), *The Gospels and the Scriptures of Israel* (JSNT SS, 104), Sheffield, 1994, pp. 280-307, esp. p. 284; M.L. STRAUSS, *Davidic Messiah* (n. 67), p. 341-342: "When Isaiah is read as a unity, the eschato-

different OT categories. The question is how these OT figures are combined in Luke's christological synthesis. "Sometimes it is suggested that Luke's Christology is rather patchwork in character, but this is not the case with his presentation through the Old Testament. Luke has kept the fundamental portrait of Jesus as the regal, Davidic hope in forefront of almost every text. Other functions also are tied to him. The image of the servant and of the prophet also appear in places, but the messiah dominates"[88]. Maybe this predominance of the royal-messianic aspect is reflected in the fact that within the LkTN there appears to be a shift from the motif of the rejected prophet, which dominates the first part of the LkTN (Lk 9,51-62; 13,33-34) into that of the rejected king at the end of the LkTN (Lk 19,11-28.29-44). As regards Luke's prophet christology: it must be said that it is partly Moses-oriented (Lk 9,35/Dt 18,15?; Acts 3,22-23; 7,37), but the Moses typology (Jesus a prophet like Moses) is more explicit in Acts than it is in the gospel itself[89], and even there it would be an exaggeration to say that Luke is a representative of the deuteronomistic school[90]. Elijah and probably other prophets were certainly also in Luke's mind when he described Jesus as a prophet[91].

logical deliverer is at the same time Davidic king, suffering servant of Yahweh and eschatological prophet. Luke's christological presentation remarkably parallels this Isaianic portrait.... The prophet-like suffering of the messianic king was prophesied in Scripture and was a necessary stage on the 'way' to his glorious enthronement at God's right hand".

88. Cf. D.L. BOCK, *Proclamation* (n. 87), p. 293-294.

89. Cf. C.C. BLACK, review of Moessner in *Perkins Journal* 43 (1990,3-4), p. 30: "Although Jesus is explicitly cast in the role of a prophet like Moses in Acts (3:22-23 and 7:37; cf. Luke 9:35), the panoply of alleged parallels between Jesus and Moses in Luke 9:1–19:44 will strike some readers as less than convincing (e.g. pp. 60-70; 272-77). Similarly, if we are supposed to regard "the [Mosaic]prophet as the *prime* character model for the narrative world of Luke-Acts" (p. 7, emphasis mine; cf pp. 55-56), then Luke botched the job badly (cf 2:11; 9:18-22; Acts 2:36; 13:38-39)".

90. Cf. T. RÖMER & J.-D. MACCHI, *Luke, Disciple of the Deuteronomistic School*, in C.M. TUCKETT (ed.), *Luke's Literary Achievement. Collected Essays* (JSNT SS, 116), Sheffield, 1995, pp.178-187.

91. Cf. J. FITZMYER, *Luke*, p. 793: "Jesus as a new Moses is not a strong motif in the Lucan Gospel, as it is in Mt; if it is present here, it is inherited from the tradition and finds little development of it in the rest of the Lucan writings"; J. NOLLAND, *Luke*, p. 503: "Jesus is not specifically seen as a new Moses, yet Moses is his predecessor in the unfolding of the purposes of God". For possible references to the prophet Elijah, we can point to the following parallels: Jesus does miracles outside his "own country" (Lk 4,23.25-26/1 Kgs 17,1); Jesus refuses to bid fire come down from heaven and consume the unfriendly Samaritans (Lk 9,54, contrast 2 Kgs 1,10-12); Jesus demands a radical decision from his would-be followers (Lk 9,61-62/1 Kgs 19,20); Jesus has come to cast fire upon earth (Lk 3,16; 12,49/2 Kgs 1,10-12; 1 Kgs 18,38); Jesus is strengthened by an angel from heaven (Lk 22,43/1 Kgs 19,5.7); Jesus is lifted up into heaven (Lk 24,53; Acts 1,4-8; 2,1-4; cf. 2 Kgs 2,9). See G. BOSTOCK, *Jesus as the New Elisha* [4,27], in *ExpT* 92 (1980-81) 39-41; T.L. BRODIE, *Luke the Literary Interpreter. Luke-Acts as a Systematic Rewriting and Updating of the Elijah-Elisha Narrative in 1 and 2 Kings* (Diss.

Source-critical implications

Our survey has shown that sometimes the Deuteronomy hypothesis is used to enhance the plausibility of Luke's dependence on Mt (Farrer, Drury, Goulder). The central section Lk 9,51–18,14 constitutes a major problem for those who defend Luke's dependence on Mt. Indeed, we have before us a section which shows little or no agreements of order with Mt. A convenient explanation for this is thought to be given by the hypothesis that in Lk 9,51–18,14 Deuteronomy, and not Mt, is the primary basis of Luke's redaction. Moessner develops a variant of the Deuteronomy hypothesis with a clear preference for a synchronic reading and with neglect of historical-critical methodology. One wonders then why he accepts so easily that Steck's fourfold deuteronomistic scheme forms the organizing principle of Luke's travel narrative, in such a way that in fact a deuteronomistic pattern replaces Mk and Q as Luke's sources. The conclusion is quite obvious: the issue of intertextuality between OT and NT texts cannot be studied without due attention to a diachronic approach. We may formulate here a methodological principle: one cannot examine the question of OT influence on the Gospel of Luke without asking at the same time whether this influence was direct or indirect (i.e. through the sources he used). To put it in a more concrete way: (i) is Jesus' journey to Jerusalem in Luke's Gospel primarily a development of Mk 10,1-32 or do OT books, traditions or patterns play a preponderant role? (ii) did Luke get the motif of the rejected prophet directly from his OT reading or from his Q-source (cf. Lk 11,49-50; 13,34-35)?

OT influences specific for the LkTN?

A last observation to be made is that the phenomenon of OT intertextuality in Luke cannot be limited to the Travel Narrative. In other words, it seems difficult to find OT influences or uses which are linked with features specific to the LkTN. The search for possible OT influences on the LkTN, be it on the level of vocabulary, motifs, characters, or models, leads scholars to transcend each time the borders of the TN. Lk 9,1-50

Pontifical University of St. Thomas Rome, 1981), Rome, 1987; ID., *The Departure for Jerusalem (Luke 9:51-56) as a Rhetorical Imitation of Elijah's Departure for the Jordan (1 Kgs 1,1-2,6)*, in *Bib* 70 (1989) 96-109; ID. *Luke 9:57-62: A Systematic Adaptation of the Divine Challenge to Elijah (1 Kings 19)*, in *SBL Seminar Papers* (ed. D.J. Lull), Atlanta, 1989, pp. 236-245: J.D. DUBOIS, *La figure d'Élie dans la perspective lucanienne*, in *RHPR* 53 (1973) 155-176; C.A. EVANS, *Luke's Use of the Elijah/Elisha Narratives and the Ethic of Election*, in *JBL* 106 (1987) 75-83.

e.g. is considered to be a preview of the LkTN. The word group ἀνάλημ-ψις/ ἀναλαμβάνεσθαι occurs in Lk 9,51 and in Acts 1,2.11.22. The Exodus motif is already present in Lk 9,31. None of the christological models (prophet; suffering servant; king) can be confined to the LkTN alone. This is true also with respect to the OT motif of God's salvific visitation of his people, which Lk transfers to Jesus (ἐπισκοπή Lk 19,44; ἐπισκέπτομαι Lk 1,68.78; 7,16; Acts 15,14), and which finds so to speak a culminating-point in the LkTN. The only motif which clearly seems to be confined to the LkTN is "Jesus and the Samaritans" (Lk 9,51-56; 10,29-37; 17,11-19), which some scholars understand as a prelude in Jesus' life to the later Gentile mission. But in what measure does the OT, rather than the experience of the early Christian mission, play a role here[92]?

---

92. On the meaning and the OT roots of the "Samaritans" motif in Luke, see D. RAVENS, *Luke and the Restoration of Israel* (JSNT SS, 119), Sheffield, 1995, pp. 72-106: "Chapter 3: The role of the Samaritans and the unity of Israel".

APPENDICES

I. **C.F. EVANS**, "The Central Section of St. Luke's Gospel", in D.E. NINEHAM (ed.), *Studies in the Gospels. Essays in Memory of R.H. Lightfoot*, Oxford, 1955, pp. 37-53; cf. ID., *Saint Luke* (TPI NT Comm.), Philadelphia/London, 1990, pp. 34-36.

1.	Dt 1,1-46/Lk 10,1-3.17-20; CPTC	sending forerunners
2.	Dt 2–3,22/Lk 10,4-16; PTP	inhospitable kings and cities
3.	Dt 3,23-4,10/Lk 10,21-24. P	special revelation
4.	Dt 5,1–6,25/Lk 10,25-27; P/T	the summary of the Law
5.	Dt 7,1-26/Lk 10,29-37; C	relations with foreigners
6.	Dt 8,1-3/Lk 10,38-42; P	spiritual food
7.	Dt 8,4-20/Lk 11,1-13; T	no privation
8.	Dt 9,1–10,11/Lk 11,14-26; T	casting out wicked people and demons
9.	Dt 10,12–11,32/Lk 11,27-36; P	keeping God's word, light, and frontlets
10.	Dt 12,1-16/Lk 11,37–12,12; C	clean and unclean
11.	Dt 12,17-32/Lk 12,13-34; C	richness toward God
12.	Dt 13,1-11/Lk 12,35-53; P/T	reward/punishment for faithfulness/ unfaithfulness
13.	Dt 13,12-18(32)/Lk 12,54–13,5; // T	communal judgment and repentance
14.	[Dt 14,28/Lk 13,6-9;]	bearing fruit
15.	Dt 15,1-18/Lk 13,10-21; T	Sabbath release from debt, slavery, disease
16.	[Dt 16,1–17,7/Lk 13,22-35;]	feasting in Jerusalem
17.	[Dt 17,8–18,22/Lk 14,1-14;] //	food for Levites/banquet parables
18.	Dt 20,1-20/Lk 14,15-35; // P/T	excuses from battle and banquet
19.	Dt 21,15–22,4/Lk 15,1-32; // C	father and son, restoration of the lost
20.	Dt 23,15–24,4/Lk 16,1-18; P/C	slaves, usury, and divorce
21.	Dt 24,6–25,3/Lk 16,19–18,8; // P	fair treatment of poor and oppressed
22.	[Dt 26,1-19/Lk 18,9-14].	obeying the Law

// points to text-units which are not inserted in the series of parallels (Dt 14,1-21; 19; 21,1-14; 22,5-23,14; 25,4-19);

W.M. SWARTLEY, *Israel's Scripture Traditions and the Synoptic Gospels*, Peabody, MA, 1994, pp. 151-153 takes over the list of Evans, except the texts between square brackets. A correspondence of parallel thought is designated (P); one of transformation of thought, (T); reversal of the thought structure, i.e. contrast, (C).

II. **M. GOULDER**, *The Evangelists' Calendar: A Lectionary Explanation of the Development of Scripture*, London, 1978, esp. pp. 95-104.

1.	Dt 1,1–3,22/Lk 9,51–10,24;	sending forerunners
2.	Dt 3,23–7,11/Lk 10,25–11,13;	summary of Law, including prayer
3.	Dt 7,12–11,25/Lk 11,14-54;	stiffneckedness of Israel
4.	Dt 11,26–16,17/ Lk 12,1–13,9;	apostasy vs. prosperity
5.	Dt 16,18–21,9/Lk 13,10–14,24;	rejection of God's message, banquet/ battle issues
6.	Dt 21,10–25,19/Lk 14,25–16,13;	same sequence of parallels as Evans

7.	Dt 26,1–29,9/Lk 16,14–17,4;	(parallels break down)
8.	Dt. 29,10–30,20/Lk 17,20–18,14;	repentance or else wrath
9.	Dt 31,1-30/Lk 18,15-43;	the new generation
10.	Dt 32,1-52/Lk 19,1–20,18.	threats of destruction

III. **D.P. Moessner**, *Lord of the Banquet. The Literary and Theological Significance of the Lukan Travel Narrative*, Minneapolis, MN, 1989, p. 211.

Table of Contents of the Central Section and its deuteronomistic Prophet

A	B	C	D
"This Generation" – "Stiff-necked" like Their "Fathers" Crooked	Jesus Sent as Voice – Mediate Will/Instruct, Admonish/ Warn Repentance	"This Generation" Rejects Jesus-Prophet and Kills Him	Therefore God Will Rain Destruction on the Whole Crooked Nation
11,29-32.49-52 12,54-56.57-59 13,1-9.22-30.34 16,27-31 17,25-30 18,8 19,41-42.44b	9,51.52-56.57-62 10,1-12.13-15.16. 17-20.21-24.25- 28.29-37.38-42 11,1-4.5-8.9-13. 14-23.24-26.27- 28.29-32.33.34- 36.37-54 12,1.2-9.10.11-12. 13-15.16-21.22- 32.33-34.35-48. 49-53.54-56.57- 59 13,1-9.10-17.18-19. 20-21.22-30.31- 33.34-35 14,1-6.7-14.15-24. 25-33.34-35 15,1-7.8-10.11-32 16,1-9.10-12.13.14 -15.16-17.18.19 -31 17,1-3a.3b-4.5-6.7- 10.11-19.20-21. 22-37 18,1-8.9-14.15-17. 18-23.24-30.31- 34.35-43 19,1-10.11-27.28- 40.41-44	9,51.52-56.57-58 10,3.10-11.13.16.25 11,14-23.24-26.29- 32.47-54 12,49-50.54-56 13,1-9.14-17.25-30. 31-33.34 14,1.24 15,1-2 16,14-15.16.27-31 17,25-30 18,8.31-34 19,7.14.39-40	(10,12.14-15) 11,31-32.50-51 12,57-59 13,24-30.35 14,24 (16,27-31) 17,26-30 19,27.41-44

IV. The Deuteronomistic View of Israel's Prophetic History (O.H. Steck)
Nehemiah 9,26-31 = 2 Esdras 19,26-31

26 A   καὶ ἤλλαξαν καὶ ἀπέστησαν ἀπὸ σοῦ
        καὶ τὸν νόμον σου ὀπίσω σώματος αὐτῶν
    C   καὶ τοὺς προφήτας σου ἀπέκτειναν
    B   οἳ διεμαρτύραντο ἐν αὐτοῖς ἐπιστρέψαι αὐτοὺς πρὸς σέ
        καὶ ἐποίησαν παροργισμοὺς μεγάλους
27 D   καὶ ἔδωκας αὐτοὺς ἐν χειρὶ θλιβόντων αὐτούς
        καὶ ἔθλιψαν αὐτούς
    E   καὶ ἀνεβόησαν πρὸς σὲ ἐν καιρῷ θλίψεως αὐτῶν
    F   καὶ σὺ ἐξ οὐρανοῦ σου ἤκουσας
        καὶ ἐν οἰκτιρμοῖς σου τοῖς μεγάλοις ἔδωκας αὐτοῖς σωτῆρας
        καὶ ἔσωσας αὐτοὺς ἐκ χειρὸς θλιβόντων αὐτούς

28 A' καὶ ὡς ἀνεπαύσαντο ἐπέστρεψαν ποιῆσαι τὸ πονηρὸν ἐνώπιόν σου
    D' καὶ ἐγκατέλιπες αὐτοὺς εἰς χεῖρας ἐχθρῶν αὐτῶν
        καὶ κατῆρξαν ἐν αὐτοῖς
    E' καὶ πάλιν ἀνεβόησαν πρὸς σέ
    F' καὶ σὺ ἐξ οὐρανοῦ εἰσήκουσας
        καὶ ἐρρύσω αὐτοὺς ἐν οἰκτιρμοῖς σου πολλοῖς
29 (B') καὶ ἐπεμαρτύρω αὐτοῖς ἐπιστρέψαι αὐτοὺς εἰς τὸν νόμον σου
    A'' καὶ οὐκ ἤκουσαν ἀλλὰ ἐν ταῖς ἐντολαῖς σου
         καὶ ἐν τοῖς κρίμασί σου ἡμάρτοσαν
             ἃ ποιήσας αὐτὰ ἄνθρωπος ζήσεται ἐν αὐτοῖς
         καὶ ἔδωκαν νῶτον ἀπειθοῦντα
         καὶ τράχηλον αὐτῶν ἐσκλήρυναν
         καὶ οὐκ ἤκουσαν
30 F'' καὶ εἵλκυσας ἐπ' αὐτοὺς ἔτη πολλὰ
    B'' καὶ ἐπεμαρτύρω αὐτοῖς ἐν πνεύματί σου ἐν χειρὶ προφητῶν σου
    A''' καὶ οὐκ ἠνωτίσαντο
    D'' καὶ ἔδωκας αὐτοὺς ἐν χειρὶ λαῶν τῆς γῆς
31 F''' καὶ σὺ ἐν οἰκτιρμοῖς σου τοῖς πολλοῖς
         οὐκ ἐποίησας αὐτοὺς συντέλειαν
         καὶ οὐκ ἐγκατέλιπες αὐτούς
         ὅτι ἰσχυρὸς εἶ καὶ ἐλεήμων καὶ οἰκτίρμων

2 Kings 17,7-20

A

7   καὶ ἐγένετο
    ὅτι ἥμαρτον οἱ υἱοὶ Ισραηλ τῷ κυρίῳ θεῷ αὐτῶν
    τῷ ἀναγαγόντι αὐτοὺς ἐκ γῆς Αἰγύπτου ὑποκάτωθεν χειρὸς φαραω
    βασιλέως Αἰγύπτου
    καὶ ἐφοβήθησαν θεοὺς ἑτέρους
8   καὶ ἐπορεύθησαν τοῖς δικαιώμασιν τῶν ἐθνῶν
    ὧν ἐξῆρεν κύριος ἀπὸ προσώπου υἱῶν Ισραηλ
    καὶ οἱ βασιλεῖς Ισραηλ ὅσοι ἐποίησαν
9   καὶ ὅσοι ἠμφιέσαντο οἱ υἱοὶ Ισραηλ λόγους οὐχ οὕτως κατὰ κυρίου
    θεοῦ αὐτῶν

καὶ ᾠκοδόμησαν ἑαυτοῖς ὑψηλὰ ἐν πάσαις ταῖς πόλεσιν αὐτῶν ἀπὸ
πύργου φυλασσόντων ἕως πόλεως ὀχυρᾶς
10 καὶ ἐστήλωσαν ἑαυτοῖς στήλας καὶ ἄλση ἐπὶ παντὶ βουνῷ ὑψηλῷ
καὶ ὑποκάτω παντὸς ξύλου ἀλσώδους
11 καὶ ἐθυμίασαν ἐκεῖ ἐν πᾶσιν ὑψηλοῖς καθὼς τὰ ἔθνη ἃ ἀπῴκισεν
κύριος ἐκ προσώπου αὐτῶν
καὶ ἐποίησαν κοινωνοὺς καὶ ἐχάραξαν τοῦ παροργίσαι τὸν κύριον
12 καὶ ἐλάτρευσαν τοῖς εἰδώλοις οἷς εἶπεν κύριος αὐτοῖς οὐ ποιήσετε
τὸ ῥῆμα τοῦτο κυρίῳ

B

13 καὶ διεμαρτύρατο κύριος ἐν τῷ Ισραηλ καὶ ἐν τῷ Ιουδα
ἐν χειρὶ πάντων τῶν προφητῶν αὐτοῦ παντὸς ὁρῶντος λέγων
ἀποστράφητε ἀπὸ τῶν ὁδῶν ὑμῶν τῶν πονηρῶν
καὶ φυλάξατε τὰς ἐντολάς μου καὶ τὰ δικαιώματά μου
καὶ πάντα τὸν νόμον ὃν ἐνετειλάμην τοῖς πατράσιν ὑμῶν
ὅσα ἀπέστειλα αὐτοῖς ἐν χειρὶ τῶν δούλων μου τῶν προφητῶν

C

14 καὶ οὐκ ἤκουσαν
καὶ ἐσκλήρυναν τὸν νῶτον αὐτῶν ὑπὲρ τὸν νῶτον τῶν πατέρων αὐτῶν
15 καὶ τὰ μαρτύρια αὐτοῦ ὅσα διεμαρτύρατο αὐτοῖς οὐκ ἐφύλαξαν
καὶ ἐπορεύθησαν ὀπίσω τῶν ματαίων
καὶ ἐματαιώθησαν καὶ ὀπίσω τῶν ἐθνῶν τῶν περικύκλῳ αὐτῶν
ὧν ἐνετείλατο αὐτοῖς τοῦ μὴ ποιῆσαι κατὰ ταῦτα
16 ἐγκατέλιπον τὰς ἐντολὰς κυρίου θεοῦ αὐτῶν
καὶ ἐποίησαν ἑαυτοῖς χώνευμα δύο δαμάλεις
καὶ ἐποίησαν ἄλση
καὶ προσεκύνησαν πάσῃ τῇ δυνάμει τοῦ οὐρανοῦ
καὶ ἐλάτρευσαν τῷ Βααλ
17 καὶ διῆγον τοὺς υἱοὺς αὐτῶν καὶ τὰς θυγατέρας αὐτῶν ἐν πυρὶ
καὶ ἐμαντεύοντο μαντείας καὶ οἰωνίζοντο
καὶ ἐπράθησαν τοῦ ποιῆσαι τὸ πονηρὸν ἐν ὀφθαλμοῖς κυρίου
παροργίσαι αὐτόν

D

18 καὶ ἐθυμώθη κύριος σφόδρα ἐν τῷ Ισραηλ
καὶ ἀπέστησεν αὐτοὺς ἀπὸ τοῦ προσώπου αὐτοῦ
καὶ οὐχ ὑπελείφθη πλὴν φυλὴ Ιουδα μονωτάτη

C'

19 καί γε Ιουδας οὐκ ἐφύλαξεν τὰς ἐντολὰς κυρίου τοῦ θεοῦ αὐτῶν
καὶ ἐπορεύθησαν ἐν τοῖς δικαιώμασιν Ισραηλ οἷς ἐποίησαν

D'

20 καὶ ἀπεώσαντο τὸν κύριον ἐν παντὶ σπέρματι Ισραηλ
καὶ ἐσάλευσεν αὐτοὺς
καὶ ἔδωκεν αὐτοὺς ἐν χειρὶ διαρπαζόντων αὐτούς
ἕως οὗ ἀπέρριψεν αὐτοὺς ἀπὸ προσώπου αὐτοῦ

Fl. JOSEPHUS

Antiquitates 9,265-267 (Northern-Israelites)

B

καὶ τοὺς προφήτας δ' ὁμοίως ταῦτα παραινοῦντας
καὶ προλέγοντας ἃ πείσονται μὴ μεταθέμενοι πρὸς τὴν εὐσέβειαν θεοῦ,

C

διέπτυον καὶ τελευταῖον συλλαβόντες αὐτοὺς ἀπέκτειναν.

(A)

καί οὐδὲ μέχρι τούτων αὐτοῖς ἤρκεσε παρανομοῦσιν,
ἀλλὰ καὶ χείρω τῶν προειρημένων ἐπενοοῦντο καὶ οὐ πρότερον ἐπαύσαντο

D

πρὶν ἢ τοῖς πολεμίοις αὐτοὺς ἀμυνόμενος τῆς ἀσεβείας ὁ θεὸς ἐποίησεν
ὑποχειρίους...

B

– πολλοὶ μέντοι (from the tribes of Manasseh, Zabulon and Issachar) πεισ-
θέντες
οἷς οἱ προφῆται παρήνεσαν εἰς εὐσέβειαν μετεβάλοντο.
– (And all these flocked to Jerusalem to Hezekiah that they might worship God).

B and when their prophets exhorted them in like manner
and foretold what they would suffer
if they did not alter their course to one of piety toward God,
C they poured scorn upon them
and finally seized them and killed them.
(A) And not stopping even at these acts of lawliness,
they devised things still worse than those mentioned,
and did not leave off
D until God punished them for their impiety by making them subject to their
enemies...

–

B However, many...heeded the prophets' exhortations and were converted in
piety.

Antiquitates 10,38-39 (about Manasseh)

(A) ἀπὸ γὰρ τῆς εἰς τὸν θεὸν καταφρονήσεως ὁρμώμενος
πάντας τοὺς δικαίους τοὺς ἐν τοῖς Ἑβραίοις ἀπέκτεινεν,
(C) ἀλλ' οὐδὲ τῶν προφητῶν ἔσχε φειδὼ
καὶ τούτων δέ τινας καθ' ἡμέραν ἀπέσφαξεν,
ὥστε αἵματι ῥεῖσθαι τὰ Ἱεροσόλυμα.
(B) λαβὼν οὖν ὀργὴν ἐπὶ τούτοις ὁ θεὸς
πέμπει προφήτας πρὸς τὸν βασιλέα καὶ τὸ πλῆθος,
δι' ὧν αὐτοῖς ἠπείλησε τὰς αὐτὰς συμφοράς,
αἷς συνέβη περιπεσεῖν τοὺς ἀδελφοὺς αὐτῶν Ἰσραηλίτας εἰς αὐτὸν
ἐξυβρίζοντας.

(C) οἱ δὲ τοῖς λόγοις οὐκ ἐπίστευον,
    παρ' ὧν ἠδύναντο κερδῆσαι τὸ μηδενὸς πειραθῆναι κακοῦ,
(D) τοῖς δ' ἔργοις ἔμαθον ἀληθῆ τὰ παρὰ τῶν προφητῶν.

(A) For, setting out with a contempt of God,
    he killed all the righteous men among the Hebrews,
(C) nor did he spare even the prophets, some of whom he slaughtered daily,
    so that Jerusalem ran with blood.
(B) Thereupon God, being wrathful at these things,
    sent prophets to the king and the people,
    and through these threatened them with the same calamities
    which had befallen their Israelite brothers when they outraged Him.
(C) They were not, however, persuaded by these words,
    from which they might so have profited as not to experience any misfortune,
(D) but had to learn from deeds the truth of what the prophets said.

Antiquitates **9,281** (theological reflection on the fall of Northern reign)

D   καὶ τέλος μὲν τοὺς Ἰσραηλίτας τοιοῦτο κατέλαβε
A   παραβάντας τοὺς νόμους
C   καὶ παρακούσαντας τῶν προφητῶν,
B   οἳ προύλεγον ταύτην αὐτοῖς τὴν συμφορὰν
(C) μὴ παυσαμένοις τῶν ἀσεβημάτων.

D   To such an end, then, did the Israelites come
A   because they violated the laws
C   and disregarded the prophets
B   who foretold that this misfortune would overtake them
(C) if they did not cease from their impious actions.

Antiquitates **10,60** (prophecy of Hulda about the Southern reign)

D   ἀπολέσαι τὸν λαὸν καὶ τῆς χώρας ἐκβαλεῖν
    καὶ πάντων ἀφελέσθαι τῶν νῦν παρόντων ἀγαθῶν,
A   παραβάντας τοὺς νόμους
C   καὶ τοσούτῳ μεταξὺ χρόνῳ μὴ μετανήσαντας,
B   τῶν τε προφητῶν τοῦτο παραινούντων σωφρονεῖν
    καὶ τὴν ἐπὶ τοῖς ἀσεβήμασι τιμωρίαν προλεγόντων·

D   This sentence was to destroy the people and drive them out of their country
    and deprive them of all the good things which they now had,
A   because they had transgressed against the laws
C   and during so long an interval of time had not repented,
B   although the prophets exhorted them to act thus wisely
    and foretold the punishment for their impious deeds.

Tiensestraat 112   Adelbert DENAUX
B-3000 Leuven

LC 17, 20-37 ET LC 21, 8-11.20-24
ARRIÈRE-FOND SCRIPTURAIRE

Il y a plus de vingt ans déjà, E.E. Ellis donnait des règles de méthode pour comprendre comment Luc avait élaboré ses sources, en particulier pour sa visée eschatologique. À elle seule, la recherche des niveaux pré-lucaniens ou non-lucaniens d'un passage ne suffit pas à mesurer le travail rédactionnel, ni à déterminer l'intention théologique de l'évangéliste. Elle doit se préoccuper d'une question complémentaire: «dans son utilisation d'une source, dans quelle mesure et de quelle manière l'écrivain la fait-il sienne?», car «Tout le matériel chez Luc est en un certain sens 'lucanien' du fait que Luc l'intègre»[1]. Ces indications ont orienté notre perspective de travail dans le présent séminaire. Le soin apporté par Luc dans la sélection d'abord, puis dans la réécriture de ses sources, leur gestion et leur «digestion», sont à apprécier comme autant de matériaux de composition rédactionnels. Il est important de préciser comment Luc s'est ressaisi des références à l'Écriture qu'il trouvait dans ses sources. Lc 17 et Lc 21 offrent à cet égard un champ de recherche particulièrement intéressant pour le thème du présent Congrès.

Par l'attention prêtée au lecteur, les recherches contemporaines sur l'intertextualité offrent un point de vue supplémentaire dans l'analyse de la composition d'un texte par son auteur: «La lecture de l'intertexte ne se limite pas à un repérage des traces qu'il aura laissées: il s'agit aussi, pour le lecteur de jouer le rôle que le texte lui assigne. Il peut être le complice du narrateur ou de l'auteur, être convoqué en tant qu'interprète capable de percevoir ce qui n'est dit qu'à mots couverts et de comprendre la parole oblique qui use de l'intertexte comme d'un masque à lever ou d'un code à décrypter»[2]. Plus qu'à une simple recherche concordantielle sur les textes de l'Ancien Testament évoqués par Luc, cette pratique conduit celui qui la mène à devenir «lecteur complice…, partenaire nécessaire d'un jeu avec les textes»[3].

---

1. E.E. ELLIS, *La fonction de l'eschatologie dans l'évangile de Luc* (BETL, 32), in F. NEIRYNCK (éd.), *L'évangile de Luc. Problèmes littéraires et théologiques.* Mémorial Lucien Cerfaux, Gembloux, 1973, p. 142; ²1989, p. 52.
2. N. PIEGAY-GROS, *Introduction à l'Intertextualité,* Paris, 1996, p. 94.
3. N. PIEGAY-GROS, *ibid.,* p. 106.

Enfin, toujours sur le plan méthodologique, il me paraît urgent aujourd'hui de dépasser[4] les questions habituelles de «déseschatologisation» chez Luc qui ont tant occupé les commentateurs de Lc 17 et de Lc 21. La rédaction lucanienne des apocalypses s'apparente en définitive à une réflexion sur la méditation du sens de l'histoire (de la dévastation de Jérusalem), à la manière des midrashim historiques. Tel a été un des éléments majeurs de notre découverte. Pour ce faire et pour nous engager dans ce séminaire, voici un texte juif, qui, comme les apocalypses lucaniennes, part d'une question sur le lieu et le temps du Messie:

> Rabbi Josué ben Levi rencontra Élie à l'entrée de la caverne où Rabbi Simon bar Yohai s'était exilé... Il lui demanda: «Quand viendra le Messie?» Il lui répondit: «Va le lui demander». – «Mais où se tient-il?» – «À l'entrée de la cité de Rome». – «À quoi le reconnaîtrai-je?» – «Il est assis parmi les pauvres lépreux. Mais alors que tous font et défont en même temps tous leurs bandages, il défait et refait les siens un à un en se disant: 'Peut-être vais-je être appelé. Ne soyons pas en retard'». Rabbi Josué vint au Messie et lui dit: «La paix soit sur toi, mon maître». – «La paix soit sur toi, fils de Levi» lui répondit-il. Josué lui demanda: «Quand viendrez-vous mon maître?» – «Aujourd'hui» fut sa réponse. Rabbi Josué s'en revient auprès d'Élie. Ce dernier lui demanda: «Que t'a-t-il dit?» – «Il m'a menti, répondit-il, parce qu'il m'a dit qu'il viendrait aujourd'hui et pourtant il n'est pas venu». Élie lui répondit: «Voilà ce qu'il t'a répondu: *Aujourd'hui si vous écoutez ma voix*» (Ps 95,7)[5].

I. L'ARRIÈRE-FOND SCRIPTURAIRE DANS Lc 17

Pour l'essentiel, le discours de style apocalyptique de Lc 17 provient de la source Q[6]. Quoiqu'il en soit de l'appartenance ou non des versets 20-21 à la tradition ou à la rédaction[7], nous considérons le discours dans son contexte le plus large (Lc 17,20-37), afin de mesurer comment Luc se réfère à l'Ancien Testament, soit dans l'utilisation de sa source, soit dans le remaniement de celle-ci.

4. Ce qui ne signifie pas contester, ni ignorer.
5. TB Sanhedrin 98a, cité par Y.H. YERUSHALMI, *Zakhor. Histoire juive et mémoire juive*, Paris, 1984 (pour la traduction française), p. 39.
6. Les positions critiques sont rassemblées dans J.S. KLOPPENBORG, *The Formation of Q. Trajectories in Ancient Wisdom Collections*, Philadelphia, 1989[2], pp. 154-170.
7. La discussion reste encore toujours ouverte pour Lc 17, 20b-21. Appartenance à la source Q: R. SCHNACKENBURG, *Der eschatologische Abschnitt Lk 17, 20-37*, in *Mélanges bibliques en hommage au P. Béda Rigaux*, Gembloux, 1970, pp. 213-234. Composition lucanienne: R. GEIGER, *Die lukanischen Endzeitreden. Studien zur Eschatologie des Lukas-Evangeliums*, Bern – Frankfurt/M., 1973, pp. 45 ss. Niveau pré-lucanien: J. ZMIJEWSKI, *Die Eschatologiereden des Lukas-Evangeliums. Eine traditions- und redaktionsgeschichtliche Untersuchung zu Lk 21,5-36 und Lk 17,20-37*, Bonn, 1972, pp. 389 s..

1. *Un premier aperçu de l'ensemble du passage permet de préciser les lieux-clés de l'analyse*

Dès le verset 22, le thème dominant du jour du Fils de l'homme surplombe toute la péricope lucanienne. Ce verset donne en effet le ton à l'ensemble et vient comme en prologue pour orienter la documentation que Luc puise à sa source; Luc dirige en quelque sorte la relecture non seulement sur le Fils de l'homme, mais sur le thème du Jour, et sur le motif de 'voir' (le jour). Tout en se servant de sa documentation, Luc fait porter l'attention progressivement sur le personnage en son jour[8]. Certes la mention du Fils de l'homme s'éclaire par le texte de Dn 7,13-14 interprété par les premières communautés chrétiennes; mais dans le passage analysé (Lc 17,20-37), la référence au texte de Daniel lui-même ne fonctionne pas comme une citation de l'Écriture. L'identification christologique entre le personnage à venir désigné comme le Fils de l'homme et Jésus est déjà faite; ce Fils de l'homme exerce le jugement. La perspective s'ouvre ici sur le thème du *jour* dans une visée explicitement christologique destinée à placer le jour du Fils de l'homme dans la perspective du Jour de Yahwé[9], et donc du jour du jugement.

Les trois comparaisons destinées à évoquer le(s) jour(s) du Fils de l'homme (celle de l'éclair au v. 24, celle des jours de Noé aux vv. 26-27 et celle des jours de Lot au v. 28) occupent une place centrale dans la construction du discours. Chez Luc le tissu intertextuel s'étend au-delà du verset 30, comme nous le constaterons. La comparaison avec les dits de Q utilisés par Mt 24 est suggestive[10]. Matthieu n'emploie que deux des comparaisons: celle de l'éclair et celle des jours de Noé. Il relie (Mt 24,27) la mention de l'éclair au logion sur les vautours qui se rassembleront où que soit le cadavre; ces deux logia, celui de l'éclair et celui du rassemblement des vautours, pourraient bien avoir été assemblés par le motif de la rapidité du rassemblement. Matthieu a encore déplacé la comparaison avec les jours de Noé (en 24,37) pour la mettre entre le motif sur l'ignorance du jour et de l'heure (cf. Marc 13) et la conclusion finale parénétique.

---

8. Aux versets 24, 26, 30 [31: *en ce jour-là*].

9. R. GEIGER (n. 7) a particulièrement souligné ce processus d'une «Hypostasierung des k'bod Jahwes», p. 67.

10. Sur la formation de cette collection de Logia apocalyptiques de Q 17,23.24.26-30.34-35.37 je renvoie à l'analyse de J.S. KLOPPENBORG (n. 6), pp. 154-170. On y trouve également un résumé des positions d'auteurs (Geiger, Zmijewski, etc.). Le tableau de la page 154 offre une bonne vue d'ensemble des matériaux apocalyptiques dans Q et de leur insertion dans la tradition de Mc 13 par Matthieu.

Éclair	Mt 24,27	Lc 17,24
Logion sur les vautours	Mt 24,28	(Lc 17,37)
Logion sur la passion du Fils de l'homme		Lc 17,25
Noé (déluge)	Mt 24,37	Lc 17,26
Lot (Sodome)	absent de Mt	Lc 17,28

Le troisième évangile offre une organisation différente de celle de Matthieu. Luc installe ses trois comparaisons (l'éclair, les jours de Noé, les jours de Lot) en enfilade. Il respecte vraisemblablement l'ordre de la source Q. Toutefois, au verset 25, le dit sur le fils de l'homme qui «doit beaucoup souffrir et être rejeté par cette génération» se glisse entre la comparaison sur l'éclair et les comparaisons sur les jours de Noé et de Lot. Cette place du logion sur la passion du Fils de l'homme et le déplacement du logion sur les vautours à la fin du passage sont des indices du travail rédactionnel; comme l'analyse le suggèrera ultérieurement, Luc porte l'insistance sur la passion.

Luc inscrit ensuite dans sa collection de logia apocalyptiques un dit de l'apocalypse marcienne (Mc 13,15-16 par. Mt 24,17-18). Ainsi posé à la suite des trois comparaisons (éclair, déluge, Sodome), ce passage reçoit de plus une interprétation originale: «qu'il ne se retourne pas en arrière. Rappelez-vous la femme de Lot» (Lc 17,31c-32). Habilement, le rédacteur supprime les mots «prendre son manteau» (Mc 13,16: «qu'il ne retourne pas en arrière *prendre son manteau*»). Il fait de cet interdit un rappel significatif des jours de Sodome. Luc accorde donc une certaine ampleur à ces figures vétérotestamentaires, au-delà du verset 30.

Au verset 33 Luc insère le dit sur la vie à perdre ou à préserver, fermement attesté au niveau traditionnel puisqu'on le trouve dans la source Q (Mt 10,39), dans la triple tradition (Mc 8,35; Mt 16,25; Lc 9,24) et dans Jean (Jn 12,25)[11]. Mais lorsque Luc insère le dit sur la vie à perdre ou à préserver en cet endroit de l'apocalypse, il renforce encore le travail intertextuel déjà à l'œuvre dans les figures vétérotestamentaires indiquées ci-dessus. L'analyse ultérieure montrera la cohérence qui s'établit à la lecture de l'ensemble.

Les verset 34-35 proviennent de la source Q (Mt 24,40-41) et sont sans référence à l'Écriture.

Au verset 37, Luc incorpore à nouveau un logion de la source Q, le dit sur les vautours qui se rassemblent au «lieu du corps»[12]: Matthieu a

---

11. M. MORGEN, *«Perdre sa vie» dans Jean 12, 25: un dit traditionnel?* in *Revue des sciences religieuses* 69 (1995) 29-46.

12. Matthieu ne parle pas du corps, mais du cadavre. Sur le lien entre ce dit sur les vautours au lieu où il y a le corps et le verset 25 de Luc, voir *infra*; idée semblable dans J.S. KLOPPENBORG (n. 6), p. 156.

vraisemblablement gardé l'ordre original de la source Q. Il nous faudra chercher pourquoi Luc déplace ce proverbe et voir si les références à Jb 39,27-30 ou à Ha 1,8[13] sont éclairantes. Le logion sur les vautours se lit chez Luc en finale de son apocalypse (17,37) où il forme inclusion avec la question du début sur le lieu (17,20). La mise en conclusion de ce proverbe par Luc, avec une insistance nouvelle sur le topos, n'est pas étrangère à la relecture lucanienne: dans cette apocalypse du chapitre 17, l'accentuation porte à plusieurs reprises sur le lieu; Lc 21 paraît davantage orienté vers une méditation sur le temps.

Ce premier parcours du texte a déjà marqué l'importance de la composition lucanienne. Il permet aussi de situer les lieux-clés de la recherche sur l'arrière-fond scripturaire. Nous considérerons cet arrière-fond dans les trois comparaisons de Luc (éclair, déluge et Sodome). Il importera ensuite d'observer comment Luc poursuit la figure de la destruction de Sodome. Il ne sera pas inutile enfin de voir comment l'image du vautour et du corps est transformée et déplacée chez Luc, pour revenir en fin de réflexion sur la compréhension lucanienne du jour de Fils de l'homme et son lien avec le thème du lieu à voir (Lc 17,20).

2. *Comme l'éclair qui foudroie...*

L'image de l'éclair que l'on trouve en Matthieu comme en Luc (ἡ ἀστραπή) provient incontestablement de la source Q. Ce n'est pas une allusion explicite à l'Écriture, encore moins une citation. Malgré cela – surtout par parenté contextuelle avec les comparaisons suivantes (jours de Noé et jours de Lot) qui, elles, renvoient explicitement à des figures vétérotestamentaires – le motif de l'éclair suggère de porter le regard vers les théophanies de l'Ancien Testament.

Sans céder à un comparatisme lexical, on peut évoquer quelques passages dans lesquels les phénomènes orageux (orage, tonnerre, éclairs, ...) accompagnent les manifestations divines et notamment le 'Jour' du jugement: Éz 1,4.7.13; Ex 24,15 ss; Ps 97,1; etc...[14]. Il me semble particulièrement important de retenir certaines références à la puissance fulgurante de l'éclair (Ha 3,11; Dn 10,6). Luc se place dans les mêmes perspectives que les apocalypses contemporaines ou immédiatement postérieures qui organisent un développement du motif. L'apocalypse

---

13. L'image du vautour qui fond pour dévorer sa proie est utilisée pour décrire les Chaldéens, instrument de la punition de Yahwé, au temps de Nabuchodonosor, en conformité avec le contexte d'ensemble Ha 1,5-11.

14. R GEIGER, (n. 7), p. 67

johannique mentionne l'éclair (le tonnerre et de la voix) dans les chapitres destinés à établir un lien entre le Dieu Juge et le personnage qui ouvre le jugement (Fils de l'homme, Agneau, Messie)[15]. L'Apocalypse syriaque de Baruch consacre le chapitre 53 à l'imposante vision du nuage et des eaux. Dans cette description de la vision, la puissance dominatrice de l'éclair sur toute la terre est considérable:

> 1. et (quelque chose) comme un éclair apparut au faîte (du nuage)...8. je vis ensuite l'éclair que j'avais aperçu au faîte du nuage. Il saisit le (nuage) et le fit descendre jusqu'à terre....9. Cet éclair était à ce point lumineux qu'il illuminait toute la terre et restaurait les lieux où les dernières eaux, en tombant, avaient semé la ruine occupant toute la terre, il la tint en son pouvoir....11. Après cela, je vis douze fleuves qui montaient de la mer, entouraient l'éclair et lui obéissaient.

Lc 17,24 se distingue néanmoins de son parallèle matthéen parce qu'il ajoute le verbe ἀστράπτω[16] construit sur la même racine que le substantif ἀστραπή auquel Luc l'ajoute. Il est difficile de déterminer si cette construction est le fait de Luc ou si elle provient de sa source[17]. Le motif de «l'éclair éclairant» (substantif + verbe de même racine) est attesté dans certains passages de la littérature hymnique de l'Ancien Testament, en particulier au Ps 143(144),6 ἄστραψον ἀστραπὴν καὶ σκορπιεῖς αὐτούς. Le même ensemble ἀστράπειν ἀστραπήν – bien que le verbe ἤστραψεν ne soit attesté que dans certains manuscrits – se trouve encore en 2 Sm 22,15 LXX (cf. Ps 17[18],15). En tous les cas, dans ces passages, la venue de Dieu est célébrée (ou implorée) comme un jour de dispersion des ennemis: il les foudroie par l'éclair et les met en déroute. Le psaume met en relief la venue lumineuse et en même temps menaçante de l'arrivée de Yahwé; il vient ainsi en aide au roi pour le délivrer de ses ennemis[18]. Il me semble que l'on peut retenir cet aspect paradoxal[19] (lumineux et menaçant) de la venue du jour du fils de l'homme comme l'éclair dans Luc. Il évoque de cette manière le pouvoir exterminateur de l'éclair et annonce le thème du châtiment inéluctable, thème important dans les deux références suivantes (au déluge, à Sodome).

---

15. Voir l'introduction de l'agneau (Ap 4,5; 8,5) ou de l'enfant (Ap 11,19) ou encore la présentation du jugement final de la grande Babylone (Ap 16,18).

16. Autre emploi en Lc 24,4. Voir aussi le verbe composé en Lc 9,29 ἐξαστράπτω.

17. Selon M.-J. LAGRANGE (*Evangile selon saint Luc,* Paris, 1927, p. 463), Matthieu serait ici plus primitif car Luc utilise ailleurs cette redondance (verbe-substantif): en 2,8; 11,46; 23,46.

18. Voir aussi Dt 32,41 «j'aiguise mon épée comme l'éclair»...

19. J. ZMIJEWSKI, ἀστραπή, in *EWNT,* cc. 419-422 esp. 421. Cet auteur pense que l'image utilisée par Luc lui permet de décrire à la fois le paradoxe de la croix et de la gloire.

3. *Comme aux jours de Noé et de Lot*

La mention des personnages de Noé et de Lot renvoie d'emblée aux nombreuses interprétations juives, hellénistiques ou chrétiennes[20] sur le déluge et sur la destruction de Sodome. Elles se sont développées sur des registres typologiques divers (anthropologique, théologique, éthique, etc.). Nous ne saurions nous y arrêter trop longuement ici. De nombreux travaux les ont suffisamment explorées. Parmi ceux-ci, il convient de retenir l'article de J. Schlosser[21]; il a particulièrement souligné comment le recours aux figures de Noé et de Lot accentue le motif de l'*inéluctable* châtiment des impies. Je souscris pleinement à ses remarques et voudrais précisément tenter, dans cette même perspective, de caractériser le travail rédactionnel de Luc dans son emploi de l'Ancien Testament: que choisit-il d'intensifier et surtout quelle est sa manière de procéder pour mettre en relief le motif du jugement? Comparé à son parallèle matthéen[22], le texte de Luc apparaît plus structuré. Le rédacteur du troisième évangile s'appuie fortement sur la thématique du jugement déjà développée au niveau de la source Q. Dans ses références aux figures de Noé et de Lot, Luc répète à deux reprises un schéma identique qui place en acmé, au terme d'un processus, la mention du jugement destructeur et absolu (καὶ ἀπώλεσεν πάντας). Ce déploiement du jugement redoutable et total trouve son point d'ancrage dans les textes bibliques de Gn 6–7 et Gn 19. Le texte de Luc offre deux fois de suite le même schéma: a) Indication du *mouvement* (d'entrée ou de sortie) du patriarche; b) *Arrivée* subite de la pluie destructrice; c) Destruction *totale*. Ce schéma obéit aux narrations traditionnelles des deux anéantissements par la pluie et par le feu.

a) Dans le texte de l'Ancien Testament, tant pour Noé que pour Lot, le salut du patriarche est explicité en terme de *mouvement* d'entrée dans l'arche ou de sortie de la ville de Sodome. Noé et Lot se mettent ainsi à l'abri de la pluie destructrice. Le mouvement d'entrée ou de sortie est refuge, salut; il traduit leur obéissance à l'ordre divin. Pour Noé en Gn 6,18: «J'établirai mon alliance avec toi: 'Entre dans l'arche...'» (voir aussi Gn 7,1); pour Lot en Gn 19,16. 22: «et ils le firent sortir.....». Dès que les justes (Noé et Lot) sont à l'abri, le jugement divin sévit et s'abat sur *tous*. Dans le passage de la source Q, l'insistance ne porte guère sur

---

20. J. SCHLOSSER, *Les jours de Noé et de Lot. À propos de Luc XVII, 26-30,* in *RB* 80 (1973) 13-36; J. CAZEAUX, *La trame et la chaîne 2. Le cycle de Noé dans Philon,* New York, 1989.
21. J. SCHLOSSER (n. 20).
22. Pour la comparaison Lc 17/Mt 24, voir R. SCHNACKENBURG (n. 7).

l'obéissance de Noé (ou de Lot) à l'ordre de Dieu. Elle met plutôt en évidence le motif de la venue subite de la catastrophe au moment précis du salut du patriarche.

b) Le schéma se poursuit en effet avec l'arrivée impromptue de la pluie destructrice: «vint le déluge... il plut du feu et du soufre». Le rédacteur lucanien met en relief le long temps qui précède le salut des uns et la destruction de tous (les autres). Dans l'Ancien Testament, c'est le temps de l'impiété manifeste; dans la source Q, l'accent porte davantage sur une sorte d'insouciance un peu folâtre par rapport au lendemain: «on mangeait, on buvait, on prenait femme, on prenait mari»[23]. Cette tranquille insouciance dure jusqu'au jour où (ἄχρι[24] ἧς ἡμέρας: Mt 24,38; Lc 17,27) Noé entra dans l'arche. L'un et l'autre évangéliste a conservé de la source Q le contraste voulu entre une indolente frivolité et la brusque apparition du cataclysme. Ce même contraste se trouvait vraisemblablement dans Q 17,28-29 à propos de Lot et de Sodome. Luc l'a conservé. Toutefois le contraste lui-même entre l'insouciance et la venue du jour est quelque peu émoussé; seule la particule δέ relie le verset 28 (sur les activités antérieures) au verset 29 (sur le jour où Lot sortit). Matthieu fait ressortir le thème de la connaissance du moment; la suture rédactionnelle malhabile en 24,39 laisse deviner le raccord matthéen (καὶ οὐκ ἔγνωσαν ἕως ἦλθεν ὁ κατακλυσμός). Avec force précisions Matthieu s'attache à décrire ce temps d'avant le cataclysme diluvien, ce temps qui dure jusqu'à ce qu'arrive le déluge, ἕως ἦλθεν ὁ κατακλυσμός (v. 39). Luc garde de la source Q le contraste entre le temps d'insouciance et la venue impromptue du jour, mais il accentue davantage la totalité de l'action du jugement divin, sa venue brutale et rapide. L'ensemble lucanien est organisé pour orienter vers le jour du Fils de l'homme, jour de jugement.

c) Le schéma s'achève enfin par le motif du jugement-condamnation: καὶ ἀπώλεσεν πάντας. Luc accorde une certaine importance à la totalité de la destruction: il les fit *tous* périr. Ce motif d'une destruction totale qui décrit la puissance du jugement divin est un leit-motiv des deux récits de l'Ancien Testament, du déluge comme de l'épisode de Sodome. Les verbes variés pour dire la destruction et la mort insistent sur la radicalité de l'opération. Ainsi,

---

23. Participes présents chez Matthieu; imparfaits de l'indicatif chez Luc
24. Ἄχρι: le mot est rare chez Matthieu. Il pourrait provenir de la source Q. Sa relative fréquence dans l'œuvre lucanienne, notamment dans les Actes, montre que ce mot a pu rencontrer une attention favorable du rédacteur. En effet, il apparaît souvent en lien avec des notions temporelles significatives sur le plan eschatologique (le jour, le kairos, le chronos), comme chez Paul. Voir H.J. RITZ, in *EWNT* I, 450.

– dans l'épisode du déluge en Gn 6–7: *toute chair* avait une conduite perverse (6,12); *la fin de toute chair* (καιρὸς παντὸς ἀνθρώπου ἥκει ἐναντίον μου)[25] est venue; je vais les détruire (καταφθείρω) (6,13); je vais faire venir le Déluge...pour *détruire* (καταφθεῖραι) sous les cieux *toute chair* qui a en elle souffle de vie; *tout* ce qui est sur la terre *expiera* (τελευτήσει) (6,17); j'*effacerai* de la surface du sol *tous* les êtres que j'ai faits (7,4); alors *expira toute chair* qui se meut sur la terre... et *tous* les hommes (7,21); *tous* ceux qui avaient haleine de vie dans les narines; *tout* ce qui était sur la terre ferme *mourut* (7,22);

– dans l'épisode de la destruction de Sodome en Gn 19: nous allons la *détruire* 19,13 (ἀπόλλυμεν...ἐκτρῖψαι αὐτήν); le Seigneur va détruire la ville (19,14) (ἐκτρίβει); de peur que tu ne périsses (19,15.17) (ἵνα μὴ συναπόλῃ); il bouleversa (κατέστρεψεν) ces villes, *tout* le District, *tous* les habitants des villes et la végétation du sol (19,25) (ἐκτρῖψαι κύριον πάσας τὰς πόλεις..., 19,29).

Luc déploie la figure de la destruction de Sodome de manière originale aux versets 30 ss. C'est une des particularités de ce jeu intertextuel de Lc 17. Le rédacteur offre tout d'abord une première conclusion à ses trois comparaisons sur le jour du Fils de l'homme au verset 30: «de même en sera-t-il le Jour où le Fils de l'homme doit se révéler (le jour de son apocalypse)». Le verset 31b («et que celui qui sera au champ ne retourne pas en arrière») est emprunté à la tradition de Marc (Mc 13,16; Mt 24,18: «et que celui qui sera au champ ne retourne pas en arrière pour prendre son manteau»). Placé ici, il prolonge explicitement la figure de Sodome, comme le rédacteur lucanien le précise lui-même au verset 32: «Souvenez-vous de la femme de Lot».

Cette métaphore filée se poursuit subrepticement encore dans la suite du passage. Au verset 33 («Quiconque cherchera à préserver sa vie la perdra et quiconque la perdra la fera vivre»), Luc valorise l'opposition 'garder vivante sa *psuchè*' ou 'la perdre', en la joignant de manière originale aux traditions sur la femme de Lot[26]. Mais comment qualifier cette désobéissance, ce 'retour en arrière' auquel Luc attache particulièrement d'importance (cf. v. 31)? Faut-il comprendre que le jugement de Dieu est tel que sa vision (se retourner pour voir le désastre) est insupportable à l'homme et qu'il conduit à la mort? Et, selon le discours de Jésus en Lc 17, que l'apocalypse (17,30) du Fils de l'homme revêt elle aussi un

---

25. Sur cette expression particulière de la LXX pour rendre l'hébreu *qeç* (fin), voir la note de M. HARL, *La Bible d'Alexandrie. La Genèse*, Paris, 1986, p. 130.

26. Parmi les nombreuses variations de ces traditions, celle de Philon d'Alexandrie (QG IV, 52) présente un certain intérêt: parce qu'elle a désobéi la femme de Lot est devenue *a-psuchè*.

tel caractère terrifiant? Dans ce cas le texte lucanien ne serait pas seulement d'ordre parénétique; il se situerait bien plutôt dans une forte perspective apocalyptique, dans l'annonce d'un jour particulièrement catastrophique et terrifiant.

Le verbe 'faire périr/périr' joue un rôle important non seulement dans les deux versets sur Noé et sur Lot (v. 27 et v. 30), mais aussi dans le dit du v. 33 (déplacé ici par Luc), sur la vie que l'on risque de perdre (τὴν ψυχὴν αὐτοῦ...ἀπολέσει αὐτήν, ...) si on cherche à la préserver, mais que, en revanche, celui qui la perd (.... ὃς δ' ἂν ἀπολέσῃ) gardera vivante. Le rédacteur lucanien tisse ainsi des liens intertextuels entre l'épisode raconté par l'Ancien Testament et le moment du jugement annoncé par Jésus. Le lecteur est appelé à décoder cette thématique de la vie à garder vivante ou à perdre. Comme à Lot en Gn 19,17, il lui est dit: «sauve-toi, il y va de ta vie. Ne regarde pas derrière-toi».

d) Enfin, l'image du vautour au verset 37 n'est pas à proprement parler une référence scripturaire. Elle mérite toutefois de figurer dans notre démarche d'analyse, car ce verset permet au rédacteur lucanien de continuer sa thématique du jour du jugement, et de la vie à perdre ou à préserver, bien que de manière plus voilée. Divers auteurs ont cherché les parallèles vétérotestamentaires susceptibles de comprendre cette image du vautour. Ils renvoient souvent à Jb 39,27-30. Au verset 30 de ce passage de Job en effet, le parallélisme avec le logion néotestamentaire est frappant: «là où il y a charnier, il (l'aigle, le vautour) y est». Il s'agit vraisemblablement d'un proverbe connu. Luc parle du corps (Matthieu mentionne le cadavre). Luc ferait[27] ici une annonce de la passion, en lien avec le dit du verset 25 («mais d'abord il lui faut beaucoup souffrir»). De l'interrogation sur le jour (du Fils de l'homme) on passe au lieu du corps. Luc revient ainsi en inclusion au thème du lieu (Lc 17,20). Le logion sur la passion remplace le logion sur les vautours. Ce dernier vient en finale du passage pour évoquer le thème de la mort et de la passion à travers la figure des vautours qui s'assemblent au lieu du corps.

En conclusion, deux points sont à relever dans les opérations intertextuelles de Luc. D'une part il qualifie le jour de l'apocalypse du Fils de l'homme comme un jour de jugement: les jours du Fils de l'homme, à l'instar du jour de Yahwé présentent un caractère terrifiant. D'autre part, s'interroger sur la venue du ou des jour(s) du Fils de l'homme implique une prise en considération de la passion, du corps comme lieu de mort, puis de vie pour qui sait déchiffrer le texte: cette clé de lecture vaut pour le Fils de l'homme lui-même (Lc 17,25) comme pour le disciple

---

27. J'ai proposé cette interprétation à la discussion lors du séminaire.

(Lc 17,33). Jésus conduit ses auditeurs vers une réflexion sur le véritable lieu de l'apocalypse: le Fils de l'homme en son corps. Cette visée sur la venue du salut prend en quelque sorte un relief particulier dans ce contexte tout entier polarisé par le tableau du jugement.

II. L'ARRIÈRE-FOND SCRIPTURAIRE EN LC 21

Dans cette deuxième partie du séminaire, nous nous sommes préoccupés également de la manière dont Luc utilise les références à l'Ancien Testament déjà présentes dans sa ou dans ses sources, essentiellement dans deux passages: Lc 21,8-11 et 21,20-24. En présence de phénomènes d'intertextualité, il importe surtout de voir quels sont les indices donnés par le rédacteur pour découvrir le sens des transformations qu'il opère. Or, dès le début Luc oriente son lecteur vers les modifications de sa relecture.

1. *Lc 21, 8-11*

Apparemment Luc se contente de reproduire les citations de Marc. À strictement parler les références scripturaires se répartissent en deux séries de termes: l'une, au verset 9 («il faut que cela arrive»), renvoie à Dn 2,28; l'autre au verset 10 («on se lèvera nation contre nation et royaume contre royaume») pourrait évoquer des formules semblables à celle de 2 Ch 15,6 (nation contre nation) et d'Is 19,2 (royaume contre royaume). Ce sont les mêmes citations que Marc 13,7. L'originalité de Luc se laisse saisir dans les menues divergences à propos des versets qui entourent ces citations. Notons les principales retouches, dans l'introduction au verset 8, dans la transformation du vocabulaire par l'insertion des adverbes temporels au verset 9, et enfin dans l'amplification de la poésie apocalyptique accordée à la conclusion du passage, au verset 11.

Le verset 8 commence par une introduction similaire à celle de Marc: Jésus recommande de ne pas se laisser égarer. En 8b Luc diffère légèrement de Marc; il ajoute «et le temps est proche». Faut-il comprendre cet ajout comme une insistance sur le *kairos*? La suite de la lecture semble aller dans ce sens.

Le verset 9 présente plusieurs menues divergences.

Au verset 9a, Luc précise le terme trop vague de 'rumeur' (Mc/Mt) par le mot plus évocateur et plus approprié de ἀκαταστασία (ruine, désordre, révolution). Ce terme «peut évoquer plus précisément des 'insurrections', des 'révoltes'. Il s'applique fort bien à la Révolte juive, qui s'est terminée par la destruction du Temple en 70»[28].

En 9b, Luc remplace le très rare verbe θροέω (au passif: effrayer) de Mc/Mt par le verbe πτοέω, hapax de Luc (Lc 21,9 et 24,37), mais fréquent dans la LXX. Dans le livre des Chroniques, ou chez Jérémie ce dernier verbe est utilisé à plusieurs reprises en parallélisme synonymique avec φοβέομαι. Ainsi lors de la victoire de Josaphat en 2 Ch 20,15.17 «ne craignez pas, ne vous effrayez pas»; en plein cœur du combat ou de la catastrophe cette injonction affirme que c'est en fin de compte Dieu qui mène les opérations: «ce combat n'est pas le vôtre, mais celui de Dieu». La planification temporelle des événements chez Luc se rapproche de cette thématique théologique du Livre des Chroniques visant à situer les événements dans le plan de Dieu. Luc avertit son lecteur sur une interprétation correcte du *kairos*. C'est différent dans le passage correspondant de Marc où les événements annoncés constituent le commencement des douleurs: «Cela c'est le commencement des douleurs» (Mc 13,8). Autrement dit, chez Luc l'insistance porte sur le temps comme accomplissement, chez Marc comme une mise en route.

Mais les divergences portent surtout dans l'introduction de la référence scripturaire en 9c: «car il faut que cela arrive *d'abord,* mais ce n'est pas *aussitôt* la fin». Chez Luc deux adverbes (πρῶτον et εὐθύς) entourent l'expression de Daniel (Dn 2,28 en Lc 21,9). L'insistance lucanienne sur les étapes temporelles s'explique, selon J. Dupont, «par le désir de contredire plus explicitement ceux qui prétendent que 'le temps est proche'»[29]. Il supprime l'étalement dans le temps tel qu'il est proposé par Marc[30] pour lui en substituer un autre, plus achevé. Cette transformation ressort clairement de la comparaison synoptique de Marc et de Luc. La conclusion du passage de Marc (13,8b) correspond aux visées eschatologiques destinées à prédire les événements qui doivent précéder la venue du Messie à la fin des temps: «Cela, c'est le commencement des douleurs». Luc élimine cette mention conclusive sur «le commencement des douleurs»; en revanche, il place en introduction à son passage une mise en garde contre une fausse interprétation du *kairos*: «beaucoup viendront sous mon nom, qui diront: 'c'est moi', et: 'Le temps est tout proche'. N'allez pas à leur suite» (Lc 21,8).

Cette transformation l'a probablement incité à donner au verset 11 une autre conclusion à partir des éléments de sa source. Il le fait en

---

28. J. DUPONT, *Les trois apocalypses synoptiques*, Paris, 1985, p. 109.
29. *Ibid.*, p. 107.
30. Mc 13,8 «Cela c'est le commencement des douleurs» et Mc 13,10: «Il faut d'abord qu'à toutes les nations soit proclamé l'évangile».

déployant un savoir faire poétique dont il a le secret: sur la base d'un vocabulaire vétérotestamentaire Luc pastiche le style apocalyptique. Si la versification est étudiée, le vocabulaire l'est également. Luc développe les sons *oi* dans la première partie du verset, ses sons *a* dans la deuxième. Il ajoute dans la première partie du verset le terme λοιμός et construit ainsi une belle succession à partir de σεισμοί: σεισμοί μεγάλοι λιμοί λοιμοί ἔσονται. Dans la deuxième partie il emploie un terme rare φόβητρον (au pluriel φόβητρα) et il construit une autre succession euphonique en α: φόβητρά σημεῖα μεγάλα ἔσται. Il renforce enfin le balancement de sa versification par τε τε. Luc a accordé beaucoup d'importance à ce poème, construit par touches successives.

En définitive, dans ces versets 8-11, Luc reprend les mêmes allusions scripturaires que Marc, mais en les accompagnant d'autres éléments, il leur confère une perspective différente. Pour l'essentiel ce paragraphe donne une orientation nouvelle de la temporalité. Les versets suivants que nous avons retenus pour cette étude feront saisir davantage encore ce travail de la rédaction lucanienne.

2. *Lc 21, 20-24*

Dans ce deuxième passage, il s'agit à nouveau de déterminer le degré de pertinence des rapprochements de Lc 21 avec l'Ancien Testament, ou plutôt, dans la perspective qui est la nôtre, de définir et de qualifier le mode d'intertextualité de Luc.

Les versets 20-24 sont truffés de références ou d'allusions à l'Écriture. On peut citer avec la plupart des commentateurs[31] de nombreux textes prophétiques. Mentionnons les principaux: a) la référence aux jours de vengeance au verset 22; b) plusieurs allusions scripturaires au verset 24.

a) Lc 21,22: «parce que ce sont des jours de vengeance, où doit s'accomplir tout ce qui se trouve écrit». L'expression ἡμέραι ἐκδικήσεως rappelle Os 9,7 LXX ἥκασιν αἱ ἡμέραι τῆς ἐκδικήσεως (*les jours de vengeance*). On peut encore évoquer Jérémie qui parle du «jour de vengeance» en Jr 46,10 (LXX 26,10), ou du «temps de vengeance» (Jr 46,21), etc. Le mot ἐκδίκησις, qui désigne le châtiment divin, n'est pas très utilisé dans le Nouveau Testament[32]. Dans deux

---

31. Voir en particulier J.A. FITZMYER, *The Gospel According to Luke X-XXIV*, Garden City, NY, 1986, *ad loc.*, esp. p. 1342.

32. Lc 18,7.8; 21,22; Ac 7,24; Rm 12,19: citation de Dt 32; 2 Co 7,11; 2 Th 1,8; He 10,30: citation de Dt 32; 1 P 2,14.

emplois néotestamentaires de ce terme, la référence à l'Écriture (Dt 32,35)[33] est explicite: en Rm 12,19: «car il est écrit *à moi la vengeance et la rétribution*»; en Hb 10,30: «Car nous connaissons celui qui a dit: *À moi la vengeance! C'est moi qui rétribuerai!*» Ces citations, dans l'épître aux Romains comme dans l'épître aux Hébreux, sont faites d'après le TM. La LXX de Dt 32,35 traduit l'hébreu «à moi la vengance» par «le jour de vengeance». Luc se rapprocherait davantage de l'expression de la LXX.

Il n'y a donc pas de textes précis, mais une expression vétéro-testamentaire qui renvoie au châtiment divin, au Dieu juge. Luc insiste ici, comme au chapitre 17, sur le jour du jugement.

b) Lc 21,24: «Et ils tomberont sous le tranchant du glaive, et ils seront emmenés captifs dans toutes les nations, et Jérusalem sera foulée aux pieds par les nations, jusqu'à ce que soient accomplis les temps des nations».

Dans ce verset, plusieurs termes fonctionnent comme des renvois à l'Ancien Testament, sans qu'il soit possible de noter *un* texte précis. On peut se référer, avec la plupart des commentateurs, aux passages suivants:

– «Le tranchant du glaive» en Si 28,18.

– Pour l'expression «captif parmi toutes les nations», les commentateurs mentionnent habituellement Dt 28,64 LXX («Yahwé te dispersera parmi toutes les nations»). Mais dans ce passage de l'Ancien Testament, il s'agit du verbe «disperser». Luc parle de la «captivité» dans toutes les nations: αἰχμαλωτισθήσονται εἰς τὰ ἔθνη πάντα. Le verbe αἰχμαλωτίζω (emmener en captivité, faire prisonnier) n'est pas fréquent dans le Nouveau Testament[34]. Dans l'Ancien Testament, il est employé bien évidemment pour la capture des prisonniers, dans les récits de guerre. On peut relever une certaine importance de ce terme ou plus exactement d'un thème théologique dans 2 Ch 28[35], mis en relief par la comparaison avec la narration de 2 R 16. Pour le chroniste l'invasion syro-ephraïmite de 2 R 16 est clairement perçue comme un châtiment de Yahwé. Apparaît ici un thème qui sera souvent repris dans la tradition juive, celui du rôle joué par les païens, instrument de la colère de Dieu pour un temps.

---

33. Ce cantique de Moïse a connu une fortune considérable dans les traditions juives et chrétiennes. Note remarquable dans C. DOGNIEZ et M. HARL, *La Bible d'Alexandrie-LXX. Tome 5. Le Deutéronome*, Paris, 1992, pp. 320-321.

34. On le trouve ici en Luc et trois autres fois dans la littérature paulinienne (Rm 7,23 [la loi qui tient captif]; 2 Co 10,5 [la pensée captive]; 2 Tm 3,6 [ceux qui captivent des femelettes chargées de péchés]). Le substantif est mentionné dans Ep 4,8; c'est une citation très libre de LXX Ps 68,19: «il a emmené captive la captivité».

35. Versets 5b.8.11.15.17.

La suite du passage lucanien n'est peut-être pas sans lien avec ce thème. – L'expression «foulée aux pieds par les païens» poursuit en effet clairement cette perspective. Le texte est une allusion à Za 12,3 où l'on trouve le verbe καταπατεῖν = fouler aux pieds.

Les versets 22 et 24 contiennent donc des renvois assez explicites à un vocabulaire vétérotestamentaire. Mais continuer cette énumération (d'autres exemples pourraient être donnés) conduirait à un comparatisme quelque peu stérile. Je souhaite plutôt poursuivre la réflexion sur la manière originale qu'a Luc de se référer à l'Ancien Testament, dans l'ensemble de ces versets.

3. *Une méditation théologique sur le passé (la dévastation de la ville) en Lc 21,20-24*

Un regard plus attentif sur la concentration de l'auteur sur le sort de la ville et de sa dévastation, ainsi que sur le rôle des païens conduit vers une précision de l'intertextualité de Luc, et de là à une réflexion sur sa signification pour le lecteur. Plutôt qu'un passage apocalyptique visant l'annonce du futur, les paroles prophétiques mises dans la bouche de Jésus en Lc 21 relèvent d'un genre littéraire différent, davantage orienté vers une méditation théologique du passé. L'auteur lucanien invite implicitement son lecteur à le suivre dans une interprétation théologique de l'histoire. Comment se fait cette opération de lecture? Il semble que l'on puisse apporter une réponse en observant le recours de Luc à des procédés similaires à ceux de l'Ancien Testament, dans des midrashim historiques repérables dans les livres des Chroniques, ou encore de certains psaumes (Ps 78). Luc se situe sur une trajectoire qui se développe encore davantage dans des textes dits apocalyptiques, postérieurs à l'an 70 de notre ère, comme l'Apocalypse syriaque de Baruch, ou dans des genres midrashiques, comme les Paralipomènes de Jérémie[36].

Je ne retiens pas tous les détails du passage, mais cherche à déterminer l'insistance lucanienne. Elle porte essentiellement sur trois points liés entre eux: la dévastation de la ville; l'importance du temps des païens; l'accomplissement des Écritures.

a) La dévastation de la ville

«Lorsque vous verrez Jérusalem investie par des armées, alors comprenez que sa désolation est toute proche» (Lc 21,20). C'est ainsi que Luc

---

36. J. RIAUD, *Les Paralipomènes du prophète Jérémie. Présentation, texte original, traduction et commentaires*, Angers, 1994.

ouvre ce paragraphe. Il évoque la chute de Jérusalem en des termes qui ressemblent beaucoup à ceux de Marc (et de Matthieu[37]). Toutefois, de menues divergences laissent percevoir l'orientation particulière de Luc, notamment dans sa référence à l'Écriture. Luc remplace l'expression τὸ βδέλυγμα (cf. Mc et Mt) par une description de l'encerclement militaire de Jérusalem (κυκλουμένην ὑπὸ στρατοπέδων Ἰερουσαλήμ), d'une part et par la modification de l'apodose, d'autre part. Il garde le motif de la désolation (ἡ ἐρήμωσις αὐτῆς), mais il le place dans l'apodose («alors comprenez que sa désolation est proche») et il précise par le pronom (αὐτῆς) qu'il s'agit de la ruine de la cité. Luc porte donc toute l'attention sur la cité et sur sa ruine[38]. Matthieu indique la provenance daniélique de l'expression τὸ βδέλυγμα τῆς ἐρημώσεως: «Lors donc que vous verrez l'*Abomination de la Désolation* annoncée par le prophète Daniel installée *dans un Lieu saint* – que le lecteur comprenne!» (Mt 24,15). Le couple de termes «abomination» et «désolation» intervient en effet dans les traductions grecques de Dn 9,27; 11,31; 12,11 (pour 9,27 et 12,11 aussi chez Théodotion). L'abomination de la désolation désigne aussi les idoles ou les actes des païens (2 Ch 28,3). Dans les passages précités de Daniel, elle renvoie au sacrilège commis par Antiochus Épiphane qui fit ériger un autel païen sur l'autel de l'holocauste (1 M 1,54). Luc donc ne mentionne que la «désolation». L'étude de l'emploi de ce terme – voire de de ce thème de la ville – conduit vers d'autres textes encore, à savoir vers la réflexion sur la première déportation au temps de Nabuchodonosor. Les récits bibliques sur Sédécias évoquent l'encerclement de la ville par les Chaldéens: en Jr 52,7 (καὶ οἱ Χαλδαῖοι ἐπὶ τῆς πόλεως κύκλῳ) et, avec la même formule, en 4 R 25,4 (καὶ οἱ Χαλδαῖοι ἐπὶ τὴν πόλιν κύκλῳ). On connaît la relecture théologique qu'Israël a fait de cette épreuve, de la dévastation de Jérusalem lors de la première déportation et de son temps de domination par les païens; on sait comment cet événement, dévastation, temps de la domination par les païens, est interprété en accomplissement de la parole du prophète, en l'occurrence Jérémie. C.H. Dodd a souligné la fréquence significative de la 'désolation' chez Jérémie[39]. Cet auteur a surtout montré l'importance de la désolation de la ville dans les textes relatifs à la première déportation. L'analyse du passage lucanien me semble aller en effet davantage dans ce sens.

37. Matthieu suit Marc, sauf lorsqu'il précise la référence à Daniel.
38. Sur ces particularités lucaniennes, voir J.D. KAESTLI, *L'eschatologie dans l'œuvre de Luc, ses caractéristiques et sa place dans le développement du christianisme primitif*, Genève, 1969, pp. 49 ss.
39. C.H. DODD, *The Fall of Jerusalem and the 'Abomination of Desolation'*, in *More New Testament Studies*, Manchester, 1968, pp. 69-83, p. 73.

Luc retient essentiellement le thème de la dévastation, comme pour mieux se centrer sur la désolation de la ville elle-même. Il accentue encore cette focalisation sur la dévastation de Jérusalem par l'évocation de son encerclement militaire (κυκλουμένην ὑπὸ στρατοπέδων Ἰερουσαλήμ); l'évangéliste annonce ici très nettement le siège de la cité, comme l'ont souligné la plupart des commentateurs[40]. Mais les transformations de Lc 21,20 par rapport à Mc 13,14 posent dès lors la question plus précise de son renvoi à l'Écriture. L'histoire et son jugement par Dieu chez Luc se lit peut être moins dans la ligne apocalyptique de Daniel, mais elle se veut plutôt orientée par une théologie du jugement. Je pense effectivement que Luc se situe sur une trajectoire des traditions qui rejoint les historiographes ou plutôt les traditions sur la lamentation à propos de la dévastation de Jérusalem et de la captivité, parce qu'elles permettent de comprendre ce qui s'est passé comme un accomplissement de l'Écriture. Lorsque Luc ajoute au verset 24 le motif du «temps des païens» il s'inscrit dans une perspective semblable: les païens deviennent pour un temps 'exécuteurs du jugement de Dieu'[41].

b) Le temps des païens

De nombreuses traditions juives témoignent en effet d'une réflexion sur le rôle tenu par les païens dans le plan de Dieu lors de la déportation, et notamment sur le 'temps' des païens. On en trouve un exemple dans la finale du deuxième livre des Rois et surtout du Chroniste. Le Ps 79 (78) évoque aussi, du moins en arrière-fond, cette théologie où Dieu permet aux païens de devenir l'oppresseur du peuple d'Israël; le psalmiste questionne son Dieu: «jusqu'à quand cette colère?» Les Paralipomènes de Jérémie (notamment au chapitre 4)[42] racontent l'encerclement de la ville par l'armée des Chaldéens, la déportation du peuple à Babylone; ce passage mentionne ensuite la lamentation de Baruch qui s'interroge: «Pourquoi Jérusalem a-t-elle été dévastée?» La mention des païens-ennemis apparaît dans la réponse: «À cause des péchés du peuple bien-aimé, elle a été livrée aux mains des ennemis, à cause de nos péchés etc.» Les patriarches Abraham, Isaac et Jacob sont ensuite déclarés heureux, parce qu'ils n'ont pas vu l'anéantissement de la ville.

---

40. Voir entre autres J.A. FITZMYER (n. 31).
41. J. DUPONT (n. 28), p. 126.
42. J. RIAUD (n. 35), pp. 141-143.

Au niveau de la *Wirkungsgeschichte*, Luc se situe donc, du moins partiellement, sur une même trajectoire des traditions[43]. Il relit l'histoire de la chute de Jérusalem, à la manière des historiographes midrashistes de la Bible (tel le Chroniste): la ruine de la cité est à lire comme un événement théologique[44]. La transformation des allusions scripturaires et l'utilisation «des thèmes de l'Ancien Testament montre que l'accent se place, non sur le fait que Jérusalem sera détruite, mais sur l'affirmation que cette destruction sera un châtiment divin»[45].

c) L'accomplissement des Écritures: «ce seront des jours de châtiment, où tout ce qui a été écrit devra s'accomplir» (Lc 21,24).

En lien avec ce qui vient d'être suggéré à propos de la relecture lucanienne, il n'est pas inutile de relire comment s'exprime ce spécialiste de la théologie de l'histoire du peuple qu'est le Chroniste lorsqu'il évoque les jours de la désolation-dévastation (2 Ch 36,17-21). Les versets 20-21 notamment traduisent ce commentaire théologique sur le temps de servitude auprès des païens «jusqu'à...l'établissement du royaume perse, accomplissant la parole de Yahwé, (transmise) par la bouche de Jérémie: jusqu'à ce que la terre se fût acquittée de ses sabbats, tout le temps qu'elle fut dévastée, elle chôma, accomplissant les soixante dix-ans... pour que s'accomplît la parole de Yahwé (prononcée) par la bouche de Jérémie...»[46].

La place que Luc accorde à l'accomplissement du «temps des nations» (v. 24) lors de la *désolation* est à lire sur un registre traditionnel bien établi: en lien avec ces traditions relatives à l'invasion de Jérusalem par les Chaldéens et à la ville foulée aux pieds, perceptibles chez Jérémie ainsi que dans les Livres des Rois et du Chroniste, s'étendant jusqu'à l'Apocalypse syriaque de Baruch (chapitre 6 ss). Cette interprétation sera encore très sensible dans diverses relectures juives postérieures: dans les Paralipomènes de Jérémie, dans la Pesiqta Rabati[47], etc. Sans tisser des

---

43. C'est la proposition que j'ai faite dans le séminaire et que nous avons discutée. Je remercie en particulier P. Beauchamp, P. Bogaert, J.M. van Cangh et A. Vanhoye pour leur participation et pour les remarques judicieuses qui ont rendu ce séminaire passionnant et dynamique.
44. J. Dupont, (n. 28) pp. 122-123.
45. Citation de L. Hartman, dans J. Dupont, (n. 28) p. 127.
46. Jr 25–27. Dans son commentaire du passage lucanien, M.-É. Boismard accorde également une attention particulière à Jérémie et au Chroniste: voir P. Benoit et M.-É. Boismard, *Synopse des quatre évangiles en français*, t. II, Paris, 1972, p. 366.
47. Dans ce livre on trouve différents motifs que nous venons d'évoquer pour parler de la désolation de la ville. Cette dernière est ainsi décrite: «C'est une ville foulée que vous avez foulée», dans P. Bogaert, *L'Apocalypse syriaque de Baruch. Introduction, Traduction et Commentaire*, t. 1, Paris, 1969, p. 230

liens artificiels de dépendance littéraire entre tous ces textes, trop distincts dans l'espace et dans le temps, il n'en reste pas moins que l'on
peut affirmer ceci: ces passages manifestent qu'il est toujours important
de relire l'histoire de la ruine de Jérusalem (de son encerclement par
l'envahisseur) et de ce qui a suivi (le foulement de la ville par les païens)
pour comprendre l'intention divine du jugement, à la lumière des Écritures. Autrement dit, la répétition de certains 'clichés', le rappel de mots
tirés de l'Ancien Testament, la reprise certains motifs et de leur articulation[48] sont autant de matériaux caractéristiques d'une réflexion sur le
sens de l'histoire telle qu'elle se forge dans la tradition biblique et au-
delà. Comme l'écrit un écrivain juif contemporain:

> Pour les rabbins, la Bible n'était pas seulement le livre de l'histoire adve-
> nue; c'était également la révélation de la trame de toute l'histoire..... ...
> pour prendre le pouls de l'histoire, il ne fallait pas écouter les manifesta-
> tions en surface, mais entendre une histoire invisible qui avait plus de réa-
> lité que les rythmes bruyants des pouvoirs qui abusaient un monde aveugle.
> L'Assyrie était l'instrument de la colère divine contre Israël, même si elle
> ne l'avait pas compris alors. Nabuchodonosor rasa Jérusalem (586) non pas
> grâce à la puissance de Babylone, mais à cause des transgressions perpé-
> trées par Jérusalem et parce que Dieu avait permit sa chute. Face au triom-
> phalisme qui était la sagesse historique et conventionnelle des nations,
> voilà que se profilait, comme dans une réprobation silencieuse, le Serviteur
> souffrant d'Isaïe, 53. La catastrophe de l'an 70 de notre ère était due,
> comme celle de l'an 586 avant notre ère, au péché....[49]

Lc 21,20-24 porte l'interrogation sur le motif de l'accomplissement
(v. 22; v. 24). Ce motif a retenu toute l'attention de notre séminaire.
Comment faut-il comprendre chez Luc et plus particulièrement dans le
passage examiné ici cette notion d'accomplissement: comme un achève-
ment ou comme une ouverture? Nous n'avons pas réussi à clore ce débat
désormais classique, mais l'interprétation que j'ai donnée de ces versets
se raccroche à celle de la majeure partie des commentateurs sur le sens
à donner au «temps des nations», à savoir que Jérusalem est livrée aux
païens[50]; le rôle des païens lors de la dévastation de la ville s'inscrit dans
le processus du jugement divin.

En conclusion, que retenir de la manière dont Luc recourt à l'Ancien
Testament? La lecture synoptique proposée pour l'analyse de Lc 17,20-
37 et Lc 21,20-24 permet de qualifier un peu mieux cette mise en œuvre.

---

48. en l'occurrence l'encerclement de la ville, le rôle du temps des païens dans
l'accomplissement du dessein de Dieu et des Ecritures, notamment pour ce dernier point
en référence au prophète Jérémie.
49. Y.H. YERUSHALMI (n. 5), p. 37 ss.
50. J. DUPONT (n. 28), p. 126.

Luc se réfère aux Écritures, sur la lancée même de ses sources (Q ou Mc), en les «déhanchant» parfois, tantôt de façon imperceptible, tantôt de manière indubitable. Ce faisant il sollicite son lecteur et l'invite – je crois qu'on peut le dire sans trop forcer l'interprétation de l'intertextualité – à méditer sur le temps et le lieu de la venue du Christ dans l'histoire des hommes comme Fils de l'homme, sur le sens de l'histoire dans les mains de Dieu, c'est-à-dire, pour les chrétiens, sur la signification de la proximité du règne tant annoncée par Jésus, comme présence effective de Dieu.

Faculté de Théologie Catholique   Michèle MORGEN
Palais Universitaire
9, Place de l'Université
F-67 000 Strasbourg

SCHRIFTZITATE IM »LEBENSBROT«-DIALOG JESU (JOH 6)
EIN PARADIGMA FÜR DEN SCHRIFTGEBRAUCH
DES VIERTEN EVANGELISTEN

Zu der mehr »technischen« Seite des johanneischen Schriftgebrauchs (vor allem zu den Fragen, welcher biblische Text den Zitaten des vierten Evangeliums zugrunde liegt und wie deren zuweilen auffälligen Abweichungen sowohl von der Masora wie von der Septuaginta sich erklären lassen) gibt es inzwischen eine Reihe von weiterführenden Untersuchungen[1]. Völlig unklar ist nach wie vor die Frage, wo, in welchem Umfang und mit welcher Intention das vierte Evangelium sich sogenannter »Anspielungen« auf das Alte Testament bedient[2]. Bei der von diesen »technischen« Fragen nicht zu trennenden Grundsatzproblematik, welchen theologischen Stellenwert die biblischen »Schriften« im Konzept des vierten Evangelisten besitzen, kommt die Diskussion erst langsam wieder in Gang[3]. C. Dietzfelbinger hat jüngst auf die aporetische Situation

---

1. Eine umfassende Bibliographie jetzt bei A. OBERMANN, *Die christologische Erfüllung der Schrift im Johannesevangelium* (WUNT, II, 83), Tübingen, 1996. Auswahlweise seien folgende übergreifende Werke genannt: E.D. FREED, *Old Testament Quotations in the Gospel of John* (NTSup, 11), Leiden, 1965; A.T. HANSON, *The Prophetic Gospel. A Study of John and the Old Testament*, Edinburgh, 1991; B.G. SCHUCHARD, *Scripture within Scripture. The Interrelationship of Form and Function in the explicit Old Testament Citations in the Gospel of John* (SBL DS, 133), Atlanta, 1992; G. REIM, *Jochanan. Erweiterte Studien zum alttestamentlichen Hintergrund des Johannesevangeliums*, Erlangen, 1995; M.J.J. MENKEN, *Old Testament Quotations in the Fourth Gospel. Studies in Textual Form* (Contributions to Biblical Exegesis and Theology, 15), Kampen, 1996.

2. Das beginnt schon bei der Frage, was »Anspielungen« sind und wie sie von wem als solche zu erkennen sind (Beispiele in nn. 20 u. 59)! Das müßte geklärt sein, bevor man sich auf ihre Suche macht, weil sonst unabweisbar die Gefahr der Überinterpretation der johanneischen Texte droht.

3. M. HENGEL, *Die Schriftauslegung des 4. Evangeliums auf dem Hintergrund der urchristlichen Exegese*, in *JBT* 4 (1989) 249-288; DERS., *The Old Testament in the Fourth Gospel*, in C.A. EVANS – W.R. STEGNER (eds.), *Studies in Scripture in Early Judaism and Christianity* (JSNT SS, 104), Sheffield, 1994, pp. 380-395; H. HÜBNER, *Biblische Theologie des Neuen Testaments*, Bd. 3, Göttingen, 1995, pp. 152-205; OBERMANN (n. 1); C. DIETZFELBINGER, *Aspekte des Alten Testaments im Johannesevangelium*, in H. CANCIK/H. LICHTENBERGER/P. SCHÄFER (eds.), *Geschichte – Tradition – Reflexion*. FS M. Hengel, Tübingen, 1996, Vol. 3, pp. 203-218; W. KRAUS, *Die Vollendung der Schrift nach Joh 19,28. Überlegungen zum Umgang mit der Schrift im Johannesevangelium* (in diesem Band, pp. 629-636); DERS., *Johannes und das Alte Testament. Überlegungen zum Umgang mit der Schrift im Johannesevangelium im Horizont Biblischer Theologie*, vorgesehen für *ZNW* (unten nach dem Ms. zitiert): beide Texte von Kraus wurden mir erst nach Abfassung meines eigenen Beitrags bekannt.

verwiesen, daß nach einigen Forschern die alttestamentlichen Zitate für den vierten Evangelisten, der »eine Heilsgeschichte nicht mehr« kenne, lediglich von »marginaler Bedeutung« seien[4], wohingegen von anderen Forschern die biblische »Heilsgeschichte«, die in Zitaten und Anspielungen im Buch reichhaltig zur Sprache käme, gerade zur Matrix der johanneischen Christologie erklärt würde[5]. Zugespitzt formuliert: Ist für die einen das Alte Testament im vierten Evangelium nur noch »der Juden Gesetz«[6] und als solches »keine religiöse Autorität und Quelle der lebendigen, persönlichen Offenbarung Gottes mehr, sondern lediglich ein Mittel, die Gegner zu widerlegen, die noch an jener Autorität festhalten«[7], so bleibt es für die anderen auch bei Joh noch das Wort Gottes, das an Israel ergangen ist und nach 10,35 auch von den Christen nicht »aufgelöst« werden kann. Wenn für diesen Beitrag Joh 6 als Paradigma für den Schriftgebrauch des vierten Evangelisten gewählt wird, dann geschieht das aus zwei Gründen, zum einen, weil Joh 6 mit seinen zwei (!) Schriftzitaten samt haggadischer Anwesenheit von Ex 16 einen ungewöhnlich dichten Bezug zum Alten Testament unterhält[8], zum andern, weil sich an diesem Kapitel die sachliche Relevanz der Schriftzitate für die Argumentation des Evangelisten in besonders anschaulicher Weise diskutieren läßt. Auf der Frage nach der Bedeutung der »Schriften« für die johanneische Theologie soll dabei der Akzent liegen. Weiter kommt man bei diesem Unterfangen allerdings nur, wenn eine möglichst präzise Ortsbestimmung der Zitate in Joh 6 gelingt, weshalb strukturellen Fragen an erster Stelle Aufmerksamkeit zu schenken ist.

I. Funktion und Bedeutung der Schriftzitate in Joh 6

Joh 6 enthält mit *Ps 77,24b LXX* in v. 31b und mit *Jes 54,13 LXX* in v. 45 zwei Schriftzitate, über deren Herkunft in letzter Zeit eine höchst

---

4. E. Plümacher, Art. *Bibel II*, in *TRE* 6, pp. 8-22, p.18.

5. So M. Hengel, *Schriftauslegung* (n. 3) p. 263 u.ö, der ausdrücklich von alttestamentlicher »Heilsgeschichte« bei Joh spricht. Im einzelnen s. Dietzfelbinger, *Aspekte* (n. 3), p. 203.

6. Von E. Plümacher (n. 4) hervorgehoben: cf. 8,17 (»auch in *eurem* Gesetz steht geschrieben...«); 10,34 (»steht nicht in *eurem* Gesetz geschrieben...«); 15,25 (»damit das Wort erfüllt würde, das in *ihrem* Gesetz geschrieben steht...«).

7. So Kreyenbühl, zitiert bei Dietzfelbinger (n. 3), p. 204.

8. *Paarweise* begegnen Schriftzitate (jeweils mit Zitateinführungsformel) noch in 12, 38/39f und 19,36/37; die besondere Dichte von Zitaten und Schriftbezügen in 19, 24.28.36f hängt wohl mit dem Einfluß der alten Passionsgeschichte zusammen. *Vereinzeltes* Auftreten von Schriftzitaten ist in 1,23; 2,17; 7,38; 12,14f; 13,18; 15,25 zu registrieren.

detaillierte, hier nicht noch einmal zu wiederholende Diskussion geführt wurde, die aber das offensichtlich konsensfähige, vorstehende Ergebnis erbracht hat[9]. Die Texte lauten[10]:

Joh 6,31b   ἄρτον ἐκ τοῦ οὐρανοῦ ἔδωκεν αὐτοῖς *φαγεῖν*
Ps 77,24   (καὶ ἔβρεξεν αὐτοῖς μάννα   *φαγεῖν*
(LXX)   καὶ *ἄρτον*   *οὐρανοῦ ἔδωκεν αὐτοῖς*

Als Alternativen kommen nicht in Frage (1) Ex 16,4a wegen des dort verwendeten Verbs »regnen lassen« (ὕειν/הַמְטִיר)[11], (2) Ex 16,15b v.a. wegen des abweichenden Bezugs des Satzes auf die zweite statt dritte Pers. plur. (»das Brot, das der Herr *euch* zum Essen gab«) sowie (3) Neh 9,15 v.a. wegen des diesem Text eigenen Gebetskontextes (»Brot vom Himmel gabst *Du* ihnen«).

Die Abweichungen der johanneischen Gestalt des Zitats von der Septuaginta-Fassung von Ps 77,24 lassen sich am besten durch Redaktion des Evangelisten erklären[12].

Joh 6,45   καὶ ἔσονται πάντες   διδακτοὶ θεοῦ
Jes 54,13   (καὶ θήσω...)
LXX   καὶ   πάντας τοὺς υἱούς σου   διδακτοὺς θεοῦ
    (*MT:* לְמוּדֵי יְהוָה)

Kommt in 6,45 als Quelle des Zitats allein Jes 54,13 in Frage[13], so dreht der Streit sich hauptsächlich darum, ob die Masora oder die Septuaginta den Bezugstext lieferten. Wahrscheinlich ist letzteres der Fall, da dem

---

9. M.J.J. MENKEN, *The Provenance and Meaning of the Old Testament Quotation in John 6,31*, in *NT* 30 (1988) 39-56; DERS., *The Old Testament quotation in John 6,45. Source and Redaction*, in *ETL* 64 (1988) 164-172: beide Studien jetzt unter neuen Kapitelüberschriften in DERS. (n. 1), pp. 47-65 (»He Gave Them Bread from Heaven to Eat« [John 6:31], »And They Shall All Be Taught by God« [John 6:45]) (danach wird im folgenden zitiert). Außerdem SCHUCHARD (n. 1), pp. 34-38, 50-53; OBERMANN (n. 1) pp. 132-135, 151-154. Anders G. RICHTER, *Die alttestamentlichen Zitate in der Rede vom Himmelsbrot. Joh 6,26-51a*, in DERS., *Studien zum Johannesevangelium* (BU, 13), Regensburg, 1977, pp. 199-265, der annimmt, daß der Evangelist nicht das Alte Testament selbst zitiert habe, sondern eine jüdische Mannatradition, zu der das Zitat gehöre.

10. Die dem joh. Zitat und dem LXX-Text gemeinsamen Worte sind kursiv gesetzt.

11. Die konkrete Farbe des Verbs ließ wohl den Vers für den joh. Kontext als ungeeignet erscheinen. Das Verb διδόναι aus Ps 77,24 LXX entsprach dagegen perfekt der johanneischen Phraseologie (cf. 3,16). Allerdings stimmt die präpositionale Wendung (ἄρτους) ἐκ τοῦ οὐρανοῦ (Masora: לֶחֶם מִן־הַשָּׁמַיִם) in Ex 16,4 mit Joh 6,31b überein.

12. Das betrifft vor allem das ἐκ τοῦ (»aus dem [Himmel]«): dazu siehe unten! Allerdings ist im Umgang mit dem bibl. »Basistext« der Mannatradition, Ex 16 (cf. n. 19!), die Rede vom »Brot vom Himmel« (Ex 16,4: cf. n. 11!) schon nahezu topisch geworden, doch variieren die Formulierungen in den griechischen Texten (Weish 16,20: ἄρτον ἀπ᾽ οὐρανοῦ; Neh 9,15: ἄρτον ἐξ οὐρανοῦ).

13. Jer 24,7; 31,33f. (LXX 38,33f.); Joel 2,27.29; Hab 2,14 lassen sich nur motivisch assoziieren.

יְהוָה der Masora doch wohl ein κυρίου entsprochen hätte (vgl. 12,13.38)[14].

Die spezifisch johanneische Gestalt des Zitats erklärt sich zum einen durch die syntaktische Verselbständigung des in der LXX von θήσω (Jes 54,12) abhängigen doppelten Akkusativs mit Hilfe des ἔσονται, zum anderen ist sie kontextuell bedingt[15].

Folgendes kann man im Blick auf die äußere Gestalt der beiden Schriftzitate festhalten: a) Sehr wahrscheinlich orientiert der Evangelist sich beidesmal an der LXX. b) Es liegen keine Mischzitate vor[16], sondern es steht jeweils ein einzelner Schrifttext im Blickfeld. An einem Hinweis auf die möglicherweise breitere alttestamentliche Textbasis des Zitierten zeigt der Evangelist offensichtlich kein Interesse[17]. c) Die Abweichungen der johanneischen Zitate von ihren Bezugstexten finden, wie im einzelnen noch zu zeigen sein wird, ihre plausible Erklärung in der gezielten redaktionellen Bearbeitung der Texte durch den Evangelisten[18]. Damit führen die »technischen« Fragen des johanneischen Schriftgebrauchs unmittelbar hinüber zur hermeneutischen Problematik: Der Evangelist findet seinen zitierten Text offensichtlich nicht einfach nur vor, er selbst konstituiert ihn als Text, in formaler und wohl auch semantischer Hinsicht. Was das über sein Schriftverständnis im einzelnen verrät, wird im folgenden des näheren zu zeigen sein.

Außer den beiden Schriftzitaten sind noch a) *6,31a* als *eine Art haggadischen Summariums* von Ex 16[19] sowie b) *6,41* (ἐγόγγυζον οὖν οἱ

14. So OBERMANN (n. 1), p. 151. Nicht überzeugend ist dagegen seine Annahme (pp. 153.160f), das ἐλθεῖν πρός με (6,44f) sei durch den LXX-Kontext von Jes 54,13 vermittelt, nämlich 54,15, wo im Unterschied zur Masora vom Kommen von Proselyten (»Hinzukommenden«) die Rede ist; die joh. Phraseologie ist eigenständig und begegnet nicht nur hier (cf. 5,40; 6,35.37).

15. Das betrifft die Auslassung von τοὺς υἱούς σου (dazu siehe unten!).

16. Das betrifft insbesondere das Psalm-Zitat in v. 31.

17. Auch die Zitationsformel »es steht geschrieben *bei den Propheten*« in v. 45a deutet nicht in diese Richtung (siehe des näheren unten n. 122f!).

18. E.E. ELLIS, *Paul's Use of the Old Testament*, Edinburgh, 1957, p. 111 n. 2, im Anschluß an K. STENDAHL, *The School of St Matthew*, Uppsala, 1954: »Thus the Johannine method is not what is usually meant by loose citations, or those more or less freely quoted from memory. It is rather the opposite since the form of John's quotations is certainly the fruit of scholarly treatment of written OT texts«.

19. Dies ist der Grundtext der Mannatradition in der Tora; »alle weiteren Stellen des AT, die auf das Manna Bezug nehmen (so Num 11,6.7-9; Dtn 8,2-4.16; Jos 5,12; Neh 9,15.20; Ps 78,23-25; Ps 105,40) sind von der Basisstelle Ex 16 abhängig« (A. SCHMITT, *Das Buch der Weisheit. Ein Kommentar*, Würzburg, 1986, p. 127, zu Weish 16,20-29; comp. außerdem Dtn 32,13). Zu Joh 6,31a: P. BORGEN, *Bread from Heaven. An exegetical study of the concept of Manna in the Gospel of John and the writings of Philo* (NTSup, 10), Leiden, 1965, p. 22: »Such summaries of the events of the Exodus were obviously a common pattern of the haggadic tradition in Judaism, both in Palestine and in the Diaspora«.

ἸΟυδαῖοι) als Anspielung auf Ex 16,2.7.8.9.12 (das Murren der Israeliten in der Wüste[20]) zu erwähnen[21].

1. Der strukturelle Ort der Zitate in Joh 6

Drei Schritte sind im folgenden zu tun: (1) eine Diskussion der strukturbildenden Faktoren der sog. »Lebensbrotrede« 6,22-59 (65), (2) Hinweise zum Bauplan des Textes sowie (3) Schlußfolgerungen zum Ort der Schriftzitate in ihm.

1. Die strukturbildenden Faktoren in Joh 6,22-59 (65)

Daß die bislang von der Forschung präsentierten Versuche, die Struktur der sog. »Lebensbrotrede« Jesu 6,22-59 (65) zu erfassen[22], noch kein allseits befriedigendes Ergebnis erbracht haben, dürfte an der je unterschiedlichen Gewichtung der im Text wirksamen strukturbildenden Faktoren liegen. Orientiert man sich streng formal an der *dialogischen* Gestaltung des Textes mit seinen sechs Redewechseln (*Frage* der Volksmenge bzw. der Juden – *Antwort* Jesu), dann führt das zu einem anderen Gesamtbild als bei Berücksichtigung auch der vier *Amen-Worte Jesu* im Text (v. 26f; 32f; v. 47; v. 53), die gleichfalls formale Signale setzen, aber ein teilweise quer zu den Redewechseln verlaufendes Strukturmuster bilden. Bringt man *inhaltliche* Gliederungsmomente zum Zug, so kann man das zwar durch Identifizierung wiederholt auftretender signifikanter Lexeme oder Lexemverbindungen (Schlüsselworte) auch formal zu kontrollieren suchen, doch wird dann der Ermessensspielraum in jedem Fall

---

20. Cf. auch Ps 106 (105),25 (γογγύζειν). Das Verb bei Joh noch in 6,61 und 7,32. Die LXX benutzt in Ex 16 γογγυσμός und διαγογγύζειν, was nicht ausschließt, daß die »Anspielung« sich am biblischen Grundtext mit seinem Leitmotiv orientiert. Siehe auch HANSON (n. 1), pp. 87-89 (Lit.).

21. Außerdem siehe noch unten n. 59 zu 6,50/Ex 16,15!

22. P. GÄCHTER, *Die Form der eucharistischen Rede Jesu*, in ZKTh 59 (1935) 419-441; J. SCHNEIDER, *Zur Frage der Komposition von Joh 6, 27-58 (59)*, in *In Memoriam E. Lohmeyer*, Stuttgart, 1951, pp. 132-142; J.-N. ALETTI, *Le discours sur le pain de vie. Problèmes de composition et fonction des citations de l'Ancien Testament*, in *RSR* 62 (1974) 169-197; L. SCHENKE, *Die formale und gedankliche Struktur von Joh 6,26-58*, in *BZ* NF 24 (1980) 21-41; M. GIRARD, *L'unité de composition de Jean 6, au regard de l'analyse structurelle*, in *EeT* 13 (1982) 79-110; J.D. CROSSAN, *It is written: A Structuralist Analysis of John 6*, in *Semeia* 26 (1983) 3-21; J. BEUTLER, *Zur Struktur von Joh 6*, in *SNTU/A* 16 (1991) 89-104. Einen Überblick über verschiedene Gliederungsversuche bietet F.J. MOLONEY, *The Johannine Son of Man*, Rome, 1976, pp. 87-107. Eine umfassende Bibliographie zu Joh 6 jetzt in P.N. ANDERSON, *The Christology of the Fourth Gospel. Its Unity and Disunity in the Light of John 6* (WUNT, 2/78), Tübingen, 1996, pp. 287-291.

größer. Hinzu kommt, daß die vorgelegten Strukturanalysen in der Regel der selbst gesetzten Zielvorgabe folgen, die genuine Einheit der »Lebensbrotrede« Jesu zu erweisen, um so Hypothesen einer sekundären Überarbeitung von Joh 6 durch die johanneische Redaktion den Boden zu entziehen. Hält man sich aber aufgrund diverser Textphänomene für die literarkritische Option offen[23], dann wird man für die integrative Reichweite einzelner strukturbildender Elemente sowie mögliche Überlagerungen von Strukturmustern sensibel bleiben. Methodisch scheint es geraten, zunächst die zur Diskussion stehenden einzelnen Faktoren gesondert auf ihre Tragfähigkeit hin zu überprüfen.

(1) Für die Fragestellung dieses Beitrags in besonderem Maße relevant ist die These von P. Borgen, die »Lebensbrotrede«, genauer 6,32-58, sei nach Form und Inhalt als christlicher *Midrasch oder Homilie zum Schriftzitat von v. 31* (einem Mischzitat aus Ex 16,4.15 und Ps 78 [77], 24) zu begreifen[24]. Danach steht die *Zentralität des Zitats v. 31* für den nachfolgenden Text insgesamt außer Zweifel, wobei es auch dessen Struktur bestimme: Seine erste Hälfte (»Brot vom Himmel gab er ihnen«) werde in v. 32-48 (I), seine zweite Hälfte (»zu essen«) in v. 49-58 (II) ausgelegt[25]. Daß Eröffnung (v. 31-33) und Schluß der Rede (v. 58) sich homiletischen Konventionen gemäß entsprächen[26], sei überdies als Argument für die ursprüngliche Zugehörigkeit des eucharistischen Abschnitts 6,52-58 zum Text zu werten. Die Bedeutung dieser Hypothese für die Frage nach dem Stellenwert der Schriftzitate in Joh 6 liegt auf der Hand.

P. Borgens ungemein anregender Versuch hat eine lebhafte Debatte ausgelöst, in deren Verlauf seine Grundannahme eines »homiletic pattern« in 6,31ff sich durchaus als problematisch herausgestellt hat[27]. Von

---

23. M. THEOBALD, *Häresie von Anfang an? Strategien zur Bewältigung eines Skandals nach Joh 6,60-71*, in R. KAMPLING – T. SÖDING (eds.), *Ekklesiologie des Neuen Testaments*. FS. K. Kertelge, Freiburg, 1996, pp. 212-246: 236-243.

24. BORGEN (n. 19) pp. 28-58; DERS., *Observations on the Midrashic Character of John 6*, in *ZNW* 54 (1963) 231-240. Der Versuch von G. GEIGER, *Anruf an Rückkehrende. Zum Sinn des Zitats von Ps 78,24b in Joh 6,31*, in *Bib* 65 (1984) 449-464, in Ps 78 das »pattern« für Joh 6 zu erkennen, kann nicht überzeugen.

25. BORGEN (n. 19) p. 35.

26. »John 6,58 sums up the whole homily« (*ibid.*, p. 37).

27. Immerhin sind darin Borgen einige Forscher gefolgt: R. SCHNACKENBURG, *Das Johannesevangelium* (HTKNT, 4/2), Bd. 2, Freiburg, [2]1977, p. 42 (»Wenigstens der Abschnitt V. 32-51b…stellt, wie P. Borgen richtig erkannt hat, einen christlichen Midrasch über jenes Schriftwort dar, der Methoden jüdischer Schriftauslegung aufnimmt«), ähnlich R. BROWN, *The Gospel according to John* (AB), Vol. 1, New York, 1966, p. 294; G. RICHTER, *Zur Formgeschichte und literarischen Einheit von Joh 6,31-58*, in DERS., *Studien zum Johannesevangelium* (BU, 13), Regensburg, 1977, pp. 88-119; G. BORNKAMM, *Vorjohanneische Tradition oder nachjohanneische Bearbeitung in der eucharistischen Rede Johannes 6?*, in DERS., *Geschichte und Glaube*, Bd. 2, München, 1971, pp. 51-64;

den unterschiedlichen Gegenargumenten[28] sei hier nur eines profiliert, zumal ihm bislang nicht die gebührende Beachtung zuteil wurde: Borgen hatte behauptet, ab v. 48 stünde das φαγεῖν des alttestamentlichen Zitats im Mittelpunkt des Midraschs und dieses verknüpfe auch v. 49-51 und 52-58 unlösbar miteinander[29]. Doch ersteres stimmt nicht. Nicht das Motiv »*essen*«[30], sondern die Opposition »*sterben*« / »*leben*« bezeichnet die Klimax des Satzgefüges v. 47(!) – 51[31]; das Element »essen« ist in keinem ihrer Teilsätze fokussiert, sondern wird vielmehr jedesmal von Lebens- oder Sterbensaussagen überboten:

47   Amen, amen,
     ich sage euch:
     Der Glaubende hat *ewiges Leben* (ζωὴν αἰώνιον).

48   Ich bin das Brot des *Lebens* (τῆς ζωῆς);
49   eure Väter haben gegessen in der Wüste das Manna
     und sind *gestorben* (ἀπέθανον)[32].

50   *Dies* ist das Brot,
     das *vom Himmel* herabkommt,
     damit (ἵνα) man von *ihm* ißt
     und *nicht stirbt* (μὴ ἀποθάνῃ).

51   Ich bin das *lebenspendende* Brot (ὁ ἄρτος ζῶν)[33],
     das vom *Himmel* herabgekommen ist;
     wenn jemand von *diesem* Brot ißt,
     wird er *in Ewigkeit leben* (ζήσει εἰς τὸν αἰῶνα).

ALETTI (n. 22) p. 180; U. WILCKENS, *Der eucharistische Abschnitt der johanneischen Rede vom Lebensbrot (Joh 6,51c-58)*, in *Neues Testament und Kirche*. FS R. Schnackenburg, Freiburg, 1974, pp. 220-248.

28. Siehe J. BECKER, *Das Evangelium nach Johannes* (ÖTK, 4/1), Bd. 1, Gütersloh, [3]1991, p. 239. U.a. gibt er zu erwägen: »Bedenklich« ist, »daß dann ein Wort im Munde der Juden normierend für Jesu Rede wäre. Jesus läßt sich sonst nirgends in so glatter Weise eine seine Rede bestimmende Vorgabe von anderen geben«.

29. BORGEN (n. 19), p. 35: »In vv. 51b-58 the discussion of the eating is at the center. This fact ties the section closely to the exposition from v. 49 onwards, where the word 'to eat' is the main subject for the exegesis«.

30. Dieses wird im übrigen bei seinem ersten Vorkommen in v. 49 nicht als Rekurs auf das *Schriftzitat* v. 31b, sondern »nach Ausweis seines Kontextes unter wörtlichem Rückgriff auf 6,31a verwendet« (so zutreffend BECKER [n. 28] p. 240).

31. Die entsprechende Terminologie begegnet ab v. 47 gehäuft: ζωή 3 mal; ζῆν 2 mal; ἀποθνήσκειν 2 mal; ihre Abwesenheit in vv. 41-46 belegt, daß die entsprechenden Aussagen in vv. 47ff. »rhematisch« sind (cf. n. 95).

32. v. 49b = καὶ ἀπέθανον ist auch neu gegenüber v. 31a!

33. Die gewöhnliche Übersetzung »*lebendiges* Brot« assoziiert das Oppositum »*totes* Brot«; doch geht es nicht *primär* um die Gegenüberstellung »*materielles* Brot« – »Brot als Metapher für die *lebendige Person* Jesu«, sondern darum, daß dieses vom *Himmel* stammende Brot eben wegen seiner göttlichen, transzendenten Herkunft *wahres Leben* gewährt. Vgl. W. BAUER, *Griechisch-deutsches Wörterbuch zu den Schriften des Neuen Testaments*, Berlin, [6]1988, p. 681: ζῆν 4b: »d. Ptz. übertr. in Verb. mit Sachen.. v. allem, was (gottgewirktes) Leben hat od. *schafft*« (Hervorheb. v. mir), cf. Apg 7,38; 1 Petr 1,23; Hebr. 4,12 etc.

Beachtet man den in diesen Versen leitenden Gesichtspunkt von Leben und Tod, dann ist auch klar, daß der von Borgen gesetzte Einschnitt in v. 49 willkürlich ist; vieles spricht für eine Zäsur vor v. 47[34]. Andererseits tritt bei dieser Profilgebung von vv. 47-51 die Akzentverlagerung, die sich in vv. 52ff tatsächlich hin zum Motiv des »Essen« vollzieht[35], deutlich hervor. Es dürfte vorschnell sein, den »eucharistischen Abschnitt« samt seiner Ankündigung im Gelenkvers v. 51e-g unter einen angeblich durchgängig der Exegese von φαγεῖν gewidmeten Midrasch zu subsumieren[36].

(2) Ein strukturgebendes Prinzip dürfte gewiß die auch szenisch relevante Abfolge der *sechs Redewechsel* sein: Auf eine *Frage* der Volksmenge bzw. der Juden (vv. 25.28.30.42.52.[60]) oder eine *Bitte* (V. 34) folgt jeweils eine *Antwort* Jesu[37]. Gattungskritisch hat man es deshalb bei der sog. »Lebensbrotrede« eigentlich nicht mit einer Rede, sondern mit einem mehrgliedrigen Dialog zu tun[38]. Wenn dennoch in der Forschung Reserve gegenüber dieser Klassifizierung zu bestehen scheint, dann dürfte das mit der ungeklärten Frage zusammenhängen, ob denn die »Gesprächspartner« Jesu zum Fortgang seiner Rede wirklich etwas beitragen oder nicht lediglich seine Stichwortlieferanten sind bzw. seine nach eigenen Gesetzen voranschreitende Rede nur durch unpassende Zwischenrufe unterbrechen. Ganz abgesehen davon, daß man Joh 6 nicht an fremden Maßstäben bezüglich dessen, was ein »Dialog« zu sein habe, messen darf[39], so wird es sich doch zeigen, daß Jesu Antworten durch die Einwürfe seiner »Gesprächspartner« tatsächlich Profil gewinnen[40] und deshalb die Kennzeichnung des Textes als Dialog als durchaus sachgemäß erscheint. In jedem Fall besitzen die Redewechsel zäsurierende Wirkung, ohne daß allerdings damit auch schon ihre höchste Position in

---

34. Außer dem hier maßgeblichen Gesichtspunkt, daß *vor* v. 47 die Thematik von Leben und Tod keine Rolle spielt, kommen vor allem noch Beobachtungen zur Gliederungsfunktion der Amen-Worte Jesu in Joh 6 in Betracht: dazu siehe unten Punkt (3)!

35. Genauer geht es um das τὴν σάρκα φαγεῖν (τρώγειν) vv. 52.53.54.(55.)56.

36. Vorbehalte äußern u.a. auch BROWN (n. 27) p. 294; RICHTER (n. 9), pp. 88-119.

37. Danach gliedern etwa BEUTLER (n. 22), pp. 97ff., und B. SCHWANK, *Evangelium nach Johannes*, Ottilien, 1996, pp. 205ff.

38. Schon von daher ist die Bestimmung von 6,31-58 als »Homilie« oder »Midrasch« nicht sehr glücklich.

39. Die Spannweite antiker Dialog-Gattungen ist enorm: cf. R. HIRZEL, *Der Dialog. Ein literarhistorischer Versuch*, 2 Bde., Leipzig, 1895; K. BERGER, *Hellenistische Gattungen im Neuen Testament*, in ANRW 25/2, Berlin, 1984, pp. 1301-1316; DERS., *Formgeschichte des Neuen Testaments*, Heidelberg, 1984, pp. 245-256; H. KÖSTER, *Dialog und Spruchüberlieferung in den gnostischen Texten von Nag Hammadi*, in EvT 39 (1979) 532-556.

40. Die Untersuchung von 6,31-35 unten in pp. 345-357 hat diesbezüglich exemplarischen Stellenwert.

der Hierarchie der strukturgebenden Prinzipien feststünde. Gegen letzteres sprechen folgende Beobachtungen:

a) Die einzelnen Redewechsel sind von recht unterschiedlicher Länge[41]. Wollte man die Struktur von 6,22-58 durch ihre gegenseitige Zuordnung definieren, wie das Beutler mit seinem chiastischen Bauplan des Textes getan hat, dann führte das zu einem ziemlich ungleichgewichtigen Ergebnis[42]. Mit anderen Worten: Die Dialog-Geschwindigkeit schwankt beträchtlich; wechseln in der ersten Hälfte Fragen und Antworten Jesu rasch ab (vv. 25-31), so tritt ab v. 35 infolge der längeren Antworten Jesu eine größere »Ruhe« ein.

b) Die Antworten Jesu gerade in dieser zweiten Hälfte des Dialogs haben deshalb immer wieder zu der Frage geführt, ob sie nicht auch ihrerseits zu untergliedern seien, da sie verschiedene, sich voneinander abhebende Sequenzen umfassen. Dies betrifft *6,35-40* und *6,41-51*. Sollte dem so sein, dann wäre das szenische Gliederungsprinzip der Redewechsel durch ein weiteres, seinerseits die Antworten Jesu strukturierendes Prinzip überlagert. Was nun *6,35-40* betrifft, so signalisiert v. 36 in der Tat eine Zäsur im Anschluß an das vorangehende Ego-Eimi-Wort Jesu von v. 35. Abgesehen von der Plazierung von Leit-Lexemen[43] macht das der *metareflexive* Charakter des Verses deutlich, der sich darin äußert, daß Jesus hier in seinem auf v. 26 bezugnehmenden, durch ἀλλά (= aber) vom vorangehenden Spruch scharf abgesetzten Selbstzitat (»*aber ich habe euch gesagt*: Ihr habt mich gesehen und glaubt [doch] nicht«[44]) von der Glaubenseinladung v. 35 gleichsam zurücktritt, um auf neuer Ebene sogleich die Zwecklosigkeit solchen Angebots im Blick auf seine anwesende Zuhörerschaft zu konstatieren; daran schließen sich die Verse 37-40 an, die zusammen mit v. 36 eine eigengewichtige Spruchfolge

---

41. Die Längen der Antworten Jesu (ohne ihre szenische Einbettung) nach Versen: 2-1-2-6-9-6.

42. BEUTLER (n. 22), p. 102, faßt seine Analyse so zusammen: Die Rede ist »chiastisch um die erste Selbstprädikation Jesu 'Ich bin das Brot des Lebens' in v. 35 aufgebaut, als Beginn des vierten von insgesamt sechs Redegängen zwischen Jesus und der Volksmenge bzw. den 'Juden'«. Dabei zeigen »sich starke Entsprechungen zwischen dem ersten und letzten Redegang und immerhin beachtliche jeweils zwischen dem zweiten und fünften sowie dem dritten und vierten. Eine Rahmung der Rede durch vv. 22-27 und 52-59« läßt »sich vor allem aufgrund von v. 27 als Vorverweis auf vv. 52-59 wahrscheinlich machen«. In Symbolen und mit Längenangaben in Versen: A(6) – B(2) – C(4) // C'(7) – B'(11) – A'(8). Auffällig ist insbesondere das Ungleichgewicht zwischen B und B', aber auch, wenn man die zu A gehörige große szenische Einleitung v. 22-24 einmal beiseite läßt, das zwischen A und A'.

43. Dazu siehe unten!

44. SCHNACKENBURG (n. 27), p. 71, dürfte zu Recht den Bezug des Selbstzitats v. 36 auf v. 26 herausgestellt haben.

bilden[45]. Auf die Zweiteilung von *6,41-51* (= 41-46/ 47-51) wurden wir oben schon aufmerksam; weitere Beobachtungen dazu folgen.

c) Unter szenischem Gesichtspunkt verweist man zuweilen auf den in v. 41 erfolgenden Wechsel in der Bezeichnung der Gesprächspartner Jesu: Ist es bis dahin eine vom Erzähler nicht näher qualifizierte »*Volksmenge*«, die Fragen an Jesus richtet, so heißen die Fragesteller in v. 41 und v. 52 gemäß dem schon von früheren Kapiteln her bekannten Namen »*die Juden*«; von Gesprächspartnern Jesu im eigentlichen Sinn kann bei ihnen freilich deshalb nicht die Rede sein, weil der Erzähler ihre Einwürfe nicht als offene Fragen, sondern als verdecktes »Murren« und »Hadern« charakterisiert, das Jesus durchschaut. Umstritten ist, ob mit diesen »Juden« eine neben der »Volksmenge« *zweite* Gruppe gemeint ist[46] oder es sich nur um eine andere Bezeichnung für ein- und dasselbe Gegenüber Jesu handelt[47]. Sollte ersteres der Fall sein, dann könnte das als Indiz für eine *Zweiteilung* des »Lebensbrot-Dialogs« (vv. 22-40/41-59) gewertet werden. Doch ist das Profil der Fragesteller nicht derart verschieden, daß dies ihre Aufspaltung in zwei unterschiedliche Gruppen erlaubte[48]. Vielmehr dürfte das scheinbar unvermittelte Auftauchen der im Evangelium weithin mit negativen Konnotationen behafteten Bezeichnung »die Juden« in v. 41 darin begründet sein, daß Jesus den »Unglauben« seiner Zuhörer kurz zuvor ausdrücklich demaskiert hat (v. 36) und diese ihn nun auch ihrerseits durch die verständnislose Frage von v. 42 bestätigen[49]. Daß die sechs »Redewechsel« in *zwei* Gruppen zu vier und zwei aufzuteilen wären (6,22-40/41-58)[50], läßt sich im übrigen auch von anderen strukturellen Beobachtungen her nicht bestätigen.

(3) Für die Struktur des Textes von Belang sind offensichtlich die vier *Amen-Worte Jesu* (vv. 26f; 32f; 47; 53). Auch wenn deren makrokontexueller Einsatz im vierten Evangelium vielfältig ist – Amen-Worte

---

45. Auch SCHNACKENBURG (n. 27), p. 70, begreift 6,36-40 als eigenen Abschnitt, dessen Klassifizierung als »Zwischenstück« aber in Frage zu stellen ist.

46. So etwa J. SCHNEIDER, *Das Evangelium nach Johannes* (THKNT), Berlin, 1976, p. 150f (»Jetzt treten anstelle der Volksmenge die Juden.. als Gegner Jesu auf«).

47. So etwa SCHNACKENBURG (n. 27), p. 75 (kein »Wechsel des Auditoriums«); SCHWANK (n. 37) p. 219.

48. Die Zeichenforderung der Menge (v. 30) und das »Murren« der Juden (v. 41) erweisen beide als Abkömmlinge der Wüstengeneration, als Kinder »ihrer Väter« (6,49).

49. SCHNACKENBURG (n. 27), p. 75, der ebd. n. 1 noch darauf hinweist, daß »diese 'Juden'.. nach v. 42 ebenfalls als Galiläer gedacht« sind. Die πῶς – Frage der »Juden« (»*Wie* kann er das sagen..?«) entspricht im übrigen der »Wie (πῶς) kann das geschehen?« – Frage des Nikodemus in 3,9.

50. So etwa G.A. PHILLIPS, »*This Is a Hard Saying. Who Can Be Listener to it?«* *Creating a Reader in John 6*, in D. PATTE (ed.), *Narrative and Discourse in Structural Exegesis* (Semeia, 26), Chico, 1983, pp. 23-56 (cf. das Referat bei BEUTLER [n. 22], p. 91).

können Passagen eröffnen oder abschließen oder sonstwie ein Wort Jesu fokussieren[51] –, so deutet in Joh 6 manches darauf hin, daß ihnen hier zäsurierende Funktion zukommt[52]. Das *erste* Amen-Wort v. 26f markiert die *Eröffnung* der Rede Jesu insgesamt. Beim *zweiten*, v. 32f, hat die Formel ihren Sinn darin, daß sie die authentische Auslegung des zuvor zitierten Schriftworts durch Jesus als *vollmächtige* Äußerung eigenen Rechts vom Schriftwort *abhebt* und gleichzeitig zum entscheidenden Ego-Eimi-Wort in v. 35 hinüberlenkt; das geschieht semantisch so, daß die in das Amen-Wort eingezeichnete Doppeldeutigkeit (vgl. v. 33) erst durch das Ego-Eimi-Wort v. 35 aufgelöst wird[53]. Die Plazierung des *dritten* Amen-Worts in v. 47 koinzidiert mit der von diesem Vers an fokussierten Lebensthematik (s.oben!), was die Annahme einer mit ihm verbundenen Zäsur stärkt[54]. Das *letzte* Amen-Wort von V. 53 eröffnet offenkundig die große eucharistische Erklärung Jesu.

(4) Strukturierende Wirkung besitzt schließlich auch der gezielte Einsatz von wichtigen *Lexemen*, ihre Wiederholung an Wendepunkten des Dialogs. Allerdings gilt das nicht durchgängig, da Joh 6 vom Mittel, Lexeme als Signalworte für semantische Bezüge einzusetzen, gehäuft Gebrauch macht, ohne daß damit immer auch schon gliedernde Funktionen verbunden wären[55]. Beachtlich ist aber unter strukturellem Gesichtspunkt die Lexem-Kombination von »sehen« und »glauben«, die, bei geringfügigen sprachlichen Variationen, gerade in *Übergangsversen* begegnet (vv. 30.36.40.46/47). Das Motiv des »Sehens« allein findet sich überdies noch im *eröffnenden* Amen-Wort der Rede v. 26. In vv. 36

---

51. K. BERGER, *Die Amen-Worte Jesu. Eine Untersuchung zum Problem der Legitimation in apokalyptischer Rede* (BZNW, 39), Berlin, 1970, pp. 95-117.

52. Das heißt nicht, daß sich in Joh 6 darin ihr Sinn erschöpfte; die christologisch bedeutsame Vollmachtsformel »Amen, amen, ich sage euch« kann vielmehr auch die nachfolgende Deklaration Jesu verbürgen wollen, etwa in 6,47.53 seine Zusage des Lebens. Auf die makrostrukturelle Funktion der Amen-Formeln in Joh 6 machte schon BORNKAMM (n. 27) pp. 59-61 aufmerksam.

53. Dazu siehe unten pp. 345-357!

54. M. THEOBALD, *Gezogen von Gottes Liebe (Joh 6,44f). Beobachtungen zur Überlieferung eines johanneischen »Herrenworts«*, in K. BACKHAUS /F.G. UNTERGAßMEIER (eds.), *Schrift und Tradition*. FS J. Ernst, Paderborn, 1996, pp. 315-341: 317f; dort auch Argumente für die alternative Annahme einer Zäsur erst *nach* v. 47, doch wiegen die Beobachtungen zur Rolle der Amen-Worte zugunsten der postulierten Zäsur *vor* v. 47 stärker; außerdem kann man auf die *inclusio* von v. 47 (ζωὴν αἰώνιον) und v. 51b (ζήσει εἰς τὸν αἰῶνα) verweisen (nur in diesen beiden rahmenden Versen begegnet das Motiv vom *ewigen* Leben!)

55. Als Lexem-Spender für nachfolgende Erörterungen fungieren das Schriftzitat V. 31 und vor allem das Ego-Eimi-Wort V. 35 (vgl. unten); außerdem beachte man das Lexem διδόναι (V. 27.31.32 [2x].33.34.37.39.51.52).

und 40 hat das Motivpaar bezüglich der von ihm eingefaßten Sequenz *rahmende* Wirkung[56].

(5) Von Lexem-Wiederholungen kann man *Wiederaufnahmen* von Sätzen und Satzteilen unterscheiden, die Aufschluß darüber erteilen, was als auslegungsbedürftig angesehen und deshalb erneuter Betrachtung unterzogen wird. Dieserart Auslegungsprozesse sind strukturrelevant, wobei es keineswegs ausgemacht ist, daß nur den *Schriftzitaten* solche Behandlung zukommt; auch und vor allem *Jesus-Worte* erfahren eine Auslegung[57]. Die folgenden Wiederaufnahmen sind signifikant:

a) *31a* οἱ πατέρες ἡμῶν τὸ μάννα ἔφαγον ἐν τῇ ἐρήμῳ
   49a οἱ πατέρες ἡμῶν ἔφαγον ἐν τῇ ἐρήμῳ τὸ μάννα
   58c οὐ καθὼς ἔφαγον οἱ πατέρες

b) *31c* ἄρτον ἐκ τοῦ οὐρανοῦ ἔδωκεν
   32d (οὐ Μωϋσῆς) δέδωκεν (ὑμῖν) τὸν ἄρτον ἐκ τοῦ οὐρανοῦ
   32e (ὁ πατήρ μου) δίδωσιν (ὑμῖν) τὸν ἄρτον ἐκ τοῦ οὐρανοῦ

c) *33a* ὁ .. ἄρτος τοῦ θεοῦ ἐστιν ὁ καταβαίνων ἐκ τοῦ οὐρανοῦ
   38a ὅτι καταβέβηκα ἀπὸ τοῦ οὐρανοῦ
   41c ὁ ἄρτος ὁ καταβὰς ἐκ τοῦ οὐρανοῦ
   42e ὅτι ἐκ τοῦ οὐρανοῦ καταβέβηκα
   50a ὁ ἄρτος ὁ ἐκ τοῦ οὐρανοῦ καταβαίνων
   51a ὁ ἄρτος (ὁ ζῶν) ὁ ἐκ τοῦ οὐρανοῦ καταβάς
   58a ὁ ἄρτος ὁ ἐξ οὐρανοῦ καταβάς

d) *33b* καὶ ζωὴν διδοὺς τῷ κόσμῳ
   51g (ἡ σάρξ μού ἐστιν) ὑπὲρ τῆς τοῦ κόσμου ζωῆς

e) *35b* Ἐγώ εἰμι ὁ ἄρτος τῆς ζωῆς
   41c Ἐγώ εἰμι ὁ ἄρτος
   48 Ἐγώ εἰμι ὁ ἄρτος τῆς ζωῆς
   51a Ἐγώ εἰμι ὁ ἄρτος ὁ ζῶν

f) *35c* ὁ ἐρχόμενος πρὸς ἐμὲ οὐ μὴ πεινάσῃ
   37c πρὸς ἐμὲ ἥξει
   37d καὶ τὸν ἐρχόμενον πρὸς ἐμέ
   44a οὐδεὶς δύναται ἐλθεῖν πρός με
   45e ἔρχεται πρὸς ἐμέ

g) *35d* ὁ πιστεύων εἰς ἐμὲ οὐ μὴ διψήσει πώποτε
   40b πιστεύων εἰς αὐτὸν ἔχῃ ζωὴν αἰώνιον
   47c ὁ πιστεύων ἔχει ζωὴν αἰώνιον

---

56. Diese *inclusio* hat SCHENKE (n. 22) p. 27 n. 15 bei seinem Vorschlag, eine Zäsur erst nach V. 36 zu setzen, übersehen.

57. In 6,65 läßt der Erzähler Jesus selbst ein Wort aus dem »Lebensbrot« – Dialog (6,44) noch einmal paraphrasierend aufgreifen, um es unter neuer Rücksicht von ihm deuten zu lassen. Auf das Selbstzitat Jesu in 6,36 (cf. v. 26) wurden wir oben (n. 44) schon aufmerksam.

h) *39e* ἀναστήσω αὐτὸ ἐν τῇ ἐσχάτῃ ἡμέρᾳ
   40e ἀναστήσω αὐτὸν ἐγὼ ἐν τῇ ἐσχάτῃ ἡμέρᾳ
   44c κἀγὼ ἀναστήσω αὐτὸν ἐν τῇ ἐσχάτῃ ἡμέρᾳ
   54d κἀγὼ ἀναστήσω αὐτὸν τῇ ἐσχάτῃ ἡμέρᾳ

Was lassen diese Wiederaufnahmen von den im Text ablaufenden Auslegungsprozessen erkennen und was ergibt sich daraus für die Struktur des Dialogs? In welchem Verhältnis stehen Schriftwort, haggadische Überlieferung und Jesus-Worte zueinander? Dazu einige Beobachtungen:

Die entscheidenden Grundtexte des Dialogs sind (1) das Schriftzitat 6,31c samt haggadischem Summarium von Ex 16 in v. 31a, (2) das Amen-Wort 6,32f als Auslegung jenes Schriftworts sowie (3) das Ego-Eimi-Wort 6,35[58]. *Die führende Stimme in diesem keineswegs gleichberechtigten Trio besitzt ohne Zweifel 6,35.* Das ersieht man zum einen an der Wiederaufnahme des haggadischen Summariums v. 31a in *v. 49a*, welche unter dem Vorzeichen des in v. 48 wiederholten Ego-Eimi-Wortes erfolgt und lediglich *e contrario* (»leben«/»sterben«) in den übergeordneten Zusammenhang eingeflochten ist[59]. Zum anderen wird das mit diesem Summarium verbundene Schriftzitat v. 31c derart im anschließenden Amen-Wort v. 32f *aufgehoben,* daß nun alles Folgende nicht mehr *Schrift*auslegung genannt zu werden verdient, vielmehr Auslegung dieses Amen-Worts bzw. des in v. 35 nachfolgenden *Jesus-Worts* ist, auf das jenes vorbereitet und von dem es dem Rang nach noch überboten wird (siehe unten!). So orientieren sich alle folgenden Bezugnahmen auf das zentrale Brot-Symbol vorrangig entweder an v. 35 oder v. 33, nicht aber am Schriftzitat, denn das später durchgehend benutzte christologisch hochbedeutsame καταβαίνειν (siehe in der Liste oben unter c!) fehlt noch im Schriftzitat und dürfte auch nicht einfach *exegetisch* aus ihm abgeleitet sein, wie P. Borgen meinte[60], sondern besitzt im Rahmen des mit der Menschensohnthematik verbundenen Abstieg-

---

58. Außer Konkurrenz läuft der viermalige Refrain 6,39e.40e.44c.54d (oben unter h), der als *Kommentarsatz* zur Zusage des »ewigen Lebens« (40.54) gedacht ist, also im Unterschied zu den übrigen Wiederaufnahmen nicht selbst eine fortschreitende Kommentierung erfährt. Er dürfte auf eine nachträgliche Redaktion zurückgehen (BECKER [n. 28] zu Joh 6), was unten exemplarisch an 6,44 gezeigt werden soll.

59. Ob das dem ἐγώ εἰμι ὁ ἄρτος v. 48 korrespondierende οὗτός ἐστιν ὁ ἄρτος.. v. 50 eine Anspielung auf Ex 16,15 (οὗτος... ὁ ἄρτος, ὃν ἔδωκεν κύριος ὑμῖν φαγεῖν) enthält?

60. BORGEN (n. 19), p. 21: »this fragment in John seems to be taken from the haggadic traditions about the manna«. Bei Philo kommt καταβαίνειν im Zusammenhang mit der Manna-Tradition aber nicht vor.

Aufstieg-Schemas (κατα-ἀναβαίνειν) eigene Quellen[61]. Gattungskritisch ist damit ein weiteresmal die Annahme widerlegt, Joh 6 sei ein Schrift-Midrasch oder eine Schrift-Homilie; viel eher haben wir einen spezifisch christlichen Texttyp vor uns: eine *szenisch dramatisierte Auslegung von Jesus-Worten*!

2. Zum Bauplan des »Lebensbrot«-Dialogs[62]

Mit dem zuletzt entwickelten Gedanken ist das entscheidende Strukturprinzip des Textes erkannt, welches das an sich wichtige szenische Gliederungsprinzip der Redewechsel noch einmal überlagert und die Kohäsion einzelner Episoden zu größeren Gruppen grundlegt; als *formales* Prinzip ist es zu deren Erhebung geeigneter als lediglich inhaltliche Erwägungen.

Das *Kernstück* des »Lebensbrot«-Dialogs besteht demnach aus dem Ego-Eimi-Wort v. 35[63] und dessen Auslegung in den vv. 36-51b. Letztere orientiert sich an den Formelementen des Ego-Eimi-Spruchs[64], wobei sie diese in umgekehrter Richtung aufgreift: Zuerst widmet sie sich dem »Ruf zur Entscheidung« (in den vv. 36-40/41-46), dann der »Selbstprädikation«, die sie in v. 48 (51) ausdrücklich wiederholt und kommentiert. Die zweiteilige Explikation des »Rufs zur Entscheidung« v. 35c.d in den vv. 36-40/41-46 ist als solche an den Signalwörtern identifizierbar: Stehen die vv. 36-40 unter dem Vorzeichen »wer an mich *glaubt*« (v. 35d)[65], so entfalten die vv. 44-46 das parallele, nur seiner metaphorischen Gestalt nach davon abweichende Motiv »wer *zu mir kommt*«

---

61. Kritisch auch RICHTER (n. 9), p. 224: »Gegen Borgen wird man bei dieser Terminologie wohl kaum von einer Übernahme von haggadischen Fragmenten sprechen dürfen. Die Vorstellung des Herabkommens oder Herabgesandtseins Jesu ist für den Evangelisten durch die himmlische Herkunft Jesu ja schon von vornherein gegeben«. Ist ὁ καταβαίνων ἐκ τοῦ οὐρανοῦ v. 33a doppeldeutig (bezieht es sich auf das Himmelsbrot oder Jesus? Siehe unten n. 107), so stellt 6,35 klar, daß beide Größen miteinander identisch sind; alle späteren Bezugnahmen auf 6,33a (vgl. oben in der Liste unter c!) lassen das eindeutig erkennen. Auch von daher wird man sagen müssen, daß das Rätselwort v. 33a den Bezugspunkt für jene Wiederaufnahmen bildet, nicht aber das Schriftzitat v. 31c.

62. Zum folgenden siehe die Gliederungstafel auf pp. 342-343!

63. Zur These, daß das Ego-Eimi-Wort V. 35 das Zentrum des Dialogs bildet, paßt die Beobachtung, daß es das absolute ἐγώ εἰμι aus 6,20 aufgreift. Durch das im gegenwärtigen Zusammenhang unmotivierte Stichwort des »Dürstens« stellt das Ego-Eimi-Wort v. 35 überdies auch eine Brücke zu Joh 4 her.

64. Diese Sprüche haben einen *zweiteiligen* Aufbau: Eingangs steht die Selbstprädikation (»Ich bin« samt Bildwort), dann folgt »der daraus sich ergebende Ruf zur Entscheidung, bei dem die Einladung (etwa als konditionales Partizip) und die Heilszusicherung, die immer auf die Gabe ewigen Lebens zuläuft, zu erkennen sind« (BECKER [n. 28], p. 251 mit Lit).

65. Zur entsprechenden *inclusio* vgl. oben n. 56!

(v. 35c; vgl. vv. 44f). Charakteristisch für beide Sequenzen ist einmal, daß sie die Auslegung des Jesus-Worts an die szenische *Dialog-Situation* zurückbinden, d.h. Jesu Glaubenseinladung jeweils mit dem faktischen Unglauben seiner Zuhörerschaft konfrontieren (vgl. vv. 36. 41f), sodann zweitens, daß sie gerade mit Hilfe dieser szenischen Konfiguration – den »Ruf zur *Entscheidung*« aus dem Grundwort (v. 35c.d) gleichsam unterlaufend – den *Gnadencharakter* von Glauben und Zu-Jesus-Kommen eindrucksvoll herausarbeiten[66]. Wichtig dürfte die Erkenntnis sein, daß mit v. 51b die Auslegung des Ego-Eimi-Worts v. 35 *definitiv* zum Abschluß gekommen ist; alle Teile des Spruches wurden bis dahin von der Auslegung aufgegriffen und berücksichtigt, so daß eigentlich – abgesehen von einem dem Proömium des Dialogs (vv. 25-31) entsprechenden Abschlußteil (siehe unten) – keine weiteren Erörterungen Jesu mehr zu erwarten sind. Der Kreis hat sich gerundet.

Damit dürfte sich der *Exkurs-Charakter* des eucharistischen Redewechsels (vv. 52-58) unter *strukturellem* Gesichtspunkt bestätigt haben; v. 51c ist »Gelenk« – oder »Übergangsvers« zu diesem Stück, in dem das in v. 50f noch metaphorisch für »glauben« stehende Motiv »essen«[67] in eucharistischem Verständis beim Wort genommen und fokussiert wird (τρώγειν). Die Einsicht in den Bauplan der »Lebensbrot« – Dialogs spricht somit nicht gegen die literarkritische Ausscheidung dieses Stücks (6,51c-58), im Gegenteil: Seine konzeptionelle Anlage würde bei Durchführung dieser Operation nur an Transparenz gewinnen. Doch muß das hier nicht weiter erörtert werden[68].

Dem Corpus des Dialogs vorangestellt ist ein *Proömium*, das (mit seiner szenischen Einleitung) die vv. 22-31 umfaßt[69]. Anbindung des Textes an die vorangegangenen Szenen von Kap. 6 (in v. 26), Ankündigung der im

---

66. Beachte insbesondere v. 37 (»alles, was mir der Vater gibt, kommt zu mir«) sowie v. 44f! Zu v. 37 siehe zuletzt O. Hofius, *Erwählung und Bewahrung. Zur Auslegung von Joh 6,37*, in Ders. / H.C. Kammler, *Johannesstudien. Untersuchungen zur Theologie des vierten Evangeliums* (WUNT, 88), Tübingen, 1996, pp. 81-86. Ebd. p. 85 werden die vv. 37-40 zu Recht als »Kommentar« zum Offenbarungswort v. 35 gedeutet.

67. Man beachte die entsprechende Metaphorik des Grundwortes v. 35 (»nicht mehr hungern – dürsten«)!

68. Dazu sei auf Theobald (n. 23), pp. 237f. 240f verwiesen.

69. Es ist das Verdienst von Beutler (n. 22), p. 97, noch einmal mit Nachdruck auf die vv. 22ff als szenische Eröffnung des mit v. 25 beginnenden Dialogs hingewiesen zu haben. Wenn andererseits viele Ausleger das Offenbarungswort v. 35 als den eigentlichen Beginn der »Lebensbrotrede« begreifen, dann haben sie durchaus etwas Richtiges erkannt. Man wird das Problem so lösen können, daß man zwischen einem *hinführenden* Abschnitt und dem *Hauptteil* des Dialogs unterscheidet. Letzterer wird mit Amen-Wort v. 32 eröffnet, das zum Ego-Eimi-Wort v. 35 zielstrebig hinführt. Umgekehrt wächst dieses aus den vorangehenden Versen hervor, so daß eine Zäsur unmittelbar *vor* v. 35 sich nicht empfiehlt (siehe unten!).

STRUKTUR DES LEBENSBROT-DIALOGS   Joh 6,22-59 (65)

	Dialog. Struktur/Dialogpartner	Worte Jesu	Worte der Schrift (haggad. Trad.)	Leit-Lexeme
Szenische Überleitung (V. 22-24)				KAFARNAUM
A. Anfangsteil (V. 25-31)	1. *Redewechsel* (V. 25-27) Frage (πότε) *Volksmenge* Antwort	Amen-Wort (V. 26)		sehen Leben/Menschensohn
	2. *Redewechsel* (V. 28f) Frage (τί) (Volksmenge) Antwort			glauben
	3. *Redewechsel* (V. 30-33) Frage (τί) (Volksmenge)		(V. 31a: Ex 16) Ps 78,24b: V.31	sehen/glauben
B. Hauptteil V.32-51 — 1. *Kernwort* V.35 samt Hinführung (V.32-35)	Antwort 4. *Redewechsel* (V.34-40) Bitte Antwort: (1) V.35 (Volksmenge)	Amen-Wort (V. 32) Ego-Eimi-Wort (V.35)		Leben/kommen/glauben
2. *Auslegung* (V.36ff) a) V.36-40: ad 35d	(2) V.36-40			sehen/glauben
	5. *Redewechsel* (V.41-51) Frage (verdeckt) *Juden* Antwort: (1) V.43-46 (2) V.47-51	(Ego-Eimi: V.41)	(»murren«: Ex 16)	
b) V.41-46: ad 35c			Jes 54,13: V.45	kommen
c) V.47-51: ad 35b		Amen-Wort (V.47) Ego-Eimi (V.48.51)	(V. 49: Ex 16)	Leben/sterben sehen/glauben

	Dialog. Struktur/Dialogpartner	Worte Jesu	Worte der Schrift (haggad. Trad.)	Leit-Lexeme
Exkurs (ad vocem φαγεῖν) (V.51c-58)	6. *Redewechsel* (V.52-58) *Juden* Frage (verdeckt) Antwort	Amen-Wort (V.53)	(V.58: Ex 16)	essen essen/trinken - Leben - Menschensohn
Szenischer Abschluß (V. 59)				KAFARNAUM
Rahmenszene (V.60-65) (C. Schlußteil)	7. Redewechsel (V.60-65) *Jünger* Frage (verdeckt) Antwort	a) pauschaler Rückblick (V.63) b) spezieller Rückblick (V.65 cf. 44)	(»murren«: Ex 16)	Menschensohn/ Aufstieg

Hauptteil des Dialogs entfalteten Themen (in den vv. 27.29) sowie erste Charakterisierung der Dialogpartner Jesu sind die entsprechenden (proömialen) Kennzeichen dieses Abschnitts[70]. Der *Schlußteil* des Dialogs dürfte in 6,60-66 vorliegen. Vor allem der metareflexive Charakter dieser Verse[71] deutet daraufhin: Nicht mehr die konkrete Metaphorik des »Lebensbrot«-Dialogs samt deren Auslegung, sondern die soteriologische Qualität der in ihm gesprochenen »Worte« überhaupt (»sie sind Geist und Leben«) ist Gegenstand der Verse. Überdies ergeben sich Bezüge zwischen Schlußteil und Proömium[72], wodurch sich der Eindruck einstellt: Der »Lebensbrot«-Dialog ist gerundet; mit seinen drei Abschnitten Proömium, Corpus und Schlußteil, die im übrigen Erwartungen zu entsprechen scheinen, die man gewöhnlicherweise mit der Disposition von Reden verbindet, bietet er eine ausgewogene und wohlproportionierte Konzeption.

3. *Zur Stellung der Schriftzitate im »Lebensbrot«-Dialog*

Den Bauplan des Dialogs zu durchschauen ist Voraussetzung dafür, den Stellenwert der beiden Schriftzitate in ihm sachgerecht bestimmen zu können. Die Struktur des Dialogs diktieren diese nicht, auch wenn die Reichweite des Psalmzitats in v. 31 größer zu sein scheint als die des offensichtlich nur seine unmittelbare Umgebung tangierenden Jesaja-Zitats in v. 45. Zumindest das erste Zitat, das Jesus von der »Volksmenge« entgegengehalten wird, steht im Sog der polemischen Auseinandersetzung des johanneischen Jesus mit den »Juden«; bezeichnenderweise gehört es nach dem Bauplan des Dialogs noch in dessen hinführenden Teil und tritt also gegenüber den Worten Jesu von v. 32f und v. 35, die den Hauptteil des Dialogs beherrschen, in das zweite Glied. Ob der Evangelist einen Zusammenhang zwischen den beiden Schriftzitaten hergestellt wissen wollte[73], ist schwer zu sagen; möglicherweise sah er zwischen ihnen das mehr *formale* Band, das darin besteht, daß dem Ps 78,24 vorausgehenden haggadischen Summarium der grundlegenden *Tora*-Perikope (Ex 16) mit Jes 54,13 ein *Propheten*-Text zur Seite gestellt sein sollte[74]. *Inhaltlich* dürfte kein unmittelbarer Faden zwischen ihnen geknüpft sein, vielmehr sind beide dem zentralen Ego-Eimi-Wort Jesu v. 35 unterstellt: Profiliert

---

70. Dazu wie zum folgenden siehe Theobald (n. 23), pp. 216.222-225.
71. Deutlich wird dieser an der auf den Dialog insgesamt *zurückblickenden* Wendung: »die Worte, *die ich zu euch gesagt habe*« (v. 63).
72. Man beachte etwa die Rede vom »Menschensohn« in 6,27 und 6,62!
73. So Obermann (n. 1), p. 167; Aletti (n. 22), pp. 191-193.
74. Schnackenburg (n. 27), p. 75: »Zur Schriftlesung aus dem 'Gesetz' kommt eine Prophetenlesung hinzu, die in eschatologischer Perspektive dem Volk neuen Mut und Zuversicht zuspricht«.

Ps 78,24 (mit Ex 16 als Bezugstext der Tora) den Hintergrund der Selbstprädikation Jesu (»ich bin das Brot des Lebens«), so expliziert Jes 54,13 (»von Gott gelehrt«) den Gnadencharakter des im Rahmen der Heilszusicherung jenes Wortes thematisierten »Kommens zu Jesus«. Mit v. 35 als dem zentralen Logion des Dialogs sind es folglich die »Geist und Leben« in sich bergenden »Worte« Jesu (v. 63), um deren Auslegung es in Joh 6 vorrangig geht; die Schriftworte besitzen ihnen gegenüber nur einen minderen Status. Die These von P. BORGEN, die »Lebensbrotrede« sei als Kommentar zum Psalm-Zitat in v. 31 zu verstehen, dürfte damit widerlegt sein.

2. Hermeneutik des Schriftgebrauchs in Joh 6

1. Psalm 78(77), 24

Drei Aspekte helfen, den johanneischen Umgang mit Ps 78 (77),24 zu erschließen: *formale* (1), *inhaltliche* (2) und zuletzt (3) *hermeneutische* Gesichtspunkte.

(1) Wie schon die Verbindung von haggadischem Summarium (Ex 16) und Schrifttext verrät, kommt letzterer nicht isoliert, sondern als schon *ausgelegter*, d.h. in einer bestimmten, wenn auch nur schwer greifbaren *Auslegungstradition* stehend zur Sprache. Das betrifft vor allem das von der Volksmenge gegen den Kontext des Zitats stillschweigend vorausgesetzte Subjekt des Satzes *Mose*, was aus der anschließenen correctio dieser Annahme durch Jesus unzweifelhaft hervorgeht[75]. Auch Jesus bietet in

---

75. So zu Recht MENKEN (n. 1), p. 54, und RICHTER (n. 9), pp. 211-219. Beide verdeutlichen, daß diese Auslegung keine Erfindung des vierten Evangelisten, sondern ihm vorgegeben ist, was methodisch bedeutet, daß sie Joh 6,31f als judaistische Quelle ernst nehmen: »The crowd obviously represent a point of view current among Jews in the environment of the fourth evangelist« (p. 56). Demgegenüber ist die dem AT unbekannte Vorstellung von *Mose* als dem Spender des Manna erst in rabbinischen Quellen belegt (B.J. MALINA, *The Palestinian Manna Tradition. The Manna Tradition in the Palestinan Targums and Its Relationship to the New Testament Writings* [AGSU, 7], Leiden, 1968, p. 87 n. 6). Doch die verwandte, zeitig greifbare Vorstellung, Gott habe das Manna auf *Fürbitte des Mose* hin gewährt (Philo, Migr. 121; Josephus, Ant. 3,1,6; Ps-Philo, Ant.Bibl. 20,8: Richter [n. 9], pp. 217-219), bietet immerhin eine Brücke. Eine andere baut MENKEN, wenn er aus hellenistisch-jüdischen (v.a. Philo, *Vit. Mos.* I, 155f; cf. I, 201f; II, 267) und samaritanischen Mose-Traditionen schließt: »There were evidently Jewish (and Samaritan) milieux with a Moses-centered piety, in which there was a tendency to deify Moses, and to consider his working of wonders as resulting from his participation in God's power. In such an atmosphere, the ascription of the manna miracle to Moses would only be a logical step« (p. 61). Derartige Deifikationstendenzen bezüglich der Mosegestalt erklären nach MENKEN auch den Umstand, daß die Tradition vom Manna spendenden Mose erst so spät in den Quellen auftaucht; jüdische Vorbehalte hätten zu ihrer Unterdrückung geführt.

v. 32f faktisch eine Auslegung von Ps 78 (77),24 (nach Meinung des Evangelisten die einzig richtige), doch ist Jesu Stellungnahme formal nicht als Auslegung des Schriftworts, sondern als vollmächtige Äußerung eigenen Rechts (»amen, amen, ich sage euch«) präsentiert. Das wird auch daran ersichtlich, daß in v. 32 die dem Schrifttext gemäße Ersetzung des Subjekts Mose durch »mein Vater« sich nicht unter ausdrücklichem Rekurs auf jenen Schrifttext[76], sondern auf der Basis eigener Sachlogik vollzieht (vgl. unter 2). Daraus folgt: *Der Evangelist stellt in v. 31f nicht einfach Schriftauslegung gegen Schriftauslegung, sondern läßt Jesu vollmächtiges Wort die Schriftauslegung des galiläischen Volkes transzendieren*[77].

Andererseits wird nun dadurch, daß Jesu Amen-Wort vom Evangelisten als Äußerung eigenen Rechts *im Gegenüber* zum Schriftwort begriffen wird, dieses nicht einfach überholt oder als vorläufig abgetan[78]. Im Gegenteil: Erst im Licht des Jesus-Worts gibt dieses Schriftwort seinen wahren Sinn preis, ja in ihm wird dieser erst Wirklichkeit, weshalb man sagen muß: Das Jesus-Wort überholt das Schrift-Wort nicht, es konstituiert vielmehr allererst seinen Sinn mit der Folge, daß jenes Schriftwort allein im Horizont des Jesus-Worts Bestand hat. Ablesen läßt sich solche völlige In-Dienst-Nahme des Schrift-Worts durch das Jesus-Wort schon an der Gestaltung des Zitats: Wenn nämlich dieses in Abweichung vom LXX-Text nicht ἄρτον οὐρανοῦ, sondern ἄρτον ἐκ τοῦ οὐρανοῦ lautet, dann ist das nicht mit einer bewußten Bezugnahme des Evangelisten

---

76. C.K. BARRETT, *The Gospel according to St. John*, London, 1978, p. 290, schließt sich BORGEN (n. 19), pp. 61-67, an, wenn er feststellt: »John has employed the *Al-tiqri* method of exegesis. This takes the form... אלא... תקרי אל (Do not read... but...). The most important points are: (1) The name Moses is negatived: Do not read Moses (gave you bread), but God (gave you bread). (2) The Hebrew is repointed: Do not read נתן (*nathan*, has given, δέδωκεν), but נותן (*nothen*, gives, or will give, δίδωσι, διδούς, or δώσει)«. So interessant diese These ist, die entsprechende *exegetische* Teminologie fehlt aber in v. 31, eben weil dieser Vers *formal* nicht als Schriftauslegung, sondern als Amen-Wort eigenen Rechts fungiert.

77. Solche Abfolge von Schriftbezug und Amen-Wort Jesu erinnert an die sog. »Antithesen« der matthäischen Bergpredigt: Wie diese nicht in ihrer Funktion einer radikalisierenden Auslegung der »Thesen« aufgehen, weil sie mit ihrem dem »es wurde den Alten gesagt« *gegenüberstehenden*, autoritativen »Ich aber sage euch« christologisch zu beschreibende Vollmacht voraussetzen, so ist auch der Sprecher des Amen-Worts Joh 6,32f. nicht ein der Schrift *unterstellter* Lehrer, sondern der »Menschensohn« und »Sohn Gottes«, der als eschatologischer Gesandter Gottes *unmittelbar* dessen Heilswillen den Menschen kundtut.

78. So aber DIETZFELBINGER (n. 3), p. 205, wenn er bei seiner Auslegung von 6,32 lediglich den Aspekt des »Widerspruch(s) zu Ps 78,24« und den übrigen Mannatexten betont. Der korrespondierende Aspekt der Anverwandlung oder Aneignung des Schrifttextes durch den Evangelisten für die eigenen Belange ist aber genauso wichtig; beides geht hier Hand in Hand.

auch auf Ex 16,4 (LXX)[79] und/oder Neh 19,15 (LXX) zu erklären, also mit dessen mutmaßlicher Sensibilität für die Polyphonie alttestamentlicher Manna-Texte, sondern hängt damit zusammen, daß er seine christologische Grundüberzeugung bezüglich Jesus als des »*aus dem Himmel*« (ἐκ τοῦ οὐρανοῦ) herabgestiegenen Menschensohns in den Schrifttext zurückprojiziert hat[80]; dieser spricht nach seiner Meinung immer schon vom »Brot aus dem Himmel« im freilich jetzt erst aufgedeckten vollen christologischen Verständnis[81]. Deshalb ist auch der über das Schriftwort hinausgehende Artikel τόν in v. 32[82] anaphorisch zu deuten: *Das* Brot vom Himmel, *von dem* das von euch beigebrachte Psalm-Zitat in Wahrheit spricht, hat euch nicht Mose gegeben... Mit anderen Worten: Die Volksmenge zitiert zwar das Psalm-Wort, versteht aber überhaupt nicht, was sie zitiert! Nicht erst in v. 34[83] verfängt sie sich in Mißverständnissen, schon in v. 31 verrät sie ihr völliges Unverständnis der Schrift, wenn sie diese im Licht ihrer eigenen Auslegungstradition begreift. Das Schrift-Wort versteht aber nur, wer über es hinausgeht und sich auf den Standort des Jesus-Worts begibt, um sich von diesem als dem authentischen Offenbarungswort sagen zu lassen, was der wahre Sinn des Schrift-Worts ist.

(2) *Inhaltlich* läßt sich die Konfrontation des Jesus-Worts mit dem von der Volksmenge reklamierten Schriftzitat als Destruktion eines fälschlicher-

79. So aber etwa SCHNACKENBURG (n. 27), p. 54: Der Evangelist »kombiniert Ps 78,24 mit Ex 16,4 (ἐκ τοῦ οὐρανοῦ) und 16,5 (φαγεῖν)... er kombiniert nur die beiden Ex-Stellen, und zwar nach MT (wo in V. 4 die Einzahl steht), und er hat dabei die ganze Erzählung Ex 16 im Sinne«. Letzteres sei nicht bestritten, wohl aber, daß die vorliegende Textform des Zitats sich aus der *Kombination* unterschiedlicher Schrifttexte erklärt und dies noch unter Bezugnahme auf den griechischen *und* hebräischen Text. Das dürfte doch zu komplex gedacht sein.

80. Vgl. außer 6,38.41.42.50.51.58 vor allem 3,13 und 3,31! MENKEN (n. 1), p. 53: »The former expression (s.c. ἄρτον οὐρανοῦ) could be misread as only saying that he belongs to the heavenly sphere; the second one (s.c. ἄρτον ἐκ τοῦ οὐρανοῦ) unmistakably indicates that he was with God in heaven and has come down from there to the world«. Allerdings schließt MENKEN Einfluß von Ex 16,4 LXX nicht aus: »Already in pre-Christian Judaism, the connection of two analogous passages from Scripture (i.e., passages that have at least one word in common and that mostly also have a similar content) was a current practice, not only in exegesis, but also in the rendering of texts« (p. 52).

81. Das Psalmwort bezieht sich im Verständnis des Evangelisten also nur *scheinbar* auf das Manna! Unzutreffend deshalb BARRETT (n. 76), p. 290: »It would be hard for John to deny what the Old Testament positively asserts, that the manna was bread from heaven, and the emphatic position in the next clause of ἀληθινός does not deny that the bread supplied by Moses was bread from heaven but asserts that as such it was a type of the heavenly bread given by Jesus«. Was hier verkannt wird, ist die völlige Neukonstituierung des Textsinns von Ps 78(77),24 durch den Evangelisten samt Destruktion seines ursprünglichen Sinns (Manna!). Auch das hermeneutische Modell der Typologie (Manna = »a type of the heavenly bread given by Jesus«) ist hier fehl am Platz.

82. V. 32: οὐ Μωϋσῆς δέδωκεν ὑμῖν τὸν ἄρτον ἐκ τοῦ οὐρανοῦ.

83. V. 34: »Herr, gib uns allezeit dieses Brot (τὸν ἄρτον τοῦτον)!«

weise mit diesem verbundenen jüdischen Erwartungshorizonts und Frei-
setzung seines eigentlichen Sinns beschreiben. Zunächst: Welcher Erwartungshorizont prägt die vorangehende Zeichen-Forderung der Volksmenge, die ja ihren Rekurs auf die Manna-Tradition begründet (v. 30f)?

Offensichtlich ist die Anfrage der Menge von einem Analogie-Den-
ken bestimmt: Wie Mose durch das Manna-Wunder als Prophet Gottes
beglaubigt wurde, so soll nun auch Jesus ein entsprechendes Zeichen
wirken, um so den von ihm erhobenen Anspruch, eschatologischer Bote
Gottes zu sein (v. 29), zu bekräftigen. Der implizite Rekurs auf Mose
knüpft an der in 6,14[84] von der Volksmenge zunächst zustimmend auf-
gegriffenen Erwartung an, Jesus sei der zweite Mose bzw. der endzeitliche Prophet Gottes nach Dtn 18,15.18[85]. Hinter der Analogie Mose-
Jesus steht somit die umfassendere heilsgeschichtliche zwischen der Zeit
Israels in der Wüste und der mit dem Auftreten jenes Propheten zu
erwartenden Endzeit. Problematisch ist dabei nur die Frage, inwiefern
die Menge ein »Zeichen« verlangen kann, wo ihr doch das der wunderbaren Speisung bereits gewährt wurde und sie dieses auch als Beglaubi-
gung des »Propheten, der in die Welt kommen sollte«, gedeutet hat;
worin unterscheidet sich das von ihr darüber hinaus erwartete »Zeichen« von jenem ihr schon gewährten[86]? Wahrscheinlich ist die Antwort auf diese Frage darin zu suchen, daß jetzt in v. 30f »an die Erneuerung des Mannawunders im Sinn einer *andauernden* Speisung, das heißt
an den *vollen, sichtbaren* Anbruch des messianischen Zeitalters« gedacht ist[87]. Die Menge möchte einen »Beweis, daß wirklich die messianische Heilsfülle angebrochen ist; nicht nur ein einzelnes Wunder wollen sie sehen, sondern das goldene Zeitalter dauernden Überflusses«[88].
Folgende Textsignale deuten in diese Richtung:

a) Wenn es in *6,15* heißt, die Menschen beabsichtigten, Jesus, den sie
für »den Propheten« hielten, zum »*König*« über sich zu erheben, dann
verbindet der Evangelist damit offensichtlich die Motivation, sie wollten

---

84. »Als nun die Menschen das Zeichen sahen, das er gewirkt hatte, sagten sie: 'Das
ist wirklich der Prophet, der in die Welt kommen soll'«.

85. MENKEN (n. 1), p. 57. Zur Vorstellung, daß sich das Manna-Wunder in der Endzeit wiederholen wird, siehe v.a. syrBar 29,8 (»es wird zu jener Zeit geschehen, daß aus
der Höhe Mannaschätze wiederum herniederkommen, sie werden zehren dann davon in
jenen Jahren, weil sie es sind, die ans Ende der Zeit gekommen sind«); Apk 2,17; Or Sib
7,148f.; Midrasch zu Kohelet 1,9.

86. Eine Übersicht über die bislang versuchten Lösungen dieses Problems bietet
M.J.J. MENKEN, *Some Remarks on the Course of the Dialogue: John 6,25-34*, in *Bijdragen* 48 (1987) 139-149.

87. So J. BLANK, *Das Evangelium nach Johannes* (1a), Düsseldorf, 1981, pp. 355f
[Hervorheb. v. mir]

88. SCHWANK (n. 37), p. 212.

jemandem, der *auf Dauer* ihr leibliches Wohlergehen garantieren könnte, die besagte königlich-messianische Würde antragen.

b) Der johanneische Jesus bestätigt das, wenn er in *6,26* erklärt: »Ihr sucht mich nicht, weil ihr Zeichen gesehen habt, sondern weil *ihr von den Broten gegessen habt (ἐφάγετε) und satt geworden seid (ἐχορτάσθητε)*«. *Diese* Erfahrung ist es, die bei ihnen nach Mehr schreit.

c) In v. 34 verraten sie selbst, Jesu Verkündigung mißverstehend, ihre tiefere Absicht: »Herr, *allezeit* (πάντοτε) gib uns dieses Brot!«[89].

d) Wenn es schließlich im Ego-Eimi-Wort *6,35* heißt: »Wer zu mir kommt, den wird nicht mehr hungern (οὐ μὴ πεινάσῃ)«, dann wird das als Metapher für den Lebens-Hunger insgesamt zu verstehen sein, den Jesus zu stillen verspricht[90], kann aber im Duktus des Gesprächs gleichzeitig auch als Signal der *Unterbrechung* an die Dialogpartner aufgefaßt werden: Ist ihr leiblicher Hunger unstillbar, so erlangen sie die Erfüllung ihres darin sich äußernden Lebens-Hungers nur im Überstieg in eine *andere* Dimension[91]. So reflektiert dieses Unterbrechungssignal noch einmal *e contrario* das Verharren der Volksmenge in den eng gezogenen Grenzen ihrer eigenen materiellen Bedürfnisse.

Auf diesem Hintergrund wird dann auch das (Miß-)Verständnis des Psalm-Worts im Mund der Volksmenge plastisch: Sie intendiert ein wirkliches φαγεῖν (6,26.34) und sieht im »Brot vom Himmel«, dessen eigentliche Bedeutung verkennend, lediglich eine »vergängliche Speise«[92]. Dabei erwartet sie, bestimmt von einem eschatologischen Erfüllungsdenken, daß solche Speise, vorausgesetzt, die Endzeit sei mit dem Propheten Jesus tatsächlich angebrochen, nicht ausgehen dürfe, sondern »allezeit« vorhanden sein müsse. So das Bild, das der Evangelist, gewiß unter Anknüpfung an zeitgenössische jüdisch-apokalyptische Vorstellungen, hier in Szene setzt[93], um es aber unverzüglich zu destruieren und

---

89. Zu ergänzen ist entsprechend dem Schriftzitat, das die Volksmenge hier in eine Bitte verwandelt, das φαγεῖν.

90. Das dürfte die einzig angemessene Deutung des Logions sein, wenn man es ohne seinen Kontext, als isoliertes Wort, interpretiert (dazu unten n. 109!). Im Duktus des Gesprächs gewinnt es aber neue Nuancen.

91. BEUTLER (n. 22), p. 101: Jesus verheißt »eine Nahrung, die keinen Hunger und keinen Durst mehr zuläßt«. Beachtlich ist die Parallele 4,13f: »Jeder, der von diesem Wasser trinkt, *wird wieder Durst haben*; wer aber von dem Wasser trinkt, das ich ihm geben werde, *wird nicht mehr Durst haben in Ewigkeit*«.

92. So die (Ab-)Wertung des Evangelisten in v. 27; die Opposition lautet: »die Speise, die bleibt für das ewige Leben«.

93. Daß dabei der Evangelist in seiner Umgebung wirklich vertretene Ansichten einfach *abgebildet* hätte, dürfte eher unwahrscheinlich sein. Das beträfe etwa die noch eigens zu reflektierende Frage, ob er hier auf eine unter Judenchristen verbreitete Prophetenchristologie bezugnimmt; jedenfalls hätte er sie dann nicht als alternative *christliche* Variante

gleichzeitig seine eigene Vorstellung vom »Leben in Fülle« (10,10) mit Hilfe des Wortes Jesu aufzubauen. Wie vollziehen sich nun Destruktion des fremden und Aufbau des eigenen Bildes? Wie sieht die Logik von v.32f aus[94]?

v. 31f:

A 'Αμὴν ἀμὴν λέγω ὑμῖν,
B *οὐ Μωϋσῆς*   δέδωκεν ὑμῖν τὸν ἄρτον ἐκ τοῦ οὐρανοῦ
C *ἀλλ' ὁ πατήρ μου* δίδωσιν ὑμῖν τὸν ἄρτον ἐκ τοῦ οὐρανοῦ τὸν ἀληθινόν.
D ὁ γὰρ ἄρτος τοῦ θεοῦ ἐστιν ὁ καταβαίνων ἐκ τοῦ οὐρανοῦ
           καὶ ζωὴν διδοὺς τῳ κόσμῳ.

Das Amen-Wort ist zweigliedrig: Es umfaßt einen Obersatz in Gestalt einer *correctio* (B/C) sowie einen mit γάρ angeschlossenen Begründungssatz (D); der Obersatz ist als Zusage formuliert (»mein Vater gibt euch…«), während der Begründungssatz ein Urteil oder eine Definition (mit ἐστίν) enthält.

Mit dem vorangehenden Schriftzitat ist das Amen-Wort eng verzahnt. Nimmt man zur Beschreibung seiner Informationsstruktur die »Thema-Rhema«-Relation zur Hilfe[95], so wird man sagen können: Aus dem

---

des Glaubens, sondern als Spielart des *Unglaubens* der *Juden* dargestellt. Worauf es ihm bei seiner fiktiven Erzählung entscheidend ankommt, ist die Destruktion *diesseitiger* Heilsvorstellungen zugunsten seines christologisch begründeten umfassenden ζωή – Verständnisses.

94. Zu den unterschiedlichen Deutungsmöglichkeiten der beiden Verse siehe BARRETT (n. 76), pp. 289f, S. PANCARO, *The Law in the Fourth Gospel. The Torah and the Gospel, Moses and Jesus, Judaism and Christianity according to John* (NTSup, 42), Leiden, 1975, pp. 461-466, sowie M. KOTILA, *Umstrittener Zeuge. Studien zur Stellung des Gesetzes in der johanneischen Theologiegeschichte* (AASF.DHL, 48), Helsinki, 1988, p. 168f.

95. Vgl. W. DRESSLER, *Einführung in die Textlinguistik* (Konzepte der Sprach- und Literaturwissenschaft, 13), Tübingen, 1973, p. 41: »In der Terminologie der Funktionellen Satzperspektive kann Thema erstens soviel wie Ausgangspunkt oder Basis des Satzes bedeuten, ähnlich dem *topic* der meisten amerikanischen Linguisten. Uns interessiert hier aber mehr die kontextuelle bzw. ko-textuelle (textuelle, textinterne) Bedeutung von Thema als das Bekannte oder Gegebene im Gegensatz zu Rhema als der neuen Information. Ein Thema wird also kontextuell aus der Situation oder ko-textuell aus einem vorangegangenen Textstück (desselben Textes) durch Kopierung gewonnen. Im zweiten Fall gehört das Thema also dem Bedeutungsfeld (Wortfeld) eines oder besonders des vorangegangenen Satzes an«. Zur »Funktionellen Satzperspektive« vgl. auch R.-A. DE BEAUGRANDE/W. DRESSLER, *Einführung in die Textlinguistik* (Konzepte der Sprach- und Literaturwissenschaft, 28), Tübingen, 1981, 21.81-83.155. Umfassende Informationen zur jüngeren linguistischen Diskussion der sprachlichen Informationsstruktur (Thema vs. Rhema, Topik vs. Kommentar, Fokus vs. Hintergrund) bieten A. DIßE, *Informationsstruktur im Biblischen Hebräisch. Sprachwissenschaftliche Grundlagen und exegetische Konsequenzen einer Korpusuntersuchung zu den Büchern Dtn, Ri und 2 Kö*, Diss. Tübingen, 1996, pp. 106-144, sowie W. GROSS, *Die Satzteilfolge im Verbalsatz alttestamentlicher Prosa* (FAT, 17), Tübingen, 1996, pp. 55-72. Die Anwendung der »Thema-Rhema« – Struktur auf den Joh-Text besitzt hier lediglich heuristischen Wert; den Einzug in die Grammatik des Neutestamentlichen Griechisch hat die »Funktionelle Satzperspektive« noch nicht gehalten.

Schriftzitat übernommen ist zunächst (τὸν) ἄρτον ἐκ τοῦ οὐρανοῦ (B/C) als »Thema«. Die neue Information von B/C oder das »Rhema« ist dann in der akzentuierten, weil voranstehenden correctio »nicht Mose, sondern mein Vater« enthalten; die Subjekt-Leerstelle des Zitats wird hier pointiert gefüllt.

Für das Objekt von B/C τὸν ἄρτον ἐκ τοῦ οὐρανοῦ hat das folgende Konsequenz: Es besitzt genau die Bedeutung, die man schon für das johanneisch interpretierte Psalmzitat voraussetzen darf bzw. umgekehrt: Dieses spricht nicht vom »Manna«, sondern meint mit ἄρτον ἐκ τοῦ οὐρανοῦ bereits das »wahre« (ἀληθινός: C) himmlische Brot. »Thematischer« Ausgangspunkt des Amen-Worts ist demnach das nach dem Psalm-Zitat »aus der Welt Gottes« stammende Brot, über das jetzt eine neue Aussage (»Rhema«) getroffen werden soll: Nicht Mose – ein *Mensch* – hat solches himmlische Brot vermittelt, das tut allein *Gott*. Nun würde man die Schärfe dieser correctio verkennen, wollte man deuten: »Nicht Mose gab euch das Himmelsbrot, sondern schon damals war Gott der eigentliche Geber«[96]. Zunächst steht das gar nicht im Text. Sodann ist nicht nur auf die deutlich voneinander abgehobenen Zeiten in B/C zu achten (»nicht Mose *gab*« – »mein Vater *gibt*«), sondern auch darauf, daß in C nicht unspezifisch »Gott«, sondern »mein Vater« Subjekt ist. Dieser *gibt* aber jetzt seinen »*Sohn*«, was allerdings in C/D nach Art eines Rätsels verschlüsselt ist, was noch genauer zu bedenken sein wird. Für B bedeutet das: Inbezug auf das Manna-Wunder in der Wüste wird hier implizit verneint[97], daß es bei ihm »Brot *vom Himmel*« zu essen gab; das Manna konnte nichts anderes als »vergängliche Speise« (6,27) sein, was auch von den Broten und Fischen zu gelten hat, die Jesus der Volksmenge gereicht hatte. Der lebensspendene Gott – so darf man zugespitzt formulieren – war in jenes Wunder der Mosezeit nicht involviert! Ist eine derartige Kritik der biblischen Tradition in B nur implizit enthalten, so tritt sie am Ende der C-Zeile im überschießenden Attribut τὸν ἀληθινόν, das neben dem »rhematischen« ἀλλ᾿ ὁ πατήρ μου gleichfalls fokussiert sein dürfte, in den Vordergrund: Nicht das Manna, sondern allein das vom Vater gespendete Brot verdient »*in Wahrheit*« Brot vom Himmel genannt zu werden[98].

---

96. SCHWANK (n. 37), p. 212. Wie Schwank eine ganze Reihe weiterer Forscher, die KOTILA (n. 94), p. 168 n. 24, teilweise aufgelistet hat!

97. Implizit deshalb, weil der Fokus in B, wie gesagt, auf »Mose«, nicht auf ἄρτον ἐκ τοῦ οὐρανοῦ ruht. Der Satz lautet nicht: »Mose gab euch *nicht* das Brot aus dem Himmel (sondern nur vergängliche Speise: Manna)«, sondern: »*Mose* gab euch nicht..., sondern *mein Vater* gibt euch...«.

98. Hinzu kommt noch unterstützend der Wechsel von der Vergangenheit ἔδωκεν zur Gegenwart δίδωσιν: »Nicht damals in der Mosezeit verwirklichte Gott seine Heilsgabe;

Möglicherweise besitzt B noch eine weitere Sinnschicht, worauf die vom Aorist des Schriftzitats abweichende Perfektform δέδωκεν hinweisen könnte[99]; diese bezeichnet ja des öfteren ein Geschehen der Vergangenheit, *das in der Gegenwart nachwirkt*[100]. Zum Manna-Wunder als einem abgeschlossenen Ereignis der Vergangenheit will sie deshalb nicht recht passen. Deshalb kann man hier vielleicht daran erinnern, daß Ex 16 im Frühjudentum verschiedentlich einer vertiefenden Interpretation unterzogen wurde, die in der Gabe des Manna mehr als nur eine vergängliche Speise, nämlich ein Sinnbild für Gottes Wort und seine Weisheit gesehen hat. Gottes Wort und Weisheit haben sich aber nach Ansicht des Judentums vornehmlich in der durch Mose übermittelten Tora inkarniert[101]. Könnte es danach unter der plausiblen Voraussetzung, daß schon in B mit dem »Brot vom Himmel« die wahre Gottesspeise gemeint ist, nicht so sein, daß der Satz torakritisch zu verstehen ist und besagen soll: Nicht Mose hat euch das Brot vom Himmel gegeben (also die Weisheit oder das Wort Gottes, aus dem der Mensch in Wahrheit zu leben vermag[102]), sondern mein Vater gibt euch jetzt dieses Brot? Möglich ist das, zumal in der nachfolgenden exklusiven Inanspruchnahme soteriologischer Lebensvermittlung durch Christus, der von sich selbst sagt: »*Ich* (allein!) bin das Brot des Lebens!« (v. 35) die

das tut er jetzt in der Sendung Jesu« (DIETZFELBINGER [n. 3], p. 205). Offensichtlich ist der sich hier vollziehende »destruierende Angriff auf die Tradition« auch in v. 49: »Wäre das Manna wirklich Brot vom Himmel gewesen, dann wären die Väter in der Wüste nicht gestorben, sondern es wäre ihnen das in 11,25f. beschriebene Leben zuteil geworden« *(ibid.).* Hat v. 49 zwar Rückhalt an der biblisch-frühjüdischen Überlieferung vom Ungehorsam der Wüstengeneration, die das Land nicht betreten durfte, vielmehr vorher sterben mußte (vgl. Num 14,23.28-30; Dtn 1,35; Ps 95,7-11; LibAnt 20,3; vgl. auch 1 Kor 10,5; Hebr 3,16-19), so hat der Evangelist diese Überlieferung doch zweifach radikalisiert: Zum einen meint »*sie starben*« nicht nur den physischen, sondern den ewigen Tod, zum anderen insinuiert die Rede von »euren« (v. 49) bzw. »unseren Vätern« (v. 31), daß die Ἰουδαῖοι in ihrer Heillosigkeit abseits von Christus in deren Geschick mit eingeschlossen sind.

99. Bei der von B D L W al und Clemens v. Alex. gebotenen Variante ἔδωκεν dürfte es sich um eine sekundäre Angleichung an das Zitat in v. 31 handeln. Gleiches ist in umgekehrter Richtung auch dort zu beobachten: ℵ W Θ f[13] pc lesen δέδωκεν.

100. So E.G. HOFFMANN – H. SIEBENTHAL, *Griechische Grammatik zum Neuen Testament*, Riehen, 1985, §200 d.

101. Den biblischen Ausgangspunkt für diese Traditionen bilden v.a. Dtn 8,2f und Weish 16,26 (dazu SCHMITT [n. 19], p. 128: »Das Manna wird zum Symbol und zur Chiffre für das göttliche Wort, das die eigentliche Existenzgrundlage des Menschen darstellt«). Cf. Philo, Mut. 253-263; aus der rabb. Überlieferung: Mek. Ex 13,17; Ex Rab. 25,7. BORGEN (n. 19), pp. 111-115; PANCARO (n. 94), pp. 455ff.

102. Die Perfektform δέδωκεν würde dann den jüdischen Anspruch widerspiegeln, in der *Gabe* der durch *Mose* vermittelten Tora auch und gerade in der *Gegenwart* »Brot vom Himmel« zu besitzen. Mit 6,32 cf. 1,17 (ὁ νόμος διὰ Μωυσέως ἐδόθη...) und 7,19 (οὐ Μωυσῆς δέδωκεν ὑμῖν τὸν νόμον;). 22!

Bestreitung konkurrierender Ansprüche, also vor allem des jüdischen, der meint, in Gottes Tora das Leben zu haben[103], impliziert ist. Schwierig bei dieser Interpretation bleibt, daß die so gedeutete Negation von v. 32 (»nicht Mose...«) in der vorangehenden Äußerung der Volksmenge selbst keinen positiven Anknüpfungspunkt hat, weil diese sich nicht an der *Tora* als »Brot vom Himmel«, sondern an dem durch Mose gewirkten *konkreten Manna-Wunder* orientiert[104]. Andererseits besteht in jedem Fall eine Diastase zwischen der Äußerung der Volksmenge in v. 30f und der Antwort Jesu in v. 32, da letztere nicht am Erwartungshorizont der Volksmenge, sondern am tieferen (johanneischen) Sinn des Schriftzitats ansetzt. So stehen sich die Frage nach der endzeitlichen Wiederholung des Manna-Wunders und die Behauptung der Lebensbrot-Gabe in der Person des Menschensohns schroff gegenüber. Von daher ist es dann auch denkbar, daß in der Negation des den Horizont sprunghaft weitenden Amen-Worts – »nicht Mose hat euch das Brot vom Himmel gegeben« – eine Anspielung auf die Tora und den mit ihr jüdischerseits (fälschlicherweise) verbundenen Anspruch auf Lebensvermittlung gegeben ist. Doch läßt sich das trotz des überraschenden Perfekts δέδωκεν am Text nicht zweifelsfrei festmachen, zumal die dann gegebene Komplexität der Aussage nicht unproblematisch wäre.

Die Informationsstruktur des Begründungssatzes v. 33 (= D) sieht folgendermaßen aus: Sein Subjekt, ὁ ἄρτος τοῦ θεοῦ, nimmt das Objekt des vorangegangenen Satzes, τὸν ἄρτον τοῦ οὐρανοῦ τὸν ἀληθινόν, auf[105] und beinhaltet folglich das »Thema« des Nominalsatzes; die neue Information, das »Rhema«, ist mit dem Prädikatsnomen gegeben, das schon wegen seiner Zweigliedrigkeit einen besonderen Akzent trägt[106]. Hinzu kommt, daß es semantisch ambivalent ist: Entweder kann man zu ὁ καταβαίνων.. καὶ διδούς entsprechend dem Subjekt des Satzes ἄρτος ergänzen (»das Brot Gottes ist *das* [Brot], *welches* vom Himmel herab-

---

103. Dazu jüngst F. AVEMARIE, *Tora und Leben. Untersuchung zur Heilsbedeutung der Tora in der frühen rabbinischen Literatur* (TSAJ, 55), Tübingen, 1996, pp. 594-596 zu Joh.

104. Allerdings ist die Tora-Perspektive möglicherweise schon vorher in der Frage der Menge v. 28 (»was sollen wir tun, um die *Werke* Gottes [ἔργα] zu wirken [ἐργαζώμεθα]?«) präsent.

105. Der Genitiv τοῦ θεοῦ entspricht der Herkunftsangabe ἐκ τοῦ οὐρανοῦ, die noch durch das nachgetragene Attribut ἀληθινόν verstärkt ist.

106. Die beiden Partizipialaussagen korrespondieren miteinander, wie schon ihre Ergänzungen ἐκ τοῦ οὐρανοῦ -κόσμῳ verraten: während sonst des öfteren Himmel (οὐρανός) und *Erde (γῆ)* ein (kosmologisches) Paar bilden (vgl. Mt 6,10; Joh 3,31; Eph 1,9 etc.), stehen sich hier οὐρανός und κόσμος *gegenüber*. Der Gesichtspunkt ihrer Gegenüberstellung ist nicht kosmologischer, sondern theo-logischer Natur: Die (Menschen-)Welt gelangt aus sich selbst heraus nicht zur ζωή, diese muß ihr »aus dem Himmel«, d.h. von Gott her »gegeben« werden!

kommt…«) oder es personal deuten (»das Brot Gottes ist *derjenige, welcher* vom Himmel herabkommt…«)[107]. Deutet die sächliche Auflösung mehr in die Richtung einer Definition (für das »Brot *Gottes*« ist wesentlich, daß es »vom Himmel« stammt, also von *Gott* gereicht wird und wahres »Leben« spendet), so besitzt die personale Auflösung eher Verweischarakter, der mit der Bezeichnung der gemeinten Person in v. 35 dann auch eingelöst wird. Versteht die Volksmenge in v. 34 das Amen-Wort im ersten Sinn[108], so *miß*versteht sie es offenkundig; den tieferen Sinn des Wortes, der in der Identität des Brotes mit der Person Jesu selbst besteht, begreift sie nicht. *Das Amen-Wort v. 32f ist demnach ein johanneisches Rätsel,* das über seinen Charakter als Kommentarwort zum Schriftzitat hinaus auf seine Auflösung durch das Jesus-Wort in v. 35 angewiesen ist. *Damit wird dann aber auch das Schriftzitat selbst mit seinem tieferen Sinn zu einem Rätselwort, das allein durch Jesu Erklärung, sein Ego-Eimi-Wort in v. 35, entschlüsselt wird.* Liest man dieses im Duktus des Dialogs vv. 30ff, dann kann nur sein dreifaches Personalpronomen fokussiert sein:

> *Ich* (ἐγώ) bin das Brot des Lebens;
> wer *zu mir* (πρὸς ἐμέ) kommt, den wird nicht mehr hungern,
> und wer *an mich* (εἰς ἐμέ) glaubt, den wird niemals mehr dürsten.

»Thema« der Selbsprädikation ist die Wendung »Brot des Lebens«[109]; die neue Information oder das »Rhema« ist die Aussage, die über dieses »Brot des Lebens« getroffen wird, also dessen Identifikation mit dem ἐγώ Jesu. Dieses ist fokussiert, weil es anderen »Orten«, die »Brot«

---

107. So zutreffend SCHWANK (n. 37), p. 211: »Die Fassung von v. 33 ist im Griechischen gewollt doppeldeutig. 'Das Brot' ist im Griechischen männlich (ho ártos); daher kann sich 'der Herabsteigende' sowohl auf das Brot als auch auf den Menschensohn beziehen«. Zur Artikelsetzung beim Prädikatsnomen in Joh siehe HOFFMANN – SIEBENTHAL (n. 100) §135a (I2b).

108. »Herr, gib uns allezeit *dieses Brot* (τὸν ἄρτον τοῦτον)!« bezieht sich zweifellos auf den vorausgehenden Satz in einem sächlichen Sinn; dabei wird dann ζωή auf leibliches Wohlergehen reduziert und (ἄρτος) ἐκ οὐρανοῦ als wunderbares Brot gedeutet.

109. Sie nimmt ἄρτον ἐκ τοῦ οὐρανοῦ bzw. ἄρτος τοῦ θεοῦ aus v. 32f auf und verknüpft sie mit ζωὴν (δίδους τῷ κόσμῳ) v. 33. Allerdings dürfte die Wendung nicht aus dieser Kombination ad hoc entstanden sein, sondern wird einen eigenen traditionsgeschichtlichen Ursprung besitzen, der mit der überlieferungskritisch zu sichernden Selbständigkeit des Ego-Eimi-Wortes zusammenhängt. R. SCHNACKENBURG, *Das Johannesevangelium* IV (HTKNT, 4/4), Freiburg, 1984, p. 125: »die geprägte Wendung 'Brot des Lebens'… läßt sich weder im jüdischen Midrasch noch in der jüdischen hellenistischen Spekulation über das Manna nachweisen«. Wahrscheinlich wird man in 6,35 »vorgegebene Tradition zu sehen« haben (so zu Recht BECKER [n. 28], p. 248). – Als isoliertes »Herrenwort« der joh. Tradition gelesen böte 6,35 im übrigen andere Akzentuierungen als im Duktus des vorliegenden Kontextes; ohne diesen wäre »Brot des Lebens« fokussiert bzw. im Nachsatz das jeweils pointiert negierte (οὐ μὴ… πώποτε) Verb (πεινάσῃ/διψήσει).

versprechen, entgegengesetzt ist: »Das Brot des Lebens bin *ich* (und sonst nichts!)«. Entsprechend sind die Nachsätze zu lesen: »Wer *zu mir* kommt (und nicht *von mir unterschiedenes* Brot sucht), *dessen* Hunger (und Durst) werden gestillt«. Also nicht die Befriedigung der leiblichen Bedürfnisse (das φαγεῖν) verspricht »Leben« (ζωή) im Vollsinn, sondern allein der Glaube an *Jesus als das lebenspendende Brot Gottes*. Die Identifikation Jesu mit dem »Brot« von Ps 78 (77),24 zieht zudem eine Neubewertung seines φαγεῖν nach sich, die hier aber nicht explizit gemacht wird: Das »Essen« vollzieht sich im »Hinzu-Treten« zu Jesus, im Glauben an ihn, nicht in einer wörtlich gemeinten Nahrungsaufnahme (siehe aber v. 50f, außerdem die Analogie in 4,14).

Zielpunkt des bisherigen Dialogs (und Ausgangspunkt für seinen Fortgang) ist also das Ego-Eimi-Wort v. 35. Dieses entschlüsselt das als Rätsel begriffene Schriftwort, ohne daß der Evangelist auf den Gedanken käme, es als Kommentarwort dem Schriftwort zu unterstellen. Die Relationen dürften genau umgekehrt zu bestimmen sein.

(3) Zwei *hermeneutische Schlußfolgerungen* zum Umgang des Evangelisten mit der Schrift lassen sich aus der bisherigen Analyse ableiten: (a) Wegen der Analogielosigkeit des Christus-Geschehens und der exklusiven Bindung der Lebensvermittlung an seine Person sieht der Evangelist sich dazu gezwungen, *typologisches Denken*, das auf der Entsprechung von Endzeit und Israels Wüstenzeit aufbaut, zu zerbrechen[110]. Letztere wird soteriologisch entleert und von der allein in Christus erschlossenen Dimension ἐκ τοῦ οὐρανοῦ abgekoppelt. Was im Manna-Wunder geschah, war lediglich leibliche Speisung, welche die Tiefendimension wahrer ζωή nicht erreichte; auch die von Mose gegebene Tora vermag diese nicht zu vermitteln. Wer deshalb auf der Basis der grundlegenden Erfahrungen Israels in der Wüstenzeit die heilvolle Endzeit projektiert, verfehlt sie. Gleiches gilt für das Verständnis des Heilbringers: Der Prophet Mose ist als Modell für diesen untauglich; dessen göttlich-transzendente Herkunft bedarf anderer sprachlicher Vermittlung[111]. Katalysatorisch wird bei diesem Vorgang der Zerbrechung typologischer Schematik die Ablösung apokalyptisch-eschatologischen Denkens durch weisheitlich orientiertes gewirkt haben[112]; letzteres ist allerdings von

110. Anders z.B. BARRETT (n. 76), p. 290: »The manna was in fact a valuable *type* of the bread of life« (Hervorheb. v. mir). Cf. n. 81! Außerdem ALETTI (n. 22), p. 170.

111. Der Evangelist zieht die Kategorien »Menschensohn« (6,27.62) und »Sohn« vor; zu letzterer ist insbesondere als Rahmenaussage 6,32 heranzuziehen: »*mein Vater gibt* euch das wahre Brot vom Himmel«, mit anderen Worten: Als Sohn Gottes ist Jesus *die* Gabe Gottes selbst an die Menschen.

112. Zu ersterem siehe insbesondere syr Bar 29,8 (oben in n. 85), zu zweitem die Belege oben in n. 101! Zur katalysatorischen Rolle der Weisheitstraditionen für die

christologischer Exklusivität aufgesogen, derzufolge jetzt Jesus allein die Person gewordene Weisheit Gottes genannt zu werden verdient. (b) Mit dem Zerbrechen des (heilsgeschichtlich-) typologischen Denkens verbunden ist die *Ablösung des Schrifttextes von der* traditionell mit ihm verbundenen *Geschichte*: Ps 78 (77),24 bezieht sich in Wahrheit *nicht* auf die Wüstenzeit Israels, sondern exklusiv auf das Christusgeschehen; *der Schrifttext wird damit dem vorfindlichen Israel genommen.* Wird er dadurch ortlos? Offensichtlich nicht! Er wird nur anders gepolt und erhält als neuen Referenten eben die *Christus*geschichte. Damit wird er aber auch zu einem *Rätsel*; es versteht ihn nur, wer um seinen eigentlichen Referenten weiß, den der Schrifttext selbst nicht preisgibt[113]. Ist sein eigentlicher Sinn (dem gegenüber sein wörtliches Verständnis nur *Miß*-Verständnis genannt zu werden verdient)[114] ihm ursprünglich eingestiftet, dann setzt das die für den vierten Evangelisten doch voll nicht fragliche Annahme voraus (die freilich in Joh 6 nicht reflektiert wird), daß der Schrifttext immer schon an Gott als seinen eigentlichen *auctor* gebunden ist[115]. Die Reduktion der Schrift Israels auf die Dimension des *Textes* (also ihre Ablösung von der hinter ihr stehenden Geschichte Israels) sowie das Verständnis dieses *Textes* exklusiv unter dem Aspekt seines *Verweischarakters* auf eine Zukunft außerhalb seiner selbst[116] ist

---

johanneische Christologie siehe M. THEOBALD, *Gott, Logos und Pneuma.* »*Trinitarische*« *Rede von Gott im Johannesevangelium*, in H.-J. KLAUCK (ed.), *Monotheismus und Christologie. Zur Gottesfrage im hellenistischen Judentum und im Urchristentum* (QD, 138), Freiburg, 1992, pp. 41-87, esp. 68-73.

113. Wenn ALETTI (n. 22), p. 191 feststellt: »L'Ecriture joue donc comme *code* permettant de lire le *passé* (ce qui s'est produit est une action divine) et le *présent*, c'est-à-dire l'authenticité des paroles et des actes de Jésus«, dann dürften damit die hermeneutischen Verhältnisse im Evangelium geradezu auf den Kopf gestellt sein. Die Schrift besitzt bei Joh nicht die Selbständigkeit, die ihr hier zugeschrieben wird; maßgebend für das Verständnis der Zitate (wie ihre textliche Konstituierung) ist der *Code* der Jesus-Worte! Das schließt freilich nicht aus, daß es neben diesem Hauptstrang johanneischer Schrifthermeneutik vereinzelt auch anders orientierte Passagen gibt, wobei an Streitgespräche Jesu mit Gegnern zu denken ist, die mit ihrem Rekurs auf die Schrift als *Basis* der jeweiligen Argumentation an den entsprechenden synoptischen Typ von Streitgesprächen anschließen: cf. 7,19-24 (Sabbatheilung); 8,17 (Zeugenregel); 10,34-36. Bezeichnenderweise sind es diese Argumentationen *ad extram*, in denen die Rede von »*eurem* Gesetz« im vierten Evangelium vor allem begegnet (siehe oben n. 6). In ihnen verweist sie auf die apologetisch-rhetorische Gesprächsstrategie Jesu, seine Gegner mit deren *eigenen* Waffen zu schlagen.

114. Es ist also keineswegs so, daß der Evangelist neben dem »tieferen« Verständnis des Schriftwortes auch noch dessen »literarischen« Sinn als legitim zuließe.

115. Das hält auch die Parenthese in 10,35 unmißverständlich fest: »und es kann die Schrift nicht aufgelöst werden (καὶ οὐ δύναται λυθῆναι ἡ γραφή)«. Cf. auch 7,23 (ἵνα μὴ λυθῇ ὁ νόμος Μωϋσέως).

116. Mit anderen Worten: Der *Text* des Zitats wird semantisch vom Evangelisten (man denke an seine redaktionellen Retuschen!) völlig neu konstituiert.

johanneisch auf den Begriff der μαρτυρία zu bringen (vgl. 5,39), was später noch zu bedenken sein wird.

2. *Jes 54,13*

Das Zitat von Jes 54,13 in v. 45 gehört, wie oben festgestellt, zu dem Abschnitt des »Lebensbrot«-Dialogs, in dem der Evangelist das »Zu-Jesus-Kommen« als Element des zentralen Ego-Eimi-Worts v. 35 einer näheren Betrachtung oder Auslegung unterzieht (6,41-46). Entsprechend dem zu Beginn dieser Episode in Szene gesetzten »Unglauben« der »Juden«[117] ist dabei der leitende Gesichtspunkt der, daß »Glauben« an Jesus angesichts der gegen ihn sprechenden menschlichen Widerstände nur als von Gottes Gnade gewirkter »Schritt zu Jesus hin« (ἔρχεσθαι πρὸς ἐμέ) begreiflich wird. Um Funktion und Bedeutung des Schriftzitats in diesem Zusammenhang bestimmen zu können, sind folgende Arbeitsgänge notwendig: (1) eine literarkritische Vorbemerkung zu v. 44c, (2) formale Beobachtungen zur Stellung des Schriftzitats im Kontext, (3) inhaltliche Erwägungen sowie (4) hermeneutische Schlußfolgerungen.

(1) Der futurisch-eschatologische Refrain »und ich werde ihn auferwecken am letzten Tag« v. 44c ist literarkritisch einer nachträglichen Redaktion (= R) des Evangeliums gutzuschreiben[118]. Um nur eine Beobachtung zu nennen: Der Refrain unterbricht den theo-zentrischen Zusammenhang zwischen v. 44b (ὁ πατὴρ...) und dem nachfolgenden Schriftzitat (διδακτοὶ θεοῦ). In keinem Fall geht es an, wegen einer angeblichen Analogie der Zukunftsperspektive im Refrain (ἀναστήσω) und im Schriftzitat (καὶ ἔσονται) die Zugehörigkeit jenes Refrains zum ursprünglichen Text als erwiesen anzusehen[119]. Wollte man das ἔσονται des Zitats im Licht des futurisch-eschatologischen ἀναστήσω deuten, wie das Obermann vorschlägt, führte das nur zu einer Überfremdung des genuinen Textduktus von 6,45f.

---

117. Hierzu beachte man die Notiz zu ihrem »Murren« und ihrer (freilich nicht offen an Jesus gerichteten) Frage, in der sie ihren eigentlichen Glaubens-Anstoß artikulieren. Dieser besteht darin, daß für sie die *Menschheit* Jesu (»Ist das nicht Jesus, der Sohn Josefs, dessen Vater und Mutter wir kennen?«) seinem *göttlichen* Anspruch zu widerstreiten scheint (»Wie kann er jetzt sagen: Ich bin vom Himmel herabgekommen?«).

118. Die Diskussion der einzelnen Argumente bei THEOBALD (n. 54), p. 319.

119. So OBERMANN (n. 1), p. 158: »Das Futur ἔσονται ist inhaltlich damit zu erklären, daß es dem Zitat – analog zu 6,44b (!) – eine eschatologische Ausrichtung verleiht«. Dazu siehe unten n. 125!

(2) Der nähere Kontext des Schriftzitats sieht also folgendermaßen aus:

43b		Murrt nicht untereinander!
44a	(A)	Niemand (οὐδείς) kann *zu mir kommen*,
b	(B)	wenn nicht (ἐὰν μή) der *Vater*, der mich gesandt hat, ihn zieht.
45a	(C)	Es steht geschrieben bei den Propheten:
b		'Und alle (πάντες) werden Gottesgelehrte sein.'
45c	(B')	Jeder (πᾶς), der vom *Vater* gehört und gelernt hat,
d	(A')	*kommt zu mir.*
46a		*Nicht* (οὐχ), daß den Vater jemand gesehen hat,
b		es sei denn (εἰ μή) derjenige, der von Gott ist;
c		dieser hat den Vater gesehen.

Formal fällt zur Zitateinführungsformel v. 45a auf, daß diese asyndetisch (ἔστιν γεγραμμένον) an v. 44 angehängt ist; gleiches gilt vom nachfolgenden Satz v. 45c (πᾶς ὁ ἀκούσας...) im Verhältnis zum vorangehenden Zitat. Was das bedeutet, kann man an der vom Autor des Textes nicht gewählten Alternative ersehen, die Zitateinführungsformel mit einem καθὼς (γεγραμμένον...) unmittelbar an v. 44 anzuschließen; in diesem Fall wäre nämlich die primäre Zuordnung des Zitats zum vorangehenden Text eindeutig gewesen[120]. So aber ist dem Text eine Offenheit eingestiftet, die es erlaubt, das Zitat als Stütze *sowohl* von v. 44 *als auch* von v. 45c.d zu begreifen. Letzterem wird der Weg nicht nur durch den schon erwähnten asyndetischen Anschluß von v. 45c geebnet, sondern auch dadurch, daß v. 45c mit »hören« (ἀκούειν) und »lernen« (μανθάνειν) zum Wortfeld der »Lehre« (v. 45b: διδακτοί) gehörige Begriffe aufbietet und damit den Anschluß an das voranstehende Zitat signalisiert. Eine förmliche Auslegung des Schriftzitats bieten v. 45c und d aber nicht; deren *christologische* Pointe (wer wirklich vom *Vater* gehört und von ihm gelernt hat, der findet den Weg auch zum *Sohn*!) hat am *theozentrisch* orientierten Zitat gerade keinen Anhalt; gleiches gilt im übrigen für die entsprechende Aussage von v. 44a.b als möglichen Bezugstext für das nachfolgende Zitat. So gewinnt man den Eindruck, daß (a) das im Zentrum des Spruchs v. 44f stehende Zitat Licht werfen soll sowohl auf das, was *voransteht*, wie das, was *folgt*, daß aber (b) davon zunächst nur die unmittelbar rahmenden Versteile (B/B') betroffen sind, die entsprechend dem Zitat (διδακτοὶ θεοῦ) von *Gottes* aktivem Handeln (»der Vater.. zieht«) bzw. von *ihm* als dem Lehrer der Menschen handeln. Dieses Ergebnis einer eher formalen Ortsbestimmung des Zitats

---

120. Zitateinführungsformeln mit καθώς finden sich 1,23 (hier folgt ausnahmsweise die Formel dem Zitat); 6,31; 7,38; 12,14. An diesen Stellen (1,23 ist eine Ausnahme), aber auch *überall* sonst im Ev, wo die Erfüllungsformel (»damit die Schrift erfüllt würde...«) benutzt wird (cf. n. 135 unten!), *geht der Bezugstext dem Zitat voraus.* Von daher könnte man schließen, daß dem auch in 6,45 (v. 44 = Bezugstext) so sei.

im Kontext bestätigt im übrigen die andernorts entwickelte Hypothese, der Evangelist habe in das Zentrum eines von ihm aus der Tradition seiner Gemeinde übernommenen »Herrenworts« (vv. 44a.b.45c.d) das Schriftzitat redaktionell eingefügt[121]. Mit welcher Absicht er das getan hat, ist jetzt zu diskutieren.

(3) Zunächst sind *inhaltliche* Fragen zu klären. Plausibel ist die Annahme, daß mit dem angegebenen pauschalen Fundort des Zitats ἐν τοῖς προφήταις nicht indirekt auf weitere *Sach*parallelen zum Jesaja-Zitat in anderen Prophetenbüchern hingewiesen wird[122], dabei vielmehr an die »Propheten« als Teil des Schriftkanons gedacht ist[123]. Dementsprechend dürfte es dem Evangelisten hier um eine Charakterisierung des Zitats als eines *prophetischen* Zeugnisses gehen. Zu dieser Annahme paßt das der syntaktischen Struktur der LXX-Vorlage gemäße, aber vom Evangelisten selbst in das Zitat eingebrachte prophetische Futur ἔσονται[124], das er den präsentischen Aussagen von v. 44a und 45d zufolge in der *gegenwärtigen* (nachösterlichen) Begegnung der Glaubenden mit Jesus zur Erfüllung gelangen sieht. Eine darüber hinausreichende Perspektive, die das zukünftige Ziel aller Menschen anvisiert[125], hat am Text keinen Anhalt[126].

---

121. THEOBALD (n. 54), pp. 319-323. Dort finden sich die entsprechenden überlieferungs- und redaktionskritischen Argumente.

122. So aber R. BULTMANN, *Das Evangelium des Johannes*, Göttingen, [10]1968, p. 172 n. 2; in Frage kämen v.a. Jer 31,33f (LXX 38,33f); Mi 4,2; Ez 36,26f (zu weiteren Stellen vgl. RICHTER (n. 9), p. 249. Doch scheint der Evangelist an einem Hinweis auf die sonstige Fundierung des Zitierten in der »Schrift« nicht interessiert zu sein.

123. RICHTER (n. 9), p. 246f (mit Hinweis auf entsprechende rabbinische Zitatkonventionen); erwogen auch von FREED (n. 1), pp. 17f. Zuletzt OBERMANN (n. 1), pp. 156-158. Daß ein Hinweis auf die »Propheten« sonst in den Zitationsformeln des Evangeliums nicht mehr begegnet (vergleichbar ist aber 12,38, wo mit Bedacht vom »Wort des *Propheten* Jesaja« die Rede ist), verleiht der Wendung an unserer Stelle durchaus Gewicht. Im übrigen paßt die Zitationsformel von 6,45 mit ihrem Hinweis auf das »Geschrieben«-Sein (ἔστιν γεγραμμένον) durchaus in das Spektrum der übrigen Zitationsformeln, die in der Regel auf die *Schriftlichkeit* des biblischen Zeugnisses abheben: cf. 2,17; 6,31; 7,38; 10,34; 12,14.16; 13,18; 19,24.28.36f; anders RICHTER (n. 9), pp. 246.259f.

124. Auch in 2,17 (Ps 69,10) dürfte das von der Vorlage abweichende Futur auf ihn zurückgehen. Beachtlich sind auch die Futura in den Zitaten 7,38 (ῥεύσουσιν) und 19,37 (ὄψονται) (Sach 12,10), von deren *gegenwärtiger* Erfüllung im Christusgeschehen der Evangelist jeweils überzeugt ist.

125. So OBERMANN (n. 1), p. 166, der von einer »grandiose(n) Vorstellung universaler Hoffnung« spricht und im Blick auf Jesu Gesprächspartner, die »Juden«, feststellt: Diese werden »nicht bei ihrer Nichterkenntnis behaftet und wegen dieser negativ klassifiziert. Vielmehr wird ihnen zugesagt, einmal alle (πάντες) im Zustand der erkennenden Gottgelehrten, nämlich der διδακτοὶ θεοῦ zu sein«. Doch klingt das eher nach Röm 11, in Joh 6,45 steht es (leider!) nicht.

126. Das gälte selbst dann, wenn man v. 44c nicht literarkritisch ausscheiden würde; denn der das Zitat aufnehmende Satz v. 45c/d blickt nun einmal nicht in die Zukunft eines »jüngsten Tages«.

»Rhematisch« sind im Zitat wohl beide Elemente: sein viel umrätseltes Subjekt πάντες und sein Prädikatsnomen διδακτοὶ θεοῦ[127]: Die aus ihnen gebildete Aussage soll mit der hinter ihr stehenden Schriftautorität das rahmende Jesus-Wort stützen. Ein unbeschränkter Universalismus läßt sich aus dem πάντες nicht ableiten; wohl signalisiert die Auslassung des υἱούς σου (»Söhne« Jerusalems) aus der LXX-Vorlage eine bewußte Öffnung der Heilsgemeinde zur Welt der Völker, doch darf man die inhaltliche Füllung des πάντες durch die kontextuelle Einbindung des Zitats nicht übersehen. Dann aber ist bei der mit πάντες bezeichneten *Ganzheit* auf der Linie des inklusiven πᾶν von vv. 37a.39a an die im Ratschluß Gottes gesetzte Zahl all derer gedacht, die dieser seinem »Sohn« anvertraut hat und von denen keiner verloren gehen soll[128]. Von dieser Heilsgemeinde (aus Juden und Heiden), deren Zahl in Gottes Vorherwissen verborgen ist (und deshalb auch nicht einfach mit der vorfindlichen Gemeinde identifiziert werden kann)[129], heißt es sodann, daß alle zu ihr Gehörigen (gemäß den Propheten) »Gottesgelehrte« sein würden. Was mit dieser Wendung gemeint ist, ist nicht einfach zu sagen[130]. Wahrscheinlich denkt der Evangelist gemäß der assoziierten frühjüdischen Erwartung, daß im künftigen Äon Gott *selbst* die Tora lehren wird[131], an eine dem Menschen gewährte neue Gottunmittelbarkeit, die sich für ihn in der vom Parakleten nachösterlich er-innerten Begegnung mit Jesus ereignet; jedenfalls besagt das für ihn v. 45c.d, wo es heißt: »jeder, der vom Vater gehört und (von ihm) gelernt hat, kommt zu mir«. Da es nach dem Kommentarsatz von v. 46 an Jesus, dem einzig wahren Gotteszeugen, vorbei keine authentische Gotteskenntnis gibt, die diese Bezeichnung verdiente, wird jenes in v. 45c thematisierte »Hören« und »Lernen« in der Schule Gottes nicht als »Propädeutikum« im Vorfeld der Begegnung mit Jesus zu denken sein, sondern als inneres Von-Gott-Bewegtwerden in der Dynamik des »Zu-Jesus-hin-Kommens« selbst:

127. Auch wenn διδακτοὶ θεοῦ semantisch mit dem »Ziehen« des Vaters in Verbindung steht, ist es doch nicht als dessen (unbetonte) Wiederaufnahme (»Thema«) zu interpretieren; es bietet einen neuen Gesichtspunkt. Zudem ist v. 45b durch seine Einführung in v. 45a von seiner Umgebung als Metatext abgehoben, geht also nicht ohne weiteres im Informationsfluß der Verse auf.
128. Diesen Bezug von v. 45 auf v. 37/39 hat OBERMANN (n. 1), pp. 158ff, übersehen, wenn er »als primäre Bezugsgröße für πάντες die Gesprächspartner Jesu« annimmt, »das heißt 'die Juden' bzw. die sich hinter 'den Juden' verbergende Volksmenge«. Dazu wie zum folgenden THEOBALD (n. 54), pp. 337ff.
129. Deshalb kann man dem Text auch keine esoterisch verengte Perspektive nachsagen.
130. Dazu siehe zuletzt die Diskussion bei OBERMANN (n. 1), pp. 162ff.
131. Rabbinische Belege bei BORGEN (n. 19), p. 150. Vgl. auch Jer 31,33f; Ez 36,26f. Zur Auslegung von Jer 31,33f in rabbinischer Überlieferung siehe H. LICHTENBERGER/S. SCHREINER, *Der neue Bund in jüdischer Überlieferung*, in *TQ* 176 (1996) 272-290.

Man hört vom Vater und lernt von ihm, *indem* man sich auf Jesus, seinen Sohn, einläßt und sich zu ihm hinziehen läßt; dessen Wort ist es, durch welches man authentisch von Gott lernt.

(4) Damit sind wir bei den *hermeneutischen* Konsequenzen der Analyse angelangt. Wiederum ist ein *Schriftwort* einem *Jesus-Wort* zugeordnet, wobei diese Zuordnung im Schriftwort selbst verankert ist, insofern es von sich aus auf eine neue Weise *gott*unmittelbaren Belehrt-Werdens verweist, wie sie nach dem Evangelisten in der Begegnung mit dem Wort des *Gottes*sohnes Wirklichkeit geworden ist. Als (prophetisches) Zeugnis fügt sich das Schriftwort in die oben zu v. 31 angedeuteten Koordinaten: Es ist ganz Christuszeugnis, auch wenn es die christologische Komponente nicht explizit enthält. Allerdings ist diese seine Zuordnung für diejenigen, die den eigentlichen Sinn des Zitats begreifen, im futurischen ἔσονται offenkundig. Mit diesem weist der Text ausdrücklich über sich hinaus in eine Zukunft, die für den Evangelisten in Jesus Gegenwart geworden ist.

Möglicherweise verbindet dieser mit dem Schriftzeugnis aber noch einen weiteren Aspekt, die Relativierung der Tora durch die Schrift selbst. Wenn diese nämlich prophetisch eine qualifiziert neue Weise eines von Von-Gott-Belehrt-Werdens ansagt, nimmt sie sich selbst in eben dieser Funktion der Belehrung ins zweite Glied zurück[132]: *Hermeneutischer Schlüssel der Schrift kann nur das Wort des eschatologischen Gesandten Gottes sein.*

II. Das Paradigmatische im Schriftgebrauch von Joh 6
für den vierten Evangelisten

Zwei Faktoren, so wurde deutlich, bestimmen die Koordinaten des Schriftgebrauchs in Joh 6: a) Zum einen fungieren die hier eingesetzten Schriftzitate als (prophetisches) *Christuszeugnis*, wobei dies ihr tieferer Sinn ist, der nicht an ihrer Oberfläche, sondern nach Art eines Rätsels in ihnen verborgen liegt[133]. Die Schrift ist überhaupt ein Rätsel, das man erst im nachösterlichen Licht zu entziffern lernt (2,17.22; 12,26). Als Text oder lebendige Stimme verweist sie über sich hinaus auf die Offenbarung Gottes in Christus. Das ist die positive Seite im Schriftgebrauch

---

132. Außerdem ist Inhalt des eschatologischen Von-Gott-Belehrtwerdens nicht mehr die Tora, die nach Jer 31,33 den Menschen »nach diesen Tagen« ins Herz gegeben werden soll, sondern die Erkenntnis Gottes, wie sie durch Jesus, den Christus und Sohn Gottes, vermittelt wird.

133. Offenkundig ist dies bei 6,31, es trifft aber auch für 6,45 zu.

des vierten Evangelisten. b) Die Kehrseite der Medaille ist die mit a)
verbundene Entkoppelung der Schrift als eines exklusiv christologisch
beanspruchten *Textes* von der ihm ursprünglich inhärierenden *Geschichte*
Israels. Diese wird abgestoßen und in einen Raum theologischer Irrele-
vanz entlassen: Was einst der Wüstengeneration unter Mose widerfuhr,
hat – gemessen an der soteriologischen Exklusivität des »Christusereignisses« – mit Heil oder ζωή im (johanneisch strengen) Sinne nichts zu
tun[134].

Offenkundig steht der Evangelist mit der zuerst genannten Dimension
seines Schriftgebrauchs in der frühchristlichen Tradition. Das läßt sich
möglicherweise auch überlieferungskritisch festmachen, insofern die für
sie typischen (traditionellen) Erfüllungszitate alle erst in der zweiten
Hälfte seines Buches im Zusammenhang mit der Passionsgeschichte
begegnen, die auf alter Überlieferung beruht[135]. Fragt man nach dem
spezifisch Johanneischen im Schriftgebrauch des vierten Evangelisten,
dann ist man an Faktor b) verwiesen. Dieser scheint, wie seine vielfältige Wirksamkeit im Buch zeigt, nicht im Widerspruch zu Faktor a) zu
stehen[136], sondern dürfte als dessen Radikalisierung im Kontext der
johanneischen Christologie mit ihren dualistischen Konturen zu verstehen

---

134. Ähnlich DIETZFELBINGER (n. 3), p. 212: »Innerhalb des Johannesevangeliums
werden zwei gegensätzliche Weisen des Umgangs mit dem Alten Testament praktiziert.
In der einen wird es entwertet, indem ihm der Eine entgegengestellt wird, der allein Gott
gesehen und seine Worte gehört hat; in der anderen wird es umfassend in Anspruch
genommen zur Begründung und Rechtfertigung des Weges, den Jesus in der Welt gegangen ist«.

135. W. REINBOLD, *Der älteste Bericht über den Tod Jesu. Literarische Analyse und
historische Kritik der Passionsdarstellungen der Evangelien* (BZNW, 69), Berlin-New
York, 1994, p. 90 (zu 19,36). p. 136 (zu 13,18). p. 167 Anm. 254 (zu 19,23f). 15,25;
17,12 gehören zur johanneischen Redaktion, außerdem cf. 12,38. 19,28 (nur hier erscheint
τελειοῦν für den Erfüllungsgedanken, sonst steht dafür immer πληροῦν) spielt eine Son-
derrolle: cf. KRAUS, *Vollendung* (n. 3), in diesem Band!

136. So aber DIETZFELBINGER (n. 3), der davon überzeugt ist, daß die gegensätzlichen Urteile über den johanneischen Schriftgebrauch in der jüngeren und älteren
Forschung (siehe oben n. 4ff) ihr fundamentum in re im Evangelium selbst besäßen,
dessen »Gegensätzlichkeit« in dieser Sache sich jedenfalls nicht literarkritisch auflösen
lasse: »Die zu beobachtenden Gegensätze im Umgang mit dem Alten Testament ziehen
sich durch das ganze Evangelium und können nicht redaktionell verschiedenen Autoren
zugerechnet werden« (p. 204). Seine eigene Lösung des Problems zielt dahin, die
beiden angeblich gegensätzlichen Aspekte des Alten Testaments als Niederschlag eines
kontroversen Gebrauchs der Schrift in der johanneischen Gemeinde zu verstehen,
wobei der Evangelist dadurch, daß er *beide* in sein Buch aufgenommen hat, aus-
gleichend wirken wollte. Doch von einem entsprechenden Streit in der johanneischen
Gemeinde hören wir aus den Quellen, einschließlich Johannesbriefe, nichts. Die Analyse von 6,31f zeigt im Gegenteil exemplarisch, wie beide Aspekte, Desktruktion und
Neu-Konstituierung, im Sinne des Evangelisten wie zwei Seiten einer Medaille zusammengehören.

sein[137]. Greifbar ist er nicht nur am Umgang des Evangelisten mit einzelnen Schriftzitaten, sondern vor allem an den wenigen, doch signifikanten Erklärungen grundsätzlich hermeneutischer Natur wie vor allem 5,37-40/45-47, aber auch 1,17 und 1,45[138]. Aufschlußreich ist vor allem die Passage aus Kap. 5. Ohne in deren detaillierte Erörterung eintreten zu können, sei hier doch wenigstens so viel gesagt, daß sie die zu Joh 6 erarbeiteten Koordinaten bestätigt. Folgendes sei hervorgehoben: Die Funktion der »Schriften« besteht nach diesem Text ausschließlich in ihrem Zeugnis für Christus (5,39.45-47; vgl. 1,45); wer deshalb diesem keinen Glauben schenkt, hat auch den in den Schriften aufbewahrten Logos Gottes verkannt (5,38) (Faktor a). Die Kehrseite dieser exklusiven Fixierung der »Schriften« auf das in ihnen enthaltene Christuszeugnis wird in v. 37b greifbar, wo Jesus den »Juden« erklärt: »Weder habt ihr seine [s.c. des Vaters] Stimme je gehört noch seine Gestalt gesehen«. »Daß Israel Gottes Gestalt nicht gesehen habe, ist gut jüdisch-orthodox«. Daß es aber Gottes Stimme nie vernommen habe, was polemisch voransteht, setzt eine jüdische »Grundüberzeugung« außer Kraft[139]. Mit anderen Worten: Eine authentische Gotteserfahrung (sei sie auditiv *oder* visionär vermittelt) wurde den Juden überhaupt nie zuteil[140]. Was ihnen gegeben wurde, ist der *Text* der »Schriften«, der in sich den auf Christus verweisenden *Logos Gottes* enthält (5,38)[141], also ein *Text* (γεγραμμένον),

137. Überzeugend J. BECKER, *Ich bin die Auferstehung und das Leben. Eine Skizze der johanneischen Christologie*, in *TZ* 39(1983) 136-151,143f, der gezeigt hat, daß der sog. johanneische Dualismus vor allem eine »Funktion der Christologie« ist, die ihren Sinn darin hat, deren »Einmaligkeit und Exklusivität zu begründen«. Unbeschadet der Tatsache, daß der Dualismus in gewisser Weise auch »religionsgeschichtlich 'vorgegeben'« ist, wird die »Erkenntnis, daß die Welt dualistisch gespalten ist«, doch erst durch Jesus als den ausnahmslos einzigen Gottesoffenbarer freigelegt. »Indem er es ist, ist er zugleich die einzige Heilsoffenbarung, die es je gab und geben wird«. Demgegenüber ist den Menschen »die Einsicht in die menschliche Verlorenheit und damit in die dualistische 'Realität'« verborgen, »weil diese Einsicht erst Konsequenz der Offenbarung ist. Indem nämlich der Gesandte des Vaters sich selbst offenbart, enthüllt er das bisherige sorglos-monistische und optimistische Weltbild der Menschheit als Teil ihrer Unkenntnis und Verlorenheit«.

138. Außerdem 10,35: comp. n. 115!

139. J. BLANK, *Krisis. Untersuchungen zur johanneischen Christologie und Eschatologie*, Freiburg, 1964, p. 206 Anm. 66: »Das οὔτε φωνὴν αὐτοῦ steht in flagrantem Widerspruch zu den Aussagen, die besonders das Deuteronomium immer wieder einschärft«.

140. Auch wenn der Satz »zeitgenössische mystische Strömungen zurückweisen« sollte, wie SCHNACKENBURG (n. 27), p. 174, vermutet, so geht er mit seiner provozierenden *Grundsätzlichkeit* (οὔτε... πώποτε... οὔτε) über einen solchen mutmaßlichen Anlaß doch weit hinaus.

141. Dem entspricht 10,35: »jene..., an welche der Logos Gottes ergangen ist (πρὸς οὓς ὁ λόγος τοῦ θεοῦ ἐγένετο)«, wobei an diejenigen gedacht ist, denen die *Tora* zugeeignet wurde (»steht nicht *geschrieben* in *eurem* Nomos...?«) (10,34). Das Ergehen des λόγος Gottes meint also keine Auditionen Gottes im Sinne von 5,37, sondern den λόγος Gottes im Geschriebenen der Tora.

dessen Lebendigkeit allein in dem *Wort* (λόγος) besteht, das im Angesicht Christi, des einzigen authentischen Gotteszeugen (1,18; 6,46), zu sprechen anhebt. Wer meint (δοκεῖν), in den Schriften *unter Absehung von diesem* λόγος das »Leben« im eigentlichen Sinn (ζωή) zu haben, unterliegt einer schwerwiegenden Täuschung (v. 39); dieses »Leben« erschließt sich allein in Christus (v. 40). Was in den Versen 37-40 vollzogen wird, ist demnach die oben schon beschriebene Loslösung der »Schriften« als *Text* von ihrem ursprünglichen »Sitz im Leben«, der *Geschichte* Israels, die hier in ihrem Kulminationspunkt – der Moses am Sinai in Audition und Vision zuteil gewordenen Gotteserfahrung – zur Sprache kommt; ist wirkliche Gotteserfahrung und -erkenntnis exklusiv an Christus gebunden, so wird um dessentwillen jenes Mose-»Ereignis« in seinem Wirklichkeitsgehalt jetzt negiert[142] (Faktor b) mit der Folge, daß die »Schriften« in ihre Zeugenfunktion für Christus zusammengedrängt werden (Faktor a)[143]. Solche Verbindung von bejahender und verneinender Komponente als den zwei Seiten einer Medaille besitzt übrigens im johanneischen Konzept des Täufer-Zeugnisses[144] eine Strukturparallele: Der Täufer hat letztlich nicht anderes zu tun (!) als Jesu Heilbringerrolle zu bezeugen; ineins damit verneint er für sich selbst jegliche wie auch immer zu fassende messianische In-Anspruch-Nahme durch andere[145]. So verflüchtigt sich oder konzentriert sich (je nach Perspektive) seine Mission in dem einen Zug, »*Stimme*« (φωνή: 1,23/Jes 40,3) oder *Zeuge* des Christus zu sein.

---

142. MENKEN (n. 1), p. 57: »John 5:37-38 is best interpreted as directed against Jewish claims to participate in the Sinai theophany; these claims probably took Moses' ascent of Mount Sinai as an ascent into heaven«. Wenn andererseits Mose als »Gesetzgeber« (7,19; vgl. 1,17) bei Joh auf seine *Zeugenfunktion* für Christus zurückgestuft wird (cf. 1,45; 5,39.45-47), dann kommt das einer *Depotenzierung* seiner sonstigen vielfältigen religiösen Bedeutung gleich.

143. 5,39: »Und jene (s.c. die Schriften) sind es, *die über mich Zeugnis ablegen* (αἱ μαρτυροῦσαι περὶ ἐμοῦ)«. Wer ihnen nicht glaubt, gegen den wird Mose »Anklage erheben« (5,45: ἔστιν ὁ κατηγορῶν ὑμῶν Μωυσῆς). Hier wird die traditionelle Rolle des Mose als des bei Gott für Israel Fürbitte Einlegenden – »auf den ihr gehofft habt« (5,45) – (cf. Ex 32, 11-13; Sir 45, 1-5; Jub 1,19-22; LibAnt 12,8-10; 19,3.8f; AssMos 1,14; 11,11.14 etc.; D. SÄNGER, »*Von mir hat er geschrieben*« [Joh 5,46]. *Zur Funktion und Bedeutung Mose im Neuen Testament*, in KuD 41 [1995] 112-135, p. 126 n. 63) polemisch in ihr Gegenteil verkehrt. Zu 5,39 stellt SÄNGER zutreffend fest: »Entgegen jüdischer Auffassung verhilft die Tora zum Leben ausschließlich in einer sie selbst limitierenden Weise, indem sie von sich weg auf den verweist, von dem sie Zeugnis ablegt (1,45; 5,46b): von Jesus Christus, dem in die Welt herabgestiegenen Gesandten des Vaters« (p. 125).

144. Μαρτυρία und ματυρεῖν als dominante Terminologie für die Verkündigung des Täufers in 1,7f.15.19.32.34; 3,26.28; 5,33f.

145. Vgl. 1,20f.25.28.

Die Frage, ob der vorstehend kurz charakterisierte johanneische Umgang mit den »Schriften« sich im Rahmen dessen bewegt, was über den sonstigen frühchristlichen Schriftgebrauch bekannt ist, kann man natürlich im Rahmen einer johanneischen Studie allein nicht beantworten. Dennoch ergibt sich aus den hier dargebotenen Überlegungen folgende These: Mit Faktor a steht das vierte Evangelium auf dem Boden der frühchristlichen Tradition; mit Faktor b dagegen, der nicht nur die *soteriologische Relativierung der Tora* oder *die Behauptung ihrer Insuffizienz*, sondern darüber hinaus eine *heilsgeschichtliche Entleerung der in den Schriften bezeugten Geschichte Israels* (samt ihrer zentralen Institution des Tempels als des jüdischerseits behaupteten dichtesten Ortes der Gegenwart Gottes[146]) signalisiert, tritt das dem vierten Evangelium eigene spezifische Profil eines destruktiven Schriftumgangs ins Blickfeld[147]. Werden in 1,17 »Gnade und Wahrheit«, die nach jüdischem Verständnis als theologische Wesensmomente die innere Wirklichkeit der Tora ausmachen, von dieser abgetrennt, um exklusiv der Christus-Offenbarung vorbehalten zu werden, dann bleibt für jene nur ein *Vakuum an göttlicher Wirklichkeit* übrig[148]. So unangenehm diese Einsicht angesichts des heute geforderten christlich-jüdischen Gesprächs wie des innerchristlichen Ringens um die Einheit der Schrift in ihren beiden Teilen auch immer sein mag, es hilft nicht weiter, die Augen vor ihr zu

---

146. Cf. 2,19-21; 4,21.23f; 7,37-39. Vor allem J. BLANK hat diese Problematik samt ihren Konsequenzen für den christlich-jüdischen Dialog in die Mitte seines mehrbändigen Johanneskommentars gerückt. Im ersten Band (n. 87) schreibt er programmatisch zur sog. Tempelreinigungsszene: »Die eschatologische Jesus-Offenbarung bedeutet das Ende des altüberlieferten Tempelkults... Die Auseinandersetzung mit der jüdischen Tempelfrömmigkeit zieht sich durch das ganze Evangelium; sie gewinnt ihre dramatischen Höhepunkte in den Kapiteln 7-10. Die johanneische Tradition hat damit ein grundlegendes Problem aufgenommen, das in der urchristlichen Situation radikal durchgedacht und ausdiskutiert werden mußte, nämlich die Frage nach dem neuen Ort der Gegenwart Gottes, nach dem eschatologischen Kultort. Darin steckt auch die Frage nach der wahren Gemeinde, ebenso die Frage, wer nun eigentlich die wahre Offenbarung hat, die Christen oder die Juden...« (p. 201). Allerdings wird man zur genaueren historischen Profilierung des vierten Evangeliums noch hinzufügen müssen, daß in jenem Übertragungsprozeß, in dem Vorstellungen vom Jerusalemer Tempel als *dem* Ort der Gegenwart Gottes exklusiv für Jesus reklamiert wurden, diese nicht einfach negiert, sondern im christologischen Verständnis »aufgehoben« wurden, wie auch die johanneische Gemeinde sich selbst ja wohl als das wahre Israel begriffen hat (vgl. 1,12; 11,49-52; 15,1-8). Mit anderen Worten: Die Welt des vierten Evangeliums steht nicht in einfacher Opposition zur jüdischen Welt (wie wir heute aus »heidenchristlicher« Perspektive zu Unrecht zu denken geneigt sind), sondern ist selbst noch zutiefst von deren Denkvoraussetzungen imprägniert.

147. DIETZFELBINGER (n. 3), p. 205, spricht im Blick nicht nur auf 6,32 zu Recht von einem »destruierenden Angriff auf die Tradition«.

148. So auch DIETZFELBINGER (n. 3), p. 207.

verschließen[149]. Auch der Hinweis auf die historische Bedingtheit des johanneischen Konzepts durch das es prägende Trauma der Trennung von Synagoge und Ekklesia[150] vermag das *Sachproblem* der johanneischen Fassung des »Solus Christus« nicht aus der Welt zu schaffen. Bevor man sich aber diesem zuwendet, gilt es, eine textlich möglichst gut begründete Diagnose des johanneischen Schriftgebrauchs zu erstellen und konsensfähig zu machen[151]. Die wachsende Konkurrenz von *jüdischer Schrift* und *johanneischer Herrenwort-Tradition* als einer der Schrift Israels gegenüberstehenden und die Identität der christlichen Gemeinde begründenden eigenen Größe scheint dabei den Schlüssel für ein Verständnis des spezifisch johanneischen Schriftgebrauchs bereitzuhalten.

Universität Tübingen   Michael THEOBALD
Abt. Neues Testament
Liebermeisterstr. 12
D-72076 Tübingen

149. Dankenswerterweise stößt auch OBERMANN (n. 1), p. 429, diese Frage an, wenn er »das johanneische Verständnis der Schrift (und des Judentums) als eine Folge seiner [s.c. des Evangeliums] exklusiven Christologie« im Blick auf den heutigen jüdisch-christlichen Dialog für »wenig förderlich« einstuft. Von schonungsloser, befreiend wirkender theologischer Wahrhaftigkeit geprägt sind die Ausführungen von N. WALTER, *Zur theologischen Problematik des christologischen 'Schriftbeweises' im Neuen Testament*, in *NTS* 41 (1995) 338-357.

150. Darauf hebt zu Recht KRAUS, *Johannes* (n. 3), ab, wenn er (p. 20) »als die entscheidende Leistung des joh Umgangs mit der Schrift« die Stärkung der bedrängten Gemeinde »in einer von Anfechtung und Auseinandersetzung gekennzeichneten Situation« ansieht. »Der Kampf um die Schrift zwischen Juden und Christen hat in dieser Zeit der Auseinandersetzung wohl keine andere Wahl gelassen, als eben die Reklamierung der Schrift für die eigenen Belange«. Dem Schriftgebrauch des vierten Evangeliums entspreche »als sozialgeschichtlicher Ort des Joh-Ev am ehesten die aktuelle Trennung bzw. Abstoßung der joh Gemeinde von ihren jüdischen Wurzeln« (p. 24).

151. Mit WALTER (n. 149) gehe ich also davon aus, daß es sich hier lediglich um eine »Bestandsaufnahme« samt deren »Deutung« handeln kann, die »für die Frage nach der Art einer legitimen christlichen Bezugnahme auf das Alte Testament nur ein Ausgangspunkt, nur eine Vorarbeit« sein kann; »für sich allein ergibt sie nicht schon einen 'Kanon' solcher 're-lecture', sondern unterliegt zunächst einmal einer theologisch-kritischen Prüfung. Schlichter gesagt: nicht jede Form von Schriftverwendung im Neuen Testament ist allein schon dadurch, daß es sie gibt, ja daß sie gelegentlich mit Nachdruck betrieben wird, theologisch zureichend legitimiert« (p. 344). Ist unserer Generation eine re-lecture des Alten Testaments verwehrt, »die zu einer christlichen Vereinnahmung der 'Schriften' Israels führte«, so ist »eine neue Definition des Verhältnisses der Kirche zum Alten Testament« gefordert, »die dem Eigenrecht Israels an seinen 'Schriften' gerecht wird und doch zugleich daran festhält, daß auch für die Christenheit ein relatives, aber doch legitimes Recht am Alten Testament als einem Teil des christlichen Bibelkanons zu begründen ist« (p. 357).

THE USE OF THE SEPTUAGINT
IN THREE QUOTATIONS IN JOHN
JN 10,34; 12,38; 19,24

I. Introduction

In a study of the textual form of John's Old Testament quotations[1], I have recently argued that most Johannine quotations that are not free paraphrases of the OT text[2], come from the LXX; in a few cases, the LXX text did not fit the evangelist's purposes, and in these cases he made use of the Hebrew text or of an extant early Christian version[3]. The remaining eleven quotations were derived from the LXX, and in the majority of these, John edited the LXX text in various ways, in agreement with current exegetical rules and for christological reasons[4]. However, in three quotations (10,34; 12,38; 19,24) he left his LXX text untouched. If my theory on John's use of the LXX in his OT quotations is correct, his complete adoption of the LXX in these three cases means that he did not see reasons to change the LXX text.

The three quotations read as follows:

(a) Jn 10,34 = Ps 81,6 LXX: ἐγὼ εἶπα· θεοί ἐστε, "I said: You are gods". The MT of Ps 82,6 has: אֲנִי־אָמַרְתִּי אֱלֹהִים אַתֶּם.

(b) Jn 12,38 = Isa 53,1 LXX: κύριε, τίς ἐπίστευσεν τῇ ἀκοῇ ἡμῶν; καὶ ὁ βραχίων κυρίου τίνι ἀπεκαλύφθη; "Lord, who has believed our report[5]? And to whom has the arm of the Lord been revealed?" The MT reads here: מִי הֶאֱמִין לִשְׁמֻעָתֵנוּ וּזְרוֹעַ יהוה עַל־מִי נִגְלָתָה.

(c) Jn 19,24 = Ps 21,19 LXX: διεμερίσαντο τὰ ἱμάτιά μου ἑαυτοῖς καὶ ἐπὶ τὸν ἱματισμόν μου ἔβαλον κλῆρον, "They divided my garments among them, and for my clothing they cast lots". The MT has in Ps 22,19: יְחַלְּקוּ בְגָדַי לָהֶם וְעַל־לְבוּשִׁי יַפִּילוּ גוֹרָל.

---

1. M.J.J. MENKEN, *Old Testament Quotations in the Fourth Gospel. Studies in Textual Form* (Contributions to Biblical Exegesis and Theology, 15), Kampen, Kok Pharos, 1996. Here referred to as MENKEN (n. 1).

2. I consider the quotations in Jn 7,42; 8,17; 12,34 as free paraphrases.

3. The Hebrew text has been used in 12,40 (except for the last three words, which come from the LXX) and 13,18, an early Christian version in 19,37.

4. Jn 1,23; 2,17; 6,31.45; 7,38; 12,15; 15,25; 19,36.

5. In translating "our report", I simply adopt a usual rendering; it will appear below how far this translation is really adequate.

In the case of the second and third quotation of this series, the selection of this particular OT passage was apparently governed by tradition[6]; that fact, however, does not exclude the possibility that the fourth evangelist used the OT texts in his own way and for his own purposes.

The first question to be asked is whether these three quotations have indeed been derived from the LXX[7]. Because in all three instances there is agreement between LXX and Hebrew text, one could argue that a correct translation of the Hebrew text into Greek would easily yield the wording we now find in the LXX; in that case, it would be impossible to tell whether the Greek translation which we find in the Fourth Gospel comes from the LXX, from another Greek translation or from the pen of the evangelist who himself translated the Hebrew into Greek. We can, however, make some observations which strongly suggest that the three quotations were really derived from the LXX:

(a) As regards the source of the quotation in 10,34, I do not think that the translation of the Hebrew nominal clause אתם אלהים by the Greek verbal clause θεοί ἐστε is very significant[8]. In Greek, nominal clauses with a subject in the 1st or 2nd pers. are rare[9]; the translation ὑμεῖς θεοί may therefore be considered as theoretically possible, but unusual in practice. The translation we actually find in both the LXX and John, is the most obvious translation (cf. also Isa 41,23 LXX). What is significant in Jn 10,34, is the evangelist's use here of εἶπα; elsewhere, he always uses εἶπον (1,15.30.50 etc.) for the 1st pers. aor. ind. The peculiar, un-Johannine form used in the quotation clearly comes from Ps 81,6 LXX[10].

(b) That Jn 12,38 agrees with Isa 53,1 LXX in having the dative τίνι where the MT has עַל־מִי, which one would expect to have been translated by ἐπὶ τίνα (so Theodotion according to ms. 86) or some such

---

6. Paul adduces Isa 53,1a in Rom 10,16, and Isa 53,1 is advanced as part of a larger quotation in 1 Clem 16,3; Justin, *Apol.* 1,50,5; *Dial.* 13,3; 42,2; 114,2; 118,4. For Ps 22,19, the relevant texts are mentioned below, under IV. As far as we can detect, John had no Christian predecessors in quoting from Ps 82; some decades later, Justin makes use of the psalm (*Dial.* 124), but in quite a different way. On the traditional character of John's use of Scripture, see MENKEN (n. 1), pp. 209-212.

7. I here reiterate and expand on what I wrote in MENKEN (n. 1), pp. 14-15.

8. E.D. FREED, *Old Testament Quotations in the Gospel of John* (NTSup, 11), Leiden, Brill, 1965, p. 61, mentions the change of a nominal into a verbal clause as an exception to an otherwise exact translation.

9. See E. SCHWYZER, *Griechische Grammatik 2: Syntax und syntaktische Stilistik*, ed. A. DEBRUNNER (Handbuch der Altertumswissenschaft 2/1.2), Munich, Beck, 1950, pp. 623-624; *BDR*, [16]1984, §128; N. TURNER, *Syntax*, vol. 3 of J.H. MOULTON, *A Grammar of New Testament Greek*, Edinburgh, Clark, 1963, pp. 294-310.

10. About the variant reading εἶπον in Jn 10,34, see MENKEN (n. 1), p. 15, n. 13.

expression, is probably not very significant[11]: the Hebrew variant reading אל־מי is found in Isa 53,1 in 1QIsaᵃ (and indirectly in Vg), and the confusion of the Hebrew prepositions אל and על is common[12]. Another point is relevant: both John's quotation and Isa 53,1 LXX begin with κύριε; the Hebrew text has no equivalent. This circumstance clearly indicates that John here draws from the LXX. A second indication is that for "to reveal" John uses in this case ἀποκαλύπτειν, whereas he normally has φανεροῦν (Jn 1,31; 2,11 etc.). Had the evangelist himself translated, he would no doubt have used the latter verb.

(c) If John (or somebody else) had translated the quotation from Ps 22,19 in Jn 19,24, he would have had at least four opportunities to deviate from the LXX. He could have translated חלק piel, "to divide", by μερίζειν instead of the compound διαμερίζειν (see, e.g., 3 Kgdms 18,6 LXX), or have chosen a translation such as διαιρεῖν (see, e.g., Isa 9,2 LXX) or διαδιδόναι (see Gen 49,27 LXX; cf. Jn 6,11)[13]. He could also have chosen alternative translations for בגד, "garment", now translated as ἱμάτιον, and for its synonym לבוש, now translated as ἱματισμός: for both Hebrew words, στολή would have been an adequate rendering (see, e.g., Gen 27,15 LXX), and the two Greek words could also have been used in inverted order. He could (just as Symmachus did) have used λαγχάνειν instead of βάλλειν κλῆρον. At all four points, John's translation is in exact agreement with Ps 21,19 LXX. The only possible explanation for this fourfold agreement is that the quotation comes from the LXX. In addition, there is the fact that in both Jn 19,24 and Ps 21,19 LXX the Hebrew imperfects have been rendered by Greek aorists[14].

I conclude that in the three quotations in question, John has simply adopted the text of the LXX. A corollary of my assumption that in quoting from the OT, John made use of the LXX, modifying it or departing from it where it did not serve his purposes, is that he left the LXX text unchanged in these three quotations because he did not see any reason to change it. It is this corollary that I wish to examine in this paper. The

11. It is considered as significant by C. GOODWIN, *How Did John Treat His Sources?*, in *JBL* 73 (1954) 61-75, p. 62, n. 7.

12. See P. JOÜON – T. MURAOKA, *A Grammar of Biblical Hebrew* (Subsidia Biblica, 14), Rome, Biblical Institute, 1991, §133b.

13. Cf. B.G. SCHUCHARD, *Scripture within Scripture. The Interrelationship of Form and Function in the Explicit Old Testament Citations in the Gospel of John* (SBL DS, 133), Atlanta, Scholars, 1992, p. 127.

14. Cf. FREED, *OT Quotations in the Gospel of John* (n. 8), p. 100; S. PANCARO, *The Law in the Fourth Gospel. The Torah and the Gospel, Moses and Jesus, Judaism and Christianity according to John* (NTSup, 42), Leiden, Brill, 1975, p. 340, n. 100; D.J. MOO, *The Old Testament in the Gospel Passion Narratives*, Sheffield, Almond, 1983, p. 253; SCHUCHARD, *Scripture within Scripture* (n. 13), p. 127.

hypothesis I intend to test is that in Jn 10,34; 12,38; 19,24, the LXX text of the quotations does indeed suit the Johannine context: it offered the evangelist precisely what he needed.

II. THE QUOTATION FROM PS 82,6 IN JN 10,34

In Jn 10,22-39, the evangelist narrates a dispute between Jesus and "the Jews" during the feast of Dedication in the temple (10,22-23). Although the story may be based on the tradition of Jesus' interrogation by the high priest, it is in its present state clearly a Johannine creation, for reasons of style, vocabulary, and theology[15]. The Jews ask Jesus to tell them plainly whether he is the Christ; Jesus answers them by referring to his words and works, but he has to establish that the Jews, not belonging to his sheep, do not believe. His answer ends with the statement that he and the Father are one (10,24-30). The Jews then pick up stones in order to stone him for blasphemy: although he is a human being, he makes himself God (10,31-33). Jesus retorts with the following words:

> Is it not written in your law[16], "I said: You are gods"? If he called them gods to whom the word of God came, and Scripture cannot be nullified, do you say of him whom the Father consecrated and sent into the world, "You are blaspheming", because I said, "I am the[17] Son of God"? (10,34-36)

Finally, Jesus refers to his works once again; the Jews try to seize him, but he escapes (10,37-39).

Without evidence to the contrary, I shall presuppose that John has Jesus here use Scripture as the authoritative utterance of God[18]. That is at

15. This is generally recognized; notable exceptions are R. BULTMANN, *Das Evangelium des Johannes* (KEK), Göttingen, Vandenhoeck & Ruprecht, 1941, p. 297, and J. BECKER, *Das Evangelium des Johannes 1* (ÖTK, 4/1), Gütersloh, Mohn – Würzburg, Echter, 1979, pp. 336, 339, who consider 10,34-36 as an addition by the ecclesiastical redactor, apparently because they missed the logic of the passage. For the Johannine style of the passage, see E. RUCKSTUHL – P. DSCHULNIGG, *Stilkritik und Verfasserfrage im Johannesevangelium. Die johanneischen Sprachmerkmale auf dem Hintergrund des Neuen Testaments und des zeitgenössischen hellenistischen Schrifttums* (NTOA, 17), Freiburg Schw., Universitätsverlag–Göttingen: Vandenhoeck & Ruprecht, 1991, pp. 189-190, 223.

16. About "your law" in the introduction to a quotation from a psalm, see MENKEN (n. 1), pp. 18 (with n. 21), 141.

17. When a determinate predicate noun precedes the verb, it usually lacks the article, cf., e.g., Mt 13,37-39; Jn 1,49; 8,12 beside 9,5; see *BDR*, §273; TURNER, *Syntax* (n. 9), pp. 182-184, with the reference, in both grammars, to E.C. COLWELL, *A Definite Rule for the Use of the Article in the Greek New Testament*, in *JBL* 52 (1933) 12-21. In P[45], the article is supplied. In the case of Jn 10,36 the context shows unmistakably that Jesus here speaks of himself as *the* Son of God.

18. So rightly, a.o., R. SCHNACKENBURG, *Das Johannesevangelium 2* (HTKNT, 4/2), Freiburg, Herder, 1971, p. 389; H.N. RIDDERBOS, *Het Evangelie naar Johannes. Proeve*

least the evident status of Scripture in early Judaism and early Christianity, a status it also enjoys elsewhere in the Fourth Gospel, as is clear from the other OT quotations (1,23; 2,17, etc.), from the references to the fulfilment of Scripture (17,12; 19,28), and also from various passages in which the Scriptures are said to testify to Jesus, to furnish proof of his having been sent by God (see 1,45; 2,22; 5,39.46; 20,9). Jesus' emphatic assertion "Scripture cannot be nullified" (10,35; cf. 7,23) betrays the same conviction. There is no reason to consider Jesus' appeal to Scripture in the argument of 10,34-36 as a mere *argumentum ad hominem*, something the Johannine Jesus himself does not take seriously; the use of Ps 82,6 is not just an accommodation to the level of Jesus' opponents, to fight them with their own weapons.

I shall also presuppose that the use of Ps 82,6 in this context was anyhow recognizable and comprehensible for John's audience and for those with whom they were arguing. Such a presupposition implies that we have to connect the exegesis of Ps 82 in John as well as possible with its explanation in John's Jewish environment, insofar as we know or can reconstruct this explanation.

A simple reading of John's text reveals a few important things about John's exegesis of the psalm. In 10,33, the Jews blame Jesus for making himself God although he is a human being. This is a theme which recurs in various wording throughout the Fourth Gospel (see 5,18; 6,41-42; 7,25-31; 8,52-53; 19,7); the Jews consider Jesus' humanity as a fact, whereas his coming from God and his unity with him constitute the point of contention. For the evangelist, on the other hand, the statements that Jesus is a human being and that he comes from God and is one with him, are both true (see esp. 1,14)[19]. Jesus reacts to the reproach of 10,33 by adducing and explaining Ps 82,6; this reaction makes sense only when the Johannine Jesus considers human beings as those addressed by God with the words "You are gods". If the Johannine Jesus would suppose the quotation to refer to superhuman, heavenly beings, his argument would lose its force. The psalm verse is supposed to support precisely the assertion that the human being Jesus can rightly claim to be God's Son.

A continued straightforward reading of John's text gives us in 10,35 a specification, by John's Jesus, of those to whom God directed the words "You are gods": God "called them gods to whom the word of God came". To understand John's interpretation of the psalm verse, it is

van een theologische exegese 1, Kampen, Kok, 1987, p. 432; differently BULTMANN, *Johannes* (n. 15), p. 297.

19. See M.M. THOMPSON, *The Humanity of Jesus in the Fourth Gospel*, Philadelphia, Fortress, 1988.

essential to know who those are πρὸς οὓς ὁ λόγος τοῦ θεοῦ ἐγένετο, "to whom the word of God came". "The word of God" from v. 35 cannot refer to God's speech in Ps 82,6, because in that case the wording of v. 35a is unnecessarily complicated and becomes tautological: God called gods those whom he called gods[20]. In the OT and in early Jewish and early Christian literature, the expression "The word of the Lord came to ..." clearly and unequivocally indicates a special revelation of God to certain privileged human beings, especially prophets. The Hebrew phrase ויהי דבר־יהוה אל and the like, and its Greek equivalent ἐγένετο λόγος (or ῥῆμα) κυρίου πρός and the like, are used in the OT (MT and LXX) of persons such as, e.g., Abraham (Gen 15,1), Samuel (1 Sam 15,10), Nathan (2 Sam 7,4), Solomon (1 Kings 6,11), Elijah (1 Kings 17,2), Isaiah (2 Kings 20,4; Isa 38,4), Hosea (Hos 1,1), Jonah (Jonah 1,1; 3,1), Zechariah (Zech 1,1.7); the expression is used very frequently of the prophets Jeremiah (e.g., Jer 1,4.11.13; Dan 9,2) and Ezekiel (e.g., Ezek 1,3; 3,16; 6,1). In early Jewish and early Christian literature, we find the same phrase concerning figures such as Noah (1 Enoch 67,1), Baruch (2 Baruch 1,1), John the Baptist (Lk 3,2), or Paul (Apocalypse of Paul 3). It usually reads "The word of *the Lord* came to ..."; rarely we find "The word of *God* came to ..." (1 Kings 12,22 MT; 1 Chron 17,3 MT; Jer 1,1-2 LXX; Lk 3,2). It is not surprising that the latter expression is used in Jn 10,35: in the Fourth Gospel, κύριος is said of God in 12, 13.38 only, and both times the word is immediately derived from the OT (Ps 118,26; Isa 53,1 LXX). As John normally reserves the title κύριος for Jesus (see, e.g., 1,23; 6,23), it is only to be expected that he speaks of "the word of *God*" in 10,35. Anyhow, in the light of the standard use of the expression "The word of the Lord came to ..." we may suppose that for John, those "to whom the word of God came" are individual recipients of special divine revelation, especially prophets[21].

20. So rightly PANCARO, *Law* (n. 14), pp. 178-179.

21. So also RIDDERBOS, *Johannes 1* (n. 18), pp. 432-433; however, he does not explain the application of Ps 82,6 to precisely these persons. According to A. HANSON, *John's Citation of Psalm LXXXII*, in *NTS* 11 (1964-65) 158-162; ID., *John's Citation of Psalm LXXXII Reconsidered*, in *NTS* 13 (1966-67) 363-367; ID., *The Prophetic Gospel. A Study of John and the Old Testament*, Edinburgh, Clark, 1991, pp. 144-149, "the Word of God" in Jn 10,35 is the pre-existent Logos who addressed Israel at Sinai (see below), and is now incarnate in Jesus; if the address of the pre-existent Word made human beings into gods, how much more can Jesus be called the Son of God. However, John does not dwell on activities of the Logos between creation and incarnation, and when he has Jesus speak about his "existence" before the incarnation, he has him use the first person (e.g., 3,11; 8,26.38), not the title of Logos. John does not know of a Logos who is to a certain degree independent of Jesus. See further M.J.J. MENKEN, review of HANSON, *Prophetic Gospel*, in *NT* 34 (1992) 403-406, pp. 405-406; also PANCARO, *Law* (n. 14), pp. 185-187.

Now that we have established two aspects of John's exegesis of Ps 82,6, we have to focus our attention on the various ways in which Ps 82 was explained in John's environment. We know of three basic types of early exegesis of Ps 82[22]:

(1) According to one explanation, the psalm is a description of a scene in God's heavenly court: the gods mentioned in vv. 1b.6 are heavenly beings or angels, sometimes evil angels[23]. The LXX goes a step in this direction by translating בעדת-אל, "in God's council", in v. 1a by ἐν συναγωγῇ θεῶν, "in the congregation of the gods". The Peshitta has ml'k', "angels", for both אל in v. 1a and אלהים in v. 1b. A similar interpretation has been preserved by Origen, according to whom God is addressing evil angels in Ps 82,6 (Homilies on Exodus 8,2)[24]. In Qumran texts, we find עדת אלים, "the congregation of the gods" (e.g., 1QM 1,10; 1QDM 4,1; 4QShirShabb[a] 2,9; 4 QM[a] 11,1,12)[25]; as far as I can see, the only OT passage that can have inspired this expression, is Ps 82,1. This type of interpretation of Ps 82 is close to what seems to be the original meaning of the psalm, when it is read against the background of Ugaritic, Phoenician and Aramaic parallels: the God of Israel is judging the gentile gods, who are considered as present in the divine council (cf. Ps 89,6-8; Job 1,6; 2,1; 15,8)[26].

The earliest known extended exegesis of Ps 82, preserved in 11QMelch[27], also belongs to this type, with the significant addition that the central figure among the heavenly beings is Melchizedek. He is considered as the subject of v. 1, the god who stands up in the divine council and

22. See the surveys in J.H. NEYREY, "I Said: You Are Gods" : Psalm 82:6 and John 10, in JBL 108 (1989) 647-663, pp. 647-649; SCHUCHARD, Scripture within Scripture (n. 13), pp. 62-63; A. OBERMANN, Die christologische Erfüllung der Schrift im Johannesevangelium. Eine Untersuchung zur johanneischen Hermeneutik anhand der Schriftzitate (WUNT, 2/83), Tübingen, Mohr, 1996, pp. 173-176.

23. Relevant materials were collected by J.A. EMERTON, The Interpretation of Psalm lxxxii in John x, in JTS NS 11 (1960) 329-332; ID., Melchizedek and the Gods: Fresh Evidence for the Jewish Background of John X. 34-36, in JTS NS 17 (1966) 399-401.

24. See for other patristic texts EMERTON, Psalm lxxxii in John x (n. 23), 331-332.

25. In the Qumran writings, angels are often called אלים or אלהים, "gods" (see, e.g., the various texts of the Songs of the Sabbath Sacrifice [4Q400-405, 11Q17]; 1QH 10,8; 1QM 1,11; 14,16; 15,14; 17,7).

26. See, e.g., H.-J. KRAUS, Psalmen 2 (BKAT, 15/2), Neukirchen, Neukirchener, 1978[5] (orig. 1960), pp. 733-739; H.-D. NEEF, Gottes himmlischer Thronrat. Hintergrund und Bedeutung von sôd JHWH im Alten Testament (Arbeiten zur Theologie, 79), Stuttgart, Calwer, 1994, pp. 13-27; W.S. PRINSLOO, Psalm 82: Once Again, Gods or Men?, in Bib 76 (1995) 219-228.

27. See A.S. VAN DER WOUDE, Melchisedek als himmlische Erlösergestalt in den neugefundenen eschatologischen Midraschim aus Qumran Höhle XI, in OTS 14, Leiden, Brill, 1965, pp. 354-373; M. DE JONGE – A.S. VAN DER WOUDE, 11Q Melchizedek and the New Testament, in NTS 12 (1965-66) 301-326.

judges in the midst of the gods; these gods are either good angels who side with Melchizedek, or evil angels, "Belial and the spirits of his lot" (see 11QMelch 2,10-14). It is important to see that in this explanation the scene of the psalm is in heaven, and that Melchizedek has the central position in the divine council. Melchizedek is here an angelic being, but a special angelic being (cf. Heb 7,1-3). We may assume that the Qumran sectarians responsible for 11QMelch knew the story about Abram's meeting with Melchizedek (Gen 14,18-20); it is at least found in 1Qap Gen 22,14-17. So they probably considered Melchizedek as an angel who once appeared as a human being on earth or as a human being who was exalted to angelic status[28].

(2) In rabbinic literature, we meet the view that the gods of Ps 82 are human judges: God is thought to be present when they are in session, at least as long as their judgment is just (see b. Ber. 6a; b. Soṭa 47b; b. Sanh. 6b, 7a; Tg. Ps 82; Midr. Ps 82). This type of explanation concentrates on the beginning of the psalm.

(3) Another type of explanation is also found in rabbinic literature, and it concerns vv. 6-7 of the psalm. According to this interpretation, God called the Israelites gods at Mount Sinai, when they accepted the Torah; it meant that death had no power over them. But after their worship of the golden calf, the next verse of the psalm ("However, you shall die like men, and like any of the princes you shall fall") applied to them (see, e.g., Mek. Exod 20,19, Baḥodesh 9; Sipre Deut 32,20, Piska 320; b. 'Abod. Zar. 5a)[29].

How do these types of interpretation of Ps 82 relate to what we observed earlier about Jn 10,34-36? We saw that the words "You are gods" were addressed, according to John, to individuals who received a special divine revelation, especially prophets; that rules out the second and third types of interpretation, in which judges and Israel at Mount Sinai were supposed to be the gods of the psalm[30]. Neither judges nor

---

28. In other Jewish writings of the period, Melchizedek is considered as a human being (see, e.g., Philo, *Abr.* 235; Josephus, *Ant.* 1,180), albeit a very special one (see, e.g., 2 Enoch 71). See M.C. ASTOUR, *Melchizedek (Person)*, in *ABD* 4, pp. 684-686; J. REILING, *Melchizedek*, in K. VAN DER TOORN a.o. (eds.), *Dictionary of Deities and Demons in the Bible*, Leiden, Brill, 1995, cc. 1047-1053.

29. See for these and other materials: Str-B 2. 543; NEYREY, *"I Said: You Are Gods"* (n. 22), pp. 655-659.

30. The second type of explanation is supposed to constitute the background of Jn 10,34-36 by: J.H. BERNARD, *A Critical and Exegetical Commentary on the Gospel according to St. John*, ed. A.H. MCNEILE (ICC), Edinburgh, Clark, 1929, p. 367; R. JUNG-KUNTZ, *An Approach to the Exegesis of John 10:34-36*, in *CTM* 35 (1964) 556-565, pp. 561-565; R.E. BROWN, *The Gospel according to John (i-xii)* (AB, 29), Garden City,

Israel as a whole can be considered as individual recipients of special revelation. Another problem with these types of exegesis is that we cannot be certain that they were current in the time the Fourth Gospel was composed, i.e., towards the end of the 1st century C.E.

It seems that the first type of exegesis of the psalm, according to which the gods are heavenly beings[31], also does not correspond to the explanation that John's Jesus gives: we observed that Jesus' argument in Jn 10,34-36 makes sense in its context only if the scriptural quotation applies to human beings. In this type of exegesis, however, there appeared

NY, Doubleday, 1966, pp. 409-410; B. LINDARS, *The Gospel of John* (NCBC), London, Oliphants, 1972, p. 374; M.-É. BOISMARD, *Jésus, le Prophète par excellence, d'après Jean 10,24-39*, in J. GNILKA (ed.), *Neues Testament und Kirche*. FS R. Schnackenburg, Freiburg, Herder, 1974, pp. 160-171 (with Moses as the supreme judge and prophet); S.L. HOMCY, *"You are Gods"? Spirituality and a Difficult Text*, in *JETS* 32 (1989) 485-491, pp. 488-491 (on p. 489, he also seems to assume the presence of the third type in John); W.G. PHILLIPS, *An Apologetic Study of John 10:34-36*, in *BS* 146 (1989) 405-419, p. 409; SCHUCHARD, *Scripture within Scripture* (n. 13), pp. 64-65. The third type of interpretation is considered to constitute the background of Jn 10,34-36 by: A. SCHLATTER, *Der Evangelist Johannes. Wie er spricht, denkt und glaubt. Ein Kommentar zum vierten Evangelium*, Stuttgar, Calwer, 1930, p. 244; C.K. BARRETT, *The Gospel according to St John*, London, SPCK, ²1978, pp. 384-385; HANSON, *John's Citation of Psalm LXXXII* (n. 21); ID., *John's Citation of Psalm LXXXII Reconsidered* (n. 21); ID., *Prophetic Gospel* (n. 21), pp. 144-149; J.S. ACKERMAN, *The Rabbinic Interpretation of Psalm 82 and the Gospel of John*, in *HTR* 59 (1966) 186-191; SCHNACKENBURG, *Johannesevangelium 2* (n. 18), p. 390; J. RIEDL, *Das Heilswerk Jesu nach Johannes* (Freiburger theologische Studien, 93), Freiburg, Herder, 1973, pp. 260-261; PANCARO, *Law* (n. 14), pp. 184-185; M. HENGEL, *Die Schriftauslegung des 4. Evangeliums auf dem Hintergrund der urchristlichen Exegese*, in *Jahrbuch für Biblische Theologie* 4 (1989) 249-288, p. 262; NEYREY, *"I Said: You Are Gods"* (n. 22); K. WENGST, *Bedrängte Gemeinde und verherrlichter Christus. Ein Versuch über das Johannesevangelium*, Munich, Kaiser, 1990, pp. 120-121; D.A. CARSON, *The Gospel according to John*, Leicester, Inter-Varsity – Grand Rapids, Eerdmans, 1991, p. 398; H. THYEN, *Die Erzählung von den bethanischen Geschwistern (Joh 11,1–12,19) als "Palimpsest" über synoptischen Texten*, in F. VAN SEGBROECK a.o. (eds.), *The Four Gospels 1992*. FS F. Neirynck (BETL, 100), Leuven, Leuven University – Peeters, 1992, pp. 2021-2050, esp. 2031-2032; OBERMANN, *Christologische Erfüllung* (n. 22), pp. 176-182 (who explicitly broadens the circle of the addressees so that it encompasses the Johannine Jews). According to G. REIM, *Studien zum alttestamentlichen Hintergrund des Johannesevangeliums* (SNTS MS, 22), Cambridge, Cambridge University, 1974, pp. 24-25, John presupposes a sapiential interpretation of Ps 82,6, in which the verse was applied to all those who now accept the Word of God coming to them; Reim does not adduce any evidence for this type of interpretation.

31. This type of exegesis is supposed to be the background of Jn 10,34-36 by: EMERTON, *Psalm lxxxii in John x* (n. 23); ID., *Melchizedek and the Gods* (n. 23); J.-A. BÜHNER, *Der Gesandte und sein Weg im 4. Evangelium. Die kultur- und religionsgeschichtlichen Grundlagen der johanneischen Sendungschristologie sowie ihre traditionsgeschichtliche Entwicklung* (WUNT, 2/2), Tübingen, Mohr, 1977, pp. 393-395; W. LOADER, *The Christology of the Fourth Gospel. Structure and Issues* (BBET, 23), Frankfurt/M, Lang, 1989, pp. 164-165; J. ASHTON, *Understanding the Fourth Gospel*, Oxford, Clarendon, 1991, pp. 147-150.

to exist a variant according to which a former human being, albeit a very special one (Melchizedek), was present in the divine council. This kind of explanation was certainly extant at the time John wrote his gospel; does it constitute a background against which the interpretation of Ps 82,6 in Jn 10,34-36 can be understood[32]?

To my mind, it does indeed: there is ample evidence in the OT, in early Jewish and in early Christian literature that individual human recipients of special revelation were supposed to be present in the heavenly council. We meet already in the OT the idea that the revelation given by prophets goes back to their attendance of God's council[33]. In 1 Kings 22,19-22 we find the story of the prophet Micaiah, the son of Imlah, who tells the king of Israel how he saw the Lord sitting on his throne amidst the host of heaven, and how he heard the conversation between the Lord and the heavenly spirits. According to Jer 23,18.22, a true prophet has been standing in the divine council, and has seen and heard there God's decisions so that he is able to pass them on to the people (cf. also Jer 15,19; Amos 3,7). The call visions of Isaiah (Isa 6,1-13) and Ezekiel (Ezek 1,1-3,15) presuppose a similar idea: the prophet is standing amidst the heavenly ones, and converses with God. In the latter case, the closing passage (3,12-15) makes quite clear that the prophet is indeed imagined to be in God's presence and brought back to earth afterwards. In the vision of Dan 7, Daniel sees the heavenly council; that he is seen as attending, is evident from v. 16: when he wishes to know the meaning of his vision, he approaches one of those who are "standing", i.e., one of the angels around God's throne (cf. v. 10). We are dealing here with descriptions of visions, in which the visionary is supposed to be attending, in some real sense, that which he sees: God in the midst of the heavenly beings.

In early Jewish and early Christian literature, we encounter a similar idea[34]: prophets and prophet-like figures have visions in which they make tours of heaven, during which they behold, as far as that is possible, God in the midst of his angels, and sometimes participate in the angels' worship of God; in many cases, the description ends with the return of the visionary to earth. According to 1 Enoch 14,8-25, Enoch ascends to the throne of God, and comes in the presence of "the Great Glory" (v. 20) and his holy ones (vv. 22-23). Similar scenes are found in the "Book of the Similitudes" (1 Enoch 39-40; 46-47; 60,1-6; 71). In 2 Enoch 3-21,

32. Cf. BÜHNER, *Gesandte* (n. 31), p. 394; ASHTON, *Understanding the Fourth Gospel* (n. 31), p. 149.

33. See NEEF, *Gottes himmlischer Thronrat* (n. 26), pp. 15, 17, 41-45, 59-60.

34. See M. HIMMELFARB, *Ascent to Heaven in Jewish and Christian Apocalypses*, New York – Oxford, Oxford University, 1993, esp. pp. 9-71.

Enoch relates his journey, accompanied by angels, through the various heavens; finally, in the tenth heaven he beholds the Lord with his angels, and he becomes like one of them (ch. 22). God reveals him many mysteries (chs. 23-35), and for the final thirty days of his earthly life, Enoch returns to earth to instruct his sons (chs. 36-38)[35]. In chs. 9-30 of the Apocalypse of Abraham, the vision Abraham had, according to Gen 15, is retold. Led by the angel Iaoel, Abraham ascends to heaven (chs. 15-17), he joins in the worship by the angels (chs. 17-18), and after having received many revelations from God himself (chs. 19-29), he returns to earth (ch. 30). The extant fragments of the Apocalypse of Zephaniah ascribe similar experiences to Zephaniah. The prophet seems to be dead (ch. 1)[36], but in reality he is travelling through heaven in the company of angels (chs. 2-12). In the course of his journey, he puts on an angelic garment, and, as one knowing the language of the angels, he prays with them (8,3-4). In 4QM[a] 11,1,14.18, it is apparently a human being who says, in language that is somewhat reminiscent of Ps 82: "I am counted among the gods and my dwelling is in the holy congregation.... I am counted among the gods, and my glory is with the sons of the king"[37].

Philo also knows about such heavenly ascents[38]. Moses, who entered on Mount Sinai into the darkness in which God was (Exod 20,21), is the type of the prophetic mind ascending into heaven, to behold what can be seen of God, to become divinely inspired, and to be divinized (*Mos.* 1,158; *Spec. Leg.* 1,37-50; *QE* 2,29.40)[39]. It should be noted that divine inspiration is for Philo the mark of real prophecy (*Her.* 249.258-266). Philo does not reserve such ascents for real prophets or prophet-like figures; he speaks in general terms about the human soul ascending on high, dancing with the celestial bodies, on its way to the Great King (*Op.* 69-71; see also *Spec. Leg.* 1,207; *QG* 4,130). Elsewhere, he speaks of angels and the divine Logos as escorting the soul on its journey

35. See also the comparable story about Enoch's transformation into the principal angel Metatron in 3 Enoch 3-15, and about R. Ishmael's ascent to the presence of God in the seventh of the heavenly palaces, where he sings in the angelic choir, in 3 Enoch 1.

36. The burial scene of ch. 1 could also imply that the prophet has really died; however, the analogy with 4 Baruch 9,7-14 (Jeremiah seems to be dead during his heavenly journey, but his soul returns into his body) makes one surmise that Zephaniah is only apparently dead; differently HIMMELFARB, *Ascent to Heaven* (n. 34), p. 52.

37. Translation from F. GARCÍA MARTÍNEZ, *The Dead Sea Scrolls Translated. The Qumran Texts in English*, Leiden, Brill, 1994, p. 118.

38. See P. BORGEN, *Heavenly Ascent in Philo: An Examination of Selected Passages*, in J.H. CHARLESWORTH – C.A. EVANS (eds.), *The Pseudepigrapha and Early Biblical Interpretation* (JSP SS, 14 = Studies in Scripture in Early Judaism and Christianity, 2), Sheffield, Sheffield Academic, 1993, pp. 246-268.

39. Moses' divinization was a widespread idea, see MENKEN (n. 1), pp. 57-60.

(*Mig.* 168-175). He also ascribes such an ascent to himself (*Spec. Leg.* 3,1-2). In spite of Philo's generalization of the heavenly ascent into something within reach of the human mind, its association with prophetic figures remains perceptible.

In addition to this range of early Jewish texts, there are similar passages in early Jewish writings which were subsequently christianized and in early Christian writings. In Testament of Levi 2-5, Levi tells about his ascent to the uppermost heaven, where God is enthroned in the midst of worshipping angels; God appoints Levi as high priest, and he is brought back to earth (cf. ch. 8). Chs. 6-11 of the Ascension of Isaiah contain a description of the prophet Isaiah's heavenly journey. While his body remains on earth, his mind is taken up for a vision (6,10-15; cf. 4 Baruch 9,7-14); an angel from the seventh heaven accompanies him through the various heavens, each of them inhabited by a host of angels (chs. 7-9). In the sixth heaven, Isaiah joins in the heavenly worship of the Trinity by the angels (8,17-18), and in the seventh heaven, he worships the Trinity again, this time together with the righteous and the angels (9,27-42). He then witnesses the descent and ascent of Christ, and returns to earth (chs. 10-11). According to Rev 4,2-5,14; 7,9-8,5; 11,16-18; 15,2-8; 19,1-10, the seer John, who is, in his visionary experience, in heaven (cf. 4,1), witnesses the heavenly worship of the angels, of the four living creatures, of the twenty-four elders, and of the martyrs. In the Apocalypse of Paul 44, Paul witnesses such heavenly worship.

So the idea that individual human recipients of special revelation ascended to heaven and participated there in angelic worship of God, was alive in John's time; that is indeed evident from the various texts just referred to, most of which are pre-Johannine or (roughly) contemporaneous with John. I recall at this point that we observed above that according to the earliest known interpretation of Ps 82 (in 11QMelch), Melchizedek, a former human being, although a very special one, was supposed to attend the divine council and to be called "god". When we now combine these findings, it is to my mind very plausible that in the environment of the Fourth Gospel Ps 82 was applied to individual human recipients of special divine revelation, who were supposed to have been present among the heavenly ones. Those persons of whom it could be said that "the word of God came to them" had been among the angels in heaven, had participated in their worship of God, and God had addressed them with the words "You are gods" (Ps 82,6). We do not of course have a direct testimony of this interpretation of Ps 82, but the interpretation in 11QMelch is relatively close to it, and we should take into account that the textual materials that have been preserved represent only a part of all traditions and ideas that must have been current. I would like to emphasize that my reconstruction of the explanation of Ps 82,6 that is supposed in Jn 10,35 is a plausible reconstruction, based on textual materials that have been preserved, and making Jn 10,35 comprehensible.

The fourth evangelist himself and his audience probably had a somewhat moderated idea of the reality of the heavenly journeys ascribed to the individual recipients of special revelation. John clearly denies that anyone has ascended to heaven except the Son of Man who came down from heaven (3,13); he also denies that anyone has ever seen God (1,18; 5,37; 6,46) except one who has seen Jesus (12,45; 14,9). On the other hand, the Johannine Jesus says to his disciples: "You will see heaven opened, and the angels of God ascending and descending on the Son of Man" (1,51), he declares that Abraham saw his day (8,26), and the evangelist remarks, in a clear allusion to Isa 6,1, that Isaiah saw the glory of Christ (12,41). His view of the unique position of Jesus made it impossible for hím to admit that anyone except Jesus had or has immediate access to God, but he does not exclude some visionary participation in the heavenly world. In this way it is possible that in his call vision, Isaiah saw the glory of the pre-existent Christ.

I conclude that according to the explanation of Ps 82,6 in Jn 10,35, God has called gods those human individuals who received special divine revelation in their visionary presence among the heavenly ones. John's Jesus now uses this scriptural statement, which cannot be nullified[40] according to v. 35b, as the first half of an argument *a minore ad maius*, or, in Jewish terms, a קל וחמר argument. The second half follows in v. 36: if those human beings were called gods, there is no reason to accuse Jesus of blasphemy because he calls himself the Son of God. In this connexion, Jesus qualifies himself as "him whom the Father consecrated and sent into the world". In John's gospel, Jesus' having been sent by the Father is tantamount to his coming from him, as is evident from the parallelism between the two expressions in 7,29; 8,42; 17,8

---

40. The clause οὐ δύναται λυθῆναι ἡ γραφή means that the scriptural statement cannot lose its validity, cannot be revoked, see H.G. LIDDELL – R. SCOTT – H.S. JONES, *A Greek-English Lexicon*, Oxford, Clarendon, 1940, s.v. λύω II.4.b; BERNARD, *St. John* (n. 30), p. 368; W. BAUER, *Das Johannesevangelium* (HNT, 6), Tübingen, Mohr, ³1933, p. 147; RIDDERBOS, *Johannes 1* (n. 18), p. 433 (with n. 27); CARSON, *John* (n. 30), p. 399. It does not mean here that Scripture has to be fulfilled in Christ (in the sense of Jn 12,38 etc.), as is supposed by, e.g., JUNGKUNTZ, *Approach* (n. 30); HANSON, *John's Citation of Psalm LXXXII* (n. 21), pp. 161-162 (who considers Ps 82,8 as the passage to be fulfilled); RIEDL, *Heilswerk Jesu* (n. 30), p. 262. Parallels to John's use of λύειν in 10,35 are to be found in Mt 5,17 (where καταλύειν is opposed to πληροῦν in the sense of "fulfilling by teaching"); Mk 7,13 (with ἀκυροῦν); Rom 3,31 (where καταργεῖν is used in opposition to ἱστάνειν).

(cf. 3,31-34; 6,57-58; 17,3-5). Jesus' consecration by the Father has then to mean that the Father had set him apart for his mission. In the Johannine context, Jesus' consecration and mission into the world imply his pre-existence with God.

Now the logic of the argument becomes clear. If God called "gods" the individual human recipients of special revelation with their visions, there is no reason to deny the title "the Son of God" to the envoy who comes from God. In the former case, the distance between subject and predicate is, so to say, greater than in the latter. Prophets and prophet-like figures are human beings, they did not pre-exist with God, only at a certain point in their lives did they ascend on high in a vision, in which they did not see God himself, but nevertheless they were called gods (in a general sense); Jesus, on the other hand, though he is fully human, did pre-exist with God, even before creation (see 1,1; 17,5.24), he descended from heaven and is the only one who has really seen God (1,18; 6,46), so he can claim, without any problem, to be the Son of God (in the specific sense). As so often in John, Jesus responds to Jewish objections to his claim to be of divine origin by explaining it, not by detracting from it (see, e.g., 5,16-47; 6,41-58)[41]. In 10,35-36, his divine origin is not demonstrated but presupposed[42], as is confirmed by the reaction of the audience in 10,39. What is demonstrated is that, against the background of Ps 82,6 and its explanation, the divine envoy may rightly call himself the Son of God.

It may well be that a certain difference of level between "God" and "Son of God" plays a role here. Ps 82,6 reads in its entirety: "I said: You are gods, and all of you sons of the Most High". In Jn 10,34, Jesus adduces only the first half of the verse; he omits the parallel second half. At the same time, he is accused by the Jews of making himself "God" (v. 33), while he claims to be "the Son of God" (v. 36). The latter title has been used by the Johannine Jesus of himself (see 5,25; possibly 3,18[43], and cf. Jesus' frequent self-designation as "the Son", in, e.g., 5,19-23); the former title is used twice of him in the Fourth Gospel, in words of the evangelist (1,1.18[44]) and of Thomas (20,28). It seems that for John, to call Jesus "God" is the ultimate confession, occurring only on the fringes of the gospel, whereas to call him "the Son of God" is much more usual. So we may suppose that John has Jesus quote the first

41. Similarly NEYREY, "*I Said: You Are Gods*" (n. 22), p. 654.
42. Cf. PHILLIPS, *Apologetic Study* (n. 30), pp. 414-419; CARSON, *John* (n. 30), p. 399.
43. Depending upon whether Jesus or the evangelist is to be considered here as the speaker.
44. If μονογενὴς θεός is the correct reading there.

half only of Ps 82,6, because the omission of the second half strengthens the argument: if prophets and the like are called not just "sons of God" but "gods", how much more is Jesus entitled to call himself not "God" but only "the Son of God"[45].

A final point of importance is that Jesus' words in Jn 10,35-36 clearly allude to Jer 1,4-10, the story of the call of Jeremiah[46]. This story begins with the words "The word of the Lord came to me" (v. 4; LXX: καὶ ἐγένετο λόγος κυρίου πρός με). God then says to the prophet, that he consecrated him (LXX: ἡγίακά σε, v. 5)[47], and that he will send him (ἐξαποστείλω σε, v. 7). Jeremiah is the only OT figure about whom it is said in one and the same context that the word of the Lord came to him, that God consecrated him and that he will send him. The Johannine Jesus takes up terms used of Jeremiah: he, "whom the Father consecrated and sent into the world" and who is "the Son of God", is greater than Jeremiah and others, "to whom the word of God came" and who were called "gods". The allusion to Jeremiah is explicable: Jeremiah is a prophet about whom it is strongly suggested in the OT itself that he was in the divine council (Jer 23,18.22), and the story of his call is easily interpreted as taking place there. He belongs pre-eminently to those "to whom the word of God came"; no wonder then that the terms in which Jesus here speaks about himself, are derived from Jeremiah's call story.

The LXX text of Ps 81(82),6 indeed offered John what he needed. The interpretation of the psalm verse which he puts into the mouth of his

45. See RIDDERBOS, *Johannes 1* (n. 18), p. 432, n. 23. Some scholars (e.g., C.H. DODD, *The Interpretation of the Fourth Gospel*, Cambridge, Cambridge University, 1953, p. 271 with n. 3; HANSON, *John's Citation of Psalm LXXXII* [n. 21], pp. 159-162; FREED, *OT Quotations in the Gospel of John* [n. 8], pp. 63, 65; SCHNACKENBURG, *Johannesevangelium 2* [n. 18], pp. 389-390; LINDARS, *John* [n. 30], pp. 374-375; NEYREY, *"I Said: You Are Gods"* [n. 22], pp. 653-654) consider John's omission of Ps 82,6b ("and all of you sons of the Most High") as inappropriate, or think that the quotation of v. 6a was supposed to evoke v. 6b as well. They overlook the function of the difference between "gods" and "sons of God" in the argument. Jesus says that if God called prophets and the like "gods", he is much more entitled to call himself "the Son of God". HOMCY, *"You Are Gods"?* (n. 30), pp. 490-491, thinks that vv. 6b-7 of the psalm are also behind Jesus' words, so that those meant in Jn 10,35a are not gods but men, while v. 6a has been manifested in Jesus; one wonders in this case why the evangelist has Jesus adduce precisely v. 6a. PANCARO, *Law* (n. 14), pp. 175-177 (followed by SCHUCHARD, *Scripture within Scripture* [n. 13], p. 67, n. 34, cont. p. 68; similarly OBERMANN, *Christologische Erfüllung* [n. 22], p. 182), explains the omission of the second half of the psalm verse by John's wish to avoid calling anyone except Jesus "Son of God", and to avoid the suggestion that "all" are children of God; to my mind, he plays down the difference, for the evangelist, between "God" and "the Son of God".

46. See esp. BOISMARD, *Jésus, le Prophète par excellence* (n. 30), pp. 162-163.

47. See also Sir 49,7; according to Sir 45,4, God consecrated Moses.

protagonist can be connected in a plausible way with what we know about contemporaneous Jewish interpretation, and it inserts itself smoothly into Johannine christology.

III. THE QUOTATION FROM ISA 53,1 IN JN 12,38

When concluding his account of Jesus' public ministry, John establishes in retrospect that although Jesus had done so many signs, "they did not believe in him". He considers this lack of belief as the fulfilment of a prophecy of Isaiah (Isa 53,1): "Lord, who has believed our report? And to whom has the arm of the Lord been revealed?" (12,37-38). He then adduces another prophecy of Isaiah (6,10) to explain their unbelief: it is due to God's activity (12,39-40). Although several scholars consider 12,37-38 as part of a signs source used by the evangelist[48], the verses are in their present form clearly Johannine[49], and should be considered as an integral part of the Fourth Gospel.

Whereas the wording of the quotation in Jn 12,40 strongly deviates from the LXX, and is in fact, except for the last three words, an independent translation from the Hebrew[50], the quotation in 12,38 agrees completely with the LXX. This state of affairs leads to the assumption that the textual form of Isa 53,1 in the LXX was precisely what the evangelist needed.

To verify this assumption, we have to ask some questions. As we have seen, the vocative κύριε at the beginning of Isa 53,1 LXX has no equivalent in the Hebrew text. So our first question should be: what significance did the evangelist attach to this vocative?

The other questions originate from reading the quotation in v. 38 as part of its immediate Johannine context. In the preceding v. 37, we are told that in spite of the performance of so many signs by Jesus, they did not believe in him. The ensuing quotation from Isa 6,10 in v. 40, serving to explain their unbelief (v. 39), has been modified by the evangelist: the lines on "ears" and "hearing" have been omitted, and the sequence of

48. See the survey in G. VAN BELLE, *The Signs Source in the Fourth Gospel. Historical Survey and Critical Evaluation of the Semeia Hypothesis* (BETL, 116), Leuven, Leuven University – Peeters, 1994 (the relevant references are easily found via the "Selected Index of Biblical References", under 12,37-38).

49. See RUCKSTUHL – DSCHULNIGG, *Stilkritik* (n. 15), p. 193; R. KÜHSCHELM, *Verstockung, Gericht und Heil. Exegetische und bibeltheologische Untersuchung zum sogenannten "Dualismus" und "Determinismus" in Joh 12,35-50* (BBB, 76), Frankfurt/M, Hain, 1990, pp. 126-127.

50. See MENKEN (n. 1), pp. 99-122.

lines has been changed so that a line dealing with the "eyes" is twice followed by a line on the "heart". The modifications in the quotation of v. 40 are obviously connected with the content of v. 37: the reason they did not believe, in spite of so many signs, is that God has denied them the right way of seeing Jesus' signs and thus the faith (seated in the human heart) that ought to be its consequence. Both v. 37 and v. 40 are determined by the Johannine connection between seeing Jesus' signs and belief in him[51]. Now the first member of the quotation in v. 38 ("Lord, who has believed our report?") is often understood as referring to belief in Jesus' words, and the second member ("And to whom has the arm of the Lord been revealed?") to the revelation that takes place in his signs. Whereas a reference to Jesus' signs in the second line is quite plausible[52], a reference to belief in his words in the first line does not fit well with the immediate context of the quotation, which deals with seeing and faith. In my study of John's OT quotations, I have therefore proposed to read the first line of the quotation in v. 38 as about faith, and the second one as about seeing: for John, the decisive word in the first line was not ἀκοῇ but ἐπίστευσεν, so that the two lines together concern the un-belief resulting from seeing Jesus' signs in the wrong way[53]. Read in such a way, the quotation from Isa 53,1 suits its context, provided that we find acceptable answers to two questions. What precisely does ἡ ἀκοὴ ἡμῶν mean: is it an indication of Jesus' words, or of something else? And why did the evangelist leave the sequence of lines unchanged here, seemingly suggesting that faith precedes seeing, whereas he changed the sequence in the quotation of v. 40, to make it suit his purposes?

Our first question was: what significance did John attach to κύριε? By prefixing this vocative to Isa 53,1, the LXX translator introduced a change in relation to the Hebrew text: he made a rhetorical question into a question addressed to God. The LXX translation can be read as a com-plaint to God about the lack of belief in the message of the speaker. The

51. For details, see MENKEN (n. 1), pp. 105-108.
52. So also W. BITTNER, *Jesu Zeichen im Johannesevangelium. Die Messias-Erkennt-nis im Johannesevangelium vor ihrem jüdischen Hintergrund* (WUNT, 2/26), Tübingen, Mohr, 1987, p. 193, n. 4. Cf. the use of "the arm of the Lord" in various OT texts to indi-cate God's power, e.g., Exod 6,6; Ps 44,4; Isa 52,10; the same use is found in the NT, see Lk 1,51; Acts 13,17.
53. See MENKEN (n. 1), p. 108, with the references in nn. 34-36; so also SCHUCHARD, *Scripture within Scripture* (n. 13), p. 89, and OBERMANN, *Christologische Erfüllung* (n. 22), p. 224 (both referring to my earlier version of this argument in *BZ* NF 32 [1988] 198). BULTMANN's identification of signs and words (*Johannes* [n. 15], p. 346, followed by W. ROTHFUCHS, *Die Erfüllungszitate des Matthäus-Evangeliums. Eine biblisch-theolo-gische Untersuchung* [BWANT, 88], Stuttgart, Kohlhammer, 1969, p. 155; KÜHSCHELM, *Verstockung* [n. 49], p. 172) is a theological theory that does not do justice to John's text.

change is somewhat awkward: the speaker now speaks to "the Lord" about "the arm of the Lord"; this awkwardness betrays the secondary character of the insertion. By considering Isa 53,1 LXX as fulfilled in the unbelief in spite of Jesus' signs, John identifies Jesus with the referent of ἡμῶν: Isaiah's word that ἡ ἀκοὴ ἡμῶν was not believed, is fulfilled in the fact that they did not believe in Jesus. Any other referent of ἡμῶν would detach the quotation from its context and make it free floating[54]. The Lord, to whom Jesus is supposed to speak, is then God, his Father[55]. The quotation in v. 38 becomes an address to the Father by the Son who establishes that his signs met with unbelief; it aligns with other Johannine passages in which Jesus directly addresses his Father (11,41-42; 12,27-28; 17,1-26) and which testify, in John's view, to the unity of the Father and the Son (see, e.g., 8,16.29; 10,30; 16,32). Although John could have used the quotation if it had not contained κύριε, the addition of this vocative suited his christological view well.

I continue with the second question: in the quotation as John uses it, what is the meaning of ἡ ἀκοὴ ἡμῶν, usually translated by "our report" or something of the kind? In the Hebrew text of Isa 53,1, שמעתנו means something like "what we heard and tell to others"[56]; the LXX translation ἡ ἀκοὴ ἡμῶν may well have the same meaning[57]. In Jn 12,38, however, this meaning is hardly compatible with the context of the quotation: it would imply that the quotation is about the words Jesus has heard from the Father and has conveyed to his audience (see Jn 3,32; 8,26.40; 15,15), whereas, as we already observed, the context is about seeing Jesus' signs and believing in him. One could suppose the plural ἡμῶν to refer to Christian missionaries preaching about Jesus' ministry, including his signs[58], but the difficulty is then that Jesus is no longer the primary referent

54. Precisely that happens in the explanation of OBERMANN, *Christologische Erfüllung* (n. 22), pp. 226-230, who considers the Johannine witnesses on behalf of Jesus (John the Baptist, Moses, etc.) as the referent of ἡμῶν, after having made (on pp. 224-225) God and the exalted Christ together into the person addressed with κύριε. That a plural in a quotation is interpreted as referring to one person, does not only occur here, but also in, e.g., Jn 1,23 (= Isa 40,3), see MENKEN (n. 1), pp. 28-29.

55. When using a part of Ps 118,26 in Jn 12,13, the evangelist also recognizes God in the κύριος.

56. See L. KOEHLER – W. BAUMGARTNER, *Hebräisches und aramäisches Lexikon zum Alten Testament*, 3rd ed. by J.J. STAMM a.o., vol. 4, Leiden, Brill, 1990, s.v. שמועה: "das von uns Gehörte", "Kunde".

57. See LIDDELL – SCOTT – JONES, *Lexicon* (n. 40), s.v. ἀκοή I.2: "thing heard, tidings"; cf. SCHLATTER, *Johannes* (n. 30), p. 274.

58. Cf. Paul's use of Isa 53,1a LXX in Rom 10,16, and see BAUER, *Johannesevangelium* (n. 40), p. 165; E.C. HOSKYNS, *The Fourth Gospel*, ed. F.N. DAVEY, London, Faber & Faber, ²1947 (orig. 1940), p. 428; M.-É. BOISMARD – A. LAMOUILLE, with G. ROCHAIS, *L'évangile de Jean* (Synopse des quatre évangiles en français, 3), Paris, Cerf,

of ἡμῶν: it becomes impossible to include him in this pronoun, for he does not proclaim his own signs in John. It is, however, quite possible to interpret ἡ ἀκοὴ ἡμῶν in another way. The genitive ἡμῶν, translated above as a subjective genitive, can equally well be read as an objective genitive, resulting in the translation "the report about us", or something similar. The substantive ἀκοή is in fact often used in this way; in Mt 14,1, for instance, ἡ ἀκοὴ Ἰησοῦ means "the fame of Jesus", "the rumour about Jesus", and there are many more examples of this usage[59].

If we assume this usage in the first member of the quotation in Jn 12,38, we can translate: "Lord, who has believed the report about us?" The clause inserts itself now very well into its context: it concerns the lack of belief in spite of the report about Jesus, i.e., about his signs[60]. In John's gospel, the report about a sign of Jesus has the same effect of arousing belief or unbelief as the sign itself. That is evident in the aftermath of the healing of the paralytic (5,10ff) and of the man born blind (9,13ff); in both cases, the Jews or the Pharisees respond to a sign they have heard of, but not seen themselves. It is very clear in the case of the raising of Lazarus. After the miracle, some of the Jews go to the Pharisees and tell them what Jesus has done (11,46); this report occasions a meeting of the Sanhedrin, starting with the question of how to react to Jesus' signs, and ending with the decision to kill him (11,47-53). Later, we hear of a positive reaction to the report about the same miracle: "Therefore the crowd came out to meet him, because they had heard that he had done this sign" (12,18). In other passages, it is impossible to determine whether John presupposes the reaction to be based on witnessing Jesus' miracles or on hearing of them (7,31; 10,25-26.38; 12,11). The (first) conclusion of John's gospel shows that the gospel narrative, as a report about Jesus' signs, is supposed to have the same effect as the signs themselves: "These [signs] have been written down that you may believe that Jesus is the Christ, the Son of God" (20,31; cf. 15,27; 17,20).

1977, p. 329; KÜHSCHELM, *Verstockung* (n. 49), pp. 58, 174-175, 177-178; R. BRANDSCHEIDT, *Prophetischer Verstockungsauftrag und christlicher Glaube. Die alttestamentlichen Zitate in Joh 12,37-43*, in *TTZ* 102 (1993) 64-76, p. 67. It will appear below that the Christian proclamation of Jesus is secondarily present in the quotation, but not in the way supposed by the authors just mentioned.

59. Other examples from the NT: Mt 4,24; 24,6; Mk 1,28; 13,7; from the LXX: Tob 10,12; Hos 7,12; Nahum 1,12; Isa 52,7; Jer 6,24; 27(50),43; 44(37),5; from Josephus: *Ant.* 6,103; from pagan Greek literature: Homer, *Odyssey* 2,308; 4,701; Thucydides, 1,20. Hebr. שְׁמֻעָ(וֹ)ה can also be used with an objective genitive, see 2 Sam 4,4.

60. R.T. FORTNA, *The Fourth Gospel and Its Predecessor. From Narrative Source to Present Gospel*, Philadelphia, Fortress, 1988, p. 138, identifies ἡ ἀκοὴ ἡμῶν with "the pre-Johannine account of Jesus' signs".

So the evangelist most probably read Isa 53,1a as concerning unbelief in relation to the report about Jesus' signs. But we still have a problem: why did John not change the sequence of lines in the quotation just as he did in quoting from Isa 6,10, so that the revelation of the arm of the Lord precedes faith? It is of course true that by leaving the quotation of v. 38 as he found it, he created a chiasm in 12,37-38: in v. 37, a reference to Jesus' performing of signs is followed by a reference to unbelief, whereas in v. 38 we find the reverse order. It is, however, equally true that in v. 40 he modified the chiasm originally present in Isa 6,10[61], so that such a strictly formal answer is not sufficient.

It seems to me that a valid answer to the question lies in the observation that the connection between seeing and believing in v. 40 differs from the one in vv. 37-38. In v. 40, God prevents people from seeing in the right way and from the faith that follows from seeing rightly; the relationship between not seeing and not believing is a consecutive one. In vv. 37-38, on the other hand, the relation between seeing and not believing is a concessive one: although they saw or heard about Jesus' signs, they did not believe in him. Or, if we use the words of the quotation in v. 38, and transform the questions into statements: they did not believe the report about Jesus, although the arm of the Lord was revealed to them. Whereas in the consecutive connection the order of the elements is fixed, it can vary in the concessive connection, and that is exactly what happens in vv. 37 and 38. That the two questions of the quotation in v. 38 have indeed a concessive relation, becomes even more clear when we realize that the answer to the first one should be "none of them", and to the second one "all of them": nobody believed, although the revelation was given to all[62].

I conclude that the quotation from Isa 53,1 LXX in Jn 12,38 suits its Johannine context well, on the condition that we suppose ἡ ἀκοὴ ἡμῶν to mean "the report about us". The addition of κύριε in the LXX lent itself to be interpreted within the framework of the Johannine view of the intimate relationship of the Father and the Son.

IV. THE QUOTATION FROM PS 22,19 IN JN 19,24

Like the synoptic passion narratives, that of the Fourth Gospel contains a short description of the division of Jesus' clothes by the soldiers

61. See MENKEN (n. 1), pp. 105-106.
62. Whether or not this agrees with the original meaning of Isa 53,1, is quite another matter; we are dealing here with John's reading of the verse.

(Jn 19,23-24; Mt 27,35; Mk 15,24; Lk 23,34). Ps 22,19, probably in the version of the LXX (= Ps 21,19), has clearly inspired the wording of the scene in the Synoptic Gospels. The psalm verse is not explicitly quoted there, but the allusion is unmistakable, especially in Matthew and Mark[63]. The synoptics take the synonymous parallelism of the verse into account. Dividing Jesus' garments and casting lots for his clothing are not two different activities, but refer to one act: the soldiers divide Jesus' clothes by casting lots for them.

In John, the soldiers do two things: they divide Jesus' clothes into four parts, one for each soldier, and they draw lots for his tunic, a seamless one, woven in one piece from top to bottom. In these two different acts, the two members of Ps 21,19 LXX have been fulfilled: the words "They divided my garments among them" in the division of Jesus' clothes into four parts, and the words "And for my clothing they cast lots" in drawing lots for his tunic. John's description of what the soldiers do has not been influenced by the wording of the psalm verse; instead, the words from the psalm are quoted in full, introduced by a fulfilment formula.

Does Ps 21,19 LXX suit the Johannine context? It certainly does insofar as all elements of the quotation have their counterpart in the preceding narrative. A juxtaposition of quotation and narrative makes this clear:

quotation	*narrative*
διεμερίσαντο	ἐποίησαν τέσσαρα μέρη
τὰ ἱμάτιά μου	τὰ ἱμάτια αὐτοῦ
ἑαυτοῖς	ἑκάστῳ στρατιώτῃ μέρος
καὶ ἐπὶ τὸν ἱματισμόν μου	καὶ τὸν χιτῶνα... περὶ αὐτοῦ
ἔβαλον κλῆρον	λάχωμεν

The question arises, however, why John does not acknowledge the synonymous parallelism of Ps 22,19, but makes the two members of the verse refer to two different realities. This question becomes even more pressing as soon as we observe that the other early Christian authors (up to and including Justin), about whom we know that they interpreted Ps 22,19 as referring to the division of Jesus' clothes, apparently recognized and respected the parallelism[64]. We have already seen that the syn-

63. Mt 27,35: διεμερίσαντο τὰ ἱμάτια αὐτοῦ βάλλοντες κλῆρον; Mk 15,24: διαμερίζονται τὰ ἱμάτια αὐτοῦ βάλλοντες κλῆρον ἐπ᾽ αὐτά; Lk 23,34: διαμεριζόμενοι δὲ τὰ ἱμάτια αὐτοῦ ἔβαλον κλήρους. In Mt 27,35, the *v.l.* with the explicit quotation is most probably due to the influence of Jn 19,24.

64. The instances in which an author adduces or alludes to one member only of the psalm verse (Barn 6,6; ActPil 10,1; Justin, *Apol.* 1,38,4) are not immediately relevant here. The same holds good for the lengthy quotation from the psalm in Justin, *Dial.* 98.

optics take the parallelism into account; they consider Jesus' clothes as the object of both dividing and casting lots, and they connect the two activities syntactically as finite verb and adverbial participle. EvPet 12 reads: καὶ τεθεικότες τὰ ἐνδύματα ἔμπροσθεν αὐτοῦ διεμερίσαντο καὶ λάχμον ἔβαλον ἐπ' αὐτοῖς, "and having put his clothes before him, they divided them and cast lots for them". The circumstance that Jesus' clothes are the object of both dividing and casting lots makes it probable that the two coordinated clauses indicate the same reality: dividing by casting lots[65]. In *Apol.* 1,35,8, Justin explains Ps 21,19b LXX (quoted by him in 1,35,5, with a change in the word order): ἔβα-λον κλῆρον ἐπὶ τὸν ἱματισμόν αὐτοῦ καὶ ἐμερίσαντο ἑαυτοῖς οἱ σταυρώσαντες αὐτόν, "those who crucified him cast lots for his cloth-ing and divided [it] among them". The clothing is again the object of both casting lots and dividing, and only the second member of the psalm verse is explained by the two parallel actions of the soldiers. In *Dial.* 97,3, Justin explains the entire verse as follows: οἱ σταυρώσαντες αὐ-τὸν ἐμέρισαν τὰ ἱμάτια αὐτοῦ ἑαυτοῖς, λάχμον βάλλοντες ἕκαστος..., "those who crucified him divided his garments among them, each one drawing lots ...". The construction of the clause is comparable with that of Mt 27,35 and Mk 15,24, and it again betrays that Justin is aware of the meaning of the synonymous parallelism. In *Dial.* 104,1, he adduces the entire verse once more, and in 104,2 he remarks that he has already shown (in 97,3) that those who crucified Jesus ἐμέρισαν ἑαυτοῖς... τὰ ἱμάτια αὐτοῦ, "divided his garments among them"; again, Justin explains the two members of the psalm verse as referring to one action. In all these instances, the synonymous parallelism of Ps 22,19 is obviously perceived[66].

On the other hand, the exegetical practice of making, if necessary, two parallel lines refer to two distinct realities was considered as legitimate in early Judaism and early Christianity. A few examples may elucidate this. For Matthew, the two parallel indications of the mount of the com-ing king from Zech 9,9 refer to two donkeys (21,2-7), and the same

65. Καί is used here epexegetically, see *BDR*, §442.6a; somewhat differently M. DIBELIUS, *Die alttestamentlichen Motive in der Leidensgeschichte des Petrus- und des Johannes-Evangeliums*, in ID., *Botschaft und Geschichte. Gesammelte Aufsätze 1: Zur Evangelienforschung*, ed. G. BORNKAMM, Tübingen, Mohr, 1953, pp. 221-247, esp. 230 (orig. in W. FRANKENBERG – F. KÜCHLER [eds.], *Abhandlungen zur semitischen Religions-kunde und Sprachwissenschaft*. FS W.W. Graf von Baudissin [BZAW, 33], Giessen, Töpelmann, 1918, pp. 125-150).

66. Cf. SCHUCHARD, *Scripture within Scripture* (n. 13), p. 126. These early Christian par-allels to Jn 19,23-24 show that there is no use in denying that John ignores the parallelism, as is done by D.A. CARSON, *John and the Johannine Epistles*, in D.A. CARSON – H.G.M. WILLIAMSON (eds.), *It is Written: Scripture Citing Scripture*. FS B. Lindars, Cambridge, Cambridge University, 1988, pp. 245-264, esp. 250; ID., *John* (n. 30), pp. 613-614.

evangelist sees in the offer of both wine mixed with gall and sour wine a realization of the two parallel lines of Ps 69,22 (27,34.48). Justin interprets the two parallel lines which he reads in Ps 81,7 LXX (ἰδοὺ δὴ ὡς ἄνθρωποι ἀποθνῄσκετε, καὶ ὡς εἷς τῶν ἀρχόντων πίπτετε) as connected with the disobedience of Adam and Eve, and the fall of the serpent respectively (*Dial.* 124,3). An early example from rabbinic literature can be found in the discussion between Bar He He and Hillel on Mal 3,18 in b. Ḥag. 9b: in the OT text, there is a clear parallelism between "the righteous and the wicked" and "the one who serves God and the one who does not serve him", but Hillel declares that both the one who serves God and the one who does not can be righteous[67].

Jn 19,23-24 is not the only instance of applying to Ps 22,19 the exegetical device of ignoring the synonymous parallelism. In Tg. Ps 22,19, the two Hebrew words for clothing, בגד and לבוש, are rendered by לבושא, "garment", and פגתא, "cloak", respectively; this rendering might suggest that the two members are considered as indicating two distinct activities[68]. In Midr. Ps 22, v. 19a of the psalm is interpreted as being about either taking "Esther's royal cloak and coat" or taking "Esther's ring and Esther's armour", while v. 19b means, according to R. Huna, "that they were casting lots for the royal cloak, which it is not seemly for commoners to use"[69]. Any direct link between John and these Jewish texts is of course very improbable, but they help to show that John's interpretation of the parallelism was an acceptable one.

I return to the question as to why John makes the two parallel members of Ps 22,19 refer to two different realities. In a general sense, his interpretation of the verse apparently remains within the parameters of OT exegesis at the beginning of the era, but it is uncommon in comparison with other early Christian interpretations of this specific verse. We should also take into account that it is somewhat uncommon within John's gospel itself. In quoting from the OT, John retains the members of a synonymous parallelism only in a few cases. Mostly, he reduces the parallel members to only one member (at the same time slightly modifying his OT text, if necessary). There are some cases in which we have reasons to presume that the evangelist's christology is the motive for the omission

---

67. The interpretation of Qoh 1,15 earlier in b. Ḥag. constitutes another example of this exegetical device; see D.I. BREWER, *Techniques and Assumptions in Jewish Exegesis before 70 CE* (TSAJ, 30), Tübingen, Mohr, 1992, pp. 166-167.

68. See FREED, *OT Quotations in the Gospel of John* (n. 8), p. 103, n. 2; R.E. BROWN, *The Death of the Messiah. From Gethsemane to the Grave. A Commentary on the Passion Narratives in the Four Gospels* (AB Reference Library), London, Chapman, 1994, p. 954, n. 41.

69. Transl. W.G. Braude; see HANSON, *Prophetic Gospel* (n. 21), p. 209.

(1,23 = Isa 40,3[70]; 10,34 = Ps 82,6[71]; 13,18 = Ps 41,10[72]), but usually John simply omits those parts of the parallel lines that are not immediately relevant to the new, Johannine, context of the quotation (2,17 = Ps 69, 10; 6,31 = Ps 78,24; 6,45 = Isa 54,13; 7,38 = Ps 78,16.20ab; 12,15 = Zech 9,9; 12,34 = Ps 89,37; 15,25 = Ps 35,19 or 69,5; 19,36 = Ps 34,21; 19,37 = Zech 12,10). Apart from the quotation under discussion, there are only two OT quotations in John in which the evangelist has retained members of a synonymous parallelism: 12,38 = Isa 53,1, and 12,40 = Isa 6,10; in the latter quotation, he twice kept only two out of three parallel lines. We observed above that in both instances the members of the parallelism that are now found in John's text are interpreted separately in the context: of every pair of parallel lines, one line refers to seeing Jesus' signs, and the other to belief in him. There are no reasons to suppose that the lines of the parallelism, read as referring to distinct realities, induced the evangelist to adapt the context to the quotation. John's idea of "seeing and believing" is found not only in 12,37-40, but at several other places of his gospel as well (see, e.g., 2,11; 4,48; 20,8.24-31); neither the idea itself nor its various wordings have been derived from the OT texts.

From this survey, we may conclude that John normally reduces the lines of a synonymous parallelism to one line only, and that if he retains more than one line, he treats the lines as referring to different realities, because he recognizes in them an idea he already had[73]. The implication of this conclusion for our study of the quotation from Ps 22,19 in Jn 19,24 is clear: we may surmise that the evangelist retained the two parallel lines of the psalm verse because, when interpreted as indicating two distinct realities, they suited his narrative.

This surmise can be confirmed by the following observation. We established earlier that all elements of the quotation have their counterpart in the preceding narrative. With one exception (τὰ ἱμάτιά μου/αὐτοῦ), however, there is no verbal correspondence between quotation and narrative. If the story of Jn 19,23-24c had been derived from the quotation in 19,24ef (at either the Johannine or the pre-Johannine level)[74], one would expect a higher degree of verbal agreement.

70. See MENKEN (n. 1), pp. 26-35.
71. See above, under II.
72. See MENKEN (n. 1), p. 137.
73. Cf. R.J. HUMANN, *The Function and Form of the Explicit Old Testament Quotations in the Gospel of John*, in *Lutheran Theological Review* 1 (1988-89) 31-54, pp. 42-43, 45.
74. So DIBELIUS, *Alttestamentliche Motive* (n. 65), pp. 231-232 (pre-Johannine level); BAUER, *Johannesevangelium* (n. 40), p. 223 (Johannine level); BULTMANN, *Johannes* (n. 15), p. 519 (pre-Johannine); BARRETT, *St John* (n. 30), pp. 550-551 (Johannine); B. LINDARS,

That the story was not derived from the quotation, does not necessarily mean that it comes from tradition; it only means that the evangelist did not create it from the quotation. Although the story contains some Johannine features (narrative οὖν, ἦν δέ followed by the subject of the clause, the parenthesis at the end of v. 23[75]), there are also traits of the story that do not seem to come from the evangelist: τὰ ἱμάτια αὐτοῦ (cf. the parallels), ἕκαστος used as an adjective (contrast Jn 6,7; 16,32, and most other NT occurrences), the expression ἐκ τῶν ἄνωθεν, which in this precise form does not occur elsewhere in John[76]. The resumption of v. 18 at the beginning of v. 23 may point to a return, by the evangelist, to traditional materials. The connection between story and quotation betrays the hand of the evangelist: the introductory formula ἵνα ἡ γραφή πληρωθῇ, and the elliptical use of ἵνα, are characteristic of John[77]. A comparison of John and the synoptics shows in addition that the nucleus of the story (soldiers dividing Jesus' clothing) and the relationship with Ps 22,19 have to be traditional. So we may provisionally conclude that in Jn 19,23-24c the evangelist has edited traditional material, and that the traditional link with Ps 22,19 inspired his explicit fulfilment quotation[78].

New Testament Apologetic. The Doctrinal Significance of the Old Testament Quotations, London, SCM, 1961, pp. 91-92, 267-268 (Johannine); ID., *John* (n. 30), p. 577 (Johannine, possibly pre-Johannine); C.H. DODD, *Historical Tradition in the Fourth Gospel*, Cambridge, Cambridge University, 1963, pp. 40-41 (uncertain); FREED, *OT Quotations in the Gospel of John* (n. 8), p. 103 (Johannine); A. DAUER, *Die Passionsgeschichte im Johannesevangelium. Eine traditionsgeschichtliche und theologische Untersuchung zu Joh 18,1-19,30* (SANT, 30), Munich, Kösel, 1972, p. 191 (pre-Johannine); R. SCHNACKENBURG, *Das Johannesevangelium 3* (HTKNT, 4/3), Freiburg, Herder, ²1976, pp. 316-317 (pre-Johannine); E. HAENCHEN, *Das Johannesevangelium*, ed. U. BUSSE, Tübingen, Mohr, 1980, pp. 551-552, 558 (Johannine?); J. BECKER, *Das Evangelium des Johannes 2* (ÖTK, 4/2), Gütersloh, Mohn – Würzburg, Echter, 1981, pp. 588-589 (pre-Johannine). Scholars who consider the derivation as pre-Johannine, usually adduce the argument that the evangelist himself does not misinterpret synonymous parallelisms elsewhere; however, John's treatment of OT quotations in 12,38.40 (see above) shows that things are different. Because the synoptics relate the division of Jesus' clothes in wordings that are strongly reminiscent of Ps 22,19 (see above), the argument against the derivation of Jn 19,23-24c from the quotation is also valid for a derivation from the synoptics (which was recently advocated by M. SABBE, *The Johannine Account of the Death of Jesus and Its Synoptic Parallels [Jn 19,16b-42]*, in *ETL* 70 [1994] 34-64, pp. 58-60).

75. G. VAN BELLE, *Les parenthèses dans l'évangile de Jean. Aperçu historique et classification. Texte grec de Jean* (SNTA, 11), Leuven, Leuven University – Peeters, 1985, p. 320, considers καὶ ἐποίησαν... μέρος in v. 23 as a parenthesis as well; that is, however, not the only possible explanation of the clause.

76. John has ἄνωθεν in 3,3.7.31; 19,11, always in the sense of "from heaven", and ἐκ τῶν followed by an adverb of place in 8,23.

77. For the Johannine features in 19,23-24, see RUCKSTUHL – DSCHULNIGG, *Stilkritik* (n. 15), p. 200; VAN BELLE, *Parenthèses* (n. 75), pp. 98-99; SABBE, *Death of Jesus* (n. 74), p. 58, n. 78.

78. Cf. DAUER, *Passionsgeschichte* (n. 74), pp. 182-185 (although not all his stylistic arguments are equally convincing).

In this connection a relevant question is whether the evangelist attached a special, symbolic meaning to the double action of the soldiers. If he did, that would enhance the probability that he himself made a single action of the soldiers into a double one. Interpreters have perceived two different symbolic meanings in the fact that Jesus' tunic was seamless, woven in one piece from top to bottom, and that it was not torn by the soldiers[79]. Some have considered the seamless tunic which was not torn as depicting Jesus as high priest (on the basis of such passages as Exod 39,27 = 36,34 LXX; Josephus, *Ant.* 3,161), while for others it was a symbol of unity (on the basis of Jn 10,16; 11,50-52; 17,21-22; 21,11; cf. the use of σχίσμα in 7,43; 9,16; 10,19)[80]; the presence of both kinds of symbolism at the same time has also been defended[81]. The first type of symbolism does not find much support in the rest of the Fourth Gospel[82]. The second one concurs with an evident interest of John, but its presence in Jn 19,23-24 is not clear. Both symbolic readings suffer from the difficulty that "one is still forced to deal with the symbolic import of having this undivided tunic *taken away* from Jesus"[83]. So it seems best to forgo these symbolic interpretations, and to consider the passage together with the quotation as showing that also this humiliation of Jesus was in agreement with God's will as revealed in Scripture[84]. There is therefore no reason to assume that John himself was responsible for the story of the double action of the soldiers; he found it most probably in his tradition.

John adduced Ps 21(22),19 LXX in its entirety because he saw the division of Jesus' garments into four parts and the drawing of lots for his tunic as an exact fulfilment of the two members of the verse, read as two independent statements. Ignoring the synonymous parallelism was a common exegetical device; John used it to give a scriptural explanation to an existing story, not to create a story[85].

79. See the discussions in DAUER, *Passionsgeschichte* (n. 74), pp. 186-191; BROWN, *Death of the Messiah* (n. 68), pp. 956-958.

80. The latter interpretation goes back at least to Cyprian (*De catholicae ecclesiae unitate* 7).

81. See F.-M. BRAUN, *Jean le Théologien 2: Les grandes traditions d'Israël et l'accord des écritures selon le quatrième évangile* (EBib), Paris, Gabalda, 1964, pp. 98-101.

82. It was defended recently by J.P. HEIL, *Jesus as the Unique High Priest in the Gospel of John*, in *CBQ* 57 (1995) 729-745; on Jn 19,23-24, see pp. 741-744.

83. BROWN, *Death of the Messiah* (n. 68), p. 958 (italics his).

84. Similarly OBERMANN, *Christologische Erfüllung* (n. 22), pp. 294-297. He adds to Jesus' humiliation his "Gottesferne"; however, this motif seems to be absent in John, and is hardly compatible with the christology of this gospel (see 8,16.29; 16,32; 19,28-30).

85. For this conclusion, cf. M.-J. LAGRANGE, *Évangile selon saint Jean* (EBib), Paris, Gabalda, 1936⁵ (orig. 1925), pp. 491-492; BERNARD, *St. John* (n. 30), pp. 629-630; BRAUN, *Jean le Théologien 2* (n. 81), p. 101; ROTHFUCHS, *Erfüllungszitate* (n. 53), pp. 159-160;

V. Conclusion

I started with the assumption that in quoting from the OT in Jn 10,34; 12,38; 19,24, the evangelist left his normal OT text, the LXX, unchanged because it offered him exactly what he needed. The circumstance that in his other quotations he either edited his LXX text or replaced it by another version led to this assumption.

We have seen that in all three cases the LXX indeed offered him what he needed. In 10,34 he had Jesus adduce a few words from Ps 81,6 LXX to prove that, if Scripture called individual human recipients of special divine revelation "gods", Jesus did not commit blasphemy when he called himself "the Son of God". In Jn 12,38, the evangelist quoted from Isa 53,1 LXX to show its fulfilment in the unbelief of those who witnessed Jesus' signs. He quoted from Ps 21,19 LXX in 19,24 because he saw the verse fulfilled in what the soldiers at the cross did with Jesus' clothing.

In 10,34 and 19,24, another adequate Greek translation of the Hebrew text would probably have served John as well; in 12,38, the prefixed κύριε made the LXX more suitable than the Hebrew text, because it made it possible to understand the verse as an address of the Father by the Son. Anyhow, the LXX was John's Bible, so we had to ask how far that version suited him.

The above study of three quotations has also shown once more that John has carefully determined the size of his quotations, that is, that he quotes just what he needs in his context, no less and no more, mostly just one line, and more than that only if he can give every line its own interpretation. Given his first century exegetical methods and his convictions concerning Jesus' significance, the fourth evangelist is an accurate interpreter of Scripture[86].

Oude Arnhemseweg 315   Maarten J.J. Menken
NL-3705 BG Zeist

R.E. Brown, *The Gospel according to John (xiii-xxi)* (AB, 29A), Garden City, NY, Doubleday, 1970, p. 920; Pancaro, *Law* (n. 14), pp. 340-341; Moo, *OT in Gospel Passion Narratives* (n. 14), pp. 254-257; Carson, *John and the Johannine Epistles* (n. 66), pp. 249-250; Id., *John* (n. 30), pp. 611-615; Humann, *Function and Form* (n. 73), pp. 42-43; Schuchard, *Scripture within Scripture* (n. 13), p. 131, n. 32.

86. I thank Dr J.M. Court for improving the English style of this article.

DIE TEMPELMETAPHORIK

ALS EIN BEISPIEL VON IMPLIZITEM REKURS AUF DIE BIBLISCHE TRADITION IM JOHANNESEVANGELIUM

Im Johannesevangelium wird entweder aus der Schrift direkt zitiert oder auf sie indirekt angespielt. Letzteres war nicht erst R. Schnackenburg[1] aufgefallen, als er im Johannesevangelium alttestamentliche Zitate, »sprachliche Anklänge«, »Gedanken« und »Bildzüge« verwendet fand und m. E. zurecht daraus schlußfolgerte, daß »ohne den tragenden Grund des AT […] dieses Ev nicht denkbar« sei. Vielmehr hatte schon A.H. Franke[2] nach Vorarbeiten von B. Weiß[3] angemerkt: »Um des Verfassers Leben und Heimat im Schriftwort des A.T. darzuthun, dazu bieten sich uns viel bessere Instanzen als seine Zitate…. In zahlreichen Fällen reproduzirt er alttestamentliche Schriftworte mehr oder weniger getreu, ohne irgendwie darauf hinzudeuten, dass es sich um solche handle«. Seiner Meinung nach stammen viele der im Johannesevangelium zitierten Schriftstellen aus der urchristlichen Tradition[4], so daß die impliziten Schriftanspielungen

---

1. R. SCHNACKENBURG, *Das Johannesevangelium* (HTKNT IV.1), Freiburg, Herder, [3]1972, pp. 105f.

2. A.H. FRANKE, *Das alte Testament bei Johannes. Ein Beitrag zur Erklärung und Beurtheilung der johanneischen Schriften*, Göttingen, Vandenhoek & Ruprecht 1885, p. 260; Dies wird neuerdings ausdrücklich bestätigt von M. HENGEL, *Die Schriftauslegung des 4. Evangeliums auf dem Hintergrund der urchristlichen Exegese*, in JBT 4 (1989) 249-288, p. 282: »Der eigentliche Schwerpunkt der Verwendung des Alten Testaments liegt jedoch…bei den sehr viel zahlreicheren Anspielungen und der Übernahme alttestamentlicher Motive«.

3. B. WEISS, *Der johanneische Lehrbegriff in seinen Grundlagen untersucht*, Berlin, W. Hertz, 1862, pp. 101-191; vgl. ID., *Lehrbuch der Biblischen Theologie des Neuen Testaments*, Berlin, W. Hertz, [3]1880, pp. 659-665; vgl. E. RIEHM, Rez.: *Der johanneische Lehrbegriff in seinen Grundzügen untersucht von Dr. Bernhard Weiß*, Berlin, 1862, in TStKr 37 (1864) 531-562, p. 558 faßt seine Meinung über den joh. Deutehorizont nach dem Studium der Schrift von B. Weiß in die Worte: »seinem ganz im alten Testament wurzelnden Denken«.

4. Nach FRANKE (Anm. 2), pp. 258ff., verweisen z.B. 1,23 = Is 40,3 auf Mk 1,3 parr.; 7,42 par. Mt 2,5f.; 12,15 par. Mt 21,5; 12,38 par. Röm 10,16; 12,40 par. Mt 13,14f.; Apg 28,26f.; 19,37 par. Off 1,7; messianische Deutung des Ps 69 in 2,17; 15,25; 19,28 ist par. Mt 27,34.48; Röm 11,9f.; 15,3; Apg 1,20; ebenso vgl. Ps 22 u.a. in 19,24 mit Mt 27,43.46; Hebr 2,12; bzw. Ps 34 in 19,36 und 1 Petr 2,3; 3,10ff.; doch bedeutet dies noch nicht, daß er von ihnen direkt abhängig ist, sondern »dass die christliche Gemeinde von Anfang an bestimmte Schriftstellen und Zusammenhänge, welche der evangelischen Geschichte in besonderer Weise zum Zeugniss dienen konnten, besonders energisch in's Auge gefasst und immer wieder verwerthet hat«.

eher auf den Ort und die Art verweisen könnten, woher der Autor stammt und argumentiert. Expliziter und zugleich impliziter Umgang mit der Schrift aber ist nicht nur dem Johannesevangelium eigentümlich, sondern kennzeichnet sowohl die biblischen Spätschriften[5] als auch die sogenannten Apokryphen und Pseudepigraphen des AT, was zuletzt D. Dimant[6] erneut bewußt gemacht hat und das analog auch für manche Schriften aus der Bibliothek von Qumran[7] gilt. Als Musterbeispiele für den impliziten Schriftgebrauch im Johannesevangelium gelten seit längerem[8] u.a. die bewußte Anspielung auf die eherne Schlange Num 21,4-9 (vgl. 2 Kön 18,4[9]; Weish 16,5f.) als österliches Rettungszeichen in 3,14 sowie das Anhauchen[10] der Jünger in 20,22[11], womit die Neugeburt (1,12f.33; 3,3-6; 14,19) der Jünger

---

5. Vgl. neuerdings R.G. KRATZ, *Die Suche nach Identität in der nachexilischen Theologiegeschichte. Zur Hermeneutik des chronistischen Geschichtswerkes und ihrer Bedeutung für das Verständnis des AT*, in J. MEHLHAUSEN (ed.), *Pluralismus und Identität* (VWGT, 8), Gütersloh, 1995, pp. 279-303.

6. D. DIMANT, *Use and Interpretation of Mikra in the Apocrypha and Pseudepigrapha* (CRINT, II.1), Assen/Maastricht – Philadelphia, Van Gorcum – Fortress Press, 1988, pp. 379-419.

7. Vgl. u.a. G.J. BROOKE, *Exegesis at Qumran. 4QFlorilegium in its Jewish Context* (JSOT SS), Sheffield, JSOT Press, 1985; M. FISHBANE, *Use, Authority and Interpretation of Mikra at Qumran* (Compendia Rerum Judaicarum ad Novum Testamentum, II.1), Assen/Maastricht – Philadelphia, Van Gorcum – Fortress Press, 1988, pp. 339-377.

8. Vgl. u.a. F.A. LAMPE, *Commentarius analytico-exegeticus tam literalis quam realis Evangelii secundum Joannem*, vol. I, Basel, E. & J.R. Thurnisios, 1725, p. 603f.; F. SCHLEIERMACHER, *Das Leben Jesu. Vorlesungen an der Universität zu Berlin im Jahre 1832*, Hrsg. K.A. RÜTENIK, Berlin, G. Reimer, 1864, p. 265; F. LÜCKE, *Commentar über das Evangelium des Johannes*, vol. 1, Bonn, E. Weber, ²1833, pp. 470-473; E. W. HENGSTENBERG, *Das Evangelium des heiligen Johannes*, vol.1, Berlin, G. Schlawitz, ²1867, pp. 203-207; A. SCHLATTER, *Der Evangelist Johannes: Wie er spricht, denkt und glaubt. Ein Kommentar zum vierten Evangelium*, Stuttgart, Calwer Vereinsbuchhandlung, 1930, pp. 95-97; R. BULTMANN, *Das Evangelium des Johannes* (KEK), Göttingen, Vandenhoek & Ruprecht, ¹⁸1968, p. 109 Anm. 1, sieht charakteristischerweise die typologische Verwendung des Motivs durch die christliche Tradition dem Evangelisten vermittelt. SCHNACKENBURG (Anm. 1), p. 408, beharrt auf einer eigenständigen Meditation des Autors über die Stelle Num 21,8f.; R.E. BROWN, *The Gospel According to John* (AB, 29), Garden City, NY, 1966, p. 133; E. HAENCHEN, *Das Johannesevangelium – ein Kommentar*, Hrsg. U. BUSSE, Tübingen, J.C.B. Mohr (P. Siebeck), 1980, pp. 224.228, vergleicht V. 14 mit einem Schriftbeweis.

9. In 2 Kön 18,4 wird – von den neutestamentlichen Kommentatoren wenig beachtet – im Rahmen der Kultreform des Königs Hiskija das kupferne Schlangenbild des Mose als ein Kultgegenstand noch einmal erwähnt, den der König zerstören ließ, obwohl die Israeliten ihm »bis zu jener Zeit Rauchopfer darbrachten«. Auch dieses Totem gehört mit in das weite Umfeld der Tempelmetaphorik des Evangelisten.

10. Gen 2,7 LXX verwendet dasselbe Verb wie 20,22. Die Intertextualität zwischen 20,22 und Gen 2,7 war schon Augustinus, *De civitate Dei*, XIII,24, aufgefallen.

11. Vgl. u.a. FRANKE (Anm. 2), p. 263; L. GOPPELT, *Typos. Die typologische Deutung des Alten Testaments im Neuen*, Gütersloh, Bertelsmann, 1939, p. 221; SCHNACKENBURG (Anm. 1), vol. 3, 1975, pp. 385f.; U. BUSSE, *Aspekte biblischen Geistverständnisses*, in *BN* 66 (1993) 40-57, pp. 52-56.

als Kinder Gottes im »heiligen« Geist vom Auferstandenen vollzogen wird. Ein viel diskutiertes Beispiel aus der frühjüdischen Literatur für dessen analogen Schriftgebrauch ist 4Q174 Kol III (= 4QFlor I, 1-9), wo in freier Wiedergabe[12] von 2 Sam 7,10 dieser u.a. in dem Sinne von Ex 15,17f. (מקדש) neu interpretiert wird, daß Gott nämlich sein eschatologisches Haus (הבית) selbst bauen wird.[13] Auf diesen Aspekt des johanneischen Schriftgebrauchs wollen wir uns hier im wesentlichen beschränken.

I

Die Mehrzahl der Ausleger teilt die Auffassung, dieses Phänomen objektiv typologisch[14] deuten zu sollen, als ob in der geschilderten Heilsvergangenheit keimhaft eine geschichtliche Dynamik angelegt gewesen sei, die im Jesusgeschehen – positiv von der Prophetie, negativ vom Gesetz her – ihr Ziel erreicht habe und den damals noch ausstehenden Vollsinn[15] des Geschehens bzw. des ehemaligen Schriftwortes nun

12. So jedenfalls J. MAIER, *Die Qumran-Essener: Die Texte vom Toten Meer II* (UTB, 1863), München/Basel, E. Reinhardt, 1995, p. 104 Anm. 140.

13. Vgl. zur Diskussion neuerdings J. J. COLLINS, *The Scepter and the Star: The Messiahs of the Dead Sea Scrolls and Other Ancient Literature* (AB.RL), New York, NY, Doubleday, 1995, pp. 106-109, 128-129.

14. Man beachte die Definition der Typologie bei F.C. BAUR, *Kritische Untersuchungen über die kanonischen Evangelien, ihr Verhältniß zu einander, ihren Charakter und Ursprung*, Tübingen, L.F. Fues, 1847, p. 273: »Sobald das Bild zur Wahrheit, der Typus zur Sache selbst geworden ist, hat das Bild, der Typus, seine Bestimmung erreicht und erfüllt, er ist für sich betrachtet, zu einer völlig bedeutungslosen Form geworden. Derselbe Moment, in welchem in dem gekreuzigten Christus das bildliche Passahlamm zum wahren und wirklichen wurde, ist der Wendepunkt, in welchem das Judenthum aufhörte zu seyn, was es bisher war, seine absolute Bedeutung ihr Ende hatte, und das Christenthum als die wahre Religion an die Stelle desselben trat«.

15. Dazu gehört auch der Hinweis auf das Argument von einem angeblichen Offenbarungsfortschritt in der Schrift, auch wenn er gegen das Argument der Tübinger Schule vom Gegensatz zwischen dem A- und NT gerichtet ist: vgl. u.a. C.E. LUTHARDT, *Das johanneische Evangelium nach seiner Eigenthümlichkeit geschildert und erklärt*, Nürnberg, C. Geiger, 1852, p. 153; W.M.L. DE WETTE, *Kurze Erklärung des Evangeliums und der Briefe Johannis*, 4, vermehrte Auflage hrsg. von B.B. BRÜCKNER, Leipzig, Weidmann'sche Buchhandlung, 1852, p. XII; J. KÖSTLIN, *Die Einheit und Mannigfaltigkeit in der neutestamentlichen Lehre*, in *JDT* 3 (1858) 85-154, p. 152; WEISS (Anm. 3 = »Lehrbegriff«), p. 107; J.H. SCHOLTEN, *Das Evangelium nach Johannes. Kritisch-historische Untersuchung, aus dem Holländischen übersetzt*, Berlin, G. Reimer, 1867, pp. 143. 251; H.J. HOLTZMANN, *Die Gnosis und das johanneische Evangelium*, in *Die Anfänge des Christentums*, Berlin, A. Haack, 1877, 112-134, p. 116; F. DÜSTERDIECK, *Über das Evangelium des Johannes*, in *TStKr* 66 (1893) 783-796, p. 792; C. WEIZSÄCKER, *Das apostolische Zeitalter der christlichen Kirche*, Tübingen/Leipzig, J.C.B. Mohr (P. Siebeck), [3]1902, p. 522.

endlich erfülle. Einmal abgesehen davon, daß man gut beraten ist, zwischen dem späteren Ausleger und dem ursprünglichen Verfasser zu unterscheiden, kann man aber für den ersteren auch ein Denkmuster annehmen, in dem jener sich – aufgrund der unangefochtenen Autorität[16] der Schrift – seiner subjektiven Deutung des Jesusgeschehens zu versichern suchte. Niedergeschrieben wird sie zum Bestandteil der Kommunikation des Autors mit seiner Lesergemeinde[17]. Falls diese seiner Deutung zustimmen, bilden sie eine Konsensgemeinschaft. D.h. die vorgeschlagene Deutung gilt zuerst nur für diese Gruppe und hat somit immer noch einen subjektiven, wenn auch nun mehr als kollektives Deutemuster einen gruppenspezifischen Charakter. Wenn man nun die Schrift als Deuteuniversum und Autorität spendende Basis der Interpretation wegnimmt, indem man sie in ihrer Bedeutung halbiert, minimalisiert oder gänzlich in Frage stellt, wird das Deutemuster selbst unweigerlich hinfällig. Damit ist das Problem markiert, was es in diesem Aufsatz exemplarisch zu lösen gilt, will man nicht die These vom stark antijüdischen Johannesevangelium auf sich beruhen lassen.

Methodologisch korrekt muß der positive Beweis geführt werden, daß die Schrift im Johannesevangelium als unumkehrbarer Deutehorizont des Jesusgeschehens verwendet wird. Dies sollte aber nicht an den durch eine christliche Auslegungstradition besonders belasteten Weissagungs- und Erfüllungszitaten geschehen, sondern an einem ausgewählten Element der johanneischen Bildsprache, indem alle Aspekte des Bildes in der Schrift wie ihre Wiederaufnahme im Evangelium zusammengeführt und anschließend im Sinne der Problemstellung bewertet werden.

II

Mehr als gleichgewichtig in seiner Bedeutung mit der Schrift war für das antike Judentum der Tempel und sein Kult. Obwohl er eine religiöse

---

16. N. FRYE, *The Great Code. The Bible and Literature*, New York/London, H.B. Jovanovich, 1982, p. 78, betont zu Recht: »Primitive Christians wanting evidence were told to read 'Scriptures,' meaning the Old Testament«. Dies gilt auch für die biblischen Spätschriften, vgl. KRATZ (Anm. 5), p. 298, der zutreffend feststellt: »Sie alle suchen – implizit oder explizit – die wörtliche und/oder sachliche Übereinstimmung mit den zitierten Texten, die damit in ihrem autoritativen Rang bestätigt werden und Autorität verleihen«. Es geht ihnen rezeptionsgeschichtlich eben um »die Herleitung der Gegenwart aus der Vergangenheit«(p. 299).

17. Zu dieser Konzeption vgl. grundsätzlich schon U. BUSSE, *Johannes und Lukas: Die Lazarusperikope, Frucht eines Kommunikationsprozesses*, in A. DENAUX (ed.), *John and the Synoptics* (BETL, 101), Leuven, 1992, pp. 281-306.

Realität außerhalb der Schrift war, war er ein Kernstück ihrer Reflexion und blieb es auch bei den Gruppen, die ihn in ihrer Zeit als profanisiert ansahen. Auch wurde sie nicht eingestellt, als der zweite Tempel zerstört war. Darin ist sich der Autor des Johannesevangeliums mit den Rabbinen (vgl. u.a. bTGit 55b-56b) und den Apokalyptikern (vgl. 4 Esr; syr. Bar) seiner Zeit einig. Schon lange ist die Bedeutung der Tempelmetaphorik für die Theologie und Christologie des Johannesevangeliums erkannt. A. Neander[18] fand, »die Formen des jüdischen Kultus« seien »vorbildliche Symbole für <dessen>[19] christliche(n) Anschauungen«, ohne dies weiter zu belegen. Erst B. Weiß[20] sah sich in seiner Korrektur von einer der Thesen bei K.R. Köstlin[21], der den Tempel nur als irgendeinen geweihten Ort ansehen wollte, der von Jesus geschützt werden mußte (2,13ff.), gezwungen, den in Anspruch genommenen Text genauer zu betrachten. Er wies darauf hin, daß Jesus gerade umgekehrt, wie jener behauptet hatte, den Tempel positiv »Haus seines Vaters« (2,16) nennt. Der Autor bleibe also im Rahmen der alttestamentlichen Vorstellungen und betrachte den Tempel als Haus Gottes. Außerdem füllt er die Lakune weiter mit Hinweisen auf die ständigen Tempelwallfahrten Jesu und sieht auch die Hohepriesterwürde 11,51 vom Autor anerkannt. H.J. Holtzmann[22] ergänzte mit Bezug auf die Arbeit von C. Wittichen trotz schwerer Bedenken den Hinweiskatalog um den auf das jüdische Opferritual, auf das die Reinigungs- und Heiligungsvorstellung sowie die Opfervorstellungen in der Gestalt Jesu als dem Passalamm (1,29.36; 11,51f.) im Evangelium basiere. Franke[23] bestätigte den bis dahin erreichten Befund, präzisierte und ergänzte ihn. Nach 2,21 und 7,38 bezeichnet der Evangelist »Jesu Leib als den Ort, an welchem Gott Wohnung genommen (...), so ist damit ausgesprochen, dass die Erkenntniss der Geistigkeit Gottes (4,24) die Annahme nicht ausschliesst,

18. A. Neander, *Geschichte der Pflanzung und Leitung der christlichen Kirche durch die Apostel*, Gotha, F. A. Perthes, [5]1862 [[1]1832], pp. 469f. Ob er der Vorreiter für diese Auslegungstradition ist, ist hier nicht so sehr von Belang.
19. Im Zitat stand ursprünglich »seine«. Dies wurde vom Verf. geändert.
20. Weiss (Anm. 3 = *Lehrbegriff*), p. 113f., wiederholt von ihm in Id. (Anm. 3 = *Lehrbuch*), p. 662f.; ähnlich urteilt W. Beyschlag, *Das Leben Jesu*, 2 vol., Halle, E. Strien, 1885-1886, I, pp. 114f., über das Verhältnis des Evangelisten zum AT.
21. K.R. Köstlin, *Der Lehrbegriff des Evangeliums und der Briefe Johannis und die verwandten neutestamentlichen Lehrbegriffe*, Berlin, G.Bethge, 1843, p. 53.
22. H. J. Holtzmann, Art.: *Johannes der Apostel*, in D. Schenkel (Hrsg.), *Bibellexikon III*, Leipzig, 1870, p. 336; C. Wittichen, *Der geschichtliche Charakter des Evangeliums Johannis in Verbindung mit der Frage nach seinem Ursprunge. Eine kritische Untersuchung*, Elberfeld, R. L. Friderichs, 1868, pp. 6f.; vgl. aber auch die bei diesem viel wichtigeren pp. 17-20.
23. Franke (Anm. 2), pp. 23.75f.85.109.135.207f.210.303.

dass Gott an besonderem Orte in besonderer Weise gegenwärtig sein könne«[24]. Wenn Gott Jesus zum vollkommenen Tempel erhoben habe, dann sei er auch das Gefäß, aus dem Ströme lebendigen Wassers fließen werden, die als Gnadengaben den endzeitlichen Tempel nach Ez 47,1-12 u.a. zu charakterisieren seien. Doch seien für diese Metaphorik noch weitere alttestamentlich bezeugte Orte der Gottgegenwart bzw. der Kommunikation zwischen Gott und Israel im Evangelium mitheranzuziehen. Besonders verweist er dabei auf die Vorstellung vom Begegnungszelt, 1,14, auf die Anspielung auf Jakobs Traum in Bethel (1,51) und die Wohnungen, die für die Jünger in der Wohnstätte Gottes im Himmel (14,2f.) von Jesus hergerichtet würden. Damit ist von ihm schon erkannt, daß die Erde Gottes Wohnsitz – wie in Is 6 (vgl. 12,37-41 sowie Ez 1) – nicht fassen kann und die reinen Gläubigen mit dem Paradiessymbol Israels, dem Weinstock (15,1ff.), zu vergleichen sind[25]. Obwohl dieser Erkenntnisstand von A. Schlatter[26] geteilt wurde, wird die Analyse dieses Problemkomplexes in der deutschsprachigen Exegese nicht intensiv fortgesetzt, sondern erst von L. Hartman[27] an einem konkreten Text, aber nun mit einem neuen methodologischen Ansatz 1989 wieder aufgenommen. Er möchte aus einer am Leser und Text orientierten Perspektive die Bedeutung des Tempelworts 2,21 erschließen, indem er den für einen antiken Christen mit einem Tempel verknüpften Assoziationskomplex analysiert.

Ausgangspunkt seiner Überlegungen ist der Aspekt, daß in der Antike ein Tempel die Wohnstatt einer Gottheit war, wie auch immer man sich ihre Gegenwart darin vorzustellen habe. Er sei der privilegierte Ort, wo Mensch und Gottheit miteinander kommunizierten. Der Mensch vollziehe deshalb dort seine kultischen Handlungen, die Gottheit gebe dort ihren Willen kund und schenken den Bittenden Heil und Segen. Er sei auch immer ein wichtiger Versammlungsplatz für antike Gesellschaften gewesen. Unter dem vorläufigen Absehen von dem Tempel als Asylort und als eschatologischer Tempel des Heils appliziert er nun diese grundlegenden Vorstellungen auf die Aussagen im Johannesevangelium. Der Tempel, der in Jesu Leib errrichtet werde, verweise auf dessen Passion und Auferstehung. Deshalb wäre gemäß 16,7 Jesu Anabasis notwendig.

---

24. S. 109.211.271f.311.

25. S. 100.206-208.249.314.

26. A. SCHLATTER, *Die Sprache und Heimat des vierten Evangelisten* (BFCT, 6/4), Gütersloh, C. Bertelsmann, 1902; ID., *Der Evangelist Johannes: Wie er spricht, denkt und glaubt. Ein Kommentar zum vierten Evangelium*, Stuttgart 1930, pp. 23f. 48f. 75. 80-82. 123f. 200.

27. L. HARTMAN, *»He Spoke of the Temple of His Body« (Jn 2:13-22)*, in *SEÅ* 54 (1989) 70-79.

Als himmlische Wohnstatt Gottes würde sie 10,38 und in Kap. 14 betrachtet. Deshalb werde Jesus auch als der »Heilige« Gottes von den Elf 6,69 bezeichnet. Lokale Kultorte würden in ihm aufgehoben, 4,21ff.. Da er sich opfere, käme dies jedem Glaubenden zugute (3,36; 6,35f.; 7,37f.) und begründe so ein erneuertes Gott-Mensch-Verhältnis (15,4f.). Auch als Offenbarungsort wäre er etabliert, weil nur er Gott kenne und dessen Willen autentisch interpretiere (u. a. 1,18). Als neuer gesellschaftlicher Treffpunkt werde er in 17,22 betrachtet. Kurzum: »When the Johannine Christians believed that they 'in' Christ had a new temple, this meant totally new conditions of man's relationship to God«. Die Übertragung dieser Vorstellung auf das Jesusgeschehen sei für den antiken Christen eine gute Erklärunghilfe für die Substanz seines Glaubens. »For they knew better than we what a temple was«[28].

III

Auf der Grundlage der bislang geleisteten Vorarbeiten zur Tempelmetaphorik im Johannesevangelium läßt sich trefflich weiterbauen. Die zentralen Gliederungspunkte zum Phänomen antiker Tempel[29] bei L. Hartman, Wohnstatt Gottes, Kultort, Lehrort, Offenbarungsort und Treffpunkt zwischen Himmel und Erde, sind gezielter auf die Stellen zu applizieren, die schon seit längerem als implizite Anspielungen auf den Jerusalemer Tempel und dessen Kult galten, bzw. um weitere Stellen zu ergänzen, die bislang übersehen wurden. Zugleich sind sie mit analogen Aussagen aus der Schrift und der frühjüdischen Literatur zu vergleichen, so daß ihr Assoziationshorizont erkenn- und besser verstehbar wird. Da zudem die Bezugspunkte über das gesamte Evangelium verstreut zu sein scheinen, ist damit zu rechnen, daß die Tempelmetaphorik ein wesentlicher Bestandteil eines umfassenderen Metaphernnetzwerkes ist, mit dem das Jesusgeschehen soteriologisch vertieft ausgedeutet werden soll. Deshalb legt es sich nahe, dem Erzählfortschritt des Evangelisten zu folgen, um so die inhaltliche Anreicherung bzw. Verdichtung des Bildkomplexes besser verfolgen zu können.

---

28. Beide Zitate finden sich bei HARTMAN (Anm. 27), p. 79.
29. Man sollte jedoch den Hinweis von E. BICKERMANN, *Der Gott der Makkabäer. Untersuchungen über Sinn und Ursprung der makkabäischen Erhebung*, Berlin, Schocken, 1937, p. 97, beachten, der auf den entscheidenden Unterschied zwischen griechischer und westsemitischer Tempelkonzeption hingewiesen hat: »Dieser [...] ist eine Wohnstätte Gottes, die jedem Besucher zugänglich ist,.... Der westsemitische Tempel ist dagegen vom Prinzip der Absonderung des Heiligen beherrscht«.

a. Der erste Text, der ein bezeichnendes Licht schon auf die johanneische Tempelinterpretation wirft, steht im dritten, den Logos-Prolog beschließenden Bekenntnisteil (Vv. 14-18). Hier melden sich die Vv. 12f.
gemäß zu Kinder Gottes Gewordenen als Zeugen des Jesusgeschehens
selbst zu Wort[30], indem sie das geschichtliche Ereignis, dem sie ihren
neuen Heilszustand verdanken, erstmals theologisch resümieren. Es wäre
ein grobes Mißverständnis der Kernaussage von V. 14, dieses Ereignis
auf ein punktuelles Datum im Leben Jesu (etwa bei seiner Geburt oder
Taufe) zu reduzieren. Vielmehr signalisiert die häufig vernachlässigte
zweite Teilaussage des Verses, »er zeltete unter uns« (vgl. Sir 24,7-12),
einen bewußten Rückblick auf ein eine gewisse Zeit andauerndes
Geschehen, das mit dem in V. 15 erstmalig konkret zitierten Zeugnis des
Johannes, des vorösterlichen Paradezeugens, begann, aber jetzt im formulierten Wir-Zeugnis als historisch abgeschlossen gelten kann. Denn
man lebt bereits von den Früchten, die damals geschenkt wurden und
deren Bedeutung man reflektieren und zugleich bezeugen will. Das gesamte Jesusgeschehen wird als geschichtlich konkrete Inkarnation des
Logos betrachtet, der als Partner und Fachmann Gottes bei der Schöpfung über sie einzigartig kundig ist und permanent ihr seine Hilfe anbietet.
Dieser war nach der Auffassung der Wir-Gruppe in Jesus ein Leben lang
inkarniert. Um den im ersten Teilvers formulierten umfassenden Sachverhalt anzusprechen und zu präzisieren, aktualisiert der Autor die Vorstellung vom Begegnungszelt (אהל מועד)[31] der Sinaigeschichte (Ex 24,
16; 25,8; 26; 29,43-46; 40,35) und der in ihm wohnenden (שכן) göttlichen
Gegenwart, die die Schrift und das Frühjudentum mit einem überirdischen,
wunderbaren Glanz (כבוד) umschreibt, der Gott umgibt und ihn so un-
sichtbar (vgl. V. 18) für menschliche Augen macht. Es ist nun auffällig,
daß das geschichtliche Geschehen, in dem der ferne Schöpfergott im
fleischgewordenen Logos so nahe gekommen war, daß man in ihm den
göttlichen Herrlichkeitsglanz zu sehen meinte, daß dieses nicht wie dort mit
dem Substantiv (σκηνή)[32], sondern mit dem Verb »zelten«[33] umschrieben

---

30. Dazu ausführlicher M. THEOBALD, *Die Fleischwerdung des Logos. Studien zum
Verhältnis des Johannesprologs zum Corpus des Evangeliums und zu 1 Joh* (NTAbh, NF,
20), Münster, Aschendorff, 1988, pp. 247-267.
31. Vgl. M. GÖRG, *Das Zelt der Begegnung. Untersuchung zur Gestalt der sakralen
Zelttradition Altisraels* (BBB, 27), Bonn, 1967; M. METZGER, *Himmlische und irdische
Wohnstatt Jahwes*, in *UF* 2 (1970) 139-158; B. JANOWSKI, *»Ich will in eurer Mitte wohnen«. Struktur und Genese der exilischen Schekina-Theologie*, in *JBT* 2 (1987) 165-193,
pp. 184f.; H. GESE, *Der Johannesprolog*, in ID., *Zur biblischen Theologie. Alttestamentliche Vorträge* (BEvT, 78), München, 1977, 152-201, pp. 181ff..
32. Gemäß der LXX.
33. Präzisierung der Ausführungen von JANOWSKI (Anm. 31), p. 192.

wird. Es genügt zur Erklärung wohl nicht allein die Auskunft[34], der Autor habe keine zusammengesetzte Verben[35] gemocht, sondern der Rückverweis auf die spezifische Zelttradition (und nicht etwa auf 1 Kön 6,11-13 bzw. Ez 43,7-9)[36] setzt voraus, daß der Ort der göttlichen Gegenwart mobil vorgestellt werden soll. Das kann sich einmal auf den erzählten, historischen Jesus und dessen »Umhergehen« (περιπατεῖν)[37] oder kontextgemäß vielmehr auf die Kata- und Anabasis des Logos/Jesus beziehen, so daß das gesamte Wirken Jesu von diesen beiden Bewegungen[38] umfangen gedacht ist. Der johanneische Jesus wird also bereits im Prolog als das sichtbare Zeichen der heilvollen Gegenwart Gottes in Israel gedeutet. Er ist auf seine Weise die »Wohnstatt« Gottes. Aber dies besagt noch nicht, daß er Gott selbst, sondern eher dessen geschichtlich einmalige Manifestation in den Augen seiner Zeugen war. Auch sollte der Mittelvers mit der folgenden Zeugnisaussage korreliert werden, daß man in diesem begrenzten Zeitraum seine »Herrlichkeit« habe sehen können[39]. Die Aufnahme der biblischen *Kabod*-Konzeption[40] ruft erneut die Vorstellung von der heilsamen Gegenwart Gottes in der Gestalt von Ex 34,6 רב חסד ואמת wach.

34. SCHLATTER (Anm. 26 = *Kommentar*), p. 23.

35. Normalerweise übersetzt die LXX κατασκηνοῦν: vgl. 2 Chr 6,1f; Sach 2,10; Joel 3,17; Ez 37,27; vgl. aber den Gebrauch des Substantivs in Lev 26,11; Ex 25,9; Jos., Ant 3,219, verwendet ὁμόσκηνος.

36. Bzw. auf die Ladevorstellung, die schon in der Schrift nicht zusammengehören: vgl. J. MAIER, *Das altisraelitische Ladeheiligtum* (BZAW, 93), Berlin, 1965, p. 3.

37. Typisch johanneische Ausdrucksweise: vgl. 1,36; 6,19.66; 7,1 etc..

38. Vgl. in Kap. 6 die katabatischen Formulierungen (6,33.38.41.42.50.51.58), bis in 6,62 endlich der Aufstieg des Menschensohns in der Rede Jesu an seine Jünger thematisiert wird.

39. Vgl. dazu besonders C.R. KOESTER, *The Dwelling of God. The Tabernacle in the OT, Intertestamental Jewish Literature, and the NT* (CBQ MS, 22), Washington, DC, 1989, pp. 100-115.

40. Dazu J. MAIER, *Zwischen den Testamenten. Geschichte und Religion in der Zeit des zweiten Tempels* (NEB.E, 3), Würzburg, Echter, 1990, pp. 196f. 205; Vgl. auch J. PEDERSEN, *Israel. Its Life and Culture*, 2 vol., London, H. Milford, 1926, II, p. 261; C.C. NEWMAN, *Paul's Glory-Christology, Tradition and Rhetoric* (NTSup, 69), Leiden, Brill, 1992, pp. 17-153, kommt in seiner gründlichen Untersuchung der Wortgeschichte von δόξα zu dem Ergebnis, daß die LXX vorrangig δόξα als Übersetzung von *kabod* wähle, habe u.a. seinen Grund in der Konnotation des Worts mit dem Phänomen königlicher Majestät (pp. 143f.) sowie der Epiphanie, ohne direkt auf die Epiphanien heidnischer Gottheiten Bezug nehmen zu müssen (p. 151) und betone deshalb besonders »the divine presence« (p. 152). Geht man zusätzlich noch davon aus, daß der Evangelist des Hebräischen kundig gewesen ist, ist damit zu rechnen, daß er die Urbedeutungen der Vokabel als »movement-terminology« (p. 73) »füllen«, »wohnen«, »sich erheben« sowie substantiviert als »Gewicht«, »Bedeutung« etc. ebenfalls noch kennt und diese überall noch mitschwingt. Dann wäre mit dem Begriff auch neben der kultischen, die soteriologische Dimension der jesuanischen »Herrlichkeit«, nämlich sein »Bedeutung« für das menschliche Heil immer mitbedacht.

b. Die noch versteckten Anspielungen auf die mit einem heiligen Ort, wo Gott auf seine Weise präsent ist, verknüpften Vorstellungen werden sogleich im narrativen Hauptteil des Evangeliums fortgesetzt. Zwar werden im Verlauf der Erzählung noch zwei weitere »Gesandtschaften« der Jerusalemer Obrigkeit (7,32.45; 18,3-12) erwähnt werden, sie bestehen aber aus Polizisten bzw. Amtsdienern. Die erste (1,19.24) jedoch setzt sich aus Priestern, Leviten[41] und zusätzlich wohl noch aus Pharisäern zusammen. Sie sollen Jesus nicht verhaften, sondern die Personalien des irdischen Zeugen par exellence, Johannes (vgl. 1,19a), feststellen und seine Berufsauffassung überprüfen. Verdeckt wird dem Leser so mitgeteilt, daß man in Jerusalem an ganz bestimmten Personen, die in eschatologisch qualifizierter Zeit erwartet wurden, ein hohes Interesse hat und Johannes aufgrund seiner Tauftätigkeit (V. 25) in den Verdacht geraten ist, eine solche zu sein. Die geprägte Wendung »Priester und Leviten« bezeichnet aber nun das Tempelpersonal[42], so daß das auffällige Interesse an und die Observation seiner Person vom Tempel ausgeht. Mit der auffälligen Aktion gleich zu Beginn der Erzählhandlung wird stillschweigend schon die Möglichkeit vorbereitet, daß es später zu einem Konflikt[43] zwischen den Interessen des Tempelpersonals und denen der Gottgesandten kommen kann. Doch bis es soweit ist,

c. bedarf es noch weiterer erzählerischer Vorbereitungen, um den Verlauf desselben besser zu motivieren. Der von Gott bestimmte Zeuge Johannes bekennt nach der ergebnislosen Personenkontrolle zuerst dem Leser[44], daß der auf ihn zukommende Jesus das »Lamm Gottes« sei, »das die Sünde der Welt trägt«. Diese Anspielung auf eine kultische Praxis impliziert zugleich auch einen Hinweis auf die Sühne- bzw. Heilsfunktion des Tempels[45] für Israel. Nun gibt es verschiedene Ableitungsvorschläge für diese

---

41. Nach 1QM gehören zur Voraussetzung eines Sieges im eschatologischen Kampf zwischen den Söhnen des Lichts mit denen der Finsternis unbedingt Reinheit (hier vermittelt durch eine Taufe) und die Führung durch Priester und Leviten.

42. So auch schon FISCHER, *Ueber den Ausdruck Ιουδαιοι im Evangelium Johannis. Ein Beitrag zur Charakteristik desselben*, in *TZT* (1840) 96-133, p. 107, der sie »als Wächter des Cultus« bezeichnet. Die Arbeit von A.J. SALDARINI, *Pharisees, Scribes and Sadducees in Palestinian Society*, Wilmington, M. Glazier, 1988, pp. 187-198, ist zu historisch orientiert, um diese intertextuelle Assoziation zu bemerken.

43. Vgl. FRANKE (Anm. 2), pp. 169f. 177; F. OVERBECK, *Das Johannesevangelium. Studien zur Kritik seiner Erforschung*. Aus dem Nachlaß hrsg. C. A. BERNOULLI, Tübingen, J.C.B. Mohr (P. Siebeck), 1911, p. 284, 393, 420. Doch darf man den Konflikt nicht wie im vorigen Jahrhundert zumeist säkular im engen Konflikt mit der jüdischen Nation einschränken. Vielmehr geht es um deren religiöse Erwartungshaltung.

44. Es wird in 1,29 noch keine Zuhörerschaft erwähnt!

45. Dazu allgemein MAIER (Anm. 40), pp. 280f..

spezifisch johanneische Vorstellung. Wenn man einmal den Sündenbockritus am Jom kippur als am wenigsten wahrscheinlich übergeht, bleiben noch drei weitere Ableitungsmöglichkeiten: 1. Von dem zweimal täglich vollzogenen Brandopfer von Sühnopferlämmern gemäß Num 28,3f., 2. von dem hier metaphorisch gedeuteten Opfer des leidenden Gottesknechts (Is 53,7) oder 3. von Passalammopfer nach Ex 12,7-27. Die Kultmetaphorik bedarf hier noch keiner dezidierten Entscheidung für eine der drei Möglichkeiten[46]. Dem Autor ist erst einmal an der programmatische Anspielung auf eine kultische Praxis und deren heilvollem universalen Sinn gelegen: Jesus hat eine entscheidende Sühne- bzw. Heilsfunktion für die Welt und nicht nur für Israel (vgl. V. 31b), wo er geschichtlich auftritt. Der sich anbahnende Konflikt zwischen den Tempelautoritäten und Jesus könnte folglich für die Frage entscheidend werden, inwiefern Israel zur Welt gehört und wie diese umfassendere Größe sich entsühnen, d.h. in den Stand der Reinheit[47] und Heiligkeit vor Gott versetzen läßt oder nicht.

d. Zum kultischen Vorstellungsbereich gehört auch der Bezug auf den Jakobstraum von der Himmelsleiter auf den Tempelstufen[48] in Bethel (1,51; vgl. Gen 28,12; 35,7). Mit der Anspielung faßt der Autor einerseits die Bedeutung der Episode von der Jüngersammlung 1,35ff. zusammen, andererseits weckt der Autor noch mehr Erwartungen bei seinen Lesern als bei den ersten Jüngern Jesu mit dessen Versprechen, sie Größeres sehen zu lassen[49]. Bei einem sorgfältige Vergleich übernehmen die Jünger aus der ursprünglichen Vision die Rolle des Jakobs[50], die bis in den Himmel ragende Leiter (LXX: κλίμαξ) bleibt unerwähnt, wird aber metaphorisch ersetzt, weil Engel auf ihr hinauf- und von dort, d.h. »auf[51] dem Menschensohn«, hinabsteigen. Die Jünger befinden sich also in einer Situation wie einst Jakob in Bethel. Sie werden zu sehen

46. Vgl. u.a. GOPPELT (Anm. 11), p. 227; E.E. ELLIS, *Biblical Interpretation in the NT Church* (Compendia Rerum Iudaicarum ad Novum Testamentum II.1), Assen/Philadelphia, 1988, pp. 691-725, p. 714.

47. So gewinnt die Unterscheidung zwischen Wasser- und Geisttaufe (vgl. 1,31-33 mit 1,25-27) eine zusätzliche Bedeutung. Beides sind kultische Tätigkeiten im johanneischen Sinn, wobei die letztere die erstere übertrifft, jene aber noch nicht überflüssig macht.

48. Vgl. R.E. CLEMENTS, *God and Temple*, Oxford, 1965, p. 13.

49. Mit der Wiederaufnahme des Verbs im Futur »sehen« aus V. 50f verknüpft er ein individuelles mit einem kollektiven Versprechen.

50. So schon FRANKE (Anm. 2), p. 208, 314; vgl. neuerdings D. BURKETT, *The Son of Man in the Gospel of John* (JSNT SS, 56), Sheffield 1991, pp. 112-119.

51. Man beachte den Akkusativ im Urtext! In der LXX steht der Dativus locativus, hier der Akkusativ in der Grundbedeutung »darüber hin« (vgl. Bauer/Aland, WNT[6], p. 583).

bekommen, wie Jesus Himmel und Erde miteinander verbindet, indem er die Kommunikation zwischen den beiden mithilfe der Engel ermöglicht. Damit wird die bislang erkennbare johanneische Tempelkonzeption um einen weiteren Aspekt angereichert. Für ihn läßt sich kein naives Tempelverständnis, etwa im Sinne von einem ständigen Wohnsitz Gottes auf Erden, mehr ausmachen, sondern Gottes ferne Wohnstatt (vgl. 12,41 mit Is 6) ist der Himmel. Er ist der Welt fern und hält mit ihr über Engel Kontakt, die sich auf der »Jesusleiter« auf- und abwärts bewegen. Was einst (vgl. Gen 28,17) der Tempel in Bethel repräsentierte, nämlich Gottes Haus und »Pforte des Himmels«[52] zu sein, diese Funktion wird nun auf Jesus übertragen. Die Anspielung auf die biblische Betheltradition brauchte vom Autor nicht näher bezeichnet zu werden, weil schon in der frühjüdischen Aufnahme der Jakobsgeschichte ihre Kenntnis beim Leser[53] vorausgesetzt wird. Viel zentraler für den Verständnishorizont der Ansage ist die Reaktion Jakobs auf die Vision, indem er an dem Traum-Ort einen Tempel[54] errichten bzw. in Zukunft errichten will. Damit ist zugleich auch immer eine dem Ort entsprechende Kultpraxis[55] inklusive Reinheitsvorschriften[56], die der Heiligkeit des Ortes entsprechen, mitgedacht. Da die ersten Jünger die Rolle Jakobs übernommen haben, ist dies auf irgendeine Weise mitzubedenken.

e. Der Sachverhalt wird dem Leser in der Perikope vom »erneuerten Tempel« 2,13-22 endgültig klar. Diese besteht aus drei Erzählbausteinen:

---

52. Vgl. M. MÜLLER, *Der Ausdruck »Menschensohn« in den Evangelien. Voraussetzungen und Bedeutung*, Leiden 1984, pp. 206f.; GOPPELT (Anm. 11), p. 224.

53. In Jub 27,19-27, der interpretierenden Nacherzählung aus dem 2. Jh. v.u.Z., wird das Geschehen erst am Erzählschluß V. 26 in Bethel lokalisiert; vgl. u.a. H.M. WAHL, *Die Jakobserzählungen der Genesis und der Jubiläen im Vergleich*, in VT 44 (1994) 524-546, p. 536.

54. Die umgehend vollzogene Errichtung eines Kultortes durch Jakob, Gen 28,18f., wird in Jub 27,27 auf einen späteren Zeitpunkt (vgl. Jub 32,20-22) vertagt. In 4Q385 Frg. 2 [4QPs-Ez^a] findet sich eine Parallelaussage zu 1,51: Auf die Frage »Wie wird ihnen ihre Verbundenheit vergolten werden?« wird geantwortet: »Und JHWH sagte (4) zu mir: 'Ich werde die Israeliten schauen lassen und sie werden erkennen, daß ich JHWH bin.'« Setzt man die johanneische Forderung an die Jünger, in Jesus zu bleiben, hinzu, sticht die Parallelität ins Auge und bestätigt die futurische Ausrichtung beider Aussagen (vgl. Ps 14,2-7).

55. Diesen Sachverhalt lassen auch 11Q19 Kol. XXIX,8-10 und 5Q13 Frg. 2 erkennen; vgl. J. MAIER, *Die Tempelrolle vom Toten Meer* (UTB, 829), München/Basel, 1978, pp. 89f. und ID., *Die Qumran-Essener: Die Texte vom Toten Meer I* (UTB, 1862), München/Basel, 1995, pp. 299, 392.

56. Vgl. 2,1-11, speziell V. 6.

der eigentlichen Tempelreinigung, die aus den Synoptikern[57] übernommen wurde, dem doppelten Motiv von der Erinnerung der Jünger (Vv. 17.22) und der Diskussion Jesu über seine Aktion mit »den Juden« (Vv. 18-20). Denn Vv. 21f. bilden zusammen mit V. 17 einen das Vorgehen und das Gespräch Jesu beschließenden, in Parenthese gesetzten, Kommentar des Evangelisten, der dem Leser jetzt schon das Mißverständnis »der Juden« über das entscheidende Jesuslogion vom Niederreißen und Wiederaufbau des Tempels ebenso aufklären hilft wie den in der Episode zwar anwesenden, aber wie danebenstehend beschriebenen Jüngern eine Frist[58] einräumt sowie das Mittel nennt, wann und womit sie den tieferen Sinn der Vorgehensweise Jesu endgültig verstehen. Die Umarbeitung der Tempelreinigungsepisode zu einer dramatischen Symbolhandlung, bei der sogar Rinder vertrieben werden, soll sicherstellen, daß der Tempelbezirk von allen Geschäften – und seien sie auch dem Kult dienlich – freigehalten wird[59]. Zugleich läßt Jesus verlauten, daß er als Sohn des Hausherrn dazu ein Recht hat. Darauf reagieren jedoch nicht die betroffenen Händler, sondern die schon in 1,19b genannten »Juden«, d.h. das Tempelpersonal. Sie fragen jedoch im Unterschied zu den Synoptikern nicht direkt nach seiner Legitimation, seiner »Vollmacht«, sondern wollen mit einigem Recht die Symbolhandlung, das Zeichen[60], erklärt haben. Er antwortet mit dem charakteristisch überarbeiteten Tempelwort. Schon die Eröffnung mit einem konzessiven Imperativ im Aorist[61] und der Wechsel

---

57. Der letzte Versuch von M.A. MATSON, *The Contribution to the Temple Cleansing by the Fourth Gospel*, in *SBL SP* 31 (1993) 489-506, wie von vielen seiner Vorgänger, eine von den Synoptikern unabhängige Tradition wahrscheinlich zu machen, scheitert schon daran, daß er eigenständige theologische Interpretamente des Autors überliest. So ist z.B. die Aussage, »das Haus meines Vaters« (V. 16) ein zentrales joh. Theologumenon (vgl. F.J. MOLONEY, *Reading John 2:13-22: The Purification of the Temple*, in *RB* 97 (1990) 432-452, und M.J.J. MENKEN, *»De ijver voor uw huis zal mij verteren«. Het citaat uit Ps 69:10 in 2:17*, in FS B. Hemelsoet, Kampen, Kok, 1994, pp. 157-164). Der hier niederländisch zitierte Beitrag von Menken (wie ein weiterer vom gleichen Verfasser) findet sich nun leichter zugänglich und in Englisch in ID., *Old Testament Quotations in the Fourth Gospel. Studies in Textual Form* (CBET, 15), Kampen, Pharos, 1996, pp. 37-45.
58. Auffällig ist die Erzähltechnik des Autors, historisch zurückzublenden: vgl. 1,30; 10,36 u.a..
59. Siehe zu dem vorausgesetzten Geschäftsleben im Tempel: J. NEUSNER, *Money-Changers in the Temple: the Mishnah's Explanation*, in *NTS* 35 (1989) 287-290; E.P. SANDERS, *Jesus and Judaism*, Philadelphia, 1985, pp. 61-71; S. SAFRAI, *Die Wallfahrt im Zeitalter des Zweiten Tempels*, Neukirchen, 1981, pp. 185ff. 201ff.; S. APPLEBAUM, *Economic Life in Palestine* (Compendia Rerum Judaicarum ad Novum Testamentum, I.2), Assen/Amsterdam 1976, p. 683; m.E. soll dieser Aspekt die Aussage von 4,23f. vorbereiten.
60. Nicht ohne Absicht ist ihre Frage präsentisch formuliert.
61. Vgl. E.A. ABBOTT, *Johannine Grammar*, London, 1906, §2439 (III-V) und BDR §387,2.

des Subjekts läßt aufhorchen. Wenn sie (und nicht er!) den Tempel auflösen, werde er ihn binnen dreier Tage wiedererrichten! Damit läßt er
durchblicken, daß die Symbolhandlung noch keineswegs das Zeichen
selbst war, sondern auf etwas verweisen soll, das noch aussteht. Zwar
deutet er für den kundigen Leser mit dem Wortspiel zwischen »errichten« und »auferstehen« an, was er wirklich meint. Doch »die Juden«
bleiben in ihrem Denken der Ebene der historischen Realität verhaftet
und vergleichen die bisherige Bauzeit des herodianischen Tempels mit
den angesagten drei Tagen. So mißverstehen sie Jesus gründlich. Der
Erzähler fühlt sich deshalb verpflichtet, für den Leser ausdrücklich anzumerken, daß Jesus mit dem Tempel metaphorisch seinen Leib gemeint
habe, d.h. sein zukünftiges gewaltsames Geschick. Zusammen mit der
Auferstehung (V. 22a) wird dies das Zeichen schlechthin sein, daß Jesus
setzen wird, um seinen Anspruch auf seines Vaters Haus zu legitimie-
ren[62]. Nun kann man auch die narrative Strategie des Erzählers, neben
der eigentlichen Handlung zwei Protokollnotizen über die Reaktionen
der anwesenden Jünger einzufügen, besser würdigen. Schon die Notiz in
V. 17 wird als Erinnerung eingestuft. Die Aktion Jesu habe in ihnen das
Schriftwort wachgerufen: »Der Eifer um Dein Haus wird mich verzehren!« Zweifellos wird hier Ps 68 (69),10LXX mit wenigen Abänderun-
gen zitiert[63]. Angepaßt an die Erzählsituation wird der Aorist des Verbs
in der LXX-Vorlage in das Futur gesetzt: Es heißt nun nicht: 'er habe
sich', sondern 'er werde sich verzehren'. Sie sehen also nicht die Schriftstelle nach dem Schema »Verheißung und Erfüllung« (vgl. 12,38 etc.)
in der auffälligen Handlungsweise Jesu erfüllt, sondern sie schliessen
aus der Aktion[64], daß ihr Herr sich für die Sache Gottes von nun an bis
zum Äußersten einsetzen wird. Damit wird indirekt ein Zusammenhang
schon zwischen der Symbolhandlung und dem späteren Tod Jesu hergestellt. Aber der Schwerpunkt der Aussage liegt für den Autor erkennbar
in ihrer Programmatik. Die Jünger sehen eine Zeit mit Jesus vor sich, die
vom Eifer für sein Vaterhaus geprägt sein wird. Auch aus der Jünger-
perspektive hat das Vorgehen Jesu also Verweischarakter. Sie sehen in
ihr seine innerste Motivation aufgedeckt. Der Endpunkt des Wirkens

---

62. Obwohl man die Vollmachtsfrage in der johanneischen Überarbeitung der Tempelreinigungsszene vergeblich sucht, ist sie bei ihm nicht gänzlich übergangen. Der Leser
wird ihr spätestens in 10,18 begegnen, wo deutlich wird, daß er die Vollmacht hat, sich
sein freiwillig hingegebenes Leben selbst zurückzugeben.

63. Vgl. M.J.J. MENKEN (Anm. 57), pp. 157-164.

64. Es wird hier klar, daß der Verfasser die Jünger Jesu als jüdisch sozialisiert ansieht.
Sie leben so intensiv aus der Schrift, daß ihnen eine zur miterlebten Situation passende
Schriftstelle aus der Erinnerung ins Bewußtsein steigt und diese deren Programmatik
erhellt.

Jesu, der Tod am Galgen zusammen mit seiner Auferstehung, kommen jedoch erst im parallel formulierten Abschlußvers 22bc in den Blick. Wenn Jesus nach dem Hinweis auf die Schrifterfüllung (19,28)[65] mit den Worten: »es ist vollbracht« stirbt, heißt das: der Eifer für dich, Vater, hat mich verzehrt! Erst dann erweitert sich nämlich ihre Erinnerung an Ps 68,10LXX noch um das Wort Jesu, der Leib des Auferstandenen sei der erneuerte Tempel, in dem Gott und Mensch sich treffen können, wie es Jesus schon in 1,51 anzudeuten versuchte. Die kunstvolle Zusammenfassung in V. 22de[66] mit der besonderen Rückblende (vgl. 1,30; 10,36 u.a.) auf die Erinnerung der Jünger läßt den tieferen Sinn der provokanten Aktion Jesu im Tempel für den Leser über die »Jüngerschiene« transparent werden. Nicht nur »die Juden«, sondern auch die Jünger haben noch eine Geschichte mit Jesus vor sich. Sie wird für letztere vom Eifer Jesu für die Sache Gottes bestimmt sein und die anderen werden, indem sie den »Tempel«[67] zerstören, zusammen mit jenen das Zeichen schlechthin zu sehen bekommen, das Jesus selbst setzen wird. »Darum liebt mich mein Vater: Daß ich mein Leben einsetze, damit ich es abermals nehme. Keiner entreißt es mir, sondern selber – von mir aus – setze ich es ein«. (10,17f.). Die Symbolhandlung verweist folglich auf das noch ausstehende Zeichen von Tod und Auferstehung Jesu, wodurch der Auferstandene als erneuerter Tempel, d.h. Ort der gnädigen Gegenwart Gottes, für die Jünger offenbar wird. Textgemäß folgt in V. 22 die Zusammenfassung der Perikope: die Jünger glauben seit ihrem Osterwiderfahrnis der Schrift und den Worten Jesu. Die biblische Ableitung des Gedankengangs aus der frühjüdischen Schriftinterpretation führt zu zwei Quellen: einmal zur eschatologischen Erwartung eines neuen, von Gott selbst errichteten Tempels gemäß Ez 37,15-28 bzw. Ez 40-48[68] und zum anderen

---

65. Wichtig ist der Hinweis von MENKEN (Anm. 57), p. 160, auf Ps 69,22, um 19,28 adäquater verstehen zu können.

66. Der Schriftglaube bezieht sich auf V. 17 und der unverstellte Glaube der Jünger an Jesu Wort auf V. 19f.. Aus beiden setzt sich unzerbrüchlich ihr österlicher Glauben zusammen.

67. Man beachte, daß hier »Tempel« ναός, anderenorts τόπος (מקום) heißt: Ersteres deckt sich mit dem Sprachgebrauch des Josephus, u.a. Bell 5,207; Ant 15,390.421, der für das eigentliche Hauptgebäude (Debir [?] und Chekal) das Substantiv gebraucht, sonst für die Tempelanlage insgesamt τό ἱερόν. Der hebr. Spezialbegriff für den Tempel als »Ort« schlechthin: vgl. 4,20; 11,48; 14,2. Dazu lese man neuerdings A. OBERMANN, Die christologische Erfüllung der Schrift im Johannesevangelium (WUNT, 2/83), Tübingen, 1996, p. 122 Anm. 51; H. SCHWIER, Tempel und Tempelzerstörung. Untersuchungen zu den theologischen und ideologischen Faktoren im ersten jüdisch-römischen Krieg (66-74 n.Chr.) (NTOA, 11), Fribourg/Göttingen, 1989, pp. 56.62.

68. Vgl. u.a. Is 2,2-4 par. Mich 4,1-4; Joel 4,16f.; Sach 2,14f.; 8,3; Mal 3,1; äth. Hen 90,29; Jub 1,17.29; 4,24-26; 1QM 2,3; 7,11; 4Q174 1,2f. usw..

zu der Überzeugung der Essener, daß ihr *Jachad*, d.h. eine Gruppe von auserwählten Menschen, vorübergehend den Tempel[69] ersetzen könne, solange der Tempel in Jerusalem ihrer Meinung nach profanisiert sei. Daß Menschen einen »Tempel« bilden können, ist also gedanklich in Qumran vorgebildet. Ob aber Jesus mit dem nicht von Menschen Hand gebauten, eschatologischen Tempel Gottes am Ende der Tage identifiziert werden soll, bleibt fraglich[70]; denn schon der Prolog betrachtet das Logos/Jesusgeschehen als bereits vergangenes. Die weitere Lektüre wird Klarheit schaffen.

f. Die Episode Jesus mit der Samariterin am Jakobsbrunnen (vgl. 4,4-44 mit 1,51) gibt einen ersten Aufschluß. Denn Vergangenheit und Gegenwart Samariens stehen dort auf dem Prüfstand. Dessen Gebrochenheit kann abgeholfen werden, wenn man Jesus nur richtig versteht und dadurch die Zukunft gewinnt. Die Samariterin bekennt ihn als Propheten (V. 19)[71], dem sie den bestimmenden Antagonismus zwischen ihrem und dem jüdischen Volk als neutrale Instanz vorlegen zu können meint: Wo ist der Ort, an dem man Gott legitim verehrt? Hier auf dem Garizim oder in Jerusalem? Jesus antwortet mit einem Weder-Noch. Obwohl zugegebenermaßen »das Heil aus den Juden« stammt[72], werde hier und jetzt wie auch in aller Zukunft[73] der Vater (vgl. 2,16) in »Geist und Wahrheit« an keinem mit einem ausschließenden religiöse Anspruch

---

69. U.a. 1QS 9,6; vgl. W. PASCHEN, *Rein und Unrein. Untersuchungen zur biblischen Wortgeschichte* (SANT, 24), München, 1970, pp. 134-152 G. KLINZING, *Die Umdeutung des Kultus in der Qumrangemeinde und im NT* (SUNT, 7), Göttingen, 1971, pp. 50-93; MAIER (Anm. 55 = *Qumran-Essener I*), p. 190 Anm. 517; J. ROLOFF, *Die Kirche im NT* (NTD.E, 10), Göttingen, 1993, pp. 110-117, sowie neuerdings W. KRAUS, *Das Volk Gottes. Zur Grundlegung der Ekklesiologie bei Paulus*, Tübingen, 1996, pp. 174-176.

70. Vgl. COLLINS (Anm. 13), p. 111; auch er unterscheidet zwischen einem Interimstempel, wie ihn die Tempelrolle beschreibt, und dem eschatologischen Tempelneubau Gottes. FRANKE hingegen (Anm. 2), p. 210, meint, der Jesus-Tempel könne nicht zerstört werden.

71. Daß dies nicht hinreichend ist, belegen Vv. 25f.,41f..

72. Hier wird erkennbar, daß der johanneische Jesus sich als Jude fühlt; vgl. WEISS (Anm. 3 = *Lehrbegriff*), p. 115; FRANKE (Anm. 2), p. 82; H.J. HOLTZMANN, *Lehrbuch der neutestamentlichen Theologie*, 2 vol., Freiburg/Leipzig 1897, II, p. 357; Diese Beobachtung wirft die Frage auf, ob die mehrfach wiederholte These von OBERMANN (Anm. 67), pp. 122 Anm. 51, 125f. 421, zu dem Problem, die Bedeutung des Tempels in Jerusalem sei »entschränkt«, den joh. Textbefund wirklich umfassend erklärt.

73. Nach 3,36 – dort noch verdeckt – wird hier zum ersten Mal Gegenwart und Zukunft sperrig miteinander korreliert. Dies ergibt nur Sinn, wenn die Episode als repräsentativ und illustrativ zugleich für zukünftige Entwicklungen betrachtet wird. M.J.J. MENKEN, *De genezing van de Lamme en de omstreden Christologie in Joh 5*, in *Coll.* 18 (1988) 418-435, p. 426, merkt dazu an: »Het deelhebben aan Gods eigen leven en nu is voor de gelovige realiteit, maar onder de condities van 'de wereld' (vgl. 17,9-19). De definitieve voltooiing van Gods heil ligt nog in de toekomst (vgl. 17,24)«.

ausgestatteten Ort angebetet. Damit taucht am biblischen Deutehorizont die Versöhnung von Ephraim und Manasse mit Juda auf[74]. Es wird von nun an ein Gottesdienst vollzogen werden, in dem alle religiösen Unterschiede miteinander ausgesöhnt sind, weil Gott begonnen hat, solche zu suchen, die ihn auf diese Weise verehren. Da aber Gott definitiv Geist ist (V. 24), sind die, welche ihn so verehren, mit ihm auf eine noch näher zu definierende Weise[75] verwandt bzw. gehören zu seinem Bereich[76]. Auch diese Konzeption hat sein Vorbild in der biblischen Tradition. Der Vorstellung von der Analogie zwischen Gott als Geist und seiner Verehrung in »Geist und Wahrheit« entspricht in der frühjüdischen Tradition die von der makellosen und einheitlichen Heiligkeit Gottes, der sich Menschen nur in einem entsprechend reinen Zustand[77] (vgl. 11,55; 13,10; 15,2f.) nähern[78] durfte. Wer dies bewußt oder unbewußt mißachtete, rief den Zorn Gottes (vgl. 3,36) hervor. Die Gott gemäße Heiligkeit wurde dinglich und sachlich im Opferkult und geschichtlich durch dessen Erwählung möglich. Letzteres setzt 4,23 voraus. Wie die in die Heilsgeschichte Israels (vgl. 1,11) eingebettete erneute Erwählung geschieht, die in 4,20-26 angekündigt wird, wird wiederum nicht ausgeführt, sondern der Leser bleibt erneut auf seine weitere Lektüre verwiesen. Aus dem direkten Kontext ergibt sich für ihn nur, daß auch Samaritaner erwählt werden können (V. 42) und die Jünger Jesu ohne eigene Verdienste die göttliche Erwählungsernte (4,35-38) miteinbringen werden. Hier wird analog zur Kultpraxis des Tempels eine zukünftige angekündigt, die jetzt zwar schon gültig ist, aber erst bei der (mehrdeutig formulierten) Zerstörung (2,19.21f.) »dieses Tempels« umfassend in Kraft gesetzt wird.

---

74. Vgl. H. THYEN, »Das Heil kommt von den Juden«, in FS G. Bornkamm, 1980, 163-184, pp. 170. 176, und H.W. BOERS, Neither on this Mountain nor in Jerusalem. A Study of John 4 (SBL MS, 35), Atlanta, 1988, p. 180.

75. Die Forderung wurde schon in 3,3-5 erhoben und in 1,12f. als Faktum angesehen. So steht dies in der Erzählzeit des Autors noch aus. Es ist dieselbe Tendenz, die man bislang in allen besprochenen Texten bemerken konnte.

76. Zur johanneischen Wahrheitskonzeption vgl. 17,17-19.

77. Dazu ausführlicher: E.S. GERSTENBERGER, Das 3. Buch Mose, Leviticus (ATD, 6), Göttingen, 1993, pp. 88-104. 194-223, und D. KELLERMANN, Art. Heiligkeit, II. AT, in TRE 14 (1985) 697-703; Beachte auch die Definition von SCHWIER (Anm. 67), p. 55: »Gebraucht man 'heilig' und 'rein' in unterschiedlicher Bedeutung, so bezeichnet 'heilig' einen von Gottes Heiligkeit abgeleiteten Zustand und 'Reinheit' eine an die Kultteilnehmer gerichtete Forderung, die der Heiligkeit korrespondieren soll«. Vgl. F. SCHMIDT, La pensée du Temple. De Jérusalem à Qumrân. Identité et lien social dans le judaïsme ancien, Paris, Les Éditions du Seuil, 1994.

78. U.a. Is 52,1; 1QH 14,27f. [*VI,27f.]; 4Q174 Kol III [=4QFlor] 1,3f.; bTBB 75b; Off 21,27; 22,14f..

g. Der Jerusalemer Tempel war seit alters[79] – so könnte es auch im Jesus-Tempel sein – ein Ort der Schriftgelehrsamkeit[80]. Ein Hinweis darauf findet sich nach einer allgemeineren Vorbereitung in 6,45, wo sie als Kennzeichen derer gewürdigt wird, die zu Jesus kommen, bald darauf in der konfliktreichen Episode am Laubhüttenfest (Kap. 7-8). Jesus selbst wird als Schriftgelehrter im Tempel (7,15) vorgestellt. Die bei seiner Belehrung Anwesenden kommen zu dem Schluß, daß es doch bemerkenswert sei, daß er zwar nie in eine entsprechende Schule gegangen sei, aber die Schriftauslegung trotzdem perfekt beherrsche. Zwar lehrte Jochanan ben Zakai nicht wie der johanneische Jesus im Tempel, aber doch in dessen Reichweite[81], so daß auch für die mit ihm beginnende formative Phase des rabbinischen Judentums die Zentralität des Tempels für das Torastudium gewahrt bleibt. Gerade weil der Tempel zerstört ist, werden in der rabbinischen Tradition seine entsühnenden Hauptfunktionen auf das Torastudium und sittliches Verhalten[82] übertragen. Exemplarisch für das erstere ist Pirke Abot 3,4[83]. Dort wird Is 28,8 wegen seiner Verwendung von מָקוֹם[84] zitiert, dem Ort schlechthin, d.h. der Tempel.

79. Vgl. Is 2,3; Mich 4,2; 1 Esr 8,22; Jub 11,16f.; 19,14; 45,16; 2 Makk 2,13-15; Lk 2,42ff.; Jos. Ant 3,38; 8,395; 11,128; 12,142; c.Ap. 2,23; MAbot 1,12; Sifre Dt 356 S. 423.
80. Gegen die einseitige Beschreibung bei SANDERS (Anm. 59), p. 64, der Tempel sei im Bewußtsein des Frühjudentums nur als Opferkultstätte verankert gewesen. Siehe vielmehr R.T. BECKWITH, Formation of the Hebrew Bible (CRINT, II.1), Assen/Maastricht-Philadelphia, 1988, 39-86, pp. 40-45; J. MCCAFFREY, The House With Many Rooms: The Temple Theme of Jn 14,2-3 (AnBib, 114), Rom 1988, p. 122; A.DEMSKY/M. BAR-ILAN, Writing in Ancient Israel and Early Judaism (CRINT, II.1), 1988, p. 23. Viele Hinweise aus der rabbinischen Literatur, die aber hier nicht weiter ausgebreitet werden können, verdanke ich meiner Kollegin in Utrecht, Universitätsdozentin Dr. Ch. Safrai, der ich herzlich zu danken habe.
81. Vgl. J. NEUSNER, A Life of Rabban Yohanan ben Zakkai (SPB, 6), Leiden, 1962, p. 44; Ob damit eine tempelkritische Haltung signalisiert werden soll, ist hier weniger von Belang als der Hinweis, daß er trotzdem weiter »im Schatten des Tempels« lehrte.
82. Exemplarisch: ARN/A 4: »Einmal ging R. Jochanan ben Zakai von Jerusalem fort und R. Joschua folgte ihm und sah den Tempel in Ruinen liegen. 'Wehe über uns!' schrie R. Joschua, 'der Ort, wo die Sünden Israels gesühnt wurden, liegt in Trümmern!' 'Mein Sohn', sagte R. Jochanan zu ihm, 'sei nicht traurig. Wir haben eine andere Entsühnung, die genau so effektiv ist wie jener.' 'Und was ist es?' 'Es sind die Werke der Barmherzigkeit, wie sagt doch die Schrift: Barmherzigkeit will ich und nicht Opfer!'«
83. »R. Simeon ben Jochai hat gesagt: Die Drei, die an einem Tisch zusammen gegessen und darüber keine Worte der Tora gesprochen haben, sind wie solche, die vom Totenopfer gegessen haben, wie geschrieben steht: 'Alle Tische sind voll von Erbrochenem, sind voll von Kot' (Is 28,8) ohne Gott. Aber jene drei, die an einem Tisch zusammengegessen und darüber Worte der Tora gesprochen haben, sind wie solche, die vom Tisch Gottes gegessen haben, wie geschrieben steht: 'Und er sagte zu mir: Das ist der Schaubrottisch, der vor dem Herrn steht' (Ez 41,22)«. (vgl. äth. Hen 89,73).
84. In anderen strata der Mischna, der weiteren rabbinischen Literatur wie bei Philo wird wie hier »der Ort« kennzeichnenderweise zum Metonym für die Gottesbezeichnung: so schon E. SCHÜRER, Der Begriff des Himmelreiches aus jüdischen Quellen erläutert, in JPT 2 (1876) 166-187, pp. 168-171.

Ebenso wird dort Ez 41,22 nur aufgegriffen wegen der Erwähnung des Schaubrottisches im Tempel. Das Torastudium hat also die Funktionen übernommen, die früher dem Tempelkult zugesprochen wurden. Torastudium ist abgeleiteter Tempelkult. Dies wirft die Frage auf, ob die johanneische Theologie nicht einem analogen Denkmuster gefolgt ist. Dies ist ebenfalls erst später beantwortbar.

h. Vorher aber wird dem Leser im Ansatz die in 4,23f. aufgetauchte Frage, wer die Gottesverehrer »in Geist und Wahrheit« sind, beantwortet. In 7,37-39 wird nämlich der entsprechende Faden wiederaufgenommen und eine nur dem Leser zugängliche Vorschau gegeben. Gemäß dem in Kap. 7 und 8 strittigen Aussageziel, nämlich die spezifische Heilsrelation zwischen Jesus und dem Gläubigen zu bestimmen, wird Jesus zum Spender und der Glaubende zum Empfänger des Geistes[85]. Doch dies endgültig bewerkstelligen zu können, ist die Frucht seines Lebens. Damit fällt auch das letzte Hindernis für die Identifikation der biblischen Anspielung V. 38. Wenn nämlich Jesu Wort anschließend auf den erwarteten Propheten wie Mose (Dt 18,18-22) bezogen wird, dann kommen nur solche Schriftstellen in Frage, die in Bezug auf die Exoduspassage stehen. Menken[86] hat mit überzeugenden Argumenten die Passagen benannt, die am ehesten dem Wortlaut in V. 38 gerecht werden: Es ist Ps 77 (78)16.20[87], der mit Sach 14,8 und möglicherweise mit Ps 114,8 redaktionell kombiniert wurde. Damit wird der Geistträger Jesus in den Mittelpunkt gestellt, der jedes Gläubigen Durst (vgl. 4,10; 6,35) als Heilsfrucht seines Lebens und Sendung ab Ostern (vgl. 6,63) stillen wird. Die Metapher von der Einladung an Durstende ist ebenfalls Teil der Zion- bzw. der Tempelmetaphorik[88], die damit die uralte Vorstellung von den Paradiesströmen[89] als Segensströme, die vom Tempel ausgehen, aktualisiert.

---

85. So schon mit Recht H. ODEBERG, *The Fourth Gospel Interpreted in its Relation to Contemporaneous Religious Currents in Palestine and the Hellenistic-Oriental World*, Uppsala, 1929, p. 284.

86. M.J.J. MENKEN, *The Origin of the OT Quotation in Jn 7:38*, in *NT* 38 (1996) 160-175 [bzw. vgl. Anm. 57 pp. 187-203]

87. Ps 77 (78),16.20 enthält den Grundbestand der Wörter aus V. 38 *Ströme, fließen* und *Wasser*; Sach 14,8 fügt *lebendig* hinzu; ob man nun *aus seinem Inneren* als eine Exegese aus Ps 114,8 bezeichnen muß oder ob hier nicht schon 19,31ff. hineinspielt, kann hier offen bleiben, da alles Wesentliche hinreichend geklärt ist.

88. Vgl. u.a. Is 33,20f.; 44,3; Joel 4,18; Hag 1,6; Sach 14,8; Ez 47,1ff.; Ps 46 [45],5[4]; 63 [62],2f.; äth. Hen 26,1-5; 1Q28b [=1QSb] Kol I,6; 1QH XVI [= VIII,4]; 11Q19 Kol XXXII, 12-14; 4Q286 Frg. 5; 4Q500; 4Q431 [vgl. 1QH XXVI,4];[Num 21,16-18; 1 Kön 7,23-26; Sir 24,23-31].

89. Vgl. u.a. CLEMENTS (Anm. 48), pp. 67-73; SCHWIER (Anm. 67), p. 74; FRANKE (Anm. 2), p. 311; T. A. BUSINK, *Der Tempel von Jerusalem von Salomo bis Herodes*, 2 vols., Leiden, 1969/1980, II p. 1418; GOPPELT (Anm. 11), p. 223.

Auffällig ist Ez 47[90], wo erst nach der Erwähnung des Kults (Ez 46, 20ff.) die segensreiche Tempelquelle genannt wird. Dementsprechend erhalten in der Tat erst die im österlichen Licht Glaubenden, 20,22, den Geist von Jesus, der vorher seine Lebensaufgabe im Gehorsam vollendet hat. Die Jünger werden so zu seinen Geschwistern (vgl. 20,17) und können auf diese Weise in die Gemeinschaft mit Jesu Vater eintreten.

i. Dies wird nach einer geschickten Vorbereitung mit der Israel und seine Leitungseliten symbolisierenden biblischen Herde- und Hirtenmetaphern (Kap. 10)[91] und der Jesu Tod einleitenden Lazaruserweckung (vgl. 11,4) in 11,47–12,23 erneut thematisiert und zugleich präzisiert. Die Hohenpriester im Verbund mit den Pharisäern befürchten wegen des Erfolgs Jesu den »Ort« (4,20) und das Volk[92] an die Römer (V. 48) zu verlieren. Deshalb schlägt der amtierende Hohepriester von Gott geleitet vor, ihn an deren Stelle als »Bauernopfer« zu opfern. Der politische Pragmatismus des Hohenpriesters gewinnt, indem er ihn bald in die Tat umsetzt, für den Autor tiefere Signifikanz. Deshalb fügt er direkt, Vv. 51f., kommentierend hinzu, dies habe jener geäußert um anzudeuten, daß Jesus »nicht nur für (ὑπέρ) das Volk allein stürbe, sondern auch, um die zerstreuten Kinder Gottes (vgl. 1,11) in eins zusammenzuführen«. Damit beantwortet er dem Leser zugleich zwei bislang offen gebliebene Fragen: Zum einen ist das Zeugnis des Täufers (1,29), Jesus sei »das Lamm Gottes, das die Sünde der Welt trage«[93], wirklich funktional im Sinne einer kultischen Opfermetapher zu verstehen. Denn ein Mensch bringt sich selbst als Opfer zum Heil aller, die Gott aus der Welt (vgl. 6,51; 10,11.15.18; 16,7; 18,14) sich erwählt hat, dar. Zum anderen wird

---

90. Dazu neuerdings W. ZWICKEL, *Die Tempelquelle Ez 47. Eine traditionsgeschichtliche Untersuchung*, in *EvT* 55 (1995) 140-154.

91. Vgl. J. BEUTLER/R.T. FORTNA (eds.), *The Shepherd Discourse of John 10 and its Context* (SNTS MS, 67), Cambridge, 1991; neuerdings L. SCHENKE, *Das Rätsel von Tür und Hirt. Wer es löst, hat gewonnen!*, in *TTZ* 105 (1996) 81-100, p. 95; Neben den Belegen aus der biblischen Tradition, die im zuerst genannten Sammelband genannt sind, beachte auch den frühjüdischen Gebrauch dieser Metaphorik: zentral dafür z.B. ist 1 Hen 89f.; dazu ausführlich: P.A. TILLER, *A Commentary on the Animal Apocalypse of I Enoch* (SBL.EJL, 4), Atlanta, 1993, pp. 36-60.

92. In 2 Makk 5,19 werden in markanter Weise beide ebenfalls miteinander verbunden: »Aber der Herr hat nicht das *Volk* erwählt wegen des *Ortes*, sondern den *Ort* wegen des *Volkes*«.

93. Das Verb αἴρειν wird in 1,29 und in 11,48 gleichermaßen verwendet. Letzteres wird in V. 50 mit ἀποθνῄσκειν und ἀπόλλυμι näher erläutert. Man kann die Gefahr, die Basis seiner Macht zu verlieren, dadurch aufheben, indem man einen für alle opfere. Dieser Aspekt wird darauf Vv. 51f. ganz im Sinn von 1,29 universal ausgedehnt: Jesus rettet nicht nur die ihm vom Vater aus dessen Eigentumsvolk Gegebenen, sondern alle Kinder Gottes.

der Leser damit zugleich auf die biblische Analogie des leidenden Gerechten Is 53,4ff. bzw. 43,4 verwiesen[94]. Jesus ist in seiner kultischen Opferlamm-Funktion mit dem leidenden Gerechten soteriologisch vergleichbar[95]. Anschließend (11,55; 12,1) wird knapp mitgeteilt, viele aus dem Lande hätten sich rechtzeitig zur Wallfahrt aufgemacht[96], um sich vor dem Passafest noch pflichtgemäß zu heiligen, d. h. sich von allem Profanen, u. a. durch Waschungen und Torastudium, abzusondern[97], um der Gegenwart Gottes im Tempel gerecht werden zu können. Erhellend formuliert dies R. Hillel[98], der gesagt hat: »Zu dem Ort (למקום), den mein Herz liebt, dorthin führen mich meine Füße. Wenn du zu meinem Haus (לביתי) kommst, werde ich zu dem deinen kommen! Wenn du zu meinem Haus nicht kommst, komme ich auch nicht zu dem deinen! Wie geschrieben steht (Ex 20,24[21]): Überall, wo ich meinen Namen (שמי) verehren lasse, dort [sei es in einer Synagoge, sei es zu Hause] werde ich zu dir kommen und dich segnen«. Wenn man das Schriftzitat als jüngere Ergänzung, veranlaßt durch die Zerstörung des Tempels, überliest, dann gewinnt man einen Einblick in das Motivationszentrum der Wallfahrer: Gottes verborgene Gegenwart im Tempel spendet Segen weit über Jerusalem hinaus, wenn man ihn dort besucht und von Herzen verehrt. Deshalb fragen sich die Wallfahrer auch im Tempelbezirk[99], ob Jesus wohl kommen würde, obwohl er zur Fahndung ausgeschrieben sei (Vv. 56f.). Damit gibt der Evangelist ein Stichwort, daß seit 2,14ff. virulent, von 7,11 an als Selbstverständlichkeit vorausgesetzt wird, daß nämlich Jesus zu allen Wallfahrtsfesten sein »Vaterhaus« aufsucht und so zuerkennen gibt, daß der Tempel für ihn der zentrale Bezugspunkt[100] ist. Doch diesmal haben

---

94. Dazu u.a. W. GRIMM, *Die Preisgabe eines Menschen zur Rettung des Volkes. Priesterliche Tradition bei Johannes und Josephus*, in FS O. MICHEL, Göttingen, 1974, pp. 133-146.

95. Aus den drei zu 1,29 skizzierten Deutemöglichkeiten sind damit schon zwei bestätigt. Es bleibt nur noch die Präzisierung offen, ob das für das tägliches Tamidopfer oder für das Passaopfer verwendete Tier gemeint ist. Dies wird Joh 19,31ff. klären.

96. Vgl. Jos. Ant. 4,203f., wo er aus seiner Sicht die Gründe zur Wallfahrt nach Jerusalem angibt.

97. Vgl. u.a. Ex 19,10-15 als Basistext; Ex 31,13; Lev 20,8-21,8.15.23; 1QSa 1,25f.; 1QS 1,8; 5,23; bTBer 14b/15a; ARN/A 2; Zum thematischen Gesamtkomplex siehe J. MILGROM, *Studies in Cultic Theology and Terminology* (SJLA, 36), Leiden, 1983; ID., *Deviations from Scripture in the Purity Laws of the Temple Scrolls*, in S. TALMON (ed.), *Jewish Civilization in the Hellenistic-Roman Period* (JSP SS, 10), Sheffield, 1991, pp. 158-167.

98. TSukk 4,3 (bTSukk 53a).

99. Mit τό ἱερόν ist wohl wie bei Josephus die Tempelanlage insgesamt gemeint.

100. Dieser ist nicht nur für den joh. Jesus Heimat (vgl. 4,42; bzw. FRANKE (Anm. 2), pp. 23.76.304), sondern schon Ez 5,5;38,12;43,14 [חיק הארץ =»Schoßgrund«]; Ps 50[49],2 (vgl. äth. Hen 26,1-5; Jos. Bell 5,212-214; bTJoma 54b; TanB, Kedoschim §10), sprechen von Jerusalem und dem Zionsberg als »Nabel der Welt«, dem kosmischen Zentrum schlechthin.

sich auch Fremde (12,20) eingefunden, um Gott am Passa ebenfalls zu
»verehren« (vgl. 4,19-26).[101] Sie werden jedoch nicht zu ihm vorgelassen, da – aus dem Kontext klar erkennbar – die erneuerte Kultpraxis
noch nicht in Kraft gesetzt ist. Jesus bedarf noch der Einwilligung seines
Vaters, die dieser ihm 12,23-28 erteilt, u. z. wiederum wie 4,35ff.
begleitet von einer Saat-Ernte-Metapher (V. 24), die auf die nachösterlichen Jünger appliziert wird. Jünger nämlich im Vollsinn des Wortes
kann jemand aus der Sicht des Autors erst werden, wer dessen Verherrlichung und anschließende Rückkehr[102] abwarten kann. Dies trifft mit
Blick auf 4,35ff., 10,16, 11,52 besonders auf die Fremden zu. Deshalb
werden sie zu Lebzeiten Jesu auch nicht zu ihm vorgelassen[103]. Der tem-
poräre Vorbehalt und Verweis auf das Ostergeschehen und die darauf
folgende Zeit signalisiert dem schriftkundigen Leser nur, daß er aus seinem Deutehorizont die Zioneschatologie für ein rechtes Verständnis des
Ostergeschehens aktivieren soll. Dies kommt nicht überraschend, da
vorher die synoptische Einzugsepisode 12,12-19 schon unter diesem
Aspekt überarbeitet worden war. Dazu gehört aber auch das Motiv von
der endzeitlichen Völkerwallfahrt nach Zion u. z. offensichtlich in der
Variante, daß die Heiden weder vernichtet[104] noch Israels Sklaven[105], sondern gleichberechtigt an der eschatologischen Verehrung Gottes und dessen
gnädiger Heilszuwendung teilhaben[106] werden. Aber die beabsichtigte

---

101. Nach Jos. Ant 20,41 konnte ein Heiden den einen Gott auch ohne Beschneidung
verehren bzw. ihm im Tempel ein Opfer darbringen lassen: vgl. dazu E. SCHÜRER, *The
History of the Jewish People in the Age of Jesus Christ*, G. VERMES/F. MILLAR/M. BLACK
(eds.), 4 vol., Edinburgh, Clark, 1973-1987, II pp. 309-313.

102. Zu diesem Komplex ausführlicher U. BUSSE, *Die »Hellenen« Joh 12,20ff. und
der sogenannte »Anhang« Joh 21*, in F. VAN SEGBROEK ET AL. (eds.), *The Four Gospels
1992*, FS F. NEIRYNCK III (BETL, 100C), Leuven, 1992, pp. 2083-2100; Hinzuweisen ist
auch auf 16,7 und 20,17, wo auf die Notwendigkeit der Anabasis Jesu für die Jünger-
schaft aufmerksam gemacht wird.

103. Die Schwierigkeiten wie begrenzten Möglichkeiten von Heiden in das Eigentumsvolk z. Z. Jesu einzutreten, darüber geben neuerdings W. KRAUS (Anm. 69), pp. 45-
110, D.R. SCHWARTZ, *Studies in the Jewish Backgroand of Christianity* (WUNT, 60),
Tübingen 1992, pp. 102-116, T.L. DONALDSON, *Proselytes or 'Righteous Gentiles'? The
Status of Gentiles in Eschatological Pilgrimage Patterns of Thought*, in JSP 7 (1990) 3-
27 und N. LOHFINK, *Bund und Tora bei der Völkerwallfahrt (Jesajabuch und Ps 25)*, in
ID./E. ZENGER, *Der Gott Israels und die Völker. Untersuchungen zum Jesajabuch und zu
den Psalmen* (SBS, 154), Stuttgart, 1994, pp. 37-83, Auskunft.

104. U.a. Jub 15,16-32; 4 Esr 12,33; 13,38; syr. Bar 40,1; ApkAbr 31,2; 4Q491 Frg.
15; 1QM passim.

105. U.a. Is 18,7;60,1-22;66,18-21; Hag 2,21f.; Sir 36,11-17; PsSal 17,30f.; Jub
32,19; 1QM XII 14; 1Q16 Frg. 9-10; 4Q504 Kol. IV,2; TgIs 25,6-10.

106. U.a. Sach 2,11;14,16-19; Ps 87; Tobit 13,10-13;14,6f.; Is 54,15LXX; Am
9,12LXX; äth. Hen 10,21;90,32; OrSib 3.702-726; 4Q177 [MidrEschat^B, Catena^A] XI
15; Philo, Vit.Mos. II.44; Quaest in Ex II.2: οἰκείωσις δὲ τῆς πρὸς τόν ἕνα καὶ
πατέρα τῶν ὅλων τιμῆς.

Erzählprogression verbietet es dem Autor, dies jetzt schon auszuführen. Erst in 21,11 wird er mit der Erwähnung der symbolischen Zahl von 153 Fischen auf die universale Sammlungsbewegung[107] der Glaubenden aus allen Völkern, die mit der österlichen Jüngerbeauftragung verbunden ist, auf dieser Thematik zurückkommen.

j. Schon früher war bemerkt worden, daß der Evangelist keine naive Wohntempel-Konzeption verficht, sondern sich der Transzendenz Gottes bewußt bleibt. Dies wird nochmals deutlich in 12,37-41, wo er auf die Berufungsvision des Propheten Isaia in Kap. 6 der Isaiarolle zu sprechen kommt. Der irdische Tempel bietet dort nur Platz für den »Saum seines Gewandes«. Gott selbst kann er nicht fassen. Sein wahrer, aber zugleich ferner Wohnort ist der Himmel[108]. Doch seine Gegenwart im irdischen Tempel ist visionär gesichert und legitimiert den Propheten mit Offenbarungswissen. Beide Orte sind folglich in diesem Denkmodell aufeinander bezogen. Der irdische Tempel entspricht in seiner Heiligkeit dem himmlischen Tempel, so daß Gott, obwohl unverfügbar, im ersteren geheimnisvoll gegenwärtig und nahe ist[109]. Die Kluft zwischen Himmel und Erde zu überbrücken, dies war auch der Auftrag Jesu (vgl. 1,51). Wenn er aber – wie bereits lange angekündigt – zu seinem Vater in dessen eigentliche himmlische Wohnstatt zurückkehrt, stellt sich die Frage, wie seine jetzigen wie zukünftigen Anhänger nach seinem Weggang mit Gott weiterhin in Verbindung bleiben können, d.h, wozu[110] er – analog zu seiner wiederholten Anabasis zum Zionsberg und seiner Vaterstadt – in die himmlische Wohnstatt Gottes reisen will und ob er von dort zurückkehrt, um die Verbindung nicht abreißen zu lassen. Diese Frage wird u. a. in 14,2f. mithilfe der Tempelmetaphorik zu beantworten versucht. Nach Jesu Ankündigung verreist er bald, aber mit dem aufmunterndem Versprechen an die Jünger, zu der eigentlichen Wohnstatt seines Vaters, um den Seinen (vgl. 7,33f.; 8,21f.; 12,26; 17,24) dort eine dauerhafte Bleibe zu schaffen, und nach seiner Rückkehr sie alle zu sich zu nehmen[111]. Hier werden ein temporärer und ein

107. Dies ist ein weiteres zentrales Motiv der Zionseschatologie: vgl. u.a. Philo, Praem 164-172.

108. Vgl. auch 1 Kön 8,27.39;22,19; 2 Chr 2,6;20,5;30,27; Ps 11,4; Is 66,1; 4Q286 Frg.1; 4Q403 Frg. 1; 4Q491 Frg. 11 Kol 1; 4 Esr 8,20; äth Hen 84,2; TLevi 5,1.

109. Vgl. u.a. 0QShirShab, eine Agende für die himmlische wie irdische Sabbatliturgie, die Auskunft gibt über das zeitgenössische Kultverständnis der Priester.

110. Im Johannesevangelium ist nicht mehr der Grund für Jesu Tod Anlaß der Reflektion, sondern dessen soteriologisches Gewicht.

111. Zu diesem anspruchsvollen Text vgl. G. FISCHER, *Die himmlischen Wohnungen. Untersuchungen zu Joh 14,2f.* (EHS.T, 38), Bern/Frankfurt, Lang, 1975; J. BEUTLER,

lokaler Aspekt[112] miteinander verknüpft. Der lokale verweist auf die nachexilische Vorstellung[113] von den endzeitlichen Wohnungen (der Gerechten)[114] im himmlischen analog zum irdischen Tempel (Ez 40,17; 1 Chr 28,11f.; 5Q15 Frg. 1 Kol. II,6; 11Q19 Kol. 44. 5f.). Das Rückkehrmotiv variert die urchristliche Parusievorstellung im Hinblick auf das Ostergeschehen (20,17ff.) und qualifiziert erneut die nachösterliche Zeit als eschatologische Interimsperiode[115], in der alle die gesammelt werden, welche zu den Kindern Gottes gehören, damit sie anschließend (möglicherweise nach einem Bluttod, vgl. 21,18f.) dort in Ruhe[116] bis zur Parusie verweilen können, wo auch Jesus derweilen ist. Daß dazu auch erwählte Heiden gehören können, davon gehen schon vor Johannes nicht nur 2 Makk 1,27-29, sondern schon Is 2,2-4 (par. Mich 4,1-4); 60,1-13 u.a. aus.

»Habt keine Angst«. Die erste johanneische Abschiedsrede (Joh 14) (SBS, 116), Stuttgart 1984, pp. 30-44; J. MCCAFFREY (Anm. 80); A. STIMPFLE, *Blinde sehen. Die Eschatologie im traditionsgeschichtlichen Prozeß des Johannesevangeliums* (BZNW, 57), Berlin, 1990, pp. 147-216; F.F. SEGOVIA, *The Farewell of the Word. The Johannine Call to Abide*, Minneapolis 1991, pp. 81-84; M. WINTER, *Das Vermächtnis Jesu und die Abschiedsworte der Väter. Gattungsgeschichtliche Untersuchung der Vermächtnisrede im Blick auf Joh 13-17* (FRLANT, 161), Göttingen, 1994, p. 146; A. DETTWILER, *Die Gegenwart des Erhöhten. Eine exegetische Studie zu den johanneischen Abschiedsreden (Joh 13,31-16,33) unter besonderer Berücksichtigung ihres Relecture-Charakters* (FRLANT, 169), Göttingen, 1995, pp. 141-157; D.F. TOLMIE, *Jesus' Farewell to the Disciples. John 13:1-17:26 in Narratological Perspective* (BISer, 12), Leiden, 1995; C. HOEGEN-ROHLS, *Der nachösterliche Johannes. Die Abschiedsreden als hermeneutischer Schlüssel zum vierten Evangelium* (WUNT, 2/84), Tübingen, 1996, pp. 98f..

112. Indem der Autor in V. 2 »Haus meines Vaters« (vgl. 2,16) und »Ort« (ὁ τόπος) (vgl. 4,20) gebraucht, spielt er unmißverständlich auf den Tempel an.

113. Der von STIMPFLE (Anm. 111), pp. 166f., erneuerte Versuch, diese Vorstellung aus einem gnostischen Kontext abzuleiten, ist mit DETTWILER (Anm. 111), p. 152, aufgrund fehlender Parallelen wenig überzeugend.

114. Vgl. u.a. äth. Hen 39,4-8;41,2;48,1 (vgl. Joh 7,37f.!);71,5-9.16; slHen 61,2f.; ApkAbr 17,16; 29,15; Jub 4,26; 8,19 (der Garten Eden als göttlicher wie adamitischer Wohnbezirk!).

115. Dies bestätigt ein Ergebnis der Dissertation von J. NEUGEBAUER, *Die eschatologischen Aussagen in den johanneischen Abschiedsreden. Eine Untersuchung zu Joh 13-17* (BWANT, 140), Stuttgart, Kohlhammer, 1995, p. 161; Dies legt auch der Sprachgebrauch von 4QMidrEschat[a.b] nahe, den A. STEUDEL, *Der Midrasch zur Eschatologie aus der Qumrangemeinde (4QMidrEschat [a.b]). Materielle Rekonstruktion, Textbestand, Gattung und traditionsgeschichtliche Einordnung des durch 4Q174 (»Florilegium«) und 4Q177 (»Catena A«) repräsentierten Werkes aus den Qumranfunden* (STDJ, 13), Leiden, 1994, pp. 161-163.214, herausgearbeitet hat.

116. Vgl. zur Vorstellung vom Tempel als Ruheort in der jüdischen Literatur MCCAFFREY (Anm. 80), p. 69.

k. Die Bildrede[117] 15,1-8 vom Weinstock und seinen Reben nimmt ihr Bildrepertoire[118] aus der biblischen Tradition[119] und appliziert es aus göttlicher Sicht auf das Verhältnis Jesu zu seinen Freunden (Vv. 11-15)[120]. Die Schwierigkeit, daß es problematisch sei, die in der Schrift überwiegend auf Israel bezogene Metapher vom Rebstock[121] auf eine Person – in diesem Fall auf Jesus – zu übertragen, war schon in Ez 17, dort auf den König Zidkija angewandt, überwunden worden. Ein weiteres Problem, daß nämlich Jesus und die gärtnerische Kunst des Winzers[122] allein das Gedeihen und den Fruchtertrag der Reben garantieren, läßt sich wiederum am ehesten mithilfe der hier deutlich eingewobenen Tempelmetaphorik erklären. Denn nicht nur ein keineswegs zu unterschätzendes architektonisches Detail des Jerusalemer Tempels, daß dort an der Vorhalle eine goldene Weinstockabbildung[123] angebracht war, sondern der johanneische Text selbst weist auch auf sie hin. Die Arbeit des Winzers wird mit κλῆμα αἴρειν bzw. καθαιρεῖν[124] umschrieben. Diese sind – gemessen an der Fachsprache der antiken Winzer[125] – impräzise

---

117. Vgl. J.G. VAN DER WATT, »Metaphorik« in Joh 15,1-8, in BZ 38 (1994) 67-80; ID., Interpreting Imagery in John's Gospel. John 10 and 15 as a Case Studies, in FS J.P. LOUW, Pretoria, 1992, 272-282.

118. Vgl. R. BORIG, Der wahre Weinstock. Untersuchungen zu Joh 15,1-10 (SANT, 16), München, 1967, pp. 79-128; R.E. BROWN, The Gospel According to John (AB, 29A), Garden City, NY, 1970, pp. 669-672; SCHNACKENBURG (Anm. 1) III, pp. 118-121.

119. U.a. Hos 11,1; Is 5; 18,5; Jer 2,21; Ez 15; 17,6-8; 19.10-14; Joel 1,7; Ps 80,9-15; 4Q500; 6Q11; Der Versuch von W. BAUER, Das Johannesevangelium (HNT, 6), Tübingen, 1933, pp. 189-191, und R. BULTMANN es aus gnostischen bzw. mandäischen Quellen abzuleiten, ist heute mit vollem Recht fast vollkommen aufgegeben.

120. So schon FRANKE (Anm. 2), p. 249.

121. Vgl. u. a. R. BISSCHOPS, Die Metapher als Wertsetzung – Novalis, Ezechiel, Beckett (DASK, 23), Bern/Frankfurt, P. Lang, 1994, pp. 213-219.

122. Dazu neuerdings: G.W. DERICKSON, Viticulture and John 15:1-6, in BS 153 (1996) 34-52, der jedoch den neusten editierten Text P.Oxy 3354 (vol. 47, 1980, pp. 108-114) außer Acht gelassen hat.

123. Vgl. BUSINK (Anm. 89) II, pp. 1146-1148; SCHNACKENBURG (Anm. 118), p. 120; BORIG (Anm. 118), p. 108.

124. Der weitere Hinweis auf die Arbeit des Winzers in V. 6, »es werde die Rebe hinausgeworfen«, nimmt wiederum nur den Gedankengang von 6,37 – kontextgemäß negativ gewendet – auf. Dieser Arbeitsgang gehört ebenfalls zu denen, die in den Pachtverträgen, aber in anderer Begrifflichkeit, verzeichnet sind.

125. Man erwartet Begriffe wie ξυλοτομία = lat. pampinatio, βλαστολογία, διάτασις φύλλων, ἀνάλημψις βλαστῶν, φυλλολογίαι etc.; zur Arbeit des Winzers und die Fachterminologie für seine Tätigkeiten vgl. PLINIUS, HN 17.35; POxy 729.1631.1692.3354 sowie M. SCHNEBEL, Die Landwirtschaft im hellenistischen Ägypten (MBPF, 7), München, C.H. Beck'sche Verlagsbuchhandlung, 1925, pp. 239-281, und Z. SAFRAI, The Economy of Roman Palestine, London/New York 1994, pp. 126-136; Weitere Hinweise findet man auch neuerdings bei U. BUSSE, In Souveränität – anders. Verarbeitete Gotteserfahrung in Mt 20,1-16, in BZ 40 (1996) 61-72.

Ausdrücke. Speziell das Verb »reinigen« in Verbindung mit dem Adjektiv »rein« in V. 3 signalisieren, daß der wachgerufene Assoziationskomplex auf zwei Aussagen übertragen werden soll: einmal auf die Abhängigkeit der Reben vom Weinstock und auf das beide betreffende, vom Winzer anvisierte Ertragsziel, viele hochwertige Trauben zu ernten. Die für diesen besonderen »Ernteerfolg« benötigte »Reinheit« verweist auf die kultische Reinheitsforderung, d.h. auf das entscheidende und biblisch geforderte Kriterium für den Verkehr mit Gott. Das exakt dies gemeint ist, dafür sprechen noch weitere Beobachtungen. Bekanntlich war schon 12,24-26 in der soteriologischen Deutung von Jesu baldigen Tod davon die Rede, daß das Samenkorn nur dann Frucht bringe, wenn es in die Erde versenkt werde, verbunden mit dem dort noch schwer verständlichem Wort vom Diener, der gefälligst dort zu sein habe, wo sich sein Herr gerade befinde. Mit dem Rollentausch Jesu in der Fußwaschungsszene jedoch, der dort einen Sklavendienst[126] leistet, und dessen für den Leser noch rätselhaftem Wort an Petrus 13,10, jeder außer einem unter den Jüngern sei »rein«, wird die hiesige Aussage besser verständlich. Denn 15,3a nennt die Kondition in kulttechnischer Begrifflichkeit, unter der erst die Jünger loyal zu Jesus und ihm im Dienst gleichgestellt – eben wie wirkliche Freunde (Vv. 13-16) – gemeinsam[127] den Ertrag erbringen, der von ihnen zusammen erwartet wird: Jeder, der Jesu Wort akzeptiert, ist – kultmetaphorisch ausgedrückt – rein, d.h. er erfüllt also die »Hausordnung Gottes«[128] und damit eines der beiden Kriterien, die bereits 2,22 als Basis des österlichen Jüngerglaubens benannt worden waren. Wer diese Kondition erfüllt, nämlich Jesu Wort hört und für sich als sein Leben bestimmend akzeptiert, darf im Jesus-Tempel an Gottes Gnadengegenwart sowie an dessen Heilsgaben partizipieren. Wer darüber hinaus bleibend loyal zu Jesus steht, wird überreiche Frucht bringen.

l. In diesem Argumentationszusammenhang wird nun vom Haß der Welt (15,18f.) gesprochen, die eine andere Vorstellung von Freundschaft[129] hat als Jesus, der die Jünger gerade wohl deshalb »aus der Welt« erwählt (vgl. 13,18 mit 17,6f.16) und sie so in jene Schicksals- und Ertragsgemeinschaft mit ihm eingebunden hat, von der bereits in

126. Zur Sklavenmetaphorik im Johannesevangelium vgl. neuerdings U. BUSSE, *The Relevance of Social History to the Interpretation of the Gospel According to John*, in *Skrif en Kerk* 16 (1995) 28-38.
127. Dies weist auch auf 4,35f. zurück!
128. So die treffende Definition der Reinheit bei GERSTENBERGER (Anm. 77), p. 191.
129. Vgl. 15,19b mit V. 14.

15,1ff. gesprochen wurde. Diese wird sie bald auf eine kaum bestehbare Probe (16,32f.) stellen, wenn er nicht etwas zu ihrer Unterstützung (vgl. 18,8f.) unternimmt. Überraschend wird diese Aktion – 12,31 aufgreifend – zum Abschluß der Abschiedsrede, 16,33, terminologisch in martialischer Sprache[130] knapp, aber prägnant erfaßt. Jesus spricht von seinem Sieg, den er über die Welt davongetragen habe. Ob nun ein juristischer, was 12,31 und 18,28–19,16a nahelegen, oder ein militärischer Sieg gemeint ist, eine solche Frage ist hier ohne Belang. Vielmehr muß erörtert werden, ob Kriegsmetaphorik generell zum Deutehorizont des Tempels gehört. Schon in den sogenannten Zionspsalmen (Ps 46.48 und partiell Ps 76)[131] wird JHWH als Schutzgott seiner Stadt auf dem Zion besungen, der dem »Zionsschema« gemäß u. a. den Völkersturm auf sie durch seine siegreiche Symmachie abwehrt. Die Vorstellung bleibt über 2 Chr 20,1-30, die Makkabäerbücher (vgl. u. a. 1 Makk 3–4; 2 Makk 10,16), äth. Hen 56,5-8; 90,13-19 und essenischen Schriften (u. a. 4Q161 [=4QpIs^a]; 0QCD XX,33f.; 1QM passim) erkennbar bis nach der Zerstörung des zweiten Tempels (vgl. 4 Esr 13,1-13; Off 11,1f. 20,9) lebendig. Auf sie kann der Evangelist zurückgreifen, um seine Vorstellung vom soteriologischen Gewicht der Passion Jesu für dessen Anhänger zu verdeutlichen. In ihr wird die den Jüngern Furcht einjagende Welt besiegt. Das gewaltsame Geschick Jesu ist also nicht nur ein historisches Einzeldatum, sondern hat auch eine fortdauernde Wirkung. Indem die jüdischen Leitungseliten ihre unzerbrüchliche Loyalität dem römischen Cäsar gegenüber (19,15) erklären, hätten sie nicht nur in den Augen der Qumran-Essener, die in 4Q167, Frg. 7 [= 4QpHos^b], ein Pesher zu Hos 6,7, sagen können: »'Und sie – wie Adam übertraten sie seinen Bund'. Die Deutung [–] haben verlassen den Gott und [wa]ndelten nach (den) Vorschriften [der Völker(?)...]« (vgl. 2 Chr 36,11-21), sondern vor allem aus johanneischer Perspektive haben sie sich uneingeschränkt zum Repräsentanten der Welt bekannt und damit ihre Loyalität dem lebendigen Gott und seiner Königsherrschaft (vgl. 3,3-6 mit 18,36) aufgekündigt und sind so seinem Zorn (3,36) verfallen und werden »in Blindheit

---

130. Vgl. dazu auch J.-W. TAEGER, »*Gesiegt! O himmlische Musik des Wortes!*« *Zur Entfaltung des Siegesmotivs in den johanneischen Schriften*, in ZNW 85 (1994) 23-46, pp. 25-28, der aber das Siegesmotiv auf die Situation der johanneischen Gemeinde appliziert wissen will. Der Motivhintergrund selbst wird nicht weiter erörtert.

131. Vgl. neuerdings: F.-L. HOSSFELD/E. ZENGER, *Die Psalmen* I (NEB, 29), Würzburg, 1993, pp. 284-289, 294-299; vorher u.a.: M. HENGEL, *Die Zeloten. Untersuchungen zur jüdischen Freiheitsbewegung in der Zeit von Herodes I. bis 70 n.Chr.* (AGJU, 1), Leiden, 1961 ²1976, pp. 277-296, 308-318; O. BÖCHER, *Die heilige Stadt im Völkerkrieg. Wandlungen eines apokalyptischen Schemas*, in FS O. MICHEL, Göttingen, 1974, 55-76; SCHWIER (Anm. 67), pp. 74-90.

(d.h in Sünde) sterben« (vgl. 9,39-41 mit 19,11). Da sie so durch ihr Verhalten die von Gott entfremdete Welt repräsentieren[132], wird im Sterben und Auferstehen Jesu diese besiegbar. Aus der Perspektive des Autors ist folglich das Passionsgeschehen von einer tiefen Ironie geprägt, da die jüdische Führungselite zur Zeit Jesu willens war, um den Tempel und das Volk für sich zu retten, dem durch seinen Bund und durch heilsame Gegenwart im Tempel dem Volk verbundenen Gott ihre Loyalität zugunsten einer weltlichen Macht aufzukündigen, hat sie durch eigenes Versagen[133] Jesus paradoxerweise möglich gemacht, in seinem Passionsleib einen Ersatztempel für Gottes Gegenwart zu errichten. Er bestätigt so die alte Überzeugung der Tempeltheologie von der Unbesiegbarkeit Gottes.

m. Bekanntlich erweiterte der Evangelist die Passionsgeschichte um eine Schlußszene (19,31-37). In ihr soll wohl die Heilsbedeutung des Todes Jesu eindringlich und hochsymbolisch zugleich zum Ausdruck gebracht werden. Doch ist diese Perikope eine wahre crux interpretum. Schon Bultmann[134] meinte, dieser Text sei erst nachträglich in das Johannesevangelium eingebaut worden. Denn er enthalte aus seiner Sicht keine echte johanneische Theologie, da er ganz vom Thema »Schrifterfüllung« geprägt sei. Deshalb gab es für ihn genügend Hinweise für eine sekundäre kirchliche Redaktion. Darum schlug er vor, V. 34b »und sofort floß Blut und Wasser heraus« und V. 35 mit der Beteuerung der Augenzeugenschaft ihr zu zuweisen. Somit hat er die anstößigsten Verse aus dem ursprünglichen Text ausgeklammert. Wellhausen[135] und Loisy waren vor ihm aber noch einen Schritt weiter gegangen. Sie hatten V. 34a, die Notiz vom Lanzenstich, der in der Thomasperikope 20,24-29 vorausgesetzt wird, und V. 37 mit dem letzten Schriftzitat der Liste von sekundären Zutaten noch hinzugefügt. Doch schon Bultmann wandte dagegen

---

132. So auch neuerdings K. BECKMANN, *Funktion und Gestalt des Judas Iskarioth im Johannesevangelium*, in *BTZ* 11 (1994) 181-200, p. 187 Anm. 15; vorher schon u. a. A. HILGENFELD, *Die johanneische Theologie und ihre neueste Bearbeitung. 2. Die johanneische Auffassung der geschichtlichen Religion*, in *ZWT* 6 (1863) 96-116. 214-228, p. 219; W. BOUSSET, Art. *Johannesevangelium*, in *RGG*[1] III (1912) 608-636, p. 627; BRÜCKNER (Anm. 15), p. XVII.

133. Es ist eine Grundüberzeugung Israels, daß die mehrfache Zerstörung des irdischen Tempels auf eigenes Fehlverhalten zurückzuführen ist: vgl. nur 4Q174 Kol III [= Frg, 1+21+2],5f.: »(Er) wird ständig über ihm (d.h. dem Tempel) erscheinen. Und nicht werden wieder Fremde es zerstören, wie sie vordem zerstört haben (6) das Heilig[tum I]sraels durch dessen Versündigung«.

134. R. BULTMANN, *Das Evangelium des Johannes* (KEK, II[19]), Göttingen, 1968, pp. 523-526.

135. J. WELLHAUSEN, *Das Evangelium Johannis*, Berlin, 1908, pp. 88-90; A. LOISY, *Le quatrième Évangile*, Paris, ²1921, pp. 490-495.

ein, daß das rätselhafte Motiv »Blut und Wasser« im doppelten Schriftbezug Vv. 36f. nicht wiederaufgegriffen sei; denn jene Zitate würden
nur auf V. 33 »Brechen der Füße« sowie auf V. 34a, auf den »Lanzenstich« anspielen. Deshalb müßten die Vv. 36-37 ursprünglich direkt auf
V. 34a gefolgt sein. V. 34b habe der kirchliche Redaktor hinzugefügt,
um auf die spätere kirchliche Praxis der sakramentalen Heilvermittlung
mit »Blut und Wasser« anzuspielen. Die kirchlichen Basissakramente
Taufe und Eucharistie würden so geschickt mit der Kreuzigung verknüpft. Doch wirft eine solche Auslegung schwerwiegende Probleme
auf: In V. 34b wäre – gegen jede frühkirchliche Regel – die Eucharistie
vor der Taufe genannt. Schon 1 Joh 5,6, wo es heißt: »Dieser ist es, der
durch Wasser und Blut gekommen ist, Jesus Christus – nicht im Wasser
allein, sondern im Wasser und Blut«, hätte die Reihenfolge besser
bewahrt. Auch sind nach 6,51-58 nicht »Blut« allein, sondern »Fleisch
und Blut« zusammen Speisen. Der Redaktor müßte – wollte man Bultmann folgen – also hier verkürzt geredet haben. Deshalb legt G. Richter[136] eine andere Deutung vor. Für ihn setzt V. 34b ein deutliches Signal für eine antidoketische Polemik. Indem Blut und Wasser aus der
Seite Jesu geflossen seien, solle sein wirklicher Tod zweifelsfrei festgestellt werden. Richter rekurriert ebenfalls auf 1 Joh 5,6. Er wäre der
eigentliche Schlüssel zur Deutung von 19,34c. Denn er besage, Jesus sei
wirklich wie alle Menschen gestorben. Er habe also nicht – wie einige
Doketen behaupteten – zum Schein bei der Jordantaufe einen Leib ange-
zogen um ihn bei der Kreuzigung wieder aus- und sein wahres göttliches
Wesen anzuziehen. Das Beharren des Autors auf Jesu wahre Leiblich-
keit richte sich also gegen die Annahme, Jesus habe als Gottessohn nur
einen Scheinleib besessen. Doch auch diese Deutung wirft nur weitere
ungeklärte Fragen auf. In 1 Joh 5,6 ist die Aufzählung – wie schon ausgeführt – umgekehrt. Dort signalisiert der gewählte komplexive Aorist[137],
daß »Wasser und Blut« nicht auf zwei unterschiedliche Heilsereignisse,
eben auf Taufe und Abendmahl hinweisen soll, sondern beide sind kom-
plementäre Zeichen[138] von Jesu Heilsbedeutung insgesamt. In 1 Joh 5,6

---

136. G. RICHTER, *Blut und Wasser aus der durchbohrten Seite Jesu (Joh 19,34b)*, in
ID., *Studien zum Johannesevangelium*, Hrsg. J. HAINZ (BU, 13), Regensburg, 1977, pp. 120-
142; vgl. auch U. SCHNELLE, *Antidoketische Christologie im Johannesevangelium. Eine
Untersuchung zur Stellung des vierten Evangeliums in der johanneischen Schule* (FRLANT,
144), Göttingen, 1987, pp. 230.256.

137. F. VOUGA, *Die Johannesbriefe* (HNT, 15/III), Tübingen, 1990, pp. 72f.; H.-J. VENETZ,
»Durch Wasser und Blut gekommen«. Exegetische Überlegungen zu 1 Joh 5,6, in FS E.
SCHWEIZER, Göttingen, 1983, pp. 345-361, p. 347.

138. Vgl. W. THÜSING, *Die Erhöhung und Verherrlichung Jesu im Johannesevangelium* (NTAbh, 21), Münster, 1960, p. 170

steht zudem das Kommen Jesu im Mittelpunkt, hier aber nur dessen
Tod. Einen dritten Lösungsvorschlag unterbreiten darum R. Schnackenburg[139] und J. Becker. Sie meinen, der Perikope gehe es nur um die Darstellung des ganz natürlichen Todes Jesu. Sein Tod sei infolge eines Lan-
zenstichs eingetreten. Dieser sollte nur bestätigen, was der Soldat erfahren
wollte, ob nämlich Jesus wirklich tot sei, und sich so ein Beinbrechen
bei ihm erübrige. Doch auch diese, für moderne, medizinisch gebildete
Menschen weitaus annehmbarere Aussage läßt fragen: Warum muß eigentlich auf den Tod Jesu noch ausdrücklich hingewiesen werden? Hat die
Auskunft 19,30 noch nicht ausgereicht? Besteht wirklich nur ein schrift-
gelehrtes bzw. apologetisches Interesse zu zeigen, daß alles nach einem
heilsgeschichtlichen Fahrplan abgewickelt oder mit antidoketischer Tendenz berichtet wurde? Es geht dem Verfasser offensichtlich gar nicht so
sehr um den Nachweis der Wirklichkeit des Todes Jesu, sondern vielmehr um die Bedeutung desselben. Wenn aber das, was in den Vv. 31-37
ausgeführt wird, keinen eindeutigen Anhalt in der medizinisch vermes-
senen Thanatologie hat, dann ist nach der symbolischen Bedeutung des
Geschehens zu fragen. Dazu hat der Leser auch jede Berechtigung, weil
ihm noch einige Fragen unbeantwortet geblieben sind. In 8,28 hatte der
Autor angedeutet, daß »die Juden«, wenn sie Jesus »erhöht« hätten
(vgl. 3,14), erkennen würden, daß jener der Sohn Gottes ist. Nun hat der
Evangelist gegen die synoptische Tradition »die Juden« vor Josef von
Arimathäa aktiv werden lassen, indem sie nun selbst um die Entfernung
der Gekreuzigten vor dem Rüsttage »jenes«[140] großen Sabbats bitten.
Dazu müssen diese aber erst gestorben sein. Deshalb folgt konsequent
die Aktion des crurifragii, um dadurch das Siechtum der Erniedrigten zu
verkürzen. Da Jesus aber bereits gestorben ist, werden ihm die Beinkno-
chen nicht zerschlagen. Diese Aussage muß der Autor direkt angestrebt
haben, damit er sinnenfällig machen konnte: Jesus ist das wahre, passa-
taugliche Lamm, dem ja nach den Vorschriften der Tora kein Knochen
je gebrochen sein durfte (Ex 12,46; Num 9,12). Die sonst nicht überlieferte Übung eines Hinrichtungskommandos, den Tod eines Gekreuzigten
mit einem Lanzenstich zu verifizieren, davon zu berichten, die Idee kam

---

139. SCHNACKENBURG (Anm. 1) III, 1975, pp. 333-345; J. BECKER, *Das Evangelium des Johannes* (ÖTK, 4/1.2), Gütersloh/Würzburg, 1979-1981, II, p. 599; neuerdings wiederholt von C.R. KOESTER, *Symbolism in the Fourth Gospel – Meaning, Mystery, Com-
munity*, Minneapolis, 1995, p. 181.

140. Der betonte Hinweis auf »*jenen* Sabbat« nimmt eine ähnliche Formulierung in
11,51 wieder auf, wo vom Hohenpriester »jenes Jahres« gesprochen worden war. Beide
Akzente wollen keineswegs die historische Exaktheit bzw. eine damals gerade üblich
gewordene einjährige Amtsführung des Hohenpriesters, sondern vielmehr die soteriologische Bedeutung der erzählten Ereignisse unterstreichen.

dem Schreiber wohl zuerst, als er 7,38f. und 12,32 (vgl. 18,32) niederschrieb:»Wie die Schrift sagt: Aus seinem Leib werden Ströme lebendigen Wassers fließen« und »wenn ich von der Erde erhöht sein werde, dann werde ich alle zu mir ziehen«. Das kann nur heißen, wenn Jesus tot ist, werden alle ihren Durst stillen können. Die Aussage wiederum weist zurück auf 4,10.14 (vgl. 6,35), wo Jesus sich als die Gabe Gottes bezeichnet, die der Samariterin ihren Durst für immer stillen könne, wenn sie nur glaube. Das Motiv schwang bekanntlich auch in 7,37 mit, wo man lesen konnte:»Dürstet da einer, er komme zu mir! Und trinken soll, wer glaubt!« Aber Jesus kann erst die Glaubensgeschichte mit der Geistgabe eröffnen, wenn er seinen Auftrag gehorsam erfüllt hat; denn in 7,39, dem entscheidenden Kommentarwort, hatte der Evangelist ausgeführt: »Das aber sprach er über den Geist, den die an ihn Glaubenden empfangen sollten. Denn noch war Geist nicht da, weil Jesus noch nicht verherrlicht (d.h. erhöht) war«. Die Geistgabe aber wird erst 20,22 erzählt. Um diesen Aspekt zu verdeutlichen, käme die Crurifragiumsszene verfrüht[141]. Deshalb wird hier zunächst die Aussage von 8,28 verdeutlicht. Woran sollten »die Juden« (19,31) nämlich erkennen, daß Jesus tatsächlich der Sohn Gottes ist? Auf diese offenen Frage gibt der Autor hier eine angemessene Antwort. Die »Erhöhung« Jesu fand am Rüsttag des Passafestes statt. Die Passachronologie, auf die seit 11,55[142] beständig hingewiesen wurde, die auffällige Erwähnung des Zeitpunkts der sechsten Stunde 19,14, an dem die Passalämmer geschlachtet wurden, gerade im Zusammenhang mit der dramatischen Zuspitzung des Pilatusprozesses, wo der Hohepriester seine Loyalität gegenüber dem Tempel aufkündigt, weiterhin der markante Verweis auf den Ysopstengel[143] 19,29, sowie letztendlich das unterbliebene crurifragium, alle diese Hinweise sollen gebündelt verdeutlichen, daß Jesus wirklich als leidender Gerechter[144] die Funktion

141. Deshalb spricht BROWN (Anm. 118), II, p. 951, auch von einer Prolepse.
142. So schon FRANKE (Anm. 2), pp. 24.85.307; u.z. 12,1; 13,1.30; 18,28; 19,14.31.
143. So mit Recht der Verweis von KOESTER (Anm. 139), p. 197, auf Ex 12,27; – Wichtig ist auch der Hinweis in dem Artikel אזוב der von S.J. ZEVIN (ed.), *Encyclopedia Talmudica. A Digest of Halachic Literature and Jewish Law from the Tannaitic Period to the Present Day Alphabetically Arranged*, 3 vol., Jerusalem 1969-1978, I, pp. 523-526, p. 523:»The Torah orders the use of hyssop in four instances:« Ex 12,22; Lev 14,4; Num 19,6.18 (bTSuk 37a). Alle vier Fälle sind kultisch orientiert; Hyssop ist notwendig beim Bestreichen der Türpfosten (Ex 12), beim Ritus zur Reinigung von Aussätzigen, Reinigungswasserherstellung und zur Beseitigung von Leichenunreinheit.
144. Vgl. für den alttestamentlichen Aspekt der Stellvertretung die Ausführungen von B. JANOWSKI, '*Er trug unsere Sünden'. Jesaja 53 und die Dramatik der Stellvertretung*, in *ZTK* 90 (1993) 1-24; M.E. ist Jesus aufgrund seines Menschseins für den Autor mit einem leidenden Gerechten, aber aufgrund seiner soteriologischen Funktion mit dem Passalamm vergleichbar. Vgl. auch J.G. VAN DER WATT, »*Daar is de Lam van God...*« *Plaasvervangende offertradissies in die Johannesevangelie*, in *Skrif en Kerk* 16 (1995) 142-158.

des Passalamms Gottes übernommen hat, das die Sünde der Welt trägt[145] (1,29). Wenn nun unmittelbar mit dem Lanzenstich »Blut und Wasser« aus dessen Innerem[146] geflossen ist, müssen diese beiden Elemente konsequenterweise zuerst mit dem Opferkult des Tempels verglichen werden, u. z. kontextgemäß besonders mit dessen sühnenden, d. h. vor allem auch mit dessen soteriologischen Funktion (vgl Ex 12,6 mit Ez 16,6; Mek zu Ex 12,6). Blut war generell das zentrale kultische Sühnemittel (vgl. Lev 17,11-14), da es als Symbol des Lebens galt, das Gott allein zu geben fähig ist[147]. Zugleich ist das Blut des Passalammes in der rabbinischen Tradition als »Leben aus dem Blut« das Zeichen für die Befreiung aus Ägypten[148]. Dieses symbolische Element für den Entfremdung von Gott beseitigenden Tod Jesu mußte zuerst erwähnt werden, weil nicht nur in Ez 46 der Kultdienst zuerst genannt wurde, bevor in Ez 47 von der göttlichen Reaktion darauf in Gestalt von einer zeichenhaften Wüstenbewässerung sowie Umwandlung des Toten Meeres in einen Süßwassersee als symbolisches Geschehen für die sich anschließende kosmische Heilspende gesprochen werden konnte, sondern auch noch aus einem anderen Grund, da ausdrücklich komplementär von austretendem Blut und Wasser aus der Seite Jesu geredet wird. Damit soll auf fließendes Wasser, also auf »lebendiges« Wasser im Unterschied zu kultischem Reinigungswasser (vgl. 2,6), hingewiesen werden, um ein solch naheliegendes Mißverständnis auszuschließen. Es geht dem Autor vielmehr um die symbolische Inkraftsetzung[149] dessen, was Jesus in 4,10.14f.; 6,35.51-58; 7,37 für die Stunde seiner Erhöhung angekündigt hatte. Deshalb greifen auch die beiden, die Perikope beschließenden Schriftzitate in Vv. 36f. diesen doppelten Gesichtspunkt noch einmal auf: Jesus ist schriftgemäß gleichermaßen das wahre Passalamm wie auch das in 3,14 angesagte Rettungszeichen, auf daß man schauen mußte, um gerettet zu werden. Eine solche symbolische Aufgipfelung der Ausführungen durfte nicht ohne einen in der urchristlichen Tradition festverankerten Zeugen sein, auf den sich die christliche Leserschaft glaubend verlassen konnte. Deshalb wird, obwohl fest in den Erzählzusammenhang integriert, der

---

145. Aus meiner Sicht wird auch die Tat der jüdischen Leitungseliten, Jesus hinrichten zu lassen, von diesem anschließend gesühnt.

146. Vgl. F.G. UNTERGASSMAIR, Art. κοιλία, in *EWNT* II (1981) 744-745, p. 745, der auf die Kirchenväterexegese verweist, in der konstant 7,38 »Inneres« mit »Herz« gleichgesetzt, d.h. als Prolepse auf 19,34 gedeutet werde.

147. Vgl. MAIER (Anm. 40), p. 233, und GERSTENBERGER (Anm. 77), pp. 214.220.

148. Vgl. ShemR 17,3; PesR 86b; PRE 29.

149. So auch R.E. BROWN, *The Death of the Messiah – From Gethsemane to the Grave: A Commentary on the Passion Narratives in the Four Gospels* (AB.RL), New York, 1994, II, pp. 1173-1188, p. 1177.

V. 35 um eine umfassende Zeugenaussage ganz im Sinne der Wir-Gruppe erweitert. Denn vorher (V. 32) war schon von einer Anzahl Soldaten die Rede, die den Auftrag »der Juden«, die Gekreuzigten vor »jenem großen Sabbat« zu entfernen, ausführen sollten. Dabei ist besonders auf jenen Soldaten zu achten, der den Lanzenstich ausführte, um sicher zu gehen, daß Jesus wirklich schon tot sei. Eine solche Aktion führt zumeist der durch, der den Auftrag erhalten hatte, das Sterben der Gekreuzigten zu beschleunigen: ein Offizier. Wenn man die Kenntnis der Synoptiker beim Autor wie bei seiner christlichen Leserschaft – wie ich sie annehme – voraussetzt, dann kann man den anonymen Zeugen sogleich identifizieren: Es ist der Centurion[150], von dem Markus den Ausspruch überliefert: »Wahrlich dieser war der Sohn Gottes« (Mk 15,39). Mit diesem Zeugnis stimmen nun wirklich alle vom Autor benannten Zeugen, der Täufer 1,34, der Vater Jesu 5,36ff., der hiesige Centurion und umfassend die Wir-Gruppe 1,14-18, überein. In dem letzten Stück der Passionsgeschichte werden also alle im Evangelium im Ansatz formulierten und weitergesponnenen »roten Fäden« der Tempelmetaphorik zu einer soteriologischen Antwort gebündelt: Jesus ist als Sohn Gottes dessen Passalamm, daß die Sünde der Welt unter Einschluß »der Juden« getragen und sie so erneut befreit (16,33) hat.

IV

Die wesentlichen Aspekte der Tempelmetaphorik[151] im Johannesevangelium zu untersuchen, war ein aufschlußreiches Unterfangen. Es konnte an einem zentralen Beispiel demonstrieren, wie biblische Vorstellungen, Motive und Theologumena vom Autor adaptiert werden, um eines seiner zentralen Anliegen, die soteriologische Bedeutung des Jesusgeschehens zu illuminieren, argumentativ zu erhärten. Dies geschieht auf literarisch brilliante und theologisch umfassende Weise. Der Leser ist ununterbrochen gefordert, seine Schriftkenntnisse und tempeltheologischen Assoziationen zu aktivieren, um der Argumentation des Autors folgen und so auf der Höhe seiner Deutung des Jesusgeschehens bleiben zu können. Deshalb werden von ihm fortlaufend gerade die Aspekte des Jerusalemer

150. Zum selben Befund kommt H. THYEN, *Noch einmal: Johannes 21 und »der Jünger, den Jesus liebte«*, in FS L. HARTMAN, Oslo, 1995, pp. 147-189, pp. 177f..
151. Wegen des Umfanges der Thematik konnten hier zwei weitere Bereiche noch nicht vorgestellt werden, die aber unbedingt zum Bereich der jüdischen Tempelvorstellung hinzugehören: das sogenannte hohepriesterliche Gebet Joh 17 und vor allem die deuteronomische Konzeption vom »Einwohnen des Namens«, die ebenfalls das angestrebte Argumentationsziel hätten weiter illuminieren können.

Tempels für die Metapher aktiviert, welche dessen heilende und versöhnende Funktion für die Gesellschaft auf ausdifferenzierende Weise zu akzentuieren vermögen. Fast schon in Umkehrung von 1 Chr 17,14, wo im Unterschied zu dessen Vorlage 2 Sam 7,16 aus der Wohnstatt und dem Königtum Davids »Haus und Königreich Gottes« wird, wird nun die Heilswende für den Leser mit dem Jesus-Tempel verknüpft. Der in Jesus erneuerte Tempel sichert die Kommunikation zwischen Himmel und Erde und garantiert so weiterhin die wohlwollende Nähe Gottes.

Zu diesem interpretativen Verfahren paßt die moderne literaturwissenschaftliche Theorie von der »Intertextualität« besser als die der Typologie. Es sei denn, man versteht letztere als eine historisierende Metapher, die nun nicht mehr eine Leerstelle im einzelsprachigen Lexikon schließt, sondern einen Deutenotstand für ein geschichtliches Ereignis und dessen fortdauernde Bedeutung und pneumatische Wirksamkeit behebt. Die Schrift als Bildspender ist es letztlich, die der theologischen Überzeugung und der Argumentation des Evangelisten Gewicht und Plausibilität, d.h. Autorität bei seiner Leserschaft verleiht. Dies aber formulierte er selbst viel treffender schon in Joh 2,22 (vgl. 17,8), indem er dort die Schrift mit Jesu Wort in engste und gleichwertige Beziehung setzt: »*Sie glaubten der Schrift und dem Wort Jesu*«.

Gesamthochschule Essen   Ulrich BUSSE
Fachbereich 1
D-45117 Essen

OFFERED PAPERS

INTERTEXTUALITÄT
EIN BEISPIEL FÜR SINN UND UNSINN 'NEUER' METHODEN

I. EINLEITUNG

1. Vor einem Jahrzehnt wäre kaum jemand auf den Gedanken gekommen, bei der Frage nach der Verwendung der Schriften des Alten
Testaments im Neuen Testament von »Intertextualität« zu sprechen.
Doch heute taucht das Wort »Intertextualität« in diesem Zusammenhang
zu Recht auf. Denn seit 1987 gibt es an der Theologischen Fakultät der
Universität Tilburg in den Niederlanden das Forschungsprogramm »Intertextualität und Bibel«: Ganz bewußt wurde nach Wegen gesucht, »um
Theorien der Intertextualität für die Exegese von Bibeltexten zu opera-
tionalisieren«[1], und man hat sich dabei, wie die bisherigen Veröffentli-
chungen zeigen, vor allem mit alttestamentlichen Zitaten und Anspielungen
im lukanischen Doppelwerk beschäftigt[2]. Außerdem erschien 1989 Hays'
Buch *Echoes of Scripture in the Letters of Paul*, dessen Arbeitshypo-
these lautet, »that certain approaches to intertextuality that have developed
within literary criticism prove illuminating when applied to Paul's letters«;
außerdem ist er davon überzeugt, »that the literary critic's 'hearing aid'
can disclose important elements of Paul's thought that have been left un-
explored by other critical methods«[3]. Sowohl die an dem niederländischen

---

1. So formuliert J.Ch. BASTIAENS es im Vorwort seiner im Rahmen dieses Forschungs-
programms verfaßten Dissertation: *Interpretaties van Jesaja 53. Een intertextueel onder-
zoek naar de lijdende Knecht in Jes 53 (MT/LXX) en in Lk 22:14-38, Hand 3:12-26,
Hand 4:23-31 en Hand 8:26-40* (TFT-Studies, 22), Tilburg, University Press, 1993, S.V
(von mir übersetzt). Hinzuweisen ist besonders auf W. WEREN, *Intertextualiteit en bijbel*,
Kampen, J.H. Kok, 1993: Neben dem programmatischen Aufsatz, der den Titel des Buches
geliefert hat (9-34), enthält dieses sieben bereits früher veröffentlichte intertextuelle
Arbeiten.
2. BASTIAENS (389 Anm. 91) nennt neben einem Aufsatz von W. WEREN *(Psalm 2
in Luke-Acts: An Intertextual Study,* in S. DRAISMA [ed.], *Intertextuality in Biblical
Writings. Essays in honour of Bas van Iersel,* Kampen, Kok, 1989, 189-203; auf
Holländisch in dem in Anm. 1 genannten Buch, 157-180) vier Aufsätze von H. VAN
DE SANDT: *The Fate of the Gentiles in Joel and Acts 2,* in *ETL* 66 (1990) 56-77; *Why
is Amos 5,25-27 Quoted in Acts 7,42f.?* in *ZNW* 82 (1991) 67-87; *An Explanation of
Acts 15,6-21 in the Light of Deuteronomy 4,29-35,* in *JSNT* 46 (1992) 73-97; *Didache
3,1-6: A Transformation of an Existing Jewish Hortatory Pattern,* in *JSJ* 23 (1992)
21-41.
3. R.B. HAYS, *Echoes of Scripture in the Letters of Paul,* New Haven, London, Yale
University Press, 1989, 15.XII.

Forschungsprogramm Beteiligten als auch Hays verstehen also »Intertextualität« als eine neue exegetische Methode, und sie setzen diese neue Methode ein im Rahmen der alten Frage nach der Verwendung der Schriften des Alten Testaments im Neuen Testament[4].

4. Einen knappen Forschungsüberblick vom 2.-20. Jhdt. bietet E.E. ELLIS, *The Old Testament in Early Christianity. Canon and Interpretation in the Light of Modern Research*, Tübingen, Mohr, 1991: Ch.II »Old Testament Quotations in the New: A Brief History of the Research«, 51-74.

Anzumerken ist freilich, daß Ellis wie manch anderer auch nicht ausreichend beachtet, wie sehr seit je bei der Frage nach den atl. Zitaten im NT Apologetik und/oder Polemik eine Rolle spielen. So hatte der atl. Schriftbeweis »von seinen Anfängen her vorzugsweise seinen Platz in den Auseinandersetzungen des Christentums mit dem Judentum« (A. VON UNGERN-STERNBERG, *Der traditionelle alttestamentliche Schriftbeweis »de Christo« und »de evangelio« in der alten Kirche bis zur Zeit Eusebs*, Halle, Max Niemeyer, 1913, 300). Christen, wie z.b. schon Justin, hielten den Juden vor, die Weissagungen der Schrift hätten sich in dem Messias Jesus erfüllt und die Christen seien das wahre Israel; die Juden, wie z.B. Trypho und seine Freunde, wandten ein, die Christen hätten die Schriftzitate willkürlich ausgewählt (Justin, Dial. 27), ihre Exegese sei »gekünstelt« (Justin, Dial. 79) und widerspreche ihrem ursprünglichen Sinn: So sei in Jes 7,14 nicht von einer »Jungfrau« die Rede, sondern von einer »jungen Frau«, und es werde dort die Geburt des Hiskia geweissagt, nicht aber die Geburt Jesu (Justin, Dial. 67). Diese Einwände beeindruckten Justin nicht; er nahm einen Doppelsinn der Schrift an und interpretierte die Zitate unbekümmert typologisch-allegorisch. Mehr als eineinhalb Jahrtausend lang verfuhren Generationen von Christen ähnlich wie Justin. Das änderte sich erst im 17. + 18. Jhdt., als die historisch-kritische Methode aufkam und die Deisten (Anthony Collins, Hermann Samuel Reimarus) den Weissagungsbeweis unter Rückgriff auf die Argumente der Juden destruierten (siehe P. STEMMER, *Weissagung und Kritik. Eine Studie zur Hermeneutik bei Hermann Samuel Reimarus*, Göttingen, Vandenhoeck & Ruprecht, 1983: »I. Kritische Hermeneutik und kirchliche Lehre im Widerstreit. W. Whiston und A. Collins«, 12-32; »VI. Der Primat der kritischen Hermeneutik und die Destruktion der christlichen Religion. H.S. Reimarus' 'Apologie'«, 147-171). Nicht umsonst liest man im 19. Jhdt. bei A. THOLUCK, *Das Alte Testament im Neuen Testament. Ueber die Citate des Alten Testaments im Neuen Testament*, Vierte vermehrte Auflage, Gotha, Friedrich Andreas Perthes, 1854 gleich als dritten Satz des »§.1. Geschichtliche Einleitung« die folgenden Worte: »So viel sieht jeder ein – sagt dann am Ende des vorigen Jahrh. der Fragmentist (vom Zweck Jesu und seiner Jünger [Lessing hatte dieses Fragment des Reimarus 1778 anonym veröffentlicht]...) – daß, will man den Satz: *dieser Spruch* [des AT] *redet von Jesu von Nazareth*, nicht aus dem N.T. auf guten Glauben voraussetzen, kein einziger Spruch etwas beweise, sondern daß sie vielmehr natürlicherweise von ganz anderen Personen, Zeiten und Begebenheiten reden« (1). Jedoch, so stellt Tholuck dann zufrieden am Ende des §1 fest, indem er auf die »Betrachtungsweise« der »überwiegende(n) Mehrzahl der Exegeten in den letzten zwanzig Jahren« blickt: »Einerseits wird zugestanden, daß die angeführten alttest. Aussprüche im Zusammenhange eine andere historische Beziehung haben, andererseits wird bestritten, daß gegen die Anführungen im N.T. der Vorwurf bodenloser Willkühr erhoben werden könne. Es wird auf den organischen Parallelismus der alt- und neutestamentlichen Oekonomie hingewiesen, vermöge dessen auch den einzelnen Beziehungen auf alttestamentliche Stellen eine gewisse Wahrheit zukomme.... die einzelne Beziehung auf das A.T. und zufällig scheinende Parallele (wurzelt) in dem tieferen Boden des einheitlichen Princips beider Testamente« (8-9). Heute, etwa anderthalb Jahrhunderte später, wird kaum noch jemand bei der Frage nach den atl. Zitaten im NT von einem »organischen Parallelismus« und dem »einheitlichen Princip der beiden Testamente« reden wollen.

2. Über Sinn und Unsinn einer neuen Methode entscheiden auch in der Exegese die konkreten Ergebnisse, die mit dieser neuen Methode erzielt worden sind[5], nicht jedoch theoretische Reflexionen. Deshalb äußere ich mich nur kurz über Intertextualität im allgemeinen und gehe dann auf die Form und die konkreten Ergebnisse der intertextuellen Arbeit in dem niederländischen Forschungsprogramm »Intertextualität und Bibel« ein. Hays' Buch lasse ich beiseite, weil sich das diesjährige Colloquium Biblicum Lovaniense mit den Evangelien beschäftigt und nicht mit Paulus[6].

3. »Je mehr ein Begriff kursiert, desto schillernder wird meist sein Inhalt. Dies gilt in besonderer Weise für den Begriff der Intertextualität« – mit diesen Worten leiteten 1985 Broich und Pfister den Sammelband *Intertextualität* ein und führten den Begriff der Intertextualität auf Julia Kristeva zurück: Sie habe ihn am Ende der 60er Jahre geprägt, »um das, was sich *zwischen* Texten abspielt, d.h. den Bezug von Texten auf andere Texte zu umschreiben»[7]. Broich und Pfister wenden sich dann energisch gegen einen »poststrukturalistische(n) Intertextualitätsbegriff«, denn der verdanke »seine revolutionären Implikationen ja gerade seiner undifferenzierten Universalität«, und sie plädieren für einen »enger gefaßte(n) Begriff, der es ermöglicht, Intertextualität von Nicht-Intertextualität zu unterscheiden und historisch und typologisch unterschiedliche Formen

---

5. An diesem Punkt sehe ich keinen Unterschied zwischen der Arbeitsweise der Naturwissenschaften und dem Vorgehen der wissenschaftlichen Exegese des Alten und Neuen Testaments. Ich setze freilich voraus, daß diese Exegese den biblischen Texten nur das entnehmen will, was sie sagen, und daß sie nicht die eigenen Gedanken in sie hineinliest oder aus ihnen heraushört. Deshalb scheint es mir bedenklich, wenn HAYS (s. Anm. 3) ausdrücklich betont, Exegese sei »a modest imaginative craft, not an exact science«, und es gebe nur »certain rules of thumb«, um »intertextual echoes« in den Paulusbriefen zu identifizieren (29).

6. Außerdem gibt es bereits eine intensive Diskussion über HAYS' Buch. Siehe H. HÜBNER, *Intertextualität – die hermeneutische Strategie des Paulus. Zu einem neuen Versuch der theologischen Rezeption des Alten Testaments im Neuen*, in *TLZ* 116 (1991) 881-897, und in dem Sammelband W.S. GREEN, J.A. SANDERS (eds.), *Paul and the Scriptures of Israel* (JSNT SS., 83), Sheffield, Academic Press, 1993 die Beiträge von C.A. EVANS, *Listening for Echoes of Interpreted Scriptures* (47-51), J.A. SANDERS, *Paul and Theological History* (52-57), W.S. GREEN, *Doing the Text's Work for It: Richard Hays on Paul's Use of Scripture* (58-63) und J.C. BEKER, *Echoes and Intertextuality: On the Role of Scripture in Paul's Theology* (64-69).

Im übrigen hat G.R. O'DAY, *Jeremiah 9:22-23 and 1 Corinthians 1:26-31. A Study in Intertextuality*, in *JBL* 109 (1990) 259-267 darauf hingewiesen, daß »most of the discussion of intertextuality in literary criticism derives from T.S. Eliot's seminal essay 'Tradition and the Individual Talent' [1919]« (259 Anm. 1), und daß HAYS der Untersuchung von J. HOLLANDER, *The Figure of an Echo. A Mode of Allusion in Milton and After*, Berkeley, University of California Press, 1981 besonders viel verdankt (260 Anm. 11).

7. U. BROICH, M. PFISTER (eds.), *Intertextualität. Formen, Funktionen, anglistische Fallstudien*, Tübingen, Max Niemeyer, 1985, IX.

der Intertextualität voneinander abzuheben«[8]. In dem niederländischen Forschungsprogramm »Intertextualität und Bibel« spielt Broich/Pfisters Sicht eine große Rolle.

II. DIE FORM UND DIE KONKRETEN ERGEBNISSE DER INTERTEXTUELLEN ARBEIT DES NIEDERLÄNDISCHEN FORSCHUNGSPROGRAMMS

1. Weren, der geistige Vater dieses Unternehmens[9], formuliert in seinem Aufsatz über Ps 2 im lukanischen Doppelwerk folgendes Programm[10]: Grundlegend sei die Hypothese, »daß die expliziten Zitate als pars pro toto funktionieren«; denn, und hier zitiert er Pfister: »Mit dem pointiert ausgewählten Detail wird der Gesamtkontext abgerufen, dem es entstammt, mit dem knappen Zitat wird der ganze Prätext in die neue Sinnkonstitution einbezogen«[11]. Die Analyse soll sich dann auf drei Fragen konzentrieren: »a) Was ist der Platz und die Funktion der zitierten Elemente in ihrem ursprünglichen literarischen Kontext? b) Was ist der Platz und die Funktion der zitierten Elemente in ihrem neuen literarischen Kontext im lukanischen Doppelwerk? c) Welcher Zusammenhang besteht zwischen den verschiedenen Verweisen auf Ps 2 im lukanischen Doppelwerk?« Wenn Weren im Zusammenhang der Analyse von »zitierten Elementen« und »Verweisen« spricht, so zeigt er damit an, daß für ihn zwischen »explizitem Zitat« und »Anspielung« kein Unterschied besteht.

Bastiaens übernimmt Werens Programm in seiner Dissertation. Ihr etwas merkwürdiger Titel und Untertitel sind von diesem Hintergrund her zu sehen: »Interpretationen von Jesaja 53. Eine intertextuelle Untersuchung des leidenden Gottesknechtes in Jes 53 (MT/LXX) und in Lk 22:14-38, Apg 3:12-26, Apg 4,23-31 und in Apg 8,36-40«[12]. Es geht eben nicht allein darum, welche Zitate und Anspielungen auf Jes 53 im lukanischen Doppelwerk zu finden sind und welche Rolle sie in ihm spielen – diese

---

8. BROICH, PFISTER (s. Anm. 7), X.

9. Siehe BASTIAENS (Anm. 1), 389 Anm. 91.

10. WEREN, *Psalm 2 in Luke-Acts* (s. Anm. 2), 190: »My hypothesis is that the explicit quotations function as a *pars pro toto*:… (Pfisterzitat [s. Anm. 12]). My analysis is concentrated around three questions: a) What is the place and function of the cited elements in their original literary context? b) What is the place and function of the cited elements in their new literary context in Luke-Acts? c) What coherence is there between the various references to Ps 2 in Luke-Acts?«

11. M. PFISTER, *Konzepte der Intertextualität*, in BROICH, PFISTER (eds.), *Intertextualität* (s. Anm. 7), 1-30, 29.

12. S. Anm. 1.

Fragen behandelt Bastiaens in den Kapiteln IV-VI[13] –, sondern auch darum, wie der Gottesknecht in Jes 53 (MT), in Dan 11-12, SapSal 1-6 und in Jes 53 (LXX) interpretiert wird – dieser Frage gelten die Kapitel II+III[14] –, kurz, um den Text und Kontext von Jes 53 im Alten Testament müht Bastiaens sich genausoviel wie um die Zitate und Anspielungen auf Jes 53 im lukanischen Doppelwerk. Zentral ist auch für ihn die Frage: »Spielt der Kontext von MT/LXX Jes 53 eine aktive Rolle bei der Interpretation der entsprechenden Zitate oder Anspielungen in den Texten des lukanischen Doppelwerks? oder: In welchem Maße wirkt der ursprüngliche Kontext bei der Bedeutung des Zitats/der Anspielung im neuen Kontext mit?«[15] Nicht ganz konsequent ist es, wenn Bastiaens wenig später hervorhebt, daß sich seine »Aufmerksamkeit primär auf die Frage richtet, welche neuen Bedeutungen dadurch geschaffen werden, daß der eine Text den anderen in sich aufnimmt«[16]. Denn bei der ersten Frage liegt der Akzent eindeutig auf dem alten Kontext, bei der zweiten Frage ebenso eindeutig auf dem neuen Kontext. Einen Unterschied zwischen »explizitem Zitat« und »Anspielung« macht Bastiaens übrigens genausowenig wie Weren.

2. Von Werens und Bastiaens' konkreten Ergebnissen greife ich je ein Beispiel heraus, an dem die Eigenart ihrer Arbeitsweise besonders gut zu erkennen ist.

a) Weren hält zu dem Zitat von Ps 2,1-2 in Apg 4,25-26 fest, daß dessen Interpretation in Apg 4,27-28 »die ursprüngliche Bedeutung der Worte des Psalms an einer Reihe von Punkten entscheidend veränderte«: Ps 2 spreche von dem Widerstand fremder Völker und Herrscher gegen den Zionskönig, in Apg 4,27 komme der Widerstand gegen Gottes Messias auch von Israel selbst und mit Herodes und Pilatus würden Einzelpersonen erwähnt; in Ps 2 planten die Gegner, sich von Gott und seinem Gesalbten zu befreien, in Apg sei der Plan bereits ausgeführt, und zwar nur gegen Jesus, Gott aber erscheine in Apg 4,28 als der, der all dies vorherbeschlossen hat[17]. Außerdem erwähnt Weren Dibelius' Meinung, daß »die Lektüre von Ps 2,1f. die Überzeugung vom Zusammengehen der beiden

---

13. »Hoofdstuk IV: De interpretatie van MT/LXX Jes 53 in Lk 22:14-38 en Hand 8:26-40« (195-279); »Hoofdstuk V: De interpretatie van MT/LXX Jes 53 in Hand 3:12-26 en Hand 4,23-31« (281-353); »Hoofdstuk VI: »Expliciete en impliciete ontleningen aan MT/LXX Jes 53: een onderlinge vergelijking« (355-381).

14. »Hoofdstuk II: De interpretatie van de knecht in MT Jes 53« (29-93); »Hoofdstuk III: De interpretatie van de knecht in Dan 11-12, WijsSal 1-6 en in LXX Jes 53« (95-194).

15. BASTIAENS (s. Anm. 1), 25.

16. BASTIAENS, (s. Anm. 1), 27.

17. WEREN, *Psalm 2 in Luke-Acts* (s. Anm. 2), 197-198.

Potentaten im Prozeß Jesu produziert« hätte[18], und daß die Beteiligung des Herodes am Prozeß gegen Jesus nicht historisch sei, sondern auf Ps 2 basiere. Weren wirft Dibelius vor, er diskutiere Ps 2 nur, um die Koalition zwischen Herodes und Pilatus zu erklären, und notiere nicht die zahlreichen anderen impliziten Hinweise auf Ps 2 im lukanischen Passionsbericht (in Lk 22,66-71; 23,1-25.32-42). Zu ihnen stellt Weren selbst dann jedoch auch nur fest: »Häufig sind die ursprünglichen Bedeutungen und Beziehungen in Ps 2 völlig umgekehrt«[19].

Bemerkenswerterweise interessiert Weren sich nicht im geringsten für die in der Forschung längst festgestellten Spannungen zwischen Apg 4,25-27 und dem lukanischen Passionsbericht und für die traditionsgeschichtliche Frage, die sich daraus ergibt. In Apg 4 betätigen sich Herodes und Pilatus als 'Rädelsführer' gegen Jesus, im lukanischen Passionsbericht bezeugen sie seine Unschuld; in Apg 4 sind auch die Heiden an der Tötung Jesu beteiligt, im lukanischen Passionsbericht sind es nur die Jerusalemer Juden. Diese Differenzen machen es wahrscheinlich, daß Apg 4,25-27 vorlukanische Tradition enthält[20].

b) Bastiaens sagt bei dem Zitat von Jes 53,7-8 in Apg 8,32-33 zum oft notierten Fehlen von Jes 53,8d (»wegen der Freveltaten meines Volkes wurde er zum Tode geführt«) das folgende: »Eines der wesentlichen Charakteristika des Gottesknechtes, nämlich, daß er die Sünden der anderen trage, komm(e) in Apg 8,26-40 nicht vor, weil es überhaupt nicht um die Sünde des Eunuchen geh(e)…, sondern um… (seine) Inkompetenz (als Eunuch)…: Er… (sei) inkompetent, Jes 53 zu verstehen, und inkompetent, als ein vollwertiges Mitglied in die Heilsgemeinschaft aufgenommen zu werden. Das erste… (könne) Philippus jetzt verändern, das zweite… (werde) möglich, weil die 'Nachkommenschaft' Jesu aus einer neuen Heilsgemeinschaft besteht, in die auch der Eunuch als vollwertiges Mitglied aufgenommen werden kann. Jesu Tod… (habe) diese neue Heilsgemeinschaft möglich gemacht und die Hindernisse beseitigt, die der Taufe des Eunuchen im Wege standen«[21].

Wenn ich Bastiaens richtig verstanden habe, dann beruht seine ganze Interpretation auf der nirgends von ihm ausgeführten Annahme, in Apg 8,26-40 werde verdeutlicht, daß Dtn 23,1 (»Kein irgendwie Entmannter

---

18. M. Dibelius, *Herodes und Pilatus*, in *ZNW* 16 (1915), 113-126, 125, zitiert von Weren, *Psalm 2 in Luke-Acts* (s. Anm. 2), 200, (Dibelius' Aufsatz ist nachgedruckt in M. Dibelius, *Botschaft und Geschichte*. Erster Band, Tübingen, Mohr, 1953, 278-292).

19. Weren, *Psalm 2 in Luke-Acts* (s. Anm. 2), 201.

20. Siehe M. Rese, *Die Aussagen über Jesu Tod und Auferstehung in der Apostelgeschichte – Ältestes Kerygma oder lukanische Theologumena?* in *NTS* 30 (1984) 335-353, 351 Anm. 41.

21. Bastiaens (s. Anm. 1), 357, vgl. 268.

darf in die Gemeinde des Herren eintreten.«) für die christliche Gemeinde nicht mehr gilt, weil mit dem Erscheinen des Messias Jes 56,4-5 erfüllt sei (»Denn so spricht der Herr: Den Verschnittenen (Eunuchen), die meine Sabbate halten und tun, was mir wohlgefällt, und an meinem Bund festhalten, ihnen will ich in meinem Haus und in meinen Mauern Denkmal und Namen geben...«)[22]. Wie dem auch sei, mit solchen und auch anderen an den Text herangetragenen Spekulationen ist in keiner Weise erklärt, warum Jes 53,8d in Apg 8,33 nicht mitzitiert wird, und die Deutung dieses Sachverhalts mit dem Hinweis auf des Lukas Scheu vor einer Sühnedeutung des Todes Jesu[23] ist nicht widerlegt.

III. KRITISCHE WÜRDIGUNG

1. Eigentlich sollte ich mich darüber freuen, daß heute nach der Verwendung der Schriften des Alten Testaments im Neuen Testament unter der Überschrift »Intertextualität« gefragt wird. Denn das bedeutet, daß man sich auch für die *Bedeutung* der Schriftzitate in ihrem neuen Kontext interessiert, und nicht nur für den *Text* oder die *Form* der Zitate, wie das noch vor einer Generation weithin der Fall war. Als ich damals forderte, daß auch nach der *Bedeutung* der Zitate in ihrem jetzigen Kontext gefragt werden müsse, fühlte ich mich wie ein Rufer in der Wüste[24]. In diesem Zusammenhang möchte ich ausdrücklich betonen: Was Weren über Ps 2,1-2 im Kontext von Apg 4 schreibt, das ist gut beobachtet und belegt, wie sorgfältig intertextuell gearbeitet werden kann.

---

22. Diese Auslegung wird vertreten von K. BORNHÄUSER, *Studien zur Apostelgeschichte*, Gütersloh, »Der Rufer« Evangelischer Verlag, 1934, 94.96. E. HAENCHEN, *Die Apostelgeschichte* (MeyerK), Göttingen, Vandenhoeck & Ruprecht, [7]1977 wendet zu Recht dagegen ein, »diese Stelle (sc. Jes 56,4-5) wird nicht erwähnt« (300 Anm. 5).

23. Siehe z.B. H.J. CADBURY, *The Making of Luke-Acts* (1927), Nachdruck London, SPCK, 1961, 280: »But Luke strikingly omits passages in Mark which might seem to suggest a doctrine of atonement... That elsewhere Luke uses part of Isaiah LIII as a prooftext for Jesus' death does not prove that he adopted from it the special theological explanation which later Christians have found in the unquoted parts of the same passage«. Vgl. M. RESE, *Alttestamentliche Motive in der Christologie des Lukas*, Gütersloh, Gerd Mohn, 1969, 98.

24. Siehe M. RESE, *Die Funktion der alttestamentlichen Zitate und Anspielungen in den Reden der Apostelgeschichte*, in J. KREMER (ed.), *Les Actes des Apôtres. Traditions, rédaction, théologie* (BETL, 48), Gembloux, Leuven, Duculot, University Press, 1979, 61-79. Damals betonte ich freilich auch, daß »man *Text* und *Form* der Zitate behandeln kann, ohne nach ihrer *Bedeutung* im jetzigen Kontext zu fragen«, während »die letztere Frage zugleich auch eine Beachtung von *Text* und *Form* der Zitate« voraussetzt (61 Anm. 1).

Gleichwohl ist meine Freude sehr gemischt, und zwar sowohl wegen bestimmter Aspekte des methodischen Ansatzes des niederländischen Programms als auch wegen der meisten konkreten Ergebnisse.

2. Beim methodischen Ansatz scheint mir die grundlegende Hypothese, »daß die expliziten Zitate als pars pro toto funktionieren«, aus mehreren Gründen falsch zu sein, ganz abgesehen davon, daß sie forschungsgeschichtlich nur Dodds Hypothese von der »Bibel der Urkirche«[25] wiederholt, anscheinend ohne das zu wissen.

a) Weren beruft sich für seine grundlegende Hypothese und für sein Forschungsprogramm zu Unrecht auf Pfister und Broich. Nicht umsonst hält Pfister fest, daß »ein Zitat als *argumentum ad auctoritatem* von geringer intertextueller Intensität« ist[26] – und was sind »explizite Zitate« aus den Schriften des Alten Testaments im Neuen Testament anderes als Berufungen auf eine übergeordnete Autorität, sei diese Autorität allgemein Gott oder die Schriften oder ein Teil aus ihnen (Tora, Psalmen, Propheten) oder Moses oder David –. Zum intertextuellen »Spiel« bleibt bei »expliziten Zitaten«, die durch eine Zitationsformel eingeleitet werden, kein Raum. Wenn Weren und Bastiaens in ihren Untersuchungen nicht zwischen »explizitem Zitat« und »Anspielung« unterscheiden, so haben sie schlicht nicht beachtet, was Broich zu Recht betont, nämlich, daß »Zitat und Anspielung ja eigentlich verschiedene, sogar einander entgegengesetzte Formen von Intertextualität sind«[27].

b) Beim niederländischen Programm »Intertextualität und Bibel« werden die Argumente all jener nicht ernst oder überhaupt nicht zur Kenntnis genommen, die meinen, im frühen Christentum seien die Schriften des Alten Testaments atomistisch gebraucht worden. Schon vor zwei Generationen stellte Cadbury fest: »In their atomistic use of Scripture the early Christians were very different from the modern theologian«[28].

c) Schließlich scheint mir Bastiaens' Inkonsequenz bei der Zielbestimmung seiner Untersuchung widerzuspiegeln, daß bei dem niederländischen Forschungsprogramm nicht ausreichend bedacht wurde, ob man sich bei der Frage nach der Verwendung der Schriften des Alten Testaments im

25. C.H. DODD, *According to the Scriptures. The Sub-Structure of New Testament Theology*, Digswell Place, James Nisbet and Company Ltd, 1952. Zur Kritik an Dodds Hypothese siehe RESE, *Alttestamentliche Motive* (s. Anm. 23), 221-223.

26. PFISTER, *Konzepte* (s. Anm. 11), 29.

27. U. BROICH, *Formen der Markierung von Intertextualität*, in BROICH, PFISTER (eds.), *Intertextualität* (s. Anm. 7), 31-47, 34.

28. H.J. CADBURY, *The Titles of Jesus in Acts*, in F.J. FOAKES JACKSON, K. LAKE, *The Beginnings of Christianity. Part I. Vol. V. Additional Notes*, London, Macmillan, 1933, 354-374, 369.

Neuen Testament mehr vom alten Kontext oder mehr vom neuen Kontext leiten lassen soll.

3. Was die konkreten Ergebnisse betrifft, so habe ich meine Kritik an Weren und Bastiaens bereits im Zusammenhang mit den beiden Beispielen geäußert. Ich möchte sie jetzt nur noch in zwei allgemeinen Sätzen zuspitzend zusammenfassen:

a) Traditionsgeschichtliche (diachrone) Fragen werden von Weren und von Bastiaens offensichtlich nicht ausreichend berücksichtigt.

b) Die durch die synchrone Analyse gewonnenen Ergebnisse sind besonders bei Bastiaens nicht frei von Willkür und stehen in der Gefahr, in die Texte mehr hineinzulesen, als in ihnen steht.

4. So gesehen ist die praktische Anwendung von »Intertextualität« im Zusammenhang mit der Frage nach der Verwendung der Schriften des Alten Testaments im Neuen Testament eher ein Beispiel für den Unsinn dieser neuen Methode als für ihren Sinn. Jedoch: Das müßte nicht so sein!

Rudolf-Harbig-Weg 23   Martin RESE
D-48149 Münster

ERWÄGUNGEN ZUM GESETZESVERSTÄNDNIS IN Q
ANHAND VON Q 16,16-18[1]

1. Vorbemerkungen

In dem folgenden Beitrag soll die Frage nach der Beurteilung des jüdischen νόμος innerhalb der Jesusüberlieferung aus einer bestimmten Perspektive beleuchtet werden. Dabei wird davon ausgegangen, daß die Zwei-Quellen-Theorie (ZQT) – trotz verschiedentlich vorgebrachter Kritik sowie alternativer Lösungsmodelle – weiterhin das plausibelste Modell zur Erklärung der synoptischen Frage darstellt[2]. Für die Analyse der Jesusüberlieferung bedeutet dies, daß Mk- und Q-Texte ausgehend von ihrer Einbindung in die jeweilige Konzeption zu analysieren sind, bevor Aussagen über ihren Ort innerhalb der Jesusüberlieferung oder gar der Verkündigung des historischen Jesus selbst getroffen werden können. In bezug auf Q ist vor diesem Hintergrund des weiteren zu bemerken, daß

---

1. Die Angaben der Q-Stellen folgen, wie es heute weithin üblich ist, der lk Kapitel- und Verseinteilung. Die Angabe Q 16,16-18 meint also die aus Lk 16,16-18 sowie den entsprechenden Mt-Parallelen zu rekonstruierenden Q-Verse. Dieses Verfahren hat seine Grundlage in der Beobachtung, daß die Q-Akoluthie in der Regel bei Lk besser bewahrt ist als bei Mt, der Mk- und Q-Stoff des öfteren zu größeren thematischen Komplexen zusammengearbeitet hat.

2. Vornehmlich im angelsächsischen Raum sind alternative Modelle entwickelt worden. Verwiesen sei auf die Erneuerung der Griesbach-Hypothese durch W. Farmer sowie auf die von A. Farrer und M. Goulder vertretene These, Lk habe Mk *und* Mt gekannt. Affinitäten zu einer Traditionshypothese sind in den Ansätzen von E.P. Sanders sowie R. Riesner zu konstatieren. Einen Sonderfall innerhalb der ZQT stellt schließlich die von A. Fuchs und seinen Schülern entwickelte Deuteromarkus-Theorie (der Q-Stoff sei bereits vor Mt und Lk in Mk eingearbeitet worden) dar. Auf diese Lösungsmodelle kann hier nur hingewiesen werden. Eine Begründung für die Plausibilität der ZQT – vornehmlich in Auseinandersetzung mit Farmer – findet sich bei J.S. Kloppenborg, *Theological Stakes in the Synoptic Problem*, in F. van Segbroeck u.a. (eds.), *The Four Gospels. FS F. Neirynck* (BETL, 100), Leuven, 1992, pp. 93-120. In Auseinandersetzung mit der Griesbach-Hypothese sowie mit Goulder hat zudem C. Tuckett jüngst die Existenz von Q noch einmal begründet. Cf. Id., *Q and the History of Early Christianity. Studies on Q*, Edinburgh, 1996, pp. 1-39 (zuerst in: R.A. Piper [ed.], *The Gospel behind the Gospels. Current Studies on Q*, Leiden/New York/Köln, 1995, pp. 19-47).

Für eine detaillierte Diskussion der methodischen Problematik um die synoptische Frage in Auseinandersetzung mit dem Lösungsmodell der »Formgeschichte« sowie alternativer Ansätze, die hier nicht vorgeführt werden kann, verweise ich auf die entsprechenden Ausführungen meiner Habilitationsschrift: J. Schröter, *Erinnerung an Jesu Worte. Studien zur Rezeption der Logienüberlieferung in Markus, Q und Thomas*, Habil. masch., Berlin 1996 (erscheint demnächst in WMANT).

trotz eines fehlenden Manuskriptes die Gestalt einer derartigen Schrift
aus den entsprechenden Mt- und Lk-Texten bis zu einem Grad zu erheben ist, der diese als Quelle mit selbständigem Profil – sowohl was die
Auswahl der Stoffe als auch was die inhaltliche Konzeption betrifft – in
Erscheinung treten läßt. Q kommt somit als vierte Quelle neben die drei
synoptischen Evangelien zu stehen und sollte auch in dieser Weise behandelt werden[3].

Aufbauend auf diesen Voraussetzungen soll im folgenden nach der in
Q vertretenen Stellung zur Tora gefragt werden. Dies legt sich von daher
nahe, als Q – wie sich noch zeigen wird – diesbezüglich eine von Mk
charakteristisch unterschiedene Position bezieht. Gehört Mk nämlich
eher in eine Tempel und Gesetz kritisch gegenüberstehende judenchristliche Richtung, so ist Q gerade an dem Aufweis der Konvergenz von
νόμος und Verkündigung Jesu interessiert und arbeitet auf diese Weise
der später von Mt programmatisch ausgebauten Forderung des περισ-
σεύειν der δικαιοσύνη gegenüber derjenigen der Schriftgelehrten und
Pharisäer (Mt 5,20) vor. Ein Blick auf Q kann somit dazu verhelfen, Entwicklungen verständlich zu machen, die auf eine strikte Bewahrung jüdischer Traditionen, gerade insofern sie die Stellung zur Tora betreffen,
auch im späteren Gegenüber von ἐκκλησία und συναγωγή sowie dem
damit verbundenen programmatischen Überschritt zur Heidenmission ausgerichtet waren.

Das Stichwort νόμος begegnet innerhalb von Q nur in den Versen 16,
16 und 17, davon einmal in der Zusammenstellung ὁ νόμος καὶ οἱ προφῆται (Lk) bzw. οἱ προφῆται καὶ ὁ νόμος (Mt). Diese Verse bieten sich
somit als Ausgangspunkt für eine Frage nach dem Verhältnis von Q zur
Tora geradezu an. Des weiteren ist es aufschlußreich, einen Blick auf
das Ehescheidungslogion und seine Verarbeitung in Q zu werfen. Aufgrund der bei der Behandlung von Q-Texten notwendigen rekonstruk-
tiven Arbeit ist dabei auch auf die Verarbeitung der Verse durch Matthäus
und Lukas einzugehen.

---

3. Die mit der Untersuchung von H.E. TÖDT, *Der Menschensohn in der synoptischen
Überlieferung*, Gütersloh, 1959 (²1963) einsetzende neuere Q-Forschung hat diesbezüglich mittlerweile zu beachtlichen Ergebnissen geführt. Dies läßt sich etwa daran ablesen,
daß bereits bei P. VIELHAUER, *Geschichte der urchristlichen Literatur*, Berlin/New York,
1975, sowie dann in den Einleitungen von W. SCHMITHALS, *Einleitung in die drei ersten
Evangelien*, Berlin, 1985, sowie von U. SCHNELLE, *Einleitung in das Neue Testament*,
Göttingen, 1994, je ein eigenes Kapitel zu Q zu finden ist, womit die in älteren Einleitungen – etwa bei A. JÜLICHER/E. FASCHER, W.G. KÜMMEL oder A. WIKENHAUSER –, aber
auch im Arbeitsbuch von H. CONZELMANN/A. LINDEMANN anzutreffende Tendenz, Q
lediglich innerhalb der Rubrik »Die synoptische Frage« zu verhandeln, eine nicht unwe-
sentliche Modifikation erfahren hat.

2. ERWÄGUNGEN ZU Q 16,16-18

2.1. Zur Position der Logien in Q. Beobachtungen zur redaktionellen Verarbeitung durch Matthäus und Lukas

Aufgrund der Differenzen zwischen Mt und Lk ist es zunächst notwendig, nach dem Ort sowie dem zu vermutenden Wortlaut der Logien in Q zu fragen. Dazu ist ein Blick auf die jeweilige redaktionelle Verarbeitung zu werfen. Dies soll so geschehen, daß zunächst auf Mt 5,17-20 geblickt (a), sodann nach der Funktion von Lk 16,16-18 in ihrem Kontext gefragt wird (b), um schließlich auf die Frage eines ursprünglichen Q-Kontextes von 16,16 bei Mt einzugehen (c)[4].

Es erhebt sich zunächst die Frage, ob Matthäus hier einen ursprünglichen Q-Zusammenhang, der bei Lukas noch zu greifen ist, aufgelöst oder aber Lukas die Spruchgruppe erst selbst komponiert hat. In letzterem Fall wäre noch einmal neu nach dem Ort der Logien in Q zu fragen. Die Relevanz für die hier verfolgte Fragestellung liegt dabei darin, daß zunächst geklärt werden muß, ob bereits in Q die Rede von νόμος καὶ προφῆται als einer bis zu Johannes reichenden Epoche durch das Logion von der bleibenden Gültigkeit des νόμος weitergeführt wurde oder aber ob dies erst aus der lk Redaktion heraus verständlich gemacht werden kann.

a) In der Forschung ist, vornehmlich im Gefolge von H. Schürmann[5], nicht selten die Ansicht vertreten worden, Lukas gebe in 16,16-18 – möglicherweise bereits seit 16,14 oder sogar seit 16,9 bzw. 16,1 – die Q-Vorlage wieder[6]. Allerdings ist zu beachten, daß Schürmann nach der traditions-

---

4. Für den Nachvollzug der folgenden Argumentation (wie für die exegetische Arbeit an Q-Texten überhaupt) sei auf das sehr hilfreiche Arbeitsbuch von F. NEIRYNCK verwiesen: *Q-Synopsis. The Double Tradition Passages in Greek. Revised Edition with Appendix,* Leuven, [2]1995.

5. Cf. H. SCHÜRMANN, *»Wer daher eines dieser geringsten Gebote auflöst ...« Wo fand Matthäus das Logion Mt 5,19?* in ID., *Traditionsgeschichtliche Untersuchungen zu den synoptischen Evangelien,* Düsseldorf, 1968, pp. 126-136.

6. Für einen Q-Kontext von 16,16-18 plädieren etwa D. KOSCH, *Die eschatologische Tora des Menschensohnes. Untersuchungen zur Rezeption der Stellung Jesu zur Tora in Q* (NTOA, 12), Freiburg (CH)/Göttingen, 1989, pp. 427-444; D.R. CATCHPOLE, *The Quest for Q,* Edinburgh, 1993, pp. 232-238; J.S. KLOPPENBORG, *Nomos and Ethos in Q,* in J.E. GOEHRING u.a. (eds.), *Gospel Origins and Christian Beginnings.* FS J.M. Robinson, Sonoma, 1990, pp. 35-48, esp. 43-46; W.D. DAVIES/D.C. ALLISON, *The Gospel According to Matthew* (ICC) II, Edinburgh, 1991, pp. 252-254; p. 406. Des weiteren hat R.A. PIPER, *Wisdom in the Q-tradition. The Aphoristic Teaching of Jesus* (SNTS MS, 61), Cambridge, 1989, pp. 86-99, eine Vorlage hinter Lk 16,9-13 zu erweisen versucht. Am weitesten geht SCHÜRMANNS Vorschlag (n. 5), der eine Vorlage hinter Lk 16,1-18 vermutet.

geschichtlichen Herkunft Mt 5,19 fragt, einem Logion also, das keine Lk-
Parallele besitzt und somit nicht zum sicheren Bestand von Q gerechnet
werden kann. Es ist somit fraglich, ob ein derartiges Logion als Ausgangspunkt dafür dienen kann, einen ursprünglichen Q-Zusammenhang zu eruieren[7]. Auch wenn man die vormt Existenz eines Logions hinter Mt 5,19
annimmt[8], ist damit noch nicht erwiesen, daß es innerhalb eines Q-Zusam-
menhanges tradiert worden ist, in dem auch 5,18 gestanden hat. Des weiteren dürften weder der Versuch, Mt 5,20 als Verarbeitung von Lk (Q) 16,15
und 16 aufzuweisen[9], noch derjenige, in 5,17 Reminiszenzen an Lk 16,16 zu
entdecken[10], als gelungen zu bezeichnen sein. Das Vorkommen der diesbezüglich von Schürmann genannten Wendungen besagt nämlich nicht mehr,
als daß in beiden Spruchgruppen die Thematik des Gültigkeitsbereiches
von Gesetz und Propheten im Gegenüber zu den Pharisäern diskutiert wird.
Als gemeinsames Logion läßt sich dabei lediglich 5,18/Lk 16,17 eruieren.
Dagegen dürfte es sich in vv. 17 und 20 um Logien der mt Redaktion handeln[11], die somit die Spruchgruppe 5,17-20 rahmen, welche Mt unter Rückgriff auf das Q-Logion 5,18 sowie auf das aus der mündlichen Tradition
stammende Logion hinter 5,19 selbst zur Einleitung der Antithesen der
Bergpredigt komponiert hat.

Ist somit der Versuch, eine gemeinsame Q-Vorlage hinter Mt 5,17-20
und Lk 16,14-18 auf der Grundlage des Mt-Textes zu erweisen, kaum als
plausibel anzusehen, so ist in einem nächsten Schritt zu fragen, ob sich Lk
16,16-18 unabhängig von einer derartigen These als Q-Kontext wahrscheinlich machen läßt. Dazu ist auf die Logik der Zusammenstellung dieser Verse im lk Kontext einzugehen[12].

b) Lk wendet sich in K.16 der Thematik des rechten Umgangs mit dem
Reichtum zu. Diese wird in 16,1-9 und 19-31 anhand zweier Gleichnisse illustriert, die jeweils mit der Wendung ἄνθρωπός τις ἦν πλούσιος eingeführt
werden[13]. In beiden kommt zum Ausdruck, daß der Umgang mit irdischem

---

7. Es ist zu beachten, daß Schürmann seine Argumentation von der – nicht näher
begründeten – Annahme her aufbaut, Matthäus habe 5,19 bereits mit 5,18 (= Lk 16,17) im
Zusammenhang gelesen, was auf die hinter Mt liegende Q-Vorlage verweise, ibid.,
pp. 127-128.

8. So etwa U. Luz, Die Erfüllung des Gesetzes bei Matthäus (Mt 5,17-20), in ZTK 75
(1978) 398-435, esp. pp. 408-409.

9. So Schürmann, Ibid., p. 130. Er verweist dazu auf das in Mt 5,20 und Lk 16,15
begegnende Thema der ungenügenden pharisäischen Gerechtigkeit, zum anderen auf die
Formulierung als Einlaßspruch (εἰσέλθητε εἰς τὴν βασιλείαν), die eine Analogie zu
dem εἰς αὐτὴν (βασιλείαν) βιάζεται in Lk 16,16 darstelle.

10. Schürmann, Ibid., p. 131, verweist hierzu auf die Wendung ὁ νόμος καὶ οἱ
προφῆται, die Matthäus bei der Formulierung von 5,17 beeinflußt habe.

11. Cf. etwa U. Luz, Das Evangelium nach Matthäus (EKK, I/1), Zürich/Neukirchen-
Vluyn, ³1992, pp. 229-230.

12. Cf. hierzu M. Klinghardt, Gesetz und Volk Gottes. Das lukanische Verständnis
des Gesetzes nach Herkunft, Funktion und seinem Ort in der Geschichte des Urchristentums (WUNT, 2/32), Tübingen, 1988, pp. 15-29; P. Hoffmann, Studien zur Theologie der
Logienquelle (NTAbh NF, 8), Münster, ³1982, pp. 54-56.

13. Man kann darüber streiten, ob das erste Gleichnis in v. 7; 8a; 8b oder erst in v. 9
endet. Unter der Voraussetzung, daß vorlk Tradition und lk Verarbeitung nicht literarkritisch voneinander zu trennen sind, ist diese Diskussion jedoch weniger relevant. Deutlich

Besitz von unmittelbarer Relevanz für das Ergehen im Endgericht ist[14]. Die dazwischen stehende Logiengruppe 16,10-18 verknüpft das Thema »Reichtum« mit demjenigen der Bewahrung des νόμος. In vv. 10-13 wird hierzu zunächst die Unvereinbarkeit von δουλεύειν θεῷ und δουλεύειν μαμωνᾷ (v. 13) herausgestellt. Damit wird deutlich, daß der in v. 9 geforderte Umgang mit dem μαμωνᾶς τῆς ἀδικίας seine Kriterien von dem Dienst für Gott her erhält. Die dort bereits angeklungene Aufforderung, den μαμωνᾶς so zu gebrauchen, daß er endzeitlichen Nutzen bringt, wird hier somit dadurch zugespitzt, daß eine Orientierung an dessen irdischem Nutzen als nicht vereinbar mit einem δουλεύειν θεῷ behauptet wird.

V. 14 nimmt, hieran anknüpfend, die im lk Reisebericht immer wieder anzutreffende Pharisäerpolemik auf[15]. Im vorliegenden Vers werden sie als geldgierig (φιλάργυροι) bezeichnet. In der hierauf Bezug nehmenden Rede Jesu wird evident, daß die Thematik des Umgangs mit dem μαμωνᾶς in direktem Zusammenhang mit der Frage nach der Geltung des νόμος steht. Wenn nämlich in bezug auf die Pharisäer gesagt wird, daß sich ihr δικαιοῦν nur auf Menschen, nicht jedoch auf Gott beziehe (v. 15), so wird dies durch vv. 16-18 als Ausdruck eines Ungenügens gegenüber den seit der Zeit der βασιλεία in veränderter Weise geltenden Forderungen des νόμος interpretiert. Der Vorwurf, der gegen die Pharisäer erhoben wird, erklärt sich somit aus der im Hintergrund stehenden Konzeption des νόμος, bezüglich dessen zwei Stadien unterschieden werden. Nach Lukas gibt es – das macht v. 16 deutlich – einen grundsätzlichen Unterschied zwischen der Zeit von νόμος

ist jedoch, daß es sich – wie häufig bei Lk – um eine Erzählung handelt, in der das exemplarische Moment von dem metaphorischen kaum zu trennen ist. Im vorliegenden Fall besteht die Pointe in der Klugheit des οἰκονόμος (cf. 16,8: φρονίμως ἐποίησεν). Daß es sich um eine »unmoralische« Geschichte handelt, bedeutet bezüglich des metaphorischen Charakters keinen Unterschied zu den sog. »Beispielerzählungen«, denn selbstverständlich wird hier nicht zum Betrug aufgefordert, ebensowenig wie die Erzählung vom barmherzigen Samariter dazu auffordert, einen unter die Räuber Gefallenen zu suchen. Innerhalb von vv. 8-9 vollzieht sich jedenfalls die Verschiebung von der Ebene des erzählten Falles zu deren Anwendung, ähnlich wie etwa in 12,20-21 oder 14,24. Vor dem Hintergrund dieser Beobachtungen wäre einmal danach zu fragen, ob Lk nicht auf eine ganz eigene Weise fiktive und reale Bestandteile innerhalb einer Reihe von Gleichniserzählungen miteinander verschränkt und die Kategorie »Beispielerzählung« somit nicht nur auf die vier seit Jülicher traditionell hierzu gerechneten Texte, sondern auch auf 14,16-24; 16,1-9 und 18,1-8 anzuwenden wäre.

14. In 16,9 wird das Gleichnis vom ungerechten Verwalter durch die Wendungen ὅταν ἐκλίπῃ und αἰώνιοι σκηναί direkt auf das Eschaton bezogen. Das Gleichnis vom reichen Mann und armen Lazarus macht durch V. 25 unmittelbar deutlich, daß durch irdischen Reichtum endzeitlicher Lohn verwirkt wird, wie umgekehrt irdischen Defiziten eschatologischer Ausgleich korrespondiert.

15. Man kann geradezu sagen, daß Lukas auf die Pharisäer als Negativschablone alle diejenigen Eigenschaften projiziert, vor denen er seine Leser warnen möchte. Eröffnet wird dies in 11,37-52 mit den Weherufen, bevor sie dann in 12,1 der Heuchelei gezogen, in 14,7-24 als ehrsüchtig, in 15,2 als unbarmherzig gegenüber den ἁμαρτωλοί und in 18,10-14 als selbstgerecht dargestellt werden. Aufschlußreich für die hiesige Stelle ist schließlich, daß in 14,2-6 bereits die Thematik der rechten Auslegung des νόμος (hier des Gebotes der Sabbatruhe) zur Sprache gekommen war. Für eine historische Rekonstruktion des Profils der Pharisäer wird man die lk Stilisierung somit wohl nur mit großer Vorsicht heranziehen können.

καὶ προφῆται und derjenigen der βασιλεία τοῦ θεοῦ. Dieser impliziert, daß der νόμος eine Neudefinition erfährt. Genau hierzu dient die Fortsetzung durch 16,17-18: Der νόμος gilt weiterhin, nun jedoch in seiner Interpretation durch die Lehre Jesu[16]. Somit ist ein Anschluß an 16,19-31 erreicht: Die Wiederaufnahme des Themas »Reichtum« illustriert nunmehr, daß der Umgang mit dem Besitz als Haltung gegenüber dem νόμος interpretiert wird[17], an dem sich zu orientieren unmittelbare Relevanz für die Beurteilung im Endgericht besitzt.

Zusammenfassend läßt sich somit urteilen, daß Lukas das Thema des unter veränderten Bedingungen weiterbestehenden νόμος an dieser Stelle einführt, um dessen Relevanz in der Zeit der βασιλεία zu explizieren. Dieses macht er inhaltlich an der Haltung gegenüber irdischem Reichtum deutlich, woraus umgekehrt zu folgern ist, daß der rechte Umgang mit dem μαμωνᾶς für Lukas eine unmittelbar aus dem νόμος resultierende Forderung ist, der die Pharisäer nicht genügen. Es zeigt sich somit, daß Lukas den νόμος unter den Bedingungen der Verkündigung der βασιλεία als ein Phänomen versteht, das Offenheit gegenüber religiös und sozial Deklassierten ausdrücklich verlangt. Auf dieser Linie liegt dann auch seine Verarbeitung der Gesetzesthematik in der Apg, wenn dort gerade umgekehrt von den Heidenchristen die Einhaltung ritueller Reinheitsvorschriften verlangt wird (so in Apg 15,20). In der Behandlung der νόμος-Thematik läßt sich bei Lukas also die Intention erkennen, sowohl kultische als auch ethische Forderungen mit dem Ziel der Beschreibung von dessen Funktion als Maßstab für eine neue Gemeinschaft aus Juden und Heiden aufzunehmen.

Es kann somit als äußerst unwahrscheinlich bezeichnet werden, daß Lukas in 16,16-18 auf eine bereits vor ihm zusammengestellte Logiengruppe zurückgegriffen hat. Vielmehr ist die Komposition in der beschriebenen Weise auf die für ihn spezifische Verarbeitung der Gesetzesthematik zurückzuführen. In einem letzten Schritt ist darum danach zu fragen, ob die Parallele zu Lk 16,16 in Mt 11,12-13 für einen Q-Kontext in Anspruch genommen werden kann[18].

16. Aus der Überlieferung des Ehescheidungsverbotes bei Mk, Q und Paulus dürfte hervorgehen, daß es sich hier um einen frühen Topos der Jesusüberlieferung handelt. Lukas führt dieses Gebot hier an, um deutlich zu machen, auf welche Weise die Aussage über das Fortbestehen des νόμος aus v. 17 konkret zu verstehen ist. Dabei konnte über das Verbot von Ehebruch und Heirat einer Geschiedenen eine Verknüpfung jüdischer Reinheitsvorschriften mit paganer Ethik, in der die Thematik ehelicher Treue ebenfalls im Horizont kultischer Reinheit diskutiert wurde, erreicht werden. Cf. dazu KLINGHARDT (n. 12), pp. 89-96.

17. Cf. bes. 16,29-31, wo mit Μωϋσῆς καὶ προφῆται auf v. 16 rekurriert wird.

18. Für die Logien in Mt 5,18 und 5,32 ist ein Q-Kontext von vornherein auszuschließen. Zu 5,18 wurde oben bereits Stellung genommen. In bezug auf 5,32 ist deutlich, daß es sich um eine der von Mt komponierten Antithesen handelt, die bei ihm diejenige über das Verbot des Ehebruches (5,27-30) unter Verarbeitung des Q-Logions fortsetzt. Dabei ist es nicht so eindeutig, wie in der Regel behauptet wird, daß erst Mt die Unzuchtsklausel in das Logion eingefügt habe. In der Regel wird hierfür auf die Parallele in 19,9 verwiesen, wo Mt die Wendung μὴ ἐπὶ πορνείᾳ in seine Verarbeitung von Mk 10,2-12 eingefügt hat. Dies kann freilich auch auf der Grundlage eines Logions geschehen sein, das Mt in 5,32 bereits aus der Tradition übernommen hat. Hierauf wird zurückzukommen sein.

c) Ansatzpunkt für eine solche Frage ist die Beobachtung, daß Matthäus dieses Logion innerhalb desjenigen Q-Komplexes überliefert, in dem es um das Verhältnis von Jesus und Johannes dem Täufer geht (Q 7,18-35/Mt 11,2-19). Dieser wird in 11,10 (Q 7,27) mit dem Zitat aus Ex 23,20/Mal 3,1 als der Vorläufer Jesu beschrieben, woran sich die hier diskutierten Verse bei Mt anschließen. Das zuweilen zu lesende Argument, es sei nicht einsichtig zu machen, warum Lk diese Verse aus einem derartigen Zusammenhang versetzt und die Spruchgruppe 16,16-18 seinerseits erst geschaffen haben solle[19], wird schon angesichts der oben unter b) herausgestellten deutlich erkennbaren lk Verarbeitung der νόμος-Thematik in 16,16-18 fraglich. Dazu ist die Beobachtung zu ergänzen, daß Lk in 7,29-30, also an derjenigen Stelle, an der bei Mt die Analogie zu Q 16,16 folgt, eine Notiz darüber einfügt, daß die Pharisäer im Gegensatz zu λαός und τελῶναι die Johannestaufe verweigerten. Da diese bei Lk als Kritik an falschem Vertrauen auf die Abrahamskindschaft (so in 3,7-9 = Q) und damit zugleich als die die Verkündigung der βασιλεία durch Jesus vorbereitende Umkehrtaufe verstanden wird, bedeutet die Verweigerung dieser Taufe zugleich eine Nicht-Anerkennung der damit verbundenen Konsequenzen in bezug auf die Neuqualifizierung des νόμος, wie sie oben ausgeführt wurde.

In der mt Einordnung setzen die Logien in 11,12-13 dagegen die Verhältnisbestimmung von Jesus und Johannes seit 11,2 fort. In einer gegenüber Lk 16,16a und b anderen Reihenfolge wird zunächst von dem mit dem Auftreten des Johannes datierenden βιάζεσθαι der βασιλεία gesprochen, bevor dann in v. 13 οἱ προφῆται καὶ ὁ νόμος auf die Zeit bis zu Johannes begrenzt werden. Die Differenz besteht demzufolge hauptsächlich darin, daß in der mt Version mit dem Auftreten des Johannes das βιάζεσθαι, bei Lk dagegen das εὐαγγελίζεσθαι der βασιλεία datiert[20]. Betrachtet man dies vor dem Hintergrund der vorangehenden, unstrittig als Q-Komposition zu identifizierenden Verse 11,2-11 (Q 7,18-19.22-28), so ergibt sich, daß Mt 11,12-13 die Aussage über das in 11,11 (Q 7,28) formulierte Verhältnis zwischen Jesus und Johannes in bezug auf die βασιλεία organisch fortsetzen: Obwohl Johannes der Größte unter den Menschen ist, ist er in bezug auf die βασιλεία Jesus untergeordnet[21]. Dennoch gilt, daß mit der Bußpredigt des Johannes, die den Anfang von Q darstellt, der Anbruch der βασιλεία datiert. Somit gibt es gute Gründe, die Einordnung von Q 16,16 in Mt

---

19. Cf. etwa KLOPPENBORG (n. 6), p. 44, in Anknüpfung an J. WEIß.

20. Bei Lukas wird Johannes dadurch von Jesus unterschieden, daß seine Funktion als Bußprediger, der der βασιλεία-Verkündigung Jesu den Weg bereitet, besonders herausgearbeitet wird. Dies geht schon aus dem gegenüber Mk und Mt erweiterten Jes-Zitat in Lk 3,1-6 sowie aus der bereits erwähnten, gegenüber Q erweiterten Bußpredigt in 3,10-14 hervor. Johannes hat also in bezug auf die βασιλεία eine von Jesus deutlich unterschiedene Funktion, wogegen er bei Mt diesem gerade parallelisiert wird. Für letzteres ist darauf zu verweisen, daß in Mt 3,2 bereits die dann in 4,17 von Jesus aufgenommene Verkündigung der anbrechenden βασιλεία als Tätigkeit des Johannes geschildert wird.

21. Dabei ist μικρότερος nicht – wie zumeist in der Exegese dieser Stelle – superlativisch, sondern komparativisch verstanden, denn es geht im Kontext um eine Verhältnisbestimmung von Jesus und Johannes. Dagegen leuchtet es wenig ein, daß Johannes als geringer gegenüber allen anderen Menschen in bezug auf die βασιλεία bezeichnet werden soll, zumal im unmittelbar folgenden Gleichnis von den spielenden Kindern wiederum eine Gleichstellung mit Jesus erfolgt.

11,12-13 bereits für Q anzunehmen[22]. In der Konzeption von Mt und Q wird die Zeit seit Johannes aufgrund des seitdem eingetretenen gewaltsamen Konfliktes um die βασιλεία[23] von derjenigen von Propheten und Gesetz unterschieden. Diese Unterscheidung bedeutet eine Zusammenordnung von Johannes und Jesus, die auf der in Mt 11,2-14 (Q 7,18-19; 21-28; 16,16) entwickelten Differenzierung aufbauend nunmehr beide nebeneinander stellt. Damit jedoch ist die hier bei Mt erfolgende Verhältnisbestimmung insofern von derjenigen des Lk verschieden, als in jener Johannes und Jesus eine je eigene, aus der Akzentuierung ihrer Botschaft zu entnehmende Funktion innerhalb der βασιλεία haben, wogegen sie bei diesem dadurch unterschieden sind, daß das mit dem Auftreten Jesu verbundene εὐαγγελίζεσθαι der βασιλεία auf der Vorbereitung durch die Johannespredigt aufbaut, die somit das Bindeglied zwischen der Verkündigung Jesu und Gesetz und Propheten darstellt. Auch das lk Interesse ist somit keineswegs auf eine Einteilung der Geschichte in heilsgeschichtliche Epochen gerichtet, vielmehr geht es hier darum, die Frage nach der Gültigkeit des νόμος unter den Bedingungen der Basileiaverkündigung Jesu zu klären[24].

Aus diesen Überlegungen lassen sich folgende Schlüsse ziehen: Die Frage nach dem Gültigkeitsbereich des νόμος wird in Q im Zusammenhang mit derjenigen nach dem Verhältnis von Johannes und Jesus diskutiert. In der mt Version des Logions, die nach der hiesigen Option auch

22. In diesem Sinne entscheiden sich auch HOFFMANN (n. 12), pp. 50-79; A.D. JACOBSON, *The First Gospel. An Introduction to Q*, Sonoma, 1992, pp. 114-120.
23. In diesem Sinne ist das βιάζεται in Mt und Q zu verstehen (cf. auch G. SCHRENK, βιάζομαι, βιαστής, in *TWNT* 1, pp. 608-613, esp. pp. 610-611). Grundsätzlich gibt es diesbezüglich folgende Interpretationsmöglichkeiten: 1) βιάζεσθαι kann in passivem Sinn verstanden und dann a) positiv auf das »Erstürmtwerden« der βασιλεία oder b) negativ auf die Gewalt, die dieser angetan wird, bezogen werden. Oder aber man versteht 2) βιάζεσθαι in medialem Sinn und interpretiert das Logion als Aussage über das Sich-Durchsetzen des Gottesreiches seit den Tagen des Johannes. Die Lösung 2) scheitert sowohl daran, daß sich – wie gezeigt – das hierbei vorausgesetzte Verständnis einer zeitlichen Periodisierung weder für Mt noch für Lk verifizieren läßt, wie auch daran, daß sich eine derartige positive Bedeutung von βιάζεσθαι nicht belegen läßt. Für Mt, der hier Q folgen dürfte, ist eine solche Deutung schon von daher ausgeschlossen, als die anschließende Formulierung καὶ βιασταὶ ἁρπάζουσιν αὐτήν auf jeden Fall auf eine gewalttätige, also negativ bewertete Handlung zu beziehen ist, ein Bedeutungswechsel zum vorausgehenden βιάζεται jedoch schwerlich einsichtig zu machen ist. Innerhalb von Lösung 1) legt sich die Deutung mit negativer Konnotation von der Wortbedeutung her nahe, insofern nämlich ein positives Verständnis von βιάζεσθαι auch hierfür nur schwerlich zu belegen ist und sich mit dem Nachsatz schlecht verträgt. Intendiert ist somit offensichtlich eine Aussage über mit dem Auftreten des Johannes beginnende gewaltsame Aktivitäten, die im Zusammenhang mit der βασιλεία stehen. Hierauf liegt der Akzent des Mt- und des Q-Logions. Dagegen handelt es sich bei Lk um eine Aussage über das Hineindrängen der Menschen *in die* βασιλεία, wodurch der Akzent hin zu der lukanischen Sicht der sich zu den Völkern ausbreitenden Gottesherrschaft verschoben wird.
24. In diesem Sinne auch W. SCHMITHALS, *Das Evangelium nach Lukas* (ZBK, 3/1), Zürich, 1980, p. 170: »Jegliche Abtrennung von Epochen der Heilsgeschichte liegt Lukas fern: Johannes der Täufer verbindet Gesetz und Propheten mit der Verkündigung der Gottesherrschaft«.

für Q vorauszusetzen ist, wird dabei das gegenüber der Zeit von Propheten und Gesetz Neue in dem gewalttätigen Konflikt um die βασιλεία, nicht jedoch in einer Differenzierung zwischen Jesus und Johannes gesehen. Dieser Konflikt wird als in der Kontinuität des προφητεύειν von προφῆται καὶ νόμος sich ereignender beschrieben (cf. hierzu das begründende γάρ in Mt 11,13). Diese Konzeption wird von Matthäus übernommen, bei Lukas dagegen durch eine veränderte Behandlung der Frage nach der Qualifikation des νόμος in der Zeit der βασιλεία ersetzt. Lukas hat demnach deutlich erkennbare Gründe, die ihn zur Umstellung von Mt 11,12-13 bewogen haben. Die beiden anderen Logien (Lk 16,17/ Mt 5,18; Lk 16,18/Mt 5,32) sind dagegen auch bei Matthäus in Kompositionen eingebunden, die als redakionell zu beurteilen sind. Über ihren Ort in Q kann darum keine Aussage mehr getroffen werden. Im folgenden sind die Logien ausgehend von diesem Befund hinsichtlich ihres Beitrages für das Verständnis des νόμος in Q auszulegen.

2.2. Zu Q 16,16

Neben dem oben Ausgeführten sprechen folgende Gründe dafür, daß der Q-Wortlaut des Logions im wesentlichen bei Mt erhalten sein wird:

1) Die Rede vom mit dem Auftreten des Johannes beginnenden gewaltsamen Konflikt um die βασιλεία ordnet sich in die Konzeption von Q ein, derzufolge die Boten der βασιλεία – wozu nach Q sowohl Johannes und Jesus als auch die von Jesus ausgesandten Träger der Q-Botschaft gehören – bei der Ausrichtung ihres Auftrags den Anfeindungen und Verfolgungen der ablehnenden Teile Israels ausgesetzt sind[25]. Dagegen hat eine Absetzung der Verkündigung der βασιλεία von Gesetz und Propheten sowie von Johannes dem Täufer innerhalb der Konzeption von Q keinen Platz.

2) Die Wendung οἱ προφῆται καὶ ὁ νόμος begegnet in dieser Reihenfolge nur hier im NT und ist auch ansonsten nicht zu verifizieren. Sie stellt angesichts der damit bezeichneten Schriftengruppen die ungewöhnlichere Fassung gegenüber Lk 16,16 dar. Auch Mt schreibt an denjenigen Stellen, an denen er frei formuliert, ὁ νόμος καὶ οἱ προφῆται (so in 5,17;

---

25. Daß die Auseinandersetzung mit dem ablehnenden Israel ein wesentliches Moment der Konzeption von Q darstellt, ist spätestens seit der Untersuchung von D. LÜHRMANN, *Die Redaktion der Logienquelle,* Neukirchen, 1969, in der Q-Forschung allgemein akzeptiert. Zu dieser Auseinandersetzung sowie zur Rede von der Verfolgung wegen der Verkündigung und des Bekenntnisses zu dem Menschensohn Jesus cf. Q 7,31-35; 11,14-26.29-32; 11,39-52; 6,22-23; 10,3; 10,12-15; 12,2-12.

7,12; 22,40)[26]. Es kann darum angenommen werden, daß sich der hiesige Wortlaut dem Q-Logion verdankt.

3) Mt überliefert – akzeptiert man die obige Argumentation – seit 11,2 einen Q-Kontext, wogegen Lk in 16,16-18 nach der hier vertretenen Position eine eigene Spruchgruppe komponiert hat. Dies macht es zusätzlich wahrscheinlich, daß Mt auch in der sprachlichen Gestalt des Logions Q näher steht als Lk.

Für das Verständnis des νόμος in Q trägt das Logion unter den genannten Voraussetzungen folgendes bei: Der seit der Verkündigung Johannes' und Jesu ausgebrochene Konflikt um die βασιλεία ereignet sich in Kontinuität zu dem, was von Propheten und Gesetz geweissagt worden war. Der νόμος kommt hier somit – neben den Propheten – als Größe in den Blick, auf deren Grundlage die Q-Boten sich ihre eigene Situation des Konfliktes, in den sie aufgrund ihrer Botschaft von der anbrechenden βασιλεία geraten sind, deuten. Sie interpretieren diesen Konflikt als Erfüllung der dortigen Voraussagen und deuten ihre eigene Zeit damit als eine solche, in der sich die geweissagten Drangsale der Endzeit ereignen[27]. Der νόμος und die Propheten stellen hier somit für die Q-Boten den Deutungshorizont ihrer eigenen Situation dar.

2.3. *Zu Q 16,17*

Das Logion besagt zunächst in beiden Fassungen, daß eine Änderung oder gar Aufhebung des Gesetzes unmöglich ist. Die sprachlichen Unterschiede lassen sich dabei folgendermaßen auswerten.

Während sich bei Mt eine zeitliche Konditionierung mit ἕως ἄν findet, ist das lk Logion auf eine Mk 10,25 (Mt 19,24; Lk 18,25) vergleichbare Weise als Sentenz formuliert[28]. Es ist unwahrscheinlich, daß

---

26. Die Wendung begegnet sonst immer mit der Voranstellung des νόμος (für die LXX cf. 2 Makk 15,9; für das hellenistische Judentum 4 Makk 18,10; im NT noch Apg 13,15; 24,14; 28,23). Die hiesige, auffällige Formulierung könnte sich von daher erklären, daß das Element des προφητεύειν betont werden soll. So auch DAVIES/ALLISON (n. 6), pp. 256-257.

27. Hierfür spricht etwa, daß der Kampf, den nach apokalyptischen Traditionen in der Endzeit selbst Familienmitglieder gegeneinander führen werden (so etwa äthHen 100,1-2), in Q 12,52-53 als Folge der Botschaft Jesu gedeutet wird, die die Q-Gruppe unmittelbar betrifft.

28. Bezüglich der Diskussion, welche der beiden ἕως ἄν-Formulierungen als mt Redaktion anzusehen ist, ist einerseits zu bedenken, daß die mit Lk übereinstimmende Wendung vom παρελθεῖν τὸν οὐρανὸν καὶ τὴν γῆν es zunächst nahelegt, daß Mt diese Formulierung aus dem Q-Logion übernommen hat. Andererseits hat K. BERGER, *Die Amen-Worte Jesu. Eine Untersuchung zum Problem der Legitimation in apokalyptischer Rede* (BZNW, 39), Berlin, 1970, esp. pp. 73-74, diese Beobachtung durch eine weitere präzisiert, die für den traditionsgeschichtlichen Hintergrund von Mt 5,18 von Belang ist. BERGER geht nämlich aufgrund eines Formschemas, welches aus einer Amen-Einleitung,

beide ἕως ἄv-Formulierungen auf Matthäus zurückzuführen sind (cf. auch n. 28). Näherliegend ist die Annahme, daß sie auf unterschiedliche Varianten des Logions zurückgehen, die Matthäus miteinander kombiniert hat. In diesem Fall wäre also auch für das Q-Logion eine Formulierung mit ἕως ἄv vorauszusetzen[29]. Unabhängig davon, wie man sich hier entscheidet, gilt jedoch, daß durch die Aussage vom Vergehen von Himmel und Erde die Unmöglichkeit einer Einschränkung der Geltung des νόμος zum Ausdruck gebracht wird. Von dem Logion in 16,16 unterscheidet sich das hiesige also zunächst dadurch, daß hier vom νόμος im Sinne konkreter Anweisungen gesprochen wird, die weiterhin in Kraft bleiben.

Für die inhaltliche Einordnung dieses Logions in die Jesusüberlieferung ist ein Vergleich mit der Analogie in Mk 13,30-31 aufschlußreich. Zunächst wird erkennbar, daß das Logion im Kontext apokalyptischer Belehrung tradiert werden konnte. Mk 13,30-31 gehört zu denjenigen Worten, in denen die Jünger über die Zeit bis zur Wiederkunft des Menschensohnes belehrt werden. Aus der sprachlichen Struktur lassen sich des weiteren Hinweise für die Deutung des Q-Logions eruieren. Setzt man nämlich aus den genannten Gründen voraus, daß auch dieses eine ἕως ἄv-Formulierung enthalten hat, so bringt Q hier die unveränderte Geltung des Gesetzes bis zum Wiederkommen Jesu als des Menschensohnes zum Ausdruck[30].

Ein zweiter aus dem Vergleich mit Mk 13,30-31 sich ergebender Aspekt folgt aus der Differenz zu der dort behaupteten ewigen Geltung

einer folgenden Negation mit οὐ μή und prophetischem Futur sowie einem mit ἕως oder μέχρις formuliertem Temporalsatz bestehe und sich vornehmlich in Mk 9,1; 13,30; 14,25; Mt 10,23 (in ähnlicher Weise auch in Mt 5,26 und Joh 13,38) feststellen lasse, davon aus, daß in Mt 5,18 die zweite ἕως ἄv-Formulierung (ἕως ἄν πάντα γένηται) ursprünglich, die erste (ἕως ἄν παρέλθῃ ὁ οὐρανὸς καὶ ἡ γῆ) dagegen von Matthäus sekundär hinzugefügt worden sei. Das von Berger herausgearbeitete Schema macht es in der Tat wahrscheinlich, daß hinter Mt 5,18 der Einfluß einer zu der Q-Version alternativen Fassung des Logions liegt. Die plausibelste Lösung scheint darum zu sein, daß Mt ein derartiges Logion mit der Q-Fassung kombiniert hat. (Anders KLINGHARDT [n. 12], p. 19, n. 15: Die Formulierung vom Vergehen von Himmel und Erde sei nicht von einem Q-Logion her, sondern auf der Grundlage von Mk 13,30-31 in Mt 5,18 eingefügt worden. Da man jedoch kaum annehmen wird, daß das Logion, das vom Nicht-Vergehen einer κεραία des νόμος [diff. Mk: der λόγοι Jesu] spricht, zweimal unabhängig voneinander entstanden ist, verliert sich die traditionsgeschichtliche Rückfrage bei Verzicht auf die Annahme eines Q-Logions im Dunkel.)

29. So urteilt etwa auch A. HARNACK, *Sprüche und Reden Jesu. Die zweite Quelle des Matthäus und Lukas*, Leipzig, 1907, p. 42, der als Wortlaut des Q-Logions ἕως ἄv παρέλθῃ ὁ οὐρανὸς καὶ ἡ γῆ, ἰῶτα ἓν ἢ μία κεραία οὐ μὴ παρέλθῃ ἀπὸ τοῦ νόμου rekonstruiert. Anders dagegen die Entscheidung des International Q Project, in *JBL* 109 (1990) 501, die der Lk-Fassung folgt.

30. E. SCHWEIZER, *Noch einmal Mt 5,17-20*, in *Das Wort und die Wörter*. FS G. Friedrich, Stuttgart u.a., 1973, pp. 69-73, nimmt unter Rekurs auf BERGER an, daß das Logion ursprünglich in einer Endzeitrede der judenchristlichen Gemeinde gestanden habe, die

der *Worte Jesu*, angesichts derer die in Q betonte Gültigkeit des νόμος als für die Q-Rezeption charakteristisches Element hervortritt. Die Frage nach dem traditionsgeschichtlichen Zusammenhang beider Varianten ist dabei nicht ohne weiteres zu beantworten. So ist etwa das Urteil von Kosch, Q 16,16 und 16,18 seien authentische Jesusworte, 16,17 dagegen ein eingefügtes Kommentarwort[31], ein Urteil, das eine bestimmte – nämlich gesetzeskritische – Akzentuierung der Verkündigung Jesu bereits voraussetzt, die dann nachträglich von Q abgeschwächt worden sei. Allerdings könnte auch die Betonung der Gültigkeit von Jesu Lehre bei Mk gerade einer gegenüber Tempel und Gesetz kritischen Darstellung der Verkündigung Jesu entspringen, was angesichts etwa von 11,22-25, wo die neue Haltung gegenüber Gott kritisch vom Tempel abgesetzt wird, durchaus plausibel erscheint. Gegenüber einem derartigen Urteil bezüglich der Konvergenz einer der Fassungen mit der Verkündigung des irdischen Jesus ist also durchaus Zurückhaltung angebracht.

Festhalten läßt sich somit, daß Q für eine Richtung innerhalb der frühen Rezeption der Jesusüberlieferung steht, für die die bleibende Gültigkeit des νόμος ein aktuelles Thema war. Q bezieht innerhalb der Diskussion um die Frage nach dem Verhältnis des νόμος zur Verkündigung Jesu eine Position, die sich von denjenigen des Markus oder Paulus dadurch unterscheidet, daß hier in einer intensiven Diskussion mit dem pharisäischen Judentum[32] die Gruppe der Jesusnachfolger selbst den Anspruch erhebt, den νόμος auf angemessene Weise zu interpretieren. Dies soll im folgenden durch den Blick auf die Interpretation einer konkreter Regelung, nämlich derjenigen in Q 16,18, in den Blick kommen.

---

damit gegen freiere Auffassungen vom Gesetz, wie sie etwa im Stephanuskreis existierten, protestiert habe. Von daher sei es dann in die Q-Überlieferurng aufgenommen worden. Auch wenn diese Rekonstruktion wohl noch zu sehr der aus dem lk Geschichtsbild entnommenen Gegenüberstellung judenchristlich – heidenchristlich verpflichtet ist, so dürfte doch die aus der sprachlichen Struktur und dem Inhalt des Logions sich ergebende Intention zutreffend erfaßt sein. Für die an der Bewahrung des νόμος ausgerichtete Version des Logions läßt sich somit als frühchristlicher Traditionskreis gerade die Q-Überlieferung selbst feststellen.

31. Cf. ID. (n. 6), p. 443; ähnlich SCHWEIZER (n. 30), p. 71: Die Redequelle habe mit dem Logion, wie auch sonst, Jesu Kritik am Gesetz abgeschwächt.

32. Die Pharisäer sind eindeutig diejenige Gruppe innerhalb des Judentums, mit der sich Q hauptsächlich konfrontiert sieht. Dies geht vornehmlich aus der Anti-Pharisäerrede in Q 11,29-52 hervor, in der in diesen eine ungenügende Beachtung der Vorschriften des νόμος vorgeworfen wird. Möglicherweise werden bereits in der Gerichtspredigt des Täufers in Q 3,7 die Pharisäer angesprochen (so R. URO, *John the Baptist and the Jesus Movement: What does Q tell us?* in PIPER [n. 2], pp. 231-257, esp. p. 234, sowie jetzt auch TUCKETT [n. 2], p. 116), obwohl dies aufgrund des divergierenden Textes (Matthäus nennt als Adressaten Φαρισαῖοι καὶ Σαδδουκαῖοι, Lukas οἱ ὄχλοι) unsicher bleibt.

2.4. Zu Q 16,18

Unter 2.1 wurde bereits dargelegt, daß nach der hier vertretenen Auffassung der Ort des Logions bei Lk auf die spezifische Verarbeitung der νόμος-Thematik im Horizont der Frage nach dessen Geltung unter den Bedingungen der Basileiaverkündigung zurückzuführen ist. Dies ist bei der nun zu diskutierenden Frage nach der sprachlichen Gestalt des Q-Logions zu berücksichtigen. Für die Nachzeichnung der traditionsgeschichtlichen Entwicklung des Logions ist dabei zunächst auf folgendes zu achten:

1) In allen Versionen der Synoptiker kommt eine Form von μοιχᾶσθαι bzw. μοιχεύειν vor. Es geht also immer um das Thema Ehebruch. Bei Paulus (1 Kor 7,10-11) ist dies nicht der Fall.

2) Die synoptischen Versionen sind weiter dadurch gekennzeichnet, daß jeweils in einem zweigliedrigen Logion zwei Formen des Ehebruchs beschrieben werden. Dabei unterscheiden sich die Mk- und die Q-Version in folgender Weise:

2.1) Nur in Mk 10,12 kommt die Möglichkeit in den Blick, daß sich die Frau vom Mann trennen kann. Damit befindet sich Markus in Übereinstimmung mit Paulus, bei dem die von der Frau ausgehende Trennung sogar denjenigen Fall darstellt, an dem er seine Anweisung entwickelt, wogegen das Nicht-Entlassen durch den Mann erst im Anschluß an diese genannt wird.

2.2) Die unmittelbaren Versionen des Q-Logions, also Mt 5,32 und Lk 16,18, sind dagegen dadurch gekennzeichnet, daß in einem zweigliedrigen Parallelismus sowohl das Entlassen der Frau als auch die Heirat einer Entlassenen als Formen des Ehebruchs gekennzeichnet werden. In beiden Fällen stellt also die Trennung einen vom Mann ausgehenden Akt dar.

2.3) Das Verbot der Wiederheirat ist offensichtlich kein ursprünglicher Bestandteil des Q-Logions, sondern von Mk 10,11-12 her sowohl in Mt 19,9 als auch in Lk 16,18 aufgenommen worden. Daraus folgt, daß die Pointe des Q-Logions anders zu bestimmen ist als diejenige bei Markus. Das Fehlen des Verbotes der Wiederheirat macht nämlich deutlich, daß Ehebruch hier dadurch entsteht, daß eine Frau geheiratet wird, die bereits zuvor mit einem Mann zu tun gehabt hat. Genau hierin liegt der Grund dafür, daß Matthäus in 5,32 schreibt, daß der Mann *die Frau* durch das Entlassen zu einer solchen macht, die die Ehe bricht (ποιεῖ αὐτὴν μοιχευθῆναι), nicht jedoch selbst zum Ehebrecher wird. Damit kann nämlich nur gemeint sein, daß der Ehebruch dadurch entsteht, daß die Frau *als Entlassene* wieder heiratet, was offensichtlich vorausgesetzt ist.

Dagegen wird der Mann, in Korrespondenz hierzu, erst dadurch selbst zum Ehebrecher, daß er eine Entlassene heiratet.

3) Nur bei Mt gibt es die »Unzuchtsklausel«, daß nämlich eine Frau nicht entlassen werden darf παρεκτὸς λόγου πορνείας (5,32) bzw. μὴ ἐπὶ πορνείᾳ (19,9).

Aus diesen Beobachtungen lassen sich folgende Schlußfolgerungen ableiten:

1) Die paulinische Version steht nur in einem weiteren traditionsgeschichtlichen, jedoch in keinem engeren sprachlichen Zusammenhang mit der synoptischen Überlieferung[33]. So ist hier etwa – entgegen dem in den synoptischen Versionen durchgängig anzutreffenden ἀπολύειν – von χωρισθῆναι die Rede. Auch findet sich bei Paulus kein Hinweis darauf, daß die Trennung von Frau und Mann im Horizont der Regelungen der Tora diskutiert wird. Gemeinsam mit den bereits genannten Differenzen weist dies darauf hin, daß Paulus frei aus ihm bekannter Jesusüberlieferung zitiert. Die mit Mk gemeinsame Erwähnung der Möglichkeit des Sich-Trennens der Frau weist in einen von dem Q-Logion verschiedenen kulturellen Raum, insofern hier ausdrücklich mit der Möglichkeit gerechnet wird, daß die Trennung auch von der Frau ausgehen kann. Diese Praxis ist in einem stärker hellenisierten Judentum zu suchen und widerspricht der gängigen jüdischen Rechtsauffassung[34].

2) Sowohl das Verbot der Heirat einer Entlassenen als auch die bei Mt überlieferte »Unzuchtsklausel« lassen sich dagegen nicht auf der Grundlage jüdischen Scheidungsrechtes erklären, sondern diskutieren die Ehefrage im Horizont von Reinheitsvorstellungen[35]. Anders als bei

---

33. Dieser Zusammenhang läßt sich nicht über das in Mk 10,11-12 par Mt bzw. Q 16,18 überlieferte Logion über Ehescheidung und Wiederheirat, sondern über das in Mk 10,9 anzutreffende Wort über die Unauflöslichkeit der Ehe (ὃ οὖν ὁ θεὸς συνέζευξεν ἄνθρωπος μὴ χωριζέτω) greifen, insofern es auch bei Paulus um das μὴ χωρίζεσθαι bzw. die Versöhnung nach erfolgter Trennung geht. Cf. hierzu auch M. und R. ZIMMERMANN, *Zitation, Kontradiktion oder Applikation? Die Jesuslogien in 1 Kor 7,10f. und 9,14: Traditionsgeschichtliche Verankerung und paulinische Interpretation*, in ZNW 87 (1996) 83-100, esp. pp. 94-96.

34. Diese leitet sich von Dtn 24,1-4 her, wo die Trennung als nur vom Mann ausgehende diskutiert wird. Das hier begegnende Verbot der Rückkehr zu dem ersten Mann nach einmal erfolgter Trennung wird etwa auch von Philo, SpecLeg 3,30-31, vertreten.

35. Cf. hierzu auch K. BERGER, *Die Gesetzesauslegung Jesu. Ihr historischer Hintergrund im Judentum und im Alten Testament, Teil I: Markus und Parallelen* (WMANT, 40), Neukirchen-Vluyn, 1972, pp. 508-575, esp. pp. 561-567. Im Hintergrund stehen zum einen die sexuellen Reinheitsvorschriften aus Lev 18, die im nachexilischen Judentum vielfältig rezipiert worden sind, zum anderen die bei Lev 21,7.14-15 (cf. auch Ez 44,22) eigentlich nur für Priester geltende Weisung, keine Ehebrecherin oder Geschiedene zu heiraten. In der traditionsgeschichtlichen Entwicklung tritt unter dem Einfluß dieser Texte

Mk geht es hier nicht um eine Begründung aus der Schöpfungsordnung, die dort gegen die Tora gestellt wird, sondern um eine Regelung des Sexuellen, die die atl. Reinheitsgebote für Priester ausweitet und sie darüber hinaus zur grundsätzlichen Behandlung der Ehefrage heranzieht[36]. Eine aufschlußreiche Analogie in der Behandlung der Ehefrage ist diesbezüglich in Qumran anzutreffen, wo – unter Bezugnahme auf Gen 1,27 (cf. Mk 10,6); Dtn 17,17 – zu Lebzeiten zwei Frauen zu haben als Unzucht (זנות) und damit als Verstoß gegen Reinheitsgebote gegeißelt wird[37]. Hier werden also die beiden Begründungen des ursprünglichen Schöpfungswillens (cf. Mk 10,3-9) sowie das Reinheitsgebot (cf. Mt 5,32 [Q]) gemeinsam angeführt, die dann in der synoptischen Überlieferung auseinandertreten. Innerhalb der letzteren liegen Mk 10,11-12 und Mt 5,32 somit am weitesten auseinander.

3) In bezug auf das Q-Logion läßt sich weiter festhalten, daß die mt »Unzuchtsklausel« genau auf der Linie der bereits festgestellten Intention liegt. Q könnte diese Klausel somit durchaus bereits enthalten und Matthäus dadurch veranlaßt haben, die Ausnahmeregelung auch in den Mk-Text einzufügen[38]. Neben der sprachlichen Beobachtung, daß Matthäus in den Mk-Text mit μὴ ἐπὶ πορνείας eine stärker gräzisierte Fassung einfügt, als sie in dem Logion in 5,32 begegnet, spricht hierfür

der Aspekt der Reinheit bei der Diskussion des Themas »Ehescheidung« in verschiedenen jüdischen Texten deutlich in den Vordergrund.
36. Cf. BERGER (n. 35), pp. 564-566. Ersteres findet sich etwa in Josephus, Ant 3,276 (die Priester dürfen keine Dirne, Sklavin, Kriegsgefangene, Gastwirtin oder von ihrem früheren Mann Verstoßene heiraten); Philo, Somn 2,185 (Auslegung von Lev 21,17.13: der Hohepriester ist Mann einer Jungfrau, die auch eine solche bleibt, ähnlich Josephus, Ant 3,277); letzteres in Jub 33,9 (Jakob nähert sich Bilha nicht mehr, weil Ruben sie durch seinen Beischlaf mit ihr für jeden anderen Mann verunreinigt hat); PsSal 8,10 (Eidesabkommen [συνθῆκαι μετὰ ὅρκου] über den Verkehr mit der Frau des Nächsten werden als Ehebruch bezeichnet); TestRub 3,15 (Jakob rührt Balla nach der Gottlosigkeit [ἀσέβεια], die Ruben an ihr verübt hat, nicht mehr an); TestLevi 9,10 (Levi soll sich eine Frau nehmen, die jung, ohne Makel und Befleckung ist und nicht aus einem fremdstämmigen Geschlecht stammt); Josephus, Ant 4,244 (Verbot für alle jungen Männer Israels, eine Frau zu heiraten, die keine Jungfrau oder eine Sklavin ist); Herm mand 4,1,4-10 (ein Mann sündigt solange nicht, wie er ohne Wissen mit einer ehebrecherischen Frau zusammenlebt; wenn er sie entläßt und eine andere heiratet, begeht er Ehebruch). Die bei Josephus, Ant 3,277 noch auf den Hohenpriester bezogene Forderung, die Jungfrau als solche zu bewahren, wird bei Paulus, 1 Kor 7,37-38 bereits als das grundsätzlich als κρεῖσσον zu Bewertende genannt.
37. Cf. CDC 4,20-5,2. In 5,9-11 werden die eigentlich für Männer geschriebenen Inzestgesetze auch auf Frauen ausgedehnt, was noch einmal die Tendenz zur Verallgemeinerung der atl. Bestimmungen zeigt. Cf. weiter 11QTempel 57,15-19 (keine fremdstämmige Frau, nicht mehr als eine Frau, Wiederheirat ausschließlich im Fall des Todes der ersten Frau).
38. Die Unzuchtsklausel wird etwa auch von LUZ (n. 11), p. 269, als vormt beurteilt, wenngleich er in bezug auf einen Q-Text zurückhaltend bleibt.

auch, daß die Scheidung bei Unzucht sich auf der Grundlage der genannten jüdischen Reinheitsvorstellungen gerade als Intention des Q-Logions verständlich machen läßt, insofern nämlich der gemeinsame Bezugspunkt der Klausel und des Verbotes, eine Entlassene zu heiraten, darin liegt, daß in beiden Fällen die Frau für den Mann unrein geworden ist und darum für die Ehe nicht mehr zur Verfügung steht. Damit jedoch liegt hier eine Rezeption der Regelungen des jüdischen νόμος vor, die sich grundsätzlich von derjenigen bei Mk unterscheidet. Die bereits in Dtn 24,1 zugebilligte Regelung, daß der Mann die Frau wegen einer דבר ערות entlassen kann (LXX: ὅτι εὗρεν ἐν αὐτῇ ἄσχημον πρᾶγμα), wird in Q (und Mt) nämlich in Übereinstimmung mit einer Traditionslinie, in der kultische Reinheit und Ehe in enge Beziehung zueinander gesetzt werden, zur Grundlage der Definition von Ehebruch erhoben[39]. Bei Mk dagegen wird die Bestimmung aus Dtn 24,1 (γράψει αὐτῇ βιβλίον ἀποστασίου καὶ δώσει εἰς τὰς χεῖρας αὐτῆς) den Schöpfungsaussagen aus Gen 1,27 und 2,24 konfrontiert und dadurch als Zugeständnis an die σκληροκαρδία der Juden dargestellt. Anders gesagt: Während Mk an eine von der Schöpfungsordnung geforderte Treuepflicht gegenüber dem Ehepartner appelliert, die auch durch das Ausstellen eines Scheidebriefes nicht unterlaufen werden kann, ist für Q und Mt die Frage der Ehescheidung im Horizont des Zusammenhangs von Sexualität und Reinheit zu diskutieren, was konkret bedeutet, daß Sexualverkehr mit *einem* Mann die Frau für alle anderen zur Unreinen macht. Zugespitzt läßt sich aus Mt 5,32 nämlich folgern, daß es nicht verboten ist, eine Frau wegen Unzucht zu entlassen und daraufhin eine Nicht-Geschiedene zu heiraten. Beide Positionen knüpfen somit auf je unterschiedliche Weise an Vorstellungen an, die sich im Judentum des Zweiten Tempels auf der Grundlage von Lev 18 und 21 bzw. Dtn 24 entwickelt hatten.

4) Die oft anzutreffende Behauptung, die verschiedenen Versionen des Ehescheidungs-Logions ließen sich auf ein absolutes Scheidungsverbot Jesu zurückführen, der damit die Regelungen des jüdischen Gesetzes verschärft habe[40], läßt sich so nicht verifizieren. Festzuhalten ist vielmehr, daß Umgang mit einer unrein gewordenen Frau in Q, Entlassen und Wiederheirat von Frau und Mann bei Mk als Ehebruch definiert werden. Paulus dagegen spricht nur von Alleinbleiben oder Versöhnung

---

39. Es ist eine bereits verschiedentlich geäußerte Annahme, daß die Wendung λόγος πορνείας aus Mt 5,32 eine Rezeption des in Dtn 24,1 angegebenen Scheidungsgrundes darstellt, cf. BERGER (n. 35), pp. 512-513; LUZ (n. 11), p. 274, n. 32. Es könnte ein nicht über die LXX vermittelter Rückgriff auf die atl. Tradition vorliegen, der bereits für Q reklamiert werden kann.

40. Cf. etwa G. STRECKER, *Die Antithesen der Bergpredigt (Mt 5,21-48 par)*, in ZNW 69 (1978) 36-72, esp. pp. 52-56.

als möglichen Konsequenzen der Trennung, klammert also die Thematik Ehebruch von vornherein aus. Welche dieser Positionen auf die Verkündigung Jesu zurückzuführen ist, läßt sich nicht einfach durch ein Subtraktionsverfahren ermitteln, in welchem der kleinste gemeinsame Nenner als das historisch Ursprüngliche deklariert wird. Vielmehr muß mit der Möglichkeit gerechnet werden, daß *eine* der hier sichtbar werdenden Begründungen aus der Verkündigung Jesu stammt.

In bezug auf die zur Diskussion stehende Frage zeigt sich somit, daß innerhalb der Jesusüberlieferung eine Linie existiert, für die die Auseinandersetzung um die Auslegung der Tora auf eine grundsätzlich andere Weise erfolgt, als dies bei Mk der Fall ist. Dies soll nunmehr in einigen abschließenden Bemerkungen etwas präzisiert werden.

3. Zusammenfassung

Aus der Analyse von Q 16,16-18 ist deutlich geworden, daß der mit dem Auftreten des Johannes datierende Anbruch der βασιλεία sowie der damit im Zusammenhang stehende Konflikt, in dem die Q-Boten gegenwärtig stehen, als ein in Kontinuität zu Propheten und Gesetz stehendes Ereignis gewertet wird (16,16). Des weiteren wurde deutlich, daß die Q-Überlieferung die unveränderte Gültigkeit des Gesetzes als einen in der Jesusüberlieferung verankerten Topos betrachtet und ihre eigene Aufnahme und Fortsetzung dieser Verkündigung von dieser Überzeugung getragen ist (16,17). Schließlich wurde anhand der spezifischen Gestalt des Scheidungsverbotes in 16,18 erkennbar, daß die konkrete Rezeption der Regelungen des νόμος im Horizont einer Tradition erfolgt, in welcher jüdische Reinheitsvorstellungen eine Rolle spielen und die sich diesbezüglich von der markinischen Aufnahme unterscheidet. Die konsequenteste Fortsetzung dieser Ansätze der Q-Überlieferung findet sich dagegen bei Matthäus, dessen Entwurf sich an vielen Stellen konzeptionell eher als Deutung der Mk-Erzählung im Lichte von Q verstehen läßt als umgekehrt[41].

Es dürfte somit gerade die Q-Überlieferung dafür verantwortlich zeichnen, daß auch in der späteren Entwicklung der Jesusüberlieferung das

---

41. Diese These kann hier nur angedeutet werden. Markant ist freilich, daß bei Matthäus mit der Hinwendung zu den ἔθνη ein entscheidender Schritt über Q hinaus erfolgt. Gerade an den diesbezüglichen Stellen zeigt sich jedoch, wie Matthäus diesen Vorgang als einen solchen versteht, der keinesfalls selbstverständlich ist, sondern auf dem erstaunlichen Glauben der Heiden sowie der Ablehnung Jesu durch »Israel« gleichermaßen basiert. Gerade für das MtEv dürfte somit die in der Forschung lange Zeit heftig diskutierte Alternative »judenchristlich/heidenchristlich« zu kurz greifen.

Element der Bewahrung des νόμος lebendig geblieben ist. Sowohl Matthäus als auch Lukas haben diese Frage auf je eigene Weise diskutiert und in ihren Konzeptionen weitergeführt. Es läßt sich von daher zumindest anfragen, ob die Sicht, daß Jesus selbst der Tora kritisch gegenübergestanden habe und gegenläufige Tendenzen als spätere Angleichungen seiner Verkündigung an das jüdische Gesetz durch judenchristliche Kreise zu beurteilen seien, nicht noch einmal zu überdenken wäre. Möglicherweise läßt sich der Streit um die rechte Interpretation des νόμος ja als ein der Jesusüberlieferung von Beginn an inhärentes Element wahrscheinlich machen, das erst durch die Orientierung an den paulinischen Aussagen über das Gesetz[42] in den Hintergrund gedrängt worden ist[43].

Waisenstr. 28
D-10179 Berlin

Jens SCHRÖTER

---

42. Ob sich diese als primär *gesetzeskritisch* verstehen lassen, wäre freilich noch einmal eigens zu fragen.
43. Cf. hierzu auch die Ausführungen von K. BERGER, *Jesus als Pharisäer und frühe Christen als Pharisäer,* in *NT* 30 (1988) 231-262.

INTERPRETATION OF SCRIPTURE AS AN INDICATOR
OF SOCIO-HISTORICAL CONTEXT

THE CASE OF THE ESCHATOLOGICAL DISCOURSES IN MARK AND Q

Recent scholarship has shown a particular interest in the study of Q, and in reconstructing its socio-historical context. The assumption behind much of this research has been that Q is the earliest and most authentic reflection of the thought of Jesus and his first followers, and that the synoptic evangelists including Mark reflect later developments in the Jesus tradition[1]. Some recent scholars have argued that Mark distorted the Jesus traditions through introducing eschatological conceptions and expectations to what were originally non-eschatological sapiential traditions[2]. Other scholars postulate that the Q traditions themselves were fundamentally reshaped through the introduction of eschatological motifs by a later redactor[3].

Eschatology is deeply rooted in the Hebrew religious tradition, and unequivocally attested in the prophetic and apocalyptic traditions preserved in Scripture[4]. Eschatological conceptions would therefore have been familiar to any first century Jew sympathetic to the prophetic and apocalyptic traditions, and expectations of divine intervention in history were widely held in Palestine and beyond[5]. This does not mean that apocalyptic eschatology, insofar as that is a speculative literary exercise, was fundamental to the thought of most Jews of the period. There was nevertheless the widespread expectation that divine justice would be brought about through intervention by the God of Israel in terrestrial history, not necessarily on

---

1. The dependence of Mark on Q has been argued by J. LAMBRECHT, *Der Redaktion der Markus-Apokalypse*, Rome, 1967. The priority of Q is also argued by A. D. JACOBSON, *The First Gospel*, Sonoma, CA, 1992. However, neither of these scholars maintains that Mark and the other synoptic evangelists fundamentally alter the sense of the Jesus traditions in their use of Q, as do some authors with whose work this paper will be particularly concerned.

2. See especially B. L. MACK, *A Myth of Innocence*, Philadelphia, PA, 1988.

3. J. S. KLOPPENBORG, *The Formation of Q*, Philadelphia, PA, 1987; B. L. MACK, *The Lost Gospel*, San Francisco, CA, 1993. Cf. also J. M. ROBINSON & H. KOESTER, *Trajectories through Early Christianity*, Philadelphia, PA, 1971.

4. See especially S. L. COOK, *Prophecy and Apocalypticism*, Minneapolis, MN, 1995; P. D. HANSON, *The Dawn of Apocalyptic*, Philadelphia, PA, 1975.

5. For discussion see J. J. COLLINS, *The Apocalyptic Imagination*, New York, 1984; C. C. ROWLAND, *The Open Heaven*, London, 1982; E. P. SANDERS, *Judaism: Practice and Belief 63 BCE – 66 CE*, London, 1992.

a cosmic scale, nor even necessarily with absolute finality, but nonetheless decisively. Such an eschatological consciousness pervades the New Testament, and is particularly prominent in Revelation and the letters of Paul as well as the synoptic Gospels[6]. Scholars since Schweitzer[7] have recognised eschatology as fundamental to the Jewish context of Jesus' ministry and teaching. It is therefore perhaps not surprising that the recent tendency towards relegation of eschatological motifs to the status of secondary interpolations in the Jesus tradition has led at least some scholars to question whether Jesus espoused any Jewish consciousness at all, and whether he stood in continuity with and revered the Hebrew Scriptures[8].

This location of the Jesus movement in the context of an hellenistic Cynicism, in which his Jewish ethnic, religious, and cultural identity are reduced to an incidental detail, seems to rest on a series of untenable assumptions. The first, already alluded to above, is that the gospel of Mark can be dated substantially later than Q[9]. Secondly, the identification

---

6. For discussion see G.R. BEASLEY-MURRAY, *Jesus and the Last Days,* Peabody, MA, 1993; E.S. FIORENZA, *The Book of Revelation,* Philadelphia, PA, 1984; B.W. LONGE-NECKER, *Eschatology and the Covenant,* Sheffield, 1991; ROWLAND (n. 5).

7. A. SCHWEITZER, *Von Reimarus zu Wrede,* Tübingen, 1906.

8. See especially MACK (n. 2). This tendency is most notably represented in historical Jesus studies by J.D. CROSSAN, *The Historical Jesus,* San Francisco, CA, 1991. See also L.E. VAAGE, *Galilean Upstarts: Jesus' First Followers according to Q,* Valley Forge PA, 1994.

9. A post-70 date for Mark is defended by S.G.F. BRANDON, *The Date of the Markan Gospel,* in *NTS* 7 (1961) 126-141; H. CONZELMANN, *Geschichte und Eschaton nach Mc 13,* in *ZNW* 50 (1959) 210-221; M.D. HOOKER, *The Gospel according to Saint Mark,* Peabody MA, 1991; LAMBRECHT (n. 1), and others. G. THEISSEN, *Lokalkolorit und Zeitgeschichte in den Evangelien,* Göttingen, 1989, likewise dates the final redaction of Mark to the post-70 period, but dates the crucial eschatological discourse very much earlier, to the early 40's CE. An early date for Mark 13 is also argued by N.H. TAYLOR, *Palestinian Christianity and the Caligula Crisis,* in *JSNT* 61 (1996) 101-124; 62 (1996) 13-41, and for the Gospel of Mark as a whole by E.P. TROCMÉ, *La formation de l'Évangile selon Marc,* Paris, 1963. Perhaps the most common dating for Mark, however, is to the period between c. 64 and 70 CE, A.Y. COLLINS, *The Beginning of the Gospel,* Minneapolis, MN, 1992; F. HAHN, *Die Rede von der Parusie des Menschensohnes Markus 13,* in R. PESCH & R. SCHNACKENBURG (eds.), *Jesus und der Menschensohn,* Freiburg, 1975, pp. 240-266; M. HENGEL, *Studies in the Gospel of Mark,* London, 1985, pp. 14-30; W. MARXSEN, *Der Evangelist Markus,* Göttingen, 1959. The date of Q is virtually impossible to establish, and whether it can be identified as a single document, and the stage in its history when the traditions were committed to writing, are all debatable. An early date is suggested, at least for a substantial part of the eschatological discourse, by D.R. CATCHPOLE, *The Quest for Q,* Edinburgh, 1993, pp. 254-255. This would compare with the dating suggested for the non-eschatological sections by KLOPPENBORG (n. 3) and MACK (n. 3), and with THEISSEN's dating of Q as a whole. A somewhat later date for Q as a whole, but ascribing it to the period before 70 CE, is argued by D. LÜHRMANN, *Die Redaktion der Logienquelle,* Neukirchen-Vluyn, 1969. For a comprehensive treatment of the dating of Q, see C.M. TUCKETT, *Q and the History of Early Christianity,* Edinburgh, 1996. The balance of evidence would clearly seem to suggest that Mark and Q should be seen as broadly contemporaneous, and that neither can be accorded absolute priority over the other.

of distinct strata within Q, with the eschatological passages assigned to the later stratum known as Q^2, seems likewise to rest on questionable presuppositions, and certainly to exceed the available evidence[10]. The eschatological pericopae are dated late because it is assumed that the earliest traditions were non-eschatological, and on the same basis texts in the hypothetical Q^1 are interpreted in exclusively sapiential terms so as to be devoid of eschatological overtones. A third untenable presupposition, upon which the second is substantially founded, is that of a dichotomy between the wisdom and prophetic-apocalyptic traditions in Israel. Such a disjunction has been shown to be unsustainable in scholarship[11]. Fourthly, the dichotomy between Judaism and Hellenism which has quite rightly been moderated in scholarship largely through the influence of M. Hengel[12], has come to be collapsed entirely, at least so far as Galilee is concerned, so that Jesus and his followers are denied any distinctively Jewish characteristics[13]. The notion of the dissipation of ethnic, religious, and cultural identity in first century Galilee not merely assumes that the co-existence between diverse communities necessarily led to coalescence in their identities, but it overlooks the absence of any Galilean institutions which could form the basis of a new collective religious and cultural identity[14]. Jesus was undoubtedly a Galilean, but he was none the less self-consciously Jewish, and shared in the heritage and identity of the community whose

---

10. The division of Q into rigidly defined strata is argued most cogently by KLOPPENBORG (n. 3). A similar reconstruction is offered by MACK (n. 3). Cf. also R. URO, *Sheep among the Wolves*, Helsinki, 1987. The unity of Q is defended by A.D. JACOBSON, *The Literary Unity of Q*, in *JBL* 101 (1982) 365-389. TUCKETT (n. 9) argues for the gradual accumulation of traditions rather than distinct strata.

11. D.C. ALLISON, *A Plea for a Thoroughgoing Eschatology*, in *JBL* 113 (1994) 651-668; C. E. CARLSTON, *Wisdom and Eschatology in Q*, in J. DELOBEL (ed.), *Logia. Les Paroles de Jésus – The Parables of Jesus*, Leuven, 1982, pp. 101-119; R. A. HORSLEY, *Innovation in Search of Reorientation: New Testament Studies Rediscovering its Subject Matter*, in *JAAR* 62 (1994) 1127-1166; G. VON RAD, *Weisheit in Israel*. Neukirchen-Vluyn, 1970; M. SATO, *Wisdom in the Sphere of Prophecy*, in R.A. PIPER (ed.), *The Gospel behind the Gospels*, Leiden, 1995, pp. 139-158; J. Z. SMITH, *Wisdom and Apocalyptic*, in B. A. PEARSON (ed.), *Religious Syncretism in Antiquity*, Missoula, MT, 1975, pp. 131-156.

12. M. HENGEL, *Judentum und Hellenismus*, Tübingen, 1973.

13. H. O. GUENTHER, *The Sayings Gospel Q and the Quest for Aramaic Sources: Rethinking Christian Origins*, in J. S. KLOPPENBORG & L. E. VAAGE (eds.), *Early Christianity, Q, and Jesus*. in *Semeia* 55 (1992) 41-76; MACK (nn. 2-3). *Pace*, S.V. FREYNE, *Galilee from Alexander the Great to Hadrian*, Wilmington, DE, 1980; HENGEL (n. 12); H.C. KEE, *Early Christianity in the Galilee: Reassessing the Evidence from the Gospels*, in L.I. LEVINE (ed.), *The Galilee in Late Antiquity*, New York, 1992, pp. 3-22.

14. MACK (n. 2), p. 65; (n. 3), pp. 51-68; GUENTHER (n. 13). *Pace*, D.R. EDWARDS, *The Socio-Economic and Cultural Ethos of the Lower Galilee in the First Century. Implications for the Nascent Jesus Movement*, in LEVINE (n. 13), pp. 53-74; S.V. FREYNE, *Urban-Rural Relations in First Century Galilee*, in LEVINE (n. 13), pp. 75-91.

centre, however remote, was the Temple in Jerusalem[15]. It is also worth noting in this regard that Paul was well aware of Jesus' Jewish identity and his observance of the Law[16], and finds no historical precedent for his ideology of unity in Christ between Jew and Gentile[17] in the Galilean Jesus movement. We should therefore expect that Gospel traditions reflecting Jesus' historical ministry should be pervaded with a Jewish eschatological consciousness, and should affirm the prophetic expectation that the God of Israel would intervene imminently and effectively in human history, and thereby establish a new and just world order.

The Jesus movement stood in continuity with the prophetic-eschatological tradition rooted in the Hebrew Scriptures, and to this Q bears eloquent testimony[18]. An eschatological consciousness is apparent not only in the conflation of sayings preserved in Lk 17,22-37[19], and the judgement saying in Lk 13,34-35[20], but also in such sayings as the Beatitudes which imply future divine intervention and reversal of fortune: "those who are poor, hungry and mourning in the present are promised a reversal of their present suffering state in an eschatological future"[21]. Q is furthermore quite self-consciously Jewish, and presupposes Torah observance in the community, and far more so than can be extrapolated from Mark[22].

15. S.V. FREYNE, *Galilee, Jesus, and the Gospels*, Philadelphia, PA, 1988, esp. pp. 176-213; E.P. SANDERS, *Jesus and Judaism*, London, 1985, pp. 133-156; G. VERMES, *Jesus the Jew*, London, 1973; *The Religion of Jesus the Jew*, Minneapolis, MN, 1993, pp. 119-150. For the contrary view see CROSSAN (n. 8); MACK (n. 3), pp. 51-68.

16. Rom 1,3; Gal 4,4. In the course of his long struggle for equal access for Gentiles to fellowship with Christian Jews, Paul was unable to cite the example of the historical Jesus in support of his position. This is particularly significant, given that Paul was at times in conflict with relatives and disciples of Jesus, Gal 2,11-14. For discussion see N. H. TAYLOR, *Paul, Antioch and Jerusalem*, Sheffield, 1992, esp. pp. 123-139.

17. 1 Cor 12,13; Gal 3,28. For discussion see E. P. SANDERS, *Paul, the Law, and the Jewish People*, London, 1983; N. H. TAYLOR, *Paolo: Fariseo, Cristiano e Dissonante*, in *Religione e Società* 24 (1996) 22-39; F. B. WATSON, *Paul, Judaism and the Gentiles*, Cambridge, 1986.

18. The overtly eschatological orientation of Q is defended by CARLSTON (n. 11), pp. 114-117; R.A. EDWARDS, *A Theology of Q*, London, 1976, pp. 371-379; P. HOFFMANN, *Studien zur Theologie der Logienquelle*, Münster, 1972, esp. pp. 34-49; JACOBSON (n. 1), pp. 72-76; LÜHRMANN (n. 9), pp. 69-83; SATO (n. 11); TUCKETT (n. 9), pp. 150-152; 175-194.

19. M.E. BORING, *The Continuing Voice of Jesus*, Louisville, KY, 1991, pp. 228-29; cf. EDWARDS (n. 18), pp. 140-142; H.L. EGELKRAUT, *Jesus' Mission to Jerusalem*, Frankfurt, 1976, pp. 186-188; KLOPPENBORG (n. 3), pp. 154-168; LÜHRMANN (n. 18), pp. 69-94; TUCKETT (n. 9), pp. 159-60.

20. CARLSTON (n. 11), p. 105; EDWARDS (n. 18), pp. 132-133; P. HOFFMANN, *The Redaction of Q and the Son of Man*, in PIPER (n. 11), pp. 159-198, esp. p. 191; T. W. MANSON, *The Sayings of Jesus*, London, 1957, pp. 126-128.

21. TUCKETT (n. 9), p. 141. Cf. CATCHPOLE (n. 9), p. 86; MANSON (n. 20), pp. 46-49. *Pace*, VAAGE (n. 8), pp. 55-65.

22. TUCKETT (n. 9), pp. 393-424. Cf. also JACOBSON (n. 10); URO (n. 10).

This is not to deny that there are significant differences of substance and emphasis, as well as of agenda, among the various strands in the gospel tradition, or that these need to be seriously considered. Q and Mark both presuppose a mythology which anticipates future divine intervention, judgement and deliverance, in which a figure described as ὁ υἱὸς τοῦ ἀνθρώπου plays a prominent part. The eschatology of Mark, however, is quite evidently and inextricably bound up with expectation of the desolation of the Temple; a motif which is a great deal less prominent in Q, but nonetheless present. The lower profile of the Temple in Q does not in itself imply that the central institution of Palestinian Judaism was insignificant to the religiosity of the Q community, even if it was somewhat peripheral to the daily life of the Galilean Jesus movement[23]. I wish to propose that the place of the Temple in the eschatological conceptions of the Mark and Q communities is crucial to understanding the differences between them, and in particular their respective appeals to Scripture, and that the differences in their socio-historical contexts can to some extent at least account for this. Before exploring this thesis, however, some consideration of the "son of man" figure is necessary[24].

The precise meaning of the expression ὁ υἱὸς τοῦ ἀνθρώπου and its various possible Hebrew and Aramaic antecedents is widely debated. That the Greek renders a Semitic original, however, is surely beyond doubt. The cumbersome, and superficially redundant, phrase presupposes a social and historical context in which Semitic idiom continues to enjoy currency[25]. The use of the term ὁ υἱὸς τοῦ ἀνθρώπου therefore indicates a proximity to Aramaic-speaking Jewish Palestine, where such a convoluted mode of expression would have been meaningful. I would wish to argue further that it presupposes a social and historical context in which the Hebrew Scriptures are revered.

We need to consider the possible meanings of ὁ υἱὸς τοῦ ἀνθρώπου in Q 17,22-37. A generic sense would seem most unlikely in this context, as a specific, even if not readily identifiable, figure is designated, rather than humanity in general. A circumlocutory sense is not independently

23. CATCHPOLE (n. 9), p. 279; FREYNE (n. 15), pp. 219-239; SANDERS (n. 5), pp. 47-72; (n. 15), pp. 61-76; *Pace*, CROSSAN (n. 8); JACOBSON (n. 1), p. 231; MACK (n. 3), p. 174.

24. For fuller discussion see P.M. CASEY, *Son of Man*, London, 1979; J.A. FITZMYER, *The New Testament Title "Son of Man" Philologically Considered*, in *A Wandering Aramaean*, Missoula, MT, 1979, pp. 143-160; *Another View of the "Son of Man" Debate*, in *JSNT* 4 (1979) 56-68; B. LINDARS, *Jesus Son of Man*. London, 1983; G. VERMES, *The Use of* bar nash/bar nasha *in Jewish Aramaic*, in *Post-Biblical Jewish Studies*, Leiden, 1975, pp. 147-165; *"The Son of Man" Debate*, in *JSNT* 1 (1978) 19-32; *The Present State of the "Son of Man" Debate*, in *JJS* 29 (1978) 123- 134.

25. Cf. C.M. TUCKETT, *On the Stratification of Q*, KLOPPENBORG & VAAGE (n. 13), pp. 213-222, esp. 218-222.

attested in the first century[26], and the identification of Jesus with the "son of man", at whatever level of the tradition, would not in any case depend upon its being a self-designation in this context, but rather on the christological understanding of the community. A recent theory has argued that the meaning derives from Palestinian colloquial usage, in which the term was applied to heirs or aspirants to legitimate, as opposed to imperial, royal power[27]. It is difficult to see how this could apply in texts referring to sudden, cataclysmic, judgement rather than to wars of liberation, however. This does not exclude the possibility that the Jesus tradition appropriated and reinterpreted Galilean colloquial expressions, but it does not adequately account for the usage in this text. An indefinite sense of the term could be meaningful only if the text is deliberately enigmatic, if not esoteric, and presupposes a definite identification of the person referred to as "the son of man", known at least to a select group within the community. This requires that the phrase derives its meaning from a body of tradition within which the enigmatic and esoteric usage is clearly understood, interpreted, and applied. I would therefore argue with scholars such as Lindars and Tuckett that the usage of ὁ υἱὸς τοῦ ἀνθρώπου in the Q eschatological discourse is dependent upon, and in continuity with, the Jewish apocalyptic-eschatological tradition associated with Daniel[28]. One should not, however, overlook the cautions of Casey that the influence of Daniel may be very indirect[29]. As with the *Similitudes of Enoch* and 4 Ezra, "son of man" or "human-like figure" is not so much a formal title as a cryptic but unambiguous designation of the eschatological judge[30]. While allusions to Daniel are a great deal less explicit in Q 17 than in Mark 13, both Mark and Q reflect continuity with that tradition, in which ὁ υἱὸς τοῦ ἀνθρώπου designates an eschatological judge and redeemer figure.

While both Mark and, however indirectly, Q stand in continuity with the apocalyptic-eschatological tradition rooted in the Hebrew Scriptures, significant differences remain in their explicit citations of the Biblical texts. Mark 13 resonates with citations of and allusions to passages in the Hebrew Bible, in particular the eschatological sections

---

26. FITZMYER (n. 24). For the contrary view see VERMES (n. 24).
27. D.E. OAKMAN, *Rulers' Houses, Thieves, and Usurpers*, in *Forum* 4 (1988) 109-123.
28. LINDARS (n. 24), pp. 93-99; TUCKETT (n. 9), pp. 266-276.
29. CASEY (n. 24), pp. 189, 195-196.
30. *I Enoch* 46,1-8; 48,2-8; 62,2-12; 69,27.29 (70,1; 71,14.17); 4 Ezra 13,3.5.51. So CASEY (n. 24), pp. 100-102; COLLINS (n. 5), pp. 147-150; G.W.E. NICKELSBURG, *Jewish Literature between the Bible and the Mishnah*, Philadelphia, PA, 1981, p. 215. Similarly, the "anointed one" in 2 Baruch 29,3; 30,1; 39,7; 40,1; 70,10; 72,2.

of Daniel[31]. Allusions to Scripture in the Q apocalypse are relatively sparse, and refer not to the prophetic- apocalyptic-eschatological traditions but to the Genesis myths of the flood[32] and the destruction of Sodom and Gomorrah[33]. At first sight this may suggest a fundamental difference of interest and inspiration between future expectations and past recollections of divine intervention on earth. However, cataclysmic events of the past as well as present experience of distress inspire the imagery employed in apocalyptic literature, and the Genesis narratives are recalled precisely to compare the past events related therein with the future events to come as suddenly, as unexpectedly, and as cataclysmically, through direct divine intervention in terrestrial history. This is not to suggest that primordial past and eschatological future can be identified, however closely related they may be as representing the implementation of the divine will on earth[34]. Furthermore, the Genesis texts are cited not to recall any ideal primaeval state, but to illustrate the suddenness with which the future eschatological judgement would be unleashed[35]. The question remains, why, when Mark cites the most eschatologically explicit portions of the Hebrew Bible, should Q choose to illustrate future predictions by appeal to the myths of cosmic destruction in Genesis? It is at this level, not so much in their interpretation of Scripture as in their selection of texts to employ, that Mark and Q seem to differ. Both stand in continuity with the prophetic-apocalyptic-eschatological tradition; both expect a future eschatological judgement and deliverance presided over by the figure cryptically referred to as the "son of man". I wish to suggest that the difference in the use of Scripture in these passages can be accounted for in terms of the social and historical contexts of their respective traditions.

Mark locates the closing stages of the ministry of Jesus, culminating in his death and resurrection, in Jerusalem. The account of Jesus' death is bound up with symbolism of the destruction of the Temple[36]. Irrespective

---

31. Mk 13,8 > 2 Chron 15,6; Isa 19,2; Mk 13,12 > Micah 7,6; Mk 13,14 > Dan 9,27; 11,31; 12,11; Mk 13,19 > Dan 12,1; Mk 13,22 > Deut 13,2; Mk 13,24 > Isa 13,10; 34,4; Mk 13,26-27 > Dan 7,13-14; Mk 13,30 > Deut 30,3-4. For discussion see BEASLEY-MURRAY (n. 6); CASEY (n. 24), pp. 165-178; L. GASTON, *No Stone on Another*, Leiden, 1970; L. HARTMAN, *Prophecy Interpreted*, Lund, 1966.

32. Lk 17,26-27 > Gen 7,6-10.

33. Lk 17,28-29.32 > Gen 19,1-29.

34. For discussion see HANSON (n. 4); *Old Testament Apocalyptic Revisited*, in *Interpretation* 25 (1971) 454- 479.

35. TUCKETT (n. 9), pp. 295-296.

36. For discussion see B.D. CHILTON, *The Temple of Jesus*, University Park PA, 1992, pp. 91-159; GASTON (n. 31); R.G. HAMERTON-KELLY, *The Gospel and the Sacred*, Minneapolis, MN, 1994; W.H. KELBER, *The Kingdom in Mark*, Philadelphia, PA, 1974; J.D. KINGSBURY, *Conflict in Mark*, Minneapolis, MN, 1989, pp. 75-88; E.S. MALBON, *Narrative Space and Mythic Meaning in Mark*, San Francisco, 1986; TAYLOR (n. 9).

of the connection between the Markan Passion traditions and the primitive Jerusalem church[37], Mark relates the death of Jesus to the anticipated destruction of the Temple. This is reflected in Markan eschatology, and it is accordingly biblical texts concerned with the state of the Temple and how anticipated divine intervention would remedy the situation that are cited and reinterpreted in Mark 13[38]. Whereas Daniel awaits the restoration and purification of the Temple, Mark sees the shrine as having ceased to function effectively with Jesus' death, and awaits fulfilment of Jesus' prediction of the destruction of the Temple[39] in the course of the unfolding eschatological judgement.

Q, on the other hand, is traditionally located in Galilee, as reflecting continuity with Jesus' historical ministry in northern Palestine[40]. Temple and cult are therefore understandably less prominent in the eschatology of Q than of Mark, and accordingly not associated with the death of Jesus as they are in Mark. Q 13,35, in continuity with the Hebrew prophetic tradition and the preaching of Jesus in Galilee, professes in general terms the belief that Jerusalem and the Temple would be destroyed in an act of divine judgement. The eschatological discourse in Q 17,22-37 in particular, and Q as a whole in general, reflects an expectation that God would intervene in history to overturn the prevailing order and establish a new and just dispensation[41]. However, there is no inextricable link between the death of Jesus and the destruction of the Temple as there is in Mark. Nor does the destruction of the Temple in Q 13,34-35 have an eschatological significance comparable with that attributed it in Mark 13,2.14-20. It is therefore readily understandable, I would suggest, that eschatological passages of Scripture concerned with the sanctity of the Temple should be of less immediate interest to the Q community than they were to Mark. Informed by different stages in the ministry of Jesus, Mark and Q perceive his death differently in relation to the institutions of Judaism. Their interpretation of Scripture to understand the death of Jesus, and the future judgement and redemption they anticipated, was influenced accordingly. Nevertheless there is no substantial difference between the

---

37. Cf. THEISSEN (n. 9), pp. 166-199; TROCMÉ (n. 9), pp. 224-239.

38. See n. 36.

39. Mk 11,15-17; 13,1-2. Cf. Mk 14,58; 15,29. For discussion see COLLINS (n. 9); HENGEL (n. 9); MARXSEN (n. 9); SANDERS (n. 15), pp. 61-76; TAYLOR (n. 9). For a different view see MACK (n. 2), pp. 291-92, and those scholars who argue for a post-70 date for Mark (n. 9).

40. Cf. CROSSAN (n. 8); JACOBSON (n. 1), p. 231; MACK (n. 3); TUCKETT (n. 9), p. 102-103; VAAGE (n. 8).

41. Cf. D. LÜHRMANN, The Gospel of Mark and the Sayings Collection Q, in JBL 108 (1989) 51-71, esp. p. 69.

eschatological expectations of the Markan and Q communities: both await the coming of Jesus, "son of man", as eschatological judge and redeemer, and both identify Jerusalem, not exclusively but representatively of Temple-oriented Judaism, as the epicentre of God's judgement[42].

To conclude, therefore, I wish to argue that the interpretation of Scripture in the eschatological sections of Mark and Q reflects no fundamental differences of substance between the two traditions. Both stand in continuity with the Hebrew prophetic-apocalyptic-eschatological tradition. The difference in emphasis between their use of this tradition to interpret their future expectations is attributable to the difference in their historical and social origins and their relative proximity not to Jesus but to the Temple with whose purity and restoration Daniel is concerned. Both Mark and Q are fundamental to our understanding of primitive Christianity, including its acute eschatological consciousness, and we cannot legitimately pose a radical dichotomy between them.

Department of Theology and Religious Studies   N. H. TAYLOR
University of Swaziland
Kwaluseni Campus
PB Kwaluseni
Swaziland

---

42. Cf. P. HOFFMANN, *The Redaction of Q and the Son of Man*, in PIPER (n. 11), pp. 159-198; LÜHRMANN, (n. 41).

INTERTEXTUALITY
AND ITS USE IN TRACING Q AND PROTO-LUKE

Intertextuality is not primarily about quotations and allusions. It is about transforming whole books. Quotations, even if constitutive, are partly decorative – cherries on the top. The essential continuity is deeper – in the mass of the text. Such is the case with literature at large, and there is increasing evidence that such also is the case with the gospels' use of the OT. Intertextuality is about taking boldly in one's hands the writing of another age or another author and rendering that work into a new idiom. It is the Akkadians' reworking of the writings of Sumer, Genesis' re-shaping of stories such as *Atrahasis*, Rome's wholescale appropriation and transformation of the literary heritage of Greece. Quotations and allusions are simply the tip of the phenomenon – like the few fish that occasionally break above the surface of the ocean. The real riches lie beneath, hidden to the observer on the shore, but massive and vivid to the diver who plunges into the depths.

By and large, NT research is still on the shore; it still has not deeply engaged the foundational literary procedure of the first centruy AD – namely the systematic transforming of whole books. This non-engagement is understandable. The using of older texts – usually referred to in NT times as imitation (Gk. *mimēsis*, Lat. *imitatio*) – is alien to the modern age[1]. Since the eighteenth century the emphasis has been on novelty and individuality. The idea of imitation, which once was central to philosophy, art, literature and conduct, has today been discouraged. During the nineteenth and twentieth centuries, when biblical research was blossoming, the study of literary imitation was almost totally neglected. Even now, when the practice of using older texts is being rediscovered, there is still, at some level, a confusion or a reluctance about accepting it on its own terms. Instead, use is made of "intertextuality", a misnomer – drawn from modern philosophy, and partly alien to ancient imitation.

At one level of course terminology does not matter; better a misnomer than unawareness, and, given the context, this paper will continue to use it. But using "intertextualiity" tends to exclude or downgrade ancient terms

---

1. On imitation, see T.L. BRODIE, *Greco-Roman Imitation of Texts as a Partial Guide to Luke's Use of Sources*, in C.H. TALBERT (ed.), *Luke-Acts. New Perspectives from the SBL*, New York, Crossroad, 1984, pp. 17-46.

such as *imitatio*, and so the ban on imitation, so strong since around 1800, remains in force. Modern terminology is like a buffer, a final barrier against plunging into the depths of the ancient practice, against taking it on its own terms.

The Tyranny of the Matthew-Mark Model

In place of the complexity of *imitatio*, a simplistic model has been installed – the Matthew-Mark model. In NT research the Matthew-Mark dependence stands like a monument at the gateway to the New Testament. Those who enter practise with this model, and so, implicitly, it has become the governing paradigm, the decisive model for what is meant by wholescale literary dependence. Frequently, other kinds of dependence are not considered seriously. Yet, in the *imitatio* which pervaded NT times, near-verbatim reproduction, especially of the Matthew-Mark type, was the exception, not the rule.

The difficulty of moving beyond the Matthew-Mark model is illustrated in Johannine research. John belongs to essentially the same genre as Matthew, Mark and Luke – that of gospel – and in all the literature of the first century there is scarcely one author who, when writing, did not use the works of those who were predecessors within the same genre[2]. For decades, however, research isolated John from the other works of his own genre, including Mark. The reasons for this were complex[3], but one of the factors was the dominance of the Matthew-Mark model. The implicit logic was clear: the Matthew-Mark model defines what is meant by literary dependence; John's relationship to Mark does not fit that model; therefore John's relationship to Mark is not one of literary dependence (the relationship is to be explained by other factors – oral traditions and lost documents, especially a signs source). Now, however, evidence is emerging that John did in fact use Mark. He absorbed Mark completely, as did Matthew and Luke, but he did so in a way that was different, more radically transformative[4].

2. See esp. J. HIGGINBOTHAM (ed.), *Greek and Latin Literature*, London, Methuen, 1969.
3. See especially, F. NEIRYNCK, *John and the Synoptics*, in M. DE JONGE (ed.), *L'Évangile de Jean. Sources, rédaction, théologie* (BETL, 44), Leuven, University Press, 1977; ²1987, pp. 73-106; ID., *John and the Synoptics: 1975-1990*, in A. DENAUX (ed.), *John and the Synoptics* (BETL, 101), Leuven, University Press – Peeters, 1992, pp. 3-62.
4. See T.L. BRODIE, *The Quest for the Origin of John's Gospel. A Source-Oriented Approach*, New York/Oxford, Oxford University, 1993.

Apart from the emergence of the John-Mark model, there are other instances of the radical reshaping of OT texts. First, within the OT itself, evidence is emerging for diverse process of rewriting: Deuteronomy, for instance, reworks the Genesis treatment of women[5]; and inner-biblical hermeneutics have begun to reveal multiple processes of transformation[6]. Furthermore, in the relationship between the OT and the NT, there are signs of NT writers engaging long passages, even whole books. This is emerging concerning Paul. In Paul's text, the OT is not secondary; it is constitutive[7]. Likewise with Matthew; his quotations from Deuteronomy are but the tip of a much greater involvement with that book[8].

Within this new context, this transforming of whole texts, it is appropriate to look afresh at two old problems – Proto-Luke and Q.

Proto-Luke and Q: From Stalemate to Intertextuality

Around 1890 two new terms emerged in NT research – Q (1890)[9] and Proto-Luke (1891)[10]. Both terms designated hypothetical documents which, if real, had a major role in the gospels' formation. But so far it has not been possible to identify reliably the nature and content of these documents.

In the case of Proto-Luke, essentially two methods, two criteria, have been used in trying to trace its shape[11]:

(1) *The identification of semitism (using Luke-Acts alone)*. The Proto-Luke hypothesis started with Paul Feine's observation that parts of Luke-Acts are distinctly semitic. This led to the idea that Luke-Acts had two

---

5. C. CARMICHAEL, *Women, Law and the Genesis Traditions*, Edinburgh, Edinburgh University, 1979.

6. M. FISHBANE, *Biblical Interpretation in Ancient Israel*, Oxford, Clarendon, 1985.

7. D.-A. KOCH, *Die Schrift als Zeuge des Evangeliums. Untersuchungen zur Verwendung und zum Verständnis der Schrift bei Paulus* (BHT, 69), Tübingen, Mohr (Siebeck), 1986, pp. 92-101, 284; R.B. HAYS, *Echoes of Scripture in the Letters of Paul*, New Haven/London, Yale University, 1989, p. 16.

8. T.L. BRODIE, *Fish, Temple Tithe, and Remission: The God-based Generosity of Deuteronomy 14–15 as One Component of Matt 17:22–18:35*, in *RB* 99 (1992) 697-718.

9. F. NEIRYNCK, *The Symbol Q (= Quelle)*, in *ETL* 54 (1978) 119-125.

10. P. FEINE, *Eine vorkanonische Überlieferung des Lukas im Evangelium und Apostelgeschichte*, Gotha. Friedrich Andreas Perthes, 1891.

11. For the history of Proto-Lukan research, see esp. Vincent TAYLOR, *Behind the Third Gospel*, Oxford, Oxford University, 1926, pp. 2-32, 182-215; Allen F. PAGE, *Proto-Luke Reconsidered*, (Diss), Chapel Hill, NC, Duke University, 1968, pp. 2-35; Lloyd GASTON, *No Stone on Another. Studies in the Significance of the Fall of Jerusalem in the Synoptic Gospels*, Leiden, Brill, 1970, pp. 244-256.

stages – an early semitic stage, Proto-Luke; and a later, more hellenistic, stage, giving the present Luke-Acts. To distinguish the original Proto-Luke, it seemed that what was needed was to go carefully through Luke-Acts and identify those parts of Luke-Acts which were markedly semitic. Feine identified, tentatively, several such passages, from Luke 1 to Acts 12. But working with Luke-Acts alone, it was not possible to be sure which texts were semitic and which were not; often the distinction was not clear, and so decades later the project floundered.

(2) *Comparison with Mark (using Luke and Mark)*. A varied theory of Proto-Luke began with the observation that, if the Markan material is removed from Luke's gospel (especially from Luke's passion narrative), Luke's account still forms an essentially complete gospel – so much so that Luke, before using Mark, seems to have had a gospel of his own.

As for Q, the modern Q theory rests on the following: Matthew and Luke, apart from sharing Mark, also share many other texts, texts containing so much agreement that, *provided neither of these evangelists copied from the other*, they must have shared a further source. The hypothetical further source is named Q.

The possibility of one evangelist copying from the other remains unresolved. Two arguments in particular suggest that there was no such copying: (1) Within each of their gospels there are doublets – episodes which occur twice – and these are easier to explain if each evangelist used two sources – Mark and Q. (2) If there was copying, it has not been possible to say who copied from whom. At times it is Luke who seems to have the older version, at other times Matthew. But these arguments are not reliable. There are other ways of accounting for doublets – as research on Genesis, for instance, suggests[12]. And the ambiguity about the relative ages of Luke and Matthew can be solved by taking account of Proto-Luke: the passages from Proto-Luke appear older; those from canonical Luke-Acts appear later. The implication: Matthew used Proto-Luke; and canonical Luke, writing later, used Matthew.

Apart from questions about Q's existence, there are serious problems, among those who accept it, about the criteria for establishing its content[13]. The result is that the theory of Q, valuable though it may be, is beset by radical doubts. To some degree it is like Proto-Luke: its existence, while probable, has not been clinched; and its shape remains uncertain.

Accompanying the uncertainty there is a form of isolation; research on Proto-Luke and Q generally takes place within a context that is quite

---

12. See T.D. ALEXANDER, *Are the wife/sister incidents of Genesis literary compositional variants?*, in *VT* 42 (1992) 145-153.

13. See A. DENAUX, *Criteria for Identifying Q-Passages*, in *NT* 37 (1995) 105-129.

limited. Proto-Lukan study has often been confined to the context of Luke-Acts and Mark. The investigation of Q, though meticulous and voluminous, has largely been restricted to the context of the Synoptic gospels, especially the context of Matthew and Luke (Q in effect is sometimes equated with the material shared by Matthew and Luke, "the double tradition"). And, compounding the isolation, often those who study Proto-Luke and Q respectively do not refer to one another. Among the exceptions to isolation has been the placing of Q within the wider context of wisdom – wisdom's tradition or "trajectory"[14].

Intertextuality brings a change. It means that the quest for Proto-Luke, instead of being traced, in vain, to the vague idea of what is semitic, can be traced slowly but surely to a specific text – the Septuagint. In other words, the criterion in adjusted: instead of semitism identify septuagintism (Lukan studies have generally shown alleged semitisms to be septuagintisms). The Septuagint is not at all vague; it is a specific book which can be checked in detail.

Likewise with Q and "wisdom tradition:" instead of speaking of wisdom tradition or wisdom trajectory in a vague way, it is best to do everything possible to check specific wisdom writings, especially those of the Septuagint. To some degree this has already been done; Q has been connected, for instance, with Sirach. But the process can be developed.

Applying Intertextuality to the Quest for Proto-Luke

When the criterion for tracing Proto-Luke is adjusted – when instead of semitism one seeks septuagintism – then the process becomes clearer. What one finds is that, while almost all of Luke-Acts has occasional faint echoes of the Septuagint, there is one strand, quite distinctive, where the presence of the Septuagint is pervasive. The texts in that strand are as follows: Luke 1,1–4,27[15] (except 3,7–9; 4,1–13); 7,1–8,3; 9,51–10,20; 16,1–9.19-31; 17,11–18,8; 19,1–10; chs. 22–24 (except 22,31–65); Acts 1,1–15,35. Such apparently was Proto-Luke.

This proposal is not made lightly. Over twenty years of research have shown the present writer that these texts involve a systematic reworking of whole narratives from the Septuagint – especially the Elijah-Elisha

14. See esp. J.M. ROBINSON, 'LOGOI SOPHON;' On the Gattung of Q, in H. KOESTER and J.M. ROBINSON, Trajectories through Early Christianity, Philadelphia, Fortress, 1971, pp. 71-113; J.S. KLOPPENBORG, The Formation of Q. Trajectories in Ancient Wisdom Collections, Philadelphia, Fortress, 1987, pp. 263-316, esp. pp. 281-82; B. WITHERINGTON, Jesus the Sage. The Pilgrimage of Wisdom, Edinburgh, T. & T. Clark, 1994, esp. pp. 75-116.

15. Not 1,1-4,30 as in BRODIE, The Quest (n. 4), p. 169.

narrative, Judges, and, to some degree, Chronicles[16]. Not all the research has been published, and to that extent this proposal is premature; but for the sake of those who wonder where this research is leading, it is useful to sketch the larger picture.

An example of this systematic intertextuality occurs, for instance, in the relationship between Luke 16,1–19,9 and much of Judges. In outline:

Judges 6–18	Luke 16,1–19,9
Two Gideon Stories **(mostly about power)** Livelihood crisis; downing of symbols of power (6,1–8,3). *[Angel; night action.* Reversal: mean are punished; poor come to power (8,4–35).	**Two Related Parables** **(about possessions)** The steward's livelihood crisis; downing of bills/possessions (16,1–9). *cf. Luke 1–2].* The rich man and Lazarus (16,19–31).
The Evil Kingdom Deathly kingdom of Abimelech; with illustrative fable (ch 9).	**The Kingdom of God** Kingdom of God; with illustrative healing (17,11–37).
A Woman Dies The maverick judge (Jephthah) and the defenceless woman (his daughter) (chs 10–12). *[Samson, chs 13–16.*	**A Woman Vindicated** The maverick judge and the widow (18,1–8). *cf. Luke 1–2…].*
A False Shrine/House Dan's quest for a home with God goes very wrong (chs 17–18).	**A True House** Zacchaeus's desire (to see Jesus) and justice brings salvation to his house (19,1–9).

16. See, by T.L. BRODIE, *Luke the Literary Interpreter. Luke-Acts as a Systematic Rewriting and Updating of the Elijah-Elisha Narrative in 1 and 2 Kings* (Diss), Rome, Pontifical University of St Thomas, 1981 (pub. 1987: University Microfilms, Michigan); *The Accusing and Stoning of Naboth (1 Kgs 21:8-13) as One Component of the Stephen Text (Acts 6:9-14; 7:58a)*, in *CBQ* 45 (1983) 417-432; *Luke 7:36-50 as an Internalization of 2 Kings 4, 1-37: A Study in Luke's Use of Rhetorical Imitation*, in *Bib* 64 (1983) 457-485; *Greco-Roman Imitation* (n. 1); *Towards Unravelling Luke's Use of the Old Testament: Luke 7.11-17 as an Imitatio of 1 Kings 17.17-24*, in *NTS* 32 (1986) 247-267; *Towards Unravelling the Rhetorical Imitation of Sources in Acts: 2 Kgs 5 as One Component of Acts 8,9-40*, in *Bib* 67 (1986) 41-67; *The Departure for Jerusalem (Luke 9:51-56) as a Rhetorical Imitation of Elijah's Departure for the Jordan (2 Kgs 1,1–2,6)*, in *Bib* 70 (1989) 96-109; *Luke 9:57-62: A Systematic Adaptation of the Divine Challenge to Elijah (1 Kings 19)*, in D.J. LULL (ed.), *SBL 1989, Seminar Papers*, pp. 236-45; *Luke-Acts as an Imitation and Emulation of the Elijah-Elisha Narrative*, in E. RICHARD (ed.), *New Views on Luke and Acts*, Collegeville, MN, Liturgical, 1990, pp. 78-85; *Not Q but Elijah: The Saving of the Centurion's Servant (Luke 7:1-10) as an Internalization of the Saving of the Widow and her Child (1 Kgs 17:1-16)*, in *IBS* 14 (1992) 54-71; *Again Not Q: Luke 7:18-35 as an Acts-oriented Transformation of the Vindication of the Prophet Micaiah (I Kings 22:1-38)*, in *IBS* 16 (1994) 2-30. Note also, *A New Temple and a New Law. The Unity and Chronicler-based Nature of Luke 1:1–4:22a*, in *JSNT* 5 (1979) 21-45.

Close analysis of most of this outline has been published elsewhere[17].

Proto-Luke's reworking involves not only christianization, but also distillation and, very often, reversal. Incidents which in Judges are highly negative have been turned around: the kingdom becomes positive; the woman is no longer the victim; and the quest for a home with a shrine, which in Dan's case goes awry, goes well for Zacchaeus – though in a christianized idiom. Judges' emphasis on power gives way to a Lukan emphasis – possessions. In general, Luke follows the original order, but some of the material on Gideon and Samson – especially about angelic annunciations and birth – has been moved to other places, particularly to the infancy narrative (Luke 1–2).

Overall, the texts identified as belonging to Proto-Luke have their own coherence – coherence of sources and genre. They are like an elaborate version – contemporized and christianized – of the twopart Elijah-Elisha narrative. It is not yet a gospel; that will come with Mark. The later work (canonical Luke-Acts) will use new sources – Mark, other Christian material, and it will also make further use of the Septuagint, especially of Deuteronomy (in the travel narrative, 9,51–ch. 18)[18]. But the two uses of the Septuagint – in Proto-Luke and canonical Luke-Acts – are distinct. Proto-Luke has its own coherence and character.

Towards Applying Intertextuality to the Quest for Q

The beginning of the emergence of Proto-Luke has implications for Q. First, concerning specific texts. Some texts which frequently are assigned to Q (e.g. Luke 7,1-10; 7,18-35; 9,57-62; 10,2-12) may be accounted for more reliably as reworkings of the Elijah-Elisha narrative[19]. This is true independently of the idea of Proto-Luke; the crucial link is simply with the text of 1 and 2 Kings. The relationship to the OT text is intricate, and unravelling it requires great patience – much more than is needed when invoking an unseen source such as Q. Yet, in the final analysis, the relationship to the OT text is more certain than the appeal to an unseen Q; it is less dependent on hypothesis, and more subject to verification.

Second, concerning Q as a whole. The more far-reaching implication is that Q research would do well to reexamine its starting point, its frame

17. T.L. BRODIE, *Reopening the Quest for Proto-Luke: The Systematic Use of Judges 6–12 in Luke 16:1–18:8*, in *The Journal of Higher Criticism* 2 (1995) 68-101.

18. D.P. MOESSNER, *Lord of the Banquet. The Literary and Theological Significance of the Lukan Travel Narrative*, Minneapolis, Fortress, 1989.

19. See the pertinent references in n. 16.

of reference. Much Q research sets its compass almost exclusively by the double tradition; but the example of the preceding paragraph – the inclusion in Q of texts which in fact are rooted in a distinct use of the Elijah-Elisha narrative – indicates that this compass leads to misjudgements.

As for a new compass, or at least a complementary one, intertextuality provides help. If intertextuality can identify Proto-Luke, then perhaps the same is true of Q. James Robinson, while working largely by the double tradition, is open to a greater emphasis on OT wisdom texts[20].

The proposal here – given in the context of intertextuality – is as follows: part of Q's *content* comes not only from Sirach but also from Deuteronomy. (Q's *form* is another question, more akin perhaps to the short collections in Proverbs 30–31 or Balaam's oracles in Numbers 23–24). Some of the reasons for invoking Deuteronomy are as follows:
1. Sirach, often connected with Q[21], is itself grounded in the law, including Deuteronomy (see esp. Sir 24,23; Deut 33,4), and a full investigation of Q's link to Sirach leads to the question of Q's relationship to Deuteronomy.
2. Deuteronomy, "a *summa theologica*"[22], synthesized much of the OT. It bridged the gaps between the Law, the prophets and the (wisdom) writings. The call to hear, for instance, so distinctive of wisdom (e.g., Prov 1,8; 4,1.10; 8,32; Wis 6,1; Sir 3,1; 15,24; 23,7) is first patterned in Deuteronomy (5,1; 9,1; 20,3; 27,9). Deuteronomy itself in fact may be regarded as a wisdom writing[23].
3. Deuteronomy had a special status among Jews. It contained two of the three texts which Jews wore on their bodies (in phylacteries), including the *Shema* (Deut 6,4-9), "the principal Jewish confession of faith"[24].
4. Deuteronomy is the book most quoted by Jesus.
5. Deuteronomy is formative for the NT. "Few OT books are quoted or alluded to as frequently in the NT as Dt; in Mt and Heb in particular, its influence is dominant"[25]. Deuteronomy (18,18-19) supplied the essential background for the eschatological prophet-like-Moses[26] and for the

20. ROBINSON (n. 15). Robinson has confirmed this openness in conversation (Chicago, SBL meeting, Nov 18, 1994).

21. See n. 14.

22. W.L. MORAN, *Deuteronomy*, in *NewCathCommHS* 1969, 225a.

23. M. WEINFELD, *Deuteronomy and the Deuteronomic School*, Oxford, Clarendon, 1972, pp. 244-281.

24. J. BLENKINSOPP, *Deuteronomy*, in *NJBC* 1990, 6:22.

25. J. BLENKINSOPP, *Deuteronomy*, in *JBC* 1968, 6:4.

26. See W.A. MEEKS, *The Prophet-King. Moses Traditions and the Johannine Christology* (NTSup, 14), Leiden, Brill, 1967, esp. pp. 24, 45-47; 1-5); M.-É. BOISMARD, *Moïse ou Jésus. Essai de christologie johannique* (BETL, 84), Leuven, Leuven Univeristy – Peeters, 1988, pp. 1-5.

emphasis – pivotal to Romans and Matthew – on righteousness (*dikaio-syně*).

6. Deuteronomy's essential content (a collection of discourses) provided a monumental model for anyone who wanted to arrange a new collection of sayings or *logia*. Deuteronomy's title, "These...words (*děbārîm*, LXX, *logoi*)", confirms this. If the Gospel of Thomas ("These are the hidden words...") deserves consideration in discussing Q, all the more does Deuteronomy.

Overall then it is plausible to connect the Logia/Q to Deuteronomy. Deuteronomy is not alien or distant. It is central to Judaism, to Jesus and to the NT. With it, complementing it, are other later sources, especially Sirach.

Conclusion

The purpose of this paper was to indicate that intertextuality, understood broadly, can eventually help in recovering Proto-Luke and Q. The evidence referred to here varies greatly between Proto-Luke and Q. In the case of Proto-Luke, the case is substantiated by a significant amount of published detailed analysis. In the case of Q, there is no such detailed backing; all that is given – apart from highlighting some central problems with the present Q hypotheses – is a broad suggestion, especially concerning Deuteronomy. Taken on their own, the observations concerning Q scarcely warrant a reorientation in Q research. But, when taken in conjunction with the data concerning Luke-Acts, they are worthy of consideration.

Dominican House of Studies   Thomas L. BRODIE
Tallaght, Dublin 24, Ireland

FALSCHE ZITATE BEI MATTHÄUS UND LUKAS

Unter den zahlreichen Stellen, in denen die Evangelisten mehr oder weniger deutlich auf das Alte Testament verweisen, finden sich auch ausdrückliche Zitate, besonders häufig bei Mt (25mal) und Lukas (14mal)[1]. Sie werden formelhaft eingeleitet, etwa mit τὸ ῥηθὲν ὑπὸ κυρίου προφήτου λέγοντος, γέγραπται oder γεγραμμένον. Um der methodischen Sauberkeit willen werden im folgenden ausschließlich Schriftzitate mit diesen Einleitungen untersucht; auch noch so deutliche Bezüge zu Bibelstellen, wie etwa in den Antithesen der Bergpredigt, werden hingegen nicht berücksichtigt. Als 'falsch' gelten Zitate dann, wenn sie weder mit der LXX noch mit dem Masoretentext übereinstimmen (siehe unten). Wörter oder Wortgruppen werden geändert, ergänzt oder weggelassen, manchmal auch mehrere, voneinander unabhängige Stellen miteinander kombiniert, wie etwa Mt 15,4: Ex 20,12 und 21,17; Mt 21,5: Jes 62,11 und Sach 9,9; Mt 21,13: Jes 56,7 und Jer 7,11; Lk 4,18: Jes 58,6 und 61,1; Lk 20,28: Dtn 25,5 und Gen 38,8. Manchmal wird auch ein Schriftzitat behauptet, das sich nicht verifizieren läßt. Selbstverständlich ist vorauszuschicken, daß dieses Thema eine moderne, neuzeitliche Fragestellung ist, die die historisch-kritischen Maßstäbe in die Entstehungszeit der Evangelien zurückprojiziert. »Die moderne Exegese führte gleichsam einen Zangenangriff gegen die Exegese des Matthäus«[2]. Mit diesem peiorativen Titel soll aber kein Vorwurf verbunden sondern vielmehr die Art und Weise der Bibelbenutzung von Mt und Lk beziehungsweise die jeweilige Aussageabsicht besser rekonstruiert werden.

1. *Matthäus*

In der Mehrzahl der Zitate gibt Mt den alttestamentlichen Text im wesentlichen genau wieder. An drei Stellen korrigiert er sogar die LXX

1. H. HÜBNER, *Biblische Theologie des Neuen Testaments III,* Göttingen, 1995, p. 121, zählt nur *fünf* und zieht daraus fälschlich den Schluß (gegen Lukas 24,27!): »Das Geschriebensein der Zitate ist anscheinend für Lukas von sekundärer Bedeutung«.

2. R. PESCH, *»Er wird Nazoräer heißen«. Messianische Exegese in Mt 1-2,* in F. VAN SEGBROECK U.A. (eds.), *The Four Gospels 1992.* FS F. Neirynck (BETL, 100), Leuven, 1992, pp. 1386-1401, hier 1391 f.

mit einer eigenständigen Übersetzung des MT, am auffälligsten in 2,15 mit τὸν υἱόν μου (Hos 11,1 בני, LXX: τὰ τεκνὰ αὐτοῦ) und in 12,18-21, wo er die in der LXX eingefügten Worte Ιακωβ und Ισραηλ mit dem MT wegläßt[3].

Die auffälligsten Änderungen am AT hat Mt an folgenden Stellen vorgenommen.

Mt 1,23 (Jes 7,14)

Mt ändert die Anrede (2. pers. sing.) zu einer Aussage (3. pers. pl.), denn »die Gemeinde ist der Ort, an dem Jesus von Nazaret als der 'Immanuel' erkannt wird; in Änderung von Jes 7,14 läßt der Evangelist nicht die Jungfrau-Mutter ihren Sohn Immanuel nennen, sondern die Glieder des Gottesvolkes: 'Sie werden seinen Namen rufen: Immanuel'«[4]. Daß das Zitat nicht direkt zum vorangegangenen Text paßt (τὸ ὄνομα αὐτοῦ Ἰησοῦν), soll hier nicht besprochen werden[5].

Mt 2,6 (Mi 5,1)

An dieser Stelle hat Mt mehrfach die atl. Vorlage korrigiert. Zunächst ersetzt er אפרתה mit γῆ Ιουδα, weil seine Leser offenbar mit Ephrata nichts verbinden können. Dann fügt er οὐδαμῶς ein, womit er, zumindest grammatikalisch, die Aussage Michas ins Gegenteil verkehrt. Statt ὀλιγοστός (hebr.: צעיר) wählt er das Adjektiv ἐλαχίστη. באלפי übersetzt er mit ἡγεμόσιν[6]; dem folgt ἡγούμενος für מושל (LXX ἄρχοντα). Damit hat er wesentlich am Text manipuliert. Außerdem erweitert er den Text mit einem zusätzlichen Zitat von 2 Sam 5,2, was er nicht angibt.

---

3. A. WEISER, *Theologie des Neuen Testaments II,* Stuttgart-Berlin-Köln, 1993, p. 89, stellt fest, daß »der Wortlaut zum Teil der hebräischen Bibel nähersteht als in den übrigen Zitaten, bei denen Mattthäus der LXX folgt«. Vgl. D. HAGNER, *Matthew 14-28* (World Biblical Commentary, 33b), Dallas, 1995, p. 813: »The quotation as Matthew gives is somewhat closer to the Hebrew than to the LXX«. Anders E. SCHWEIZER, *Das Evangelium nach Mt* (NTD, 2), Göttingen, ⁴1986, p. 17: »Da Mt sonst nicht auf den hebräischen Text zurückgreift...«

4. PESCH (n. 2), p. 1388. J. GNILKA, *Matthäus II* (HTKNT), Freiburg-Basel-Wien, 1992, p. 21: »die in der Kirche versammelten Christusbekenner«. W. ROTHFUCHS, *Die Erfüllungszitate des Mt-Evangeliums* (BWANT, 88), Stuttgart, 1969, p. 58, führt den Plural auf Maria und Josef zurück.

5. *ibid.,* pp. 57-60, vgl. U. LUZ, *Das Evangelium nach Matthäus* (EKK, I/1), Zürich, ²1989, p. 105.

6. SCHWEIZER (n. 3), p. 17: »Die Verlesung eines einzigen hebräischen Buchstabens ergab 'Fürsten' statt 'Tausendschaften', was dann den nah verwandten Ausdruck 'Führer' nach sich gezogen hat« (Denkt SCHWEIZER an אלוף – Hauptmann?)

2,23

ist wohl der umstrittenste Vers in diesem Zusammenhang, da sich dafür überhaupt keine genaue alttestamentliche Stelle als Pendant auffinden läßt[7]. Allenfalls könnte Ri 13,5 (נזיר; LXX: ναζιραῖον) als Vergleich herangezogen werden, stimmt aber mit ναζωραῖος nicht ganz überein. Abgesehen davon verbindet Mt Jesus mit dem Stadtnamen Nazaret, der mit dem Begriff Nazir nichts zu tun hat. Möglicherweise hat Mt aber auch an Jes 11,1 (נצר – Sproß) gedacht[8]. Damit wäre – wie schon in 2,6 – ein weiterer messianischer Unterton intendiert.

Mt 4,10 (Q 4,8)

Im Zitat von Dtn 6,13 wird μόνῳ ergänzt. Diese Erweiterung verschärft deutlich die atl. Aussage im Sinne des ersten Gebots, ist andererseits wohl auch kontextbedingt.

Mt 26,31 (Sach 13,7)

Dieses Schriftzitat übernimmt Mt von Mk 14,27 (vgl. auch Joh 16,32: σκορπισθῆτε). Grammatikalisch ist der Wortlaut zwar verändert – πατάξω statt πατάξετε (MT: הך) –, doch inhaltlich entspricht die Aussage der alttestamentlichen, wo Gott ein Schwert beauftragt, in seinem Namen den Hirten zu schlagen. Allerdings hat die Stelle bei Sacharja einen starken kritischen Unterton gegenüber dem – nicht näher umschriebenen – Hirten, während sich im ntl. Zitat die Kritik gegen die Schafe richtet.

Mt 27,9

Eine lange Sequenz wird eingeleitet mit der Formel: ἐπληρώθη τὸ ῥηθὲν διὰ Ἰερεμίου τοῦ προφήτου λέγοντος. Um die Schwierigkeiten mit diesem »Zitat« zu umgehen, liest sy[hmg] statt Ιερεμιου: Ζαχαριου und h[r2] Ησαιου; einige Minuskeln lassen Ιερεμιου ersatzlos weg. NESTLE-ALAND nennt als Marginalie Sach 11,12f und mit »??« Jer 18,2-12; 19,1-15 und 32,6-9, wohl mehr als Reminiszenz denn als Zitat. Ausgangspunkt dieses intertextuellen Paradebeispiels[9] ist τριάκοντα ἀργυροὺς von Sach 11,12. Im folgenden Vers steht in der LXX χωνευτήριον

---

7. Weder in E.NESTLE/K.ALAND, *Novum Testamentum Graece,* Stuttgart, [27]1993 noch in K.ALAND/B.METZGER u.a., *The Greek New Testament,* Münster, [4]1993, ist das Zitat als solches im Druck hervorgehoben.

8. LUZ (n. 5), p. 133.

9. S. VAN TILBORG, *Matthew 27,3-10. An Intertextual Reading,* in S. DRAISMA (ed.), *Intertextuality in Biblical Writings.* FS B. van Iersel, Kampen, 1989, pp. 159-174. P. COLELLA, *Trenta Denari,* in *RivBib* 21 (1973) 325-327.

(Schmelzofen) für hebr. יוֹצֵר (Töpfer), oder für אוֹצָר (Schatzkammer; so liest die Peschitta[10]). Zu Töpfer assoziierte Mt Jer 18,2[11]; dieser Vers leitet eine Perikope ein, in der Jahwe Unheil[12] für Israel verheißt. Die gedankliche Kette geht weiter über den zerschlagenen Krug (Jer 19,1-13) zum Ackerkauf (Jer 32,6-9). Der Abschluß hat damit überhaupt nichts zu tun, sondern kommt von Ex 9,12. Inhaltlich fällt auf, daß die Ereignisse um Judas sich in zwei wesentlichen Punkten von Sach 11,12-17 unterscheiden: Der Prophet akzeptiert das Geld und bringt es in den Tempel, die Hohenpriester hingegen weisen es zurück und geben es nicht in den Tempelschatz.. Man muß daher davon ausgehen, daß es Mt nur um den Begriff der Schrifterfüllung an sich gegangen ist: »The main goal in the pericope is obviously the fulfillment quotation«[13].

2. Lukas

Der dritte Evangelist benützt das AT viel seltener als Mt; wenn er es aber tut, leitet er das Zitat fast immer mit γέγραπται ein. Im gesamten Reisebericht (9,51–19,27) findet sich mit Ausnahme von 10,27 (**ohne** γέγραπται) kein einziges Zitat.

Lk 2,23-24 (Ex 13; Lev 12,8)

Verglichen mit der ausladenden, umständlichen Formulierung von Ex 13,2.12.15 hat Lukas gestrafft und vereinfacht. Lag in Ex die Betonung einmal auf der Eigenschaft »männlich«, dann auf »erstgeboren«, hat er es zusammengefaßt. Dann fügt er ein zusätzliches Zitat an: in Lev 12,8 ersetzt er δυὸ mit ζεῦγος, welches Wort im NT nur noch Lk 14,19 vorkommt. Trotz des ausdrücklichen Zitats ist Lukas »als Hellenist nicht genau über die Gesetzesvorschriften informiert. Er denkt an eine 'Reinigung' nicht nur der Wöchnerin (αὐτῶν in V. 22)«[14], wie dies im zitierten Text aus Lev vorgesehen ist.

---

10. SCHWEIZER (n. 3), p. 329; GNILKA (n. 4), p. 446.
11. HAGNER (n. 3), p. 814: »Matthew may have had a separate tradition about the amount of 'thirty', but perhaps it is more likely that he imports this detail from the Zachariah quotation«.
12. Nach GNILKA (n. 4), p. 449, ist für Mt »Jeremia der klassische Unheilsprophet«.
13. HAGNER (n. 3), p. 815. Vgl. SCHWEIZER (n. 3), p. 330: »So ist die ganze Geschichte im wesentlichen aus dem als Weissagung gelesenen Alten Testament entstanden«. GNILKA (n. 4), p. 446: »für unseren Geschmack außerordentlich kühn«.
14. G. SCHNEIDER, Das Evangelium nach Lukas (ÖTK, 3/1), Gütersloh, 1977, p. 71.

Lk 3,4-6 (Jes 40,3-5)

Lukas verlängert das Zitat von Jesaja 40 im Vergleich zu Mt und Mk um die beiden Verse 40,4-5. Es ist bemerkenswert, daß er die Wörter τοῦ θεοῦ ἡμῶν durch ein einfaches αὐτοῦ ersetzt. Dies geschieht offensichtlich deshalb, weil er mit κύριος ausdrücklich Jesus meint, den er aber nicht mit θεοῦ ἡμῶν bezeichnen will[15]. In V. 6 fällt auf, daß Lk Jes 40,5a wegläßt: καὶ ὀφθήσεται ἡ δόξα κυρίου. Außerdem ist darauf hinzuweisen, daß das typische Lk-Wort σωτήριον (vgl. 2,30; Apg 28,28) nur in LXX, nicht aber im MT steht.

Lk 4,18-19 (Jes 61,1-2; 58,6)

Diese Verse, die in der lukanischen Christologie im Hinblick auf das AT eine »Schlüsselstellung«[16] einnehmen, kombinieren Jes 61,1; 58,6; zuletzt 61,2a. Auffällig sind hier zwei Auslassungen. Von 61,1c unterschlägt der dritte Evangelist ἰάσασθαι τοὺς συντετριμμένους τῇ καρδίᾳ, obwohl ihm sonst gerade das Heilen Jesu so wichtig ist (vgl. 5,17; 6,19; 9,2.11.42; 14,4; 22,51; teilweise diff par). Grund dafür ist nach Martin RESE »das Geistverständnis des Lukas…. durch die Streichung will Lukas anzeigen, daß der Geist des Herrn prophetischer Geist und nicht wunderwirkende Macht ist«[17]. Weiters fehlt in V. 19 καὶ ἡμέραν ἀνταποδόσεως von Jes 61,2, offenkundig, weil ihm an der »Trennung von Freudenbotschaft und Ansage des Gerichts«[18] gelegen war.

Lk 19,46 (Jes 56,7)

Hier fehlt – im Unterschied zu Markus – der Hinweis auf die Heiden (πᾶσιν τοῖς ἔθνεσιν), »vielleicht, weil erst der Auferstandene zu ihnen führt oder weil Lukas nur die wahre Bestimmung des Tempels als Ort der Lehre Jesu betonen will«[19].

Lk 20,28 (Dtn 25,5)

In der Sadduzäerfrage übernimmt Lk das (stark verkürzte) Zitat zur Regelung der Leviratsehe mit einer kleinen Änderung (ἄτεκνος) aus der

---

15. *Ibid*, p. 84: »Wahrscheinlich sieht Lukas in Jesus den 'Herrn'«, und *ibid, p.* 97: »Das Verhältnis Jesu zu Gott ist bei Lukas durch eine enge Verbundenheit, aber auch durch eine grundsätzliche Unterordnung des 'Sohnes' unter den Vater gekennzeichnet«.

16. M. RESE, *Alttestamentliche Motive in der Christologie des Lukas* (SNT, 1), Gütersloh, 1969, p. 143.

17. *Ibid.*, p. 145. Vgl. *ibid.,* p. 152: »…daß dem Heilen Jesu nicht so große Bedeutung zukommt wie seinem Wirken in Verkündigung und Vergebung«.

18. *Ibid.,* p. 152.

19. E. SCHWEIZER, *Das Evangelium nach Lukas* (NTD, 3), Göttingen, ³1993, p. 200.

Mk-Tradition, in der auch schon das Wort ἀναστήσει (aus Gen 38,8) enthalten war.

3. Auswertung des Befundes

Die dargelegten Beobachtungen und deren Analyse lassen unter anderem vier Schlußfolgerungen zu.

a) Die Nachprüfung der von Mt und Lk angeführten Zitate im ursprünglichen Kontext hat an mehreren Stellen gezeigt, daß die Septuaginta den uns bekannten hebräischen Masoretentext nicht einfach nur übersetzt. Sie verwendet aber weit mehr als nur einzelne neue Vokabel, die dem Original nicht entsprechen, sondern strafft beziehungsweise erweitert und interpretiert damit die Vorlage, teilweise in eigenwilliger, aktualisierender Weise. Das bedeutet, daß schon innerhalb des Judentums selbst der ursprüngliche Bibeltext nicht als wörtlich fixiert angesehen wurde; außerdem, daß damit die Kategorien 'richtig' oder 'falsch' für den Benutzer des Mt oder Lk bereits im Ansatz verschwimmen.

b) Wie der synoptische Vergleich exemplarisch ergeben hat, haben Mt und Lk den teilweise sehr freien Umgang mit dem Alten Testament nicht erst selbst initiiert, sondern stützten sich dabei auf eine allgemeine urchristliche Praxis. Schon bei Q und Mk werden beim Zitieren der Bibel Ergänzungen, Streichungen und kleine Korrekturen vorgenommen. Freilich nimmt die Häufigkeit atl. Zitate bei Lk und vor allem bei Mt deutlich zu. Man darf schließen, »daß eine Phase der Anspielungen durch eine Phase der Zitate abgelöst wird, welche jeweils die intensive Auseinandersetzung mit dem nicht-christlich verbliebenen Judentum einläutet«[20].

c) Matthäus nimmt das AT auf vielfältige Art und Weise in Gebrauch, um nicht zu sagen, er vereinnahmt es: teils in freien Anspielungen, teils in ausdrücklichen Zitaten; einerseits übersetzt er eigenständig aus dem (welchem?) hebräischen Text, andererseits benützt er die LXX. Die Schrift wird als Steinbruch verwendet, verschiedene, nicht zusammengehörige Verse mosaikartig zusammengesetzt. Die entscheidenden Abweichungen können entweder damit erklärt werden, daß er aus dem Gedächtnis zitiert[21], oder ganz bewußt und ausdrücklich manipuliert. In den meisten Fällen gibt er dadurch den ursprünglichen Aussagen einen völlig neuen Sinn,

---

20. K. BERGER, *Theologiegeschichte des Urchristentums, Theologie des Neuen Testaments*, Tübingen-Basel, 1994, p. 18.

21. SCHWEIZER (n. 3), p. 329. Anders ROTHFUCHS (n. 4), p. 89: »Die hier und da begegnenden auffälligen Hapaxlegomena lassen eine dem Evangelisten schriftlich vorliegende Form der Prophetenworte vermuten«.

wie »sie in der von Mt geltend gemachten Deutung so niemals gedacht waren«[22]. Außerdem ist festzuhalten, daß »das Verhältnis zwischen den Zitaten und ihrem Kontext durch eine gegenseitige Beeinflussung charakterisiert«[23] ist. Schließlich ist festzuhalten, daß die meisten Zitate einen zumindest apologetischen, wenn nicht bewußt polemischen Zweck verfolgen[24].

d) Lukas kann im Vergleich mit Mt als wesentlich korrekter bezeichnet werden. Eine Nachprüfung ist auch deswegen einfacher, weil er ausschließlich die LXX benützt. Seine Eingriffe in den Text bestehen vor allem in ganz bewußten Auslassungen, »um seiner theologischen Konzeption Rechnung zu tragen«[25], was allerdings an manchen Stellen nicht schon auf den ersten Blick überzeugt. Erst bei näherer Betrachtung des lukanischen Gesamtwerkes ist zu rekonstruieren, in welcher Weise er mit seinen Auslassungen seine Grundprinzipien realisiert.

e) Der urchristliche, neutestamentliche Schriftgebrauch – und der von Mt (und Lk) im besonderen – geschieht nicht im Sinne des gegenwärtig zunehmenden Fundamentalismus. Zwar werden die einzelnen Sätze aus dem jeweiligen Kontext gerissen, aber sie sollen nicht als einzelne »Beweise« bestimmte Sachverhalte belegen oder begründen. Vielmehr geht es darum, in einem neuen (eben christlichen) Gesamtblick die alten Texte völlig neu zu verstehen. Dabei werden kleine Elemente mosaikartig zu einem ganzheitlichen (Kunst-)Werk zusammengefügt. Der neutestamentliche Umgang mit dem Alten Testament kann daher geradezu als Paradigma für **Intertextualität** angesehen werden.

4. *Hermeneutisch-theologische Rückfragen*

Es kann selbstverständlich nicht darum gehen, in einer modernen Kritik wie ein akademischer Lehrer Mt (und Lk) Zitationsfehler nachzuweisen, um ihre christo- bzw. theologische Argumentationskette zu widerlegen. Die Vorstellung, die Evangelisten hätten mit Konkordanz und publizierten Bibelausgaben genau gearbeitet, ist sicherlich eine unzulässige Rückprojektion der Moderne ins 1. Jhdt. Insofern ist Rudolf PESCH

22. N. WALTER, *Zur theologischen Problematik des 'christologischen Schriftbeweises' im Neuen Testament,* in *NTS* 41 (1995) 338-357, p. 350.
23. ROTHFUCHS (n. 4), p. 89.
24. Vgl. *ibid*, p. 180.
25. HÜBNER (n. 1), p. 120.

in seiner (Selbst-)Kritik an der historisch-kritischen Methode recht zu geben[26]. Es seien aber doch zwei Rückfragen erlaubt:

a) Ist die Argumentation von Pesch nicht eine petitio principii? Läuft es nicht auf eine Zirkelargumenation hinaus, wenn er die Exegese des Mt als »eschatologische«[27], als »messianische«[28] oder als »Glaubens-apologetik des Evangelisten und seiner Gemeinden«[29] bezeichnet und daraus folgert: »nur eine Sicht mit den Augen des Glaubens, nur eine theologische Geschichtsdeutung und Geschichtsschreibung kann ihr gerecht werden«[30]?

b) Legitimiert Pesch nicht – ohne es ausdrücklich zu formulieren – die antijudaistische Grundtendenz des Mt? Es ist deutlich geworden, daß sich beim ersten Evangelisten »die Schrift verselbständigt«[31], daß **nur** die Christen das AT richtig lesen. Damit soll zwar der urkirchliche Umgang mit der jüdischen Bibel »keineswegs pauschal als illegitim gebrandmarkt werden«[32], aber »daß eine solche Re-lecture des Alten Testaments durch die christliche Kirche und Theologie, die zu einer Vereinnahmung der 'Schriften' Israels führte, spätestens unserer Generation nicht mehr erlaubt ist, dürfte auf der Hand liegen«[33].

Arsenal 7/4/3   Georg GEIGER
A-1030 Wien

---

26. Vgl. oben n. 2.
27. PESCH (n. 2), p. 1388.
28. *Ibid.*, p. 1390.
29. *Ibid.*, p. 1389.
30. *Ibid.*, p. 1402.
31. BERGER (n. 19), p. 18.
32. WALTER (n. 22), p. 354
33. *Ibid.*, p. 357, vgl. auch p. 353.

DIE VERWENDUNG DER SCHRIFT IN MT 4,1-11

Mit Hilfe der Schrift wird im Gespräch zwischen Jesus und dem Diabolos in Mt 4,1-11 nicht – wie sonst in Streitgesprächen (Mt 19,3-9; 22,23-33) – ein bestimmtes Einzelproblem erörtert, sondern das zentrale Thema der Gottessohnschaft Jesu. Die folgenden Überlegungen betreffen das im Schriftgebrauch Jesu implizierte Sohnesverständnis und speziell die in seinem dritten Schriftzitat erkennbare Abweichung von der alttestamentlichen Vorlage. Läßt diese eine Deutung im Gesamtkontext des Matthäusevangeliums zu?

1. Innerhalb des Matthäusevangeliums sind (abgesehen von Mt 3,15) die im wesentlichen aus Schriftzitaten bestehenden Antworten Jesu an den Versucher zugleich seine ersten Worte. Auch seine letzten Worte als Sterbender am Kreuz stammen aus der Schrift (Mt 27,46 = Ps 22,2). In beiden Fällen reagiert Jesus mit Hilfe der Schrift auf eine Infragestellung seiner Gottessohnschaft. Im ersten Fall geschieht diese durch den Diabolos, im zweiten durch Lästerer und Spötter unter dem Kreuz (Mt 27, 40.43). Die das irdische Wirken Jesu gleichsam umrahmenden Schriftworte verweisen auf die besondere Bedeutung der Schrift in der persönlichen Gottesbeziehung Jesu.

2. In sprachlicher Hinsicht lehnen sich die beiden ersten Schriftzitate Jesu (Mt 4,4.7) im wesentlichen an den Wortlaut der Septuaginta an[1]. Im dritten Zitat (Mt 4,10) zeigen sich jedoch zwei gravierende Unterschiede: Anstelle des in Dtn 6,13 (und 10,20)[2] sowohl in der Septuaginta als auch im masoretischen Text verwendeten Verbums »fürchten« (φοβέομαι, ירא) steht προσκυνέω; durch das zusätzliche μόνῳ akzentuiert Matthäus ferner die Exklusivität des auf Gott bezogenen Dienens[3].

---

1. Das Zitat aus Dtn 8,3 in Mt 4,4 hält sich (abgesehen von der Auslassung von τῷ) wortwörtlich an die Septuaginta, die ihrerseits (durch die Verwendung von ῥῆμα und θεός) an dieser Stelle jedoch ziemlich vom masoretischen Text abweicht. Auch das Zitat aus Dtn 6,16 in Mt 4,7 folgt genau der Septuaginta, die sich (durch die Wiedergabe der Aufforderung »ihr sollt den Herrn euren Gott nicht versuchen« im Singular) gleichfalls vom masoretischen Text unterscheidet.

2. Ob Matthäus Dtn 6,13 oder 10,20 zitiert, läßt sich kaum entscheiden. Ein Argument dafür, daß eher die erste Stelle gemeint ist, ist die Nähe zu 6,16 und 6,4-5 (Schᵉmaᶜ-Israel – von Mt in 22,37 aufgegriffen).

3. Daß der Codex Alexandrinus in Dtn 6,13 und 10,20 gleichfalls προσκυνήσεις hat sowie den Zusatz μόνῳ, kann als christliche Interpolation bewertet werden. Cf. R.H. GUNDRY, *The Use of the Old Testament in St. Matthew's Gospel* (NTSup, 18), Leiden, Brill, 1967, pp. 68-69; R.H. GUNDRY, *Matthew*, Grand Rapids, Eerdmans, ²1994, p. 58;

3. In der zweiten Versuchung zitiert der Diabolos Ps 91,11a und (verbunden durch ein καί) v. 12 im Wortlaut der Septuaginta, die an dieser Stelle sachlich gleichlautend ist mit dem masoretischen Text. Der Grund für die Auslassung von v. 11b (»dich zu behüten auf all deinen Wegen«) liegt möglicherweise darin, daß das Zitat speziell auf die Szene bei der Tempelzinne[4] bezogen ist (und nicht auf das ganze irdische Leben Jesu).

4. Im Hinblick auf Jesu Gottessohnschaft und sein Passionsgeschick[5] wird Schrift gegen Schrift zitiert. Im Sinne des Diabolos ist es schriftgemäß, daß der Gottessohn vor Gefahren und Leid geschützt bleibt. Jesu Sohnesanspruch wäre durch die Schrift widerlegt, sollte ihm Leid zustoßen. Für Jesus hingegen entspricht es der Schrift, daß er sein Vertrauen konsequent auf Gott setzt, ohne den in Ps 91,11-12 verheißenen Schutz zu verlangen (vgl. Mt 26,53-54!). Sein Leidensgeschick bedeutet sogar – wie sich später zeigen wird (Mt 26,24.31.54.56) – Erfüllung der Schrift.

5. Die von Jesus verwendeten Schriftworte (Dtn 8,3; 6,16; 6,13 [10,20]) werfen nicht nur Licht auf seine singuläre Beziehung zu Gott (Sohnschaft), sondern auch auf seine besondere Beziehung zum Volk Israel. Dies zeigt sich darin, daß er sich Weisungen der Schrift zu eigen macht, die seit jeher dem ganzen Volk gelten. Wie für Israel spielt auch für ihn die Schrift eine zentrale Rolle im Leben. Sein in den drei Schriftworten ausgedrücktes Sohnes- und Selbstverständnis hebt sich im Grunde nicht ab von der für ganz Israel eigentümlichen Gottesbeziehung, sondern es wurzelt in ihr. Was für das Volk Israel gilt, gilt auch für ihn. Wie für Israel in der Wüste ist auch für ihn Gottes Wort Nahrung, die man zum Leben ebenso braucht wie Brot. Wie Israel weiß auch er in lebensbedrohlicher Gefahr sich aufgerufen, Gott uneingeschränkt Vertrauen zu schenken, ohne an seinem Schutz zu zweifeln und ohne einen Beweis seiner rettenden Liebe zu fordern. Das Hauptkennzeichen der Religion Israels ist die exklusive Verehrung Jahwes. Ähnlich liegt in der alleinigen Anbetung Gottes und im

---

W.D. Davies – D.C. Allison, *The Gospel According to Saint Matthew*, Vol. 1 (ICC), Edinburgh, Clark, 1988, p. 373. In der Septuaginta wird sonst nirgendwo das hebräische Verbum »(sich) fürchten« (ירא) mit »anbeten« (προσκυνέω) wiedergegeben. Innerhalb von Dtn wird ירא konsequent mit φοβέομαι übersetzt (an 13 Stellen). Dem Verbum προσκυνέω liegt in der Septuaginta in den meisten Fällen שׁחה, sich beugen, niederwerfen, zugrunde (innerhalb von Dtn an den Stellen: 4,19; 5,9; 8,19; 11,16; 17,3; 26,10; 29,26; 30,17).

4. G. Schwarz, *TO ΠΤΕΡΥΓΙΟΝ ΤΟΥ ΙΕΡΟΥ (Mt 4,5 / Lk 4,9)*, in *BN* 61 (1992) 33-35, schlägt mit guten Gründen vor, die Tempelzinne zu definieren als eine »Schulter« des Daches der Vorhalle des Heiligtums.

5. Die Ansicht, daß die Szene auf der Tempelzinne bereits einen Vorverweis auf die Passion Jesu enthält, stützt sich besonders auf Mt 27,40, wo ausdrücklich an die Worte des Diabolos (»wenn du Sohn Gottes bist...« [Mt 4,3.6]) erinnert wird. Ähnlich wie Mt 27,40 enthält auch 27,43 die bereits vom Diabolos vertretene Auffassung, daß Gottessohnschaft unvereinbar ist mit Leidens- und Todesgeschick. Die Sohnesthematik in Mt 27,40.43 ist Sondergut des Matthäus.

ganz auf Gott gerichteten Dienst ein Hauptmerkmal des Sohnesverständnisses Jesu.

6. Betrachtet man Jesu Zitate nicht isoliert, sondern als Rückgriff auf die deuteronomistischen Paränesen Dtn 6–8 (10), die ihrerseits reflektierende und aktualisierende Wiederaufnahmen des Exodusgeschehens sind, so legt es sich nahe, Jesu Aufenthalt in der Wüste in typologischer Entsprechung zum Wüstenaufenthalt Israels zu sehen[6]. Für eine Israeltypologie spricht vor allem auch das Erfüllungszitat aus Hos 11,1 in Mt 2,15. Israel ist während des Wüstenaufenthaltes in seinen Versuchungen (durch Gott) im Gottvertrauen schwach geworden. Jesus ist Antityp Israels, insofern die Versuchungen (durch den Diabolos) sein Vertrauen und seinen Gehorsam gegenüber Gott nicht erschüttern.

7. Die – bereits in (2) erwähnten – Änderungen im Zitat von Dtn 6,13 (10,20) (προσκυνέω, μόνος)[7], durch die im unmittelbaren Kontext ein Kontrast zur Vorstellung der Anbetung des Diabolos (Mt 4,9)[8] gebildet wird, haben auch eine eigene Funktion im Gesamtkontext des Matthäusevangeliums. Während Lukas προσκυνέω nur noch in Lk 24,52 gebraucht, findet sich dieses Verbum bei Matthäus öfters. Es drückt eine besondere Haltung gegenüber Jesus aus, die verschiedene Personen bekunden: die Magier (Mt 2,2.8.11), der Aussätzige (Mt 8,2), der Synagogenvorsteher (Mt 9,18), die Jünger im Boot (Mt 14,33), die kanaanäische Frau (Mt 15,25), die Mutter der Zebedäussöhne (Mt 20,20), die Frauen am Ostertag (Mt 28,9) und schließlich die Jünger am Berg in Galiläa (Mt 28,17)[9]. Ein Gleichnis schildert die Proskynese des Knechtes vor seinem König (Mt 18,26). In Mt 27,29 läßt sich gegenüber Mk 15,19 eine Streichung von προσκυνέω erkennen, ebenfalls in Mt 8,29 gegenüber Mk 5,6. Als Grund

---

6. Über die Zitate hinaus weist Mt 4,1-11 folgende Gemeinsamkeiten mit Dtn auf: die Zahl 40 (Dtn 9,9.18 [40 Tage und Nächte]; vgl. Ex 24,18; 34,28; 1 Kön 19,8) sowie die Vorstellungen von Wüste (Dtn 8,2.4) und Versuchung (Dtn 8,2.16).

7. Da das Schriftzitat in Mt 4,10 identisch ist mit jenem in Lk 4,8, darf man annehmen, daß Matthäus es in dieser Form bereits aus einer gemeinsamen Vorlage (Q?) übernimmt. Anders betrachtet W. WILKENS, *Die Versuchung Jesu nach Matthäus*, in *NTS* 28 (1982) 479-489, Mt 4,1-11 als eigene Bildung des Mt, von der Lk 4,1-13 sekundär abhängig ist.

8. Innerhalb des Neuen Testamentes findet sich eine vergleichbare Vorstellung nur in Offb 13,4.8.12.15 (Anbetung des Drachen, des ersten Tieres und seines Bildes) – vgl. auch 14,9.11; 16,2; 19,20; 20,4.

9. Die Szene auf dem Berg in Galiläa (Mt 28,16-20) läßt sich jener am Berg der Versuchung (Mt 4,8-10) gegenüberstellen. Dabei wird deutlich, daß im Kontrast zum Ansinnen des Diabolos (»dies alles [πᾶς] werde ich dir geben [δίδωμι]...« – Mt 4,9) Jesus, und zwar als der Auferstandene, allein durch Gott universale Vollmacht und Herrschaft erhält («gegeben wurde mir [δίδωμι – passivum divinum] alle [πᾶς] Vollmacht im Himmel und auf der Erde« – Mt 28,18). Die Szene am Berg der Versuchung zeigt, daß Proskynese allein Gott gebührt. Das Verhalten der Jünger am Berg in Galiläa ist ein Zeugnis dafür, daß nicht nur Gott, sondern auch Jesus Proskynese verdient.

dafür kann man vermuten, daß dieses Verbum bei Mt immer wirkliche Huldigung und Anbetung bezeichnet. Die der Person Jesu entgegengebrachte Proskynese kann als ein Charakteristikum der matthäischen Christologie verstanden werden. In semantischer Hinsicht ist ein spezieller Aspekt von προσκυνέω hervorzuheben: Das fußfällige Huldigen, bzw. das (anbetende) Niederfallen[10] ist verknüpft mit der Vorstellung von der Gegenwart dessen, dem die Huldigung erwiesen wird. Während das Fürchten (φοβέομαι) oder Verehren auch auf jemanden bezogen sein kann, der abwesend ist, setzt das Niederfallen und Huldigen eine Anwesenheit voraus. »Die Proskynese bedarf einer vor Augen stehenden Majestät, vor der sich der Anbetende beugt«[11]. Dies ist auch zu beachten bei den Zeugnissen einer Proskynese vor dem Auferstandenen.

Im Vergleich mit den übrigen Proskynese-Stellen bei Matthäus läßt sich sagen: Das dritte und besonders bedeutsame Schriftwort in der Versuchungserzählung, das modifizierte Zitat von Dtn 6,13 in Mt 4,10, hebt die exklusive Theozentrik dessen hervor, dem seinerseits von verschiedenen Personen und Gruppen sowohl in seinem irdischen Wirken als auch nach Ostern Huldigung entgegengebracht wird. Proskynese wird somit dem erwiesen, dessen gesamtes Wirken und Leben Ausdruck der Huldigung und Anbetung Gottes ist.

Zusammenfassung: Sowohl das Faktum, daß Jesus seine Antworten an den Versucher in Schriftworte kleidet, als auch der Inhalt dieser Zitate läßt erkennen, daß Jesu singuläre Sohnesbeziehung tief verwurzelt ist in der für das Volk Israel vom Beginn seiner Existenz an kennzeichnenden Gottesbeziehung. Die Änderung im dritten Schriftzitat trägt im Kontext des gesamten Matthäusevangeliums zur Erkenntnis bei, daß Jesus an Gottes Hoheit und Verehrungswürdigkeit partizipiert.

Institut für Neutestamentliche Bibelwissenschaft   M. HASITSCHKA
Universität Innsbruck
Karl-Rahner-Platz 3
A-6020 Innsbruck

Die dritte Versuchung Jesu (Mt 4,8-10) mit den erzählerischen Elementen des sehr hohen Berges und des Zeigens aller Reiche der Welt sowie der Vorstellung, daß der Teufel die Reiche einfach »geben« kann, ist schwieriger zu interpretieren als die Parallelszene bei Lukas (Lk 4,5-8). Schärfer als Lukas akzentuiert Matthäus auch die Anbetungsthematik (»niederfallend«; »geh fort, Satan!«). Meines Erachtens hat Lukas die Szenenfolge umgestellt. Er reiht, um das für ihn wichtige Thema Jerusalem hervorzuheben, die dritte Versuchung, die bei Matthäus den Höhepunkt bildet, als zweite Szene ein.

10. Wie in Mt 4,9 ist auch in Mt 2,11 und 18,26 προσκυνέω mit πίπτω verbunden.

11. H. GREEVEN, προσκυνέω, in *TWNT* VI 759-767, p. 766.

MATTHEW'S USE OF HOSEA 6,6
IN THE CONTEXT OF THE SABBATH CONTROVERSIES[1]

The Matthean Sabbath controversies have traditionally been interpreted in such a way as to prove the continued Sabbath observance of the Matthean community on the basis of the love commandment as proclaimed by Jesus[2]. Apologetics with regard to Sabbath-observance is, however, not the primary concern of Mt 12,1-14. The use of Hos 6,6 in the exegetical argument of the first Sabbath controversy and the allusions it brings with it opens much larger perspectives with regard to christology and community identity.

"I take pleasure in compassion rather than sacrifice": The explicit quotation from the prophet Hosea cited in the first of the Matthean Sabbath controversies (Mt 12,1-8) offers rich ground for intertextual interpretation. The quotation is not simply a text interpreted out of context of the prophetic book. Rather, its use in Mt 12,7 *presupposes* the Hosean prophetic message. Further, the quotation in chapter 12 also functions as a citation of Mt 9,14, as well as to participate in the first-century discussion around the meaning of Hos 6,6. The presence of the quotation in the Gospel text, then, provides the reader with a multitude of interpretative contexts, which allow for a complex of meanings and allusions in the passage. The following analysis of the first Matthean Sabbath controversy, drawing on three interpretative contexts, will show that the quotation does not primarily function as an exhortation, but is to be understood prophetically, as a christological argument in the context of the Matthean struggle to separate from the Jewish mother-community.

Before drawing on contextual and intertextual meaning to interpret Mt 12,1-8, it is necessary to focus on the passage itself, and the exegetical argument which it brings. The first Sabbath controversy is introduced by the disciples picking grain in the field[3] on a Sabbath. The Pharisees see this

---

1. I am indebted to S.C. Barton and L.T. Stuckenbruck, Durham, for their helpful comments on an earlier draft of this paper.
2. Cf. e.g. R. S. McConnell, *Law and Prophecy in Matthew's Gospel. The Authority and Use of the Old Testament in the Gospel of Matthew* (Theologische Dissertationen, II), Basel, 1969, pp. 68-72; G. Barth, *Matthew's Understanding of the Law*, in G. Bornkamm et al. *Tradition and Interpretation in Matthew*, Philadelphia, 1963, pp. 58-164, esp. 80-85; U. Luz, *Das Evangelium nach Matthäus* (EKK, I), Zürich/Neukirchen-Vluyn, 1989/1990, vol. 2, pp. 233-234.
3. Probably according to the system of Peah. Lev 19,9, Deut 23,24-25. Cf. M. Casey, *Culture and Historicity. The Plucking of the Grain (Mark 2.23-28)*, in *NTS* 34 (1988) 1-23, p. 2.

and accuse them of doing that which is impermissible on the Sabbath. Jesus' defence of his disciples includes first a haggadic argument already present in the Markan tradition Matthew preserves (vv. 3-4) concerning David and his men eating the shewbread from the Temple[4]. Matthew's redaction of the passage makes the parallel between David and the disciples clear: in both cases hunger led to the doing of something which was not lawful[5]. Here, the question of Sabbath is irrelevant[6]: David and the men who were with him broke the law when they were hungry. Likewise the disciples were hungry and broke the law. Human need overrides the commandment. The haggadic argument is followed by a halakhic argument which is added by Matthew (v. 5)[7]. It points to the priests' service on a Sabbath being exempt from the Sabbath law. The second example, related to the first by the mention of the temple and the priests, is an inference *a minori ad maius* ending in the statement which Matthew has added in v. 6: something greater than the temple is here[8]. If temple service is exempt from the Sabbath law, then certainly that which is greater than temple service will also be excused. The statement needs clarification, however: What is there that is greater than the temple?[9] This clarification

4. 1 Sam 21,7.

5. Οὐκ ἔξεστιν ποιεῖν ἐν σαββάτῳ (v. 2)// οὐκ ἐξὸν ἦν αὐτῷ φαγεῖν (v. 4) Matthew underlines this parallel further by adding πεινάω and ἐσθίω to the source, in the description of the disciples' action. Cf. I. BROER, *Anmerkungen zum Gesetzesverständnis des Matthäus*, in K. KERTELGE (ed.), *Das Gesetz im Neuen Testament*, Freiburg (Br.), 1986, p. 139; G. BARTH (n. 2), p. 81.

6. There is nothing in the tradition which suggests that David and his men broke the *Sabbath* law. The rabbinic tradition early inferred that the incident took place on the Sabbath, because of the reference to the shewbread which was to be arranged every Sabbath (Lev 24,5-8). Cf. H.L. STRACK and P. BILLERBECK, *Das Evangelium nach Matthäus erläutert aus Talmud und Midrasch*, München, 1922, p. 618f. The Rabbis excused David because, being pursued by Saul, he was in mortal danger. Matthew's argument, however, is *not* dependent on the supposition that David ate bread on the Sabbath.

7. It is possible that Matthew has added the argument to the original text, because Jewish exegesis demands an example from the law to build a halakhah, a requirement not met by the first example. Cf. M.D. GOULDER, *Midrash and Lection in Matthew*, London, 1974, p. 328; U. LUZ (n. 2) vol. 2, p. 231.

8. Mt 12,6 λέγω δὲ ὑμῖν ὅτι τοῦ ἱεροῦ μεῖζόν ἐστιν ὧδε.

9. It is precisely with regard to this sentence that scholarship is divided in the interpretation of the passage. Luz, pointing to the tightness of the Matthean argumentation, and the neuter of the adjective, concludes that it is the mercy (ἔλεος) of the Hosean citation to which "the greater" in v. 6 refers. V. 6 is, however, a Matthean construction reminiscent of Q's καὶ ἰδοὺ πλεῖον Ἰωνᾶ (Σολομῶνος) ὧδε, which is found in Mt 12,41.42. There the neuter πλεῖον obviously has a christological reference. LUZ, (n. 2) vol. 2, p. 231 questions a too quick christological interpretation also here, however. Greek usage of the neuter allows for a lack of correspondence between the neuter and the word to which it relates in cases such as this, especially as the "something" in fact is not specified in the argument. As R. GUNDRY, *Matthew. A Commentary on His Literary and Theological Art*, Grand Rapids, MI, 1982, p. 223 points out: "The neuter gender of μεῖζον stresses

is given in vv. 7-8. In verse 7 ("if you knew what it is: 'I take pleasure in compassion rather than sacrifice', you would not condemn the innocent"), Matthew, in the words of Jesus, first brings a denunciation of the Pharisees, then offers a point of correspondence between the disciples and the temple priests. The denunciation of the Pharisees is dual: first, they have not understood[10]; secondly, as a result of their incomprehension, they have condemned the blameless[11]. The point of correspondence between the temple priests and the disciples is their being without guilt despite breaking the Sabbath law[12]. Following the quotation, the concluding v. 8: κύριος γάρ ἐστιν τοῦ σαββάτου ὁ υἱὸς τοῦ ἀνθρώπου, constitutes the qualifying statement to v. 6 and forms the climax of the Matthean argument. It is ὁ υἱὸς τοῦ ἀνθρώπου who is the Lord of the Sabbath and who is greater than the temple. The disciples, owing service to him, are innocent of breaking the Sabbath law.

The exegetical argument of the first Sabbath controversy has thus been shown to be primarily christological. The quotation from Hos 6,6 "Mercy, I want, rather than sacrifice", as it occurs in Mt 12,7, gives content to the christological pronouncement of the Sabbath controversy. Compassion, ἔλεος, is a guiding principle of the ministry of Jesus. If Jesus, upon this principle, does not condemn the disciples' behaviour, then the Pharisees, if they would understand, should not do so either. Jesus demands from them the insight to recognise the compassion of God in Jesus. This compassion is further illustrated in the second Sabbath controversy, where Jesus heals the man with the withered hand. The citation from Hos 6,6, therefore, serves also as an introduction to the second of the Sabbath controversies (Mt 12,9-14).

In the second Sabbath controversy Jesus enters *their* synagogue where a man with a withered hand is found, and *they* question him whether it

the quality of superior greatness rather than Jesus' personal identity". Thus, the adjective has a christological reference.

10. This is the greatest offence of the Pharisees. Lack of understanding, or not recognising the nature of Jesus' ministry, is a theme parallel to the christological one in Mt 11–13 (cf. e.g. Mt 11,15.16-19.25-30; 13,14). The repeated use of γινώσκω in the first 8 verses of Mt 12: "Do you not know", "do you not know", and "if you knew what it means", all refer back to 11,25-30, where "these things" are hidden from the wise, but revealed to children. To those to whom it has been revealed it is also given to recognise the father in the son (Mt 11,27).

11. The accusation does not include an exhortation to be merciful, i.e. as a reference to the love commandment (contra McCONNELL [n. 2], pp. 68-72). The issue at stake here is the ability to recognise the father through the son, or through the deeds of the son (cf. Mt 11,19. 27).

12. Mt 12,5: τοῖς σάββασιν οἱ ἱερεῖς ἐν τῷ ἱερῷ τὸ σάββατον βεβηλοῦσιν καὶ ἀναίτιοί εἰσιν//Mt 12,7: εἰ δὲ ἐγνώκειτε τί ἐστιν, Ἔλεος θέλω καὶ οὐ θυσίαν, οὐκ ἂν κατεδικάσατε τοὺς ἀναιτίους.

is permissible to heal on the Sabbath[13]. The repetition of "ἔξεστιν" ties the present pericope with the previous, explicitly raising the question of the lawfulness to heal on a Sabbath[14]. The sentence introducing Jesus' response is identical to that of Mt 12,3. He points out that anyone would lift his sheep out of a pit on the Sabbath, and a human being is much more (διαφέρω) than a sheep. Matthew otherwise uses διαφέρω only where it occurs in Q: Mt 6,26 (you are worth more than the birds of the sky and the seeds of the earth) and 10,31 (more than sparrows). The insertion of the phrase here duplicates the Q-tradition[15] and functions to bring the two previous occurrences into mind. The healing of the withered hand, as well as other good deeds towards human beings on the Sabbath, are to be understood as an expression of God's compassion. Therefore, Jesus concludes, it is lawful to do good on the Sabbath. Mercy, concern for the human being, fulfils the Sabbath commandment[16]. The second controversy illustrates in practice the mercy of Jesus' ministry.

When turning to the textual contexts which will inform the interpretation of Mt 12,1-8, it is first necessary to examine closer the context of the Sabbath controversies themselves. The controversies have been removed from their original context of disputes over purity and other laws in Mark[17] to its present place, where they introduce a set of new conflicts with the

13. Matthew's preference for the verb ἐπερωτάω rather than παρατηρέω (to watch closely), underlines the feeling of hostility on the part of the Jewish leaders which is already there in the Markan account. Cf. W. SCHENK, Die Sprache des Matthäus. Die Text-Konstituenten in ihren makro- und mikrostrukturellen Relationen, Göttingen, 1987, p. 261. The verb has no formal subject, the indefinite "they" of "their synagogues" (12,9), are those who condemn. It is worth noting that this Matthean stereotype (αὐτῶν as a way to distinguish their synagogues, their leaders, their cities) is only prevalent in the first part of the Gospel, ending in 13,58 with Jesus' inability to do any powerful deeds because of their unbelief (Mt 4,23; 7,29; 9,35; 10,17; 11,1; 12,9; 13,54; 13,58).

14. In Mark this is only implicit, as they watch him carefully to see whether he would heal.

15. SCHENK (n. 13), p. 183.

16. Therefore, it is too simple to conclude that the redactionally omitted phrase from Mk 2,27: Τὸ σάββατον διὰ τὸν ἄνθρωπον ἐγένετο καὶ οὐχ ὁ ἄνθρωπος διὰ τὸ σάββατον was too radical or "gentile" oriented for Matthew. Cf. E. SCHWEIZER, Das Evangelium nach Matthäus (NTD, 2), Göttingen, [16]1986, p. 180. Differently D. HILL, On the Use and Meaning of Hos VI.6 in Matthew's Gospel, in NTS 24 (1977-78) 107-119, p. 114, suggests that Matthew's omission of the statement is grounded in Matthew's knowledge of the view that the Sabbath was a gift from God to the human being. It was used to strengthen the Sabbath commandment in Jewish teaching rather than to soften it. Matthew's redaction of the whole of the two controversies, which actually form one unit, shows an understanding of Jesus' ministry where the concern for the human being corresponds with the purpose of the Sabbath commandment. The Sabbath controversies as a unit in Matthew, may consequently be interpreted as an expansion of the omitted Markan phrase.

17. With Pharisees over eating with tax collectors and sinners, with the disciples of John concerning fasting, with the Pharisees again concerning Sabbath observance.

Pharisees. It is to be assumed that this change of context serves a purpose in the Matthean Gospel narrative. It is appropriate, therefore, to inquire about the link between Mt 12 and that which precedes. In chapters 11-13 of Matthew's Gospel, the wider context of the controversies in chapter 12, two themes are prevalent: the christological affirmation, and the invitation to see, hear, and understand[18]. The first of these is of interest to the present analysis.

In the verses immediately preceding the controversies we find Wisdom's invitation to the weary, with promise of rest and an easy yoke[19]. Knowing that Sabbath in the Septuagint often is translated with ἀνάπαυσις, and that ἀνάπαυσις was the purpose of the Sabbath[20], one can conclude that it is the idea of rest which ties Wisdom's invitation with the question of the Sabbath[21]. Furthermore, the Sabbath commemorates God's liberation in the past[22], and anticipates future redemption[23]. The ministry of Jesus as the giver of rest is at the beginning of Mt 11-13 described in terms which announce the eschatological hope of redemption in the Hebrew Scriptures: "the blind receive sight, the lame walk, the lepers are cleansed and the dead are raised up" (Mt 11,5). The associations between Jesus, Sabbath rest and the eschatological hope adds force to the christological argument of the Sabbath controversies. In his ministry of mercy and healing the true purpose of the Sabbath rest is present. This is something greater than the temple. In Jesus' ministry, one may recognise God's redemptive work (cf. Mt 11,27). The christological affirmation is developed in the fulfilment quotation following the Sabbath controversy (Mt 12,18-21). Citing the first servant song of Isaiah, Matthew describes Jesus as God's chosen one, who has received God's Spirit, and who works in humility for the poor and needy.

18. See n. 10.
19. Although this contrast is obviously present in the Gospel (Mt 23,4), the Sabbath controversies are not introduced here with the primary purpose to contrast the heavy burdens of the Pharisaic rules concerning Sabbath observance with the light load of Jesus. Contra R. SCHNACKENBURG, "Siehe da mein Knecht, den ich erwählt habe..." (Mt 12,18). Zur Heiltätigkeit Jesu im Matthäusevangelium, in L. OBERLINNER & P. FIEDLER (eds.), Salz der Erde Licht der Welt. FS A. Vögtle, Stuttgart, 1991, pp. 203-222, p. 217; and J.C FENTON, The Gospel of St Matthew, Harmondsworth, 1966, p. 187.
20. Ex 23,23; Deut 5,14.
21. Cf. SCHWEIZER (n. 16), p. 181.
22. Deut 5,15.
23. Zech 14,7. For this three dimensional scope of Sabbath observance, see S. BACCHIOCCHI, From Sabbath to Sunday, Rome, 1977, p. 23. Bacchiocchi also points out that in Judaism the Sabbath functioned as typology for the messianic redemption in several ways, in: S. BACCHIOCCHI, Sabbatical Typologies of Messianic Redemption, in JSJ 17 (1986) 155-167. T. FRIEDMAN, The Sabbath: Anticipation of Redemption, in Judaism 16 (1967), p. 445, points to Isa 56,1-7; 58,13-14; 66,20-24, where the same terminology is used to describe both the Sabbath and the end of days.

Although the saying "I take pleasure in compassion rather than sacrifice" is originally derived from the Book of Hosea, Mt 12,7 also cites Mt 9,14 as a result of the double occurrence of the saying in the Gospel. It is interesting to note that the citation actually connects material of Mt 9 and Mt 12 which is found together in the Gospel of Mark. Several common factors indicate that the repetition of the quotation in Mt 12 has a specific purpose. First, the quotation is introduced similarly in both contexts, where τί ἔστιν emphasises the need for understanding. Jesus' reproach in chapter 12: "if you had known" refers back to chapter 9, where the Pharisees are requested to "go and learn". Second, the antagonists in both occurrences are the Pharisees. In Matthew they are a stereotypical entity representing the religious leaders of Israel. Finally, but perhaps decisively, the citation is in both passages preceded and followed by a christological pronouncement.

In Mt 9, the Hosean citation is inserted into Markan material where the disciples are questioned about the practice of Jesus in eating with tax collectors and sinners. Jesus himself answers "It is not the powerful who need a healer, but those who are worthless", and "I did not come to call the righteous, but sinners". The quotation is inserted by the Matthean redactor between the two statements, and like in Mt 12, interrupts the apparent logic of the pericope. Clearly, the issue in question is the mission or practice of Jesus. Compassion is given content in Jesus' praxis: healing, forgiving sins (Mt 9,6), fellowship with and calling of "tax collectors and sinners" to discipleship (Mt 9,9-13)[24]. Christologically interpreted then, the quotation illustrates the meaning of Mt 5,17: "Do not believe that I came to bring an end to the law or the prophets: I did not come to abolish, but to fulfil"[25].

The christological emphasis naturally reduces the importance of the contrasting element of the quotation: sacrifice. Mt 9 does not give an indication as to the significance of this contrast, rather, the Pharisees are invited, in a teacher-pupil manner, to go and learn what it means. This significance is subsequently revealed to them in Mt 12, where the citation occurs again, following a statement about the temple. Sacrifice, as a celebration which takes place in the presence of God in the temple[26], is less significant now that the word of the prophet has been fulfilled, and

24. It cannot be by chance that Matthew inserts the calling of the tax collector called Matthew before the pericope concerning tax collectors and sinners, which ends with Jesus' statement: "I did not come to call the righteous but sinners."

25. Cf. Luz (n. 2), vol. 2, p. 45.

26. Deut 12,5-12. "זבח", *TDOT*, vol. IV, p. 25.

the presence of God is found in Jesus' ministry of compassion and mercy[27]. That Matthew thought in these terms about the temple is confirmed in Mt 23, where the statement "Behold, I will leave your house desolate" (v. 38) coincides with the exit of Jesus from the temple (Mt 24,1). In the narrative of Matthew, then, Mt 9,13 prepares for the second occurrence of Hos 6,6 by already placing it in a context of christological pronouncement. The question at stake is ultimately the question of the presence of God.

Hos 6,6 is the only quotation which is repeated in the Gospel. Consequently the passage may be assumed to be of special importance for Matthew. Two final intertextual or interpretative contexts may point to the particular importance of the quotation for Matthew or the Matthean community in the midst of the struggle of separation from the Jewish mother-community.

In the original context of the citation in the book of Hosea, ἔλεος is connected with the covenant as faithfulness to God[28]. Hos 6,6 is part of a prophetic speech of judgement of Israel for its disloyalty. Words of judgement constitute most of the book of Hosea. The purpose of the prophetic judgement, however, is ultimately the repentance of God's people. In repeatedly using the quotation, in the context of controversies with the Pharisees, Matthew is alluding to the Hosean judgement upon Israel. Here, as in the prophetic book, threat of judgement implies an invitation to repentance. The lack of understanding among the Pharisees leads eventually to their denunciation, patterned on prophetic judgement in chapter 23. In the employment of Hos 6,6 is implied a prophetic judgement against those who do not recognise in Jesus the mercy of God[29].

---

27. The connection between θυσία and the temple is often denied or overlooked, and the contrast ἔλεος// θυσία is understood to contrast the love commandment of Jesus with the legalism of the Pharisees, and, consequently, Judaism as a whole. Cf. e.g. McCONNELL (n. 2), p. 72; O.L. COPE, *Matthew. A Scribe Trained for the Kingdom of Heaven* (CBQ MS, 5), Washington DC, 1976, p. 68; GOULDER (n. 7), p. 37; D. HAGNER, *Matthew 1-13* (WBC, 33a), Dallas, 1993, p. 239. The consecutive reference to the priests duty in the temple on the Sabbath (i.e. sacrifice), Jesus greatness as greater than the temple, and the contrast compassion/sacrifice, however, seems to emphasise that θυσία here actually means the obvious: sacrifice in the temple cult.

28. C.L. SEOW, *Hosea, Book of*, in *ABD*, vol. III, 296.

29. While assuming that a specific problem of Matthean community is dealing with the separation from the mother community, a fact that is illustrated through the extraordinary harsh judgement on the Jewish leaders, it is difficult to conclude with HILL that Hos 6,6 is used atomistically in the Gospel as a source of halakhah. Although HILL (n. 16), pp. 114-116, uses the Hosea reference to analyse the meaning of חסד in terms of covenant loyalty in the book of Hosea, he prefers to understand the use of Hos 6,6 in Matthew plainly on the level of proper Sabbath observance.

The inner Matthean connections between the use of Hos 6,6 in controversies with the Pharisees, together with chapter 23 of the Gospel, hints at an explanation for the destruction of the temple; it is a theme which provides a link to a final interpretive context for the Sabbath controversies. Looking at the destroyed temple, Yoḥanan ben Zakkai is reported to have quoted Hos 6,6, referring to compassion as a redemptive power equal to sacrifice[30]. The use of the same citation in connection with temple practice in Matthew, as well as the Rabbinic tradition of Yoḥanan, suggests Hos 6,6 as a text particularly relevant to the Jewish community after the destruction of the temple[31]. In inserting the passage into the christological argument of the Sabbath controversies, Matthew as a part of the Jewish community attempts to make sense of the destruction of the temple. Significant, however, is that for Matthew, Jesus as Immanuel is the fulfilment of the compassion spoken of in Hosea.

Both the prophetic implications of judgement, and the alternative use of Hos 6,6 as applicable in understanding the destruction of the temple, mirror the crisis of the Matthean community regarding the separation from the synagogue. The heightening of the conflict with the Pharisees and the scribes in the Gospel story illustrates this crisis. The greatest fault of the Pharisees is that they do not understand, despite what they see in Jesus[32]. But even their inability to understand has a paradigm in Scripture. So Israel's disloyalty (Hos 6,6//Mt 12,7) and blindness (Isa 6,9//Mt 13,14) is the scriptural pattern of which the "Scribes and the Pharisees" become representative.

The analysis of Matthew's use of Hos 6,6 in the context of the Sabbath controversies has shown that there is more at stake in Jesus' defence of the disciples' behaviour than an apologetic of the later church over against the Pharisaic movement concerning the church's loosening up of the Sabbath command. Matthew's interpretation of the event is primarily christological. Jesus is Immanuel, "God with us": something more than the temple. The composer of the first Gospel sees the two accounts of Sabbath controversies as revolving around the question of the true reason for keeping the Sabbath. The concern of the Pharisees as depicted in Mt 12,1-14 is the proper keeping of the Sabbath command. In Matthew's understanding, ἀνάπαυσις is the purpose of the Sabbath. The essence of Sabbath observance is as pointed out above, the proleptic presence of the

30. Cf. STRACK-BILLERBECK (n. 6), p. 500.
31. Though any literary dependence between Matthew and Yoḥanan cannot be speculated on account of the problems of dating rabbinic literature, the context of Hos 6,6 in Matthew does show a common concern.
32. Mt 11,5; 11,25; 12,7.

"rest" of the age to come. Through the placing of the Sabbath controversies in the present context, Matthew brings the Sabbatical promise of liberation and rest in connection with the ministry of Jesus[33]. This is practically depicted in the healing of the man with the withered hand: his hand was made whole like the other. Further, and quite significantly, this is set forth in the Matthean addition which at first glance seems an awkward argumentation: Behold something more than the Temple is here. True Sabbath is found in the ministry of Jesus who is "the one who is to come" (Mt 11,3), replacing the temple as God's resting place among God's people.

Department of Theology   Lena LYBÆK
University of Durham
Durham DH7 8RZ
England

---

33. Despite the presence of the eschatological idea here, Jesus' defence of the disciples is not to be understood as a concession to this age. The christological emphasis does not do away with Sabbath observance in the Matthean community. The practice of Sabbath observance is presupposed in Matthew, and the Matthean community probably still observed the Sabbath, cf. LUZ (n. 2) p. 233. The christological accent is much more to be understood as similar to the question of fasting in Mt 9,14-15: while the "bridegroom", or the true Sabbath is present, there is an exemption from the rule, like with the priests in the Sabbath temple service.

A STRANGE SALVATION
INTERTEXTUAL ALLUSION IN MT 27,39-44

I

The work of many scholars has contributed to an understanding of the use of the Old Testament by the writers of the New Testament, although their interest has been primarily in the classification of the borrowings in an effort to come to historical critical judgments on the sources, forms, and redactions of the New Testament. Critical emphasis has remained on the intentional use of the Old Testament by gospel redactors because quotation, whether explicit or implicit, is easily recognizable. The writer or redactor chooses to make reference to another text; the critic's job then is primarily to verify the source. Allusions that are not marked in some way, and echoes, are harder to work with, for a variety of reasons. Because they are difficult to prove, and indeed may only exist in the mind and ear of the reader, allusions are often dismissed as "unintentional", and therefore not within the scope of critical inquiry. Max Wilcox comments twice that they "may be little more than the sort of language early Christian pious people used, without any deeper intention"[1]. Larger structures are equally difficult to handle. Typological criticism has a long history, but only recently have scholars begun to explore the ways in which genre and narrative structure may be part of a study of literary connection or dependence[2]. Modern literary critics are likely to discuss these relationships in terms of intertextuality, a term coined by Julia Kristeva[3], in which various codes combine in a text to make meaning possible. Ellen van Wolde aptly points out that intertextuality as a method is not the comparative study of texts by a new name, although certain critical efforts might lead to that conclusion; intertextual method "becomes significant only when it causes a change in our understanding of texts"[4].

---

1. M. WILCOX, *On Investigating the Use of the Old Testament in the New Testament*, in E. BEST and R.McL. WILSON (eds.), *Text and Interpretation*. FS M. Black, Cambridge, 1979, pp. 231-245, esp. 237.

2. See particularly G.W.E. NICKELSBURG, *The Genre and Function of the Markan Passion Narrative*, in *HTR* 73 (1980) 156-163; and T.L. DONALDSON, *The Mockers and the Son of God (Matthew 27.37-44): Two Characters in Matthew's Story of Jesus*, in *JSNT* 41 (1991) 3-18.

3. J. KRISTEVA, *Séméotikè: Recherches pour une semanalyse*, Paris, 1969.

4. E. VAN WOLDE, *Trendy Intertextuality?* in S. DRAISMA (ed.), *Intertextuality in Biblical Writings*. FS B. van Iersel, Kampen, 1989, pp. 43-50, p. 43.

While studies in allusion indicate connections between texts and suggest nuances of meaning when various connotations are possible, it is not typically concerned with the effects of recontextualization. Kristeva has argued that intertextuality is not simple borrowing, but the intersection of two systems of meaning which conflict[5]. By thinking intertextually, then, we may be able to see how Matthew appropriates a text, for which Jewish scriptures provide an important intertext, and turns it to Christian polemical uses.

The Passion narrative in the gospel of Matthew provides a good place to start because the source and redaction critical issues are simpler here than in other parts of the text. Matthew follows Mark closely, and in the pericope under consideration adds material for which we also have written sources. The ways in which Matthew differs from Mark, and the use to which Matthew puts his sources, indicate, more clearly than is sometimes the case, Matthew's redactional activity. This material has been ably investigated by a number of biblical critics whose interests range from text- and source-critical issues to literary criticism; their findings provide the basis for my own intertextual explorations[6]. Some have seen connections between Matthew and the Wisdom of Solomon, although the interpretive implications have not been fully examined[7]. In this short paper, I want to focus on the intertexts for Mt 27,39-44, the mockers at the cross. This pericope provides a limited context in which first to establish Matthew's allusive borrowing of Old Testament words and images, and then to analyze the structural parallels with the Wisdom of Solomon and the political effects of his intertextual rewriting.

5. J. KRISTEVA, *The System and the Speaking Subject*, in T. MOI (ed.), *The Kristeva Reader*, New York, 1986, pp. 24-33.

6. Among the commentators whose work has been particularly significant in this regard are O.L. COPE, *Matthew: A Scribe Trained for the Kingdom of Heaven*, Washington, 1976; W. D. DAVIES, *Reflections About the Use of the Old Testament in the New in Its Historical Context*, in *JQR* 74 (1983) 105-136; C.H. DODD, *According to the Scriptures: The Substructure of NT Theology*, London, 1952; J.A. FITZMYER, *The Use of Explicit Quotations in Qumran Literature and in the NT*, in *NTS* 7 (1961) 297-333; R.H. GUNDRY, *Matthew: A Commentary on His Literary and Theological Art*, Grand Rapids, MI, 1982; and *The Use of the Old Testament in St. Matthew's Gospel*, Leiden, 1975 <1967>; D.A. CARSON & H.G.M. WILLIAMSON (eds.), *It is Written: Scripture Citing Scripture*. FS B. Lindars, Cambridge, 1988; F. J. MATERA, *The Plot of Matthew's Gospel*, in *CBQ* 49 (1987) 233-253; D.J. MOO, *The Old Testament in the Gospel Passion Narratives*, Sheffield, 1983; D.P. SENIOR, *Matthew's Special Material in the Passion Story: Implications for the Evangelist's Redactional Technique and Theological Perspective*, in *ETL* 63 (1987) 272-294; and *The Passion of Jesus in the Gospel of Matthew*, Wilmington, DE, 1985; K. STENDAHL, *The School of St. Matthew and Its Use of the Old Testament*, Lund, 1954.

7. DONALDSON (n. 2), p. 8; and J.P. MEIER, *The Gospel According to Matthew: An Access Guide*, New York, 1980, p. 347.

II

The first section of the Wisdom of Solomon provides a number of references to language which echoes in Matthew 27. The listener is warned to trust and not to tempt God, μὴ πειράζουσιν (1,2), for God will condemn the blasphemer, βλάσφημον (1,6), and vengeance will not pass by the wicked, whose counsel is described as devilish: ἐν διαβουλίοις ἀσεβοῦς (1,8-9). Their mouths tell lies: στόμα καταψευδόμενον (1,11). The creation, on the other hand, is whole: σωτήριοι (1,14).

The second chapter describes the thoughts and plans of the wicked, who do not believe in immortality and who oppress the righteous man who does (2,1-4). Having no hope, they live for the moment and attempt to destroy the man whose life is a rebuke to them: ὀνειδίζει ἡμῖν ἁμαρτήματα νόμου (2,12). The righteous man calls himself the child of the Lord, παῖδα κυρίου (2,13), and claims that God is his father, πατέρα Θεόν (2,16). The wicked resolve to test him to see whether he is indeed God's son: εἰ γάρ ἐστιν ὁ δίκαιος υἱὸς Θεοῦ (2,18), believing that if he is, God will help and deliver him, ῥύσεται αὐτὸν (2,18), from his enemies. They torture him and put him to a shameful death (2,19-20).

The rest of the section continues with the condemnation of the wicked and the vindication of the righteous, with a warning to rulers typical of kingship tracts. God, although he tests the righteous man, vindicates him because he pleased God and was loved by him: εὐάρεστος Θεῷ γενόμενος ἠγαπήθη (4,10). The wicked who derided him, ὀνειδισμοῦ (5,4), are ultimately witnesses to his strange salvation: ἐπὶ τῷ παραδόξῳ τῆς σωτηρίας (5,2). Having thought him destroyed without honor, they see him among the sons of God, ἐν υἱοῖς Θεοῦ (5,5). Much of this language echoes in the mockery in Matthew, some of it directly, and some through other gospel intertexts, particularly the Temptation narrative, where obedience is stressed. The pericope begins with an introduction in 27,39: "And the passers-by blasphemed him, shaking their heads...": Οἱ δὲ παραπορευόμενοι ἐβλασφήμουν αὐτὸν κινοῦντες τὰς κεφαλὰς αὐτῶν. The commentators are quick to recognize an allusion to LXX Ps 21,8 in the shaking of the heads: "All the onlookers mocked me; they spoke with their lips, they shook their heads...": πάντες οἱ θεωροῦντές με ἐξεμυκτήρισάν με, ἐλάλησαν ἐν χείλεσιν, ἐκίνησαν κεφαλήν. Seeing and mocking are important elements of the LXX verse, along with the shaking of the head, a gesture of derision. The use of the verse in the gospels is typical of the way the language of the Old Testament is used in the New; there would seem to be a pool of associated words and images that belong to a given motif, in this case, the language of impious mockery. Various verbs connoting "to mock" are found in contexts which include shaking the head, reproaching, and blaspheming; and the form may include a rhetorical question tinged with irony[8]. So, while Matthew's verse does not explicitly quote scripture or the Wisdom of Solomon, the language recalls these texts. The use of "passers-by" instead of "onlookers", and the ironic question, may indicate a stronger connection to Lamentations than has been suggested. In the Old Testament context, the lament over the destruction of Jerusalem in 587 B.C.E. emphasizes that the sins of the people have incurred God's wrath, resulting in the triumph of Israel's enemies. Like the wisdom tradition reflected in the Wisdom of Solomon, Lamentations explores the relationship of suffering and sin, affirming God's justice and hope in God's ultimate salvation. In Wis 2, however, the sin is not that of God's people, who then must suffer, but rather the sin is of the enemies of God's chosen one, an innocent victim who suffers at the hands of his enemies and is later vindicated. These echoes resonate in Matthew. For his community, which has experienced the destruction of the Temple, the subtle implication is that the wickedness of those in power caused the destruction. Furthermore, the mockery of the enemies of Israel in Lamentations is followed by a description of them, in which they literally consume their victims, with images of open mouths and gnashing teeth: κατεπίομεν αὐτήν, and Διήνοιξαν ἐπὶ σὲ στόμα αὐτῶν πάντες οἱ ἐχθροί σου (Lam 2,16). This complex of images echoes also in LXX Ps 21,14-22 where the speaker perceives himself to be surrounded by vicious enemies who are likened to dangerous wild animals, bulls, lions, and, especially, dogs: indeed, the gospel account may allude to this image[9].

The verb "to blaspheme" ordinarily means to speak impiously of God or profanely of sacred things. In the synoptic gospels the verb suggests that God has been dishonored in some way by impious speech. When others interpret Jesus' words as "blasphemy", their interpretation is based on the assumption that Jesus does not have the authority he claims; that is to say, from Matthew's perspective, they are mistaken. Those who mock Jesus "blaspheme" because, without realizing it, they are speaking impiously, in the context of the narrative. Thus the use of the verb subtly

---

8. 2 Ki 19,21 (LXX 4 Ki 19,21), for example, includes all these elements; cf. Isa 37,22; Sir 13,7. In the passage from 2 Kings, God wonders aloud whom the Assyrians might have blasphemed and then promptly answers the question. Similarly, the mockery in Lam 2,15, occasionally suggested as a source for Mt 27,39, takes the form of an ironic question, and like LXX Ps 21, also stresses the involvement of all the passers-by: πάντες οἱ παραπορευόμενοι...ἐκίνησαν τὴν κεφαλὴν αὐτῶν.

9. COPE (n. 6), pp. 102-103.

reinforces the presentation of Jesus as Son of God and Christ, claims that will also be made more explicitly in this pericope.

The following verse (27,40) alludes to the trial of Jesus, where he is accused of threatening to destroy the Temple: "This fellow said, 'I am able to destroy the Temple of God, and to rebuild it in three days'": ὁ καταλύων τὸν ναὸν καὶ ἐν τρισὶν ἡμέραις οἰκοδομῶν, echoing δύναμαι καταλῦσαι τὸν ναὸν τοῦ Θεοῦ καὶ διὰ τριῶν ἡμερῶν οἰκοδομῆσαι (26,61). At the cross, the same charges are repeated, beginning with the accusation of hostility to the Temple and power over it. But Jesus was charged at the trial as a Messianic pretender[10]. Caiaphas places the title "Son of God" in a Messianic context, where ὁ Χριστὸς implies the righteous and victorious king predicted in Zech 9,9-10, an intertext for Jesus' entry into Jerusalem. At the cross, however, Matthew omits the title, leaving only "Son of God". The passers-by had challenged Jesus to prove his identity by saving himself from death: "Come down from the cross": κατάβηθι ἀπὸ τοῦ σταυροῦ (27,40). Matthew had defined Jesus' entire mission at the beginning of the gospel: "for he will save his people from their sins": αὐτὸς γὰρ σώσει τὸν λαὸν αὐτοῦ ἀπὸ τῶν ἁμαρτιῶν αὐτῶν (1,21). Here the mockers, ironically, evaluate Jesus' success in fulfilling that purpose: he saved others. In the mouths of the mockers, save means heal, deliver, rescue from death; it is the language of the Exodus and the Psalms. To the Matthean community it is a creedal statement: Jesus saved others, but saved them by his own death. The mockers' words have an ironic effect, although they are not spoken ironically. Thus from the beginning, Jesus' role as Son of God has been associated with his ability to save others from sin.

The taunt continues with what D.P. Senior calls "without a doubt the central issue of the Matthean crucifixion and death account": "if you are the Son of God": εἰ υἱὸς εἶ τοῦ Θεοῦ (27,40)[11]. In the context of the narrative, the title recalls the language of the trial scene, as noted above;

10. M. de Jonge sees two complexes of related terms, each including the term "Son of God"; the complexes indicate the range of connotations available: "It is probable ... that the notions of Messiah/Son of David/Son of God, and wise and righteous man/perfectly obedient servant of God/pious charismatic/Son of God, were constitutive for the earliest stages of the Christian use of the term". His description suggests the existence of a language pool, like that used in impious mockery, of terms related to Son of God, used in different combinations to indicate different connotations and different emphases. De Jonge is probably correct in seeing the connection; the interpretation then depends on the emphasis found in individual contexts. M. DE JONGE, *The Use of ὁ Χρίστος in the Passion Narratives*, in J. DUPONT (ed.), *Jésus aux origines de la christologie* (BETL, 24), Leuven, 1973, pp. 169-192, esp. 169.

11. D.P. SENIOR, *The Passion of Jesus in the Gospel of Matthew*, Wilmington, DE, 1985, p. 132. Cf. R.H. GUNDRY, 1982 (n. 6), p. 283.

placed here it is also a reminder of the Temptation narrative, where it is Satan himself who makes the identification (4,3.6). Satan tests Jesus, using biblical quotes, and Jesus responds by quoting scripture himself, making reference specifically to three verses from Deuteronomy (Deut 8,3; 6,16 and 6,13). The Old Testament context of these verses is Moses' speech to the Israelites, enjoining them to obedience by recalling the forty years in the wilderness, when God tested them (Deut 8,2). He then tells them to "obey willingly and faithfully" (Deut 8,3). The quotes from Deut 6 recall another quotation, Mt 22,37, where the Shema appears as the first of the "great commandments". Thus Jesus' responses in the Temptation, evoked in the mocking, indicate the importance of faithful obedience in understanding the Son of God title. The allusion reinforces the extremely negative portrayal of Jesus' opponents in Matthew as satanic and bestial. The mocking continues in Mt 27,41-42, with the appearance of the entire Sanhedrin, chief priests and elders, along with scribes. The Temple authorities provide a response to the earlier challenge of the passers-by that Jesus save himself, denying that Jesus has the power to do so: "He saved others, he cannot save himself": ἄλλους ἔσωσεν, ἑαυτὸν οὐ δύναται σῶσαι (27,42). Their taunt ends with the suggestion, that as king of Israel, Jesus should come down from the cross: "...he is the king of Israel; let him come down now from the cross...": βασιλεὺς Ἰσραήλ ἐστιν, καταβάτω νῦν ἀπὸ τοῦ σταυροῦ (27,42). Their statement contains the Christian confession of Jesus as Messiah, although they are speaking ironically. The Temple authorities assert that they will believe in him if they are given a sign, although Jesus had said that there would be no sign given (Mt 12,39; 16,4). But whereas the mockers will believe that Jesus is the Messiah-king if he saves himself, they are doubly mistaken: they do not expect that he will be vindicated, and the content of their idea of the Messiah is shown to be wrong. Matthew, then, stresses that it is as Son of God that Jesus dies; his presentation links the two terms, "Son of God," and "King of Israel".

The mocking concludes with an implicit quotation of the Old Testament: "He trusted in God; let him deliver him, if he desires him; for he said 'I am the son of God": πέποιθεν ἐπὶ τὸν Θεόν, ῥυσάσθω νῦν εἰ θέλει αὐτόν· εἶπεν γὰρ ὅτι Θεοῦ εἰμι υἱός (27,43). The language of trust and hope in God's deliverance of those who trust is the core of a complex of terms related in Matthew to the Son of God title. The title is associated in this gospel with trust and obedience under testing, which may well include suffering. Jesus rebukes Satan with the words "Go away, Satan": ὕπαγε σατανᾶ (4,10), echoed when Peter refuses to accept the possibility that the "Son of the living God" might suffer and die: "Get behind me,

Satan": ὕπαγε ὀπίσω μου, σατανᾶ (16,21-2)[12]. Thus this pericope is linked with the Temptation narrative, echoing Deuteronomy, and with the motif of righteous suffering. The quotation of LXX Ps 21,9 here functions to recall the motif of trust in God's deliverance of the faithful from mortal enemies; followed in context by the Son of God title, it suggests a further connection with the language of the Wisdom of Solomon.

On the surface, then, Matthew has drawn on two complexes of terms and images, one related to the language of impious mockery, and the other to the Son of God title. This vocabulary, found also in the Wisdom of Solomon, echoes the language of the Psalms, Lamentations, 2 Kings, Exodus, and Deuteronomy, both by direct allusion and by allusion to other Matthean passages, especially the Temptation narrative. By making use of this language, Matthew, no doubt intentionally, has created an interpretative context for the pericope which would be readily recognizable to those Greek-speaking readers and hearers of his gospel who were familiar with Jewish scriptures. The use of language in the Wisdom of Solomon suggests a close connection, one that will be reinforced when we examine similarities in narrative structure.

III

The structure of Matthew's text suggests a deeper level of intertextual borrowing, one not confined to the allusive use of individual words and phrases. The structure of the Passion narrative generally bears resemblance to a generic form identified by G.W.E. Nickelsburg as "Stories of Persecution and Vindication"[13]. Nickelsburg convincingly shows that the genre of the Passion follows this pattern, which he argues is an intertext for the Passion in Mark and in a pre-Markan narrative source. We might expect to find a similar generic intertext for Matthew, and indeed that is the case. In Nickelsburg's analysis, the protagonist typically must make a crucial decision between obedience and disobedience and the decision to obey may be ascribed to trust in God[14]. The form as it appears in the Wisdom of Solomon is concentrated particularly in chapters 2 and 5. In the Wisdom of Solomon, "the enemies of the righteous man mock his claim to be a 'child of God', his Father, and make his death an ordeal to determine the truth of this claim"[15]. According to Nickelsburg's

12. Cf. DONALDSON (n. 2), pp. 8-9.
13. NICKELSBURG (n. 2), pp. 155-67.
14. *Ibid.*, pp. 159-60.
15. *Ibid.*, p. 162.

classifications, the Wisdom of Solomon begins with the elements of provocation and conspiracy (2,12-16), and moves directly to the ordeal (2,17-19). The trial and condemnation which ordinarily precede the ordeal, as well as the expression of the protagonist's trust in God, follow here (2,20 and 3,9). The reactions of the observers are a "variable" in the genre, according to Nickelsburg, which "often add a novelistic touch or serve other functions"[16]; they are omitted here. The rescue which is expected does not occur, and the righteous man "appears" to die (3,2-4). Usually the protagonist is rescued before death, although in the Wisdom of Solomon, as in the gospels, "the rescue occurs after and in spite of death"[17]. The righteous man is vindicated and exalted (5,1.4-5), the reaction of the observers is recorded (5,2), and punishment is meted out (5,9-14).

The elements of provocation and conspiracy develop throughout the first part of Matthew's gospel; Jesus' obedience and trust in God, emphasized especially in the Temptation narrative, provoke the anger of his enemies, who conspire to eliminate him, and finally accuse him in a trial. His condemnation leads to crucifixion and death, after which he is vindicated and exalted. The mocking at the cross in Matthew includes the elements Nickelsburg identifies as "ordeal" and "reactions". The ordeal serves "to test the veracity of [the protagonist's] claims or the validity of his behavior", and the antagonists express "their certainty that these claims or this behavior will be shown to be false or wrong. The element is always paired (usually explicitly) with the protagonist's vindication after his rescue from death"[18]. In Matthew's gospel, Jesus is mocked as "Son of God", a claim that is explicitly vindicated by the centurion after his death (27,54).

There are, then, strong narrative connections between the pattern of persecution and vindication Nickelsburg describes and the Passion narrative. The wicked, deriding and killing the righteous man who is later vindicated by God, provide an intertext which suggests, if the context of the source is respected, that Jesus is primarily to be taken, as Gundry intuitively does, as the suffering just man who is vindicated in his death and shown to be indeed God's Son[19]. The shared language and the similarities in the narrative structure lead the reader to make a connection between texts that otherwise might not seem to have similarities. The combination of similarities of both surface and deep structures, both

16. *Ibid.*, p. 161.
17. *Ibid.,* p.161.
18. *Ibid.*, pp. 160-161.
19. GUNDRY, 1982 (n. 6), p. 566.

with different groups of intertexts, may argue for Matthew's use of the the text of Wisdom of Solomon, in spite of the differences in the order of the generic elements. But once we have recognized these relationships, what difference does it make?

IV

In the Wisdom text, the righteous man suffers at the hands of the ungodly, who have made a covenant with death, rejecting the promise of immortality for those who are righteous (1,12-15). God had made a covenant with Abraham, promising that Abraham and his descendants would be God's people and would live in the land; God made a covenant with David, promising that his kingdom would not fall. The history of Israel is the story of those covenants with God which define Israel as God's people. God may test the people and may punish them for unrighteousness, but the covenant is eternal. So in the Wisdom text, one of the righteous people of God is tortured and condemned to a shameful death by the ungodly, those who have not covenanted with God but with death. God's ultimate vindication of him provides a word of hope for God's people.

Perhaps a century later, Matthew revises this history. Jesus' genealogy traces him back to Abraham and to David, placing him in the line of those who have been given God's promise. By placing Jesus in this lineage and making his purpose that of saving people from their sins, Matthew portrays Jesus as the inheritor of God's promise to Israel. By framing the story of his death in terms of the persecuted righteous man, Matthew is able to present all those who do not believe in him as enemies of God: not just Romans, but Jews: those passing by, the Jewish leaders, and even the two others who were crucified at the same time, the "robbers" who may represent other groups resistant to the Jewish establishment. The people of Israel, insiders or outsiders, with the exception of those who follow Jesus, are no longer the chosen people of God. The promise of the covenant, in Matthew's telling, passes from the original recipients of the promise to the righteous Son of God and those who follow him. While in the Wisdom text, God's vindication provides hope in what seems to be a hopeless situation, Matthew has used this text as a curse upon the people for whom it was a word of hope. The gospel thus neutralizes Israel's hope by portraying the people of God as both the enemies of God and the persecutors of the righteous children of God. Those who were once the recipients of God's promise, and those who were the guardians of righteousness in Israel, have been transformed by this text into Israel's enemies. While they may seem to thrive, God's vindication of Jesus is assured by the generic intertext, as is the eternal condemnation of those who are Jesus' enemies. Thus Matthew's text uses Jewish scripture against the Jews.

Should, then, we say that Christian tradition is inescapably anti-Semitic? J.G. Gager points out that history is written by the winners, and that in this case, the Christian writings that remain represent and reinforce the anti-Judaizing views of those who felt that acceptance of Christian belief required repudiation of Judaism[20]. He distinguishes anti-Judaism from anti-Semitism; anti-Judaism "is primarily a matter of religious and theological disagreement. This is not to deny that Christian statements about Judaism sometimes manifest strong negative feelings, at times even hatred. Nonetheless, the undeniable family ties between Christianity and Judaism shaped Christian attitudes toward Judaism in a way that was never true for pagans". Anti-Semitism, then as today, designates hostility toward Jews and Judaism from the point of view of complete outsiders[21]. Matthew's gospel is part of a polemical argument in the early Church, attempting to define Christianity over against Judaism, while at the same time, appropriating the symbols and scripture of Judaism. Gager argues that the Christian tradition, including modern scholarship, has too unquestioningly accepted the point of view argued in the gospel, pointing out that "much of Christian scholarship has been shaped by the legacy of early Christian anti-Judaism"[22]. Anti-Semitism is our response as outsiders to what was once an internal battle. And anti-Semitism in the twentieth century has had unthinkable consequences.

There is, then, a need to recognize the ways in which the Christian gospels, particularly that of Matthew, participated in the anti-Judaic polemic, and to reinterpret the negative presentation of Judaism in Christian texts and tradition. This is, in Gager's words, "an enormously difficult task"[23], but the theological stakes are high. Lloyd Gaston puts it well: "A Christian Church with an anti-semitic New Testament is abominable, but a Christian Church without a New Testament is inconceivable"[24]. This reading of Mt 27,39-44 is an attempt to use an awareness

20. J.G. GAGER, *The Origins of Anti-Semitism: Attitudes Toward Judaism in Pagan and Christian Antiquity*, New York and Oxford, 1985, p. 7.
21. *Ibid.*, p. 8.
22. *Ibid.*, p. 31.
23. *Ibid.*, p. 34.
24. L. GASTON, *Paul and the Torah*, in A. DAVIES (ed.), *Anti-Semitism and the Foundations of Christianity*, New York, 1979, p. 48.

of intertextuality to discern the use of Jewish scripture against the Jews and the appropriation of its symbols in a redefined system which overturns its original values and substitutes their opposites. Through the intertext of the Wisdom of Solomon, Matthew uses Jewish writings against the people for whom it functioned as scripture, infecting the scriptures, as it were, with a virus which would prove destructive of Judaism while at the same time allowing Christianity to appropriate them as the Christian Old Testament, in Mark's words, a "new teaching" whose canon will include even the Wisdom of Solomon. In Matthew's hands, the scriptural intertext is in the service of an anti-Judaic bias which invites modern readers to read along and which continues to create and justify Christian anti-Semitism in our time.

University of Sheffield   Susan Lochrie GRAHAM

MK 12,28-34: ÜBEREINSTIMMUNG IM KERN DER SACHE

1. *Einleitung*

Wenn das Thema dieses Kongresses das Alte Testament in den Evangelien ist, dann geht es wohl nicht nur um expliziten oder impliziten Umgang mit der Schrift, sondern auch um eine Einstellung oder Haltung: Interpretation von Heiligen Texten und Schriften ist eine der naheliegendsten Formen von Weisheit im Zeitalter des Zweiten Tempels[1]. Diese Einstellung hat dem Judentum eine Menge von termini technici der Schriftauslegung und exegetischen Techniken beschert, die bereits im Neuen Testament vorgezeichnet sind[2].

In diesem Beitrag soll deshalb der Frage nachgegangen werden, ob es möglich und sinnvoll ist, im Neuen Testament nach einer Kontinuität und damit nach dem Gemeinsamen zwischen authentisch jüdischer Tradition und dem Neuen Testament zu suchen.

Dieser Artikel will sich der oben formulierten Frage aber nicht global widmen, sondern von einem Textbeispiel, Mk 12,28-34, ausgehend, einige Argumenten für die behauptete Kontinuität anführen[3]. In dieser Perikope diskutiert Jesus mit einem Schriftgelehrten die Bedeutung des ersten Gebots. Jesus antwortet mit einer Kombination aus Dtn 6,5 und Lev 19,18[4].

---

1. Siehe z.B. M. HENGEL, »*Schriftauslegung*« *und* »*Schriftwerdung*« *in der Zeit des Zweiten Tempels* in ID-H. LÜHR (Hsg.), *Schriftauslegung im antiken Judentum und im Urchristentum* (WUNT, 73), Tübingen, 1994, pp. 1-71, bes. pp. 1-8.

2. Siehe z.B. R.N. LONGENECKER, *Biblical Exegesis in the Apostolic Period*, Grand Rapids, 1977.

3. Diese Kontinuität scheint eigentlich selbstverständlich. Nur wenn man von einem theologischen a priori, d.h. von einem absoluten »Bruch« zwischen Juden- und Christentum oder von der klassische Einleitungsthese ausgeht, daß Markus ein in Rom ansässiger Heidenchristen gewesen sei, kann sie negiert oder bezweifelt werden. Für ein ebenmäßig Urteil, siehe z.B. R. PESCH, *Das Markusevangelium* (HTKNT, II,1), Freiburg-Basel-Wien, ³1980, pp. 12-15. Konsequent könnten aus dieser These folgenden Fragen abgeleitet werden: Welches jüdische Material müssen wir bei einer Untersuchung berücksichtigen? und Worin genau besteht Kontinuität und Diskontinuität zwischen Jesus und dem (späteren rabbinischen) Judentum? Aufgrund der beschränkten Länge des Artikels liegt es auf der Hand, daß ich nicht ausgedehnt auf methodische Fragen eingehen kann.

4. Zur historisch-kritischen Untersuchung von Markus 12,28-34, siehe J.-G. MUDISO M. MUNDLA, *Jesus und die Führer Israels: Studien zu den sog. Jerusalemer Streitgesprächen* (NTAbh, 17), Münster, 1984, pp. 110-141; und J. KIILUNEN, *Das Doppelgebot der Liebe in synoptischer Sicht: Ein redaktionskritischer Versuch über Mk 12,28-34 und die Parallelen* (AASF, B/259), Helsinki, 1989.

Der Schriftgelehrte stimmt dem zu: er spricht Jesus sogar ein Kompliment aus und wiederholt dessen Antwort mit eigenen Worten[5].

Besonders drei interpretative Elemente aus Mk 12,28-34 sind für unsere Thematik zentral. Dabei handelt es sich um protorabbinische Elemente die – wie sich zeigen wird – sich durchaus mit Elementen aus dem späteren rabbinischen Judentum vergleichen lassen[6]. So kann einerseits gezeigt werden, daß zwischen bestimmten neutestamentlichen Passagen und späterem rabbinischen Denken eine größere Kontinuität besteht als häufig angenommen wird. Außerdem sollen weitere Belege angeführt werden, die eine angemessenere Beurteilung der Hintergründe der Passage stützen.

Es handelt sich dabei um die folgenden drei Elemente: (1) Der Ausdruck συζητέω, der sich mit dem rabbinischen technischen Ausdruck דרש (vgl. *midrash*) vergleichen läßt. (2) Die Art und Weise, wie zwei Toratexte zusammengebracht werden, läßt an eine der hermeneutischen Regeln Hillels denken, der sogenannten *geserah schawah*. (3) Wir finden in dieser Passage, genauso wie an anderen Stellen im Neuen Testament, eine Art Zusammenfassung des Gesetzes, die mit dem *kelal gadol* vergleichbar ist.

---

5. In der Sekundärliteratur zu dieser Stelle liest man oft, daß sie den Geist des hellenistisch-jüdischen Denkens atme: G. BORNKAMM, *Das Doppelgebot der Liebe*, in: ID., *Geschichte und Glaube* I, München, 1968, pp. 37-45, bes. 37.38.39; C. BURCHARD, *Das doppelte Liebesgebot in der frühen christlichen Überlieferung*, in ID. – B. SCHALLER (Hg.), *Der Ruf Jesus und die Antwort der Gemeinde*. FS. J. Jeremias, Göttingen, 1970, pp. 39-62, bes. 51-55; K. BERGER, *Die Gesetzesauslegung Jesu* (WMANT, 40), Neukirchen-Vluyn, 1972, pp. 131-176. B. GERHARDSSON, *The Hermeneutic Program in Matthew 22:37-40*, in R. HAMERTON-KELLY–R. SCROGGS (Hg.), *Jews, Greeks and Christians. Religious Cultures in Late Antiquity*. FS. W.D. Davies, Leiden, 1976, pp. 129-150, tendiert auch in diese Richtung, aber weist zurecht darauf hin, daß man nicht zu voreilig zwischen hellenistisch und jüdisch trennen sollte, siehe schon E. SCHÜRER, *Geschichte des Jüdischen Volkes im Zeitalter Jesu Christi*, III, Leipzig, [3]1898, pp. 135-136: »Zwei Hauptgruppen lassen sich in dieser bunten Mannigfaltigkeit zunächst unterscheiden; die palästinische und die hellenistische. Wir wählen diese Bezeichnungen in Ermangelung von besseren.... Es ist dabei aber nachdrüklich zu betonen, daß die Grenze zwischen beide Gruppen eine fließende ist und die Bezeichnungen sehr *cum grano salis* zu verstehen sind«. Vielleicht hat die Zuschreibung an das hellenistische Judentum damit zu tun, daß Bornkamm, Burchard und Berger sich um das rabbinische Judentum bemühen. In Bezug auf Berger merkt Gerhardsson in *The Hermeneutic Program*, p. 134, Anm. 13, bei seiner Betrachtung von Mt 22,37-40 dann auch zu Recht an, daß dieser dem rabbinischen Denken vor allem dem *Schma* so wenig Aufmerksamkeit widmet. Dieses gilt auch in Bezug auf Mk 12,28-34. Es ist auffallend, daß Berger sich z.B. sehr stark auf hellenistisch-griechische Quellen konzentriert, aber – so vermute ich – seine Auffassungen bezüglich des rabbinischen Judentums vor allem auf Sekundärliteratur, meistens wohl auf Strack-Billerbeck, zu beruhen scheinen. Siehe *Die Gesetzesauslegung Jesu*, p. 78, Anm. 2; p. 131, Anm. 1; p. 141, Anm. 1 und 2.

6. Zum Begriff »protorabbinisch«, siehe z.B. J. WEINGREEN, *From Bible to Mishna*, Manchester, 1976, p. 132: »The term proto-rabbinic suggests that the rabbinic legislative machinery was not a post-biblical innovation; its antecedents can be traced back to the activity of the deuteronomic legislator«; vgl. P. SIGAL, *The Halakah of Jesus of Nazareth according to the Gospel of Matthew*, Lanham–New York–London, 1986, pp. 2-9.

In angemessener Kürze läßt sich das formale Verhältnis dieser drei Elemente zueinander folgendermaßen charakterisieren: von einem für die Beschreibung der Begegnung typischen Verb über die Anwendung einer exegetischen Technik hin zum inhaltlichen Kern[7].

2. Ein exegetischer »terminus technicus«

Im Neues Testament kommt das Verb συζητέω zehn Mal vor. In den Übersetzungen fällt auf, daß, wenn der Ausdruck in einer Diskussion unter jüdischen Autoritäten (Schriftgelehrten u.s.w.) oder mit Jesus gebraucht wird, er häufig mit einem Wort aus der Streitsphäre übersetzt wird. Bezieht es sich dagegen auf eine Diskussion unter den Jüngern Jesu, übersetzt man das Verb mit einem Ausdruck aus dem Umfeld des Gesprächs. Bauers *Wörterbuch* referiert ebenfalls beide Übersetzungsmöglichkeiten: »sich besprechen«: Mk 9,10 und Lk 24,15; »disputieren«; »streiten«: Mk 8,11; 9,14; 12,28; Apg 6,9; 9,29[8]. Jedoch ist eher anzunehmen, daß dieser semantische Konnotationsunterschied künstlich aufgebaut und die Übersetzung mit z.B. »streiten« aufgrund einer zu negativen Betrachtungsweise der jüdischen Autoritäten zu negativ eingefärbt ist. Vielmehr liegt es philologisch näher, daß zwischen den Fällen, in denen negativ, und denen, in welchen positiv übersetzt wird, ein gemeinschaftlicher Nenner besteht: Das Verb wird nämlich überwiegend bei denjenigen Kontakten und Unterhaltungen Jesu mit Menschen gebraucht, in denen zuweilen Jesu Lehre und besonders seine Interpretation der Schrift zur Debatte steht. Συζητέω hat also vor allem mit Lernen und Lehren in polemische und in nicht-polemische Gesprächssituationen zu tun[9]. Es kann auch im Streit und vom Streiten gelernt werden. Hinzu tritt, daß Streitgespräche nicht immer auf unüberwindliche Feindschaft hinweisen müssen.

Mk verwendet συζητέω erstmals in 1,27. Dort wird Jesu Auftreten als »lehren« charakterisiert (1,21-22). Das sabbatliche Ereignis in der

---

7. Es würde den Rahmen dieses Artikels sprengen, diese Elemente in die Gesamtstruktur von Mk 12,28-34 zu situieren. Es würde lohnenswert sein, das Vorkommen von ἐπερωτάω in den synoptischen Schriften näher zu untersuchen. Schon eine oberflächliche Lektüre läßt vermuten, daß dieses Verb oft in Lehrsituationen gebraucht wird. Dadurch läßt es sich meines Erachtens mit dem Verb πειράζω vergleichen. Es erinnert nämlich an einen rabbinischen Brauch, Lehrer zu hinterfragen, um ihren Standpunkt zu erfahren. Siehe z.B. Sɪɢᴀʟ, *The Halakah of Jesus*, p. 163, Anm. 15.

8. Nach W. Bᴀᴜᴇʀ, *Wb*[6], s.v., p. 1548.

9. Ich beschränke mich in diesem Beitrag auf den Gebrauch des Ausdruckes bei Mk und verweise bezüglich des Gebrauches in Lukas und der Apostelgeschichte auf mein Artikel *Some Traces of a Semantical Field of Interpretation in Luke 24,13-35*, in meinem Buch: *Five Studies on Interpretation of Scripture in Luke-Acts* (SNTA, 14), Leuven, 1989, pp. 56-72.

Synagoge von Kafarnaum, eine Diskussion über die Vollmacht Jesu (1, 21-27) liefert das passende Dekor dazu. Der Evangelist sagt jedoch nicht, was Jesu Lehre beinhaltet. Er beschreibt vielmehr deren Wirkung: das Erstaunen der Anwesenden (1,22) über sein machtvolles Auftreten. Nachdem Jesus den unreinen Geist des Mannes ausgetrieben hat, reagieren alle Anwesenden wiederum mit Staunen und Fragen. Ihre Reaktion wird mit dem Verb συζητέω charakterisiert. Sie mündet in Fragen, die erkennbar einen Kommentar zu Jesu Lehre aus »Vollmacht« geben sollen. Dies ist ein erster Hinweis im Evangelium, daß das Verb bewußt im Zusammenhang mit »lehren« verwendet wird.

Darüber hinaus kennzeichnet in Mk 8,11 das Verb die Diskussion zwischen Jesus und den Pharisäern. Die Pharisäer begehren ein Zeichen aus dem Himmel. Was für ein Zeichen kann das sein? Die Antwort darauf findet man im Kontext. Die kurze Passage verbindet nämlich die Erzählung von der zweiten wunderbaren Brotvermehrung (8,1-9) mit Jesus Auslegung derselben (8,14-21; vor allem 8,19). So kann die Zeichenfrage zum Kommentar über Jesu Wirken werden. In der vorangegangenen Erzählung ist Jesus in die Fußstapfen seines prophetischen Vorgängers Elisa (2 Kön 4,38-44) getreten. Auch die Frage nach dem Zeichen ist also implizit eine Frage nach Jesu Auftreten und Lehre (cf. Mk 1,27). Die überarbeitete lukanische Fassung Lk 11,29 bestätigt dies. Dort wird das explizit, was bei Mk noch implizit blieb. Jesus sagt dort nämlich, daß diesem Geschlecht nur das Zeichen des Jona gegeben werde. Anschließend deutet Jesus wiederum das Gesagte, daß Jona damals ein Zeichen für die Bewohner Ninives gewesen sei, worauf jene sich bekehrten. Aus denselben Gründen kam die Königin des Südens, um die Weisheit Salomos zu hören. Wenn Lk hier das Auftreten Jesu mit dem eines Jona und Salomo vergleicht, und dies damals zum Zeichen für jenes Geschlecht wurde, bedeutet dies für ihn analog, daß Jesu Auftreten als Umkehrprediger wie Jona und Weisheitslehrer wie Salomo das einzige Zeichen ist, daß seine Zeitgenossen empfangen sollen.

Zum dritten und vierten Mal kommt συζητέω in Mk 9,10.14 vor. Nachdem in Mk 9,2-9 Jesus mit Petrus, Jakobus und Johannes den Berg bestiegen haben und dort mit Elia und Mose, den zwei großen Gestalten der Schrift, gesehen wurde, sagt Jesus beim Hinabsteigen, daß »sie niemandem sagen sollten, was sie gesehen haben, bis der Menschensohn von den Toten auferstanden ist«. Das Stichwort (»auferstehen«; 9,9; cf. 8,31) ruft eine Diskussion (συζητοῦντες) zwischen den Jüngern/ Schülern um die Frage »was ist das, Auferstehen von den Toten?« (Mk 9,10) – eingeführt wiederum mit dem Verb »συζητέω« – hervor. Sowohl aus neutestamentlichen Belegen (Mk 12,18, vgl. auch Mt 22,31;

Apg 23,6-8) wie aus der rabbinischen Literatur wissen wir, daß in der
mündlichen Tora die Lehre der Auferstehung der Toten ein wichtiger
Streitpunkt war (vgl. z.B. *m.Sanh* 10.1)[10]. So wird also eine Frage, die ihren
Ursprung in der mündlichen Tradition hat, zum Ausgangspunkt des
Gesprächs unter den Jüngern. Dies wird wiederum durch das Verb
συζητέω gekennzeichnet. In der Fortsetzung 9,11 wird auf das Kommen
Elias verwiesen, eine Reminiszenz an Mal 3,23. Jesus bezieht sich in
seiner Antwort nämlich auf die Schriften (»und wie geschrieben steht?«
Mk 9,12). Kurzum, es ist überaus deutlich, daß in dieser Passage eine
zentrale Frage aus der mündlichen Tradition in den Kontext der Lehre
Jesu aufgenommen wurde. Damit wird die Schriftinterpretation des
markinischen Jesus – besser gesagt seine Schriftanwendung – problematisiert. Wenn in 9,10 die interne Diskussion mit συζητέω charakterisiert
wird und die sich direkt anschließende Diskussion vor allem über die
Anwendung der Schrift geht, dann liegt es nahe, daß es auch in 9,10 um
die Lehre Jesu, u.z. um den biblischen Hintergrund der Totenauferstehung
geht. Gerade dies soll der Ausdruck συζητέω, angesichts des Frageein-
halts, suggerieren. Wiederum beschreibt das Verb eine Situation, in der
nach der Bedeutung eines Themas der mündlichen Lehre gefragt wird.

Direkt danach finden wir unser Verb erneut wieder: In Mk 9,16 ist es
Jesus, der die Schriftgelehrten fragt, warum sie sich besprechen (συζη-
τεῖτε). Es bezieht sich auf die Unterhaltung zwischen den Jüngern und
den Schriftgelehrten (Mk 9,14). Würde auch eine Diskussion über die
Schrift und ihre Auslegung in diesem Gespräch unter Schülern des Leh-
rers Jesus (9,17) und den Schriftgelehrten nicht fehl am Platze sein, so
kann doch in diesem Fall nicht direkt gefolgert werden, daß es sich um
eine spezifische Diskussion über Schriftauslegung handelt.

Wir kommen nun zur zentralen Stelle des hier erörterten Problems.
Mk 12,28 zeigt noch einmal, daß συζητέω gerade im Kontext von Tora-
Interpretation eine bedeutende Rolle spielt. Das Verb bezieht sich hier
auf das fortschreitende Streitgespräch zwischen Jesus und den Saddu-
zäern (es dreht sich wiederum um das Problem der Auferstehung der
Toten), aber es is doch auch damit typisch für die Atmospäre vom 12,
28-34. Die Frage wird jetzt aber konkreter gefaßt: Ist dieses Thema in
der Schrift begründet oder nicht (vgl. Mk 12,18-27 mit 9,10-14)? An
beiden Textstellen geht es um die Begründung der Auferstehung der
Toten (9,10; 12,18.25-26). In beiden wird die Diskussion darüber mit
dem Verb συζητέω gekennzeichnet. Im einen Fall sind zwar die Schüler

---

10. Zur (früh)jüdischen Auferstehungsvorstellung siehe z.B. H.C.C. Cavallin, *Life
after Death. Paul's Argument for the Resurrection of the Dead in I Cor 15 Part I: An
Enquiry into the Jewish Background* (CB.NT, series 7:1), Lund, 1974, pp. 171-186.

das Subjekt, im anderen die Sadduzäer und Jesus, dennoch ist es möglich, daß das Verb in beiden Fällen dieselbe Bedeutung hat. Daß συζητέω sich zudem in 12,28 auf Schriftauslegung bezieht, erweist sich aus dem Kontext. Sowohl in 12,18-27 als auch in 12,28-34 spielen Schrifttexte und Schriftauslegung die Hauptrolle. Das Stichwort »der Dornbusch« (12,26) verweist mit Ex 3,1ff. darauf, daß in dieser Passage eine sehr spezifische Art von Schriftauslegung angewendet werden soll: Jede Perikope der Torah hat nämlich ihre eigenen Stichworte: »either the introductory word to the pericope in question or – more usually – of some decisive word from the pericope itself, a word which was sometimes a quite adequate indication of its contents«[11]. Aus der Umschreibung dieser speziellen Passage entnimmt man, genau wie die Sadduzäer, auf welchen Text Jesus sich bezieht: Die Diskussion in Mk 12 wird von jüdischen Menschen geführt, die erkennbar an der Tora des Moses geschult sind, und sie behandelt zudem ein zentrales (nach-)biblisch eschatologisches Thema. Wir sehen also, daß der Ausdruck συζητέω sich in Mk auf »lernen« sowie »lehren« und vielleicht sogar auf die Schriftinterpretation insgesamt bezieht.

Um einen Vergleichspunkt für einen möglicherweise gemeinsamen Hintergrund zu gewinnen, ist es methodisch sinnvoll, das hebräische Verb דרש zu betrachten. Sowohl דרש wie ζητέω bedeuten primär: »suchen; fragen«. דרש hat sich bei den späteren Rabbinen zu einem terminus technicus für Schriftauslegung entwickelt[12]. Die LXX übersetzt דרש unterschiedlich, überwiegend jedoch mit ζητέω bzw. Derivaten von ζητέω. Im Griechischen hat sich möglicherweise eine ähnliche Entwicklung wie im Hebräischen vollzogen, u.z. an einer von ζητέω abgeleiteten Form.

Die hier zur Diskussion gestellte These lautet folglich, daß die Verwendung des Wortes συζητέω bei Mk dem späteren rabbinischen Benutzung von דרש verwandt und in gewissem Sinn schon eine Präfiguration davon ist[13]. Mk 12,18-34 ist also von der gleichen Grundstimmung wie die Diskussion bei den späteren Rabbinen durchzogen.

---

11. Siehe B. GERHARDSSON, *Memory and Manuscript. Oral Tradition and Written Transmission in Rabbinic Judaism and Early Christianty* (Acta Seminarii Neotestamentici Upsaliensis, 22), Uppsala, 1961, pp. 143-144.

12. Siehe z.B. W. BACHER, *Die exegetische Terminologie der jüdischen Traditionsliteratur*, Budapest, 1899; repr Darmstadt, 1965, pp. 25-27.

13. Der frühchristliche Apologet Justinus Martyr benutzt ebenfalls συζητέω im Kontext von Jesu Diskussionen mit den Pharisäern (e.g. Dial. 102.5; vgl. 107.1; 120.5; siehe 93.5).

3. *Eine hermeneutische Regel*[14]

Die im Folgenden weiterverfolgte These muß nun lauten, daß die Art und Weise in der zwei Toratexte miteinander verbunden werden, ein früher Hinweis auf die Anwendung einer der sieben Regeln *(middot)*, die die Tradition Hillel zuschreibt, nämlich die *geserah schawah* ist[15]. Der Name *geserah schawah* ist wahrscheinlich am ehesten mit »gleiche Verordnung« zu übersetzen, wenn auch die genaue Etymologie noch nicht abschließend geklärt ist[16]. Außerdem ist strittig, wie diese Regel im einzelnen angewendet wurde. Auf jeden Fall ist deutlich, daß bei der Anwendung dieser Regel zwei Schriftpassagen miteinander in der Absicht verbunden werden, daß sie sich eben auf der Grundlage, daß ein Wort an zwei Stellen vorkommt, gegenseitig auslegen. Häufig wird dazu noch angemerkt, daß auch die Kontexte, in denen diese Passagen auftauchen, das gleiche Thema haben sollten[17].

Weitere Beispiele für diese Arbeitsweise findet man auch sonst in NT wie auch bei Pseudo-Philo[18]. Gerhardsson weist in Bezug auf Mt 22,37 darauf hin, daß die hebräische Konsekutivform ואהבת in der ganzen hebräischen Bibel nur in Dtn 6,5; 11,1 und Lev 19,18.34 vorkommt und daß diese verbale Voraussetzung dazu einlud, die zwei Gebote miteinander zu verbinden[19]. Mit Recht setzt Gerhardsson in einer entsprechenden Anmerkung voraus, daß auch Mt 22,37-40 in die Erörterung einbezogen werden muß, wenn man die Entstehungsgeschichte der Middot im Allgemeinen und die der *geserah schawah* im Besonderen untersuchen will[20].

Allerdings muß man dann auch m.E. die vermutliche Vorlage, Mk 12, 28-34, in die Untersuchung miteinbeziehen. Schon in diesem Text werden

---

14. Die Anwendung dieser Regel ist kein Argument, um *nur* eine spezifisch palästinische Prägung von Mk 12,28-34 aufzuzeigen. Die Regeln Hillels sind eine Zusammenstellung der gemeinantiken Schlußverfahren.

15. H.L. STRACK-G. STEMBERGER, *Einleitung in Talmud und Midrasch*, München, 1982, siebente, völlig neu bearbeitete Auflage, pp. 27-30 gibt eine Übersicht dieser Middot; siehe auch W. SIBLEY TOWNER, *Hermeneutical Systems of Hillel and the Tannaim: A Fresh Look*, in *HUCA* 53 (1982) 101-135; M. CHERNICK, *Internal Restraints in Gezerah Shawah's Implication*, in *JQR* 80 (1990) 253-282. Zur weiteren Literaturhinweisen zur *geserah-schawah* im Neuen Testament, siehe z.B. SIGAL, *The Halakah of Jesus*, pp. 60-63.

16. STEMBERGER, *Einleitung*, p. 28.

17. Zu dieser Problematik, siehe D. BOYARIN, *Intertextuality and the Reading of Midrash* (Indiana Studies in Biblical Literature), Bloomington/Indianapolis, 1990.

18. NT: LONGENECKER, *Biblical Exegesis*, (Anm. 2) z.B. p. 97. 117. Pseudo-Philo: LAB 48,3 und 50,2: L. GINZBERG, *The Legends of the Jews*, Vol. VI, Philadelphia, ⁴1954, p. 213, Anm. 135.

19. *The Hermeneutic Program*, p. 138. Ich möchte nebenbei anmerken, dass uns der Text von Mt natürlich nur in Griechisch überliefert ist, aber dass wir auch in der LXX die Form ἀγαπήσει nur in diesen Texten antreffen.

20. *The Hermeneutic Program*, p. 138, Anm. 18.

nämlich die beiden Schrifttexte auf die gleiche Art und Weise aufeinander bezogen. Weil in Mk schon die beiden Toratexte in Beziehung zu einander gesetzt werden, kann man die in der Auslegung verbreitete Kennzeichnung »hellenistisch« bezüglich dieser Passage noch weiter relativieren.

4. *Zusammenfassung des Gesetzes*

Man kann in dieser Passage – wie auch an anderen Stellen des Neuen Testaments – eine Zusammenfassung des Gesetzes, die vergleichbar mit den *kelal gadol* ist, sehen. Für Mk 12,28-34 wurde nämlich schon aufgezeigt, daß das Verb συζητέω eine Sphäre der Diskussion und Lehre bzw. der Schriftanwendung konnotiert. In diesem Rahmen paßt die Frage nach dem größten Gebot nahtlos hinein.

Wie bereits hingewiesen, wird in der gegenwärtigen Auslegung die Frage diskutiert, ob der »Sitz im Leben« der Mk-Passage hellenistisch oder palästinisch-jüdisch sei[21]. Innerhalb dieser Diskussion paßt auch die Überlegung, inwieweit die Frage in Mk 12,29 »Welches ist das erste Gebot unter allen?« ein *kelal gadol* ist.

Zur Diskussion steht nun, was ein *kelal gadol* eigentlich ist[22]. P. Lenhardt und P. von der Osten-Sacken, die im großen und ganzen auf Max Kadushin zurückgreifen[23], weisen darauf hin, daß *kelal gadol* in einem halachischen Kontext eine Bezeichnung für eine Hauptregel bei bestimmten Geboten oder Verboten darstellt, so z.B. in *m.Shab* 7,1: »... eine Hauptregel haben (welche, die Rabbinen bezüglich des Sabbats, d.h. bezüglich der am Sabbat verbotenen Arbeiten angegeben).....«. Doch trifft man in *Bereschit Rabba* zu Gen 5,1 auch in einem haggadischen Kontext den Begriff *kelal gadol* an[24].

---

21. Siehe Anm. 4.

22. Von כלל = »zusammenfassen«; גדל = »groß«.

23. *Nächstenliebe*, in P. LENHARDT – P. VON DER OSTEN-SACKEN, *Rabbi Akiva Texte und Interpretationen zum rabbinischen Judentum und Neuen Testament*, (ANTZ,1), Berlin, 1987, pp. 174-199; hier bes. 181-183.

24. »Dies ist das Buch der Nachkommen des Adam. Am Tage, da Gott schuf den Menschen – in der Ähnlichkeit Gottes machte er ihn (Gen 5,1). Ben Asai sagt: 'Dies ist das Buch der Nachkommen des Adam (Gen 5,1) – (dies ist) eine Hauptregel (גדל כלל) in der Tora'. R. Akiva sagt: 'Sondern du sollst deinen Nächsten lieben wie dich selbst (Lev 19,18) – (dies ist) eine umfassendere Hauptregel als jene; (denn sie hat den Sinn,) daß du nicht sagst: Weil ich verachtet werde, soll (auch) mein Mitmensch verachtet werden'. Rabbi Tanchuma sagt: 'Wenn du so handelst, dann sei dir im klaren, wen du verachtest, »in der Ähnlichkeit Gottes machte er ihn'' (Gen 5,1)«. Diese Übersetzung stammt aus: VON DER OSTEN-SACKEN, *Nächstenliebe*, in *Rabbi Akiba*, p. 175.

Diesbezüglich äussern sich Lenhardt und von der Osten-Sacken, Kadushin zitierend, folgendermaßen:»Der Begriff *kelal gadol* (umfassende Regel) ist für diesen Zweck vorzüglich geeignet. Es ist ein halachischer Begriff, der größere Weite oder Inklusivität anzeigt; freilich bezieht er sich hier (in *BerRab*) nicht auf halachische Gegenstände, *Kelal gadol* ist hier deshalb als ein Kunstbegriff gebraucht, um Aufmerksamkeit für den ausgewählten Vers zu erregen, um diesen Vers zu betonen«[25]. Eine *kelal gadol* ist kein »letztes Kriterium«, sondern eine betonte Hervorhebung bestimmter herausragender biblischer Aussagen oder Tendenzen in einem Zusammenhang, der sie um so wirksamer macht, kurzum: sie ist eine herausgehobene Regel oder Richtschnur.

Was bedeutet das nun für die Frage in Mk 12,29 und Jesu Antwort darauf in 12,30-31? Vielleicht ist es gut, noch einmal auf Gerhardsson's These zurückzukommen. Er merkte ja zu Mk 12,28-34 an, daß die Kombination von Dtn 6,5 und Lev 19,18 im rabbinischen Judentum nicht gefunden werden könne[26]. Dies hindert ihn jedoch nicht, Mt 22,37-40 gerade mit rabbinischem Material zu vergleichen. Auch wenn das griechische ἐντολή nicht das Gleiche ist wie das hebräische *kelal*, so meint er doch, daß Rabbi Akivas Antwort, gegeben in Sifra Lev 19,18, in dem Maße mit Mt 22,37-40 übereinstimme, daß ein Vergleich sinnvoll erscheine (*kelal gadol betorah*; in Mt 22,36 ἐντολὴ μεγάλη ἐν τῷ νόμῳ)[27]. Damit läßt er erkennen, daß bei Mt eine Art *kelal gadol* formuliert wird und der Mt-Text deshalb rabbinisch geprägt ist[28].

25. *Nächstenliebe*, in *Rabbi Akiva*, p. 182.

26. *The Hermeneutic Program*, pp. 131-132. Im Gegensatz zur Behauptung Gerhardsson weist D. Flusser, *A New Sensitivity in Judaism and the Christian Message*, in *HTR* 61 (1968) 107-127, reprinted in: Id., *Judaism and the Origins of Christianity*, Jerusalem, 1988, pp. 469-489, darauf hin, daß z.B. schon im Jubiläenbuch (36,4-6) durch eine Art Paraphrase von Dtn 6,5.13 und Lev 19,18 eine Verbindung zwischen 'den Herrn lieben' und 'den Nächsten lieben' geschaffen wird ('den Herrn lieben' wird dabei allerdings durch den gewissermaßen auswechselbaren Ausdruck 'den Herrn fürchten' angedeutet). Flusser verweist auch auf Ben Sirach, der ebenfalls das Gott Dienen aus Liebe mehr oder weniger mit dem Gottesdienst aus Furcht vergleicht. Ebenfalls in 27,30–28,7 sind diese Motive zu finden (siehe auch Sir 34). So vermutet Flusser, daß es purer Zufall sei, daß das Doppelgebot nicht in der rabbinischen Tradition angetroffen wird. Der Herausgeber der niederländischen Übersetzung verweist in einer Anmerkung auf eine persisch-jüdische Handschrift, die erst 1978 veröffentlicht wurde, in der neben bekanntem Material auch eine Reihe bisher unbekannte Midraschim zu finden sind, indem Dtn 6,5 und Lev 19,18 verbunden werden, siehe D. Flusser, *Tussen oorsprong en schisma*, Hilversum, 1984, 2 ed., pp. 61-80, Anm. 7a. Den Text kann man finden in: E.E. Urbach, *Sefer Pitron Tora*, Jerusalem, 5738/1978, p. 79v. Auf diese Weise scheint Flusser also bestätigt zu werden.

27. *The Hermeneutic Program*, p. 137; Sifra Lev 19,18 ist eine vermutlich ältere Parallel vom GenRab.

28. *The Hermeneutic Program*, p. 135. Ich frage mich, ob ich aus seinen Worten eine gewisse Enttäuschung hören muß und ob er die Version von Mt weniger schätzt als die von Mk, weil Mk eine wichtigere Frage (a conception of life) als Mt aufgreift (a question

Diese Feststellung muß auch auf den Mk-Text zutreffen. Denn es erscheint unwahrscheinlich, daß Mt in dieser Hinsicht stark von seiner Vorlage abgewichen ist. Es muß daher konstatiert werden, daß auch bei Mk eine Art *kelal gadol* gemeint sein muß.

Wenn man den oben angeführten Text aus *BerRab* mit dem Mk-Text vergleicht, fällt auf, daß in beiden Texten eine innere Spannung zwischen dem Verhältnis von Gott und Mensch auf der einen Seite und dem von Mensch zu Mensch auf der anderen Seite besteht. Doch im Text von *BerRab* wird ebenfalls ein Relation zwischen dem Thema von der »Ähnlichkeit Gottes« aus Gen 5,1 und dem Thema der Nächstenliebe hergestellt. Parallel zu Mk 12,31.33 wird auch hier Lev 19,18 zitiert und darüber hinaus ebenfalls ein entsprechender Vergleich angestellt. Werden bei Mk die beiden Gebote mit allen anderen verglichen, so wird in *BerRab* das eine Gebot mit dem anderen, jedoch schon unter der Fragestellung, welches der beiden Gebote besser als alle anderen sei, verglichen. Es ist unbezweifelbar deutlich, daß große Unterschiede zwischen den rabbinischen und neutestamentlichen Texten bestehen, aber in beiden Texten wird eine Richtschnur gegeben. Obwohl in *BerRab* (und Mt) expliziter benannt, fallen sowohl in Mt und *BerRab* als auch in Mk Gottes- und Nächstenliebe zusammen. Gerade so aber ist die *kelal gadol* (*BerRab*) definiert: es ist das erste Gebot (Mk 12,29) bzw. das große und erste Gebot (Mt 22,36-39).

Wenn man also feststellen kann, daß die Antworten von Jesus und dem Schriftgelehrten in Mk 12 sich mit einer *kelal gadol* vergleichen lassen, muß gleichzeitig aber vor einer Gefahr gewarnt werden, nämlich die *kelal gadol* gegen andere Gebote auszuspielen; denn gerade das wird ja in 12,28-34 bewußt vermieden. Es werden die kultischen Gebote eben nicht abgeschrieben, sondern höchstens relativiert[29]. Es würde aber den Rahmen dieses Beitrages sprengen, hierauf noch näher einzugehen.

---

concerning the order of precedence of God's word); siehe p. 134; vgl. »In the Matthean version the scribe's question has thus been reduced (*sic*!) to an exegetical problem« (auch p. 134).

29. Christen neigen dazu, zuviel Nachdruck auf die sogenannte kultische Einseitigkeit des Judentums zur Zeit Jesu zu legen. Sie denken, daß Jesus, aber auch Stephanus, den Tempel und Tempelkult ablehnten (vgl. 1 Kön 8.27). Meines Erachtens verwirft Stephanus den Tempel nicht, sondern relativiert den Tempel in der Nachfolge der Propheten. Siehe meinen Artikel *Prophets and Law: Paul's Change as Interpreter of Scripture in Acts*, in *Five Studies*, pp. 73-96 (Anm. 9), bes. 78-80. Stephanus war nicht der einzige Jude seiner Zeit, der den Status des Tempels relativierte, z.B. die Erzählung über Jochanan ben Zakkai, der zur Zeit der Tempelverwüstung auf die sühnende Wirkung von Taten der Nächstenliebe hingewiesen hat, siehe *'Abot R. Nat* I Kapitel 4 (Version A). Siehe auch J. HERZER, *Alttestamentliche Traditionen in den Paralipomena Jeremiae als Beispiel für den Umgang frühjüdischer Schriftsteller mit 'Heiliger Schrift'* in HENGEL, *Schriftauslegung* (Anm. 1) pp. 114-132, hier 132. Anm. 58.

5. Schlußfolgerungen

Obwohl nur auf einige wenige Details in Mk 12,28-34 eingegangen werden konnte, konnte gezeigt werden, daß sich durchaus überzeugende Argumente finden lassen, die gegen die oft geäußerte Auffassung sprechen, daß diese Perikope hellenistisch, d.h. wohl implizit nichtrabbinisch, sei. Sie lasse sich deshalb nicht mit dem späteren rabbinischen Judentum vereinbaren[30]. Es genügt schon die hier vorgelegte Materialsammlung, um daraus die Schlußfolgerung ziehen zu können, daß in Mk 12,28-34 eine argumentative Gemeinsamkeit zwischen Jesus und den Schriftgelehrten im Kern der Sache vorliegt. Eigentlich ergibt sich das schon aus der Atmosphäre dieser Perikope, in der Jesus und der Schriftgelehrte deutlich miteinander übereinstimmen und einander in ihrer Meinung sogar bekräftigen. Das wird noch durch die Beobachtung unterstützt, daß die Ausdrucksweise wie die hermeneutischen Prinzipien dieser Passage viele Berührungspunkte mit den Auslegungsprinzipien eines späteren Judentums aufweisen, ein Judentum, das sich in den rabbinischen Schriften spiegelt.

Früher wurde in der christlichen Exegese allzuoft die unüberwindbare Feindschaft zwischen Jesus und den Schriftgelehrten betont. In dieser Perikope tritt jedoch ein Jesus auf, der auf einfühlsame Weise gerade mit einem dieser Schriftgelehrten über das wahre Fundament des Lebens spricht, was jenen zu Komplimenten über die gelungene Argumentationskette veranlaßt.

Bilderdijkkade 63 B   Bart J. Kᴏᴇᴛ
NL-1053 VJ Amsterdam

---

30. Übrigens hätte man auch noch auf die Tatsache eingehen können, daß die Kultkritik sicher nicht typisch, geschweige denn besonders kennzeichnend für das sogenannte hellenistische Judentum, sondern gerade ein durchgängiges Element ist, das sich innerhalb des Judentums von der Zeit der Profeten über z.B. Jesus bis hin zum späteren rabbinischen Judentum hindurchzieht. Siehe Anm. 30.

DESCRIBING THE PAROUSIA

The Cosmic Phenomena in Mk 13,24-25

Verses 24-27 of the apocalyptic discourse in Mk 13 contain a description of the parousia. This *description* (that it is not just an announcement of the parousia is one of the major problems) is largely influenced by OT imagery and wording: the whole of verses 24b-25 (except for ἐκ τοῦ οὐρανοῦ and σαλευθήσονται) and part of v. 26 (τὸν υἱὸν τοῦ ἀνθρώπου ἐρχόμενον ἐν νεφέλαις and καὶ δόξης) are printed in italics in N²⁷, and identified as literal quotations from Isa 13,10 (v. 24b), 34,4 (v. 25) and Dan 7,13-14 (v. 26); in the margin there are additional references to Joel 2,10; 3,4; 4,15 LXX (v. 24b), and Zech 2,6 and Deut 30,4 (v. 27).

The quotations are not introduced by a quotation-formula; they are "allusive quotations". This is not exceptional in a text that wants to imitate apocalyptic style. Indeed, "the apocalyptic style is characterized by allusive references and this in a way which seems to imply a deliberate unwillingness to cite exactly"[1]. Nor is it exceptional to find several such quotations in this kind of text: "it is just these texts that are abounding in allusions which with supreme freedom and skill have been woven into the context"[2]. There seems to be no difficulty with the presence or with the identification of the OT texts in 13,24-27. And yet, there are quite some problems with the interpretation of the passage. First I will briefly deal with the section as a whole; then I will focus on the interpretation of the imagery in vv. 24b-25.

1. *Theophany or Judgement?*

It is a common observation in studies on Mk 13 that there is a certain tension in vv. 24-27. Whereas the purpose of the passage apparently is to announce the salvation of the elect (v. 27), the wording in vv. 24-25

---

1. K. STENDAHL, *The School of St. Matthew and Its Use of the Old Testament* (ASNU, 20), Uppsala, 1954, p. 79 (on Mt 24); cf. p. 158.

2. *Ibid.*, p. 158. Of the forty allusive quotations in Mt with a parallel in Mk listed by R.H. Gundry, twelve are from Matthew's version of the eschatological discourse, including Mt 24,29-31 par. Mk 13,24-27 (24,6a.b.7.13.15a.b.21.24.29.30.31.34): cf. *The Use of the Old Testament in St. Matthew's Gospel. With Special Reference to the Messianic Hope* (NTSup, 18), Leiden, 1967, pp. 28-66, esp. 46-56; see also p. 148.

is borrowed from texts which refer to the coming judgement. Isa 13,10 and 34,4 and the passages of Joel belong to the so-called "Day of Yahweh" traditions and are used in the Old Testament to announce or to express the judgement which is to come upon the enemies of Israel. Basically two solutions are to be mentioned[3]. One way to deal with the problem is to give full emphasis to the result of the parousia as described in v. 27. Thus, for L. Hartman the formulation of the parousia of the Son of man is modelled after the OT descriptions of the theophany of the Almighty on the "Day of Yahweh for the 'gathering' of his people"[4]. The cosmic phenomena describe the terrifying effect of the coming of the Son of man which is pictured in v. 26 and will result in the salvation of the elect (v. 27). The parousia of the Son of man is inspired by the theophany of Yahweh as described in the Day-of-Yahweh traditions, but it is essentially a salvific action.

In *Naherwartungen* R. Pesch has criticized the understanding of the images of vv. 24-25 as a theophany and has presented an interpretation that is said also to retain the unity of the passage, yet to make better sense of the OT background. Vv. 24b-25 are to be explained as metaphors of the day of God's judgement: "Ihr Aussagegehalt läßt sich schlicht so umschreiben: In jenen Tagen nach der großen Drangsal kommt der Gerichtstag"[5]. V. 26 offers the theological interpretation of these

---

3. I do not further discuss the assumption that vv. 24-25 are the cosmic counterpart of the disasters that are mentioned in vv. 5-22 (see the criticism by R. PESCH, *Naherwartungen. Tradition und Redaktion in Mk 13*, Düsseldorf, 1968, pp. 158-160: J. Schmid; H. Conzelmann, H. Tödt), though this view continues to find some support: cf. T.J. WEEDEN, *Mark. Traditions in Conflict*, Philadelphia, PA, 1971, p. 89; H. BAARLINK, *Die Eschatologie der synoptischen Evangelien* (BWANT, 120), Stuttgart, 1986, p. 62; C.C. BLACK, *An Oration at Olivet*, in D.F. WATSON (ed.), *Persuasive Artistry*. FS G. Kennedy, Sheffield, 1991, pp. 66-92, esp. 76.
    I think one also misses the point when arguing that 13,24-25 merely announces an important turning point in history (references in J. MATEOS, *Marcos 13. El grupo cristiano en la Historia*, Madrid, 1987, p. 346 n. 506), or the judgement of the heavenly powers (see, e.g., GUNDRY, *Mt*, p. 487 and below n. 23), of Jerusalem and the Jewish nation (so, e.g., R.T. FRANCE, *Jesus and the Old Testament*, London, 1971, pp. 230-234) and/or of pagan religions: so MATEOS, pp. 348-355, esp. 353; see now also B. van Iersel's interpretation of how the original readers of Mk must have understood vv. 24-25. "It is probable that the Roman audience understood these words of Jesus first of all as announcing the end of the idols of the Greco-Roman pantheon": cf. *The Sun, Moon, and Stars of Mark 13,24-25 in a Greco-Roman Reading*, in *Bib* 77 (1996) 84-92, esp. p. 89 (see also below n. 43), and contrast his commentary (*Reading Mark*, Edinburgh, 1989, p. 167).
    4. *Prophecy Interpreted. The Formation of Some Jewish Apocalyptic Texts and of the Eschatological Discourse Mark 13 Par.* (ConBib NT, 1), Lund, 1966, p. 165; cf. p. 157.
    5. *Naherwartungen*, p. 162. It is worth emphasizing that in Pesch's view the metaphors characterize (the day of) God's coming, but they do not describe the judgement itself (see below n. 10).

metaphors (admittedly, while using apocalyptic vocabulary, as in vv. 24-25): "Der Menschensohn kommt, der Menschensohn kommt zum Gericht". Yet, this judgement is balanced by a positive element, since the Son of man will also bring about the salvation of the elect (v. 27)[6].

The interpretation of Pesch is based on two arguments. The first has to do with the background of 13,24-25. The *Gerichtsmetaphorik* in these verses stems from passages which belong to the traditions of the "Day of Yahweh". "Die Zitatkontamination bei Markus besteht also aus Texten, die vom Tag Jahwes, dem Tag des allgemeinen Weltgerichts sprechen"[7]. The second argument is about v. 26. The description of the judgement in Isa 13,9-12 and 34,1-17 is followed by the announcement of salvation for the people of Israel (Isa 14,1-2 and Isa 35). This schema may have influenced the structure of vv. 26-27[8]. This understanding of v. 26 as a reference to the judgement of the end time can also be derived from the parallels to 13,26 in Mk 14,62 and 8,38[9].

In his Commentary on Mark, Pesch repeated his interpretation of 13,24-27, but with an interesting nuance. He admits that the reference to the coming judgement in v. 26 is expressed rather weakly. "Die Gerichtsaussage [in v. 26] ist (nach der reichen Gerichtsmetaphorik der VV 24-25) knapp gehalten, weil das Schwergewicht auf die Heilszusage von V 27 fallen soll"[10]. Pesch's explanation of vv. 24-27 has been taken up by

---

6. *Ibid.*, pp. 168 and 172-174. For a similar interpretation (without reference to Pesch), see L. GASTON, *No Stone on Another* (NTSup, 23), Leiden, 1970, pp. 31-32.

7. *Naherwartungen*, p. 165.

8. *Ibid.*, pp. 164-166, esp. 166: "Ist dort [v. 27] von der Sammlung der Erwählten die Rede, so redet 13,26 gemäß dem alten Schema 'Gericht zum Unheil und Heil' vom Kommen des Menschensohnes zum Weltgericht". Cf. *Mk* II, pp. 302 and 304 (on the double καὶ τότε in vv. 26-27).

9. "Vom Kommen des Menschensohnes ist nur in den drei Logien 8,38; 13,26; 14,62 die Rede, Mk 8,38 und 14,62 sprechen eindeutig vom Kommen zum Gericht. Nur 13,26 und 14,62 reden vom 'Sehen' der Ankunft des Menschensohnes. Es legt sich nun unbedingt nahe, 13,26 zumindest im gegenwärtigen Kontext, im Licht von 14,62 zu interpretieren" (*Naherwartungen*, p. 168; cf. p. 170 and *Mk* II, p. 304). This last observation should not be misunderstood. For Pesch, 13,26 may itself have influenced 14,62 (except perhaps for ὄψονται). He refers to A. Suhl, who points out that Mark redacted 14,62 "im Anschluß an" and "in Übernahme des Gedankens von Mk 13,26", but who does not say that ὄψονται/ὄψεσθε refers to the coming judgement. Cf. A. SUHL, *Die Funktion der alttestamentlichen Zitate und Anspielungen im Markusevangelium*, Gütersloh, 1965, pp. 54-56.

10. *Mk* II, p. 304; and again on the same page: "Die knappe Parusieschilderung... bleibt, wie V 27 zeigt, weiter am Geschick der zugesprochenen Auserwählten orientiert... in dessen Nachfolge über das Strafgericht, das die Welt trifft, sehr zurückhaltend gesprochen wird". Compare also pp. 302-303 and his article on *Markus 13*, in J. LAMBRECHT (ed.), *L'Apocalypse johannique et l'Apocalyptique dans le Nouveau Testament* (BETL, 53), Leuven, 1980, pp. 355-368, p. 359. It remains remarkable that the theological implementation of the metaphors of judgement in v. 26 is so indirect, whereas vv. 24-25, in Pesch's opinion, picture God's judgement in such strong images.

A. Vögtle[11]. His influence is also clearly visible in the commentary of J. Gnilka. The OT passages represent the parousia as judgement, and that judgement itself is briefly indicated in v. 26 with the verb ὄψονται as in *1 Enoch* 62,3.10[12].

There are two more noticeable differences from *Naherwartungen* in these later publications. It is now stated less clearly that vv. 24-25 are metaphors (cf. below, n. 31). Pesch has also changed his view on the sign character of these verses. In 1968 he had still argued: "Es gibt Zeichen für die Nähe des Endes, keine Zeichen für das Ende selbst" (p. 178); he now describes the function of vv. 24-25 as "Zeichen des Endes" (signs of the end: p. 366). This complicates the question and introduces an understanding of the cosmic catastrophe which he had rejected earlier (see *Naherwartungen*, p. 159: ctr. F.C. Grant; cf. also p. 162 n. 654 and 166 n. 679), but for which he refers to parallels in the Pseudepigrapha (*Markus 13*, p. 366: "geläufig"). But Pesch himself wrestles with this understanding: "Zeichen und Endvollendung fallen zusammen, denn der Herr kommt 'plötzlich'" (*Mk* II, p. 303). On this last point, see the comments by F. NEIRYNCK, *Marc 13. Examen critique de l'interprétation de R. Pesch*, in J. LAMBRECHT (ed.), *L'Apocalypse johannique*, pp. 369-401, esp. 377 and 391-393 (= *Evangelica*, 1982, pp. 573; 587-589) and his quotation from Lagrange: "Il ne s'agit donc point de prodromes marqués par les transformations des astres, mais de fortes images pour marquer que Dieu entre en scène" (cf. below, n. 33). Compare also T. GEDDERT, *Watchwords. Mark 13 in Markan Eschatology* (JSNT SS, 26), Sheffield, 1989, p. 227. In the line of Pesch: M. MYLLYKOSKI, *Die letzten Tage Jesu*, 2, Helsinki, 1994, pp. 203-204 ("sichere Begleiterscheinungen") and p. 206 ("letztes Glied in der Ereignisabfolge vor der Parusie"); J. LIETAERT PEERBOLTE, *The Antecedents of the Antichrist* (JSJSup, 49), Leiden, 1996, p. 43. On Brandenburger, see below, n. 23.

11. See *Das Neue Testament und die Zukunft des Kosmos*, Düsseldorf, 1970, pp. 69-71: "kosmologische Metaphern, die in ihre eigentliche Aussage übersetzt besagen wollen: der Tag des Gerichts kommt und wird für die davon Betroffenen schrecklich sein" (p. 70). Cf. also in one of his last publications: *Die "Gretchenfrage" des Menschensohnproblems. Bilanz und Perspektive* (QD, 152), Freiburg, 1994, pp. 101-119, esp. pp. 102-103: Pesch's judgement is "sorgsam abgewogen". In this chapter Vögtle critically examines a suggestion of P. Hoffmann (in the FS Vögtle, 1991, 165-202, p. 196 n. 74) to consider Mk 13,26 as the oldest NT Son-of-man saying and Dan 7,13 as its background. He argues that the Christian appropriation of the Son-of-man concept occurred through the influence of *1 Enoch* (ch. 62) rather than of Dan and that this is reflected in Lk 17,24. For a discussion of Vögtle's views on Mk 13,26-27, see M. STOWASSER, *Mk 13,26f und die urchristliche Rezeption des Menschensohnes. Eine Anfrage an Anton Vögtle*, in *BZ* 39 (1995) 246-252.

12. "Vor diesem biblischen Hintergrund erfüllen die Bilder die Funktion, das Gericht an den Frevlern zu veranschaulichen. ... Es ist darum nicht zutreffend zu sagen, daß nach Markus nur die Rettung der Auserwählten im Blickpunkt steht" (*Mk* II, p. 200); "es kann in aller Kürze gesagt werden, daß sich das Gericht an ihnen vollzieht, indem sie ihn sehen" (p. 201).

Many others have been influenced by Pesch: see, e.g., E. LOHSE, *Christus als der Weltenrichter*, in G. STRECKER (ed.), *Jesus Christus in Historie und Theologie*. FS H. Conzelmann, Tübingen, 1975, p. 481 ("vorausgesetzt, aber nicht ausdrücklich genannt"); J.M. NÜTZEL, *Hoffnung und Treue. Zur Eschatologie des Markusevangeliums*, in P. FIEDLER – D. ZELLER (eds.), *Gegenwart und kommendes Reich. Schülergabe A. Vögtle*, Stuttgart, 1975, pp. 82-84; X. LÉON-DUFOUR, *L'annonce de l'Évangile* (Introduction à la Bible, 3/2), Paris, 1976, p. 56; M.D. HOOKER, *Trial and Tribulation in Mark XIII*, in *BJRL* 65 (1982-83) 78-99, here p. 92; cf. *Mk*, 1991, pp. 318-319; C. BREYTENBACH, *Nachfolge und Zukunftserwartung nach Markus* (ATANT, 71), Zürich, 1984, pp. 296-298; D.

J. Dupont, on the other hand, sides with Hartman. He comments on vv. 24-25: "L'ébranlement des astres marque la venue du Tout-Puissant en personne; il ne se confond pas avec le jugement destructeur qui sera l'effet de son intervention. Les images reprises dans le texte de Marc sont celles qui signalent une théophanie, non pas celles qui décriraient métaphoriquement un massacre général"[13]. As for v. 26, Dupont argues that Pesch too readily assumes that the parallels in Mk 8,38 and 14,62 can only be explained as announcing the coming of the Son of man for judgement. Both texts certainly are quite menacing, but they do not speak of vengeance or destruction. They refer to the perception of the Son of man in glory[14]. Moreover, Pesch's understanding of v. 26 does not fit the context of the discourse. The disasters which are announced in 13,5-22 are not described in terms of judgement and no one is held responsible for them. The other aspect, the fate of the elect, is extensively dealt with in the preceding (vv. 9-13 and 19-20); and they are also addressed in the final part of the discourse (vv. 28-37)[15]. "Le seul but assigné à la venue du Fils de l'homme est le rassemblement des élus"[16]. In 1977 Dupont could still note that this used to be the common opinion on vv. 24-27[17].

LÜHRMANN, *Mk*, 1987, p. 224; J. ROLOFF, *Weltgericht und Weltvollendung in der Offenbarung des Johannes*, in H.-J. KLAUCK (ed.), *Weltgericht und Weltvollendung* (QD, 150), Freiburg, 1994, 23-53, esp. 38-39; LIETAERT PEERBOLTE, *The Antichrist*, p. 44 (but "once this is acknowledged, it becomes all the more remarkable that there is no description whatsoever of a victory of Christ over his eschatological adversary").

13. *La ruine du Temple et la fin des temps dans le discours de Marc 13*, in ACFEB (ed.), *Apocalypses et théologie de l'espérance* (Lectio Divina, 95), Paris, 1977, pp. 207-269, esp. 251; repr. ID., *Études sur les Évangiles synoptiques*, 1 (BETL, 70-A), Leuven, 1985, pp. 368-433, esp. 412.

14. "Il me semble que la portée de l'affirmation [14,62, and also 8,38] est essentiellement christologique:... elle leur [the Jews] déclare qu'ils seront eux-mêmes les témoins de la gloire divine de celui qu'ils s'apprêtent à condamner" (*La ruine du Temple*, p. 251 = 412); cf. p. 252 on 8,38. And the same is true for 13,26: "Si Mc 13,26 ne dit rien d'un pouvoir que le Fils de l'homme aurait à exercer en sévissant contre les pécheurs, il n'y a pas lieu d'introduire cette perspective dans un texte qui tient avant tout à placer ce Fils de l'homme dans une position proprement divine" (p. 252 = 413).

15. *Ibid.*, pp. 247-249 (= 408-410). Cf. L. HARTMAN, *La Parousie du Fils de l'homme* (AssSeign, 2/64), Paris, 1969, 47-57, p. 51.

16. *Ibid.*, p. 252 (= 413).

17. Cf. his list of authors on p. 244 = 405 n. 91 and the one in W. KELBER, *The Kingdom in Mark*, Philadelphia, PA, 1974, p. 123 n. 43. Among earlier authors not mentioned there, see esp. J. WEISS, *Die Schriften des Neuen Testaments*, I, Göttingen, 1907, p. 198: "von dem Vernichtungs-Gericht über die Feinde Gottes... ist nicht die Rede, auch nicht von der Errichtung des ewigen Reiches der Heiligen, wie bei Daniel, sondern bloß von der Sammlung der Auserwählten". Compare also E. HAENCHEN, *Mk*, ²1968, p. 449; U. WILCKENS, *Gottes geringste Brüder – zu Mt 25,31-46*, in E.E. ELLIS, et al. (eds.), *Jesus und Paulus*. FS W.G. Kümmel, Göttingen, 1975, p. 369. And more recently: NEIRYNCK, *Marc 13*, p. 378 = 574 (with reference to Dupont); J. ERNST, *Mk*, 1981, p. 386; H.

In his monograph on Mk 13, E. Brandenburger has tried to solve the dilemma and proposed a kind of compromise between both explanations. His starting point is the explanation of Pesch, "der einzige Ansatz, in den Vv. 24-27 überhaupt ein Sinngefüge zu entdecken"[18]. With Pesch, he recognizes the presence of the motif of judgement, but it is restricted to v. 26 and it is only a secondary aspect in a text which is thoroughly marked by the Theophany genre. "Kennzeichnend für die Texteinheit ist vielmehr die durchgehende Prägung durch Motive, die für das Sinngefüge – oder die Gattung – der *Theophanie* konstitutiv sind"[19]. Vv. 24-27 consist of two subsections. The first two verses describe the parousia of the Son of man. Vv. 26-27 are separated from the preceding and describe in two acts (double καὶ τότε) the purpose of that parousia: it will bring judgement for "them" (v. 26: impers. pl. ὄψονται) and salvation for the elect (v. 27)[20]. Brandenburger clearly distinguishes between both parts of the section. V. 26 deals with the coming judgement, "aber daraus folgt nicht schon, daß die Vv. 24f selbst vom Gerichtstag sprechen"[21]. One of the motifs in passages which belong to the Theophany tradition is that of "der weltordnend einschreitenden und erscheinenden Jahwe / Gott-

GIESEN, *Christliche Existenz in der Welt und der Menschensohn. Versuch einer Neuinterpretation des Terminwortes Mk 13,30* (SNTU, 8), Linz, 1983, pp. 18-69, esp. 41-42: Giesen argues, against the opinion of "die meisten Autoren", that "die apokalyptischen Bilder hier vielmehr die Bedeutung der in V. 26f geschilderten Szene über den Menschensohn unterstreichen (dürften). Wenn der Menschensohn in Macht eingesetzt ist, hat die Endzeit begonnen" (see also his discussion with Gnilka on the interpretation of Mk 15,33 and 13,24-25); G.R. BEASLEY-MURRAY, *Jesus and the Kingdom of God*, Grand Rapids, MI, 1986, p. 331 and *Jesus and the Last Days. The Interpretation of the Olivet Discourse*, Peabody, MA, 1993, pp. 423-424; M.A. TOLBERT, *Sowing the Gospel*, Minneapolis, MN, 1989, p. 266; A. YARBRO COLLINS, *The Eschatological Discourse of Mark 13*, in *The Four Gospels 1992*. FS F. Neirynck (BETL, 100), Leuven, 1992, II, pp. 1125-1140, here 1136-1137 (taking up an argument that is sometimes found in this respect: "if the judgment is already implied in vv. 14-23, it is not necessary here"); U.B. MÜLLER, *Apokalyptik im Neuen Testament*, in F.W. HORN (ed.), *Bilanz und Perspektiven gegenwärtiger Auslegung des Neuen Testaments*. FS G. Strecker (BZNW, 75), Berlin, 1995, pp. 144-169, esp. 152-155.

18. E. BRANDENBURGER, *Markus 13 und die Apokalyptik* (FRLANT, 134), Göttingen, 1984, p. 56. In n. 119 he also refers to the "weit verbreitete Auslegungstradition" to interpret the section only in a positive way; cf. p. 64 n. 136. In that light, his observation on the "atomistic" exegesis of vv. 24-27 is somewhat surprising, as not only Pesch but also Hartman has precisely been trying to establish such "ein positiver Gedankenzusammenhang" (p. 55).

19. *Ibid.*, p. 58; cf. also p. 56: "Der leitende Gesichtspunkt ist der des Kommens des Menschensohns vom Himmel her". This also means that Mk 13,24-27 cannot be explained only from such Son-of-man passages as Dan 7, *1 Enoch* 62, or *4 Ezra* 13. Cf. the detailed survey of the parallels and differences between these texts and 13,24-27 (pp. 56-58).

20. *Ibid.*, p. 61; cf. p. 102 n. 213.

21. *Ibid.*, p. 56 n. 118; with reference to PESCH, *Naherwartungen*, p. 166.

könig". In vv. 24-27 this is expressed with the verb ὄψονται (v. 26). "To see" the theophany of Yahweh / the Son of man is a first step (p. 62: "ein erster, vorläufiger Akt"; cf. p. 64) in the judgement which will come over those who have opposed Him. The realization of the judgement itself, however, is not expressed in v. 26[22].

Like Pesch, Brandenburger regards vv. 24-25 as the signs of the end[23]. He has correctly pointed out the influence of the Theophany genre on Mk 13,24-27, but with his interpretation of v. 26 he faces the same difficulties as Pesch. In the Old Testament the coming of Yahweh to judge the world is explicitly characterized as such[24]. In v. 26 that judgement would be present only indirectly at most[25]. It would function in the overall perspective of the theophany which is regarded as an act of salvation. Only ὄψονται is "negativ qualifiziert"[26]. The subject of ὄψονται would

22. For a similar interpretation, see now Brandenburger's student, A. Scriba, *Die Geschichte des Motivkomplexes Theophanie. Seine Elemente, Einbindung in Geschehensabläufe und Verwendungsweisen in altisraelitischer, frühjüdischer und frühchristlicher Literatur* (FRLANT, 167), Göttingen, 1995, pp. 196-197 and 219. Compare also W. Zager, *Gottesherrschaft und Endgericht in der Verkündigung Jesu. Eine Untersuchung zur markinischen Jesusüberlieferung einschließlich der Q-Parallelen* (BZNW, 82), Berlin, 1996, pp. 147-149 and 297-303.

23. *Markus 13*, pp. 100-101: "ein vorauslaufendes Begleitgeschehen" (see above n. 10 and below n. 31). Compare Zager, *Endgericht*, p. 148, who goes beyond Brandenburger, however, when he also considers the possibility that the cosmic phenomena represent the judgement over the heavenly powers which precedes, as an autonomous act, the judgement on earth (see above n. 3). Though he admits that it is perhaps not common in the "spätjüdische (in his terminology: frühjüdische) Apokalyptik" (an observation made by Neirynck, cf. above n. 10), Brandenburger agrees with Pesch that there is some evidence for the use of cosmic phenomena as signs of the end (p. 101: *4 Ezra* 5,4; *OrSib* 3,796-806; also *4 Ezra* 6,11-24). However, the origin of this use is not decided ("Man kann fragen, ob dieses Motiv aus dem Traditionskomplex der Theophanie oder des Tages Jahwes stammt") and in any case: "Das Verfahren des Markus geht erheblich darüber hinaus". See my article on *Persecution and Eschatology. Mk 13,9-13*, in *The Four Gospels 1992* (above n. 17), II, pp. 1141-1159, esp. 1149 n. 31. Brandenburger's interpretation of vv. 24-25 holds together with his understanding of τότε in vv. 26-27 as indicating stages in the realization of the parousia. This is clearly seen by Gundry, *Mk*, p. 783: "because in v. 26 τότε means 'then' in the sense of 'at that time', not 'then' in the sense of 'next', the celestial disasters do not count as signs that the Son of man is about to come, but as events that take place as he comes".

24. Brandenburger refers to Deut 33; Ps 68; 96,13; 98,9; 102,13-14; Isa 26,21; Micah 1,3; also *1 Enoch* 1,3-4; *AssMos* 10 (*Markus 13*, p. 59 n. 122). See below p. 542 (Isa 13,10; 34,4).

25. Cf. *ibid.*, p. 56: "Der Gerichts*gedanke* ist zwar durchaus vorhanden" (italics mine); see also p. 102: "nur eben angedeutet".

26. *Ibid.*, p. 64. "In Mk 13,24-27 dominiert deutlich der Gedanke der Wende zum Heil. ... Der nur in ὄψονται anklingende Gedanke des Vernichtungsgerichts ist vom positiv orientierten Theophaniegedanken her umgriffen" (*ibid.*, p. 58); cf. pp. 51, 60 and 102: "die Voraussetzung für die Durchsetzung des Heils". Brandenburger observes that in this Mark was true to the perspective of his source (cf. below n. 109).

be those that are to be condemned[27]. The judgement is not described but formulated from the viewpoint of the sinners. In seeing the Son of man they realize that they will be judged[28]. But in the OT passages that speak of "seeing the theophany of the Lord" the subject of the verb is clearly not restricted to this group only, and there is a neat distinction between the act of seeing and the realization of the judgement[29]. Consequently, one cannot conclude that this "außerordentlich knapp angedeutetes Motiv" (ὄψονται) was probably easily understood by the audience as a reference to judgement[30].

In *Naherwartungen*, Pesch had rightly argued that vv. 24-25 are metaphors[31]. But metaphors of what? The cosmic phenomena in vv. 24-25

In a more recent contribution on concepts of judgement in Judaism and in the New Testament, Brandenburger characterizes Mk 13,24-27 par., *1 Enoch* 1,3-8, *AssMos* 10, and *4 Ezra* 6,13-20 as "Erlösungs- oder Heilsgericht" (pp. 24-26), which is to be distinguished from the "Vernichtungsgericht" of Isa 13,9-13 and Joel 2,1-11 (pp. 26-28); cf. *Gerichtskonzeptionen im Urchristentum und ihre Voraussetzungen. Eine Problemstudie*, in *SNTU* 16 (1991) 5-54; repr. in *Studien zur Geschichte und Theologie des Urchristentums* (SBAB, 15), Stuttgart, 1993, pp. 289-338; see already his article on *Gericht Gottes*, in *TRE* 12 (1984) 469-483. Compare also K. MÜLLER, *Gott als Richter und die Erscheinungsweisen seiner Gerichte in den Schriften des Frühjudentums*, in H.-J. KLAUCK (ed.), *Weltgericht und Weltvollendung* (above n. 12), pp. 23-53, esp. 38-39.

27. Zager (*Endgericht*, p. 300 n. 346) argues on the basis of Mt 24,30 and Lk 21,27 that the subject of ὄψονται is "die gesamte Menschheit – mit Ausnahme der Auserwählten". Contrast GUNDRY, *Mk*, p. 745: "people in general will see Jesus' coming" (cf. p. 783).

28. "Es ist ein überraschtes Erkennenmüssen, das Schmerz, Scham und Erschrecken auslöst" (*ibid.*, p. 63).

29. Brandenburger refers to Ps 97,4.6; 98,2-3; Isa 66,18; Ezek 38,23; 39,21-23; and also to *1 Enoch* 62,3 (p. 60 n. 129). He recognizes that there are some important differences between this last passage and Mk 13,26. "Es fehlt aber das Theophaniemotiv, und nur im zweiten Akt der Handlung wird das Vernichtungsgericht vollzogen (62,10-12).... (Das Motiv des Sehens) ist hier ebenfalls auf Gottes 'Herrlichkeit' gerichtet, allerdings auf den Herrlichkeitsthron des Richter-Gottes, auf dem jetzt der Menschensohn sitzt" (p. 63).

30. *Ibid.*, p. 62. For other proposals to do away with the dilemma, see J.R. DONAHUE, *Are You the Christ?*, Missoula, MT, 1973, p. 133 (vv. 24-25 were part of a description of the coming judgement which was replaced by Mark with vv. 26-27); K. TAGAWA, *Marc 13*, in *Foi & Vie CahBib* 16 (1977) 11-44, esp. 38 ("Marc a abrégé maladroitement la tradition"); and more recently GEDDERT, *Watchwords*, pp. 226-231: Mk leaves it open whether or not the final judgement has already taken place with the fall of Jerusalem. If so, no other judgement is to be expected and vv. 24-27 only describe the parousia of the Son of man to gather the elect; if not, these verses also denote judgement. Mark is "brilliantly ambiguous". But what evidence is there that Mark in 13,14-20 understood the fall of Jerusalem and its temple as the execution of God's judgement (cf. above n. 3), and if he did so, can he possibly have understood it to be identical with the final judgement?

31. For this reason his treatment of vv. 24-27 has been called "the most impressive section in *Naherwartungen*" (BEASLEY-MURRAY, *Jesus and the Last Days*, p. 425). In his Commentary, however, Pesch has changed his mind under the influence of F. Hahn who argues for a "realistic" interpretation (*Mk* II, p. 302); cf. *Die Rede von der Parusie des*

either describe the parousia as the day of God's judgement through the
Son of man, and the tone of the whole passage is markedly negative, or
they express the theophany of the Son of man, an event incomparable
and utterly terrifying alike, but in which the salvation of the elect will be
realized (v. 27). Pesch interprets v. 26 from vv. 24-25 and he regards
v. 27 as some sort of complement. He can claim to stick closer to the
original function and meaning of the wording of vv. 24-25 in the Old
Testament and this remains an attractive aspect of his hypothesis. Hartman
and Dupont point out that Mark 13 is not about vengeance and judgement.
Vv. 24-27 describe the parousia of the Son of man and his concern for
the elect. They assume that the Old Testament was handled quite freely,
but they have to admit that the choice of the wording in vv. 24-25 is
remarkable[32]. For Brandenburger, too, the wording in vv. 24-25 remains
a problem. Can we do more than note the difficulty? Or is it enough to
state with M.-J. Lagrange that the choice of the images after all is of less
importance[33]?

According to Pesch vv. 24-25 are much closer to the text of the Old
Testament than are comparable passages in Jewish apocalyptic litera-
ture[34]. He concludes from it that 13,24-25 is clearly meant to reflect the
original meaning of the OT imagery: "ein weiteres Argument für die
Annahme, daß der markinischen Text Gerichtsmetaphorik bieten will"[35].
The texts behind Mk 13,24-25 do indeed belong to the Day-of-Yahweh

Menschensohnes Markus 13, in R. PESCH – R. SCHNACKENBURG (eds.), *Jesus und der
Menschensohn*. FS A. Vögtle, Freiburg, 1975, p. 240-266, esp. 265-266: "Mk 13,24f
(hat) durchaus noch eine reale und nicht nur eine metaphorische Bedeutung, wenngleich
diese Bedeutung nicht ohne weiteres mit dem wortwörtlichen Sinn der hier vorausgesetzten Vorstellung zusammenfallen dürfte". See also Gnilka's "in der Mitte vom
Metaforik und Realistik" (*Mk* II, p. 200) or Hooker's "it is more than metaphorical, less
than literal... the language of myth" (*Trial*, pp. 92-93). For critical remarks, compare
NEIRYNCK, *Marc 13*, p. 378 (= 574); BRANDENBURGER, *Markus 13*, p. 55; and BEASLEY-
MURRAY, p. 425. For references to earlier authors defending a realistic understanding of
the images, see MATEOS, *Marcos 13*, p. 346 n. 505.

32. "Marc ne parle ici ni de l'écrasement du mal ni du jugement du monde, bien que
les passages vétérotestamentaires utilisés dans les vv. 24-25 pour décrire la scène de la
Parousie traitent tous du jugement divin" (HARTMAN, *La Parousie*, p. 51). And the same
goes for Dupont: "La netteté de cette orientation [of v. 27] est d'autant plus remarquable
que les images apocalyptiques traditionnelles utilisées dans ce dernier passage auraient
facilement conduit à présenter l'avènement du Fils de l'homme en fonction d'un jugement" (*La ruine du Temple*, p. 253 = 414).

33. Cf. M.-J. LAGRANGE, *L'avènement du Fils de l'homme*, in *RB* 13 (1906) 382-411,
p. 388: "Les images importent peu...; c'est un scénario expressif qui pourrait être rem-
placé par un autre". In his commentary on Mk, he speaks of "termes courants" (p. 345).

34. *Naherwartungen*, pp. 163-164. He refers more particularly to *1 Enoch* 102,2; *Ass
Mos* 10,5; and *OrSib* 3,796-806.

35. *Ibid.*, p. 164.

traditions. But how close is close: is it really correct to say that vv. 24-25 are so close to the wording of their sources (and how has one to explain the differences that exist after all)? And, moreover, does Pesch not jump from one conclusion to another?

2. The OT Background

Mk 13,24-25 is routinely described as a contamination or a conflation of Isa 13,10 and 34,4[36], with possibly also some influence of other passages (see below n. 61). Mk 13,24-25 clearly depends upon the Greek textual tradition of the Old Testament and not on the Hebrew, but it does not merely reproduce the text of the LXX[37]. No doubt Isa 13,10 LXX is the key text behind vv. 24b-25a. It reads: οἱ γὰρ ἀστέρες τοῦ οὐρανοῦ καὶ ὁ Ὠρίων καὶ πᾶς ὁ κόσμος τοῦ οὐρανοῦ τὸ φῶς οὐ δώσουσι, καὶ σκοτισθήσεται τοῦ ἡλίου ἀνατέλλοντος, καὶ ἡ σελήνη οὐ δώσει τὸ φῶς αὐτῆς[38]. One difference immediately strikes the eye. Whereas the passage in the prophet follows the order stars-sun-moon, the sequence in Mark is sun-moon-stars, and the intermediate element (καὶ ὁ Ὠρίων... οὐ δώσουσι) is lacking. The wording of v. 24b ὁ ἥλιος σκοτισθήσεται καὶ ἡ σελήνη οὐ δώσει τὸ φέγγος αὐτῆς is very close to that of Isa 13,10b. There are, however, two differences: φέγγος is substituted for φῶς, and the participle of the genitive absolute τοῦ ἡλίου ἀνατέλλοντος has been dropped and consequently ἥλιος has become the

36. PESCH, *Naherwartungen*, p. 164 (contamination); BEASLEY-MURRAY, *Jesus and the Last Days*, p. 423 n. 136 (conflation).

37. As it is well known, T.F. Glasson has argued that vv. 24-25 are taken from the LXX and concluded from it that the quotation is not an authentic part of the teaching of Jesus: cf. *Mark xiii and the Greek Old Testament*, in *ExpT* 69 (1957-58) 213-215; see also his *Theophany and Parousia*, in *NTS* 34 (1988) 259-270, 270 n. 14; compare N. PERRIN, *The Kingdom of God in the Teaching of Jesus*, London, 1963, p. 133. For dependence upon the Hebrew, see FRANCE, *Jesus and the OT*, pp. 242, 255-256; cf. also GUNDRY, *Use of the OT*, pp. 51-52; H.C. KEE, *The Function of Scriptural Quotations and Allusions in Mark 11–16*, in E.E. ELLIS, et al. (eds.), *Jesus und Paulus* (above, n. 16), pp. 165-188, 169. Note also the change in Pesch, without further comment, from "am griechischen AT orientiert" (*Naherwartungen*, p. 160; cf. 161) to "eine am MT orientierte Kontamination" (*Mk* II, p. 302). Cf. NEIRYNCK, *Marc 13*, p. 392 (= 588) n. 66.

38. Cf. J. ZIEGLER (ed.), *Isaias* (Septuaginta, 14), Göttingen, 1939, pp. 170-171. There are a few variant readings of secondary importance (note, e.g., the omission of αὐτῆς, *v.l.* φέγγος for φῶς² in ms. 106, obviously an assimilation with the text of the gospel, and the plural σκοτισθήσονται, with οἱ ἀστέρες as its subject), and there is some evidence of the text of the younger translators (Σ τὰ ἄστρα αὐτοῦ for Ὠρίων and Σ Θ ὁ ἥλιος ἐν τῇ ἐξόδῳ αὐτοῦ for the gen. abs.). Isa 13,10 LXX does not differ markedly from MT except for the paraphrase with καὶ ὁ Ὠρίων. According to ZIEGLER, *Untersuchungen zur Septuaginta des Buches Isaias* (ATA, 12/3), Münster, 1934, p. 64, (πᾶς) ὁ κόσμος τοῦ οὐρανοῦ is a gloss from Isa 24,21.

subject of the main verb (order subject-verb). None of these differences can be explained from the Hebrew text[39].

Mk 13,25a combines elements of Isa 13,10a and of 34,4b. Isa 34,4 LXX reads: καὶ ἑλιγήσεται ὁ οὐρανὸς ὡς βιβλίον, καὶ πάντα τὰ ἄστρα πεσεῖται ὡς φύλλα ἐξ ἀμπέλου καὶ ὡς πίπτει φύλλα ἀπὸ συκῆς[40]. The LXX traditions of 34,4b agree to translate "the starry host (shall) fade away" as πάντα τὰ ἄστρα πεσεῖται. It is such a wording that must have provided the link between Isa 13,10 (ἀστέρες) and 34,4 (ἄστρα)[41]. The form of the noun in Mk 13,25 (οἱ ἀστέρες), and possibly also the expression (ἐκ) τοῦ οὐρανοῦ, comes from 13,10 (οἱ ἀστέρες τοῦ οὐρανοῦ), the verb from 34,4[42]. The expression "the stars (of heaven) will fall" does not occur elsewhere in the LXX. In the context of Isa 34,4 and in combination with the reference to the eclipse of the sun and the moon (Isa 13,10), there can be no discussion about its meaning. It is found with the same meaning in Rev 6,13 (καὶ οἱ ἀστέρες τοῦ οὐρανοῦ ἔπεσαν εἰς τὴν γῆν, after v. 12 ὁ ἥλιος ἐγένετο μέλας; in 8,10 the image is different). Πίπτω may have been preferred to avoid the repetition of οὐ δώσουσιν/-σει τὸ φῶς of 13,10 (said of the stars and of the moon)[43]. It seems more difficult to explain the periphrastic construction. It is not used in 13,10 or 34,4. The future of εἰμι occurs four times in Isa 13,12.14 (twice in the plural and twice in the singular), in three of the instances with a participle as its subject. Could there be some influence from these verses[44]?

39. Ἀνατέλλω renders MT *bṣ't*; its omission is more significant than the agreement on the case of ἥλιος. Ctr. FRANCE, *Jesus and the OT*, p. 242.

40. ZIEGLER, 1939, pp. 243-244. Compare MT 34,4 (NEB): "All the host of heaven shall crumble into nothing, the heavens shall be rolled up like a scroll, and the starry host fade away, as the leaf withers from the vine and the ripening fruit from the fig-tree". The text of the Hebrew is not without problem: H. WILDBERGER, *Jesaja* (BKAT, 10), Neukirchen, 1979; NEIRYNCK, *Marc 13*, p. 392 n. 66.

41. If the assumption that both passages have been combined in 13,24-25 is taken seriously, there is no need to turn to the Hebrew (diff. FRANCE, *Jesus and the OT*, p. 256).

42. Hartman has pointed out that key-word association (cf. ἀστήρ-ἄστρον) is a common midrashic procedure (*Prophecy Interpreted*, p. 157). Pesch observes that Isa 34,4 probably depends upon 13,10 (*Naherwartungen*, p. 165 n. 672, with reference to G. Fohrer).

43. The combination of σκοτίζω/οὐ δίδωμι φῶς and πίπτω is not found in the Isa passages. Cf. MATEOS, *Marcos 13*, p. 347. It is not excluded that there could be some secondary influence of Isa 14,12-13 (LXX πῶς ἐξέπεσεν ἐκ τοῦ οὐρανοῦ ὁ ἑωσφόρος ὁ πρωὶ ἀνατέλλων;... εἰς τὸν οὐρανὸν ἀναβήσομαι, ἐπάνω τῶν ἄστρων τοῦ θεοῦ θήσω τὸν θρόνον μου) which has been paraphrased as ὑψώθησαν ἕως τῶν ἄστρων εἶπαν οὐ μὴ πέσωσιν in *PsSol* 1,5 and as ἐξ ἄστρων πέπτωκας ἐς οὐρανὸν οὐκ ἀναβήσῃ in *OrSib* 5,72, but Isa 14,12-13 is certainly not the primary text behind Mk 13,24-25 (ctr. VAN IERSEL, *Mark 13,24-25*, pp. 88-89: v. 25a has nothing to do with Isa 34,4; MATEOS, pp. 348-349).

44. Pesch refers to the influence of the Greek OT (in his view: on Mark's *Vorlage*) but it is not clear whether he has specifically in mind Isa 13,12.14 (*Naherwartungen*,

The real problem, however, is with Mk 13,25b which contains a reading of Isa 34,4a that does not go back to the LXX. The Alexandrian tradition of Isa 34,4a begins with καὶ ἑλιγήσεται ὁ οὐρανὸς ὡς βιβλίον (absent from Mk 13,24-25) and leaves out the very beginning of the verse according to MT ("All the host of heaven shall crumble into nothing")[45]. LXX B has a more complete text that includes a rendering of that part of the Hebrew: καὶ τακήσονται πᾶσαι αἱ δυνάμεις τῶν οὐρανῶν (on v.l. σαλευθήσονται, see below n. 64). According to Eusebius of Caesarea that is precisely the reading of Theodotion. We are particularly well informed about the differences in the rendering of Isa 34,4 by the younger translators through his Commentary on Isaiah. Eusebius observes that all three have rendered the beginning of the verse as it is found in the Hebrew original and he quotes their translation[46]. They also differ from LXX for the second half of 34,4[47]. Their rendering of 34,4a is even quoted twice. And though there seems to be a slight difference between the two quotations of the text of Symmachus[48], Eusebius' witness is more complete and also seems to be more accurate than the information which is found in the margin of some LXX manuscripts that ascribe the reading of Theodotion in 34,4a to οἱ γ′ (Q^mg) or to α′σ′θ′ (Syh^mg), or even to α′σ′θ′ο′ (86^mg). Ziegler has rightly emphasized the importance of this information[49]. He has also pointed out that

p. 160). Again it is a more complex explanation to argue for dependence upon the Hebrew with the observation (in itself correct) that *nbl* is sometimes rendered by πίπτω (so FRANCE, *Jesus and the OT*, p. 256), only because 13,25 "is not verbally identical with the LXX". The important thing is that Mark has the same verb πίπτω as in 34,4 LXX and not one of the other verbs which are used in the LXX to render *nbl* (e.g., ἀποβάλλω).

45. On the influence of the reading with ἑλιγήσεται on later Christian authors and art, see H. HUNGER, Ἑλιγήσεται ὁ οὐρανὸς ὡς βιβλίον, in *Kleronomia* 1 (1969) 79-82.

46. Καὶ τακήσονται πᾶσα στρατιὰ τῶν οὐρανῶν (Aquila); καὶ τακήσεται πᾶσα ἡ δύναμις τοῦ οὐρανοῦ (Symmachus); and καὶ τακήσονται πᾶσαι αἱ δυνάμεις τῶν οὐρανῶν (Theodotion). Cf. J. ZIEGLER (ed.), *Der Jesajakommentar* (GCS, 56), Berlin, 1975, pp. 220-221 (on Isa 34,4). It is no doubt a mistake when I.L. SEELIGMANN, *The Septuagint Version of Isaiah*, Leiden, 1948, p. 15, attributes the reading of LXX B to Aquila.

47. Instead of πάντα τὰ ἄστρα πεσεῖται-fin. (cf. above), they read καὶ πᾶσα στρατιὰ αὐτῶν ἀπορρεύσει ὡς ἀπορρεῖ (LXX πίπτει; but the Lucianic tradition has ἐκρεῖ) φύλλον ἀπὸ ἀμπέλου καὶ ὡς ἀπόπτωμα ἀπὸ συκῆς (Aquila); καὶ πᾶσα ἡ δύναμις αὐτῶν πεσεῖται ὡς πίπτει φύλλον ἀπὸ ἀμπέλου καὶ ὡς ἀπόπτωμα ἀπὸ συκῆς (Symmachus); καὶ πᾶσα δύναμις αὐτῶν πεσεῖται ὡς πίπτει φύλλα ἀπὸ ἀμπέλου καὶ ὡς πτῶμα ἀπὸ συκῆς (Theodotion).

48. The first time the article ἡ is missing and the genitive is in the plural (τῶν οὐρανῶν); or is this an inadvertence of the editor? Cf. ZIEGLER, 1975, p. xxxix and 220.

49. "Auch deshalb ist der neue Jesaja-Kommentar wichtig, weil Eusebius genau und gewissenhaft, ohne Zeit und Raum zu sparen, die einzelnen Wiedergaben des Aquila, Symmachus und Theodotion getrennt aufgeführt hat. ... Ein gutes Beispiel bietet Is 34,4a" (ZIEGLER, 1975, p. xxxix).

the rendering of 34,4a by the younger translators, as given by Eusebius, agrees with what we know of their translation techniques[50]. Eusebius adds that the reading of Theodotion was introduced later on in the LXX: μὴ κείμενον δὲ ἐν τῇ τῶν Ἑβδομήκοντα ἑρμηνείᾳ τό· καὶ τακήσονται πᾶσαι αἱ δυνάμεις τῶν οὐρανῶν, μετὰ ἀστερίσκων ἐκ τῆς τῶν λοιπῶν ἑρμηνείας προσετέθη[51]. It is found in the text in some manuscripts of the Hexaplaric tradition (B-V and 109-736). "Die Quellen dieser Zusätze waren gewöhnlich die jüngeren Übersetzungen, namentlich Theodotion"[52]. The reading pervaded the Lucianic tradition[53]. Theodoretus of Cyr also appears to have read this form of Isa 34,4[54].

50. Aquila follows the Hebrew original most strictly, even to produce a text such as τακήσονται πᾶσα στρατιά. Symmachus and Theodotion have complied with the rules of Greek grammar, either by changing the verb into the singular (Σ) or the noun into the plural (Θ); cf. ZIEGLER, 1975, p. XL. It is also to be observed that they all three have repeated the noun of 34,4a in their rendering of 34,4b (Α πᾶσα στρατιά; Σ πᾶσα δύναμις; Θ πᾶσαι δυνάμεις in 4b but the sing. in 4a, due to his preference to alter the subject and not the verb in 4a), and that they agree on the verb τακήσονται/-σεται in 4a; the same verb was already used by Theodotion in 34,3b: ἐκτακήσονται τὰ ὄρη for βραχήσεται..., and it led Eusebius to a comment on the interpretation of δυνάμεις: αἱ γὰρ δυνάμεις τῶν οὐρανῶν ὄρη νοούμεναι τακήσεσθαι λέγονται, or, Eusebius adds, are they not rather to be interpreted as does Paul in Eph 6,12 (cf. ZIEGLER, 1975, p. 221)?

51. ZIEGLER, 1975, p. 221. It is of less importance for our purpose whether this observation is to be understood as if the reading was missing in the pre-Hexaplaric tradition and was introduced (by Origen) in the Hexapla (so ZIEGLER, 1975, p. XL; cf. also R.R. OTTLEY, The Book of Isaiah according to the Septuagint, Cambridge, 1906, II, p. 276), or whether it means that Eusebius did not find it in his Hexaplaric manuscript (this is the usual meaning of ἡ τῶν Ἑβδομήκοντα ἑρμηνεία) and that he himself is responsible for introducing it (so R.G. JENKINS, The Biblical Text of the Commentaries of Eusebius and Jerome on Isaiah, in Abr Nahrain 22 [1983-84] 64-78, p. 73: though Ziegler's is "a natural enough assumption"). "Certainly ἐκ τῆς τῶν λοιπῶν ἑρμηνείας προσετέθη implies that the reading in question has been excerpted from 'the three' and added" (JENKINS, p. 73). It is not the only mention of the asterisk (it is also found in the margin of Q 86 Syh at Isa 34,4) in the Commentary of Eusebius (ctr. ZIEGLER, 1975, p. XXXVIII): there is another one at Isa 41,13.

52. ZIEGLER, 1939, p. 60; with reference to Isa 22,25 and 34,4.

53. All its most important representatives and some manuscripts of a related text type, such as 233 and 403′. Cf. ZIEGLER, 1939, pp. 76-77. It is also attested in some other minuscles of a mixed type: 538 and 770, both of the 12th c. (ibid., p. 243; see also p. 83).

54. Cf. A. MÖHLE, Theodoret von Kyros. Kommentar zu Jesaia (Mitteilungen des Septuaginta-Unternehmens, 5), Berlin, 1932, p. 137: (καὶ) τακήσονται αἱ δυνάμεις τῶν οὐρανῶν, καὶ εἱλιχθήσεται ὡς βιβλίον ὁ οὐρανὸς καὶ πάντα τὰ ἄστρα τοῦ οὐρανοῦ πεσεῖται ὡς πίπτει φύλλα ἀπὸ ἀμπέλου καὶ ὡς ἐκρεῖ φύλλα ἀπὸ συκῆς. But the only existing manuscript of his CommIsa (cod. K, 14th c.) is deeply influenced by the Lucianic recension (cf. MÖHLE, p. XV, who has used manuscripts of that tradition to emend K in several instances). Moreover, Theodoretus heavily depended on Eusebius, whose interest in the reading of Theodotion may have been taken by Theodoretus as an indication that Eusebius regarded this reading as the most correct translation, even though Eusebius does not state this explicitly. On the influence of Eusebius on Theodoretus, see ZIEGLER, 1975, p. XLIX.

The addition of Isa 34,4a in LXX B is an interpolation[55]. Yet there is no reason to reckon with (additional) influence of the Hebrew on v. 25b. There is no evidence for the translation of *mqq* ("crumble") with σαλεύω (Mk). It is not enough to say that there is "no mistranslation of the Hebrew" and that *ṣb' hšmym* is frequently rendered by δύναμις[56]. Ἡ δύναμις τοῦ οὐρανοῦ (in the singular) is found six times in the LXX[57]. In each case it is the rendering of *ṣb' hšmym*[58]. The exceptional rendering of *ṣb' hšmym* with αἱ δυνάμεις and the plural of οὐρανός is found only in the Greek tradition of Isa 34,4a (Th)[59]. Why would one who undeniably relies on a Greek version have returned to the Hebrew at 34,4a? It is a more probable solution to accept dependence on a recension with a "mixed" text form which is close to or identical with that of Theodotion for 34,4a (with pl. αἱ δυνάμεις) and which agrees with that of the LXX for 34,4b (with πάντα τὰ ἄστρα πεσεῖται; note that Th here reads πᾶσα δύναμις αὐτῶν)[60]. One should realize, however, that Mk 13,24-25 is the only witness for such a recension (LXX B-V are influenced by the reading of Th) and that even this text form does not explain all the differences between Mk 13,24-25 and the Isaiah passages.

Theodoretus also quotes Isa 34,4b after Mt 24,29a in his commentary on Isa 24,22 (MÖHLE, p. 100). At Isa 66,15 (p. 260), he quotes Mt 24,30b followed by a quotation in which he combines Mt 24,30a with 24,29a and to which is added Isa 34,4b. This kind of combinations may explain the addition of τοῦ οὐρανοῦ after πάντα τὰ ἄστρα in his quotation of 34,4 at the beginning of his comment on that verse (p. 137; cf. Mt 24,29 οἱ ἀστέρες πεσοῦνται ἀπὸ τοῦ οὐρανοῦ), as well as the omission of πᾶσαι before αἱ δυνάμεις in his quotation of 34,4a (diff. Theodotion; cf. Mt 24,29 αἱ δυνάμεις without πᾶσαι). In his commentary on Isa 66,21-22 Eusebius had quoted Mt 24,35a in combination with Isa 34,4a (ZIEGLER, p. 408).

55. T.F. Glasson still considered αἱ δυνάμεις τῶν οὐρανῶν to be the reading of the LXX (*Mark xiii*, p. 213). See the remark by HARTMAN, *Prophecy Interpreted*, p. 157 n. 38.

56. FRANCE, *Jesus and the OT*, p. 255.

57. 2 Kings 17,16; 21,3.5; 23,4.5; 2 Chron 18,18 (here without ἡ). Compare also Sir 17,32 δύναμιν ὕψους οὐρανοῦ αὐτὸς ἐπισκέπτεται.

58. As in the Hebrew it is always accompanied with the adjective πᾶς (*kl*), and, except for 2 Chron 18,18 (nom.), it is always in the dative (*l*). In addition *(l)kl ṣb' hšmym* is also rendered by LXX as πάντα τὸν κόσμον τοῦ οὐρανοῦ (Deut 4,19; cf. above), παντὶ τῶν ἐκ τοῦ κόσμου τοῦ οὐρανοῦ (Deut 17,3), πᾶσα ἡ στρατιὰ τοῦ οὐρανοῦ (1 Kings 22,19, but cf. above 2 Chron 18,18; 2 Chron 33,3.5, but see 2 Kings 21,3.5; Jer 8,2; 19,13; Zeph 1,5, without πᾶς) or αἱ στρατιαὶ τῶν οὐρανῶν (Neh 9,6). In Dan 8,10 LXX renders it as τῶν ἀστέρων τοῦ οὐρανοῦ and its repetition as ἀπὸ τῶν ἀστέρων καὶ ἀπὸ αὐτῶν. Ode 12,15 has σὲ ὑμνεῖ πᾶσα ἡ δύναμις τῶν οὐρανῶν. Cf. also Ps 32,6 LXX par MT: οἱ οὐρανοὶ ἐστερεώθησαν καὶ... πᾶσα ἡ δύναμις αὐτῶν.

59. FRANCE, *Jesus and the OT* (p. 255 n. 46), refers still to Ps 103(102),21 and 148,2, but "the heavens" is missing there (in both πᾶσαι αἱ δυνάμεις αὐτου for *kl ṣb'*).

60. Cf. SCRIBA, *Theophanie*, p. 199: "offensichtlich nicht die ursprüngliche LXX Fassung, sondern eine frühe Rezension". Compare also ZAGER, *Endgericht*, p. 299 n. 338.

It is remarkable that four of these differences – the substitution of φέγγος for φῶς, the mention of ἥλιος in the nominative and followed by a verb denoting "darkening" instead of the genitive absolute with ἀνατέλλω, the inversion of the order of the triad stars-sun-moon (Isa 13,10), and the mention of the shaking of the heavens – occur together in another passage from the Day-of-Yahweh tradition, Joel 2,10 (cf. also 3,4; 4,15 LXX)[61]. In Joel 2,10 the coming of "a mighty, countless host" is announced: πρὸ προσώπου αὐτῶν συγχυθήσεται ἡ γῆ καὶ σεισθήσεται ὁ οὐρανός, ὁ ἥλιος καὶ ἡ σελήνη συσκοτάσουσι, καὶ τὰ ἄστρα δύσουσι τὸ φέγγος αὐτῶν[62]. This verse may have influenced the change of order (sun-moon-stars) and of the construction with ἥλιος, and also the choice of φέγγος for φῶς[63]. As to the fourth differ-

61. The influence of this passage on Mk 13,24-25 has been minimized by Pesch (*Naherwartungen*, p. 163 n. 660), Dupont (*La ruine*, p. 249: "Les contacts sont moins précis"), and Gundry (*Mk*, p. 783), and is not even mentioned by Brandenburger (*Markus 13*, p. 58) and Scriba (*Theophanie*, p. 199). But see J. LAMBRECHT, *Die Redaktion der Markus-Apokalypse. Literarische Analyse und Strukturuntersuchung* (AnBib, 28), Rome, 1967, pp. 177-178 and D. WENHAM, *The Rediscovery of Jesus' Eschatological Discourse*, Sheffield, 1984, pp. 309-310 ("the Joel passages were the primary influence"), though both underestimate the influence of Isa 13,10; 34,4; see also C.H. DODD, *According to the Scriptures*, London, 1952, p. 48; GASTON, *Stone*, p. 32 ("perhaps"); KEE, *Function*, p. 169 (allusion); BEASLEY-MURRAY, *Jesus and the Last Days*, p. 423.
Some authors refer to the (subsidiary) influence of Ezek 32,7-8 (e.g., KEE, p. 169), but this passage contains nothing that is not also found in the passages from Isa and Joel and the verbal parallels are less impressive (different verbs are used). References to Amos 8,9 or Dan 8,10 offer interesting parallels but these texts are not the source of Mk 13,24-25.
62. Cf. Joel 3,4 LXX: ὁ ἥλιος μεταστραφήσεται εἰς σκότος καὶ ἡ σελήνη εἰς αἷμα πρὶν ἐλθεῖν ἡμέραν κυρίου τὴν μεγάλην καὶ ἐπιφανῆ; and 4,15 LXX: ὁ ἥλιος καὶ ἡ σελήνη συσκοτάσουσι, καὶ οἱ ἀστέρες δύσουσι φέγγος αὐτῶν. This last passage is a nearly literal repetition of 2,10b. Note the difference: ἀστέρες-ἄστρα, as in the combination of Isa 13,10 and 34,4 in Mk 13,24-25. Note also the repetition of 2,10a.11a (καὶ κύριος δώσει φωνὴν αὐτοῦ) in 4,16: ὁ δὲ κύριος... δώσει φωνὴν αὐτοῦ, καὶ σεισθήσεται ὁ οὐρανὸς καὶ ἡ γῆ. In Joel 3,4 and 4,15 the cosmic images are immediately followed by a reference to the salvation of Israel (3,5; 4,17).
63. France holds that influence of Joel 2,10 for φέγγος is "not impossible" (*Jesus and the OT*, p. 242 n. 10), but he does not envisage it for ἥλιος. According to Pesch (*Naherwartungen*, p. 164), the omission of the participle with ἥλιος may be due to the change of order. If the stars are mentioned first, the chronology is that of night – morning (the rising sun) – evening/night. Pesch reads φέγγος also in Isa 13,10 (p. 160), but this must be a mistake. The variant reading with φέγγος in 13,10 is probably an assimilation with Joel 2,10, or rather with Mk 13,24/Mt 24,29 (so Ziegler), and cannot be used as an argument against the possible influence of Joel 2,10 on Mk 13,24 (ctr. ZAGER, *Endgericht*, p. 299 n. 338). The variant reading οὐ δώσουσιν for δύσουσι in Joel 2,10 (Ziegler in his edition of Joel LXX refers to Isa 13,10; Mt 24,29; Mk 13,24) proves that the assimilation may have worked in both directions and that the two texts have always been regarded as close parallels. Cf., e.g., H.W. WOLFF, *Dodekapropheton*, 2 (BKAT, 14/2), Neukirchen, 1969, pp. 55-56 (2,10 and the influence of Isa 13).

ence, the shaking of heaven and earth is mentioned in Isa 13,13[64], but there is no such direct link between the two images in Isa 13,10.13 as there is in Mk. Vv. 24-25a are closely linked together through the image of the eclipse of the heavens, and in v. 25b another image is combined with it: καὶ αἱ δυνάμεις αἱ ἐν τοῖς οὐρανοῖς σαλευθήσονται. This connection of the shaking and of the eclipse of heavens, however, is found in Joel 2,10, though the wording differs: the passage does not have the formulation with αἱ δυνάμεις or the verb σαλεύω.

The combination of the two passages from Isa and, even more so, the agreements with Joel 2,10 suggest that 13,24-25 is the result of a freely formulated (the shaking) conflation of related OT texts[65]. With regard to the addition of αἱ δυνάμεις τῶν οὐρανῶν (τακήσονται) in v. 25b, this raises in turn the question whether not also different recensions may have been conflated. If so, Mk 13,24-25 does not reproduce an otherwise unknown Greek version, but it combines, at one point, the reading of the LXX, which remains its basic text, with an element from another (proto-Theodotionic) recension which also renders Isa 34,4a. Individual elements of vv. 24-25 may be relatively close to the text of certain OT passages (σαλεύω is an important exception), but the result of the conflation is after all a quite different text.

3. *The Interpretation of 13,24-25*

This brings me to my second point. Is it enough to use images which occur in passages that deal with the Day of Yahweh to conclude that

---

64. Ὁ γὰρ οὐρανὸς θυμωθήσεται καὶ ἡ γῆ σεισθήσεται ἐκ τῶν θεμελίων αὐτῆς διὰ θυμὸν ὀργῆς κυρίου σαβαωθ τῇ ἡμέρᾳ, ᾗ ἂν ἐπέλθῃ ὁ θυμὸς αὐτοῦ. On θυμόω, cf. below n. 93.

There is a variant reading σαλευθήσονται for τακήσονται in 34,4 in the LXX manuscript 403′ that contains the addition from Theodotion in 34,4a (cf. above). Ziegler rightly considered it to be an assimilation with Mt 24,29 / Mk 13,25 (1939, p. 243). The whole of the Lucianic tradition, together with a few independent manuscripts (46 106 130 and again 403′) and Theodoretus, reads σαλευθήσεται instead of θυμωθήσεται in Isa 13,13 (cf. Ziegler 1939, p. 88: "als paralleles Verbum zu σεισθήσεται"). Ziegler does not mention the possible influence of Mt 24,29 / Mk 13,25 also in this case, though 403′ (at Isa 34,4) and 106 (with the *v.l.* φέγγος at 13,10; cf. above) clearly were assimilated to the text of the New Testament; the Sahidic version of 13,13 (σκοτισθήσεται for θυμωθήσεται) shows that this verse has been assimilated to 13,10.

65. Perhaps the omission of the paraphrase in Isa 13,10a and of the comparisons in Isa 34,4ab has also been inspired by Joel 2,10. There, the description is reduced to its essentials. There is no reason to assume that these omissions would go back to a text form different from LXX (proto-Th), since Th has a transcription of part of Isa 13,10a (χισιλεεμ) and retains the comparison in 34,4b. Similarly, the reading ὁ ἥλιος in Mk 13,24 (instead of the gen.) is not to be connected with that of Th (and S) who both add ἐν τῇ ἐξόδῳ αὐτοῦ.

vv. 24-25 must be "metaphors of judgement"? The representations of the Theophany of Yahweh and of the Day of the Lord have influenced each other and they have several motifs and images in common[66]. According to Jeremias, the eclipse of the heavenly bodies is one of three motifs that have been introduced in descriptions of the theophany from the Day-of-Yahweh tradition[67]. In the oldest stratum, in Amos 5,18-20, the Day of Yahweh was not yet further described and only characterized as "darkness" (18 καὶ αὐτή ἐστι σκότος καὶ οὐ φῶς; cf. v. 20)[68]. This may have been developed later on into the motif of the eclipse of the heavens[69]. In Isa 13,10; Joel 2,10 and 4,15 (and also in Ezek 32,7) the motif is expressed in the specific form of the darkening of the sun, the moon, and the stars. In Isa (and in Ezek) the order is stars-sun-moon, and the strength of the expression is weakened because of the addition in v. 10a. Mk 13,24-25 is closer to Joel. The motif is not frequently used in the Theophany tradition. It is found in Hab 3,11 without the characteristic wording (σκοτίζω/άω or the like) and in a reduced form ("sun and moon" only, though this is also the case in some Day-of-Yahweh passages: cf. Amos 8,9; Jer 4,23)[70]. *AssMos* 10,5, however, the only other example mentioned by Jeremias of a Theophany text that contains the motif of the eclipse, does have the triad and the characteristic verbs in its description of the theophany as is the case in Mk[71].

66. Cf. J. JEREMIAS, *Theophanie. Die Geschichte einer alttestamentlichen Gattung* (WMANT, 10), Neukirchen-Vluyn, 1965, ²1977, p. 97: "In sehr enger Beziehung zur Gattung der Theophanieschilderungen steht die Tradition vom 'Tage Jahwes'". After more than thirty years, this is still the standard work on Theophany as is fully recognized by Scriba who has recently studied the whole complex again: *Theophanie* (above n. 22), pp. 9-10.

67. The other two are "die Verwüstung des Landes und die Vernichtung der Menschen" (JEREMIAS, *Theophanie*, pp. 98-99).

68. The motif of darkness occurs also in connection with Theophany (cf. WILDBERGER, *Jesaja*, p. 517).

69. "(Es) ist doch leicht vorstellbar, daß die Aussage, der 'Tag Jahwes' werde erschreckende Finsternis bringen, die von Anfang in der Tradition zu Hause ist, jene Ausführung über das Versagen der Gestirne nach sich zog" (JEREMIAS, *Theophanie*, p. 98).

70. Hab 3,11 MT "The sun forgets to turn in his course, and the moon stands still at her zenith" / LXX ἐπήρθη ὁ ἥλιος, καὶ ἡ σελήνη ἔστη ἐν τῇ τάξει αὐτῆς. In the second half of the verse MT and LXX differ even more. On the text of this notoriously difficult passage, see now SCRIBA, *Theophanie*, pp. 225-230.

71. Cf. J. TROMP, *The Assumption of Moses. A Critical Edition with Commentary* (SVTP, 10), Leiden, 1993, p. 18: "Sol non dabit lumen et in tenebris convertet se cornua lunae et confringentur, et tota convertit se in sanguine; et orbis stellarum conturvavitur". Tromp points out that "both concepts, the Day of the Lord and the theophany, have been combined" in *AssMos* 10,3-7 (p. 234: vv. 3 and 7), but he agrees that 10,4-6 describes the theophany of God ("the upsetting of the natural order") and not His judgement (p. 232). There is no reason to assume that *AssMos* 10,4-6 was "probably well known to the Evangelists, and may have influenced" Mk 13,24-25 (so B.P.W. STATHER HUNT, *Primitive Gospel Sources*, London, 1951, p. 71 n. 3).

The influence also worked the other way around, and Jeremias points out two important features of the Theophany genre which have found their way into descriptions of the Day of Yahweh. The first is that of "the voice of Yahweh", which is found in its original form in Amos 1,2, but shows up in Joel 2,11 and 4,16 LXX[72]. The second one is that of the shaking of heaven and earth, which is a constant motif in theophanies[73] and is also found in Isa 13,13 and Joel 2,10; 4,16. The same imagery can be used to describe the coming of the Lord and the fulfilment of His judgement. This is of great importance in studying Mk 13,24-25.

But there must of course also be ways to distinguish between both uses in the application and/or perhaps also the formulation of the motifs. Therefore, I propose to further examine some of the differences between Mk 13,24-25 and its sources. A first observation, though obvious and frequently mentioned, remains worth repeating: Mk 13,24-25 does not speak of a judgement on earth[74] or of the "Day of the Lord" (LXX ἡμέρα κυρίου)[75]. On this point Mk 13,24-25 contrasts very strongly with the passages from Isa and Joel[76]. The imagery is identical in Isa – Joel and in Mk, but what it represents is not. In short, Mk 13,24-27 is not a summary of the "Gerichtsschilderung" of Isa 13 and parr., but a "fragment"[77]. It retains only one element which occurs also in connec-

72. It is an indication that the passages in Joel are in some respects closer to the Theophany tradition. This may be the real importance of the influence of Joel on Mk 13,24-25.

73. "Das Beben von Bergen, Himmel und Erde (gehört) unlöslich zu den Theophanieschilderungen" (JEREMIAS, *Theophanie*, p. 100).

74. See, e.g., the comment of Dupont (above n. 13).

75. It may be that this last expression was felt by a Christian author to be less appropriate to describe the parousia of the Son of man, but it could certainly have contributed to strengthen the connotation of the parousia with judgement and it was not unknown in that context in Christian tradition both before and after Mark. Cf. 1 Cor 1,8; 5,5; 2 Cor 1,14 (in the first and third with explicit application to Jesus); 1 Thess 5,2 ἡμέρα κυρίου ὡς κλέπτης (cf. Mk 13,34); 2 Pet 3,10 (followed by ἡ τοῦ θεοῦ ἡμέρα in v. 12; cf. also Rev 16,14); and esp. the quotation of Joel 3,4 LXX in Act 2,20 πρὶν ἐλθεῖν ἡμέραν Κυρίου τὴν μεγάλην καὶ ἐπιφανῆ. See also 2 Thess 2,2 and ἡμέρα ('Ιησοῦ) Χριστοῦ in Phil 1,6.10; 2,16.

76. Cf. Isa 13,6.9 LXX: ἐγγὺς γὰρ ἡ ἡμέρα κυρίου... ἰδοὺ γὰρ ἡμέρα κυρίου ἀνίατος ἔρχεται θυμοῦ καὶ ὀργῆς θεῖναι τὴν οἰκουμένην ὅλην ἔρημον καὶ τοὺς ἁμαρτωλοὺς ἀπολέσαι ἐξ αὐτῆς; 34,5.8: καταβήσεται καὶ ἐπὶ τὸν λαὸν τῆς ἀπωλείας μετὰ κρίσεως... ἡμέρα γὰρ κρίσεως κυρίου; and also Joel 2,11b: διότι μεγάλη ἡμέρα κυρίου, μεγάλη καὶ ἐπιφανὴς σφόδρα (cf. 3,4 LXX); and also 4,14: ὅτι ἐγγὺς ἡμέρα κυρίου ἐν τῇ κοιλάδι τῆς δίκης. The contrast is even stronger when the cosmic signs are regarded as a part of the destruction itself: cf. O. KAISER, *Der Prophet Jesaja* (ATD, 18), Göttingen, 1973, p. 17: "Das absolute Dunkel (wird) selbst zu einem Teil des Gerichts". I wonder, however, whether that is meant in Isa 13,10.

77. This characterization goes back to E. Lohmeyer: "Merkwürdig, die Zeilen sprechen nur von dem Himmelsgewölbe, als seien Erde und Menschen nicht vorhanden oder unberührt in diesen Katastrophen des Firmaments. Der Spruch ist also, gewollt oder ungewollt, ein Fragment. ... Wo diese apokalyptischen Katastrophen uns sonst geschildert

tion with the Day of Yahweh – the cosmic phenomena –, and these are not used to characterize that Day as the day of the judgement of the Lord, but to describe the coming of the Son of man.

The formulation of vv. 24-25 also contains certain traces which reveal that the images do refer to the Theophany of the Lord. This is perhaps not yet the case for the motif of the eclipse which was borrowed from the descriptions of the Day of Yahweh (cf. above on Hab 3,11 and *Ass-Mos* 10,5), though it is noteworthy that one of the very rare references to the falling down of the stars from heaven in Biblical and Pseudepigraphical literature (besides Isa 34,4 Th) occurs in the context of an account of the theophany of Yahweh in the burning bush[78]. But there are such traces for the second motif.

The shaking of the heavens is expressed in Mk 13,25b as αἱ δυνάμεις αἱ ἐν τοῖς οὐρανοῖς σαλευθήσονται. The expression is not found elsewhere in the New Testament besides Mk 13,25 and parr. *Ṣb' hšmym* and its Greek parallels occur in the Old Testament mostly as the object of worshipping[79]. Only in Isa 34,4 is it said that "the heavenly host shall crumble into nothing" (*mqq*) on the Day of the Lord, and here the expression is not rendered by the LXX[80]. The combination with the motif of the eclipse of the sun, moon, and stars suggests that αἱ δυνάμεις in v. 25b takes up, in a more general way, the subjects of vv. 24b-25a[81]. This may explain the use of the plural. Mark has the plural of

werden, da bedeuten sie den Höhepunkt der 'Drangsal' oder den Beginn des Gerichts. Hier fehlt Beides, und das Bruchstückhafte der Überlieferung ist von Neuem offenbar. In der ungeheuren Leere und Finsternis erscheint 'mit vielem Glanz' der Menschensohn auf Wolken" (*Mk*, p. 279). Even if the passage would be "ein ungewolltes Fragment", the absence of a reference to judgement is striking.

78. In the *Exagoge* of the jewish-hellenistic author Ezechiel Tragicus (text preserved in Eusebius, *Praep. Ev.* 9,29,5,12), the episode of Ex 3,2-4 is preceded by an account of a dream of Moses in which he sees the Lord at Mt Zion and is put on His throne from where he contemplates heaven and earth, "and a multitude of stars fell down at his knees" (καί μοί τι πλῆθος ἀστέρων πρὸς γούνατα ἔπιπτ'... κἀμοῦ παρῆγεν ὡς παρεμβολὴ βροτῶν). "L'épisode est évidemment inventé, car l'Exode n'offre rien de pareil, mais il ne constitue, pensons-nous, qu'un dédoublement de la théophanie du buisson ardent": L. CERFAUX, *Influence des mystères sur le judaïsme alexandrin avant Philon*, in *Le Muséon* 37 (1924) 29-88, here p. 44 (= *Recueil L. Cerfaux*, I, 1954, p. 86).

79. 2 Kings 21,5 par 2 Chron 33,5; in Jer 19,13 and Zeph 1,5 as worshipping "on the roofs". Often also in combination with the sun, moon, and/or stars (Deut 4,19; 17,3; Jer 8,2), with the cult of Baal (2 Kings 17,16; 21,3; 23,4 par 2 Chron 33,3), or with both (2 Kings 23,5). In 1 Kings 22,19 par 2 Chron 18,18 the heavenly host stands near to God's throne; in Neh 9,6 it worships him.

80. Together with Zeph 1,5, it is the only passage that belongs to the tradition of the Day of Yahweh.

81. This is the common understanding of αἱ δυνάμεις in v. 25b. Cf. PESCH, *Naherwartungen*, p. 165; GNILKA, *Mk* II, p. 201. For P. JOÜON, *"Les forces des cieux seront ébranlées"*, in *RSR* 29 (1939) 114-115, αἱ δυνάμεις refer to "les forces par lesquelles les

οὐρανός also in 1,10.11; 11,25; 12,25. The formulation in 11,25 (ὁ πατὴρ ὑμῶν ὁ ἐν τοῖς οὐρανοῖς) is identical with that of 13,25[82]. But perhaps there is also some influence of the Theophany tradition. The motif of the shaking of the heavens occurs in the two passages that are considered by Jeremias to be the best representatives of the oldest form of that tradition (Judg 5,4; Ps 67(68),8-9)[83]. In the second of these οὐρανός is in the plural in the LXX. It is of course possible that this is due to the LXX translators of the Psalms since more than half (28 out of 51) of the occurrences of οὐρανός in the plural are from the Psalms. But the Psalms also contain some of the best examples of a description of the theophany of the Lord. And if not all of them do mention the shaking of the heavens[84], the motif is found with the plural of οὐρανός in Ps 143(144),5 κλῖνον οὐρανοὺς καὶ κατάβηθι, and again in Ps 17(18),9 οὐρανὸν (S² -οὺς) ἔκλινεν καὶ κατέβη, and also in its source, 2 Sam 22,10 ἔκλινεν οὐρανούς[85]. On the other hand, when the same motif occurs in descriptions of the Day of Yahweh, it is used in the singular (cf. Joel 2,10; 4,16; Isa 13,13, but see Aquila οὐρανοὺς κλονήσω). The resumptive use of δύναμις in Mk may account for the expression in v. 25b (following a recension that renders the full text of Isa 34,4). But there is also a remarkable agreement with the Theophany tradition in the plural of οὐρανός.

The influence of that tradition becomes fully apparent at the end of v. 25b, with the verb σαλεύω. "It is a standard term in OT descriptions of theophany"[86]. Beasley-Murray calls it "a curious fact" that the verb is used here, as it does not occur in the Day-of-Yahweh passages behind vv. 24-25. This would be a clear indication that the parousia is to be understood as a theophany. I think that is a correct conclusion, even though in none of the Theophany passages referred to by Beasley-Murray is σαλεύω used with οὐρανός as its subject. It is said of the earth or its foundations[87],

cieux se maintiennent dans une parfaite immobilité" (see LAMBRECHT, *Redaktion*, pp. 175-176). For different opinions, cf. above n. 3. B. STANDAERT, *L'évangile selon Marc*, Brugge, 1978, p. 234, sees a double parallelism in vv. 24-25 (αα σκοτισθήσεται / α'β οὐ δώσει τὸ φέγγος, and bβ' ἔσονται πίπτοντες / b'α' σαλευθήσονται), but such a structure disregards the meaning of οἱ ἀστέρες... πίπτοντες in v. 25a (connected with 24) and of αἱ δυνάμεις in v. 25b (resuming the subjects of v. 24-25a).

82. Cf. LAMBRECHT, *Redaktion*, p. 175 n. 4.

83. Cf. JEREMIAS, *Theophanie*, pp. 10-11.

84. Ps 49(50),6 and 96(97),6 have ἀναγγελοῦσιν οἱ οὐρανοὶ τὴν δικαιοσύνην.

85. Many of the other instances of the plural of οὐρανός in Pss and in other books are doxologies and standard formulas of exhortation to praise the Lord.

86. BEASLEY-MURRAY, *Jesus and the Last Days*, p. 424.

87. Cf. Amos 9,5 ὁ θεὸς... ὁ ἐφαπτόμενος τῆς γῆς καὶ σαλεύων αὐτήν; Hab 3,6 ἔστη καὶ ἐσαλεύθη ἡ γῆ; Ps 76(77),19 and 113(114),7 ἐσαλεύθη ἡ γῆ. And Job 9,6 ὁ σείων τὴν ὑπ᾽ οὐρανὸν ἐκ θεμελίων, οἱ δὲ στῦλοι αὐτῆς σαλεύονται. G.L. ARCHER

of the mountains and the hills[88], or of both the earth and the mountains (cf. below n. 92).

The shaking of the heavens is expressed in Hebrew, and rendered by the LXX, with a variety of verbs. In passages from the Theophany tradition one finds ἐξίστημι and στάζω for MT *ntf*[89], συνταράσσω for MT *rgz*[90], and κλίνω for MT *nṭh*[91]. But once, in a passage that is not mentioned by Beasley-Murray, one also finds σαλεύω. Sir 16,18-19 LXX reads ἰδοὺ ὁ οὐρανὸς καὶ ὁ οὐρανὸς τοῦ οὐρανοῦ, ἄβυσσος καὶ γῆ ἐν τῇ ἐπισκοπῇ αὐτοῦ σαλευθήσονται· ἅμα τὰ ὄρη καὶ τὰ θεμέλια τῆς γῆς ἐν τῷ ἐπιβλέψαι εἰς αὐτὰ τρόμῳ συσσείονται[92].

In passages on the Day of Yahweh the motif is expressed with θυμόω for MT *rgz* in Isa 13,13 (cf. above n. 64) and with σείω for MT *r'š* in Joel 2,10; 4,16 (σεισθήσεται ὁ οὐρανός). Θυμόω is a common rendering for *rgz* (cf. above n. 90: 2 Sam 22,8), but it is hardly appropriate in a combination with οὐρανός and seems to have been influenced by the second half of v. 13[93]. Σείω also is a common rendering of *r'š*, especially for 'the shaking of the earth', in Day-of-Yahweh (Isa 13,13) and more often in Theophany passages (Judg 5,4; 2 Sam 22,8; Ps 67(68),8)[94]. The only other occurrences of σείω (*r'š*; Act.) with

– G. CHIRICHIGNO, *Old Testament Quotations in the New Testament*, Chicago, IL, 1983, pp. 99-100, while denying Mk 13,25b "all quotation status, since it finds no clear source either in the MT or LXX", nevertheless refer to Job 9,6 because σείω "is very close" to σαλεύω.

88. Judg 5,5 ὄρη ἐσαλεύθησαν; Micah 1,4 σαλευθήσεται τὰ ὄρη; Isa 64,1 Th ὄρη ἐσαλεύθησαν (LXX τακήσονται); Nahum 1,5 οἱ βουνοὶ ἐσαλεύθησαν.

89. Judg 5,4A ὁ οὐρανὸς ἐξεστάθη and B ὁ οὐρανὸς ἔσταξεν δρόσους; in both recensions the text continues as καὶ αἱ νεφέλαι ἔσταξαν (*ntf*) ὕδωρ· ὄρη ἐσαλεύθησαν (only here for *zll*) ἀπὸ προσώπου κυρίου. See also Ps 67(68),8 οἱ οὐρανοὶ ἔσταξαν ἀπὸ προσώπου τοῦ θεοῦ. A more common translation of *ntf* is (ἀπο)στάζω (2/5) or (ἀπο)σταλάζω (2/1).

90. 2 Sam 22,8 καὶ ἐταράχθη καὶ ἐσείσθη ἡ γῆ, καὶ τὰ θεμέλια τοῦ οὐρανοῦ συνεταράχθησαν (A ἐτ.) καὶ ἐταράχθησαν, ὅτι ἐθυμώθη κύριος αὐτούς. The parallel in Ps 17(18),8 has τῶν ὀρέων for τοῦ οὐρανοῦ and an interesting variation of verbs: καὶ ἐσαλεύθη (*n'š*) καὶ ἔντρομος ἐγενήθη ἡ γῆ, καὶ τὰ θεμέλια τῶν ὀρέων ἐταράχθησαν καὶ ἐσαλεύθησαν (*n'š* hitp.), ὅτι ὠργίσθη αὐτοῖς ὁ θεός. In LXX *rgz* is frequently rendered by (συν)ταράσσω (1/8), by (παρ)οργίζω and θυμόω, twice by σείω (below n. 94), and once by σαλεύω: Ps 76(77),19.

91. 2 Sam 22,10 par. Ps 17(18),9, and Ps 143(144),5 (cf. above). Though there are other instances of (ἐκ)κλίνω for *nṭh*, the verb does not occur elsewhere with οὐρανός.

92. The verb should be read with ἄβυσσος καὶ γῆ and with ὁ οὐρανὸς καὶ ὁ οὐρανὸς τοῦ οὐρανοῦ (= οὐρανοί: cf. TestLevi 3,9). MT *mwṭ* is probably corrupt: cf. JEREMIAS, *Theophanie*, p. 22.

93. The younger translators all three have the verb in the first pers. Act. Ind. fut. with οὐρανόν (A -ούς) as its object. Θ retains θυμόω and A introduces his favorite κλονέω (not in LXX), but Σ has ταράσσω, which is no doubt the better choice.

94. For other instances of σείω said of the earth, see Job 9,6 and Prov 30,21 LXX (*rgz*); Isa 24,18 (*r'š*) and 20 (*nwd*[bis] hitp., only here; LXX ἔκλινε καὶ σεισθήσεται); Jer

οὐρανός (sg.) besides Joel 2,10 and 4,16 are in Hag 2,7(6) σείσω τὸν οὐρανόν and 2,22(21) σείω τὸν οὐρανόν. These two passages represent a later development of the Theophany genre in which the shaking of the heaven has become almost an independent motif that is used to characterize the theophany of the Lord as a universal event and as "ein neues Heilshandeln"[95].

On the assumption that v. 25b goes back to a reading such as the one in Isa 34,4a Th/LXX B (τακήσονται), the omission of τήκω is no surprise. The image of Isa 34,4a is strange (*mqq*/τήκω of the heavenly host). Τήκω never is used with "the heavens" as subject and the textual tradition of Isa 34,4a LXX shows that the copyists have suggested variant readings for it (cf. above). But the verb occurs in a combination with σαλεύω in descriptions of the Theophany of the Lord[96]. Τήκω and σαλεύω are not unrelated in that tradition.

The survey has shown that there is a wide variety, both in the Hebrew and in the Greek, in the use of the verb to express the shaking of the heavens. Σείω figures in the description of the Theophany in Hag 2,6.21. It is also found in both passages from Joel, and that may have been the very reason not to use it in 13,24-25. If it was the intention to differentiate from the Day-of-Yahweh tradition, σαλεύω provided a good alternative. This verb, which may have been suggested by τήκω, is frequently used in Theophany descriptions and the only instance in which it occurs with the heaven(s) as its subject is in such a context (Sir 16,18). Σαλεύω may be decisive proof that in Mk 13,24-25 the parousia is thought of as a theophany of the Son of man in glory.

8,16; 27(50),46; 28(51),29; 29(49),21 (all *r'š*); and Dan 2,40 LXX; 1 Macc 1,28; 9,13. In the description of the theophany in Nahum 1,5 it is said of the mountains (*r'š*): τὰ ὄρη ἐσείσθησαν ἀπ᾽ αὐτοῦ, followed by καὶ οἱ βουνοὶ ἐσαλεύθησαν (cf. above n. 88).

95. "Aus dem Beben der Berge ist ein Beben des gesamten Universums geworden; sie erzittern nicht mehr vor Jahwes Kommen, sondern ihre Erschütterung ist die Ankündigung dafür, daß Jahwe eine neue Wende des Geschickes seines Volkes herbeiführt" (JEREMIAS, *Theophanie*, pp. 68-69).

96. Cf. Micah 1,4 σαλευθήσεται τὰ ὄρη... καὶ αἱ κοιλάδες τακήσονται ὡς κηρός; Nahum 1,5-6 τὰ ὄρη ἐσείσθησαν ἀπ᾽ αὐτοῦ, καὶ οἱ βουνοὶ ἐσαλεύθησαν· καὶ ἀνεστάλη ἡ γῆ... καὶ τίς ἀντιστήσεται ἐν ὀργῇ θυμοῦ αὐτοῦ; ὁ θυμὸς αὐτοῦ τήκει ἀρχάς, καὶ αἱ πέτραι διεθρύβησαν ἀπ᾽ αὐτοῦ; Hab 3,6 ἐσαλεύθη ἡ γῆ... διεθρύβη τὰ ὄρη βίᾳ, ἐτάκησαν βουνοὶ αἰώνιοι; Isa 64,1-2a Th οὐκ ἐρήξας οὐρανούς καὶ κατέβης ἀπὸ προσώπου σου ὄρη ἐσαλεύθησαν, ὡς ἔκκαυσιν πυρὸς ἐτάκησαν ὕδατα ἐξεκαύσας πῦρ and LXX ἐὰν ἀνοίξῃς τὸν οὐρανόν, τρόμος λήμψεται ἀπὸ σοῦ ὄρη, καὶ τακήσονται ὡς κηρὸς ἀπὸ πυρὸς τήκεται; Ps 96(97),4-5 ἐσαλεύθη ἡ γῆ. τὰ ὄρη ἐτάκησαν; Jdt 16,15 ὄρη γὰρ ἐκ θεμελίων σὺν ὕδασιν σαλευθήσεται, πέτραι δ᾽ ἀπὸ προσώπου σου ὡς κηρὸς τακήσονται. In Isa 34,4 τήκω renders *mqq*. It is one of thirteen verbs that are translated by τήκω in LXX. Among them are also *mwg* and *mmm*, which both are rendered by σαλεύω in Theophany passages: cf. *mwg* Ps 45(46),5 and Amos 9,5 (qal); Nahum 1,5 (hitp.); *mmm* Micah 1,4 (ni.).

4. *The Parousia in Mk 13*

There are negative (no mention of judgement) and positive indications (the origin of the motif of the shaking of the heavens, the verb σαλεύω, and perhaps also the plural of οὐρανός) that vv. 24-25 are to be interpreted from the Theophany tradition. But it remains yet to be explained why the coming of the Son of man is expressed with cosmic signs. It is often said that the images do not matter. I would rather say: it is the imagery that is of interest, not the texts from which they are borrowed. In its most common form the appearance of Yahweh in the Theophany passages of the Old Testament is located on earth (often it is a mountain) and expressed by a relatively "natural" event (usually a storm)[97]. The eclipse and the shaking of the heavens introduce an aspect of universalism[98], which is particularly appropriate in the context of an apocalyptic discourse describing the theophany of the Son of man as an eschatological event[99].

In Jewish tradition the cosmic signs were used only with regard to God. In vv. 24-27 they describe the appearance of the *Son of man* as a universal and eschatological event. It is "der entscheidende Unterschied"[100]. The section is a Christian composition. This is now also widely recognized by authors who argue that Mark has incorporated in chapter 13 a written document which included vv. 24-27[101]. For Hahn

---

97. Cf. T. Hiebert, art. *Theophany in the OT*, in *Anchor Bible Dictionary*, 6, pp. 505-511, esp. 505 and 508: mountains are the location of "the most significant theophanies"; and "the most common natural form of divine appearance in Israelite literature is the thunderstorm". "Als Zielort der Theophanie gilt verbreitet der Berg Zion" (Scriba, *Theophanie*, p. 42). The idea is that God comes to reside in the temple and this is considered an act of salvation or restoration. "Früh und verbreitet ist der Motivkomplex der Jahwe-Theophanie mit... der Erscheinung des Wettergottes im Gewitter zur Machtsdemonstration (verbunden worden)" (*ibid.*, pp. 14-21, here 14).

98. Cf. the quotation of Jeremias on Hag 2,6.21 (above n. 95).

99. Commenting on the developments in the representation of the Theophany in Christian texts, Scriba observes: "Die Eschatologisierung der Theophanievorstellung (hat wohl) eine zunehmende Distanz zur theophanen Deutung von Naturphänomenen wie Erdbeben und Gewitter geschaffen" (*Theophanie*, p. 195). For Gundry, *Mk*, p. 745, the images "provide a black curtain against which the glory of the Son of man's coming shines out all the more"; cf. also P.S. Minear, *Some Archetypal Origins of Apocalyptic Predictions*, in *Horizons* 1 (1979) 105-135, here 108.

100. Vögtle, *Die "Gretchenfrage"*, p. 105.

101. It used to be a common assumption in the *Vorlage*-hypothesis that Mark relied on a Jewish text which had its origin in the Caligula crisis of 40 A.D. (G. Hölscher, *Der Ursprung der Apokalypse Mrk 13*, in *TBl* 12 [1933] 192-202) and had eventually been misused in Mark's community (so Pesch, *Naherwartungen*, pp. 207-214). G. Theissen, who continues to defend the connection with Caligula, admits nevertheless that the document was a Christian one from the outset: it was their response to the crisis (not resistance but flight in the expectation of the imminent parousia), an attitude which con-

and Pesch the origin of the document is evident from such clearly Christian verses as 13,9b.11.13.28-31[102]. Brandenburger, who limits the *Vorlage* to 13,7-8.14-20.24-27 and rightly differentiates between his position and that of Hahn and Pesch[103], argues that the text must have originated in a milieu that still could be impressed by the imminent destruction of the temple, yet did no longer think of a rescue from this threat in terms of contemporary Jewish expectations[104]. "Bestimmend ist für die Vorlage das Fluchtmotiv; und das bedeutet, daß sich für sie im Ausstrahlungsbereich des Tempelfrevels und des Zion schlechterdings nur Unheilsgeschehen ereignen kann. ... Es gibt hier eben keine explizite Aussage eines Vernichtungsgerichts über die gegen Heiligtum und Gottesvolk frevelnde Weltmacht Rom... Es findet sich vor allem auch nicht die geringste Andeutung über den in Herrlichkeit wieder auferbauten Zion". The Jewish-Christian community of Jerusalem qualifies as a possible "Trägerkreis" for such expectations as those of vv. 24-27[105].

Vv. 24-27 witness to the ongoing christological interpretation of the figure of the Son of man in the Early Church, and this especially also with regard to his theophany. "Es besteht also Grund zur Annahme, in solcher Ausbildung der Menschensohnanschauung ein urchristliches Charakteristikum zu sehen"[106]. The expectation of the theophany of the

tributed to increase the gap with the Jews: *Lokalkolorit und Zeitgeschichte in den Evangelien. Ein Beitrag zur Geschichte der synoptischen Tradition* (NTOA, 8), Freiburg–Göttingen, 1989, pp. 133-176, esp. 174. See now also N. TAYLOR, *Palestinian Christianity and the Caligula Crisis*, in *JSNT* 61 (1996) 101-124 and 62 (1996) 13-41: 13,24-27 reflects the experience of "delayed *parousia* hopes in the aftermath of the Caligula crisis" (p. 37).

102. HAHN, *Die Rede*, p. 260; PESCH, *Mk* II, p. 266.

103. BRANDENBURGER, *Markus 13*, p. 65 n. 138.

104. Flavius Josephus provides a good illustration of how the Jewish population of Jerusalem and its leaders thought of the ending of the war. In BJ 6,288-304 he reports about a series of portents which happen to the temple and are mistakenly interpreted by the Jews as indications of God's help. The section is preceded by the account of the death of 6000 people who had taken refuge in a portico of the outer court. And Josephus comments that they had been misled by false prophets to expect the parousia of Yahweh to occur in the temple at that critical moment (6,285). The portents which are recalled in 6,288-304 illustrate that this help was to be provided by Yahweh manifesting himself in the temple. O. Michel points out that, though Josephus puts the blame on the Zealots, "die jüdischen Führer selbst unter dem Einfluß der apokalyptischen Weissagung standen und im subjektiven Sinn nicht Verführer des Volkes waren, wie Josephus meint" (O. MICHEL – O. BAUERNFEIND, *De Bello Iudaico. Der Jüdische Krieg*, II,2, Darmstadt, 1969, p. 179).

105. BRANDENBURGER, *Markus 13*, pp. 68-69. Cf. SCRIBA, *Theophanie*, pp. 209-210.

106. BRANDENBURGER, *Markus 13*, p. 70. "Der Ausbau der urchristlichen Menschensohnanschauung (ist) in einem wichtigen Teilbereich unter dem Leitgedanken der Theophanie erfolgt" (*ibid.*, p. 71); on the development of this identification of the Son of man with Christ, see also his *Das Recht des Weltenrichters. Untersuchung zu Matthäus 25,31-46* (SBS, 99), Stuttgart, 1980, pp. 35-55.

Son of man functions within the assumptions and the aims of the *Vorlage* as they are formulated by Brandenburger. But there are no indications that this description of the parousia of the Son of man has originally been conceived as an answer or as a reaction to current Jewish eschatological expectations with regard to the fate of the temple or its vindication by God. In so far, the imagery of vv. 24-27 is not linked exclusively to the alleged *Vorlage*. Rather, vv. 24-27 reflect the way Christians came to think about the parousia of the Risen Lord as the Son of man. For Vögtle, e.g., the section certainly was not part of a Jewish, and nor of a Jewish-Christian apocalypse[107]. Moreover, even those who argue that there are few undisputed traces of Markan redaction in vv. 24-27 and that there is no evidence that Mark was responsible for the composition of the whole section[108], have no reason to assume a priori that, if Mark took over the description from oral tradition or even from a written document, he felt bound to his source, so as to allow no changes to it[109]. In that perspective, it is important to observe, first, that Mark does not speak of judgement or of the Day of Yahweh, and second, that the universal character of the images and the description of vv. 24-27 (with moreover a focus on salvation) is in line with what Mark has to say in v. 10 about the mission "to all nations" which has to precede the parousia[110]. Perhaps that is the most one can say with regard to Mark's han-

107. Cf. *Die "Gretchenfrage"*, p. 105 and 106 ("eine ältere judenchristliche Vorlage"); cf. already *Die Zukunft des Kosmos*, p. 69.

108. But see J. LAMBRECHT, *Redaktion*, pp. 175 and 192-193, who regards the variation in the choice of the verbal forms in vv. 24-25 as the result of Mark's redaction, and who also points to the periphrastic construction in v. 25a ("markinisch") and to the paraphrase of the genitive with αἱ ἐν τοῖς οὐρανοῖς. One cannot say that the periphrastic construction is not common in Mark (so PESCH, *Naherwartungen*, p. 160). Pesch describes the change from the singular to the plural of οὐρανός in a way in which others would argue for Markan redaction (p. 161: "Markus verwendet οὐρανός im Singular und im Plural. Vielleicht ist der Übergang [in V. 25]... ein Hinweis darauf, daß die beiden Verse als synthetischer Parallelismus verstanden sein wollen"). For J. MARCUS, *The Way of the Lord. Christological Exegesis of the Old Testament in the Gospel of Mark*, Edinburgh, 1993, p. 15, Mk 13,24-26 is one of many passages which illustrate that "the fusion of two or more scriptural passages into one conflated citation is a characteristic Markan method of biblical usage"; cf. already, KEE, *Function*, pp. 175-178.

109. See my *Persecution and Eschatology* (above n. 23), p. 1158. Mark has added several sections to his source (esp. in Brandenburger's reconstruction of the *Vorlage*). With regard to vv. 24-27, one may agree with Brandenburger and others that the addition of v. 23 and of the second time reference in v. 24 (μετὰ τὴν θλῖψιν ἐκείνην), which are generally ascribed to Markan redaction, do not substantially change the pattern of his source (*Markus 13*, p. 85; see also PESCH, *Naherwartungen*, pp. 158 and 174, and *Mk* II, p. 311).

110. Regardless of the origin of the verse, it is widely accepted that v. 10 was most probably no part of the *Vorlage* and may have been inserted in the chapter by Mark (cf. BRANDENBURGER, *Markus 13*, p. 32). The preaching of the gospel has been interpreted as

dling of vv. 24-27, but it may be a significant indication of how he understood the parousia of the Son of man.

The transfer of certain motifs from one tradition to another begins already in the Old Testament, and the texts that are behind Mk 13,24-25 are the very illustration of this (cf. above on the influence of Theophany motifs in Joel). The eclipse and the shaking of the heavens can be used in quite distinct contexts. What turns them into "metaphors of judgement" is the explicit mention of God's judgement (as in Isa 13,6.9-10; 34,4-5.8; Joel 2,10-11; 4,15-16). When these motifs are taken out of that context, as in Mk 13,24-27, the connotation is lost. The section is more than a somewhat random collection of OT passages. The texts behind vv. 24-25 have been chosen because of the images they contain. But they have been quoted selectively and they have been reformulated (esp. σαλεύω) so that they might be used to express the "unimaginable" (Beasley-Murray) but universally recognizable theophany of the Son of man to assemble the elect which, according to Mark, is expected to happen in the end time[111].

Berglaan 32   Joseph VERHEYDEN
B-3001 Leuven   Senior Research Associate FSR (FWO)

a criterion for judgement of the persecutors, but even authors who argue that v. 26 refers to the judgement of the end time point out that the "Gerichtsgedanke" of v. 10 differs from that of v. 26 (*ibid.*: "V. 24-27 als Pendant zu V. 7f.14-20"). However, there is perhaps a more fundamental connection between v. 10 and vv. 24-27. "Mk 13,10 setzt eine Tradition voraus, nach welcher die Völkermission durch den Hinweis auf die nahe Heilswende gerechtfertigt wurde und ihren eigentlichen Impuls erhielt": G. DAUTZENBERG, *Das Wort von der weltweiten Verkündigung des Evangeliums (Mk 13,10) und seine Vorgeschichte* (ErfTS, 59), Leipzig, 1989, pp. 150-165, esp. 159.

111. In a recent article, F.G. Downing has gathered evidence from pagan (Latin) literature of the first century AD dealing with "the end of the world" (esp. Seneca and Pliny): cf. *Cosmic Eschatology in the First Century: "Pagan", Jewish and Christian*, in *L'Antiquité Classique* 64 (1995) 99-109 (partially reproduced in *Common Strands in Pagan, Jewish and Christian Eschatologies in the First Century*, in *TZ* 51 [1995] 169-211). If, as he contends, "people at large in the Mediterranean world of late antiquity would recognise the imagery" of Mk 13,24-25 (107 = 202; he also refers to Rev 6,12-14 and 2 Pet 3,3-13), it should be added that most of them probably understood only part of it. The imagery describes the parousia of the Lord at the end of time.

The argument for vv. 24-25 should be completed with an analysis of v. 26 (and 27). For Pesch, the interpretation of v. 26 is related to that of vv. 24-25. This means that if my interpretation of vv. 24-25 is correct, it should direct the understanding of v. 26.

LUKE'S USE OF *ΜΙΜΗΣΙΣ*?

RE-OPENING THE DEBATE

Introduction[1]

The purpose of this paper is to focus on the thesis, mainly proposed by Thomas Louis Brodie, that Luke used an ancient rhetorical technique, known as *imitatio* or μίμησις, to imitate narratives from his Jewish Scriptures. Brodie did his doctorate on *Luke the Literary Interpreter* (1987)[2] and published some articles on this issue since 1979[3] in which he tried to identify (sometimes too eagerly?) some places in Luke's gospel where Luke probably made use of this technique. The question is: Did Luke make use of μίμησις or not? The use of μίμησις by Paul can be proved from his letters[4]. But when turning to the Lukan literature the matter seems to be somewhat more complicated. The term itself, for instance, is not found in the Lukan literature. Without taking a definite position to either side, I would rather like to keep the debate going and to contribute to this debate by supplying more data which need to be taken into account when this issue is discussed. But let us first look at the theory of μίμησις.

1. Μίμησις as an Ancient Technique

The word group μιμέομαι is absent in the works of Homer and Hesiod and only appears during the 6th century BC in poetry and prose[5]. It became

---

1. This paper was first presented as a draft during a seminar at the Department of Greek and Latin studies at the Rand Afrikaans University on 6 June 1996. Collegues in the department deserve a special word of thanks for their comments which helped in the shaping of this contribution. The shorter version, as read at the *Colloquium Biblicum Lovaniense* in 1996, is published here. A longer and more expanded version will be published elsewhere.

2. T.L. BRODIE, *Luke the Literary Interpreter. Luke-Acts as a Systematic Rewriting and Updating of the Elijah-Elisha Narrative in 1 and 2 Kings*, Rome, 1987.

3. Cf., for instance, T.L. BRODIE, *A New Temple and a New Law*, in *JSNT* 5 (1979) 21-45; ID. *Luke 7,36-50 as an Internalization of 2 Kings 4,1-37: A Study in Luke's Use of Rhetorical Imitation*, in *Biblica* 64 (1983) 457-485; ID. *Greco-Roman Imitation of Texts as a Partial Guide to Luke's Use of Sources*, in C.H. TALBERT (ed.), *Luke-Acts: New Perspectives from the Society of Biblical Literature Seminar*, New York, 1984, pp. 17-46.

4. Cf. for instance: 1 Thess 1,6; 2,14; 2 Thess 3,7.9; 1 Cor 4,16; 11,1; Eph 5,1; Phil 3,17. See also W.J. ONG, *Mimesis and the Following of Christ*, in *Religion and Literature* 26/2 (1994) 73-77.

5. W. MICHAELIS, s.v. μιμέομαι in: G. KITTEL, *TWNT* IV, Stuttgart, 1942, p. 661.

particularly prominent in the works of Plato[6]. McKeon, who summarised the use of μίμησις in antiquity, particularly in Plato and Aristotle, points out that it is difficult to confine Plato's use of this term into one particular meaning. It is used in a universal sense, sometimes "in a broader sense to include all human activities" and sometimes "applied even more broadly to all processes – human, natural, cosmic, and divine"[7]. Plato used μίμησις to distinguish three kinds of poetic style: "pure narrative, in which the poet speaks in his own person without imitation, as in the dithyramb; narrative by means of imitation, in which the poet speaks in the person of his characters, as in comedy and tragedy; and mixed narrative, in which the poet speaks now in his own person and now by means of imitation"[8]. Alternative or related terminology to μίμησις started to appear. This terminology included: εἰκάζειν (copy), ὅμοια (resemblances), τύπος (pattern), ἀφομοιοῦσθαι (assimilate), πλάττειν (mold), παραδείγμα (model), εἴδωλον (image), etc. It is important to note also that all verbal accounts were seen as imitations and that, according to Plato, things which are familiar were easier to imitate than those which were unfamiliar. The unfamiliar is difficult to imitate in action, and even more difficult in words[9]. Even the "component parts of poems, discourses, and dialogues are imitations,"[10] and therefore "one should make one's thought clear by means of verbs and nouns, modeling (ἐκτυποῦν) opinion in the stream that flows through the lips as in a mirror or in water"[11]. For Aristotle, however, "the term is restricted definitely to a single literal meaning"[12]. He repeatedly cites the phrase that "art imitates nature". But the use of μίμησις was not only applied to the natural arts – also to the literary word. Isocrates said in this regard around 400 BC: "*The teacher...must...set such an example (παραδεῖγμα) of oratory that the students who...are able to pattern (μιμήσασθαι) after him will...show a degree of grace and charm which is not found in others*".

2. *Possible Traces of μίμησις in the Lukan Literature?*

In comparison with studies on quotations and phrases, only a few studies were conducted in the past on the motifs as units which were taken over by writers from their known literature. This despite the fact that studies on the motifs seem to be the field where the real struggle took place to determine

6. See, for instance, his *Epistulae, Cratylus, Timaeus, Sophista, Respublica,* etc.
7. R. McKEON, *Literary Criticism and the Concept of Imitation in Antiquity,* in *Modern Philology* 34 (1936) 1-35, here p. 3.
8. *Ibid.,* 5. Cf. Plato's *Respublica* III, 392D-394C.
9. Cf. *Timaeus* 19D-20B.
10. R. McKEON, *Concept of Imitation,* p. 8.
11. *Ibid.,* p. 12. Cf. *Theaetetus* 206D.
12. *Ibid.,* p. 16.

the extent and function of material used from the Jewish "Scriptures" in the documents of what is known today as the "New Testament". The gospel according to Luke presents itself as a very good case study. Not only are explicit quotations found here, but it is also drenched with broader motifs from those Jewish Scriptures. Most scholars, however, agree that Luke's knowledge of these Scriptures came from the Greek Septuagint versions. The question is now: Did Luke made use of the *Jewish* hermeneutical methods, or did he make use of the *Greek* methods, e.g. the rhetorical technique, μίμησις, when he used and re-interpreted the material from his Jewish Scriptures? The question inevitably leads one back again into the tough debate about *who Luke was* – a Jew or a Greek? If he was a Jew, which this author believes, then he definitely was a *Hellenistic* Jew. He probably grew up outside the borders of Palestine and was taught the Jewish Scriptures in its translated Greek form ("Septuagint" version) since his childhood. But, he also must have had, like somebody such as Josephus[13], a thorough training in, or exposure to, Greek and Roman literature, philosophy and rhetoric. This is clear from his use of the Greek language and the quotation from the *Phaenómena* of the Greek poet Aratus, in Acts 17,28.

Kurz[14] mentioned that "what we know of the Greco-Roman rhetorical and educational practice of *imitation* of earlier sources indicates, rather, a concern to apply traditional material creatively to new situations and themes. One aspect of this in historiography is the expectation that new authors will rewrite their sources in their own style. If T. Brodie is right in identifying this ancient rhetorical technique in Luke's gospel, then it should be present in the *manner* (or form), rather than the *matter* (or contents) of what his source texts contained. This means that it would not be so much the contents of the material which will overlap, as the overall structure, or pattern, which will resemble that of the literature which was used when compiling his gospel. This seems indeed to be the case in motifs such as the examples listed below:

The motif of infertility

The nativity stories in Lk 1–2 which seemed to be based on the birth narratives of the patriachs and Samson in the Septuagint version. As some of these examples were published elsewhere[15], I will only summa-

---

13. Cf. T. RAJAK, *Josephus: The Historian and His Society*, Philadelphia, 1983, p. 43.

14. W.S. KURZ, *Intertextual Use of Sirach 48.1-16 in Plotting Luke-Acts*, in C.A. EVANS & W.R. STEGNER (eds.), *The Gospels and the Scriptures of Israel* (JSNT SS, 104), Sheffield, 1994, pp. 308-323, here 310.

15. Cf. G.J. STEYN, *Die manifestering van LXX-invloed in die "Sondergut-Lukas"*, in *HTS* 45/4 (1989) 864-873.

rize the Abraham/Sarah —> Zechariah/Elizabeth synopsis and that of Samson.

(a) Abraham/Sarah —> Zechariah/Elizabeth

Genesis 11-18	*Luke 1,5-25*
Sarah is στεῖρα (11,30)	Elizabeth is στεῖρα (1,7)
Abraham and Sarah are advanced in years, προβεβηκότες (18,11)	So are Zechariah and Elizabeth, προβεβηκότες (1,7)
Abraham is approached by God: εἶπεν... ὁ θεὸς (17,16)	Zechariah is approached by God: εἶπεν δὲ... ὁ ἄγγελος (1,13)
The message is: a son will be born and his name should be... ἰδοὺ Σάρρα ἡ γυνή σου τέξεταί σοι υἱὸν, καὶ καλέσεις τὸ ὄνομα αὐτοῦ (17,19)	The same message: καὶ ἡ γυνή σου Ἐλισάβετ γεννήσει υἱόν σοι καὶ καλέσεις τὸ ὄνομα (1,13)
Abraham doubted God's promise (although not in this context!): κατὰ τί γνώσομαι ὅτι (15,8)	Zechariah doubted God's message: κατὰ τί γνώσομαι τοῦτο (1,18)
Abraham mentioned that he and Sarah are old (17,17)	Zechariah mentioned the same reason (1,18)
Abraham said later: μὴ ἀδυνατεῖ παρὰ τῷ θεῷ ῥῆμα (18,14)	Mary said later: ὅτι οὐκ ἀδυνατήσει παρὰ τοῦ θεοῦ πᾶν ῥῆμα (1,37)

Luke refers explicitly to Abraham in his nativity stories, in the Magnificat (1,55) and the Benedictus (1,73). We read later in the Nunc Dimittis: Νῦν ἀπολύεις τὸν δοῦλόν σου, δέσποτα, κατὰ τὸ ῥῆμά σου ἐν εἰρήνῃ (Lk 2,29) – which reminds one of the words of Abraham: συ δὲ ἀπελεύσῃ πρὸς τοὺς πατέρας σου μετ' εἰρήνης (Gen 15,15).

(b) Samson

	Judg 13, 2-5.24-25	Lk 1,7-80
Infertility	v.3	v.7
Announcement of pregnancy and birth of a son	v.3	vv.13,31
Abstaining from alcohol	v.4	v.15
Saviour of the people of Israel	v.5	vv.16,68,71
Set aside for their task from their mothers' womb	v.5	v.15
Grew up and "Spirit of the Lord drove them"	vv.24-25	vv.15,80

The motif of God testing his son

The Lukan temptation narrative (Lk 4,1-11) is another example of how the structure of an old narrative is used and filled with new contents. Although this is not "Lukan material", but "Q-material" which indicates that Luke and Matthew used the same source here, Luke has a different order from that of Mt 4,1-11, probably because he follows the sequence of events as described in Deut 6-8, where God's "other son" was tested. This motif was discussed in more detail elsewhere[16].

The motif of another Elijah

This motif has been touched upon several times in the past[17]. Traces of the tradition can be found in Mal 3,1.22-23 and in Mt 11,13-14; 17,10-13. Elements of this tradition have been taken up by Luke in the message of the angel to Zechariah (Lk 1,17) and in the Benedictus (1,76). The *crux* of this motif is found in Lk 7,24-28 where, by means of an explicit quotation from Mal 3,1 and presented as *verba ipsissima* of Jesus, this section is applied to John the Baptist.

Other elements of this "other Elijah" are also applied to Jesus himself. The resurrection story of the son of the widow of Nain by Jesus (Lk 7,11-17) seems to be based on the same structure as the resurrection narrative of the son of the widow of Sarphat by Elijah in the Septuagint version, 3 Kings 17,17-24. This was discussed in more detail elsewhere by Crockett[18], Nützel[19] and Brodie[20].

	3 Kings 17,17-24	*Luke 7,11-17*
A widow	καὶ ἰδοὺ ἐκεῖ γυνὴ χήρα	καὶ αὐτὴ ἦν χήρα
Her son	ὁ υἱὸς τῆς γυναικὸς τῆς κυρίας τοῦ οἴκου	μονογενὴς υἱὸς τῇ μητρὶ αὐτοῦ
The son died	θανατῶσαι τὸν υἱόν μου	ἐξεκομίζετο τεθνηκὼς
At the gate of the city	εἰς τὸν πυλῶνα τῆς πόλεως	ἤγγισεν τῇ πύλῃ τῆς πόλεως
The son is resurrected	καὶ ἀνεβόησεν τὸ παιδάριον	καὶ ἀνεκάθισεν ὁ νεκρὸς καὶ ἤρξατο λαλεῖν
The son is "given back"	καὶ ἔδωκεν αὐτὸν τῇ μητρὶ αὐτοῦ	καὶ ἔδωκεν αὐτὸν τῇ μητρὶ αὐτοῦ
Audience recognises the "man of God"	ἰδοὺ ἔγνωκα ὅτι ἄνθρωπος θεοῦ εἶ σύ	προφήτης μέγας ἠγέρθη ἐν ἡμῖν

16. G.J. STEYN, *Intertextual Similarities between Septuagint Pretexts and Luke's Gospel*, in *Neot* 24/2 (1990) 229-246.

17. E.g. C.A. EVANS, *Luke's Use of the Elijah/Elisha Narratives and the Ethic of Election*, in *JBL* 106 (1987) 75-83.

18. L.C. CROCKETT, *The Old Testament in the Gospel of Luke: With Emphasis on the Interpretation of Isaiah 61.1-2*, PhD, Michigan, 1966.

19. J.M. NÜTZEL, *Elijah- und Elischa-traditionen im Neuen Testament*, in *BiKi* 41 (1986) 160-171.

20. See T.L. BRODIE, *Towards Unravelling Luke's Use of the Old Testament: Luke 7.11-17 as an Imitatio of 1 Kings 17.17-24*, in *NTS* 32 (1986) 247-267.

The motif of the "Spirit of God" from the scroll of Isaiah

Isa 11,1-2 states that: καὶ ἐξελεύσεται ῥάβδος ἐκ τῆς ῥίζης Ιεσσαι καὶ ἄνθος ἐκ τῆς ῥίζης ἀναβήσεται. καὶ ἀναπαύσεται ἐπ᾽ αὐτὸν πνεῦμα τοῦ θεοῦ, πνεῦμα σοφίας καὶ συνέσεως, πνεῦμα βουλῆς καὶ ἰσχύος, πνεῦμα γνώσεως καὶ εὐσεβείας.

	Luke
The Spirit is present with John the Baptist	1,15.17
The Spirit impregnated Mary	1,35
The Spirit let Zechariah rejoice	1,67
The Spirit strengthens John	1,80
The Spirit is present at Jesus' baptism	3,22
The Spirit leads Jesus into the desert	4,1
The Spirit leads Jesus into Galilee	4,14
Jesus applies Isa 61 on himself	4,18

Conclusion

1. There is no doubt, on the one hand, that definite traces of narratives, story structures and even phraseological resemblances from Luke's Scriptures – particularly his LXX Scriptures – are to be found in the Lukan material. It must be said, however, and on the other hand, that similar traces are also to be found in other early Christian writers, and even before them already in the Jewish sources themselves. Therefore, before resemblances, such as these which were mentioned, are labelled as being due to μίμησις particularly, more proper comparisons between Luke's re-writing of narratives, copying of speeches or sections from prophetic literature, will have to be made with similar trends in other literature.

2. The traces of story structures, patterns or speeches cannot be denied. But how do these differ from what we currently classify as allusions? More research is needed to determine the extent and cohesiveness of these traces. If this cannot be proven, then we will have to agree that these are mere elements or motifs known from the tradition.

3. Should a case be made that Luke deliberately copied the structure and style of stories and speeches from his Scriptures in order to create and present the life and work of Jesus, then one must still clearly distinguish between the use of μίμησις by Luke as a literary technique, and the person and character of Jesus as an imitation of outstanding elements from the characters known from Luke's Scriptures. Luke's Jesus then becomes a character who obtains all the features of prominent figures in his Scriptures. He then reflects these characteristics in his ministry, like

a face is reflected in water or in a mirror – within the Platonic concepts of μίμησις.

Although this looks very tempting, much more research needs to be done before a more objective, measured and controlled choice could be made with regard to the fact whether Luke used μίμησις or not.

Rand Afrikaans University   Gert J STEYN
Department of Greek and Latin Studies
P.O. Box 524
2006 Aucklandpark
Johannesburg, South Africa

THE DOUBLE COMMANDMENT OF LOVE IN LK 10,27

A DEUTERONOMISTIC PILLAR OR LUKAN REDACTION OF MK 12,29-33?

Certain studies on the Lukan travel narrative (Lk 9,51–19,28) consider Lk 10,25-28 and 18,18-30 as two "Deuteronomistic pillars"[1]. The 'Shema' (Deut 6,4-5) in Lk 10,27 and the Decalogue (Deut 5,6-21) in 18,20 are supposed to be an important argument in favour of the "Deuteronomy hypothesis" which states that Luke used mainly or even exclusively the book of Deuteronomy as a model for his composition of the travel narrative[2]. A number of questions remain, however: in what sense are these pericopes inspired by Deuteronomy? Where did Luke read the quotations in the first place: in Deuteronomy or in Mark? Lk 18,20 has a clear parallel in Mk 10,19, but what can be said about the lawyer's quotation of Deut 6,5 and Lev 19,18 in Lk 10,27?

I. THE TEXT FORM OF THE QUOTATIONS IN LK 10,27 (AND PARALLELS)

This paper focuses on Lk 10,27 in which a lawyer (νομικός) recites the double love commandment. The formulation of the Old Testament quotations in Lk 10,27 is rather awkward. As a matter of fact, Luke does not cite the 'Shema' of Deut 6,4, but he offers a narrow combination of the command to love God of Deut 6,5 with the love command towards

---

1. D.P. MOESSNER, *Lord of the Banquet. The Literary and Theological Significance of the Lucan Travel Narrative,* Minneapolis, MN, 1989, p. 124: "It has been pointed out that the Central Section is framed or buttressed by the Deuteronomic 'pillars' of the Shema, 10:26-27 (Deut. 6:4-5), and the Decalogue, 18:20 (Deut. 5:6-21)". On p. 238, n. 163, Moessner contends that M.D. Goulder is the first to use this terminology in M.D. GOULDER, *The Chiastic Structure of the Lucan Journey,* in F.L. CROSS (ed.), *Studia Evangelica II* (TU, 87), Berlin, 1964, 195-202, p. 196. Goulder refers to C.F. EVANS, *The Central Section of St. Luke's Gospel,* in D.E. NINEHAM (ed.), *Studies in the Gospels. Essays in Memory of R.H. Lightfoot,* Oxford, 1955, pp. 37-53, who does not use that terminology. The 'pillar'-terminology, however, has already been employed by A.M. FARRER, *On Dispensing with Q,* in D.E. NINEHAM (ed.), *Studies,* 1957, pp. 55-86, here 79: "The Scribe's Question and the Rich Man's Question are the twin pillars which mark out the extent of St. Luke's Deuteronomy" (he is also referring to Evans, who does not use this terminology).

2. According to EVANS, *Central Section,* pp. 42-50, Luke followed the order of the book of Deuteronomy to compose his travel narrative: Lk 10,25-28 accords with Deut 6. Moessner defends a more thematic approach (four "Deuteronomistic" tenets). Between the Deuteronomistic pillars Lk 10,25-28 and Lk 18,18-30 the evangelist composes an "eschatological *Halakah*" (MOESSNER, *Banquet* [n. 1], pp. 124-127).

one's neighbour – a verbatim quotation of Lev 19,18b. Luke's rendering of Deut 6,5 differs profoundly from the text of the LXX. The evangelist offers four instead of three human faculties: he adopts καρδία and ψυχή, but replaces δύναμις by ἰσχύς and adds διάνοια. Moreover, Luke uses the LXX preposition ἐξ only once and seems to prefer ἐν as the Greek rendering of the Hebrew בְּ. If Luke wants to build a "Deuteronomistic pillar", he certainly intends to crown it with a Lukan capital.

To explain Luke's intentions in Lk 10,27 a synchronic approach needs to be supplemented by a comparison with the formulation of the double love commandment in Mk 12,29-33 par. Mt 22,37-39[3]. The three versions agree on the literal quotation of Lev 19,18. In Mk 12,29 and Mt 22,37 it is Jesus and not the scribe who recites the commandment, and both evangelists make a distinction between the first and the second commandment. Matthew and Luke agree against Mark in the omission of the 'Shema' in Mk 12,29b (Deut 6,4) and both lack the scribe's repetition of the double commandment in Mk 12,32-33. For the formulation of Deut 6,5 each evangelist goes his own way. Mark uses the preposition ἐξ (Mk 12,30.33) and in Mk 12,30 he mentions four human faculties as in Lk 10,27 but in a different order (καρδία – ψυχή – διάνοια – ἰσχύς). In Mk 12,33 the scribe refers to only three faculties: he drops ψυχή and substitutes διάνοια for σύνεσις. In Mt 22,37 Matthew uses the preposition ἐν three times and mentions καρδία, ψυχή and διάνοια, without a counterpart for δύναμις (LXX) or ἰσχύς (Mk and Lk). Thus, the use of ἐν and the positioning of διάνοια at the end of the series of human faculties are also to be considered as minor agreements of Matthew and Luke against Mark.

The text-critical problem of Lk 10,27 can be considered in the light of this synoptic diversity. D f[1] l 2211 pc and it read ἐν[4] four times and A C W Θ Ψ f[13] 33 𝔐 lat sy[(c)] ἐκ four times[5]. Some manuscripts have three human faculties instead of four: καὶ ἐν ὅλῃ τῇ ἰσχύϊ σου is lacking in 1241 bo[ms], καὶ ἐν ὅλῃ τῇ διανοίᾳ σου in D it Mcion[6]. The text of N[27]

---

3. For a presentation of the texts in comparison with the LXX, see K. BERGER, *Die Gesetzesauslegung Jesu. Ihr historischer Hintergrund im Judentum und im Alten Testament. Teil I: Markus und die Parallelen* (WMANT, 40/1), Neukirchen-Vluyn, 1972, pp. 177-183: "Die Gestalt des Textes Dt 6,4.5 in der synoptischen Überlieferung". Comp. G. DAUTZENBERG, *Sein Leben bewahren. Ψυχή in den Herrenworten der Evangelien* (SANT, 14), München, 1966, pp. 114-123; T. HOLTZ, *Untersuchungen über die alttestamentlichen Zitate bei Lukas* (TU, 104), Berlin, 1968; K.J. THOMAS, *Liturgical Citations in the Synoptics,* in *NTS* 22 (1974-75) 205-214, pp. 209-212.

4. Accepted as the original reading by HOLTZ, *Untersuchungen* (n. 3), p. 65.

5. 070 reads ἐκ before ἰσχύς.

6. Accepted by C.M. Tuckett as the original reading (*infra,* n. 16). But see DAUTZENBERG, *Leben* (n. 3), p. 121: "… sein Fehlen in D it, Mcion wird von den übrigen Zeugen nicht gestützt und dürfte auf biblizistische Streichung zurückzuführen sein".

(ἐξ... ἐν... ἐν... ἐν...) is undoubtedly to be preferred as *lectio difficilior* (𝔓⁷⁵ B Ξ 070 *l* 844 *pc*)⁷. The omission of the article τῆς before καρδίας (𝔓⁷⁵ B Ξ 070 *l* 844; within brackets in N²⁷) and of καί before ἐν ὅλῃ τῇ ψυχῇ σου (𝔓⁷⁵ B) is worth consideration⁸.

II. Hypotheses Concerning the Source(s) of Lk 10,27

The remarkable quotation in Lk 10,27 is only one aspect of the much debated problem of Luke's source(s) in Lk 10,25-28⁹. Luke's version of the double love commandment figures in Luke's travel narrative and not in the Jerusalem section as Mk 12,28-34 par. Mt 22,34-40 do. Moreover, there is supposed to be a disuse of the Markan source in Luke's context (the "great interpolation")¹⁰. The minor agreements in Lk 10,25-28 par. Mt 22,34-40¹¹ also give rise to different hypotheses which have been repeated in recent study. Our short survey will be limited to the afore-mentioned recent studies.

With reference to T.W. Manson's opinion that "great teachers constantly repeat themselves"¹², C.A. Kimball (1994) ascribes Lk 10,27 to Luke's special source ('L'): Lk 10,25-28 is too different in comparison with Mt and Mk, and Jesus likely combined the two Old Testament texts prior to Mt 22,34-40 par. Mk 12,28-34¹³. The lawyer repeated what he knew as Jesus' opinion.

---

7. Dautzenberg, *Leben* (n. 3), p. 121: "Die Mischform ist an sich *lectio difficilior*"; I.H. Marshall, *The Gospel of Luke. A Commentary on the Greek Text* (NIGTC), Exeter, 1978, p. 443: "... the harder reading and transcriptionally more probable".

8. Dautzenberg, *Leben* (n. 3), p. 122; Marshall, *Luke* (n. 7), p. 443: "The inclusion of τῆς before καρδίας is doubtful"; see also J. Kiilunen and F. Neirynck (*infra*, n. 44).

9. A recent review of opinions concerning Lk 10,25-28 can be found in J. Kiilunen, *Das Doppelgebot der Liebe in synoptischer Sicht. Ein redaktionskritischer Versuch über Mk 12,28-34 und die Parallelen* (AASF, B, 250), Helsinki, 1989, pp. 13 and 17-18; A. Ennulat, *Die ›Minor Agreements‹. Untersuchungen zu einer offenen Frage des synoptischen Problems* (WUNT, 2,62), Tübingen, 1994, pp. 278-280.

10. For the terminology see J.C. Hawkins, *Three Limitations to St. Luke's Use of St. Mark's Gospel,* in W. Sanday (ed.), *Studies in the Synoptic Problem,* Oxford, 1911, pp. 27-94, esp. 29-59: "The Disuse of the Marcan Source in St. Luke ix.51–xviii.14".

11. The other important minor agreements are νομικός, (ἐκ)πειράζων and διδάσκαλε in Lk 10,25 par. Mt 22,35-36; ἐν τῷ νόμῳ in Lk 10,26 par. Mt 22,36.

12. T.W. Manson, *The Sayings of Jesus as Recorded in the Gospels According to St. Matthew and St. Luke Arranged with Introduction and Commentary,* London, 1937 (*The Mission and Message of Jesus. Part II*), ²1949; reprint 1954, p. 260.

13. C.A. Kimball, *Jesus' Exposition of the Old Testament in Luke's Gospel* (JSNT SS, 94), Sheffield, 1994, pp. 120-123. For the text form of the quotations in Lk 10,27, see pp. 123-125. Comp. J.A. Fitzmyer, *The Gospel according to Luke X–XXIV* (AB, 28A), Garden City, NY, 1985, pp. 877-878, who also ascribes Lk 10,25-28 to 'L'.

According to J. Nolland (1993), Luke and Matthew used a second source, but "Luke's Markan source is available for inspection" (Mk 12,28-34 and 10,17-22)[14]. The fact that Lk 10,27 is a single love commandment (to both God and neighbour) together with the agreements with Matthew suggests that Luke is following this second source quite closely in Lk 10,27[15]. The inversion of the order of the last two human faculties, however, is due to Lukan redaction: Luke restores the Old Testament sequence and builds a chiastic structure with the natural pairings καρδία – διάνοια and ψυχή – ἰσχύς. The source mentioned only three elements (as in Mt 22,37): Luke supplements διάνοια from Mk 12,30 or from Deut 6,5.

Luke's and Matthew's second source is often identified with Q, as is the case in C.M. Tuckett's recent study on Q (1996)[16]. Sometimes Lk 10, 25-28 is considered as a faithful reproduction of the Q text[17], but most scholars admit the influence of Mk 12,28-34[18]. Questions remain, how-

---

14. J. NOLLAND, *Luke 9:21–18:34* (WBC, 35B), Dallas, TX, 1993, p. 580. He is not without hesitation in offering his hypothesis: "… with perhaps an additional second form from the tradition shared with Matthew". Comp. T. SCHRAMM, *Der Markus-Stoff bei Lukas. Eine literarkritische und redaktionsgeschichtliche Untersuchung* (SNTS MS, 14), Cambridge, 1971, pp. 47-49; MARSHALL, *Luke* (n. 7), pp. 440-441. See also C.M. Tuckett, *infra*, n. 16.

15. NOLLAND, *Luke II* (n. 14), p. 583. The single love commandment "seems to be a response to the problem posed by a tradition that gave an answer with two commandments to a question requiring the identification of a single commandment. This is a problem Luke had no need to address since he uses a quite different form of question".

16. C.M. TUCKETT, *Q and the History of Early Christianity. Studies on Q,* Edinburgh, 1996, pp. 416-418. Comp. his *The Temptation Narrative in Q,* in F. VAN SEGBROECK et al. (eds.), *The Four Gospels 1992.* FS F. Neirynck (BETL, 100), Vol. 1, Leuven, 1992, pp. 479-507, esp. 485-486. Tuckett refers to his earlier analysis of the great commandment pericope in *The Revival of the Griesbach Hypothesis. An Analysis and Appraisal* (SNTS MS, 44), Cambridge, 1983, pp. 125-133. In this analysis, however, he is not clearly referring to Q, but speaks about a "common source" (p. 127; see p. 213, n. 12: Q or a non-Markan tradition). For Tuckett, the agreement between Lk 10,25-28 and Mk 12,28-34 is mostly confined to their OT quotations (Lk 10,27 and Mk 12,30). Tuckett accepts the omission of ἐν ὅλῃ τῇ διανοίᾳ σου in Lk 10,27 D 1241 it and Marcion, however, and proposes a coherent text with three faculties and without the only significant agreement between Mark and Luke (p. 126): "If this is so, then the only verbal point of contact between Luke and Mark is the use of ἰσχύς instead of the LXX's δύναμις, and this might be due to independent reminiscence by both writers of 2 Ki xxiii. 25" (pp. 126-127).

17. See especially C. BURCHARD, *Das doppelte Liebesgebot in der frühen christlichen Überlieferung,* in E. LOHSE et al. (eds.), *Der Ruf Jesu und die Antwort der Gemeinde.* FS J. Jeremias, Göttingen, 1970, pp. 39-62, esp. 46-51; J.D. CROSSAN, *Parable and Example in the Teaching of Jesus,* in *NTS* 18 (1971-72) 285-307, pp. 287-291; A.J. HULTGREN, *The Double Commandment of Love in Mt 22:34-40. Its Sources and Compositions,* in *CBQ* 36 (1974) 373-378, p. 373. Comp. M. KLINGHARDT, *Gezetz und Volk Gottes. Das lukanische Verständnis des Gesetzes nach Herkunft, Funktion und seinem Ort in der Geschichte des Urchristentums* (WUNT, 2,32), Tübingen, 1988, pp. 136-139.

18. See especially R.H. FULLER, *Das Doppelgebot der Liebe. Ein Testfall für die Echtheitskriterien der Worte Jesu,* in G. STRECKER (ed.), *Jesus Christus in Historie und*

ever, concerning the place of Q 10,25-28 within the order of Q[19], and the reconstruction of the Q text[20]. Nevertheless, R.H. Fuller proposed a reconstruction in 1975, which is accepted by R. Pesch[21]. According to Fuller, Q lacks the citation of the 'Shema' of Deut 6,4, mentions three human faculties as in Mt 22,37 and Deut 6,5 (also in Mk 12,33) and uses the preposition ἐν. Matthew and Luke adopt Mark's διάνοια, while Q probably reads ἐν ὅλῃ τῇ ἰσχύϊ σου as in Lk 10,27. There is no distinction between the first and the second commandment in Q. The reconstruction of Lev 19,18 is obvious.

Recently, a reconstruction of Q 10,25-28 has been offered by U. Mell (1994) and J. Lambrecht (1995). Mell's reconstruction of the quotation of Deut 6,5 in Q 10,27 does not differ from the one offered by Fuller[22]. According to Lambrecht καὶ ἐν ὅλῃ διανοίᾳ concluded the enumeration in Q[23]. It is not impossible that Q mentioned a concluding remark after

Theologie. FS H. Conzelmann, Tübingen, 1975, pp. 317-329, esp. 318-320; G. SELLIN, *Lukas als Gleichniserzähler. Die Erzählung vom barmherzigen Samariter (Lk 10,25-37)*, in *ZNW* 65 (1974) 166-189; 66 (1975) 19-60, pp. 20-23; M. SATO, *Q und Prophetie. Studien zur Gattungs- und Traditionsgeschichte der Quelle Q* (WUNT, 2,29), Tübingen, 1988, p. 22; J. LAMBRECHT, *The Great Commandment Pericope and Q*, in R.A. PIPER (ed.), *The Gospel Behind the Gospels. Current Studies on Q* (NTSup, 75), Leiden, 1995, 73-96, pp. 76-78.

19. SATO, *Q und Prophetie* (n. 18), p. 39; LAMBRECHT, *Great Commandment* (n. 18), p. 88: "In regard to the precise position of the great commandment pericope in Q, it would perhaps be better simply to confess our ignorance because of lack of clear data".

20. A Q version of Lk 10,25-28 is not accepted in D. LÜHRMANN, *Die Redaktion der Logienquelle* (WMANT, 33), Neukirchen-Vluyn, 1969, p. 32, n. 1; S. SCHULZ, *Q. Die Spruchquelle der Evangelisten*, Zürich, 1972; A. POLAG, *Fragmenta Q. Textheft zur Logienquelle*, Neukirchen-Vluyn, 1979, p. 99; R. LAUFEN, *Die Doppelüberlieferungen der Logienquelle und des Markusevangeliums* (BBB, 54), Bonn, 1980, p. 89; J.S. KLOPPENBORG, *The Formation of Q. Trajectories in Ancient Wisdom Collections* (Studies in Antiquity & Christianity), Philadelphia, PA, 1987, p. 82 (hesitating); *Q Parallels. Synopsis, Critical Notes and Concordance*, Sonoma, CA, 1988, p. 81; F. NEIRYNCK, *Q-Synopsis. The Double Tradition Passages in Greek* (SNTA, 13), Leuven, 1988, ²1995; D.R. CATCHPOLE, *The Quest for Q*, Edinburgh, 1993, p. 265; B.L. MACK, *The Lost Gospel. The Book of Q & Christian Origins*, San Francisco, 1993; H.T. FLEDDERMANN, *Mark and Q. A Study of the Overlap Texts* (BETL, 122), Leuven, 1995.

D. ZELLER, *Kommentar zur Logienquelle* (SKK NT, 21), Stuttgart, 1984, p. 70, and SATO, *Q und Prophetie* (n. 18), pp. 22 and 39, take account of the possibility of Q 10,25-28.

21. FULLER, *Doppelgebot* (n. 18), pp. 319-322. Comp. R. PESCH, *Das Markusevangelium*. II. Teil. *Kommentar zu Kap. 8,27–16,20* (HTKNT, 2,2), Freiburg – Basel – Wien, 1977, p. 245, n. 25.

22. U. MELL, *Die "anderen" Winzer. Eine exegetische Studie zur Vollmacht Jesu Christi nach Markus 11,27–12,34* (WUNT, 77), Tübingen, 1994, pp. 315-316. See esp. p. 315, n. 21: "Das vierte, nachgetragene Glied der Formel (διάνοια) von Lk 10,27 sowie die erste Formulierung mit ἐκ + Gen. stammen von Mk"; p. 316, n. 33: "Ist das vierte Glied der Formel bei Lk nach Mk ergänzt, so lag in Q eine dreigliedrige Formel vor. Mt hat ἰσχύς nach Mk mit διάνοια ausgetauscht" (referring to Fuller).

23. LAMBRECHT, *Great Commandment* (n. 18), pp. 83-87. To reconstruct the Q text Lambrecht also takes into account Mk 12,28-34, according to his hypothesis that Mark knew and used Q. See p. 83: "It is possible that some features of Q have been preserved only in Mark".

Deut 6,5 (as in Mt 22,38) and a distinction between the first and the second commandment (as in Mt 22,39). Moreover, the verb ἀγαπήσεις is mentioned twice (as in Mt 22,39 and Mk 12,31). The narrow combination of the commandments in Lk 10,27 is due to the influence of Mk 12,33[24]. Given the uncertainties, Lambrecht prefers to offer a text in English. A synopsis of the three reconstructions can now be offered:

Fuller (1975)	Mell (1994)	Lambrecht (1995)
ὁ δὲ εἶπεν πρὸς αὐτόν·	ὁ δὲ ἔφη αὐτῷ·	He said to him,
ἀγαπήσεις κύριον τὸν θεόν σου		"You shall love the Lord your God
ἐν ὅλῃ τῇ καρδίᾳ σου		with all your heart,
καὶ ἐν ὅλῃ τῇ ψυχῇ σου		and with all yous soul,
καὶ ἐν ὅλῃ τῇ ἰσχύϊ σου,		and with all your mind.
		[This is the greatest commandment.]
		[And a second is like it,]
καὶ τὸν πλησίον σου ὡς σεαυτόν.		You shall love your neighbour as yourself
		[There is no other commandment greater than these]".

A. Ennulat (1994) finds only weak support in Lk 10,27 par. Mt 22,39 for the Deuteromark hypothesis[25]. Deut 6,4 may have been omitted in Luke's and Matthew's version of Mark, but the differences in the quotation of Deut 6,5 are due to their redactional activity[26].

According to M.D. Goulder (1989) and R.H. Gundry (1982, 1992), Lk 10,27 is a clear instance of Luke's dependence on Matthew. Goulder points out that "Luke wanders between his authorities for the quotation of Deut 6,5"[27]: Mk 12,29-33, Mt 22,37-39, and Deut 6. Like Matthew he omits the 'Shema' (Deut 6,4) and mentions the preposition ἐν three times. He retains the preposition ἐκ of Mark and the LXX once. Matthew's citations are regularly influenced by the Hebrew text, but Luke's never are. Since Luke's text reads most probably ἐξ... ἐν... ἐν... ἐν... "the natural

---

24. *Ibid.*, p. 77.

25. ENNULAT, *Die ›Minor Agreements‹* (n. 9), pp. 285-286.

26. *Ibid.*, p. 285: "Da für Lk gewisse kompositorische Verbindungslinien zu 18,18ff. bestehen, ist es zumindest auffällig, daß er diese Verbindungslinie über die Monotheismus-formel (Lk 18,19!) nicht nutzt. Oder hat er sie nicht mehr in seinem MkText gelesen?". This minor agreement gets Ennulat's category "II". With respect to Deut 6,5 Ennulat states: "Einfacher erscheint mir eine Ableitung sowohl der mt als auch der lk Textform direkt aus Mk 12,30.... Schwierig zu erklären bleibt das erste ἐξ ὅλης... in Lk 10,27" (pp. 285-286).

27. M.D. GOULDER, *Luke. A New Paradigm* (JSNT SS, 20), 2 Vols., Sheffield, 1989, p. 485. The hypothesis of Luke's dependence on Mt has been defended earlier by R.T. SIMPSON, *The Major Agreements of Matthew and Luke against Mark*, in *NTS* 12 (1965-66) 273-284, pp. 279-280.

explanation seems to be that Luke began with Mark = LXX, and was then influenced by memories of Matthew's redaction"[28]. Luke has Mark's four human faculties, but the reversion of the order of διάνοια and ἰσχύς is due to influence of Mt 22,37. On the whole, Lk 10,27 "seems a clear instance of mixed citation from memory"[29].

In Gundry's opinion, the omission of Deut 6,4 is a "Matthean foreign body" in Lk 10,27. Whereas Matthew's Jewish-Christian public can take monotheism for granted, Luke's Gentile audience should be interested in the 'Shema': "So his agreement with Matthew in omitting the monotheistic introduction favours Matthean influence"[30]. Matthew prefers the prepositon ἐν because of its closer conformity with the Hebrew בְּ. Luke starts with ἐκ but switches to ἐν: "The switch suggests that he is conflating Mark and Matthew"[31].

F. Neirynck has recently (1994, 1995) criticized Gundry's "Matthean foreign bodies" in Luke 10,25-28[32]. Neirynck considers the quotation in Lk 10,27 in the light of Luke's editing of Mk 12,29-33 in combination with Luke's acquaintance with Septuagintal texts. This hypothesis is defended in J. Kiilunen's study on the great commandment pericope (1989), and also with some variations in the work of M. Ebersohn (1993)[33]. Two commentators on Luke have changed their initial opinion on Lk 10,25-28: J.

28. GOULDER, Luke II (n. 27), p. 486.

29. Ibid., p. 485.

30. R.H. GUNDRY, Matthean Foreign Bodies in Agreements of Luke with Matthew against Mark. Evidence that Luke Used Matthew, in VAN SEGBROECK et al. (eds.), The Four Gospels 1992 (n. 16), Volume 2, pp. 1467-1495, esp. 1482. Comp. R.H. GUNDRY, Matthew. A Commentary on His Literary and Theological Art, Grand Rapids, MI, 1982, reprint: 1983; ²1994 (A Commentary on His Handbook for a Mixed Church under Persecution), pp. 448-449. See also Gundry's answer to F. Neirynck's critical remarks (infra, n. 32) in A Rejoinder on Matthean Foreign Bodies in Luke 10,25-28, in ETL 71 (1995) 139-150.

31. GUNDRY, Bodies (n. 30), p. 1482; compare Matthew (n. 30), p. 449. Gundry suggests that διάνοια in Mt 22,37 can result from reading the third Hebrew element as מַדְּעֲךָ instead of מְאֹדְךָ: "But Matthew omits the reference to strength in order to maintain the triplicity of the 'tones'" (p. 449). See also GUNDRY, The Use of the Old Testament in St. Matthew's Gospel with Special Reference to the Messianic Hope (NTSup, 18), Leiden, 1967, pp. 22-25.

32. F. NEIRYNCK, Luke 10:25-28: A Foreign Body in Luke?, in S.E. PORTER, P. JOYCE and D.E. ORTON (eds.) Crossing the Boundaries. FS Michael D. Goulder (Biblical Interpretation Series), Leiden – New York – Köln, 1994, pp. 149-165, esp. p. 164. See Neirynck's answer on Gundry's Rejoinder (n. 30) in The Minor Agreements and Lk 10,25-28, in ETL 71 (1995) 151-160. On Lk 10,25-28 see also F. NEIRYNCK, The Minor Agreements and Q, in PIPER (ed.), The Gospel Behind the Gospels (cf. n. 18), pp. 49-72, esp. 61-64.

33. KIILUNEN, Doppelgebot (n. 9), esp. pp. 61-67 (on Lk 10,27); compare pp. 42-46 (on Mt 22,37-39); M. EBERSOHN, Das Nächstenliebegebot in der synoptischen Tradition (Marburger Theologische Studien, 37), Marburg, 1993, pp. 145-147. See also E. LINNEMANN, Gleichnisse Jesu. Einführung und Auslegung, Göttingen, 1961, ²1962, pp. 62-64; H. ZIMMERMANN, Das Gleichnis vom barmherzigen Samariter: Lk 10,25-37, in G. BORNKAMM and K. RAHNER (eds.), Die Zeit Jesu. FS H. Schlier, Freiburg – Basel – Wien, 1970, 58-69, pp. 61-62; H.L. EGELKRAUT, Jesus' Mission to Jerusalem: A Redaction

Ernst (special source) and H. Schürmann (Q) now opt for Luke's reworking of Mk 12,28-34[34].

III. Mk 12,29-33 AND THE SEPTUAGINT: THE SOURCES OF Lk 10,27

Luke's remarkable use of the prepositions in Lk 10,27 does not necessarily refer to a special source, a Q version or the influence of Mt 22,37. It is rather commonly accepted that Luke adopts the preposition ἐκ under the influence of Mk 12,30.33 (and Deut 6,5 LXX)[35]. His use of ἐν may be inspired by Deut 6,6 (LXX) and 2 Kings 23,25 (and its counterpart 2 Chron 35,19b)[36]:

Deut 6,5	καὶ ἀγαπήσεις κύριον τὸν θεόν σου
	ἐξ ὅλης τῆς καρδίας σου
	καὶ ἐξ ὅλης τῆς ψυχῆς σου
	καὶ ἐξ ὅλης τῆς δυνάμεώς σου
Deut 6,6	καὶ ἔσται τὰ ῥήματα ταῦτα,
	ὅσα ἐγὼ ἐντέλλομαί σοι σήμερον,
	ἐν τῇ καρδίᾳ σου
	καὶ ἐν τῇ ψυχῇ σου
2 Kings 23,25	ὅμοιος αὐτῷ οὐκ ἐγενήθη ἔμπροσθεν αὐτοῦ βασιλεύς,
	ὃς ἐπέστρεψεν πρὸς κύριον
	ἐν ὅλῃ καρδίᾳ αὐτοῦ
	καὶ ἐν ὅλῃ ψυχῇ αὐτοῦ
	καὶ ἐν ὅλῃ ἰσχύι αὐτοῦ
	κατὰ πάντα τὸν νόμον Μωυσῆ, καὶ μετ' αὐτὸν οὐκ
	ἀνέστη ὅμοιος αὐτῷ

Critical Study of the Travel Narrative in the Gospel of Luke, Lk 9:51–19:48 (Europäische Hochschulschriften, 23/80), Frankfurt/M – Bern, 1976, pp. 85-86; P.J. FARLA, Jezus' oordeel over Israël. Een form- en redaktionsgeschichtliche analyse van Mc 10,46–12,40, Kampen, 1978, pp. 249-253; J.-G. MUDISO MBA MUNDLA, Jesus und die Führer Israels. Studien zu den sog. Jerusalemer Streitgesprächen (NTAbh, Neue Folge, 17), Münster, 1984, pp. 118-119. Comp. E. KLOSTERMANN, Das Lukasevangelium (HNT, 5), Tübingen, [2]1929, pp. 480-481; G. SCHNEIDER, Das Evangelium nach Lukas (ÖTKNT, 3,1-2), 2 Vols., Gütersloh – Würzburg, 1977, [2]1984, p. 247; W. SCHMITHALS, Das Evangelium nach Lukas (Zürcher Bibelkommentare NT, 3,1), Zürich, 1980, p. 127; W. WIEFEL, Das Evangelium nach Lukas (THKNT, 3), Berlin, 1988, p. 207.

34. J. ERNST, Das Evangelium nach Lukas (RNT), Regensburg, [2]1993, p. 260; H. SCHÜRMANN, Das Lukasevangelium. 2. Teil. Erste Folge: Kommentar zu Kapitel 9,51–11,54 (HTKNT, 3,2/1), Freiburg – Basel – Wien, 1994, pp. 128 and 129-140.

35. See already KLOSTERMANN, Lukasevangelium (n. 33), p. 481; and also DAUTZENBERG, Leben (n. 3), p. 121; BERGER, Gesetzesauslegung (n. 3), p. 182; THOMAS, Citations (n. 3), p. 213; EGELKRAUT, Mission (n. 33), p. 86; FARLA, Jezus' oordeel (n. 33), p. 249; KIILUNEN, Doppelgebot (n. 9), p. 65; NEIRYNCK, Luke 10:25-28 (n. 32), p. 164; LAMBRECHT, Great Commandment (n. 18), p. 78.

36. Contra EBERSOHN, Nächstenliebegebot (n. 33), p. 146, who thinks that also in Luke the preposition ἐν is a "Angleichung an den hebräischen Text".

According to Gundry it is unlikely that 2 Kings 23,25 influenced Lk 10,27, "for it speaks of turning to the Lord rather than of loving the Lord your God and it had not attained the prominence of Deut 6,4-5"[37]. Luke and Mark, however, mention ἰσχύς and not δύναμις, and Luke's reversion of the Markan sequence (διάνοια – ἰσχύς) restores the order of 2 Kings 23,25[38].

In any case, Deut 6,6 and 2 Kings 23,25 prove the diversity of the use of the prepositions in the LXX. Such variety heightens the possibility that different versions of the daily recited love commandment existed[39]. This suggestion is not so hypothetical when the variants in the transcriptional tradition of Deut 6,5 (LXX) are considered: codex B[r] reads διάνοια as first human faculty; codex A has καρδία. Moreover, in other passages the LXX varies in the wording of the faculties: 2 Kings 23,25 uses ἰσχύς and not δύναμις; Josh 22,5b mentions only two elements and uses διάνοια instead of καρδία[40]. Younger texts such as 2 Macc 1,3-4; 4 Macc 13,13 and Sir 6,26; 7,27-30 paraphrase the love command and maintain the variation in the wording of the faculties. Dautzenberg states "daß sich in dieser Spätzeit das intrumentale ἐν für בּ durchhält"[41]. In this sense the use of ἐν is acceptable within Luke's acquaintance with Septuagintal texts.

As Luke is editing Mk 12,29-33 he combines the three human faculties of the LXX with the fourfold Markan formula, which results in the sequence ἐξ... ἐν... ἐν... ἐν... He may have retained the additional fourth element διάνοια to emphasize the Markan demand for total

---

37. GUNDRY, *Rejoinder* (n. 30), pp. 149-150.

38. BERGER, *Gesetzesauslegung* (n. 3), p. 182: "Die gegenüber Mk umgestellte Reihenfolge läßt zweifellos Beschäftigung mit der Schrift erkennen; die Wortfolge καρδία – ψυχή – ἰσχύς begegnet in der LXX in 4 Kg 23,25". Comp. FARLA, *Jezus' oordeel* (n. 33), p. 249; KIILUNEN, *Doppelgebot* (n. 9), p. 65. The fact that διάνοια is the last element in Mt 22,37 and Lk 10,27, can be considered a mere coincidence.

39. DAUTZENBERG, *Leben* (n. 3), p. 114; FARLA, *Jezus' oordeel* (n. 33), p. 249: ".. of zelfs vanuit verschillende in omloop zijnde versies van deze, voor het jodendom centrale tekst, die tweemaal daags, en niet noodzakelijk in het Hebreeuws, maar ook in het Grieks werd gebeden"; SCHÜRMANN, *Lukasevangelium II/1* (n. 34), p. 139; NEIRYNCK, *Luke 10:25-28* (n. 32), p. 164: "Luke can be influenced by an alternative version of Deut. 6:5, in conformity with the Hebrew בּ". BERGER, *Gesetzesauslegung* (n. 3), p. 182, goes too far when he states: "Keiner der Synoptiker hat sich offenbar um den Wortlaut von Dt 6,5 LXX gekümmert".

40. Josh 22,5b ἀγαπᾶν κύριον τὸν θεὸν ὑμῶν,
πορεύεσθαι πάσαις ταῖς ὁδοῖς αὐτοῦ,
φυλάξασθαι τὰς ἐντολὰς αὐτοῦ
καὶ προσκεῖσθαι αὐτῷ καὶ λατρεύειν αὐτῷ
ἐξ ὅλης τῆς διανοίας ὑμῶν
καὶ ἐξ ὅλης τῆς ψυχῆς ὑμῶν.

41. DAUTZENBERG, *Leben* (n. 3), p. 117.

dedication to God[42]. The transition to ἐν can also be considered as a stylistic improvement[43]. Luke employs a structure "1+3": the first element functions as a title and the other three elements accord with the Old Testament threefold formula. That structure becomes more obvious when the reading without article and καί is accepted (𝔓[75] B)[44]:

ἐξ ὅλης [τῆς] καρδίας σου
[καὶ] ἐν ὅλη τῇ ψυχῇ σου
καὶ ἐν ὅλη τῇ ἰσχύϊ σου
καὶ ἐν ὅλη τῇ διανοίᾳ σου

Luke's version of the love commandment Deut 6,5 is a clear example of the evangelist's tendency to combine Mark with the LXX: "Mk bot die vier Komponenten, LXX ihre Reihenfolge, die beiden zusammen die Präpositionen"[45].

In comparison with Mt 22,37-39 and Mk 12,29-33 Luke reproduces the double commandment in brief. This may be the consequence of the introductory character of the pericope, but Luke found a close combination of the two commandments in Mk 12,33 where Deut 6,5 and Lev 19,18 are connected with καί in one sentence[46]. Luke retains the verb ἀγαπάω only once: the ἀγαπήσεις sentence offers a clear answer to the lawyer's question τί ποιήσας (Lk 10,25 comp. Lk 18,18 par. Mk 10,17)[47]. Such an accent on the practical consequences of the love commandment also explains Luke's omission of Deut 6,4 and of the distinction between the first and the second commandment. The evangelist evaluated the 'Shema' as an inadequate answer to the question τί ποιήσας[48].

42. D. LÜHRMANN, *Das Markusevangelium* (HNT, 3), Tübingen, 1987, p. 206; PESCH, *Markusevangelium II* (n. 21), p. 240; KIILUNEN, *Doppelgebot* (n. 9), pp. 65-66; LAM-BRECHT, *Great Commandment* (n. 18), p. 86, n. 42 (hesitating).

43. DAUTZENBERG, *Leben* (n. 3), p. 122: "Einem Stilisten wie Lukas ist eine stärkere Markierung der unterschiedenen Glieder zuzutrauen, die auch die innere Motivierung des Wechsels erkennbar macht"; KIILUNEN, *Doppelgebot* (n. 9), p. 66; NEIRYNCK, *Luke 10:25-28* (n. 32), p. 164; *The Minor Agreements and Lk 10,25-28* (n. 32), p. 159.

44. DAUTZENBERG, *Leben* (n. 3), p. 122; KIILUNEN, *Doppelgebot* (n. 9), p. 66; NEIRYNCK, *Luke 10:25-28* (n. 32), p. 164; *The Minor Agreements and Lk 10,25-28* (n. 32), p. 159.

45. KIILUNEN, *Doppelgebot* (n. 9), p. 66. Comp. BERGER, *Gesetzesauslegung* (n. 3), p. 179: "Der Lukastext zeigt ein solches Bild, und sein Text wird zurückzuführen sein auf eine Beschäftigung mit Mk und der LXX zugleich".

46. KIILUNEN, *Doppelgebot* (n. 9), p. 62; SCHÜRMANN, *Lukasevangelium II/1* (n. 34), pp. 134 en 138; NEIRYNCK, *Luke 10:25-28*, p. 159.

47. SCHMITHALS, *Lukas* (n. 33), p. 127; KIILUNEN, *Doppelgebot* (n. 9), p. 62; EBER-SOHN, *Nächstenliebegebot* (n. 33), p. 147; NOLLAND, *Luke* (n. 14), p. 583; NEIRYNCK, *Luke 10:25-28* (n. 32), p. 164. See also SCHÜRMANN, *Lukasevangelium II/1* (n. 34), p. 134. Moreover Schürmann comments that Deut 6,4 "keine ἐντολή ist" (p. 139).

48. NEIRYNCK, *Luke 10,25-28* (n. 32), p. 164; *The Minor Agreements and Lk 10,25-28* (n. 32), p. 158.

Moreover, the point of the parable of the Samaritan makes it clear that Luke is more interested in the coherence of the double love commandment than in the monotheistic creed[49]. Perhaps Luke considers the Jewish character of the 'Shema' unsuited to his Gentile audience[50], but above all he wants to emphasize the importance of the *double love* commandment[51]. For this reason he drops the Markan distinction between a first and a second commandment[52] and alters Mk 12,32-33 where the double commandment seems to consist of the monotheistic creed in combination with the love commandment.

It remains an open question as to which commandment Luke gives more weight. In any case, the catchword πλησίον is the link between Lk 10,25-28 and the parable in 10,29-37: the second commandment of Lev 19,18 may receive some emphasis. Moreover, the formula τοῦτο ποίει καὶ ζήσῃ in Lk 10,28 not only forms an inclusion with Lk 10,25, but echoes Lev 18,5 (LXX)[53]. Not only Deuteronomy but also Leviticus seem to have played a not unimportant role for Luke's redaction of the pericope of the double love commandment.

---

49. EBERSOHN, *Nächstenliebegebot* (n. 33), p. 147: "Die Auslassung steht bei ihm im Zusammenhang mit seiner Fortsetzung des Gesprächs 10,29-37, wo es primär um das *Halten* der Gebote geht".

50. NEIRYNCK, *Luke 10:25-28* (n. 32), pp. 163-164. Comp. J. GNILKA, *Das Matthäusevangelium. II. Teil. Kommentar zu Kap. 14,1–28,20 und Einleitungsfragen* (HTKNT, 2), Freiburg – Basel – Wien, 1988, p. 258. Even FITZMYER, *Luke II* (n. 13), pp. 877-878, contends that the omission of Deut 6,4 "could be easily explained by Luke's redactional concern for the predominantly Gentile audience for whom he was writing".

51. FARLA, *Jezus' oordeel* (n. 33), p. 252: "Dt 6,4 verstoort enigszins de parallellie tussen de beide geboden, een parallellie, die in Mt door de kwalificatie van het tweede gebod als gelijk aan het eerste, en in Lc door de samenvoeging tot één gebod nog wordt onderstreept". Comp. EBERSOHN, *Nächstenliebegebot* (n. 33), p. 153: "... nur hier also liegt wirklich ein *Doppel*gebot vor"; SCHÜRMANN, *Lukasevangelium II/1* (n. 34), p. 139.

52. KIILUNEN, *Doppelgebot* (n. 9), pp. 62-63: "Dabei ist die Ansicht zu nennen, Lukas wolle durch den Gebrauch eines gemeinsamen Prädikats dem 'Missverständnis' einer markinischen Abstufung des Schwergewichts der beiden Gebote entgegenwirken. Eine Überprüfung dieser Ansicht könnte bei den vielen in Lk zu beobachtenden Stellen ansetzen, wo eine sachliche Zusammengehörigkeit und Gegenseitigkeit der Gottes- und Nächstenliebe zum Vorschein kommt". On the other hand NOLLAND, *Luke* (n. 14), p. 583, means that "this is a problem Luke had no need to address since he uses a quite different form of question".

53. Lev 18,5 καὶ φυλάξεσθε πάντα τὰ προστάγματά μου καὶ πάντα τὰ κρίματά μου καὶ ποιήσετε αὐτά, ἃ **ποιήσας ἄνθρωπος ζήσεται** ἐν αὐτοῖς· ἐγὼ κύριος ὁ θεὸς ὑμῶν. See KLOSTERMANN, *Lukasevangelium* (n. 33), p. 482; J.M. CREED, *The Gospel according to St. Luke. The Greek Text with Introduction, Notes and Indices*, London, 1930; reprint: 1965, p. 152; MARSHALL, *Luke* (n. 7), p. 444; SCHNEIDER, *Lukas I* (n. 33), p. 248; KIILUNEN, *Doppelgebot* (n. 9), p. 68; SCHÜRMANN, *Lukasevangelium II/1* (n. 34), p. 136: "Dabei spricht Jesus mit den Worten des Pentateuch".

IV. Conclusion

We return to our initial question: can Lk 10,27 be considered a Deuteronomistic pillar? In fact, even in the "great interpolation" Mk 12,28-34 seems to be Luke's first source: there he finds the unique combination of the love commandments in Deut 6,4-5 and Lev 19,18. Editing Mk 12,29-33, Luke omits Deut 6,4 and retains Deut 6,5 in a "Markan" formulation while he adopts the preposition ἐν inspired by other passages in the LXX. Thus, the evangelist deliberately makes his formulation of the love commandment less Deuteronomistic.

Defenders of the Deuteronomy hypothesis should take into account that Luke also emphasizes Lev 19,18 (πλησίον) and Lev 18,5 (τοῦτο ποίει καὶ ζήσῃ). Perhaps Lk 10,27 can be called a biblical or Pentateuchal pillar, but not without mentioning that Luke focuses on the *Markan* combination of the double love commandment.

Abdij Averbode   Filip NOËL
Abdijstraat 1
B-3271 Averbode

(ETERNAL) LIFE AND FOLLOWING THE COMMANDMENTS
LEV 18,5 AND LUKE 10,28[1]

In Luke 10 Jesus motivates his opinion about the manner to obtain eternal life[2]. He argues with the help of words which are reminiscent of a statement we find in Lev 18,5 and in some other texts of the Old Testament. The saying of Lev 18,5 is quoted by Paul in Gal 3,12 and in Rom 10,5. First of all we will discuss Luke 10,28 and Lev 18,5. Then we discuss Gal 3,12 and Rom 10,5 and their relation to Lev 18,5. Finally we compare Luke 10,28 with Gal 3,12 and Rom 10,5 and make some concluding observations on the use of the Old Testament in these texts.

I

In Luke 10 a lawyer asks Jesus which are the requirements to inherit eternal life. Jesus refers to the law, ὁ νόμος, in his answer (10,26). Then the lawyer recites the so-called great commandment: "you shall love the Lord your God with all your heart, and with all your soul, and with all your strength, and with all your mind, and your neighbour as yourself". The texts of Lev 19,18 and Deut 6,5 are combined in his answer. Though only the great commandment is recited, it is clear that the whole law is summarized with these words[3]. Then Jesus says: τοῦτο ποίει καὶ ζήσῃ[4]. Thus, Jesus argues that people will inherit (eternal) life by doing the words of God[5]. In his question the lawyer speaks of *eternal* life, τί ποιήσας ζωὴν αἰώνιον κληρονομήσω. In his answer Jesus uses just the verb "to live" to refer to "eternal life". We find the same difference between question and answer in Matt 19,16-19[6]. In John 11,25 the same

---

1. I would like to thank Ms. drs. J.W. van Arenthals for her critical remarks on this text.
2. In this paper we cannot discuss the complications with regard to the synoptic problem. We speak only about the way Jesus reasons in Luke 10,28.

3. H. SCHÜRMANN, *Das Lukasevangelium* (HTKNT, III/2/1), Freiburg, 1993, p. 134: "Gottes- und Nächstenliebe zusammen sind in unserem Text also die Zusammenfassung der Tora".

4. The variants in the manuscripts are not important for this paper.

5. Cf. H. BRAUN, in *TWNT* VI, 477: "Lk 10,28, wo die Erlangung des Lebens an das *Tun* der Gebote gebunden ist […]".

6. Cf. Mark 10,17-22.

verb ζάω is used in the sense of life including life after death: ὁ πιστεύων εἰς ἐμὲ κἂν ἀποθάνῃ ζήσεται. So the verb ζάω can be used in the sense of eternal life[7]. We can conclude that according to Luke 10,28 in Jesus' opinion "doing the commandments" is the condition for inheriting eternal life[8]. It has nothing to do with exegesis when Schürmann says: "Freilich weiß Gal 3,12ff; Röm 10,5ff das korrigierend zu ergänzen"[9].

I have to say here something about "Jesus and the Law". The literature about this subject is immense[10]. I restrict myself to some remarks. Jesus points out to the lawyer the way to obtain eternal life with the help of words from the Torah. That means that the law is valued positively by Jesus. There is not any indication in this text that the law is disqualified by him. In Matt 19,17 Jesus says: εἰ δὲ θέλεις εἰς τὴν ζωὴν εἰσελθεῖν, τήρει τὰς ἐντολάς. And then he quotes some commandments from the Decalogue. Jesus alludes to words as found in Lev 18,5[11], though the text of the Septuagint is quite different: ἃ ποιήσας ἄνθρωπος ζήσεται ἐν αὐτοῖς[12]. Usually scholars distinguish between quotations, allusions and reminiscences, "language colouring from the OT"[13]. We speak of an allusion when a text of the Old Testament is referred to consciously. Though the decision to differentiate between allusions and reminiscences is sometimes arbitrary, it seems to me that Jesus in Luke 10,28 refers to Lev 18,5. The crucial words of Lev 18,5 ποιέω and ζάω are used here.

7. See R. BULTMANN, in *TWNT* II, p. 865: "Weil die zukünftige ζωή die eigentliche ist, kann sie […] einfach ζωή ohne Attribut genannt werden, wie auch ζῆν ohne nähere Bestimmung in diesem Sinne gebraucht werden kann". Bultmann mentions Luke 10,28 as an example for his statement.

8. See again H. BRAUN (n. 5), p. 477: "Lk 10,28, wo die Erlangung des Lebens an das *Tun* der Gebote gebunden ist […]". G. SCHNEIDER, *Das Evangelium nach Lukas* (ÖTK, 3/1), Gütersloh, 1984², p. 248 speaks of the "theoretischen Konsens zwischen Jesus und dem Gesetzeslehrer".

9. SCHÜRMANN (n. 3), p. 136. See also HUGO GROTIUS, *Annotationes in Novum Testamentum* I, Erlangen, 1755 I, p. 804: "Stricte ποιεῖν dicitur de factis externis: late porrigitur etiam ad internos animi motus", in fact it is spoken about external things: broadly it refers to the inner motions of the spirit.

10. See I. BROER (ed.), *Jesus und das jüdische Gesetz*, Stuttgart, 1992; G. KLEIN, *Das Gesetz*, in *TRE* 13, 1984, pp. 58-75.

11. See H. SCHÜRMANN (n. 3), p. 136; cf. E. HÜHN, *Die alttestamentlichen Citate und Reminicenzen im Neuen Testamente*, Tübingen, 1900, p. 57.

12. See J.W. WEVERS, *Leviticus* (Septuaginta, Vetus Testamentum Graecum, Auctoritate Academiae Scientiarum Gottingensis editum, vol. II/2), Göttingen, 1986, p. 202. Cf. E. VERHOEF, *Er staat geschreven …*, Diss. Vrije Universiteit Amsterdam, 1979, pp. 78-80, for the complicated tradition of this text.

13. E.E. ELLIS, *Paul's Use of the Old Testament*, Edinburgh, 1957, pp. 10-11; cf. T. BAARDA, *The Gospel Quotations of Aphrahat the Persian Sage* I, Diss. Vrije Universiteit Amsterdam, 1975, pp. 290-291.

And in the preceding verses some commandments are spoken of. The fact that Jesus argues with words of his tradition is not very striking as he quotes texts from the Torah, from the Psalms and from the Prophets quite often[14]. Such a quotation from the Torah makes this argument much stronger. Moreover, discussion partners were expected to quote the Scripture[15].

The statement we find in Lev 18,5 was used quite often: see LXX Ezek 20,11.13.21; 2 Ezra 19,29[16]. In Ezek 20 and in 2 Ezra the lessons Israel can learn from history are spoken about. Perhaps this statement has been quoted from an older tradition[17]. The meaning of these words in Lev 18,5 is clear. The Israelites are asked to obey the commandments given in this chapter and in return God promises "life" for those who do[18]. Sometimes "life" is related with "to inherit the land" (Deut 4,1), in other texts this "life" is connected with "blessings" (Deut 30,16), with "go well" and with "live long" (Deut 5,33 [MT 30]). In Lev 18 "life" is spoken of in contrast with the death penalty; see Lev 18,29; 20,9-10. The verb חיה is used here in the sense of "the life of people here on earth". There is no reason to interpret this word in these texts in the sense of "eternal life"[19].

It seems, however, that in later times this word was interpreted in the sense of eternal life. Philo quotes the words of Lev 18,5 in *De congressu quaerendae eruditionis gratia*, 86-87[20]. He concludes after this quotation: thus the true life (ἡ πρὸς ἀλήθειαν ζωή) is the life of him who walks according to the ordinances of God. Here already we see a shift in the meaning of the Old Testamentwords. "Life" is not life in contrast to death, but "life" is here something like the life of the pious man. In the Damascus Document 3,15.16 the same Old Testament text has been quoted. The author argues that people should obey the commandments

14. See the study from Hühn (n. 11) and see the survey in G.L. ARCHER, G. CHIRICHIGNO, *Old Testament Quotations in the New Testament*, Chicago, 1983.

15. Cf. R.N. LONGENECKER, *Biblical Exegesis in the Apostolic Period*, Grand Rapids, 1975, pp. 19-20 and M. BONEY, *Paul's Use of the Old Testament*, Diss. Ann Arbor Michigan, 1956, pp. 20-21.

16. Cf. W. ZIMMERLI, *Ezechiel* (BKAT, XIII/1), Neukirchen-Vluyn, 1969, p. 447.

17. ZIMMERLI (n. 16), p. 447: argues that it "wohl aus dem Heiligtums-Zulassungsrecht stammen dürfte".

18. H. BRAUN, in *TWNT* VI, p. 468: "das Normale ist [...], trotz aller prophetischen Gerichtspredigt, jedenfalls in der Thora und der Weisheitsliteratur, die Fähigkeit des Israeliten und Juden zum gebotenen *Tun* [...] Von solchem rechten *Tun* der Thora hängt das Leben, dh für den großen Teil des AT, das zeitliche Heil ab".

19. Cf. H. RINGGREN, in *TWAT* II, pp. 886-888. See above the statement of H. Braun.

20. See L. COHN, P. WENDLAND, *Philonis Alexandrini Opera quae supersunt* III, Berlin, 1898, pp. 89- 90.

of God and he who does them will live by them: he is destined for eternal life, לחיי נצח, (3,20)[21]. In this text the word חיה is interpreted in the sense of eternal life. In later times the Jewish scholar Rasji explained the words of Lev 18,5 in the same way, וחי בהס:לעולס הבא, and he will live by them referring to the future world.

In the same positive way we must read these words in Luke 10. Though the question about eternal life is a question to put Jesus to the test (10,25), Jesus' answer is a serious answer. He does not question the possibility of obeying the law, but just asks the lawyer to do the commandments. Then he will live. As we have to understand these words as an answer to the lawyer, ζάω has here the meaning: to live eternally[22].

Later on, these words of the Tenach were quoted by the rabbis on several occasions. In Baba Qama 38a these words are used to prove that even a gentile who occupies himself with the study of the Torah will receive a reward, for it is written: the man who does these [commandments], will live by them, אשר יעשה אותם האדם וחי בהם. Then the rabbi defends that even the gentile will receive a reward if he does the commandments, because of the use of האדם, the man, instead of "priests" or "levites"[23]. The words of God were seen as a means of obtaining life, not as a way to death. See the Babylonian Talmud, Aboda Zara 27b and 54a: וחי בהם ולא שימות בהם, he will live by them, but he will not die by them[24]. In Midrash Rabba Ex 30,22 we read a quotation from Ez 20,25: "I gave them statutes which were not good and ordinances whereby they would not live (לא יחיו בהם), but with regard to the commandments it is said: the man who does, shall live by them". So it is thought to be possible to live according to the commandments and that people who do so, will have life. The biggest difference is that in Lev 18,5 life here on earth is meant whereas in the later texts life is interpreted in the sense of eternal life[25]. We can say that apart from this difference the way people use the words we find in Lev 18,5 and in other texts, is in accordance with the meaning of these words in Lev 18,5: there is a great reward for those people who obey the words of the Lord.

---

21. See E. LOHSE, *Die Texte aus Qumran*, Darmstadt, 1964, pp. 70, 72.

22. Comp. Sir 15,15-20.

23. We read the same argument in the Babylonian Talmud in Sanh 59a; Aboda Zara 3a; see also Bamidbar Raba 13,16.

24. See also the Palestinian Talmud Shabbat 14,4; Qohelet Rabba 1,8.

25. See for example Hermas, Visions 3.8.5: ὅταν οὖν τὰ ἔργα τῆς μητρὸς αὐτῶν πάντα ποιήσῃς, δύνασαι ζῆσαι, when thus you do all the works of their mother, you can live, in: M. WHITTAKER, *Der Hirt des Hermas* (GCS, 48), Berlin, 1956, p. 15.

II

In Gal 3 the situation is very different for several reasons. First of all we must reckon with the polemical context of this letter. In Luke 10 we read about a conversation between Jesus and a lawyer. In the epistle to the Galatians Paul is very sharp to his opponents who in his opinion bend the gospel. The point under discussion, not yet very different from the question in Luke 10, is: in which way do we receive righteousness before God? In Gal 2,6 Paul claims that the apostles in Jerusalem did not burden him with any commandments; the only thing he had to do was to care for the poor (Gal 2,10). In Gal 2,11-14 we read the famous passage about Paul's conflict with Peter. The main point under discussion is living like the heathens, ἐθνικῶς, in contrast with ἰουδαΐζειν, living in the Jewish way. According to Paul the latter is not a good way of life. Living in the Jewish way means living for the purpose of receiving righteousness by the works of the law. In 2,16 this way of life is contrasted with the life through faith in Jesus Christ. Apparently Paul has heard that there were preachers in Galatia who claimed that people will receive righteousness by doing the works of the law. The central question is: how do we receive righteousness? Or in other words: in what way will people be justified at the eschatological judgment by God and so inherit eternal life? It is impossible, Paul argues, to be justified by the works of the law, the only way is to be justified through faith (Gal 2,16). In this text, and more specifically in Gal 3, Paul constructs an antithesis between "faith" and "(the works of) the law".

He argues in the following way[26]. In Gal 3,6-9 Paul wants to prove that only through faith in Jesus Christ people will be justified. Through this faith in Jesus Christ people will receive the Spirit (3,2.5). According to Paul, even Abraham was justified through his faith (3,6). And therefore it could be said that "in Abraham all the peoples will be blessed" (3,8), because in the same way as Abraham all the peoples will be justified through their faith. In 3,10-12 it is argued that the law cannot justify at all. On the contrary, the law brings a curse over people, because cursed is everyone who does not live according to the law (3,10; a quotation from Deut 27,26). Paul presupposes that nobody obeys the words of the law. It is faith which gives life (3,11; Hab 2,4). And then Paul states in 3,12 ὁ δὲ νόμος οὐκ ἔστιν ἐκ πίστεως, ἀλλ᾿ ὁ ποιήσας αὐτὰ ζήσεται ἐν αὐτοῖς. It is clear that in this text "faith" and "law" are opposites of each other. With the help of Lev 18,5 Paul argues that people

26. See for this passage VERHOEF (n. 12), pp. 45-86; 172-193.

do *not* get righteousness by (doing) the law, as nobody lives according to the law. Paul uses the words of Lev 18,5 to describe the disputed principle of receiving righteousness by doing the works of the law. It is clear that in this way the words of Lev 18,5 have a meaning different from the meaning in the context of Lev 18[27].

Here Rom 10 must be mentioned as well. The scope of this passage is slightly different from that in Gal. Paul speaks in Rom 10 about the Jews who are ignorant of the righteousness which God gives and who look for their own righteousness. In 10,5-6 Paul contrasts the righteousness of the law with the righteousness of the faith. "Both exclude each other"[28]. The righteousness of the law is described with the words of Lev 18,5: he who does these (commandments) will live by them. This antithesis becomes even stronger by the introductory formulas. In v. 5 Paul introduces the words of Lev 18,5 with: Moses writes about the righteousness of the law. In v. 6 Paul continues: but the righteousness of faith speaks in a different way. After this introductory formula we find an accumulation of quotations ending with the conclusion (v. 8): this is the word of faith that we preach.

In both texts, Rom 10,5 and Gal 3,12, Paul speaks about (the works of) the law as opposed to faith as two oppposite ways by which people try to be justified. But the way of the law is in his opinion the wrong way. It is impossible to get righteousness by doing the works of the law. The only way is by faith in Jesus Christ.

III

Paul's opinion differs strikingly from Jesus' answer to the lawyer in Luke 10. It is surprising to read in Ellis' book with regard to these texts: "Paul finds close affinity with the teachings of the Lord Jesus"[29]. Whereas Jesus says with the words of the law: do this and you will live, Paul disqualifies the law, because it does not give what it promises. The law is set aside by him, or even stronger: the law brings a curse over all the people (see Gal 3,10.13). It is presupposed by him that nobody really obeys the law.

A complicating factor is that Paul himself quotes the great commandment in the same letter to the Galatians (5,14). After the negative statements about the law in Gal 3, Paul quotes the great commandment to

27. See VERHOEF (n. 12), p. 188.
28. So H.D. BETZ, *Galatians* (Hermeneia), Philadelphia, 1979, p. 148 about Rom 10.
29. ELLIS (n. 13), p. 87.

summon the Galatians that they must live in the right way. Betz asks: "How is the entirely negative view of the Law, expressed up to 5:12, related to the positive interpretation of the concept in 5:14–6:10?"[30] We cannot speak about this verse in great detail here. Paul says that it is the ἀγάπη, the love by which the whole law is fulfilled. He seems to make a distinction between the commandment to love each other and the other commandments. Nevertheless, though the commandment to love each other is important to him, it is not the way to get righteousness.

We can conclude that Jesus' attitude towards the law is much more positive than Paul's. Paul breaks radically with the idea that the law is a means to obtain eternal life or to get righteousness, whereas for Jesus doing the law *is* the way to obtain eternal life. They both allude to the same words of Lev 18,5, but they interpret them in different ways. Jesus alludes to these words in order to argue that by doing the commandments the lawyer will receive eternal life, whereas Paul quotes them to prove that by doing the law nobody can get righteousness. His presupposition is that nobody actually obeys the law, whereas without questioning this possibility Jesus asks the lawyer to live according to the law in order to achieve eternal life. The comparison between Luke 10 and Gal 3 shows that Jesus, or more exactly, Jesus as he speaks in Luke 10 and Paul have different opinions about the right way to achieve eternal life or righteousness. According to Jesus life is dependent on following the commandments, according to Paul righteousness will be obtained only by faith in Jesus Christ.

Tolakkerweg 76   Eduard VERHOEF
NL-3739 JR Hollandsche Rading

---

30. BETZ (n. 27), p. 274. Cf. F. MUßNER, *Galaterbrief* (HTKNT, IX), Freiburg, 1974, pp. 369-370.

DER BETENDE SÜNDER VOR GOTT
Lk 18,9-14
ZUR REZEPTION VON PSALM 51(50),19

In den Texten des griechisch sprechenden Judentums und schließlich auch des Urchristentums gibt es verschiedene Möglichkeiten, das Verhältnis zwischen Gott und den »Sündern« zu beschreiben. Der Umgang Gottes mit den Verfehlungen der Menschen wird mit Hilfe eines vielfältigen Vokabulars und mit vielfältigen »Vergebungs«-Vorstellungen zum Ausdruck gebracht. Im folgenden soll gezeigt werden, welche Bedeutung eine bestimmte Vorstellung, die sich in verschiedenen jüdischen und christlichen Texten findet und die im Anschluß an Ps 51(50),19 ausgebildet wurde, für die Interpretation des Gleichnisses vom Pharisäer und Zöllner im lukanischen Sondergut gewinnen kann[1].

In der Literatur zu Lk 18,9-14 wird häufig die Hinzufügung des Q-Logions in v.14b (Q 14,11) als unsachgemäße Überfrachtung des eigentlichen Gleichnisses gesehen, da in der Erzählung weder davon die Rede sei, daß der Pharisäer sich selbst erhöht noch daß der Zöllner sich selbst erniedrigt[2]. Es kann jedoch gezeigt werden, daß der betende Zöllner im Tempel in seinem vorbildlichen und exemplarischen Verhalten vom Evangelisten Lukas als ein Mann dargestellt wird, der seine »Seele zerknirscht« und sein »Herz demütigt«. Denn Lukas entwirft das Bild von einem betenden Sünder vor Gott, das den Vorstellungen von betenden Sündern entspricht, wie sie in einigen Texten des griechisch sprechenden Judentums und Urchristentums u.a. im Anschluß an PsLxx 50,19 ausgebildet wurden. Im Gebet Asarjas, in 1 Clem 52 und im Gebet des

---

1. Die vorliegende Untersuchung ist aus Studien zu Gebets- und Redentexten des griechisch sprechenden Judentums und Urchristentums erwachsen. Im Rahmen eines Dissertationsprojektes wurden poetische Texte auf ihre Vorstellungen von »Vergebung« befragt, also auf die Konzeptionen vom Umgang Gottes mit Verfehlungen der Menschen und seinem Verhalten gegenüber den »Sündern«; siehe S. v. STEMM, *Der betende Sünder vor Gott. Studien zu Vergebungsvorstellungen in poetischen Texten des griechisch sprechenden Judentums und Urchristentums*, Diss. Berlin, 19.6.1996.

2. Sowohl die Selbstbeschreibung des Zöllners als auch die Selbstdarstellung des Pharisäers werden als angemessene Zusammenfassung der gegebenen Standpunkte beider Personen gedeutet: der erste ein rechtschaffener Mann, der keine Verfehlungen beging, und der zweite ein Sünder, ein ἁμαρτωλός. Siehe schon R. BULTMANN, *Die Geschichte der synoptischen Tradition*, Göttingen [8]1970, p. 193, und die Aufsätze von H. MERKLEIN, «Dieser ging als Gerechter nach Hause...», in *BiKi* 32 (1977) 36, und F. SCHNIDER, *Ausschließen und ausgeschlossen werden*, in *BZ* 24 (1980) 42-56.

Hohenpriesters Simon nach 3 Makk 2 beispielsweise wird die zentrale
Rolle des Gebetes deutlich, und besonders das Bußgebet hat für die
Beschreibung des Verhältnisses von Gott und Sündern in den Texten
des griechisch sprechenden Judentums und Urchristentums große Bedeutung: Der Sünder steht hier als Betender im Zentrum des Interes-
ses. Von einem Menschen, der Verfehlungen begangen hat, wird gefordert, daß er seine Verfehlungstaten bekennt und sich im Gebet an
Gott wendet.

I. Gemeinsamkeiten in den Rezeptionen von PsLxx 50,19

Die Texte von Dan 3,39; 1 Clem 52,4 und 3 Makk 2,20 rezipieren
PsLxx 50,19 in durchaus unterschiedlichen Zusammenhängen. Gemeinsam
ist ihnen aber, daß in diesen Texten nach Wegen gesucht wird, wie Menschen, die Verfehlungen begangen haben, sich vor Gott verhalten können. Es geht um das menschliche Tun angesichts der eigenen Verfehlungen. Auffällig ist zudem, daß die (weisheitliche) Feststellung in PsLxx
50,19, wonach ein zerknirschter Geist und ein demütiges Herz als Opfer
vor Gott gelten, in den Zusammenhängen der Textausschnitte von Dan
3; 1 Clem 52 und 3 Makk 2 jeweils mit einer imperativischen Spitze
versehen wird. Sowohl die beiden jüdischen Gebetstexte als auch Klemens in seinem Schreiben nach Korinth rezipieren das alttestamentliche
Wort im paränetischen Sinne.

Für das Gebet Asarjas[3] steht der mit den traditionellen Worten vorge-
zeichnete Weg, von Gott in das verheißungsvolle Verhältnis des Bundes
aufgenommen zu werden, in Verbindung mit einem Wunsch (v. 40) und
schließlich mit einer Selbstaufforderung (v. 41). Die Möglichkeit, auf die
beschriebene Weise von Gott angenommen zu werden, wird in diesem Gebet nicht nur konstatiert, sondern es wird dazu aufgefordert, sich so zu
verhalten, wie es PsLxx 50,19 vorschreibt. Das Gebet des Hohenpriesters Simon (3 Makk 2,2-20) blickt auf ein solches Verhalten, das
sich an PsLxx 50,19 als Handlungsmaßstab orientiert, schon zurück.

---

3. K. Koch, *Die Deuterokanonischen Zusätze zum Danielbuch* (AOAT, 38/I+II),
Kevelaer/Neukirchen-Vluyn, 1987, pp. 11+69 u.ö., vertritt gegen die herkömmliche Ein-
schätzung die These, daß innerhalb der griechischen Zusätze zu Dan 3 ältere aramäische
Originaltexte verarbeitet worden wären; siehe auch J.J. Collins, *Daniel: A Commentary
on the Book of Daniel* (Hermeneia), Minneapolis, 1993 [»Appendix: The Prayer of Azariah
and the Song of the Three Young Men« (pp. 195-203)]. Doch selbst für diesen Fall
nimmt Koch an, daß die Entstehungszeit des Gebetes Asarjas nicht weit vor derjenigen
des kanonischen Danielbuches (ca. 165 v.Chr.) anzusetzen sei. Auch er liest also das
Gebet als jüdischen Text aus der Zeit des Zweiten Tempels.

Denn der Hohepriester beschreibt sich selbst und sämtliche mit ihm Betenden als solche, die sich zum Gebet niedergeworfen haben und ihre Seele »zerknirschten«. Die Betenden haben sich so verhalten, wie es in PsLxx 50,19 empfohlen wird. Schließlich wird in 1 Clem 52,4 das Zitat aus PsLxx 50,19 als Erläuterung für einen Imperativ gesetzt, so daß auch hier der paränetische Zusammenhang deutlich ist. Klemens ruft die Korinther, deren Taten er mißbilligt, dazu auf, Gott Lobopfer und Gebete vorzubringen. Demnach erfordert die Absetzung der Gemeindeführung durch die Korinther ein Verhalten, wie es in PsLxx 50,19 anschaulich wird.

Werden nun die drei Texte nebeneinander betrachtet, wird die Basis für die oben angedeutete These erkennbar. Adäquaten Ausdruck findet nach Aussage dieser Texte das umschriebene und zur Forderung erhobene Verhalten im Gebet. Das Zerknirschen der Seele und das Demütigen des Herzens drückt sich im Beten zu Gott aus.

Eine Annäherung an den gemeinsamen Gehalt der genannten Textstellen ergibt sich auch über die Klärung der Terminologie. Denn es ist zu fragen, in welchem Sinne die Vokabeln συντρίβειν und ταπεινοῦν in der besonderen Kombination mit den Substantiven καρδία, πνεῦμα und ψυχή zu verstehen sind. Für die besondere Wendung ἐν ψυχῇ συντετριμμένῃ in Dan 3,39 schlägt Klaus Koch im Rückgriff auf semitischen Sprachgebrauch vor, hier einen Beleg für den Gedanken der Selbsthingabe zu sehen, da auf die Selbstopferung der drei Männer im Feuerofen angespielt werde[4]. Und tatsächlich wird συντρίβειν (wie zum Teil auch ταπεινοῦν) auch in der jüdischen Literatur zur Beschreibung von Zerstörungshandlungen und Gewalteinwirkungen verwendet[5].

Doch συντρίβειν ist nicht nur in Konstellationen mit Begriffen belegt, die Gegenstände, Gebäude, Menschen oder Völker bezeichnen und das Objekt der ausgesagten Zerstörungshandlung ausweisen. Vielmehr finden sich besonders bei den Historikern auch Abstraktbegriffe, wie beispielsweise die Hoffnung (ἐλπίς) oder die hoffende Einstellung (διανοία), die zerbrechen können[6]. Oder es wird davon berichtet, daß »Gedanken verworfen«

---

4. KOCH kann aufgrund seiner Interpretation in Dan 3,39 einen Beleg für die Bedeutung von Martyrien als Sühnehandlungen finden, da hier von der Vernichtung des Lebens der drei Männer gesprochen werde. In diesem Sinne sei die griechische Übersetzung von נפשא mit ψυχή zu verstehen; cf. *Zusätze* II, p. 54. KOCH, *Zusätze* I+II, passim, vertritt wie gesehen die Auffassung, daß ein aramäisches Textstück aus dem 10. Jahrhundert den ursprünglichen Text des Gebetes Asarjas enthält. In der ersten Zeile dieses Textes liest KOCH ואזלו תלתיהון לגו אחון נורא und übersetzt: »die Drei gingen zur/in die Mitte des brennenden Feuerofens« (*Zusätze* I, p. 28, und passim). Naheliegender ist es jedoch, das Umhergehen der Männer im Ofen als Zeichen ihrer Rettung und Unversehrtheit zu verstehen, denn ausdrücklich wird im griechischen und hebräischen Text gesagt, daß sie in den Ofen geworfen werden. Zudem fehlt der Anfang des aramäischen Textes!

5. Siehe grHen 103,10; JosAs 10,12; PsSal 8,5; 17,24; TestJob 25,10; Philo, Fug 197.201; LegGai 366; Josephus, Ant 10,79; Bell 1,43; 2,28; 5,464 u.ö.

6. Cf. Diodor Sic., 4,66,4; 16,59,3. Polybios, 21,13,2; 30,32,11, parallelisiert die Aussagen mit δυσελπίζω bzw. ἀπαλπισμός.

werden[7]. Und schließlich begegnet nicht nur im Übersetzungsgriechisch der jüdischen Texte das Substantiv ψυχή als Objekt zu συντρίβειν: Die Wendung συντρίβεσθαι ταῖς ψυχαῖς wird nämlich andernorts auch gebraucht, um die Reaktion einer großen Menge auf eine Schreckensnachricht[8] oder die Erschütterung von einzelnen zu beschreiben[9]. Es kommt jeweils zum Ausdruck, daß die äußeren Umstände auch innere Zerrüttung und Furcht bewirken[10]. Damit ist zu vermuten, daß die oben genannten Texte, die sämtlich auf PsLxx 50,19 anspielen, nicht einen semitisierenden Sprachgebrauch übernehmen, wenn dort συντρίβειν und/oder ταπεινοῦν mit καδία, πνεῦμα und ψυχή konstruiert werden. Es scheint in der griechischen Sprache durchaus üblich, innere Zerrüttungen oder psychischen Druck mit Hilfe von συντρίβειν ψυχήν und dergleichen zum Ausdruck zu bringen. Somit ist nicht das gesamte Leben eines Menschen als Objekt der mit diesen Wendungen umschriebenen Handlungen zu verstehen, sondern das Innere, die Seele, der Geist oder das Herz des Betreffenden.

Im Gebet Asarjas wird daher die aufgezeigte Alternative zu den herkömmlichen Wegen, von Gott angenommen zu werden, nicht weiter als mit jenen traditionellen Worten aus PsLxx 50 umschrieben. Das Zerknirschen der Seele und Demütigen des Geistes wird als Ersatz für die Tieropfer und als angemessenes Opfer vor Gott ausgegeben (v. 39-40). Da aber keine weiteren Angaben gemacht werden, wie das so beschriebene Opfer auszusehen hat, muß die Umsetzung für diese Zerknirschung in dem formulierten Gebet selbst gesehen werden. In diesem Gebet wird in Anlehnung an die Tradition der jüdischen Bußgebete[11] Gott angesichts seines Strafhandelns gegenüber Israel gerecht gesprochen (vv. 27-28), die eigene Schuld wird eingestanden (vv. 29-30), und die Barmherzigkeit Gottes wird angerufen, um aus der bestehenden Notsituation gerettet zu werden (v. 42); diese Gebetselemente bringen die Zerknirschung der Seele und die Demütigung des Geistes zum Ausdruck[12].

---

7. Siehe Diodor Sic., 11,78,4; Appian, BellCiv 2,14,97, vgl. Philo, QEx 2,17.

8. Cf. Diodor Sic., 16,81,3.

9. Cf. *ibid.*, 30,11,1 und siehe auch Jes 61,1.

10. Auch in Jer 23,9 wird die Furcht des Propheten wiedergegeben, wobei hier ἡ καρδία συνετρίβη zur Übersetzung von לבי נשבר dient.

11. Siehe 2 Esdr 19,6-20,1; Est 4,17[l-z]; Dan 9,4b-19; Bar 1,15-3,8, aber auch schon Ps 78; 79; 106 oder 1QS 1,24b–2,1; CD 20,28-30 und cf. O.H. STECK, *Das apokryphe Baruchbuch. Studien zu Rezeption und Konzentration »kanonischer« Überlieferung* (FRLANT, 160), Göttingen, 1993, pp. 81-83.

12. Auffällig ist zudem, daß der erhoffte Vorgang, der durch die Zerknirschung und Demütigung von Gott erwartet wird, mit dem Verbum προσδέχεσθαι benannt ist. Denn gerade dieses Verb wird im Judentum nicht nur dazu verwendet, die Auf- und Annahme von Menschen zu beschreiben, sondern auch das Erhören von Gebeten (siehe Sir 7,9; 35,11; TestJob 42,8; Josephus, Ant 6,25; 7,334)! Eindrücklich ist daher die Rezeption von Dtn 26,5-11 durch Philo. Er verwendet das Verbum προσδέχεσθαι und setzt es für εἰσακούειν in der biblischen Vorlage (εἰσήκουσεν κύριος τῆς φωνῆς ἡμῶν – Dtn 26,7): Das Annehmen und Akzeptieren des Volkes besteht darin, daß Gott die Gebete des

Diese Elemente der Bußgebete finden sich auch im Gebet des Hohenpriesters Simon nach 3 Makk 2,2-20. Indem aber hier der Vorgang der Zerknirschung der Seele noch mit dem Niederfallen (καταπεπτωκέναι) parallelisiert wird, kommt besonders anschaulich zum Ausdruck, daß die geforderte Haltung im Gebet zu Gott umgesetzt werden kann. Mit dem vorliegenden Gebet haben die um Hilfe flehenden Einwohner Jerusalems und die Priester des Tempels nach Auffassung des Hohenpriesters ihre »Seelen zerknirscht«. Sie haben Gott gerecht gesprochen (vv. 3+11), ein Sündenbekenntnis abgegeben (vv. 13-14) und um Barmherzigkeit angesichts der Not gebeten (vv. 19-20). Durch die rahmende Erzählung wird schließlich diese Auffassung sanktioniert, denn alle Gewaltmaßnahmen gegen die Bedrohung durch Ptolemaios IV. werden abgelehnt (1,23-24; siehe auch im Gebetstext 2,10). Schließlich wird die folgende Bestrafung des Eindringlings explizit auf das Erhören des Gebetes durch Gott zurückgeführt (εἰσακούσας τῆς ἐνθέσμου λιτανείας – v. 21). Das Gebet wurde entsprechend der traditionellen Worte aufgenommen, und das Gebet zeigt seine Wirkung.

Die traditionellen Elemente der Bußgebete finden sich nicht in 1 Clem 52. Doch zeigt die Rezeption von PsLxx 50,19 in 1 Clem 52,3+4, daß auch hier das Gebet als angemessene Haltung angesichts des korinthischen Fehlverhaltens gefordert wird – wie übrigens auch ähnlich schon in 1 Clem 18. Der Kontext hebt nämlich die Exhomologese, also das Sündenbekenntnis hervor (v. 1 und v. 2), und gefordert werden explizit Lobopfer bzw. Gebete, da als Opfer vor Gott ein »zerknirschter Geist« gelte. Auch hier wird damit die Zerknirschung ausdrücklich im Gebet umgesetzt. Wer wie die Korinther Verfehlungen begangen hat, ist dazu angehalten, diese im Gebet vor Gott zu bekennen, um so seinem zerknirschten Geist Ausdruck zu verleihen.

Es läßt sich daher zusammenfassen, daß in den herangezogenen Texten dem Gebet zu Gott eine entscheidende Rolle im Verhältnis des Sünders zu Gott zugemessen wird. Gemeinsam werden in diesen Texten die Menschen, die Verfehlungen begingen, dazu aufgefordert, ihre Seele oder ihren Geist zu zerknirschen bzw. zu demütigen. Gemeinsam wird davon ausgegangen, daß diese Zerknirschung in einem Gebet zu Gott seinen angemessenen Ausdruck finden kann. In der gebotenen Kürze scheint damit eine spezifische Vorstellung angedeutet zu sein, welche

---

Volkes annimmt bzw. erhört (προσδεξάμενος τὴν ἱκεσίαν ὁ πᾶσι τοῖς ἀδικουμένοις εὐμενῆς – SpecLeg 2,218). Es ist zu vermuten, daß gerade auch in Dan 3,39 das Verb προσδέχεσθαι gewählt wurde, um die Doppeldeutigkeit des gemeinten Vorganges sichtbar werden zu lassen. Die Betenden erhoffen sich, daß sie von Gott angenommen werden, indem sie als Betende erhört werden.

Rolle das Beten im Verhältnis eines Menschen, der Verfehlungen begangen hat, zu Gott spielen kann. Im Anschluß an die herangezogenen
Texte kann formuliert werden, daß sich ein solcher Mensch dann angemessen verhält, wenn er sich als betender Sünder vor Gott erweist[13].

II. DAS LUKANISCHE GLEICHNIS ALS ANLEITUNG ZUM BETEN

Im Anschluß an diese Beobachtungen zur Rezeption von PsLxx
50,19 in einigen antiken jüdischen und christlichen Texten ist nun für
das lukanische Sondergutgleichnis vom Zöllner und Pharisäer zu fragen,
welche Rolle hier das Gebet für die Darstellung der Erzählfiguren spielt
und wie die bisherigen Beobachtungen für die Auslegung des Gleichnisses fruchtbar gemacht werden können.

1. *Die Bedeutung des Gebetes für das Gleichnis vom Pharisäer und Zöllner*

Für den Inhalt des Zöllnergebetes (Lk 18,13b) ist zunächst festzuhalten, daß die kurzen Worte neben der Bitte um einen barmherzigen Umgang Gottes mit ihm, dem Zöllner, ein Sündenbekenntnis enthalten.
Denn der Zöllner bezeichnet sich selbst als ἁμαρτωλός. Zudem ist wohl
das Ziel der gesamten Gleichniserzählung in der Beschreibung der Gebetshaltung und der Gebete der beiden Erzählfiguren zu sehen. An der
Figur des Pharisäers wird nämlich hervorgehoben, daß er zwar für sich
spricht, aber dennoch frei und offen sein Gebet vorbringt (v. 11a)[14]. Der

---

13. Anzumerken ist, daß in allen Texten gemeinsam die Kritik gegenüber dem Opferkult, die in PsLxx 50 besonders in v. 18 zum Tragen kommt, vermieden wird. Im Gebet
Asarjas wird die Alternative zum Opferkult wohl allein aus der Not heraus aufgezeigt, da
ein solcher Kultus derzeit für die Betenden nicht möglich ist. Der Kultus bleibt also weiterhin hochgeschätzt, er dient als Bild, um die Funktion anderer »Heils«-Wege zu erläutern. Doch im Gebet des Hohenpriesters und im Ersten Klemensbrief wird PsLxx 50,18
schlicht übergangen. Hier ist eine Alternative nicht mehr im Blick, der Kultus wird nicht
einmal als Möglichkeit für die Sünder, sich angemessen gegenüber Gott zu verhalten,
angesprochen.

14. Ebenso wie beispielsweise bei Josephus, Ant 4,209; 8,231.337; 9,214; 11,155;
findet sich auch bei Lk (siehe 18,11; 19,8; Apg 2,14; 17,22; 27,21) in Redeeinleitungen
eine passive oder mediale Form von ἱστάναι. Es wird die Wichtigkeit der Rede durch den
eigens hervorgehobenen Akt des Hinstellens unterstrichen. Siehe zur textkritisch schwer
zu entscheidenden Folge der Worte πρός und ἑαυτόν in v. 11a schon A. JÜLICHER, *Die
Gleichnisreden Jesu*, Band II, Nachdruck der 2. Auflage (Tübingen, 1910), Darmstadt,
1976, p. 601, und J.A. FITZMYER, *The Gospel according to Luke X-XXIV. A New Translation with Introduction and Commentary* (AB, 28A), New York, 1986, p. 1186. Im Blick
auf Lk 20,5 (πρὸς ἑαυτούς) ist jedoch zu vermuten, daß auch in Lk 18,11 das Gebet des
Pharisäers als Sprechen für sich gekennzeichnet werden soll.

Zöllner wird hingegen in seiner Zurückhaltung beschrieben (v. 13a), und es wird mit dem geschilderten Gestus des Brustschlagens unterstrichen[15], daß er sich als Büßender versteht. Anders beispielsweise als die Erzählung vom Oberzöllner Zachäus (Lk 19,1-10) enthält Lk 18,9-14 darüber hinaus keine weiteren Informationen oder Beschreibungen der Erzählfiguren oder ihrer Handlungen, es geht also ausschließlich um die Gebetshaltungen und um die wörtlich wiedergegebenen Gebete des Pharisäers und des Zöllners. Daher muß geschlossen werden, daß der Zöllner aufgrund seines Gebetes sich in höherem Maße als gerecht erweist, wie es in v. 14a heißt[16]. Die gesamte Erzählung von dem Pharisäer und Zöllner kann als Erzählung vom angemessenen Beten gelesen werden.

Dies legt sich auch aus dem gegebenen lukanischen Kontext nahe. Gegenüber der vorausgehenden Erzählung von der Witwe und dem Richter hebt der Evangelist Lukas einen weiteren Aspekt an seiner Auffassung vom Gebet hervor. Er entwirft mit der Erzählfigur des Zöllners ein exemplarisches Bild, wie sich ein Mensch, der Verfehlungen begangen hat, gegenüber seinem Gott verhalten soll. Er zeichnet ihn als büßenden *Beter*, der seine Sünden bekennt und um Barmherzigkeit bittet. Dem Gebet wird die entscheidende Rolle im Rahmen der Beschreibung des Verhältnisses von Gott und Sünder zugesprochen[17].

15. Die Untersuchungen der Gebetshaltungen stellen meist einhellig heraus, daß der Akt des Brustschlagens als Kennzeichen der Reue und Buße gewertet werden müsse. Doch bleibt dies leider eine Beschreibung des Befundes; cf. beispielsweise F.J. DÖLGER, *Sol Salutis. Gebet und Gesang im christlichen Altertum*, Münster, [2]1925, p. 74, Anm 3. Nicht geklärt ist damit der Ursprung dieses Gestus, der vielleicht in einem orientalischen bzw. altägyptischen Trauergestus gesucht werden kann; siehe T. OHM, *Die Gebetsgebärden der Völker und das Christentum*, Leiden u.a., 1948, pp. 105+281.

16. Es ist fraglich, ob die in v.14a vorliegende eigentümliche Konstruktion παρ' ἐκεῖνον exklusiv interpretiert werden muß, so daß allein der Zöllner anstelle des Pharisäers gerecht gesprochen gilt (so J. JEREMIAS, *Die Gleichnisse Jesu*, Göttingen, [7]1965, p. 142, und die ihm folgenden Auslegungen). Lukanischem Sprachgebrauch scheint vielmehr zu entsprechen (siehe Lk 13,2.4), παρά τινα im komparativischen Sinne zu verwenden (siehe dazu BDR §236), so daß allein eine Steigerung, nicht aber eine Ausgrenzung impliziert ist; cf. auch B. HEININGER, *Metaphorik, Erzählstruktur und szenisch-dramatische Gestaltung in den Sondergutgleichnissen bei Lukas* (NTAbh, 24), Münster, 1991, p. 217.

17. Im Rahmen dieser kurzen Untersuchung kann nicht eingehender auf die Bedeutung des Zöllner-Gleichnisses für die lukanischen Konzeptionen vom Verhältnis der Sünder zu Gott und Jesus eingegangen werden. Mit Blick auf die Zöllner-Darstellung kann aber an der Erkenntnis festgehalten werden, daß Lukas in seinen Sünderdarstellungen häufig Taten und Verhaltensweisen von den betreffenden Menschen fordert, auch wenn dahinter noch nicht die Ausbildung eines festen Buß-Weges im Rahmen einer frühkatholischen Sakramentenlehre gesehen werden muß; siehe dazu schon H. CONZELMANN, *Die Mitte der Zeit. Studien zur Theologie des Lukas* (BHT, 17), Tübingen, [5]1964, p. 213, und insgesamt J.-W. TAEGER, *Der Mensch und sein Heil. Studien zum Bild des Menschen und zur Sicht der Bekehrung bei Lukas* (SNT, 14), Gütersloh, 1982.

2. *Die Bedeutung der Rezeptionen von PsLxx 50,19 für das Verständnis von Lk 18,9-14*

Wenn aber derart das Gebet und die Gebetshaltung im Zentrum der Gleichniserzählung stehen, legt es sich nahe, hier eine Verbindung zu den oben angedeuteten Rezeptionen von PsLxx 50,19 in jüdischen und christlichen Texten herzustellen. Denn auch für die lukanische Erzählung scheint die Vorstellung grundlegend, daß das Gebet ein angemessenes Verhalten eines Sünders vor Gott bedeutet. Derjenige erweist sich als gerecht, der das Gebet zu Gott aufnimmt und sich selbst angesichts seiner Verfehlungen als ἁμαρτωλός bekennt. Im Rahmen der direkten Beziehung Gottes zu den Menschen wird das Gebet als Instanz gesehen, welche Sündenvergebung bzw. eine »Gerechtsprechung« ermöglicht.

Demnach entwirft Lukas in seinem Gleichnis ein Bild von einem Sünder, der seine bestehende Gottesbeziehung dazu nutzt, einer Vergebung teilhaftig zu werden, indem er in einer entsprechenden Gebetshaltung und mit einem schlichten Sündenbekenntnis sowie einer Bitte um Barmherzigkeit seinem Anliegen Ausdruck verleiht. Der betende Sünder vor Gott, den Lukas hier darstellt, entspricht den (Vergebungs-) Vorstellungen, die auch in Dan 3,39; 1 Clem 52,4 und 3 Makk 2,20 für die Rezeption von PsLxx 50,19 leitend gewesen sind. Es legt sich daher die Vermutung nahe, auch das Gebet und die Gebetshaltung des Zöllners als Ausdruck für eine »zerknirschte Seele« bzw. für einen »gedemütigten Geist« anzusehen. Zwar wird im lukanischen Text das Verhalten des Zöllners nicht explizit im Blick auf PsLxx 50,19 veranschaulicht, doch kann die Hinzufügung des weiteren Deutesatzes in v. 14b genau aus dieser Vorstellung heraus verständlich gemacht werden.

3. *Die Deutung der Erzählung durch das Logion von der Selbsterniedrigung (v. 14b)*

Der abschließende Deutesatz unterstreicht nämlich nochmals die Vorstellung, daß die Gebetshaltung und das Gebet des Zöllners Ausdruck seiner Buße und Reue sind. Denn der abschließende Satz faßt die Beispielfunktion des Zöllners in Gegenüberstellung zum Pharisäer zusammen: Angesichts von Verfehlungen ist ein solch bußfertiges Verhalten gefordert, das sich in einem solchen Gebet ausdrücken kann, wie es in der Beschreibung und Selbstbeschreibung des Zöllners anschaulich wurde. Der Zöllner erniedrigt sich selbst, indem er sich in einem bußfertigen Gebet zu Gott wendet.

Terminologisch begründen läßt sich diese These, da die Beschreibung und Selbstbeschreibung des Pharisäers gut mit ὑψοῦν ἑαυτόν zusammengefaßt werden kann: Dieser setzt sich in seinem Gebet von anderen Menschen ab und stellt sein eigenes Verhalten über deren Verhalten (v. 11b-12). Die weitere Formulierung ταπεινοῦν ἑαυτόν ist zudem durchaus offen, das Einnehmen einer bußfertigen Haltung zu bezeichnen. Denn auch wenn in Lk 18,14b ein verbreitetes Q-Logion aufgenommen ist, kann weder der Ausdruck ὑψοῦν noch ταπεινοῦν ἑαυτόν als terminus technicus für eine bestimmte Handlung gelesen werden. Der Gebrauch der Wendung in Mt 23,12 auf der einen Seite und in Phil 2,8 auf der anderen ist sehr unterschiedlich. Und wieder anders scheint die gemeinsame Verwendung der Formulierung ταπεινοῦν ἑαυτόν in Mt 18,4 und im Zöllner-Gleichnis zu sein. In Mt 18,4 und in Lk 18,14 ergeht jeweils die Aufforderung, eine demutsvolle Haltung einzunehmen – wie ein Kind, um die Gottesherrschaft zu empfangen, bzw. wie ein betender Sünder.

Wird also in Lk 18,14b die Erzählung abschließend mit dem Hinweis gedeutet, daß der, der sich selbst erhöht, »erniedrigt« werden wird, und der sich selbst »erniedrigt«, erhöht werden wird, so wird kein neuer Gedanke der Erzählung hinzugefügt, sondern eine Zusammenfassung geboten: Die Bedeutung der bußfertigen Haltung, die im Gebet des Zöllners ihren Ausdruck findet, wird für das Verhältnis des Sünders vor Gott deutlich gemacht. Es werden in Form einer Erzählung zwei Menschen vor Augen geführt, von denen der eine in seiner Selbstdarstellung sich von den Sündern absetzt und seine positiven Taten herausstreicht. Dieser erhöht sich selbst. Der zweite jedoch, der schon durch die Beschreibung als Zöllner als Mensch dargestellt ist, der Verfehlungen begangen hat[18], disqualifiziert sich selbst als ἁμαρτωλός. Er nimmt also die Haltung einer Selbsterniedrigung in dem Sinne ein, als er sich betend und bekennend zu Gott wendet.

Die untersuchten Rezeptionen von PsLxx 50,19 legen es also nahe, die »Selbsterniedrigung« des Zöllners als bußfertige Wendung im Gebet zu Gott zu verstehen. Der Vorgang der Selbsterniedrigung (ταπεινοῦν

---

18. F. HERRENBRÜCK, *Jesus und die Zöllner* (WUNT, 2.41), Tübingen, 1990, pp. 225-235, und W. STENGER, »*Gebt dem Kaiser, was des Kaisers ist...!*«. *Eine sozialgeschichtliche Untersuchung zur Besteuerung Palästinas in neutestamentlicher Zeit* (BBB, 68), Frankfurt, 1988, pp. 13-25, haben jetzt wieder herausgestellt, daß die Steuerpächter in Palästina zur Zeit Jesu ebenfalls jüdischen Glaubens waren und im Rahmen des römischen Zensus-Steuer-Systems für die Besatzungsmacht die Abgaben eintrieben. So deutet auch Josephus (Ant 18,3.26; Bell 2,405ff.; 2,287ff.) an, daß in der Provinz Judäa die Oberschicht bzw. bestimmte Steuerpächter von den Römern für die Eintreibung der Steuern verantwortlich gemacht wurden; cf. E.W. STEGEMANN / W. STEGEMANN, *Urchristliche Sozialgeschichte. Die Anfänge im Judentum und die Christusgemeinden in der mediterranen Welt*, Stuttgart u.a., 1995, pp. 112-113. Daß die Steuerpächter kein gutes Ansehen genossen, sondern mit ἁμαρτωλοί in einem Atemzug genannt werden konnten, geht in den synoptischen Evangelien aus Mt 5,46; 9,10f.; Mk 2,15f. parr. u.ö. hervor.

ἑαυτόν) umschreibt damit ein solches Verhalten, wie es an der Beispiel-figur des Zöllners veranschaulicht wurde.

III. Sündenvergebung und Gebet: Eine Möglichkeit von vielen

Abschließend sei eine weiterführende Bemerkung erlaubt: Ist nämlich die Deutung zutreffend, daß es in den herangezogenen Texten – ein-schließlich des lukanischen Gleichnisses vom betenden Zöllner und Pha-risäer – darum geht, das Gebet als Ausdruck der Buße und zugleich als Möglichkeit zu etablieren, sich angesichts von eigenem Fehlverhalten angemessen gegenüber Gott zu verhalten, muß wohl die Bedeutung des Gebetes für die urchristliche Darstellung des Verhältnisses von Gott und Sündern stärker betont werden. Sowohl in jüdischen als auch in christli-chen Texten scheint angesichts von Verfehlungen die Haltung des Gebe-tes gefordert zu werden.

Die Verfehlungen und ein entsprechender Umgang Gottes mit diesen Verfehlungen wird nach dieser Konzeption streng im Rahmen des beste-henden Gott-Mensch-Verhältnisses gedacht. Weitere Instanzen, die von seiten des Menschen die Reue oder die Buße über die begangenen Taten zum Ausdruck bringen, kommen ebenso wenig in den Blick wie Instan-zen von seiten Gottes, die die zu gewährende »Vergebung« vermitteln. Als Belege für diese Konzeption lassen sich weitere zentrale urchristli-che Texte heranziehen, wobei besonders das Herrengebet hervorgehoben werden kann[19]. Denn dieser zentrale Text gründet die Vergebungshoff-nung ausschließlich in der Vater-Kind-Beziehung der Betenden, die im Gebet angerufen wird. Das Gebet enthält allein eine Bitte um Sündener-laß und macht damit deutlich, daß es keiner weiteren Vermittlung und keiner weiteren Instanzen bedarf. Die Verfehlungen werden von Gott erlassen allein aufgrund dieser Bitte um Vergebung.

Das läßt den Schluß zu, daß auch in den urchristlichen Texten nicht allein unterschiedliche Vorstellungen von der Sündenvergebung, wie dem Erlaß von Verfehlungen oder der Gerechtsprechung des Sünders und dergleichen, vorliegen. Vielmehr scheint das Urchristentum die Sündenvergebung nicht nur im Bereich der Christologie und der Sote-riologie zu thematisieren, sondern auch im Bereich der Lebensführung

---

19. Siehe aber auch die matthäische Einbettung des Vaterunsers durch Mt 6,14-15 sowie Mk 11,25 oder Jak 5,13. Stets wird allein auf ein Gebet der Betreffenden ange-spielt, welches sie angesichts ihrer Verfehlungen vorbringen. Die Gebetsworte allein ber-gen die Möglichkeit, von Gott »Vergebung«, also einen barmherzigen Umgang mit den Verfehlungen erhoffen zu dürfen. Siehe dazu auch v. STEMM, *Sünder*, p. 302.

der Christen vor Gott. Das direkte Beziehungsverhältnis derjenigen, die sich zur christlichen Gemeinschaft zählen, wird als Basis gesehen, das alltägliche Fehlverhalten und die alltäglichen Verschuldungen von Gott erlassen zu bekommen. Die oben dargestellte Vorstellung von der Bedeutung des (Buß-) Gebetes macht deutlich, daß Sündenvergebung nicht allein einen ein für alle Mal gültigen Akt umfassen muß, sondern im Rahmen der bestehenden Gottesbeziehung kann Sündenvergebung auch zum alltäglichen Gebetsanliegen werden, wie die Bitte um Brot.

Humboldt-Universität zu Berlin   Sönke VON STEMM
Institut für Urchristentum und Antike
Waisenstr. 2
D-10179 Berlin

SCRIPTURE RESISTING THE CARNIVALESQUE
IN THE LUCAN PASSION[1]

In the thematic development in Luke, John the Baptist stipulates that a tree that does not bear good fruit is cut down and consumed by fire (Luke 3,9), and Jesus asserts that trees are known by their fruit (Luke 6,44). Readers, therefore, expect to know who Jesus is by his fruits. What better occasion for such expectations to come to fruition than festival – unleavened bread – ancient reminiscences of barley harvest – Passover – divine deliverance from oppressors[2].

Which tree, however, gets cut down and thrown into the fire? If Jesus is a tree known by his fruits, in the end is he cut down and thrown into the fire? Indeed readers gain such an impression through the mockery at Jesus' crucifixion. In fact opposite evaluations of Jesus and correspondingly different constructs of the world clash in the passion. On one side, antagonists attempt to deflate Jesus' identity with the carnivalesque. On the other, Jesus wins support from several corners – including God. But direct resistance to the carnivalesque comes primarily through allusions to scripture.

"Carnivalesque" is modern language for an age-old phenomenon of creating an inverted world alongside the norm[3]. It is a lethally serious portrayal of the norm as ridiculous. My interest here is not to claim a direct relationship to something like the saturnalia, but to claim that the passion evokes cultural codes of a lethally serious inversion of the norms of the narrative.

Competing visions of the world emerge in Jesus' vow to fast in the last supper (Lk 22,16.18), which inverts the feast of Passover. More

---

1. Longer versions of this paper appear in R. BRAWLEY, *Text to Text Pours Forth Speech: Voices of Scripture in Luke-Acts* (Indiana Studies in Biblical Literature), Bloomington, IN, 1995, pp. 42-60, and in *Semeia* 69/70 (1995) 33–60: *Resistance to the Carnivalization of Jezus: Scripture in the Lucan Passion Narrative*.

2. On harvest, Passover, and liberation themes see D. SENIOR, *The Passion of Jesus in the Gospel of Luke*, Wilmington, DE, 1989, pp. 42-43, 56-57, 162-63.

3. M. BAKHTIN, *Rabelais and His World*, Bloomington, IN, 1984, pp. 5-17; ID., *Problems of Dostoevsky's Poetics*, Manchester, 1984, pp. 108, 120-176; J. KRISTEVA, *Desire in Language: A Semiotic Approach to Literature and Art*, New York, 1980, pp. 78-85. On the morphology of the carnivalesque I follow P. STALLYBRASS, *Drunk with the Cup of Liberty: Robin Hood, the Carnivalesque, and the Rhetoric of Violence in Early Modern England*, in *Semiotica* 54 (1985) 113-114.

forcefully, Jesus' advice to the disciples to take up swords predicts an in-version of inlaw and outlaw by citing a portion of Isa 53,12. Incidentally, the carnivalesque helps resolve the enigma of this text. Against Conzel-mann[4], ἀλλὰ νῦν does not mean "from this time forward". Rather, it introduces a curious period set off as an inversion of ordinary time. Against Minear[5], however, it is not Jesus who considers the disciples outlaws, but opponents. Further, appropriate to the carnivalesque, the disciples really play the part of outlaws by producing two swords. But Jesus puts an end to the swordplay and repudiates the construal of the swords as an act of holy war.

Beyond the open citation of Isa 53,12, there are covert allusions to the Isaianic context on the level of setting and plot. Isaiah juxtaposes two worlds – the world of idolatry and the world centred on God. Given Lucan references to Isaiah elsewhere[6], when Jesus' opponents abuse him, readers who know Isaiah hear echoes of Isa 50,6 LXX: "I gave my back to the whips and my jaws to slaps, and I did not turn my face away from the dishonor of spittings". Further, the plot of the passion coin-cides with the rejection of the servant in Isa 53,3 LXX: "But his appear-ance was dishonorable; abandoned more than all others, he was a man of calamity, and he knew what it was to bear weakness". Moreover, the verdict of innocence in Isa 53,8 corresponds to the reiterated verdict concerning Jesus at his crucifixion.

I use Harold Bloom's revisionary ratios to analyze ways successor texts use precursors[7]. Jesus' direct appeal to Isa 53,12 makes a claim to fulfil-ment, that is, a revisionary ratio that is a figurative play of completion. But completion means both continuity and discontinuity. Jesus' citation does not overthrow Isa 53,12. Rather, it depends on it. On the other hand, there is an implicit claim that Isaiah is unfinished, and as such it takes on a meaning that it did not have prior to its use in Luke's passion. By itself, Isa 53,12 centres on the history of Israel. By itself Jesus' passion centres on senselessness. Together, they relocate on new centres. Israel's history extends to Jesus' passion; Jesus' passion takes its meaning from the God of Israel's history. Mere completion, however, does not do justice to the revisionary relationship. Completion comes about when revisionary relationships provoke a new level of discernment, a gain in meaning, like

4. H. CONZELMANN, *The Theology of St. Luke*, New York, 1961, pp. 16, 81-82, 150.
5. P. MINEAR, *A Note on Luke xxii.36*, in *NovT* 7 (1964) 128-134.
6. On availability and recurrence as criteria for allusions see R. HAYS, *Echoes of Scripture in the Letters of Paul*, New Haven, 1989, pp. 29-30.
7. Bloom's theory of revisionary ratios is repeated in a number of his works. E.g., H. BLOOM, *The Anxiety of Influence*, Oxford, 1973; ID., *Kabbalah and Criticism*, New York, 1975.

a coil spring turning back on itself at a higher level. But the gain in meaning occurs at the expense of a loss of meaning in the precursor. Viewed through the Lucan passion, Isa 53,12 is no longer part of Israel's hope of the restoration of the nation after the exile but part of the hope of the restoration of Jesus as messiah after the crucifixion.

On the heels of the mockery of those who arrested Jesus, the council demands, "If you are the Messiah, tell us". But for Jesus, this interrogation is an inversion of a genuine inquest. The council will not regard his answer soberly: "If I tell you, you will not believe". But in competition with the cultural code of a carnival king, Jesus speaks to them of his genuine enthronement at the right hand of God. By contrast, in the carnivalesque world, he is whatever they say: "You say that I am". Jesus answers Pilate in like terms. He is whatever Pilate says. Then Herod and his soldiers mock Jesus and put an exquisite robe on him as a carnival king.

Suddenly there is a street scene. The populace transgresses the boundaries of walls and takes to the streets – a feature of the carnivalesque. The populace does not observe carnival, it lives it[8]. Then the release of Barabbas is a carnivalesque inversion of outlaw for inlaw. In addition, true to carnival, the populace parades the mock king through the streets. The wailing women are also a part of carnival that mixes the comic and the tragic, guffawing and wailing.

Again, biblical allusions resist carnivalization. In response to the wailing women, Jesus cites Hos 10,8. As with Isaiah, the context in Hosea juxtaposes the world of idolatry and the world centred on Israel's God. Ugaritic texts parallel precisely the kind of weeping going on in Hosea – the hysteria of laughter and weeping associated with the resurrection and death of a deity[9]. The people of Samaria weep over the departure of the calf of Beth-aven (Hos 10,5-8). Thus the death wish of Hos 10,8 is the destiny of people who have an idolatrous construct of the world. In Luke 23,30 Jesus anticipates a similar destiny for those who have a carnivalesque construct. So Hos 10,8 is a synecdoche for its context, another case of completion. Further, the use of Hosea shifts the centre historically and substantively. The historical shift is from the time of Hosea to the time of Jesus' passion. The substantive shift is from Hosea's confrontation with the world of idolatry to Jesus' confrontation with the carnivalesque.

8. BAKHTIN (n. 3), *Rabelais*, p. 7; ID., *Problems of Dostoevsky's Poetics*, p. 122.

9. G. WIDENGREN, *Early Hebrew Myths and Their Interpretation*, in S. HOOKE (ed.), *Myth, Ritual, and Kingship: Essays on the Theory and Practice of Kingship in the Ancient Near East and in Israel*, Oxford, 1958, p. 179.

The carnivalesque emerges strongly again in the mockery of soldiers. They offer Jesus sour wine instead of the superior beverage fit for a king saying, "If you are the king of the Jews, save yourself" – carnival king. Also the inverted citation of Ps 21,9 LXX from the leaders who mock Jesus is carnivalesque. Like the scoffers in the psalm, the leaders make deliverance a criterion of authenticity. But they twist Ps 21,8-9 LXX away from divine deliverance to Jesus' deliverance of himself, a twist that produces irony. That is, to the chagrin of the scoffers, both Psalm 21 LXX and the Lucan passion locate the power of deliverance in God. Thus, when the leaders twist Psalm 21 LXX, readers overhear hope in God.

But not too fast! Jesus dies under an inscription: "This is the king of the Jews" – carnival king. He also dies in a curious time of carnivalesque inversion. The sun's light fails, the temple curtain is torn, day becomes night, sacred becomes profane, inlaw is swapped for outlaw, God's messiah is killed. In the jaws of such inversion, Jesus casts himself in utter dependence upon God: "Father, into your hands I commit my spirit" (Luke 23,46).

Babylonian Talmud Berakot 4b-5a gives evidence that Jesus recites a Jewish bedtime prayer, though it is uncertain that the tradition goes back to the time of Jesus. In any case, Jesus casts himself in dependence upon God. Does the authorial audience know Ps 30,6 LXX so that they also hear, "You have redeemed me, Lord, God of truth" (Ps 30,6)? As a recall of the larger context of the psalm, Jesus' last words are a synecdochical marker that calls for completion. But fitting the citation into a new whole recentres both the psalm and the passion. The committal to God abandons its home in the psalms. But the psalm's confidence in the power of God to rescue shifts the passion off of senselessness, and when the committal to God comes to rest on Jesus' lips, it rises to an enhanced level of meaning.

Explicit and implicit hope in God is a key to allusions to scripture in the Lucan passion. The allusions resist the carnivalesque by juxtaposing a world that centres on God. It is conventional to speak of christological interpretation of scripture in Luke-Acts. But if Jesus is a key to understanding scripture, he gives another key – God. The Lucan appropriation of scripture is primarily theocentric. This theocentric appropriation of scripture is a figuration. Luke views the crucifixion of Jesus indirectly through scripture. But equally Luke views scripture through the crucifixion of Jesus. The juxtaposition of the two relocates the centre of each – crucifixion shifts off its centre on senselessness, scripture shifts off its centre on Israel's past to relocate on the crucifixion of Jesus. The successor recentres the precursor and opens a new vista so that readers see what they could not see before. On the other hand, the only way readers gain the new vista is to hear the voices of Isaiah, Hosea, and the psalmists. These figures of the past come to the present, but when they speak, they also speak in Luke's voice.

So do readers know who Jesus is by his fruits? Is he cut down and thrown into the fire? The carnivalesque presses on readers the notion that he is. But that notion is a part of the anticipations readers have to revise. Against their expectations that Jesus is like a flourishing tree planted by streams of water which yields its fruit in its season, Luke's passion offers a revision of messianism. The messiah is crucified. But Luke's passion is also a revision of the God of the messiah, because this is the Lord's doing.

5555 S. Woodlawn Ave.
Chicago, IL 60637, U.S.A.

Robert L. BRAWLEY

A SWORD OVER HIS HEAD OR IN HIS HAND?
LUKE 22,35-38[1]

A variety of solutions have been offered by scholars to explain Jesus' instruction to his disciples to purchase (a) sword(s)[2]. However, a survey of all the attempts at a solution of the problem is beyond the scope of this paper. The hermeneutical key used by many scholars to explain this command is based on the alleged incompatibility between the life and teachings of Jesus who summoned his followers to a peaceful life-style (e.g. Lk 6,27.29.35a), and the possibility that he contemplated violent action against his enemies, as perhaps implicated in Lk 22,35-38. The view that Jesus summoned his followers to start a rebellion against the Roman authorities, finds little support among scholars[3]. However, the reality of a discrepancy between what Jesus taught elsewhere and what he probably commanded his followers to do according to this passage, appears to resist harmonisation. To overcome this contradiction, the usual option taken was a non-literal understanding of Jesus's reference to swords[4]. Scholars who espouse a realistic understanding of the passage usually interpret the life and teachings of Jesus in terms of the Jewish nationalistic movements of his day[5].

Elsewhere attention was given to the meaning of the expression Ἱκανόν ἐστιν (Lk 22,38b), and ἱκανούσθω (an Old Testament equivalent)[6]. The present paper studies the impact of two Old Testament traditions on Jesus' instruction to buy (a) sword(s), on the one hand, and his subsequent

---

1. Previous articles by this author: *Die twee swaarde (Luk 22,35-53), 'n Poging tot verstaan*, in *NGTT* XXVII 2 (1986) 191-196; *Die twee swaarde ('n vervolg)*, in *NGTT* XXX 1 (1989) 2-5.

2. H.-W. BARTSCH, *Jesu Schwertwort, Lukas XXII.35-38*, in *NTS* 20 (1973-74) 190-203; I.J. DU PLESSIS, *Die Evangelie volgens Lukas,* Vol II (Kommentaar op die Nuwe Testament), Cape Town, Lux Verbi, 1995, pp. 698-704; E. BAMMEL & C.F.D. MOULE (eds.), *Jesus and the Politics of His Day,* Cambridge, University Press, 1984; I.H. MARSHALL, *The Gospel of Luke,* Exeter, Paternoster, 1978, pp. 824-827; P.S. MINEAR, *A Note on Luke xxii 36*, in *NT* 7 (1964) 128-134; O. BETZ, *Jesu Heiliger Krieg*, in *NT* 2 (1958) 116-137.

3. DU PLESSIS, p. 699, n. 2; BARTSCH, pp. 191-193, n. 2.

4. μάχαιραν, the short sword: W. MICHAELIS, *Sword,* in G. KITTEL & G. FRIEDRICH, (eds.), *Theological Dictionary of the New Testament* (abridged in one vol. by G. W. BROMILEY), Grand Rapids, Michigan, Eerdmans, 1985, pp. 572-573.

5. BAMMEL & MOULE (n. 2), especially E. BAMMEL, *The Revolution Theory from Reimarus to Brandon*, pp. 11-68.

6. See n. 1.

rejection of the armed struggle, on the other. The point will be argued that the intermediate pericope in Luke 22,39-46 holds a key to the understanding of the passage running from Luke 22 verse 35 to 53.

It is proposed that Jesus' instruction to his followers to buy weapons can be dealt with by bringing the Old Testament into play in a particular way. Via two indicators, the reference to swords (Lk 22,36b.38), and the citation of a passage from Isaiah (Lk 22,37 < Isa 53,12), the exegete can focus on two Old Testament traditions which have a bearing on the present passages. The passages (Lk 22,35-38.39-46.47-53) also reveal a tension between these two Old Testament traditions; this will be considered below.

Jesus' reference to swords evokes the Old Testament imagery of Yahweh as the *Divine Warrior*[7]. In this connection some exegetes probably deal with the problem in an inconsistent way when they attempt to explain away Jesus' statement on the buying of swords, which perhaps implies planned violence (Lk 22,35-38), but seem to have little concern for Yahweh's violent actions in the past (as narrated in the Old Testament), or in the future (Revelation). However, any attempt to sever Jesus' actions from those of Yahweh, is rebutted by the early application of Yahweh texts to Jesus[8]. It is important to note Jesus' declared relationship to God the Father – the reason why the Jews wanted to kill him[9]. One aspect of that relationship relates to the idea of the Divine Warrior.

The imagery of Yahweh as the Divine Warrior dominates the Old Testament to a large extent, leading some scholars to think that it is possible to write a theology of the Old Testament from this angle[10]. The context of the Divine Warrior is the so-called Holy War[11] or Yahweh War[12]. Old Testament texts representing Yahweh as Warrior include, inter alia, Exod 15,3; Deut 32,40-43; Ps 24,8; Isa 27,1; 42,13; 51,9;

---

7. But see BETZ (n. 2), pp. 116-124.

8. D.B. CAPES, *Old Testament Yahweh texts in Paul's Christology*, Tübingen, Mohr, 1992, pp. 165-167, and n. 358.

9. W. GRUNDMANN, *The Decision of the Supreme Court to Put Jesus to Death (John 11,47-57) in Its Context: Tradition and Redaction in the Gospel of John*, in BAMMEL & MOULE, pp. 299-300, 313, 317, n. 2.

10. T. LONGMAN, *The Divine Warrior: The New Testament Use of an Old Testament Motif*, in *WTJ* 44 (1982) 290-307, especially p. 306; also L. RYKEN & T. LONGMAN (eds.) *A Complete Literary Guide to the Bible*, Grand Rapids, Michigan, Zondervan, 1993, p. 105. See P.D. MILLER, *God the Warrior*, INT, 1965, pp. 39-46, especially p. 39.

11. S. A.-Moon KANG, *Divine War in the Old Testament and in the Ancient Near East*, Berlin, W. de Gruyter, 1989. See his pp. 225-235 for literature on this subject. Some think that Yahweh may be portrayed as the Avenger in some parts of the Old Testament. See F. HOLMGREN, *Yahweh the Avenger*, in J.J. JACKSON & M. KESSLER (eds.), *Rhetorical Criticism, Essays in honour of J Muilenberg* Pittsburgh, Pickwick, 1974, pp. 134-148.

12. G.H. JONES 1975, *Holy War or Yahweh War?*, in *VT* 25 (1975) 642-658.

59,17; 63,3; 66,16; Ezek 21,3.4.5. In some of these texts Yahweh is pictured as the Warrior taking action against his enemies with his sword. The violent action of the Israelites under Yahweh's command in texts like Exod 32,27-29 and Deut 13,7-12, and similar executions in Joshua-Judges, adds to the climate. Longman[13] indicated that the theme of the Divine Warrior runs through both the Old and New Testaments. Whereas Yahweh represents the Divine Warrior in the Old Testament, the New Testament identifies Jesus Christ with the Divine Warrior[14]. Longman[15] also indicated that Jesus appears as Divine Warrior in eschatological and non-eschatological passages. In the non-eschatological passages Jesus' death and resurrection cuts off from the church holy war activity similar to that of the Israelites. Jesus turns from the role of Divine Warrior to that of Saviour of the world. Longman does not, however, explain how this change took place. It is not easy to find decisive evidence of a discontinuity between Yahweh's command in, for example, Judges and Joshua to slay people with the sword, and Jesus' instruction to buy a sword. And further: Yahweh's action as Divine Warrior at the time of David's rise to power parallels the divine warriors who appeared in the rising time of each empire of the ancient Near East[16]. Jesus proclaimed the arrival of his own Kingdom (Mk 1,14). It is thus quite possible that Jesus considered his future action on the basis of this tradition of Yahweh as Divine Warrior.

Some take the reference to a sword in Mt 10,34ff not in terms of a struggle against the Roman empire, but against the godless world and Belial[17]. Betz[18] claimed that statements made in the Gospels and the Apocalypse about the eschatological Messianic struggle[19] reach back to the views held by the Qumran community, including references to the use of the sword. According to him these ideas are extended to the Apocalypse of John where the sword is a sign of Christ's triumph. He carries a sharp, two-edged sword which proceeds out of his mouth (Rev 1,16; 2,12.16; 19,15.21). As the sword of his mouth it is a spiritual sword, the sword of his Word. Here a relation between the historical (the texts concerning the slaying with the sword mentioned e.g. in Exod, Deut, Josh, and Judg) and the eschatological dimension ("the sword of his mouth" – Rev) appears strained. The Old Testament, however,

13. LONGMAN (n. 10), pp. 305-307.
14. B.A. STEVENS, *Jesus as Divine Warrior*, in *ExpT* 94.11 (1983) 326-329.
15. LONGMAN (n. 10), pp. 292-305.
16. KANG (n. 11), pp. 203, 224.
17. Mt 12,29 – BLACK, in BAMMEL & MOULE (n. 2), p. 292; BETZ (n. 2), pp. 116-137.
18. *Ibid.* (n. 2), pp. 116-117, 130.
19. BLACK, in BAMMEL & MOULE (n. 2), p. 291.

confirms this phenomenon of the oscillation between vision and reality. The idea of Yahweh (or his representative) as Divine Warrior, occurs in visionary mode (e.g. 1 Chron 21,16). It is also intertwined with a physical representation of the sword, handled by human beings (Judg 7,20). In the execution of holy war in the Old Testament, God and man's actions are very much intertwined[20]. Thus references made to the sword of Yahweh in the Old Testament, including references to himself as Warrior (e.g. Exod 15,3), reveal an ambivalence (comp. Judg 7,20-22 and Isa 31,8). Jesus perhaps acted against this background of moving between the spheres of vision and reality, creating the impression of arming with real swords, on the one hand, and on the other, moving on a theological or an eschatological level in his thinking. This perspective is confirmed by the development of thought which in its initial stages regarded Yahweh as Divine Warrior in historical terms (that is, Lord of history), followed by his portrayal as the Lord of nature and finally as the "cosmic" and "mythical" Lord beyond history in the exilic and post-exilic period[21].

Jesus' reference to twelve legions of angels at the time of his arrest (Mt 26,53), may be a revelation of his frame of mind[22]. The fact that he used the word "legion" (a Roman military unit) [23] with a superterrestrial connotation perhaps confirm that his thoughts were moving on an eschatological level. If this is taken into account, his reference to a sword (again near the time of his arrest) can perhaps also be understood on an eschatological level; Lk 22,35-38 falls in the category of eschatological warnings[24]. Thus the sword may function as a metaphor of something great to occur, namely the sword of the Lord of Hosts punishing his enemies, or rather the sword of his triumphant Messiah. The sword would then be an image of the terrible prelude to the last judgment, the manifestation of the wrath of God by the armies of heaven[25]. If an eschatological perspective is present in the passage under discussion, it is irrelevant whether the number of swords are in fact a total of two, or two each for every disciple (as

---

20. BETZ (n. 2), p. 116.

21. KANG (n. 11), p. 204.

22. See Gen 32,1-2; KANG (n. 11), p. 198-202; A. VAN SELMS, in A. VAN SELMS & A. S. VAN DER WOUDE (eds.), *Genesis deel II, De Prediking van het Oude Testament*, Nijkerk, Callenbach, 1967, pp. 129,131. Jesus's words sound ironical: The "cohort" sent to arrest him (see Jn 18,3, and LAMPE, in BAMMEL & MOULE (n. 2), p. 349) usually consisted of 600 men, the tenth part of a Roman legion of 6000 soldiers. In this way the overwhelming assistance of Yahweh is emphasized. See B. M. NEWMAN, *A Concise Greek-English Dictionary of the New Testament*, Stuttgart, United Bible Societies, 1971, p. 165.

23. H. PREISKER, *Legion*, in KITTEL & FRIEDRICH, p. 505, n. 4; NEWMAN (n. 22), p. 107.

24. LAMPE, in BAMMEL & MOULE (n. 2), pp. 337-338.

25. BLACK, in BAMMEL & MOULE (n. 2), pp. 293-295.

was the custom of the Sicarii), thus twenty-two or twenty-four, or "thousands"[26].

It is conceded that the overriding view of the Gospels confirms that Jesus was non-violent in his approach, but that Luke (22,35-38) probably allows for the possibility that Jesus, on the one hand, glancing backward in time (at the Old Testament), considered, for a brief moment, promoting his Kingdom in terms of Yahweh as the Divine Warrior, while also glancing ahead, into the future, where the idea of saints wielding power with iron rods, shattering their enemies like clay pots, prevails (Rev 1,13; 2,27.28). Revelation continues in the same vein when picturing the Messiah as punishing his enemies with the sword of his mouth (Rev 19,11-21, especially v. 15); ruling them with an iron rod (cf 2,27.28), and treading the winepress like Yahweh the Warrior (Isa 63,1-3.6). Thus both the word "sword" (in Lk 22,36) as well as the expression "the sword of his mouth" (Rev 19,15), may be taken as metaphors, or as part of eschatological expressions.

The view that Jesus associated himself with Yahweh as the Divine Warrior, and thus contemplated violent action against his enemies, must be distinguished from the policy of the Jewish nationalistic groups who wanted to rid the country of Roman rule. Naturally, the two strands of thought have been intertwined and confused in the minds of many in Israel. But Jesus had a different view of the aim of such action in comparison to these nationalistic groups. He considered himself as the Divine Warrior ready to attack God's people because of their sins (Lk 21,9.11.20.22.24). The historical background of these statements is probably the Jewish War[27]. However, God's intended punishment of his people is related to this war[28]. As Divine Warrior, God acted and will act through the sword of man.

The statements in Luke 21 confirm that Jesus announced Yahweh's intention to set in motion the events mentioned. He does not make common cause with Jerusalem/Judah. His priority is that of God the Father, to judge his people. In this way he actualizes the role of the Divine Warrior. The essays in Bammel & Moule's work are geared to rid Jesus of involvement with revolutionary parties/groups fighting for the Jewish national feeling. Apparently little attention is paid to Jesus' opposition to the Jews, that his teachings are in fact detrimental to the Jewish nation[29]. Perhaps some Jewish scholars came close to this point when they alleged

---

26. See LAMPE, in BAMMEL & MOULE (n. 2), pp. 349, 351.
27. LAMPE, in BAMMEL & MOULE (n. 2), p. 350.
28. But see BARTSCH (n. 2), pp. 199-201.
29. E. BAMMEL, *Jesus as a Political Agent,* in BAMMEL & MOULE (n. 2), p. 205.

that Jesus did not care about their national hopes[30]. Although Jesus adhered to a non-violent standpoint before and after the sword incident of Lk 22,35-38, at that particular point in time, he looked beyond the mundane, recognized God the Father in the image of the Divine Warrior, considered the sword, and thus extending the role of Yahweh the Divine Warrior, the God of Israel, to his own time and situation. Thus the real issue is not about the number of swords, or whether the swords which were in the disciples' possession were carving knives or fisherman's knives[31]. The point is that the sword of the Lord of Hosts will presently cut down his own people. On the other hand, it cannot be denied that he also had in mind the great eschatological Messianic conflict[32].

However, in the interim, Jesus opts for undergoing violence, instead of encouraging violence. The words of Jesus in Lk 22,51.53 to his followers and adversaries at the time when he was captured, perhaps confirm his decision to suspend any idea of force for the time being. This statement brings us to the next argument and the second Old Testament tradition already referred to in this paper.

The exegetical problem caused by Jesus's summons to buy swords can be looked at from another Old Testament perspective, provided by Lk 22,37, a text which contains a citation from Isa 53,12. The citation is taken from one of the so-called Servant Songs[33] which describes the suffering of the mysterious *Servant of Yahweh* (Isa 52,13–53,12). It would seem as if Luke's citation functioned as a literary device to trigger off the fulfilment of a prophecy from Isa 53,12 in the sense that Jesus would be reckoned with brigands[34]. In this way a precedent would be created for his adversaries, namely to allow himself to be caught red-handed, that is, in possession of weapons. Thus he would be accused and subsequently judged as a criminal[35]. The thrust of this citation is the innocent suffering of the Servant of Yahweh. Luke applies the plight of the Servant to Jesus.

At this point the two Old Testament traditions may be considered together. The two views (or traditions) of Yahweh as Divine Warrior, and the Servant of Yahweh, represent opposite, conflicting positions. In

30. BAMMEL, in BAMMEL & MOULE (n. 2), pp. 43-51.

31. LAMPE, in BAMMEL & MOULE (n. 2), p. 348.

32. BLACK, in BAMMEL & MOULE (n. 2), p. 291.

33. See H.H. GROSHEIDE, et. al. (eds.), *De Knecht. Studies rondom Deutero-Jesaja*, Kampen, Kok, 1978; H.H. GROSHEIDE, et al. (eds.), *De Knechtsgestalte van Christus*, Kampen, Kok, 1978.

34. MINEAR (n. 2), p. 132.

35. BARTSCH, pp. 193-196, n. 2; J. GILLMAN, *Temptation to Violence. The Two Swords in Luke 22,35-38*, in *LS* 9 (1982/3) 142-153; LAMPE, in BAMMEL & MOULE (n. 2), pp. 339-351, especially pp. 347,349.

the former, Yahweh the Warrior is the Aggressor, in the latter the Servant suffers innocently. Jesus is associated with both traditions: Warrior and Servant. As applied to Jesus's own person and situation, a certain tension develops between the two traditions. The question arises: Which tradition will get the upper hand in his mind and determine his actions? Initially the tradition of the Warrior seems to dominate the scene.

The passage intermediate between Lk 22,35-38 and 22,47-53, namely Lk 22,39-46, highlights the tension between the idea of the Warrior and the Servant, and provides a key to the understanding of the command to buy swords (vv. 35-38), and its outcome, namely Jesus' subsequent disapproval of such action (vv. 47-53)[36].

The passage of Lk 22,39-46 narrates Jesus' struggle and decision on the Mount of Olives in connection with God's will, namely that he must die a violent death for the salvation of mankind (the "turning point")[37]. In a sense the pericope represents the precursor to the cross. But the decision taking shape in Jesus' mind to submit to his Father's will, does not come easy (see vv. 42a and 42b). The way Jesus addressed his disciples on the Mount of Olives ("stay awake","get up") has some association with holy war terminology[38]. Thus it would seem that Jesus, even when he was moving towards a final decision to resign himself to God's will, still considered the way of the Divine Warrior as a means to establish his Kingdom. However, Jesus' conviction that he must act out the role of the Divine Warrior, subsequently undergoes a radical change.

In Gethsemane the bloody battle associated with the Divine Warrior as presented in the Old Testament is decisively arrested and abandoned, or at least for the time being, when Jesus submitted himself to God's will (v. 42b). Here the holy war of the Old Testament is left behind by him, a perspective which also represents a certain discontinuity with the Old Testament. Jesus abandons the role of the Divine Warrior and accepts the will of God in terms of the suffering Servant to die for the sins of the world (v. 42b). The sword will not be in his hand, but over his head[39]. Instead of Jesus using the sword, Yahweh will strike him with the sword, if there is any prospective or retrospective connection here with Zechariah[40].

36. See BAMMEL, in BAMMEL & MOULE (n. 2), pp. 49-53.
37. *Ibid.* (n. 2), p. 48.
38. 1QM 12:11ff; 1QH 6:31; Num 10,35; Judg 5,12; Zech 13,7. See Mt 26,27.41.46; Mk 14,34.38.42; BETZ (n. 2), p. 135, footnote 1.
39. "Note the reversal – Christ the Divine Warrior wins the war by being killed, not by killing" (LONGMAN (n. 10), p. 304).
40. Zech 13,7; Cf. Mk 14,27 – see BETZ (n. 2), p. 135.

The Gospel of John (18,11) cuts the proverbial Gordian knot by bringing together in the same context the cup of suffering and the rejection of the sword[41]. The cup of the Passover, previously taken by Jesus with his disciples, is at the same time the cup of suffering (Lk 22,15). This is followed by Jesus separating the coming of his Kingdom and the use of violence (Jn 18,36). This development in Gethsemane, that Jesus resigns himself to God's will, forms the background of the incident described in Lk 22,47-53 and which changes the whole atmosphere and intention in connection with the swords as stated in Lk 22,35-38. Against this background, it seems clear why in Lk 22,47-53 Peter's use of the sword (see Jn 18,10), is rejected by Jesus (Lk 22,51). It is this temptation, namely to take up the sword, that Jesus commanded his disciples to resist in prayer (vv. 40.46), the temptation which he himself overcame eventually (v. 42). Jesus' initial resistance against his coming death (v. 42a), is replaced by his submission to God's will (v. 42b).

5 Pinegrove Place   H. A. J. KRUGER
Pinetown
3610 South Africa

---

41. See D.L. CHRISTENSEN, *Transformation of the War Oracle in Old Testament Prophecy: Studies in the Oracles against the Nations*, Montana, University of Montana, 1975, pp. 193ff, for the establishment of a relation between God's wrath, the sword, and the cup.

A PENTATEUCHAL ECHO IN JESUS' PRAYER ON THE CROSS
INTERTEXTUALITY
BETWEEN NUMBERS 15,22-31 AND LUKE 23,34a

One way to evaluate Luke's attitude toward the Jews is by the use and function he attributes to scripture in telling his story. Craig Evans argues "the manner in which the evangelist [Luke] applies Scripture to the Jews should to a significant extent reveal his true perspective", i.e. towards Judaism[1]. He [Evans] has assessed the function of each OT text in Luke-Acts bearing on the evangelist's view of the Jewish people. The present discussion is much more modest and will focus on Luke 23,33-38, in particular Luke 23,34a where Jesus forgives his accusers for their part in the crucifixion, "Father, forgive them for they do not know what they do".

1. *Preliminaries*

Many studies have considered the use of the OT in Luke's Gospel, in particular chapters 1–2[2]. New attention is being given to the use of the OT in other sections, for example Luke's Travel Narrative[3]. A passage, however, which has received relatively little attention is Luke 23,33-38

---

1. C.A. EVANS, *Prophecy and Polemic: Jews in Luke's Scriptural Apologetic,* in C.A. EVANS and J.A. SANDERS (eds.), *Luke and Scripture: The Function of Sacred Tradition in Luke-Acts*, Minneapolis, Fortress, 1993, p. 171. The importance of the subject is reiterated in the recent publication of C.M. TUCKETT, *Luke* (New Testament Guides), Sheffield, Sheffield Academic Press, 1996, pp. 50-51.

2. D.L. BOCK, *Proclamation from Prophecy and Pattern: Lucan Old Testament Christology* (JSNT SS, 12), Sheffield, JSOT, 1987; T. HOLTZ, *Untersuchungen über die alttestamentlichen Zitate bei Lukas* (TU, 104), Berlin, Akademie, 1968; M. RESE, *Alttestamentliche Motive in der Christologie des Lukas* (SNT, 1), Gütersloh, Mohn, 1969; C.A. KIMBALL, *Jesus' Exposition of the Old Testament in Luke's Gospel*, (JSNT SS, 94), JSOT, 1994.

3. C.F. EVANS, *The Central Section of St. Luke's Gospel*, in D.E. NINEHAM (ed.), *Studies in the Gospels*, Oxford, Blackwell, 1955, pp. 37-53; D.P. MOESSNER, *Lord of the Banquet. The Literary and Theological Significance of the Lukan Travel Narrative*, Minneapolis, Fortress, 1989; J. DRURY, *Tradition and Design in Luke's Gospel: A Study in Early Christian Historiography*, London, Darton, Longman and Todd, 1976, pp. 138-64; J.A. SANDERS, *The Ethic of Election in Luke's Great Banquet Parable*, pp. 106-120; and C.A. EVANS, *Luke 16:1-18 and the Deuteronomy Hypothesis,* in C.A. EVANS and J.A. SANDERS (eds.) (n. 1), pp. 120-139. See J.B. GREEN & M.C. McKEEVER, *Luke-Acts and New Testament Historiography*, Grand Rapids, MI, Baker, 1994, pp. 45-52, for a catalogue of recent literature on the OT in Luke-Acts.

especially 23,34[4]. We will argue that the background to this request for forgiveness echoes a sentiment found in Num 15,22-31. In order to ensure the relevance of this investigation to the topic of intertextuality in the Gospels and to understand better Luke's attitude towards the Jews three requirements must be satisfied: (1) a suitable definition of intertextuality must be proposed; (2) sufficient evidence for the originality of the Lucan text must be provided; (3) arguments must also be proposed that the primary referent of the prayer is the Jews.

First a definition of intertextuality. Richard Hays in his *Echoes of Scripture in the Letters of Paul* defines intertextuality: "whenever a community who hearkens to earlier texts as power and evocative voices of a claim to be heard in the present, intertextual writing and reading will take place"[5]. This definition of intertextuality is based on the assumption that scripture continues in one form or another to speak in and through later texts. This process invites the reader into a kind of echo chamber so as to hear in the current text reverberations of other texts[6].

Another definition of intertextuality from the field of literary criticism is that of Julia Kristeva and Roland Barthes who are pioneers in discussions on intertextuality[7]. Kristeva and Barthes advocate the view that intertextuality is not confined to an analysis of how one author cites and alludes to another who preceded him. They consider intertextuality as far more than a historical, diachronic analysis of texts. The premise of Kristeva and Barthes is that "intertextuality thus becomes less a name for a work's relation to particular prior texts than a designation of its participation in

---

4. Two scholars who consider Luke 23,34 from the perspective of Luke's attitude to the Jews are D. DAUBE, *For They Know Not what They Do: Luke 23,34*, in *Studia Patristica 4* (TU, 79), Berlin, Akademie, 1961, pp. 58-70 and J.H. PETZER, *Anti-Judaism and the Textual Problem of Luke 23.34* in *Filologia Neotestamentaria* 5 (1992) 199-203. Other recent discussions of this passage include: J.B. GREEN, *The Death of Jesus: Tradition and Interpretation in the Passion Narrative* (WUNT, 33), Tübingen, Mohr, 1988, pp. 90-5; D.M. CRUMP, *Jesus the Intercessor: Prayer and Christology in Luke-Acts* (WUNT, 49), Tübingen, Mohr, 1992, pp. 76-96.

5. R. HAYS, *Echoes of Scripture in the Letters of Paul*, New Haven & London, Yale University Press, p. 15. This study utilizes a definition of intertextuality that focuses on citations and allusions to specific texts. Cf. Hays' statement "My working model of intertextuality seeks to incorporate a serious concern for diachronic issues, without making them the center of attention". (p. 198 n. 52).

6. R.B. HAYS and J.B. GREEN, *The Use of the Old Testament by New Testament Writers* in J.B. GREEN (ed.), *Hearing the New Testament: Strategies for Interpetation*, Grand Rapids, Eerdmans, 1995, p. 228.

7. J. KRISTEVA, *Semiotiké*, Paris, Seuil, 1969 and R. BARTHES, *S/Z*, Paris, Seuil, 1970. See also J. CULLER, *Presupposition and Intertextuality*, in *The Pursuit of Signs. Semiotics, Literature, Deconstruction*, Ithaca, Cornell University Press, 1981, pp. 100-118, for a discussion of these studies.

the discursive space of a culture"[8]. This approach seeks to explore intertextual space by taking inventory of the cultural codes or conventions
that function within a text[9]. This kind of analysis relates sociology and
anthropology as well as historical criticism of the Bible to the analysis of
texts.

Our study is neither exclusively dependent on the working model of
Hays nor does our analysis subscribe to the broader definintion of Kristeva and Barthes. We will suggest at the conclusion of our essay that a
definition of intertextuality that converges on a notion of intra-thematic
echoes may be a more accurate description of the phenomenon presented
in this essay.

The second factor is the originality of the text. The originality of Luke
23,34a has been questioned because of its omission in several important
and impressive textual witnesses (P[75] $\aleph$[a vid] B D* W Θ syr[s] bo[mss] Cyril).
While these are impressive mss witnesses against the authenticity of the
verse, several factors based on external and internal evidence suggest the
antiquity of the verse, if not its originality[10]. Internal evidence offers
equally impressive evidence for the longer reading. The mss evidence is
early and diverse: $\aleph$[*, C]A C D[b] L f[1] f[13] 23 33 565 vg syr bo[mss] Marcion,
Tatian, Hegesippus, Justin, Irenaeus, Clement of Alexandria, Origen,
Eusebius. Second, the age of P[75] (175-225 AD) is counter-balanced by
equally as old and in several instances even older witnesses than P[75].
Several Fathers who favor the inclusion of the prayer are Hegesippus,
Marcion, Tatian, Justin, Irenaeus, and Clement of Alexandria[11]. Third,
the fact that most of the old Latin and Syriac versions include the reading
strongly counteracts the combination of D and $\aleph$[a]. Fourth, the attestation

8. CULLER, *ibid.*, p. 103.
9. HAYS, (n. 5), p. 15.
10. Purponents of the longer reading include: A. HARNACK, *Probleme im Texte der
Leidengeschichte Jesu,* in *SPAW* 11 (1901) 255-261; E.E. ELLIS, *The Gospel of Luke,*
London, Marshall, Morgan and Scott, 1974, p. 267; J. SCHMID, *Das Evangelium nach
Lukas* (RNT), Regensburg, Pustet, 1960, p. 348; GREEN (n. 1), pp. 91-92; G. SCHNEIDER,
Das Evangelium nach Lukas, Gütersloh, Mohn, vol. 2, 1977, p. 483. Those who advocate
the shorter reading include: PETZER (n. 3), pp. 54-56; B. METZGER, *A Textual Commen-
tary on the Greek New Testament,* London, United Bible Societies, 1971, p. 180; J.M.
CREED, *The Gospel according to St. Luke,* London, Macmillan, 1942, p. 286; A.H.
DAMMERS, *Studies in Texts, Luke xxiii,34a,* in *Theology* 52 (1949) 138-139; W. OTT,
Gebet und Heil: Die Bedeutung der Gebetsparänese in der lukanischen Theologie (SANT,
12), München, Kösel, 1965, p. 96 n. 14. See I.H. MARSHALL, *The Gospel of Luke: A Commentary on the Greek Text* (NIGTC), Exeter, Paternoster, 1978, p. 867, for a critique of
views.
11. Hegesippus, Marcion, Tatian, and Justin were at their height in the early to mid
second century; Irenaeus was slightly later; Clement lived in the third century. Cf. CRUMP
(n. 4), p. 82.

of the shorter reading in P[75] א and B must be understood in a larger context. As significant as P[75] א and B are individually, all represent the same Alexandrian text family[12]. The significance of this Alexandrian association is increased by the surety that א and B share the same scribal tradition[13]. Indeed, it is probable that P[75] represents at least the archetype for the gospel traditon found in B[14]. Therefore, it is unwarranted to assert that א[a] and B are independent witnesses for the omission of Luke 23,34a.

These arguments based on internal evidence are strengthened by considering external factors: (1) the prayer of Stephen in Acts 7,60 presupposes the prayer of Jesus for his accuser – the former suggests a conscious paralleling of the latter, not vice versa[15]; (2) the ignorance motif found in Luke's prayer is consistent with Lucan thought elsewhere (Acts 3,17; 13,27; 17,23.30)[16]; (3) it is probable that some early scribes would have dropped the plea for forgiveness because its inclusion appears to exonerate the Jews. The thought that God would pardon the Jews, especially in light of the destruction of the temple, would be incredible to some scribes; (4) the anti-Jewish tendencies of the scribes has been documented in other passages of Luke, especially in the 'western' text tradition[17]; (5) the language of the prayer is Lukan[18]: πάτηρ cf. Lk. 2,49; 10,21; 11,2; 22,42; 23,46; ἀφὲς αὐτοὶς cf. Acts 3,17; 7,60; 13,27; 17,30; τί ποιοῦσιν cf. Lk. 6,11; 19,48. On balance we agree with Nolland and affirm Lucan awareness rather than confidence that he reproduced the tradition[19]. But if he was aware of the tradition and it fits his theological outlook, is it not plausible that Luke put it there?

The third requirement to ensure the appropriateness of the use of Luke 23,34 is that it is directed at the Jews. This essay assumes that fundamental to Lukan understanding is that he is less concerned with who "drove the

12. CRUMP, *ibid.*, p. 81.
13. *Ibid.*
14. *Ibid.*; K.W. CLARK, *The Text of the Gospel of John in Third-Century Egypt*, in *NT* 5 (1962) 24; G. FEE, *P[66], P[75], and Origen: The Myth of Early Textual Recension in Alexandria*, in R.N. LONGENECKER and M.C. TENNEY (eds.), *New Dimensions in New Testament Study*, Grand Rapids, Zondervan, 1974, pp. 30-31,44.
15. CRUMP (n. 4), p. 84.
16. GREEN (n. 4), p. 92; D.L. TIEDE, *Prophecy and History in Luke-Acts*, Philadelphia, Fortress, 1980, p. 111; DAUBE (n. 4), p. 59.
17. CRUMP (n. 4), p. 83; E. EPP, *The Theological Tendency of Codex Bezae Cantabrigiensis in Acts*, Cambridge, University Press, 1966, p. 166; G. RICE, *The Anti-Judaic Bias of the Western Text in the Gospel of Luke*, in *AUSS* 18 (1980) 51-57; E. SCHWEIZER, *The Good News according to Luke*, Atlanta, John Knox Press, 1984, pp. 359-60.
18. CRUMP, *ibid.*, p. 84.
19. J. NOLLAND, *Luke 18:35-24:53* (WBC, 35c), Dallas, Word, 1993, p. 1141 n.a-a. Cf. CRUMP (n. 4), p. 84.

nails than who instigated the affair"[20]. J. Weatherly, in the recent study *Jesus Responsibility for the Death of Jesus in Luke-Acts,* argues that Luke's Gospel implicates the Jewish religious leaders of Jerusalem in the crucifixion of Jesus and, to a much lesser extent, others, particularly Pilate, Herod and the soldiers. It is, however, never the Jews in general in the passion narrative who are implicated for the death of Jesus[21]. It is not until Acts that people of Jerusalem are implicated (2,23.36; 3,13-15; 10,39; 13,27-29). An important distinction must be noted – for Luke responsibility is placed on those who set in motion the events which led to the crucifixion and not those who performed deeds to accomplish it.

The responsibility for the death of Jesus is on the Jerusalem religious leadership and can be documented by classifying the data under four categories: (1) examples at Jesus' entry to Jerusalem (19,47; 20,19); (2) retrospective comments following the trial scene (24,20); (3) specific attributions of responsibility (22,1; 22,3-5; 23,4ff; 23,10; 23,13) surrounding the trial; (4) events regarding the crucifixion of Jesus (23,25-26; 23,33-38). In categories 1-3 above the Jewish religious establishment is repeatedly involved: chief priests, scribes, elders, temple officers who sought to destroy, trap, mock, and kill Jesus. Given all those classified who oppose Jesus during his last day the Pharisees are conspicuously absent (see 19,39)[22]. What we do find in a telling retrospective statement at 24,20 is those responsible for the death of Jesus clearly identified as "chief priests and rulers [who] delivered him up to be condemned to death, and crucified him". The *crux interpretum* regarding the death of Jesus is Luke 23,25-26. In v. 25 Pilate delivered Jesus over to "their will" (i.e those who called for his crucifixion). In v. 26 the nearest antecedent to ἀπήγαγον is αὐτῶν in v. 25. It would also appear that the same subject is implied for ἦλθον and ἐσταύρωσαν in v. 33. This example illustrates a known problem in Luke – uncertain antecedents (Lk. 5,33; 14,35; 16,4; 17,21; 21,5)[23]. The reader must go back to 23,13 (10) to see that those intended are the chief priests, scribes and rulers who wanted Pilate and Herod to declare Jesus' actions worthy of the death sentence. Consequently, in v.34a when Jesus prays for his accusers – "Father forgive them" – it is reasonable to suggest that the Jerusalem religious establishment is intended.

20. J. WEATHERLY, *Jewish Responsibility for the Death of Jesus in Luke-Acts* (JSNT SS, 106), Sheffield, JSOT, 1994, p. 68.

21. *Ibid*, p. 50

22. J.A. FITZMYER, *The Gospel According to Luke* (Anchor Bible), New York, Doubleday, 1985, vol. 1, p. 1270.

23. WEATHERLY (n. 20), p. 65; A. HARNACK, *The Acts of the Apostles*, New York, Putnam's, 1909, p. 226.

Are there others too who are directly involved in the incrimination of Jesus? Luke 23,33-38 suggests others may be candidates for his prayers. These verses suggest two agents of mockery: the leaders (Jewish) who scoffed at him saying "he can save others, let him save himself". This is a repetition of the group mentioned more generally which has already been documented at various points in our discussion. In addition, the Roman soldiers mocked Jesus saying "if you are King of the Jews, save yourself". Thus, the soldiers and the leaders joined efforts in the mockery of Jesus in contrast to the Jewish people who viewed (beheld) him sympathetically[24].

We have seen throughout that Pilate and Herod are significant characters in the story. Three times they pronounce Jesus' innocence (23,4.14-15.22). Do they bear any responsibility for the death of Jesus or are they merely fixtures in the story? In addition to the pronouncements of Jesus' innocence by Pilate and Herod there are clues that Pilate is, in some sense, culpable. Pilate is the one who turns Jesus over to be crucified. Herod does not seem to fare much better since his pronouncement of Jesus' innocence is accompanied by beating and mocking Jesus (23,11). While Luke may be intent to show that Jesus is innocent according to Roman law, the implication is that the actions of Pilate and Herod show a perversion of the Roman legal system. There are two other examples that illustrate Pilate's involvement. In Luke 23,21 the second person singular verb σταύρου is used which implies the crowd expected that Pilate would be the one to crucify Jesus. Similarly, Luke follows the traditional burial account (Lk 23,52//Mt 27,58//Mk 15,43) in which Joseph of Arimathea goes to Pilate for the body of Jesus. If Pilate had authority to dispose of Jesus' body, it is reasonable to conclude that he was the one who had direct involvement in the crucifixion of Jesus[25].

The conclusion from the above remarks is that the Jerusalem leaders associated with the temple were the instigators of the death of Jesus. They were assisted by the involvement of the Roman authorities, in particular Pilate and Herod. The people surrounding the passion narrative do not indicate direct involvement (though the story gives a different picture in Acts). Therefore, an apt formulation is "Jesus was killed by the Romans at

---

24. There is one reference in the events surrounding the passion that may suggest the people were not positive towards Jesus. In 23,13 the "people" are included with the chief priests and rulers. Pilate gives the pronouncement that he finds no crime committed by Jesus. This scene is a prelude to the cry for crucifixion in vv. 18.21.23. See WEATHERLY (n. 20), p. 78 for suitable solution. Cf. FITZMYER (n. 22), p. 1484. Luke sees a reference to the people as indication that an attempt is made to find support from the populace in opposition to the leaders.

25. WEATHERLY (n. 20), p. 96.

the behest of the Jewish leadership"[26]. Consequently, those to whom Jesus directed his prayer are the Jerusalem religious establishment.

2. *Contextualizing Luke 23,34a*

The scene of our passage (Lk 23,33-38) is Jesus on the cross between two accused criminals which Mt/Mk calls 'bandits'. The location given is the place called the "Skull" following Mk 15,22 but Luke omits the word 'Golgatha'. What is noticeable is that this is only one of the features Luke omits from the Markan account. Others include the initial offer of wine, Jesus' rejection of it, reference to the third hour, mocking of bystanders, and the allusion to Elijah. It is also apparent that Luke added new material: the prayer for his executioners, the designation of Jesus as "the chosen one", the offer of wine interpreted as an act of mockery and verbal mocking of the soldiers[27].

The passage offers various perspectives on how Jesus was viewed by those surrounding the events of the passion. This is presented in a chiastic structure beginning with the people[28]:

A   The people (sympathetically) behold (v. 35a)
B   The leaders (Jewish) cry "Save yourself, if you are the Christ" (v. 35b)
C   The soldiers (Roman) cry "If you are the king of the Jews", save yourself (vv. 36-37)
C' The titulus says, "King of the Jews" (v. 38)
B' One evildoer says "Are you not the Christ? Save yourself and us"(v. 39)
A' The other evildoer expresses sympathy/support (vv. 40-42).

The contrast is shown here between the people and the leaders[29]. The people watch and the repentant accuser on the cross asks for mercy. The leaders, soldiers and others accused person on the cross mocks and ridicules Jesus.

Second, the pericope presents the suffering Christ on the cross by allusions/echoes from several lament psalms (Pss 22, 69) and from the Isaianic Servant Song (53). Scholars have often noted the allusion in

---

26. E.P. SANDERS, *Jesus and Judaism*, London, SCM, 1985, pp. 317-318.
27. GREEN (n. 4), p. 90.
28. WEATHERLY (n. 20), p. 82.
29. This Lukan emphasis is noted in TIEDE (n. 17), pp. 111-2; R.J. CASSIDY, *Luke's Audience, the Chief Priests, and the Motive for Jesus' Death* in R.J. CASSIDY and P.J. SCHARPER (eds.), *Political Issues in Luke-Acts*, Maryknoll, NY, Orbis, 1983, pp. 150-1; U. WILCKENS, *Die Missionsreden der Apostelgeschichte* (WMANT, 5), Neukirchen-Vluyn, Neukirchener, ³1973, pp. 60-1; A. GEORGE, *Le sens de la mort de Jésus pour Luc*, in *RB* 80 (1973) 200-1.

Luke 23,34 from Ps 22,19 (LXX 21,19) of dividing of garments and casting lots. In Luke 23,35 the reference to mocking and the call for Jesus to save himself echoes Ps 22,8-9 (LXX Ps 21,8-9). Another example of an echo from the Psalms is Luke 23,36. The mention of the mocking offer of wine recalls Ps 69,21-22 (Ps 68,21-22 LXX). Each of these examples are found in the Synoptics and thus reflect tradition[30]. These echoes suggest that Jesus' experience parallels the righteous suffer of the psalms.

It is sometimes suggested that a possible echo exists between Luke 23,33 and Isa 53,12 in the mention of Jesus being crucified with two criminals. If there is a conscious echo Luke has made no effort to assimilate his language to that of the LXX since the criminals in Luke are referred to as κακοῦργοι (v 32) and Isa 53,12 uses the term ἀνόμοις. It is clear that Isa 53,12 influenced Luke at 22,37 and therefore there may be a echo of Luke 22,37 which carried forward to Luke 23,33[31].

There is a second category of material in our passage that may echo the OT – the intercessory prayer of Jesus. A text sometimes suggested as an echo of Jesus' intercessorary prayer for his executioners in Luke 23,34a is Isa 53,12[32]. Two problems emerge: (1) if an allusion does exist, it must be based on the MT not the LXX since intercession is what the hiphil פגע connotes. The LXX only speaks of being given over (παρεδόθη) because of sins. Thus, if an allusion does exist it points to a Semitic source behind the Lucan material. (2) If an allusion is based on the MT it may require understanding Isa 53,12 in a way that is outside its intended sense. Marshall maintains that Luke 23,34a gives a prayer of Jesus for his executioners which exemplifies the statement of Isa 53,12 that the Servant makes intercession for the transgressors[33]. However, the intention of the passage is to offer intercession for the transgressors by means of bearing their sin, not by offering a prayer of intercession for them such as the case at Luke 23,34a. Therefore, we maintain that if intertextuality does exist between Isa 53,12 and Luke 23,34a it is hard to hear it.

If the Isa text is not satisfactory as an OT echo for Luke 23,34a then are there other backgrounds that can be explored? One suggestion is that Num 15,22-31 may serve as the backgound to Luke's petition[34]. Luke's

---

30. Bock (n. 2) p. 146. Cf. Nolland (n. 19) pp. 1143-4.
31. Nolland (n. 19), p. 1144 is quite doubtful; Fitzmyer (n. 22), p. 1503; Bock (n. 2), p. 145 and Tiede (n. 12), p. 417 affirm both points.
32. I.H. Marshall, *Luke: Historian and Theologian*, Grand Rapids, Zondervan, 1970, p. 172; Bock (n. 2), p. 145 notes its uncertainty. See also C.G. Montefiore, *The Synoptic Gospels*, New York, Ktav, 1968, vol. 2, p. 625.
33. *Ibid.*
34. Ellis (n. 10), p. 267; Evans (n. 1), p. 183; Daube (n. 4), p. 23.

prayer to the Father is on the grounds that the Jewish accusers acted out of ignorance "they did not know what they did". However, it matters a great deal who is the intended audience in order to interpret the language of the verse. Daube argues that, if the Romans are intended, ignorance means lack of information. By contrast, if the Jews are intended, the ignorance is due to lack of understanding[35]. Thus, if Jesus is praying for the Romans it means they have not been told, the gospel has not reached them – they lack information. If the Jews are intended it means they do not grasp what they have seen and heard, they do not comprehend the truth of the gospel and the significance of Jesus' message – they lack understanding. Since we have already argued the antecedents of the prayer are the Jewish leaders it is not additional information Jesus prays for but understanding of his identity and the significance of his mission. The assumption is that had the Jerusalem leaders understood this they would not have orchestrated Jesus' death.

Num 15,22ff makes a distinction between sins committed deliberately and those committed unwittingly. Sometimes due to the multitude, variety, and minuteness of legal regulation, it was inevitable that laws would be infringed "in ignorance". Accordingly the Law created a special category of sin committed, that done unwittingly (בשגגה) or through inadvertence. For sins of this type atonement is available. The opposite to this is sinning with a high hand (ביד רמה) – wilfully and defiantly. For these sins no atonement is available[36]. A sin committed unwittingly may result from one of two causes: negligence or ignorance. Either the law is known but is violated unintentionally (Num 35,22ff; Deut 19,4-10) or the perpetrator acts without knowing wrong was committed (Gen 20,9; Num 22,34)[37].

שגגה is a technical term for inadvertent sin found almost exclusively within the OT in legislative passages (Num 15,24-29; Lev 4,2.22.27)[38]. The Hebrew roots שגג and שגה convey the idea of "erring" or "going astray" with the expressed or implied causation of ignorance. The fact that one is unaware of his wrongdoing does not excuse him. Guilt immediately attaches itself to the deed. When sin of inadvertence is known the prescribed sacrifice must be carried out to achieve communion with God. This concept of inadvertence may lie behind the Jew ignorance of crucifying Jesus[39].

35. DAUBE, ibid.

36. G.F. MOORE, Judaism in the First Centuries of the Common Era, Cambridge, Harvard University Press, 1927, vol. 1, p. 463.

37. R.L HARRIS, G.L. ARCHER, B.K. WALTKE, Theological Wordbook of the Old Testament, Chicago, Moody Press, 1980, vol. 2, p. 905.

38. The sin of inadvertence or unintentional sin can be documented also in Lev 4.2.22.27; 35,23; Num 35,11.15; Josh 20,3.9; TZeb. 1,4-5; Slav. En. 30,16; Tg. Ps. Jon. Num 15,28-31; Tg. Onk. Num 15,22-31.

39. S.J. DE VRIES, Ignorance, in IDB, vol. 2, p. 680.

Why did Jesus pray for the Jewish leaders? It was because they had committed the sin of inadvertence. They did not understand the magnitude of their actions because they did not comprehend the identity of Jesus. Rather than consider him a restorer to the religious ideal of the Jewish nations, they viewed him as a threat to the Jesus status quo and politically dangerous. In a similar vein to the OT offering for atonement of sins committed inadvertently, Jesus prays for the Jewish leaders for sins committed unwittingly. Jesus makes atonement possible for the Jewish leaders[40]. This motif of the Jewish offer of atonement for sins of inadvertence is made by Peter in Acts 3,17 and Paul in Acts 13,27. The unspoken assumption is that if the Jewish leaders fail to admit their sin of ignorance it will become a witting sin for which the Mosaic law has no explicit promise of atonement[41].

We began with the question of Luke's attitude toward to the Jews. Has Luke given up on the Jews? There is diverse opinion on how to understand Luke's intention of the Jews in his story. At the expense of oversimplification, opinion may be classified in two groups: (1) those who view the Jews either as those who accept the gospel or those who do not; (2) those who make no distinction among the Jews and thus condemn them as a group. This second view maintains that Luke writes for a church that is predominantely Gentile and that he has abandoned any mission to the Jews. Luke depicts the Jews negatively because he is pessimistic about the prospects of Jewish conversion. A recent advocate of this perspective on Luke is J.T. Sanders who maintains that Luke's hostility to the Jews is 'fundamental and systemic' – Luke does not relent on this view of the Jews and Judaism. He is thoroughly anti-Semitic, opposes the Jewish religion and hates the Jewish people[42].

Sanders' view of the Jews in Luke-Acts has been challenged by scholars which include Jacob Jervell, Gerhard Lohfink, Augustin George, and David Tiede[43]. It is argued that Luke's portrayal of the Jews only makes

---

40. EVANS (n. 1), p. 183.

41. I.H. MARSHALL, *Acts of the Apostles* (NIGTC), Exeter, Paternoster, 1978, p. 92.

42. J.T. SANDERS, *The Jewish in Luke-Acts*, Philadelphia, Fortress, 1987, pp. xvi-xvii, 47, 310, 317; *The Jewish People in Luke-Acts*, in J.B. TYSON (ed.), *Luke-Acts and the Jewish People*, Minneapolis, Augsburg, 1988, pp. 51-75. The diversity of scholarly opinion on Luke's relationship to Judaism is documented by GREEN & McKEEVER (n. 3), pp. 61-71.

43. J. JERVELL, *Luke and the Divided People of God: A New Look at Luke-Acts,* Minneapolis, Augsburg, 1972, pp. 60-62; A. GEORGE, *Israël dans l'oeuvre de Luc*, in *RB* 75 (1968) 481-525; G. LOHFINK, *Die Sammlung Israels: Eine Untersuchung zur lukanischen Ekklesiologie* (SANT, 39), München, Kösel, 1975, p.30; TIEDE, *Prophecy* (n. 17), passim and *Glory to Thy People Israel*, in *Luke-Acts and the Jews*, (n. 42), pp. 21-34. See also R.L. BRAWLEY, *Luke-Acts and Jews: Conflict, Apology, and Conciliation* (SBL MS, 33), Atlanta, Scholars Press, pp. 1-5.

sense when read from the perspective of inner Jewish struggles at the end of the first century. Luke presents not Israel's rejection or condemnation but its division over the gospel. The fulfillment of Simeon's prophecy (Lk 2,34: "He is set for the rise and fall of many in Israel") is a central to this view. Those who "rise up" within Israel become the true Israel along with the Gentiles.

The subject of Luke's attitude towards the Jews is far more complex than a few observations on a single passage can solve. Our passage, however, may serve as a pointer in a more positive direction, especially since the words are the final ones placed on the lips of Jesus before committing his spirit to the Father.

The fact that Jesus prayed for the Jewish religious establishment in spite of their inability to understand the events surrounding him as Messiah is a telling corrective to the view espoused by Sanders. Luke's passion acccount indicates that he has not given up on the Jewish leaders but prays for them. Since the prayer is unique to Luke and its background accords with OT law, the view is strengthened that Luke has not given up on the Jews. It is hard to believe that if Luke was truly anti-Judaic he would have provided this prayer for his accusers. If Luke thought they were incapable or undeserving of forgiveness he could have remained silent or appealed to Jewish opinion that advanced a harsh response to opposing God's actions. For example, consider the unforgiving words of the martyred sons of the Maccabean revolt. "Do not think that you will go unpunished for having tried to fight against God" (2 Macc 7,19) or "Keep on and see how God's mighty power will torture you and your descendents" (2 Macc 7,17). Such sentiments are not placed on the lips of Jesus. We affirm that Luke's record in the passion narrative suggests he did not give up on his people but prays for them on account of their sins of inadvertence and offers the atonement of Jesus as the means for rectifying ignorance.

4. Conclusions

We must conclude by returning to our definition of intertextuality. If the atonement of Jesus continues to be available, what sort of reverberation would have been achieved by recollecting Num 15 in reading Luke 23,34? What is the intertextual relationship between these passages? Several points of common ground exist between Num 15.22ff and Luke 23.34a. First, Num 15 indicates a provision was made for sin of inadvertence within the nation of Israel, collectively and individually. This was because of their lack of knowledge about some prescribed OT laws. In Luke's account the Jewish leaders took part in the events surrounding the crucifixion of Jesus. The "unknowing" in Luke 23,34 is the failure of the Jewish leaders to recognize Jesus as Messiah and the realization that the activities of the leaders were contrary to the purposes of God. Second, atonement is made available through the appropriation of animal sacrifice in Num 15. This will ensure restoration with God and within the community. In the Lukan account the restorative process is initiated by prayer, not through animal sacrifice. This is a note of irony that since Jesus' death is imminent, the atoning sacrifice of Jesus' death would appear to be the substitute for the sacrifice of Num 15.

How then does the intertextual relationship of these texts function? We propose it is neither at the contextual level, genre nor at the level of linguistic similarities. Rather, the echo of Num 15 functions in Luke 23,34 at the thematic level. Luke fuses together a rationale for continued prayer for the Jewish leaders with an OT legal precedent. By so doing he offers his attitude toward the Jews at the conclusion of his gospel. Whether these intertextual or intra thematic echoes would have been noticed by Luke's audience one can only surmise. We believe a level of resonance exists between our texts, especially to provide thematic coherence to the Lukan passage. Regardless, our analysis confirms that intertexuality involves reactivating past revelation under new conditions and circumstances. It also invites the reader into a kind of echo chamber to hear in the current text reverberations of past ones. Finally, our study confirms the need for ongoing discussions on the definition of intertextuality that includes both the textual, diachronic approach of Hays and the text as discursive codes of a culture as Kristeva and Barthes argue.

Near Eastern Studies Department   George P. CARRAS
University of California, Berkeley
USA

L'ACCOMPLISSEMENT DE LA PAROLE DE JÉSUS

LA PARENTHÈSE DE JN 18,9

La tournure ἵνα πληρωθῇ est utilisée dans le quatrième évangile pour marquer l'accomplissement de l'Écriture. Les parenthèses de Jn 18,9 et 18,32 font exception: le verbe πληρόω y est appliqué à une parole de Jésus. Par cette substitution l'auteur semble souligner que la parole de Jésus a la même valeur que la parole de Dieu, l'Écriture (voir 2,22). C'est ce que nous comptons examiner ici dans le cadre du colloque sur «L'Ancien Testament dans les Évangiles», en nous limitant à la parenthèse de Jn 18,9: ἵνα πληρωθῇ ὁ λόγος ὃν εἶπεν ὅτι οὓς δέδωκάς μοι οὐκ ἀπώλεσα ἐξ αὐτῶν οὐδένα.

1. La plupart des critiques littéraires ont interprété Jn 18,9 comme l'accomplissement de la parole de Jésus dans la seconde partie de la prière sacerdotale: Jn 17,12 (cf. 6,39; 10,28). Ils remarquent cependant que la citation n'est pas littérale et que la parole y a un sens différent: en 17,12 il s'agit de la sauvegarde de la foi des disciples, tandis que 18,9 parle de la sauvegarde de leur vie physique. Pour cette raison, ils considèrent Jn 18,9 comme une interpolation d'un rédacteur[1]. Parmi les exégètes récents qui soutiennent cette vue, nous pouvons mentionner R. Bultmann, R.E. Brown, S. Schulz, H.M. Teeple, S. Temple, W. Lang-

---

1. Depuis A. Schweizer (1841) cette observation était l'argument pour compter Jn 18,9 parmi les «kleine Einschaltungen» (19,35-37; 18,9; 16,30; 2,21-22; 6,64.71; 12,6), qui seraient insérées par une main secondaire dans l'évangile primitif: «neben die äccht Johannäischen, geistvollen ἵνα πληρωθῇ... gestellt, verräth sie XVIII.9 als eine Combination niedrigern Geistes». À la suite de Schweizer, J.H. Scholten (1864) accepte l'inauthenticité de 18,9 et 2,21-22 et à ces deux cas il ajoute encore les «interpolations» en 7,39; 12,33 et 18,32, qui n'expriment pas le sens exact des paroles de Jésus. Sans se référer à Scholten, H.H. Wendt a plusieurs fois (1896, 1900, 1910) attiré l'attention sur les mêmes versets (2,21-22; 7,39; 12,33; 18,9.32): ce sont des «Mißdeutungen einzelner Aussprüche Jesu» et ils sont à considérer comme «Anzeichen des Benutztseins einer Quellenschrift im vierten Evangelium». D'une manière analogue, F.W. Lewis (1909-11), J.M. Thompson (1917) et H.J. Flowers (1921) considèrent les mêmes versets comme des interprétations erronées, ajoutées ou interpolées par un éditeur. L'argument de la tension entre la préservation spirituelle (17,12) et la préservation matérielle pour attribuer Jn 18,9 à une main secondaire se retrouve encore chez B.W. Bacon (1900, 1903, 1933), J. Wellhausen (1907), E. Schwartz (1907-08), W. Bousset (1909), F. Spitta (1910), A. Meyer (1910), G.H.C. MacGregor (1928) et E. Hirsch (1931). – Pour tous ces auteurs, voir les références dans G. VAN BELLE, *Les parenthèses dans l'évangile de Jean* (SNTA, 11), Leuven, 1985.

brandtner, J. Becker et M. Myllykoski[2]. En revanche, W. Wilkens a défendu (contre Bultmann) l'origine johannique du verset: c'est l'évangéliste lui-même qui l'aurait ajouté dans son «Grundevangelium»[3]. Pour R.T. Fortna[4], A. Dauer[5], M.-É. Boismard (et A. Lamouille)[6] et W. Schmithals[7] le verset fait partie d'une addition plus large de l'évangéliste. Ainsi, A. Dauer répond à Wellhausen, Schwartz, Spitta, Hirsch et Bultmann: «Diesen Vers als 'Glosse der Red.'… auszuscheiden ist willkürlich, da er durchaus joh Sprachkolorit trägt, wie auch Bultmann… zugeben muß»[8]. Il estime que les versets 4-9 sont inserés par l'évangéliste dans la source de la passion: «Sprache, Kompositions-

2. R. BULTMANN, *Das Evangelium des Johannes* (KEK, 2), Göttingen, 1941, p. 495; R.E. BROWN, *The Gospel According to John*, II (AB, 29A), Garden City, NY, 1970, p. 811-812 (par contre, dans *The Death of the Messiah*, I [ABRL], New York, 1994, p. 289-291, Brown ne parle plus d'un ultime rédacteur pour 18,9); S. SCHULZ, *Das Evangelium nach Johannes* (NTD, 4), Göttingen, 1972, ³1978, p. 224, 225; H.M. TEEPLE, *The Literary Origin of the Gospel of John*, Evanston, IL, 1974, p. 234; S. TEMPLE, *The Core of the Fourth Gospel*, London – Oxford, 1975, p. 38, 231; W. LANGBRANDTNER, *Weltferner Gott oder Gott der Liebe* (BET, 6), Frankfurt, 1977, p. 105 n. 13 et n. 15; J. BECKER, *Das Evangelium nach Johannes*, vol. II (ÖTKNT, 4/2), Gütersloh – Würzburg, 1981, p. 541; ³1993, p. 645 (même texte); M. MYLLYKOSKI, *Die letzten Tage Jesu*, I (AASF B, 256), Helsinki, 1991, p. 171. – Noter que Becker et Myllykoski, par ex., donnent l'argument des parallèles rédactionnels pour attribuer 18,9 au rédacteur: «In jedem Fall ist V 9 der KR zuzuschreiben, da die ungenaue Zitation sich nur auf 6,39 oder (eher auf) 10,28; 17,12 (alle KR) beziehen kann» (Becker); «Nach dieser Folge unterbricht V 9 den Zusammenhang zwischen V 8 und 10. Er stammt nicht von der Hand des Evangelisten, sondern geht auf die Tätigkeit des KR zurück, wie aus entsprechenden Parallelstellen (5,39; 10,28; 17,12) zu entnehmen ist» (Myllykoski).

3. W. WILKENS, *Die Entstehungsgeschichte des vierten Evangeliums*, Zollikon, 1958, p. 78 et n. 292; comparer B. LINDARS, *The Gospel of John* (NCB), London, 1972, p. 542. Voir déjà A.E. GARVIE, *The Beloved Disciple*, London, 1922, p. XXI-XXII, 14-29, spéc. XXVII, 18: «comment by the evangelist»; J.H. BERNARD, *The Gospel according to St. John* (ICC), Edinburgh, 1928, I, p. XXXIII-XXXIV: «Evangelistic comments», et spéc. p. CLV; voir également II, p. 588.

4. Il défend que les vv. 5b-9 sont inserés par l'évangéliste dans l'évangile des signes. Cf. R.T. FORTNA, *The Gospel of Signs* (SNTS MS, 11), Cambridge, 1970, p. 115-116, 242; comparer *The Fourth Gospel and Its Predecessor*, Philadelphia, PA, 1988, p. 151, 153, 154; *The Signs Gospel*, in R.J. MILLER (éd.), *The Complete Gospels: Annotated Scholars Version*, Sonoma, CA, 1992, p. 175-193, spéc. 189.

5. Voir *infra*, nn. 8-9.

6. Ils considèrent les vv. 4-9 comme une insertion dans le Document C. Cf. M.-É. BOISMARD – A. LAMOUILLE, *L'évangile de Jean. Commentaire* (Synopse des quatre évangiles en français, 3), Paris, 1977, p. 402b: «Ce texte remonte fondamentalement à Jean II-A, mais il fut repris et amplifié par Jean II-B. Le v. 9 est de Jean II-B» (p. 403b).

7. Les vv. 5b-12a sont inserés par l'évangéliste («antidoketische Bearbeitung», vers 140) dans l'évangile primitif («Grundevangelium», fin du premier siècle, provenant d'une autre main), qui contenait 18,1.3b-5a. Cf. W. SCHMITHALS, *Johannesevangelium und Johannesbriefe* (BZNW, 64), Berlin – New York, 1992, p. 407; voir également p. 317, 405, 406-407, 414.

8. A. DAUER, *Die Passionsgeschichte im Johannes-Evangelium* (SANT, 30), München, 1972, p. 32 n. 73.

technik und theologische Motive haben deutlich gemacht, daß Johannes für das Zwischenstück 18,4-9 keine Traditionen verarbeitet hat, sondern die Szene selbst erst entworfen und gestaltet hat»[9].

2. C'est à bon droit que la plupart des auteurs récents attribuent Jn 18,9 à l'évangéliste, car les termes et tournures du verset sont de style johannique[10]: l'usage elliptique de ἵνα, les formules ἵνα πληρωθῇ ὁ λόγος et ὁ λόγος ὃν εἶπεν, le verbe δίδωμι dans le sens de «Dieu donne les disciples à Jésus», οὐκ... οὐδείς et οὐδεὶς ἐκ + génitif et, enfin, l'utilisation du pronom αὐτός supportant un *casus pendens*. Dans le cadre de cette note, c'est surtout la phrase ἵνα πληρωθῇ ὁ λόγος ὃν εἶπεν qui doit retenir notre attention[11].

La tournure ἵνα πληρωθῇ ὁ λόγος se rencontre quatre fois en Jn (12,38; 15,25; 18,9; 18,32) et nulle part ailleurs dans le N.T. Elle apparaît deux fois sous la forme ἵνα ὁ λόγος... πληρωθῇ (12,38; 18,32) et deux fois dans l'ordre inverse ἵνα πληρωθῇ ὁ λόγος (15,25; 18,9). En 12,38 et 15,25 il s'agit de l'accomplissement de l'Ancien Testament, en 18,9 et 18,32 de l'accomplissement des paroles de Jésus. L'on peut comparer ἵνα πληρωθῇ ὁ λόγος avec la tournure ἵνα ἡ γραφὴ πληρωθῇ, également propre à Jean[12], et l'expression synonymique ἵνα τελειωθῇ ἡ γραφή en 19,24, seul emploi dans le N.T. En plus, ces formules sont très proches de la caractéristique johannique ἔστιν γεγραμμένον, qu'on rencontre neuf fois en Jean[13].

9. *Ibid.*, p. 29-43, spéc. 43. C'était aussi l'opinion de son promoteur; voir R. Schnacken-burg, *Das Johannesevangelium*, III (HTKNT, 4/3), Freiburg – Basel – Wien, 1975, p. 249 (sur 18,4-8). Sur 18,9, voir p. 255.

10. Pour cette analyse stylistique, nous avons utilisé surtout les listes des caractéristiques stylistiques d'E. Schweizer (1939, ²1965), E. Ruckstuhl (1951, ²1987), W. Nicol (1992), M.-É. Boismard – A. Lamouille (1977), E. Ruckstuhl – P. Dschulnigg (1991) et W. Schenke (1993). Voir également les listes dans F. Neirynck, *Jean et les Synoptiques* (BETL, 49), Leuven, 1979, p. 45-66 (= *ETL* 53, 1977, 363-478, p. 404-425); Van Belle, *Les parenthèses* (n. 1), p. 105-155; Id., *The Signs Source in the Fourth Gospel* (BETL, 116), Leuven, 1994, p. 405-420, et les «Sprachliche Beobachtungen» sur 18,9 dans Dauer, *Die Passionsgeschichte* (n. 8), p. 32-33.

11. Sur la formule ἵνα πληρωθῇ, voir surtout C.A. Evans, *On the Quotation Formulas in the Fourth Gospel*, dans *BZ* 26 (1982) 79-83; Id., *Word of Glory* (JSNT SS, 89), Sheffield, 1993, p. 172-184; A. Obermann, *Die christologische Erfüllung der Schrift im Johannesevangelium* (WUNT, 2/83), Tübingen, 1996, p. 78-89. Sur l'hypothèse d'A. Faure, dans *ZNW* 21 (1922) 99-121, qui distinguait deux auteurs à la base des formules d'introduction des citations (cf. Van Belle, *The Signs Source* [n. 10], p. 17-20), voir la réaction de F. Smend, dans *ZNW* 24 (1925) 147-150.

12. Voir Jn 13,18; 19,24; 19,36; 17,12. À l'exception de 17,12, la formule est suivie d'une citation explicite.

13. Voir Jn 2,17; 6,31.45; 10,34; 12,14.16; 19,19.20; 20,30. Le seul autre emploi dans N.T. est Lc 4,17.

La tournure ὁ λόγος ὃν εἶπεν se lit sept fois en Jn (2,22; 4,50; 7,36; 12,38; 15,20; 18,9.32; et nulle part ailleurs dans le N.T.)[14]: avec ἵνα πληρωθῇ en 12,38; 18,9.32, avec le verbe πιστεύω en 2,22; 4,50 et avec le verbe μνημονεύω en 15,20 (comparer 2,22 ἐμνήσθησαν οἱ μαθηταὶ αὐτοῦ ὅτι τοῦτο ἔλεγεν, καὶ ἐπίστευσαν τῇ γραφῇ καὶ τῷ λόγῳ ὃν εἶπεν). La formule ὁ λόγος ὃν εἶπεν est à comparer avec ὁ λόγος ὃν ἐλάλησα (12,48), διὰ τὸν λόγον ὃν λελάληκα ὑμῖν (15,3). Voir également τὰ ῥήματα ἃ ἐγὼ λελάληκα en 6,63; τὰ ῥήματα ἃ ἐγὼ λέγω (λαλῶ S TR) ὑμῖν en 14,10. La formule ὁ λόγος ὃν εἶπεν comporte encore une caractéristique johannique plus générale: εἶπον + accusatif de la chose, qui se rencontre 39 fois en Jean et 29(+3) fois dans le reste du N.T.[15].

En plus, Jn 18,9 est un exemple des explications par lesquelles «l'évangéliste aide ses lecteurs à bien comprendre les événements qu'il raconte et les idées qu'il enseigne»[16]. Le verset est considéré depuis longtemps comme un bon exemple des «animadversiones interiectae», des «Parenthesen», des «epexegeses» et des «erläuternde Bemerkungen»[17], qui apparaissent «longe plura in uno Ioanneo»[18]. D'après la forme et le contenu, la parenthèse de Jn 18,9 a été classée dans différentes catégories[19]. Mentionnons en particulier que «l'accomplissement de l'Écriture ou de paroles de Jésus» forme une catégorie spécifique d'après J. Konings et B. Olsson[20] et

14. Comparer les tournures semblables dans Lc 22,61; Ac 20,35; 20,38; Jude 15.
15. Outre la tournure ὁ λόγος ὃν εἶπεν (sept fois), voir les caractéristiques johanniques: καὶ τοῦτο εἰπών (cinq fois: Jn 11,28; 18,38; 20,20.22; 21,19), ταῦτα εἶπεν/εἶπον (cinq fois: Jn 6,59; 9,22; 11,11; 12,41; 20,18; comparer ταῦτα λαλέω, treize fois: 8,26.28.30; 12,36; 14,25; 15,11; 16,1.4.6.25.33; 17,1.13), ταῦτα εἰπών (sept fois: 7,9; 9,6; 11,43; 13,21; 18,1.22; 20,14), τοῦτο δὲ εἶπεν (quatre fois: 7,39; 11,51; [12,6 CT]; 21,19; comparer τοῦτο δὲ ἔλεγεν, trois fois: 6,6; [8,6]; 12,33). Voir encore 3,12(bis); 4,29 = 39; 10,6.41; 11,46; 12,27 = 49; 14,26; 16,4; 18,21.
16. VAN BELLE, Les parenthèses (n. 1), p. 206-210, spéc. 206. Sur Jn 18,9, voir spéc. p. 96.
17. Les expressions sont de H.P.C. Henke, J.D. Schulze, M. Weber et K.A Credner. Voir VAN BELLE, Les parenthèses (n. 1), passim.
18. L'expression est de H.P.C. Henke.
19. Voir les classifications de H.P.C. Henke, J.D. Schulze, M. Weber, K.A. Credner, E. Stange, A.E. Garvie, T. Bromboszcz, J.H. Bernard, R. Bultmann, J.J. O'Rourke, R. Schnackenburg, R.E. Brown, J. Konings, B. Olsson et celles H.A. Lombard, C.W. Hedrick (n. 21) et C.A. Pourciau, mentionnées dans Les parenthèses (n. 1) et Les parenthèses johanniques. Un premier bilan, dans F. VAN SEGBROECK, et al. (éds.), The Four Gospels 1992. FS F. Neirynck (BETL, 100), III, Leuven, 1992, p. 1901-1933. Ajouter: T. THATCHER, A New Look at Asides in the Fourth Gospel, in BS 151 (1994) 428-439, spéc. p. 437: «Asides that explain discourse, providing the significance of what a speaker said» (2,9; 2,21; 2,22; 4,9; 4,27; 6,64; 7,39; 8,27; 11,51; 12,33; 13,29; 18,8.32; 18,40; 19,28; 21,4; 21,19; 21,23. Voir son commentaire, à la p. 432. Sur Thatcher, cf. ETL 71 (1995) 465-468, spéc. p. 468.
20. J. KONINGS, Het johanneïsch verhaal in de literaire kritiek, diss. Leuven, 1972 (dir. F. Neirynck), IIIc, p. 46*-54*; B. OLSSON, Structure and Meaning in the Fourth

que C.W. Hedrick considère comme une catégorie distincte les «asides» en 18,9 et 18,32 où le narrateur cite les paroles de Jésus comme «proof texts»[21].

Par la formule ὁ λόγος ὃν εἶπεν la parenthèse se réfère à une parole énoncée par Jésus. La parole ne semble pas être citée à la lettre, mais «provoque une série de rappels en chaîne de passages»[22]:

6,39	πᾶν ὃ δέδωκέν μοι	μὴ	ἀπολέσω ἐξ αὐτοῦ
10,28		οὐ μὴ	ἀπόλωνται εἰς τὸν αἰῶνα
17,12	καὶ οὐδεὶς ἐξ αὐτῶν		ἀπώλετο εἰ μὴ ὁ υἱὸς τῆς ἀπωλείας
18,9	οὓς δέδωκάς μοι	οὐκ	ἀπώλεσα ἐξ αὐτῶν οὐδένα.

La parole citée en 18,9 semble être le plus proche de 6,39. On y retrouve le *casus pendens* et les deux verbes δίδωμι et ἀπόλλυμι (ce dernier à la voix active; cf. la voix moyenne en 10,28; 17,12). Mais il y a aussi des différences. L'objet du verbe δίδωμι est au neutre en 6,39 et au pluriel en 18,9. L'idée que Jesus n'a perdu aucun de ceux que le Père lui a donnés (18,9) n'est pas exprimée explicitement en 6,39 mais semble être l'idée principale en 17,12: «aucun d'eux ne s'est perdu, en dehors du fils de perdition». Enfin, l'image du bon pasteur, qui donne la vie éternelle à ses brebis et qui prend garde qu'elles ne périssent jamais, répond à l'idée de la sauvegarde spirituelle exprimée en 6,39; 17,12, et c'est encore la même idée qui joue dans la présentation de la scène de l'arrestation et de la parenthèse en 18,9.

Que la parole de Jésus citée en 18,9 ne corresponde strictement à aucun de ces passages ne peut être une raison pour attribuer le verset 9 à un rédacteur postérieur. En effet, il y a dans le quatrième évangile de nom-

---

Gospel (ConBibNT, 6), Lund, 1974, p. 262-263. Voir également VAN BELLE, *Les parenthèses* (n. 1), p. 110 (catégorie 10), cf. Jn. 1,23; 2,17; 6,31; 7,38; 12,14-16; 18,9.32; 19,24.28.36-37; comparer 4,44; 10,35; 12,38; 20,9.

21. C.W. HEDRICK, *Authorial Presence and Narrator in John: Commentary and Story*, dans J.E. GOEHRING, *et al.* (éds.), *Gospel Origins & Christian Beginnings*. FS J.M. Robinson (Forum Fascicles, 1), Sonoma, CA, 1990, p. 74-93, spéc. 82.

22. C.H. DODD, *The Interpretation of the Fourth Gospel*, Cambridge, 1953, p. 424; trad. française, 1975, p. 546. Comparer T. KNÖPPLER, *Die theologia crucis des Johannes-evangeliums* (WMANT, 69), Neukirchen-Vluyn, 1994, p. 215: «Dieses die Jünger schützende Wort in V. 8b und der Erfüllungshinweis in V. 9 deuten zurück auf die soteriologischen Aussagen des vierten Evangeliums: die Jesus vom Vater gegebenen Menschen sollen nicht verloren gehen (6,39; 10,28; 17,12)». – La leçon οὓς δέδωκάς μοι en 17,11.12 au sens de «ceux que tu m'as donnés» (défendue, par. ex., par J. HUBY, dans *RSR* 27, 1937, 408-421) peut être considérée comme correction «prompted by the recollection of ver. 6 or the statement in 18.9»; voir B.M. METZGER, *A Textual Commentary on the Greek New Testament*, London – New York, 1971, p. 250 (= ²1994, p. 213). – Sur la variante ἔδωκεν en 6,39 et ἔδωκας en 18,9, voir M.J.J. MENKEN, *Old Testament Quotations in the Fourth Gospel* (Biblical Exegesis & Theology, 15), Kampen, 1996, p. 49 n. 8.

breuses exemples de «répétitions inexactes»[23] et celles-ci ne sont qu'un aspect d'un trait spécifique du style de l'évangéliste, c'est-à-dire la répétition et la variation: «Un auteur, et surtout Jean, dont la progression de l'idée est lente, explique et répète ce qu'il a dit, fait des corrections et des connexions avec d'autres parties de l'évangile dans le but d'avertir ses lecteurs de bien comprendre ce qu'il a écrit»[24]. L'argument le plus important pour attribuer 18,9 à un rédacteur postérieur est sans doute le fait qu'il y est question de protéger les disciples contre la police, tandis que dans les autres versets, et surtout en 17,12, il s'agit des dangers qui menacent leur salut spirituel. Mais l'argument n'est guère valable[25]:

> Une telle objection... traduit une impuissance à comprendre le mode de penser de l'évangéliste. Pour lui, chaque acte, chaque parole de Jésus, en quelque circonstance que se soit, comporte une signification qui dépasse cette circonstance particulière. Sans doute ne peut-on restreindre la signification de 17,12 aux dimensions de 18,9, mais l'action de Jésus au Jardin des Oliviers est un σημεῖον de l'action qu'il mène sur une plus vaste échelle et sur un plan plus élevé; et cette action sur une échelle plus vaste et sur un plan plus élevé constitue précisément le sens de son action dans le Jardin.

3. Le style johannique et le caractère parenthétique du verset ne sont pas les seuls arguments qui empêchent d'attribuer le verset 18,9 à une autre main que celle de l'évangéliste. La parenthèse s'accorde bien avec la description du Christ dans le récit de la passion johannique, qui «tend à illustrer trois thèmes majeurs: Jésus va au-devant de la mort volontairement; par sa mort il triomphe; il accomplit fidèlement la volonté de son Père»[26]. Voyons d'abord quelques traits de cette représentation dans le récit de l'arrestation. Pleinement conscient de tout ce qui va lui arriver

---

23. Cf. T.F. GLASSON, *Inaccurate Repetitions in the Fourth Gospel*, in *ExpT* 57 (1945-46) 111-112.

24. VAN BELLE, *Les parenthèses* (n. 1), p. 209.

25. DODD, *The Interpretation* (n. 22), 1953, p. 432; trad. française, p. 543-544. Comparer, par ex., A. LOISY, *Le quatrième évangile*, Paris, 1903, p. 824-825; ²1921, p. 456; E.C. HOSKYNS, *The Fourth Gospel* (éd. F.N. DAVEY), London, 1940, ²1947, p. 510.

26. H. VAN DEN BUSSCHE, *Jean* (Bible et vie chrétienne), Bruges, 1967, p. 465-466. Voir surtout J. RIAUD, *La gloire et la royauté de Jésus dans la Passion selon saint Jean*, in *Bible et vie chrétienne* 56 (1964) 28-44; DAUER, *Die Passionsgeschichte* (n. 8), p. 37-41, où il analyse «Die theologische Gestaltmotive» de Jn 18,4-9, c'est-à-dire, «a) Die starke Betonung des Wissens Jesu (V. 4); b) Leiden und Tot sind freie Tat Jesu; c) Jesu Sterben ist ein Sterben *für die Seinen* (V. 8f.); d) Die Passion als 'Erhöhung und Verherrlichung' Jesu»; comparer p. 242-246, 280-284, 312-313. Voir également D. SENIOR, *The Passion of Jesus in the Gospel of John* (The Passion Series, 4), Collegeville, MN, 1991, p. 47: «Jesus, God's powerful Word, is triumphant over death. He is not a victim from whom life is violently taken, but one who gives his life freely as an act of love for the world»; voir p. 144-159; S. LÉGASSE, *Le procès de Jésus*, II. (LD Commentaires, 3), Paris, 1995, p. 584-593.

(18,4; cf. 13,1)[27], Jésus prend l'initiative et se rend lui-même[28]: «C'est lui en effet qui, sorti du jardin au-devant de ses agresseurs, pose des questions, culbute la troupe à sa déclaration d'identité et, après sa défense des disciples et l'incident du coup d'épée, se laisse finalement appréhender»[29]. Mais en se rendant «Jésus domine tellement la situation qu'il réinstalle lui-même les soldats effondrés dans leur rôle, en prenant soin que l'arrestation se limite à sa personne»[30]. Par cette description l'évangéliste a accentué le caractère volontaire du sacrifice du Christ: «On ne me l'ôte pas [la vie]; je la donne de moi-même» (10,18). Comme le bon pasteur, Jésus donne sa vie pour ses brebis (10,11.15.17). Il est venu pour que les brebis aient la vie et l'aient en abondance (10,10); il leur donne la vie éternelle et elles ne périront jamais (10,28). La scène de l'arrestation illustre ce thème[31]. Il se rend lui-même à condition qu'on permette à ses disciples de s'en aller. En se livrant lui-même, le Christ accomplit fidèlement la volonté de son Père (14,31; cf. 4,34; 5,30; 6,38)[32]. Ainsi, «l'arrestation devient un récit d'épiphanie qui démontre la supériorité du Christ; seul actant du récit, il est décrit sous les traits du vainqueur»[33]. La parenthèse du v. 9 s'inscrit bien dans ce récit et dans une telle représentation du Christ.

(a) Les versets 4-9 forment la partie centrale du récit de l'arrestation. Jésus y prononce deux fois la formule ἐγώ εἰμι (vv. 5 = 6, 8a) et «c'est autour de ces deux affirmations que s'articule l'ensemble des vv. 4-9 en deux petits volets»[34]. Dans le premier volet (vv. 4-6), l'ἐγώ εἰμι «exprime l'autodésignation souveraine de Jésus face à ses ennemis»[35]. Dans le second (vv. 7-9), la formule «distingue Jésus de ses disciples et épargne ceux-ci» et «les vv. 7-9 ont le même propos de montrer le con-

---

27. Sur ce thème de la prescience surnaturelle, voir Van Belle, *The Signs Source* (n. 10), p. 392-393.

28. Ainsi, «le Christ est toujours décrit dans une attitude de parfaite souveraineté et de parfaite liberté par rapport à sa mort»; voir J. Zumstein, *L'interprétation johannique de la mort du Christ*, dans *The Four Gospels 1992*. FS F. Neirynck (n. 19), III, p. 2119-2138, spéc. 2135; comparer Id., *Le signe de la croix*, dans *Lumière et vie* 41 (1992), n° 209, 68-82, spéc. p. 209. Sur ce thème de Jésus qui prend l'initiative, voir également Van Belle, *The Signs Source* (n. 10), p. 392.

29. Légasse, *Le procès de Jésus*, II (n. 26), p. 586.

30. Cf. C. L'Éplattenier, *L'Évangile de Jean* (La Bible, Porte-Parole), Genève, 1993, p. 344.

31. Voir surtout M.W.G. Stibbe, *John as Storyteller* (SNTS MS, 73), Cambridge, 1992, p. 95-105; Id., *John* (Readings: A New Biblical Commentary), Sheffield, 1993, p. 179-185; J.P. Heil, *Blood and Water* (CBQ MS, 27), Washington, DC, 1995, p. 16-26.

32. Légasse, *Le procès de Jésus*, II (n. 26), p. 586, 591.

33. Zumstein, *L'interprétation johannique* (n. 28), p. 2135; Id., *Le signe de la croix* (n. 28), p. 81.

34. Neirynck, *Jean et les Synoptiques* (n. 10), p. 270.

35. *Ibid.*

trôle que conserve Jésus sur les événements: lui-même se déclare seul en cause, eux peuvent 'partir' sans être inquiétés»[36]. D'après Mc 14,50 et Mt 26,56b, les disciples prennent la fuite. Jean a modifié la scène: les disciples ne s'enfuient pas, mais Jésus lui-même a favorisé leur départ. En même temps il a transformé l'accomplissement des Écritures dans un accomplissement de la parole de Jésus[37]: par la parenthèse du v. 9, l'évangéliste caractérise cette intervention de Jésus comme un geste sauveur par lequel il accomplit sa propre parole dite auparavant.

La parenthèse sur la préservation des disciples est bien préparée dans l'introduction du récit, qui décrit les deux groupes qui entrent en scène. La présence des disciples y est mentionnée trois fois dans la description du premier groupe, où Jésus prend la tête des disciples[38]. Cette répétition fait partie de la description johannique de Jésus prenant l'initiative: «It is John, however, who underscores the theme of the structured group of Jesus and his disciples in order to focus attention here on Jesus as the Lord who approaches his passion freely»[39]. Le chef du second groupe est Judas, qui le livrait: connaissant le lieu (v. 2), il vient là de la part des grands prêtres et des phariséens, ayant pris la cohorte et les gardes (v. 3). Mais contrairement aux Synoptiques (Mc 14,44-45 et parallèles), le traître est «dépouillé de son rôle d'indicateur: simplement, 'il se tenait avec eux', inclus dans la troupe des gens qui, à la parole de Jésus, 'reculèrent et tombèrent à terre' (v. 6)»[40]. Dans la parenthèse du v. 9, il s'agit en premier lieu du premier groupe: Jésus prend garde que ses disciples soient sauvegardés. Constatant que l'intervention de Jésus est proposée comme l'accomplissement de propos qu'il a tenus auparavant,

36. *Ibid.*

37. Cf. M. SABBE, *The Arrest of Jesus in Jn 18,1-11 and Its Relation to the Synoptic Gospels: A Critical Evaluation of A. Dauer's Hypothesis*, in M. DE JONGE (éd.), *L'évangile de Jean* (BETL, 44), Leuven, 1977 ([2]1987), p. 203-234, spéc. 221-222; = M. SABBE, *Studia Neotestamentica* (BETL, 98), Leuven, 1991, p. 355-386 (387-388), spéc. 373-374; NEIRYNCK, *Jean et les Synoptiques* (n. 10), p. 270-271: «Le ἄφετε τούτους ὑπάγειν du v. 8 est un écho inversé de la finale du récit en Mc 14,50 καὶ ἀφέντες αὐτὸν ἔφυγον πάντες. Selon Jn, Jésus n'est pas 'abondonné' par ses disciples, ceux-ci ne sont pas contraints à la fuite; c'est Jésus qui commande de les 'laisser partir'. Le lamentable épilogue du récit marcien apparaît transposé en un 'accomplissement' d'une parole prononcée par Jésus avant son arrestation (v. 9). Ici encore, Jn récupère à sa manière un 'argument' des Synoptiques: ceux-ci s'efforçaient déjà d'expliquer et de corriger le caractère infâmant de l'arrestation par l''accomplissement des Écritures' (Mc 14,49; Mt 26,54.56). Jn va plus loin en employant une formule semblable à propos d'une parole de Jésus qu'il assimile à la parole de Dieu et dont il met en relief la portée rédemptrice en faveur des disciples».

38. Jn 18,1... Ἰησοῦς ἐξῆλθεν σὺν τοῖς μαθηταῖς αὐτοῦ... εἰς ὃν εἰσῆλθεν αὐτὸς καὶ οἱ μαθηταὶ αὐτοῦ. 2... ὅτι πολλάκις συνήχθη Ἰησοῦς ἐκεῖ μετὰ τῶν μαθητῶν αὐτοῦ.

39. SABBE, *The Arrest* (n. 37), p. 205 (= p. 357).

40. NEIRYNCK, *Jean et les Synoptiques* (n. 10), p. 270.

entre autres 17,12, le lecteur sait également que le chef du second groupe est perdu, qu'il est le fils de perdition. Ainsi, en se référant à 17,12, la parenthèse du v. 9 est liée à celle du v. 5b: εἱστήκει δὲ καὶ Ἰούδας ὁ παραδιδοὺς αὐτὸν μετ' αὐτῶν.

(b) La parenthèse exprime bien la christologie johannique qui met en relief «la maîtrise de Jésus sur les événements, lors même qu'il les subit, par la prescience qu'il en a et la décision qu'il prend de les affronter»[41]. En effet, en appliquant la formule ἵνα πληρωθῇ pour introduire une parole de Jésus lui-même (comparer 18,32), cette parole reçoit maintenant une autorité semblable à celle de l'Écriture[42]. L'on peut comparer 18,9 et 32 avec 2,22; 5,39 et 12,34, où la parole de Jésus est juxtaposée (ou opposée) à l'Écriture[43]. Les verbes μνημονεύω et μιμνήσκομαι s'appliquent également à l'Écriture et aux paroles de Jésus: les disciples se rappelèrent ce qui est écrit (2,17.[22]; 12,16) ou ce que Jésus a dit (2,22; 15,20; 16,4)[44]. «Jean fait appel à l'Écriture pour établir que Jésus

---

41. *Ibid.*, p. 271.

42. Plusieurs commentateurs ont souligné cette autorité semblable. Voir, par ex., J.H. Bernard (1928), F.W. Grosheide (1950), W. Hendriksen (1954), C.K. Barrett (1955, ²1978), J.N. Sanders – B.A. Mastin (1968), R.E. Brown (1970), R. Schnackenburg (1975; comparer n. 47), M.-É. Boismard – A. Lamouille (1977), J. Blank (1977), J. Becker (1981, ³1993), F.F. Bruce (1983), J.R. Michaels (1984, 1989), G.R. Beasley-Murray (1987), H.R. Ridderbos (1992), J.W. Pryor (1992), C. L'Éplattenier (1993). Voir également G. DELLING, πληρόω, dans *TWNT* 6 (1959) 285-296, spéc. p. 295; H. HÜBNER, γραφή, dans *EWNT* 1 (1980) 628-638, spéc. c. 636-637; OBERMANN, *Die christologische Erfüllung* (n. 11), p. 389; J. BEUTLER, *The Use of «Scripture» in the Gospel of John*, dans R.A. CULPEPPER – C.C. BLACK (éds.), *Exploring the Gospel of John*. FS D.M. Smith, Louisville, KY, 1996, p. 147-162, spéc. 154. Noter que Brown (*John*, II [n. 2], p. 760), Hübner et Beutler ont rejeté l'opinion d'E.D. FREED, *Old Testament Quotations in the Gospel of John* (SupplNT, 11), Leiden, 1965, p. 51-59, qui défendait que γραφή est également utilisé «to refer to a saying of Jesus given earlier in the Gospel as in Jn 17:12; (and) to indicate the use of a Synoptic passages as in 7:42 and 20:9» (voir *infra*, n. 52). – C.K. BARRETT, *The Gospel According to St John*, London, 1955, p. 435 (²1978, p. 521) note à propos de 18,9: «only in John (here and 18.32) is it [ἵνα (ὅπως) πληρωθῇ] used of the fulfilment of words of Jesus», mais il ajoute: «cf. however Mark 13.31».

43. Comme ailleurs, l'évangéliste utilise en 2,22 et 5,39 des expressions synonymiques, c'est-à-dire γραφή/γράμμα et λόγος/ῥῆμα. En 12,34, la foule (les juifs) voit une opposition entre la loi (ἐκ τοῦ νόμου) et les paroles de Jésus (πῶς λέγεις σύ).

44. Le verbe μιμνήσκομαι est utilisé pour l'Écriture en 2,17; 12,16 et pour la parole de Jésus en 2,22, tandis que le synonyme μνημονεύω n'est utilisé que pour la parole de Jésus en 15,20; 16,4 (de même pour l'unique occurrence johannique de ὑπομιμνήσκω en 14,26). Voir A. FAURE, dans *ZNW* 21 (1922) 99-121, spéc. p. 101-102, et surtout J. ZUMSTEIN, *Mémoire et relecture pascale de l'évangile selon Jean*, dans D. MARGUERAT – J. ZUMSTEIN (éds.), *La mémoire et le temps*. FS P. Bonnard (Le monde de la Bible, 23), Genève, 1991, p. 153-170, spéc. 163; = ID., *Miettes exégétiques* (Le monde de la Bible, 25), Genève, 1991, p. 299-316, spéc. 309: «L'Écriture dont la mémoire pascale fait état est certes la Bible juif (2,17.22; 12,16), mais elle comprend également les paroles de Jésus (2,22; 14,26; 16,4)»; comparer ID., *Der Prozess der Relecture in der johanneischen Literatur*, in *NTS* 42 (1996) 394-411, p. 410.

et son œuvre sont une réalisation d'un plan tracé par Dieu»[45]. En accomplissant de fait les Écritures, le Pré-existant (1,1; 8,58) accomplit sa mission révélatrice: «ses paroles et ses œuvres lui sont dictées par le Père dans l'intimité duquel il ne cesse pas de vivre (1,18)»[46]. Le Christ johannique, c'est-à-dire celui que Dieu a envoyé, «prononce les paroles de Dieu» (3,34)[47]. Si Jean souligne à la fin de la vie de Jésus que les Écritures s'accomplissent (19,24.28.36.37)[48], il peut en même temps souligner que la parole dite par le Fils, qui est lui-même le λόγος et qui parle et témoigne de ce qu'il a vu et entendu, s'accomplit (18,9.32)[49]. En effet, le Christ en se livrant accomplit la volonté de son Père, mais en protégeant ses disciples il obéit également à sa propre parole qui exprime la volonté de son Père: «Or la volonté de celui qui m'a envoyé est que je ne perde rien de ce qu'il m'a donné, mais que je le ressuscite au dernier jour» (6,39). En outre, en Jn 13,19; 14,29 et 16,4, les paroles de Jésus sont des annonces prophétiques des événements à venir[50]. Surtout dans le dernier verset, où le verbe μνημονεύω est lié à la parole de Jésus, il devient clair qu'une parole de Jésus peut s'accomplir. Enfin, si l'on accepte avec M. Sabbe que καθὼς εἶπον τοῖς Ἰουδαίοις en 13,33, se référant à la parole Jésus (7,33-34; 8,21-22), dépend de Mc 14,21 ὑπάγει καθὼς γέγραπται περὶ αὐτοῦ (par Mt 26,24; diff. Lk 22,22 κατὰ τὸ ὡρισμένον), on y retrouve un autre cas où Jean en dépendance des Synoptiques a transformé l'accomplissement des Écritures dans un accomplissement d'une parole de Jésus[51].

Concluons. Le style et le vocabulaire de la parenthèse de 18,9 sont johanniques et son contenu s'accorde avec la représentation du Christ

---

45. LÉGASSE, *Le procès de Jésus*, II (n. 26), p. 591.
46. *Ibid.*, p. 591. Voir spécialement 3,11.32; 5,19-30, 8,26.38; 12,49.
47. Comparer 14,24; 7,16-17; 8,26.28-29; 12,49; 14,10. Voir R. SCHNACKENBURG, *Die Messiasfrage im Johannesevangelium*, in *ThJ* (1966) 318-348, spéc. p. 320 n. 8: «Jesus als der eschatologische Offenbarer spricht selbst die Worte Gottes (3,34). So wird auch der 'Erfüllungsbeweis' in der Weise weitergeführt, daß sich die Worte Jesu für den Evangelisten erfüllt haben, vgl. 2,22; 18,9; ferner 13,19; 14,29; 16,4».
48. Voir D.E. GARLAND, *The Fulfillment Quotations in John's Account of the Crucifixion*, in R.B. SLOAN – M.C. PARSONS (éds.), *Perspectives on John* (NABPR Special Studies Series, 11), Lewiston, 1993, 229-250.
49. Voir également l'accomplissement de la prédiction du reniement de Pierre (13,38) en 18,27: «et le coque chanta». Cf. X. LÉON-DUFOUR, *Lecture de l'évangile de Jean*, IV (Parole de Dieu), Paris, 1996, p. 21: «En même temps qu'il souligne l'accomplissement de l'Écriture, l'évangéliste montre à trois reprises [18,9.27.32] que s'accomplit la parole dite par le Fils».
50. Voir la citation de R. Schnackenburg dans la n. 47.
51. M. SABBE, *The Footwashing in Jn 13 and Its Relation to the Synoptic Gospels*, in *ETL* 57 (1982) 279-308, spéc. p. 294; = ID., *Studia Neotestamentica* (n. 37), p. 409-438 (439-441), spéc. 424.

dans la passion johannique. En plus, la parenthèse cadre bien dans le contexte. L'évangéliste souligne que Jésus garantit souverainement la liberté de ses disciples, selon ce qu'il affirmait en 17,12 (cf. 6,39; 10,28). En appliquant la formule ἵνα πληρωθῇ à une parole de Jésus (ὁ λόγος ὃν εἶπεν), Jean souligne que la parole de Jésus a une autorité semblable à celle de l'Écriture. E.D. Freed va peut-être trop loin quand il assume que pour l'évangéliste les paroles de Jésus font partie de l'Écriture[52]. L'opinion de J. Beutler nous semble préférable: «There are no reasons for assuming that the words of Jesus are part of scripture for the fourth evangelist, but it may be said that they have a comparable authority»[53].

Platte Lostraat 274/31   Gilbert VAN BELLE
B-3010 Leuven (Kessel-Lo)

---

52. Cf. *supra*, n. 42.
53. BEUTLER, *The Use of «Scripture»* (n. 42), p. 154.

DIE VOLLENDUNG DER SCHRIFT NACH JOH 19,28

ÜBERLEGUNGEN ZUM UMGANG MIT DER SCHRIFT
IM JOHANNESEVANGELIUM

Im Johannesevangelium lassen sich bei der Frage nach dem Umgang mit der Schrift vier Aspekte unterscheiden. Auf die beiden ersten Punkte gehe ich nur ganz kurz ein. Punkt drei und vier werde ich etwas ausführlicher behandeln. In einem fünften Punkt will ich mich kurz mit einigen hermeneutischen Konsequenzen befassen.

1. *Die Schrift/das AT selbst gibt Zeugnis von Christus.* Dies läßt sich paradigmatisch an Joh 5,31-47 zeigen (vgl. 1,45; 2,22; 3,14; 5,39.45f; 7,15f.19.22.51.52; 10,35; 20,9). Es geht in diesem Text um den Anspruch Jesu, der von Gott gesandte, endzeitliche Bevollmächtigte zu sein. Wie kann dieser Anspruch begründet werden? Neben Johannes d.T. und Jesu Werken ist es Gott selbst, der sich für Jesu Legitimität verbürgt, ja bereits verbürgt hat (5,37). μεμαρτύρηκεν ist dabei der zusammenfassende Ausdruck für das Reden Gottes in der Schrift Israels. Wer die Schrift richtig hört, wird durch sie auf Jesus hingewiesen. Sachgerechtes Schriftstudium müßte daher zur Anerkenntnis Jesu als des Offenbarers und des Lebensspenders führen (5,39). Wer den Schriften glaubt, glaubt auch Jesus, wer den Schriften nicht glaubt, kann auch Jesus nicht glauben (5,46). Und umgekehrt: wer Jesu Worten kein Zutrauen schenkt, glaubt folglich auch nicht den Worten des Mose, denn Mose spricht von Jesus. D.h. letztlich: Wer sich Jesus verweigert, verweigert sich damit Gott selbst, hat Gott nie wirklich gehört oder erkannt. Die Schrift wird hierbei von der Geschichte Israels abgekoppelt, christologisch enggeführt und in einer Zielrichtung allein auf Jesus hin gesehen. Die ganze Schrift ist nach Joh – exklusiv – auf Jesus ausgerichtet. Es gibt kein verborgenes, erst zu entdeckendes Christuszeugnis im AT, sondern die Schrift als solche *ist* Christuszeugnis.

2. *Jesus ist der Erfüller der Schrift.* Auch einzelne Schriftworte werden erst durch ihn erfüllt. Dies läßt sich paradigmatisch an Joh 12,37-43 zeigen. Der Abschnitt bildet zusammen mit den Versen 44-50 den Abschluß der öffentlichen Wirksamkeit des Offenbarers in Israel. Alttestamentliche Belege werden dabei direkt auf Ereignisse im Leben Jesu angewendet. Dies kann erklärend (12,38) oder begründend (V. 39f) geschehen. Der Unglaube

der Juden ist hiernach eine direkte Erfüllung der prophetischen Verkündigung (Jes 53,1; Jes 6,10). Jesajas Botschaft wird hier als Aussage über die Geschichte Jesu verstanden. V. 41 gibt als johanneischer Kommentar Auskunft darüber, aus welchem sachlichen Grund der Evangelist die alttestamentlichen Schriftstellen so lesen konnte: Jesaja hat den präexistenten Christus geschaut, den λόγος τοῦ θεοῦ (vgl. 17,5.24). Sein Wort bezieht sich streng auf dessen Sendung – die Sendung des Logos. Durch die Einführung der alttestamentlichen Belege in Joh 12,37-43 werden Jesu Stellung und Wirken bzw. die Reaktionen darauf direkt in der Schrift verankert. Auch hier gilt: Die Schrift selbst ist Christuszeugnis, sie hat schon von Jesus gesprochen und seinen Weg vorgezeichnet.

Überblickt man die übrigen johanneischen Schriftzitate, so ist stets von einem christologischen Schriftgebrauch zu sprechen. Dabei kann der Akzent einmal auf der *Person* (1,51; 2,17 [7,38; 7,42]; 12,13; 12,15; 12, 27), sodann auf dem *Lehren* und *Handeln* Jesu (6,31; 6,45; 10,34) und schließlich auf seinem *Geschick* liegen (12,38; 13,18; 15,25; 19,24.28; 19,36; 19,37). Eine gewisse Besonderheit weisen 1,23 und 12,40 auf: In 1,23 erscheint Jes 40,3 im Mund Johannes d.T., um die Vorläufertätigkeit des Täufers für Jesus auszudrücken. Er weist auf Jesus, indem er von sich weg weist. In 12,40f wird auch die ablehnende Reaktion des Volkes auf Jesus als schriftgemäß dargetan. Beide Belege bedeuten jedoch gerade keinen Gegensatz zum christologischen Schriftgebrauch, sondern eine Bestätigung.

Die johanneischen Erfüllungsworte, von denen es von Kap. 12 an sechs an der Zahl gibt (12,38; 13,18; 15,25; 17,12; 19,24.36), sind sämtlich so angelegt, daß Ereignisse im Zusammenhang der Passion Jesu (Einzelheiten seines Leidensweges bzw. die weitgehende Ablehnung Jesu durch das zeitgenössische Judentum) als *Schrifterfüllung* ausgegeben werden.

Die für die expliziten Zitate geltende christologische Zielrichtung ist auch ein Kennzeichen der Aussagen *über* die Schrift (1,17; 1,45; 5, 39.45f; 7,15f; 10,35). Dabei wird einerseits die Schrift als *Vorausdarstellung* oder *Bestätigung* der Person und des Handelns Jesu verstanden (1,45; 5,39.45f; 7,42; 1,17; vgl. auch 3,14). Andererseits liefert sie *Argumentationshilfe* für Jesus (7,22; 8,17; 10,34f), der die Schrift kennt und sich darauf beruft (7,15f).

3. *Jesus erfüllt nicht nur die Schrift, sondern er vollendet sie.* Hierin liegt m.E. die eigentliche Spitze des johanneischen Schriftverständnisses. Dies wird deutlich an Joh 19,28. Anders als bei den Erfüllungsworten wird hier nicht πληρόω, sondern τελειόω gebraucht. Beide Begrifffe sind nicht einfach Synonyma, sondern haben jeweils eine qualifizierte

Bedeutung. Nach Joh handelt Jesus in völliger Analogie zum Vater und führt das von ihm begonnene Werk zu Ende. Τελειόω begegnet in diesem Zusammenhang dreimal (4,34; 5,36; 17,4; vgl. 5,17.19ff; 10,37f; 14,10f). Als der Logos Gottes kann und muß er so handeln. Die Werke wiederum weisen Jesus als Beauftragten Gottes aus (vgl. 5,36; 10,25.32.37f; 14,10f; 15,24).

Nach Joh 19,28 bezieht sich das τελειοῦν Jesu auch auf die Schrift. »*Danach, da Jesus wußte, daß alles vollbracht war, sprach er, um die Schrift zu vollenden*: '*Mich dürstet*'«. Der Ruf Jesu »*mich dürstet*« fehlt bei den Synoptikern. Nach Mk (15,36) erhält Jesus den Weinessig aufgrund seiner körperlichen Schwäche in betontem Zusammenhang mit seiner Verlassenheit am Kreuz. Ansatzweise schon Mt (27,48), aber besonders Lk (23,36) hat die Geste als Verhöhnung aufgefaßt. Bei Joh hingegen ist Jesu Ruf *nicht* Ausdruck seiner Kreatürlichkeit, sondern des *Willens zur Schriftvollendung*[1]. Dies wird durch den Kontext eindrucksvoll vorbereitet und gestützt. In kürzester Folge findet sich dreimal die Begrifflichkeit τελέω bzw. τελειόω: Nach 19,28a weiß Jesus, daß bereits alles *vollbracht* ist (τετέλεσται). Daraufhin sagt er (λέγει), damit die Schrift *vollendet* würde (ἵνα τελειωθῇ ἡ γραφή): »mich dürstet«. Als Jesus den Weinessig genommen hat, spricht er öffentlich aus »es ist *vollbracht*« (τετέλεσται).

Die syntaktische Struktur von V. 28 ist nicht eindeutig klar. Die Mehrzahl der neueren Ausleger bezieht den ἵνα-Satz auf λέγει· δίψω und sieht durch die Voranstellung des Finalsatzes dessen Inhalt unterstrichen[2]: »*Danach, da Jesus wußte, daß alles vollbracht war, sprach er, um die Schrift zu vollenden*: '*mich dürstet*'«. Doch läßt sich v.a. aufgrund der strukturellen Parallelen in Joh 6,15 und 13,1 eine Zusammengehörigkeit des ἵνα- und des ὅτι-Satzes nicht rundweg von der Hand weisen[3]. Dann wäre zu übersetzen: »*Danach, da Jesus wußte, daß alles vollbracht war, um die Schrift zu vollenden/erfüllen, sprach er*: '*mich dürstet*'«.

Dieses Verständnis hat in jüngerer Zeit R. Bergmeier erneut zu begründen versucht, es scheitert jedoch v.a. daran, daß in V. 36f erneut

---

1. M. Hengel, *Die Schriftauslegung des 4. Evangeliums auf dem Hintergrund der urchristlichen Exegese*, in *Jahrbuch Biblische Theologie* 4 (1989) 249-288, p. 279, sieht im »mich dürstet« einen Ausdruck der Kreatürlichkeit und erkennt der Stelle antidoketischen Charakter zu. Dies ist m.E. aufgrund des Kontextes ausgeschlossen. Die Stelle wird auch von Schnelle (s.u. Anm. 8) m.R. nicht als antidoketischer Beleg ausgewertet.

2. BDR, [15]1979, §478; G. Delling, Art. τελειόω, in *TWNT* VIII, 80-85, p. 83 A. 16; R. Schnackenburg, *Das Johannesevangelium*, Bd. 3 (HTKNT, IV.3), 1975, p. 330.

3. So wieder R. Bergmeier, ΤΕΤΕΛΕΣΤΑΙ *Joh 19,30*, in *ZNW* 79 (1988) 282-290, p. 285f.

von einer Schrifterfüllung die Rede ist, mit V. 28 also gar noch nicht alles vollbracht war, um die Schrift zu erfüllen. Aber auch der Kontext und der johanneische Sprachgebrauch erweisen Bergmeiers Darstellung als nicht zwingend.

Zwar besteht kein Zweifel daran, daß Jesu Passion nach Johannes insgesamt im Zusammenhang der Schrifterfüllung zu verstehen ist. Ebenso bildet Joh 19,28 mit 18,4 eine Inklusion, durch welche die Passionserzählung zusammengehalten wird[4]. V. 28 blickt daher auf den gesamten Passionskomplex zurück. Doch läßt sich hieraus – gegen Bergmeier – noch kein schlüssiges Argument für die eine oder andere Möglichkeit der Syntax von V. 28 gewinnen. Auch eine literarkritische Analyse, wie Dauer sie vorgelegt hat[5], bringt keine Interpretationshilfe, sondern verlegt das Problem nur auf eine andere Ebene. Eine Entscheidung muß der nähere Kontext und der johanneische Sprachgebrauch für τελειόω ergeben.

Vom Kontext her bezieht sich μετὰ τοῦτο zurück auf das Wort Jesu an Maria und den Jünger. Im Falle der Zusammengehörigkeit des ἵνα- und des ὅτι-Satzes würde also auch die Szene unter dem Kreuz in den Rang der Schrifterfüllung treten. Dafür gibt es m.E. keine ausreichenden Indizien. Der johanneische Sprachgebrauch weist in die gleiche Richtung: Τελειόω findet sich neben Joh 19,28 außerdem in 4,34; 5,36; 17,4; 17,23. An keiner dieser Stellen hat τελειόω den Sinn »erfüllen«, sondern bedeutet stets »vollenden«, »vollkommen machen«, »zur Vollendung bringen«. Joh 19,28 ist deshalb ebenfalls nicht im Sinn der Erfüllung, sondern der Vollendung zu verstehen[6]. V. 28 will damit nicht nur sagen, daß »das Ganze der Passion, auf das Jesus in 18,4 vorausgeblickt hatte, realisiert [ist]«[7], sondern daß Jesus die Schrift selbst durch sein Geschick zur Vollendung führt. Es erscheint somit wahrscheinlicher, mit der Mehrzahl der Exegeten den ἵνα-Satz nicht vom ὅτι-Satz abhängig zu sehen, sondern als eigenständige Aussage aufzufassen.

Das bedeutet: Selbst in der tiefsten Erniedrigung und unter den größten Qualen bleibt Jesus der Souverän und hat die Vollendung des Willens Gottes, der in der Schrift niedergelegt ist, im Blick. V. 30 konstatiert dann, daß mit dem Trinken des Weinessigs nun alles *vollbracht* ist

---

4. A. DAUER, *Die Passionsgeschichte im Johannesevangelium. Eine traditionsgeschichtliche und theologische Untersuchung zu Joh 18,1-19,30* (SANT, 30) München, Kösel, 1972, p. 202; BERGMEIER, ΤΕΤΕΛΕΣΤΑΙ, p. 286. Eine Inklusion besteht auch zwischen 19,28 und 13,1: εἰδὼς ὁ Ἰησοῦς.

5. DAUER, *Passionsgeschichte*, p. 202f.

6. Vgl. W. THÜSING, *Die Erhöhung und Verherrlichung Jesu im Johannesevangelium* (NTAbh, 21) Münster, Aschendorff, ²1970, pp. 65ff, der jedoch auch πληροῦν im johanneischen Sinn als »vollenden« verstehen will.

7. So BERGMEIER, ΤΕΤΕΛΕΣΤΑΙ, p. 286.

(τετέλεσται). Bei diesem τετέλεσται in V. 30 liegt *ein* Aspekt gewiß darin, daß die Offenbarung Gottes durch Jesus jetzt am Kreuz ihr Ziel erreicht hat[8]. Daneben steht jedoch ein weiterer: *Der Vers resümiert auch die Vollendung der Schrift selbst*[9]. So wie Jesus das Werk des Vaters vollendet, wird durch ihn auch die Schrift selbst zur Vollendung geführt. Es gilt also ein Doppeltes: Jesu in der Schrift vorgezeichnetes und von ihm selbst vorhergewußtes Geschick hat sich vollendet, aber auch ἡ γραφή, die Schrift selbst, ist vollendet.

4. *Mit der Vollendung des Geschickes Jesu rückt die johanneische Darstellung des Christusereignisses selbst in den Rang der* γραφή. Auch über den σημεῖα Jesu steht jetzt: **γέγραπται** (20,31).

Der Begriff σημεῖα in V. 31 bezieht sich zunächst auf die Selbsterweise des Auferstandenen[10]. Jedoch wirft die »österliche Selbsterschließung Jesu« Licht auf das ganze Johannesevangelium[11]. Joh 20,30 u. 31 sind zwar das »Schlußwort zur johanneischen Ostergeschichte«[12], in Korrespondenz zum Prolog (1,1-18) wird damit jedoch das rechte Verständnis des gesamten Evangeliums normiert.

Nun läßt sich das Johannesevangelium von seiner Funktion her im Anschluß an W. Meeks als »Ätiologie der johanneischen Gruppe« verstehen[13]. Die im Johannesevangelium erzählte Geschichte Jesu und die Geschichte der johanneischen Gemeinde fließen ineinander. Der fortschreitenden Entfremdung Jesu von den Juden entspricht die Entfremdung der Glaubenden von der Welt. Das Evangelium stellt somit als Ätiologie die »Basisgeschichte« der johanneischen Gemeinde dar. Das Christusgeschehen ist nach Joh die Grundgeschichte der Angehörigen des neuen Volkes Gottes, die als Jesusgläubige die »Kinder Gottes« sind. Das Evangelium liefert das »symbolische Universum« für die Existenz der johanneischen Gruppe. Das bedeutet: Von der *Funktion* her ist das Evangelium vergleichbar mit der Geschichte der Erwählung und

---

8. Vgl. U. Schnelle, *Antidoketische Christologie im Johannesevangelium* (FRLANT, 144) Göttingen, Vandenhoeck und Ruprecht, 1987, pp. 192.250.

9. Traditionsgeschichtlicher Hintergrund für V. 28 ist vermutlich Ps 69(68),22, da nur hier die beiden Begriffe ὄξος und δίψα nebeneinander begegnen; so mit Schnackenburg, *Johannesevangelium*, p. 330.

10. Vgl. dazu H.-C. Kammler, *Die 'Zeichen' des Auferstandenen*, in O. Hofius/H.-C. Kammler, *Johannesstudien* (WUNT, 88) Tübingen, Mohr, 1996, pp. 191-211.

11. Kammler, *ibid.* p. 210 (im Original kursiv).

12. *Ibid.* p. 211 (im Original kursiv).

13. W.A. Meeks, *Die Funktion des vom Himmel herabgestiegenen Offenbarers für das Selbstverständnis der johanneischen Gemeinde*, in Id. (ed.), *Zur Soziologie des Urchristentums* (Theologische Bücherei, 62) München, Kaiser, 1979, pp. 245-283, p. 279; anders Schnelle, *Christologie*, p. 84 A. 173.

Aussonderung des Gottesvolkes im AT. Mit dem bisher stets für die Schrift geltenden und jetzt auf das eigene Evangelium bezogenen γέγραπται in Joh 20,31 wird dem AT als γραφή das Evangelium *zumindest gleich – wenn nicht doch: übergeordnet*[14].

Zur Stützung dieser These lassen sich neben den σημεῖα des Auferstandenen (Joh 20,31), die als das Geschriebene gelten, worauf sich die Gläubigen berufen können, im vorliegenden Kontext folgende acht Indizien nennen:

a) Joh 1,1 bezieht sich zurück auf Gen 1,1. Der Beginn des Christusgeschehens ist somit als Schöpfungsbeginn qualifiziert. M. Hengel stellt dazu m.E. zu Recht fest, Joh wolle »eine Art neuer »heiliger Schrift« verfassen«[15].

b) Nach Joh 1,17 stehen Mose und Christus – d.h. das »Gesetz« einerseits und die »Gnade und Wahrheit« andererseits als Signaturen der alten und der neuen Ordnung – zueinander im Verhältnis einer Antithese bzw. zumindest im Verhältnis der Überbietung.

c) Für die johanneische Gemeinde gilt nicht mehr der frühere νόμος. Dieser wird meist mit einem Beiwort versehen: »euer« oder »ihr Gesetz« (8,17; 10,34; vgl. [8,5;] 15,25; 18,31f). Für die johanneische Gemeinde gilt das »neue Gebot« (13,34). Es ist durch Jesus selbst verkörpert[16]. Daß das (frühere) Gesetz für die Jünger Jesu keine Bedeutung mehr hat, geht aus den Abschiedsreden unzweideutig hervor: Nachdem Jesus in 13,34 erstmalig das »neue Gebot« erwähnt hat, beziehen sich alle folgenden Anweisungen für das Verhalten der Jünger auf eben diese ἐντολὴ καινή (14,15.21; 15,10.12.17; vgl. 1Joh 2,7f; 3,23; 4,21, weiterhin 2,10; 3,10. 11.14; 4,7 u.ö.). Dabei entspricht das »neue Gebot« inhaltlich dem alten Liebesgebot (Lev 19,18), lediglich die Begründung hat sich geändert: Es ist jetzt Jesu Vorbild und die Liebe zu ihm, die das Gebot der Nächstenliebe einhalten läßt. D.h.: Joh 10,34f, die Aussage über die Geltung der Schrift (daß sie nicht aufgelöst werden könne [λύω]), die sich gerade auf »euer Gesetz« bezieht, findet in Jesu Geschick und im Leben der Jüngergemeinde doch ihr Ziel und Ende.

d) Die Passionsgeschichten der Evangelien insgesamt, besonders aber diejenige des Joh sind als »archetypische Kultbericht[e]« in Antithese

---

14. Vgl. K. WENGST, *Bedrängte Gemeinde und verherrlichter Christus. Ein Versuch über das Johannesevangelium*, München, Kaiser, 1990 (4. Aufl. Nachwort).

15. HENGEL, *Schriftauslegung*, p. 283. Zu fragen ist jedoch, ob er damit die bisherige Schrift nur ergänzen und abschließen (so HENGEL, *ibid.*) oder gar ersetzen will.

16. Vgl. D. SÄNGER, '*Von mir hat er geschrieben*' *(Joh 5,46). Zur Funktion und Bedeutung Mose im Neuen Testament*, in *Kerygma und Dogma* 41 (1995) 112-135, p. 124 A. 52.

zur Pessach-Haggada zu verstehen[17]. Dieser Aspekt wird bei Joh verstärkt durch die sehr enge Verzahnung von eigentlicher Passionsgeschichte und übrigem Evangelium und durch die christologische Pessach-Typologie des Evangeliums (vgl. 1,29.35; 19,31-37).

e) Das Verbum πληροῦν wird in 18,9 und 18,32 auch bezüglich des Wortes Jesu gebraucht. Jesu Wort und alttestamentliches Gotteswort stehen damit auf der gleichen Stufe.

f) Nach Joh 19,28 erfolgt Jesu Ruf »mich dürstet« – wie gezeigt – darum, daß die Schrift vollendet würde (ἵνα τελειωθῇ ἡ γραφή).

g) An verschiedenen Stellen wird den Jüngern das Verständnis für die Schrift erst aufgrund der Geschichte Jesu, insbesondere seiner Auferstehung, ermöglicht: 2,17; 12,15f; 20,9[18].

h) Nach der Auferstehung fallen Wort der Schrift und Wort Jesu zusammen (2,18-22; vgl. 12,16; 20,8f).

Durch diese 8 Indizien ist die These, daß mit der Vollendung des Geschickes Jesu die johanneische Darstellung des Christusereignisses selbst in den Rang der γραφή rückt und die bisherige Schrift überbietet, m.E. hinreichend begründet.

5. Eine hermeneutische Überlegung zum Schluß: Der Umgang mit der Schrift im Johannesevangelium ist einerseits Ausdruck der johanneischen Christologie, wonach in Jesus *der* Offenbarer Gottes schlechthin erschienen ist. Andererseits spiegelt sich darin die sozialgeschichtliche Stellung der johanneischen Gruppe. Die Dimension der Heilsgeschichte ist dabei weitgehend preisgegeben. Dies zeigt sich z.B. in der johanneischen Ekklesiologie: Joh spricht von der Gemeinschaft der »Kinder Gottes«; die heilsgeschichtliche Dimension dieses Begriffes nimmt er aber – anders als etwa Paulus – nicht auf. Die Schrift wird losgelöst von der Geschichte Gottes mit Israel, dem ersten Adressaten, und dem Christusereignis als Voraussetzung zugeordnet. Die Weitergeltung alttestamentliche Grundaussagen, etwa das Festhalten Gottes an seinem Bund mit Israel, wird bei Joh nicht thematisiert. Damit nimmt Joh eine Hauptlinie alttestamentlicher Gottesverkündigung nicht auf, und der Behauptung in Joh 10,35 fehlt hinsichtlich solcher auf Israel bezogenen Schriftstellen die inhaltliche Ausführung.

17. J. BLANK, *Die Johannespassion. Intention und Hintergründe*, in K. KERTELGE (ed.), *Der Prozeß gegen Jesus* (Quaestiones Disputatae, 112), Freiburg u.a., Herder, ²1989, pp. 148-182, p. 150ff esp. A. 9.

18. Vgl. SCHNELLE, *Christologie*, p. 44; U. LUZ, *Gesetz*, in R. SMEND/U. LUZ, *Gesetz. Biblische Konfrontationen*, Stuttgart u.a., Kohlhammer, 1981, p. 120; W. SCHRAGE, *Ethik des Neuen Testaments* (Grundrisse zum Neuen Testament, 4), Göttingen, Vandenhoeck und Ruprecht, 1982, p. 288.

Um der Schrift willen und angesichts der Wirkungsgeschichte neutestamentlichen Umgangs mit ihr, wäre der johanneische Schriftgebrauch
im Gespräch mit Paulus und auch gesamtbiblisch erneut zu diskutieren.

Lange Länge 55   Wolfgang KRAUS
D-91564 Neuendettelsau

DIE WERKE DES ESCHATOLOGISCHEN FREUDENBOTEN
(4Q521 UND DIE JESUSÜBERLIEFERUNG)

I

Das durch É. Puech der Forschung zugänglich gemachte Fragment 4Q521,2[1] läßt sich aufgrund sprachlicher, formaler und inhaltlicher Kriterien als ein frühjüdischer eschatologischer Psalm verstehen[2]. Charakteristisch für diesen Text ist die poetische Neuformulierung biblischer Vorstellungen und Wendungen und ihre konsequente Umgestaltung zu futurischen Endzeitaussagen. Geradezu mosaikartig setzt er sich aus Stichwörtern und Satzteilen zusammen, die an verschiedenen Stellen der Bibel oder der frühjüdischen Literatur begegnen, ohne daß ein einziger Bibeltext wörtlich zitiert, geschweige denn ausdrücklich benannt wird. Bei den Textkomplexen, die mehrfach im Hintergrund stehen, handelt es sich jeweils um Texte mit Heilscharakter aus den Psalmen (31; 105; 107; 146), dem Jesajabuch (29; 35; 40; 42; 49; 61) und dem Deuteronomium (4; 31; 32).

Im Blick auf die anschließend zu besprechenden Texte aus der Jesusüberlieferung verdienen vor allem folgende Aussagen Beachtung:

Z. 8 gibt im Partizipialstil fast wörtlich Ps 146,7c-8b wieder. Lediglich die dreimalige Nennung JHWHs ist ausgelassen. Dies hat seinen Grund in der poetischen Neuformulierung der Aussagen von Z. 5 an, die alle auf das dort am Anfang stehende Subjekt אדני zurückverweisen. Darüber hinaus kann man noch auf andere Bibeltexte hinweisen, vor allem Jes 35,5; 42,7; 29,18; 49,8f.; 61,1 sowie Ps 105,20; 145,14.

Verschiedene Heilsverheißungen des Jesajabuches klingen auch in Z. 5f. an. Das Kommen Gottes verkündet 35,4; 40,9ff. Daß er Israel beim Namen ruft, sagt 43,1. Daß der Geist über den Armen schweben wird, erinnert an

---

1. É. PUECH, *Une apocalypse messianique (4Q521)*, in *RQ* 15 (1992) 475-522; ID., *La croyance des Esséniens en la vie future: immortalité, résurrection, vie éternelle*, Paris, 1994, II, pp. 627-692.

2. Eine ausführliche Untersuchung zu Text, biblischen Wendungen, Gattung und Ort innerhalb der frühjüdischen Literatur dieses Fragments erscheint unter dem Titel *4Q 521,2 II – Ein eschatologischer Psalm* in dem Sammelband *Mogilany 1995*, ed. Z.J. KAPERA (Qumranica Mogilanensia), Kraków, 1996 (cf. in *The Qumran Chronicle* 5 [1995] 93-96). Zusätzlich zu der dort genannten Lit. cf. jetzt noch R. BERGMEIER, *Beobachtungen zu 4 Q 521 f 2, II, 1-13*, in *ZDMG* 145 (1995) 38-48.

Jes 61,1, wenngleich dort der Geist dem gesalbten Freudenboten verliehen ist. Jes 40,31 verheißt: »Die auf JHWH hoffen, schöpfen neue Kraft« (יחליפו כח).

Auch für die Einzelaussagen in Z. 12f. finden sich biblische Anknüpfungspunkte. Das Lebendigmachen der Toten gehört nach Dtn 32,39, 1 Sam 2,6 und Hos 6,1f. zu Gottes heilendem Handeln (cf. auch Jes 26, 19). 1 Sam 2,4-9 nennt daneben eine Reihe weiterer heilsamer Taten Gottes (Kräftigung der Strauchelnden, Sättigung der Hungernden, Reichmachen und Erhebung der Armen, Bewahrung der Frommen). Sachparallelen dazu finden sich wieder in den Psalmen (31,4; 37,19; 107,9; 146,9). Subjekt des heilvollen Handelns ist in 4Q521,2 II 12f. wie in allen biblischen Aussagen über das Lebendigmachen (חיה Pi.) der Toten Gott (אדני Z. 11; cf. auch Frgm. 7, Z. 6). Im Unterschied dazu ist die Verkündigung der Frohbotschaft an die Armen nach Jes 61,1 ebenso wie das Heilen gebrochener Herzen und die Befreiung und Erlösung Gefangener Werk des endzeitlichen gesalbten Boten. Dem entspricht, daß in der Bibel das Verbum בשר nirgends mit Gott als grammatischem Subjekt verwendet wird. Freilich geht es auch in Jes 61,1 um das endzeitliche Handeln JHWHs, das im Ankommen der Botschaft geschieht (cf. Jes 40,9; 41, 27; 52,7; Ps 107,20; 147,18f.; PsSal 11,7f.).

Für die Interpretation von Z. 1f. ist der *parallelismus membrorum* entscheidend. Er legt es nahe, das Wort למשיחו als Plural zu lesen[3]. Beide Zeilen beschreiben ein Gehorsamsverhältnis, zunächst den Gesalbten, dann den Geboten der Heiligen gegenüber. Vom Gehorsam der Schöpfung gegenüber dem Messias ist weder in der Bibel noch in der frühjüdischen Literatur die Rede. Eine Identifikation des Gesalbten von Z. 1 mit dem endzeitlichen davidischen, prophetischen oder priesterlichen Messias ist daher m.E. fragwürdig[4]. Vom biblisch-jüdischen Sprachgebrauch her[5] ist die messianische Interpretation jedenfalls ebensowenig nahegelegt wie vom Kontext unseres Fragments. In Jes 61,1 ist zwar von einem endzeitlichen gesalbten Propheten die Rede. Seine Aktivität richtet sich aber nicht auf die Schöpfung, sondern auf Menschen. Zudem ruht nach 4Q521,2

---

3. BERGMEIER (n. 2) p. 39 möchte wegen des Parallelismus umgekehrt קדושים in Z. 2 singularisch verstehen als Ausdruck für Gott (»der Hochheilige«).

4. Ausführliche Begründung dafür bei NIEBUHR (n. 2). Zur weiterhin lebhaften Diskussion dieser Frage cf. BERGMEIER (n. 2) p. 39.43f. Auch sein Verweis auf Jes 1,2a, Ps 2 und äthHen 90,37 löst nicht die genannte Schwierigkeit, denn eine Herrschaft des Gesalbten über »Himmel und Erde« wird auch an diesen Stellen keineswegs behauptet.

5. Die Mehrzahl der Belege für משיח bezieht sich auf gesalbte Könige, Priester oder Propheten, sei es in der Geschichte oder in der Endzeit. Cf. M. KARRER, *Der Gesalbte. Die Grundlagen des Christustitels* (FRLANT, 151), Göttingen, 1991.

II 6 der Geist Gottes nicht auf einem Gesalbten, sondern schwebt über den Armen, und die Verkündigung der Freudenbotschaft ist hier Werk des Herrn (cf. Z. 12). Der endzeitliche Bote in Mal 3,1, der in 3,23 als der Prophet Elija identifiziert wird, ist wiederum kein Gesalbter.

In 4Q521,2 II 1 scheint mir ein priesterliches Gesalbtenverständnis am wahrscheinlichsten[6]. Demnach stehen die Gesalbten von Z. 1 im synonymen Parallelismus zu den Heiligen von Z. 2. Mit beiden Aussagen wird die gesamte Schöpfung der Autorität der Tora unterstellt, die in der Endzeit wie ursprünglich durch priesterliche Gestalten erteilt werden wird. Ein solches die Schöpfung umfassendes priesterlich-endzeitliches Toraverständnis läßt sich gut in frühjüdische Endzeiterwartungen einordnen[7].

Im Vergleich zu den biblischen »Vorlagen« wird in 4Q521 der endzeitliche Charakter der biblischen Aussagen zwar verstärkt und komprimiert. Als apokalyptisch oder messianisch kann man den Text allerdings nicht bezeichnen[8]. Wir finden weder dualistische Tendenzen noch dämonologische Züge, weder ein Epochenschema noch einen Endzeitkampf, nicht einmal Aussagen über ein künftiges Gericht. Auch qumranspezifische Züge wie die Pescher-Auslegung, die Verwendung spezifischer Selbstbezeichnungen, die Betonung exklusiver Reinheit oder Hinweise auf Gestalten der Gemeindegeschichte fehlen[9].

Innerhalb der nachbiblischen poetischen Literatur steht unser Text den frühjüdischen Psalmdichtungen inhaltlich und formal am nächsten[10]. Mit ihnen verbindet ihn nicht nur die poetische Gestalt, sondern ebenso das Vokabular und die Vorstellungswelt. Wie sie bezieht er die entscheidenden Wendungen und Motive aus der biblischen Überlieferung. Stärker und konsequenter noch als die meisten vergleichbaren frühjüdischen Texte wendet er aber den Blick auf die bevorstehende, durch Gott heraufgeführte und durch sein Wirken bestimmte Heilszeit. Gott selbst wird die überlieferten Verheißungen erfüllen und die angesammelten Hoffnungen der Frommen wahr machen. Dies werden vor allem die Schwachen, Behinderten und Bedrängten erfahren.

6. Cf. NIEBUHR (n. 2).
7. Cf. 4Q541,9 I 3-5 (TLevi ar^d); TestLev 4,2f.; 14,3; 18,2-14; Jub 31,13-17; 32,1-15.
8. Das zeigt besonders der Vergleich mit 11Q13 (Melch), cf. dazu u.
9. So auch BERGMEIER (n. 2) p. 44ff. Die Auslassung des JHWH-Namens dient der Straffung und poetischen Gestaltung der Aussage, hat also nichts mit der Vermeidung des Tetragramms in den qumranspezifischen Handschriften zu tun.
10. Cf. Sir 51,1-12, PsSal sowie die nichtkanonischen Psalmen aus 11Q Ps^a (cf. syrPs 152 und 153), die ebenso wie die »Non-canonical Psalms« (4Q380.381, cf. 4Q448,1 I) offenbar nicht erst in der Qumrangemeinschaft entstanden sind.

II

Nach Mt 11,5; Lk 7,22 beantwortet Jesus die Frage des Täufers nach seiner Person mit dem Verweis auf sein Tun: »Blinde sehen, Lahme gehen, Aussätzige werden rein, Taube hören, Tote stehen auf, Armen wird das Evangelium gepredigt«. Auch dieses Wort Jesu[11] ist ein Mosaik biblischer Wendungen, vor allem aus den Heilsverheißungen des Jesajabuches (Jes 26,19; 29,18f.; 35,5f.; 61,1 LXX). Die in der Gegenwart Jesu wahrnehmbaren Geschehnisse entsprechen dem, was in der Bibel und im Frühjudentum von Gott für die eschatologische Heilszeit zu erwarten ist. Aber nur in 4Q521 stehen wie in der Antwort Jesu Krankenheilungen, Totenauferweckung und Frohbotschaft für die Armen in einer Reihe.

Während in 4Q521,2 II 8.12f. die partizipialen Aussagen von dem Subjekt אדני (Z. 5.11) und den mit ihm verbundenen Verben in der 3.Ps.S.m.Impf. abhängig sind, also Gottes zukünftiges Handeln benennen, bezieht sich das Jesuswort auf ein gegenwärtiges Geschehen. Das Subjekt der Verben bleibt hier ungenannt. Die Aussagen über das Reinwerden Aussätziger, die Erweckung Toter und die Verkündigung an die Armen stehen im *passivum divinum*. Erst durch den Kontext werden sie explizit als Bezeichnungen für das Handeln Jesu erkennbar. Aber weder die Wendung τὰ ἔργα τοῦ Χριστοῦ (Mt 11,2)[12] noch die Prädikation Jesu als ὁ ἐρχόμενος (Lk 7,19f. par Mt 11,3; cf. Mt 3,11)[13] sind in der Bibel oder der frühjüdischen Literatur im Sinne eines messianischen Titels vorgeprägt. Die Vorstellung, daß der Messias als Wundertäter auftreten

---

11. Die Frage nach der Herkunft des Logions kann hier offen bleiben. Zur traditionsgeschichtlichen Analyse cf. W.G. KÜMMEL, *Jesu Antwort an Johannes den Täufer. Ein Beispiel zum Methodenproblem in der Jesusforschung*, in SbWGF 9 (1974) 129-159; = ID., *Heilsgeschehen und Geschichte II. Gesammelte Aufsätze 1965-1977*, ed. E. GRÄSSER und O. MERK (Marburger Theologische Studien, 16), Marburg, 1978, pp. 177-200; M. SATO, *Q und Prophetie. Studien zur Gattungs- und Traditionsgeschichte der Quelle Q* (WUNT, 2, 29), Tübingen, 1988, pp. 140-144; E. SEVENICH-BAX, *Israels Konfrontation mit den letzten Boten der Weisheit. Form, Funktion und Interdependenz der Weisheitselemente in der Logienquelle* (Münsteraner Theologische Abhandlungen, 21), Altenberge, 1993, pp. 320-332.

12. Sie ist aus dem matthäischen Erzählzusammenhang heraus zu verstehen, cf. U. LUZ, *Das Evangelium nach Matthäus. 2. Teilband Mt 8-17* (EKK, I/2), Zürich–Neukirchen-Vluyn, 1990, p. 167.

13. Cf. P. GRELOT, «*Celui qui vient*» (Mt 11, 3 et Lc 7, 19), in *Ce Dieu qui vient*. FS B. Renaud (LD, 159), Paris, 1995, pp. 275-290. Die Möglichkeit, den Ausdruck »der Kommende« auf das Kommen eines endzeitlichen Repräsentanten Gottes, sei es, der Messias oder der Menschensohn, zu beziehen, ist allerdings durch verschiedene frühjüdische Texte und Vorstellungen vorbereitet, cf. die Belege bei P. STUHLMACHER, *Biblische Theologie des Neuen Testaments I: Grundlegung. Von Jesus zu Paulus*, Göttingen, 1992, p. 61f.

werde, ist im Frühjudentum unbekannt[14] und kann auch, wie gezeigt, durch 4Q521,2 II nicht belegt werden. Daß der vom Täufer angekündigte endzeitliche Repräsentant Gottes gerade der Wundertäter Jesus aus Nazaret ist und daß die vom Täufer angekündigte Endzeit gerade so aussieht wie das Geschehen mit Jesus, ist somit eine unerwartete, erklärungsbedürftige Antwort.

Jesus wird also von den Evangelisten nicht mit einer vorgegebenen messianischen Gestalt identifiziert. Vielmehr wird sein geschichtlich wahrnehmbares Auftreten in Galiläa identifiziert mit den endzeitlichen Heilserwartungen vom Handeln Gottes. Dadurch wird ein geradezu unmessianischer Zug Jesu, der durch die Jesusgeschichte vorgegeben war, nämlich sein Wirken als Wundertäter, zum Erweis seiner Funktion als endzeitlicher Repräsentant Gottes. Voraussetzung für dieses neue Messiasbild ist zum einen das Bekenntnis zu der endzeitlichen Qualität des Kommens Jesu, in den Evangelien repräsentiert durch die Verkündigung des Täufers vom Kommenden, Stärkeren, und zum anderen das Wissen um das Wirken Jesu als Wundertäter. Die biblisch verwurzelten und im Frühjudentum lebendigen Erwartungen vom endzeitlichen Handeln Gottes werden von diesen beiden Voraussetzungen aus aufgenommen und auf das Jesusgeschehen bezogen. Wir haben damit eine charakteristische Gestalt des aktualisierenden Umgangs mit der Schrift im Urchristentum vor uns.

III

Das Zitat aus Jes 61,1f., das nach Lk 4,18f. Jesu »Antrittspredigt« in Nazaret zugrunde liegt[15], entspricht im wesentlichen dem Wortlaut der Septuaginta. Ihr folgend ist die schwierige Wendung לאסורים פקח־קח (»für die Gefesselten Öffnung«) ersetzt durch die Aussage τυφλοῖς ἀνάβλεψιν (»für die Blinden das Wieder-Sehen«). Ausgelassen ist die Zeile ἰάσασθαι τοὺς συντετριμμένους τῇ καρδίᾳ (»zu heilen die mit zerschlagenem Herzen«), eingefügt eine Wendung aus Jes 58,6: ἀπόστελλε τεθραυσμένους ἐν ἀφέσει (»Gebrochene frei zu entlassen«). Vor der Ankündigung des Tages der Vergeltung in Jes 61,2 bricht das Zitat ab. Dadurch wird es zu einer uneingeschränkten Heilszusage.

14. Cf. KARRER (n. 5) p. 323; LUZ (n. 12) p. 169.
15. Zur Bedeutung der Perikope für die lukanische Jesusdarstellung mit jeweils umfassenden Literaturhinweisen cf. F. BOVON, *Das Evangelium nach Lukas. 1. Teilband Lk 1,1-9,50* (EKK, III/1), Zürich–Neukirchen-Vluyn, 1989, pp. 204-216; M. KORN, *Die Geschichte Jesu in veränderter Zeit. Studien zur bleibenden Bedeutung Jesu im lukanischen Doppelwerk* (WUNT, 2,51), Tübingen, 1993, pp. 56-85; R. O'TOOLE, *Does Luke also Portray Jesus as the Christ in Luke 4,16-30?*, in Bib 76 (1995) 498-522.

Wie diese Textfassung entstanden ist, kann man schwer erklären[16]. Daß sie kaum frei vom Evangelisten gebildet wurde, zeigt die Auslassung der Zeile über das Heilen der zerschlagenen Herzen, die gut in den lukanischen Zusammenhang gepaßt hätte[17]. Auch die Einfügung der Zeile über die Freilassung der Gebrochenen läßt sich schwerlich auf Lukas zurückführen, denn sie hat keinerlei inhaltlichen Bezug zum lukanischen Erzählzusammenhang.

Nun zeigt allerdings schon der Vergleich zwischen dem hebräischen Text und der Septuaginta, daß in der Überlieferung des Jesajatextes ganze Sätze umformuliert werden konnten (bzw. wegen Unverständlichkeit der Vorlage mußten). Die LXX-Wiedergabe der Wendung לאסורים פקח־קח kann geradezu als Beispiel innerbiblischer Exegese angesehen werden, denn sie deutet offenbar den schwierigen hebräischen Wortlaut von vergleichbaren Aussagen des Jesajabuches her (cf. 35,5; 42,7)[18]. Aber auch die Aussagenreihe in Ps 146,7f. ist als Anregung für die interpretierende Übersetzung von Jes 61,1 in Betracht zu ziehen. Sie bietet nicht nur eine Deutungsmöglichkeit für פקח־קח im Sinne des Öffnens der Augen der Blinden[19], sondern verkündet zugleich die Befreiung der Gefangenen (אסורים). Damit aber rückt erneut die Aussagenreihe 4Q521,2 II 8 in den Blick, die ja offenkundig sowohl Ps 146,7f. als auch (neben anderen Stellen) Jes 61,1 rezipiert. Könnten nicht solche frühjüdischen Aussagenreihen, die durch Kombination verschiedener biblischer Wendungen entstanden sind, auch umgekehrt wieder Eingang in die Überlieferung des Bibeltextes gefunden haben? Es ist jedenfalls auffällig, daß die Wendungen über die Befreiung Gefangener und die Heilung Blinder in 4Q521,2 II 8 einerseits offensichtlich aus Ps 146,7f. übernommen worden sind, andererseits aber auch Übereinstimmungen mit dem LXX-Text von Jes 61,1 aufweisen, im Unterschied zu dessen hebräischer Vorlage.

R. Albertz hat nun unter Rückgriff auf die ursprünglichen Aussagezusammenhänge des Tritojesajabuches versucht, die Zitatgestalt in Lk 4,18f. als bewußte Uminterpretation durch den Evangelisten zu erweisen[20]. Durch Auslassung aller heilsgeschichtlichen Bezüge auf Israel und den Zion wolle

---

16. Cf. T. Holtz, *Untersuchungen über die alttestamentlichen Zitate bei Lukas* (TU, 104), Berlin, 1968, pp. 39ff.; Bovon (n. 15) p. 211f. Zum traditionsgeschichtlichen Hintergrund cf. umfassend J.A. Sanders, *From Isaiah 61 to Luke 4*, in J. Neusner (ed.), *Christianity, Judaism and Other Greco-Roman Cults.* FS M. Smith (SJLA, 12), Leiden, 1975, I pp. 75-106.

17. Cf. 4,23 ἰατρέ, θεράπευσον.

18. Cf. Sanders (n. 16) pp. 82f.

19. Anders dann wieder Ps 145,8 LXX: κύριος σοφοῖ τυφλούς!

20. R. Albertz, *Die »Antrittspredigt« Jesu im Lukasevangelium auf ihrem alttestamentlichen Hintergrund*, in ZNW 74 (1983) 182-206.

Lukas »die alttestamentliche Verheißung aus ihrer partikularen Beschränkung befreien, er will sie öffnen über das alte Gottesvolk hinaus«[21]. In der Einfügung von Jes 58,6 sieht Albertz, der sozialen Ausrichtung des Textzusammenhangs von Jes 58 entsprechend, einen Hinweis des Evangelisten darauf, »daß die Sendung Jesu auch und gerade diesen sozialen Aspekt umgreift«. Damit habe Lukas durch Streichungen und Einfügungen die schwebende, übertragene Sprache von Jes 61,1f. in soziale Richtung konkretisiert[22].

Versucht man, 4Q521,2 II in die Traditionsgeschichte zwischen Jes 61,1f. und Lk 4,18f. einzuordnen, dann lassen sich einige Aspekte der These von Albertz untermauern, andere modifizieren. In 4Q521,2 II fehlen wie im Jesajazitat in Lk 4,18f. alle auf die Heilsgeschichte Israels und sein endzeitliches Geschick bezogenen Aussagen[23]. Dies zeigt ein Vergleich mit der Rezeption von Jes 61,1 im Zusammenhang mit weiteren Bibelstellen in 11Q13 (Melch)[24].

Dort wird zunächst mit Hilfe von Jes 61,1f. die Anordnung der Tora über das Jobeljahr (Lev 25,13; Dtn 15,2) auf die Freilassung der Gefangenen am »Ende der Tage« gedeutet (II 1-4). Melchisedek wird sodann mit dem Boten identifiziert, der nach Jes 61,1f. den Gefangenen die Freilassung auszurufen hat, und erscheint als eschatologischer Rächer und Retter im Völkergericht, der den Entscheidungskampf der »Heiligen Gottes« gegen Belial und die »Geister seines Loses« anführt und mit Unterstützung der »Göttlichen« bzw. »Söhne Gottes« den Tag des Friedens für Zion heraufführt (II 5-17). Unter Rückgriff auf Jes 52,7; Dan 9,25f. und erneut Jes 61,2f. wird schließlich ein »Bote« und »Gesalbter des Geistes« verheißen, der die Trauernden trösten soll (II 18ff)[25].

Eine Verbindung von 4Q521 zu diesem Text könnte man allenfalls im Bezug auf Jes 61,1 in Kombination mit weiteren Stellen aus Jesaja und den Psalmen finden[26]. Weitere sprachliche oder inhaltliche Berührungen zwischen beiden Texten gibt es aber nicht, und die Methode der Pescher-

---

21. *Ibid.*, p. 190.

22. *Ibid.*, p. 198.

23. Die christologisch-messianische Interpretation ergibt sich erst aus dem lukanischen Kontext, cf. vv. 21.31.41.43 (s. dazu u.)!

24. Maßgeblich ist jetzt die Edition und Rekonstruktion von É. PUECH, *Notes sur le manuscrit de XIQMelkîsédeq*, in *RQ* 12 (1987) 483-513.

25. Die Identifikation Melchisedeks mit diesem Gesalbten ist aber fraglich. Eher könnte man an den endzeitlichen Propheten aus 1QS IX 11 denken, cf. F. GARCÍA MARTÍNEZ, *Messianische Erwartungen in den Qumranschriften*, in *Jahrbuch für Biblische Theologie* 8 (1993) 171-208, pp. 202f.; T.H. LIM, *11QMelch, Luke 4 and the Dying Messiah*, in *JJS* 43 (1992) 90-92.

26. Keine der übrigen in 11QMelch zitierten Stellen (Lev 25,9.13; Dtn 15,2; Ps 7,8f.; 82,1f.; Jes 52,7; Dan 9,25) hat sich aber in 4Q521 erkennbar niedergeschlagen!

Auslegung, die in 11QMelch klar erkennbar ist, wird in 4Q521 nirgends angewendet. In 4Q521 fehlen zudem alle Aussagen, die den eschatologisch-apokalyptischen Charakter von 11QMelch bestimmen. Auch die Erwartung eines individuellen endzeitlichen Gesalbten finden wir, wie gesehen, in 4Q521 nicht.

Gegenüber dem hebräischen Text von Jes 61,1f., der durchgängig das Reden des Freudenboten entfaltet, legt die Fassung des Zitates bei Lukas mit LXX und Jes 58,6 einen stärkeren Akzent auf sein Tun, nach Albertz vor allem auf dessen soziale Konkretion. Schon in 4Q521,2 II tritt aber diese konkrete Ausrichtung des Tuns auf die Kranken, Hilfsbedürftigen und sozial Schwachen noch sehr viel deutlicher hervor. Daß dabei Interpretationslinien wirksam werden, die Jes 61,1f. von Texten wie Jes 58,1-12 her verstehen, läßt sich besonders in den Zeilen 8[27] und 13[28] beobachten.

Daß im Dienste einer klar profilierten Aussage Wendungen aus verschiedenen Bibelstellen zusammengezogen werden können, zeigt gerade 4Q521,2 II. Die ganz unterschiedlichen Satzstrukturen der ursprünglichen Textzusammenhänge bilden dabei kein Hindernis. So werden die beschriebenen Taten kaum dadurch verändert, daß das Subjekt des Handelns nach dem jeweiligen Kontext in Jes 61,1f. der Freudenbote, in Jes 58,6 der gerecht handelnde Mensch, in 4Q521,2 II 8.12f. Gott und in Lk 4,18f. Jesus ist.

4Q521,2 II belegt somit, daß die Befunde, die sich bei der Untersuchung der Textgestalt des Jesajazitates in Lk 4,18f. ergeben, ganz ähnlich schon für den Umgang mit der Schrift im Frühjudentum geltend gemacht werden können. Zwischen die ursprünglichen biblischen Aussagezusammenhänge und die Aufnahme von Schriftzitaten im Neuen Testament tritt damit als dritte zu berücksichtigende Größe die freie, mosaikartige Rezeption biblischer Wendungen in frühjüdischen Texten. Sie kann zwar nicht unmittelbar den Wortlaut des Jesajazitates in Lk 4,18f. erklären, aber doch vielleicht das Milieu erhellen, in dem er zustande gekommen sein mag. Daß Lukas selbst ihn erst gebildet haben sollte, scheint mir demgegenüber weniger wahrscheinlich[29].

Das Prophetenwort von dem endzeitlichen Freudenboten entsprach gerade in der durch 4Q521,2 II repräsentierten Gestalt seiner frühjüdischen Rezeption der Darstellungsabsicht des Lukas. Indem der Evangelist den Auftritt Jesu im Synagogengottesdienst und seine Auslegung des

---

27. Cf. Jes 58,6.
28. Cf. Jes 58,7.10.11; cf. auch zu Z. 10 Jes 58,8 und zu Z. 4 Jes 58,9.
29. Verschiedene, wenig überzeugende Erklärungsversuche für die Gestaltung des Zitats durch Lukas diskutiert KORN (n. 15) pp. 68-78.

Jesajawortes an den Beginn seiner Erzählung stellt, rückt er das gesamte
Wirken Jesu in Wort und Tat unter dieses Leitwort der Schrift. Erst aus
diesem erzählerischen Zusammenhang wird die Bedeutung der Kurzpredigt
Jesu zu Jesaja 61,1f. deutlich: »Heute ist diese Schrift erfüllt worden vor
euren Ohren«. Eine christologische Deutung dieses Geschehens und damit
eine messianische Prädikation Jesu ist aber zunächst weder durch das Zitat
und die mit ihm verbundenen Vorstellungen traditionell vorgegeben noch
durch Jesu Deutung auf die Gegenwart schon explizit ausgesprochen. Sie
erfolgt erst im Rückblick auf den Anfang des Wirkens Jesu in Galiläa
am Ende des gesamten Erzählzusammenhangs Lk 4,14-44 (cf. vv. 41.43).

IV

Die Petrusrede im Haus des Kornelius (Apg 10,34-43), die die entscheidenden Inhalte der urchristlichen Jesusverkündigung zusammen-
faßt, mündet in der Berufung auf »alle Propheten«, die »bezeugen,...
daß durch seinen Namen alle, die an ihn glauben, Vergebung der Sünden
empfangen sollen« (V. 43)[30]. Dieser generelle Anspruch auf die Propheten als Zeugen für das Christusgeschehen wird implizit auch dadurch
erhoben, daß die Aussagen über den Weg Jesu durchsetzt sind mit biblischen Wendungen. Ohne daß dies durch Zitate nachgewiesen werden
müßte, erscheint so Jesus als der von den Propheten verheißene Heils-
bote der Endzeit.

Ein solcher Umgang mit der Schrift, bei dem verschiedene Wendungen und Vorstellungen aus verschiedenen Teilen und Texten der Bibel
zu einem neuen, bewußt gestalteten Text verbunden werden, steht in
Analogie zum Schriftgebrauch in 4Q521,2 II und anderen frühjüdischen
Texten. Im einzelnen ergibt die Untersuchung der biblischen Wendungen in Apg 10,34-43 zahlreiche Querverbindungen sowohl zu 4Q521,2
II als auch zu 11QMelch. Alle Bibelstellen, die in Apg 10,34-43 durch-
scheinen, stehen auch in 4Q521,2 II und 11QMelch im Hintergrund.
Von fast allen biblischen Wendungen der Petruspredigt her lassen sich
Beziehungen zu beiden Texten herstellen. Die zwei Ausnahmen betref-
fen jeweils charakteristische Ausprägungen der betreffenden frühjüdischen
Texte: In 11QMelch gibt es keine Aussagen zu endzeitlichen Heilungs-
wundern und in 4Q521,2 II fehlt die Ankündigung eines endzeitlichen
(messianischen) Richters.

30. Auf Querverbindungen zwischen Apg 10,36-38, Lk 4,18f. und 7,22 auf der Ebene
lukanischer Theologie verweist KORN (n. 15) pp. 236ff.

In Apg 10,34-43 finden wir beides. Das muß nicht bedeuten, daß die beiden hier herangezogenen frühjüdischen Texte traditionsgeschichtliche Vorstufen für den neutestamentlichen darstellen. Man könnte aber vielleicht sagen: In der Deutung des Christusgeschehens in Apg 10,34-43 werden zwei verschiedene frühjüdische Interpretationslinien biblischer Endzeiterwartungen zusammengeführt, die Hoffnung auf Gottes eschatologische Heilstaten, die u.a. durch 4Q521,2 II repräsentiert wird, und die Erwartung eines endzeitlich-messianischen Richters, wie wir sie z.B. in 11QMelch II finden. Mit einem solchen Urteil würde erneut zum Ausdruck gebracht, daß die Aussagen der Schrift über ihre Rezeption im Frühjudentum Eingang in das neutestamentliche Christuszeugnis gefunden haben[31].

Abtnaundorfer Straße 60   Karl-Wilhelm NIEBUHR
D-04347 Leipzig

---

31. Von hier aus wäre m. E. ein Urteil wie das von R. PESCH, *Die Apostelgeschichte. 1. Teilband Apg 1-12* (EKK, V/1), Zürich–Neukirchen-Vluyn, 1986, pp. 342f. (»Der Vers basiert auf einer Auslegung von Ps 107,20…, die in 37-38 fortgeführt wird, und Jes 52,7…«), zu modifizieren und präzisieren.

THE CORE OF JESUS' EVANGEL
ΕΥΑΓΓΕΛΙΣΑΣΘΑΙ ΠΤΩΧΟΙΣ (ISA 61)

The interest of this paper is to trace the historical origins of Jesus' evangel, using this archaism to distinguish his own message from the Christian "gospel" *about* him. This relates to the distinction, well-entrenched in Protestant theology, between the *historical Jesus* and the *kerygmatic Christ*[1]. Rudolf BULTMANN even pronounced that Jesus' prophetic Jewish message, unlike the *kerygma* about him, does not belong within New Testament theology[2]. One of our sub-plots will be to query this dichotomy. After a lexical survey, we shall investigate scriptural passages used in the reports of Jesus' initial appearance, notably Isa 61. This leads to studying some Qumran texts and, thence, to an investigation of John the Baptist and his possible relation to the beginnings of Jesus' career and message.

Introductory: εὐαγγέλιον, εὐαγγελίζεσθαι

The compound εὐαγγέλιον already appears in Homer and there means "rewards for good news"[3]. This usage recurs in classical and Hellenistic Greek, with the gods being included as beneficiaries in the frequent plural expression, εὐαγγέλια θυεῖν, "to offer sacrifices for good tidings"[4]. We also find the more general meaning, "good tidings"[5]. The

---

1. G.E. Lessing in his *Religion Christi* (1780) already distinguished between the "Christian religion" and the "religion of Christ"; see D. FLUSSER, *Jezus als vraag voor Joden en Christenen*, in *Concilium* 8 (1971) 110-116.

2. See the opening sentence of his *Theologie des Neuen Testaments*, Tübingen, Mohr, 1958[5], p. 1: "Die Verkündigung Jesu gehört zu den Voraussetzungen der Theologie des Neuen Testaments und ist nicht ein Teil dieser selbst."

3. Od. 14,152.166. See entry in LIDDELL and SCOTT and cf. H. KOESTER, *Ancient Christian Gospels. Their History and Development*, London, SCM – Philadelphia, Trinity, 1990, pp. 1-48. G. FRIEDRICH (J. SCHNIEWIND), εὐαγγελίζομαι κτλ., in *TWNT* 2, 705-735, exaggerates the *religious* meaning as connected with the Deutero-Isaianic messenger, the θεῖος ἄνθρωπος, and the emperor cult (see below n. 6). Acknowledging the University of California's Regents' permission, I found that the TLG CD-ROM yields 77 mentions of εὐα[/η]γγελι- up to and including the 1st cent. CE. Largest concentrations are 29 in the LXX, 23 in Plutarch, 16 in Josephus, 15 in Philo. The 134 instances in the NT eloquently express the Christian appropriation of the word.

4. E.g. Aristophanes, *Equites* 643.647.656; Xenophon, *Hist.* 1.6.37; 4.3.14; Plutarch, *Sertorius* 11.8; 26.6. According to LIDDELL and SCOTT, in Attic the plural is always used.

5. This is also the meaning of the much less frequent feminine, εὐαγγελία, 2 Sam 18,22.27; 2 Kgs 7,9; Jos. *Ant.* 18,229; and in Christian usage OrSib 1,382. Cf. the synonym, ἀγγελία.

cognate verb is primarily the middle εὐαγγελίζεσθαι, "to make one-self rewardable by bringing good news", later also the active εὐαγγελίζειν. There is nothing intrinsically religious about these words, except that both good and bad news remind of human frailty and dependence on higher powers[6]. In Philo and Josephus, the root plainly means "to inform, to bring (good) news", in the philosophical, the religious, the military, and otherwise[7]. The same situation prevails largely in the Septuagint[8]. The potential interference with the Hebrew text yields no additional connotations. The translators were particular about using the word group εὐαγγελ- for the Hebrew root בשר[9], as is seen especially when related compounds are used close by[10]. Since the equivalent noun בשורה can also mean "messenger's reward"[11], there is a close overlap.

A marked difference, however, is felt in the "soteriological" edge which these words acquire in prophetic and oracular discourse, as also in Roman imperial propaganda[12]. Classically, we read: "Behold, on the mountains the feet of him who brings good tidings (εὐαγγελιζομένου) and who announces peace" (Nahum 2,1; cf. Isa 52,7)[13]. This usage is characteristically found in Second and Third Isaiah, as in the passage which will occupy us most: "The Spirit of the Lord is upon me, there-fore that He has anointed me; *to bring good tidings to the poor* (εὐαγγελίσασθαι πτωχοῖς) did he send me, to heal those worn at

6. See below n. 12.
7. See n. 3 for statistics. FRIEDRICH (n. 3) stresses pagan influence in Philo, *Leg.* 99, and chides him and Josephus for their "non-Isaianic", matter-of-fact use of the terms.
8. 9 out of the 29 mentions being found in the story of Absalom's death, 2 Sam 18,19-31, including the active verb (v. 19f.) and the feminine εὐαγγελία (v. 20, 27).
9. FRIEDRICH *ibid.* (n. 3), 710 mentions 3 exceptions: 1 Sam 4,17; Isa 41,27; 1 Chron 16,23.
10. Next to ἀναγγέλλω or ἀπαγγέλλω, for להגיד in 2 Sam 1,20; 4,10; 18,22f; 2 Kgs 7,9; for לספר and להשמיע in Ps 95,5; Nah 2,1 [1,15].
11. 2 Sam 4,10; 18,22, בשורה = LXX εὐαγγελία, messenger's fee.
12. The Priene inscription (A. DEISSMANN, *Licht vom Osten*, Tübingen, Mohr, 1923[4], p. 293 and pl. 69) calls Augustus' "birth as a god" the first of the "*good tidings*" he brought to the world (ἦρξεν...τῶν εὐανγελίων, sic). This novel soteriological meaning (KOESTER [n. 3], p. 3f.) *parallels* Greek-Jewish and Christian usage but does not warrant a one-way causal explanation as given by KOESTER and by FRIEDRICH (n. 3), p. 723. FRIEDRICH, 706 does stress Deutero-Isaianic usage, but with theological over-valuation; he also refers to oracular usage and to εὐάγγελος as "proclaimer of oracles" (709). KOESTER under-rates the relative independence of the semantic shift in stressing the influ-ence of imperial soteriology. Rather, the soteriological edge developed in prophetic and oracular usage seems to have been appropriated by imperial propaganda.
13. Cf. the variant (or mixed quotation) of both related passages, closer to the Hebrew, in Rom 10,15; and the quote in 11QMelch 2,16; 18f. (see below). Also PsSol 11,1; Joel 3,5 καὶ εὐαγγελιζόμενοι, reading ומבשרים for ובשרידים. FRIEDRICH points to the significance of the nominalized participle.

heart, to herald release to the captives and vision to the blind" (Isa 61,1)[14].

The frequency in the New Testament[15] expresses an unprecedented interest which begs explanation. The verb is mostly used in Luke and Acts, Paul being a second best. The broader meaning is retained, such as when "good tidings are brought" to Mary, to the shepherds, or to the people[16]. The soteriological drive of prophetic usage is felt in the expression, "to bring the good tidings of the Kingdom of God"[17]. The noun, not used in Luke, appears in Mark, specifically as "the good tidings of God" or "of Jesus Christ"[18]. In Matthew, the typical expression is "the good news of the Kingdom"[19]. The noun is mostly used by Paul to denote the "good tidings about Jesus" or in other words, "the gospel". Typically, he speaks of "my gospel"[20], and of his "gospel of the foreskin" as distinct from that "of the circumcision"[21]. Yet he also preserves the broader sense when speaking of "the Gospel of God"[22]. The appropriation by Pauline tradition is expressed in the neologism εὐαγγελιστής[23].

These observations only bring out the Christian predilection for the word group. Our interest in the following will be to try and explain it.

The Core of Jesus' Evangel

In all canonical gospels, Jesus makes his first public appearance after his baptism by John, which in the synoptics is followed by the temptation in the desert. The evangelists are not quite at one about the moment of the calling of the first disciples, but they agree that this also occurred in the initial phase. They definitely part ways, however, when giving the first elaborate story of Jesus' work, which we may see as exemplary of their various portrayals of Jesus. In Mark this is the sensational *healing* in the synagogue of Capernaum and elsewhere, while John opens by demonstrating Jesus' mysterious *authority* in the changing of water into wine and the cleansing of the temple (Mk 1,21-45; Jn 2,1-25). In Matthew and Luke, the first full episode is the *teaching* to the people,

---

14. τυφλοῖς ἀνάβλεψιν for לאסורים פקח קוח. Also Isa 40,9 (2 x); 52,7 (2 x); 60,6.
15. See n. 3.
16. Lk 1,19; 2,10; 3,18.
17. Lk 4,43; 8,1; 16,16.
18. Mk 1,14; 1,1.
19. In the formulary descriptions, Mt 4,23; 9,35; and 24,14.
20. Rom 2,16; 16,25.
21. Gal 2,7.
22. Rom 1,1; 15,16; 2 Cor 11,7.
23. Acts 21,8; Eph 4,11; 2 Tim 4,5. But cf Bauer, *Wörterbuch* s.v.

but again in a different elaboration. Matthew programmatically opens with the beatitudes and the sermon on the mount (Mt 5–7), while Luke uses a singular tradition of the preaching in the synagogue at Nazareth (Lk 4,16-30). The difference is enhanced by the fact that both Mark and Matthew carry another story of Jesus in the synagogue at Nazareth (Mk 6,1-6; Mt 13,53-58), while Luke uses the beatitudes and subsequent teaching material elsewhere (Lk 6,20-49).

Precisely so, it strikes that Jesus' teaching in the first episode both in Matthew and in Luke opens in the key set by the programmatic verse of *Isa 61,1* which was just quoted. In *Luke*, this is explicitly indicated. Jesus stands up, reads the passage from the Isaiah scroll, and sits down to start his remarkable sermon to the effect that "Today this scripture has been fulfilled in your hearing" (Lk 4,21). Nor is this the only time the Isaiah verse is heard in Luke. Another very important passage for us is the question John the Baptist sends from prison: "Are you the one who is coming, or do we wait for someone else?" Jesus' answer is: "Go and tell John what you see and hear: *the blind regain vision*, the cripple walk, lepers are cleansed and the deaf hear, *the dead are raised up, the poor receive good tidings*" (Lk 7,18-23). As we shall see in a moment, the first beatitude, which in Luke is in the preceding chapter, also contains an allusion to the Isaiah passage. Judging from Luke and his traditions, the beginning of Isa 61 is basic to Jesus' preaching.

As David Flusser showed, the first three beatitudes in *Matthew* elaborate on the same passage in Isaiah[24]. This is almost explicit in the second beatitude[25], "Blessed are those who mourn, for they shall be comforted" – compare the prophet's task in Isa 61,2, "to *comfort* all *those who mourn*". But also the promise of the "Kingdom of Heaven" to "the poor in spirit" reminds of Isaiah's words. Indeed, it is possible to hear this first beatitude as an exposition of the prophet's task לבשר ענוים, "to bring good news to the meek". The Septuagint translates πτωχοῖς, "to the poor", taking in the close similarity between the Hebrew ענו "meek" and עני "poor". The third beatitude may be seen as a sort of paraphrase of the same: "Blessed are the *meek*, for they will inherit the land." There is an echo here of the ending of the previous Isaiah chapter: "Your people are wholly righteous, in eternity will they *inherit the*

24. D. FLUSSER, *Blessed are the Poor in Spirit*, in *IEJ* 10 (1960) 1-13; repr. in ID., *Judaism and the Origins of Christianity* [collected articles], Jerusalem, Magnes, 1988, 102-114.

25. FLUSSER (*ibid.*) points out that the order of the 2nd and 3rd beatitudes is inversed in some mss and in the Catholic tradition inaugurated by Jerome, and that this inverse order is both more logical and closer to the parallel in 1QH (see below). It also follows the order in Isa 61 better.

land" (Isa 60,21)[26]. More overtly, the allusion is to Ps 37,11, "The *meek* (עניים, οἱ πραεῖς) *will inherit the land*".

We see that while Isa 61 plays a central role in Jesus' initial appearance in Matthew, other passages also come in. The same happens in Luke. The passage Jesus reads from Isaiah contains an insertion from elsewhere: "To let go the afflicted in liberty" (Lk 4,18; Isa 58,6). The phenomenon is particularly striking in Jesus' answer to the Baptist's question. Nestle-Aland note allusions to Isa 29, 35, 42, 26 and, emphatically at the end, 61. If the beginning of Isa 61 is central, it is embroidered with passages from Isaiah and elsewhere. Many exegetes ascribe the phenomenon to the evangelist[27], but in view of his conservative composition procedures the influence of traditions is much more likely. We could envisage a tradition of associative reading and expounding in view of the messianic future. Since in the reports in Luke and Matthew the phenomenon is connected in different ways with the message of Jesus at his first public appearance, the question arises whether this message did by any chance arise from such a tradition.

Isaiah Readings in Qumran

A positive answer becomes likely in view of the conglomerative use made of Isaiah verses in the Qumran scrolls. Foremost is the reference to Isa 40,3 in a passage about the foundation of the community in the desert under the direction of the Interpreter, "…In order to prepare the way, as it is written: 'In the desert prepare the way of ****[28], straighten in the steppe a roadway for our God' – this is studying the Tora" (מדרש התורה)[29]. We have here a formal[30] reference to a single Isaiah verse. In other cases, we find a conglomeration of passages reminiscent of Luke and Matthew.

This concerns the verse we have been focussing on, Isa 61,1. In typical first person speech, the author of a Hymn expresses his awareness of

---

26. Our chapter division only dates from the middle ages. Moreover, 60,21 and 61,3 are linked by the expression at the end of both sentences, להתפאר...[ו]מטע.

27. E. HAENCHEN, *Historie und Verkündigung bei Markus und Lukas*, in G. BRAUMANN (ed.), *Das Lukas-Evangelium; Die redaktions- und kompositionsgeschichtliche Forschung* (Wege der Forschung 280), Darmstadt, Wiss. Buchges., 1974, pp. 287-316, esp. 296, 301.

28. The Tetragram being indicated by four dots. I follow the edition and, with some alterations, the translation of F. GARCÍA MARTÍNEZ, *The Dead Sea Scrolls Translated; the Qumran Texts in English*, Leiden, Brill, 1994.

29. 1QS 8,14, and in a more implicit version 9,19f. מדרש התורה seems to be connected with moral investigation by the community, see 8,17ff. (below) and cf. the same expression in the context of CD 20,6.

30. The quotation formula כאשר כתוב reminds of rabbinic formulae.

having been called: "You have opened a spring in the mouth of your servant", the mission being, among other things, "to *bring good tidings to the meek*, in your abundant mercy[31], [to......] from the spring [....] to *the beaten in spirit*, and the downtrodden to everlasting joy"[32]. As FLUSSER pointed out, the ענוים, the "meek" from Isa 61 are here explained from Isa 66,2, "I shall look at the poor, at the beaten in spirit", using the ambivalence of עני / ענו[33]. This illuminates the expression from the War Scroll, ענוי רוח, "the meek of the Spirit"[34]: it is a conflation of both Isaiah passages, which undoubtedly was inspired also by the "ointment of the Spirit" from Isa 61,1[35]. The reading together of Isaiah passages with a messianic interest is fully explicit in the Melchizedek fragment, where verses from Isaiah and the Psalms function in a concatenated *pesher* on Tora passages about the jubilee year: "...How beautiful on the mountains are the feet of him who brings good tidings (מבשר) and announces peace... (Isa 52,7)....The messenger is [the ano]inted of the spirit (מ[שיח הרו]ח)..."[36] It is hard not to think here of Jesus' Nazareth proclamation.

Another striking instance is what has been termed a "Messianic Apocalypse" (4Q521):

> [For the heav]ens and the earth will listen to his Messiah... For the Lord (אדני) will observe the devout (חסידים) and He will call the righteous (צדיקים) by name, and his Spirit will hover (תרחף) upon the meek (ענוים)... He who sets free those that are bound, who gives vision to the blind, who straightens out the twisted....For He will heal the badly wounded and He will make the dead revive, to the meek He will bring good tidings..[37].

The allusions are to Dt 32,1 (heaven and earth will listen), Gen 1,2 (the Spirit *hovering* over the waters), Ps 146,7f (Who gives vision to the blind, etc.), Isa 26,19 (He will make the dead revive), and of course Isa 61,1, the good tidings to the meek. The "Spirit hovering over the meek", an expression reminiscent of baptism or immersion, is probably connected again with the ointment of the Spirit in Isa 61, and if so, represents a more elaborate version of the "poor of the Spirit". As pointed

31. Taking לרוב רחמיכה as an adjunct.
32. 1QH 23[18],14f.
33. See above. LXX have here ταπεινόν!
34. 1QM 14,7.
35. FLUSSER (n. 24).
36. 11QMelch (11Q13) 2,15f.18.
37. 4Q521 frg 2, 2,1-12, according to the text published by M.O. WISE and J.D. TABOR *4Q521 "On Resurrection" and the Synoptic Gospel Tradition: A Preliminary Study*, in *JSP* 10 (1992) 150. For elaborate comments see É. PUECH, *Une apocalypse messianique (4Q521)*, in *RQ* 15 (1992) 475-522; cf. ID., *La croyance des Esséniens en la vie future*, Paris, Gabalda, 1992.

out by the first editors, the passage is a very close parallel to Jesus' answer to the Baptist[38]. In addition to the three identical expressions of the blind receiving vision, the dead being resurrected, and the meek receiving good tidings, we have in both cases the sequence of the revival of the dead and the good tidings to the meek at the end.

It is clear that at Qumran, an associative, messianist reading tradition of prophetic passages was practised, which strongly resembles the reported initial preaching of Jesus. Since this tradition presents itself as studying the Tora "to prepare the way" in the desert, in association with immersions and repentance, it is obvious to proceed to the next question. What are the possible connections with John the Baptist?

John the Baptist and Jesus

As from Exodus, the desert is the acknowledged location of purification and revelation. Thus we find desert and Exodus motifs in Isaiah, most notably in that phrase applied both to the Qumran community and John the Baptist, "prepare the way in the desert". While it is exaggerated to suppose John had been a member of the Qumran sect[39], it is clear that he must be situated not far from the physical and spiritual milieu of the desert community. The teacher of Josephus' youth, Bannus[40], reminds us that there were other "baptist" desert preachers.

In these circles, repentant immersion and messianic exposition of Tora and prophets went hand in hand. The elaborate description used for John's baptism in Mark and Luke is eloquent: "a baptism of *repentance* and *forgiveness* of sins"[41]. It has been pointed out that not only is this description confirmed by Josephus' report on John[42], but that repentance was an essential condition for immersion and re-acceptance of sinners in

---

38. See previous note.
39. Advocated in 1957 by W.H. BROWNLEE (in K. STENDAHL, *The Scrolls and the New Testament*, New York, Harper, 1957, p. 35) and reiterated by R. EISENMAN, *Maccabees, Zadokites, Christians and Qumran* (Studia Post-Biblica 34), Leiden, Brill, 1983.
40. Josephus, *Life* 11. If they had links with the desert, the "morning baptizers" mentioned by rabbinic literature and the Church Fathers would have to be added: טובלי שחרית (tYad 2,20 according to R. Shimshon me-Shantz on mYad 4,8; yBer 3,6c) or, "aramaizing", טובלי שחרין (bBer 22a; tYad 2,20 text. rec.); βαπτισταί (Justin, *Dial.* 80,4) or ἡμεροβαπτισταί (Hegesippus *apud* Eusebius, *Hist. eccl.* 4,22,7). Cf. S. LIEBERMAN, *Light on the Cave Scrolls from Rabbinic Sources*, in *PAAJR* 20 (1951) 395-404, esp. pp. 401f., repr. in ID., *Texts and Studies*, New York, Ktav, 1974, pp. 190-199, esp. 196f. On Jesus and baptist movements see C. PERROT, *Jésus et l'histoire* (coll. "Jésus et Jésus-Christ", 11), Tournai, Desclée – Paris, Groupe Mame, 1995[2].
41. Mk 1,4; Lk 3,3; cf. Acts 13,24; 19,4.
42. Josephus, *Ant.* 18,117; cf. 1QS 2,25-3,11; 4,20-22; 5,23f; 8,17f. (see below).

Qumran[43]. Another important element is the *purification by the Holy Spirit* in Qumran[44]. In the passages pertaining to repentant immersion, we even find a reference to the work of "the Spirit of truth and meekness" in "those meek of soul"[45], which reminds us of the cluster of Isaianic phrases including the "ointment by the Spirit" and the "good news for the meek". The element of the Spirit was emphasized rather by Jesus, but probably had been part of John's message[46].

We must also take into account the Lukan report of the Baptist's teaching to the masses who asked the standard question when it comes to eternal salvation: "what shall we do?" (Lk 3,10-14)[47]. John's answers are clearly meant as a betterment of life tied up with repentance and baptism[48], and hence are understood as *part of his "preparing the way in the desert"*. Indeed, in a redactional summary of John's appearance, Luke says that the Baptist "by exhorting brought good tidings (παρακαλῶν εὐηγγελίζετο) to the people" (Lk 3,18). Now it is significant that the Qumran passage about "preparing the way" as "studying the Tora" goes on to state that anyone who high-handedly transgresses a "commandment", "cannot touch the food of the holy men...until his deeds have been cleared", the implication again being that ritual purification is inoperative without repentance[49]. It seems that John's baptismal instruction is another form of this practical "studying the Tora"[50]. Also, it bears similarity with Jesus' teaching[51].

---

43. D. FLUSSER, *The Dead Sea Sect and Pre-Pauline Christianity*, in *Scripta Hierosolymitana* 4 (1958) 215-66, pp. 242-246, repr. in *Judaism and the Origins of Christianity* (n. 24), pp. 23-74. On Josephus see J.P. MEIER, *John the Baptist in Josephus: Philology and Exegesis*, in *JBL* 111 (1992) 225-37.

44. D. FLUSSER, *Tevilat Yohanan we-kat midbar Yehuda* (in *Sefer zikkaron le-Sukenik*, Jerusalem 1968) repr. with addendum on this very point in ID., *Jewish Sources in Early Christianity. Studies and Essays*, Tel Aviv, Poalim, 1979, pp. 81-112 (in Hebrew).

45. 1QS 3,7f., ... ובעגוות נפשו...,וברוח יושר וענוה...,וברוח קדושה...,וברוח עצת אמת...,כיא ברוח עצת אמת. The repeated instrumental ב, in addition to John's baptist ideology, explains the alternating [ἐν] ὕδατι and [ἐν] πνεύματι ἁγίῳ in the mss., Mk 1,8 par.

46. Cf. John's saying that "I baptize you with water, but he will baptize you with Holy Spirit", Mk 1,8. The Q version adds "Holy Spirit *and fire*" (Lk 3,16; Mt 3,11). Fire, often an apocalyptic symbol of the Spirit, is manifest in John's preaching as reported in the Q tradition (Lk 3,7-9; Mt 3,7-10).

47. Cf. the same expression Acts 2,37; 22,10, and with explicit mention of salvation, Acts 16,30; Mk 10,17 par.

48. Lk 3,12, ἦλθον...βαπτισθῆναι.

49. 1QS 8,17f. The willed transgression of מכול המצוה דבר, "from the commandment, anything", is not irreparable, in contrast to willed transgression of דבר מתורת משה, which is punished by lasting excommunication, 1QS 8,20-9,2. J. LICHT, *The Rule Scroll*, Jerusalem, Bialik Institute, 1965, p. 183f. (in Hebrew) thinks המצוה represents the code of discipline of the community.

50. For the moral implication of this term see above n. 29.

51. Cf. the story of Zacchaeus, Lk 19,8, and John's instruction 3,13f.

Now as observed earlier, the gospels concur in stating that Jesus began appearing in public after his sojourn with John the Baptist. In the "telescoped chronology" of Mark[52], this first appearance even seems to be occasioned by John's imprisonment (Mk 1,14f). However that may be, there are multiple indications of a close relationship between Jesus' public appearance and the Baptist movement[53]. Scattered over the four gospels, they seem to reflect a primitive stage of the gospel tradition. These are the most important ones: Jesus submits to John's "baptism of repentance and forgiveness of sins" (Mk 1,4-11), which signals acceptance of his authority as a prophetic Tora interpreter. Matthew and John seem to reflect later hesitation about this submission (Mt 3,14f; Jn 1,32). In Matthew, Jesus makes his appearance with the same message as the Baptist: "Repent, for the Kingdom of Heaven is at hand" (Mt 3,2; 4,17). A singular Johannine report says that Jesus also baptized (Jn 3,22-24; 4,1f). We hear of habitual exchanges between Jesus, John and their mutual disciples (Mk 2,18; Jn 1,35-41). Two of John's disciples left their master to follow Jesus, one of whom being Andrew, the brother of Jesus' foremost disciple (Jn 1,37.40). John's disciples came to Jesus to report their master's execution (Mt 14,12). In Matthew, Jesus sends out his "apostles" with the same message he took over from John (Mt 10,7; cf Lk 9,2; 10,9). The disciples of both went out to preach, even in the diaspora (Acts 19,3). In Matthew, Jesus sees the Baptist as his prophetic precursor (Mt 11,14; 17,13). Finally, there is the accredited Q passage where Jesus summarizes his messianic work both in continuity and in contradistinction to John the Baptist (Mt 11,2-6; Lk 7,18-23). Precisely here do we find the conglomerate of Isaiah quotations cited above. This cumulated evidence suggests that Jesus' sojourn with John was more than accidental. His message must have taken shape in the milieu of John's baptismal preaching and "studying the Tora" in the desert, and it even seems that he had been his disciple, until he made his own appearance. The desert is also a basic ingredient of his own life. Not only does he in the synoptic gospels undergo the "temptation in the desert" immediately after his baptism by John. Indications scattered over all gospels tell us that he often retreated to "deserted places" to pray, to teach or to baptize, thus continuing the activity of his former master[54].

52. For Mark's "telescoping" see M. BLACK, *The Arrest and Trial of Jesus and the Date of the Last Supper*, in A.J.B. HIGGINS (ed.), *Studies in Memory of T.W. Manson*, Manchester, University Press, 1959, pp. 19-33.

53. Cf. PERROT (n. 40).

54. Mk 1,12f.35.45; Jn 3,22-24; 10,40f.; Lk 4,42; 5,16; 6,12; 9,18.28f.

On the whole, what evidence we have makes it most unlikely that these various desert preachers were a uniform lot. Indeed, if Jesus was John's one time disciple, the gospels are also clear about their difference[55]. In contrast to John, Jesus is distinguished by his extensive work of healing (Mt 11,5; Jn 10,40f; 5,36). This relates to a deeper level. In some passages already referred to, Jesus sets his mission sharply off from John's. He expresses an almost overt messianic consciousness precisely in contrast to John, the greatest of prophets who nevertheless is the smallest in the Kingdom of Heaven (Mt 11,7-13; Lk 7,24-28; 16,16). In other images of speech, he distinguishes himself from John and the Pharisees as the messianic bridegroom, as the new wine and as the new cloth in contrast to the old (Mk 2,19-22par.). More than anything else, John's question sent from prison and the answer Jesus gives are eloquent. In Jesus' appearance, the messianic Isaiah prophecies are being fulfilled.

The Evangel of Jesus and the Christian Gospel

Let us pull the threads together. In Luke and Matthew, the beginnings of Jesus' appearance are marked by concatenated allusions to messianic verses in Isaiah. This strongly reminds us of the Qumran scrolls, both in the choice of Isaiah passages and in the way of conglomerating them. We hear of a community "preparing the way in the desert" by "studying the Tora", of a teacher whose task it was "to bring good tidings to the meek", of the elect being called "the meek of the Spirit", and of a messianic figure in whom God realizes the Isaianic promises. This led us to *the only documented formative period in Jesus' life*, his sojourn in the desert with John the Baptist. In addition to his submission to John's call for repentant baptism, numerous indications point to a close interrelation between the work of John and Jesus. It is plausible to see Jesus as a one-time disciple of John who went his own way. This relationship comes to a head in Jesus' answer to the imprisoned Baptist, a conglomerate of Isaiah phrases which strongly reminds of the Messianic Apocalypse from Qumran and like that document ends with the resurrection of the dead and the good tidings to the poor.

It seems that this constellation conditioned the germinal core of Jesus' evangel. Both his Lukan Nazareth sermon and the first three Matthean beatitudes circle around the beginning of Isaiah 61. It is here that we can perceive a subcutaneous affinity with the appeal which in Matthew

---

55. Cf. the antagonism between their followers, Acts 18,24-19,7 and Jn 1,8.20; 5,33-36; 10,41.

marks his appearance and which he not only took over from the Baptist but also commissioned to his apostles: "Repent, for the Kingdom of Heaven is near". In Mark's version, this involves the Isaianic "evangel": "...Jesus came to Galilee preaching *the evangel of God* and saying, The time is fulfilled and the Kingdom of God is near; repent and *believe in the evangel*" (Mk 1,14f). The appeal expresses the awareness that the messianic promises of Isaiah now are being realized. It represents the core of Jesus' evangel.

Of course, this does not explain all of the figure of Jesus. The messianic Isaiah readings and the Baptist connection are only two aspects of the extraordinary and complex personality that emerges from the gospels. Another component is his affinity with the Pharisees as expressed in his humane use of parables[56], and his lenient conception of the sabbath. Exactly how that affinity came about remains an enigma, like so much of the historical Jesus.

The above also allows us to explain the predilection for the word group εὐαγγελ- in the New Testament. It must have arisen from its prominence in the Isaiah texts cherished in the milieus of John the Baptist and of Jesus himself. Thus early Christianity appropriated the word in the soteriological meaning of prophetic and oracular usage. Another question, raised by Mk 1,14f, is whether Jesus himself would have used the noun εὐαγγέλιον or בשורה. The broad expression "evangel of God" reminds of Isaianic usage. It is also used by Paul[57] and hence belongs to basic apostolic tradition. But it is hard to prove that the phrase "believe in the evangel" was not put in Jesus' mouth by the Marcan evangelist. His opening phrase definitely reflects later Christian usage: "Beginning of the *gospel* of Jesus Christ" (Mk 1,1).

Just so, early Christian tradition used the word εὐαγγέλιον *to indicate Jesus' message and teachings*. Such is clear not only from Mark, but also from the Didache. This work of Jewish-Christian provenance shows affinities not so much with the gospel of Matthew as with one of its sources. Thus an exhortation of the readers to pray "as the Lord commanded in his evangel" is followed by Matthew's wording of the Lord's Prayer. Likewise, "As for apostles and prophets, act according to the command of the evangel" – and in this case we have no secure gospel parallels[58]. This may be taken to reflect the stage at which the teachings

---

56. D. FLUSSER, *Die rabbinischen Gleichnisse und der Gleichniserzähler Jesus*, 1: *Das Wesen der Gleichnisse*, Bern, Lang, 1981.

57. Above n. 24.

58. Did 8,2, cf. Mt 6,9ff.; Did 11,3 (but cf. Mt 10,8-15; Lk 9,3-6; 10,4-12; 1 Cor 9,14). See also Did 9,5, no one unbaptized may partake in the Eucharist, "for concerning

of Jesus were transmitted orally[59]. As far as the Didache and the New Testament are concerned, the evangel of Jesus is part and parcel of the gospel. The message of this extraordinary Jewish preacher ought to be at the very heart of New Testament theology.

Bollandistenstraat 40　　　　　　　　　　　　　　　　Peter J. TOMSON
B-1040 Brussel

this the Lord has said, 'Do not give the holy things to the dogs'" (Mt 7,6); and Did 15,3, on mutual reprimanding, prayers and alms, "you have it in the evangel..., you have it in the evangel of our Lord".

59. See most recently R.H. GUNDRY, *EYAΓΓEΛION: How Soon A Book?*, in *JBL* 115 (1996) 321-325, supporting H. KOESTER's view (n. 3, pp. 24ff.) that the "book" meaning only arose after Marcion.

INDEXES

LIST OF ABBREVIATIONS

AASF	Annales Academiae Scientiarum Fennicae
AB	Anchor Bible
ABD	Anchor Bible Dictionary
AB.RL	Anchor Bible Reference Library
AGJU	Arbeiten zur Geschichte des antiken Judentums und des Ur-christentums
AGSU	Arbeiten zur Geschichte des Spätjudentums und des Ur-christentums
AnBib	Analecta Biblica
ANRW	Aufstieg und Niedergang der römischen Welt
ANT	Apocrypha Novi Testamenti
AOAT	Alter Orient und Altes Testament
ASNU	Acta Seminarii Neotestamentici Upsaliensis
ATANT	Abhandlungen zur Theologie des Alten und Neuen Testaments
ATD	Das Alte Testament Deutsch
ANTZ	Arbeiten zur neutestamentlichen Theologie und Zeitgeschichte
AUSS	Andrews University Seminary Studies
BAR	Biblical Archaeological Review
BBB	Bonner biblische Beiträge
BBET	Beiträge zur biblischen Exegese und Theologie
BEvT	Beiträge zur evangelischen Theologie
BETL	Bibliotheca Ephemeridum Theologicarum Lovaniensium
BGBE	Beiträge zur Geschichte der biblischen Exegese
BHT	Beiträge zur historischen Theologie
Bib	Biblica
BN	Biblische Notizen
BibT	Biblical Theology
BiKi	Bibel und Kirche
BIOSCS	Bulletin of the International Organization for Septuagint and Cognate Studies
BJRL	Bulletin of the John Rylands Library
BK	Biblischer Kommentar
BKAT	Biblischer Kommentar. Altes Testament
BN	Biblische Notizen
BNTC	Black New Testament Commentaries
BS	Bibliotheca Sacra
BTB	Biblical Theology Bulletin
BTSt	Biblisch-theologische Studien
BTZ	Berliner theologische Zeitschrift
BU	Biblische Untersuchungen
BWANT	Beiträge zur Wissenschaft vom Alten und Neuen Testament
BZ	Biblische Zeitschrift
BZAW	Beihefte zur Zeitschrift für die alttestamentliche Wissenschaft

BZNW	Beihefte zur Zeitschrift für die neutestamentliche Wissenschaft
CB.NT	Coniectanea Biblica. New Testament
CBET	Contributions to Biblical Exegesis and Theology
CBQ	Catholic Biblical Quarterly
CBQ MS	Catholic Biblical Quarterly Monograph Series
CEB	Commentaire évangélique de la Bible
CGTC	Cambridge Greek Testament Commentary
CJAS	Christianity and Judaism in Antiquity Series
CNT	Coniectanea neotestamentica
Coll.	Collationes
CRINT	Compendia Rerum Iudaicarum ad Novum Testamentum
CTM	Concordia Theological Monthly
DASK	Duisburger Arbeiten zur Sprach- und Kulturwissenschaft
DBS	Dictionnaire de la Bible. Supplément
DJD	Discoveries in the Judean Desert
DSD	Dead Sea Discoveries
EB	Echter Bibel
EBib	Études bibliques
EHS	Europäische Hochschulschriften
EKK	Evangelisch-katholischer Kommentar zum Neuen Testament
EvQ	Evangelical Quarterly
ETL	Ephemerides Theologicae Lovanienses
ErfTSt	Erfurter theologische Studien
EvT	Evangelische Theologie
EWNT	Exegetisches Wörterbuch zum Neuen Testament
ExpT	Expository Times
FAT	Forschungen zum Alten Testament
FilNT	Filología Neotestamentaria
FJS	Frankfurter judaistische Studien
FOTL	The Forms of Old Testament Literature
FRLANT	Forschungen zur Religion und Literatur des Alten und Neuen Testaments
FzB	Forschung zur Bibel
GCS	Die griechischen christlichen Schriftsteller der ersten drei Jahrhunderte
HBT	Horizons in Biblical Theology
HNT	Handbuch zum Neuen Testament
HTKNT	Herders theologischer Kommentar zum Neuen Testament
HTK.S	Herders theologischer Kommentar zum Neuen Testament. Supplementband
HTR	Harvard Theological Review
HTS	Hervormde Theologiese Studies
HUC	Hebrew Union College
HUCA	Hebrew Union College Annual
IBS	Irish Biblical Studies
ICC	International Critical Commentaries
IDB	Interpreters Dictionary of the Bible
IEJ	Israel Exploration Journal
Int	Interpretation

JAAR	Journal of the American Academy of Religion
JBC	Jerome Biblical Commentary
JBL	Journal of Biblical Literature
JBT	Jahrbuch für biblische Theologie
JES	Journal of Ecumenical Studies
JETS	Journal of the Evangelical Theological Society
JJS	Journal of Jewish Studies
JPT	Jahrbücher für protestantische Theologie
JQR	Jewish Quarterly Review
JR	Journal of Religion
JSJ	Journal for the Study of Judaism
JSNT	Journal for the Study of the New Testament
JSNT SS	Journal for the Study of the New Testament Supplement Series
JSP	Journal for the Study of the Pseudepigrapha
JSP SS	Journal for the Study of the Pseudepigrapha Supplement Series
JSS	Journal of Semitic Studies
JTS	Journal of Theological Studies
JTSA	Journal of Theology for Southern Africa
KAT	Kommentar zum Alten Testament
KuD	Kerygma und Dogma
KEK	Kritisch-exegetischer Kommentar über das Neue Testament
LD	Lectio Divina
LS	Louvain Studies
LTJ	Lutheran Theological Journal
MBPF	Münchener Beiträge zur Papyrusforschung und antiken Rechtsgeschichte
MThA	Münsteraner theologische Abhandlungen
NCBC	New Century Bible Commentaries
NABPR	National Association of Baptist Professors of Religion
NEB	Neue Echter Bibel
NEB.E	Neue Echer Bible. Ergänzungsband
Neot	Neotestamentica
NGTT	Nederduitse gereformeerde teologiese tydskrif
NICOT	New International Commentary on the Old Testament
NIGTC	New International Greek Testament Commentary
NJBC	New Jerome Biblical Commentary
NRT	Nouvelle revue théologique
NT	Novum Testamentum
NTAbh	Neutestamentliche Abhandlungen
NTD	Das Neue Testament Deutsch
NTOA	Novum Testamentum und Orbis antiquus
NTS	New Testament Studies
NTSup	Supplements to Novum Testamentum
OBO	Orbis biblicus et orientalis
ÖTK	Ökumenischer Taschenbuchkommentar
OTL	Old Testament Library
OTP	Old Testament Pseudepigrapha
OTS	Oudtestamentlische Studien

PAAJR	Proceedings of the Americal Academy for Jewish Research
PL	Patrologia Latina
POT	De Prediking von het Oude Testament
PTA	Papyrologische Texte und Abhandlungen
QD	Quaestiones Disputatae
RB	Revue biblique
RExp	Review and Expositor
RGG	Religion in Geschichte und Gegenwart
RHPR	Revue d'histoire et de philosophie religieuses
RivBib	Rivista Biblica
RNT	Regensburger Neues Testament
RQ	Revue de Qumran
RSR	Recherches de science religieuse
RTL	Revue théologique de Louvain
SANT	Studien zum Alten und Neuen Testament
SBAB	Stuttgarter biblische Aufsatzbände
SBB	Stuttgarter biblische Beiträge
SBL DS	Society of Biblical Literature Dissertation Series
SBL.EJL	Society of Biblical Literature. Early Judaism and Its Literature
SBL MS	Society of Biblical Literature Monograph Series
SBLSP	Society of Biblical Literature Seminar Papers
SBS	Stuttgarter Bibelstudien
SBT	Studies in Biblical Theology
SbWGF	Sitzungsberichte der Wissenschaftlichen Gesellschaften der Johann Wolfgang Goethe-Universität Frankfurt a.M.
SCS	Septuagint and Cognate Studies
SEÅ	Svenk Exegetisk Årsbok
SémBib	Sémiotique et Bible
SJLA	Studies in Judaism in Late Antiquity
SJOT	Scandinavian Journal of the Old Testament
SJT	Scottish Journal of Theology
SNT	Studien zum Neuen Testament
SNTA	Studiorum Novi Testamenti Auxilia
SNTS MS	Society for New Testament Studies Monograph Series
SNTU	Studien zum Neuen Testament und seiner Umwelt
SPAW	Sitzungsberichte der Preußischen Akademie der Wissenschaften
SPIB	Scripta Pontificii Instituti Biblici
SPB	Studia Postbiblica
ST	Studia Theologica
STDJ	Studien on the Texts of the Desert of Judah
SUNT	Studien zur Umwelt des Neuen Testaments
SVTP	Studia in Veteris Testamenti Pseudepigrapha
SWJT	Southwestern Journal of Theology
TBl	Theologische Blätter
TDOT	Theologiocal Dictionary of the Old Testament
TFT	Theologische Fakulteit Tilburg
THKNT	Theologischer Handkommentar zum Neuen Testament
TJ	Theologisches Jahrbuch

TLZ	Theologische Literaturzeitung
TQ	Theologische Quartalschrift
TR	Theologische Rundschau
TRE	Theologische Realenzyklopädie
TS	Theological Studies
TSAJ	Texte und Studien zum antiken Judentum
TStKr	Theologische Studien und Kritiken
TToday	Theology Today
TTZ	Trierer theologische Zeitschrift
TU	Texte und Untersuchungen
TWAT	Theologisches Wörterbuch zum Alten Testament
TWNT	Theologisches Wörterbuch zum Neuen Testament
TynB	Tyndale Bulletin
TZ	Theologische Zeitschrift
TZT	Tübinger Zeitschrift für Theologie
UF	Ugarit-Forschungen
UTB	Uni-Taschenbücher
VT	Vetus Testamentum
VTS	Supplements to Vetus Testamentum
XWGT	Veröffentlichungen der wissenschaftlichen Gesellschaft für Theologie
WBC	Word Biblical Commentaries
WMANT	Wissenschaftliche Monographien zum Alten und Neuen Testament
WUNT	Wissenschafliche Untersuchungen zum Neuen Testament
YJS	Yale Judaica Series
ZAW	Zeitschrift für die alttestamentliche Wissenschaft
ZBK	Zürcher Bibelkommentare
ZDMG	Zeitschrift der morgenländischen Gesellschaft
ZNW	Zeitschrift für die neutestamentliche Wissenschaft
ZTK	Zeitschrift für Theologie und Kirche
ZWT	Zeitschrift für wissentschaftliche Theologie

INDEX OF AUTHORS

INDEX OF REFERENCES

OLD TESTAMENT

13,7	109 603
14,7	495
14,8	413
14,16-19	416

MALACHI
3,1	8 10 409 447 555 639

3,18	389
3,22-23	232 555
3,23	517 639

OLD TESTAMENT PSEUDEPIGRAPHA AND OTHER WRITINGS

3 MACCABEES
1,23-24	583
2,2-20	580
2,3	583
2,10	583
2,11	583
2,13-14	583
2,19-20	583
2,20	580 586
2,21	583

4 MACCABEES
13,13	567
18,10	450

2 ESDRAS
11,4	35
19,6–20,1	582
19,26-31	284 302
19,26	283
19,29	573

4 EZRA
5,4	531
6,11-24	531
6,13-20	532
8,20	417
12,33	416
13,1-13	421
13,3	464
13,5	464
13,38	416
13,51	464

JUBILEES
1,17	409
1,19-22	364

1,29	409
4,24-26	409
4,26	418
8,19	418
11,16-17	412
15,16-32	416
19,14	412
23,21	184
27,19-27	406
27,27	406
27,30–28,7	521
31,13-17	639
32,1-15	639
32,19	416
36,4-6	521
45,16	412

PSALMS OF SOLOMON
1,6	535
8,5	581
8,10	455
11,1	648
11,7-8	638
17	185-186
17,24	581
17,30-31	416

1 ENOCH
1,3-8	532
1,3-4	531
1,4	211
10,21	416
14,8-25	376
14,20	376
26,1-5	413 415
39–40	376
39,4-8	418

8	378	2,3	409
9,10	455	7,11	409
14,3	639	12,11	603
14,4-8	184	12,14	416
14,4	184	14,16	373
16,2	184	15,14	373
18,2-14	639	17,7	373

TAsher

7,5	184

TZebulun

1,4-5	613
4,8	35

TDan

4,2	69

TJoseph

3,9	35

QUMRAN

1QS

1,8	415
1,24–2,1	582
2,25–3,11	653
3,7-8	654
4,11	148
4,20-22	653
5,4-5	194
5,23-24	653
5,23	415
8,14	651
8,17-18	653-654
8,20–9,2	654
9,6	410
9,11	206 643
9,19-20	651

1QSa (=1Q28a)

1,25-26	415
2,11-22	206

1QSb

1,6	413

1QM   416 421

1,10	373
1,11	373

1QH

6,31	603
10,1-19	226
10,8	373
10,20-30	227
10,21-22	227
10,23-25	227
10,31-39	226
11,1-18	226
12,5-13	226
13,5-19	226
13,20–15,5	226
13,23-24	226
13,31	226
14,27-28	411
15,6-25	226
15,12	226
16,4-40	226
18,14	59
23,14-15	40
23,14-15	652

CD

1,3–2,4	283
3,15	573
3,1	573
3,20	574
4,5	184
4,15-16	69
4,15	70
4,16	70
4,19	217
4,20–5,2	455
5,9-11	455
8,12	217
8,18	217
8,20	70
9,9	68
11,20-21	68
20,6	651
20,33-34	421

NEW TESTAMENT (GOSPELS AND ACTS)

4,10	27 29 106 **481** 487 489 490 506	6,9ff.	657
4,11	29	6,9	29
4,14-16	93-94 97 104	6,10	29 353
4,15-16	98	6,11	29
4,15	77	6,12	29
4,17	447 655	6,13	29
4,23–11,1	63	6,14-15	588
4,23	494 649	6,16	36
4,24	385	6,19	29
5–7	63 105 276 650	6,20	29
5,3-6	41	6,22	29
5,3-4	38 63	6,23	29
5,3	24 29 31 33 37-39 42-44 60	6,26	29 494
		6,27	29
5,4	20 24 29 31-36 38-45 64	6,28	29
		6,29	29
		6,33	29
5,5-10	38	7,1	29
5,5	32-33 38-43	7,6	658
5,6	24 29 31 33 37-43	7,8	29
5,7-9	32-33	7,12	29 96 105 450
5,8	42-43	7,21	29
5,9	42-43	7,22	29
5,10	32-33 37 42-43	7.23	29
5,11-12	32	7,24	29
5,11	29	7,25	29
5,12	29 43	7,27	29
5,17-48	183	7,29	100 494
5,17-20	443-444	8–9	63
5,17	105 108 379 444 449 496	8	104
		8,2	489
5,18	29 179 444 446 449 450	8,11	29
		8,12	29
5,19	444	8,17	93-94 98 114
5,20	442 444	8,20	29
5,21-48	106	8,21-22	188
5,21	106	8,21	29
5,26	451	8,23-27	108
5,27-30	446	8,28-34	131
5,32	446 449 453 455-456	8,29	489
		9,6	496
5,39	29	9,9-13	496
5,42	29	9,10-11	587
5,44	29	9,13	96 106 137 497
5,46	587	9,14-15	499
5,47	26	9,14	491 496
5,48	29	9,15	41
6,2	36	9,18	489
6,5	36	9,35	494 649

17,5	106		137 288
17,10-13	555	21,16	106 119 **137-138**
17,13	655	21,17	117-118 121
18	276	21,42	106
18,4	587	22,3	29
18,12	29	22,4	29
18,15	29	22,23-33	487
18,16	111	22,31	516
18,26	489-490	22,34-40	11 561
19,3-9	487	22,36-39	522
19,4-5	106	22,36	521
19,8-9	96	22,37-40	514 519 521
19,9	446 453	22,37-39	279 560 564 568
19,16-19	571	22,37	28 506 519 560 562-
19,17	572		563 565
19,18-19	106 279	22,38	564
19,19	96	22,39	28 564
19,24	450	22,40	96 105
19,28	29	23,4	495
20,20	489	23,12	29 587
20,29-34	131	23,13	29
21	104	23,30-36	110
21,1-17	**117-141**	23,34	29
21,1-9	117-118 132	23,35	110
21,13	125	23,36	29
21,1	118	23,38	29 497
21,2-7	388	23,39	29 119
21,2-3	130-131	24-25	276
21,2	130-132	24,1	497
21,4-5	93-95 98 103 119	24,6	385
	124	24,14	649
21,3	125 130	24,15	96
21,4	119	24,18	315
21,5	119-120 **124-133** 140	24,29-31	525
	395 479	26,1	110-111
21,6-9	125	24,6	525
21,6	125	24,7	525
21,7	130-132	24,17-18	310
21,9	118-119 125 132-	24,27	309-310
	133 **134-135**	24,28	29 310
21,10-17	117	24,29	538-540
21,10-11	118 125 140	24,30	532 538
21,10	118 125 135	24,35	538
21,12-17	118	24,37	29 309-310
21,12	118 135 137 141	24,38	29 314
21,13	96 119 **135-137** 479	24,39	314
21,14	135	24,40-41	310
21,15-16	118	26,11	110
21,15	118-119 121 **134-135**	26,13	525

12,34	202	14,26-31	113
12,35-37	**201-214**	14,27	109 170 603
12,35	203-207	14,29	172-173
12,36	200 203-210 212-213	14,33	221
	221	14,34	199 227 603
12,37	203-207	14,38	227-228 603
13	464	14,41	193
13,1-2	466	14,42	193 603
13,3-37	192	14,44	193
13,5-22	526 529	14,49	108 170 624
13,7-8	548	14,50	624
13,7	317 385	14,53–15,1	215-216
13,8	318 465	14,53	218
13,9-13	193 529	14,54	218
13,9	193 548	14,55-65	218
13,10	549-550	14,55-64	231
13,11	193 548	14,55	218
13,12	193 465	14,57-58	199
13,13	548	14,58	466
13,14-20	466 532 548	14,61-62	202
13,14	323 465	14,62	199-200 208-212 221
13,15-16	310		527 529
13,16	310 315	14,64	218-219
13,19-20	529	14,65	25
13,19	465	14,66-72	218
13,22	465	14,72	36
13,23	549	15,1	218-219
13,24-27	**525-550**	15,2	231
13,24-25	**525-550**	15,16-20	231
13,24	465 525 534-535 539-	15,17-20	112
	540 549	15,19	489
13,25	525 534-540 543-546	15,22	611
	549	15,23	227-228
13,26-27	465 527-530	15,24	112 199 227-228 234
13,26	213 525-533 550		387-388
13,27	525-533 550	15,26	231
13,28-37	529	15,28	170
13,28-31	548	15,29	112 199 227-228 234
13,30-31	451		466
13,30	451 465	15,33	530
13,32	213	15,34	112 199 227-228 234
13,34	542	15,36	199 227-228 631
13,35	207	15,39	231 427
14,2	153	15,43	610
14,10	193	16,1-8	215-216
14,11	193	16,5-6	221
14,18	193 227-228	16,6	221
14,21	193	16,8	221
14,25	451	16,10	35-36

14,16-24	445	17,5-6	301
14,16-20	277	17,7-10	277 301
14,19	482	17,11–18,8	473
14,20	279	17,11-37	474
14,24	301	17,11-19	301
14,25–16,13	277 300	17,11-17	299
14,25-33	301	17,20–18,14	277 301
14,25	295	17,20-37	**308-317**
14,26	188 279	17,20-21	301 308
14,28-33	279	17,20	311 316
14,31-32	277	17,21	609
14,34-35	301	17,22-37	301
14,35	609	17,22	309
15,1-32	275 300	17,24	309-310 312
15,1-7	279 301	17,25-30	301
15,2	296 445	17,25	310 316-317
15,8-10	301	17,26-30	301 **313-317**
15,11-32	277 279 301	17,26-27	309 465
16,1–19,9	474	17,26	309-310
16,1-18	275 300	17,27	28 314 316
16,1-9	279 301 444-445 474	17,28-29	314 465
16,1-8	277	17,28	309-310
16,1	443	17,29	314
16,4	609	17,30	309 315-316
16,7	444	17,31-32	310 315-316
16,8	444-445	17,32	315-316 465
16,9	443 444-445	17,33	315-317
16,10-18	445	17,37	310-311
16,10-13	277 445	18,1-8	301 445 474
16,10-12	301	18,9-14	275 300 301 **579-589**
16,13	301 445	18,11-12	587
16,14–17,4	277 301	18,11	584-585
16,14-18	444	18,13	584-585
16,14-15	301	18,14	271 579 585-587
16,14	443 445	18,15–19,44	279
16,15	444-445	18,15-43	277 301
16,16-18	443-444 445-446 450	18,15-17	301
16,16-17	301	18,18-23	301
16,16	444 445-446 449 649 656	18,18	279 568
		18,19	564
16,17	444 446 449	18,20	279 559
16,18	277 301 446 449 453	18,24-30	301
16,19-18,8	275 300	18,25	450
16,19-31	277 301 444 446 473 474	18,31-34	301
		18,35–19,10	295
16,25	445	18,35-43	301
16,29-31	446	19,1–20,18	277 301
17,1-3	301	19,1-10	301 473 585
17,3-4	301	19,1-9	474

1,1	380 626 634	2,18-22	635
1,7-8	364	2,18-20	407
1,8	656	2,19-21	365
1,11	414	2,19	411
1,12-13	396 402 411	2,21-22	407 411 617
1,12	365	2,21	399 620
1,14-18	402 427	2,22	371 407-409 420 428
1,14	371 400 402		617 620 625-626 629
1,15	364 402	3,3-6	421
1,15	368	3,3-5	411
1,17	352 363 365 400 630	3,3-6	396
	634	3,3	391
1,18	364 379-380 401-402	3,7	391
	626	3,9	336
1,19	364 404	3,11	626
1,20-21	364	3,12	620
1,20	656	3,13	347 379
1,23	328 358 364 367 371-	3,14	424 426 629-630
	372 384 390 395 621	3,18	380
	630	3,22-24	655
1,24	404	3,26	364
1,25	364 404	3,28	364
1,28	364	3,31-34	380
1,29	399 404 414-415 426	3,31	347 353 391
	635	3,32	384 626
1,30	368 407 409	3,34	626
1,31	369	3,36	401 410 421
1,32	364 655	4,1-2	655
1,33	396	4,4-44	410
1,34	364 427	4,9	620
1,35-41	655	4,10	413 425-426
1,35	635	4,13-14	349
1,36	399 403	4,14-15	426
1,37	655	4,14	355 425
1,40	655	4,19-26	416
1,45	363-364 371 629-630	4,19	410
1,50-51	405	4,20-26	411
1,50	368	4,20	409 414 418
1,51	379 400 405 409-410	4,21ff.	401
	417 630	4,21	365
2,1-25	649	4,23-24	365 413
2,6	426	4,23	411
2,9	620	4,24	399 411
2,11	369 390	4,25-26	410
2,13-22	399 406	4,27	620
2,16	399 407 410	4,29	620
2,17	328 359 361 367 390	4,34	623 631-632
	395 407-408 671 619	4,35-38	411 416
	621 625 630 635	4,35-36	420

6,47-51	333-334 342	7,32	331 404
6,47	331 333-334 336-338 342	7,33-34	417 626
		7,36	620
6,48	338-339 342	7,37-39	365 413
6,49-58	332	7,37-38	401 418
6,49-51	333	7,37	425-426
6,49	333-334 336 339 342 352	7,38-39	425
		7,38	328 358-359 367 390 413 621 630
6,50-51	355	7,39	425 617 620
6,50	331 347	7,42	395 630
6,51-58	333 341 343 423 426	7,43	392
6,51	195 334 337-338 340-342 347 403 414	7,45	404
		7,51	629
6,52-59	335	7,52	629
6,52-58	332-333 341 343	8,5	634
6,52	334 336-337	8,6	620
6,53	331 334 336-337 343	8,16	384 392
6,54	334. 339	8,17	328 356 630 634
6,55	334	8,21-22	417 626
6,56	334	8,23	391
6,57-58	380	8,26	379 384 620 626
6,58	332 343 347 403	8,27	620
6,59	343 620	8,28-29	626
6,60-66	344	8,28	392 424 620
6,60-65	343	8,29	384
6,60	334	8,30	620
6,61	331	8,38	626
6,62	344 355 403	8,40	384
6,63	343 345 413 620	8,42	379
6,64	617 620	8,52-53	371
6,65	338 343	8,58	626
6,66	403	9,6	620
6,69	401	9,16	392
6,71	617	9,22	620
7,1	403	9,39-41	422
7,9	620	9,41	166
7,11	415	10	414
7,15-16	629-630	10,6	620
7,15	412	10,10	623
7,16-17	626	10,11	414 623
7,19-24	356	10,15	414 623
7,19	352 629	10,16	392 416
7,20	629	10,17	409 623
7,22	352 630	10,18	408-409 414 623
7,23	356 371	10,19	392
7,25-31	371	10,22-39	370
7,28	399	10,22-23	370
7,29	379	10,24-30	370
7,31	385		

13,27-29	609	19,3	655	
13,27	608 614	19,4	653	
13,38-39	298	19,9	295	
14,10	48	19,23	295	
14,13	267	20,35	620	
14,42	267	20,38	620	
15,14	299	21,8	649	
15,20	446	21,10-11	267	
15,31	35	21,13	36	
15,40–16,1	267	21,17	267	
16,30	654	22,4	295	
17,22	584	22,10	654	
17,23	608	23,6-10	285	
17,27	269	23,6-8	517	
17,20	608	24,14	295 450	
18-19	261	24,22	295	
18,24–19,7	656	27,21	584	
18,25-26	295	28,21	450	
18,25	261	28,26-27	145 395	
19,1	261	28,28	290 483	
19,3-4	261			

BIBLIOTHECA EPHEMERIDUM THEOLOGICARUM LOVANIENSIUM

SERIES I

* = Out of print

*1. *Miscellanea dogmatica in honorem Eximii Domini J. Bittremieux*, 1947.

*2-3. *Miscellanea moralia in honorem Eximii Domini A. Janssen*, 1948.

*4. G. PHILIPS, *La grâce des justes de l'Ancien Testament*, 1948.

*5. G. PHILIPS, *De ratione instituendi tractatum de gratia nostrae sanctificationis*, 1953.

6-7. *Recueil Lucien Cerfaux. Études d'exégèse et d'histoire religieuse*, 1954. 504 et 577 p. FB 1000 par tome. Cf. *infra*, n°s 18 et 71 (t. III).

8. G. THILS, *Histoire doctrinale du mouvement œcuménique*, 1955. Nouvelle édition, 1963. 338 p. FB 135.

*9. *Études sur l'Immaculée Conception*, 1955.

*10. J.A. O'DONOHOE, *Tridentine Seminary Legislation*, 1957.

*11. G. THILS, *Orientations de la théologie*, 1958.

*12-13. J. COPPENS, A. DESCAMPS, É. MASSAUX (ed.), *Sacra Pagina. Miscellanea Biblica Congressus Internationalis Catholici de Re Biblica*, 1959.

*14. *Adrien VI, le premier Pape de la contre-réforme*, 1959.

*15. F. CLAEYS BOUUAERT, *Les déclarations et serments imposés par la loi civile aux membres du clergé belge sous le Directoire (1795-1801)*, 1960.

*16. G. THILS, *La «Théologie œcuménique». Notion-Formes-Démarches*, 1960.

17. G. THILS, *Primauté pontificale et prérogatives épiscopales. «Potestas ordinaria» au Concile du Vatican*, 1961. 103 p. FB 50.

*18. *Recueil Lucien Cerfaux*, t. III, 1962. Cf. *infra*, n° 71.

*19. *Foi et réflexion philosophique. Mélanges F. Grégoire*, 1961.

*20. *Mélanges G. Ryckmans*, 1963.

21. G. THILS, *L'infaillibilité du peuple chrétien «in credendo»*, 1963. 67 p. FB 50.

*22. J. FÉRIN & L. JANSSENS, *Progestogènes et morale conjugale*, 1963.

*23. *Collectanea Moralia in honorem Eximii Domini A. Janssen*, 1964.

24. H. CAZELLES (ed.), *De Mari à Qumrân. L'Ancien Testament. Son milieu. Ses écrits. Ses relectures juives* (Hommage J. Coppens, I), 1969. 158*-370 p. FB 900.

*25. I. DE LA POTTERIE (ed.), *De Jésus aux évangiles. Tradition et rédaction dans les évangiles synoptiques* (Hommage J. Coppens, II), 1967.

26. G. THILS & R.E. BROWN (ed.), *Exégèse et théologie* (Hommage J. Coppens, III), 1968. 328 p. FB 700.

27. J. COPPENS (ed.), *Ecclesia a Spiritu sancto edocta. Hommage à Mgr G. Philips*, 1970. 640 p. FB 1000.

28. J. COPPENS (ed.), *Sacerdoce et célibat. Études historiques et théologiques*, 1971. 740 p. FB 700.

29. M. DIDIER (ed.), *L'évangile selon Matthieu. Rédaction et théologie*, 1972. 432 p. FB 1000.
*30. J. KEMPENEERS, *Le Cardinal van Roey en son temps*, 1971.

SERIES II

31. F. NEIRYNCK, *Duality in Mark. Contributions to the Study of the Markan Redaction*, 1972. Revised edition with Supplementary Notes, 1988. 252 p. FB 1200.
32. F. NEIRYNCK (ed.), *L'évangile de Luc. Problèmes littéraires et théologiques*, 1973. *L'évangile de Luc – The Gospel of Luke*. Revised and enlarged edition, 1989. x-590 p. FB 2200.
33. C. BREKELMANS (ed.), *Questions disputées d'Ancien Testament. Méthode et théologie*, 1974. *Continuing Questions in Old Testament Method and Theology*. Revised and enlarged edition by M. VERVENNE, 1989. 245 p. FB 1200.
34. M. SABBE (ed.), *L'évangile selon Marc. Tradition et rédaction*, 1974. Nouvelle édition augmentée, 1988. 601 p. FB 2400.
35. B. WILLAERT (ed.), *Philosophie de la religion – Godsdienstfilosofie. Miscellanea Albert Dondeyne*, 1974. Nouvelle édition, 1987. 458 p. FB 1600.
36. G. PHILIPS, *L'union personnelle avec le Dieu vivant. Essai sur l'origine et le sens de la grâce créée*, 1974. Édition révisée, 1989. 299 p. FB 1000.
37. F. NEIRYNCK, in collaboration with T. HANSEN and F. VAN SEGBROECK, *The Minor Agreements of Matthew and Luke against Mark with a Cumulative List*, 1974. 330 p. FB 900.
38. J. COPPENS, *Le messianisme et sa relève prophétique. Les anticipations vétérotestamentaires. Leur accomplissement en Jésus*, 1974. Édition révisée, 1989. XIII-265 p. FB 1000.
39. D. SENIOR, *The Passion Narrative according to Matthew. A Redactional Study*, 1975. New impression, 1982. 440 p. FB 1000.
40. J. DUPONT (ed.), *Jésus aux origines de la christologie*, 1975. Nouvelle édition augmentée, 1989. 458 p. FB 1500.
41. J. COPPENS (ed.), *La notion biblique de Dieu*, 1976. Réimpression, 1985. 519 p. FB 1600.
42. J. LINDEMANS & H. DEMEESTER (ed.), *Liber Amicorum Monseigneur W. Onclin*, 1976. XXII-396 p. FB 1000.
43. R.E. HOECKMAN (ed.), *Pluralisme et œcuménisme en recherches théologiques. Mélanges offerts au R.P. Dockx, O.P.*, 1976. 316 p. FB 1000.
44. M. DE JONGE (ed.), *L'évangile de Jean. Sources, rédaction, théologie*, 1977. Réimpression, 1987. 416 p. FB 1500.
45. E.J.M. VAN EIJL (ed.), *Facultas S. Theologiae Lovaniensis 1432-1797. Bijdragen tot haar geschiedenis. Contributions to its History. Contributions à son histoire*, 1977. 570 p. FB 1700.
46. M. DELCOR (ed.), *Qumrân. Sa piété, sa théologie et son milieu*, 1978. 432 p. FB 1700.
47. M. CAUDRON (ed.), *Faith and Society. Foi et société. Geloof en maatschappij. Acta Congressus Internationalis Theologici Lovaniensis 1976*, 1978. 304 p. FB 1150.

48. J. KREMER (ed.), *Les Actes des Apôtres. Traditions, rédaction, théologie,* 1979. 590 p. FB 1700.
49. F. NEIRYNCK, avec la collaboration de J. DELOBEL, T. SNOY, G. VAN BELLE, F. VAN SEGBROECK, *Jean et les Synoptiques. Examen critique de l'exégèse de M.-É. Boismard,* 1979. XII-428 p. FB 1000.
50. J. COPPENS, *La relève apocalyptique du messianisme royal. I. La royauté – Le règne – Le royaume de Dieu. Cadre de la relève apocalyptique,* 1979. 325 p. FB 1000.
51. M. GILBERT (ed.), *La Sagesse de l'Ancien Testament,* 1979. Nouvelle édition mise à jour, 1990. 455 p. FB 1500.
52. B. DEHANDSCHUTTER, *Martyrium Polycarpi. Een literair-kritische studie,* 1979. 296 p. FB 1000.
53. J. LAMBRECHT (ed.), *L'Apocalypse johannique et l'Apocalyptique dans le Nouveau Testament,* 1980. 458 p. FB 1400.
54. P.-M. BOGAERT (ed.), *Le livre de Jérémie. Le prophète et son milieu. Les oracles et leur transmission,* 1981. 408 p. FB 1500.
55. J. COPPENS, *La relève apocalyptique du messianisme royal. III. Le Fils de l'homme néotestamentaire.* Édition posthume par F. NEIRYNCK, 1981. XIV-192 p. FB 800.
56. J. VAN BAVEL & M. SCHRAMA (ed.), *Jansénius et le Jansénisme dans les Pays-Bas. Mélanges Lucien Ceyssens,* 1982. 247 p. FB 1000.
57. J.H. WALGRAVE, *Selected Writings – Thematische geschriften. Thomas Aquinas, J.H. Newman, Theologia Fundamentalis.* Edited by G. DE SCHRIJVER & J.J. KELLY, 1982. XLIII-425 p. FB 1000.
58. F. NEIRYNCK & F. VAN SEGBROECK, avec la collaboration de E. MANNING, *Ephemerides Theologicae Lovanienses 1924-1981. Tables générales. (Bibliotheca Ephemeridum Theologicarum Lovaniensium 1947-1981),* 1982. 400 p. FB 1600.
59. J. DELOBEL (ed.), *Logia. Les paroles de Jésus – The Sayings of Jesus. Mémorial Joseph Coppens,* 1982. 647 p. FB 2000.
60. F. NEIRYNCK, *Evangelica. Gospel Studies – Études d'évangile. Collected Essays.* Edited by F. VAN SEGBROECK, 1982. XIX-1036 p. FB 2000.
61. J. COPPENS, *La relève apocalyptique du messianisme royal. II. Le Fils d'homme vétéro- et intertestamentaire.* Édition posthume par J. LUST, 1983. XVII-272 p. FB 1000.
62. J.J. KELLY, *Baron Friedrich von Hügel's Philosophy of Religion,* 1983. 232 p. FB 1500.
63. G. DE SCHRIJVER, *Le merveilleux accord de l'homme et de Dieu. Étude de l'analogie de l'être chez Hans Urs von Balthasar,* 1983. 344 p. FB 1500.
64. J. GROOTAERS & J.A. SELLING, *The 1980 Synod of Bishops: «On the Role of the Family». An Exposition of the Event and an Analysis of its Texts.* Preface by Prof. emeritus L. JANSSENS, 1983. 375 p. FB 1500.
65. F. NEIRYNCK & F. VAN SEGBROECK, *New Testament Vocabulary. A Companion Volume to the Concordance,* 1984. XVI-494 p. FB 2000.
66. R.F. COLLINS, *Studies on the First Letter to the Thessalonians,* 1984. XI-415 p. FB 1500.
67. A. PLUMMER, *Conversations with Dr. Döllinger 1870-1890.* Edited with Introduction and Notes by R. BOUDENS, with the collaboration of L. KENIS, 1985. LIV-360 p. FB 1800.

68. N. LOHFINK (ed.), *Das Deuteronomium. Entstehung, Gestalt und Botschaft / Deuteronomy: Origin, Form and Message*, 1985. XI-382 p. FB 2000.

69. P.F. FRANSEN, *Hermeneutics of the Councils and Other Studies*. Collected by H.E. MERTENS & F. DE GRAEVE, 1985. 543 p. FB 1800.

70. J. DUPONT, *Études sur les Évangiles synoptiques*. Présentées par F. NEIRYNCK, 1985. 2 tomes, XXI-IX-1210 p. FB 2800.

71. *Recueil Lucien Cerfaux*, t. III, 1962. Nouvelle édition revue et complétée, 1985. LXXX-458 p. FB 1600.

72. J. GROOTAERS, *Primauté et collégialité. Le dossier de Gérard Philips sur la Nota Explicativa Praevia (Lumen gentium, Chap. III)*. Présenté avec introduction historique, annotations et annexes. Préface de G. THILS, 1986. 222 p. FB 1000.

73. A. VANHOYE (ed.), *L'apôtre Paul. Personnalité, style et conception du ministère*, 1986. XIII-470 p. FB 2600.

74. J. LUST (ed.), *Ezekiel and His Book. Textual and Literary Criticism and their Interrelation*, 1986. X-387 p. FB 2700.

75. É. MASSAUX, *Influence de l'Évangile de saint Matthieu sur la littérature chrétienne avant saint Irénée*. Réimpression anastatique présentée par F. NEIRYNCK. Supplément: *Bibliographie 1950-1985*, par B. DEHANDSCHUTTER, 1986. XXVII-850 p. FB 2500.

76. L. CEYSSENS & J.A.G. TANS, *Autour de l'Unigenitus. Recherches sur la genèse de la Constitution*, 1987. XXVI-845 p. FB 2500.

77. A. DESCAMPS, *Jésus et l'Église. Études d'exégèse et de théologie*. Préface de Mgr A. HOUSSIAU, 1987. XLV-641 p. FB 2500.

78. J. DUPLACY, *Études de critique textuelle du Nouveau Testament*. Présentées par J. DELOBEL, 1987. XXVII-431 p. FB 1800.

79. E.J.M. VAN EIJL (ed.), *L'image de C. Jansénius jusqu'à la fin du XVIIIe siècle*, 1987. 258 p. FB 1250.

80. E. BRITO, *La Création selon Schelling. Universum*, 1987. XXXV-646 p. FB 2980.

81. J. VERMEYLEN (ed.), *The Book of Isaiah – Le livre d'Isaïe. Les oracles et leurs relectures. Unité et complexité de l'ouvrage*, 1989. X-472 p. FB 2700.

82. G. VAN BELLE, *Johannine Bibliography 1966-1985. A Cumulative Bibliography on the Fourth Gospel*, 1988. XVII-563 p. FB 2700.

83. J.A. SELLING (ed.), *Personalist Morals. Essays in Honor of Professor Louis Janssens*, 1988. VIII-344 p. FB 1200.

84. M.-É. BOISMARD, *Moïse ou Jésus. Essai de christologie johannique*, 1988. XVI-241 p. FB 1000.

84A. M.-É. BOISMARD, *Moses or Jesus: An Essay in Johannine Christology*. Translated by B.T. VIVIANO, 1993, XVI-144 p. FB 1000.

85. J.A. DICK, *The Malines Conversations Revisited*, 1989. 278 p. FB 1500.

86. J.-M. SEVRIN (ed.), *The New Testament in Early Christianity – La réception des écrits néotestamentaires dans le christianisme primitif*, 1989. XVI-406 p. FB 2500.

87. R.F. COLLINS (ed.), *The Thessalonian Correspondence*, 1990. XV-546 p. FB 3000.

88. F. VAN SEGBROECK, *The Gospel of Luke. A Cumulative Bibliography 1973-1988*, 1989. 241 p. FB 1200.

89. G. THILS, *Primauté et infaillibilité du Pontife Romain à Vatican I et autres études d'ecclésiologie,* 1989. XI-422 p. FB 1850.
90. A. VERGOTE, *Explorations de l'espace théologique. Études de théologie et de philosophie de la religion,* 1990. XVI-709 p. FB 2000.
91. J.C. DE MOOR, *The Rise of Yahwism: The Roots of Israelite Monotheism,* 1990. XII-315 p. FB 1250.
92. B. BRUNING, M. LAMBERIGTS & J. VAN HOUTEM (eds.), *Collectanea Augustiniana. Mélanges T.J. van Bavel,* 1990. 2 tomes, XXXVIII-VIII-1074 p. FB 3000.
93. A. DE HALLEUX, *Patrologie et œcuménisme. Recueil d'études,* 1990. XVI-887 p. FB 3000.
94. C. BREKELMANS & J. LUST (eds.), *Pentateuchal and Deuteronomistic Studies: Papers Read at the XIIIth IOSOT Congress Leuven 1989,* 1990. 307 p. FB 1500.
95. D.L. DUNGAN (ed.), *The Interrelations of the Gospels. A Symposium Led by M.-É. Boismard – W.R. Farmer – F. Neirynck, Jerusalem 1984,* 1990. XXXI-672 p. FB 3000.
96. G.D. KILPATRICK, *The Principles and Practice of New Testament Textual Criticism. Collected Essays.* Edited by J.K. ELLIOTT, 1990. XXXVIII-489 p. FB 3000.
97. G. ALBERIGO (ed.), *Christian Unity. The Council of Ferrara-Florence: 1438/39 – 1989,* 1991. X-681 p. FB 3000.
98. M. SABBE, *Studia Neotestamentica. Collected Essays,* 1991. XVI-573 p. FB 2000.
99. F. NEIRYNCK, *Evangelica II: 1982-1991. Collected Essays.* Edited by F. VAN SEGBROECK, 1991. XIX-874 p. FB 2800.
100. F. VAN SEGBROECK, C.M. TUCKETT, G. VAN BELLE & J. VERHEYDEN (eds.), *The Four Gospels 1992. Festschrift Frans Neirynck,* 1992. 3 volumes, XVII-X-X-2668 p. FB 5000.

SERIES III

101. A. DENAUX (ed.), *John and the Synoptics,* 1992. XXII-696 p. FB 3000.
102. F. NEIRYNCK, J. VERHEYDEN, F. VAN SEGBROECK, G. VAN OYEN & R. CORSTJENS, *The Gospel of Mark. A Cumulative Bibliography: 1950-1990,* 1992. XII-717 p. FB 2700.
103. M. SIMON, *Un catéchisme universel pour l'Église catholique. Du Concile de Trente à nos jours,* 1992. XIV-461 p. FB 2200.
104. L. CEYSSENS, *Le sort de la bulle Unigenitus. Recueil d'études offert à Lucien Ceyssens à l'occasion de son 90e anniversaire.* Présenté par M. LAMBERIGTS, 1992. XXVI-641 p. FB 2000.
105. R.J. DALY (ed.), *Origeniana Quinta. Papers of the 5th International Origen Congress, Boston College, 14-18 August 1989,* 1992. XVII-635 p. FB 2700.
106. A.S. VAN DER WOUDE (ed.), *The Book of Daniel in the Light of New Findings,* 1993. XVIII-574 p. FB 3000.
107. J. FAMERÉE, *L'ecclésiologie d'Yves Congar avant Vatican II: Histoire et Église. Analyse et reprise critique,* 1992. 497 p. FB 2600.

108. C. BEGG, *Josephus' Account of the Early Divided Monarchy (AJ 8, 212-420). Rewriting the Bible*, 1993. IX-377 p. FB 2400.

109. J. BULCKENS & H. LOMBAERTS (eds.), *L'enseignement de la religion catholique à l'école secondaire. Enjeux pour la nouvelle Europe*, 1993. XII-264 p. FB 1250.

110. C. FOCANT (ed.), *The Synoptic Gospels. Source Criticism and the New Literary Criticism*, 1993. XXXIX-670 p. FB 3000.

111. M. LAMBERIGTS (ed.), avec la collaboration de L. KENIS, *L'augustinisme à l'ancienne Faculté de théologie de Louvain*, 1994. VII-455 p. FB 2400.

112. R. BIERINGER & J. LAMBRECHT, *Studies on 2 Corinthians*, 1994. XX-632 p. FB 3000.

113. E. BRITO, *La pneumatologie de Schleiermacher*, 1994. XII-649 p. FB 3000.

114. W.A.M. BEUKEN (ed.), *The Book of Job*, 1994. X-462 p. FB 2400.

115. J. LAMBRECHT, *Pauline Studies: Collected Essays*, 1994. XIV-465 p. FB 2500.

116. G. VAN BELLE, *The Signs Source in the Fourth Gospel: Historical Survey and Critical Evaluation of the Semeia Hypothesis*, 1994. XIV-503 p. FB 2500.

*117. M. LAMBERIGTS & P. VAN DEUN (eds.), *Martyrium in Multidisciplinary Perspective. Memorial L. Reekmans*, 1995. X-435 p. FB 3000.

118. G. DORIVAL & A. LE BOULLUEC (eds.), *Origeniana Sexta. Origène et la Bible/Origen and the Bible. Actes du Colloquium Origenianum Sextum, Chantilly, 30 août – 3 septembre 1993*, 1995. XII-865 p. FB 3900.

119. É. GAZIAUX, *Morale de la foi et morale autonome. Confrontation entre P. Delhaye et J. Fuchs*, 1995. XXII-545 p. FB 2700.

*120. T.A. SALZMAN, *Deontology and Teleology: An Investigation of the Normative Debate in Roman Catholic Moral Theology*, 1995. XVII-555 p. FB 2700.

121. G.R. EVANS & M. GOURGUES (eds.), *Communion et Réunion. Mélanges Jean-Marie Roger Tillard*, 1995. XI-431 p. FB 2400.

*122. H.T. FLEDDERMANN, *Mark and Q: A Study of the Overlap Texts*. With an *Assessment* by F. NEIRYNCK, 1995. XI-307 p. FB 1800.

123. R. BOUDENS, *Two Cardinals: John Henry Newman, Désiré-Joseph Mercier*. Edited by L. GEVERS with the collaboration of B. DOYLE, 1995. 362 p. FB 1800.

*124. A. THOMASSET, *Paul Ricœur. Une poétique de la morale. Aux fondements d'une éthique herméneutique et narrative dans une perspective chrétienne*, 1996. XVI-706 p. FB 3000.

125. R. BIERINGER (ed.), *The Corinthian Correspondence*, 1996. XXVII-793 p. FB 2400.

*126. M. VERVENNE (ed.), *Studies in the Book of Exodus: Redaction – Reception – Interpretation*, 1996. XI-660 p. FB 2400.

*127. A. VANNESTE, *Nature et grâce dans la théologie occidentale. Dialogue avec H. de Lubac*, 1996. 312 p. FB 1800.

128. A. CURTIS & T. RÖMER (eds.), *The Book of Jeremiah and its Reception – Le livre de Jérémie et sa réception*, 1997. 332 p. FB 2400.

129. E. LANNE, *Tradition et Communion des Églises. Recueil d'études*, 1997. XXV-703 p. FB 3000.

130. A. Denaux & J.A. Dick (eds.), *From Malines to ARCIC. The Malines Conversations Commemorated*, 1997. ix-317 p. FB 1800.
131. C.M. Tuckett (ed.), *The Scriptures in the Gospels*, 1997. xxiv-721 p. FB 2400.

ORIENTALISTE, KLEIN DALENSTRAAT 42, B-3020 HERENT